Encyclopedia of World Cultures

Volume III

SOUTH ASIA

ENCYCLOPEDIA OF WORLD CULTURES

David Levinson
Editor in Chief

North America
Oceania
South Asia
Europe (Central, Western, and Southeastern Europe)
East and Southeast Asia
Soviet Union (Eastern Europe and Russia) and China
South America
Middle America and the Caribbean
Africa and the Middle East
Bibliography

The Encyclopedia of World Cultures was prepared under the auspices and with the support of the Human Relations Area Files at Yale University. HRAF, the foremost international research organization in the field of cultural anthropology, is a not-for-profit consortium of twenty-three sponsoring members and 300 participating member institutions in twenty-five countries. The HRAF archive, established in 1949, contains nearly one million pages of information on the cultures of the world.

Encyclopedia of World Cultures
Volume III
SOUTH ASIA

Paul Hockings
Volume Editor

G.K. Hall & Co.
Boston, Massachusetts

MEASUREMENT CONVERSIONS

When You Know	Multiply By	To Find
LENGTH		
inches	2.54	centimeters
feet	30	centimeters
yards	0.9	meters
miles	1.6	kilometers
millimeters	0.04	inches
centimeters	0.4	inches
meters	3.3	feet
meters	1.1	yards
kilometers	0.6	miles
AREA		
square feet	0.09	square meters
square yards	0.8	square meters
square miles	2.6	square kilometers
acres	0.4	hectares
hectares	2.5	acres
square meters	1.2	square yards
square kilometers	0.4	square miles

TEMPERATURE

$°C = (°F - 32) \times .555$

$°F = (°C \times 1.8) + 32$

© 1992 by the Human Relations Area Files, Inc.

First published 1992
by G.K. Hall & Co., an imprint of Macmillan Inc.
866 Third Avenue
New York, NY 10022

10 9 8 7 6 5 4 3 2 1
Macmillan, Inc., is part of the Maxwell Communication Group of Companies.

Library of Congress Cataloging-in-Publication Data

(Revised for volume 3)
Encyclopedia of world cultures.

    Includes bibliographical references and indexes.
    Filmography: v. 1, p. 407-415.
    Contents: v. 1. North America / Timothy J. O'Leary,
David Levinson, volume editors   --v. 3. South Asia /
Paul Hockings, volume editor.
    1. Ethnology--Encyclopedias. I. Levinson, David,
1947-
GN307.E53 1991   306'.03   90-49123
ISBN 0-81611-808-6 (alk. paper)
ISBN 0-81688-840-X (set : alk. paper)
ISBN 0-81611-812-4 (v. 3 : alk. paper)

The paper used in this publication meets the minimum requirements of American National Standard for Information Sciences—Permanence of Paper for Printed Library Materials. ANSI Z39.48-1984. ∞™
MANUFACTURED IN THE UNITED STATES OF AMERICA

Contents

Contributors

Akbar S. Ahmed
Faculty of Oriental Studies
University of Cambridge
Cambridge
United Kingdom

Pathan

Brenda Amunsen-Hill
Office of Campus Program
University of Illinois at Chicago
Chicago, Illinois
United States

Bhutanese; Sikkimese

Marcus Banks
Institute of Social and Cultural Anthropology
University of Oxford
Oxford
United Kingdom

Jain

N. G. Barrier
Department of History
University of Missouri
Columbia, Missouri
United States

Sikh

Helene Basu
Institut für Ethnologie
Berlin
Germany

Sidi

Joseph C. Berland
Berland House
Oxford
United Kingdom

Kanjar; Qalandar

Gerald D. Berreman
Department of Anthropology
University of California
Berkeley, California
United States

Pahari

Peter J. Bertocci
Department of Sociology and Anthropology
Oakland University
Rochester, Michigan
United States

Bengali

Nurit Bird-David
Department of Sociology and Anthropology
Tel Aviv University
Tel Aviv
Israel

Nayaka

S. K. Biswas
Indian Statistical Institute
Calcutta, West Bengal
India

Bhuiya

James Brow
Department of Anthropology
University of Texas at Austin
Austin, Texas
United States

Vedda

Marine Carrin-Bouez
Laboratoire d'Ethnologie et de Sociologie Comparative
Université de Paris X—Nanterre
Nanterre
France

Santal

Thomas Hylland Eriksen
International Peace Research Institute
Oslo
Norway

Mauritian

James F. Fisher
Department of Anthropology
Carleton College
Northfield, Minnesota
United States

Brahman and Chhetri of Nepal

Stephen Fuchs
Institute of Indian Culture
Bombay, Maharashtra
India

Gond

Kamala Ganesh
Bombay, Maharashtra
India

Vellala

B. B. Goswami
Anthropological Survey of India
Calcutta, West Bengal
India

Mizo

John T. Hitchcock
Department of Anthropology
University of Wisconsin
Madison, Wisconsin
United States

Magar

Paul Hockings
Department of Anthropology
University of Illinois at Chicago
Chicago, Illinois
United States

Anglo-Indian; Aryan; Badaga; Bihari; Brahman; Chinese of South Asia; Dard; Europeans in South Asia; Hill Tribes; Hindu; Indian Christian; Kalasha; Kanarese; Kashmiri; Kohistani; Kshatriya; Malayali; Muslim; Neo–Buddhist; Refugees in South Asia; Scheduled Castes and Scheduled Tribes; Sudra; Thug; Untouchables; Vaisya

Shigeru Iijima   **Thakali**
Department of Humanities and Social Sciences
Tokyo Institute of Technology
Tokyo
Japan

Hiroshi Ishii   **Newar**
Institute for the Study of Languages and Cultures of Asia
    and Africa
Tokyo University of Foreign Studies
Tokyo
Japan

K. Ishwaran   **Lingayat**
Department of Sociology
York University
North York, Ontario
Canada

George Kurian   **Syrian Christian of Kerala**
Department of Sociology
University of Calgary
Calgary, Alberta
Canada

Murray Leaf   **Punjabi**
University of Texas at Dallas
Dallas, Texas
United States

Frederic K. Lehman   **Chin**
Department of Anthropology
University of Illinois at Urbana-Champaign
Urbana, Illinois
United States

Nancy E. Levine   **Nyinba**
Department of Anthropology
University of California at Los Angeles
Los Angeles, California
United States

Owen M. Lynch   **Jatav**
Department of Anthropology
New York University
New York, New York
United States

June McDaniel   **Baul; Bengali Shakta; Bengali Vaishnava**
Department of Religious Studies
College of Charleston
Charleston, South Carolina
United States

Ernestine McHugh   **Gurung**
Department of Anthropology
University of California at San Diego
La Jolla, California
United States

Triloki Nath Madan   *Pandit of Kashmir*
Institute of Economic Growth
University of Delhi
Delhi
India

L. K. Mahapatra   *Oriya*
Sambalpur University
Sambalpur, Orissa
India

Clarence Maloney   *Divehi; Tamil*
Louis Berger, International, Inc.
New Delhi
India

Joan P. Mencher   *Nambudiri Brahman; Nayar*
Department of Anthropology
Herbert H. Lehman College
City University of New York
Bronx, New York
United States

W. D. Merchant   *Bania; Castes, Hindu; Maratha; Parsi*
Department of Social and Behavioral Sciences
South Suburban College
South Holland, Illinois
United States

Promode Kumar Misra   *Peripatetics*
Department of Anthropology
North-Eastern Hill University
Shillong, Meghalaya
India

Brian Morris   *Hill Pandaram*
Department of Social Anthropology
Goldsmiths' College
University of London
London
United Kingdom

Nils Finn Munch-Petersen   *Divehi*
Louis Berger, International, Inc.
New Delhi
India

Serena Nanda   *Hijra*
Department of Anthropology
John Jay College of Criminal Justice
City University of New York
New York, New York
United States

William A. Noble   *Irula*
Department of Geography
University of Missouri
Columbia, Missouri
United States

Alfred Pach III
Department of Medical Education
University of Illinois at Chicago
Chicago, Illinois
United States

Nepali

Hugh R. Page, Jr.
Department of Religious Studies
California State University
Sacramento, California
United States

Abor; Baiga; Bondo; Burusho; Khasi; Lakher; Nagas; Purum; Sadhu

Vishvajit Pandya
Westminster College
Fulton, Missouri
United States

Andamanese

Robert Parkin
Institut für Ethnologie
Freie Universität zu Berlin
Berlin
Germany

Munda

Robert Paul
Department of Anthropology
Emory University
Atlanta, Georgia
United States

Sherpa

Bryan Pfaffenberger
Department of Anthropology
University of Virginia
Charlottesville, Virginia
United States

Sinhalese; Tamil of Sri Lanka

Mohammed Habibur Rahman
Department of Sociology
University of Dhaka
Dhaka
Bangladesh

Chakma

Aparna Rao
Institut für Völkerkunde
Universität zu Köln
Köln
Germany

Jat

Sankar Kumar Roy
Department of Anthropology
Gauhati University
Guwahati, Assam
India

Garo

Ghanshyam Shah
Centre for Social Studies
South Gujarat University
Surat, Gujarat
India

Gujarati

K. Suresh Singh
Director
Anthropological Survey of India
New Delhi
India

Kol

Bruce Elliot Tapper
The American Occupational Therapy Association, Inc.
Rockville, Maryland
United States

Telugu

Paul Titus
Department of Anthropology
University of California at Riverside
Riverside, California
United States

Pathan

Stephen A. Tyler
Department of Anthropology
Rice University
Houston, Texas
United States

Koya

Piers Vitebsky
Scott Polar Research Institute
University of Cambridge
Cambridge
United Kingdom

Sora

Anthony R. Walker
Department of Anthropology
Ohio State University
Columbus, Ohio
United States

Toda

Shalva Weil
School of Education
Hebrew University of Jerusalem
Mount Scopus, Jerusalem
Israel

Bene Israel; Cochin Jews

Richard Kent Wolf
Musicology Division
College of Music
University of Illinois at Urbana-Champaign
Urbana, Illinois
United States

Kota

Michael Woost
Department of Anthropology
University of Texas at Austin
Austin, Texas
United States

Vedda

Eleanor Zelliot
Department of History
Carleton College
Northfield, Minnesota
United States

Chitpavan Brahman; Mahar

Preface

This project began in 1987 with the goal of assembling a basic reference source that provides accurate, clear, and concise descriptions of the cultures of the world. We wanted to be as comprehensive and authoritative as possible: comprehensive, by providing descriptions of all the cultures of each region of the world or by describing a representative sample of cultures for regions where full coverage is impossible, and authoritative by providing accurate descriptions of the cultures for both the past and the present.

The publication of the *Encyclopedia of World Cultures* in the last decade of the twentieth century is especially timely. The political, economic, and social changes of the past fifty years have produced a world more complex and fluid than at any time in human history. Three sweeping transformations of the worldwide cultural landscape are especially significant.

First is what some social scientists are calling the "New Diaspora"—the dispersal of cultural groups to new locations across the world. This dispersal affects all nations and takes a wide variety of forms: in East African nations, the formation of new towns inhabited by people from dozens of different ethnic groups; in Micronesia and Polynesia, the movement of islanders to cities in New Zealand and the United States; in North America, the replacement by Asians and Latin Americans of Europeans as the most numerous immigrants; in Europe, the increased reliance on workers from the Middle East and North Africa; and so on.

Second, and related to this dispersal, is the internal division of what were once single, unified cultural groups into two or more relatively distinct groups. This pattern of internal division is most dramatic among indigenous or third or fourth world cultures whose traditional ways of life have been altered by contact with the outside world. Underlying this division are both the population dispersion mentioned above and sustained contact with the economically developed world. The result is that groups who at one time saw themselves and were seen by others as single cultural groups have been transformed into two or more distinct groups. Thus, in many cultural groups, we find deep and probably permanent divisions between those who live in the country and those who live in cities, those who follow the traditional religion and those who have converted to Christianity, those who live inland and those who live on the seacoast, and those who live by means of a subsistence economy and those now enmeshed in a cash economy.

The third important transformation of the worldwide cultural landscape is the revival of ethnic nationalism, with many peoples claiming and fighting for political freedom and territorial integrity on the basis of ethnic solidarity and ethnic-based claims to their traditional homeland. Although most attention has focused recently on ethnic nationalism in Eastern Europe and the Soviet Union, the trend is nonetheless a worldwide phenomenon involving, for example, American Indian cultures in North and South America, the Basques in Spain and France, the Tamil and Sinhalese in Sri Lanka, and the Tutsi and Hutu in Burundi, among others.

To be informed citizens of our rapidly changing multicultural world we must understand the ways of life of people from cultures different from our own. "We" is used here in the broadest sense, to include not just scholars who study the cultures of the world and businesspeople and government officials who work in the world community but also the average citizen who reads or hears about multicultural events in the news every day and young people who are growing up in this complex cultural world. For all of these people—which means all of us—there is a pressing need for information on the cultures of the world. This encyclopedia provides this information in two ways. First, its descriptions of the traditional ways of life of the world's cultures can serve as a baseline against which cultural change can be measured and understood. Second, it acquaints the reader with the contemporary ways of life throughout the world.

We are able to provide this information largely through the efforts of the volume editors and the nearly one thousand contributors who wrote the cultural summaries that are the heart of the book. The contributors are social scientists (anthropologists, sociologists, historians, and geographers) as well as educators, government officials, and missionaries who usually have firsthand research-based knowledge of the cultures they write about. In many cases they are the major expert or one of the leading experts on the culture, and some are themselves members of the cultures. As experts, they are able to provide accurate, up-to-date information. This is crucial for many parts of the world where indigenous cultures may be overlooked by official information seekers such as government census takers. These experts have often lived among the people they write about, conducting participant-observations with them and speaking their language. Thus they are able to provide integrated, holistic descriptions of the cultures, not just a list of facts. Their portraits of the cultures leave the reader with a real sense of what it means to be a "Taos" or a "Rom" or a "Sicilian."

Those summaries not written by an expert on the culture have usually been written by a researcher at the Human Relations Area Files, Inc., working from primary source materials. The Human Relations Area Files, an international educational and research institute, is recognized by professionals in the social and behavioral sciences, humanities, and medical sciences as a major source of information on the cultures of the world.

Uses of the Encyclopedia

This encyclopedia is meant to be used by a variety of people for a variety of purposes. It can be used both to gain a general understanding of a culture and to find a specific piece of information by looking it up under the relevant subheading in a summary. It can also be used to learn about a particular region or subregion of the world and the social, economic, and political forces that have shaped the cultures in that region. The encyclopedia is also a resource guide that leads readers who want a deeper understanding of particular cultures to additional sources of information. Resource guides in the encyclopedia include ethnonyms listed in each summary, which can be used as entry points into the social science literature where the culture may sometimes be identified by a different name; a bibliography at the end of each summary, which lists books and articles about the culture; and a filmography at the end of each volume, which lists films and videos on many of the cultures.

Beyond being a basic reference resource, the encyclopedia also serves readers with more focused needs. For researchers interested in comparing cultures, the encyclopedia serves as the most complete and up-to-date sampling frame from which to select cultures for further study. For those interested in international studies, the encyclopedia leads one quickly into the relevant social science literature as well as providing a state-of-the-art assessment of our knowledge of the cultures of a particular region. For curriculum developers and teachers seeking to internationalize their curriculum, the encyclopedia is itself a basic reference and educational resource as well as a directory to other materials. For government officials, it is a repository of information not likely to be available in any other single publication or, in some cases, not available at all. For students, from high school through graduate school, it provides background and bibliographic information for term papers and class projects. And for travelers, it provides an introduction into the ways of life of the indigenous peoples in the area of the world they will be visiting.

Format of the Encyclopedia

The encyclopedia comprises ten volumes, ordered by geographical regions of the world. The order of publication is not meant to represent any sort of priority. Volumes 1 through 9 contain a total of about fifteen hundred summaries along with maps, glossaries, and indexes of alternate names for the cultural groups. The tenth and final volume contains cumulative lists of the cultures of the world, their alternate names, and a bibliography of selected publications pertaining to those groups.

North America covers the cultures of Canada, Greenland, and the United States of America.
Oceania covers the cultures of Australia, New Zealand, Melanesia, Micronesia, and Polynesia.
South Asia covers the cultures of Bangladesh, India, Pakistan, Sri Lanka and other South Asian islands and the Himalayan states.
Europe covers the cultures of Europe.

East and Southeast Asia covers the cultures of Japan, Korea, mainland and insular Southeast Asia, and Taiwan.
Soviet Union (Eastern Europe and Russia) *and China* covers the cultures of Mongolia, the People's Republic of China, and the Union of Soviet Socialist Republics.
South America covers the cultures of South America.
Middle America and the Caribbean covers the cultures of Central America, Mexico, and the Caribbean islands.
Africa and the Middle East covers the cultures of Madagascar and sub-Saharan Africa, North Africa, the Middle East, and south-central Asia.

Format of the Volumes

Each volume contains this preface, an introductory essay by the volume editor, the cultural summaries ranging from a few lines to several pages each, maps pinpointing the location of the cultures, a filmography, an ethnonym index of alternate names for the cultures, and a glossary of scientific and technical terms. All entries are listed in alphabetical order and are extensively cross-referenced.

Cultures Covered

A central issue in selecting cultures for coverage in the encyclopedia has been how to define what we mean by a cultural group. The questions of what a culture is and what criteria can be used to classify a particular social group (such as a religious group, ethnic group, nationality, or territorial group) as a cultural group have long perplexed social scientists and have yet to be answered to everyone's satisfaction. Two realities account for why the questions cannot be answered definitively. First, a wide variety of different types of cultures exist around the world. Among common types are national cultures, regional cultures, ethnic groups, indigenous societies, religious groups, and unassimilated immigrant groups. No single criterion or marker of cultural uniqueness can consistently distinguish among the hundreds of cultures that fit into these general types. Second, as noted above, single cultures or what were at one time identified as single cultures can and do vary internally over time and place. Thus a marker that may identify a specific group as a culture in one location or at one time may not work for that culture in another place or at another time. For example, use of the Yiddish language would have been a marker of Jewish cultural identity in Eastern Europe in the nineteenth century, but it would not serve as a marker for Jews in the twentieth-century United States, where most speak English. Similarly, residence on one of the Cook Islands in Polynesia would have been a marker of Cook Islander identity in the eighteenth century, but not in the twentieth century when two-thirds of Cook Islanders live in New Zealand and elsewhere.

Given these considerations, no attempt has been made to develop and use a single definition of a cultural unit or to develop and use a fixed list of criteria for identifying cultural units. Instead, the task of selecting cultures was left to the volume editors, and the criteria and procedures they used are discussed in their introductory essays. In general, however, six criteria were used, sometimes alone and sometimes in combination to classify social groups as cultural groups: (1) geographical localization, (2) identification in the social science literature as a distinct group, (3) distinct language, (4) shared traditions, religion, folklore, or values, (5) maintenance of group identity in the face of strong assimilative pressures, and (6) previous listing in an inventory of the world's cultures such as _Ethnographic Atlas_ (Murdock 1967) or the _Outline of World Cultures_ (Murdock 1983).

In general, we have been "lumpers" rather than "splitters" in writing the summaries. That is, if there is some question about whether a particular group is really one culture or two related cultures, we have more often than not treated it as a single culture, with internal differences noted in the summary. Similarly, we have sometimes chosen to describe a number of very similar cultures in a single summary rather than in a series of summaries that would be mostly redundant. There is, however, some variation from one region to another in this approach, and the rationale for each region is discussed in the volume editor's essay.

Two categories of cultures are usually not covered in the encyclopedia. First, extinct cultures, especially those that have not existed as distinct cultural units for some time, are usually not described. Cultural extinction is often, though certainly not always, indicated by the disappearance of the culture's language. So, for example, the Aztec are not covered, although living descendants of the Aztec, the Nahuat-speakers of central Mexico, are described.

Second, the ways of life of immigrant groups are usually not described in much detail, unless there is a long history of resistance to assimilation and the group has maintained its distinct identity, as have the Amish in North America. These cultures are, however, described in the location where they traditionally lived and, for the most part, continue to live, and migration patterns are noted. For example, the Hmong in Laos are described in the Southeast Asia volume, but the refugee communities in the United States and Canada are covered only in the general summaries on Southeast Asians in those two countries in the North America volume. Although it would be ideal to provide descriptions of all the immigrant cultures or communities of the world, that is an undertaking well beyond the scope of this encyclopedia, for there are probably more than five thousand such communities in the world.

Finally, it should be noted that not all nationalities are covered, only those that are also distinct cultures as well as political entities. For example, the Vietnamese and Burmese are included but Indians (citizens of the Republic of India) are not, because the latter is a political entity made up of a great mix of cultural groups. In the case of nations whose populations include a number of different, relatively unassimilated groups or cultural regions, each of the groups is described separately. For example, there is no summary for Italians as such in the Europe volume, but there are summaries for the regional cultures of Italy, such as the Tuscans, Sicilians, and Tirolians, and other cultures such as the Sinti Piemontese.

Cultural Summaries

The heart of this encyclopedia is the descriptive summaries of the cultures, which range from a few lines to five or six pages in length. They provide a mix of demographic, historical, social, economic, political, and religious information on the cultures. Their emphasis or flavor is cultural; that is, they focus on the ways of life of the people—both past and present—and the factors that have caused the culture to change over time and place.

A key issue has been how to decide which cultures should be described by longer summaries and which by shorter ones. This decision was made by the volume editors, who had to balance a number of intellectual and practical considerations. Again, the rationale for these decisions is discussed in their essays. But among the factors that were considered by all the editors were the total number of cultures in their region, the availability of experts to write summaries, the availability of information on the cultures, the degree of similarity between cultures, and the importance of a culture in a scientific or political sense.

The summary authors followed a standardized outline so that each summary provides information on a core list of topics. The authors, however, had some leeway in deciding how much attention was to be given each topic and whether additional information should be included. Summaries usually provide information on the following topics:

CULTURE NAME: The name used most often in the social science literature to refer to the culture or the name the group uses for itself.

ETHNONYMS: Alternate names for the culture including names used by outsiders, the self-name, and alternate spellings, within reasonable limits.

ORIENTATION
Identification. Location of the culture and the derivation of its name and ethnonyms.
Location. Where the culture is located and a description of the physical environment.
Demography. Population history and the most recent reliable population figures or estimates.
Linguistic Affiliation. The name of the language spoken and/or written by the culture, its place in an international language classification system, and internal variation in language use.

HISTORY AND CULTURAL RELATIONS: A tracing of the origins and history of the culture and the past and current nature of relationships with other groups.

SETTLEMENTS: The location of settlements, types of settlements, types of structures, housing design and materials.

ECONOMY
Subsistence and Commercial Activities. The primary methods of obtaining, consuming, and distributing money, food, and other necessities.
Industrial Arts. Implements and objects produced by the culture either for its own use or for sale or trade.
Trade. Products traded and patterns of trade with other groups.
Division of Labor. How basic economic tasks are assigned by age, sex, ability, occupational specialization, or status.
Land Tenure. Rules and practices concerning the allocation of land and land-use rights to members of the culture and to outsiders.

KINSHIP
Kin Groups and Descent. Rules and practices concerning kin-based features of social organization such as lineages and clans and alliances between these groups.
Kinship Terminology. Classification of the kinship terminological system on the basis of either cousin terms or genera-

tion, and information about any unique aspects of kinship terminology.

MARRIAGE AND FAMILY

Marriage. Rules and practices concerning reasons for marriage, types of marriage, economic aspects of marriage, postmarital residence, divorce, and remarriage.

Domestic Unit. Description of the basic household unit including type, size, and composition.

Inheritance. Rules and practices concerning the inheritance of property.

Socialization. Rules and practices concerning child rearing including caretakers, values inculcated, child-rearing methods, initiation rites, and education.

SOCIOPOLITICAL ORGANIZATION

Social Organization. Rules and practices concerning the internal organization of the culture, including social status, primary and secondary groups, and social stratification.

Political Organization. Rules and practices concerning leadership, politics, governmental organizations, and decision making.

Social Control. The sources of conflict within the culture and informal and formal social control mechanisms.

Conflict. The sources of conflict with other groups and informal and formal means of resolving conflicts.

RELIGION AND EXPRESSIVE CULTURE

Religious Beliefs. The nature of religious beliefs including beliefs in supernatural entities, traditional beliefs, and the effects of major religions.

Religious Practitioners. The types, sources of power, and activities of religious specialists such as shamans and priests.

Ceremonies. The nature, type, and frequency of religious and other ceremonies and rites.

Arts. The nature, types, and characteristics of artistic activities including literature, music, dance, carving, and so on.

Medicine. The nature of traditional medical beliefs and practices and the influence of scientific medicine.

Death and Afterlife. The nature of beliefs and practices concerning death, the deceased, funerals, and the afterlife.

BIBLIOGRAPHY: A selected list of publications about the culture. The list usually includes publications that describe both the traditional and the contemporary culture.

AUTHOR'S NAME: The name of the summary author.

Maps

Each regional volume contains maps pinpointing the current location of the cultures described in that volume. The first map in each volume is usually an overview, showing the countries in that region. The other maps provide more detail by marking the locations of the cultures in four or five subregions.

Filmography

Each volume contains a list of films and videos about cultures covered in that volume. This list is provided as a service and in no way indicates an endorsement by the editor, volume editor, or the summary authors. Addresses of distributors are provided so that information about availability and prices can be readily obtained.

Ethnonym Index

Each volume contains an ethnonym index for the cultures covered in that volume. As mentioned above, ethnonyms are alternative names for the culture—that is, names different from those used here as the summary headings. Ethnonyms may be alternative spellings of the culture name, a totally different name used by outsiders, a name used in the past but no longer used, or the name in another language. It is not unusual that some ethnonyms are considered degrading and insulting by the people to whom they refer. These names may nevertheless be included here because they do identify the group and may help some users locate the summary or additional information on the culture in other sources. Ethnonyms are cross-referenced to the culture name in the index.

Glossary

Each volume contains a glossary of technical and scientific terms found in the summaries. Both general social science terms and region-specific terms are included.

Special Considerations

In a project of this magnitude, decisions had to be made about the handling of some information that cannot easily be standardized for all areas of the world. The two most troublesome matters concerned population figures and units of measure.

Population Figures

We have tried to be as up-to-date and as accurate as possible in reporting population figures. This is no easy task, as some groups are not counted in official government censuses, some groups are very likely undercounted, and in some cases the definition of a cultural group used by the census takers differs from the definition we have used. In general, we have relied on population figures supplied by the summary authors. When other population data sources have been used in a volume, they are so noted by the volume editor. If the reported figure is from an earlier date—say, the 1970s—it is usually because it is the most accurate figure that could be found.

Units of Measure

In an international encyclopedia, editors encounter the problem of how to report distances, units of space, and temperature. In much of the world, the metric system is used, but scientists prefer the International System of Units (similar to the metric system), and in Great Britain and North America the English system is usually used. We decided to use English measures in the North America volume and metric measures in the other volumes. Each volume contains a conversion table.

Acknowledgments

In a project of this size, there are many people to acknowledge and thank for their contributions. In its planning stages, members of the research staff of the Human Relations Area Files provided many useful ideas. These included Timothy J. O'Leary, Marlene Martin, John Beierle, Gerald Reid, Delores Walters, Richard Wagner, and Christopher Latham. The advisory editors, of course, also played a major role in planning the project, and not just for their own volumes but also for the project as a whole. Timothy O'Leary, Terence Hays, and Paul Hockings deserve special thanks for their comments on this preface and the glossary, as does Melvin Ember, president of the Human Relations Area Files. Members of the office and technical staff also must be thanked for so quickly and carefully attending to the many tasks a project of this size inevitably generates. They are Erlinda Maramba, Abraham Maramba, Victoria Crocco, Nancy Gratton, and Douglas Black. At Macmillan and G. K. Hall, the encyclopedia has benefited from the wise and careful editorial management of Elly Dickason, Elizabeth Kubik, and Elizabeth Holthaus, and the editorial and production management of Ara Salibian.

Finally, I would like to thank Melvin Ember and the board of directors of the Human Relations Area Files for their administrative and intellectual support for this project.

DAVID LEVINSON

References

Murdock, George Peter (1967). _Ethnographic Atlas_. Pittsburgh, Penn., University of Pittsburgh Press.

Murdock, George Peter (1983). _Outline of World Cultures_. 6th rev. ed. New Haven, Conn., Human Relations Area Files.

Introduction

The diversity of South Asia, which covers a major sector of tropical and subtropical Asia, is quite apparent as one reads through the dozens of descriptive accounts published here, most written by an acknowledged expert on the community, caste, tribe, or sect in question. Some groups are tiny, others number in the millions; some are maritime, others live high in the mountain ranges; most have long flourished in the mainstream of major Indian civilizations, although a few are so remote that they have been effectively cut off from any civilizational influence until the present century, by mountains or deserts if not by preference.

Geography and Agriculture

Contemplation of the huge numbers of people now living in South Asia prompts me to point out that this volume deals with about 20 percent of the world's population (which stood at almost 5 billion in 1986, the year in which the population of South Asia passed the 1 billion mark). The rough geographic limits encompassing this mass of people and cultures are the Helmand River in the west, the Chindwin River in the east, the Indian Ocean to the south, and the Tibetan reaches of the Brahmaputra River to the north. We have not treated Tibet as a part of this territory, as it is today administered as a province of China, and it is not included in the population estimates given below. For convenience, however, Mauritius has been dealt with in this volume.

The land area covered by this volume is 4,430,789 square kilometers (not including Mauritius, Afghanistan, or Tibet). The average population density at present is about 260 persons per square kilometer, although this figure rises to around 155,000 persons per square kilometer in parts of Bombay and Calcutta, the two largest cities. However, there are some extensive tracts with very light population, notably the Thar Desert, the Himalayan Mountains, the Karakoram and the Hindu Kush (see map 2).

If there is a single factor uniting geography and culture throughout tropical Asia, it is that much of eastern India, Bangladesh, Sri Lanka, and in general the lowland areas of Southeast Asia are devoted to the intensive cultivation of one staple crop, rice (*Oryza sativa*). Evidently it was indigenous to southern China and Vietnam but spread south and west from there during the Neolithic period, until in ancient times it had occupied most of the land suited to its cultivation in the tropical areas, which up to that point had been densely for-ested. Today, while large tracts of that tropical forest do still remain in some parts of Southeast Asia that are unsuited to rice, many thousands of square kilometers in the formerly forested Gangetic Plain have become small irrigated paddy fields, terraced in the hillier parts to make use of the slopes. Because of its growing needs rice is ideally suited to these tropical forest lands: unlike any other cereal crop, rice needs a hot growing season, inundation of the field during part of the growth period, and hence an abundant supply of water from rivers or heavy rainfall. The two monsoons answer this need fully. Where irrigated paddy is grown, one finds the densest rural populations in the world, as for example in Kerala State and Bangladesh. Cultivation of the crop is labor-intensive, using humans even more than it does water buffalo.

Ideal though these geographical conditions might be for rice cultivation, they are by no means found throughout the entire South Asian area. The floodplains of the larger rivers, with their alluvial soil and plentiful water, were sometimes canalized and terraced where necessary; but much of the land is mountainous and climatically unsuited to the cultivation of even those varieties of rice that need no irrigation. To the extent that agriculture can be practiced on the mountains, it consists of the farming of several species of millet that are indigenous to those regions. In general millets (*Panicum* and *Sorghum*) require rather less sun and less rainfall: some cultivation of millets in swiddens is still fairly widespread in the northeast extremity of India. A third staple crop on the Indian subcontinent is wheat, but its growth is restricted to Pakistan and northern India. Elsewhere the climate is generally too wet for wheat. Barley too is an important staple in north and central India, though nowhere else in our area.

During the nineteenth century colonial commercial interests introduced several extremely valuable new plantation crops, largely through private initiative: first indigo, in Bengal, and shortly after that tea, coffee, and rubber, which between them revolutionized the economy of much of South Asia and changed the landscape almost beyond recognition. Sugarcane and spices have also long been of economic importance. Indeed, it was the great need for spices that first attracted the Romans to south India and much later the Dutch to Sri Lanka and Indonesia.

While we might well expect such a vast area to show considerable climatic variation, most of the Indian subcontinent experiences only three climatic types (Aw, Afi, and Cwa in the Köppen system). Translated into figures, this means that everywhere except on the mountains the average temperature of the coldest month of the year is at least 18° C (64.4° F) and a dry season occurs in the winter. The Himalayas and other high mountains, on the other hand, are of the Cwa climatic type, which is characterized by the average temperature of the coldest month falling somewhere between 18° and −3° C (64.4° and 26.6° F), while that of the warmest month is over 10° C (50° F). The dry season is still in the winter and summers are both hot and wet, the warmest month having an average temperature of about 22° C (71.6° F) and the wettest month being at least ten times as rainy as the driest one in winter.

Political History

The years 1947–1948 saw an immense political upheaval in the subcontinent that laid the essential framework for the modern political scene. Up to that date some two-fifths of the area had been ruled by nearly 600 kings and princes, the largest of whose territories, Nepal and Hyderabad, were equal in extent to several European nations. At the same time the remaining three-fifths was ruled by one king, namely George VI, a constitutional monarch who was both king of England and emperor of India. His rule embraced not only "nonprincely" India but also Burma and Ceylon (now known as Myanmar and Sri Lanka respectively), as well as Mauritius. By the terms of the independence agreements of that period, India absorbed all of the princely states except Nepal and Bhutan into its polity, but it was split into three new units: the Indian republic, West Pakistan, and East Pakistan. Sri Lanka and Myanmar (then called Ceylon and Burma) also became independent republics in 1948. The two parts of Pakistan, 1,400 kilometers apart from each other, formed a single republic, but from its early years Pakistan's national integrity was in peril, and in 1971 it split up altogether, East Pakistan becoming the independent nation of Bangladesh.

Today therefore South Asia contains two kingdoms (Nepal and Bhutan), three secular republics (Bangladesh, India, and Sri Lanka), and two Islamic republics (Pakistan and the Maldives). Three outlying archipelagoes—the Andaman, Nicobar, and Lakshadweep islands—are all administered by India. In addition this volume deals with the Republic of Mauritius, which is 3,500 kilometers southwest of Colombo but has a sizable South Asian population. It became independent in 1968.

It is not easy to summarize the political systems of these states, for they have varied greatly, but it is certain that the states themselves are viable entities. With the exception of Bangladesh breaking away from Pakistan, the political units today are precisely those set up at independence. Since that time India and Sri Lanka have run parliamentary democracies; Pakistan, Bangladesh, and the Maldives have been Islamic democracies alternating with military dictatorships of a form common in the Middle East. Nepal's kingship has been much constrained by parliamentary government, which has created a de facto constitutional monarchy.

Socialist rhetoric and Islamic orthodoxy have been prominent guidelines for many of these governments through the years. Regrettably, though, another procedure for political change has been added to the "Westminister system": assassination. If one includes suspicious air crashes in the scenario, then India has seen two prime ministers and an "heir apparent" killed; Pakistan has hanged one president and seen another die in a plane crash; Bangladesh has lost two presidents to assassination; and in Sri Lanka as well as Bhutan one prime minister has been assassinated. The grim model for all of these acts of desperation was no doubt the shocking assassination of Mahatma Gandhi in 1948, an event that showed extremists of all sorts that if a person were willing to die, he or she could probably take a major national leader along with him. This was still just as true in 1991.

The Nations of South Asia

Although the focus of this volume is the distinct cultural groups of South Asia, it is necessary to provide some basic information about the nations in which these people live. These nations are shown on map 1, with capital cities also indicated.

Bangladesh (People's Republic of Bangladesh), formerly the Eastern Province of Pakistan, became an independent nation in 1971. It occupies a territory of some 144,000 square kilometers and is bordered on the west, north, and east by India and by Myanmar (formerly Burma) on the southeast. In 1990 the population was estimated at 118,000,000. Dhaka (formerly Dacca) is the capital city, with Chittagong, Khulna, Rajshahi, and Barisal being other major urban centers. The official language is Bangla (Bengali), with 98 percent of the population being ethnic Bengalis and 87 percent Muslims. Bangladesh is among the poorest nations in the world with an annual per capita income of U.S. $113 in 1986. In 1988, 1989, 1991, and on many other occasions Bangladesh has suffered the effects of monsoons and cyclones that have killed tens of thousands and left millions homeless.

Bhutan (Kingdom of Bhutan) is located in the eastern Himalayan Mountains and is bordered by India on the south and west, Sikkim on the west, and China (Tibet) on the north. It occupies 47,000 square kilometers, in three distinct regions of high mountains in the north, valleys in the center, and forests in the south. An independent nation and democratic monarchy since 1949, its affairs are closely managed by India. In 1990 the population was estimated at 1,500,000. Dzongka is the official language, with Nepali and English also widely spoken. The capital is Thimphu. Seventy-five percent of the people are Buddhist and Buddhism is the official state religion.

India (Republic of India) is the largest and most populous of the nations of South Asia. The 1991 census of India lists 844 million inhabitants (probably an undercount) or 16 percent of the world's population. India occupies some 3,166,000 square kilometers. It became a democratic republic in 1950 and is comprised of twenty-four states and seven union territories. It is a member of the British Commonwealth of Nations. The population of India is composed of an incredibly diverse mix of different religions, language groups, cultures, and social categories. New Delhi is the capital.

Maldives (Republic of Maldives) is an island nation composed of over 2,000 islands (201 inhabited) located in the Indian Ocean 640 kilometers southwest of Sri Lanka. The land area covers 300 square kilometers, with no island having an area greater than 13 square kilometers and none rising over 2 meters above sea level. The population in 1991 was 228,000 with 57,000 living in the capital city of Male. The national language is Divehi and the state religion is Islam.

Mauritius is an island nation located 1,280 kilometers off the east coast of Madagascar in the Indian Ocean. It is composed of the main islands of Mauritius and Rodrigues and the smaller islands of Agalega and Saint Brandon. The population in 1990 was estimated at 1,142,000 with about 160,000 in the capital of Saint Louis. The official language is English, although French and Creole are widely spoken as well. Mauritius is a member of the British Commonwealth of Nations and is governed by a governor-general who represents Queen Elizabeth II.

Nepal (Kingdom of Nepal) is a land-locked nation bordered on the north by China and on the south by India. It covers 147,180 square kilometers and had an estimated population of 19,000,000 in 1990. Kathmandu is the capital, with other large cities being Patan, Morung, and Bhaktapur. One of the few Asian countries never under European control, Nepal is an absolute monarchy, divided into fourteen administrative zones and seventy-five districts. The national language is Nepali and Hinduism is the national religion.

Pakistan (Islamic Republic of Pakistan) is the westernmost nation in South Asia and is bordered by India on the east, China and Afghanistan on the north, and Iran on the west. It occupies about 800,000 square kilometers and in 1990 had an estimated population of 113 million. Islamabad is the capital, with the largest cities being Karachi, Lahore, Faisalabad, Rawalpindi, Hyderabad, and Multan. Urdu is the national language, with English used in business and government and provincial languages commonly used as well. Islam is the official state religion and 97 percent of the people are Muslims. Pakistan is divided administratively into six provinces (including Gilgit and Azad Kashmir), the Federal Capital Territory, and the tribal areas of the northwest.

Sri Lanka (Democratic Socialist Republic of Sri Lanka), formerly Ceylon, is an island located off the southeast coast of India. It occupies some 65,610 square kilometers. In 1990 the population was estimated at 17,135,000. Colombo is the capital city, with other major urban centers being Dehiwela-Mount Lavinia, Jaffna, Trincomalee, Kandy, and Kotte. Sri Lanka is divided into nine administrative districts. Sinhala (spoken by the Sinhalese majority) and Tamil are the official languages, with English also being widely spoken.

The Flux of Civilizations

But what unity is there amidst this diversity? Tropical geography has certainly been a crucial and limiting factor, determining which staple crops can be grown in each region; but almost as influential has been the long and insidious thrust of civilization emanating from empires and kingdoms alike. For South Asia has been the home to several major civilizations in succession, each being the historical and cultural elaboration of a world religion of great antiquity and wide popular appeal. Not all of these civilizational influences were indigenous to the area, but all of them had great impact.

First there was the Indus Civilization, covering a vaster area than any other empire of ancient times. We know practically nothing of its language, religion, or philosophy, but it is quite evident that this well-organized urban civilization owed much to early Bronze Age Mesopotamia. Probably a proto-Dravidian language was spoken, and there is evidence of the worship of Shiva in the form of a linga (phallic emblem). If correctly understood, these factors would make the Indus Civilization an ancestor of the Dravidian Civilization in the southern parts of India.

Next we may identify the Hindu phase. Arising from the earlier Brahmanism of Vedic and post-Vedic India, Hinduism

as it is now to be found throughout India, Nepal, and Sri Lanka took its recognizable form around the sixth to seventh centuries A.D. At about the same time Indian mariners had embarked on their only phase of foreign ventures, spreading their influence eastward to touch, if not actually establish, the medieval kingdoms of Burma, Thailand, Malaya, Cambodia, southern Vietnam, southern Borneo, Sumatra, Java, Bali, and Lombok.

Another major Indian philosophical and religious system, Hinayana Buddhism, was even more influential in those countries, yet paradoxically it had all but disappeared from its homeland by about the sixth century A.D. Nepal and Tibet, in contrast, had all along retained a Mahayana form of Buddhism, albeit intermingled with Hindu and animistic practices. Buddhism was to provide a permanent philosophical framework for most of the mainland cultures that stretched between Tibet in the west and Vietnam in the east; indeed, its influence has stretched beyond the purview of this particular volume to become one of the main religious and philosophical strands in the civilizations of China and Japan. The Buddhism of Sri Lanka, Myanmar, and Thailand owes little to China because it was carried to those lands by monks coming from India, and its texts were in the Pali language, written in a script derived from that used for Sanskrit.

For the past thousand years another great civilizing force, coming from well beyond the subcontinent, has been associated with the spread of Islam. Reaching our area first with the Arab invasions of what is now Pakistan in A.D. 711, Islam spread across India and Southeast Asia not only by the sword but also with the trading vessels that linked the northern half of the Indian Ocean with the western Pacific Ocean. Today the most populous Islamic lands in the world are to be found in South and Southeast Asia, namely Pakistan, India, Bangladesh, Malaysia, and Indonesia. Other religions that left their mark on Indian civilization—Jainism and Sikhism—were of no importance farther east, but in their several eras they certainly contributed much to Indian life and thought.

The fifth and final influence to be noted has been the more recent European one: it effectively began with Vasco da Gama's voyage to south India from Portugal in A.D. 1498. One hesitates to identify this as a Christian influence, even though that was the religion of these colonial conquerors, because the impact of Christian evangelists in most areas has not been very great. In fact today Christians in South Asia number some 24 million, always coexisting with the neighboring Hindus or Muslims. The real impact of European civilization has been administrative, educational, technical, and commercial, and the recently ended colonial period in South Asia saw every country of this region—with the exceptions of Afghanistan, Nepal, and some princely states in India—under fairly direct imperial administration. This state of affairs had ended before 1950; but the modern infrastructure of highways, railways, ports, government buildings, air services, postal service, schools, universities, political and commercial institutions, and a vast civil service was firmly in place by that time and has altered the face of these countries forever.

This picture of an area under the influence of so many historically distinct civilizations must be recognized as a partial one: it is not the whole story. The fact is that here, in ancient times and in recent, many people have commonly subsisted through simple farming or food-collecting strategies, with no reliance whatever on long-distance maritime trade, often with no familiarity with any of the great religions, and with no participation in any city-centered polity. These people primarily compose the tribal groups that this volume describes in considerable detail.

Religions

All of these influences persist throughout this vast region to this day and are reflected in the latest estimates for religious adherence. For all of South Asia, it is probable that in 1991 there were about 735 million Hindus, 315 million Muslims, 24 million Christians, and 21 million Buddhists. These figures are only estimates, of course; and they do not quite cover the entire estimated population of 1,119,000,000 as it also includes about 17 million Sikhs, 4 million Jains, and some 5 million "tribal animists," Zoroastrians, and nonbelievers. What these figures do reflect, then, is the persisting influence of the diverse philosophies mentioned above.

Categorization of Cultures

The conventional way of classifying the social groups of South Asia has been, for well over a century, to treat them all as either tribe or caste. This classification is in fact a relic of British administrative procedures in the region, and was not really one that anthropologists developed, although they have inherited it. But the bipartite classification was long ago enshrined in the "castes and tribes" handbooks for the various regions, the titles of which are listed at the end of the appendix to this volume. Although now very out-of-date, these handbooks have never been updated, only reprinted; and the terms "tribe" and "caste" remain to designate two fundamental kinds of sociocultural unit in the region. The problem with this dichotomy is where to draw the dividing line. Evidently Hinduism, without being a proselytizing faith, has for many centuries been recruiting new members into caste society by attracting isolated tribal people, especially peripatetics, into the status of Untouchable castes. This is still going on, as tribal groups Sanskritize their worship and enter the Hindu fold. When is such a group to be called a caste, when a tribe?

An ad hoc classification that perhaps better expresses the kinds of sociocultural unit that occur in South Asia is the following, which still acknowledges the tribe/caste distinction:

1.   Castes
1.1   Hindu
1.2   Muslim
2.   Modern Urban Classes
2.1   laboring classes, often immigrant
2.2   Westernized elite, including religious isolates, such as:
2.21 Sikh
2.22 Jain
2.23 Christian
2.24 Jew
2.25 Parsi
3.   Hill Tribes
3.1   groups speaking Munda, Indo-Aryan, or Dravidian languages
3.2   Paleo-Mongoloid, Tibeto-Burman–speaking people of Nepal and northeastern India
3.3   Islamic pastoral tribes
4.   Peripatetics

This volume includes descriptions of groups representative of all these categories.

Biological and Cultural Variety

Although there is no dearth of racial theories to explain the variety of peoples in the subcontinent, these have not accounted satisfactorily and scientifically for the well-studied facts of physical anthropology. The cultural and genetic impact of some dozens of invading peoples who, over the past four millennia, have moved into the area and stayed there, has left a patchwork quilt of different ethnic groups, various physical types, varying complexions, and multiple languages and cultural forms, which together defy any simplistic theory. Although it was once fashionable to explain the caste system, the "racial types," and indeed the very history of India and Pakistan in terms of the historic alignment of Aryan versus Dravidian, such ideas have scant explanatory force today in the light of present anthropological knowledge.

Since the castes, tribes, and religious communities that make up this patchwork (and form the subject of this volume) are so numerous and so diverse, one needs to look at the combined effects of geography and of history, effects that have persisted through the centuries, to understand the diversity. That Pakistan and northern India are the area of longest Muslim impact, that Sri Lanka and Bhutan are the only Buddhist lands in the subcontinent, that Bangladesh differs from West Bengal mainly in its high numbers of Muslim people, and that tribal groups are mostly concentrated in relatively inaccessible, hilly terrain are all contemporary ethnographic facts that only make sense in terms of geographical features and historical influences.

Languages

There is no space to outline the history of the subcontinent here, and innumerable studies are available that do this very adequately. Those features of regional history most relevant to an understanding of a caste or tribal culture will be mentioned under the heading "History and Cultural Relations" in most articles of this volume. The articles frequently name states in India or Pakistan. These are not merely administrative entities; for, since the 1950s, the state boundaries, especially the Indian ones, have reflected the reality of cultural units: they are linguistically defined states. It is thus easy for anyone to remember that Kashmiri is spoken in Kashmir, Sindhi in Sindh, Marathi in Maharashtra, Tamil in Tamil Nadu, etc. Not so evident from the modern state names are the facts that Hindi is spoken in Uttar Pradesh, Malayalam in Kerala, Telugu in Andhra Pradesh, and Hindi with numerous tribal languages in Madhya Pradesh. We refer here essentially to the dominant and official state languages, for each state can also show some dozens of minority (immigrant) languages and localized tribal languages. Some of the language groups are among the most populous on Earth (as gauged by number of speakers in 1981): Hindi then had 250 million, Bengali 160 million, Telugu 52 million, Punjabi 51 million, Tamil and Marathi 50 million each, and Urdu 40 million, to name just those at the top of the list. This linguistic complexity is made all the more daunting by the use of at least a dozen distinct scripts throughout the subcontinent. Government in the Republic of India proceeds in 15 languages, including the nearly ubiquitous English. Things are simpler in Bangladesh (with Bengali and English), while Sri Lanka uses Sinhalese, Tamil, and English. But Pakistani government is also encumbered with a total of 6 official languages, including English. For the whole South Asian subcontinent at least 150 languages have been enumerated by censuses, along with several hundred more mutually intelligible dialects. Some 20 of the languages have a highly developed, often venerable, literary tradition.

The South Asian languages belong to four different families: Indo-Aryan, which is a branch of the Indo-European Family, roughly distributed through Pakistan, Nepal, northern India, Bangladesh, and Sri Lanka; Dravidian, found in southern India, western Pakistan, and Sri Lanka; Tibeto-Burman, found among the Himalayan peoples of Nepal, Bhutan, and northeast India; and Munda, found mainly in the central Indian hills where Indo-Aryan abuts on the Dravidian zone. In the past scholars often treated these language families as racial categories, which was fallacious. But it is nonetheless true in a general way that people in Pakistan and northern India who speak Indo-Aryan are of fairer complexion than others, indeed are physically similar to Middle Easterners; that Dravidians are usually darker in complexion than other Indians; and that those speaking Tibeto-Burman languages have Paleo-Mongoloid features.

Religious and Economic Diversity

There are certainly other factors that add to South Asia's diversity—the dominant religion, for one. India is 83 percent Hindu and Nepal 90 percent Hindu; Pakistan is 97 percent Muslim and Bangladesh 87 percent Muslim; and Sri Lanka is 70 percent Buddhist. Yet the numerous minority religions in all of these countries cannot be ignored, either in their political significance or their cultural impact. India, for example, with only 11 percent Muslims, still has one of the largest Muslim populations of any country on Earth—only slightly less than those of Pakistan and Bangladesh.

Economic diversity, based largely on geographical factors, also helps explain the cultural diversity of South Asian countries. For instance, just to mention the most basic staples, we can state that Pakistan and India both produce wheat, rice, and cotton, with spiked millet (*bajra*), durra, pulses, and oilseeds playing nearly as prominent a role in agriculture. Bangladesh is mainly a flat, rice-producing country. Sri Lanka also grows much rice, but there the plantation crops of coconuts, tea, and rubber account for more than half of the cropped area. It is notable that several of the most important crops have been introduced by Europeans from other parts of the world, especially tea, rubber, coffee, and maize.

The local economy of a particular caste or tribe today, as most of our articles imply, is based on the balance between four variable factors: land, labor, crops, and domestic animals. It is like a game of chess, in which movement can occur in several different ways: the fields can be moved, in the sense of shifting cultivation; or the animals can be moved around by herders; or the labor force can move, as it does with hunters, vagrants, and migrant farm laborers; or the crops can be circulated, as they sometimes are to promote the fertility of particular, long-cultivated fields. In premodern times even whole villages were shifted, as marauding brigands or unscrupulous tax demands made a certain place uninhabitable. Today there is rarely enough land available for the luxury of

transhumance or shifting cultivation (though a few articles here still do report such movements). But those not tied to a piece of land may still move around within their region, as peripatetics, itinerant peddlers and artisans, carters, religious mendicants, or urban migrants. (This volume supplies descriptions of examples of each.)

The Caste System

Giving coherence and meaning to the long human adaptation to this varied land is an ancient social system based firmly on the idea of differentiation of people into caste groups. In all of the South Asian countries it is the most pervasive form of social organization, although it is not widely found in the tribal societies, and some of the biggest cities are now in the process of moving toward a system of social classes. *Caste* is a term that comes from the Portuguese word *casta*, meaning "race, category," and it has been applied to cover the two indigenous terms *varṇa* and *jāti* (see Castes, Hindu). Although the characteristic endogamy of each jāti or caste is a primary and obviously ancient feature of all the Hindu social groups discussed in this volume, it is an institution that is also to be found among Muslims, Buddhists, Jews, and Christians, most of whom are in fact descended from people converted from Hinduism.

Although for half a century (1881–1931) the census of India strove not only to count heads but to lay out the skeleton of the caste system throughout what are now the republics of India, Pakistan, and Bangladesh, nobody really knows how many jatis there are or what their precise ranking is. The uncertainty about the total number springs from the phenomenon of *subcastes*, endogamous groups that (although separate nowadays) probably formed parts of a larger caste before some political or ideological rift occurred within it. Castes then are normally made up of subcastes, and these in turn are formed of exogamous clans and lineages.

Yet many educated Indians will say there are only four castes! The reason for this disparity is that in ancient times scholars had divided Hindu society up into four ranked categories, or varnas, which are still recognized today. These are, in descending order: the Brahmans or priestly castes; the Kshatriyas, who were warriors and sometimes rulers; the Vaisyas, who were landowners and traders; and finally the Sudras, who were basically farmers. The first three of these categories are often referred to as the "twice-born" because their boys, unlike those of the Sudras, are supposed to go through a ceremonial rebirth when they adopt the wearing of the sacred thread: it is an initiation into adulthood, though it may come as early as 7 years. This rough varna model of society, it should be noted, makes no reference to the Untouchables or Harijans, nor to the tribal people. (Today there are perhaps 79 million tribal people in South Asia, the exact number depending on how one defines tribe.)

A jati (Hindi and Sanskrit for "race, people, caste, tribe, kind") is thus the regional, kin-based social unit within which any Indian is born, marries, and dies. Its members share a common language and subculture, a traditional occupation, and a well-established position in the local caste hierarchy. A particular jati may, over many decades, change its position somewhat in that hierarchy, yet individual members of the jati cannot really leave it to alter their own position and fortunes in society. Only in very recent times has it become possible for families to leave their traditional homes, move to cities far away, even overseas, and so begin a process of upward mobility in a class-structured society. This modern urban migration does much to explain the present massive populations of Bombay and Calcutta (12.5 million and 10.8 million, respectively, in 1991), as well as the millions of Indian and Pakistani immigrants to Great Britain, North America, and other English-speaking regions.

It was primarily the Hindu religious code that maintained the social order through its teachings about reincarnation. There are still hundreds of millions who believe that the soul of a person who does many good deeds will one day be reincarnated into another newborn of a higher varna category, whereas the soul of an evil person will be reincarnated as an Untouchable or even some kind of animal. In essence one has only oneself to thank for one's present social status, since it is an effect of deeds (karma) one did in a previous life. With such a pervasive belief, it has proven impossible to legislate caste out of existence, and so today its inequalities coexist with a national ideal of political democracy in India, Pakistan and Bangladesh.

In summary, according to Gerald Berreman, "a caste system occurs where a society is made up of birth-ascribed groups which are hierarchically ordered and culturally distinct. The hierarchy entails differential evaluation, rewards, and association."

The Coverage of This Volume

There is no way in which we might have covered, even schematically, all the castes and tribes of South Asia. At a conservative guess there are over 3,000 castes and subcastes, with perhaps 500 tribes in addition to these. Of course, in counting them much would depend on where the boundaries were drawn; and these boundaries are usually a little more fluid than the ethnographic literature suggests. It should not therefore be surprising that totaling up the number of castes and tribes has never been a serious anthropological enterprise, and the appendix to this volume is certainly not a definitive list.

At the outset, I was faced with the task of selecting from these thousands of disparate social units a relatively small number that might represent the cultural diversity—religious, ethnic, social, and economic—of the subcontinent. Since statistical sampling did not seem a reasonable way to proceed, the selection of social units to be included in our coverage depended very much on what study had already been done. Fortunately the ethnography of South Asia has been very richly covered, especially in India, Nepal, and Sri Lanka. As a starting point, just under four dozen "peoples" that had been included in the World Ethnographic Sample were deemed, by that fact alone, worthy of inclusion here (though in several cases no appropriate living author could be found).

A second procedure was to strive for coverage of castes and tribes that, no matter how large or how small, figure prominently in the ethnographic literature. The Todas, for example, numbering a mere one thousand today, would have been included even if they had not been in the World Ethnographic Sample, simply because of the excellent monographs of W.H.R. Rivers, M.B. Emeneau, Prince Peter, and A.R. Walker.

A third requirement was to ensure that major cultural

categories such as the Tamils and Bengalis were covered, if only because they often numbered tens of millions of people. This will often mean that the volume has one such broad article on, say, Tamils, as well as more specific articles on Vellalas and Sri Lankan Tamils, who are actually Tamils too. I thus saw no difficulty in including articles on groups of different scale and size.

A final factor, a very important one, that helped determine our coverage was which authors might be available. In some cases professional anthropologists volunteered to write about a particular caste or tribe with which they were familiar, and of course such offers were never refused. In other cases, however, the obvious person to write about a particular social group—the "authority" on them, so to speak—was unavailable or deceased. In the latter instances, where some sort of lacuna in our coverage seemed unavoidable—or where a geographical gap became apparent in some extensive tract of territory that remained untouched by our coverage—the project staff came into play. These were people at the HRAF office, especially Hugh R. Page, Jr., and anthropology students at the University of Illinois, in Chicago, who worked with the editor to produce articles based on already published ethnographic literature. These articles had the effect of balancing and supplementing our coverage of the South Asian societies by other professional scholars. The articles have followed the format established in volume 1 for the entire encyclopedia; but we have included in this volume one lengthier article, on Magar, which concentrates on a particular Hindu village and gives a fair sense of the religious, economic, and interpersonal details that have been noted throughout the subcontinent, but for which space is otherwise not available here.

Reference Resources

The best single-volume introduction to all aspects of South Asian culture and society is edited by Robinson (1989). Basham (1963, 1975) are two excellent surveys of the history and culture. For an anthropological survey of the subcontinent, Tyler (1973) and Maloney (1974) are both fairly good; and a more detailed survey of the literature on South Asian society is Mandelbaum (1970), which has the virtue of paying serious attention to regional variations in social organization. There are innumerable other books that deal—as these do—with caste society: a general introduction is provided by Lannoy (1971), and two of the most useful are Hutton (1963) and Dumont (1970). They may be supplemented with Raheja's recent survey article (1988). For specific, though never up-to-date, cultural details about the several thousand castes, subcastes, and tribes that make up South Asian society, one should consult the relevant handbook listed at the end of the appendix to this volume. Maloney (1980) is a study of the Republic of the Maldives, while Benoist (1978) is a handy account of Mauritian society. An interesting cultural history of the Indian Ocean, which pays particular attention to the island groups, is Toussaint (1966). A long history of Indian anthropology has been published by Vidyarthi (1979), but it lacks balance. Much more reliable is the extensive survey of anthropology and sociology edited by Srinivas et al. (1972–1974).

There are numerous excellent cultural histories of the Indian subcontinent, the most detailed of which is the multivolume set edited by Majumdar et al. (1951–1969). Also very reliable are the Cambridge histories (Johnson et al. 1987–; Kumar et al. 1982; Rapson et al. 1922–1937). Standard single-volume histories include Smith (1958), Thapar and Spear (1965–1966), and Majumdar, Raychaudhuri, and Datta (1961). A brief modern account is by Kulke and Rothermund (1986). Sri Lanka, which has quite a distinct history, is covered by Codrington (1939). Extremely useful for cultural as well as historical studies is the atlas edited by Schwartzberg (1978). An even more up-to-date atlas is edited by Muthiah (1987), but it only covers the Republic of India. Of regional geographies, Spate et al. (1972) and Singh (1971) may be recommended.

Two good surveys of South Asian languages are Sebeok (1969) and Shapiro and Schiffman (1981); Masica (1976) is also helpful. Of course, bilingual dictionaries exist for every major language. For Asian words that have crept into the English language, Yule and Burnell (1903) makes fascinating browsing. There are numerous modern English-language novels written by South Asians that poignantly reveal features of ordinary life in the subcontinent. Without claiming any favorites, we will simply point to the work of Ahmad Ali, Mulk Raj Anand, Bankim Chandra Chatterjee, Nirad C. Chaudhuri, Anita Desai, Ruth Prawer Jhabvala, Hanif Kureishi, Manohar Malgonkar, Kamala Markandaya, Ved Mehta, W. D. Merchant, Rohinton Mistry, R. K. Narayan, Raja Rao, Salman Rushdie, Kushwant Singh, and Rabindranath Tagore (their many books are not listed in the following bibliography). Of British literature dealing with the old India there is a massive amount: most outstanding surely are Rudyard Kipling's short stories, E. M. Forster's *A Passage to India* (1924), and Leonard Woolf's *Village in the Jungle* (1913).

A fine introduction to Indian religions and philosophy was edited by de Bary (1958), a new edition of which was recently prepared. Very similar in its coverage of Hinduism and Buddhism, and like the preceding volume featuring many translations from the classics, is Radhakrishnan and Moore (1957). Another succinct introduction to Indian philosophy is Bishop (1975). A concise dictionary of Hinduism is Stutley and Stutley (1977); Garrett (1871–1873), though old, may also be recommended.

The natural history of the subcontinent has been studied in incredible detail, and so there are, for example, excellent handbooks on the flora of each region (most of them now quite old, however). A superb new encyclopedic survey that covers flora, fauna, geography, geology, and climatology in a single volume is edited by Hawkins (1986). Also very useful for its botanical, zoological, and historical information (although not for its out-of-date economic data) is Watt (1908), which is a one-volume abridgment of *A Dictionary of the Economic Products of India* that he wrote in 1885–1893. A modern encyclopedia that covers much the same subject matter is *The Wealth of India* (1948–).

Two excellent guidebooks to the historical monuments of South Asia, equally useful to the tourist and the scholar, have been edited by Williams (1975) and Michell and Davies (1989).

Numerous bibliographies of South Asian topics are available. A useful bibliography of bibliographies for the region is by Drews and Hockings (1981). Patterson (1981) has provided the most detailed bibliography for the whole subcontinent. For Sri Lanka, however, one may consult Goonetileke (1970).

Acknowledgments

The editor thanks the many dozens of contributors—European, Asian, and American—who have organized their special knowledge into the format we proposed for this encyclopedia. William J. Alspaugh, a South Asian bibliographer at the Regenstein Library, University of Chicago, kindly provided many of the references listed in the appendix. In addition, the help of Joyce Drzal, at the University of Illinois in Chicago, provided up-to-date information on the distributors for all films listed in the filmography. Their assistance, together with that of numerous anthropology students at the University of Illinois, is gratefully acknowledged.

References

Basham, A. L. (1963). *The Wonder That Was India*. Rev. ed. New York: Hawthorn Books. Numerous reprints.

Basham, A. L., ed. (1975). *A Cultural History of India*. Oxford: Clarendon Press. Reprints. London: Oxford University Press, 1983, 1989.

Benoist, Jean (1978). "L'Île Maurice—la Réunion." In *Ethnologie Régionale*. Vol. 2, *Asie—Amérique—Mascareignes*, edited by Jean Poirier, 1867–1899. Paris: Encyclopédie de la Pléiade, Éditions Gallimard.

Berreman, Gerald D. (1979). *Caste and Other Inequities: Essays on Inequality*. New Delhi: Manohar Book Service.

Bishop, Donald H., ed. (1975). *Indian Thought: An Introduction*. New York: John Wiley & Sons.

Codrington, H. W. (1939). *A Short History of Ceylon*. Rev. ed. London: Macmillan.

de Bary, William Theodore, et al., eds. (1958). *Sources of Indian Tradition*. New York: Columbia University Press. Reprint. 1963. Rev. ed., edited by Ainslie T. Embree and Stephen Hay. 2 vols. 1988.

Drews, Lucy B., and Paul Hockings (1981). "Asia Bibliographies . . . South Asia." In *Anthropological Bibliographies: A Selected Guide*, edited by Margo L. Smith and Yvonne M. Damien, 106–121. South Salem, N.Y.: Redgrave Publishing.

Dumont, Louis (1970). *Homo Hierarchicus: An Essay on the Caste System*. Translated by Mark Saintsbury. Chicago: University of Chicago Press.

Garrett, John (1871–1873). *A Classical Dictionary of India Illustrative of the Mythology, Philosophy, Literature, Antiquities, Arts, Manners, Customs, &c. of the Hindus*. 1 vol. + supplement. Madras: Higginbotham. Reprint in 1 vol. 1973. New York: Burt Franklin.

Goonetileke, H. A. I. (1970). *A Bibliography of Ceylon: A Systematic Guide to the Literature on the Land, People, History,* and Culture Published in Western Languages from the Sixteenth Century to the Present Day. 2 vols. Bibliotheca Asiatica, no. 5. Zug: Inter Documentation.

Hawkins, R. E., ed. (1986). *Encyclopedia of Indian Natural History.* Delhi: Oxford University Press; Bombay: Bombay Natural History Society.

Hutton, John H. (1963). *Caste in India: Its Nature, Function, and Origins.* 4th ed. London: Oxford University Press.

Johnson, Gordon, et al., eds. (1987-). *The New Cambridge History of India.* 4 pts. in numerous volumes. Cambridge: Cambridge University Press.

Kulke, Hermann, and Dietmar Rothermund (1986). *A History of India.* Totowa, N.J.: Barnes & Noble.

Kumar, Dharma, Tapan Raychaudhuri, et al., eds. (1982). *The Cambridge Economic History of India.* 2 vols. Cambridge: Cambridge University Press.

Lannoy, Richard (1971). *The Speaking Tree: A Study of Indian Culture and Society.* New York: Oxford University Press. Reprint. 1974.

Majumdar, R. C., et al., eds. (1951-1969). *The History and Culture of the Indian People.* 11 vols. Bombay: Bharatiya Vidya Bhavan. 2nd ed. 1970-1988.

Majumdar, R. C., H. C. Raychaudhuri, and Kalikinkar Datta (1961). *An Advanced History of India.* London: Macmillan.

Maloney, Clarence (1974). *Peoples of South Asia.* New York: Holt, Rinehart & Winston.

Maloney, Clarence (1980). *People of the Maldive Islands.* Madras: Orient Longman.

Mandelbaum, David G. (1970). *Society in India.* 2 vols. Berkeley: University of California Press.

Masica, Colin P. (1976). *Defining a Linguistic Area: South Asia.* Chicago: University of Chicago Press.

Michell, George, and Philip Davies (1989). *The Penguin Guide to the Monuments of India.* 2 vols. New York: Viking Penguin; London: Penguin.

Muthiah, S., et al., eds. (1987). *A Social and Economic Atlas of India.* New Delhi: Oxford University Press.

Patterson, Maureen L. P. (1981). *South Asian Civilizations: A Bibliographic Synthesis.* Chicago: University of Chicago Press.

Radhakrishnan, Sarvepalli, and Charles A. Moore, eds. (1957). *A Source Book in Indian Philosophy.* Princeton: Princeton University Press. Numerous reprints.

Raheja, Gloria G. (1988). "India: Caste, Kingship, and Dominance Reconsidered." *Annual Review of Anthropology* 17:497-522.

Rapson, E. J., et al., eds. (1922-1937). *The Cambridge History of India.* 5 vols. Cambridge: Cambridge University Press.

Robinson, Francis, ed. (1989). *The Cambridge Encyclopedia of India, Pakistan, Bangladesh, Sri Lanka, Nepal, Bhutan, and the Maldives.* Cambridge: Cambridge University Press.

Schwartzberg, Joseph E., ed. (1978). *A Historical Atlas of South Asia.* Chicago: University of Chicago Press.

Sebeok, Thomas A., et al., eds. (1969). *Current Trends in Linguistics.* Vol. 5, *Linguistics in South Asia.* The Hague and Paris: Mouton.

Shapiro, Michael C., and Harold F. Schiffman (1981). *Language and Society in South Asia.* Delhi: Motilal Banarsidass.

Singh, R. D. (1971). *India: A Regional Geography.* Varanasi: Benares Hindu University.

Smith, Vincent A. (1958). *The Oxford History of India.* Revised by Percival Spear et al. Oxford: Clarendon Press; numerous reissues.

Spate, O. H. K., et al. (1972) *Indian and Pakistan.* 3rd ed. London: Methuen.

Srinivas, M. N., et al., eds. (1972-1974). *A Survey of Research in Sociology and Social Anthropology.* 3 vols. Bombay: Popular Prakashan.

Stutley, Margaret, and James Stutley (1977). *Harper's Dictionary of Hinduism: Its Mythology, Folklore, Philosophy, Literature, and History.* New York: Harper & Row.

Thapar, Romila, and Percival Spear (1965-1966). *A History of India.* 2 vols. Harmondsworth: Penguin.

Toussaint, Auguste (1966). *History of the Indian Ocean.* Chicago: University of Chicago Press.

Tyler, Stephen A. (1973). *India: An Anthropological Perspective.* Pacific Palisades: Goodyear.

Vidyarthi, L. P. (1979). *Rise of Anthropology in India: A Social Science Orientation.* Atlantic Highlands, N.J.: Humanities Press.

Watt, George (1885-1893). *A Dictionary of the Economic Products of India.* London: W.H. Allen. Reprint. 1889-1896. 6 vols. in 10. Calcutta: Superintendent of Government Printing. Reprint. 1972. Delhi: Periodical Publications.

Watt, George (1908). *The Commercial Products of India, Being an Abridgement of "The Dictionary of the Economic Products of India."* London: Dutton. Reprint. 1966. New Delhi: Today & Tomorrow's Printers & Publishers.

The Wealth of India: A Dictionary of Indian Raw Materials and Industrial Products. (1948-1990) Delhi: Council of Scientific and Industrial Research.

Williams, L. F. Rushbrook, ed. (1975). _A Handbook for Travellers in India, Pakistan, Nepal, Bangladesh & Sri Lanka (Ceylon)._ 22nd ed. London: John Murray.

Yule, Henry, and A. C. Burnell (1903). _Hobson-Jobson, A Glossary of Coloquial Anglo-Indian Words and Phrases, and of Kindred Terms, Etymological, Historical, Geographical, and Discursive._ Rev. ed. London: John Murray. Reprint. 1968. New York: Humanities Press; numerous reissues.

PAUL HOCKINGS

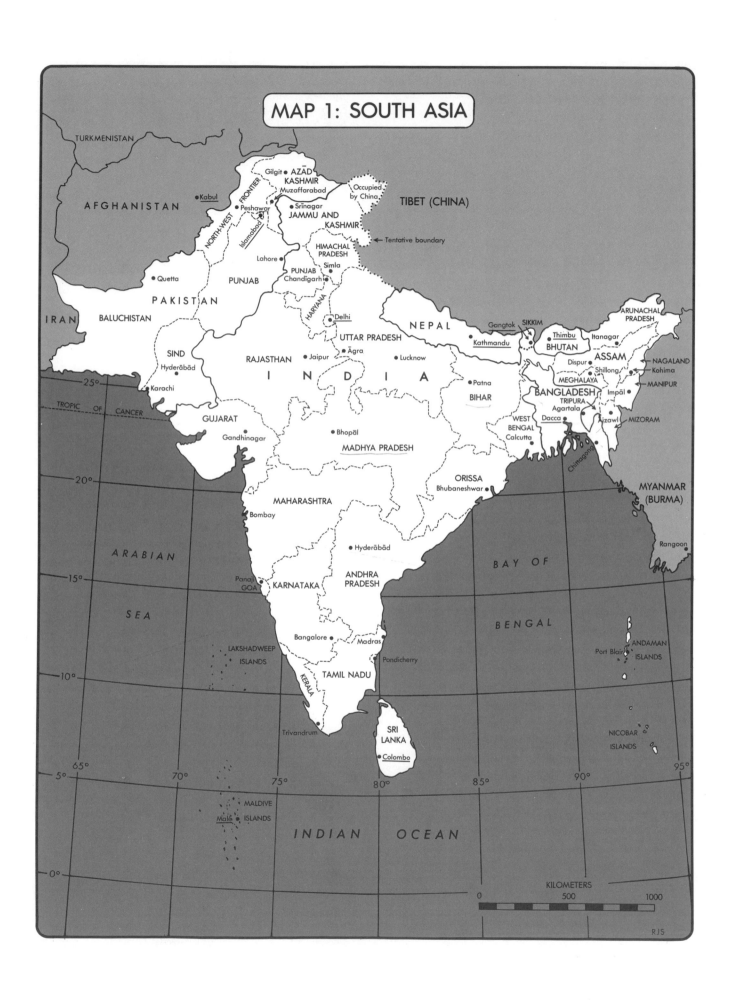

MAP 1: SOUTH ASIA

TURKMENISTAN

AFGHANISTAN

• Kabul

IRAN

PAKISTAN

BALUCHISTAN

Quetta •

NORTH-WEST FRONTIER

Peshawar •

Islamabad

SIND

Hyderābād •

Karachi •

Gilgit •   AZAD KASHMIR

Muzaffarabad •

• Srinagar

JAMMU AND KASHMIR

Occupied by China

TIBET (CHINA)

← Tentative boundary

HIMACHAL PRADESH

Lahore •

PUNJAB

Simla •

PUNJAB

Chandīgarh •

HARYANA

Delhi

• Jaipur

RAJASTHAN

• Āgra

UTTAR PRADESH

• Lucknow

I   N   D   I   A

NEPAL

Gangtok •   SIKKIM

Kathmandu

Thimbu •   Itanagar •

BHUTAN

ARUNACHAL PRADESH

Dispur •   ASSAM

← NAGALAND

Shillong •   Kohima •

MEGHALAYA   ← MANIPUR

• Patna

BIHAR

BANGLADESH

Impāl •

TRIPURA

Agartala •

Dacca

Aizawl •   ← MIZORAM

25°

TROPIC   OF   CANCER

GUJARAT

Gandhinagar •

• Bhopāl

MADHYA PRADESH

WEST BENGAL

Calcutta

Chittagong

20°

ORISSA

Bhubaneshwar •

MYANMAR (BURMA)

MAHARASHTRA

Bombay •

A R A B I A N

• Hyderābād

BAY   OF

ARUNACHAL

Rangoon •

15°

Panaji •

GOA

KARNATAKA

ANDHRA PRADESH

B E N G A L

S E A

Bangalore •   • Madras

Pandicherry •

LAKSHADWEEP

ISLANDS

TAMIL NADU

Port Blair •   ANDAMAN

ISLANDS

10°

KERALA

Trivandrum •

SRI LANKA

Colombo

NICOBAR

ISLANDS

5°

65°   70°   75°   80°   85°   90°   95°

• MALDIVE

Malé •   ISLANDS

I N D I A N   O C E A N

KILOMETERS

0   500   1000

0°

RJS

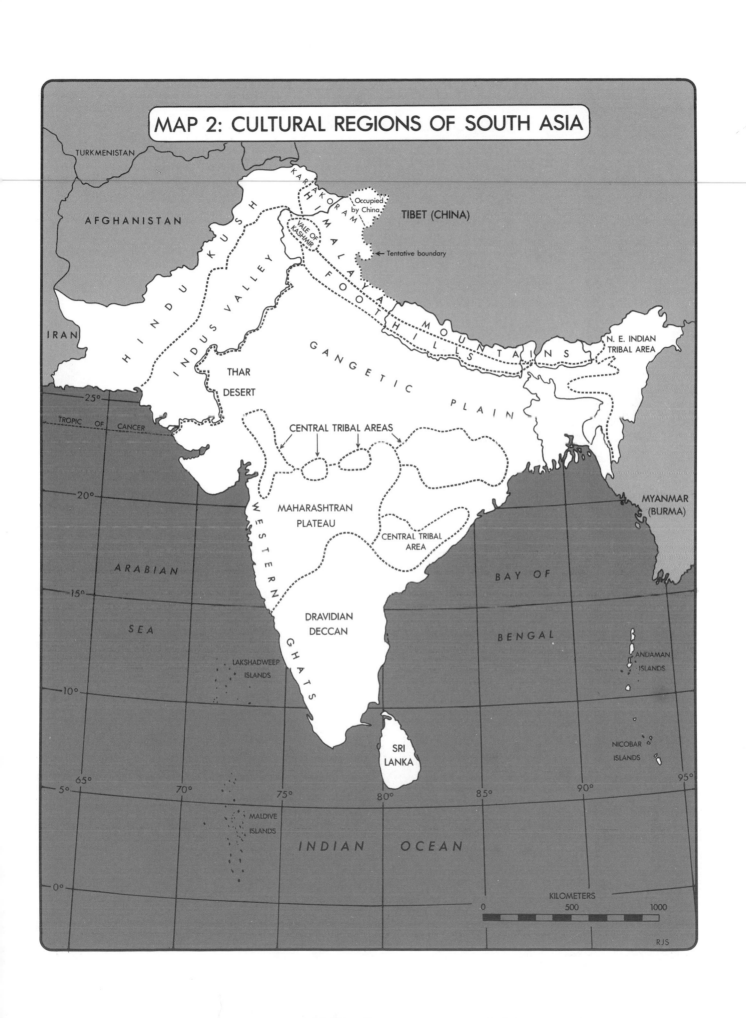

MAP 2: CULTURAL REGIONS OF SOUTH ASIA

TURKMENISTAN

AFGHANISTAN

KARAKORAM

HIMALAYA

Occupied
by China

TIBET (CHINA)

VALE OF
KASHMIR

HINDU KUSH

← Tentative boundary

IRAN

INDUS VALLEY

FOOTHILL

MOUNTAINS

N. E. INDIAN
TRIBAL AREA

THAR

DESERT

GANGETIC

PLAIN

25°

TROPIC   OF   CANCER

CENTRAL TRIBAL AREAS

20°

MAHARASHTRAN
PLATEAU

CENTRAL TRIBAL
AREA

MYANMAR
(BURMA)

ARABIAN

WESTERN

BAY   OF

15°

SEA

GHATS

BENGAL

ANDAMAN
ISLANDS

DRAVIDIAN
DECCAN

LAKSHADWEEP
ISLANDS

10°

NICOBAR
ISLANDS

SRI
LANKA

5°

65°   70°   75°   80°   85°   90°   95°

MALDIVE
ISLANDS

INDIAN   OCEAN

0°

KILOMETERS

0   500   1000

RJS

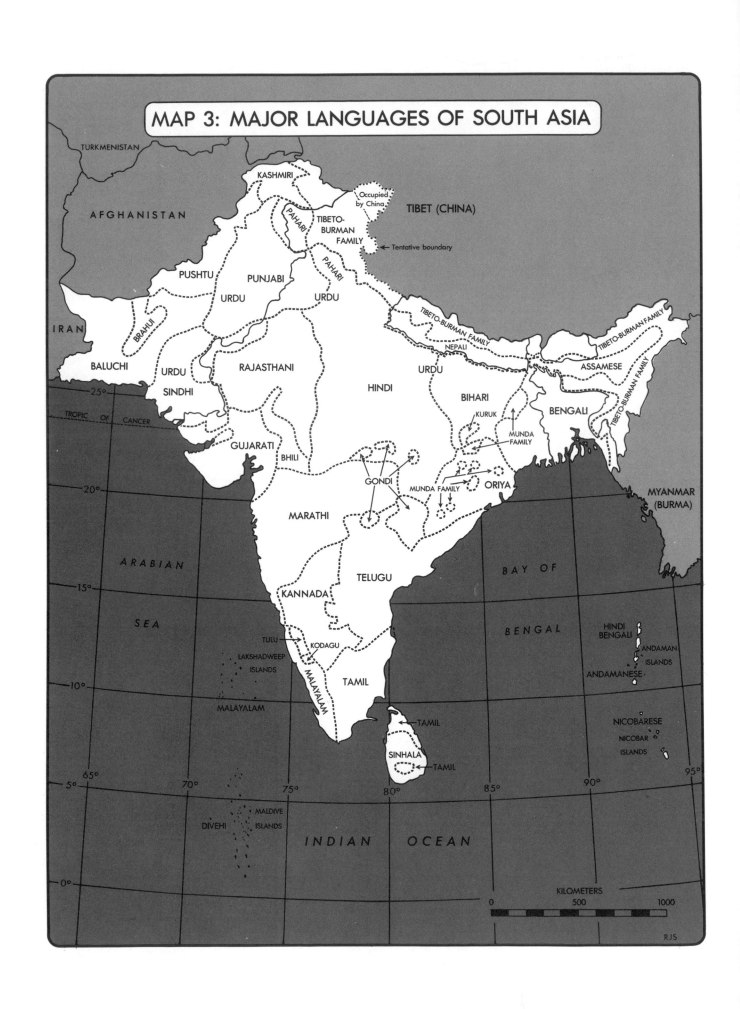

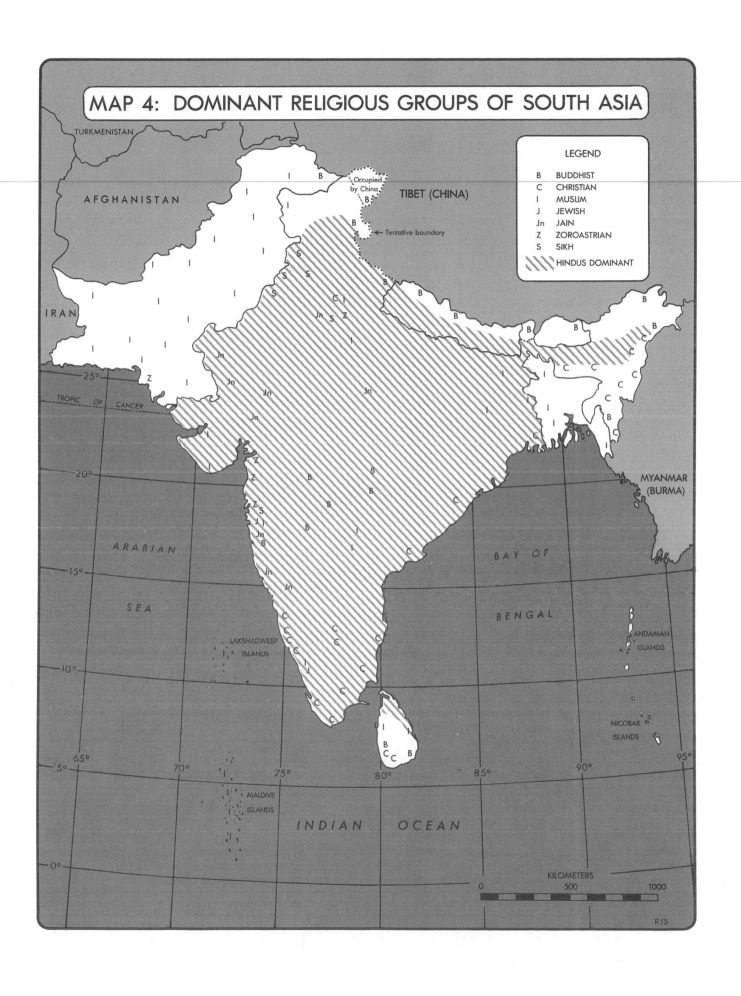

MAP 4: DOMINANT RELIGIOUS GROUPS OF SOUTH ASIA

LEGEND

B   BUDDHIST
C   CHRISTIAN
I   MUSLIM
J   JEWISH
Jn   JAIN
Z   ZOROASTRIAN
S   SIKH
  HINDUS DOMINANT

TURKMENISTAN

AFGHANISTAN

TIBET (CHINA)

Occupied by China

← Tentative boundary

IRAN

TROPIC OF CANCER

MYANMAR (BURMA)

ARABIAN SEA

BAY OF BENGAL

ANDAMAN ISLANDS

LAKSHADWEEP ISLANDS

NICOBAR ISLANDS

MALDIVE ISLANDS

INDIAN OCEAN

KILOMETERS

0   500   1000

RJS

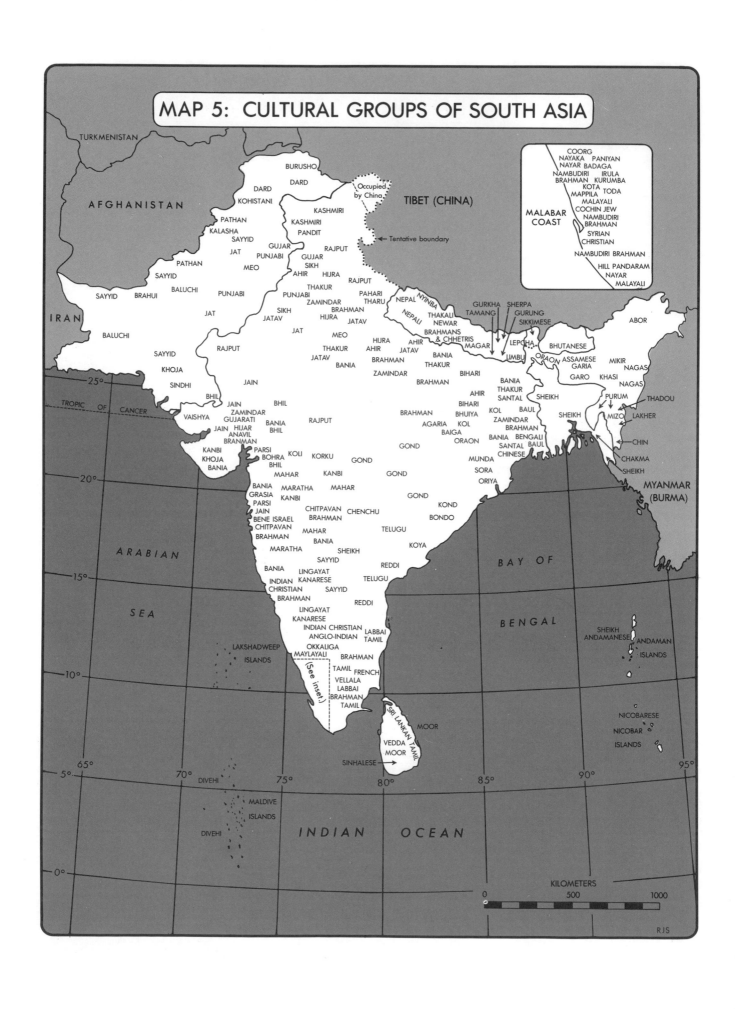

MAP 5: CULTURAL GROUPS OF SOUTH ASIA

Encyclopedia of World Cultures

Volume III

SOUTH ASIA

Abor

ETHNONYMS: Abuit, Adi, Tani

Orientation

Identification. The name "Abor" is applied, in a general sense, to all of the hill tribes that live in the area surrounding the Assam Valley. In a more specific sense, it refers to those peoples inhabiting the southern reaches of the Himalayan range in Arunachal Pradesh. The Abor label refers to fifteen related groups (Padam, Minyong, Pangis, Shimong, Ashing, Pasi, Karko, Bokar, Bori, Ramo, Pailibo, Milan, Tangam, Tangin, and Gallong), of which the Padam, Minyong, and Shimong are the most numerous. Abor settlements are also found in Tibet and China. The etymology of the word has been the subject of considerable debate. Two interpretations represent the range of opinion about the origin of the word. The first holds that *abor* is of Assamese origin and is derived from *bori,* meaning "subject, dependent," and the negative particle *a-*. Thus, "Abor" suggests one who does not submit allegiance (i.e., one who is hostile, barbarous, or savage). The alternative view connects the word with Abo, the primordial man in Abor mythology. The final *-r* is taken to be similar to final *-rr* in tribal designations such as Aorr, Simirr, and Yimchungrr, which means "man." In the 1960s, the Abor began calling themselves Adis because of the negative connotations of their former name (*see* Adi in the Appendix).

Location. Abor communities in India are concentrated on the banks of the Siang and Yamne rivers. Their territory, totaling some 20,000 square kilometers, has the India-Tibet border as its northern boundary, Pasighat as its southern boundary, and Gallong country and the Siyom river as its western boundary. The region's geographic coordinates are 28° and 29° N, by 95° and 96° E.

Demography. According to the 1971 census there were 4,733 Abor. A United Bible Societies survey suggests a total Adi-speaking population of 84,026 in 1982.

Linguistic Affiliation. The Abor speak Adi (also called Miri, Abor, Arbor, or Mishing), a language of the Tibeto-Burman Stock belonging to the Sino-Tibetan Phylum.

History and Cultural Relations

The Abors immigrated to their Indian homeland from the north crossing the Himalayas into the Assam Valley. Eventually they retreated into the highland regions that they currently occupy. The cause of this migration is unknown, although natural causes and political upheaval have been suggested as possible catalysts. It is also not known whether they migrated as a solid body at a single point in history, or in smaller subgroups over a period of several hundred years. Between 1847 and 1862, the British government tried unsuccessfully to conquer all of Abor territory. Following the failure of several military endeavors, a treaty was reached that guaranteed limited British hegemony and uninhibited trade and communication on the frontier. In spite of occasional treaty violations, an uneasy peace was maintained. After the final British military action against the Abor (in response to the murder of the assistant political officer and a companion) in 1912, the hills north of Assam were divided into western, central, and eastern sections for administrative purposes. The last of these were collectively given the name of Sadiya Frontier Tract. In 1948, the Tirap Frontier Tract was divided into the Mishmi Hills District and the Abor Hills District. Finally, in 1954, the name of the Abor Hills District was changed to the Siang Frontier Division. Since this time, the Abor have undergone considerable acculturation, which has resulted in a number of changes in the nature of village life, the local economy, social structure, and political organization.

Settlements

Villages are usually built on hilltops (though in the plains, Abor tend to follow the local practice of building villages on level land). Preference is given to those locations that afford access to a river by a sloping incline on one side and the protection of a very steep decline on the other side. Houses are built on elevated platforms. They are arranged in rows extending from the top to the bottom of the hill, and are constructed so that the rear side of the house faces the hill itself. Public buildings in a typical village include the *moshup* (bachelors' dormitory), the *rasheng* (single females' dormitory), and granaries. In older villages, stone walls with wooden reinforcements are found. Major building materials are bamboo, wood, thatching grass, and cane.

Economy

Subsistence and Commercial Activities. The major subsistence activities are hunting, fishing, gathering, agriculture, and barter of surplus crops for basic necessities and luxuries. Slash-and-burn (or *jhum*) agriculture is the norm. Forest and undergrowth are cut, dried, and burned, after which seeds are planted. Soil fertility is maintained for a period of one to three years using this method. Agricultural land is graded according to latent fertility, and crops are assigned accordingly.

Major crops include rice, five varieties of Job's tears, four types of finger millet, foxtail millet, maize, and *namdung* (*Perilla ocimoides*, the seed of which is eaten whole or ground). Green vegetables grown include mustard, country bean, pumpkins, white gourds, small onions, soybeans, flat beans, eggplants, bitter gourds, french beans, small mustard plants, potatoes, tomatoes, and *enge* (*Colocasia antiquorum*). Fruits grown include jackfruit, oranges, papayas, bananas, and pineapples. Condiment crops are limited to chilies, ginger, and sugarcane. Cotton is the most important of the several fiber crops grown. Finally, tobacco is also raised. Gayals, dogs, pigs, goats, and chickens are the most important of the animals domesticated by the Abor. The Abor do not have a currency of their own with any item of value (i.e., having a practical or decorative use) being used as money. Metal items are valued by the Abor, and the metal cauldron (*danki*) imported from Tibet is particularly treasured.

Industrial Arts.   Bamboo, wood, cane, clay, stone, glass, metal, cotton, and wool are used as raw materials. Manufactured items include yarn, woven cloth, personal attire (e.g., for daily, ceremonial, and military use), ornaments (e.g., for ear, neck, waist, and wrist), household furniture, baskets, utensils for the preparation and storage of food (e.g., bamboo containers, wooden gourds, and metal pots), and implements of war (e.g., bows, arrows, swords, shields, helmets, spiked wristlets, and bamboo spikes or *panjis*).

Trade.   Surplus goods are bartered by the Abor in exchange for various necessities and luxury items. Market relationships exist among the Abor themselves and trade routes link them with markets in Nayi Lube (Tibet), Along, Pangin, and Pasighat (the latter three being in Siang Frontier Division). For example, raw hides and chilies are traded by the Boris in Tibet for rock salt, woolen cloth, raw wool, Tibetan swords and vessels, ear ornaments, and brass bangles. They exchange salt, iron, and some utensils for other items with neighboring groups. With the establishment of Along, Pasighat, and Pangin as administrative centers, Abor traders from throughout the region come to these towns to barter their goods. In addition to barter, currency is also used as a medium of exchange.

Division of Labor.   While some tasks such as child care and cooking are shared in some cases by men and women, gender-based demarcation of responsibilities is followed in others. For example, weaving is the province of women, while the cutting and burning of trees and brush for jhum is a male task. Generally speaking, women assume primary responsibility for cooking, maintenance of domestic animals, and the seeding, weeding, and harvesting of jhum fields.

Land Tenure.   Each village has its own territorial boundaries. Within these, the land belongs to the families inhabiting the village. Roy has suggested that clan ownership of land obtains in some older villages, though this is not the general norm. Lal and Gupta suggested that in Minyong villages, the dominant clan(s) is (are) the majority landholder(s). Theoretically all land belongs to the village. However, the families that constitute a village have the right to cultivate the land that they claim as their own.

Kinship, Marriage and Family

Kin Groups and Descent.   Descent is patrilineal. Each of the constituent Abor groups traces its descent from a single mythical ancestor and is composed of a number of clans. These clans are divided into various subclans (groups of families that are the basic Abor social unit). Clan exogamy, strictly adhered to at one time, has become less the norm for the Abor due to population increase and dispersion. Subclans, however, have remained strictly exogamous. Larger divisions may exist between the clan and group levels (e.g., among the Minyong, who are divided into two moieties).

Marriage.   Monogamous unions are the norm, though polygyny is also practiced. Divorce is frequent and easily obtainable. Premarital sexual exploration is encouraged. Freedom of choice in mate selection is the norm, but parentally arranged marriages also occur. Postmarital residence does not fall neatly into any category, but it seems to be bilocal (the newly married couple settling with the parents of either the bride or the groom) in the beginning of the union and neolocal after the birth of the first child. In some cases, the youngest son of a family may remain in the home of his father along with his wife and children.

Domestic Unit.   The typical unit is made up of a husband and wife, together with their children. However, a number of variations in basic Minyong family composition have been noted. Absolute authority resides with the male head of the household. Joint families are rare because the allegiance of male and female offspring is transferred, first to the male and female dormitories, then to their own families, as the life cycle progresses. While monogamous unions are the Abor norm, polygynous arrangements are known. Consequently, households with cowives are not rare.

Inheritance.   The inheritance of all property descends through the male line. Sons share equally in the real property (land) of their father's estate. The same is true of the family house, though the youngest son inherits his father's house if he has chosen not to establish his own residence after marriage. The care of the father's widow is the responsibility of the youngest son. All other property owned by the father—such as beads inherited from his father, implements used in hunting and warfare, and clothing woven for him by his wife—is divided equally among his sons. Some of his personal effects (though none of real value) are used to decorate his grave. Ornaments that a woman brings with her into a marriage and those given to her by her husband remain hers and are inherited by her daughters and daughters-in-law.

Socialization.   The chief agents of socialization are a child's parents, the moshup (men's dormitory), and the rasheng (women's dormitory). In the home, gender-specific roles and responsibilities are introduced by the parents, and children spend their days engaged in household and subsistence activities. After a child is able to crawl, it is placed under the care of its elder siblings. Once the child has reached adolescence, responsibility for socialization shifts to the moshup and rasheng, where children spend evenings after their round of daily domestic chores is over. The dormitories serve as the training ground for men and women until they are married and are able to establish their own households.

Sociopolitical Organization

Social Organization. The primary allegiance of an individual is to his or her family. The cohesion of larger groups within the society, such as subclans, clans, and moieties, can also be occasioned by disputes and conflicts that threaten one or more of the constituent members of these larger groups. Among the Abor's primary institutions must be included jhum agriculture, the nuclear family, the moshup, and the rasheng. The anticipated secondary institutions (i.e., core religious beliefs, ritual cults, and folklore corpus) also obtain among the Abor. Traditionally, social status was achieved through the accumulation of wealth. Today, education and occupation are also viewed as signs of status.

Political Organization. Each village is an autonomous unit whose affairs are administered by a council (*kebang*). Council membership consists of clan representatives and individual village members. Every aspect of village life is governed by the kebang. This includes the mediation of local disputes. Groups of villages are organized into *bangos*, which are governed by a bango council. Disputes between bangos are mediated by a *bogum bokang* (a temporary interbango council made up of bango elders from the same group).

Social Control. Sources of conflict within Abor society include marital and familial disputes, divorce, theft, assault, and inheritance disputes. The resolution of conflict and the regulation of behavior within the society are the responsibility of the village kebang, the bango council, and the bogum bokang. Order is maintained through a system of customary law that deals with matrimonial and familial affairs, property rights, personal injury, and inheritance. Provision is made for the use of ordeals when the mediation of disputes by humans proves unsuccessful.

Conflict. Disputes between the Abor and neighboring peoples are no longer resolved by means of armed conflict. Internal (i.e., within the various Abor groups) and external (i.e., with neighboring peoples) warfare were effectively eliminated after the initiation of British rule. Conflict between villages is handled by the bango council and the resolution of interbango conflict is the responsibility of the bogum bokang.

Religion and Expressive Culture

Religious Beliefs. Abor religion is characterized by a belief in a host of spirits (*uyu*), both beneficent and malevolent. Of these, the Epom (offspring of Robo, father of evil spirits) figure prominently. They are the adversaries of human beings (who are believed to be the offspring of Robo's primordial brother, Nibo) and are said to induce accidents. The souls of those who have not been properly buried or who died unnatural deaths become *urams* (evil spirits who join the Epom in combat against humanity). Other notable evil spirits include the *nipong* (spirit of a woman who dies during pregnancy) and the *aying uyu* (lowland evil spirits whose assaults are directed against men and women of all ages). Among the more important benevolent spirits, Benji Bama (controller of human destiny) must be noted, and each natural force is believed to possess a spirit that must be held in check through proper personal conduct and the performance of certain rituals. In addition, the Abor believe in several eternal beings (e.g., Seti, the earth, and Melo, the sky) who were in existence before creation and are removed from the affairs of humanity. These beings belong to a higher order than the spirits, and they figure prominently in Abor creation myths.

Religious Practitioners. The Abor have two categories of religious practitioners: the *epak miri* (diviner) and the *nyibo* (medicine man). Through the use of incantations, herbs, divination, and spiritual discernment, they determine which spirits are responsible for their misfortune and appease these malevolent forces through the invocation of a familiar spirit. This spirit possesses the body of the practitioner and assists the soul of the epak miri or nyibo in locating the spirit that must be appeased and in arranging for a suitable propitiatory act of the individual who has been afflicted. The nyibo establishes contact with the world of spirits by recounting creation stories, while the epak miri utilizes dance and song. No special social significance is attached to either office, though the epak miri is allowed to wear special beads on ceremonial occasions.

Ceremonies. Ceremonial activity accompanies the major events in the human life cycle and is also associated with affairs of state, the life of the moshup and rasheng, subsistence activities, warfare, and health care. Song and dance are of great importance on these occasions. The epak miri, who is also the guardian of tribal myths, histories, genealogies, and other traditional lore, is the central figure during these ritual observances.

Arts. In addition to those artifacts manufactured by the Abors that have a utilitarian or ornamental purpose, tattooing is also practiced by many groups. Abor oral literature includes a number of myths, legends, folktales, traditional ballads (*abangs*), religious ballads (*ponungs*), and political narrations (*abes*). The recent introduction of writing has contributed to an increase in this literature. While musical compositions are few in number, dance is a highly developed art form among the Abor.

Medicine. In traditional Abor thought, sickness is believed to have its basis in the malevolent activity of forces in the spirit world and treatment consists of the ministrations of the epak miri. It is his or her job to ascertain from the spirit world which spirit has been offended and how expiation is to be made.

Death and Afterlife. It is believed that life continues beyond the grave, in a land where each of the uyus has its individual abode. When one dies, his or her soul is taken to the domain of the uyu who was the cause of death. An individual enjoys the same status and life-style that he or she had while alive. For this reason the deceased is provided with food, drink, possessions, and other tools and provisions to ensure comfort in the afterlife.

Bibliography

Chowdhury, J. N. (1971). *A Comparative Study of Adi Religion*. Shillong: North-East Frontier Agency.

Duff-Sutherland-Dunbar, G. (1905). *Abor and Galong*. Memoirs of the Royal Asiatic Society of Bengal, 5 (extra number). Calcutta.

Fürer-Haimendorf, Christoph von (1954). "Religious Beliefs and Ritual Practices of the Minyong Abors of Assam, India." *Anthropos* 49:588–604.

Fürer-Haimendorf, Christoph von (1962). *The Apa Tanis and Their Neighbours*. London: Routledge & Kegan Paul.

Lal, Parmanand, and Biman Kumar Das Gupta (1979). *Lower Siang People*. Calcutta: Government of India.

Roy, Sachin (1960). *Aspects of Padam-Minyong Culture*. Shillong: North-East Frontier Agency.

Simoons, Frederick J., and Elizabeth S. Simoons (1968). *A Ceremonial Ox of India: The Mithan in Nature, Culture, and History*. Madison: University of Wisconsin Press.

Srivastava, L. R. N. (1962). *The Gallongs*. Shillong: North-East Frontier Agency.

HUGH R. PAGE, JR.

Agaria

ETHNONYMS: Agariya, Agharia

Although the Agaria are not a homogeneous group, it is believed they were originally a Dravidian-speaking branch of the Gond tribe. As a separate caste, however, they do distinguish themselves from others by their profession as iron smelters. Their population was 17,548 in 1971, and they were widely dispersed across central India on the Maikal range in Mandla, Raipur, and Bilaspur districts of Madhya Pradesh. There are other castes of Agarias among the Lohars as well. The Agaria's name comes from either the Hindu god of fire Agni, or their tribal demon who was born in flame, Agyasur.

The Agaria live in their own section of a village or town, or sometimes they have their own hamlet outside of a town. Some travel from town to town working their trade as well. As already indicated, the traditional occupation of the Agaria is iron smelting. They get their ore from the Maikal range, preferring stones of a dark reddish color. Ore and charcoal are placed in furnaces that are blasted by a pair of bellows worked by the smelters' feet and channeled to the furnace through bamboo tubes, a process that is kept up for hours. The clay insulation of the kiln is broken up and the molten slag and charcoal are taken and hammered. They produce plowshares, mattocks, axes, and sickles.

Traditionally both men and women (in Bilaspur men only) collect the ore and make the charcoal for the furnaces. At dusk the women clean and prepare the kilns for the next day's work, by cleaning and breaking up the pieces of ore and roasting them in an ordinary fire; the tuyeres (cylindrical clay vents for delivering air to a furnace) are rolled by hand and made by the women as well. During smelting operations the women work the bellows, and the men hammer and fashion the ore on anvils. The construction of a new furnace is an important event involving the whole family: the men dig the holes for the posts and do the heavy work, the women plaster the walls, and the children bring water and clay from the river; upon completion, a mantra (prayer) is recited over the furnace to ensure its productiveness.

There are two endogamous subcastes among the Agaria, the Patharia and the Khuntias. These two subgroups do not even share water with each other. The exogamous divisions usually have the same names as the Gonds, such as Sonureni, Dhurua, Tekam, Markam, Uika, Purtai, Marai, to name a few. Some names such as Ahindwar, Ranchirai, and Rattoria are of Hindi origin and are an indication that some northern Hindus possibly have been incorporated into the tribe. Individuals belonging to a section are believed to constitute a lineage with a common ancestor and are therefore exogamous. Descent is traced patrilineally. Marriages are usually arranged by the father. When a boy's father decides to arrange a marriage, emissaries are sent to the girl's father and if accepted presents will follow. Contrary to Hindu marriage customs, marriage is permitted during the monsoons when iron smelting is postponed and there is no work. A bride-price is generally paid a few days before the ceremony. As with the Gonds, first cousins are permitted to marry. Widow marriage is accepted and is expected with one's late husband's younger brother, particularly if he is a bachelor. Divorce is allowed for either party in cases of adultery, extravagance, or mistreatment. If a woman leaves her husband without being divorced, the other man by custom is obligated to pay a price to the husband. Even among the widely dispersed subgroups of the Agaria there traditionally has been discrimination: among the Asur, marriage was sanctioned by custom with the Chokh, although both groups refused to marry with the Hindu Lohar subgroup, owing to their lower status.

The family god is Dulha Deo, to whom offerings of goats, fowl, coconuts, and cakes are made. They also share the Gond deity of the forest, Bura Deo. Lohasur, the iron demon, is their professional deity, whom they believe inhabits the smelting kilns. During Phagun and on the day of Dasahia the Agaria make offerings of fowl as a sign of devotion to their smelting implements. Traditionally, village sorcerers were recruited during times of sickness to determine the deity who had been offended, to whom an atonement would then be offered.

Bibliography

Elwin, Verrier (1942). *The Agaria*. Oxford: Humphrey Milford, Oxford University Press.

Russell, R. V., and Hira Lal (1916). "Agaria." In *The Tribes and Castes of the Central Provinces of India*, by R. V. Russell and Hira Lal. Vol. 2, 3–8. Nagpur: Government Printing Press. Reprint. 1969. Oosterhout: Anthropological Publications.

JAY DiMAGGIO

Ahir

ETHNONYMS: Gahra, Gaolan, Gaoli, Gerala, Goala, Golkar, Mahakul, Rawat

The Ahir are a caste of cowherds, milkers, and cattle breeders widely dispersed across the Gangetic Plain, especially in the more easternly part (Bihar, Bengal, and eastern Madhya Pradesh). The Ahir must number well over a million today: they numbered 750,000 in the Central Provinces and Berar in 1911, ranking as the sixth-largest caste in terms of numbers. In many castes there is a separate division of Ahirs, such as the Ahir Sunars, Sutars, Lohars, Shimpis, Salic, Guraos, and Kolis. The name "Ahir" is derived from "Abhira," a tribe mentioned several times in inscriptions and the Hindu sacred books. "Goala," meaning a cowherd or "a protector of cows," is the Bengali name for the caste, and the term "Gaoli" is now used in Madhya Pradesh State to signify a dairy worker.

Some dialects named after the Abhira or Ahirs are still spoken. One, known as Ahirwati, is spoken in the Rohtals and Gurgaon districts, the Punjab, and near Delhi. The Malwi dialect of Rajasthani is also known as Ahiri; there is a dialect of Gujarati called Khandeshi, also known as Ahirani. These linguistic survivals are an indication that the Ahirs were early settlers in the Delhi country of the Punjab, and in Malwa and Khandesh.

The Ahir were apparently one of the immigrant tribes from central Asia who entered India during the early Christian era. The Ahir have been for centuries a purely occupational caste, mainly recruited from the indigenous tribes. As cattle must graze in the forest during hot weather, there is a close relationship between Ahirs and many of the forest tribes. Many Ahir in Mandla, for example, are barely considered Hindus, because they live in Gond villages (a forest tribe).

Only about 30 percent of the Ahirs are still occupied in breeding cattle and dealing in milk and butter. About 4 percent are domestic servants, and nearly all the remainder were cultivators and laborers in 1931. Formerly the Ahirs had the exclusive right to milk cows, so that on all occasions an Ahir had to be hired for this purpose even by the lowest caste.

The caste has exogamous sections, which are of the usual low-caste type, with titular or totemistic names. The marriage of persons belonging to the same section and of first cousins is prohibited. A man may marry his wife's younger sister while his wife is living. The practice of exchanging girls between families is permissible.

The Ahir have a special relation to the Hindu religion, owing to their association with the sacred cow, which is itself revered as a goddess. Among the special deities of the Ahirs is Kharsk Deo, who is always located at the place of assembly of the cattle. Mater Deo is the god of the pen. A favorite saint is Haridas Baba. The main festival is the Diwali, falling about the beginning of November. All people observe this feast by illuminating their houses with many small saucer-lamps and with fireworks.

Bibliography

Blunt, E. A. H. (1931). *The Caste System of Northern India.* London: Oxford University Press. Reprint. 1969. Delhi: S. Chand.

Darling, Malcolm (1947). *The Punjab Peasant in Prosperity and Debt.* 4th Ed. Bombay: Oxford University Press. Reprint. 1977. New Delhi: Manohar.

Rose, H. A. (1911). *A Glossary of the Tribes and Castes of the Punjab and North-West Frontier Provinces.* Vol. 1. Lahore: Superintendent, Government Printing. Reprint. 1970. Patiala: Languages Department, Punjab.

Russell, R. V., and Hira Lal (1916). "Ahir." In *The Tribes and Castes of the Central Provinces of India,* by R. V. Russell and Hira Lal. Vol. 2, 18–38. Nagpur: Government Printing Press. Reprint. 1969. Oosterhout: Anthropological Publications.

Siraj ul Hassan, Syed (1920). "Ahir." *Castes and Tribes of H.E.H. the Nizam's Dominions.* Vol. 1, 1–7. Bombay: Reprint. 1990. New Delhi: Vintage Books.

JAY DiMAGGIO

Anavil Brahman

ETHNONYM: Grhastha Brahman

Anavil Brahmans are *grhastha* or "homeowner" Brahmans, which means they cannot perform priestly functions. They are traditionally landowners. There are also *bhikshuka* or mendicant priests among Anavil Brahmans. There seems to be a clear distinction between these two kinds of Anavil Brahmans, along with a certain amount of ambivalence that results from the contrast between the independence of the Anavil Brahmans as self-supporting landowners and the village priest's "obligation" to beg.

The Anavil Brahmans have been large landowners for at least three centuries. It is not clear from historical sources when the Anavil Brahmans settled in Gujarat. In the nineteenth century some Anavil Brahmans left the central part of the state and moved to the sparsely populated hills in the east (Mahuva, Vyara) where they employed the aboriginal, tribal population of the area as laborers.

There are two types of agricultural land: irrigated and nonirrigated. In the southern part of the Surat District in Gujarat, the land is well irrigated, and hence this is the traditional rice-growing region. Another cultivated cash crop from the district is ginger, as well as various other spices. In the north cotton is the main cash crop.

Within the endogamous unit, the *jati*, are two distinguishable groups of unequal social status: the Desai descendants of tax farmers, and the non-Desai. Non-Desai farmers strive to marry their daughters to Desai men but at the cost of large dowries. Hypergamy is also practiced. This system permits a woman to marry a man of a higher but not a lower social status than her own. Anavil Brahmans have a preference for patrilocality, patrilineal systems of inheritance, and residence in joint family groups. Brahmanic ideals lead to a preference for dowry marriage. The laws of Manu distinguish eight different forms of marriage, of which four are actually variations of the dowry marriage; and it is these four that are theoretically recommended to Brahmans.

Bibliography

Marriot, McKim (1968). "Caste Ranking and Food Transactions: A Matrix Analysis." In *Structure and Change in Indian Society,* edited by Milton Singer and Bernard S. Cohn, 133–171. Chicago: University of Chicago Press.

Van der Veen, Klaas W. (1972). *I Give Thee My Daughter.* Assen: Van Gorcum & Comp. N.V.

LeSHON KIMBLE

Andamanese

ETHNONYM: Mincopie

Orientation

Identification.   The Andamanese are the indigenous tribes of Negrito hunters and gatherers of the Andaman Islands. In 1908, the term "Andamanese" referred to thirteen distinct tribal groups, each distinguished by a different dialect and geographical location. Today only four tribes remain and are referred to collectively as "Andamanese." The four extant tribes are the Ongees of Little Andaman Island, the Sentinelese of North Sentinel Island, the Jarwas of the Middle Andamans, and the Great Andamanese of Strait Island.

Location.   The Andaman Islands, which comprise an archipelago of 348 islands, are located in the Bay of Bengal between 10°30′ and 13°30′ N and 92°20′ and 93°0′ E. The total land area is 8,293 square kilometers, of which about 7,464 square kilometers are covered with tropical rain forests. The northern and central islands are hilly, while the southern islands are surrounded by offshore coral reefs and are crisscrossed with tidal creeks. The southwestern and northwestern monsoons create a rainy season that lasts approximately nine to ten months each year; annual precipitation is 275 to 455 centimeters. The only dry season on the islands begins in February and ends in March.

Demography.   In 1800, the total tribal population on the islands was estimated at approximately 3,575. In 1901, the estimate dropped to 1,895, and in 1983, the total tribal population was 269. Of the 1983 estimate only the count of 9 Great Andamanese and 98 Ongees was accurate. The Jarwas and the Sentinelese are isolated by topography and by each tribe's hostility toward outsiders. Since 1789, the population of nontribal peoples on the islands has steadily increased. The total number of outsiders on the islands was 157,552 in 1983 compared to the 269 tribals. The intrusion of outsiders and diseases introduced by them, such as measles, ophthalmia, and venereal disease, has contributed directly to the overall decline in tribal population and its disproportionate male/female ratio. The islands' expanding timber industry and the settlement of increasing numbers of nontribals, primarily from mainland India, also have reduced the total area available for use by the tribals.

Linguistic Affiliation.   Areal linguistic connection of Andamanese with South and Southeast Asian language areas has not been systematically established. Andamanese as a language family is composed of two main groups: Proto–Little Andamanese, which includes Ongee, Jarwa, and Sentinelese; and Proto–Great Andamanese. Proto–Great Andamanese is further subdivided into three groups: Bea and Baie of South Andamans; Puchikwar, Kede, Juwoi, Koi, and Jko of Middle Andamans; and Bo, Chari, Jeru, and Kora of North Andamans. Early ethnographic accounts suggest that each of the tribal groups on the islands spoke mutually unintelligible languages. Yet linguistic records, compiled by the island's administrators and more recent research, suggest a great degree of overlap in terms used by each group.

History and Cultural Relations

The Andamanese are believed to share a cultural affinity with some of the Orang Aslis of insular Southeast Asia. It has been argued that the Andamanese arrived from the Malay and Burmese coasts by land in late quaternary times or, at a later time, by sea. There is also speculation that the Andamanese came from Sumatra via the Nicobar Islands. However, the precise origins of the Andamanese remain scholarly speculations that have not been thoroughly investigated and researched. The early recorded history of the islands began in earnest with the British in 1788. Rapid changes in trade winds in the area, monsoons, and coral reefs surrounding the islands caused many shipwrecks; those few who survived shipwrecks were killed by the Andamanese. In an effort to establish a safe harbor for their ships, the British made many unsuccessful attempts to pacify the islanders. In 1859, the British established Port Blair, a penal settlement on Middle Andamans; the location was chosen because it was fortified by its isolation and by Andamanese hostility. Over a period of time the Great Andamanese, who occupied the forests surrounding Port Blair, were pacified and even cooperated with British authorities in tracking down escaped convicts. Today the islands form a part of the Union Territory of India. The British imperial administration established "Andaman homes" (large permanent residences under a supervisor) for the tribals in an effort to foster a cordial relationship through exposure to European civilization. By 1875, Andamanese culture had come under scientific scrutiny, as anthropologists finally realized that this was a group of people dangerously close to extinction. From 1879, under the direction of British scholars, Andamanese culture was documented, cataloged, exhibited, and written about, especially with regard to linguistics and physical anthropology. Since Indian independence in 1947, many different plans for the social welfare and economic development of the islands and the tribal population have been implemented. Today the remaining four tribal groups are under the government-controlled institution called Andaman Adim Jan Jati Vikas Samiti. Government planners, administrators, and social workers face a dilemma in determining what kinds of changes in the traditional worldview of the remaining tribal groups, especially the Ongees, should be effected. The Jarwas and the Sentinelese have remained largely outside the framework of structured and prolonged welfare activities. The Great Andamanese, who of the four groups have had the longest period of contact with outsiders, are the most dependent on outsiders and their goods; they also are the smallest group, with practically no memory of their own language and traditions.

Settlements

Andamanese settlement patterns are based on seasonal changes. During the relatively dry season (from October to February) simple thatched lean-to huts are set up in a circular formation close to the coastal area by four families or more. All huts face the central campground created by the surrounding huts. Usually the separate huts for the unmarried men and newly married couples do not form a part of the huts surrounding the campground. During the months of May to September, the Andamanese move from the coast to the forest where pigs are hunted and honey, fruit, and tubers are collected. Violent rainstorms, which occur from May to September, make it impossible for the Andamanese to hunt turtles, dugongs, or fish from their canoes. The move from the coast to the forest is marked by a change in settlement pattern: though camps are set up in the forest as they are at the coast, only four or five families stay in one camp. As the wet season ends, each family moves to its clan's traditional hut, which is circular and houses from fifteen to twenty sleeping platforms. A clan's hut is stationary and is maintained throughout the year by the men of the clan. With the exception of a clan's hut, all housing is temporary. A clan's hut, usually 5 to 7 meters in diameter, has a woven thatched roof and side walls. Permanently installed sleeping platforms for each nuclear family are arranged circularly within each hut. Housing, in the forest and at the coast, is usually dismantled before leaving a campsite. At each new campsite—selected for its proximity to fresh water and firewood—a new sleeping platform, about 70 centimeters above the ground, is constructed for each hut. Each family retains its sleeping mats and log headrests and moves them to each new campsite. The government of India has constructed wooden houses situated on 2-meter stilts for the Great Andamanese and the Ongees. Some families use these, but among the Ongees they are not very popular and the structures are used primarily for storage.

Economy

Subsistence and Commercial Activities. Hunting and gathering, predicated on a seasonal translocationary pattern, characterize Andamanese culture. The Jarwas and Sentinelese are still completely dependent on hunting and gathering activities. Among the Ongees, however, plantation cultivation of coconuts has become important since its introduction in 1958. Although the Ongees gather the coconuts, they do not want to be involved with, nor do they participate in, any form of agricultural activity. The Ongees are paid for gathering coconuts by the welfare agency with food rations

and industrial products from mainland India. Consequently, the forest products they consume increasingly are being replaced by imported products. Among the Great Andamanese hunting is only an occasional activity. They are paid a monthly allowance by the government and also receive wages for taking care of the citrus fruit plantations. Fishing in the sea is usually done with bows and arrows while standing in knee-deep water, especially during low tide, and it is a year-round activity. Occasionally lines and hooks are used to fish in the sea. Hand-held nets are used to fish and to gather crabs and other shellfish from the island's inland creeks. Fish is an important part of Andamanese culture; in the different dialects the term for "food" is the same as that for "fish." Traditionally the northern groups caught sea turtles in large nets, but this is not done by the southern groups. Ongees paddle out to sea in their dugout outrigger canoes to hunt sea turtles and dugongs with harpoons. During the wet season the Andamanese hunt pigs in the forest with bows and detachable arrowheads. Dogs, introduced to the island in 1850 and the only domesticated animals among the Andamanese, are sometimes used to track down the pigs. Throughout the year there is a strong dependence on gathering a variety of items, such as turtle eggs, honey, yams, larvae, jackfruit, wild citrus fruits, and wild berries.

Industrial Arts. Traditionally the Andamanese were dependent on the forest and the sea for all resources and raw materials. Raw materials such as plastic and nylon cords have now been incorporated into Andamanese material culture: plastic containers are used for storage; nylon cords are used as string to make nets. These items are usually discarded by passing ships and fishing boats and are then washed up onto the islands. The Indian government distributes as gifts to the Ongees, Jarwas, and Sentinelese metal pots and pans, and as a consequence metal cookware has nearly replaced the traditional hand-molded clay cooking pots that were sun-dried and partially fire-baked. The Ongees continue to make clay pots but use them primarily for ceremonial occasions. Ongees grind metal scraps, found on the shore or received from the government, on stones and rocks to fashion their cutting blades and arrowheads. Prior to the introduction of metal in 1870 by the British, the Ongees made adzes and arrowheads from shells, bones, or hard wood. Although iron is highly valued by the Ongees, they do not use iron nails to join objects. Ongees still join objects by carving or tying rattan rope, cane strips, or strands of nylon cord. Smoking pipes, outrigger canoes, and cylindrical containers for holding honey are among the many items carved by the Ongees.

Trade. Traditionally trade within a group was conducted between the bands identified as pig hunters (forest dwellers) and turtle hunters (coastal dwellers). The pig hunter band traded clay paint, clay for making pots, honey, wood for bows and arrows, trunks of small trees for canoes, and betel nuts in exchange for metal gathered from the shore, shells for ornaments, ropes and strings made from plant fibers and nylon, and edible lime gathered by the turtle hunters. The bands would take turns serving as host for these organized events of exchange. Historically the Andamanese gathered honey, shells, and ambergris to trade with outsiders in return for clothes, metal implements, or even cosmetics. Under the imperial administration trade with outsiders was the means of entry for opium and liquor into the Northern Andamanese community. According to the Ongees in the days before coconut plantations and the help of the welfare agencies, they and their ancestors would travel by canoe northward to Port Blair to exchange with other Andamanese for the sugar and tobacco received from the British administration.

Division of Labor.   Only men hunt pigs, dugongs, and turtles. Both men and women perform all other activities of day-to-day life, including child care, cooking, and the gathering of food resources and raw materials.

Land Tenure.   Traditionally, among the Andamanese certain territories were identified as belonging to a specific band. In the Northern and the Middle Andamans it was frequently necessary to pass through another's territory. The trespassers were obliged to behave as guests in another's territory and, in return, the owners of a given territory were obliged to behave as cordial hosts. Thus, a feeling of mutual interdependence and a value for hunting and gathering in each other's part of the island has created a process of shared production and consumption. Among the Ongees of Little Andaman, where no other tribal group resides, the island is divided into four major parts and identified with two pairs of mythical birds, each of which is associated with land or water. The four divisions of land represent the four Ongee clans. Each section of the island is further subdivided into sections of land associated with a lineage. These land divisions, known as *megeyabarrotas,* are identified with a person's matrilineage and, depending on whether the territory is in the forest or on the coast, with either the turtle hunters (*eahambelakwe*) or the pig hunters (*ehansakwe*). Ongees prefer to hunt and gather in their own megeyabarrota but there are no restrictions on hunting in someone else's megeyabarrota. If one does hunt in another's megeyabarrota one is obliged to offer and share first with the owners any resource taken. A person's identity with a megeyabarrota plays a crucial role in Ongee rituals and ceremonies; for example, consummation of a marriage must occur in the wife's megeyabarrota, and a dead person's bones must be kept in the *berale* (circular hut) of a descendant's megeyabarrota.

Kinship

Kin Groups and Descent.   The present small size of the population and the limited information available on the Northern and Middle Andamans makes it difficult to create a comprehensive picture of Andamanese kinship. Earlier ethnographic accounts present the basic tribal division as the "sept," but Radcliffe-Brown's observations lead us to believe that groups came together to ensure friendly relations. On the basis of Ongee ethnographic material and early descriptions of the Andamanese, it is beyond a doubt that the Andamanese have bilateral descent groups.

Kinship Terminology.   The kinship system is cognatic and terminology, on the whole, specifies classificatory relations. Prefixes are affixed to classificatory terms of reference that also emphasize senior and junior age differentials.

Marriage and Family

Marriage.   Marriage is arranged by the elders within the prescribed group, that is, between turtle hunters and pig hunters. A man's patrilineal relatives take gifts and demand a daughter from a man's matrilineal group. Among the Ongees, population decline often makes it impossible for a young man to marry his classificatory cross cousin, and consequently he sometimes must marry a much older woman who is his mother's classificatory cross cousin. Monogamy is a strict rule. An older man or woman who has lost a spouse receives priority for marriage. Levirate marriage is acceptable. Marriage is a highly valued status. Both Man and Radcliffe-Brown imply that residence is ambilocal, but some of Radcliffe-Brown's remarks indicate a tendency towards virilocal residence. Among the Ongees a newly married couple stays with the wife's matrilineal relatives at least until a child is born. After a child is born the couple may move to live with the husband's siblings and their families. Divorce is rare and is considered immoral after the birth of a child.

Domestic Unit.   The nuclear family is the major group around which all activities revolve. The nuclear family includes a married couple's own children as well as any adopted children.

Inheritance.   Men and women inherit rights and obligations primarily from their matrilineal lineage. Tools and canoes may be inherited from the father's side.

Socialization.   Customarily children are given in adoption. The responsibility of early socialization of the child rests with the child's matrilineal relatives. Once a young boy is ready for initiation his training and education become the responsibility of his father and his paternal relatives. After a girl's first menstruation she is even more closely aligned with her matrilineal relatives. Children of both sexes are taught about the forest while they accompany their elders on various hunting and gathering activities. Through play and the making of toy canoes, bows and arrows, shelters, and small nets, children are introduced to the basic requisite skills.

Sociopolitical Organization

Social and Political Organization.   Traditionally speakers of a dialect resided as an independent and autonomous group in a specific part of the islands. Each local group was further divided up, especially in the Northern and the Middle Andamans, into twenty to fifty people who, depending on the season, lived either at the coast or in the forest. Marriage alliances and adoptions between coastal and forest dwellers controlled conflict; those social controls were supplemented by the dictates of the elders.

Social Control.   The Andamanese value system is the basic means for maintaining social control. Direct confrontation is avoided, and "going away"—that is, leaving the source and scene of conflict for a short time—is encouraged. Usually a person expresses resentment by breaking or destroying some piece of property at the campsite and then staying in the forest for a few days. While the offended person is gone, other campmates fix up the destroyed property and wait for that person, who is taken back without recriminations.

Conflict.   Occasionally neighboring groups would have a conflict of interests; however, hostility never escalated beyond the level of avoidance. When problems between groups would arise, women, through informal channels of negotiation, were instrumental in the resolution of tension. Resolution was usually marked by a feast in which the groups in conflict would participate. Between neighboring groups with different identities that were marked by different spoken dialects, the peacemaking ceremony consisted of a sequence of shared feasts held over a period of time. The imperial administrators of the islands acknowledged the position of influence held by some of the elders, and thus titles such as _raja_ were introduced and functionary chiefs created. The position of raja was always held by an elder who could speak the administration's language of Hindustani.

Religion and Expressive Culture

Religious Beliefs.   The basic belief system of the Andamanese may be characterized as animistic. All living things are believed to be endowed with power that affects human beings. The universe is a multilayered structure, a configuration of various places through which spirits and the smell and the breath of humans, animals, and plants move. Restriction of movement is regarded as a major threat to the order of nature, since each place within space is associated with a distinct type of spirit that permits or restricts the movements of all living things.

Formless, boneless, and smell-absorbing spirits live in different parts of the forest and the sea and may be divided into two main categories: those associated with natural phenomena and those of the dead. Natural phenomena, such as earthquakes, thunder, rainbows, waterspouts in the sea, and storms, mark the arrival at and departure from the islands of the spirits associated with the winds coming from different directions. The second significant category of spirits, those of the dead, may be further subdivided into benevolent and malevolent spirits. When a person dies his body undergoes a sequence of burial rites; a secondary burial rite transforms a dead person's spirit into a benevolent spirit who helps the living. Persons who die and do not receive the appropriate burial rites become a class of malevolent spirits who cause harm. The Andamanese, and specifically the Ongees, share an identity and space with the spirits; that is, spirits are formed from dead Andamanese and both spirits and the living compete in hunting and gathering the same resources on the islands.

Religious Practitioners.   The only distinguishable practitioner is the spirit communicator who communicates with ancestral spirits while dreaming or being in a state of unconsciousness. Frequent contact with spirits endows the _okojumu_ or _okopaid_ (medicine man) with supernatural powers. Among the Ongees such a specialist is called _torale_ and he or she is consulted by the community to locate resources, cure the sick, and plan the group's routine and ceremonial activities. Ongees believe that anyone can become a torale, but only an apprenticeship under an experienced torale provides one with the skill to navigate to and from the spirit world.

Ceremonies.   Major ceremonies are held for the initiation of young men and women and at the time of death. There is a continuity between these ceremonies: initiation completes the child, who is closer in identity to the spirits prior to initiation, and makes him a full human being; the funerary ceremonies transform the human being into a full spirit. Singing, dancing, and feasts form an integral part of these occasions and other rites of passage. These ceremonies entail certain food restrictions and prescriptions for the participating individual and his or her family. Ceremonial singing and dancing frequently accompany changes in residence, from forest to sea or sea to forest, and the change of seasons. The launching of a new canoe is also marked by ceremonies.

Arts.   The primary art form practiced by the Andamanese is clay painting of the body and the face. Each lineage has its own distinct design that is painted on the faces of men and women. The paint is made of red, white, or yellow clay mixed with water and/or pig fat. Intricate geometric patterns are applied to the body and the face with fingers or wooden comb-like instruments. Body painting accompanies almost all ceremonies; face painting is an everyday affair. Usually the woman paints each member of her family. Men and women make and wear ornaments made of shells and different plant materials to wear at organized singing sessions. The singing sessions are of the call-and-response style, and any individual may lead the songs. The elders will also sing traditional songs to which new lines are never added. The subject matter for traditional songs is historical and mythological events. Ongees regard traditional songs as a form of "weeping and crying" and the songs are sung in a formalized "crying" style. Storytelling, with dramatic enactments and highly stylized discourse, is another form of expression that brings campmates, especially the children, together. Among the Ongees some individuals are acknowledged to be better storytellers than others and are frequently called upon to perform. With the exception of the Great Andamanese who use sounding boards to accompany their singing and dancing, no musical instruments are used among the Andamanese. The dance steps are all a traditional body of choreographed movements that are performed on specific ceremonial occasions. Rhythm for dancing is usually accomplished by hand clapping and the slapping of the foot against the body and ground. Men and women always dance separately.

Medicine.   The Andamanese believe that the body gets sick when it becomes either too hot or too cold. Extremes in body temperature result in the release (hot) or solidification (cold) of body fluids and smell. The spirit communicator diagnoses the illness and usually attributes it to spirits. Depending upon the diagnosis, an illness is cured through the application of clay paints, mixed with other substances, in conjunction with the body either being tied with a cord around the affected part or being cut to make it bleed. Massage is also used to cure. As a preventive medicine, the Andamanese wear amulets made out of the bones of dead relatives that are believed to ward off any malevolent spirit who may cause sickness.

Death and Afterlife.   When a person dies his "body internal" is believed to escape into either the forest or the sea. Thus a dead coastal dweller becomes a spirit of the sea (_jurua_) and a dead forest dweller becomes a spirit in the forest (_lau_). Those who die in accidents or those whose dead body did not receive the appropriate ceremonial burial become malevolent spirits who cause sickness and death among human beings. Through secondary burial the bones of the dead person are recovered and made into amulets and body ornaments that attract the spirits of benevolent ancestors who will help and keep safe his living human relatives. The Ongees believe that the spirits of dead ancestors are attracted to the islands and, through a series of events, are transformed into the fetuses in human mothers. Thus the spirits of the ancestors become the children of the Ongees.

Bibliography

Cipriani, Lidio (1966). *The Andaman Islanders*. New York: Praeger.

Man, E. H. (1885). *On the Aboriginal Inhabitants of the Andaman Islands*. London: Anthropological Institute.

Pandya, Vishvajit (1897). "Above the Forest: A Study of Andamanese Ethnoanemology, Cosmology, and the Power of Ritual." Ph.D. dissertation, University of Chicago.

Portman, M. V. (1859). *History of Our Relations with the Andamanese*. Calcutta: Government Printing Press.

Radcliffe-Brown, A. R. (1922). *The Andaman Islanders*. Cambridge: Cambridge University Press.

VISHVAJIT PANDYA

Anglo-Indian

ETHNONYMS: Castee, East Indian, Eurasian, Goan, Goanese, Mustee

This term has been used in two distinct senses. Up to about 1900 it meant a British person (whether of English, Scottish, Irish or Welsh ancestry) who had been born in India ("country born") and resided there. But since 1900 the term "Anglo-Indian" has been applied to those previously known as Eurasians who were of mixed European and Indian descent (they had been known in earlier times as "East Indians"). Anglo-Indians in this latter sense are found today in all cities of India, as well as in Britain, Canada, and Australia. The last census count of them, in 1951, identified 11,637 in the Republic of India.

The English have been going to India for 1,000 years. Possibly the first English visitor was Swithelm or Sigelinus, an envoy sent by King Alfred to visit the tomb of St. Thomas in A.D. 884. He is said to have returned home safely. An equally dramatic journey was that of Thomas Coryate, whose celebrated walk from Somerset to Ajmere took three years. But by 1615, when he reached India, English visitors were becoming commonplace due to expanding trade with the Mogul Empire. While there is no evidence that Swithelm left any progeny in India, many later European visitors did. It was customary in Indian inns in the Middle Ages to provide a female companion for the pleasure of distinguished travelers. By the nineteenth century, the number of British residents was into the thousands, and most were male. Until the opening of the Suez Canal in 1869 it was common for unmarried Britons to keep an Indian mistress/housekeeper who would raise their children. After the opening of the canal, the journey became much shorter and easier, and thus many women went to India and married Englishmen. From then on the Eurasian community became a stable, largely endogamous unit.

From then until now, these Anglo-Indians have been characterized by (1) Christian religion, (2) English mother tongue, (3) European life-style at home, (4) Western dress, and (5) employment in particular administrative and service professions that typically require fluency in English and a high-school education (e.g., the post office, railways, teaching, police, and nursing professions). The popular singer Engelbert Humperdinck is an Anglo-Indian.

In Goa and other Portuguese enclaves within the Indian subcontinent, there was from the sixteenth until the twentieth century free and regular intermarriage of settlers with local Konkani-speaking women. The history of their descendants paralleled that of other Eurasians in India. Portuguese born on Indian soil were called "Castees" (from the Portuguese *castico*, a term no longer used); whereas Creoles were called "Mustees" or "Mestiz" (from the Portuguese *mistices*). In recent decades these Goanese of partial European ancestry have been assimilated into the Anglo-Indian community, though not without some resentment on the part of color-conscious Anglo-Indians. Goanese speak English, live in cities, and are Roman Catholics. It is often not recalled that the Goanese had another kind of link with Anglo-Indians: until the early nineteenth century one could buy slave girls in Goa, and some British residents of India did just that.

Bibliography

Gaikwad, Vijay Singh Rameshwar Rao (1967). *The Anglo-Indians: A Study in the Problems and Processes Involved in Emotional and Cultural Integration*. Bombay: Asia Publishing House.

Gist, Noel P., and Roy Dean Wright (1973). *Marginality and Identity: Anglo-Indians as a Racially Mixed Minority in India*. Leiden: E. J. Brill.

Schermerhorn, Richard Alonzo (1978). "Anglo-Indians: An Uneasy Minority." In *Ethnic Plurality in India*, by Richard Alonzo Schermerhorn, 210–237. Tucson: University of Arizona Press.

PAUL HOCKINGS

Aryan

ETHNONYM: Vedic Indians, now usually known to linguists as Indo-Aryan or Indo-Iranian

These early speakers of Vedic Sanskrit, an Indo-European language, invaded the Indian subcontinent from the northwest in about 1500 B.C., although there is considerable disagreement about this date. Their descendants today form the great bulk of the population in Nepal, Pakistan, northern India, Bangladesh, and Sri Lanka, though they do not identify themselves primarily as Aryans.

The term, *arya* in Sanskrit, means "noble," no doubt in reference to their dominant position in the society they invaded so long ago. They introduced to the Indo-Gangetic Plain the horse-drawn chariot and the Brahmanic religion still known to us from the four sacred books called Vedas. The earlier Indus Valley civilization, in all probability not Aryan in its language, was already destroyed or moribund by the time of their arrival. Archeologically, their early presence in India is marked by the distribution of Painted Gray Ware. The lands they occupied were called Aryavarta and are dealt with in the oldest Sanskrit literature, which is our chief source on the early Aryans.

Although the term "Aryan" has been used by European writers since 1835, it has fallen into disfavor among recent scholars because of its abuse by Nazi propagandists half a century ago, who imagined that northern and central Europeans were the purest representatives of an "Aryan race." Today the term "Aryan" is still used in discussion of early Indian history and in relation to the Subfamily of Indo-Aryan languages. The last word on usage was in fact written over a century ago by Max Müller: "I have declared again and again that if I say Aryans, I mean neither blood nor bones, nor hair nor skull; I mean simply those who speak an Aryan language. . . . To me an ethnologist who speaks of the Aryan race, Aryan blood, Aryan eyes and hair, is as great a sinner as a linguist who speaks of a dolichocephalic dictionary, or a brachycephalic grammar."

For many centuries after their arrival in the Indo-Gangetic Plain, the Aryans lived as horsemen and cattle herders, clearing patches in the forests and inhabiting small villages, rather than living in the ancient towns that their ancestors had probably helped bring to ruin. Only with the start of the Indian Iron Age (about 700 B.C.) did Aryan towns begin to emerge; this development presumes a background of settled farming in the plains by that era.

There has been much speculation about the subsequent development of northern Indian society and the Aryans' further colonization of the subcontinent; about relations between them and the conquered "Dasas" or "Dasyu" (names meaning "slaves" and probably referring to remnants of the earlier Indus Valley population); and about the rise of the caste system. During the Vedic period (about 1500 to 800 B.C.) the Aryans developed the enormously elaborate rituals of Brahmanism, the forerunner of Hinduism; and they formed a stratified society in which the rudiments of the caste system were already apparent. Thus there was a priestly caste (Brahmana), a ruling noble caste (Rajanya), a warrior caste (Kshatriya), and the menial caste (Sudra). Prior to the Mauryan Empire (321 to 185 B.C.) there was no organized Aryan government with a class of bureaucrats to administer the land throughout India. Instead, there were numerous ruling chieftains (*rajan*) who commanded their armies and were assisted by *purohitas*, men who counseled and protected the rulers with their magical skills. As larger kingdoms emerged the purohita became like a combined archbishop and prime minister, consecrating the king, giving him political counsel, and performing major sacrifices for him. The introduction of iron technology led to urbanization, and by 500 B.C. many of these kingdoms had an important merchant class in the towns who were already using copper and silver coins. Siddhārtha Gautama, the Buddha, came from the ruling family of one such kingdom (Kosala, now in Bihar State).

See also Castes, Hindu

Bibliography

Burrow, Thomas (1975). "The Early Aryans." In *A Cultural History of India,* edited by A. L. Basham, 20–29. Oxford: Clarendon Press.

Childe, Vere Gordon (1926). *The Aryans: A Study of Indo-European Origins.* London: Kegan Paul, Trench, Trübner & Co., Ltd. Reprint. 1987. New York: Dorset Press.

Thapar, Romila (1980). "India before and after the Mauryan Empire." In *The Cambridge Encyclopedia of Archaeology,* edited by Andrew Sherratt, 257–261. Cambridge: Cambridge University Press.

PAUL HOCKINGS

Assamese

ETHNONYMS: none

The term "Assamese" is often used to refer to those who are citizens of Assam: Mymensinghy settlers (from Bangladesh) and tea-garden laborers are thus included in its coverage. The term can also be used to describe the indigenous or long-settled inhabitants of this northeast Indian state.

The Brahmaputra Valley population reached 12.5 million in 1971; at the time of the 1961 census there were 16,307 inhabited villages in Assam with an average population of a little more than 500. About 12 million people spoke Assamese in 1981. The people of Assam have been described as small in stature with dark yellow complexion, an indication of their Mongoloid origin. Their language was in premodern times the easternmost member of the Indo-European Family.

The Assamese for centuries have occupied a peripheral position, both geographically and politically, in relation to the rest of India. The country was originally ruled by the Ahoms, a Shan people who migrated from upper Myanmar (Burma), at the beginning of the thirteenth century. These people variously applied the terms "Assam," "Asam," or "Aham" to their country. The Ahoms maintained chronicles of the main events of their reign. Assam originally consisted of six districts of the lower Brahmaputra or Assam Valley. But when in 1822 a chief commissionership of Assam was created by the British it was extended to include two districts in the Surma Valley, six hill areas, and two frontier tracts. Villagers associate on the basis of membership of a local center of devotional worship called a "name house" (*nam ghar*), whose members describe themselves as "one people" (*raij*). There are usually several name houses in a village. Assamese households can be graded into five economic categories, chiefly on the basis of income. Villages are also made up of families from a number of distinct castes.

Rice is the staple in Assam. If a harvest is good the people may relax and enjoy their abundance for the months ahead. Their lives revolve around rice production. They have built their houses so that their fields can be easily viewed as their crops grow; the granary is positioned at the front of each house so a farmer can rise in the morning and see his store of rice before anything else.

Within the Assamese religion a form of Hinduism exists with two contrasting emphases, that of caste and that of sect. In caste one finds polytheism, hierarchy, membership by birth (inherited status), collective ideas of humanity (caste groups), mediation of ritual specialists, rites conducted in Sanskrit through priests, complexity and extravagance of ritual, multiplicity of images, and salvation through knowledge or works. In sects one can find monotheism, egalitarianism among believers, membership by invitation (acquired status), individual ideas of humanity (individual initiates), direct access to scriptural revelation, worship conducted in the vernacular by the congregation, simplicity of worship, incarnation of God in the written word, and salvation through faith and mystical union.

Bibliography

Cantlie, Audrey (1984). *The Assamese*. London and Dublin: Curzon Press.

Census of India 1961. Vol. 3, *Assam*. New Delhi: Manager of Publications.

LeSHON KIMBLE

Badaga

ETHNONYMS: Badacar, Badager, Baddaghar, Bergie, Budaga, Buddager, Buddagur, Burga, Burgher, Vadaca, Vadacar, Vuddaghur, Wuddghur (all former spellings)

Orientation

Identification. The name "Badaga" (northerner) was given to this group because they migrated from the plains of Mysore District, just to the north of the Nilgiri Hills, in the decades following the Muslim invasion that destroyed the great Hindu empire of Vijayanagar in A.D. 1565. Badaga is also a common name for the Gaudas, who are by far the largest phratry in this community. In the nineteenth century the name was spelled in various ways. The Badagas are the largest community in the Nilgiri Hills of Tamil Nadu State (formerly Madras) in southern India, between latitude 11° and 11°30' N.

Location. The Badagas occupy only the small Nilgiris District at the junction of Kerala, Karnataka, and Tamil Nadu states, but they share their territory with many other tribal groups and an even larger number of fairly recent immigrants from the plains of south India. The district area is 2,549 square kilometers, about the same as the state of Rhode Island. Although the majority of Badagas are still small-scale farmers, there is now a sizable middle class living in the four main British-built towns on the plateau, and the community can boast several thousand college graduates. Badaga doctors, lawyers, teachers, and government officials are very plentiful, and there are also a few professors, agronomists, and politicians. Although still largely a rural population, they have as high a rate of literacy (in Tamil and English) as the inhabitants of Madras City. A few households can boast cars and imported videotape players. Several dozen doctors, engineers, and architects have recently settled with their families in America.

Demography. The Badagas number an estimated 145,000 (1991), about 19 percent of the district population of 630,169 (as of 1981). Progressive attitudes have made the Badagas an unusually successful farming community. Population figures from the official censuses bear out this success: in 1812 there were reportedly only 2,207 Badagas; by 1901 there were 34,178; today, about 145,000. By developing intensive cash-crop cultivation they have managed to accommodate this greatly increased labor force and improve their standard of living. With birth control in practice now for some twenty years, the annual population growth rate is down to about 1.5 percent (our estimate).

Linguistic Affiliation. All Badagas—and only Badagas—speak Badaga, or more correctly Badugu, a Dravidian language. It is now a distinct language, but it was originally derived from sixteenth-century Kannada (or Canarese), which belongs to the South Dravidian Subfamily. Today it contains many words of English and Tamil origin, as well as many from Sanskrit. In premodern times the language served as a lingua franca among the various Nilgiri tribes.

History and Cultural Relations

The early Badagas, refugees from the Muslim invaders of Mysore, had to cut their farmsteads out of the Nilgiri forests. They continued some slash-and-burn cultivation there until the 1870s. By that time the land demands of British tea and coffee planters, then resident for half a century, had created a market for farmland, which tempted many Badagas to sell some of their land. But most of their land was retained. By the early twentieth century they were pursuing advanced education and some urban professions.

For many years now the Badagas have been adapting to their own use certain alien customs and techniques. Nowhere is this more evident than in agriculture.

Settlements

The villages, each inhabited only by Badagas of a particular clan and usually containing no more than several hundred people, consist of parallel rows of stone or brick houses with tiled roofs. They lie along the slope of a hill on its leeward side, for protection from the westerly monsoon. The fields spread out all around. Up to a half-dozen temples and shrines for different Hindu gods are found in each village. Modern villages have electricity and piped water to communal taps, but not long ago the water supply was a nearby stream or at best a channel running into the village from a stream. One other universal feature is a village green, important as a council place, playground, dance ground, funeral place, and general grazing area for the calves. The traditional Badaga two-room houses, still in common use, are built in groups of a dozen or less to form a continuous line along a level piece of ground. They are now made of whitewashed brick and have tiled or corrugated-iron roofs, but the traditional building material was wattle and daub. Scarcely any thatched roofs now remain.

Economy

Subsistence and Commercial Activities. In general Badagas use fields around the villages to practice mixed farming of millets, barley, wheat, and a variety of European vegetables, two of which—the potato and cabbage—have now assumed major commercial importance. Millets were the staple until this century, and they were sometimes cultivated in forest clearings by the slash-and-burn technique. Badaga farmers use no irrigation; instead, they rely on the rainfall of two regular monsoon seasons. During this century they have gradually shifted from subsistence farming of traditional grains to cash-crop farming of potatoes and cabbages. After several seasons of disease, potatoes were recently superseded by numerous small plantations of tea (which was first introduced here by the British in 1835) and cabbage fields. Crops of European origin are now grown on machine-made terraces with the help of chemical fertilizers, truck transport, improved seed, and even crop insurance; similar techniques are used on the tea plantations, which must maintain world market standards. Herds of buffalo and cows are kept for dairy purposes; these are less numerous than in the past, and they are never kept for meat, even though most people are not vegetarians. Poultry are frequently kept and ponies occasionally. Beekeeping is practiced now, but in earlier days only wild honey was collected in the forests. Although potatoes and purchased rice are the staples nowadays, the Badagas traditionally ate wheat and various millets. Their mixed farming produces a good variety of both local and European crops, and their diet also may be complemented with some wild forest plants. Most Badagas are nonvegetarian, eating mutton and occasional wild game. There is no evidence of opium addiction, although this was an opium-producing community in the last century. Illicit liquor is produced.

Industrial Arts. Although Badagas have been doing building and urban trades for about a century, until 1930 they looked to the Kotas to supply all of their needs in pottery, carpentry, leather, blacksmithing, silver ornaments, thatching, and furniture. Badagas include no specialized artisan phratries or subcastes.

Trade. This community is well known for its complex symbiosis with the Toda, Kota, and Kurumba tribes of the Nilgiris. Some Badaga villages also maintain exchange relations with the Irulas, Uralis, Paniyans, and Chettis of the surrounding slopes. The closest ties are with the seven nearby Kota villages. Until 1930 every Badaga family had a Kota associate who provided a band of musicians whenever there was a wedding or funeral in that family and who regularly furnished the Badagas with pottery, carpentry, thatching, and most leather and metal items. In return for being jacks-of-all-trades to the Badagas (who had no specialized artisans in their own community), the Kotas were supplied with cloth and a portion of the annual harvest by their Badaga associates. The Todas, a vegetarian people, were the only group in the Nilgiri Hills whom the Badagas were willing to accept as near equals. The two communities used to exchange buffalo and attend each other's ceremonies. Some Todas still supply their associates with baskets and other jungle-grown produce, as well as clarified butter (_ghee_). In return the Badagas give a portion of their harvest. Since 1930 the relationship has become attenuated, as with the Kotas, largely because the Badaga population has increased out of all proportion to the Todas and Kotas; and also because the Badagas are distinctly more modernized. The Kurumbas are seven tribes of jungle gatherers, gardeners, and sorcerers on the Nilgiri slopes. Each Badaga village has a "watchman," a Kurumba employed to protect them from the sorcery of other Kurumbas. He also takes part in some Badaga ceremonies as an auxiliary priest and supplies his Badaga friends with baskets, nets, honey, and other jungle products. The Badaga headman levies for him a fixed quantity of grain from each household in the village. Irulas and Uralis are thought to be sorcerers like the Kurumbas, if less effective ones, and are treated similarly. Some Chettis are itinerant traders who sell knickknacks on a fixed circuit of Badaga villages once a month, and have done so for several centuries. They also have minor ceremonial connections with the Badagas. Paniyans are agrestic serfs on the land of certain Badagas and Chettis who inhabit the Wainad Plateau directly west of the Nilgiris proper. In addition to the economic exchanges described above, the Badagas buy all kinds of goods in the district's town markets that were started by the British administrators around 1820.

Division of Labor. A rigid sexual division of labor is apparent. Men do the heavy field work of plowing, sowing, and threshing, while women do the lighter work of weeding and help at harvest. All dairy operations are conducted by men or boys. Women are responsible for preparing food. Children find much of their time taken up with school, although girls are also expected to help in the home.

Land Tenure.   According to legend, Badagas acquired their first land as gifts from the Kotas and Todas already settled in the area; as time passed they simply cleared new plots from the forests. Until 1862 such swidden cultivation was still common, but henceforward it was prohibited by state law. This regulation has not been a great hardship, however, because the richer and more valuable fields are the permanent ones close to each village. Irrigation is very rare but terracing is now widespread. House sites often have gardens attached. For more than a century each farmer has registered all of his land holdings with the local government and has paid an annual land tax proportional to the amount of land and the quality of the soil. Government also registers nonfarm land for such purposes as a village site, public grazing, cremation ground or cemetery, temple site, roadway, or government forest.

Kinship

Kin Groups and Descent.   Each village belongs to just one clan and commonly contains several lineages made up of numerous extended families. About a century ago a new Badaga Christian phratry emerged, which is now made up of numerous clans each following the usual rules of exogamy. A male always belongs to his father's extended family, lineage, clan, phratry, and village. This is also true of girls, but only up to a point: once they marry they usually move to a new village and are merged with the social units of their husbands. There are no family names, though lineages, clans, and phratries usually have names, and villages always do.

Kinship Terminology.   Badagas have a Dakota-type terminology. The cousin terminology is of the bifurcate-merging (Iroquois) type.

Marriage and Family

Marriage.   The favored marriage partner is a cross cousin, preferably a father's sister's daughter, or else a mother's brother's daughter. But other, more distant relatives are acceptable, provided clan exogamy is observed. Beyond this the Badagas have what are, for Hindus, some unusual regulations. Most remarkable perhaps is that hypogamy is as acceptable as hypergamy; marriages may occur between couples coming from certain clans of different status, yet in these cases it does not matter whether the groom is from the higher or the lower clan. Generation level is recognized as a distinguishing feature of men alone; women may change their generation levels if they marry successive husbands belonging to different generations. It is even theoretically possible for a man to marry a woman and her daughter and granddaughter simultaneously, provided he does not thereby marry his own offspring. All three wives would thus attain the generation level of their cohusband. Gerontogamy—old men taking young wives—is not at all uncommon. Although a dowry has become a requirement during the past few years, it is not a traditional part of the Badaga marriage arrangements. Instead a bride-wealth of up to 200 rupees was, and still is, paid by the groom's family. This sum does not purchase the girl but is payment for the ornaments she brings with her to the wedding, and hence it has increased over the years with the price

of gold. Every Badaga village belongs to one particular clan or another and hence is exogamous: at marriage a bride has to leave her natal village and move to her husband's. Polygyny is acceptable, though not nearly as common as monogamy. The newly married couple always takes up residence in the husband's natal village, either under his father's roof in a patrilocal extended family, or in a new house built nearby. It is very common for them to sleep in a small room built on the veranda of the father's house until the first child comes, when they make arrangements to get their own house. Although a young wife may repeatedly visit her own parents for short periods, especially to give birth, the married couple never live with them. Divorce and remarriage are easy for men, even for women, and are acceptable practices. Widows can remarry without adverse comment. Divorce is quite common, with the children and all property belonging to the husband.

Domestic Unit.   Both nuclear and extended families occur, but the small size of the houses places restrictions on large extended families. They usually split up once the patriarch of the family has died. A nuclear family may often include a mother or close collateral relative who is widowed. Although household servants are now rare, until about fifty years ago there were indentured children from poor Badaga homes working as domestic serfs.

Inheritance.   Property is impartible until the owner's death, and then the land can be divided equally between his male heirs, normally his sons. Although an agreement on the partition of the land may be written down and signed by the beneficiaries, there are still many disputes over the inheritance of land. The general principles of inheritance are: male heirs should divide the land and cattle equally among themselves, or, alternatively, they should maintain them as a joint property if they continue to be a joint household; females do not inherit anything; and the family's home goes to the youngest brother among the heirs. This latter practice of ultimogeniture allows the widowed mother of those heirs to be housed and cared for by a younger and hopefully vigorous son. If a wealthy man leaves other houses too, these are divided up among his other sons. In poorer families the house is somehow partitioned among the sons and their wives, but the youngest son is nonetheless the owner and has to be compensated by them for the space they use. Headmanship of a village or group of villages is hereditary, and it passes from one incumbent (before or after his death) to his brother and then to the eldest son of the deceased man. Some household articles or money may be given to a wife or daughters by a dying man, at his request.

Socialization.   Babies are breast-fed for a year, then weaned on solid food; in fact they begin eating boiled rice at 3 to 5 months. For about a century children have gone to local schools, from the age of 6. Younger children usually stay near home during the day, even though their parents may be out working in the fields. Grandparents and other elders stay in the village to mind and educate the small children. In later years the children help with housework and cultivation when needed and when school obligations permit. The main childhood ceremonies are naming (before the fortieth day), head shaving, ear boring, starting at school, nostril piercing, milking initiation (for boys at age 7 or 9), and girls' puberty rites. Tattooing (formerly done on girls) is no longer practiced.

Sociopolitical Organization

India is a constitutional and democratic republic, and the Badagas have been involved in electing representatives to the state legislature since 1924. But their own traditional sociopolitical organization also is still alive.

Social Organization. The community is divided into a number of phratries. It is not correct to call these units subcastes, for they are not altogether endogamous and they have no forms of occupational specialization. They are like subcastes, however, in that they form a hierarchy, with the conservative Lingayat group, the Wodeyas, at the top and the headmen's official servants, the Toreyas, at the bottom. Between these two extremes there are one phratry of vegetarians and three phratries of meat eaters. It is arguable that meat eaters and vegetarians constitute two moieties. The Christian Badagas, started by the first Protestant conversion in 1858, now constitute a separate meat-eating phratry ranked below the Toreyas but respected for their progressive habits. Each phratry is made up of several exogamous clans: two each in the case of Toreyas, Bedas, and Kumbaras, three in the case of Wodeyas, and more in the other cases.

Political Organization. Traditionally Badagas lived in a chiefdom, and they are still under a paramount chief. This is a hereditary position always held by the headman of Tuneri village. Below him are four regional headmen, each in charge of all Badaga and Kota villages within one quarter (*nadu*) of the Nilgiri Plateau. At the most local level a village has its own headman, and several neighboring villages (any number up to thirty-three) constitute a commune. Each commune takes its name from its leading village; its headman is also the commune headman.

Social Control. The Badaga council system still has some influence, although its judicial authority has been greatly undermined by modern courts of law and the Indian legal system. Each headman has his own council, made up in the case of communes by the constituent village headmen; the regional council is made up of the commune headmen; and the paramount chief's council, rarely called together, consists of all the headmen from all levels. The legal procedure requires that a dispute or crime be considered first by the hamlet council—with the headman's judgment being final—but a decision can be appealed up through the hierarchy of councils. Major land disputes and cases of murder formerly would be brought to the paramount chief after consideration by councils at a lower level. In early times the headmen could dictate severe punishments, including ostracism and hanging. Today the headmen are mainly involved in small disputes and in ceremonial duties, and the district magistrate's court handles more serious cases.

Conflict. Although intervillage feuding and factionalism are still common, and the massacring of supposed Kurumba sorcerers sometimes occurred in the last century, warfare as such was unknown between the Nilgiri peoples in pre-British days, although it often occurred on the adjacent plains of south India. Badagas have no offensive weapons, only the nets and spears that were once used in hunting. A few now own shotguns for the same purpose.

Religion and Expressive Culture

Religious Beliefs. Except for perhaps 2,500 Christians (Protestants and Roman Catholics in similar proportions, converts since 1858), all Badagas are Hindus of the Shaivite persuasion. A sizable minority are however of the Lingayat sect, which is almost confined to Karnataka State (formerly Mysore). This is a medieval sect, which adopted Shiva as its only deity and which still worships him through a phallic symbol, the *linga*. Among Badagas the sect is represented in the entire membership of several clans, namely Adikiri, Kanakka, Kongaru, and the three which make up the Wodeya phratry. The Hindu Badagas, including these Lingayat clans, worship quite a number of gods, all of which are sometimes explained as "aspects" of Shiva. These include Mahalinga and Mariamma (the smallpox goddess), together with many deities unknown outside the Badaga community, among them the ancestral Hiriodea and his consort, Hette.

Religious Practitioners. Most villages have two or three kinds of priest. In addition, the Lingayat clans have gurus to perform their special life-cycle rituals, and various Christian missionaries, priests, and nuns work in the villages too. Men of Woderu clan, one of the three clans of the high-ranking Wodeya phratry, function as village priests for all non-Lingayat villages. The position is hereditary and usually life-long. All Wodeyas are vegetarian and form an endogamous unit, thus maintaining the high standards of purity expected of priests. The Haruva clan, some of whom claim descent from Brahmans, are a non-Lingayat group who also supply some hereditary priests (even though it is widely felt that the claim to Brahman descent is unsubstantiated). In addition some villages have an accessory priest from a Kurumba tribe who, like the other two sorts of priest, helps in the performance of a few annual ceremonies. Haruva priests usually perform regular temple worship and also the life-cycle ceremonies for individual families. All priests are traditionally paid through a levy of grain or other produce from each house in the village they serve. There is no hierarchy of the priesthood, except that the Lingayat gurus, spiritual advisers who perform life-cycle rituals, do belong at the lowest level in a nationwide Lingayat hierarchy. Because menstruation is considered an impurity, women never serve as priests. Some however become possessed during ceremonies and speak for the gods. A few men exorcise ghosts, although this service is often performed for the afflicted by non-Badaga exorcists and charm makers (*mantravadis*).

Ceremonies. Each village celebrates about a dozen festivals during the year. The most important are Dodda Habba, "Great Festival," which begins the agricultural year in November, and Deva Habba, "God Festival," which celebrates the harvest in July. Mari Habba is intended to keep smallpox away for the year and is celebrated in a few villages by a firewalking ceremony in which the devotees walk unscathed across glowing charcoal with no protection for their feet. Life transitions are marked by ceremonies, including those mentioned above associated with child rearing, weddings, and funerals. On rare occasions each Badaga commune used to hold a huge memorial ceremony (*manevale*) in honor of a whole generation of the dead, once the last member of it had passed away. This ceremony was last performed in 1936.

Arts. While the verbal arts are highly developed in the forms of sung epic poetry, tales, proverbs, and riddles, no visual arts are practiced at all. Even embroidery for Badaga shawls is done by women of the Toda tribe.

Medicine. Over the centuries the Badagas have developed their own folk medicine: its practice is largely in the hands of women, and it depends heavily on mixtures of local herbs. Spells are relatively unimportant in curing, though crucial in ghost exorcism.

Death and Afterlife. The funeral is the most important of life-cycle ceremonies and the only one to be conducted by the village and its headman rather than by one's own family. Its ritual can last for a total of 11 days, culminating in the release of the soul from the village environment.

See also Kota; Kurumbas; Toda

Bibliography

Hockings, Paul Edward (1978). *A Bibliography for the Nilgiri Hills of Southern India.* 2 vols. New Haven, Conn.: Human Relations Area Files.

Hockings, Paul Edward (1980a). *Ancient Hindu Refugees: Badaga Social History, 1550–1975.* The Hague: Mouton Publishers; New Delhi: Vikas Publishing House.

Hockings, Paul Edward (1980b). *Sex and Disease in a Mountain Community.* New Delhi: Vikas Publishing House; Columbia, Mo.: South Asia Books.

Hockings, Paul Edward (1982). "Badaga Kinship Rules in Their Socio-Economic Context." *Anthropos* 77:851–874.

Hockings, Paul Edward (1987). "The Man Named Unige Mada (Nilgiri Hills, Tamilnadu)." In *Folktales of India*, edited by Brenda E. F. Beck, Peter J. Claus, Praphulladatta Goswami, and Jawarharlal Handoo, 125–129. Chicago: University of Chicago Press.

Hockings, Paul Edward (1988a). "The Badagas." In *Blue Mountains: The Ethnography and Biogeography of a South Indian Region*, edited by Paul Hockings, 206–231. New Delhi: Oxford University Press.

Hockings, Paul Edward (1988b). *Counsel from the Ancients: A Study of Badaga Proverbs, Prayers, Omens, and Curses.* Berlin: Mouton de Gruyter.

Jagor, Andreas Feodor (1876). "Die Badagas im Nilgiri-Gebirge." [Verhandlungen der Berliner Gesellschaft für Anthropologie, Ethnologie und Urgeschichte 1876.] Printed in *Zeitschrift für Ethnologie* 8:190–204.

Jagor, Andreas Feodor (1914). *Aus Fedor Jagor's Nachlass mit Unterstützung der Jagor-Stiftung herausgegeben von der Berliner Gesellschaft für Anthropologie, Ethnologie und Urgeschichte unter Leitung von Albert Grünwedel. Südindische Volksstämme.* Vol. 1. Berlin: Dietrich Reimer.

Thurston, Edgar, and Kadamki Rangachari (1909). "Badagas." In *Castes and Tribes of Southern India*, edited by Edgar Thurston and Kadamki Rangachari. Vol. 1, 63–124. Madras: Government Press.

PAUL HOCKINGS

Baiga

ETHNONYMS: Bhuiya, Bhumia, Bhumiaraja, Bhumij, Bhumija, Bhumijan

Orientation

Identification. The Baiga (who call themselves Bhumiaraja or Bhumijan) are a Munda or Kolarian people (part of the Bhuiya tribe) located in the central highlands of India. The name "Baiga" means "sorcerer, medicine man" and is applied in this sense to the priests of the Chota Nagpur tribe. The Bhuiyar of Mirzarpur are also called Baiga, as are any individuals who serve in the capacity of village priest in this immediate region (cf. the usage of the Pardhan, Ghasiya, Kharwar, and Gond). The Kol and Gond consider the Baiga as priests having knowledge of the secrets of the region's soil. They also recognize the Baiga as a more ancient people than themselves and respect their decisions in boundary disputes. It is believed that the Baiga migrated from Chhattisgarh into the Satpura Hills on the western borders of the plains, and were among the earliest residents of the Chhattisgarh Plains and the northern and eastern hill country.

Location. The locus of Baiga culture is an area formerly part of the Central Provinces of India and now part of Madhya Pradesh. It extends from about 22° to 24° N and 80° to 82° E.

Demography. In 1971 there were 178,833 Baiga.

Linguistic Affiliation. The Baiga have lost all trace of their native Austroasiatic language and have assimilated the speech of their neighbors. Verrier Elwin (1939) reported that in Bilaspur they adopted Chhattisgarhi, in Mandla and Jubbulpore they spoke a modified Eastern Hindi, in Balaghat they spoke Marathi, Hindi, Gondi (or a combination of Marathi, Hindi, and Gondi), and Baigani (a language of Indo-Aryan Stock belonging to the Indo-European Phylum).

History and Cultural Relations

Baiga contact with other peoples and knowledge of regions beyond their own has been minimal. Many have never heard of major urban areas adjacent to their immediate environs, such as Nagpur, Delhi, and Bombay. Relations with the British during colonial rule were favorable overall; the only substantial point of contention between the two parties was limitations placed on *bewar* (shifting agriculture) by the British. As India sought independence from British rule, mythological traditions about Mahatma Gandhi began to emerge, superhuman status being ascribed to him by the Baiga. Nevertheless, Gandhi's attitude toward alcohol prohibition did result in some negative Baiga sentiment. Christian missionary efforts have met with little success among the Baiga. Elwin observed that traditional village life had begun to decay (because of prohibitions against bewar and hunting, the effects of the Hindu caste system, and the pressures imposed by forced modernization) and that the Baiga no longer produced those items necessary for daily survival.

Settlements

The Baiga build villages either in the form of a large square or with houses aligned on the sides of a broad street (approximately 10 meters in width). Villages are located in areas convenient for cultivation with consideration also being given to the aesthetic value and degree of isolation of the intended site. Village locations vary (jungles, high hills, and valleys), but, whenever possible, a location atop a steep hill (with limited access by footpath) is preferred. The village boundary (_mero_) is marked by a large expanse of land (approximately 30 meters wide) and is delimited by intermittently placed piles of stones. The boundary is reinforced by a magic wall intended to protect against wild animals and disease. The village burial place (_marghat_) is located within this boundary. The fourth side of the village (which is open) is protected by either a bamboo or cactus hedge. Individual residence units within the village are detached structures connected by narrow roads. Surrounding the village one finds _bari_ (land set aside for the cultivation of tobacco, maize, and sweet potatoes). Pig houses (_guda_) are attached to each house within the village square. Cattle sheds (_sar_) are similar in structure to and barely distinguishable from human habitations. Platforms (_macha_) for drying and storing maize are found in the center or at the side of the village square. Granaries, corporate houses, temples, and shrines are absent from Baiga villages. A small compound (_chatti_) for use by travelers and officials is located outside the village square. Often these squares are dominated by a single family and its relatives; members of other families build their houses in small groups at some distance from the main area of habitation. A typical Baiga house is rectangular in shape. It usually has a small veranda and a single entrance. The interior is divided into two parts by grain bins or a bamboo wall. The first room contains stands for water pots and a fire kept burning for warmth. The inner room has a hearth for cooking, behind which is a place for the gods (_deosthan_). Access to the inner room by outsiders is prohibited. The veranda of the house contains the rice husker, pestle, and grindstone.

Economy

Subsistence and Commercial Activities. The Baiga raise pigs (which are held in particularly high esteem), poultry, goats, and cattle (cows, bullocks, and buffalo). Dogs and cats are kept. The Baiga also grow several kinds of tobacco for personal use and import an alcoholic beverage manufactured from the corolla of the _mahua_ tree (_Bassia latifolia_). _Ganja_ is used frequently but opium use is rare. Rice, various kinds of grain (_kodon_, _kutki_, and _siker_), sweet potatoes, cucumbers, _dal_ (lentils), maize, roots, leaves, herbs, and young bamboo shoots are among the items grown or gathered for consumption. _Pej_ (the broth in which rice or grain has been boiled) is a staple. The following fruit trees are among those grown by the Baiga: mountain black plum, mango, forest mango, white

teak, coromandel ebony, wild fig, banyan, Indian quince, and sebasten plum. Leaves of the butter tree, which are ground to produce chutney, are also gathered. Fish is consumed, and all meats are considered to be acceptable for consumption. The following animals are hunted: sambar deer, blackbuck, barking deer, hares, mongooses, peacock, and various wildfowl. The Baiga also hunt rats (seventeen varieties of which have been noted) and gather eggs. Bewar is practiced. An area of forest is selected, its trees cut (leaving stumps about a foot high) and allowed to dry, then burned. Seed is sowed after the first rain. Land cultivated in this manner is worked for an average of three years. In addition to hunting, fishing, animal domestication, and agriculture, the Baiga derive income from the manufacture of bamboo products, from the cultivation and sale of honey, and by hiring themselves out as laborers.

Industrial Arts. The Baiga do not spin fibers or weave cloth. Clothing is purchased in local markets. Few implements are manufactured by Baiga artisans. Iron implements such as the axe (_tangia_), sickle (_hassia_), arrowheads, digging tools (_kudari_ and _sabar_), wood plane (_basula_), drilling tool (_bindhna_), and a grass-clearing tool (_raphi_) are purchased from the Agaria, the Lohar, or other neighboring peoples. Many kinds of bamboo and leaf baskets are manufactured by the Baiga for personal use. Wooden beds are also produced locally.

Trade. The Baiga rely on trade to secure iron implements, salt, blankets, alcoholic beverages, and articles of clothing from neighboring peoples. Trade activity seems limited to these items. Otherwise, the Baiga are in large part self-reliant.

Division of Labor. There exists no clear division of labor based on gender. Women may engage in almost all of the activities undertaken by men. Men and women share the responsibility for cooking (the husband assuming full responsibility when the wife is menstruating), gathering water, fishing, and woodcutting. Only men are allowed to hunt, and women are not permitted to make _khumris_ (wicker hoods lined with _mohlain_ leaves, used when it rains) or thatch roofing for houses. Women may participate in cultivation by clearing and lighting the field debris. Women may not, however, touch plows. Women are also prohibited from killing pigs, goats, and chickens.

Land Tenure. The garden lands immediately surrounding the village and the fields used for bewar appear to be considered as the property of the individual members of particular households.

Kinship

Kin Groups and Descent. The Baiga are strictly endogamous, though Baiga men who take non-Baiga wives may have their spouses admitted to the tribe by the performance of certain rites. The tribe is divided into several relatively endogamous _jat_. Each of these jat occupies a separate territory and there is considerable intergroup rivalry over the issue of superiority. The various jat include the Binjhwar (also Binchwar), Mondya, Bheronnthya, Muria Baiga, Narotia, Bharotia, Nahar, Raibhaina, Kathbhaina, Kondwan (or Kundi), Gondwaina, Bhumia, Kurka Baiga, Sawat Baiga, and Dudhbhaina. These jat are also subdivided into exogamous _garh_ and _goti_, the former being of greater importance than the latter. The garh is a unit based on residence. It is believed that originally every Baiga man was attached to a specific jungle or hill and was required to secure mates for his daughters from other jungles or hills, thereby preventing incest. These garh are not totemic. Elwin suggests that the Baiga kinship system emphasizes classification over other concerns. Descent is patrilineal.

Kinship Terminology. Iroquois kinship terminology is employed for first cousins.

Marriage and Family

Marriage. Premarital relations between men and women are common and socially sanctioned. Formal engagement takes place at any age, though frequently after puberty. The engagement process in initiated by the male. The consent of his desired spouse and her parents (along with payment of the bride-price) are required before the betrothal may take place. The chief actors in the ceremony are the *dosi* (two old men who are related to the bride and groom and perform the greater part of the religious ceremonies) and the *suasin* (young unmarried sisters or cousins of the bride and groom). The ceremony takes place over several days and includes feasting, the taking of omens, the anointing and bathing of the bridal pair, a number of ceremonial processions, the construction of a booth (*marua*), the tying of the bridal pair's clothes in a ceremonial knot, and the giving of gifts (by the bridegroom's father to the bride's paternal grandmother, her mother, her brother, the dosi, and the suasin). The couple spend their first night together in the jungle and perform the *beni chodna* ceremony, part of which includes the ceremonial bathing of one another. The ceremony described above may be performed only once in life. A less elaborate ceremony (having no social stigma attached to it) called the *haldi-pani* or *churi-pairana* marriage may be performed more than once. The latter ceremony is roughly equivalent to marriage in a registry office. It may precede the more elaborate form described above. Its use depends on the preference of the parties involved. Divorce is allowed and polygamy is practiced to a somewhat limited extent. Postmarital residence is patrilocal. Baiga norms also permit the marriage of a grandparent to a grandchild.

Domestic Unit. The size and composition of the typical domestic unit vary. There is evidence of nuclear and extended family structure (e.g., father, mother, elder son, elder son's wife, younger son, and younger son's wife, forming a residential unit).

Inheritance. The practice of shifting cultivation and the nomadic tradition of the Baiga have contributed to a rather ambiguous stance toward property and inheritance. The corpus of Baiga possessions includes axes, cooking utensils, various ornaments, and cash. The home and all of its contents belong to the male head of the family. After marriage, everything that a wife earns belongs to her husband. If she runs away from or divorces her husband, she forfeits claim to anything that her present husband has given her. However, whatever possessions she has brought with her into the union from her parents' home remain with her. A widow is able, in some instances, to retain a portion of her deceased husband's property. Such property would remain in the widow's possession should she choose to remarry. The earnings of sons and daughters also belong to their father. Should a father approve of his son's choice of a mate, then he may elect to give a certain amount of his personal property (e.g., cooking utensils, axes, and cloth) to his son if the son has elected to establish a separate household. Otherwise, the earnings of the son and those of his wife belong to the son's father. The male head of household is empowered, during his lifetime, to apportion all property according to his discretion. When a man dies, his property is inherited by his son or sons. Provision is made for stepsons to receive a smaller portion. A son who remains with his father and maintains him until the time of the father's death will receive a slightly larger portion of the father's property. Widows are generally maintained on the estates of their deceased husbands until such time as they are remarried, and each widow is entitled to a share in her husband's estate equal to a son's share. Frequently daughters also receive a small portion of a deceased father's property. If a man is survived only by nephews and grandsons, his property is equally divided among them. Should he be survived only by an adopted son, then that adopted son receives all of the adoptive father's property.

Socialization. Child rearing is shared equally by both parents. A child is suckled by the mother for three years, then weaned. From that point on, children are allowed a great deal of freedom, sexual and otherwise. As there are no children's dormitories, children are allowed to explore and experiment freely within their households and within the larger society.

Sociopolitical Organization

Social Organization. As has already been noted above, the Baiga are divided into several endogamous jat, which are themselves subdivided into exogamous garh and goti. Social relationships between the different jat are governed by a series of detailed and rather complicated regulations. Few, if any, caste prejudices are held by the Baiga, though some have been known to avoid untouchables and those who consume beef (out of fear of offending their Hindu neighbors).

Political Organization. Baiga villages appear to be governed autonomously, with leadership being exercised by the village headman (*mukkadam*). Other village officials include the landlord (*malguzar*) and watchman (*katwar*). Legal disputes and tribal offenses are handled by the *panch*, a group composed of key village members who convene with a quorum of five.

Social Control. Traditional Baiga jurisprudence governs tribal life to a greater extent than regulations established by national authorities. This jurisprudence is concerned chiefly with the maintenance of tribal integrity and prestige. Control is maintained by tribal excommunication, fines, and imprisonment. These matters are decided by both informal procedures (i.e., by nonstructured consultation of various community members) and formal procedures (i.e., by the village panch). Tribal consensus, obtained by both formal and informal structures, regulates social behavior.

Conflict. Christian missionaries and Hindu culture have had minimal direct influence on the Baiga. Material culture, however, has been affected by Hindu influence. The Baiga are almost completely dependent on neighboring peoples for the manufacture of the goods that they consume, and their relations with these peoples (as well as with the British and Indian governments) have not been characterized by long-standing conflict. The only major issue of contention has been that of Baiga agricultural practice.

Religion and Expressive Culture

Religious Beliefs.   The Baiga worship a plethora of deities. Their pantheon is fluid, the goal of Baiga theological education being to master knowledge of an ever-increasing number of deities. Supernaturals are divided into two categories: gods (_deo_), who are considered to be benevolent, and spirits (_bhut_), who are believed to be hostile. Some Hindu deities have been incorporated into the Baiga pantheon because of a sacerdotal role that the Baiga exercise on behalf of the Hindus. Some of the more important members of the Baiga pantheon include: Bhagavan (the creator-god who is benevolent and harmless); Bara Deo/Budha Deo (once chief deity of the pantheon, who has been reduced to the status of household god because of limitations placed on the practice of bewar); Thakur Deo (lord and headman of the village); Dharti Mata (mother earth); Bhimsen (rain giver); and Gansam Deo (protector against wild animal attacks). The Baiga also honor several household gods, the most important of which are the Aji-Dadi (ancestors) who live behind the family hearth. Magical-religious means are used to control both animals and weather conditions, to ensure fertility, to cure disease, and to guarantee personal protection.

Religious Practitioners.   Major religious practitioners include the _dewar_ and the _gunia_, the former of a higher status than the latter. The dewar is held in great esteem and is responsible for the performance of agricultural rites, closing village boundaries, and stopping earthquakes. The gunia deals largely with the magical-religious cure of diseases. The _panda_, a practitioner from the Baiga past, is no longer of great prominence. Finally, the _jan pande_ (clairvoyant), whose access to the supernatural comes by means of visions and dreams, is also important.

Ceremonies.   The Baiga calendar is largely agricultural in nature. The Baiga also observe festivals at the times of Holi, Diwali, and Dassara. Dassara is the occasion during which the Baiga hold their Bida observance, a sort of sanitizing ceremony in which the men dispose of any spirits that have been troubling them during the past year. Hindu rites do not, however, accompany these observances. The Baiga simply hold festivals during these times. The Cherta or Kichrahi festival (a children's feast) is observed in January, the Phag festival (at which women are allowed to beat men) is held in March, the Bidri ceremony (for the blessing and protection of crops) takes place in June, the Hareli festival (to ensure good crops) is scheduled for August, and the Pola festival (roughly equivalent to the Hareli) is held in October. The Nawa feast (thanksgiving for harvest) follows the end of the rainy season. Dassara falls in October with Diwali coming shortly thereafter.

Arts.   The Baiga produce few implements. Thus there is little to describe in the area of the visual arts. Their basketry may be so considered, as may their decorative door carving (though this is rare), tattooing (chiefly of the female body), and masking. Frequent tattoo designs include triangles, baskets, peacocks, turmeric root, flies, men, magic chains, fish bones, and other items of importance in Baiga life. Men sometimes have the moon tattooed on the back of a hand and a scorpion tattooed on a forearm. Baiga oral literature includes numerous songs, proverbs, myths, and folktales. Dancing is also an important part of their personal and corporate lives; it is incorporated into all festal observances. Important dances include the Karma (the major dance from which all others are derived), the Tapadi (for women only), Jharpat, Bilma, and Dassara (for men only).

Medicine.   For the Baiga, most illness is traceable to the activity of one or more malevolent supernatural forces or to witchcraft. Little is known of the natural causes of disease, though the Baiga have developed a theory about venereal diseases (all of which they place within a single classification). The most frequent cure cited for the cure of sexually transmitted diseases is sexual intercourse with a virgin. Any member of the Baiga pantheon may be held responsible for sending sickness, as may the _mata_, "mothers of disease," who attack animals and humans. The gunia is charged with the responsibility of diagnosing disease and with the performance of those magical-religious ceremonies required to alleviate sickness.

Death and Afterlife.   After death, the human being is believed to break down into three spiritual forces. The first (_jiv_) returns to Bhagavan (who lives on earth to the east of the Maikal Hills). The second (_chhaya_, "shade") is brought to the deceased individual's home to reside behind the family hearth. The third (_bhut_, "ghost") is believed to be the evil part of an individual. Since it is hostile to humanity, it is left in the burial place. The dead are believed to live in the same socioeconomic status in the afterlife that they enjoyed while alive on earth. They occupy houses similar to those inhabited by them during their actual lifetimes, and they eat all of the food that they gave away when they were alive. Once this supply is exhausted, they are reincarnated. Witches and wicked persons do not enjoy such a happy fate. However, no counterpart to the eternal punishment of the wicked found in Christianity obtains among the Baiga.

See also Agaria; Bhuiya

Bibliography

Chattopadhyaya, Kamaladevi (1978). _Tribalism in India._ New Delhi: Vikas Publishing House.

Das, Tarakchandra (1931). _The Bhumijas of Seraikella._ Calcutta: University of Calcutta.

Elwin, Verrier (1939). _The Baiga._ London: John Murray.

Elwin, Verrier (1968). _The Kingdom of the Young._ London: Oxford University Press.

Fuchs, Stephen (1960). _The Gond and Bhumia of Eastern Mandla._ Bombay: Asia Publishing House.

Misra, P. K. (1977). "Patterns of Inter-Tribal Relations." In _Tribal Heritage of India._ Vol. 1, _Ethnicity, Identity, and Interaction,_ edited by S. C. Dube, 85–117. New Delhi: Vikas Publishing House.

Roy, Sarat Chandra (1935). _The Hill Bhuiyas of Orissa—with_

Comparative Notes on the Plains Bhuiyas. Ranchi: Man in India Office.

Russell, R. V., and Hira Lal (1916). "Baiga." *The Tribes and Castes of the Central Provinces of India.* Vol. 2, 77–92. London: Oxford University Press. Reprint. 1969. Oosterhout: Anthropological Publications.

HUGH R. PAGE, JR.

Baluchi

ETHNONYMS: Baloch, Baluch

Orientation

Identification.   The Baluchi are predominantly Sunni Muslim, seminomadic pastoralists, whose homelands straddle the Iran-Pakistan border as well as including a small portion of southern Afghanistan.

Location.   Baluchistan is the name of the westernmost province of Pakistan, as well as of the transnational territory of the traditional Baluchi homeland. This larger region was carved up by the imperial powers concerned more with ease of administration than with recognition of the territorial limits of the inhabitants. The traditional Baluchi territory extends from the southeastern portion of the Iranian Plateau across the Kirman Desert to the western borders of Sind and the Punjab, and from the Gumal River in the northeast to the Arabian Sea in the south. This is a largely inhospitable land, much of it barren desert or harsh mountainous terrain. Baluchi territory lies outside the monsoon belt, and annual rainfall is very low, not exceeding 16 centimeters. Throughout the region, winters are harsh and cold, and summers are very hot. In the mountains, the rains come in October and March, while in the lowlands they come in July and August.

Demography.   Population figures for the Baluchi are somewhat suspect, in part because of the unreliability of census-taking procedures across the three major political units that now control Baluchi territory, and partly because the criteria for ascribing Baluchi identity are not tightly defined. On the strength of linguistic criteria, there are an estimated 5 million or so Baluchi speakers living in eastern Iran, southern Afghanistan, and in Pakistan. However, Baluchi have in some areas become linguistically assimilated to neighboring peoples while retaining a specifically Baluchi cultural identity; this means that if sociocultural rather than purely linguistic criteria were used, the population count could easily exceed 9 million. Many Baluchi have migrated to Pakistan's Sind and Punjab provinces, and to the emirates of the Persian Gulf.

Linguistic Affiliation.   The Baluchi language is a member of the Indo-Iranic Language Family, having some affinity with Kurdish. There are three distinct divisions: Eastern, Western, and Southern Baluchi. Until the nineteenth century the language had no written form, because Persian was the language of official use. Illiteracy is extremely high among the Baluchi.

History and Cultural Relations

Legend has it that the Baluchi people are directly descended from Amir Hamza, one of Mohammed's uncles, and migrated into the transnational region of Baluchistan from somewhere in the vicinity of Aleppo, in Syria. The migrations that brought them to their current territory began as long ago as the fifth century and were more or less complete by the end of the seventh. Prior to the twelfth century, theirs was a society of independent, more or less autonomous seminomadic groups, organized along principles of clan affiliation rather than territorial association. As the population of the region increased, access to land assumed greater and greater importance, giving rise to a system of tribes, each with a territorial base. The first successful attempt to unite several Baluchi tribal units was accomplished by Mir Jalal Han, who set up the First Baluchi Confederacy in the twelfth century, but this unity did not long survive his rule. Warfare between various Baluchi tribes and tribal confederacies was frequent during the fifteenth century, largely owing to economic causes. By the sixteenth century the Baluchis were roughly divided up into three separate political entities: the Makran State, the Dodai Confederacy, and the khanate of Baluchistan (the Kalat Confederacy). In the eighteenth century, Mir Abdullah Khan of the Kalat Confederacy succeeded in reuniting all of Baluchistan, providing a centralized government based on *Rawaj,* the customary law of the Baluchi people. The arrival of the British in the region had profound effects on the future trajectory of Baluchi development. Uninterested in the region economically, the British were solely concerned with establishing a buffer zone that could forestall the encroachment of the Russians upon the rich prize of India. To further this end, the British relied on the manipulation of Baluchi tribal leaders, cash handouts, and the establishment of garrisons, but they paid no attention to the economic development of the region itself.

Settlements

The Baluchi have two types of settlements, consistent with their seminomadic way of life. Village settlements are clusters of mud houses, loosely oriented around the house of the local chief. These permanent settlements are found in the mountains and valleys, and they are occupied chiefly in the summer. In winter the people migrate to the plains and the coastal areas, seeking pasturage for the livestock that are central to the traditional Baluchi economy. During this time, the Baluchi live in tents, moving freely across the landscape as conditions favor the care of their herds, and settlements are smaller, consisting of closely related kin.

Economy

Subsistence and Commercial Activities.   The traditional Baluchi economy is based on a combination of subsistence farming and seminomadic pastoralism (cattle, sheep, and goats). Because of the harshness of the environment, agriculture is somewhat limited, but it nonetheless constitutes a significant part of the economy. The principal crop is wheat.

Wild fruits and vegetables also form a part of the household economy, and chickens may be raised as well. When the local economy cannot provide adequate opportunities, young men may migrate out in search of paid labor.

Industrial Arts. The Baluchi are a self-sufficient lot, as a whole, and they rely on their own skills to construct their houses and many of the tools necessary in their day-to-day life. Rugs are woven for household use and as items of trade also.

Division of Labor. The entire household participates in the work of tending the family's herd, but in other aspects of the economy there is a division of labor by sex: women work in groups to thresh and winnow the grain harvest, while plowing and planting are men's work. The gathering of wild foods, water, and firewood is done by groups of women.

Land Tenure. By tradition, land is not privately owned but rather is vested in the subsection of the tribe to which one belongs. It therefore is inalienable by the individual. However, during the British period, tribal leaders often managed to have title to some property conveyed in their own names.

Kinship

Baluchi kinship is patrilineal, tracing descent through one of several lineages, ultimately back to the putative apical ancestor, Amir Hamza. Clan membership is based on familial ties, while tribal membership has a more specifically territorial referent. For both males and females, one remains a member of one's patrilineal group for life—even after marriage, for example, a woman's "real" home is that of her father, and her position in her husband's house brings to her only very limited rights.

Marriage and Family

Baluchi marriages are arranged between the bride's father and the prospective groom upon the payment of a bride-price consisting of livestock and cash. On marriage, a woman passes from the control of her father to that of her husband. Marriage is monogamous and is expected to be for life. Adultery was traditionally punishable by the death of both parties involved. Marriage to a non-Baluchi is rigidly proscribed. Postmarital residence is patrilocal.

Inheritance. All heritable property passes from father to sons.

Socialization. Baluchmayar, or "the Baluchi Way," is the guiding principle of proper conduct for the Baluchi people. It is a sort of honor code, entailing the extension of hospitality, mercy, refuge, and honesty to one's fellows, and it is reaffirmed in the oral traditions of Baluchi song and poetry. Children learn proper behavior through observing their elders and through being subject to taunt and gossip should they behave badly.

Sociopolitical Organization

Baluch society is organized both into kin-based clans and territorially defined tribes. One could claim a rough correspondence between the clan and the social hierarchy as distinct from the tribe and the more specifically political sphere, but this correspondence is not absolute. The Baluchi people are an amalgam of many large units, or chieftaincies, each one of which is itself composed of a nested set of smaller organizational units. From largest to smallest, these constituent units can best be understood as clans, clan sections, and subsections—with smaller segments of this last division being the level that most closely corresponds to actual settlement units. At each level of this hierarchy, leadership is in the hands of a male elder. At the least comprehensive level, such leadership is as likely to be achieved as inherited, but over time authority at the more inclusive levels has devolved to the elders of what have become hereditary "chiefly clans" (_Sardarkel_). By the fifteenth century, the Sardarkel formed the organizational foci of a loosely understood feudal system, which had developed into a set of semiautonomous sovereign principalities by the eighteenth century. During the imperial period, the Sardarkel served as mediators between British and local interests, losing a great deal of their original autonomy in the process. However, as a result of their participation in securing the interests of the ruling power, much land and wealth accrued to these groups, establishing a new and more purely economic basis for their leadership role, as well as allowing them to develop something of a monopoly over access to the larger political systems within which the Baluchi people now found themselves. As a "stateless" people, the Baluchi political presence is today somewhat attenuated. In the 1970s and 1980s, a number of groups sprang up in the name of Baluchi nationalism, but their activities have been largely of a guerrilla nature and, as yet, they have been unable to secure international support for their cause.

Social Control. Although Muslim, the Baluchi do not invoke _Sharia_ (Islamic law) to deal with social transgressions. Rather, secular authority is vested in the traditional tribal leaders (_Sardars_) and conducted according to Rawaj, which is based on the principles of Baluchmayar. The ultimate traditional sanction was provided by the mechanism of the blood feud, invoked by the clan to avenge the wrongful death of one of its members. Capital punishment was also traditionally applied in cases of adultery or the theft of clan property. Refusal to comply with the socially prescribed norms of hospitality is punishable by fines imposed by the local elders. Pardon for many social infractions can be obtained by the intercession of female representatives of the offender's family. In the case of all offenses except that of adultery, the offender may seek refuge in the household of a nonrelated clan, which obligates the household providing sanctuary to fight to the death to defend the refugee. Petitions for such sanctuary must be granted, according to the code of Baluchmayar. Formal public taunting, in verse as well as in direct speech, provides a further mechanism by which compliance with the Baluchi code of behavior is enforced.

Conflict. The warrior tradition of the Baluchi extends back throughout their history, reaching its fullest flowering in the eleventh to fourteenth centuries, at a time coincident with their need to establish a settlement base from which to conduct their seminomadic way of life. During the imperial period the British imposed a policy of pacification upon the region and enforced it by maintaining a substantial garrison presence. The Baluchi reputation for producing fierce warriors is today recalled primarily in the activities of the "free fighters" of the Baluchi nationalist movement.

Religion and Expressive Culture

Religious Beliefs. The Baluchi today are Sunni Muslims but, according to many of the traditional ballads of the Baluchi, they have in the past claimed to be followers of Caliph Ali and thus were once Shia Muslims. Prior to the coming of Islam, the Baluchi were probably followers of Zoroaster, and traces of earlier, non-Islamic beliefs are still retained in current religious observance. In any case, and unlike the situation found in much of the Muslim world, religious belief and practice are considered to be a private affair—there is no Baluchi concept of a "religious state." Secular authority is quite distinct from the spiritual authority vested in religious leaders. It appears that their religious orientation (Sunni versus Shia) has something of a political component to it: when Iran was aligned with the Sunni sect of Islam, the Baluchi professed for Shia; whereas, when Iran embraced Shia, the Baluchi promptly realigned themselves as Sunni.

Religious Practitioners. Religious instruction and observance are led by the local mullah.

Arts. Although the Baluchi are largely an illiterate people and their language was until quite recently unwritten, they have a long tradition of poetic composition, and poets and professional minstrels have been held in high esteem. Their oral literature consists of epic poetry, ballads of war and romance, religious compositions, and folktales. Much composition is given over to genealogical recitals as well. This poetic creativity traditionally had a practical as well as aesthetic aspect—professional minstrels long held the responsibility of carrying information from one to another of the scattered Baluchi settlements, and during the time of the First Baluchi Confederacy these traveling singers provided an important means by which the individual leaders of each tribe within the confederacy could be linked to the central leadership. The earliest securely dated Baluchi poem still known today dates to the late twelfth century, although the tradition of such compositions is no doubt of much greater antiquity.

Bibliography

Baloch, Inayatullah (1987). *The Problem of Greater Baluchistan: A Study of Baluch Nationalism.* Stuttgart: Steiner Verlag Wiesbaden.

Pastner, Stephen L. (1978). "Baluch Fishermen in Pakistan." *Asian Affairs* 9:161–167.

Pehrson, Robert N. (1966). *The Social Organization of the Marri Baluch.* Viking Fund Publications in Anthropology, edited by Fredrik Barth, no. 43. New York: Wenner-Gren Foundation for Anthropological Research.

Salzman, Philip C. (1971). "Movement and Resource Extraction among Pastoral Nomads: The Case of the Shah Nawazi Baluch." *Anthropology Quarterly* 44:185–197.

Wirsing, Robert (1981). *The Baluchis and Pathans.* London: Minority Rights Group.

NANCY E. GRATTON

Bania

ETHNONYMS: Agarwal, Agarwala, Agarwal Marwadi, Aggarwal, Agrawal, Bani, Banik, Banikar, Baniya, Banjig, Barnik, Mahajan, Marwadi Bania, Marwari, Oswal, Sahukar, Sarnabanik, Seth, Sonarbania, Sowcar, Subarnabanik, Vani, Vania

Orientation

"Bania" is a functional term applied to bankers, moneylenders, and dealers in grain, ghee, groceries, and spices. The name *vania* (or *bania*) is derived from the Sanskrit word *vanij*, "a merchant." An interesting aspect of this group is that some of them are Hindus by religion while a substantial number are Jains.

Bania are found all over India, in towns and villages, with large concentrations in Maharashtra, Gujarat, Rajasthan, West Bengal, and Madhya Pradesh. An extremely large group, Banias are distinguished by their well-defined traditional occupation and a distinctive social status. More Banias adhere to their traditional occupation in modern India than any other caste or group. They are considered to be Vaisyas, the third great division of the Aryan twice-born groups. They wear the sacred thread and are strict observers of the taboo against eating meat. They are divided into several endogamous subcastes. The important ones, like the Oswals and Agarwals, are of Rajput or Kshatriya stock and come from Rajputana, Bundelkhand, or Gujarat. Others migrated centuries ago to different parts of the country, where they have become endogamous and have taken on a new local name. Because of their need to keep accounts, Banias have long been a literate group, and they are credited with special mental and moral characteristics by other castes. Like all mercantile classes, they display energy, shrewdness, and intelligence. Consequently they have been employed by Rajput princes as counselors and high officers of the state. From early childhood Bania boys are trained to keep accounts and are taught to view profit as the only creditable outcome of any transaction. To this end, they receive training in mental arithmetic, including fractional tables, interest tables, and other complex calculations. For petty accounts Banias traditionally used the *rekha* system, which is based on fourths, tied to the old currency in which 12 paise = 1 anna and 16 annas = 1 rupee. They are capitalists par excellence, and even at the beginning of their trading careers they are able to turn over their inventory at a very high rate by dint of hard work. Their career is reflected in such proverbs as, "He comes with a *lota* (water pot) and goes back with a *lakh* (100,000)," and "If a Bania gets a rupee, he will have an income of 8 rupees a month."

Economy

The Banias' relationship with members of other castes is tinged with envy. As moneylenders they provide an essential function, especially for cultivators; but they are seen as ruthless usurers. The cultivators, usually illiterate, rarely get fair treatment from the Banias. They do not understand figures or the result of paying compound interest at 25 or 50 percent. They must have money at planting time and to live on while their crops are growing. The result is that frequently the land, if salable, passes to the Bania, and the borrower declines from landowner to tenant or tenant to day laborer. There are many proverbs, in most Indian languages, warning against the Banias and their cunning. Nevertheless without them the traditional farming economy would be impossible. The Banias are willing to lend on security that is unacceptable to banks, and frequently on none at all. They are willing to wait indefinitely for the repayment of principal, especially if the interest is paid. This means that debts can be postponed in a bad year and repayment accelerated in a good one.

The introduction of cash as the basis of all transactions and the changes in the laws governing the proprietary and transferable rights in land have added tremendously to the Banias' prosperity and to their clients' perception of their rapacity. But in their defense it must be said that although the interest they charge is exorbitant by modern banking standards, it is merely a carryover from earlier peasant agrarian conditions when the entire transaction was made in grain. A 25–50 percent rate of return in grain does not yield more than a reasonable profit to the lender. But when in recent times cash has been substituted for grain, interest may far outstrip any income that the investment has generated for the borrower. Furthermore, whereas in earlier times a loan of seed was essentially for planting, most of the loans today are consumer loans taken for expenses like dowries and marriage expenses.

Like any commercial class, the Banias had to have a high standard of probity. It was not unusual for people to place their money in a rich Bania's hands for safekeeping. Bankruptcy was considered disgraceful and punished. The duty of paying ancestral debts is taken seriously, since Banias believe that their condition in the next life depends on the discharge of all claims in this one. The Banias are well known for keeping caste funds to which all of them contribute to enable any impoverished member to start afresh. Today the Marwaris are extremely generous in their subscriptions for the maintenance of educational institutions and temples.

Marriage

The marriage rules vary among the local groups; but on the whole the subcastes are endogamous, and they in turn are divided into exogamous units that are sometimes called *gotras*. Widow remarriage and divorce are not allowed. Although it is not customary to pay dowry or bride-price, a marriage requires the youth's father to make ritual prestations to the girl. Bania weddings involve great expense, and feasting may last eight days.

Religion

All Banias are Jains or Vaishnava Hindus, and both follow the life-cycle rituals prescribed by Hinduism. One of the gods they specifically worship is Ganapati, the lord of wealth and prosperity. They also revere all life and are loath to kill any animal. Their diet reflects this strict taboo, and most of them abstain from all kinds of meat and alcoholic drink. Many of them, especially the Jains among them, will also eschew onions, garlic, and other tubers, since this involves taking the life of a plant. Most of the animal asylums in India (*panjarapol*) are supported by donations from Jain Banias. Gauri, the mother of Ganapati (or Ganesh), is worshiped by a bridal couple. In Rajasthan Gauri is worshiped as the corn goddess about the time of the vernal equinox, especially by women.

At Divali, in addition to Ganapati, the Banias worship Lakshmi, the goddess of wealth. She is considered to be the deified cow, and as such is the other main source of wealth both as the mother of the bull, which is the tiller of the soil, and the giver of milk from which ghee is made. Divali is also the beginning of the accounting year, and a ceremony venerating the new account books and invoking Lakshmi is conducted. The other important festival is Holi, when Marwaris make an image out of mud of Nathu Ram, who was supposed to be a great Marwari. The image is mocked and beaten with shoes; after two or three days it is broken up and thrown away. Mock contests between men and women and the throwing of colored powder are universal features of Holi. Banias both Jain and Hindu usually begin the day with a visit to the local temple.

The dead are as a rule cremated, and the ashes thrown into a sacred river or stream. A period of mourning is observed for an odd number of days. Professional mourners may be employed. The mourning period is followed by a feast given to local members of the caste.

See also Jain; Vaisya

Bibliography

Darling, Malcolm Lyall (1925). *The Punjab Peasant in Prosperity and Debt.* London: Oxford University Press. 4th ed. 1978. Columbia, Mo.: South Asia Books; New Delhi: Manohar Book Service.

Enthoven, Reginald E. (1922). "Vanias." In *The Tribes and Castes of Bombay*, edited by Reginald E. Enthoven. Vol. 3, 412–442. Bombay: Government Central Press. Reprint. 1975. Delhi: Cosmo Publications.

Risley, Herbert Hope (1891). "Subarnabanik." In *The Tribes and Castes of Bengal*, edited by Herbert Hope Risley. Vol. 2, 261–266. Calcutta: Bengal Secretariat Press. Reprint. 1981. Calcutta: Firma K. L. Mukhopadhyay.

Russell, R. V., and Hira Lal (1916). "Bania." In *The Tribes and Castes of the Central Provinces of India*, by R. V. Russell and Hira Lal. Vol. 2, 111–161. London: Macmillan. Reprint. 1969. Oosterhout: Anthropological Publications.

W. D. MERCHANT

Baul

ETHNONYMS: none

Bauls are a religious and cultural group of India, best known for their songs and poems to the god who dwells within. The term "Baul" is usually understood to mean "madman" or religious ecstatic, and Bauls often describe themselves as crazy for God.

Bauls are found primarily in the state of West Bengal in

India and in Bangladesh. There are three major communities or lineages (*sampradayas*). The first is associated with the Birbhum District, which is traditionally considered to be the source of the Baul tradition in West Bengal. This community is in the western part of the state, and it inhabits the districts of Birbhum, Burdwan, Bankura, and Midnapore. It shows many influences, including Tantric Buddhism and Shaktism (goddess worship). The second community is known as the Navadvipa sampradaya, which shows strong Bengali Vaishnava influence and is found primarily in the Nadia and Murshidabad districts. The third group is the Muslim Bauls or fakir sampradaya, found primarily in Bangladesh.

Bauls may live as religious ascetics or as laypeople. The householder Bauls live as married couples and perform daily rituals in their homes. The ascetic Bauls take initiation, often as renunciant vows (*sannyasa diksha*), and may wander through the countryside or live in the ashram or *akhara* (monastery). These ashrams are frequently supported by the local villagers. Bauls who wander from village to village may also contribute from their earnings from begging (*madhukari*) or singing.

There are great gatherings of Bauls at festivals called *melas* or *mahotsavas*, at which hundreds of Bauls meet to sing and share stories. There are large tents and awnings, incense, fires, and flowers. Some of the largest of the gatherings are in Birbhum, in Jayadeva-Kenduli, Gopalnagar, Dubrajpur, and Bilvamangala. Baul singers are usually men, and they play a variety of instruments to accompany the songs. The most common is the *gopijantra* or *ektara*, a one-stringed instrument made from gourd and split bamboo. They may also play the *dotara*, a two-stringed lute with a long neck, as well as various drums, and sometimes small cymbals or a harmonium.

Bauls usually dress in orange or saffron, to show their association with the religious life. Men wear the *alkhalla*, a robe of coarse cloth, small bells at the ankles, long hair (often in a topknot), and beards, and sometimes *rudraksha* beads (sacred to the god Shiva). Women may wear simple white or saffron saris and no jewelry.

Bauls have a system of religious theology and practice that is characterized by the belief that God exists physically within the world, especially within the human body. This differs from more traditional Indian religious thought (both Vedic and dharmic) that understands the body as more distant from the gods and emphasizes the importance of purity and transcendence of the physical world. For Bauls, the body is pure because the god is present. The teacher or guru is important because he can guide the student toward the vision of the god within (*bhagavata darshan*).

Baul religious belief and practice are expressed in song, there is no revealed text and no single founder. Some songs emphasize spontaneity (*sahaja*) and the states of religious ecstasy and creativity that come of their own accord, without effort. These states are highly valued by Bauls. Other songs describe the role of disciplined religious practice (*sadhana*), which seeks to induce the state of ecstasy (*bhava*).

Baul practice shows tantric influence, both in the importance of having a female partner and in its acceptance of sexuality as a path to religious experience. The god is associated with creativity and is understood to dwell physically in the sexual fluids of the body. These fluids meet during sexual ritual, which takes place when the male and female essences are believed to be strongest. At this time, the male and female aspects of the divine are understood to be fully present, and the god (often understood to be a divine couple, the god and goddess) can be perceived by the performers of the ritual. Many poetic metaphors are used to describe this process: the union of water and milk, catching the fish at high tide, the piercing of the moons. When the deity is fully manifest in the body, the body is recognized as a microcosm of the universe. As a Baul proverb states, "What is not in the body is not in the universe."

Baul beliefs are derived from many sources. Tantric Buddhism was strong in Bengal from perhaps the fifth century A.D. until the Muslim conquest in the early thirteenth century. Sufism or Islamic mysticism then arose in the area and became intermingled with the rising tide of devotional Vaishnavism (in Bengal, focusing on the relationship between Krishna and his mistress Radha) and its tantric offshoot, Sahajiya Vaishnavism. Shakta religion, the worship of the goddess (in forms such as Kali or Devi), grew from an esoteric meditative tradition to widespread devotional love, and it was also a strong influence on the Baul tradition. Shaktism was incorporated in the Baul songs both as worship of the physical woman and as imagery from Kundalini yoga. In Baul song and poetry, the deity may be called Bhagavan, Radha/ Krishna, Shiva/Shakti, Allah, the man of the heart, the unknown bird, the great bliss (*mahasukha*), or infinite light.

Today, Bauls are both religious practitioners and entertainers, and they may sing both religious and secular songs. With the popularity of Christianity among Westernized Indians, some Baul songs now include Christian elements as well as more traditional ones.

Bibliography

Bhattacarya, Deben, trans. (1989). *Songs of the Bards of Bengal*. New York: Grove Press.

Capwell, Charles (1974). "The Esoteric Belief of the Bauls of Bengal." *Journal of Asian Studies* 33:255–264.

Dasgupta, Alokeranjan, and Mary Ann Dasgupta (1977). *Roots in the Void: Baul Songs of Bengal*. Calcutta: K. P. Bagchi.

Karim, Anwarul (1980). *The Bauls of Bangladesh*. Kushtia: Lalan Academy.

McDaniel, June (1989). *The Madness of the Saints: Ecstatic Religion in Bengal*. Chicago: University of Chicago Press.

JUNE McDANIEL

Bene Israel

ETHNONYMS: Beni Israel, Shanwar Teli

Orientation

Identification. The Bene Israel Indian Jews lived in Bombay and in villages on the Konkan Coast, south of Bombay, in Maharashtra State. Today less than 5,000 Bene Israel live in India, and more than 30,000 live in Israel. The Bene Israel claim that they originated in Israel and were shipwrecked off the Indian coast in the year 175 B.C. The name "_Bene Israel_" means "Children of Israel" in Hebrew, bolstering their origin claims.

Location. In India the Bene Israel originally lived in more than 100 villages along the Konkan Coast, such as Pen, Ashtame, and Navgaon. In the nineteenth century they moved to Bombay and set up small colonies in other cities in India (e.g., Ahmedabad, Poona, and Delhi), leaving only a few hundred families in the Konkan.

After 1948 the Bene Israel community (all but 5,000) gradually moved to Israel, where they live exclusively in urban settlements. At first, the Bene Israel had difficulty adjusting to a climate colder than India's, but this problem passed.

Demography. The Bene Israel population increased from 6,000 in the 1830s to 20,000 in 1948. Since then, due to natural increase and the decline of infant mortality in Israel, an estimated 32,000 Bene Israel live in Israel; less than 5,000 remain in India.

Linguistic Affiliation. The Bene Israel speak Marathi, an Indo-Aryan language, although it is dying out among the younger generation in Israel. In addition, the more educated speak English. In Israel, the Bene Israel speak modern Hebrew.

History and Cultural Relations

The Bene Israel claim that they are members of "lost" tribes that reached India as long ago as 175 B.C. According to their tradition, their ancestors were shipwrecked off the Konkan Coast and lost all their holy books; they only remembered the Shema, the Jewish prayer expressing faith in God. They lived among the Hindus and adopted several of their customs. When discovered by a Jewish outsider, David Rahabi, possibly in the eighteenth century, they observed the Sabbath, dietary laws, circumcision, and many of the Jewish festivals, but they had no synagogue. Navyacha San, the New Year, was only celebrated for one day; the rationale for several Jewish fast days appeared to have been forgotten; and Hannukah (the Feast of Lights) was unknown, since it had developed after the Bene Israel departure from the land of Israel.

From 1750 onward, the Bene Israel embarked upon a process of adjusting to mainstream Judaism. They gradually moved from the Konkan villages to Bombay and other cities as their involvement with the British Raj increased. Their first synagogue, named "Gate of Mercy," was established in Bombay in 1796. The Bene Israel were also assisted in their religious life by Cochin Jews from the Malabar Coast, who acted as cantors, ritual slaughterers, and teachers. In the second half of the nineteenth century, the Bene Israel of Bombay were joined by some Jews from Baghdad (including the Sassoon family), who served as a reference model of normative Judaism. Paradoxically, the arrival of Christian missionaries in the Konkan from 1810 promoted the Bene Israel rapprochement with world Jewry by introducing them to the Hebrew Bible and other religious texts in Marathi translation.

After the British withdrew from India in 1947 and the State of Israel's establishment in 1948, Bene Israel began emigrating to Israel. By 1960, it became clear that certain rabbis in Israel would not marry Bene Israel to other Israelis on Jewish legal (_halakhic_) grounds, alleging that there were doubts concerning their Jewishness. Between 1962 and 1964, the Bene Israel organized a series of strikes and demonstrations in Israel involving the whole community to demand status as "full Jews." In 1964, the Chief Rabbinate withdrew its halakhic objections and declared the Bene Israel "full Jews in every respect."

Settlements

In India, the Bene Israel tended to live in typical tenement buildings in Bombay, although the upper middle classes lived in private houses. In Israel, many Bene Israel live in apartment blocks (called _shikunim_) in "development towns."

Economy

The traditional occupation of the Bene Israel in the Konkan villages was that of oil pressing. They were known as _Shanwar Telis_ or "Saturday oilmen" because, as Jews, they refrained from pressing oil on Saturdays. In the towns, Bene Israel were primarily employed as clerks. Only in the Konkan villages did the Bene Israel sell the oil they pressed to other members of the village or neighboring villages. Otherwise they were and are employed in the services. In recent decades only a minority of the Bene Israel were still living in the Konkan villages, engaged in cultivation and agriculture and industries indirectly associated with their traditional occupation of oil pressing. The majority of those still in India are employed either as white-collar workers or as mechanics and skilled laborers in factories and workshops. A significant minority were employed in India in the professional category as doctors, teachers, and lawyers. As a result of their previous ties with the British, many Bene Israel members are still to be found in the armed forces and the transportation and communication industries. Almost 50 percent of the women work outside the home in Israel.

Kinship

Kin Groups and Descent. The Bene Israel strictly observed "caste" endogamy, marrying only other Bene Israel and, later, other Jews. However, there was no intermarriage between Gora (White) and Kala (Black) Bene Israel, the former claiming descent from the original families who were shipwrecked off the Konkan Coast and the latter being the descendants of mixed marriages with Hindus, possibly even Untouchables.

Kinship Terminology. In India, Bene Israel kinship terminology reflects local Marathi terminology, whereas in Israel the Bene Israel terms _dod_ (uncle) and _doda_ (aunt) refer to parent's siblings without specification of maternal/paternal linearity.

Marriage and Family

Marriage. The Bene Israel traditionally prefer cross-cousin marriage in order to ensure that wealth and prestige are retained within the family. Postmarital residence is ideally patrilocal, although actually there are variations from the ideal. Divorce is completely disapproved of and was extremely rare in India, although in Israel it is on the increase. Widow remarriage was also discouraged in India. The incidence of polygamy is sharply declining among the Bene Israel; and in Israel, where polygamous marriages are forbidden under contemporary Jewish religious law, there are only a few Bene Israel polygamous families in the whole country.

Domestic Unit. In India, the ideal pattern of family living among the Bene Israel was a structure based on a complex network of rights and duties between members that is usually described as "joint." In its ideal form, the joint family has its basis in common property; members live in a single household and share common resources. Most Bene Israel joint families are lineal, whereby sets of two husband-wife pairs (with children) belonging to different generations live together. In addition, there is a collateral joint family composed of a man, his wife, and their unmarried children and a man's married brother(s) with wife (or wives) and children. The "augmented family" refers to a lineal joint family where the senior male member has died. "Family with dependents" refers to a unit composed of husband, wife, and their unmarried children and other kin such as the wife's brother, who could not be said to constitute an augmented family. "Nuclear families," composed of a husband and wife with or without unmarried children, represent a high percentage of families, particularly in Israel but also in India too, depending upon the stage in the life cycle. In many cases, the phenomenon of "proximal housing," whereby patrikin live in separate yet adjacent or neighboring apartments, enables families to operate in a joint fashion by adhering to the ideal of mutual cooperation without making coresidence a requirement.

Inheritance. A man's estate is divided among his widow and sons, although an amount is kept aside for unmarried daughters' dowries.

Socialization. Socialization of the child is carried out within the joint family, all female members helping to raise the young child and male members acting as discipliners. The mother's brother is particularly loved. A high value is placed on education. Today in Israel all Bene Israel attend regular schools with other Israeli children. Boys have a Bar Mitzvah ceremony at the age of 13.

Sociopolitical Organization

Social Organization. In a manner not surprising to anyone familiar with the literature on caste, the Bene Israel were incorporated into the caste system. Although they themselves did not subscribe to the Hindu religion and mystic beliefs, they referred to themselves and were regarded by others as a caste. Caste features not only influenced external relations with non-Jews but also pervaded Jewish life internally in India. Thus the Bene Israel were divided into two *jatis* or sub-castes called "Whites" and "Blacks," or Gora and Kala. The White Bene Israel claimed direct descent from the seven couples who landed on the Konkan Coast, while the Black Bene Israel were said to be the descendants of unions between Bene Israel men and non–Bene Israel women. Until the twentieth century, Gora and Kala neither intermarried nor interdined: their relationship was characterized by their belief in the concept of pollution. As late as the 1970s a weak distinction between Gora and Kala was reported to have been preserved in very limited Bene Israel circles, but with the breakdown of caste, particularly in urban surroundings, jati divisions have lost much of their significance.

Political Organization. There never was a single Bene Israel leader, but different factions supported different social and charitable causes. The Stree Mandel, established as a women's organization, is still active today, even in Israel. The Home for Destitutes and Orphans was established in 1934. During the twentieth century, sports clubs, Zionist organizations, and credit associations were set up, and many were carried over to Israel. The Bene Israel also published a large number of communal periodicals.

Religion and Expressive Culture

Religious Beliefs. The Bene Israel, as Jews, believe in one all-powerful God. Their beliefs, for example with respect to afterlife, were also influenced by Hinduism.

Religious Practitioners. The task of guiding the community in religious matters was traditionally entrusted to three leaders from three particular families. Their positions were inherited over several generations. By the nineteenth century, Cochin Jews from south India served among the Bene Israel as teachers, cantors, and ritual slaughterers. The Bene Israel never had any rabbis or priests (*cohanim*) themselves.

Ceremonies. When first "discovered," probably in the seventeenth century, the Bene Israel were found to be practicing circumcision and the dietary laws as prescribed in the Bible; they observed many Jewish festivals and recited the Shema, the confession of the Jewish faith, at every ceremonial occasion. From the nineteenth century, they began to come in line with the religious customs of other Jews. Today they practice Judaism like other Jews, although certain rites, such as the prewedding *mehendi* (henna) ceremony, are clearly influenced by Hindu custom.

Arts. Bene Israel sing and dance as other Maharashtrians. They also act out special *kirtan* (religious singing) of distinctly Biblical character, in which they sing about and act as Old Testament figures.

Medicine. Bene Israel believe in the efficacy of scientific medicine; some also receive homeopathic treatment.

Death and Afterlife. The Bene Israel believe in an afterlife, influenced both by Hindu and Jewish belief. The dead are buried according to Jewish custom in a special Jewish cemetery. If a person has committed suicide, he or she is buried just outside the walls of the cemetery.

See also Cochin Jew

Bibliography

Israel, Benjamin J. (1984). *The Bene Israel of India.* Bombay: Orient Longman.

Kehimkar, Hayeem S. (1937). *The History of the Bene Israel of India.* Tel Aviv: Dayag Press.

Roland, Joan (1989). _Jews in British India._ Waltham, Mass.: Brandeis University Press.

Strizower, Schifra (1971). "Verbal Interaction among the Bene Israel." _International Journal of the Sociology of Language_ 13:71–85.

Weil, Shalva J. (1988). "The Influence of Caste Ideology in Israel." In _Cultural Transition,_ edited by M. Gottesman, 150–161. Jerusalem: Magnes Press.

SHALVA J. WEIL

Bengali

ETHNONYMS: Bangali, Bangladeshi (formerly Bengalee, Baboo)

Orientation

Identification. The Bengali people speak the Bengali (Bangla) language and live in the Bengal region of the Indian subcontinent located in northeastern South Asia, and most follow either the Hindu or the Muslim faith. The Bengal region is divided politically between the nation of Bangladesh and the Indian state of West Bengal. Bengalis themselves refer to their region as _Bangla desh,_ meaning simply "the Bengali homeland," a term adopted by the people of eastern Bengal when they won sovereign independence for the nation of Bangladesh in 1971. The native ethnic term for themselves is Bangli—of which "Bengali" is an anglicization. However, Bengalis who are citizens of Bangladesh will also most readily call themselves Bangladeshi.

Location. Lying at the north of the Bay of Bengal and roughly between 22° and 26° N and 86° and 93° E, the Bengal region consists largely of a vast alluvial, deltaic plain, built up by the Ganges River and watered also by the Brahmaputra River system originating in the eastern Himalaya Mountains. As in much of South Asia, monsoon winds bring a rainy season that can last from April to mid-November. Bengal's total area is approximately 233,000 square kilometers, of which about 38 percent (just under 89,000 square kilometers) is in India, the remaining 62 percent (144,000 square kilometers) constituting the nation of Bangladesh.

Demography. According to the last available (1981) censuses, India's West Bengal contained some 47 million people (35 percent) and Bangladesh 86 million people (65 percent) claiming to be primary speakers of the Bengali language, with the total of around 133 million constituting the "core" ethnic Bengali population. To this total must be added at least another 7 million Bengali speakers living in adjacent or nearby states of India—Assam, 3 million; Bihar, 2 million; Tripura, 1.4 million; Orissa, 378,000; Meghalaya, 120,000; and Nagaland, 27,000—forming a kind of "Bengali diaspora" that, although concentrated in northeastern South Asia, is actually worldwide, with large numbers of Bengalis living as immigrants in the United States, United Kingdom, and Canada. In sum, Bengalis comprised a population of about 140 million in 1981, one which can be expected to have grown by at least 25 percent by the time data from 1991 censuses becomes available. Bengali speakers make up 85 percent of the population of West Bengal, which otherwise is home to an additional 9 million non-Bengali people. Most of these are from other parts of India, living in the metropolis of Calcutta, the state capital, but there are significant numbers of non-Bengali people locally classed as "tribals" in rural West Bengal as well. Bangladesh is far more homogeneous; all but 1 percent of its people identify themselves as Bengali. Most of the remaining 900,000 consist of non-Bengali ethnic groups also locally designated as "tribal," and the majority of these are speakers of Tibeto-Burman and other minority languages, often living in border areas of the country. Some speakers of dialects of Hindi-Urdu remain in Bangladesh as well. Overall population densities in West Bengal were recorded at 615 people per square kilometer in 1981, ranging from 466 in some rural areas to 56,462 in urban localities (especially Calcutta). In Bangladesh overall densities reached 624 persons per square kilometer by 1981, rising to 2,179 in the urban areas (especially Dhaka, the nation's capital), but also registering a quite high 693 persons per square kilometer in part of the countryside.

Linguistic Affiliation. Like most of the languages of northern South Asia, Bengali belongs to the Indo-Iranian (sometimes also called Indo-Aryan) Branch of the Indo-European Family. Descended from ancient Sanskrit, Bengali contains forty-seven sounds: eleven vowels, twenty-five consonants, four semivowels, and seven "breath sounds" (including sibilants and aspirates). Its script, also Sanskrit-derived, contains fifty-seven letter symbols. The Bengali language is associated with a long literary tradition, pride in which is a major factor in Bengali ethnic and national identity. A Bengali, Rabindranath Tagore, was the first Asian to receive the Nobel Prize for literature (in 1913). The literary language with which educated speakers are familiar is, however, quite distinct from the urban and rural speech of the less well educated. The eastern dialects of Bengali, notably those spoken in the Sylhet and Chittagong districts of Bangladesh, differ quite noticeably from those heard in West Bengal.

History and Cultural Relations

Bengal is mentioned as a distinct region of South Asia in some of the earliest Hindu texts, and throughout the first millennium A.D. it was governed by a succession of Buddhist and Hindu rulers. Islamic armies arrived in the region in the late twelfth and early thirteenth centuries, and gradual Muslim conquest—culminating in Mughal rule after 1576—set the stage for widespread conversion of the local population to Islam, especially in eastern Bengal. Not long thereafter, European contact with, and competition for power on, the Indian subcontinent began, and the British period of India's history is usually dated from England's takeover of the administration of Bengal in 1757. Lasting until 1947, British rule had a profound impact on Bengali culture and society, especially with the introduction of English as the medium of higher education after 1835. Hindus responded more rapidly than did Muslims to opportunities provided by English education, and the nineteenth and early twentieth centuries saw the rise of a highly Westernized elite, mostly, but not exclusively, Hindu in composition, whose intellectual attainments were coupled with efforts at sociocultural and political reform. Bengali elites provided major leadership to the Indian nationalist movement as a whole, which began to develop in force after the mid-1800s. Bengali Hindus tended to support a nationalist party called the Indian National Congress in its vision of a free, secular India to follow British rule. But most Bengali Muslims believed, as did many Muslims throughout India at that time, that they had benefited less than Hindus under British rule and feared that they would suffer discrimination in a free India dominated by the country's Hindu majority. The Muslims of Bengal were thus more attracted to another nationalist organization, the Muslim League, which in 1940 advocated a separate postindependence state for Muslims, to be known as Pakistan. The British acceded to India's independence in 1947, at which time the subcontinent was partitioned into two separate nation-states: India, with a Hindu majority, and Pakistan, with a Muslim majority. The predominantly Hindu western districts of Bengal then comprised the Indian state of West Bengal, whereas the mainly Muslim districts of eastern Bengal formed the eastern province of Pakistan (called East Pakistan). Pakistan's national unity was based on common religious identity of its citizens as Muslims, but it was undermined by the nation's linguistic diversity and growing conflict between the country's ethnic groups. Over time the Bengali Muslims of East Pakistan came into increasing confrontation with the non-Bengali Muslim groups of West Pakistan, where a preponderance of the economic wealth and political power of the country was concentrated. In 1971 the schism between East and West Pakistan erupted into a civil war—a national liberation struggle from the Bengali point of view—resulting in the breakup of Pakistan and the emergence of Bangladesh as a new nation. This history helps to explain why the Bengali population is divided into its two major political entities: the Hindu-majority Indian state of West Bengal, with its capital at Calcutta; and the Muslim-majority independent nation-state of Bangladesh, with its capital at Dhaka.

Settlements

Throughout the Bengal region the officially recognized unit of rural settlement is known as a *mauza* or "revenue village," which has surveyed boundaries determined during the British imperial period for purposes of taxation and general administration. There are more than 40,000 such villages in West Bengal, and some 68,000 in Bangladesh, but it is important to recognize that these officially designated villages do not necessarily always correspond to actual rural communities as locally and socially defined. Peasant communities range from 100 to 1,000 people, and a typical village in the low-lying Bengal delta consists of one or more hamlets (*para*) of peasant homesteads (*bari*) built on land deliberately raised so as to avoid monsoon flooding. Along canals and other waterways the pattern of settlement is more linear, and in areas of the country where monsoon inundations are especially great the pattern tends to be more dispersed. Peasant homesteads are usually composed of extended families, broken down into households most often consisting of a man and his dependents, who form an independent landholding and/or cultivat-

ing and consuming unit. Interspersed throughout one finds a network of periodic rural markets, and in the multivillage area served by each local market—what some anthropologists have called the "standard marketing area"—the market functions not only as the focus of commercial activity but also as the social and political center that unites the village communities served by the market into a certain degree of wider regional identity. Dwellings are most commonly constructed from the dense mud of the Bengal Delta and local, indigenous construction engineering is sometimes sophisticated enough to allow the raising of homes of two and three stories in height. Animal shelters and fruit-bearing trees are common fixtures in a homestead area, and the excavation of mud for construction often results in a human-made pond that serves the residents as a source of fish as well as water for bathing and laundering. Thatch grass typically provides roofing, but wealthier families can afford roofs of corrugated iron; the poorest families often have homes primarily made of bamboo only.

Economy

Subsistence and Commercial Activities. Statistical data for 1981 indicate that some 83 percent of the people in the Bengal region as a whole resided in the rural areas (89 percent in Bangladesh, 74 percent in West Bengal), and it is unlikely that the rural-urban distribution of the population or the occupational breakdown of the labor force has changed markedly over the past decade. Two-thirds (67 percent) of the labor was engaged in agriculture, more so in Bangladesh (74 percent) than in West Bengal (55 percent). The region is largely homogeneous in the kinds of crop its people grow, wet rice agriculture being the hallmark of the Bengali economy. There are three cropping seasons: (1) a spring season marked by the onset of monsoon rains in April, during which varieties of rice classed as *aus* are typically grown along with jute, the region's major commercial crop, until mid-July; (2) the *aman* season, which accounts for the bulk of annual rice production, lasting to November; and (3) the dry winter season, lingering through March, in which types of rice called *boro*, which can grow under irrigated conditions, are sown, along with pulses and oilseeds. Wheat and potatoes represent relatively recent food crop innovations in Bengal. The raising of farm animals for food and labor is not usually an occupational specialization, although whether or not a farm family will possess any of the animals commonly found throughout Bengal—cows, oxen, bullocks, water buffalo, and goats—will depend on its wealth. Some small-scale fishing may be engaged in by farm families with homestead ponds, but extensive fishing is an occupational specialty of particular Hindu castes or castelike groups among Muslims.

Industrial Arts. Preindustrial manufacture and the provision of nonagricultural goods throughout Bengal has always been carried out by specialized, mostly Hindu, artisan caste groups—weavers, potters, blacksmiths, carpenters, and so forth. Because Bengali villages usually are small, it is rare for a full complement of artisan castes to be present in them, but these artisans are usually sufficiently dispersed throughout standard marketing areas to make their wares generally available. It should also be emphasized that industrial manufacturing is widespread in Bengal, concentrated primarily in its major cities.

Trade. As noted above, periodic local markets dot the Bengal countryside, and these in turn are linked to permanent, daily markets in larger provincial towns and ultimately to major urban commercial centers. Many peasants engage in petty marketing to supplement their primary occupation, but large-scale accumulation and transportation of major crops, especially rice and jute, and artisan products are typically carried out by wholesalers who move from market to market. As elsewhere in South Asia, some Hindu caste groups specialize in certain kinds of trade and commercial transactions (e.g., those related to gold and other jewelry or specific consumption items other than rice). Because Bengal possesses a labyrinthine network of rivers, providing boat transportation to and between riverside centers is a major activity for many. Commerce is overwhelmingly male-dominated, since adult women are usually required to limit their activities to their homesteads and immediate surroundings and thus are not permitted to engage in significant trading activity.

Division of Labor. The division of labor by both gender and occupational specialization is highly marked throughout South Asia, including Bengal, particularly so in the rural areas. Regardless of a rural family's occupational specialty, men engage in activities that take place outside the home, while women are limited to those that can be performed within its confines. Thus, for example, in rice-farming families men perform all the work in the fields—plowing, planting, weeding, and harvesting—and once the crop is brought into the homestead women take up the tasks of threshing, drying, and husking the crop. A similar kind of intra- (versus extra-) homestead division of labor by gender occurs in families with nonagricultural occupational specializations. Not surprisingly, domestic and child-rearing tasks fall within the women's domain as well. The degree to which women are permitted to work outside the home is, however, related to the economic and social status of the family. A poor or landless farmer's wife may spend part of her day processing agricultural goods in a wealthier household, for example, to supplement her family's meager income, and among the lower-ranked service castes (see below) the taboo on women working outside the home is considerably less strict. In the urban middle class and upper classes, it is by no means uncommon for women to have a profession, especially in the teaching and medical fields (nearly all gynecologists are women), and to work outside the home. The other major feature of the Bengali division of labor is occupational specialization by caste, already mentioned and discussed more fully below. In traditional Bengali Hindu society, nearly every occupation is carried on by a ranked hierarchy of specialized caste groups—not only the artisan and trading occupations already discussed but also personal and domestic service functions (e.g., barbering, laundering, latrine cleaning) as well as nonmenial tasks such as those related to public administration and, of course, the priesthood. There is some caste-based specialization among Muslims as well. In the modern sectors of Bengal's economy, the division of labor is not formally organized by caste. But the caste hierarchy tends to be visible in the distribution of the work force nonetheless; the professions and management jobs are likely to be taken up by persons of higher caste background, whereas laborers and lower-level service workers are most often members of the traditionally lower-ranked castes.

Land Tenure. Land has always been individually owned and small family farms, typically little more than a single hectare in size, are found throughout Bengal. Farm holdings are often highly fragmented, consisting on average of between seven and nine separate plots per holding. Recent land tenure surveys from Bangladesh indicate that around 80 percent of the cultivated area is owned by only 35 percent of the landowning households; 30 percent of rural households are landless and 10 percent more own farms of less than half a hectare. No significant land reform has been attempted in Bangladesh in the past forty years. Two decades ago, only 20 percent of the landholdings in West Bengal accounted for some 60 percent of the total cultivated area, and a large number of cultivating families were landless laborers, tenants, and sharecroppers as well; since then West Bengal has made a significant effort at land reform with some beneficial results.

Kinship

Kin Groups and Descent. The commonest kin group in rural Bengal is the homestead-based patrilineal extended family, whose members jointly own homestead land and may—but usually do not—also own agricultural land in common. The homestead is typically composed of a senior male head, his married sons with their families, unmarried children and grandchildren, and other dependents.

Kinship Terminology. In conventional classifications, the Bengali kinship terminology is of the bifurcate collateral type in terms of first ascending generation terminology, and it is of the Sudanese type from the point of view of cousin terminology. Thus, each of Ego's parental siblings is denoted by a separate term, and so therefore is each parental sibling's child (i.e., "cousin" in English terms). In this respect, Bengali terminology does not differ from that found across north India and the Middle East. Although both Bengali Hindu and Bengali Muslim terminologies share the same pattern, Muslims employ seven kinship terms that are found in Urdu and in several cases are actually derived from Arabic and Persian, all of which languages are distinctively identified with Islamic rather than Hindu civilization. (Recent discussions of Bengali kinship, however, suggest that the conventional anthropological classification system has limited utility for understanding the basic cultural categories of kinship in Bengali culture.)

Marriage and Family

Marriage. Bengali marriages are arranged, but Hindu and Muslim marital practices differ in certain key respects. Among Hindus, considerations of caste rank are important; that is, marriage usually occurs between persons of the same caste. Hypergamous unions—between members of closely ranked castes, with women marrying upward—are not forbidden. But hypogamous marriages—in which a woman marries a man of a lower caste—are strongly discouraged and rarely occur. Because of the egalitarian ideology of Islam, caste-related restrictions are not formally required for Muslims. But since Bengali Muslim society as a matter of fact reflects some castelike features, social rank is also a strong consideration in the selection of mates, and there are some low-ranked Muslim occupational groups that are perforce highly endogamous. Among Hindus also lineage exogamy is the basic rule and matrilateral cousin marriage is also forbidden. By contrast, as Islam raises no barrier to cousin marriage, its occurrence among Bengali Muslims is common, although empirical studies show that it is neither pervasive nor necessarily preferred. Similarly polygyny, rare and strongly discouraged among Bengali Hindus, is of course permitted to Bengali Muslims, although its actual rate of occurrence is not high. Divorce among high-caste Hindus is strongly discouraged and, at least until recently, has always brought great stigma. Islam discourages but nonetheless permits divorce, and thus its rate among Bengali Muslims is much higher than among Bengali Hindus. Finally, among high-caste Hindus, widow remarriage—despite a century of legislation outlawing the ancient custom of proscribing it—is still greatly frowned upon. Islam places no barrier on remarriage for either sex after spousal death or divorce, although the incidence of remarriage of elderly Muslim widows is not high. For both Hindus and Muslims patrilocal/virilocal postmarital residence patterns are much preferred and almost universally practiced, at least in the rural areas. Neolocal nuclear-family households are much more common among urban professional families in both West Bengal and Bangladesh.

Domestic Unit. Throughout rural Bengal the patrilineally extended family homestead is subdivided into its natural segments, called *paribar*, consisting of men, their wives, their children, and other dependents, who form the basic subsistence-producing and consuming kinship units. The economic and social "jointness" of the paribar is underlined by the sharing of a common kitchen or hearth, as well as the ownership or control of land and/or other productive assets, if any.

Inheritance. Among Bengali Hindus, inheritance is governed by the *dayabhaga* system of customary law in which a man has sole rights in all ancestral property until his death and can in principle pass it on to his survivors in any manner that he wishes. Unless he makes a will to the contrary, upon his death a man's sons are to inherit equally all property as a matter of survivorship, not a matter of right; his wife and daughters have no claim by right to any of his property, but they do have the right to maintenance so long as they are dependent on their sons or brothers. Among Muslims inheritance is of course governed by Islamic law, which permits a man's female dependents to inherit a portion of his property; since sons are expected to be the sole providers for their families, the law permits them to receive more of a father's property than do daughters. In actual Bengali Muslim (at least rural, peasant) practice, however, daughters commonly forgo or are deprived of their inheritance of immovable property in favor of their brothers, assuming that if they need to return to their natal homes after widowhood or divorce their brothers will take care of them. Although joint retention and use of the father's property by his sons is the cultural ideal for both Hindus and Muslims, in practice the subdivision of a man's property begins not long after his death, and the formation or further proliferation of the domestic units discussed above begins.

Socialization. Children learn proper behavior from parents and older siblings, gradually becoming differentiated according to gender as they mature. The pattern of older children caring for their younger siblings is widespread. While small children of both sexes are warmly indulged, as girls approach physical maturity their movements outside the household are gradually curtailed in anticipation of the relative restrictions that both high-caste Hindu and Muslim adult women will experience for most of their child-bearing years. Schools abound throughout Bengal, but whether and how long a child will attend depend much upon gender as well as the social standing and financial condition of the family. Schools for religious education—Hindu *pathsalas* for boys and Islamic *madrassas* open to both sexes—are found everywhere and commonly attended, at least during childhood years.

Sociopolitical Organization

West Bengal is a federal state within the Republic of India, with its own elected governor and legislature; it also sends representatives to a bicameral national parliament. Bangladesh is an independent sovereign republic with an elected president and a unicameral, elected national assembly (the Jatiya Sangsad).

Social Organization. Bengali Hindu society is organized along the lines of the Hindu caste system, in which every individual is a member by birth of a corporate, ranked, endogamous occupational group, called a caste (*jati*). One's place in society is determined by the rank of one's caste, and the latter is determined by the relative prestige—measured by the degree of ritual purity or impurity—associated with the caste's traditional occupation. The castes traditionally associated with religious leadership are considered to be the most pure ritually and so have the highest rank. At the bottom of the hierarchy are found those castes whose occupations, because they involve direct or indirect contact with such defiling substances as blood and human excreta or may be associated with death in some way, are considered to be the most ritually impure. The customs governing much of the individual's existence are those of his or her caste community; the wealth of one's family is also correlated with one's caste ranking; the probability that a person will receive a high degree of education is also related to caste status, and of course most people marry a member of their caste as well. Individual upward social mobility is highly restricted in this kind of social system, but it is possible for a whole caste to elevate its actual rank in its local hierarchy if its members become wealthy and attempt to emulate norms and customs of the higher castes. Certain castes found elsewhere in India, notably those associated in the past with royalty (i.e., the Kshatriya varna) and the performance of traditional ruling functions, have not been historically present in Bengal. Anywhere from six to a dozen caste groups might be found in a typical Bengali Hindu village, but villages in Bengal tend to be less highly stratified, in the sense that they tend to have a smaller number of castes than Hindu communities in other parts of India. In the most populous southern areas of the Bengal Delta, Hindu village communities are often dominated numerically and politically by one of several low-ranked cultivating castes: the Namasudras, the Mahisyas, and/or the Pods. In part because Islam is an egalitarian religion and in principle forbids hereditary distinctions of social rank, one does not find among Bengali Muslims whole communities organized along the lines of caste, and the social system is more open and fluid from the point of view of social mobility. The vestiges are still found of a traditional South Asian Muslim system of social rank that distinguished between "noble" (*ashraf*) and low-ranked (*ajlaf* or _atraf_) status groups, and some of the latter still exist and tend to be occupationally endogamous. Today, however, Muslim village communities, at least in Bangladesh, are most often populated by ordinary cultivators, among whom well-marked castelike distinctions are not found and who emphasize distinctions in wealth as the basis for social rank.

Political Organization. West Bengal is divided into sixteen districts, and below the district level (as everywhere in India) there is a three-tiered council system known as _panchayati raj_, whose purpose is to administer village and multivillage affairs and to carry out development projects consistent with statewide plans and goals. Each village elects a village assembly (_gram sabha_), whose executive body is the village council (_gram panchayat_). Usually these village councils are controlled by the numerically and/or economically dominant caste group in the villages electing them. Several village councils in turn elect an area council (_anchal panchayat_), which has jurisdiction over the village councils. The heads of the various area councils, along with nominated members of the state legislative assembly, form the district council (_zilla parishad_), which, linked to the state government, has control over the entire local government system. Parallel to the local councils at each level is a three-tiered judicial system as well. In Bangladesh, which undertook administrative reforms in 1982, the 68,000 officially designated "villages" or _mauzas_ are amalgamated into around 4,300 unions with governing councils known as _union parishads_ constituting the lowest levels of the national government and administration, to which the villagers elect members. Unions are further grouped into nearly 500 _upazillas_ or "subdistricts," governed by _upazilla parishads_, whose memberships are composed by the chairmen of the union parishads (except that the chairman of an upazilla parishad is directly elected). Upazillas in turn are united into some sixty-four districts, and these again into four divisions. The key to this administrative scheme is supposed to be the upazilla parishad, which has many local decision-making powers, especially those relevant to community development. Social scientists who have studied the local government system in Bangladesh have found that it is usually dominated by the more wealthy sections of the peasantry and locally powerful village elites.

Social Control. In both West Bengal and Bangladesh, formal social control mechanisms are provided by the units of local government described above, in conjunction with police and civil court administration. However, informal mechanisms have traditionally been important as well. Among Hindus, intervillage caste _panchayats_ (councils), headed by the elders, regulate marriages and otherwise govern the affairs and mediate disputes of the members of the same caste in several adjacent villages. Among Muslims, similar traditional councils, called _samaj_, of village elders perform similar functions, and sometimes these groups may encompass several contiguous villages. These traditional sociopolitical groupings may overlap with the official units of local government described above, in that the leaders of these indigenous groups are sometimes elected to membership in the governmental bodies too.

Conflict. Anthropologists have conducted many studies of conflict in South Asian villages, including those of Bengal. They have found that conflict often occurs not only between the various castes but also between factions, each composed of members of various caste groups. Competition for scarce land is a major source of conflict, as well as rivalry between landowners for power and influence in local, regional, and even state and national affairs. Wealthy landowning families will often exercise control over their tenants and the landless people who work on their land, relying on the support of the latter in conflict situations. The outcomes of elections for both local and upper-level councils are influenced by factional conflict, as are the polls in each constituency for state and national legislative bodies.

Religion and Expressive Culture

Hinduism and Islam are the two major religions of Bengal, and religious identification was the basis for the political division experienced by the Bengalis with the departure of British rule in 1947. In West Bengal, Hindus constituted 77 percent of the population in 1981, and Muslims 22 percent. Some 85 percent of Bangladeshis are Muslim, about 14 percent Hindu. Less than 1 percent of Bengalis are Christians; one can also find a few isolated Bengali Buddhist villages in southern Bangladesh.

Religious Beliefs. Bengali Hinduism by and large conforms to the orthodox Vedantic variety of that faith, although in response to the cultural impact of the British in the last century there emerged certain modernistic variants (e.g., the Brahmo Samaj, to which some Westernized high-caste elites were drawn). The Shaivite cult, focusing on worship of the god Shiva and his female counterparts, is widespread among the upper castes, while Vaishnavism, involving devotion to the Lord Krishna, is popular among the lower castes. Bengali Muslims belong overwhelmingly to the Sunni division of Islam and generally conform to the Hanafi school of Islamic law. Popular religion in Bengal often displays syncretism, a mixing of both Hindu and Muslim folk beliefs, deities, and practices. Bengal is famous for its wandering religious mendicant folk musicians (e.g., the Bauls, who disdain caste and conventional Hindu/Muslim religious distinctions in their worship and way of life). In addition to formal worship at Hindu temples and Muslim mosques, popular worship involving religious folk music is widespread, especially at Vaishnavite gatherings (_kirtan_) and among Muslim followers of several Sufi orders (_tarika_) present in Bengal. Bengali Muslims are also known for their practice of "pirism," the cultic following of Muslim saints or holy men (called _pirs_).

Religious Practitioners. The Hindu clergy is drawn from the highest (Brahman) castes and is thus a matter of birthright, although not all Brahmans actually practice as priests (_pandit, purahit_). Practitioners within the Hindu system also include persons who withdraw from conventional society to become religious mendicants in search of personal salvation (_sadhus_). By contrast, in Bengali Islam, recruitment to the clergy is voluntary; any man who has the desire and opportunity to study the Quran (for which he must learn to read the classical Arabic language) can eventually become the worship leader (mullah or imam) of a local mosque if so chosen by the congregation. Further study of the Quran and of Muslim law (the _sharia_) may qualify a man to be a religious leader with a wider following, greater stature, and sometimes significant political influence.

Ceremonies. The Bengali Hindu religious calendar is replete with worship ceremonies (*puja*) devoted to the deities of both the Great and Little Traditions. Especially important is the annual festival (or *gajan*) of the Lord Shiva, as are those of his counterpart goddesses, Kali and Durga. The goddesses Lakshmi (of wealth and good fortune) and Saraswati (of learning and culture) also have annual ceremonies. Important folk deities propitiated by Hindus and Muslims alike include the "goddesses of the calamities"—Sitala, goddess of smallpox; Olabibi, goddess of cholera; and Manasa, goddess of snakes—all of whom have their annual festivals. Bengali Muslims celebrate the major festivals of Islam: the Id al-Fitr, which marks the end of the Muslim month of fasting (Ramadan); the Id al-Adha, or "feast of the sacrifice," coterminous with the annual pilgrimage (*haj*) to Mecca and commemorating the story of the prophet Ibrahim's willingness to sacrifice his son at God's command. Even though Bengali Muslims are Sunnis, they also observe the festival of Muharram, usually associated more prominently with the Shia division of Islam, in which the death of Hussain, grandson of the Prophet Mohammed and martyr of the faith, is mourned. Bengalis also celebrate the well-known Hindu rite of spring called Holi; for members of all religious faiths, the annual new year ceremony on the first day of the Hindu (and Bengali) month of Baisakh, coming between April and May and marking the onset of spring, is a joyous occasion.

Arts. Urban Bengali elite culture has produced one of South Asia's finest literary traditions, including not only the novel, short story, and poetry but drama and film as well. Some of India's best classical musicians and greatest exponents of the dance have been Bengalis. Bengalis have also made major contributions to Indian and world cinema. Rural Bengal has an old and well-developed folk literature, including narrative poetry (*puthi*), drawn from history, myth, and legend, as well as a very popular itinerant theater (called *jatra*). There is also a strong tradition of religious folk music, particularly associated with the more devotional and mystical practices of popular Hinduism (e.g., worship of the goddess Kali and the Lord Krishna) and of popular Islam (e.g., the devotional gatherings of the various Sufi orders). Terra-cotta temple and mosque architecture throughout Bengal is much admired, and there is a folk tradition of painting, seen in Hindu religious scrolls and in the flowery, and often obscure, religious symbols (*alipana*) commonly daubed in white rice paste on the walls and floors of homesteads by Hindu village women. Finally, despite industrialization and the spread of commercially manufactured products throughout the region, the Bengali rural economy still depends on the services of traditional craftspeople—weavers, potters, carpenters, blacksmiths, metalworkers, and the like—whose wares often represent a high quality of both technique and aesthetic design.

Medicine. Although modern scientific medicine has long been known and accepted in Bengal, the homeopathic, allopathic, and the Hindu Ayurvedic and Muslim Unani medical traditions continue to exist as alternatives. There also remains a host of folk beliefs and curing practices among both the urban immigrant poor and the peasantry as a whole. Folk healers (*ojha* or *fakir*) are commonly called upon to treat everything from temporary illnesses and chronic diseases to bone fractures and snakebite, as well as to counteract ethnopsychiatric afflictions resulting from sorcery and ghost possession. Folk curing practices stress the use of magical verses (mantras), often combined with indigenous medicinal concoctions. Traditional healers also provide amulets for protection against devilry and sorcery, the wearing of which is ubiquitous not only among the peasantry and the urban poor but also among the Bengali middle classes as well.

Death and Afterlife. Bengali Hindus, of course, accept the doctrine of samsara, or the transmigration of souls from one earthly life to another. Funerary cremations, practiced by nearly all Hindu castes, are thought to release the individual's spiritual essence or soul from its transitory physical body. Bearing the influence (karma) of all the actions of its just terminated earthly embodiment, the soul then is reincarnated into a new worldly form and way of life shaped by those past actions. Normally a man's eldest son carries out the funerary rites, lighting the funeral pyre after first placing a burning stick in the mouth of the deceased. Muslim beliefs require that at death the person be ritually bathed, shrouded, and buried in a coffin with the head facing the holy city of Mecca, after which there follows a funerary prayer ceremony ideally led by either a relative or a recognized leader of the local Muslim community. The dead are thought to enter an indefinite transitional state—during which the wicked begin to experience punishment and the virtuous to receive their reward—between time of death and an eventual Day of Destruction, upon which the world will come to an end. There will then be a Day of Judgment, whereupon all beings will be restored to life, and humans will be brought before God (Allah) to have their lifetime deeds—which have been recorded by Allah's angels in a Great Book—reviewed and counted. Should one's good deeds outbalance the evil one has done, Resurrection Day will lead to everlasting life in Heaven; if vice versa, the outcome is a purifying, remedial period in Hell, whereupon, purged of its past iniquities, the soul may qualify for entry into Paradise.

See also Baul; Bengali Shakta; Bengali Vaishnava

Bibliography

Aziz, K. M. Ashraful (1979). *Kinship in Bangladesh.* Monograph Series, no. 1. Dhaka: International Centre for Diarrhoeal Disease Research.

Bertocci, Peter J. (1980). "Models of Solidarity, Structures of Power: The Politics of Community in Rural Bangladesh." In *Ideology and Interest: The Dialectics of Politics*, Political Anthropology Yearbook no. 1, edited by Myron J. Aronoff, 97–125. New Brunswick, N.J.: Transaction Books.

Chaudhuri, Nirad (1951). *The Autobiography of an Unkown Indian.* London: Macmillan.

Davis, Marvin (1983). *Rank and Rivalry: The Politics of Inequality in Rural West Bengal.* Cambridge: Cambridge University Press.

Inden, Ronald B., and Ralph W. Nicholas (1977). *Kinship in Bengali Culture.* Chicago: University of Chicago Press.

Islam, A. K. M. Aminul (1974). *A Bangladesh Village: Political Conflict and Cohesion.* Cambridge, Mass.: Schenkman. Reprint. 1990. Prospect Heights, Ill.: Waveland Press.

Östör, Ákos (1980). *The Play of the Gods: Locality, Ideology, Structure, and Time in the Festivals of a Bengali Town.* Chicago: University of Chicago Press.

Raychaudhuri, Tarak C., and Bikash Raychaudhuri (1981). *The Brahmins of Bengal.* Calcutta: Anthropological Survey of India.

Roy, Manisha (1972). *Bengali Women.* Chicago: University of Chicago Press. Reprint. 1975.

PETER J. BERTOCCI

Bengali Shakta

ETHNONYMS: none

Shaktas are the worshipers of the goddess, called Shakti or Devi, in India. Popular Shaktism in Bengal is primarily an oral tradition, organized around living teachers (gurus) and sacred places (*shakta pithas*). Shaktas as a group include both laypeople and religious ascetics. Laypeople usually worship images of the goddess in the household with daily rituals (*pujas*). Ascetics may live in temples or ashrams, out in the woods, or at sacred sites. They frequently dress in red clothing, wear long and matted hair (*jata*), and have rosaries (*malas*) made of bone or *rudraksha* berries.

Shaktism in India is primarily of two types—the Shrikula (the lineage or family of the goddess Shri) and the Kalikula (the lineage of the goddess Kali). The first type, located primarily in southern India, sees the goddess as the embodiment of good fortune, fertility, and wealth, and it respects the Brahmanic tradition (the mainstream Hindu tradition, which emphasizes caste and purity). The main form of the goddess here is called Shri or Lakshmi. The second type is seen mostly in northern India, especially in West Bengal, Assam, Bihar, and Orissa. The focus of the Kali lineage is upon the goddess as the source of wisdom and liberation, and it stands in opposition to the Brahmanic tradition, which it views as overly conservative and denying the experiential part of religion. Kali and Tara are the main forms of the goddess, though there are ten different forms that are worshiped (the ten *mahavidyas* or "great wisdom" figures). There is also worship of local goddesses, such as Manasha, the snake goddess, and Sitala, the smallpox goddess, as well as rituals to more well-known pan-Indian goddesses (such as Sarasvati, Durga, Radha, Parvati, and Gayatri Devi). These goddesses are described in stories in Bengali and Sanskrit sacred texts. All of them may be understood as aspects of *shakti*, the feminine power of creation and transformation.

Two of the major centers of goddess worship in West Bengal are Kalighat in Calcutta and Tarapith in Birbhum District, with different styles of Shakta practice in each. In Calcutta, the emphasis is on devotion to the goddess as Kali, the loving mother who protects her children and whose fierceness guards them. She is outwardly frightening (with dark skin, pointed teeth, and a necklace of skulls) but inwardly beautiful. She can guarantee a good rebirth or great religious insight, and her worship is often communal (especially at festivals, such as Kali Puja and Durga Puja). Worship may involve contemplation of the devotee's union with or love of the goddess, visualization of her form, chanting mantras (sacred words), prayer before an image or symbol (yantra) of the goddess, and giving offerings.

At Tarapith, whose major religious focus is a cremation ground, the goddess is called Tara, "the one who saves," and Ugratara, "the fierce one." She is the goddess who gives liberation (*kaivalyadayini*). The forms of ritual practice (*sadhana*) performed here are more yogic and tantric (esoteric) than devotional, and they often involve sitting alone at the burning ground, surrounded by ash and bone. There are shamanic elements associated with the Tarapith tradition, including conquest of the goddess, exorcism, trance, and control of spirits.

Both Kalighat and Tarapith are considered by Bengali Shaktas to be *pithas*, seats or dwelling places of the goddess. The idea of the pithas is based upon the story of Sati, which is found in different variants in several medieval texts known as Puranas. Sati was the wife of the god Shiva, and her father held a sacrificial ceremony to which Shiva was not invited. She went there and died of the insult to her husband. Shiva came to find her, went mad with grief at her death, and danced a dance of destruction with Sati's corpse in his arms. The gods feared that he would destroy the world, so they cut her body into pieces, which fell to earth. Shiva stopped his destructive dance, and the world was saved. The places where pieces of the body fell came to be known as pithas, places where the goddess would dwell forever.

Bengali Shaktism as a religion is strongly connected with Shaivism, or worship of Shiva, the husband of the goddess. While most texts speak of them as equal (or of Shiva as superior), in practice the Shaktas focus their worship on the goddess, and Shiva is often seen as inferior or dependent, the servant or gatekeeper of the goddess. The term *shakti* means creative power, the power to bring into being, and Shiva would otherwise be a corpse (*shava*) without the power of the goddess to enliven him. One of the most frequently seen statues of Kali in Calcutta is the image of the goddess stepping on her husband, who is lying down like a corpse.

One form of ritual frequently practiced by Shaktas is Kundalini yoga. This involves meditation to awaken the goddess Kundalini, who sleeps in the lowest *chakra* (energy center) of the body, at the coccyx, and leading her up the spine into the chakra at the top of the head, where she unites with the god Shiva (and the meditator attains liberation). This practice makes use of breath control and the visualization of spiritual channels and deities within the body.

Although goddesses are mentioned in such ancient texts as the Vedas and Puranas, Shaktism was an esoteric religion practiced mainly by yogis and tantric ascetics until the eighteenth century. At that time there was a rise of Shakta devotion (*bhakti*), encouraged by the songs of such poets as Ramprasad Sen and Kamalakanta Bhattacarya. They made the religion accessible to laypeople who were not initiated into the complex meditative practices of the tantric lineages and who wished to worship the Divine Mother with love and offerings. For popular Shaktism, the goal was not liberation but an afterlife in the goddess's paradise.

In recent days, Bengali Shaktism has been strongly influenced by the nineteenth-century saint, Ramakrishna Paramahamsa of Dakshineshwar. Ramakrishna was priest of a Kali temple and worshiped the goddess throughout his life, but he also claimed to have attained spiritual realization through other paths, such as Vaishnavism, Islam, and Christianity. Modern popular Shaktism echoes this universalist sentiment, that the ultimate aim of all religions is the same. The altars of modern Shakta devotees are often filled with symbols from the different religions of the world.

See also Baul; Bengali Vaishnava

Bibliography

Bhattacarya, Narendra Nath (1974). *The History of the Sakta Religion.* New Delhi: Munshiram Manoharlal Publications.

Hawley, John Stratton, and Donna M. Wulff (1982). *The Divine Consort: Radha and the Goddesses of India.* Boston: Beacon Press.

Kinsley, David (1977). *The Sword and the Flute: Kali and Kṛṣṇa, Dark Visions of the Terrible and Sublime in Hindu Mythology.* Berkeley: University of California Press.

McDaniel, June (1989). *The Madness of the Saints: Ecstatic Religion in Bengal.* Chicago: University of Chicago Press.

Sinha, Jadunath, trans. (1966). *Rama Prasada's Devotional Songs: The Cult of Shakti.* Calcutta: Sinha Publishing House.

JUNE McDANIEL

Bengali Vaishnava

ETHNONYMS: none

Vaishnavas are worshipers of the Hindu god Vishnu, and different subgroups worship him in his various forms and incarnations (avatars). Often these forms are associated with places—he is worshiped as Jagannath at Puri, as Rama at Ayodhya, and as Vithoba at Pandarpur. In West Bengal, he is worshiped as Krishna.

Bengali Vaishnavism, or Gaudiya Vaishnavism (after Bengal's older name, "Gaur"), is unique in India in several ways. It claims that Krishna is the supreme deity, rather than an incarnation of Vishnu, and that he is in eternal play (*lila*) with his beloved consort Radha. The major human focus is the fifteenth-century saint/avatar Caitanya, who is believed to be a joint incarnation of Krishna and Radha (they were born together in a single body, in order to share each other's experiences intimately). Caitanya is himself worshiped as a form of the deity. There is also an emphasis upon the role of aesthetics and the belief that the divine is best understood through emotional and erotic (though sublimated) experience. Krishna's consort Radha and her friends the *gopis* (milkmaids who loved Krishna during his rural childhood) are believed to be the ideal devotees, and worshipers seek to feel the intensity of love that the milkmaids felt for Krishna. After death, the devotee hopes to enter Krishna's paradise, to participate forever in his adventures.

The geographic focus of Bengali Vaishnavism is Nadiya District, especially the town of Navadvipa, held as sacred because it was Caitanya's birthplace. While there are Vaishnava groups throughout West Bengal, the Navadvipa area has some of the largest and best-known communities.

Vaishnavas generally live according to three major lifestyles. One style is that of laypeople, who hold Krishna as their god and worship him (usually with his consort Radha) at the household altar and participate at temple festivals. Another approach is that of the monastic devotee, an initiate who lives in community in a *math* or monastery (which is vegetarian and usually follows strict purity rules). A third option is for the Vaishnava ascetic to live separately, in a meditation hut (*bhajan-kutir*) or in the woods. Devotees or *bhaktas*, whether monk or ascetic, are usually initiated into a guru lineage (a line of religious leaders or teachers) and vow to lead a religious life. They may rise at 4 A.M. to begin chanting the day's several *lakhs* of mantras (one lakh is 100,000 repetitions), eating little, with shaven head, saffron or white robes, and the *tilaka* marks of white clay on the face and body. There are fewer women Vaishnava ascetics, and these are most frequently widows. They dress in white or saffron saris, keep their heads and faces covered, and spend the day in prayer and chanting.

Vaishnava religious activity revolves around the forms and images of Krishna. There are temple gatherings, festivals, worship ceremonies (*pujas*), and processions for chanting (*kirtan*). Devotees dance, sing, play music, chant, and recite the stories of Krishna's exploits. These celebrations differ from more traditional Hindu ceremonies (both Vedic and dharmic) in which there are strict ritual requirements, and participation is restricted by caste and status. For Bengali Vaishnavas, spontaneous love (*prema*) is most important, and Krishna's perfect milkmaid devotees were neither *Brahmans* (the priestly caste) nor ritual specialists. The god may be loved as a young child, a divine lover, a master, or a friend, residing in the statue or within the teacher or guru. More private ritual activity can involve visualization of Krishna or Caitanya and their associates (*lila smarana*) and inner or mental worship of the deity.

The Vaishnavite movement arose in the eleventh and twelfth centuries A.D. in Bengal, though it existed earlier in south India (where many scholars believe that the sacred text for all Vaishnavas, the *Bhagavata Purana*, originated). The greatest Bengali exponent of Vaishnavite bhakti was Caitanya, who would go into frenzies of joy and sorrow when thinking of Krishna. He was not a theologian but rather a person in the throes of divine madness. His associates and later followers wrote the theologies for Bengali Vaishnavism, which became the basis for later factional splits within the group. The major tension was between adaptation to orthodox Vedic Hinduism and the devotional (bhakti) enthusiasm and nonconformity. One group of Caitanya's followers, the Gosvamins of Vrindavana, were scholars who wrote in Sanskrit and emphasized the more conservative aspects of Vaishnavism. Other of Caitanya's associates emphasized his more radical side, especially his joint incarnation and the ways he broke barriers of caste and tradition to express his passionate love, as the milkmaids left their husbands to follow Krishna. This is the aspect of bhakti devotion that emphasizes the radical equality of all people before Krishna, regardless of law and custom, caste and status. The more conservative approach tends to be found in the monasteries and among Vaishnava scholars (pandits), while the more radical approach tends to be found among the forest dwellers and wanderers.

There are two offshoots of Gaudiya Vaishnavism that are worth mentioning. One is Sahajiya or Tantric Vaishnavism, in which sexuality comes to play a major role in both belief and practice. The other is the International Society for Krishna Consciousness (ISKCON), better known as Hare Krishnas, whose members have carried and adapted Bengali Vaishnava beliefs to the Western world.

See also Baul; Bengali Shakta

Bibliography

Chakravarti, Ramakanta (1985). _Vaisnavism in Bengal._ Calcutta: Sanskrit Pustak Bhandar.

De, Sushil Kumar (1981) _Early History of the Vaisnava Faith and Movement in Bengal._ Calcutta: Firma K. L. Mukhopadhyay.

Dimock, Edward C. (1989). _The Place of the Hidden Moon: Erotic Mysticism in the Vaisnava-Sahajiyā Cult of Bengal._ Chicago: University of Chicago Press.

McDaniel, June (1989). _The Madness of the Saints: Ecstatic Religion in Bengal._ Chicago: University of Chicago Press.

Singer, Milton, ed. (1971). _Krishna: Myths, Rites, and Attitudes._ Chicago: University of Chicago Press.

JUNE McDANIEL

Bhil

ETHNONYMS: none

Orientation

Identification. The Bhils are the third-largest (after the Gonds and Santals) and most widely distributed tribal group in India. Although their racial origin remains undetermined, they have been variously classified as Gondids, as Proto-Australoid Veddids, and as a subsection of the "Munda race." The name "Bhil" is believed to have been derived from _villu_ or _billu_, which in most Dravidian languages is the word for "bow," in reference to the weapon that, until recent times, they seemed almost always to be carrying. Many Urdu speakers, however, equate the term "Bhil" with the English "aboriginal," leading to speculation that the term is a generic one associated with a number of tribes in contiguous areas bearing cultural similarities. Recent work on the Bhils appears to indicate that what has always been treated as one tribal group in fact is heterogeneous in nature. This is reflected in the 1961 census by the numerous tribes that are to be found under the name of "Bhil." It seems best to consider the term "Bhils" as covering a number of subtribes that include the Barelas, Bhagalia, Bhilalas, Dhankas, Dholi, Dublas, Dungri, Gamits or Gamtas, Garasias, Mankars, Mavchis, Mewasi, Nirle (Nilde), Patelia, Pathias, Pavadas, Pawra, Rathias, Rawal, Tadvis, Talavias, Vasavas, and Vasave. The Dhankas, Tadvis, Pavadas, and the Gamits or Gamtas may refer to themselves as separate tribes, or at least as distinct from the main stock, with the Dhankas even having an origin myth that upholds their derivation from the Rajputs. The Bhilalas are generally acknowledged as a mixture of Bhils and Rajputs. Yet the members of each tribe regard themselves as belonging to an ethnic unit separate from their neighbors and have developed a shared tribal consciousness. The areas inhabited by the Bhils remain some of the more remote and inaccessible parts of India today. Their unique scattered settlement pattern has hindered government efforts to provide services as has their general distrust of government officials. Recent studies of the progress made by the Hindu Bhagat movement appear to indicate that there may be a process of transformation from tribal group to caste under way among the Bhils.

Location. The area occupied by the Bhil is the forested lands of the Vindhya and Satpura hills in the western portion of central India between 20° and 25° N and 73° and 77° E. Straddling the borders of Andhra Pradesh, Gujarat, Madhya Pradesh, Maharashtra, and Rajasthan states, most of this territory, traditionally referred to as "Rewakantha" (a Gujarati term for the drainage of the Rewa, another name for the Narmada River), is the homeland of peoples collectively referred to as the Bhil.

Demography. A total number of 5,172,129 people are to be found under the heading of "Bhils including other subtribes" in the 1971 census. The largest concentration, 1,618,716 strong, is found in Madhya Pradesh. In Gujarat there are 1,452,987 Bhils, while there are 1,431,020 in Rajasthan. In Maharashtra 678,750 registered as members of the tribal group. The Bhils as a whole recorded an astounding 64.5 percent increase in population (from 2,330,278 to 3,833,331) during the decade 1951–1961, but this remarkable rate may be in large part attributable to the reclassification of the tribal group in the census. Between 1961 and 1971, the Bhil population registered a much more moderate 45.9 percent growth rate.

Linguistic Affiliation. The numerous and varied Bhili dialects spoken by the Bhil belong to the Indo-Aryan Family of languages and exhibit divergent levels of Rajasthani and Gujarati influence. A radius of 32 to 48 kilometers appears to be the limit of each dialect's boundaries.

History and Cultural Relations

Although empirical evidence is lacking, the Bhil are credited with the earliest occupation of their area; with successive immigrations of Rajputs and conflicts with periodic waves of

Muslim invaders believed to have driven them farther into the refuge of the forested central Indian highlands. The Rajputs, in feuds, periods of truce, and even alliances against the Muslims, were a constant source of interaction. By the end of the tenth century, most of Rewakantha was under the rule of either Bhil or Koli (a neighboring tribal group) chieftains. Between the eleventh and fourteenth centuries, the Bhil were supplanted by chiefs of Rajput or mixed descent. In recognition of the Bhil's prior occupation of the land, many Rajput ascensions of the throne in recent times necessitated validation by the performance of a *tika* or consecration ceremony, by representatives of the Bhil chiefs of the area. Around 1480, Rewakantha came under Muslim administration, leading to conversion to Islam among many Bhils. However, these Tadvi Bhils, as they came to be known, maintain many of the traditions as well as the religious beliefs of the past. A political system of rulership is ascribed to the Bhils from the earliest times. From the sixteenth century, which coincides with the Rajput supplantation, the Bhil political leadership fragmented into several chieftainships, leading to speculation that the Hindu encroachment, driving the Bhil into the hinterland, was a dynamic force that led to sociopolitical change. During the eighteenth century, deprived of their lands and finding their subsistence base greatly reduced, the Bhils resorted to looting and pillaging in large, armed bands. This led to conflict with the Maratha invaders and local rulers who retaliated by attempting to eradicate them. The Bhils were killed by the hundreds, and the survivors took refuge even deeper in the hills; this move resulted in greater disintegration of their leadership but increasing self-reliance and individualism. These developments are reflected in today's egalitarian structure of social relations, quite different from the system of rulership that is believed to have existed prior to the successive waves of immigration into Rewakantha. It took the intervention of the British imperial administration to restore peace and order in the Rewakantha territory, enticing the Bhils back through the extension of an amnesty and persuading them to settle down as cultivators. An agreement hammered out by a Mr. Willoughby, a British political agent and Kumar Vasava of Sagbara, a powerful Bhil chief, ensured a semiautonomous status for the Bhil under Rajput territorial administration and provided them with land for cultivation, loans with which to purchase seed and bullocks, as well as rights to resources of the forest. Similar pacts were worked out in Khandesh. At present, the Bhils are a settled agricultural people whose short history of brigandage undeservedly besmirches their image on occasion. Those who have lost their lands now work as laborers. Extensive deforestation that has now reduced the forest to portions of the eastern highlands has considerably diminished Bhil dependence on forest resources.

Settlements

A Bhil village, whose boundaries are clearly marked by bundles of grass tied to trees along paths and roads, is composed of anywhere from three to forty families inhabiting houses set far apart from each other. A man's grown son may, on occasion, build his hut next to his father's, but generally a distance of 70 to 230 meters separates individual houses. Clusters of homes, usually made up of related families, are not, however, infrequent. The Bhil erect their houses on the tops of the hills with their fields surrounding them, thereby allowing them to maintain constant security over their crops. Where fields extend farther from the households, the Bhil build improvised field houses. The scattered pattern of household distribution results in Bhil villages occupying an area of about 3 to 4 square kilometers. Each village has land reserved for communal use, such as for cattle pasture, for roads, for a village cemetery, and for the community threshing floor. Most Bhils live in rectangular two-storied structures of timber frame with bamboo walls daubed with a plaster made of water, clay, and cattle dung, material valued for its cooling and insect-repelling properties. The windowless abode is provided with an entrance on the front wall that is usually the only opening into the building, although a rear entry for the exclusive use of the resident family may at times be built in. The roof is generally thatched with grass or teak leaves and bamboo, material that often requires annual replacement. Built 0.5 to 1.0 meter above the ground on a plinth of earth and stone or timber, the structure is essentially a cattle shed and domicile, with regional variations on the division and utilization of space.

Economy

Subsistence and Commercial Activities. As hunters and gatherers, the Bhils traditionally relied primarily on the bow and arrow, although spears, slings, and axes were also used. Game hunted by the Bhils included rabbits, foxes, deer, bear, lizards, pigs, birds, rodents, and wild cats. The same weapons were also used for fishing, along with weir baskets, stone and bamboo traps, nets, and poisons. Edible plants, tubers, and fruits gathered from the forest supplemented their diet or their income, as also did honey, wild fruits, and firewood. The *mahua* tree (*Bassia latifolia*) is an important source of berries and flowers. When they converted to agriculture, the Bhils used slash-and-burn techniques until the method was declared illegal to prevent extensive destruction of the forests. Today fields are farmed continuously, although the lands that were allocated to the Bhils, as enticement to settle down in the nineteenth century, were generally poorer fields that lacked water. Crops planted include maize, millet, cucumbers, cotton, eggplants, chilies, wheat, chickpeas, wild rice, lentils, barley, beans, tobacco, and peanuts. Many Bhils today are landless and make a living working as laborers, primarily in clearing forests and in road repair. The primary draft animal is the bullock, of which each family owns at least a pair, as well as cows with which they may be bred. Buffalo are rare, but goats are kept for their milk and meat, as are pigs and chicken. Most Bhils are nonvegetarian, consuming all forms of game and raising pigs, poultry, and goats for their meat. Although all families own herds of cattle, they are never eaten but are kept for their milk, from which curds and ghee may be made. Maize, rice, wheat, and assorted kinds of millet are staples in the Bhil diet, supplemented with the various vegetables they grow as well as a variety of edible forest products.

Industrial Arts. The Bhil have no tradition of weaving cloth, making pottery, or metalworking and are dependent on trade for the procurement of the products of these crafts.

Trade. The Kotwals, a caste of basket weavers, are an important trading partner from whom the Bhils obtain mats, baskets, winnowers, and grain containers woven from the bark of bamboo. Clothing is bought ready-made. Earthenware vessels need to be traded for from neighboring potter castes. Vohra and Vania traders that set up shop in weekly markets are the Bhils' primary sources for iron implements, spices, salt, and ornaments. For all these products, the Bhil trade excess agricultural produce, such as grain and vegetables, as well as products of the forest, such as wild honey and mahua flowers. The uncertain nature of the Bhil economy has on many occasions made them dependent on moneylenders for funds to make it through periods of scarcity, as well as to pay for ceremonies associated with important ritual occasions. For these loans, collateral may be in the form of future crop harvests or indentured labor.

Division of Labor. The father, as head of the household, controls the pooled income of all members of the family and distributes the daily work among them. The mother assigns and supervises the work among her daughters and daughters-in-law. These duties include the preparation of the family meal and its delivery to the men in the fields. Drawing water from its source, milking the cows, cleaning the cattle shed, and gathering firewood and wild fruits are some of women's daily work. In agriculture, the women assist in transplanting, weeding, and harvesting. The children are generally assigned the task of taking the cattle out to pasture. The agricultural work of plowing and sowing is done by the men and hunting is primarily a male activity.

Land Tenure. The peaceful solution to the conflict between the Bhils and their neighbors in the late nineteenth century provided the tribals with land for cultivation. Shifting agriculture that the Bhils practiced was ended by government measures that brought pressure to settle permanently and farm the lands allocated to them. Landholdings range from 1.2 to 6 hectares with fruit and nontimber trees considered as part of the property if the owner's father had harvest rights to them. Timber trees are the property of the state. Property taxes are paid to the government annually and the Bhils rarely fall behind in these payments, for fear of offending the goddess of earth and bringing misfortune upon their crops.

Kinship

Kin Groups and Descent. Within each 32- to 40-kilometer radius, the limits of a tribal and dialectal boundary, the Bhil are divided into _ataks_ (clans), patrilineal exogamous descent groups. Clans are led by chiefs who have paramount power in matters concerning the clan or caste. These clans may be segmented, with each portion distributed among similar divisions of other clans over a wide area. A process of fission appears to be quite actively involved, resulting in dispersion of the polysegmentary clans. Clanship appears to have practically no regional or corporate function. The structural importance of clanship is limited, apparently, to serving as guidelines for determining the extent of exogamy as well as for purposes of identification in reckoning descent. Within the clans are generally vicinage-based _nal_, or lineages, that are corporate in character. Disputes between members of the lineage are resolved by male elders of the lineage who also control activities within the group. In theory, the lineage reserves residual rights to its members' property. Examples of both cognitive and unilineal descent systems occur among the Bhils. Males always belong to their father's joint or extended family, lineage, clan, and village. Upon marriage into a lineage, women are assumed into their husband's kinship group.

Kinship Terminology. Among the Bhils of the Ratanmal hill area of Vadodara District in Gujarat, kinship terminology is classificatory. A man's relatives fall into at least one of four categories: (1) his patrilineage, (2) other cognatic kinsmen, descended from women of his lineage, which include his father's sister as well as his own sister, (3) his _haga_, or wife's relatives now related to him by marriage, and (4) his _haga-sambandhi_, a term for those not directly related to him who are cognatically or affinally related to his immediate relatives. In the Panch Mahals and Sabar Kantha districts of Gujarat, descriptive kinship terms also occur for such categories as grandfather (the older father or aged father) and grandmother (the older mother or aged mother), for whom there are no classificatory names. The Bhils in the former state of Rajpipla (now Nandod taluk of Bharuch District, Gujarat) and in West Khandesh, Dhule District, Maharashtra, reflective of preferential cross-cousin marriage, have one term, _mama_, by which they refer to their father's sister's husband or mother's brother.

Marriage and Family

Marriage. Extensive regional variations of the marriage restrictions exist, although clan exogamy is strictly enforced everywhere. In some areas, such as Sabar Kantha and the Panch Mahals, cross-cousin marriage with the daughter of one's father's sister is permitted or even preferred. Polygyny among the Bhils is quite frequent. In the Ratanmal area, where lowland Bhils express displeasure at the thought of marrying off their daughters to the highland Bhils, a high incidence of this intermarriage occurs nevertheless, almost all as a result of elopement. This practice invariably results in dissatisfaction and bitterness, especially where negotiations for the bride-wealth are involved. Bhils marry young, at around 14–16 years for boys and 11–13 years for girls. A boy's first wife is expected to be a virgin. Residence is not established until after the girl's first menstruation, and the couple remain in most respects highly dependent on their parents for guidance and assistance for several more years. Clan exogamic injunctions are strictly enforced. Additionally, tribal endogamy is preferred, therefore intermarriage is often spatially restricted to a 35- to 40-kilometer radius. Although polygyny is accepted, the high bride-price to be paid, especially for a virgin first wife, is an important reason for the prevalence of monogamy among the Bhils. Sororal unions often occur among polygynous marriages, but although leviratic alliances are allowed they are quite rare. Most marriages fall in one of five categories: contract marriages, elopements, mutual attraction, marriage by service, and abduction.

A married woman sets up residence in her husband's village, in a new house built near his father's homestead. A son is generally given some farmland and a few head of cattle with which he may subsist and provide for his own family. The new couple function as a distinct economic unit and are expected soon to be independent of his parents, but mutual assistance occurs frequently, especially in such farming activities as plowing, sowing, and harvesting. It is not uncommon for related men to cultivate land jointly with the express purpose of sharing the harvest equally. Among polygynous families, each wife is entitled to her own abode, but all are considered members of one household. The senior wife maintains a position of authority and determines the equitable distribution of the labor requirements of the homestead. The annulment of a marriage is formally recognized by all parties with the return of the bride-wealth. The dissolution of a marriage is often initiated by the woman, who, dissatisfied with her husband, abandons him, frequently eloping with another man.

Domestic Unit. The basic coresidential unit is the nuclear family, comprising a couple and their unmarried children. Within polygynous families, several contiguous homes may constitute the homestead. As sons marry, the nuclear family loses its commensal nature but solidarity continues as a joint family evolves with corporate characteristics, wherein the patriarch maintains ultimate control and authority over the landholdings.

Inheritance. Upon the death of the patriarch, his property and debts are divided among his sons, the size of the allotment increasing in direct proportion to a son's seniority. A daughter receives an inheritance only if she has no male siblings, although her father's brother's sons may receive an allotment as well. Property owned by her is inalienable and reverts back to the lineage upon her death if she in turn has no heirs. In instances where there are no direct heirs, the property is inherited by the deceased person's closest collaterals.

Socialization. Although formal submissiveness is rarely stressed, discipline is maintained by frequent beatings or threats, and the child is expected to contribute to the household economy very early, often accompanying the parents in their daily rounds by the age of 6. Babies are weaned from the mother's breast and fed solid food after 10 to 11 months. Among the Bhils, the shaving of the head occurs when the child reaches the age of 5 years.

Sociopolitical Organization

The Bhils' history of interaction with the British imperial government is characterized by alternating periods of submission and of sporadic, isolated rebellion. The overall objectives of their uprisings were to protest the erosion of agrarian and forest rights as well as to demand the attainment of higher social status and political self-determination. Tribal peoples were among the last to become politicized and thus their participation in national politics was much delayed. Until the early 1940s, awareness of tribal concerns among Indian leaders, with the exception of Mahatma Gandhi and Rajendra Prasad, was rare, and tribal issues were never addressed in resolutions passed in Congress.

Social Organization. Among the Bhils, a social distinction is conceptualized by the different subtribes, including a division between Ujwala (or pure) Bhils in Kotra Bhomat and Kalia (impure) Bhils. A cleavage is also evident between the plains and hill Bhils, with the former considering themselves superior. Bhil villages consist of two or more extended families (tad in Ratanmal), each with a depth of six to seven generations and inclusive of cognates such as sisters' children, a pattern that tends to promote cooperation and unity among the extended family. In Ratanmal, a village's population may be made up entirely of members of one lineage, but in many villages several lineages may be represented and one lineage, claiming descent from the village founder and thus ownership of the village, becomes the dominant lineage. The members of the subordinate lineages in this case enjoy restricted privileges, and their rights to the lands they till, in theory at least, are subject to revocation by the dominant lineage. Dominant (bhaibeta) lineages reserve for their use the most fertile lands, the choicest pastures, most fruit trees, and other valuable trees even when they stand on the subordinate (karhan) lineage's plots of land. In general, the karhan are considered as mere tenants and are excluded from participation in the management of the affairs of the village. Bhils recognize the concept of caste purity and impurity in transactions with artisan castes; and among Hinduized Bhils, their dependence on ritual specialists such as sweepers and handlers of cattle carcasses has increased. Among the Bhils of Khandesh and Rajpipla, care of their cattle is entrusted to the Gori, members of an Untouchable caste.

Political Organization. Each village is under the leadership of a headman (vasawo in Gujarat; gammaiti among the Palia Bhils; gaddo among the Kalia Bhils; tadavi in Ratanmal; mukhi in Kotra Bhomat), a hereditary position whose functions include being the head both of the dominant lineage and of the local pancha or village assembly. The headman represents not only the lineage but also the village in functions beyond the community, and he is also the local conduit for transactions between the villagers and the government. He is assisted by one or two functionaries whom he generally appoints from among his kin. In some large Bhil villages in Gujarat, the pardhan (another hereditary office, but confirmed by the government) is subordinate only to the vasawo. During a headman's absence, he assumes many of the functions of the vasawo's office relating to government. The amount of power vested in the office of the headman varies greatly on a regional basis, but his dependence on the village panchayat (council) is constant in Bhil society.

Social Control. The village council is composed of all the senior men of the village, and when they meet on important matters that concern the village, its members are of equal status, be they members of the dominant lineage or of the subordinate lineages. Indeed, since almost all important matters are discussed within the council before a decision is reached regarding their resolution, the subordinate lineages, which often are numerically and economically stronger, are able to assert themselves politically as equals of the dominant lineage. The headman settles disputes, imposes sanctions on dissidents, gives advice, arranges the settlement of debts, and mediates conflicts within the family. The presence of the headman is essential in validating any transaction, with negotiations being sealed and held binding by the eating of opium. Where serious punishment such as ostracism, banishment, or trials by ordeal are indicated, council acquiescence and support is essential before the headman delivers the verdict. Serious crimes that would have merited these punishments in the past, however, are at present brought before a local magistrate.

Conflict. Apart from their history of resistance to successive waves of invasion and domination by Rajputs, Muslims, Hindus, and the British, the Bhils had a brief period of brigandage and a series of rebellions during which their martial skills were put to the test. Their most efficient weapons of war were those that they employed for exploiting the forest environment—their bows and arrows. They sometimes also carried muskets, swords, and daggers.

Religion

Religious Beliefs. The Bhils have traditionally been classified as animists; this classification is reflected in the 1901 census, wherein 97.25 percent were labeled as animists and the remainder were associated with the Hindu faith. The process of Hinduization has, however, been a long-term process, and the lower level of Hindu belief integrates much animistic belief for which the Bhils would have found much affinity. There are localized deities, such as Wagh deo, the tiger god. Nandervo, the god of agriculture, is paid homage to after the rains have brought a new growth of grass. Shrines to lesser gods are built on slightly elevated and secluded land that is believed to preserve their sanctity by keeping them away from the pollution of the lower regions. Images of deities are also kept near their agricultural fields, to be propitiated with offerings to ensure the safety and quality of the crops. Today Christianity, Islam, and Hinduism are the major faiths that the Bhils adhere to, with the latter two having had the most impact on the belief systems. Among the Ratanmal Bhils, Hinduism is widespread, with four main elements predominating. (1) The few Hindu gods that they have adopted are powerful but benevolent rather than malevolent. (2) They believe in the existence of an afterlife where one's senior relatives maintain authority and control over events in this life, even in death. (3) There are many spirits of the earth, some that unite in bands with maleficent intentions and require personal devotion and regular propitiation. (4) There are malicious individuals among them that wield supernatural powers in the form of witchcraft and sorcery that must be neutralized. Bhagwan is the predominant name for the supreme deity among the Bhils, although in Ratanmal he is also referred to as Mahaveda. Kalika, the "earth mother," is another deity who evokes reverence and fear. Holi, an important postharvest festival, is celebrated for her. A person who did not die of natural causes—a murder or a suicide, for example—is believed to become a malevolent spirit who will consume people. Twins and babies with unusual features or deformities are believed to be manifestations of an evil spirit that must be destroyed immediately lest they be a source of danger to their kin (the practise is now illegal). Two Muslim sections of the Bhils are the Tadvi of Madhya Pradesh and the Nirle or Nilde in Maharashtra. They maintain, apart from the main body of Islamic faith, a belief in a _pir_ or guardian spirit of the village for whom a shrine (_mazar_) is built, and this is the focal point for the annual _urs_ or _jatra_ festivals that celebrate the death anniversary of the spirit.

Religious Practitioners. A priest (_badava_) among the Ratanmal Bhils plays the role of medium, diviner, and healer as well as worshiper. Only males may become priests as women are considered to be ritually impure and also believed to have insufficient strength of character. A person is born a priest but requires a long period of training under a master who imparts the wisdom and technical intricacies of the priesthood. The culmination of the rigorous period of discipline is a trial by ordeal. He may then undergo possession or induce possession in others. In essence, he officiates in functions that involve the gods. Below him are the more numerous priests who do not possess the spiritual strength to undergo the ordeal

and as such are competent only in rituals that involve malignant ghosts. Lowest in rank are those who only possess powers that allow them to divine the causes of illness, heal certain diseases, or offer sacrifices and worship. Priests are generally no match for witches and are immune to witches' powers only if they are under the possession of a deity. To deal with these dangerous and formidable persons, villagers call on the aid of a witch doctor (_kajalio badava_) who has developed the power of divining the witches and sorcerers, neutralizing their powers, and, on occasion, destroying them. Sorcerers are believed to be persons who have trained for priesthood but, lacking the moral fortitude to resist, have succumbed to temptations to use their skills for personal gain (either monetary or in terms of power over others). Witches are believed to be persons (usually women) with low moral integrity who, lacking spiritual strength, have become agents of evil spirits in exchange for the occult powers of flight and transformation.

Ceremonies. Apart from the main festivals of Holi and urs mentioned above, as well as rituals associated with childrearing, other festivals celebrated by the Ratanmal Bhils include the Akhatrij, when offerings are made to Mahadeva, the god of destruction; Indraj, the sky god; and Hadarjo Kuvar, the guardian spirit of fertility of the earth and women. These are joyous occasions marked by feasts, singing, and dancing. An _anabolkham_ or ghost ritual, in contrast, is marked by tension, performed as a gesture of appeasement or propitiation to a spirit and is prompted by a series of unfortunate events. _Gundaru kadvanu_ (exorcism of the cattle shed) is one major ghost ritual that takes place in a clearing in the jungle, during which offerings are made to all punitive and malignant spirits. In such rituals, active participation is limited to the headman, a ritual specialist, and a priest, while others attending maintain distance and silence. Women of all ages are barred from being present or anywhere near the site. In the Panch Mahals, the Bhils observe Gol Gadhedo six days after Holi. In a central place in the village, a pole is raised at the top of which some jaggery (crude sugar, or _gur_) is tied. Men attempt to climb the pole and reach the gur even as the women, drunk and armed with sticks, try to deny them access to the pole. He who succeeds in reaching the gur is considered clever and throws the prize down to the crowd. The Muslim Tadvi Bhils continue to observe local and regional festivals such as Adhujee, Holi, Dassara, and Divali (the lamp festival) but have minimized their religious significance.

Arts. There is very little representational art among the Bhils. Rough wooden posts of carved human figures are sometimes used as memorials to the deceased. Some Bhils sport tattoos, many in the form of crescent moons, stars, and flowers. Music is perhaps the area of greatest artistic elaboration, with songs playing a central role in the celebration of festivals and in such ceremonies as weddings.

Medicine. In Gujarat most diseases have an associated god who must be appeased to relieve illness. For epidemics, Bhils may resort to building a toy cart that they consecrate and take to another village, whose people in turn take it to the outskirts of another, and so on, until the cart has reached a remote portion of the forest. By doing so they hope to drive out the plague. Since Bhils believe that illness is caused by the displeasure of the spirits, they are indifferent to practitioners of modern medicine.

Death and Afterlife. The traditional method of disposing of the body was by burial, but Hindu influence has made cremation much more prevalent with a secondary burial of the charred remains. People raise memorial markers made of either stone or wood, with heroic figures often carved into the material. Ceremonies are performed three and twelve days after cremation, and food is set out for the deceased up to a year after death. All the dead of a house are offered food during important occasions. The Ratanmal Bhils believe in an afterlife where the spirits, endowed with human attributes that correspond to those of their past life, hover about the area that they lived in and maintain interest in their surviving kin. Thus, "good" persons who died of natural causes are believed to become benevolent spirits. Those who were mean or spiteful, practiced witchcraft, or died violently are believed to become malevolent spirits that cause misfortune among the living.

Bibliography

Ahuja, Ram (1966). "Marriage among the Bhils." *Man in India* 46:233–240.

Bhandari, Bhagwat (1989). *Tribal Marriages and Sex Relations: Customary Laws of Marriage in Bhil and Garasias Tribes.* Udaipur: Himanshu.

Carstairs, G. Morris (1954). "The Bhils of Kotra Bhomat." *Eastern Anthropologist* 7:169–181.

Koppers, Wilhelm (1948). *Die Bhil in Zentralindien.* Wiener Beiträge zur Kulturgeschichte und Linguistik, vol. 7. Vienna: Institut für Völkerkunde. Translated by Theodore Ziolkowski. *The Bhil in Central India.* 1958. New Haven, Conn.: Human Relations Area Files.

Moore, Grace Wood (1965). *Bhil Cultural Summary.* New Haven, Conn.: Human Relations Area Files.

Naik, T. B. (1956). *The Bhils: A Study.* Delhi: Bharatiya Adimjati Sevak Sangh.

Nath, Y. V. S. (1960). *Bhils of Ratanmal: An Analysis of the Social Structure of a Western Indian Community.* Baroda: Maharajah Sayajirao University.

Navlakha, Surendra Kumar (1959). "The Authority Structure among the Bhumij and Bhil: A Study of Historical Causations." *Eastern Anthropologist* 13:27–40.

Rao, Adityendra (1988). *Tribal Social Stratification.* Udaipur: Himanshu.

ANGELITO PALMA

Bhuiya

ETHNONYMS: Bhui, Bhuihar, Bhuiyar, Bhumia, Bhumiya, Bui

Orientation

Identification. The Bhuiya are one of the most widespread tribes of India. Their name is derived from the Sanskrit word *bhūmi*, "land." The ethnonyms are applied either in the sense of autochthons or of some connection with land. The Bhuiya are classified into a southern division, with Orissa State as its center, and a northern, with Bihar State, particularly the Chota Nagpur region, as its center. The southern division of the tribe is more backward than its northern counterpart. The two divisions together contain various groups. For example, the Katti, Dandsena, Hake, Dake, and Naksiya are just descriptive names. The Musahar, Rajwar, Rikhiasan, and Pawanhans are distinguished on the grounds of their varying mythical origins. Some groups, such as Bhatudi, Saonti, and Santali, share many common social and cultural traits with the Bhuiya and long ago attained the status of separate communities. The other groups are the Das or Mal (Pauri Bhuiya), who are swidden cultivators; and the Paik, Rajkoli, and Parja, who are agriculturists, farmers, and agricultural laborers, respectively. The Ghatwar or Tikait is a landowning community. The economically most backward group, the Hill Bhuiya (Pauri), are the focus of this entry.

Location. The Bhuiya tribe is found in the states of Orissa, Bihar, West Bengal, Assam, Uttar Pradesh, Madhya Pradesh, and Tamil Nadu. The main concentration of the tribe is in the former northern princely states of Orissa. The tribe represents various stages of cultural development, ranging from the primitive Hill Bhuiya to the Hindu-influenced Bhuiya landowning sections. The Pauri group is located roughly between 21° and 22° N and 85° and 86° E. Jungle-clad hills and high woodland valleys in the northwest of Keunjhar, northeast of Bonai, and north of the Pal Lahara subdivision in Orissa form their home. The settlements are situated generally on higher elevations at about 600 to 1,050 meters above sea level. The climate is at certain times unhealthy. Lack of roadways has kept most of the inhabited Pauri villages cut off from the outside world. During the monsoon, approach to most of the villages is difficult.

Demography. In 1971 the population of the tribe was 1,312,472 (probably an undercount), making it one of the largest tribal groups in the world. The literacy of the tribe as a whole in 1981 was 22.5 percent, but only about 5 percent of the hill group were literate at that time. The economic benefit of education is still not appreciated by that group.

Linguistic Affiliation. Opinions differ about the linguistic affinity of the tribe. The Bhuiya speak an Indo-Aryan language.

History and Cultural Relations

The Bhuiya tribe believe that they were born out of the mother earth and have several legends about their origin. According to a legend, the goddess chose the Bhuiya tribe to be the owners of land and cultivation to be their livelihood. Another legend suggests that formerly all sections of the tribe were of royal origin and enjoyed equal status, but some of them lost the purity of their royal blood and were degraded to a lower status. Social mobility both up and down is indicated. Some sections of the Bhuiyas disclaimed the tribal name and assumed names indicative of higher social status, while others sank lower in social position than most of their congeners elsewhere. Some tribes ethnoculturally distinct from the Bhuiyas, and also a few Hindu castes of high social status, take pride in adopting Bhuiya nomenclature. The latter are titular Bhuiya.

Settlements

The settlement is generally surrounded by hills and forests. Villages are located either in valley regions, on hill slopes, or on tableland. Each village has preferentially chosen a large tract of forest land within which the village shifts from time to time to facilitate swidden cultivation, food gathering, and hunting. A village or a small group of villages is separated from other villages by a considerable distance through jungles or ravines. A few villages recently have been connected with main routes by jeep tracks for mining, quarrying, and forestry works. Depending on the site, villages are either arranged lineally or are dispersed in a pattern. The size of a village also usually depends on its location. Plains villages are bigger, with sixty or more houses; however, villages located on a hilltop or on its slopes may be smaller, with perhaps only five to twenty houses. A grouping of three or four huts on a rectangular courtyard, a backyard kitchen garden, and a cattle shed on one side together constitute a Bhuiya house. Rectangular huts with thatched, sloped roof, and mud walls are common. The homestead is kept clean. Not only the size and the plan of a Pauri house but also its inner arrangements are determined functionally. A hut is divided into three distinct portions: an innermost part, for storage of grains and sheltering small domestic animals and birds; the middle part, with a family hearth and a secluded place (_bhitar_) meant for ancestral spirits; and the outer portion, used as a livingroom. The council house, an occasional guest house, as well as a bachelor's dormitory, all grouped in one commodious hut called the _mandagahr_ or _darbar gahr_, are in the center of a village. The village tutelary goddess represented by a carved wooden pillar on one side, musical instruments used by the unmarried boys, and straw-packed bundles of grain are all common sights inside the manda garh. The dormitory organization is weakening in some areas. Very near to the manda garh is the seat of the village mother goddess. The Pauris change their village site occasionally for economic considerations connected with swidden cultivation, successive crop failure, epidemic deaths, and menace from wild animals, as well as for religious reasons. Some villages have definite sites to which they shift on rotation. The selection of a new site for habitation partly depends on the suitability of water sources and the number and size of hill forests for cultivation; but, above all, the proposed site must withstand several tests for good omens.

Economy

Subsistence and Commercial Activities. The main economic activities are tuned to swidden cultivation (_kamani_) of paddy, other cereals, lentils, and vegetables. The livelihood is supplemented by food collection, hunting, fishing, and wage earning. Minor forest products, such as resin, lac, honey, firewood, wild creepers for rope, etc., also supplement the economy for both trading and domestic use. There has been recent change in the direction of permanent wet cultivation in the valleys. The cultivable land falls into several categories depending on duration of its use, water management, location, and purpose. A family generally cultivates a patch of forest land consecutively for a period of three years, and then leaves it for ten to fifteen years, depending on the availability of forest land and demographic pressure, to renew itself sufficiently for a fresh cycle of cultivation. Pauri livestock include cows, bullocks, buffalo, goats, sheep, and poultry. The first two categories of beast are used for draft; the others are used for nonagricultural purposes, namely, as sacrifices for the propitiation of deities, as provisions for a family's own consumption and the entertainment of guests, and as resources to be sold in hard economic times.

Industrial Arts. The crafts of basket and mat making are common in the Pauri country for both domestic consumption and trading, primarily through the tribal markets.

Trade. The Pauri Bhuiyas live at a subsistence level; hence, trading activities are very limited and are restricted to products they grow on their land and some minor forest products they collect.

Division of Labor. The family's economic and other activities are shared by able-bodied adult members. Children also assist in the domestic chores in several ways. Lighter work is generally assigned to elderly persons and the women. The women are prohibited from plowing, sowing, leveling, roof thatching, tree climbing, and hunting. Daily cooking and many other indoor household activities are women's jobs. The periodic employment of outside labor on a wage basis becomes necessary, particularly during the cutting of trees for cultivation and weeding and harvesting operations.

Land Tenure. Except for permanent paddy plots and kitchen gardens, the Pauri right to land use is usufructuary. Some virgin forest patches are controlled by the village community. Land disputes are rare, but if one does occur it is settled through divinatory methods and collective judgment.

Kinship

Kin Groups and Descent. All members who are related to each other by birth or by marriage, even if they are not all living together at the same place, form the kin group. Descent is patrilineal, and the members of each kin group believe they have descended from a common ancestor. The clan or maximal descent group (_khilli_) is divided into lineages and sublineages.

Kinship Terminology. A classificatory system for addressing kin is used. Thus the same relationship term is used for addressing persons of the same generation and sex in many cases.

Marriage and Family

Marriage. Monogamous marriage is the rule. A second marriage is normally permissible after the death of the first wife. The tribe is endogamous, but villages inhabited by the tribal community are exogamous, since most villages are peopled by one khilli. Marriage within the same khilli is forbidden. The marriageable boys and girls of agnatic villages are wedded only to those villages where suitable cognitive partners are available.

Marriage by elopement and capture are both common and marriage by arrangement has become more frequent recently. Cross-cousin and sororate marriages are uncommon, but not widow remarriage.

The patrilocal Pauri family is nuclear, composed of parents and their unmarried children. The grown-up sons live separately with their wives after marriage. A man may divorce his wife on grounds of neglect of household duties, quarrelsomeness, and carrying on intrigue. Children born out of wedlock are taken care of by their father. A divorced woman may remarry.

Domestic Unit. Members who live under the same roof and share food from the same kitchen form the domestic unit. More often it is the smallest unit, the family, which also performs economic and ritual functions in common. Pauri families vary between three and ten members. Some family democracy is maintained, but the authority is patripotestal.

Inheritance. Sons inherit property equally after the death of their father. Unmarried daughters of a deceased person are maintained until marriage and then marriage expenses are met by their brothers. A son adopted from agnatic kin only is eligible to inherit the property of a deceased person.

Socialization. Children are reared up to the age of 7–8 years by their parents within the family, after which boys and girls are encouraged to join the respective dormitory organizations. The latter occupy an important position in Pauri society and play a significant role in sociocultural life. The dormitories act as schools where the young people are initiated into tribal tradition and the art of community living.

Sociopolitical Organization

Social Organization. Three most important components of the Pauri Bhuiya social organization are family, descent group (khilli), and village. People relate to each other in a network based on consanguinity and affinity. They also differentiate themselves in many other ways. The eldest male member of the family functions as its head and exercises control and authority, commanding respect from all other members. The control and authority passes down to one's eldest son. The head enjoys special status both in his family and in the village, as other elders do. A number of smaller lineages constitute a khilli. The lineage members are obliged to help each other in social, economic, and ritual pursuits. Marriage is prohibited between boys and girls of the same khilli and also within the same village. Every Pauri village has a definite territory with a boundary and is a well-knit social entity. Village cohesiveness continues in spite of the recent introduction of private property in land in the plains area. Established intervillage relationships for performing various sociopolitical functions are common among the tribe.

Political Organization. When occasional disputes arise within and between villages, the council of elders decides the course of action. Intravillage disputes are settled by the elders, including the sacerdotal head (dihuri), under the chairmanship of the village headman (naik). Intervillage disputes either are decided by the elders of disputing villages or are referred to the larger territorial organization. Everyone participates in decision making until a consensus is reached. The political organization, in conformity with the value system of Pauri society, regulates the behavior pattern of the disputants and transgressors. The office of village head is hereditary. The village *panchayat*, a new statutory body, has recently been introduced side by side with the traditional council of elders, primarily for village welfare activities. The waves of national party politics have not reached Pauri country.

Social Control. Several recent changes in interpersonal relationships are the result of a change in the social setting from ethnic homogeneity and village exogamy to ethnic heterogeneity and village endogamy. The common ownership of land under swidden cultivation and private ownership of valley land for cultivation are acknowledged. Common ritual practices bind Pauri society into a single entity. The organic control of community life is guided by an egalitarian outlook of the people.

Conflict. Except for conflicts of a minor nature, harmonious relations between persons and also between social groups are maintained. Still, when disputes over land control, incestuous relations, adultery, divorce, or homicide do arise, the village council of elders and the larger territorial council—for intravillage and intervillage disputes, respectively—decide the issues through deliberation.

Religion and Expressive Culture

Religious Beliefs. The universe is dominated by numerous deities and spirits, both good and evil, and these possess unequal powers. These supernatural beings are ordered hierarchically and are classified as supreme, nature, and village deities, general tribal gods, and ancestral spirits. Both male and female deities exist. The sun god and his consort, the earth goddess, are supreme deities. They are remembered on each ritual occasion, but there is no specific ceremony for their worship. The Pauri Bhuiya have adopted many Hindu deities.

Religious Practitioners. Priesthood is hereditary and is held by a male who represents the seniormost branch of the original village family. The priest propitiates the deities on behalf of the villagers and is the chief official in all communal worship.

Ceremonies. Most of the festivals are closely associated with different aspects of economic activities. Some festivals are borrowed from the Hindus. Social and religious ceremonies are occasions when interactions and meetings of people take place. Almost all rituals have sacred and secular aspects, yet they are extremely stereotyped in their details.

Arts. Dancing and singing, especially by the youth, are an integral part of Pauri life. External influences have affected many aspects of the cultural heritage. Yet the vibrant *changu* (tambourine) dance of the villagers in front of the community hall is very common after the day's toil and particularly on festive occasions.

Medicine. People, crops, and cattle are believed to be protected from diseases by the village tutelary deity. The propitiation of other deities also is thought to help protect people from diseases. The men have great inclination for folk doctors and their medicine. Most diseases are due to malnutrition and unsanitary conditions. Modern methods of treatment, though mostly beyond their reach, have begun to influence the hill tribe. Many curative rituals are performed by the shaman. The black magic of a sorcerer that afflicts individuals is countered either by the medicine man or by a more powerful sorcerer.

Death and Afterlife. The Pauri Bhuiyas believe that death occurs when gods and goddesses are utterly displeased or when black magic is performed by a sorcerer. They also believe that life does not come to an end with death. The soul is called back into the house to rest in the family's inner tabernacle, which is meant to propitiate ancestral spirits, and is offered food and water during auspicious occasions. The blessings of ancestral spirits are invaluable in the life of the Bhuiyas.

See also Baiga

Bibliography

Dalton, Edward Tuite (1872). "Bhuiyas or Bhuniyas of Keonjhur." In _Descriptive Ethnology of Bengal_. Calcutta: Superintendent of Government Printing. Reprint. 1960. Calcutta: Indian Studies Past and Present.

Patnaik, N., Almas Ali, S. P. Rout, and K. B. Debi (1980). _Handbook of the Pauri Bhuiya: An Anthropological Study of the Bhuiya Tribe of Orissa_. Bhubaneswar: Tribal and Harijan Research Cum-Training Institute.

Roy, Sarat Chandra (1935). _The Hill Bhuiyas of Orissa—with Comparative Notes on the Plains Bhuiyas_. Ranchi: Man in India Office.

Russell, R. V., and Hira Lal (1916). "Bhuiya." In _The Tribes and Castes of the Central Provinces of India_, by R. V. Russell and Hira Lal. Vol. 2, 305–319. London: Oxford University Press. Reprint. 1969. Oosterhout: Anthropological Publications.

S. K. BISWAS

Bhutanese

ETHNONYMS: Bhote, Bhotia, Bhutia

Orientation

The name "Bhutan" is derived from the compound _bhotente_, the _ente_ or "borderland" of Bhot. The Bhutanese know their country as "Druk-yul," the land (_yul_) of the thunder dragon (_druk_). The country's association with the dragon is explained by the evolution of the early sects of Buddhism in Tibet and its adjoining territories. It was the Indian saint Padma Sambhava, "the lotus-born," known in Tibet as Guru Rimpoche or "precious teacher," who was primarily responsible for the introduction of Buddhism into Bhutan, Sikkim, and Tibet in the eighth century A.D.

Bhutan has an area of 47,182 square kilometers. It is flanked on the north by Tibet, on the south by Bengal and Assam, on the east by Arunachal Pradesh and on the west by Sikkim. In 1990 the estimated population of Bhutan was 1,566,000, the second most populous Himalayan kingdom after Nepal. At least another 100,000 live in West Bengal and Nepal. However, its density of population, about 32 persons per square kilometer, is the lowest of the three Himalayan kingdoms. Bhutan's population is entirely rural. The kingdom has no towns, no banks, and no shops worthy of the name. Thimbu is the capital, built up with Indian aid, and is just a cluster of houses around the _dzong_, a fortress built in the architectural style of the _potala_ or palace of the Dalai Lama at Lhasa. In the north and center of the country Tibetan is spoken, in the southeast Sangla; both are Tibeto-Burman languages. In the southwest live Rai, Gurung, and Limbu settlers from Nepal, and some Nepalese Brahmans and Chhetris, all of whom speak Nepali.

Economy

Bhutan's economy is based on agriculture. The main crops are rice, wheat, maize, and millet. The country is heavily forested, but the absence of good communications has prevented any effective exploitation. The forests of teak and sal (_Shorea robusta_) along the southern foothills are within easy reach of railheads in India. That rail system provides a way for timber to be dispatched to a ready market. The larger proportion of Bhutan's forests is inaccessible. These forests consist of conifers extending over mountain ranges rising to a height of 3,600 meters and more. Bhutan does have limestone, gypsum, and other valuable mineral deposits that will provide raw material for setting up industries, but the field of horticulture is the most significant source of advancement for the country. The Bhutan apple is much favored in India, and the climate is also ideally suited for the cultivation of peaches, plums, and apricots. Some liqueur is manufactured.

Kinship, Marriage and Family

The king has worked on modernizing the social structure of Bhutan. For example, besides declaring serfdom illegal, he has abolished polyandry and restricted polygamy to a maximum of three wives per man. Before taking a new wife, the man must obtain the permission of his first wife, who is free to seek a divorce and maintenance for life from the husband. The age for marriage has been raised to 16 for women and 21 for men. Once married the bride does not necessarily leave her home; it all depends on the strength of the two families as an agricultural labor force. The groom moves in if the bride's family's labor needs are greater. If both families have ample labor, then the couple may stake out their own plot of land and home.

Sociopolitical Organization

Bhutan is divided into fifteen districts, each with its own dialect, that grew out of history and tradition and formerly were isolated by the mountain ranges. This geographic pattern of fertile valleys surrounded by mountains gives the background to the whole administrative and political concept of the country. One-quarter of Bhutan's people are Nepalese immigrants, and there are strict restrictions against their settling north of a specified middle line running from east to west across the entire country. The Bhutanese have seen how in neighboring Sikkim the original inhabitants have been gradually outnumbered by Nepalese immigrants, and they are determined to stop the process in their own country before it assumes unmanageable proportions. The Nepalese are a polygamous people and a household of three or four wives and a dozen to fifteen children is not an uncommon phenomenon. The Bhutanese worry that, unless restrictions are set on further settlement, the Nepalese will in time emerge as the majority community, as in Sikkim, and seek to exert political and cultural dominance. Twenty-five percent of the 130 members of the Tsongdu (the national assembly) are government officers appointed to the assembly by the king. Included in the membership are influential lamas and the abbot of the chief monastery at Pimakha, who is a member of the ruler's council of eight ministers. The rest of the body consists of village headmen elected for five-year terms from all over the kingdom. Each family in the villages has one vote.

Religion and Expressive Culture

The dominant religious cult in Bhutan is that of the Red-Hat sect (Kargyupa), a Tibetan lamaistic order of Mahayana Buddhism. Tibetan shamanism in the form of Bon, a more ancient religious tradition, is also practised. Only among the Nepalese immigrants does one find Hinduism, or a combination of that tradition with Tibetan lamaism, being followed. The idea of ablution has diffused here from India. The inherent idea is that purification of the body leads to the purification of the mind as well. The Bon practice salutation, circumambulation, and offering of water; devotions are part of the Buddhist mode of worship in Bhutan. The offering of sacrifices is accompanied by ritual dances and dramatic representations. The special dance sequences known as *acham*, where trained and inspired actors impersonate gods and goblins, wearing appropriate masks and mimicking mystery actions, are essentially frameworks for offering the *torma* (see below). These dances are described by some Western scholars as "devil dances," because the chief purposes of these performances are to exorcise evil spirits and secure blessings or, allegorically speaking, to drive out bad luck and usher in the good year and good luck. Whenever a domestic or public rite of greater importance is to be performed, lamas expert in ritual are called to prepare the altar and appropriate accessories and to conduct the elaborate worship. An indispensable part of all such ritual performances is the torma, figures made of dough and butter, shaped to symbolize deities and spirits and presented to the deities invoked.

See also Brahman and Chhetri of Nepal; Gurung; Lepcha; Limbu; Rai

Bibliography

Chakravarti, Balaram (1980). *A Cultural History of Bhutan.* Chittaranjan: Hilltop Publishers.

Karan, Pradyumna P. (1967). *Bhutan, a Physical and Cultural Geography.* Lexington: University of Kentucky Press.

Jenkins, William M. (1963). *The Himalayan Kingdoms: Bhutan, Sikkim, and Nepal.* Princeton: D. Van Nostrand.

Olschak, Blanche C. (1971). *Bhutan: Land of Hidden Treasures.* New York: Stein & Day.

Rustomji, Nari (1978). *Bhutan: The Dragon Kingdom in Crisis.* New York: Oxford University Press.

BRENDA AMENSON-HILL

Bihari

ETHNONYMS: none

The name "Bihari" subsumes several hundreds of Hindu castes, inhabiting the state of Bihar in northeastern India. They number about 85 million (1991) and speak Bihari, which is an eastern dialect of Hindi. About one in every six Biharis is a follower of Islam. Located in the middle of the Gangetic Plain and receiving good rainfall most years, Bihar's economy is based almost wholly on agriculture. In ancient times, this area was the birthplace of both Buddhism and Jainism. In recent years, the state's history has been marked by radical politics and violence. This unrest may be a result of Bihar's status as the most backward state of India, which is attributable to scant industrialization combined with the low average literacy rate of 38.5 percent in 1991 (the rate is appreciably lower for females).

Bibliography

Grierson, George Abraham (1885). *Bihar Peasant Life, being a discursive catalogue of the surroundings of the people of that province, with many illustrations from photographs taken by the author.* Calcutta: Bengal Secretariat. Reprint. 1975. Delhi: Cosmo Publications.

PAUL HOCKINGS

Bohra

ETHNONYMS: Bohora, Daudi Bohra, Lotia, Vohora

Orientation

The Bohra, who numbered 118,307 in 1901, are found today in large numbers in the Surat and Bharuch districts of Gujarat State, in Bombay city, and in all major trade centers of India. Their religious and political center is at Surat, where the high priest of the Daudi Bohra, the main section of the community, resides. Although the Daudi Bohras (also known as the Lotias, from their word for "water pot," because their turban is traditionally shaped like one) represent the largest and most widespread class of Bohras, there are several other divisions of trading Bohras: Alia, Jaafari, Nagoshi, and Sulaimani Bohras. In addition to the trading Bohras there is a large and equally prosperous group of village Bohras whose occupation is farming. The origin of the name "Bohra" is believed to be traceable to the class of Hindu Bohras who are still found in Jodhpur District, Rajasthan. One theory suggests the word is derived from the Gujarati word meaning "to trade," the occupation of the first Hindu converts to Islam. Many Barias and Nagar Brahmans to this day bear the surname "Bohora."

The Daudi and most of the other Bohras speak Gujarati, an Indo-European language; many living in large cities such as Bombay also speak Urdu and English.

History and Cultural Relations

All Bohras can be traced to converts made by Shiite missionaries of the Ismaili sect in the eleventh century. Some of them claim to come from Egyptian-Arab and Yemen-Arab ancestors. Others maintain they are entirely of Hindu blood; according to the Sunni Bohras they were converted from many castes. The Alia Bohras take their name from Ali, who founded the sect in A.D. 624. The Alias strongly resemble the Sulaimani Bohras in their appearance and customs; the Daudi Bohras are the wealthiest, most organized, and most ubiquitous sect of Bohras. The main difference between them and the other Muslims is that they pay special veneration to Ali, to his sons, Hassan and Hussain, and to their high priest, the mullah sahib of Surat. The Jaafari Bohras trace their name to Jaafar Sherazi who converted them to the Sunni faith (they are also known as Patanis after their headquarters in that city). Jaafari Bohras are the descendants of those Daudi Bohras who changed to the orthodox (Sunni) faith during the reign of Muzaffar I, governor of Gujarat in A.D. 1391. Nagoshis or "nonfleshites" are a very small schism founded around A.D. 1789. The founder was excommunicated because he proposed a peculiar doctrine, the most noteworthy feature being that to eat animal flesh was sin. The Nagoshis have now almost disappeared. The Sulaimani Bohras are the descendants of the converts made in Arabia in the sixteenth century by a missionary sent by a Surat Bohra. They received their name due to a dispute surrounding the succession of the high priest of the Gujarat Bohras in A.D. 1588: based on the merits of a letter from the high priest sent to Sulaiman of the Yaman priesthood, he claimed to be the successor to the high priest; however, only a very small minority accepted his claim and so Sulaiman went back to Arabia. This small minority who upheld his claims were thus called Sulaimanis. The Sunni Bohras are the descendants of Hindu converts of the unarmed castes who converted at the close of the fourteenth and during the fifteenth centuries. Throughout the twentieth century the Daudi Bohras have been split by factional strife, the orthodox followers of the high priest frequently rioting against reformists, attacking them in their homes or even in the mosque, divorcing them by fiat, refusing to permit burial of the dead, throwing acid on individuals, etc. The police have commonly been powerless to stop such behavior.

Economy

Almost all Daudi, Alia, and Sulaimani Bohras live by trade. Some are merchants with large dealings with the Middle East, China, Thailand, and Zanzibar, and many are local traders in hardware, silks, hides, horns, and cattle. Most, however, are traditionally town and village shopkeepers, selling hardware, cloth, stationery, books, groceries, and spices; a few— especially in the larger cities like Bombay, Surat, Ahmedabad, and Baroda—are confectioners; and many are also in government service. Many Jaafari Bohras are also traders and silk weavers. Traditionally, most of the Sunni Bohras are peasant farmers and landholders. All the Bohra groups have a high proportion of college-educated people in the professional classes as well. As Muslims the Bohras abstain from alcohol or other drugs and pork or pork products. The Bohras are noted for their rich beef, fowl, and fish curries. The preferred cooking medium is ghee (clarified butter).

In accordance with Muslim tradition, women work mainly in the home running the household and caring for children. The poorer peasant farmers and their womenfolk work in the fields side by side. With increased education some Bohra women have moved into academia and the professions. Men still head the family business, however.

Kinship and Marriage

Bohra descent is patrilineal. Traditionally the Daudi and Jaafaris have been endogamous; however, the other Bohra groups do marry other Muslims outside their own groups, except in some of the more remote villages of the Sunni where they would seldom marry outside their own class, a remnant of their Hindu heritage. Cross-cousin marriage is usual but polygyny, although permissible, is rare.

Sociopolitical Organization

The traditional head of the Daudi Bohras is the mullah of Surat. Sometimes even claiming a divine status, the head mullah is the absolute authority in all issues of religious and civil importance. Discipline in religious matters generally is enforced by fines; cases of adultery, drunkenness, and other serious offenses traditionally were punished by fines, flogging, and excommunication or ostracism. Every settlement of Daudis has its mullah or a deputy of the head mullah. In addition there are four grades of mullahs: Mayan, which means literally "the permitted" (to rule); Mukasir, "the executor"; Mashaikh, "the elder"; and Mullah, "the guardian." They earn their livelihoods as schoolmasters or by some craft. Traditionally mullahs are trained for their duties in a college in Surat. Every Daudi settlement has its school taught by the local mullah and a Muslim lay teacher. Much of the absolute authority of the mullahs, however, has in recent years been challenged by a reformist movement, which has led in some instances to social boycott of the reformers by the orthodox followers.

Religion

The Daudi Bohras are Shias of the Mustaalian division of the great Ismaili sect. The main differences between their beliefs and practices and those of regular Muslims are: the Daudi Bohras pay special attention to Ali, to his sons, Hassan and Hussain, and to their high priest, the Mullah Sahib of Surat; they pay special attention to circumcision; they reject the validity of the three caliphs, Abu Bakr Sidik, Umar, and Usman; and at death a prayer for pity on the soul and the body of the deceased is laid in the dead man's hand. The Jaafari Bohras are Sunnis in faith. They have no religious head, but many traditionally have followed spiritual guides. Many of them are known as Kabarias from being devoted to the *kabar* or grave of Pir Muhammad Shah at Ahmedabad. As already stated, the Nagoshis' founder held the peculiar doctrine that animal food was sinful; otherwise their religious sect is very much like the Alia sect. The Sulaimani Bohras only differ from the Daudi in their recognition of the religious head of the sect. Their high priest traditionally lives in Najram in the Hifa in Arabia. The Alia Bohras strongly resemble the Sulaimani Bohras in their religious practices. Many Sunni Bohras traditionally have spiritual guides, who are given much respect, and many also still keep to certain Hindu practices. They give death and marriage dinners; they sometimes give Hindu names to their children or modify Muslim ones. Some Sunni Bohras, however, are followers of the Gheit-Mukallid teachers of the Wahabi sect, who follow strict Muslim customs.

Bibliography

Engineer, Asghar Ali (1980). *The Bohras*. Sahibabad: Vikas Publishing House.

Enthoven, Reginald E., ed. (1920). "Bohoras." *The Tribes and Castes of Bombay*. Vol. 1, 197–207. Bombay: Government Central Press. Reprint. 1975. Delhi: Cosmo Publications.

Insaf, Saifuddin (1986). *The Bohra Controversy (As Reflected through Newspapers)* (in Gujarati). Surat: Central Board of Dawoodi Bohra Community Publications.

JAY DiMAGGIO

Bondo

ETHNONYMS: Bonda Gadaba, Bondo Poroja, Porja, Remo

Orientation

Identification. The Bondo are an Austroasiatic people who inhabit the area northwest of the Machkund River in the state of Orissa, India. While the cultural relationship between the Bondo and neighboring peoples (e.g., the Poroja and Gadaba) has been debated, largely because of substantial differences in appearance, personal adornment, social norms, and religious beliefs, Verrier Elwin has concluded that a sufficient degree of cultural commonality exists between the Bondos and Gadabas to warrant the suggestion that both groups are descendants of a common ancient Austroasiatic progenitor. The classic ethnographic account of Bondo culture is Elwin's 1950 study.

Location. The locus of Bondo culture extends from approximately 18° 20' to 18° 30' N and 82°20' to 82°30' E. The Bondo homeland (sometimes known as Bara-jangar-des) is a hilly habitat that overlooks the Machkund Valley and the Malkangiri Plain. The average annual rainfall is approximately 150 centimeters. Settlements fall into three geographic groupings: the Bara-jangar group (also known as Mundlipada or Serayen); the Gadaba group (northeast of Mundlipada); and the Plains group. The first of these areas is the most important. It is the Bondo capital and is also believed to have been the ancient Bondo homeland. It has also been suggested that the twelve villages that bring yearly tribute to the ruler of this place are the original Bondo settlements (each having been founded by one of twelve brothers).

Demography. In 1971 there were 5,338 Bondos, 75,430 Gadabas, and 227,406 Porojas.

Linguistic Affiliation. The Bondo speak a language of Munda Stock belonging to the Austroasiatic Phylum.

History and Cultural Relations

The early prehistory of the Bondo is unclear because there exist no physical remains upon which to base a reconstruction of their origin. It is believed that their original home is northeast of their present habitat. Elwin concurs with Christoph von Fürer-Haimendorf's suggestion that the Bondo belong to the group of neolithic Austroasiatic peoples who cultivated rice by means of irrigation and terracing, domesticated cattle for sacrificial and dietary purposes, and erected megaliths (e.g., dolmens, stone circles, and menhirs).

Settlements

Generalizations regarding the nature of Bondo villages are not easily made. The typical Bondo village is built either along or ascending a hillside, reasonably close to a spring. The placement of individual domiciles follows no set pattern and there are no regular thoroughfares within village boundaries. The grouping of houses according to clan obtains at times, but for the most part social and other distinctions have no impact on the arrangement of houses. The *sindibor* (the stone platform that is the locus of village social and religious ceremonies) is placed at some shady spot within the village. Villages are not fortified and tend to be surrounded by gardens containing an assortment of trees, spice plants, and other plants. Fields for cultivation are located in the general proximity of the village. Public structures within the village confines include manure pits and male and female dormitories. The typical Bondo house, composed of mud, wood, and thatching grass, contains two main rooms and a veranda. Attached to the outside of the house is a place for pigs. Cattle, goats, and chickens are also housed in the vicinity of the house.

Economy

Subsistence and Commercial Activities. Bondos engage in most of the major subsistence activities. Wild birds are caught, rats and hares are hunted, fish and crabs are netted or trapped, pigs, cattle, goats, and chickens are domesticated, and crops are grown. Roots, tubers, wild vegetation, bamboo shoots, mushrooms, fruit, red ants, date-palm grubs, dung beetles, and silkworms (for medicinal purposes) are collected for consumption. However, the most important part of the Bondo subsistence cycle is agriculture. Three types of cultivation are practiced: dry cultivation of plowed fields on a level grade; shifting (slash-and-burn) cultivation on steep hills; and wet cultivation (of rice) on terraced and irrigated fields. The following crops are planted in the hill tracts: pulses, cucumbers, castor-oil bush, and millet. Dry rice, ragi, and Niger seed (_Guizotia abyssinica_, a native of Africa that yields cooking oil) are grown in level ground. Axes (to cut trees and brush), hoes (for turning soil after the sowing of seeds), and dibbles (for drilling holes to plant various seeds) are used in the cultivation of hillsides. The plow is the major implement used in dry cultivation. Canals, gutters, plows, and levelers are the implements for wet cultivation. A few necessities and luxuries are obtained by the Bondo from outside sources (e.g., a small number of cooking vessels, iron implements, personal ornaments made of beads, and a small quantity of colored cloth).

Industrial Arts. The Bondo community is almost wholly self-sufficient. The following are manufactured internally: cloth, personal ornaments (made of bark and leaves), gourds, alcoholic beverages, pipes (for tobacco smoking), coats (of bark or leaves), and umbrellas (of bark or leaves).

Trade. The following are procured through trade: pots and cooking vessels (in limited number), brass and bead ornaments, iron implements (from local blacksmiths), and colored cotton.

Division of Labor. Men and women share various tasks. According to Elwin women assume a disproportionate share of this commonly shared labor. The clearing of fields, carrying of water, care of children, weaving of cloth, husking, grinding, preparation of household floors, bearing of wood (during the Hindu month of Jeth), extraction of fiber from _kereng_ (_Calotropis gigantea_) bark for yarn, and the cutting of hair (of adult women) are among the duties assumed by women. Women are also allowed to divine the causes of sickness, but they are not permitted to prescribe treatment for specific maladies. There are ritual restrictions that prevent men from performing some of these duties. Men plow, bear burdens requiring the use of a carrying pole, make mats, hunt, offer sacrifice, divine and treat sickness, cut trees, and play drums and the majority of other musical instruments during festival observances. Correspondingly, there are ritual prohibitions that prevent many of these tasks from being performed by women.

Land Tenure. Individual families are considered by other Bondo to "own" several tracts of land on the hillsides, which they cultivate in rotation. They have no real legal title to this land, even though they sometimes mortgage it or sell it to others. In the recent past poor people sometimes rented such hillside clearings by paying meat and liquor to the supposed owner.

Kinship

Kin Groups and Descent. At least three exogamous affiliations have been noted within Bondo society: the _soru_ (that division represented by all of the members of a particular village); the _kuda_ (exogamous patrilineal clans of which several exist within a village, and the names of which are drawn from the titles of village officials); and the _bonso_ (totemic divisions of which there are two—the _ontal_, "cobra," and the _killo_, "tiger"). Elwin considers this subdivision of Bondo society into two large moieties to be the oldest and most basic of Bondo subdivisions, the kuda and soru systems having been adopted or developed secondarily. Exogamy at the soru and kuda levels is strictly observed. Freedom of choice in the selection of mates and the numerical inequities characteristic of the two bonso divisions (the ontal being the larger of the two) have led to the ignoring of the rule of exogamy at this level.

Kinship Terminology. Iroquois kinship terminology is employed for first cousins.

Marriage and Family

Marriage. Young men and young women are permitted freedom of choice in the selection of mates. The female dormitory serves as the locus in which male-female relationships are established and nurtured. A female dormitory in a village is generally off-limits to the young men of that village. As a result, part of the male courting ritual involves intervillage travel. While parental consent is required, Bondo unions are based upon the mutual affection of the marital partners. Bondo women prefer men several years younger than themselves as marital partners. Elwin cites the desire not to wed an older man, the belief that a younger man would be either a harder worker or a more obedient partner, and the fear of defloration as possible reasons for this. Extramarital liaisons do occur. Such a relationship between a man and his younger brother's wife is not ritually prohibited. It is believed that the age disparity in Bondo marriages has led to the acceptance of this type of extramarital relationship because the parties involved would be closer in age than those in the marital union. Marital dissolution is rare, though divorce is allowed and may be initiated by either party. The remarriage of widows is not prohibited. Postmarital residence is patrilocal. Polygyny is sanctioned.

Domestic Unit. The typical domestic unit consists of a nuclear family (with limited evidence of polygyny).

Inheritance. Anecdotal data suggests that real property is inherited by sons from their fathers.

Socialization. The socialization of children is shared jointly by parents, though women are in fact the chief agents of socialization. Children are also allowed a considerable amount of freedom from a young age. The _ingersin_ (girls' dormitory) and the _selani-dingo_ (boys' dormitory) are important social institutions. Young men assist at ceremonies associated with life crises (e.g., weddings and burials) and the hunt, while young women prepare cups and platters manufactured from leaves, cook, and prepare rice beer. Of these, the ingersin also serves as a center for mate selection. It is here that young men come in search of spouses.

Sociopolitical Organization

Social Organization. Bondo life is centered on a cycle of yearly agricultural activities. Stratification by age or other categories does not obtain. Although it is likely that some method exists for achieving status within the community,

Elwin has not devoted much attention to it. Instead, he has characterized Bondo society as one in which freedom and independence act as leveling forces that reduce the importance of the hierarchical ranking of individuals in the social order. One important Bondo social institution, that of the *moitur/ mahaprasad* friendship, must be noted. This is a ceremonial alliance established for mutual support.

Political Organization. The autonomous village is the most basic of Bondo political units. Village officials include the *naiko* (headman), *bariko* (village watchman), and the *sisa* (village priest). The headman is assisted by a council of elders. Officials in a Bondo village, according to Elwin, encounter certain difficulties in the carrying out of their duties because of the emphasis placed on the rights of the individual in Bondo society. Officials are appointed by the populace on an annual basis. Provision is also made for their removal from office should their work prove unsatisfactory to the electorate.

Social Control. In addition to the means usually employed by the state to maintain order and to discourage antisocial behavior (e.g., legal prosecution and imprisonment), Bondo cosmology uses the potential retribution of supernaturals for offenses against tribal customs (e.g., customs relating to exogamy, incest, and marital fidelity) as an additional means of social control.

Conflict. External relations are stable, though historically tensions have been noted between the Bondo and both the Didayis (whose villages were at one time targets of Bondo raids) and the Doms (upon whom Bondo robbers formerly preyed). Antagonism toward the Doms may have been caused, at least in part, by Dom attempts to force the Bondo to adopt Hinduism and abandon aspects of their traditional culture.

Religion and Expressive Culture

Religious Beliefs. Hinduism has had a profound impact on Bondo religion. Its impact may be noted in the structure of the pantheon and the nature of ceremonial. The Bondo religious system represents a syncretic blending of indigenous beliefs with Vaishnavite Hinduism. Bondo retain belief in a supreme being (Mahaprabhu) who is identified with the sun, under whom is arranged a hierarchy of demigods, who exercise influence over natural phenomena (e.g., streams and forests) and domestic habitations. Furies and the spirits of the recently deceased are believed to have the ability to destroy crops, send wild animals, disturb cattle, and inflict disease on humans. It is believed that the demigods dwell in trees and stones and so the Bondo have erected stone shrines in their honor. The most important of all stone shrines is the sindibor, dedicated to mother earth, which is the site of most important social and religious ceremonies. The services of a shaman are used to discern the nature of any difficulty when the malevolent activity of supernaturals is believed to be the cause. Priests officiate at the rituals necessary to alleviate this distress and restore prosperity. Religious ceremonial includes an array of magicoreligious acts (e.g., incantations and manual gestures) and ceremonial accoutrements (e.g., decorated altars, booths, leaf cups, plates, ceremonial dolls, and carts).

Religious Practitioners. The egalitarian spirit of Bondo society, according to Elwin, has prevented a proliferation of sacerdotal officials from taking place. There exist, nonethe-

less, two levels of priestly activity. The first takes place at the household level (e.g., at funerals and certain festival observances), while the second takes place at the village level. Those that fall into the latter category are the responsibility of the sisa. Each village has at least two such priests (a chief priest and his assistant) and at least two unmarried boys who serve as liturgical assistants. The sisa's authority is limited to his own sindibor. His duties include the performance of sacrifice on public occasions and during festivals. His home houses the *kinding-sagar* (sacred drum) and his spouse has ritual duties associated with the brewing of a special kind of rice beer. She is also associated with the hunt. The sisa must be appointed annually (by popular election) and may be removed from office should he fail to dispatch his duties properly. The *dissari* (shaman/medicine man) also plays an important role in the religious life of the Bondo. The individuals who function in this capacity are believed to be descendants of the original inhabitants of the land and as such are felt to be acquainted with the deities indigenous to the area. The claim to the dissari title must be substantiated by the quality (i.e., accuracy and efficiency) of the claimant's counsel and prognostications. This is not an institution unique to the Bondo. This office is found among many of the Bondo's neighbors (e.g., the Gour, Didayi, Gadaba, and Kond). The ministrations of the dissari are required for the most part during times of distress (e.g., sickness and domestic trouble). The dissari determines the nature of a problem by means of trance and prescribes measures for the alleviation of the problem. These may be performed by a member of the afflicted party's household or by the dissari. While the hereditary transfer of the offices of sisa and dissari is possible, there is no Bondo law mandating that such action must occur. Sorcerers (usually male) are also known among the Bondo. Among their supposed repertoire of powers (which are believed to be largely evil in nature and negative in manifestation) is the ability to conjure up violent storms.

Ceremonies. Magicoreligious ceremonies accompany almost all stages of the Bondo agricultural calendar. Some of the more important of these are: the Sume Gelirak festival (held in January and associated with the reaping and threshing of the rice harvest); the Giag-gige festival (held in April and associated with the completion of work in the fields); the Gersum-gige festival (held in July and associated with the weeding of the fields); the Feast of First Fruits (held in August or September and associated with the maize crop); the Dassera festival (held in October and associated with the reaping of millet); and the Gewursung festival (held in October or November and corresponding to the Hindu festival of Diwali). In form and practice, Bondo ceremonial includes the following elements: the construction of ritual appurtenances (e.g., booths, carts, dolls, and altars); the presentation of sacrifices (e.g., fruit, grain, eggs, fish, crabs, fowl, cattle, goats, and pigs); a sacrificial feast; the use of special gestures (on the part of the officiant); and repetition (presumably of manual acts and spoken formulas) in order to guarantee the efficacy of the ritual.

Arts. Dance is an important element of certain Bondo ceremonial observances (e.g., weddings, festivals, and funerals). Instrumental music accompanies dancing on these occasions. Instruments include drums, gongs, horns, and flutes. Vocal music is also included in these rites. The corpus of Bondo songs is substantial. Compositions reflect usage in a variety of social settings (e.g., the hunt and courtship). The visual arts include carving, decorative weaving, and tattooing (to a limited extent). Items for personal adornment (chiefly bracelets and necklaces) are manufactured for the Bondo by Ghasia and Kammar metalworkers. Finally, Bondo oral literature also contains a substantial number of folklore motifs.

Medicine. The Bondo acknowledge the existence of several disease-causing gods (e.g., those related to smallpox, pneumonia, cholera, and stomachache). These show evidence of Hindu influence. In addition, even Mahaprabhu, who is seen as a benevolent force primarily, may also cause sickness. It is the responsibility of the dissari to diagnose and prescribe the ritual means of relief for illness.

Death and Afterlife. It is believed that after death, the human *sairem* (ghost) and *jiwo* (soul) are separated from the body. The sairem wanders aimlessly in the afterlife until the *gunum* ceremony (in which a stone memorial is erected) is performed. Upon the performance of this ritual, the ghost is admitted into the company of the Bondo departed. The jiwo rises to dwell in the presence of Mahaprabhu until it is reincarnated. These beliefs show a blending of indigenous and Hindu elements.

Bibliography

Elwin, Verrier (1950). *Bondo Highlander.* London: Oxford University Press.

Elwin, Verrier (1964). *The Tribal World of Verrier Elwin.* New York and Bombay: Oxford University Press.

HUGH R. PAGE, JR.

Brahman

ETHNONYMS: none

The Brahmans are a sacerdotal elite found everywhere in Hindu Asia, even as far east as Bali and Lombok in Indonesia. While in any one area they may be identified as the highest caste, there are in fact some hundreds of endogamous Brahman castes throughout South Asia; and so the Brahmans should more correctly be seen as a caste block, or in Sanskrit terms a *varna.* They have always been the highest-ranking of the four varnas or categories that make up Hindu society. Brahmans have traditionally been priests, either in temples or to particular families (*purohita*). Nevertheless, many Brahmans still follow other traditional occupations such as teacher, scribe or government clerk, and landowner.

The essential attributed character that all Brahmans share depends on: (a) their supreme level of purity, which is usually expressed in a vegetarian diet (though there are fish-eating Brahmans in Bengal); and (b) their literacy in Sanskrit and other languages, combined with their knowledge of

Hindu liturgy. The various Brahman castes are distinguished from each other first in terms of mother tongue (e.g., Tamil Brahmans, Konkani Brahmans). Then they are distinguished in terms of philosophical sect (e.g., Smarta Brahmans, Madhava Brahmans, Sri Vaishnava Brahmans). Thirdly, they may be distinguished in terms of the precise locality that was their homeland (e.g. Kongudesa Brahmans, those who came from the old Kongu territory, which is now Coimbatore District, in Tamil Nadu).

See also Anavil Brahman; Castes, Hindu; Chitpavan Brahman; Kshatriya; Nambudiri Brahman; Pandit of Kashmir; others listed in the Appendix.

Bibliography

Enthoven, Reginald E. (1920). "Brahman." In *The Tribes and Castes of Bombay,* edited by R. E. Enthoven. Vol. 1, 213–254. Bombay: Government Central Press. Reprint. 1975. Delhi: Cosmo Publications.

Nanjundayya, H. V., and L. K. Ananthakrishna Iyer (1928). "Brahman." In *The Mysore Tribes and Castes,* edited by H. V. Nanjundayya and L. K. Ananthakrishna Iyer. Vol. 2, 297–549. Mysore: Mysore University.

Rangachari, Kadambi (1931). *The Sri Vaishnava Brahmans.* Bulletin of the Madras Government Museum, New Series, General Section, 2, no. 2. Madras: Government Press.

Raychaudhuri, Tarak C., and Bikash Raychaudhuri (1981). *The Brahmans of Bengal: A Textual Study in Social History.* Calcutta: Anthropological Survey of India.

Russell, R. V., and Hira Lal (1916). "Brahman." In *The Tribes and Castes of the Central Provinces of India.* Vol. 2, 351–400. Nagpur: Government Printing Press. Reprint. 1969. Oosterhout: Anthropological Publications.

Thurston, Edgar, and Kadambi Rangachari (1909). "Brahman." In *Castes and Tribes of Southern India.* Vol. 1, 267–393. Madras: Government Press.

PAUL HOCKINGS

Brahman and Chhetri of Nepal

ETHNONYM: Bahun

Orientation

Identification. Brahman and Chhetri are high Hindu Nepalese castes. They have played a more dominant role than have any other group in the formation of the modern Nepalese state. Their moral values and social and political strength continue to play a commanding part in contemporary Nepalese life. Brahmans are known in Nepali as "Bahuns." Chhetri is the Nepali equivalent of Kshatriya, the second of the four *varnas* into which classical Indian society was divided.

Location.   Brahmans and Chhetris are found throughout Nepal. Those living in the Terai (the low, level strip in the southern part of the country) are much like their counterparts across the border in northern India. This article describes those who inhabit the middle hills of Nepal. Here the climate of their villages depends primarily on elevation, which varies from 300 meters or so in the valley bottoms to as high as 2,500 to 3,000 meters on the hillsides and tops of ridges.

Demography.   Because the Nepalese census does not record the caste status of citizens, it is impossible to know how many Brahmans and Chhetris inhabit the country; but probably the two castes together constitute the largest group in Nepal. Their percentage of the population declines from the western hills, where they comprise well over half the population, to the east, where they are usually one among many minorities.

Linguistic Affiliation.   Brahmans and Chhetris speak the national language, Nepali, as their mother tongue. This is an Indo-European language closely related to Hindi and other North Indian languages. Like Sanskrit, the language from which it is descended, Nepali is written in the Devanagari script, which is a syllabary rather than an alphabet. The rate of literacy among Brahman men, whose traditional priestly role required them to read sacred Hindu texts, is well above the national average.

History and Cultural Relations

Brahmans are thought to have begun emigrating to the far western Nepalese hills in the twelfth century after they were dislodged by Muslim invasions in India. In the Nepal hills they encountered the Khas, people of the same general background as the Brahmans, who nevertheless ranked low in the caste order because of their deviance from orthodox caste rules. Both the Khas and the progeny of unions of Brahman men and Khas women, called Khatri, were granted the status of Chhetri. The existence of Matwali Chhetris (those who drink liquor), who do not wear the sacred thread, is evidence that not all Khas were accorded Chhetri status.

Settlements

Brahmans and Chhetris live in villages, hamlets, and isolated homesteads. The walls of their small houses are constructed from stone or mud brick, painted red ocher around the base, whitewashed above, and topped with a thatched roof. The floors and interior walls are made from a mixture of cow dung and mud, which dries to a clean, hard surface. The houses of those living in towns, such as Kathmandu, the capital, are larger and are made of brick and cement.

Economy

Subsistence and Commercial Activities.   Rural Brahmans and Chhetris keep a few cattle and raise crops in their terraced fields. Brahmans also act as family priests, and Chhetris serve in both the Nepalese army and the Gorkha (Gurka) brigades of the British and Indian armies. In urban areas both castes are prominent in government service, financial services, and politics.

Industrial Arts.   Any needs that Brahmans and Chhetris experience for craft and industrial products are met by lower-ranked artisan castes, such as blacksmiths, tailors, and leather workers.

Trade.   In rural areas Brahmans and Chhetris typically rely on others, such as Newar shopkeepers, for their commercial requirements.

Division of Labor.   Only Brahman males may act as priests, but much of the daily household *puja* (worship) is done by women. The day-to-day agropastoral activities of Brahman and Chhetri families are shared between men and women. Both sexes work in the fields, but overall women spend more hours per day in agricultural and domestic labor than men. They perform most of the child care, preparation and cooking of food, and weeding and tending of crops. Men do the plowing and maintain the terrace walls. Both are active at harvest time.

Land Tenure.   Brahmans and Chhetris are often landowners. Fields are often terraced and mostly have been fractionated into small plots through inheritance over generations. Large-scale absentee landlordism is not common in the hills of Nepal.

Kinship

Kin Groups and Descent.   Brahmans and Chhetris are members of two kinds of clans, the *thar* (indicated as a surname) and the *gotra;* the former is exogamous if a relation can be traced, but the latter is strictly exogamous. Descent and inheritance follow the male line exclusively.

Kinship Terminology.   All first cousins are addressed by sibling terms. Siblings are designated as either older or younger brothers or sisters: there is no generic term for brother or sister. Unrelated persons, including strangers, are also often addressed by kinship terms.

Marriage and Family

Marriage.   Most marriages are monogamous, but polygynous unions were traditionally frequent and are still occasionally found. Second and subsequent wives are often members of other ethnic groups, such as the Gurungs, Magars, Tamangs, Sherpas, and Newars, but not low-caste artisan groups. With the exception of Thakuris, the self-proclaimed aristocrats among the Chhetris who practice matrilateral cross-cousin marriage, cousin marriage is not practiced. Brahman girls traditionally married by the age of 11, and Chhetri girls a few years later; but educated urban dwellers now marry in their late teens or early twenties. Grooms are normally a few years older than their brides. Village exogamy is usually observed, and parents arrange their children's marriages with the help of an intermediary. An astrologer also is consulted to ensure that the couple make a good match. The boy's family priest, in consultation with the bride's family, sets an auspicious date and time, based on the lunar calendar (several months of the year are inauspicious for marriage). The entire wedding ceremony lasts a full day, from the time the members of the groom's party arrive at the bride's home till they leave the next day with the bride. The most important part of the ritual is *kanyadan*, the gift of the bride to the groom by her parents. A married woman always wears vermilion powder in the parting of her hair, so long as her husband is alive.

Domestic Unit. The newly married couple ideally, and usually, live with the groom's family, along with his parents, brothers and their wives (if any), and unmarried sisters. A new bride enters this household in a lowly position, and her mother-in-law usually gives her the most onerous chores. Her status rises after she has given birth to a child, particularly if it is a son. Eventually she herself succeeds to the powerful position of mother-in-law.

Inheritance. Except for what a daughter may receive as dowry, all property, particularly all landed property, is inherited by sons. If a joint family is dissolved before the senior parents die, a woman is entitled to a share of her husband's property.

Socialization. Mother and child are considered polluting until the eleventh day after birth, when a purifying ceremony is conducted and the baby is given a name. The first feeding of rice, called *pasni*, is given after 5 months for a girl and 7 months for a boy. A boy's head is shaved at about 7 years of age (a small tuft of hair is left on the back as a sign that he is a Hindu), and he is formally initiated into full caste membership when he receives the sacred thread, either at the time of the haircut or a few years later. At her first menstruation a girl is removed to another house, where she is shielded from the sight of any men in her family and from the sun. Both parents participate in raising their children, but women perform most of the child care, especially in the preteen years. Fathers act as disciplinarians as their children grow older.

Sociopolitical Organization

Social Organization. A caste system prevails, with the Brahmans and Chhetris occupying a very high position in it.

Political Organization. Village political life tends to follow its own dynamic, regardless of changes in the national political scene. Village affairs tend to be managed by formal or informal councils of village elders in which Brahmans and Chhetris, by virtue of their status as landholders and their relatively higher education, often play prominent roles. Nationally the king, whose ancestor unified the country in roughly its present form at the end of the eighteenth century, has always been a Thakuri, an aristocratic section of Chhetris. The Rana family, which provided all prime ministers from 1846 till 1950 and is still powerful in the government and army, is also Chhetri. The movement to overthrow the Ranas and subsequent political movements aimed at democratic or socialist reform have frequently been led by Brahmans and Chhetris.

Social Control. Until 1963 Nepal's Mulki Ain (national code) explicitly stated which activities were proper for each caste group and prescribed penalties for infractions of the law. Since the code's revision in 1963, the Mulki Ain treats all citizens equally under the law.

Conflict. Those conflicts that cannot be settled through informal means at the village level are referred to the legal and judicial system of Nepal.

Religion and Expressive Culture

Religious Beliefs. All Brahmans and Chhetris are Hindus and subscribe to most of the basic Hindu beliefs. At a minimum these include three notions. One is dharma—the idea that each person has a specific duty, moral code, and set of behaviors which are entailed by virtue of membership in a group (such as a caste group). Another idea is that of karma—sometimes likened to "cause and effect," because it explains whatever present state of affairs exists in terms of the events in previous lives that produced it. The third is *moksha* (salvation)—release from the round of rebirths that reincarnation involves.

Religious Practitioners. Brahmans may act as family priests (for Brahman and Chhetri households, but not for other castes and ethnic groups), as well as officiate at shrines and temples and at rituals associated with major festivals. They also handle all the rituals performed during marriage. They are generally present on religious occasions and read excerpts from the Vedas or other Sanskrit texts. They also recite from the Puranas and from the two great Hindu epics, the *Ramayana* and the *Mahabharata*.

Ceremonies. All Brahmans and Chhetris are Hindus and observe festivals, perform rituals, and worship deities associated with Hinduism. One of the more important annual festivals is Dasein (or Durga Puja), in which the goddess Durga (Kali) is worshiped over a fortnight in the month of October. Many ritual offerings and animal sacrifices are made at this time, and there is much feasting and visiting among immediate family and extended kin. On the tenth day of the fortnight each individual male and female pays respect to senior relatives, who then reciprocate by placing a colored *tika* on the forehead of the junior person. Also observed is Phagu (called Holi in India), the spring rite of Hindu culture related to fecundity and the god Krishna. It comes in the month of Phagun (February–March) and is a riotous time when men, women, and children sing, dance, and throw colored powder and water at each other. Other annual festivals include Tihar (Dipavali, the festival of lights), Janai Purnima (changing of the sacred thread), and Tij-panchami (a purificatory rite for women). Rituals in addition to those mentioned above (under Socialization and Marriage) include worship of the household god (*kuldevta*), worship of brothers by sisters (*bhai tika*, celebrated during Tihar), and daily (morning and sometimes evening) worship of various of the Hindu deities, including Ganesh, Shiva, Vishnu, Ram, Krishna, Saraswati, Durga, Parvati, Narayan, Bhairab, and many others. Some Chhetris of west Nepal worship Mashta through shamans (*dhamis* or *jhankris*) and know little or nothing about traditional Hindu deities and festivals.

Arts. Brahmans and Chhetris are not known for their artistic interests or abilities. Music, dance, and visual and plastic arts are traditionally the domain of other, generally lower castes, and except among educated urban people Brahmans and Chhetris do not indulge themselves in these activities. Their simple, mostly undecorated houses reflect this lack of artistic bent.

Medicine. Brahmans and Chhetris will accept medical help from any available source, whether it is an Ayurvedic doctor (a specialist in herbal medicine), a passing Buddhist lama with a reputation for effective medicines, a shaman who prescribes treatment after going into a trance, or a practitioner trained in modern scientific medicine.

Death and Afterlife. Someone whose death appears to be imminent is taken to a riverbank to die, as all rivers are considered sacred. Even if death occurs elsewhere, within hours the corpse is cremated beside the river, into which the ashes are finally cast. Mourning restrictions (including elimination of salt and other items from the diet) for the death of a close relative are observed for thirteen days. Men shave their heads and are considered polluting during this time. At the end of the mourning period a big feast takes place. Food and other items for the deceased in the next life are given as gifts to the officiating priest. For one year a monthly *shraddha* ceremony is performed. Thereafter an annual shraddha ceremony commemorates the person who has died. Without funeral rites—which must be performed by a son—the deceased cannot proceed to either Heaven or Hell and instead will plague survivors as an evil spirit.

Bibliography

Bennett, Lynn (1983). *Dangerous Wives and Sacred Sisters: Social and Symbolic Roles of High-Caste Women in Nepal*. New York: Columbia University Press.

Bista, Dor Bahadur (1987). *People of Nepal*. 5th ed. Kathmandu: Ratna Pustak Bhandar.

Fürer-Haimendorf, Christoph von (1966). "Unity and Diversity in the Chhetri Caste of Nepal." In *Caste and Kin in Nepal, India, and Ceylon*, 11–67. London: Asia Publishing House.

Hitchcock, John T. (1978). "An Additional Perspective on the Nepali Caste System." In *Himalayan Anthropology: The Indo-Tibetan Interface*, edited by James F. Fisher, 111–120. The Hague: Mouton Publishers.

Prindle, Peter H. (1983). *Tinglatar: Socio-Economic Relationships of a Brahmin Village in East Nepal*. Kathmandu: Ratna Pustak Bhandar.

Sharma, Prayag Raj (1971). "The Matwali Chhetris of Western Nepal." *Himalayan Review* 4:43–60.

JAMES F. FISHER

Brahui

ETHNONYMS: none

The Brahui are a group of tribes who live primarily in Baluchistan and Sind provinces of Pakistan. Their numbers have been placed at anywhere from 861,000 to 1.5 million in Pakistan with about 200,000 in Afghanistan and 10,000 in Iran. Brahui is a Dravidian language and, as such, is distinct from the languages of the neighboring Pathan, Baluch, and Sind peoples. It is reported that many Brahui are bilingual in Baluchi and that Brahui contains numerous loanwords from Baluchi and Sindhi. The heart of Brahui territory is the district of Kalat, in Baluchistan. Politically, the Brahui are best described as a loose confederation of tribes, which was ruled from about 1700 to Pakistan's independence in 1947 by the Ahmadzais dynasty. Tribal membership is based on patrilineal descent and political allegiance, although both membership and alignments are somewhat fluid. Tribes are governed by the *sadar*, a hereditary chief, who today plays the role of intermediary between the largely rural population and the national government. Since independence, the Brahui have been slowly drawn into the national political and economic systems, though these integrative processes are far from complete.

The traditional economy for many Brahui was based on pastoral nomadism, with a shift to transhumant pastoralism beginning about 100 years ago, and more recently a shift to settled agriculture. As nomads, they dwelt in tents made of goat hair, and lived chiefly on the products of the herd. From March to October they grow cereals, fruits, and vegetables; in November they move south to sell cattle and handicrafts, or work as seasonal laborers. Many have settled on irrigated land in Sind.

The Brahuis are nearly all Sunni Muslims. Some of them take multiple wives, and divorce is unusual. Men prefer to marry a brother's daughter. Women are not strictly veiled. The men are often armed with rifles, swords, and shields.

Bibliography

Swidler, Nina (1984). "Brahui." In *Muslim Peoples: A World Ethnographic Survey*, edited by Richard V. Weekes, 177–180. Westport, Conn.: Greenwood Press.

Wilber, Donald N. (1964). *Pakistan: Its People, Its Society, Its Culture*. New Haven: HRAF Press.

SAIDEH MOAYED-SANANDAJI AND SARWAT S. ELAHI

Burusho

ETHNONYM: Hunzukuts

Orientation

The Burusho are a mountain people inhabiting a small number of rocky terraces in the independent Pakistani states of Hunza and Nagir. The region is mountainous and is characterized by deep valleys carved by the Hunza River. The geographical focus of the Burusho homeland extends from 36°00' to 37°10' N and from 74°10' to 75°40' E. The area is dry and quite barren and the terraces occupied by the Burusho require considerable ingenuity to be rendered habitable. The major portion of the area occupied by them falls within the boundaries of Hunza. In 1959 the population of Hunza totaled some 25,000 persons. This figure represents a significant increase from the figures of 1894 (6,000) and 1934 (15,000).

Burushaski, a language unrelated to any language spoken in the region, is the lingua franca. Burushaski is believed to be a survival of an aboriginal language once spoken in much of northern India before the arrival of Aryan settlers. The dialect of Burushaski spoken in Hunza is thought to be a pure form of its archaic (i.e., pre-Aryan) progenitor, while the dialect spoken in Nagir is believed to have been influenced partially by Shina, the native language of the state of Nagir. A few Arabic and Persian loanwords can be found in Burushaski as a result of the influence of Islam in the region.

History and Cultural Relations

Legend records that the original inhabitants of the Hunza region were three soldiers in the army of Alexander the Great. These soldiers and their families were left behind because of physical infirmity. The soldiers themselves are said to have been the founders of the first three Hunza villages (Baltit, Ganesh, and Altit). The ruling families in Hunza and Nagir claim, unofficially, direct descent from Alexander the Great. There is also lore ascribing European ancestry to the original inhabitants of Hunza. The physical characteristics of the Burusho seem to verify this. Before the arrival of the British, the people of Hunza conducted raids throughout central Asia. The _mirs_ (rulers) of Hunza have enjoyed favorable relations with their neighbors in China over the years. In 1947, Hunza and other regions originally part of Kashmir were seized by Pakistan. The area is now part of the Gilgit Agency in Pakistan.

Settlements

Villages are built on shelves several hundred feet above the Hunza River gorge (approximately 2,500 to 3,000 meters above sea level) and are heavily fortified. Access to individual villages in this area is obtained by traveling on narrow roads that are also located high above the river basin. Homes are never built on arable land. Construction materials consist of stone, rock, or clay. Doors, roofs, supporting pillars, and a few other household features are made of wood. The lower floor of a home has two sections: a courtyard (uncovered) for animals; and a living space for human use. Homes are built in close proximity to one another and are in a sense located almost on top of one another.

Economy

Subsistence and Commercial Activities. The Burusho engage in most subsistence activities. Small breeds of cattle, yaks, goats, and sheep are kept (goats and cattle for meat and dairy purposes). Ducks, crows, golden eagles, vultures, chickens, pheasants, chickores (red-legged partridges), pigeons, and doves are hunted. A small number of wild fruits are gathered. Cats are kept as household pets. Agriculture is at the heart of the Burusho cycle of subsistence. Crops include potatoes, garlic, beans, peas, carrots, tomatoes, leafy vegetables, mulberries, apples, walnuts, almonds, plums, pears, cherries, grapes, millet, wheat, barley, rye, buckwheat, rice, spices, cucumbers, tobacco, and flax. Fields are terraced on mountainsides. These are irrigated by a complex system of drainage conduits. Wooden agricultural implements are the norm, though iron-tipped plowshares, iron hoes, spades, forks, shears, and sickles are also used.

Industrial Arts. Some of the more important items made by the Burusho are convex iron grills (for cooking), wooden trays (for flour kneading), goat's-hair products (rugs, saddlebags, and ropes), animal-skin boots, handiwork (in stone, bone, and horn), moccasins, woolen garments, baskets, farming implements of iron and wood, woven cloth, blankets, and various utensils (for food preparation, consumption, and storage).

Trade. Trade between the Burusho and their neighbors has been negligible since antiquity. In exchange for personal services (as laborers, porters, and burden bearers), Chinese caravanners provided cooking implements, cloth, tea, silk, and other commodities to Burusho traders. The Burusho also obtain food from Nagir by means of barter and the exchange of money (though cash has always been in scarce supply in Hunza). The Burusho obtain salt (once mined locally at Shimshal) from Pindi and Gilgit. Most luxury items from India, Turkestan, and central Asia are purchased by the Burusho at markets in Gilgit.

Division of Labor. Occupational specialization based on gender designations does not obtain. Men and women share in such varied activities as threshing, winnowing, load carrying, and in the socialization of children. Family cooperation in most matters is the Burusho norm. Although there is no formal prohibition against the performance of certain tasks by either gender, heavier work tends to be done by males (e.g., wall construction, plowing and irrigation), while other tasks are assumed by females (e.g., child rearing, care of vegetable patches, and the management of the household food supply).

Land Tenure. The majority of Hunza families are freeholders. Land remains in these families from generation to generation. Taxes are not levied against a landowner during his lifetime or upon his death. In antiquity, the mirs owned parcels of village land and these were farmed by means of forced labor. In this century, reforms have led to the leasing of this land to tenant farmers who pay a small fixed fee to the mir once the land begins to produce its yield.

Kinship, Marriage and Family

Kinship. The Burusho population contains four major clans and several minor ones. The major clans are centered on the city of Baltit while the minor clans are dispersed in other settlements. Mixed marriages (i.e., between the Burusho and other ethnic groups) are rare. Patrilineal descent is the norm. Hawaiian-type kin terms for first cousins are used.

Marriage. The practice of child marriage does not obtain among the Burusho. The average marital age is 16 years of age for a female and 18 years of age for a male. The marriage of first cousins is avoided but not prohibited. Bride-price varies with social class. Marriages are held once each year (usually on 21 December when snow is on the ground) and the ceremony is performed in the house of the bride's father. In theory, parents have complete authority in the mate selection for their children. In practice, however, the will of the male and female to be wed is ascertained before the marriage is arranged. A man and woman will not be wed against their will. Divorce is allowed but is difficult to obtain. Divorce is granted to a man only on the grounds of adultery. A wife may not divorce her husband. She may appeal to the mir to have her husband divorce her. Children remain with the mother (until they reach the age of 10) if a divorce is granted. During this time, the husband is required to provide child support. Widows must wait three months and seven days after the death of a spouse before remarrying. The wait for a widower is two months and seven days. Polygyny is not prohibited.

Domestic Unit.   Small extended families (the procreated family of one individual in the senior generation and those of at least two in the next generation) with limited polygyny are the norm.

Inheritance.   The father of a family owns all of the family property. He may choose to divide his property among his off-spring before his death or it may be divided after he dies. Upon his death, his estate is divided equally among his sons. Sons may choose to work any land inherited together (i.e., as a group) or they may divide it among themselves. Sons by second wives inherit a grandson's share. The youngest son inherits the family dwelling. Provision is usually made so that the eldest son inherits the best land. A daughter is not permitted to inherit property. She may be allowed the use of certain property during her lifetime. Unmarried daughters must be cared for (including the provision of a dowry) by the estate of a deceased father. Apricot trees (and their produce) are often willed to daughters.

Socialization.   The socialization of children is a responsibility shared by both parents, with the bulk of it being assumed by the mother. Siblings also share in this task. In 1934, a public school system was donated and put into place by the Aga Khan, thus placing part of the burden for child rearing on teachers.

Sociopolitical Organization

Burusho society contains five classes: the Thamo (royal family); the Uyongko/Akabirting (those who may occupy offices of state); the Bar/Bare/Sis (land cultivators); the Shadarsho (servants); and the Baldakuyo/Tsilgalasho (bearers of burdens for the Thamo and Uyongko). The Bericho (Indian blacksmiths and musicians), who maintain their own customs and speak their own language (Kumaki), are also an important part of Burusho social structure. Age and gender stratification do not obtain among the Burusho.

The head of state is the mir, whose authority in all matters is absolute. He is assisted in the dispatch of his duties by a grand vizier. Mirs are responsible for the distribution of justice as well as the maintenance of local customs and tribal festivals. A village *arbob* (chief) and *chowkidar* (sergeant at arms) are appointed for each village. *Khalifas* are appointed by the mir to preside at important occasions in the life of the individual and the community. It has been noted that at one time retainers to certain villagers were paid by the British government for occasional services and that certain officials within a village were charged with the care of visitors.

The threat of deportation (for the purpose of engaging in public service to the mir or for the completion of public works) and the imposition of fines are the primary means of maintaining social control. External relations between the Burusho and other peoples have been stable. Intervillage rivalry is channeled nonviolently into polo matches. Although the attitudes of the Burusho toward their neighbors in Nagir are less than friendly, armed conflict is far from normal. Both Hunza and Nagir supported the military action that led to the annexation of the region to Pakistan.

Religion and Expressive Culture

Religious Beliefs and Practices.   The Burusho have been Muslim for more than 300 years. They are adherents of the Ismaili sect (headed by the Aga Khan) and have made such modifications in religious belief and practice as to render this system of Islamic belief practicable within their social and environmental setting. No systematized eschatological system exists among the Burusho. It is generally believed that at some point in the future the living and the dead will be reunited. *Bitaiyo* (male and female prognosticators) foretell the future by inhaling the smoke of burning juniper twigs. No professional priesthood exists among the Burusho. The mir appoints several literate men as khalifas to officiate at burials, weddings, and naming ceremonies. These individuals do not perform these duties on a full-time basis. Religious ceremony plays little part in the daily life of the Burusho. Ritual prayer and fasting are practiced by some. While little is known of pre-Islamic religious practices, it is believed that at one time sacrifice was offered to the *boyo* (divinities thought to occupy a place above the fort at Hini). The communal wedding ceremony held on 21 December is also an important part of the Burusho ritual cycle.

Arts.   Embroidery and wood carving may be noted as examples of Burusho visual art. Dancing and music (both being important components of Burusho ceremonial life) are attested. The same can be said of dramatic art, performances being sponsored on certain special occasions. Burusho oral literature contains folklore (indigenous and borrowed), anecdotes, and songs.

Medicine.   A variety of natural substances (roots, herbs, and berries) is used for medicinal purposes. Access to scientific medicine is also available. The belief is still held by some Burusho that supernaturals play a major role in the cause of human illness. Indigenous medical practitioners are lacking.

Bibliography

Clark, J. (1963). "Hunza in the Himalayas: Storied Shangri-La Undergoes Scrutiny." *Natural History* 72:38–45.

Lorimer, David L. (1935–1938). *The Burushaski Language*. 3 vols. Instituttet for Sammenlignende Kulturforskning, Serie B: Skrifter, 29, 1–3. Oslo: H. Aschehoug & Co. (W. Nygaard): Cambridge: Harvard University Press.

Lorimer, E. O. (1938). "The Burusho of Hunza." *Antiquity* 12:5–15.

Lorimer, E. O. (1939). *Language Hunting in the Karakoram*. London: George Allen & Unwin.

O'Leary, Timothy J. (1965). "Burusho Cultural Summary." New Haven, Conn.: Human Relations Area Files.

Tobe, John H. (1960). *Adventures in a Land of Paradise*. Emmaus, Pa.: Rodale Books.

HUGH R. PAGE, JR.

Castes, Hindu

The caste system is a form of hierarchical, kin-based social organization of great antiquity found in South Asian societies. The term, from the Portuguese _casta_, is frequently contrasted with such other social categories as race, class, tribe, and ethnic group. In India, caste—together with the village community and the extended family—forms the main element of social structure. This system consists of hierarchically arranged, in-marrying groups that were traditionally associated with a specific occupational specialization. Interrelations between castes arose out of the need of one caste for the goods or services of another. These relations are governed by codes of purity and pollution.

The word _caste_ itself is homologous with any of three different indigenous terms. _Varna_, which was an ancient, all-India classification system consisting of a fourfold division of society, perhaps arose out of a blending of the nomadic warrior culture of Aryans with the settled urban, agrarian culture of the Indus Valley. The religious text _Rig Veda_ spells out and justifies this stratification system, putting the Brahman or priest at the top, followed by the Kshatriya or warrior, Vaisya or landowner and trader, and Shudra or artisan and servant, in that order. Later a fifth varna of Untouchables developed, called Panchama, to accommodate intercaste offspring. The word _caste_ may also be coterminous with the word _jati_, which is a hereditary occupational unit. Hindu texts say that jatis, of which there are several thousand, emerged out of intermarriages between varnas. Modern theory holds that jatis developed as other social groups like tribes or those practicing a new craft or occupational skill became integrated into the classic varna system. This process continues today as groups on the fringes of Hindu society become part of it by claiming a jati designation. Lastly, caste may refer to _gotra_, which is an exogamous descent group within a jati. It may be anchored territorially, and its members may hold property in common.

The caste system rests on the following principles. (1) Endogamy. The strictest rule of caste is marriage within the jati. Arranged marriage at adolescence ensures this. (2) Commensality. Caste members are restricted to eating and drinking only with their own kind. (3) Hereditary membership. One is born into the caste of one's parents. (4) Occupational specialization. Each caste has a fixed and traditional occupation. This makes it an economic as well as a social system. This aspect of caste is the one that has been affected most by modernization and Westernization. (5) Hierarchy. Castes are arranged in some kind of order, each caste being superior or inferior to another. Since not all castes are found in every village or every part of South Asia, and which one is superior to which others varies from region to region, hierarchy is the dynamic element of caste.

Underpinning the entire system are notions of purity and pollution. Words for these two ideas occur in every Indian language. Each term has a certain amount of semantic fluidity. _Pure_ means "clean, spiritually meritorious, holy"; _impure_ means "unclean, defiled," and even "sinful." The structural distance between castes is measured in terms of purity and pollution; higher castes are pure in their occupation, diet, and life-style. Caste rules govern intercaste relations, determining the social and physical distance that people of different castes have to maintain from each other and their rights and obligations toward others. An equally important feature of caste rank is the notion of serving and being served, of giving and receiving. Castes may be ranked by the balance between the intercaste transactions in which one caste is a giver and those in which it is a receiver of goods, services, gifts, or purely spiritual merit. The seeming contradiction between the power and position of the Brahman versus that of the king or the politically and economically dominant caste can be resolved in light of the transactional aspect of caste, which creates varied realms of differentiation and ranking.

Individuals accept their position in the caste system because of the dual concepts of karma and dharma. It is one's karma or actions in a previous life that determine one's caste position in this lifetime. The only way to ensure a better position in society next time is to follow one's dharma or caste duty. So closely are notions of salvation in Hinduism tied to caste duty that a Hindu without a caste is a contradiction in terms.

Although an individual's caste is fixed by his or her birth, the position of a caste within the system is changeable. A caste as a whole may accumulate wealth that would allow it to give up manual labor and adopt a "cleaner profession," thereby raising their comparative purity. Today the process of "Sanskritization," in which a lower caste or a tribal community imitates high-caste behavior, is an attempt to move up the caste hierarchy. The most common changes are switching to a vegetarian diet and holding public prayers using high-caste forms and Brahman priests. In daily life secularization and Western education lead to an undervaluing of caste identity on the one hand and a compartmentalization of the self on the other. The latter phenomenon occurs when an individual varies his behavior according to the context (e.g., at work he adopts a secular self without observing caste taboos, but at home he is a caste Hindu).

Caste becomes a potent force in a modern democratic political system when it becomes a caste block whose members can affect the outcome of elections. At local levels this can lead to a monopoly of power by one caste, but no caste is large enough or united enough to do so at a national level. Another modern trend is to be found among migrants from rural parts who tend to settle close to each other in the city, forming a caste neighborhood. Often they form caste associations for civic and religious purposes (e.g., celebrating Independence Day or performing religious recitals). In addition they may petition for government benefits, set up student hostels, commission the writing of a caste history, or in other ways promote the welfare of their group. In recent times some high castes have resented the privileges now flowing to low castes and have even taken the matter into their own hands in intercommunal strife.

See also Bengali; Brahman; Kshatriya; Sudra; Untouchables; Vaisya

Bibliography

Berreman, Gerald D. (1979). _Caste and Other Inequities: Essays on Inequality._ New Delhi: Manohar Book Service.

Kolenda, Pauline M. (1978). _Caste in Contemporary India: Beyond Organic Solidarity._ Prospect Heights, Ill.: Waveland Press.

Mandelbaum, David. G. (1970). *Society in India.* 2 vols. Berkeley and Los Angeles: University of California Press.

Raheja, Gloria G. (1988). "India: Caste, Kingship, and Dominance Reconsidered." *Annual Review of Anthropology* 17: 497–522.

W. D. MERCHANT

Chakma

ETHNONYM: Changma

Orientation

Identification.   The Chakma speak a dialect of Bengali or Bangla, live in southeastern Bangladesh, and are predominantly of the Buddhist faith. Although they are generally known in the anthropological literature as Chakma—and are officially so termed in Bangladesh—they usually call themselves Changma.

Location.   Bangladesh is located between 20° 34' and 26° 38' N and 88° 01' and 92° 41' E. Chakma (and another eleven ethnic minority peoples) occupy three hilly districts of Bangladesh—Rangamati, Bandarban, and Khagrachhari. This hill region is cut by a number of streams, canals, ponds, lakes, and eastern rivers; it covers a total area of about 13,000 square kilometers. Some Chakma also live in India.

Demography.   According to the 1981 census the total Chakma population in Bangladesh was 212,577, making them the largest tribal group in Bangladesh. In 1971 a further 54,378 Chakma were enumerated in neighboring Indian territory. They constitute 50 percent of the total tribal population of the southeastern hill region, although there are also many Bengali-speaking (nontribal or originally plains) people in the region who migrated there at various times in the past. As a result, Chakma now constitute less than 30 percent of the total population of that region. In 1964, this region lost its officially designated tribal status, and as a result many people from the plains migrated there.

Linguistic Affiliation.   The Chakma speak a dialect of Bangla (Bengali), which they write in the standard Bangla script. (This is the mother tongue of almost 99 percent of the total population in Bangladesh—i.e., of some 110 million people.) However, it seems likely that the Chakma once spoke an Arakanese (Tibeto-Burman) language, which they later abandoned in favor of the Indo-European tongue of their Bengali neighbors. The Chakma writer Biraj Mohan Dewan gives a figure of 80 percent for the Bangla-derived Chakma vocabulary.

History and Cultural Relations

Scholars differ on the origin and history of Chakma. One popular view among the Chakma is that their ancestors once lived in Champoknagar, although opinions differ as to its location. It is also guessed that the Chakma derived their name from Champoknagar. According to oral history the Chakma left Champoknagar for Arakan in Burma where they lived for about 100 years. They had to leave Arakan for Bangladesh in or around sixteenth century, when Bangladesh was governed by Muslim rulers, before the arrival of the British. Even if we do not believe the story of their origin in Champoknagar, we have reason to believe the Chakma lived in Arakan before they migrated to Bangladesh. They were then nomadic shifting cultivators. On their arrival in Bangladesh the Chakma chiefs made a business contract with the Muslim rulers, promising to pay revenue or tax in cotton. In return they were allowed to live in the hill region and engage in trade with the larger society. By the late eighteenth century, British authorities had established themselves in the southeastern districts of Bangladesh. The British formally recognized a definite territory of the Chakma raja (the paramount chief). In 1776, Sherdoulat Khan became the Chakma raja. He fought unsuccessfully against the British. Further fighting between the Chakma and the British took place between 1783 and 1785. In 1787, Raja Janbux Khan, son of Sherdoulat Khan, made a peace treaty with the British government, promising to pay the latter 500 *maunds* of cotton. The British recognized the office of Chakma raja throughout the rest of their rule. Different Chakma rajas maintained good relations with the authorities of central administration and the Chakma increasingly came in contact with the Bengali people and culture.

Settlements

Traditionally the Chakma build their houses about 1.8 meters above the ground on wooden and bamboo piles. With the increasing scarcity of bamboo and wood, they have started to build houses directly on the ground in the Bengali style. The Chakma have a settled village life. A family may build a house on a separate plot of land. A few families also build houses on the same plot of land. These units (clusters of houses) are known as *bari* (homestead). A number of bari constitute a hamlet (*para* or *adam*). A number of hamlets make up a *gram* or village. This is also known as a *mouza*, a "revenue village." Most houses are built on the slopes of the hills, usually near streams or canals.

Bamboo is widely used in making houses. The pillars are made of bamboo (or wood); the platform (above the ground) and walls are also of bamboo. The roof is made with bamboo and hemp. A very few Chakma have started using tin for making roofs.

Economy

Subsistence and Commercial Activities.   The economy is based on agriculture. Chakma farmers utilize three different microenvironments: flat lands, which can be irrigated, slightly higher lands, which are not usually irrigated; and relatively steep highlands. Each microenvironment is utilized for the cultivation of specific crops. In the irrigated lowlands, the Chakma grow wet rice. Here plowing is done with a single metal-blade wooden plow drawn by bullocks or water buffalo. The Chakma who learned plow agriculture from Bengalis in the mid–nineteenth century grow wet rice twice a year on the same land. The crop is harvested by hand with the help of sickles. On slightly higher lands the Chakma cultivate a variety of crops. These include root crops such as taro, ginger, and turmeric, some vegetable crops, and pulses, chilies, garlic, and onions. In the hills, they cultivate mainly dry paddy, sesame, and cotton. These crops are grown by the traditional method of shifting cultivation. Men select land for swiddens in December–January; clear off the trees and bush in February–March; burn this debris by April when dry; and start sowing after a heavy rainfall, usually in April–May. They fence their swidden fields to protect crops from pigs, cattle, goats, and buffalo and begin to harvest crops in October, continuing into November.

Because of increasing population pressure, shifting cultivation is gradually being limited. The government also discourages swidden agriculture. Instead it has been trying to motivate the Chakma and other hill peoples to grow fruits such as pineapples, bananas, and jackfruit on the hills. Many Chakma have started doing so. Silviculture (i.e., planting of timber and rubber trees) is also becoming popular.

Hunting, fishing, and collecting of different edible leaves and roots are also part of their economy. Around their houses, the villagers grow vegetables. Domestic animals include pigs, fowl, ducks, cattle, goats and water buffalo.

Industrial Arts.   The Chakma weave their own cloths and make bamboo baskets of various types.

Trade.   Surplus products are brought to the markets. Some Chakma supply products to the nontribal businessmen who buy cheap, store, and then sell dear; or they supply the cities for a higher price.

Division of Labor.   Traditionally the Chakma women cook, tend babies, clean house, fetch water, weave, and wash cloths. The men assist them in tending babies and fetching water from the canals or from waterfalls. The women also do all agricultural work side by side with the men, except for plowing and cutting big trees for shifting cultivation. They also buy and sell in the marketplace.

Land Tenure.   There was no private ownership in land even in the early twentieth century. The Chakma were at liberty to choose any hill land for swiddens or flat land (between the hills) for wet rice cultivation. The Chakma and other hill peoples are now required to take grants of land from the government and to pay a land tax to the government. The Chakma raja traditionally received a small portion of tax on swidden land.

Kinship

Kin Groups and Descent.   The *paribar* (family) is the basic kinship unit in Chakma society. Beyond the paribar and bari (homestead), multihousehold compounds are the next widest unit, the members of which may form work groups and help each other in other activities. Next are the hamlets, comprised of a number of bari. They form work groups for economic activities requiring travel, such as swidden cultivation, fishing, collecting, etc. Hamlet people are organized and led by a leader called the *karbari*. The village is the next larger group who arrange a few rituals together. Descent among the Chakma is patrilineal. When a woman marries, she leaves her own family and is incorporated into that of her husband. Property is inherited in the male line. Despite the patrilineal-

ity, some recognition is given to maternal kin. For example, an individual's mother's family will participate in his or her cremation ceremony.

Kinship Terminology.   The patrilineal nature of the Chakma kinship system is partially reflected in the kinship terminology. Thus, different terms are used to address a father's brother and a mother's brother and to address a father's sister and a mother's sister. On the other hand, in the grandparental generation the distinction between paternal and maternal kin disappears, with all grandfathers being called *aju* and all grandmothers *nanu*. In the first descending generation, there is again no distinction between patrilineal and other types of kin. Thus father's brother's children, father's sister's children, mother's brother's children, and mother's sister's children are all termed *da* (male) and *di* (female).

Marriage and Family

Marriage.   Polygynous marriages are permissible among the Chakma, although they are less common today than in the past. Marriages are usually arranged by the parents, but opinions of potential spouses are considered. If a boy and girl love each other and want to marry, the parents usually give their consent provided the rules of marriage allow them to do so. Chakma rules of exogamy forbid marriage between people belonging to the same *gutti* (or *gusthi*). This gutti may be defined as a patrilineage whose members traditionally traced descent from a common ancestor within seven generations. However, early in the present century a Chakma prince, Ramony Mohon Roy, took for his wife a woman related to him within five generations, both being descendants of the same great-grandfather. Following this example, it has now become common for marriages to be allowed with anyone not patrilineally related within four generations. The gutti seems to have been redefined accordingly. In more recent times, Chakma still say that marriage should not take place within the gutti, and yet it sometimes happens that second cousins (the descendants of the same great-grandfather) are permitted to marry. Virilocal residence after marriage is the norm and people do not look favorably upon uxorilocal residence; however, rare instances of uxorilocal residence have been reported.

Domestic Unit.   The family (paribar) usually comprises a husband and wife, together with their unmarried children. However, there are instances of married sons with their wives and children living together with their parents in one paribar. Usually all members of the paribar occupy a single *ghar* or house. However, if a paribar expands to the point where it is impossible or uncomfortable for all members to live under the same roof, one or two annexes may be added at the side of the main building. But even when the paribar members live under separate roofs, they continue to cook and eat together.

Inheritance.   Property is divided equally among the sons. The daughters usually do not inherit. Usually a younger son who cares for his parents in their old age receives the homestead in addition to his share.

Socialization.   Infants and children are raised by both parents and siblings. In a three-generation family, grandparents also take active roles in socializing and enculturating the children. They are taught Buddhist ideology at an early age. Respect for elders is stressed.

Sociopolitical Organization

Social Organization.   Chakma society is hierarchically organized on the basis of age, sex, occupation, power, religion, wealth, and education. An older person is invariably respected by a younger person. The husband is more powerful than the wife in the family; and a man is afforded more status outside the family. Power is unequally distributed in Chakma society (see below). The society is also hierarchically organized on the basis of religious knowledge and practice as follows: monks, novices, religiously devoted laymen, and commoners. Educated persons who are engaged in nonagricultural work are especially respected. Wealth also influences behavior in different aspects of social life.

Political Organization.   The entire hill region of southeastern Bangladesh (which is divided into the three political and administrative districts of Rangamati, Khagrachhari, and Bandarban) is also divided into three circles, each having its own indigenous name: Mong Circle, Chakma Circle, and Bohmang Circle. Each circle, with a multiethnic population, is headed by a raja or indigenous chief, who is responsible for the collection of revenue and for regulating the internal affairs of villages within his circle. The Chakma Circle is headed by a Chakma raja (the Mong and Bohmong circles by Marma rajas). Unlike the situation in the other two circles, Chakma Circle's chieftaincy is strictly hereditary.

Each circle is subdivided into numerous mouza or "revenue villages" (also known as gram, or "villages"), each under a headman. He is appointed by the district commissioner on the basis of the recommendation of the local circle chief. The post of headman is not in theory hereditary, but in practice usually it is. The headman has, among other things, to collect revenue and maintain peace and discipline within his mouza. Finally, each mouza comprises about five to ten para (also called *adam*). These are hamlets, each with its own karbari or hamlet chief. He is appointed by the circle chief, in consultation with the concerned headman. The post of karbari also is usually hereditary, but not necessarily so. Each hamlet comprises a number of clusters of households. The head of a household or family is usually a senior male member, the husband or father.

In addition to these traditional political arrangements (circle, village, and hamlet, each having a chief or head), the local government system (imposed by the central government) has been in operation since 1960. For the convenience of administration, Bangladesh is split into four divisions, each under a divisional commissioner. Each one is further subdivided into *zila*, or districts. The administrative head of a zila is called a deputy commissioner. Each zila consists of several *upazila* or subdistricts, headed by an elected upazila chairman (elected by the people). He is assisted by a government officer known as *upazila nirbahi*, the officer who is the chief executive there. Each upazila consists of several union *parishad* or councils. An elected Chairman heads a union parishad. Several gram make up a union parishad. This administrative setup is also found in the districts of the hill region. The Chakma and other ethnic minority hill people are increasingly accepting this local governmental system because the government undertakes development projects through this structure.

Social Control.   Traditionally the village headman would settle disputes. If contending parties were not satisfied with the arbitration, they might make an appeal to the Chakma raja, the circle chief. Traditionally he was the highest authority to settle all disputes. Today they can move to the government courts if they are not satisfied with the raja's judgments. Although Chakma were usually expected to get their disputes settled either by the headman or raja, they are now at liberty to go to these courts. In recent times, depending on the nature and seriousness of disputes, the Chakma are increasingly doing this rather than settling disputes locally.

Conflict.   In the past, the Chakma fought against the British imperial government several times but failed. In recent times (since 1975), they have become aware of their rights. They do not like the influx of the nontribal population in the hill region, and they consider it an important cause of their growing economic hardships. Therefore, since 1975, some Chakma (and a few from other tribes) have fought to banish nontribal people from the hill region. The government is trying to negotiate with the Chakma and other tribal elites to settle this matter. It has already given some political, economic, and administrative powers to elected representatives of the Chakma and other hill people. These representatives (who are mostly hill men) are trying to negotiate with the Chakma (and other) agitators on behalf of the government. Many development projects have also been undertaken by the government in the hill region, so that the economic condition of the Chakma and other ethnic peoples might improve gradually.

Religion and Expressive Culture

Religious Beliefs.   The Chakma are Buddhists. There is a Buddhist temple (*kaang*) in almost every Chakma village. They give gifts to the temple and attend the different Buddhist festivals. The Chakma follow Theravada Buddhism, their official and formal religion. Buddhism dominates their life. Indeed, it is now a unifying force in the southeastern hill region of Bangladesh, as Buddhism is the common religion of Chakma, Marma, Chak, and Tanchangya. These ethnic groups celebrate together at one annual Buddhist festival called Kathin Chibar Dan, in which they make yarn (from cotton), give it color, dry the yarn, weave cloth (for monks), and formally present this cloth (after sewing) to the monks in a function. The Chakma also believe in many spirit beings, including a few Hindu goddesses. Some of these are malevolent while others are benevolent. They try to propitiate malevolent spirits through the exorcists and spirit doctors (*baidyo*). They also believe in guardian spirits that protect them. The malevolent spirits are believed to cause diseases and destroy crops.

Religious Practitioners.   Many Chakma go to the temples to listen to the sermons of the monks and novices. They also give food to the monks, novices, and the Buddha's altar. The monks read sermons and participate in life-cycle rituals, but they do not take part in village government affairs. In addition to the monks, exorcists and baidyo are believed to mediate between humans and the world of spirits through incantations, charms, possession, and sympathetic actions.

Arts. The Chakma are noted for two arts, music and weaving. The bamboo flute is popular among young men, and girls play on another kind of flute. Songs and epic poems are sung. Weaving is an essential accomplishment of women. They make complex tapestries on a back-strap loom called a _ben_. They do their own spinning and dyeing.

Ceremonies. Chakma observe both Buddhist and non-Buddhist ceremonies. They observe the days of birth, enlightenment, and death of the Buddha; they observe Kathin Chibar Dan and other Buddhist occasions. Villagers also unite to propitiate the malevolent spirits. Individual Chakma households may also arrange rituals to counteract illness and crop damage.

Medicine. Illness is attributed to fright, spirit possession, or an imbalance of elements in the body. Most Chakma will still call in a village baidyo.

Death and Afterlife. The dead body is burnt; kin and affines mourn for a week, and then they arrange _satdinna_ to pray for peace for the departed soul. The Buddhist monk leads the cremation and satdinna.

See also Bangali

Bibliography

Bangladesh, Government of (1983). _Chittagong Hill Tracts: District Statistics_. Dhaka: Bangladesh Bureau of Statistics.

Bangladesh, Government of (1989). _Statistical Year Book of Bangladesh_. Dhaka: Bangladesh Bureau of Statistics.

Bernot, Lucien (1964). "Ethnic Groups of Chittagong Hill Tracts." In _Social Research in East Pakistan_, edited by Pierre Bessaignet, 137–171. Dhaka: Asiatic Society of Pakistan.

Bessaignet, Pierre (1958). _Tribesmen of the Chittagong Hill Tracts_. Dhaka: Asiatic Society of Pakistan.

Dewan, Biraj Mohan (1969). _Chakma Jatir Itibritta_ (The history of the Chakma). Rangamati: Kali Shankar.

Ishaq, Muhammad, ed. (1972). _Bangladesh District Gazetteers: Chittagong Hill Tracts_. Dhaka: Government of Bangladesh.

MOHAMMED HABIBUR RAHMAN

Chenchu

ETHNONYM: Jungle people

The Chenchus of Andhra Pradesh (formerly Hyderabad) inhabit the hilly country north of the Kistna River, which forms the most northerly extension of the Nallamalai Hills and is generally known as the Amrabad Plateau. It lies between 16° and 16°30' N and 78°30' and 79°15' E. The whole of the plateau belongs to the Mahbubnagar District, but a few scattered Chenchus live on the other side of the Dindi River in the district of Nalgonda. In the north the plateau rises steeply about 200 meters over the plains and in the south and east drops precipitously into the valley of the Kistna River. The Amrabad Plateau falls naturally into two definite parts: the lower ledge to the northeast, with an elevation of about 600 meters, that slopes eastwards to the Dindi River; and the higher ranges to the southwest, averaging 700 meters. On the lower ledge, where there are large cultivated areas, lie Amrabad, Manamur, and other villages inhabited by Chenchus and others. The higher ranges are a pure forest area and are almost exclusively inhabited by Chenchus. In 1971 there were 24,415 Chenchus.

The Amrabad Plateau has three seasons: the hot season, which lasts from the middle of February to the end of May, with temperatures rising to 39° C; the rainy season, early in June until the end of September; and the winter from October to February. The upper plateau is a dense forest jungle of bamboo and climbers, with heavy rainfall in the rainy season but an arid sun-baked land in the hot weather. There is a great variety of animals, such as bears, panthers, hyenas, wild cats, tigers, antelope, monkey, peacocks, jungle fowl, and snakes. In 1941 the upper plateau was declared a game sanctuary.

The economic system of the Chenchus is primarily one of hunting and gathering. The Chenchus depend on nature for nine-tenths of their food supply. Traditionally Chenchus roamed the jungles, living under trees and in rock shelters. The common food was honey, the roots of trees, plants, and the flesh of animals caught in hunting. A typical day was spent in gathering the fruits and roots to be eaten that day. Gathering may be done in small groups but is still today a solitary activity without cooperation from others. Hunting is also a solitary rather than cooperative effort that rarely produces much game. Hunting is done with bow and arrow, occasionally with a gun. No trapping or snaring is done. Very few things are cultivated—mostly tobacco, corn, and some millet—and little provision is made for "a rainy day" (i.e., there is no storing of grain). There is division of labor between the sexes: men hunt, gather honey, and make baskets; women prepare most of the food. Gathering is done by both sexes although the men may go further afield, even spending two to three days away from the community. A few buffalo cows may be kept in a village for milk but are not eaten.

Recently (ca. 1943) most Chenchus lived in houses of bamboo and thatch. A part of the population remains dependent on food collected in the forest (1943). This forces them to follow the train of the seasons and at certain times of the year to leave the villages for places with more water and increased probabilities for collection of edible plants. Permanent village sites are occupied for ten to fifteen years unless disease ravages a community and many deaths occur. The size varies from three to thirteen houses, with an average number of six or seven. The permanent house (_gada illu_) is solidly built with a circular wattle wall and conical thatched roof and bamboo roof beams. Temporary dwellings may be low grass huts or shelters constructed of leafy branches.

The principal units of social organization are the clan, the local group, and the family. There is a pronounced lack of tribal feeling with few traditions. The tribe practice clan exogamy. The clans are patrilineal. There are four principal clan groups on the upper plateau: (1) Menlur and Daserolu; (2) Sigarlu and Urtalu; (3) Tokal, Nallapoteru, and Katraj; and (4) Nimal, Eravalu, and Pulsaru. Villages are usually mixed clans. Individuals may join at will any local group with which they have relations; however, they always remain "linked" to their home village where their parents lived and where they grew up. There they are coheirs to the land, whereas a man living in his wife's village is only a "guest." The family consists of the husband, wife, and unmarried children. The husband and wife are partners with equal rights and property jointly owned. There is a concurrence of patrilocal and matrilocal marriage. In the kin group there is a spirit of cooperation and mutual loyalty that is not seen at the tribe and clan levels.

The Chenchus speak a dialect of Telugu interspersed with a number of Urdu words, as do most people of Andhra Pradesh. Increasing exposure to the plains peoples has led the Chenchus to adopt the cult of various deities of the Telugu's Hindu religion.

Bibliography

Fürer-Haimendorf, Christoph von (1943). *The Aboriginal Tribes of Hyderabad.* Vol. 1, *The Chenchus.* London: Macmillan.

SARA J. DICK

Chin

ETHNONYMS: 'kKxou and related words; Mizo (same as Lushai), Zo, Zomi. Also regional and dialect group names: Chinbok, Chinbon, Dai, Kuku, Lai (same as Haka), Laizo (same as Falam), Mara (same as Lakher), Ngala (same as Matu), n'Men, etc.

Orientation

Identification.   The Chin live in the mountains of the Myanmar (Burma)–India border and in neighboring areas of Myanmar and India. "Chin" is an English version of the Burmese name for these people (cognate with a southern Chin word, 'kKxang, "a people") who call themselves Zo (or related words), meaning "marginal people." "Chin" applies strictly to the inhabitants of Myanmar's Chin State. On the Indian side of the border the major related people are the Mizo, or Lushai, of Mizoram State. The Kuki and Hmar are their relatives in Manipur State. The Plains Chin, or Asho, live in Myanmar proper just east of Chin State.

Location.   The Chin live between 92° and 95° E, and 20° and 26° N. For the most part this is high mountain country (the highest peak is 3,000 meters) with almost no land level enough for plow cultivation; villages are found at elevations between about 1,000 and 2,000 meters. This region is not drained by any major or navigable rivers. It has a monsoon climate, with a marked wet and dry season. Annual rainfall is locally as much as 230 centimeters or more a year. In the hot season (March to June) the temperature can reach about 32° C, while in the cold season (November–February), after the monsoon rains, early-morning temperatures at the higher elevations can sink to a few degrees of frost.

Demography.   There have been no useful censuses of the Burma Chin in a couple of decades, but reasonable projections from the figures of the 1950s indicate a population there of perhaps 200,000, while the population of India's Mizoram State is roughly half a million. Outside these two major areas the Chin-related population amounts to no more than a few tens of thousands. The population is unevenly distributed, but a crude estimate of average population density is at most 80 persons per square kilometer. There are few towns of any size. The largest is Aizawl, capital of Mizoram State, with a population exceeding 100,000. Owing to the absence of flat lands and ready communications with major plains areas in India and Myanmar (Burma), the number of non-Chin peoples living in the region is negligible.

Linguistic Affiliation.   The Chin languages belong to the Kuki-Chin Subgroup of the Kuki-Naga Group of the Tibeto-Burman Family. They are all tonal, monosyllabic languages, and until the late nineteenth century, when Christian missionaries developed Roman alphabets for at least the major Chin languages (including Mizo), none of them was written. There are excellent grammars and dictionaries of such major languages as Mizo, Lai (Haka) Chin, Laizo (Falam) Chin, Tedim (Northern) Chin, and n'Men (Southern) Chin.

History and Cultural Relations

Our earliest notice of Chin is in stone inscriptions in Burma of the twelfth century, which refer to Chin living in or adjacent to the middle Chindwin River of northwestern Burma. In the next century the Chindwin Plain and the tributary Kabaw-Kale Valley were conquered and settled by the Shan (a Tai-speaking people of the region), and from then on more and more of the Chin were pushed up into the mountains (no doubt displacing their close relatives already living there). By the seventeenth century these pressures increased owing to the Burmese wars with the Kale Shan and with Manipur. This brought about major population movements within the mountain region, and the present distribution of peoples in the mountains goes back mainly to the eighteenth century. The Kuki are remnants of people who were pushed out from the main Chin areas of occupation by the ancestors of the Mizo, and who then took refuge under the protection of the maharajas of Manipur. The Chin and Mizo peoples were independent of any major state until the imperial era when, in the late nineteenth century, they were brought under British rule: the Mizo in the Lushai Hills Frontier District of India, the Chin in the Chin Hills of Burma. With the achievement of independence for India and Burma in the late 1940s, these districts became respectively the Union Territory of Mizoram (Mizoram State within the Indian Union since the late 1980s) and the Chin Special Division, now Chin State, of the Union of Burma, now Myanmar. However, in spite of their traditional freedom from any semblance of outside rule or administration before the colonial period, these peoples were dependent upon the plains civilizations of India and Burma. They got all the iron for their tools and weapons from the plains, which they reforged locally, and they looked to the plains as the source for luxury goods (preeminently brassware, some elaborate woven goods, and gold and silver) and for their ideals about more luxurious social and cultural life. Their name, Zo, reflects this sense of their relative deprivation, and their origin tales also expand on this theme, purporting to explain why the Burman or Assamese "elder brother" of their original ancestor came to have all those amenities and the Chin so few. The Chin peoples got what they needed from the plains partly through trading the produce of their forests and partly by raiding border settlements in the plains. It was this habit of raiding plains settlements (for goods, slaves, and human heads—especially Lushai raids on the tea plantations of Cachar and Assam) that caused the British, in the late nineteenth century, to occupy the Chin and Lushai territories.

Settlements

With the exception of a few administrative towns—such as Aizawl, the Mizoram capital; Haka, capital of Chin State; Falam, Tedim, Matupi, and Mindat in Chin State; and the various district administrative towns in Mizoram State—the Chin peoples live in agricultural villages ranging in size from a few dozen to several hundred houses. There are more towns and fewer very small villages in Mizoram now because from 1964 until well into the 1980s Mizoram was insurgent territory in which the Indian government instituted massive resettlement and village consolidation. Now, as traditionally, the average household has about five persons in it. Villages tend to be situated well up on the hillsides, though some are placed nearer the small streams lower down. Village location has always been a compromise between the need for defensibility and the need for access to water. Houses and villages are oriented according to the possibilities provided by the convoluted slopes. Houses are built on pilings, though in some places one end or the uphill side rests directly on the ground. Traditional houses are built of hand-hewn planks for the most part, though the poorer ones have at least their walls and floors made of split bamboo. The roof is generally thatched with grass, but in parts of northern Chin State there are some slate roofs. Nowadays corrugated iron or aluminum sheeting is used when possible. The traditional floor plan is of one main interior room—or at most two—with its central hearth, a front veranda open in front but covered by a roof gable, and frequently a shallow rear compartment for washing and various sorts of storage, which may have also a latrine hole in its floor. The major limitation on the size of a village is the accessibility of agricultural land. These people are exclusively shifting cultivators: they clear and cultivate a hill slope for one to five years or so, then leave that slope to fallow and clear another forested slope in their territory. The longer a hillside is farmed, the longer it must lie fallow until fit for use again (twenty and more years in some cases), and it is not thought manageable to have to walk more than 12 kilometers or so to one's fields, so that a village's territory extends not much above 10 kilometers from the settlement periphery. An average household can and must cultivate a field of 2 hectares or so. Traditionally, when the population of a village outgrew its effective ability to get access to farm tracts it would move as a whole, or some smaller groups would break off and move away from the parent settlement. Villages might also move because of vulnerability to raids from powerful neighbors, be-

cause of such inauspicious events as epidemics, or simply because a better site was found elsewhere. Since the imperial period villages have been forced to remain stationary, and the increasing pressure of population on the land has resulted in deforestation, erosion, and depleted fertility, as fields have had to be used more years in a row and the fallow periods have been reduced substantially. Fertility also depends upon the ash resulting from the felling and burning of forest on a new hill slope. Thus, the lengthening of the periods of use and the shortening of the fallow periods have combined to lessen the ability of forest to regenerate. Overuse and reduced forest recovery also have led to heavy growth of tough grasses replacing forest growth during fallow periods, and this too has set a severe limit on the system of shifting cultivation as the population has grown.

Economy

Subsistence and Commercial Activities. The Chin are nonpioneer shifting cultivators. Where soil and climate permit, they grow dry hill rice as their chief staple, and elsewhere, chiefly at the higher elevations in Chin State, the grain staple is one or another kind of millet, maize, or even grain sorghum, though the latter grain is mainly used only for the brewing of the coarser variety of country beer (_zu_). Cultivation is entirely by hand, and the tools involved are mainly the all-purpose bush knife, the axe, the hoe (an essentially adze-hafted implement about 45 centimeters long), and, in places where rice is grown, a small harvesting knife. Grown amidst the staple are a variety of vegetable crops, mainly melons, pumpkins, and, most important, various kinds of peas and beans, on whose nitrogen-fixing properties the longer-term shifting-cultivation cycles of central Chin State depend crucially. Cotton is also widely grown, though nowadays less so because commercial cloth has rapidly displaced the traditional blankets and clothes locally woven on the back-strap tension loom. The traditional native dyes were wild vegetable dyes such as indigo. In the southern areas a kind of flax was also grown for weaving cloth (chiefly for women's skirts). Various vegetable condiments are also commonly grown, such as chili peppers, ginger, turmeric (also used to make dye) and rozelle (_Hibiscus sabdariffa_); the Mizo in particular grow and eat a great deal of mustard greens, and nowadays all sorts of European vegetables are grown, especially cabbages and potatoes. Fruits, such as shaddocks, citrons, and guavas, and such sweet crops as sugarcane were traditionally unimportant. Today there is some commercial growing of apples, oranges, tea, and coffee; other commercial crops are also grown experimentally, but the chief hindrance to such developments is the fact that the plains markets in which they might be sold are still difficult of access. Tobacco has long been grown in all villages: it was traditionally smoked green (cured by being buried in hot sand), in clay pipes (later in hand-made cigarettes) by men, and in small bamboo water pipes with clay bowls by women. The nicotine-charged water produced by the latter is decanted into small gourd containers or other vessels kept about the person and is widely used as a stimulant, being held in the mouth and then spat out.

Livestock such as pigs and fowl (less commonly goats, cows, and the occasional water buffalo and horses) may be penned within or beneath the house; most notable is the gayal (_Bos frontalis_), a semidomesticated bovid forest browser bred for meat and for ritual sacrifice, which constitutes a major form of traditional wealth. Dogs are common village scavengers along with pigs, and some dogs are used in hunting. Little game remains today, but formerly all sorts of game were hunted including black and brown bears, all kinds of deer (preeminently barking deer, also known as muntjac), mountain goats, gaur (*Bos gaurus*), various jungle cats large and small, and even, from time to time, elephants and rhinoceroses, though these have long since gone from the hills. The Bengal tiger was rarely hunted because, as in many Southeast Asian societies, its spirit was (and still is) thought related to the human soul (the "wer-tiger" idea) and therefore had to be treated in much the same way as a severed human head—that is, it required expensive and ritually dangerous ceremonies.

Industrial Arts. The traditional manufactures, other than the reforged iron tools and weapons made with the open-hearth double-bamboo pistols bellows, were mainly things like bamboo and cane mats and baskets of all sorts and red-fired utility pottery; and the ubiquitous weaving of blankets, loincloths, and women's skirts and blouses. Some of the weaving employed silk-thread embroidery and single-damask weave, and the most elaborate forms were traditionally called *vaai* (civilized), suggesting that anything that fine must have come originally from the plains. These things could have been made by anyone, but certain persons had more than ordinary skill and only some villages were endowed with potting clays, so such persons and villages became part-time specialists in this work and traded their wares (bartering for grain or other kinds of goods) in surrounding villages. There were smiths who made the traditional silver-amalgam (later aluminum) jewelry—such as the bracelets, belts, earrings, rings, and necklaces hung with imported beads and silver rupee coins—as well as brass hairpins and other items, but those artisans were even fewer in number than the ones mentioned above. Indeed, the trade in the latter items was akin to the long-distance trade in heirloom goods, such as the great gongs from Myanmar (Burma), brass vessels from India, and other sorts of items that signified at least a nominal claim upon the goods of the vaai plains country.

Trade. All of these more expensive items constituted the basis of the prestige economy of these hills and passed not only by sale but by circulation of myriad ceremonial payments and fines (especially marriage-prices, blood-money payments, and compensation payments for defamation of status). Prestige goods and gayals—especially important for their use in sacrifices associated with the "merit feasts" by which social rank was attained or validated—were the traditional wealth of these people. Furthermore, the display or announcement of the entire array of what one currently owned or had owned in life—symbolically indicated on carved memorial posts erected for prestigious dead—was the definitive sign of one's social and ceremonial rank. More specifically, the possession of a supposedly unique object from the outside world, likely to possess a unique "personal" name of its own, was especially important. The idea behind the prestige economy is that prosperity in this world depends upon the sacrificial exchange of goods with inhabitants of the Land of the Dead, and only if one had conducted feasts of merit would one and one's descendants have wealth and well-being. Thus, too, the continuity of lineage between the dead and the living was important; it was especially important for anyone to be memorialized after his or her death. Memorial service was done not only by the display of wealth and by its figuration on memorial posts and stones but also in the composition of songs (*va hia*) commemorating a man's greatness on the occasion of one of his feasts. So greatly were wealth and possessions tied up with a person's social position that among the most heinous traditional offences in this society were theft, bastardy, and the supposed possession of "evil eye" (*hnam*, the unconscious and heritable ability to cause harm by looking enviously upon another's prosperity, or even someone's consumption of a good meal). All these situations meant that property had failed to pass by means of expected formal exchanges: it had passed instead by arbitrary expropriation, or through a child born out of wedlock without benefit of marriage-price, or by misfortune caused by murderous envy of possessions to which one had no legitimate claim.

Division of Labor. The few classes of part-time craft specialist are mentioned above. Women do more of the domestic tasks and all the traditional weaving. They are also almost exclusively the spirit mediums because male spirit familiars choose them. Men alone cut down the forests and work as smiths. There appear to be no female hunters or warriors except in legends, probably because no woman can hold in her own name a feast of celebration for the killing of a major animal, or a feast of celebration of a human trophy head or that of a tiger. (In all of these cases the point is to tame the angry spirit of the deceased animal or person and send it to serve one and one's forebears in the Land of the Dead.) A woman can, however, hold a domestic feast of merit in the name of her deceased husband, in which domestic animals are similarly sacrificed on behalf of the Land of the Dead. Nevertheless, only men can be village priests, who are mostly appointed by chiefs and headmen because they have memorized the required chants and formulas and know the ritual sequences. Priests serve as masters of ceremony at the feasts of merit and celebration and at the various kinds of rite of placation—both cyclical and sporadic—addressed to the various spirit owners of the face of the land, great and small. Almost all other tasks and activities can be undertaken by either sex; there have even been historical instances of important female chiefs, who attained office through being widowed. There are few if any exploitable natural resources in these hills and virtually no modern industry, at least nothing made for export. Aside from the salaries of teachers and government servants of all sorts and the incomes of merchants and shopkeepers, the main source of money is the wages of Chin who work on the outside—preeminently in Myanmar, in the armed forces.

Land Tenure. This aspect of Chin culture is highly variable. A village has complete ownership of its tract, and even the right to hunt in it must be requested from the village; however, it is possible to rent lands in another village's tract on an individual or a communal basis. Village tract boundaries are precisely indicated by landmarks. Frequently a given hillside tract, or even the whole village tract, will be owned by a chief or other hereditary aristocrat. The right of a chief to the dues and services of his villagers in fact derives from his ownership of the land, while the ultimate ownership by a village of its land as a whole derives from the heritable pact made by the ancestral founders of the village with the spirit owners of the land. The paramount right is ownership, since it is to some extent at least conveyable in marriage-prices or by sale, and yet it is far from an absolute paramount right. For instance, it is arguable whether conveyance of ownership through marriage payments or sale can ever be outright alienations rather than mere long-term mortgagings. At least in the Haka (Lai) area of central Chin State, individual households and persons can have heritable, even conveyable rights (within village limits, perhaps) over individual cultivation plots in one or more cultivation tracts, for which the owner owes payments to the chiefly paramount owner that are in the nature of both tax and rent. Yet should these payments not be made, the field owner technically cannot be evicted—though he may be exiled, physically assaulted, or even killed, because the failure of payment is a rejection of constituted authority. Fruit trees, honeybee hives, and other exploitable items on the land may also be individually owned and conveyed. House sites are owned subject to the right of residence in the village at the pleasure of constituted village authority. Nowadays much of the land has passed into true private ownership, especially where modern commercial crops or a patch of irrigated rice are grown, more so perhaps on the Indian side of the border than in Myanmar. But in both countries there are legal restrictions on the right of nonnative inhabitants to own land in the Chin-Lushai country.

Kinship

Kin Groups and Descent. Descent is agnatic, with eponymous clans and lineages that tend to segment frequently: in general one finds maximal lineages and major and minor segments, the minor segment often being coextensive with the household. Often only the minimal lineage segment is strictly exogamous—and the rapidity of segmentation can often override even that proscription, so that marriage between even half-siblings is in parts of Chin State not necessarily penalized—though at least the legal fiction that clans are themselves exogamous is commonly maintained. Postnuptial residence is usually virilocal, and it is viripatrilocal in the case of the son who will inherit his parent's house. Daughters always marry out of the household and noninheriting sons marry neolocally. Although polygyny is allowed, it is generally confined to aristocrats who can afford a plurality of wives or who need more than one wife to manage their households and farms or who need to make various politically motivated marriage alliances. More commonly, one wife is thought to be quite enough, and it is the rare strong character who will have several wives in a single establishment—for the Chin believe that if the wives hate one another, their fights will make the husband's life miserable, and if they agree with one another, they'll combine against him. Besides, love matches occur frequently, and often they will override the common parental arrangements for marriages of state that engage couples from infancy. (For example, a girl may simply camp on the veranda of a young man who is too shy to ask for her hand.) Chin men often love their wives, and if a man refers to his wife as _inn chung_ (the "inside of [the speaker's] house"), he is certainly fond of her and probably faithful to her. Also, marriage alliances are usually avoided because the ensuing obligations often cause men to be dominated by their wives or by the brothers of their wives.

Kinship Terminology. The terminology is bifurcate-merging, with an Omaha cousin terminology, consistent with

asymmetric alliance marriage. The men of all generations in wife-taking lineages are classed with grandfathers, but in the wife-taking lineages only those agnatically descended from the original union linking the lineages are classed with grandchildren. Members of lineages other than one's own, who are not either wife givers or wife takers, are classed with one's own lineage agnates according to sex and generation. There are separate terms for younger siblings of the same sex as the speaker and for younger siblings of the opposite sex.

Marriage and Family

Marriage. With the exception mainly of the Mizo (Lushai), the Chin peoples practice asymmetrical alliance marriage. There is no obligation to marry into a lineage to which one is already allied; indeed, save in the demographically relict Kuki groups of Manipur, diversification of marriage connections is a leading strategic principle. But it is proscribed under severe penalties—occasionally amounting to temporary exile from the community—to reverse the direction of marriage alliance (e.g., to marry a woman from a wife-taking lineage). With the Mizo the rapidity of segmentation means that affinal alliances lapse almost as soon as they are formed, and so there can be no question of their reversal. Also, inasmuch as wife givers are at least ritually dominant over wife takers, it is often necessary to cement and renew an alliance by further marriages, both because a particular wife-giving lineage may provide a useful umbrella of wealth and power and because this lineage may be unwilling to let a profitable alliance lapse (which it will after three or four generations); also, it may insist on imposing more wives with a view to taking in more marriage dues. Divorce, if the woman is said to be at fault, is cause for an attempt to recover all or much of the bride-price, either from her natal family or, if she has run off with another, from her seducer. Divorce of a woman for no good cause is difficult because it constitutes an implicit offense against the wife givers.

Inheritance. Houses, land, and other major property, as well as succession to office (priestly or chiefly), pass from father to son. Sometimes they pass by primogeniture, sometimes by ultimogeniture, and sometimes by a combination of the two (e.g., house and household goods to the younger son, office and movable estate to the older). These matters vary even from lineage to lineage. Certain classes of property that a woman brings from her natal household to her marriage (chiefly valuable jewelry and the like) pass to one of her daughters upon either the marriage of the daughter or the death of the mother. Even noninheriting sons have some right to expect their father to settle on them a portion of his estate while he is still alive, when those sons are about to establish households of their own. It is commonly thought that a noninheriting son of a chief or other powerful man is likely to become socially disaffected, footloose, volatile, and unreliable, and this sort of person is called, in Lai Chin, _mihraw-khrawlh,_ "one who is constantly looking for the main chance."

Socialization. Both parents take care of infants, as do elder siblings of either sex; it is not rare to see even a distinguished chief with a baby in a blanket on his back or a child crawling all over him, and a child carrying a baby carrying an even smaller infant is not an unknown sight. Mothers slap and scold children even to age of about 10 or 12, but the power of the father, at least over sons, is his power to withhold support and settlement. Young boys are encouraged to throw tantrums so that they may grow up a bit wild and willful. Children are weaned when the demands of the next infant are too great, or by 18 months of age. While there is a tendency for tensions between fathers and sons to arise as sons come of age and need financial independence, the emotional bonds between parents and children in general are often deep and lasting, and those between daughters and their mothers are especially poignant: if a woman becomes drunk she often weeps, and it is said then that she is "thinking of her mother."

Sociopolitical Organization

Northern and Central Chin and Mizo have hereditary headmanship or chieftainship and the associated distinction between commoner and chiefly clans and lineages. The Southern Chin (including those of Matupi) have neither institution. In the former groups some villages have a single paramount headman or chief, while others are ruled by a council of aristocratic chiefs, each of whom may have his own network of followers either locally or in the form of subordinate chiefs and headmen of client villages. It is a mistake to suppose that villages ruled by these councils are "democratic." What distinguishes a mere headman from a chief is that only the latter can have other village heads under his jurisdiction, and not every chief is the head of a whole village. The dues owed headmen are mentioned above in connection with land tenure and derive as a right from the exclusive heritable connection between the village founder and his successors and the ultimate spirit owners of the village lands. These dues consist mainly of tax/rent for the right to cultivate land and a hindquarter of any large-sized wild or domestic animal killed in the territory. Furthermore, a headman, chief, or major landowning aristocrat can demand various sorts of services from his client households, such as farm work, house building, and assistance at feasts, rites, and ceremonies. Headmen or chiefs also could demand public work and sentry/warrior/ messenger service from the young men. Acting in council with their peer household heads in the village, these leaders also constitute a formal court for adjudicating legal cases and levying fines. All these rights and offices have been abolished in recent decades. Formerly it was usual for the young people of the village, especially the young men, to be organized as a cadre for such service purposes, and in those circumstances they tended to reside, from before their teens until marriage or beyond, in a ceremonial bachelors' house (the Lai and Lushai word *zawlbuk* is its best-known name). This institution had disappeared before the middle of this century. When it still existed, either the young women visited the youths in the bachelors' house at night, or the young men roamed the village and spent the night courting at the houses of young women. Today, the power of a chief, in the strict sense, derives from either the threat or exercise of force or from the fact that satellite villages may have split off from the mother village where the chief resides. The chief's ability to demand gifts and assistance in warfare from client villages is enforced by threat of reprisal and by the fact that the chief will commonly make himself wife giver to his client headmen who are not of his own lineage. Through marriage gifts and payments he is also likely to acquire landholdings in the satellite vil-

lages. Rank differences are complicated. On the one hand, there is the principle that rank is hereditary by clans, but, on the other hand, it is jurally recognized that wealth can effectually raise the rank of a lineage segment. With wealth, one can give the necessary series of feasts of merit and celebration, with the object of persuading other born aristocrats to attend and acknowledge one's claims; there are always aristocrats who have fallen upon hard times, who are willing to accept inflated amounts for the ceremonial attendance payments and inflated bride-prices for their daughters in marriage to a born commoner. Such complicated marriage maneuvers, made possible by wealth, are necessary in order to elevate one's rank, for only a man whose major wife is of aristocratic lineage can give the higher feasts. All of this forms the basis of a naturally inflationary cycle of the prestige economy. These processes and rank ambiguities are supported by the tendency for lineages to segment rapidly, so that an upwardly mobile lineage segment can readily dissociate itself from its lineage fellows. Still, to be an aristocrat by clan membership gives one a better claim to the rank and better ritual privileges, and it is not uncommon for members of commoner clans to insist that for them the very idea of clan membership is meaningless. Chin society also used to include slaves. Some slaves were war captives, while others chose slavery as a way out of debt or as protection from revenge feuds. Slavery was strictly hereditary only through females. A female slave was considered a member of her aristocratic owner's household, with the interesting consequence that her marriage-price was often greater than that of a commoner girl, though it was never equal to that of an aristocrat's daughter even by a commoner minor wife. The Southern Chin had only small-scale feasts of merit, which secured only nonhereditary ritual prestige to the giver's household.

Social Control. There are five main sources of control: (1) the ideology that sees all social relations as defined by ritualized exchanges of property, which binds people to one another in the expectation of making property claims on each other; (2) the threat of force (feuding and revenge are common) and the associated need of mutual cooperation for defense; (3) the power of hereditary headmen to monopolize ritual access to the spirit world, directly and through appointed or hereditary village priests, without which the spirits would make life intolerable; (4) fear that one's bad reputation and actions will preclude one's going to the Land of the Dead after death; and (5) the closely related ideology of mutual assistance within the community.

Conflict. Many of the causes of feuds have already been mentioned. The most common causes of warfare between villages, however, were the following three: disputes over women; disputes over land rights (not uncommonly having to do with access to the very few and essential salt wells in the whole region and to trade routes within and to outside regions); and disputes over property, usually property claims stemming from marriage alliances and tributary relations. It was not unusual to take human heads in raids on other villages, and this headhunting constituted something of an independent motivation for warfare, since one's prosperity depended upon one's ability to aggrandize one's own forebears in the Land of the Dead and for that purpose one needed to ensure them a regular supply of slaves. This object was achieved by taking heads and celebrating them, which tamed the resulting dangerous spirits and made it possible to send them as servants to the Land of the Dead. The Southern Chin never practiced headhunting.

Religion and Expressive Culture

Religious Beliefs. The Chin-Lushai traditional pantheon is complicated. There is generally a somewhat remote creator god, sometimes with a female counterpart. Some say his realm is coextensive with the Land of the Dead. He is revered as a remote father figure, but his power consists only of a vague ability to protect one against ultimate adversity. It is in the light of these characteristics that the traditional high god served as a sort of model to which the Christian God of the missionaries was rather readily assimilated. The Chin believe the universe to be populated as well by all sorts of spirits; some of them being great and deitylike; some of them residing in other "worlds," such as the afterworld; some of them having dominion over domains large or small, locally or elsewhere; and some of them appearing as wandering ghosts, demons, and less personifiable beings. Some of the most fearsome of the last group are the ghosts of those who die by accident or violence, for they are angry and vengeful (e.g., the ghosts of women who have died in childbirth and cannot be made to leave for the Land of the Dead). The cosmos is basically divided into two parts, the sky world (including the Land of the Dead) and the earth, but since the relations between the two are an asymmetrical dependency, there are two routes between them: one upward and one through the "underworld"—the latter ambivalently associated with death and also with prosperity, owing to the fact that crops grow out of the ground. Because of this ambiguity, Chin origin tales often say that the first people came at one and the same time out of some hole or cave and from the sky world.

Religious Practitioners. Mediums, generally women, who go into trances and find out which spirits are demanding what from whom, and for what offense, and who may also find out where the soul of an ill or deranged person has wandered, have been mentioned earlier. The village priests and reciters who serve at private feasts and communal sacrifices have also been mentioned. They tend to be chiefly appointees, though one kind has to be from a commoner lineage.

Ceremonies. Feasts and celebrations occur irregularly, whenever someone finds it possible or necessary to give one: for instance, when one has killed a major game animal or when one wishes to make a more elaborate house. Some village rites take place once in every year or once every few years, depending upon the arrangement with the spirit in question. Other such rites are held when some plague or calamity seems to demand it and a medium or a diviner has identified what is to be done. There are all manner of private curing rituals, and these are held by whomever knows how, not by professionals; they tend to involve sacrifices to intruding spirits, soul recalling, and the leaving of miniature images of wealth outside the village for the spirits. There are few definite seasonal calendrical ceremonies, but village rites must be held before clearing, planting, and harvesting. All sorts of means (such as observing cracks in heated eggshells, the bile ducts in pig livers, or how a dying fowl crosses its legs) are used for divining the source of troubles and the auspiciousness of plans.

Arts. With minor exceptions, all Chin art is nonrepresentative, and many Chin used to find it hard even to recognize a drawn or painted human figure, though photographs were clear enough to them. Floral-geometric decoration is found in the weaving and in the memorial posts mentioned earlier. Some of the design figures conventionally stand for things—for example, for various kinds of possessions belonging to a person being commemorated—but none is iconic.

Disease and Curing. The first recourse in the treatment of diseases and even of wounds is the use of mediums who arrange for the placation of the spirits responsible, who might otherwise prevent recovery. Alongside this there is a wide variety of quite idiosyncratic treatment, chiefly of an herbal nature, which is mainly passed on from mothers to daughters and daughters-in-law.

Death and Afterlife. The dead are buried, and in the Southern Chin hills there is secondary reburial of the bones in a small jar. In general the blanket-wrapped corpse is interred in a stone-lined chamber in one side of a vertical pit. Those who have died a violent death and who therefore are likely to have become dangerous ghosts are buried in a separate gravesite, remote from the village and surrounding trails. The range of memorial constructions is considerable, but among them should be mentioned—in addition to the commemorative posts—the stone platforms in and around the village, on which people can rest and on which, some say, the spirit of the deceased may sometimes come and rest; and the clusters of miniature houses on tall stilts, in which periodic offerings of food and miniature furnishings are placed for the spirit of the deceased. An interesting feature of the stone platforms (in the case of deceased males), behind which the memorial posts are raised, is the line of small stones that may also be present, each representing either a human victim of the deceased or, equivalently, another man's wife seduced by the deceased. Modern memorial stones have written on them lists of the deceased's possessions in life, often in astonishing detail, down to the odd enameled tin cup or pair of woolen socks.

See also Mizo

Bibliography

Carey, B. S., and H. P. Tuck (1896). *The Chin Hills.* 2 vols. Rangoon: Government Press.

Lehman, F. K. (1963). *The Structure of Chin Society.* Urbana: University of Illinois Press.

Lehman, F. K. (1970). "On Chin and Kachin Marriage Cycles." *Man,* n.s. 5:118–125.

Lehman, F. K. (1989). "Internal Inflationary Pressures in the Prestige Economy of the Feast-of-Merit Complex." In *Upland-Lowland Contrasts in Mainland Southeast Asia,* edited by Susan B. Russell, 89–102. Northern Illinois University Center for Southeast Asia Studies Occasional Paper. DeKalb.

Parry, N. E. (1932). *The Lakhers.* London: Macmillan.

Shakespear, John (1912). *The Lushei Kuki Clans.* London: Macmillan.

Stevenson, H. N. C. (1943). *The Economics of the Central Chin Tribes.* Bombay: Times of India Press (for The Government of Burma in Exile).

F. K. LEHMAN (MARK-PA)

Chinese of South Asia

ETHNONYMS: Chini, Indian Chinese

This article refers not to Chinese soldiers, who for more than thirty years have patrolled the Tibetan border that forms the northern limit of South Asia, but rather to ethnic Chinese who have lived mainly in major South Asian cities for a century or more. In 1982 there were 700 Chinese in Bangladesh, 110,000 in India, 3,600 in Pakistan, and 3,000 in Sri Lanka. There are also 700,000 Chinese in Myanmar (Burma), who usually are classified as Chinese of Southeast Asia (rather than of South Asia). In all South Asian nations the Chinese population has increased since 1955, although, except in Myanmar, they are a small minority. Calcutta, Bombay, Madras, Delhi, and Colombo each have sizable populations, with most of the Chinese providing specialized economic services such as running shoe shops and restaurants; in Calcutta Chinese-owned tanneries are also important. Even a town the size of Ootacamund (population 100,000) has two long-resident Chinese business families.

A few Buddhist pilgrims, most notably Fa Hien (fl. A.D. 399–414), came to India from China in very early times; and early in the fifteenth century a few thousand came to the coast of Kerala, to Calicut, with the Ming expeditions; but it was only after 1865 that Chinese came in significant numbers. They worked as tea plantation laborers, carpenters, road builders, tradesmen, and seamen's launderers; also a few were convicts.

Those who migrated to South Asia came mainly from the southeastern provinces of Guangdong, Hunan, Jiangxi, and Fujian, speaking either Cantonese or Hakka (a minority language of that region). They tended to settle in the seaports of South Asia, and they have remained in some cases for five or six generations.

Although most of the Chinese businessmen speak English and another local language, they speak a Chinese language in the home and only very rarely marry a non-Chinese spouse. Most marriages are arranged in the traditional Chinese manner.

Bibliography

Chang, Sen-Dou (1968). "The Distribution and Occupations of Overseas Chinese." *Geographical Review* 58:89–107.

Poston, Dudley L., Jr., and Mei-Yu Yu (1990). "The Distribution of the Overseas Chinese in the Contemporary World." *International Migration Review* 24:480–508.

Schermerhorn, Richard Alonzo (1978). "The Chinese: A Unique Nationality Group." In *Ethnic Plurality in India,* by Richard Alonzo Schermerhorn, 290–313. Tucson: University of Arizona Press.

Thurston, Edgar (1909). "Chinese-Tamil Cross." In *Castes and Tribes of Southern India,* edited by Edgar Thurston and Kadamki Rangachari. Vol. 2, 98–100. Madras: Government Press.

PAUL HOCKINGS

Chitpavan Brahman

ETHNONYM: Konkanastha

Orientation

Identification. "Chitpavan," sometimes spelled "Chittapavan," may mean either "pure from the pyre" or "pure in heart." Another name for this Brahman caste of the Marathi-speaking area of western India is "Konkanastha," which means "being of the Konkan," the coastal strip between the Arabian Sea and the Western Ghats (mountains) south of the city of Bombay. The "pure from the pyre" meaning of Chitpavan is a reference to an origin myth claiming that the caste was created by the god Parashuram from bodies of shipwrecked sailors, purified on the pyre, restored to life, and taught Brahman rites. This myth is found in the "Sahyadri Khanda" of the *Skanda Purana,* a chapter probably compiled by a Deshastha Brahman, one of the "original" Brahmans of the Marathi-speaking area, and hence not always flattering to Chitpavans. Members of the caste are generally very fair, often have aquiline noses, and frequently possess gray, blue, or green eyes. At various times it has been speculated that they were originally Turks, Iranians, Egyptians, Greeks, Jews, Berbers, or people from farther south or north in India.

Location. The original home of the Chitpavans was around the city of Chiplun in Ratnagiri District, the northern part of the Konkan, and some derive the name "Chitpavan" from "Chiplun." In the eighteenth century members of the caste moved throughout the Desh area (the Marathi-speaking heartland, inland from the coastal mountains) and in British times to all the cities of the Marathi-speaking area, especially Pune, Sangli, and Wai, and beyond. Since Indian independence in 1947, many have migrated abroad.

Demography. No census records on castes other than Untouchables have been kept since 1931. Maureen Patterson estimates that there are now around 250,000 Chitpavans, roughly 13 percent of the Brahmans of the state of Maharashtra, less than 1 percent of that area's population.

Linguistic Affiliation. Marathi is spoken by all people native to Maharashtra; it is an Indo-European language containing elements from the Dravidian Language Family. Until recently, there was a "Chitpavani *bhasa*," a distinctive nasality in many Chitpavans' speech. The last traces may be seen in the popular didactic book of short sketches by Sane Guruji (1899–1950), _Shyamchi Ai_ (Shyam's Mother), published in 1933 and still read for enjoyment, moral tales, and its cultural importance.

History and Cultural Relations

From the beginning of the eighteenth century to the contemporary period, Chitpavans have played a part in the history of India far beyond their numbers. Unheard of before the late seventeenth century, the Chitpavans began their rise to fame with the appointment of Balaji Vishwanath Bhat as _peshwa_ (prime minister) to Shahu, the grandson of the founder of the Maratha Kingdom, Shivaji. Balaji raised the office of the peshwa to de facto rule of the Maratha Empire, and from 1713 until their defeat by the British in 1818, the peshwas ruled one of the last large independent kingdoms in India. During this period, Chitpavans from the Konkan joined the military and administrative ranks of the Maratha Empire in large numbers. Chitpavans served not only in the cities of the Marathi-speaking area but also in the other kingdoms of the Maratha expansion: Gwalior, Baroda, Indore. Even after the British victory over the peshwa, one of the important Chitpavan administrative families, that of the Patwardhans, was left to rule seven small princely states in southern Maratha territory. The peshwa himself was exiled to the north lest he form a nucleus of rebellion, and the British ruled what then became part of Bombay Presidency. Nana Saheb, the heir of the peshwa, became from his exile near Kanpur (Cawnpore) one of the important figures in the 1857 rebellion against the British.

Under British rule, the Chitpavans quickly took to English education, and most of the famous names of Maratha history from the nineteenth and early twentieth centuries are from this caste: the early reformer and essayist Hari Gopal Deshmukh (Lokahitawadi) (1823–1892); reformers and nationalists on an all-India scale Mahadeo Govind Ranade (1842–1901) and Gopal Krishna Gokhale (1866–1915), whom Gandhi called one of his gurus; the most famous Maharashtrian woman of the nineteenth century, educator and Christian convert Pandita Ramabai (1858–1922); the radical patriot Bal Gangadhar (Lokamanya) Tilak (1856–1920); the Hindu revivalist Vinayak Damodar Savarkar (1893–1966); orientalists Pandurang Vaman Kane (1880–1972) and Ramchandra Narayan Dandekar (b. 1909); economist D. R. Gadgil (1901–1971); Mahatma Gandhi's "spiritual successor," Vinoba Bhave (1895–1982); anthropologist Iravati Karve (1905–1970); cricketer D. B. Deodhar (b. 1891); and many others. Even Maharashtra's "terrorists" were Chitpavan, from the nineteenth-century rebel Wasudeo Balwant Phadke, through the Chapekar brothers in the 1890s, to Nathuram Vinayak Godse, Gandhi's assassin in 1948. The nationalist activities of the Chitpavans, both radical and moderate, caused considerable hatred and fear on the part of some Britons, and there are many references to the arrogant and "untrustworthy" Chitpavans in the Raj literature. Maharashtrians today are justifiably proud of the many contributions to Indian nationalism made by Chitpavans.

With the rise of Gandhi after 1920, the Maharashtra area ceased to be a main center of Indian political life, and such Chitpavan political figures as Tilak's successor, N. C. Kelkar, had little power on the national scene. The non-Brahman political movement brought the large caste of the Marathas to the fore, and it is claimed that Chitpavan N. R. Gadgil brought the non-Brahman leadership into the Indian National Congress to strengthen that chief nationalist group. The non-Brahmans then dominated by sheer numbers and a newfound sense of their importance in the previously Brahman-dominated political arena. By the time of Indian independence, no Brahman was important in the Congress party. Later Chitpavan political skill was exerted on the Left and on the Right, not in the moderate Indian National Congress. Important Socialists are S. M. Joshi (b. 1904), N. G. Goray (b. 1907), and currently Madhu Limaye (b. 1922), although these have not been as well known on the national stage as were Tilak, Gokhale, or Ranade.

Chitpavans dominated the Marathi-speaking area administratively, culturally, economically, and educationally—in fact, in every field except ritual religion—since their first appearance in western India in the late seventeenth century until the decades just before Indian independence. This dominance eventually resulted in a strong anti-Brahman feeling that surfaced violently after the death of Gandhi in 1948 at the hands of a Chitpavan Brahman. Rioting and destruction in Bombay, Nagpur, and a belt from Pune to Kolhapur drove Chitpavans (and often other Brahmans) to large cities, out of government service, and into still more new pursuits. Most Chitpavan families now have at least one member working in professional life in Europe or the United States.

Economy

The occupation of the Chitpavans in their original territory of the Konkan was farming, with some income from performing ritual among their own caste. However, they often were the _khots_ of a Konkani village, a position combining the headmanship and the financial work of the village. In other areas of Maharashtra, Brahmans were the village accountants, but the head of the village was of a Maratha caste. The combination of the two responsibilities put power into the hands of a single head, and there were many efforts to reform the _khoti_ system in the nineteenth and twentieth centuries. Chitpavans rarely took up agricultural work after their migration, nor did they become ritual priests except within their own caste. Many, however, became teachers and recognized Sanskrit scholars. Some of the best known Brahman scholars in the sacred city of Varanasi were Chitpavan migrants. From the nineteenth century on they have entered the professions in large numbers. The early entrance of the Chitpavans into new occupations and pursuits caused the Ratnagiri _District Gazetteer_ of the late nineteenth century to describe them as "a very frugal, pushing, active, intelligent, well-taught, astute, self-confident and overbearing class [following] almost all callings and generally with success." A 1920 census list of their occupations reads: government service, lawyers, engineers, doctors, bankers, priests, writers, landowners, and "husbandmen" (farmers). One of the first Maharashtrian industrialists was Vishnu Ramchandra Velankar (b. 1890), founder of Gajanan Weaving Mills. Recently Chitpavans have entered high-tech industry and business.

Kinship, Marriage and Family

The Chitpavan caste contains fourteen *gotras* (kin groups based on a mythical ancestor), which play a role chiefly in determining marriage patterns. One may not marry within one's gotra or with someone from an "unfriendly" gotra. Outside marriage, the most important unit is the household family, and in addition to that the *kula*, an exogamous clan usually based on a family name, is important. A most unusual feature of the caste are family histories, called *kula-vrittantas* in Marathi, each based on a clan name such as Limaye, Karandikar, Bapat, etc. Originally 60 (according to the *Sahyadri Khanda*—see above), there are now about 400 last names. Since 1914, fifty-five books covering the histories of forty-seven kulas (and involving in total 80 surnames) have been published, offering an unusual opportunity to study changes in occupation and location, the nature of household gods, the marriage patterns, etc. of these Chitpavan families. It is perhaps significant that no genealogy in the kula-vrittantas traces ancestors to a time before the Chitpavans appeared in the historical records around 1700.

In contrast to most Maharashtrian and south Indian castes, a Chitpavan may not marry his maternal uncle's daughter, and cross-cousin marriages are not usually allowed. Chitpavans have been freer than other Brahman castes to marry outside their caste, and many have married into other high-caste groups; occasionally Chitpavan men have married Western women.

Sociopolitical Organization

Chitpavans have had no caste *panchayat* as many other castes have had, but social control was firm, if informal. The reformer Justice Mahadeo Govind Ranade was made to perform penance after a nineteenth-century tea party in a Christian home, and D. K. Karve (1858–1962), founder of a widows' home and later the first women's university in India, was ostracized for marrying a widow in the late nineteenth century. Chitpavans have been fighters in the front ranks of reform as well as defenders of traditionalism.

Religion and Expressive Culture

Religious Beliefs. Although there is an image of Parashuram in the temple at Chiplun, this does not seem to have become a pilgrimage center for Chitpavans. Most Chitpavans belong to the Smarta sect of Hinduism, and they consider themselves either Rigvedis of the Ashvalayana Shaka or Yajurvedis of the Taittiriya Shaka. Each family has a special god or goddess (or both), called a *kuladaivata* or *kula-swami(ni)*, which are ritually important at the household level. The majority of these gods are Shaiva, associated with villages in the Konkan, and the goddess or *devi* is often Jogai or Jogeshvari or a Konkani goddess. The temple of Jogeshvari is one of the main goddess temples in the older part of the city of Pune (Poona), the capital of the peshwas during the Maratha period. The peshwas also had a special relationship with the elephant-headed god Ganesh, "the remover of obstacles," and in the late nineteenth century the nationalist Bal Gangadhar Tilak raised household Ganesh worship to a neighborhood function, complete with "booths" for public worship and patriotic themes. The Ganesh or Ganpati festival still has special importance in Pune and other Maharashtrian cities.

Ceremonies. Although Chitpavans were known as Sanskrit scholars and teachers and strict observers of religious rights, Deshastha Brahmans, the traditional ritual priests of the Marathi-speaking area, considered them ritually inferior. The Chitpavans never adopted the role of ritualist, except within their own caste. However, they were orthodox in many ways. Suttee, or the immolation of the widow on the pyre of her husband, was a valued ceremony among Chitpavans until it was outlawed in 1830, but it was given up totally at that time. Marriage and funeral rites for Chitpavan Brahmans resemble those for other Brahmans, but there is a special modern Chitpavan twist to the funeral experience. The elements of the funeral include: water from the Ganges being poured as a last oblation on the dying Brahman's head; the carrying of the corpse to the cremation grounds on a bamboo pyre; the bringing of fire to the grounds in a special earthen pot; the lighting of the fire by the oldest son; and the thirteen days of mourning followed by a feast for neighbors and family. All this is the subject of a very popular, darkly comedic play by a Chitpavan, Satish Alekar's *Mahanirvana*, translated in English as "The Dread Departure." A practice that is especially important to Chitpavan and other Brahman women is the Mahalakshmi *puja*, which occurs during the festival of Navratri ("nine nights"). It is a special celebration for the first five years of married life. During this festival, women join in a ritual of blowing into earthen pots, which induces hyperventilation, possession by a goddess, and at times a generally hilarious party atmosphere.

Arts. While Chitpavans have no particular traditional art or craft, they have been enormously important in bringing modernity to Maharashtrian culture. Vishnushastri Chiplunkar (1850–1882) is called the father of modern Marathi prose. Vishnu Narayan Bhatkande (1860–1936) systematized classical music, established schools for the teaching of music, and facilitated the continuance of Hindustani music under modern systems of patronage. Govind Ballal Deval (1855–1916) was a popular early dramatist, creating plays on social reform themes. Hari Narayan Apte (1864–1919) is considered the father of the modern Marathi novel, and many of the most famous writers in Marathi have come from the Chitpavan caste.

See also Maratha

Bibliography

Chitale, Venu (1950). *In Transit*. Bombay: Hind Kitabs.

Cox, Linda (1970). "The Chitpavans." *Illustrated Weekly of India* 91:6–15, 36–37.

Karve, Iravati (1958). "What Is Caste?" *Economic Weekly* 10 (January annual; 22 March; July special): 125–138; 401–407; 881–888.

Patterson, Maureen L. P. (1968). "Chitpavan Brahman Family Histories. Sources for a Study of Social Structure and Social Change in Maharashtra" In *Structure and Change in In-*

dian Society, edited by Milton B. Singer and Bernard S. Cohn, 397–411. Chicago: Aldine.

Patterson, Maureen L. P. (1970). "Changing Patterns of Occupation among Chitpavan Brahmans." _Indian Economic and Social History Review_ 7:375–396.

Patterson, Maureen L. P. (1988). "The Shifting Fortunes of Chitpavan Brahmans: Focus on 1948." In _City, Countryside, and Society in Maharashtra_, edited by D. W. Attwood et al. Toronto: South Asian Studies, University of Toronto.

Tilak, Lakshmibai Gokhale (1950). _I Follow After: An Autobiography_. Translated by E. Josephine Inkster. Madras: Oxford University Press.

ELEANOR ZELLIOT

Cochin Jew

ETHNONYMS: Cochinis, Malabar ("Black") Jews, Paradesi ("Foreign" or "White") Jews

Orientation

Identification. The Cochin Jews are one of the smallest Jewish communities in the world. They hail from the Malabar Coast in India and traditionally were divided into two castelike subgroups: "White" and "Black" Jews. Today only thirty Cochin Jews remain in Cochin. The community has mostly been transplanted to Israel, where they continue to retain unique religious customs derived from their origins in Cochin while having integrated successfully into Israeli society.

Location. In India the Cochin Jews lived in several towns along the Malabar Coast in Kerala: Attencammonal, Chenotta, Ernakulam, Mallah, Parur, Chenemangalam, and Cochin. Today some Cochin individuals remain in Parur and Chenemangalam, and a small community of thirty people live in "Jews Town" in Cochin. In Israel the Cochin Jews live primarily in agricultural settlements such as Nevatim and Mesillat Zion. A minority also live in the towns with small concentrations in Ramat Eliahu, Ashdod, and Jerusalem.

Demography. When the traveler Benjamin of Tudela visited India in about 1170, he reported there were about 1,000 Jews in the south. In 1686 Moses Pereira de Paiva listed 465 Malabar Jews. In 1781 the Dutch governor A. Moens recorded 422 families or about 2,000 persons. In 1948, 2,500 Jews were living on the Malabar coast. In 1953, 2,400 emigrated to Israel, leaving behind only about 100 "White" Jews on the Malabar Coast. Today, there are only about 250 "White" Jews in existence and as a result of exogamy they are becoming extinct; conversely, the "Black" Jews in Israel are increasing in numbers.

Linguistic Affiliation. The Cochin Jews, like their neighbors, speak Malayalam, a Dravidian language. In Israel they also speak modern Hebrew.

History and Cultural Relations

The settlement of Jews on the Malabar Coast is ancient. One theory holds that the ancestors of today's Cochin Jews arrived in south India among King Solomon's merchants who brought back ivory, monkeys, and parrots for his temple; Sanskrit- and Tamil-derived words appear in 1 Kings. Another theory suggests that Cochin Jews are descendants of captives taken to Assyria in the eighth century B.C. The most popular and likely supposition, however, is that Jews came to south India some time in the first century C.E., after the destruction of Solomon's second temple. This theory is confirmed by local South Indian Christian legends.

Documentary evidence of Jewish settlement on the southern Indian coast can be found in the famous Cochin Jewish copperplates in the ancient Tamil script (_vattezuthu_). These copperplates are the source of numerous arguments, both among scholars as to their date and meaning and among the Cochin Jews themselves as to which particular castelike subgroup of Cochin Jews are their true owners. Until recently, the Jewish copperplates were dated 315 A.D., but contemporary scholars agree upon the date 1000 A.D. In that year, during the reign of Bhaskara Ravi Varman (962–1020 C.E.), the Jews were granted seventy-two privileges. Among these were: the right to use a day lamp; the right to use a decorative cloth to walk on; the right to erect a palanquin; the right to blow a trumpet; and the right to be exempt from and to collect particular taxes. The privileges were bestowed upon the Cochin Jewish leader Joseph Rabban, "proprietor of the 'Anjuvannam,' his male and female issues, nephews and sons-in-law."

The meaning of the word "Anjuvannam" is also the subject of controversy. The theory that the word refers to a kingdom or a place has been superseded by newer theories that it was an artisan class, a trade center, or a specifically Jewish guild.

From the eighteenth century on, emissaries from the Holy Land began to visit their Cochin Jewish brethren. Indirectly, they helped Cochin Jewry to align with world Jewry and finally, as part of the "ingathering of the exiles," to request a return to Zion.

In 1949, the first Cochin Jews—seventeen families in all—sold their property. Urged on by religious fervor and deteriorating economic conditions in postindependence India, community elders wrote to David Ben-Gurion, prime minister of the newly established State of Israel, requesting that the whole community emigrate to Israel. In 1953–1954, 2,400 Cochin Jews, the vast majority of whom were "Black" or Malabar Jews, went to Israel. A small number stayed behind on the Malabar Coast; and today only a handful remain.

Economy

Subsistence and Commercial Activities. In India the Cochin Jews mainly engaged in petty trading in the towns in which they lived on the Malabar Coast. In general, the "White" Jews enjoyed a higher standard of living and included among their ranks several merchants, including international spice merchants, and professionals (lawyers, engineers, teachers, and physicians).

In Israel, the Cochin Jews are largely employed in agriculture. The first groups of these Jews to arrive in Israel were herded from place to place; in an early attempt to isolate them (from fear of contagious diseases) they were taken to outlying *moshavim* (agricultural settlements) such as Nevatim in the south. Their attempts to make a success out of Nevatim failed. By 1962, when a Jewish Agency Settlement Studies Centre sociologist conducted a survey of the *moshav*, he described the situation as one of "failure" and "economic and social crisis" expressing itself in declining output and emigration from the moshav.

Trade. In the 1970s, however, Nevatim turned into a thriving moshav, producing avocados, olives, citrus fruits, pecans, cotton, potatoes, flowers, and chickens. Today, Nevatim (with 571 Cochinis in 1982) is only one of fifteen successful Cochini moshavim. Some of these, such as Mesillat Zion near Beit Shemesh (174 Cochin Jews), are populated by a majority of Cochin Jews; while others, such as Fedia (27 Cochin Jews) and Tarom (23), are heterogeneous.

Division of Labor. In Cochin men usually had small shops selling sundry goods. These were located on the verandas of their houses. The women were engaged in domestic pursuits. In Israel men have now adopted many professional or clerical jobs.

Land Tenure. Due to lack of land on the moshav and new aspirations on the part of the younger generation, an expanding urban sector of Cochin Jews is increasingly making itself felt. "Pockets" of Cochin Jews can be found in the Ramat Eliahu neighborhood of Rishon Lezion and in Jerusalem, Ashdod, and other towns, where they are employed in white-collar and skilled occupations.

Kinship

Kin Groups and Descent. Cochin Jews observed strict caste endogamy, only marrying other Jews. However, there was no intermarriage between "White" and "Black" Jews. Even within the "White" Jewish subgroup, the "White" *meyuhasim* (privileged), who claimed direct descent from ancient Israel, did not accept their *meshurarim*, or manumitted slaves, as marriage partners. Similarly, the "Black" meyuhasim did not marry their freed slaves or proselytes. Today in Israel, more than one in every two Cochini marriages is contracted between Cochin Jews and other Israeli Jews.

Kinship Terminology. Cochin Jews in general tend to encourage cross-cousin marriage. Kinship terminology reflects local Malayalam terminology, while in Israel *dod* (uncle) and *doda* (aunt) refer to one's mother's and father's siblings without specification.

Marriage and Family

Marriage. Marriage is the most important Cochini social occasion, celebrated in India for a complete week. In Israel, celebrations are shorter due to demands of the working week.

Domestic Unit and Socialization. The young couple set up a new household and in Israel aim to socialize their children to become Israelis who are proud of their Cochini heritage. The average number of people in a family of Cochini origin in Israel was 5.7 in 1972 and 5.2 in 1982. Today the trend is toward smaller families.

Sociopolitical Organization

Social Organization. The "Black" Jews claim that they were the original recipients of the copperplates, thereby proving their high status in the South Indian context. However, the copperplates are today in the hands of the "White" Jews in the Paradesi synagogue. The term *paradesi* means "foreigner," and the "White" Jews are the descendants of Spanish, Portuguese, Iraqi, and other Jews who arrived on the Malabar Coast from the sixteenth century on, later than the first appearance of the copperplates.

After the "White" Jews built the Paradesi synagogue in 1568, no "Black" Jews were qualified to pray there. The "Black" Jews, for their part, had several synagogues that no "White" Jew would enter. To complicate matters, both "White" and "Black" Jews were internally divided into meyuhasim and nonmeyuhasim (privileged and nonprivileged).

It is not entirely clear when divisions within the community came into being. One of the earliest recorded splits was in 1344, when some of the Jews of Cranganore moved to Cochin, three years after the port of Cranganore was silted up and Cochin was founded. But it was only after Vasco da Gama's expedition when the Portuguese ruled Kerala that some European Jews settled in Cochin. They became the first "White" Jews. By the time Pereira de Paiva visited Cochin in 1686 on behalf of Amsterdam Jewry, he could report that "the 'White Jews' and the 'Malabarees' were neither intermarrying nor inter-dining."

One "White" Jew who rose to prominence under the Dutch, who had taken over in 1668, was Ezekiel Rahabi (1694–1771). For forty-eight years he acted as the principal merchant for the Dutch in Cochin. He had contacts all over the East as well as in Europe, and he signed his numerous memorandums in Hebrew.

Political Organization. The Jews' lives on the Malabar Coast were centered on the synagogue, which corporately owned estates in each settlement. The congregation was known as the *yogam* and it administered communal affairs collectively.

Social Control. The yogam acted as a social control device determining the fate of its members. In extreme cases, where social taboos were ignored, the congregation could excommunicate a member. A famous example was the case of A. B. Salem, a lawyer, who became the leader of the meshurarim in his fight for equal rights for his group. Even as late as 1952, the "White" Jews would not let his son marry a "White" Jew in the Paradesi synagogue. When his son and new daughter-in-law returned from their marriage in Bombay, all the women in the ladies' gallery of the Paradesi synagogue walked out in protest.

Religion and Expressive Culture

Religious Beliefs. The Cochin Jews believe in one deity. Their religious observances conform in every way with the Jewish norms established by the *halacha* (Jewish legal code), and they kept contact with mainstream Judaism through many generations. At the same time, since they were fully integrated into Kerala society, they were influenced by many Hindu practices and beliefs (e.g., the emphasis upon purity of descent, the wedding customs and canopy, and the "asceticism" associated with Passover preparations). Reportedly, the Cochin Jews have never suffered from anti-Semitism at the hands of their Hindu neighbors.

Religious Practitioners. The Cochin Jews never had any rabbis, but several men served as *shochetim* (ritual slaughterers) and *hazanim* (cantors) both for their own communities and for another community of Indian Jews, the Bene Israel in Bombay.

Ceremonies. Both the "White" and the "Black" Jews perform their ceremonies separately in their own synagogues and homes. However, the ceremonies are similar and distinctly Cochini, reflecting both local Hindu and Christian influences. Both groups build a *manara*, or aperion, for the wedding, usually at the groom's house. After a ritual bath the bride receives a *tali*, an Indian pendant, in imitation of local Nayar practice. The groom and bride dress in traditional wedding dress. The groom enters the synagogue on a white carpet—a custom apparently observed by "Black" and not "White" Jews—and sits near the podium until the bride's procession arrives. The groom himself—and not a rabbi, as in other Jewish communities—actually announces his betrothal and marriage to his bride.

Arts. Daily prayers were chanted according to the *shingli* custom, a unique version of the standard Jewish prayers. In addition, the Cochin Jews have a large number of folksongs that they sing regularly. Some are sung at weddings, some are lullabies, and some specifically recall the return to Zion. In 1984 the Cochin Jews in Israel staged a huge pageant relating in song and dance the story of their emigration from India and their integration into Israeli society.

Death and Afterlife. The Cochin Jews believe in an afterlife, influenced both by Jewish and Hindu beliefs. Their dead are buried in Jewish cemeteries.

See also Bene Israel

Bibliography

Katz, Nathan, and Ellen Goldberg (1989). "Asceticism and Caste in the Passover Observances of the Cochin Jews." *Journal of the American Academy of Religion* 62:53–82.

Mandelbaum, David G. (1975). "Social Stratification among the Jews of Cochin in India and in Israel." *Jewish Journal of Sociology* 17:165–210.

Velayudhan, P. A., et al. (1971). *Commemorative Volume: Cochin Synagogue, Quatercentenary Celebration.* Cochin: Kerala Historical Association.

Weil, Shalva J. (1982). "Symmetry between Christian and Jews in India: the Cnanite Christian and the Cochin Jews of Kerala." *Contributions to Indian Sociology* 16:175–196.

Weil, Shalva J. (1984). *From Cochin to Eretz Israel* (in Hebrew). Jerusalem: Kumu Berina.

SHALVA J. WEIL

Coorg

ETHNONYMS: Coorgi, Kodara

Coorg is a tiny, isolated, mountainous district in southwest India, bounded on the east by the high Mysore Plateau, averaging an elevation of 1,000 meters, and on the west by a mountainous frontier 30–50 kilometers from the western coast. Its greatest length, north to south, is about 100 kilometers, and its greatest breadth, east to west, is 65 kilometers. The Western Ghat mountain range runs from north to south and its many spurs strike out in all directions through the small province, now a district of Karnataka State. The main rivers, the Kveri and Laksmanatirtha, are shallow and unnavigable.

The Coorg year is divided into three seasons—cold, hot, and rainy—with a marked variation in rainfall in the various regions. The average yearly temperature ranges from 10° to 27° C. Coorg is primarily an agricultural country with coffee and rice being the main products. Coorg contains dense forests of bamboo, sandalwood, and cardamom. Fauna includes elephants, tigers, panthers, boars, and deer.

The early history of Coorg can be traced back to the ninth century A.D. and consists of a succession of feudal rulers leading up to the dynasty of the Lingayat rajas beginning in the 1600s. The last survivors of the dynasty were the brothers, Doddavirarajendra (died 1809) and Lingarajendra (died 1820). The heir to the throne, a daughter, Devammaji, was 10 at the time of her father's death and the throne was therefore usurped by an uncle. The uncle, Lingarajendra, was succeeded by his son Chikkavirarajendra (Vira Raja II) who was poorly accepted by his subjects. This led to the eventual annexation of Coorg by the British in 1834. The annexation led to a number of economic, political, and social reforms, one of the most prominent being the abolition of slavery.

There are three levels of territorial group; the village is the smallest and the most important. Villages, which are multicaste, contain a number of ancestral estates, each comprised of a main house of stone and wood and nearby servants' huts of mud and bamboo. The *nad*, consisting of several villages, is the next larger group. In the 1931 census 94 percent of the population of Coorg lived in such villages. Traditionally Coorg was divided into thirty-five nads and twelve *kombus*, which serve judicial purposes. Every village has a council of elders that is presided over by a headman whose position is hereditary.

There are two towns in Coorg: Mercara, (or Madikeri) with a population of 7,112; and Virarajpet, with 4,106 persons (as of 1931). Mercara lies in the north-central portion of the region. Virarajpet is the most important commercial center today. Of the total 1931 population of 163,327, 89 percent were Hindus, 8 percent Muslims, and 2 percent Christians. The number of Kodagu speakers was listed as 72,085 in the 1971 census. The primary languages spoken in Coorg are Kodagu, Kannada (Dravidian language), Hindi, and English.

Coorgs consider themselves to be Kshatriyas, who constitute the caste of rulers and soldiers in the traditional hierarchy and rank below only Brahmans. Today Coorgs are some of the prominent military leaders in India. There are more than forty main castes and tribes in Coorg. The caste system is no longer rigidly adhered to. Within a village there is a great deal of cooperation between *okkas* (family units), especially during holidays or in times of disaster or mourning; however, feuds between nads were formerly common.

The traditional nuclear unit of Coorg society is the okka or patrilineal joint family. Only male members of an okka have any rights in the ancestral estate; women born into the okka leave it upon marriage. No woman may be head of an okka. There is sexual division of labor, with men working outside and women inside the house. The sexes are generally segregated. Since independence new laws have given women full equality with men; however previous traditions such as arranged marriages are still the norm. The okka commonly consists of two to three generations of agnatically related males, their wives, and their children. All members of an okka are descended from a common ancestor and the spirits of the dead ancestors are regarded with great reverence. Each okka has an ancestral house. This ancestral house is regarded as sacred to a Coorg and has a distinctive architectural design. Ancestor shrines (*kaimada*) and ancestor platforms (*karanava*) are located near it.

For the Coorgs, the external world is divided into two parts, the sacred and the nonsacred. The sacred includes good sacredness as well as bad sacredness. The Kodagu term for ritual purity is *madi*; the term for ritual impurity is *pole*. The ritual act of *mangala* is important in Coorg culture. Every mangala marks a change in the social personality of the individual; he moves from one position in the social system to another. The rite surrounding the mangala represents approval by the social group of the individual's change in social position. The mangala formerly celebrated several kinds of events: attainment of adulthood; construction of a new house; or marriage. Today it is performed primarily at marriage. An individual example of a part of the mangala, *murta*, is the salutation offered in greeting. The festivals of village deities and the harvest festival (Huthri) are the most important celebrations of villages. Village deities are commonly known by reference to the village in which they have a shrine, and they are an all-India phenomenon. The most common in Coorg are Bhagavati (Povvedi) and Ayyappa (or Shasta). It is common for two or three villages to combine in celebrating the festival of a village deity, which can last for seven to twenty-one days.

Every stage of cultivation of the rice crop is marked by ritual, but the most important is Huthri, which is performed when the paddy sheaves are cut and harvested. Every family member returns to the ancestral home for the celebrations. The ceremony includes a purification process, the donning of traditional dress, and a salutation and offering to the elders.

Bibliography

Krishna Iyer, L. A. (1948). *The Coorg Tribes and Castes (with 27 illustrations)*. Madras: Gordon Press. Reprint. 1969. New York: Johnson Reprint Corp.

Murphy, Dervla (1985). *On a Shoestring to Coorg: An Experience of South India*. London: Century Hutchinson.

Muthanna, I. M. (1953). *A Tiny Model State of South India*. Mysore: Usha Press.

Srinivas, M. N. (1952). *Religion and Society among the Coorgs of South India*. London: Oxford University Press. Reprint. 1965. London: Asia Publishing House.

SARA J. DICK

Dard

ETHNONYMS: none

Although this name appears in the anthropological literature, it seems that there is no discrete cultural group identifiable as Dards. It is true that Pliny and Ptolemy in ancient times both referred to such a people inhabiting a tract of the upper Indus Valley in what is today Pakistan, and in that area people living on the left bank of the Indus were called Dards. The Dards, based on descriptions of the Gilgit area around 1870, are described as a hunting, herding, and farming people with: large, extended families and some polygyny; some transhumance; no extensive cereal agriculture; villages of from 400 to 1,000 inhabitants; patrilocal postmarital residence; and no localized clans but lineages or sibs spreading beyond a single community. While all of this may have been true for the inhabitants of Gilgit, there is still some question as to whether those labeled Dards are, in fact, a distinct cultural entity.

It is more appropriate to speak of the "Dardic branch," a term used by linguists to designate a small group of languages of the Indo-Aryan Subfamily spoken in and near the north of Pakistan. Of these, Kashmiri is the most important. There is also a territory there known as Dardistan, which includes Gilgit Valley, Hunza, Chitral, Yasin, Nagar, Panyal, Kohistan, the Astore Valley, and part of the upper Indus Valley between Bunji and Batera.

See also Kashmiri; Kohistani

Bibliography

Biddulph, John (1880). _Tribes of the Hindoo Koosh._ Calcutta: Superintendent of Government Printing.

Leitner, Gotlieb William (1877). _The Languages and Races of Dardistan._ Lahore: Government Central Book Depot.

PAUL HOCKINGS

Divehi

ETHNONYMS: Divehin, Dives, Maldivians

Orientation

Identification. Divehis are those who speak Divehi, the language of the Republic of the Maldives. They occupy all the Maldives and also the island of Maliku (Minicoy on the maps) to the north, which belongs to India. The people call themselves Divehi (from _dive-si,_ meaning "island-er"), and their country is Divehi Rājje (kingdom). The name "Maldives" is probably from _mālā-dīv_ ("garland-islands" in Indian languages), referring to the double chain of atolls that appears like a garland or necklace. The word _atol_ is Divehi, originally spelled with one _l._ The country was a nexus of Indian Ocean shipping, and it has remained mostly independent since ancient times.

Location. The Maldives stretch from 0° 2' S to 7° 0' N, with Minicoy at 8° 2'. Longitude is about 73° E. There are about 1,200 islands, of which 201 are permanently inhabited. The islands are low and flat, mostly less than a kilometer long with only 9 as long as 2 kilometers, ringing coral atolls. Total land area is only about 280 square kilometers, and nowhere is the land more than 2 meters above sea level. The Maldives extend for 867 kilometers north to south and claim the surrounding ocean as national territory. Maliku is the largest island, 16.5 kilometers long and lying 140 kilometers north of the Maldives proper, but it is politically cut off from other parts of the archipelago.

Demography. As of 1991 there were 228,000 Divehis—220,000 Maldivians and roughly 8,000 on Maliku. The first census was in 1911 as part of the Ceylon census, and it showed 72,237 Divehis on 217 inhabited islands. Population was previously kept in check by epidemics, famine because of storms that interrupted imports of food, and cerebral malaria, but during recent decades the population has been shooting up rapidly. The 1990 census showed a crude birthrate of 43 per 1,000 and a growth rate of 3.5 percent a year. The government has taken little initiative on family planning because of the momentum of Islamic tradition. Male has 57,000 people, a quarter of all Divehis, though it is only 1.6 kilometers long and the thin groundwater lens has become polluted, so the government tries to curb migration there. Life expectancy is about 62 years for males and 60 for females.

Linguistic Affiliation. Divehi is derived from the old Sinhala of Sri Lanka, and so it is classifiable as an Indo-Aryan language, although at the very end of the Eurasian chain of that language stock. There is an underlying component of Tamil-Malayalam. Since conversion to Islam, numerous Arabic and Persian words have been borrowed. The bounds of the language are clear, but the three southern atolls and Maliku have their own dialects. The script is unique, invented for Divehi three centuries ago from a combination of Arabic and Indian principles of script. It suits the language well and is easy to learn.

History and Cultural Relations

The Maldives were known to very early Indian seafarers, such as sailed from Gujarat in the middle of the first millennium B.C. and settled in Sri Lanka, and are mentioned in early works such as the Buddhist Jātaka tales and the Sri Lankan epics. Early settlement was evidently from Kerala, diffused through the Lakshadvīp (Laccadive) Islands by fishermen and by the kings of Kerala who made conquests by sea, according to Tamil literature of the early centuries A.D. The Maldives were perhaps touched by Indonesian culture (which passed through to Madagascar) roughly at the same time, and the islands were well known to classical Greek geographers. Persians began trading about the seventh century. The country was conquered several times by Tamil and Kerala kings in medieval centuries. The most significant settlement was by Sinhalas from Sri Lanka, perhaps by political exiles, which gave the Maldives their language, the old Sinhala script, Theravada Buddhism, and Sri Lankan beliefs and foods. This little civilization flourished especially in the tenth to twelfth centuries, held together by a Sinhala type of highly centralized kinship. On several islands there are remnants of Buddhist stupas of coral stone, described by H. C. P. Bell as being of Anuradhapura style. In the twelfth century an Arab saint who claimed that he had power to chase away a powerful jinni by reading the Quran convinced the king to convert the country to Islam and made him a sultan. The national chronicle records ninety-two sultans (and a few sultanas). Through Islam, the Maldives had the advantage of trade links all over the Indian Ocean. Ibn Battuta, the Arab chronicler, came in 1343–1344 and taught Islamic law. The Maldives were visited by the Chinese in the ninth and fifteenth centuries. The Portuguese ruled for fifteen years in the sixteenth century. The British "protected" the country from 1887 on, but they did not leave much of a cultural stamp, and they granted the Maldives independence in 1965. So the old culture is comprised of three main layers: the Tamil-Malayalam substratum with its many subtle roots; old Sinhala culture and language, which is the dominant element; and the phase of Arabic influence. But the Maldives were touched by every cultural wind that passed over the Indian Ocean. Since independence there has again been influence from Sri Lanka, through its teachers brought over to set up modern education with teaching of English. Unusually rapid change has occurred in Divehi culture in the past twenty-five years.

Settlements

The 201 inhabited islands are the larger or best fishing islands. Houses are made of local vegetation and thatch or coral stones, sometimes with imported iron or tile roofs. People desire pleasant houses, and they often arrange them on streets with the plots marked by stick fences. The island is the social and administrative unit. Everybody has official registration on his or her island and cannot change it to another island without twelve years' residence. Each island comprises an insular social community, in which its land, people, and products are preferred to those of other islands. The islands are grouped into nineteen administrative atolls. Male is the only city, with some multistoried buildings of coral stone neatly whitewashed and mostly built along the straight sandy streets. It has a pious air, with thirty-five mosques and many tombs. Nearby is the airport island of Hulule, with a runway extending on the reef. Some 60 "uninhabited" islands are now built up as profitable tourist resorts, which especially attract Europeans in winter, but the government tries to minimize their cultural influence.

Economy

Subsistence and Commercial Activities. The main traditional economic activities are trading and fishing. Bonitos and larger tuna are a mainstay of the economy, caught by pole-and-line or trolling-line from sailboats or motorized wooden boats. The famous Maldives fish is prepared by boiling, drying, and smoking. A man maximizes wealth by acquiring fishing boats because the owner gets a larger share of fish than the fishing crew. A boat owner might also obtain the right from the state to lease uninhabited islands, mainly for collecting coconuts. There are three kinds of millets grown and taro in the south. Some homes have breadfruit, mango, papaya, and banana trees, but few vegetables are eaten. Sea trade has always been a vital source of income, and now there is a modern shipping industry; profits from it and tourism accrue mostly to a few prominent families in Male. Income per capita from foreign aid is relatively high.

Industrial Arts. The most striking traditional craft is building wooden boats, both small and large ones with lateen sails, which can fish in the deep sea and carry goods to the continents. Sailing long distances without benefit of maps and charts is a remarkable traditional skill. Maldives rope twisted from coconut coir was always in demand by foreign navies. The islanders also make fine products such as mats woven from local reeds and lacquer work on turned wood. Cotton weaving, silver work, stonecutting, and brass work have mostly died out.

Trade. For many centuries the Maldives were famous as the main source of cowrie shells, used as money in Bengal and Africa. Divehis are skilled in rapid counting, necessary for handling cowries, coconuts, or fish. The traditional method was to count by twos to 96 and mark each unit of 192 by laying 2 coconuts on the side; they thereby could count rapidly to many thousands. The base number was 12, which Clarence Maloney finds significant in Maldives history. What is more peculiar is that Indo-Aryan words for 25, 50, 75, 100, and 1,000 are applied respectively to 24, 48, 72, 96, and 960, as the decimal system has been replacing the duodecimal. Weights and measures are based on multiples of 4 and 12. The main imports have been rice, wheat flour, cotton textiles, kerosene, metal products, tobacco, salt, and condiments. Now the whole country is a duty-free entrepôt, contrasting with the controlled economies of other South Asian countries, and there is modern banking.

Division of Labor. Men fish, while women prepare and dry the fish. Men grow millets, while women cultivate root crops. Men conduct interisland and overseas trade, climb coconut trees, and are the artisans in cotton, silver, lacquer, and stonework, while women weave mats and do embroidery. Women do the tedious job of twisting coir into small ropes, which men then twist into thick ropes for their boats. However, these sex roles are not absolutely fixed; there are cases of these activities being done by the other sex. Women do most of the housework and child care, but men may also do it. Boat crews and leaders of Islamic ritual and law, however, are all males.

Land Tenure. All land belongs to the state, which leases uninhabited islands or parts of islands to prominent people for collection of produce, as part of its system of control. All households in the Maldives, except on Male, can claim the right to a plot of land for a house and garden in their island of registration. In Fue Mulaku in the south, residents have the right to cultivate as much taro land as they wish.

Kinship

Kin Groups and Descent. The Divehi kinship system in origin is a combination of Dravidian and Arab with elements of North Indian kinship derived from Sri Lanka. Although these three systems are sharply at variance, they are resolved in Divehi culture. The Dravidian system is based on preferred cross-cousin marriage, and a male classifies all females as either sister (unmarriageable) or female cross cousin (marriageable). The matrilineal variant of the Dravidian system occurs most clearly in the Lakshadvīp Islands off the coast of Kerala, from which Tamil-Malayalam culture would have extended to form the cultural substratum in the Maldives. This comes through clearly in Divehi kinship terminology, the history of queens, remnants of girls' menstruation ceremonies, and other features traced out in Maloney's reconstruction of the culture history. Sinhala settlers too brought a form of Dravidian kinship, modified by features derived from North India. The present Divehi system is heavily influenced by Islamic law, so a man can marry any cousin but not a sibling's daughter, a foster sister, or a stepdaughter. There are few lateral kinship ties and no lineage depth except in a few prominent families; some Divehis do not even recall their grandparents' names.

Kinship Terminology. Divehi kin terms are few, of mixed Sinhala, Arabic, and Dravidian origin. The terms "grandfather" (*kāfa*) and "grandmother" (*māma*), and "father" (*bappa*) and "mother" (*mamma*) may be applied to other kin of their generation. The terms "elder brother" (*bēbe*) and "elder sister" (*datta*) are extended to elder cousins. Terms one uses for one's juniors, as "younger sibling" (*kokko*), "child" (*dari*), and "child-in-law" (*danbi*), do not distinguish sex. As for in-laws, all males are covered by one term (*liyanu*, of Malayalam origin) and females by another (*faliui*). In Fua Mulaku atoll there is a word for "mother's brother," *māber*, to whom a male may have a special relationship, a Dravidian remnant. There are no terms or marriage rules about cousins, any of whom can marry, as in Islam. There are hardly any ritual relationships with one's own children, and none with siblings or other kin. In this sparse system, most of the special kin relationships in the three underlying systems historically canceled each other out, compatible with the extreme frequency of divorce and remarriage.

Marriage and Family

Marriage. There is a tendency toward preferential island endogamy, because people don't like other islands and it is difficult to move. The wedding ceremony consists only of the elemental Islamic rituals. A woman does not appear at her own wedding, but her prior consent is obtained by the *katibu* who officiates. Every woman has a male guardian who signs for her marriage, and all marriages and divorces are meticulously recorded. Divorce and remarriage are remarkably common; someone might divorce and marry a neighbor, then remarry the original partner or another neighbor, while the children remain nearby. Marriage and divorce are according to Islamic law, interpreted so as to allow frequent remarriages. A man can divorce his wife by a single pronouncement, and if a woman wants a divorce she can behave in such a way that she gets it. It is common to meet people who have been divorced and remarried a dozen times; there are people who have married even 80 or 90 times in life, often to previous partners. The marriage rate in the Maldives is 34.4 per 1,000 persons per year (compared with 9.7 in United States, and 7.9 in Sri Lanka where divorce is rare). This is by far the highest rate of legal marriage and divorce of any country listed in United Nations statistics. But divorce does not induce trauma in a child, because the parent who departs the home will be a close neighbor, and the parents might remarry. So a

child grows up with a special feeling toward all the citizens of his or her island, who are all related and tend to form a marrying unit.

Domestic Unit. The family is usually nuclear and is a fluid unit. Often a woman owns the house, and in divorce the children may stay with her. Descent can be classified as bilateral and residence mostly as ambilocal or neolocal, or in a few places duolocal. People try to build houses of several rooms and a kitchen, with a fenced garden, and usually keep them tidy. Old people are not automatically entitled to special respect, especially if they cannot earn; they live either with a child or alone. By law, an aged person should be supported equally by all his grown children.

Inheritance. Islamic inheritance is observed, in which a daughter gets half the share of a son. But some people will all their property to one child in return for old-age support. A woman tends to inherit the house and a man the boats. When a woman dies, the first share of her property goes to her legal guardian (usually her father) and then in turn to husband, sons, and daughters. Because of the frequency of divorce, married couples have separate ownership of all movable and immovable property. Inheritance is settled by the Islamic judge (*qāzi*).

Socialization. Children are mostly raised benevolently, with emphasis on absence of violence and control of emotion. Aggressive play among children is not acceptable, and in the society there is hardly any physical aggression, violence, or murder. Boys may swim, play on boats, climb trees, fly kites, or walk on stilts. Girls do not do these things, but they play hopscotch, shell games, or "kitchens." Children's play is not encouraged. On most islands there is little that is new to explore, no new personalities, and no real schooling. Mothers teach children to read and write Divehi, using chalk on little slate boards, for Islamic teaching, and many islands have little schools attached to the mosques, so almost all Divehis become literate. Many children learn to intone Arabic letters in order to "read" the Quran, although without any understanding.

Sociopolitical Organization

Social Organization. In the old society there were three ranks, mostly in Male and the large southern islands, and though descendants of the old elite class still hold most political power and property, they have no hereditary privileges or titles now. Rank today is determined mostly by wealth. Divehis comprise a single tight sociopolitical system with no significant ethnic minorities, though there are minor cultural differences among the atolls, particularly the three southern atolls. The people of Maliku have been under separate administration for two centuries, and there is little outside knowledge of the society because India does not allow foreigners to visit there. India administers it along with the Lakshadvīp Islands and expects the people to go to school in Malayalam, though they still speak Divehi. In the Maldives, just one castelike group has been described. This group is the Girāvaru, Aborigines who formerly ruled Male. They lived on an eroding island, so the government moved them to Hulule, the airport island, from where they have again been displaced; now they have again been partly absorbed by another island community. They have consciously retained differences in dress, have claimed that unlike the other Divehis they had no divorce or widow remarriage, and have said their ancestors were Tamils, though they have no knowledge of such people and have never traveled outside their atoll. They have also claimed to be strictly endogamous. Other Divehis traditionally have thought of the Girāvaru as dirty, while they have thought of other Divehis as morally corrupt.

Political Organization.   The old aristocratic families from the time of the sultanate are still dominant in Male. Since independence in 1965 the country has been called a republic. It is governed by a president, who maintains tight authority through the ministries of religion and law, the system of appointed atoll and island chiefs, and finances from the tourist and shipping industries. In theory, he governs at the will of the national assembly, the Majlis, which is just now beginning to assume a modern legislative role.

Social Control.   Control is through the island offices and atoll offices, in which religious law is part of the tight state apparatus. All larger islands and atoll offices have a qāzi, who performs marriages, adjudicates disputes and inheritance, examines the accused, and enforces Sharia law as interpreted by the attorney-general. The atoll court has separate sections to deal with religious, criminal, and political violations. The court may punish an accused by giving an order for social boycott or by banishment to some island for a year or for life. Atoll and island headmen study Islamic religious law, and there are a few experts trained in Egypt.

Conflict.   Divehis are extremely reticent to show aggression or to make threats, and there is hardly any murder. But there are serious contests to seize national political power, and a loser may be banished to an island for many years. There is a historic tendency for the southern atolls to claim autonomy, but this tendency is not overt now, and there is no other organized or open conflict in the society. Divehis on small islands may have hardly any knowledge of the outside world, and they often fear strangers.

Religion and Expressive Culture

Religious Beliefs.   All Divehis are Sunni Muslims, of the Shafi tradition, and will remain so because a non-Muslim cannot marry or settle there. Every island has its mosque with the katību in charge, who is paid by the government. Most men attend Friday prayers and give to charity. Women perhaps more than men pray five times a day and read scripture. The ethos of Islam appears to be very strong, but some feel it tends to consist only of perfunctory fasting and prayers. Islamic mysticism and Sufi ideas are officially disapproved of as leading to emotionalism rather than to Sunni legal observance. Islam overlies an earlier religious system having many deities and spirits—originally Hindu, Buddhist, or Jain deities and local ghosts—but people now think of them as jinnis and deal with them by Islamic strategies. The outside world is unknown and fearsome, and people are concerned about strange lights on the ocean. There is a system of religious practice called fanḍita, which is used to chase away jinnis and fearsome lights, catch fish, heal disease, increase fertility, facilitate divination, make a person give up his or her spouse, cast out a spirit, or solve any problem in life. When a new boat is launched there is a fanḍita ritual combined with Arabic prayers for its good performance. Fanḍita is performed at several stages in growing a taro or millet crop. Black magic is also known, but it is prohibited by law. Fanḍita has many elements similar to village religion in south India and Sri Lanka. Pre-Muslim concepts of the evil eye and pollution have been absorbed into Islamic values. Menstrual pollution is strongly observed.

Religious Practitioners.   The katību of an island preaches Friday sermons, settles disputes, reports behavior deviations to the atoll office, and also runs the island office. He is assisted by a functionary to care for the mosque, make calls to prayer, and bury the dead. Fanḍita practitioners were at one time licensed by the state. Fanḍita men and women seldom go into trance, which they think Islam disapproves of; their purpose is to help others in difficult life situations. Larger islands also have astrologers.

Ceremonies.   Divehis know five calendrical systems: a nakṣatra or zodiacal system from India; an Indian solar calendar; an Arabic solar calendar; the Arabic religious calendar; which is ten days shorter than the solar year; and now the "English" calendar. Weather is keenly observed, along with fishing seasons and agricultural festivals, according to the nakṣatra (nakai) system. Other festivals are observed according to their respective calendrical systems, but the new-moon festival that came from Sri Lanka has now almost disappeared. Divehis are assiduous about observing the Ramzan holiday, enforced by the state. But at night in Ramzan the food is abundant. The two īd festivals are important, and the Prophet's birthday is celebrated by special foods. Personal ceremonies include giving a name about a week after birth, circumcision of boys at age 6 or 8, symbolic circumcision of baby girls (which may be declining), and girls' puberty ceremony as a carryover from Sri Lanka and south India. Marriage is less important as a life ceremony.

Arts.   The arts are very poorly developed because of the isolated and scattered population. Divehi music is monorhythmic and infrequently heard; Radio Maldives tends to play Hindi cinema songs. Dancing has been disfavored by Islam. There is some artistry in living crafts such as lace making, lacquer work, and mat weaving.

Medicine.   Most people seek healing from fanḍita which uses both mantras invoking Allah's power and factual advice. The diverse medical systems of India are not developed, but there are a few practitioners of the Islamic system of Unani. There is a government hospital in Male providing scientific medicine, and donors have funded the beginning of a health-care system.

Death and Afterlife.   The death ritual is important. The katību is informed and a conch shell is blown. Then the body is washed, tied, and shrouded as specified in Islam and laid in a coffin or in a leaf box. The grave is dug by family members or friends, and then the corpse is laid in with the face toward Mecca, while passages from the Quran are read. Death is not greeted with much emotion, and questions about life after death are not of much concern.

Bibliography

Bell, H. C. P. (1940). *The Maldive Islands: Monograph on the History, Archaeology, and Epigraphy*. Colombo: Government Press.

Maloney, Clarence (1984). "Divehi." In _Muslim Peoples: A World Ethnographic Survey_, Vol. 1, 232–236. Rev. ed., edited by Richard Weekes. Westport, Conn.: Greenwood Press.

Maloney, Clarence (1980). _People of the Maldive Islands._ Madras: Orient Longman.

Munch-Petersen, Nils Finn (1982). "Maldives: History, Daily Life, and Art Handicraft." _Bulletin du C.E.M.O.I._ (Brussels). 1:74–103.

Ottovar, Annagrethe, and Nils Finn Munch-Petersen (1980). _Maldiveneøet øsamfund i det Indiske Ocean_ (The Maldivian Island community in the Indian Ocean). Copenhagen: Kunstindustrimuseet.

CLARENCE MALONEY AND NILS FINN MUNCH-PETERSEN

Europeans in South Asia

ETHNONYMS: Ferangi (from "Franks"), Sahib (fem.: Memsahib; child: Chhota Sahib)

While the impact of Europe on the South Asian subcontinent has been immeasurable and dates back long before Vasco da Gama's exploratory visit in 1498, the number of Europeans resident in the area now is merely a few tens of thousands. (They move about so much that a close estimate is difficult.) But even in the heyday of British imperialism there were only about 167,000 Europeans in all of South Asia (1931 census).

Leaving aside from this discussion the Anglo-Indians and Luso-Indians of the South Asian mainland, and the Burghers of Sri Lanka, who are all in fact local people of part-European ancestry, we can identify the following categories of Europeans as being resident in South Asia today.

(1) _Diplomats and journalists._ Found only in the capital cities and other consular posts.

(2) _Development workers, etc._ Technical specialists from the World Health Organization, other United Nations agencies, the U.S. Peace Corps, etc. are regularly encountered in most South Asian countries. Students of anthropology, linguistics, and some other subjects may be found almost anywhere, though never in great numbers. Some tea and coffee plantations in India still have European managers and indeed are owned by British companies.

(3) _Retired British residents._ A small number of very elderly people who retired in India or Sri Lanka at about the time of independence are still there. (Most, however, left the subcontinent to retire in Britain, the Channel Islands, Cyprus, or Australia.)

(4) _Christian missionaries._ While the South Asian churches are essentially self-governing, several hundred European and American missionaries and Catholic priests and nuns may still be encountered in the region. They are still of some importance in education, as well as in funneling Western aid to their parishioners.

(5) _Religious seekers._ At any given time there are some thousands of Australian, European, or American people, usually fairly young, who are wandering around India, Nepal, and elsewhere in search of religious enlightenment within the broad tradition of Hindu spirituality. Some of these people have been loosely classed as "hippies." French people are particularly attracted to Pondicherry and the nearby religious center of Auroville, while others have been especially attracted to specific ashrams, to Rishikesh and other Himalayan sites, or to the Theosophical Center in Madras City.

(6) _Tourists._ The region has an enormous tourist potential, which has been slowly developed since independence, and in 1991 India, Sri Lanka, Nepal, and the Maldives have a thriving tourist industry. Unlike the religious seekers mentioned above, who may stay for many months, ordinary Western tourists usually visit for just two or three weeks. The great majority of these tourists are from western Europe and Australasia. (Many of India's tourists, on the other hand, are non-Europeans from other South Asian countries.)

The British Impact

The cultural and political impact of the British over the past two centuries in South Asia has been vast and extremely pervasive. Numerous histories of the "British period" testify to this, and it is an influence referred to in the Introduction to this volume. Space does not permit even a brief review of the administrative, legal, religious, educational, public health, military, agricultural, industrial, sporting, and communicational developments that occurred during the period of British administration of most of the subcontinent.

We may instead highlight the contribution of Europeans from India to the arts. Best known of course is the literary contribution of Rudyard Kipling (1865–1936), one of two Indian-born writers to receive the Nobel Prize for Literature (the other was Rabindranath Tagore). Of numerous professional artists to work in India, the most outstanding was the Anglo-German painter John Zoffany, who worked there from 1783 to 1790. The artistic impact of the British on Indian architecture was vast, and well documented: witness only the official buildings of New Delhi. Less recognized during the present century has been the impact of this relatively small ethnic group on the British film industry. Julie Christie, Vivien Leigh, Margaret Lockwood, Merle Oberon, and several other actors, as well as the director Lindsay Anderson, were all born and at least partly brought up in British India. One might wonder whether the ubiquity of school plays and amateur dramatic societies in that era had something to do with these careers.

See also Anglo-Indian; French of India; Indian Christian

Bibliography

Ballhatchet, Kenneth (1980). *Race, Sex and Class under the Raj: Imperial Attitudes and Policies and Their Critics, 1793–1905.* New York: St. Martin's Press.

Barr, Pat (1976). *The Memsahibs: The Women of Victorian India.* London: Secker & Warburg.

Hervey, H. J. A. (1913). *The European in India.* London: Stanley Paul & Co.

Hockings, Paul (1989). "British Society in the Company, Crown, and Congress Eras." *Blue Mountains: The Ethnography and Biogeography of a South Indian Region,* edited by Paul Edward Hockings, 334–359. New Delhi: Oxford University Press.

Kincaid, Dennis (1938). *British Social Life in India, 1608–1937.* London: George Routledge & Sons.

Moorhouse, Geoffrey (1983). *India Britannica.* New York: Harper & Row.

Nilsson, Sten (1968). *European Architecture in India, 1750–1850.* London: Faber and Faber.

Trevelyan, Raleigh (1987). *The Golden Oriole.* New York: Viking Penguin.

PAUL HOCKINGS

French of India

ETHNONYMS: French Tamils, Pondichériens, Pondicherry (name of town and territory)

There were 12,864 French nationals residing in India in 1988. Nearly all are in the Union Territory of Pondicherry in southeastern India (11,726 in 1988), with much smaller numbers in Karaikal (695 individuals), Mahé (50), Yanam (46), and 342 elsewhere in India. (These were coastal pockets belonging to the former French Empire.) While legally still citizens of France and resident aliens in India, they are ethnically Indian, about 90 percent being ethnic Tamils. Almost unaccountably, they vote in the French constituency of Nice. They form a small minority, accounting for less than 3 percent of the present population of Pondicherry.

The French in India are an artifact of the French presence there, which began in 1673 with the establishment of French India and continued until 1962 when the French territory was formally transferred to India. The French presence was always small and minor compared with the British presence and the French in India were generally ignored. Today, the majority of these French are Hindus or Christians of local or mixed family origin, and less than 50 percent of them speak French. At the same time, however, French is taught in schools attended by French Indian children and adult French classes are well attended, reflecting an interest in maintaining ties and an allegiance to France or in finding jobs with French companies. The French Indians are the wealthiest group in Pondicherry (aside from those running the Aurobindo Ashram), deriving much of their income from pension (some 20 percent are retirees), social security, welfare, and other programs of the French government. They are also entitled to emigrate to France, although few do so and the French government does not encourage the practice.

See also Europeans in South Asia; Tamil

Bibliography

Glachant, Roger (1965). *Histoire de l'Inde des Français.* Paris: Librairie Plon.

Miles, William F. S. (1990). "Citizens without Soil: The French of India (Pondicherry)." *Ethnic and Racial Studies* 13:252–273.

Ramasamy, A. (1987). *History of Pondicherry.* New Delhi: Sterling Publishers.

Scholberg, Henry, and Emmanuel Divien (1973). *Bibliographie des Français dans l'Inde.* Pondicherry: Historical Society of Pondicherry.

Garia

ETHNONYM: Assamese Muslims

Assam is an Indian state located between 26° and 28° N and 90° and 94° E. Muslim Assamese speakers number 2 million out of a total Muslim population of about 5 million in Assam. Although the basic values of the Assamese Muslims are Islamic, they share some Hindu customs and practices, which are contradictory to Islamic conventions. While intermarriage with Hindus is rare, many Assamese Muslims identify more strongly with other Assamese who are Hindu than with other Muslims. Their identity is inexorably connected with the Asamiya language and the region of Assam. Asamiya (Asambe, Asami), the native language of the Assamese, is derived from Sanskrit and is the official language of Assam State. There are two important dialects, eastern and western, which are very different in linguistic structure from each other. The language is rich in borrowed vocabulary from Hindi, Persian, Arabic, English, Portuguese, and regional tribal languages. The language uses the Bengali script.

The Asamiya-speaking Muslims of Assam developed their culture through continuous contact between Islam and native regional cultures. They have many cultural traits in common with Assamese Hindus and are less orthodox than other Indian Muslims. Assam first came into contact with Islam in 1206, when Muhammad bin Bakhtar led a military expedition to Tibet through the region. In 1532 Turbak invaded Assam with a Muslim army and was defeated by the king of the Ahoms. Those taken prisoner were settled in the region and married Assamese women, losing all their Islamic culture within a few generations and adopting local customs. In the 1630s, the Muslim saint Shah Milan, also known as Azan Faqir, opened the way for Islamic missionaries, by winning the patronage of the Ahom rulers. Between 1910 and 1931, thousands of Bengali Muslim peasants from eastern Bengal, now Bangladesh, settled in the riverine tracts of the plains. Their descendants today have adopted the Asamiya language and identify themselves as Assamese. In the last forty years, thousands more Bengali Muslims have migrated to Assam, settling there as rice farmers. Many local non-Muslims resent them because they have kept their language and customs. Many more Indian Muslims have immigrated from other regions, especially Bihar and eastern Uttar Pradesh. Most of them are urban nonfarmers.

Agrarian Assamese Muslims inhabit clustered hamlets and villages surrounded by their fields. Hindu and Muslim Assamese generally live separately; some do live together, however, keeping their separate identities but sharing some common institutions. Approximately 70 percent of Assamese Muslims are farmers by occupation. The principal crop of the region is paddy (rice) of several different local varieties. Other important crops include, maize, wheat, oilseeds such as mustard, jute, and sugarcane, and various seasonal vegetables. Many farmers also engage in small commerce, trade, and work as wage laborers. The Marias are traditionally brass workers. Most urban Muslims pursue varied occupations including the professions.

Assamese Muslims combine many Islamic and Hindu customs. Assamese Muslim families are patriarchal and patrilineal. Women are allowed to inherit one-eighth of their father's property. The kinship terminology is very similar to the Hindu. Avoidance relations between father-in-law and daughter-in-law and between husband's elder brother and younger brother's wife are practiced among both Muslims and Hindus. Marriage among Assamese Muslims entails two separate events: the ring ceremony, which is followed by the actual marriage. After the negotiations are fixed, the future groom's parents and kin visit the bride's home. The entourage brings a gold ring, silk clothes, and sweets as gifts. The marriage ceremony is consummated with the reciting of verses from the Quran by a Muslim cleric. Cross-cousin marriage is not encouraged.

Components of the Hindu caste system are present among Assamese Muslims. They are divided into a three-tier system: the Sayyids, who hold the highest status and claim to be descendants of the prophet Mohammed; the Sheikhs, composed of the local peoples, who are second in social status; the Marias, who hold the third social slot and are the descendants of the Muslim soldiers captured in the Muslim invasion of 1532.

The vast majority of Assamese Muslims are Sunni of the Hanafi juridical rite; however, they observe many local Hindu rites that put them at odds with Islamic practice. For example, many are attracted to the Vaishnavite philosophy preached in Assam by the sixteenth-century philosopher Sankaradeva.

See also Muslim; Sayyid; Sheikh

Bibliography

Ahmad, Imtiaz (1976). "For a Sociology of India." In _Muslim Communities of South Asia_, 172–178. New Delhi: Vikas Publishing House.

Ali, A. N. M. Irshad (1979). "Hindu Muslim Relations in Assam." _Man in India_ 9:261–381.

Das, B. M., and A.N.M. Irshad Ali (1984). "Assamese." In _Muslim Peoples: A World Ethnographic Survey_, edited by Richard V. Weekes, Vol. 1, 58–63. Westport, Conn.: Greenwood Press.

JAY DiMAGGIO

Garo

ETHNONYM: Achik

Orientation

Identification. The Garos living in the East and West Garo Hills districts of Meghalaya in northeastern India speak the Garo dialect. They are one of the best-known matrilineal groups in India. Here the Garos are not just another aboriginal tribe—they are the _major_ aboriginal tribe. Others are the

Hajong, the Koch, the Rabha, the Dalau, and the Banais who reside on the adjacent plains of the neighboring district. There remains an obscurity about the origin of the word "Garo." They are known as "Garos" to outsiders; but the Garos always designate themselves as "Achik" (hill men). The Garos are divided into nine subtribes: the Awe, Chisak, Matchi-Dual, Matabeng, Ambeng, Ruga-Chibox, Gara-Ganching, Atong, and the Megam. These are geographic subtribes, but they are also dialectal and subcultural groups. According to their beliefs and religion, the Garos are divided into the "Songsarek" (those who follow indigenous beliefs and practices) and the Christians.

Location. The two Garo Hills districts are situated between 25°9' and 26°1' N and 89°49' and 91°2' E, covering an area of 8,000 square kilometers. The districts border Bangladesh on the south and west and Assam on the north. Hills cover most of the district, with some adjacent fringes of plains bordering the monsoon area, producing thick vegetation on the hills. There are a number of hilly streams and rivers; except for the Simsang River, which forms a wide floodplain, none is navigable.

Demography. According to the census of India for 1971, Garos numbered 342,474. Christian Garos were 54.3 percent of the total Garo population; now they may be more than 60 percent of the total Garo population.

Linguistic Affiliation. According to Sir George Grierson's classification in *The Linguistic Survey of India*, Garo belongs to the Bodo Subsection of the Bodo-Naga Section, under the Assam-Burma Group of the Sino-Tibetan or Tibeto-Burman Language Family.

History and Cultural Relations

There remains no record of when the Garos migrated and settled in their present habitat. Their traditional lore, as recorded by A. Playfair, indicates that they migrated to the area from Tibet. There is evidence that the area was inhabited by stone-using peoples—Paleolithic and Neolithic groups—in the past. After settling in the hills, Garos initially had no close and constant contact with the inhabitants of the adjoining plains. In 1775–1776 the Zamindars of Mechpara and Karaibari (at present in the Goalpara and Dhuburi districts of Assam) led expeditions into the Garo hills. The first contact with British colonialists was in 1788, and the area was brought under British administrative control in the year 1873.

Settlements

The population in a Garo village may range from 20 to 1,000 persons. The population density tends to decrease as one moves toward the interior areas from the urban areas of the districts. Villages are scattered and distant from one another in the interior areas. These villages are generally situated on the top of hillocks. The houses are built, together with granaries, firewood sheds, and pigsties, on piles around the slope of the hillock, using locally available bamboo, wood, grass, etc. The approach to the rectangular house is always built facing the leveled surface of the top, while the rear part of the house remains horizontal to the slope. Nowadays new pile-type buildings using wood and iron as major components are being made in some traditional villages also. In addition, buildings

similar to those of the neighboring plains are constructed. The villages may remain distant from agricultural fields (*jhum*). In order to guard a crop (during agricultural seasons) from damage by wild animals, the people build temporary watchtowers (*borang*) in trees in the field. Men's dormitories exist in some villages. They act as places for meeting and recreation for the bachelors.

Economy

Subsistence and Commercial Activities. Traditionally, the Garos living in the hills subsist by slash-and-burn cultivation. The iron hoe, chopper, and wooden digging stick are essential appliances. Human hands continue to be the principal tool. Very often in some areas a plot allotted to a family remains underused because of an insufficient number of workers and the low level of technology. To survive the erratic nature of the monsoons, mixed crops—both wet and dry varieties—are planted. A shifting cultivator plants a wide assortment of crops consisting of rice (mainly dry varieties), millet, maize, and many root crops, vegetables, etc. In addition to these cotton, ginger, and chili peppers are commonly raised as cash crops. All crops are harvested in October. At present the available strips of low and flat land lying between the hillocks or hills are used for permanent wet cultivation. The variety of crops cultivated is like that of the neighboring plains peoples. Such lands are owned individually. Additional production from such plots places the villagers in a better economic condition. The expansion of the modern economy and the steady increase of population are causing constant pressure on traditionally owned plots. The same plot is used almost continuously in some areas, thus leading to a decline in annual production. This trend is evident from the 1981 census report, which estimated that about 50 percent of the Garo people are now solely dependent on shifting cultivation and the rest use a part of a jhum plot permanently for growing areca nuts, oranges, tea (on a small scale), pineapples, etc. In this changing situation a producer may not always be a consumer; and reciprocity and cooperation do not exist as dominant forces in the socioeconomic life of this population.

Industrial Arts. Each family in a traditional context acts as a self-contained economic unit. Modernization has brought some changes in the socioeconomic sphere of this population. The Garos residing in the hills did not weave cloth a few decades back; they used to procure thick cloth known as *kancha* from the plains Garos. Now that the loom has been introduced in the hill areas, they weave *dokmande* (a kind of cloth) for commercial purposes as well as for their personal use. Previously each family used to make pottery for its own domestic use, but nowadays the art is confined to a few families only who either sell it or barter it.

Trade. A few centuries ago the Garos were famous for headhunting. That practice constrained the neighboring population of the plains from entering the hills. But people must exchange their produce to meet their requirements, and both hill and plains Garos needed such trade. Hence some trade started at border points on a very limited scale. Over time, these contacts grew into organized *hutta* (weekly markets) under the initiative of the Zamindars, who were subjects of the Muslim ruler. Initially cotton was sold outright or exchanged for pigs, cattle, goats, tobacco, and metallic tools. In the beginning silent barter was possible because each party understood from long involvement the respective values of their goods. This process has continued to the present, with increasing involvement of traders from neighboring areas, and has now become fully monetized. Cotton, ginger, and dried chilies produced by the Garos are sold to the traders. The Garos in turn purchase pottery, metallic tools, and other industrial goods such as cloth from the traders.

Division of Labor. The division of labor between members of the household is as follows: the males are responsible for clearing jungle and setting fire to the debris for shifting cultivation, while women are responsible for planting, weeding, and harvesting. During the peak of the agricultural operations the men sometimes help the women. Construction and repair of the house are male duties. Men make baskets, while women carry crops from the field and firewood from jungle. Women look after the kitchen and prepare beer, and men serve the beer to guests. Women rear the children and keep the domestic animals. Both men and women sell firewood and vegetables in the market.

Land Tenure. Land for shifting cultivation is owned by the clan. Each village has a traditionally demarcated area of its own termed _adok_. This area is subdivided into plots that are used for cultivation in a cyclic order. The plots are distributed to the families. Allotment of the general plots is done by common consensus of the village elders, but the flat area for permanent wet cultivation is owned by individuals.

Kinship

Kin Groups and Descent. The Garos reckon their kinship through the mother. Individuals measure the degree of their relationship to one another by the distance of their matrilineages. For men, children of their sisters or sisters' daughters are very important kin. For women, children of their sisters' daughters are equivalent to those of their own daughters.

Kinship Terminology. The kinship terms used by the Garos form a set, which is broad enough so that each Garo can be assigned a term. The terms are arranged in a system that classifies the kin. This classification is based on nine principles, as follows: (1) sex, (2) generation, (3) relative age, (4) moiety membership, (5) collaterality, (6) inheritance, (7) type of wife, (8) intimacy of relationship, (9) speaker's sex.

Marriage and Family

Marriage. Descent is matrilineal, residence uxorilocal. The mother's brother's daughter type of cross-cousin marriage is the most widely accepted and prevalent among the people. It is a rigid custom that a man must marry a woman from the opposite _chatchi_ (moiety). The rule of chatchi exogamy stipulates that a man's mother's father will be in the opposite chatchi and a man's wife's potential husbands will be in his own chatchi. After marriage a man keeps up his relation with his _machong_ (clan). His relation with reference to his wife's machong is designated as _gachi_. Marriage establishes a permanent relation between two machong, known as _akim_. After marriage, a male moves to the residence of his wife. In the case of a _nokrom_ (husband of the heiress of property), marriage does not create a new household but rather adds a new lease on life to an old household. Even after the death or divorce of a spouse the akim relation continues. It is

the responsibility of the deceased's machong to provide a replacement spouse to the surviving partner.

Domestic Unit. The household is the primary production and consumption unit. A Garo household comprises parents, unmarried sons and daughters, a married daughter (heiress), and her husband and their children. In principle a married granddaughter and her children should be included, but in reality grandparents rarely survive to see their grandchildren married. Some households may—for short periods only—include distant relatives or nonrelated persons for various reasons.

Inheritance. Property among the Garos is inherited in the female line. One of the daughters is selected by the parents to be the heiress. If the couple have no female child, a girl belonging to the machong of the wife (preferably the daughter of her sister, whether real or classificatory) is adopted to be an heiress. She is not considered to be the absolute owner of the property. Decision about the disposal of property is taken by her husband, who is considered to be the household authority (_nokni skotong_). After the death of the father-in-law responsibility transfers to the son-in-law. If a dead man is survived by a widow, she stays in the family of her daughter and is sometimes referred to as an additional wife (_jik_) of her daughter's husband.

Socialization. Children start helping their mother to look after the infants when their mother is busy with work. Today there are different educational institutions—namely, the mission schools and other Indian establishments—that act as major agents of education.

Sociopolitical Organization

Social Organization. In Garo society the most important social group is the machong (clan). A machong is an exogamous matrilineal descent group wherein a Garo is automatically assigned by birth to the unilineal group of his mother. A chatchi (moiety) is divided into many machong. Each married couple chooses one daughter—or, if they have none, they adopt a close relative of the mother—to be heiress (_nokna dongipika mechik_) of the family. Her husband traditionally is selected from the lineage group of the father and is accepted as the nokrom of the house. He resides with his wife in her parents' house. He has to take on the responsibility of looking after his parents-in-law during their old age, and his wife inherits the property.

Political Organization. Traditionally, the Garos were not a politically organized society, and even today there exists no clear-cut political structure. Chieftainship involves religious functions only.

Social Control. The kinship system, the kinship bond, and the related value system act as an effective means of social control. Formerly the bachelors' dormitories were important agents of social control.

Conflict. Among the Garos most disputes arise over the issues of property, inheritance, and domestic quarrels within the family. Such problems are to a large extent settled by the _mahari_ (lineage) of the offended and the offender. A new situation develops when someone's cattle cause damage to another's crops. In such a situation the _nokma_ (village headman) acts as an intermediary only. If he fails to settle the dispute, the matter can go before the civil court of the district council.

Religion and Expressive Culture

Religious Beliefs.   There are two faiths prevalent among the Garos: native and Christian. People who follow the traditional faith are known as Songsarek. Difference in religion has not brought any split in the population. The traditional world of the Garos includes a number of spirits who behave like human beings but have no shape. They are Saljong, the spirit of the sun and fertility; Gaera, the spirit of strength and the thunderbolt; *Susume*, the spirit of wealth. Propitiation for each is followed by the sacrifice of an animal and an offering of beer. A Christian Garo is supposed to avoid such practices. Ogres and biting spirits (*mite*) also occur.

Religious Practitioners.   A Garo religious practitioner is known as *kamal*. The word is used to mean "specialist"; thus a midwife may be a kamal. A kamal derives neither special privilege nor prestige from his or her service to the society.

Ceremonies.   All traditional annual festivals were connected with the different stages of shifting cultivation: Agalmaka, Maimua, Rongchugala, Ahaia, Wangala, etc. Wangala is considered to be the national festival among the Garos, taking place October–December. When a member of a family becomes Christian, he refuses to participate in Songsarek festivals.

Arts.   The Garos used to make the following items: carved wooden shields (*spee*); baskets of different types; different varieties of drums—*gambil*, *kram*, and *nakik*; pipes (*adil*) made of buffalo horn; flutes of bamboo; *gonogina* (Jew's harp) made of bamboo.

Medicine.   They use a variety of herbal medicines for all sorts of ailments, and they claim to have herbal medicine for birth control also.

Death and Afterlife.   They believe that after death human beings and animals turn into spirits known as *memang* ("ghosts"). These memang are considered counterparts of human beings.

Bibliography

Burling, Robbins (1956). "Garo Kinship Terminology." *Man in India* 36:203–218.

Burling, Robbins (1963). *Rengsanggri: Family and Kinship in a Garo Village*. Philadelphia: University of Pennsylvania Press.

Dalton, Edward Tuite (1872). *Descriptive Ethnology of Bengal*. Calcutta: Superintendent of Government Printing. Reprint. 1960. Calcutta: Indian Studies Past & Present.

Das, K. N. (1982). *Social Dimension of Garo Language*. Ph.D. dissertation, Gauhati University.

Grierson, George A., ed. (1903). *The Linguistic Survey of India*. Vol. 3, pt. 2. Calcutta: Government of India. Reprint. 1967. Delhi: Motilal Banarsidass.

Majumdar, D. N. (1980). *A Study of Culture Change in Two Garo Villages of Meghalaya*. Gauhati: Gauhati University Press.

Playfair, Alan. (1909). *The Garos*. London: Nutt.

Roy, Sankar Kumar (1977). *A Study of Ceramics from the Neolithic to the Medieval Period of Assam: An Ethnoarchaeological Approach*. Ph.D. dissertation, Gauhati University.

Roy, Sankar Kumar (1981). "Aspects of Neolithic Agriculture and Shifting Cultivation, Garo Hills, Meghalaya." *Asian Perspectives* 24:193–221.

Tayang, J. (1981). *Census of India, 1981*. Series 14, *Meghalaya*, paper no. 1. Shillong: Directorate of Census Operations, Meghalaya.

SANKAR KUMAR ROY

Gond

ETHNONYM: Koi

Orientation

Identification.   The Gonds are an important and numerous tribe, residing at the present time mainly in Gondavana, "the Land of the Gonds," the easternmost districts of Madhya Pradesh, formerly the Central Provinces of India. They were first called "Gonds" (hill men) by the Mogul rulers. They call themselves Koi or Koitūr; the meaning of the latter name is unclear.

Location.   While the Gond live mainly in Madhya Pradesh, important clusters live also in the adjoining districts to the north, west, and south of Gondavana. Many of these subsections have assumed different tribal names so that their identity with the Gond tribe is not always clear.

Demography.   The latest available Census figures are from 1971, when there were 4,728,796 Gonds—one of the largest tribal groups on earth. In fact, the number of Gonds is really much higher, since many Gond communities have been fully accepted into the Hindu caste system, have adopted another name, and have completely abandoned their original tribal ways of life. While some Gond subsections thus have been lost to the tribe, some communities of different origin may have been incorporated into the Gond tribe. The Bisonhorn Marias of Bastar may be such a tribe.

Linguistic Affiliation.   If the Gonds ever had a language of their own, they have lost it completely. Half of the Gonds speak a Dravidian language called Gondi at present, which is more akin to Teluga than to Karmada. In the southern parts of Gondavana the Gonds speak a language called Parsi or Parji (Persian), also of the Dravidian family. In the northern regions the Gonds often speak the local language, a dialect of Hindi or Marathi.

History and Cultural Relations

The racial history of the Gonds is unknown. From their physical appearance it is obvious that they differ from the Aryan and Dravidian speakers settled in the country. According to B. S. Guha, they are Proto-Australoids by race like the Oraons and Maler of Chota Nagpur Plateau. It is unknown when and by which route they arrived in this part of India. At one time they must have been settled in the hills between Tamil Nadu and Karnataka, because their dialect, Gondi, is closely related to the languages of those regions. R. V. Russell and Hira Lal maintain that only between the ninth and thirteenth centuries A.D. did the Gonds come and settle in present-day Gondavana. They became progressive and wealthy farmers and were gradually transformed into Ragbansi Rajputs. When the ruling Rajput dynasties in these regions declined, Gonds established themselves as rulers at four centers. The zenith of their might was from the sixteenth to eighteenth centuries. Then the Marathas under a Bhonsle ruler of Nagpur overran their country and completely dispossessed them of their power except in the hill fastnesses, which held out against all invaders.

Settlements

The Gonds invariably live in villages. But in each village the Gonds live in a hamlet of their own. The hamlet is not a closed cluster of huts, for the Gonds' homesteads are spread over a large area within the hamlet. Each homestead houses a family, often a joint family consisting of the families of the married sons living with their parents. In the plains where the Gonds are more Sanskritized, or influenced by high Hindu culture, some have adopted Hindu ways and begun to live in closed villages, yet apart from the other castes and tribes.

Economy

All Gonds are in some way or other engaged in agriculture or work in the forest. They would not dream of accepting any other occupation. Originally they must have been nomadic hunters and food gatherers and then switched to shifting cultivation, retaining, however, their close connection with the forest. Shifting cultivation is not merely one type of agriculture but a complex cultural form, a way of life. It requires no draft animals and allows the cultivators more leisure time for work in the forest, hunting, fishing, and the collection of jungle produce. However, most Gonds have been forced to abandon shifting cultivation by the government because it is harmful to the forest, and some Gond sections had already voluntarily changed over to plow cultivation and even to terrace cultivation. They prospered economically and acquired a high social standing.

Kinship

Kin Groups and Descent. The Gonds have a pronounced patrilineal and patriarchal clan system. They call it _gotra_ or _kur_. A Gond clan comprises a group of persons who believe that they are descendants in the male line from a common ancestor. While a male can never change his clan, a woman on marriage is taken into the clan of her husband. The Gonds practice clan exogamy, considering intermarriage within a clan to be incest. They believe the gods would punish such a sin with a skin disease, worms in a wound, or leprosy. Offenders against the law of exogamy are excluded from the tribal community and can only be readmitted after separation. Many of the Gond clans bear animal or plant names, which suggests a totemic origin of the clans, and some Gond clans still observe totemic taboos. But generally, except for the observance of exogamy, the clan system has no important function. In the Mandla District at least, eighteen clans have been combined into a phratry. The combination of the clans varies locally, but the number—eighteen—is always retained. The phratry too observes exogamy, but with the payment of a fine the marriage prohibition can be waived.

Marriage and Family

Marriage. A normal marriage among the Gonds is the monogamous union of a man and a woman based on mutual choice, sanctioned by the ceremonial exchange of vows, with the approval of the tribal council, witnessed by the relatives of the partners and the village community, and concluded with a festive wedding dinner. Although the Gonds have liberal views on premarital sex, they are strict in the observance of married fidelity. They believe that adultery is punished by the ancestral spirits that can cause crop failure or an epidemic among humans and cattle. A Gond wedding is solemnized with many significant ceremonies. The essential wedding rite consists of the groom walking with his bride seven times around a wedding post erected in the center of the wedding booth. Marriage is obligatory. Originally Gond boys and girls married on reaching physical maturity. Nowadays the Gonds increasingly follow the example of the rural Hindu population and parents arrange the marriage when children are still young. The father of the groom has to pay a bride-price, the amount of which depends on the position and wealth of the two families. Cross-cousin marriages are much preferred, so much so that a youth has to pay a fine if he refuses to marry an available cross cousin. A Gond can have more than one wife, polygyny being restricted only by the capability of the man to support a number of wives. The Gonds practice the sororate and the levirate. Widow marriage is forbidden only among the Sanskritized Gonds. Gonds who are too poor to pay the bride-price and the wedding expenses contract a service marriage. Families with no sons prefer such a marriage arrangement. Other more irregular forms of marriage among the Gonds are the elopement of an unmarried girl with a boy or the capture of a girl and her forced marriage to her captor. Marriage by capture was in the past a popular form of marriage among the Gonds. The marriage must later be legalized by the relatives and village councils of the partners. The Gonds permit divorce and easily resort to it for various reasons. For instance, a man may obtain a divorce if his wife is barren, quarrelsome, or negligent in doing her assigned work. Likewise, a woman may elope with another man if her husband is a bad provider, a drunkard, or a wife beater, or if he is habitually unfaithful. A divorce requires the legal sanction of the tribal council of the village.

Domestic Unit. Gond marriages are as a rule happy and lasting if the husband is able to provide a frugal livelihood for wife and children and if the wife is competent in her household tasks and field work. Gond men and women are affectionate toward children and enjoy having large families.

Inheritance. Property, primarily land, descends patrilineally to the sons equally (unless one son should move elsewhere, in which case he forfeits his rights). Daughters inherit next to nothing from their fathers. A widow usually remains in the house, which is inherited by her youngest son (ultimogeniture). If not too old, the widow may be remarried to a close relative of her deceased husband.

Socialization. The ambition of every Gond woman is to bear a son. Barrenness in a woman is considered a curse. Pregnancy and birth are surrounded with protective rites against magic spells and evil influences. Children are generally welcome and treated with affection. Although sons are preferred, daughters are welcome too. Children grow up without much restriction, but the community teaches them correct behavior. Children are early invited to take over some tasks, first playfully, then in earnest. Boys spontaneously seem to prefer male company, while girls seem to gravitate naturally toward other females. The change to adulthood is gradual; there is no initiation ceremony. The first menstruation of a girl is not specially celebrated, but she does learn in advance what prohibitions she has to observe. Only three Gond sections in the south have youth dormitories, and only the Murias use the dormitory for the education of youth in married and civic life. The other Gond sections have no dormitory system.

Sociopolitical Organization

Social Organization. Since the Gonds are spread over a wide area, there are many local subsections that have no social contact with each other. The more Sanskritized these sections are, the higher is the social rank they claim. But the highest rank is given to the descendants of the Gond rajas and their retainers, the Raj-Gonds and Katholias. Among these two sections we find the greatest number of Gonds with substantial landholdings. Other Gond sections outside of Gondavana are the Kisans, in the south of Bihar and in the neighboring districts of Orissa. The Gonds reached even the hills along the southern bank of the Ganges. There they are known as Majwars or Majhis (headmen). Akin to the Gonds are a number of other tribes, such as the Bhattras, Koyas, Konda Kapus, Konda Deras, and Halbas. The Khonds of Orissa, another important tribe, also may originally have been Gonds.

Political Organization. The entire Gond tribe was never a political unit. Tribal solidarity does not extend beyond the confines of a subsection. The basic political unit is the Gond village community. It is a democratic organization in which the headman and other officials are chosen by the villagers. Each village has its council, with officials like the headman, the priest, the village watchman, and four or five elders. More important affairs are discussed and decided upon by all the men of the community. A village has also its servant castes, such as the Ahir (cowherds), Agaria (blacksmiths), Dhulia (drummers), and Pardhan (bards and singers). At the towns of Garha-Mandla, Kharla, Deogarh, and Chanda, the leading headmen managed to rise to the rank of rulers (rajas) and to establish dynasties that lasted for centuries. But the very fact that these rajas surrounded themselves with Hindu officials and eagerly adopted Hindu or Mogul methods of administration proves that royalty was alien to tribal democracy. In the present political situation the Gonds are, despite their numbers, politically powerless, which is partly because of this tribal disunity but also because of their comparative lack of education and drive, and their great poverty. Those few Gonds who are members of the legislative assemblies or even the national parliament (Lok Sabha) are either alienated from their tribal culture or easily manipulated by other politicians.

Conflict and Social Control. In settling disputes the court of first instance is the village council (panch), which is presided over by the headman. Usually it strives to restore harmony between the litigants rather than to implement customary law. A settlement commonly involves a fine, or excommunication in varying degrees. Those who offend against the rule of clan exogamy incur supernatural sanctions.

Religion and Expressive Culture

Religious Beliefs. The religion of the Gonds does not differ much from that of the numerous other tribes in central India. Like them, the Gonds believe in a high god whom they call either by his Hindu name, "Bhagwan," or by his tribal name, "Bara Deo," the "Great God." But he is an otiose deity and is rarely worshiped, though his name is often invoked. He is a personal god—eternal, just, merciful, maker of the fertile earth and of man—though the universe is conceived as coexisting with him. In the Gond belief system, besides this high god there also exist a great number of male and female deities and spirits that personify various natural features. Every hill, river, lake, tree, and rock is inhabited by a spirit. The earth, water, and air are ruled by deities that must be venerated and appeased with sacrifices and offerings. These deities and spirits may be benevolent, but often they are capricious, malevolent, and prone to harming human beings, especially individuals who have made themselves vulnerable by breaking a rule of the tribal code. The deities and spirits, especially the ancestor spirits, watch over the strict observance of the tribal rules and punish offenders.

Religious Practitioners. Gonds distinguish between priests and magicians. The village priest is appointed by the village council; however, his appointment is often hereditary. His responsibility is to perform all the sacrifices held at certain feasts for the village community for which he receives a special remuneration. Sacrifices and religious ceremonies on family occasions are usually performed by the head of the family. The diviners and magicians, on the other hand, are unofficial charismatic intermediaries between the supernatural world and human beings. The Gonds, like the other tribals of central India, believe that most diseases and misfortunes are caused by the machinations of evil spirits and offended deities. It is the task of the soothsayers and diviners to find out which supernatural agencies have caused the present sickness or misfortune and how they can be appeased. If soothsayers and diviners cannot help, magicians and shamans must be employed. Magicians believe that by magic formulas and devices they can force a particular deity or spirit to carry out their commands. Shamans are persons who easily fall into trances and are then believed to be possessed by deities or spirits that prophesy through their mouths. These frequent ecstasies do not seem to have any detrimental mental or physical effects on the shamans, who may be male or female. Magic may be "white" or "black": it is white if it counteracts black magic or effects a cure when a sickness has been caused by black magic. Gonds also believe in the evil eye and in witchcraft. A witch is usually a woman who by her evil power brings sickness and death to people in the neighborhood. When discovered, she is publicly disgraced and expelled from the village or even killed.

Ceremonies. The Gonds celebrate many feasts connected mainly with the agricultural seasons and with life-cycle events (birth, marriage, sickness, and death). On all festive occasions sacrifices and offerings are performed either by the official village priest, by the soothsayers and magicians, or by the head of the family that is celebrating an event. All these sacrifices are accompanied by appropriate ceremonies of symbolic significance. The offerings and sacrifices can be either animal or vegetable; it depends on the type of deity being addressed. Female deities generally demand that blood be spilled; the victims are usually chickens or goats, sometimes male buffalo, and, occasionally in the past, human beings. Vegetable offerings include fruits (especially coconuts), flowers, colored powder, and strings.

Arts. Like most tribals, the Gonds are accomplished artisans and can manufacture almost all the implements they require for their work on the farm and in the forest, all furniture in house and kitchen, and all of their ornaments and decorations. They are artistically gifted: they paint their house walls with artistic designs, and they carve memorial pillars in wood and stone for their dead. They have invented various original dances and are passionate dancers. They are good musicians on the drum, the flute, and other instruments. They are good singers, though the melodies of their songs sometimes sound monotonous and may not be of their own invention. They are inventive in composing new songs, folktales, legends, and myths and in retelling them dramatically. They have composed a great epic celebrating the origins and exploits of a culture hero named Lingo.

Medicine. The Gonds are fully aware that certain diseases have a natural cause, and they know many jungle medicines to cure such diseases. But when these remedies remain ineffective, they resort to magical devices.

Death and Afterlife. After death an adult Gond man or woman is cremated; children are buried without much ceremony. Ceremonies are performed at the funeral to prevent the soul of the deceased from finding its way back to its house and village. The Gonds believe in an afterlife. They believe each human being has two souls, the life spirit and the shadow. The shadow must be prevented from returning to its home, or it will harm the surviving relatives. The life spirit goes to Bhagwan to be judged and rewarded by reincarnation into a higher form or punished in a pool of biting worms; after a while the soul is reborn and begins a new life. Others believe that the soul joins the other ancestors of the clan, especially after a stone memorial has been erected. Still others believe that the soul is absorbed in Bhagwan or Bara Deo. The belief in the survival of the ancestral spirits is, however, quite strong. These ancestor spirits watch over the moral behavior of the living Gond and punish offenders of tribal law. Thus they act as strict guardians of the Gond community.

See also Agaria; Ahir; Baiga; Kond; Koya

Bibliography

Elwin, Verrier (1943). _Maria Murder and Suicide_. London: Oxford University Press. 2nd ed. 1950.

Elwin, Verrier (1944). _The Muria and Their Ghotul_. London: Oxford University Press.

Fuchs, Stephen (1960). _The Gond and Bhumia of Eastern Mandla_. Bombay: Asia Publishing House. 2nd ed. 1968. Bombay: New Literature Publishing Co.

Fürer-Haimendorf, Christoph von (1948). _The Aboriginal Tribes of Hyderabad_. Vol. 3, _The Raj Gonds of Adilabad_. London: Macmillan.

Fürer-Haimendorf, Christoph von, and Elizabeth von Fürer-Haimendorf (1979). _The Gonds of Andhra Pradesh: Tradition and Change in an Indian Tribe_. New Delhi: Vikas Publishing House.

Grigson, William (1938). _The Hill Marias of Bastar_. London: Oxford University Press.

Russell, R. V., and Hira Lal (1916). "Gond." In _The Tribes and Castes of the Central Provinces of India_. Vol. 3, 38–143. London: Oxford University Press. Reprint. 1969. Oosterhout: Anthropological Publications.

Singh, Indrajit (1944). _The Gondwana and the Gond_. Lucknow: University Publishers.

STEPHEN FUCHS

Grasia

ETHNONYMS: Bhil-Grasia Bhomia, Dungri-Grasia, Gara, Garasia, Girisia

Orientation

The term "Grasia" refers to the Rajput and other landholders in sections of Gujarat and Rajasth, where they hold lands given to them as _garas_ (landlords) by the chieftains for maintenance. It is said that the term "Grasia" is derived from the native term for "landlords." The Grasias are the principal inhabitants of the Bhakkar section of Pakistani Punjab, and also of parts of Kachchh District, in Gujarat. Sir John Malcolm noted that the term "Girasias" denotes "chiefs who were driven from their possessions by invaders and established and maintained their claim to a share of the revenue upon the ground of their power to disturb or prevent its collection." The word can be derived from the Sanskrit _giras_, which signifies "mouthful," and in the past it was used metaphorically to designate the small share of the produce of the country that these plunderers claimed. The Grasias are said to have come from Mewar many centuries ago, "and as they still have their internal 'Gots' or circles of affinity (such as Parmars, Chouhan, Rathoi, etc.) upon the model of a regular clan, we may perhaps assume that they are the descendants of Rajputs by Bhil women," according to P. C. Dave.

In Maharashtra State the Grasias are on the list of Scheduled Tribes as "Dungri-Grasias." The Grasias speak a dialect of their own that is close to Bhili, with Bhili being closely related to Gujarati.

Settlements

Grasia houses are found on the slopes of hills with their fields extending out in front. The houses usually each have one room and an open veranda with walls of mud or split bamboo plastered with mud. The roofs are covered with handmade flat tiles made by the Grasias themselves. Sometimes, though, the houses of the poor may have grass thatching covering the roofs.

A special shed for the cattle is often constructed on the side of or opposite to the house, and often fodder is stored on the roofs of these sheds. To shelter guests, a special shed with a tiled roof is built opposite the house of the headman.

Economy

Grasias are generally vegetarian but have been known occasionally to enjoy nonvegetarian foods. Maize is the food staple, which is grown by every Grasia who has land for cultivation. It is prepared by cooking the coarse maize flour with buttermilk and adding some salt to it. Sometimes breads of maize flour are also prepared. When little wheat and maize are available the Grasias use inferior grain like *kuro* (Italian millet?) as a substitute, and when necessary jungle roots and tubers are used.

Men primarily do the work that requires the most physical strength, such as plowing and other agricultural work, preparing fences for the fields, construction of houses, felling of trees, and some household work such as churning of the curds for butter. Women do the cooking, tend to the cattle and milk the cows, buffalo, and goats, bring drinking water, grind grain, etc., and look after the children. There are no social stigmas attached to either men's or women's work. Women veil their faces in the presence of elder male relations of their husbands, but they are generally free to move about in society like men and are not considered inferior to men. Girls share a similar freedom with boys. Once they are grown up they have the freedom to choose their own husbands. The largest sign of female social oppression is that women aren't allowed to own property on their own, not even if it was left to them by their father.

Kinship, Marriage and Family

Only extreme circumstances such as abject poverty, debilitating disease, etc. keep Grasia men and women from marrying, as the Grasias believe marriage is a necessity for all. Boys marry between the ages of 18 and 24, and girls between 14 and 18. The selection of a mate usually is without ritual and involves selecting a spouse and then living together without any marriage ceremony. This arrangement may vary in some areas because of Hindu influence. The only restrictions are that the bride-price must be paid and that the marriage can-

not be between cousins. Divorce often occurs if the boy does not like the girl. It is easy and freely permitted.

The terms *natra*, or *nata*, refer to widow remarriage, which is quite common and which involves the handing out of bread and jaggery to relatives, and the man making a payment of money to the widow's father and providing the necessary marriage clothes to the widow.

Polygyny occurs but polyandry is unknown, although most Grasia men marry only once. Because of the social structure that exists it is not necessary for him to marry for companionship or even for help in cultivation, as the average holding of a Grasia is small and he is able to do all agricultural work even if he has a small family. The main reasons for a man to take more than one wife are either that his first wife cannot bear children or that she has only female children.

Sociopolitical Organization

The Grasias work within a joint-family system where the sons stay with the family up to the time their children become adults. Only on rare occasions do the sons live separately from their parents due to domestic quarrels. Separation usually occurs, however, after the father's death. Only unmarried sisters and minor unmarried brothers continue to live with the family of one of the older brothers.

Religion

The Grasias basically worship the Hindu gods and respect the cow and are thus almost Hinduized, even though they tend to hold onto their original belief in spirits and fear ghosts, spirits of the dead, and black magic.

See also Bhil

Bibliography

Dave, P. C. (1960). *The Grasias also Called Dungri Grasias.* Delhi: Bharatiya Adimjati Sevak Sangh.

LeSHON KIMBLE

Gujar

ETHNONYMS: Gujareta, Gujjar, Gujjara

The Gujars are a historical caste who have lent their name to the Gujarat District and the town of Gujaranwala in the Punjab, the peninsula and state of Gujarat, and the area known as Gujargash in Gwalior. They numbered 56,000 persons in 1911, of which the majority belonged to the Hoshangabad and Nimar districts. (In 1971 there were 20,634 Gujars enumerated in Himachal Pradesh alone.) In those provinces the caste is principally found in the Narmada Valley. The caste is broadly divided along religious and geographic lines into the Muslim Gujars (who also share many Hindu customs with their Hindu Gujar brethren and are thus not fully accepted into the Muslim majority) in northern India and Pakistan and the Hindu population in the central regions of India. Gujars speak Gujari, a dialect of Rajasthani, an Indic language of the Indo-Iranian Sector of the Indo-European Family. In Himachal Pradesh the language is mixed with Western Pahari. Gujars write in the Urdu script.

The origins of the Gujars are unknown; however, several theories place them either as a branch of the White Huns who overran India in the fifth and sixth centuries or as a branch of the Kushan division of the Yueh-Chi tribe, which controlled much of northwestern India during the early centuries of the Christian era. In the past the Gujars were considered marauders and vagrants. Today they are law-abiding pastoralists and cultivators. Many Gujars were converted to Islam at various times and in different places, beginning with the attack of Mahmud of Ghazni on Somnath in Gujarat in 1026. The Gujars of Oudh and Meerut date their conversion to the time of Timur in 1398, when he sacked Delhi and forcibly converted them. By 1525, when Babur invaded, he discovered that the Gujar in the northern Punjab had already been converted. Until the 1700s the conversions continued under the Mogul ruler Aurangzeb, who converted the Gujar of Himachal Pradesh at the point of a sword. The Pathans and Baluchi drove the Gujar converts from their land, forcing them into a nomadic existence.

The Gujars are divided into Hindu and Muslim septs, with the latter being Sunni converts retaining some of their Hindu practices. Most keep copies of the Quran in their homes; however, like Hindus they worship a family deity. Brahman priests are consulted to determine a lucky time for the first bath for the mother after a baby is born. Id-al-Zuha (Id-al-Adha) and Id-al-Fitr are their two most important festivals. Gujar Muslims observe some of the Hindu festivals, such as Holi and Naz Panchmi. They bury their dead according to Muslim custom; however, they make fire offerings and upturn a pitcher of water near the grave as Hindus traditionally do. Gujars make offerings to the dead on Fridays, like Hindus, but instead of feeding Brahmans, Gujars follow the Muslim tradition of feeding beggars in the anticipation that the charity will reach their ancestors.

The Hindu Gujars are a successful sedentary cultivating group. The Muslim Gujars are a pastoral people, whose living depends on the raising of buffalo, which involves a semi-nomadic life-style constantly in search of pastoral land. There is little interest in secular education, which has made them vulnerable to the rapidly changing world around them.

The Gujar divide themselves into hundreds of exogamous clans, the names of which are derived from the names of founders or from places of their early settlement. Muslim Gujars count descent patrilineally, and marriage is patrilocal with consanguine marriage sought; marriage is usually arranged by parents. The payment of a bride-price by the groom's family is commonly made in cash or buffalo. A less costly arrangement is the exchange of daughters and sons in marriage. Some still conduct their marriages as Hindus. Others consult a Brahman priest to determine a lucky day for betrothal, but the mullah conducts the marriage ceremony. Divorce and remarriage are accepted. A woman may leave her husband and live with another man, who is obligated to pay compensation to the ex-husband.

Bibliography

Raheja, Gloria Goodwin (1988). _The Poison in the Gift; Ritual, Prestation, and the Dominant Caste in a North Indian Village._ Chicago and London: University of Chicago Press.

Rose, H. A. (1911). "Gujar." In _A Glossary of the Tribes and Castes of the Punjab and North-West Frontier Provinces._ Vol. 1, 306–318. Lahore: Superintendent, Government Printing. Reprint. 1970. Patiala: Languages Department, Punjab.

Russell, R. V., and Hira Lal (1916). "Gūjar." In _The Tribes and Castes of the Central Provinces of India,_ edited by R. V. Russell and Hira Lal. Vol. 3, 166–174. Nagpur: Government Printing Press. Reprint. 1975. Oosterhaut: Anthropological Publications.

Sharma, J. C., (1984). "Gujars." In _Muslim Peoples: A World Ethnographic Survey,_ edited by Richard V. Weekes. Vol. 1, 298–301. Westport, Conn.: Greenwood Press.

JAY DiMAGGIO

Gujarati

ETHNONYMS: none

Orientation

Identification. Gujaratis are the inhabitants of Gujarat, one of the federal states of the Indian Republic.

Location. Gujarat covers 195,984 square kilometers and is situated on the west coast of India between 20°6' N to 24°42' N and 68°10' E to 74°28' E. Geopolitically and culturally Gujarat can be divided into five regions: (1) north Gujarat, the mainland between Mount Abu and the Mahi River; (2) south Gujarat, the mainland between the Mahi and Damanaganga rivers; (3) the Saurashtrian Peninsula; (4) Kachchh; and (5) a hilly eastern belt consisting of the outliers of the Aravalli system, the Vindhyas, the Satpuras, and the Sahyadris. The state lies in the monsoon area with a monsoon climate. The rainfall period is confined to four months from the middle of June to the middle of October. The amount of annual rainfall varies considerably in different parts of the state. The southernmost area receives annual rainfall as high as 200 centimeters. The rainfall in central Gujarat is between 70 and 90 centimeters; and Kachchh and the western part of Saurashtra receive less than 40 centimeters. The maximum temperature in the year occurs in May, when it is as high as 40° C in north Gujarat, Saurashtra, and Kachchh. January is the coldest month of the year, when the temperature does not exceed 30° C.

Demography. At the time of the 1981 census, the population of Gujarat was 34 million. The population density averages 174 persons per square kilometer; it is highest in central

Gujarat and lowest in Kachchh. The population is growing at the rate of 2.7 percent per year. Gujarati-speaking people constitute 91 percent of the population of Gujarat, which also includes 1.5 percent Kachchh-speaking people. There are three main religious groups in Gujarat: Hindus (89.5 percent), Muslims (8.5 percent) and Jains (1 percent). A majority of the Muslims speak Gujarati, though there is a small Muslim section that speaks Urdu. Around 14 percent of the Gujarati population are tribals who predominantly live in the eastern hilly belt. Sixty-nine percent of the population live in rural areas and 31 percent live in urban areas. Ahmadabad, Surat, Vadodara, and Rajkot are large cities.

Linguistic Affiliation. Gujarati is considered by linguists to be a member of the outer circle of Indo-Aryan languages: it is partly Prakritic and partly Sanskritic in origin. A number of Arabic, Persian, Urdu, and European—particularly Portuguese and English—words have become part of the language. There are several dialects. Important among them, based on region, are Kathiawadi, Kachchh, Pattani, Charotari, and Surati. There are also caste- or community-based dialects, such as Nagari, Anavla or Bhathala, Patidari, Kharwa, Musalmani, Parsi, etc. Different tribal groups have their own dialects that bear a close affinity to Gujarati. The distinctive Gujarati script has thirty-four consonants and eleven vowels.

History and Cultural Relations

The territory was known as "Gurjara Bhoomi," "Gurjara Desh," "Gurjaratta," or "Gurjar Mandal"—meaning abode of the Gurjar people—between the fifth and ninth centuries A.D. The name of the area known as "Gujarat" was recognized from the tenth century during the Solanki period, when Mulraja laid the foundation of his kingdom with its capital at Anhilwad Patan. During British rule the area was divided into a number of native states and estates and British administrative districts, which were a part of the Bombay presidency. After independence in 1947, the native states merged into the Indian Union. A group of states formed Saurashtra State; the mainland Gujarat became a part of Bombay State and Kachchh was centrally administered. But as a result of further reorganization of the states in 1956, Saurashtra and Kachchh were dissolved as separate states and became a part of Bombay State. Then, because of demands for a separate linguistic state, Gujarat, Saurashtra, and Kachchh formed the separate state of Gujarat in 1960.

Settlements

Among 18,114 villages, 8 percent are small with a population of less than 200 persons; and 49 (0.2 percent) are large with more than 10,000 people in each. The settlement pattern of each village is either clustered or dispersed. Clustered villages are divided into subclusters consisting of a group of families belonging to the same caste or community. The dominant caste resides in the center, and traditionally Untouchable castes live on the periphery of the village. In the dispersed pattern mainly found among tribals, each family—nuclear or joint—lives on its own farm. A temple or public platform under a large tree is a central place where males from upper and middle castes meet and spend their spare time. Today, most of the middle-sized and big villages have primary schools, one or two shops, grazing land, and a cremation

ground. There are 255 towns or urban agglomerations. All but eleven of these towns have a population under 100,000. Many of them are expanded villages where caste or community clusters form neighborhood localities. Two styles of housing are common in urban and rural Gujarat. The first is the sturdy modern kind made of brick and concrete, with more than two rooms and a separate kitchen. The second is a tenement of mud, stone, and wood. The roofs are of locally made tiles or thatch. (Numerical data from 1981 census.)

Economy

Subsistence and Commercial Activities. Despite rapid industrial development, agriculture occupies a prominent place in the economy of the state. It contributes an average of 35 to 40 percent of the state's domestic products. Sixty-two percent of the workers engaged in agriculture are either cultivators or laborers. Although agriculture is not fully mechanized, use of tractors has increased considerably in recent years. The major food crops are *bajri, jowar,* rice, and wheat. Cotton, groundnut, tobacco, and sugarcane are major commercial crops: they occupy about 40 percent of the total cultivated area of the state. Cattle, buffalo, sheep, goats, chickens, horses, camels, monkeys, donkeys, and pigs are the main domestic animals. Bullocks are used for agriculture, cows and buffalo for milk. A cooperative dairy industry has developed.

Industrial Arts. Artisans in rural areas are engaged in pottery, silver- and brass-ornament making, embroidery, handloom construction and furniture making. Despite government support, these crafts are rapidly disappearing. Gujarat is one of the most highly industrialized states in India. The major industries are textiles, plastics, chemicals, and engineering. In terms of income generated from manufacturing, Gujarat ranks second in the country.

Trade. Trade is a primary occupation of Gujaratis. The Hindu and Jain Banias are the trading castes. In this century the Patidars have emerged as entrepreneurs. In addition, the Parsis and Muslim Bohras are also traders. Gujarat has been well connected by trade routes within the continent and also with other countries. Historically, the Gujaratis possessed a remarkable spirit of enterprise that led them in search of wealth to Java and Cambodia during the sixth and seventh centuries A.D. and to Siam, China, Sri Lanka, and Japan at about the end of the seventh century A.D. Some Gujaratis emigrated to Africa in the last century, and from there they have moved to Europe and the United States.

Division of Labor. Except among the tribals, work is clearly divided between men and women. Gujaratis continue to believe that "a woman's place is in the home": a woman's main tasks are cooking, washing, other household work, and child rearing. However, among the poor, women also participate in economic activities, engaging in cultivation and agricultural labor.

Land Tenure. With the introduction of various land reforms in the 1950s, land was given to the tillers. Intermediary tenures were legally abolished. Nevertheless, concealed tenancy continues. Land distribution is uneven. According to the 1976–1977 agriculture census, the average size of holdings for the state was 3.71 hectares. Nearly 46 percent of the cultivators have less than 2 hectares of land, which holdings constitute only 13 percent of the total area holdings; but only

6 percent of cultivators hold 10 hectares or more of land, which altogether constitutes nearly 25 percent of the total holdings. The Patidars and the Brahmans are rich peasants. The Kolis, the Scheduled Castes (or "SC," viewed as "Untouchables"), the tribals, and the Muslims are poor peasants and agricultural laborers.

Kinship, Marriage and Family

Kin Groups and Descent. Descent is agnatic and patrilineal.

Marriage. Among the Hindu Gujaratis, marriage is a sacrament. It is arranged by parents. Certain castes (_jatis_) follow the principle of endogamy in which a man must marry not only within his jati but also within his subjati, which is divided into _ekdas_ and _gols_ (i.e., circles). However, among certain castes exogamy restricts the circle within which marriage can be arranged. It forbids the members of a particular group in a caste, usually believed to be descended from a common ancestor or associated with a particular locality, to marry anyone who is a member of the same group. Another custom among the Rajputs, Patidars, and Brahmans is hypergamy, which forbids a woman of a particular group to marry a man of a group lower than her own in social standing and compels her to marry into a group of equal or superior rank.

Domestic Unit. The family is generally considered to be the parents, married as well as unmarried sons, and widowed sisters. The joint family is a norm particularly among the trading and landed castes and also among the Muslims in rural areas. In the traditional joint family, three generations live together. All the family members eat from one kitchen and cultivate land jointly. Even if the kitchens become separate, cooperative farming continues in many cases. A joint family may have more than thirty members, although such cases are exceptional. A typical joint family has from eight to twelve members in rural areas and six to eight members in urban areas. Joint families are becoming less common. The head of the family—the father or grandfather—exercises authority over all family members. Women and even married sons have no independence and can do little without first obtaining consent or approval from the head. This situation is now changing.

Inheritance. Among the Hindus, consanguinity is the guiding principle for determining the right of inheritance. The following are heirs in order of precedence: sons, sons' sons, sons' grandsons, the widow of the deceased, daughters, daughters' sons, mother, father, brothers, brothers' sons. Although inheritance is based on patrilineal principles, two women—the widow and the daughter—are very high on the scale of priority.

Socialization. Infants and children are raised by the mother and grandparents, though the role of the father in bringing up the children has recently increased. A girl is not closely looked after and she is involved in household chores from a very young age, whereas a boy is protected and indulged.

Sociopolitical Organization

Social Organization. Gujaratis are divided into a number of social groups. The Hindus who constitute the largest group are divided into a number of jatis, which have a hierarchical order based on the principles of purity and pollution. The Brahmans are in the highest position, while the Scheduled Castes occupy the lowest position in the hierarchy. The SCs constitute 7 percent of the population, and they are scattered throughout the state. The Brahmans constitute nearly 4 percent. The other upper castes are the Vanias (traditionally traders) and Rajputs (traditionally warriors). They and some other upper castes together represent 8 percent of the total population. The Patidars, who belong to the middle strata of the caste hierarchy and were earlier known as the Kanbis, constitute around 12 percent of the population. Comprising about 24 percent of the population, the Kolis form the largest caste cluster among the Gujaratis and are distributed throughout the state. Broadly they can be divided into Kolis of the coastal and mainland belts. The latter prefer to be identified as Kshatriyas. The other low castes, such as the Bhois, Machhis, Kharvas, etc., together constitute about 7 percent of the Gujaratis. The Scheduled Tribes, generally known as the Adivasis, constitute 14 percent of the population and are mainly in the eastern belt. There are several tribal groups, some of the major ones being the Bhils, Dhodiyas, Gamits, and Chaudharis. The jatis have traditional _panchayats_, which are councils consisting of elders that regulate social customs and resolve conflicts. The importance of such panchayats in conflict resolution has declined over the last four decades.

Political Organization. Gujarat is one among twenty-one federal states of the Indian republic. It is governed by representatives elected by universal adult franchise who constitute a _vidhan sabha_ (legislative assembly). A majority party forms the government. The head of the state is the governor, appointed by the president of India. The state government has very wide powers for maintaining law and order, levying taxes, and carrying out development work. It also shares resources with the union government. Gandhinagar is the capital city of the state. The state is divided into 19 districts, which are further subdivided into 184 _talukas_. Local self-government by elected representatives functions at village, taluka, and district level and also in towns and cities. The local government performs functions related to public amenities, education, and development. It raises resources by levying taxes and income from property and also receives aid grants from the state government. Industrial investment is strongly encouraged.

Social Control. Gujarat today has the usual institutions of a state police force and a hierarchy of law courts, ranging from the submagistrate's court to the state supreme court. In all courts the central writ is the Indian Penal Code. But in addition to these institutions, which were first developed under the British administration of the old Bombay Presidency, there is also an indigenous system of caste and village councils. The caste council is found in any village or small town where the numbers of any one caste or caste bloc are sufficient to warrant it. This council consists of the male heads of the most prominent families in the caste, and its function is to maintain equanimity with other castes by seeing that traditional patterns of behavior (the caste's dharma) are followed. Fines and minor physical punishment may be handed down to those who offend against these patterns. Public humiliation, such as a beating with sandals, is a usual punishment. There is also a village council (_gram panchayat_) which is headed by the village headman (*patel*) and contains leading representatives of each of the caste groups. Its function is partly to conduct formal community affairs, such as seasonal festivals, and partly to resolve intercaste disputes and offenses.

Conflict. Because there has been little labor unrest in recent times, Gujarat has become a relatively prosperous state. Public life has however been marred by several riots led by upper-caste students, in protest against the government policy of reserving places in the colleges for Scheduled Castes and Scheduled Tribes.

Religion and Expressive Culture

Gujarati Hindus are divided into a large number of religious sects. There are two broad categories: those who worship one or a combination of some of the great Vedic deities or of the Puranic accretions to the orthodox pantheon; and those who deny the regular deities and prohibit idol worship. The former are the Shaivites, Shaktas or Devi Bhaktas, Vaishnavites, and the followers of minor deities. The latter belong to the Arya Samaj, Kabir Panthi, and other such fairly modern sects. These sects are not mutually exclusive.

Religious Beliefs. A Gujarati Hindu attaches the greatest importance to bathing. He or she observes fasts once a week and every eleventh day in a fortnight. A Gujarati Hindu believes in Heaven, Hell, and the transmigration of the soul. One hopes to better one's position in this and the life to come by one's devotion to God, by *dan* (charity), and by *daya* (mercy toward fellow human beings and cows, etc.). Gujarati Jains, though few in number, occupy an important place in Gujarati society and the economy. Jainism rejects the authority of the Vedas and the spiritual supremacy of the Brahmans. The highest goal of Jainism is nirvana or *moksha*, the setting free of the individual from the *sanskara*, the cycle of birth and death. The Jains are divided into two sects, Digambaris and Svetambaris. The cow is worshiped and considered sacred by Hindus. Besides worshiping various idols, an average Hindu worships animals, trees, fire, etc. and believes in *bhuts* (possessing spirits). Belief in omens is also common. Hindus believe that the result of every undertaking is foreshadowed by certain signs and hints.

Religious Practitioners. The life-cycle ceremonies are performed by Brahmans. Wandering holy men, however, are revered irrespective of their caste, religion, or origin. Gujaratis also patronize men who have a reputation for being able to rid the individual of bhuts.

Ceremonies. Ceremonies are performed at birth, marriage, and death when relatives are invited for feasts. Among the important festivals are: Diwali, the festival of lamps; Hindu new year's day, which is the next day after Diwali; Utran or Sankrant, a festival of the harvest; and Navratra, a festival of the "nine nights" involving a folk dance called *Garba*.

Arts. *Ras* and Garba are important folk dances performed by both males and females. *Melas*, fairs either at pilgrimage places or on the bank of a river during certain festivals, attract a large crowd where people dance, sing, and watch bullfights or cockfights. *Bhavai* is a popular folk drama, generally performed in open spaces in villages and towns. Wood and stone sculptures decorating temples, palaces, and private buildings

are well known. Paintings called *sathia* and *rangoli*, done by using powdered chalk, are made by women at the threshold of their houses for festivals and other ceremonies. The calico printing of Gujarat is famous. Tattooing is common among certain castes in Saurashtra and north Gujarat.

Medicine. Traditionally, disease was believed to be caused by an imbalance of elements in the body, as well as by several supernatural causes such as the displeasure of a god or goddess or spirit possession. Although home remedies and concoctions of local herbs are still used, modern medicine has been increasingly accepted and used.

Death and Afterlife. Normally a corpse is not kept more than twelve hours. It is taken in a procession mainly of males to the cremation ground. There the body is laid upon the pyre with its head to the north. The chief mourner lights the pyre. The period of mourning varies from a fortnight to a year according to the age of the deceased and the closeness of the relationship. A caste dinner is given on the twelfth and thirteenth days afterward as a part of the death rites. Certain religious rituals are performed and Brahmans are given gifts according to what the mourners can afford.

See also Bhil; Bohra; Grasia; Jain; Kanbi; Khoja; Koli; Parsi

Bibliography

Desai, R. B. Govindbhai (1932). *Hindu Families in Gujarat.* Baroda: Baroda State Press.

Gujarat, Government of. Bureau of Economics and Statistics (1982). *Statistical Atlas of Gujarat.* Vols. 1–2. Gandhinagar: Government of Gujarat.

Majumdar, M. R. (1965). *Cultural History of Gujarat.* Bombay: Popular Prakashan.

Shah, Arvind M. (1973). *The Household Dimension of the Family in India: A Field Study in a Gujarat Village and a Review of Other Studies.* Berkeley: University of California Press; New Delhi: Orient Longman.

Shah, Ghanshyam (1989). "Caste Sentiments and Dominance in Gujarat." In *Dominance and State Power in Modern India*, edited by Francine Frankel and M. S. A. Rao. Delhi: Oxford University Press.

GHANSHYAM SHAH

Gurkha

ETHNONYM: Gurkhali

"Gurkha" is not the name of an ethnic group but rather the name given those Nepalese nationals who serve in the British army. Gurkhas are drawn from a number of Nepalese ethnic groups including the Gurung (who contribute the greatest percentage of their population of all the groups), Magar, Tamang, Sunwar, Limbu, and Rai. Gurkhas claim descent from the warlike Rajputs of Chittaur, in Rajasthan, saying they were driven thence to the Nepalese hills by the Muslim invasions. The Gurkha military tradition can be traced back to the sixteenth century when the kingdom of Gorkha was conquered by the first kings of the Shah Thakuri dynasty. By the end of the eighteenth century the Gurkha Kingdom, as it was then known, had expanded control over much of what is now Nepal and had begun pushing north into China and Tibet. Expansion south into India was resisted by the British (who were expanding northward), but in 1815 the Nepalese were defeated. The British were impressed by the Gurkhas and obtained permission to recruit them for the British-Indian Army. The recruits were organized into ethnic regiments and participated with distinction (on the government side) in the Indian Mutiny of 1857–58, the Second Afghan War (1878–1880), and the Boxer Rebellion (1900). By 1908 the 12,000 Gurkhas were organized into ten regiments as the Gurkha Brigade. During World War I and World War II the number of Nepalese military volunteers increased to more than 200,000 and additional units were formed. In 1947 the Gurkha Brigade was disbanded and since then various Gurkha units have served with the British army, the Indian army, the Nepal army, and the United Nations peacekeeping forces. Today, they are mainly used in the Crown Colony of Hong Kong (which will revert to China in 1997). With Britain's integration into Europe, Gurkhas are being phased out of the British army.

Gurkha veterans play a significant social and economic role in Nepalese society. They enjoy high status and are often elected community leaders, and the income from their pensions provides a steady source of cash for their families and communities. Nepalese working in India as watchmen are also sometimes referred to as Gurkha.

See also Gurung; Limbu; Magar; Nepali; Rai; Sunwar; Tamang

Bibliography

Vansittart, Eden, and B. V. Nicolay (1915). *Gurkhās*. Calcutta: Superintendent of Government Printing. Reprint. 1985. New Delhi: B. R. Publishing Corp.

Gurung

ETHNONYMS: none

Orientation

Identification. The Gurungs are a people inhabiting the foothills of the Himalayas in central Nepal. Their origins are uncertain, though linguistic evidence suggests that their ancestors may have migrated from Tibet about 2,000 years ago.

Location. The majority of Gurung villages are located on mountain slopes at elevations between 1,050 and 2,100 meters in the foothills of the Annapurna and Lamjung Himalaya and Himalchuli in Nepal at 28°0' to 28°30' N and 83°30' to 84°30' E. Toward the Himalayan range, there are wide gorges with tall craggy ridges rising above them. These are dotted with villages, set high on the mountainsides. Often there will be jungle above a village and below it a cascade of terraced fields. Winters are cold and dry, though it seldom freezes. Monsoon rains come from the south in summer. Temperatures range from about 0° to 32° C. "Gurung country" is situated between two distinct ecological zones, the alpine mountain highlands and the low subtropical valleys. Likewise it exists between two great cultural and social traditions, Tibetan Buddhism to the north and Indian Hinduism to the south.

Demography. The 1981 Nepal census reported 174,464 Gurung speakers in Nepal, making up 1.2 percent of the country's total population. These figures reflect a smaller number of Gurungs than actually exist, since they indicate only those who named Gurung as their mother tongue and not all Gurungs speak the language. The census shows Gurungs to be most numerous in the districts of Lamjung, Syangja, Kaski, Gorkha, Tanahu, Parbat, and Manang in Gandaki Zone, central Nepal.

Linguistic Affiliation. Gurung belongs to the Tibeto-Burman Language Family and resembles other languages of peoples of the middle hills of Nepal, such as Thakali and Tamang. It has a tonal structure and no written form. Most Gurungs are bilingual and tend to be fluent from childhood in Nepali, the Sanskritic language that is the lingua franca of the nation.

History and Cultural Relations

Gurung legends describe a "Ghale Raja," a king who ruled the Gurungs in ancient times. He was overthrown by the Nepali raja of a neighboring principality about the fifteenth century A.D. By the sixteenth century, Khasa kings of the Shah family had conquered most of the principalities that make up present-day Nepal. Gurungs acted as mercenaries in Khasa armies, including those of Prithvi Narayan Shah, the ancestor of the present king of Nepal, who completed unification of the kingdom of Nepal when he conquered the Kathmandu Valley in 1769. Because of their service, Gurungs enjoyed relatively high status in the new kingdom. They continued to act as mercenaries, and in the nineteenth century the Nepalese government signed a treaty allowing the British army to recruit them and other hill peoples into the Gurkha regiments, in which they continue to serve. Beyond ancient legend and documented relations with the nation-state (such as military service), little is known about the history of Gurungs.

The Gurungs are neither geographically isolated from other groups nor unaware of the social conventions and cultural values of the peoples around them. They are involved in trading relations with members of neighboring ethnic groups, including Thakalis and Tibetans, and high-caste Hindu merchants who travel through the villages selling household goods. Gurungs also have ongoing patron-client relationships with members of blacksmith and tailor service castes who live in hamlets attached to Gurung villages. Although interethnic marriage is strongly disapproved of, friendly social intercourse with members of other ethnic groups is usual, and bonds of ritual friendship (*nyel*) are forged between Gurungs and members of equal-status ethnic groups.

Settlements

Gurung villages are built high on ridges and consist of closely clustered groups of whitewashed houses with slate roofs. Houses of lineage members tend to be built alongside one another. While most Gurungs remain in rural villages, since the mid-1970s many more prosperous Gurung families have chosen to move to Pokhara, the nearest urban center, because of the greater comfort of urban living and improved access to educational facilities and medical care.

Economy

Subsistence and Commercial Activities. The main occupation of Gurungs is subsistence agriculture. Millet, wheat, barley, maize, potatoes, soybeans, and rice are grown. Some households also maintain vegetable gardens. Goats, chickens, water buffalo, and oxen are kept within the villages. Sheep and water buffalo are still grazed on high-altitude pastures, but deforestation has caused a reduction of fodder and thus in the last fifty years pastoralism has become a less significant economic activity. The rugged terrain on which Gurungs farm does not allow much agricultural surplus. The most important source of cash income for Gurungs is service in the Gurkha regiments of the British and Indian armies.

Industrial Arts. Weaving is a common activity during the slack agricultural season. Women weave carrying cloths and woolen blankets, and men weave carrying baskets, winnowing baskets, and storage baskets.

Trade. Beginning in the late nineteenth century, Gurungs played an important part in the salt trade with Tibet. This relationship was discontinued for political reasons in the mid-twentieth century. At present, some urban Gurungs engage in trade with India and others are prominent in contracting and transportation businesses around Pokhara.

Division of Labor. There is little formal division of labor among Gurungs. Men may not weave cloth and women may not weave bamboo or plow. Women generally look after the house, cook, and care for the physical needs of children. Men and women engage in most agricultural activities, as well as chopping wood for fuel and gathering fodder for livestock. Livestock in high-altitude pastures is most often tended by men. Metalwork, tailoring, and carpentry are performed by non-Gurung service castes who live in hamlets attached to Gurung villages.

Land Tenure. While forest and grazing land are communally owned, agricultural land is held privately. Rights to land are equally distributed among sons.

Kinship

Kin Groups and Descent. Lineages in Gurung society involve localized agnatic groups linked by a known ancestor. Each lineage is part of a clan. Clan affiliation cuts across locality and acts as a more generalized organizing principle in Gurung society. Descent in terms of rights to lineage resources and clan affiliation is patrilineal, but descent through the mother's line influences marriage possibilities and prohibitions.

Kinship Terminology. The Gurungs have a wide array of kin terms, which are highly differentiated and precise. Birth order and relative age are important matrices in the structure of Gurung kinship. Kin terms are used for nearly everyone with whom Gurungs interact; unrelated persons are assigned a fictive term.

Marriage and Family

Marriage. Marriage and childbearing are important to the assumption of full adult status for Gurungs. Marriages are arranged when daughters are in their mid- to late teens and sons in their late teens to twenties. In previous generations the age at marriage for girls was earlier, from about 9 to 13. Among Gurungs, cross-cousin marriage is preferred. The category of cross cousin is broad, including a large number of classificatory relatives. Residence is patrilocal, with a preference for village exogamy. Divorce can be initiated by either the man or the woman. Bride-wealth in the form of gold jewelry is given to the bride at marriage. If the husband initiates a divorce without due complaint, such as adultery, the wife has the right to keep the bride-wealth. However, if the wife causes or initiates the divorce she is required to return the bride-wealth to her husband.

Domestic Unit. Among Gurungs, the domestic unit changes over time. A household will begin as a nuclear family, and, as sons reach adulthood and marry, their brides come into the parental home and remain there while their first one or two children are small. The domestic unit is then an extended family for a period of five to ten years. As the son's children grow, he will build a separate residence, usually next to that of his parents.

Inheritance. Resources are distributed equally among sons in Gurung society. If there is no son, a daughter can inherit, and the son-in-law will come to reside in the household of his parents-in-law. The patrimony may be divided prior to the death of the father. In that case, the father can reserve a small portion. Although it runs contrary to Gurung custom, Nepalese law specifies that unmarried adult daughters should inherit a share of family property.

Socialization. Children are taught to be obedient and respectful of elders. They learn by imitation and the active encouragement of the older children, who often care for smaller ones. Corporal punishment is occasionally used, and unruly children may be isolated briefly. More often children are coaxed toward good behavior and instructed through stories about possible social and supernatural consequences of bad behavior.

Sociopolitical Organization

Social Organization. Gurung society is organized into two tiers or subgroups called the "Char Jat" or "four clans" and the "Sora Jat" or "sixteen clans." The subgroups are endogamous and within subgroups each clan is exogamous. The Char Jat group has traditionally claimed superior status to the Sora Jat group. Clans within each subgroup intermarry and otherwise treat one another as equals.

Political Organization.   Until 1962 the Gurung villages were governed by hereditary clan leaders and village headmen. In 1962 the national government instituted an electoral system whereby villages are grouped together in units of five, called *panchayats,* and divided into neighborhoods or wards from which local councillors are elected. The electorate also chooses a *pradhan panche* and *uper pradhan* (like a mayor and vice mayor, respectively) to lead the panchayat.

Social Control.   Gossip and fear of witch attack are common means of social control. The local council is able to levy fines against panchayat residents, and for serious crimes government police may be called in.

Conflict.   Disputes are often resolved by elders trusted by the parties involved. If this does not provide a solution then they may be brought before the village council or, as a last resort, to the district court.

Religion and Expressive Culture

Religious Beliefs.   The Gurungs practice a form of Tibetan Buddhism strongly influenced by the pre-Buddhist religion of Tibet, and they also observe major Hindu festivals, such as Dasain. They believe in some tenets of Buddhism and Hinduism, such as karma, yet they have a set of beliefs about an afterlife in the Land of the Ancestors and in local deities that are peculiarly Gurung. Gurungs believe their locale to be inhabited by supernatural forest creatures and by a variety of formless wraiths and spirits. Some of these exist in and of themselves, while others are believed to be the spirits of humans who have died violent deaths. Gurungs believe in the major Hindu deities and in the Buddha and bodhisattvas. Particular villages have their own deities, which are felt to be especially powerful in their immediate surroundings.

Religious Practitioners.   Practitioners of the pre-Buddhist Gurung religion, called *panju* and *klihbri,* are active in the performance of exorcisms and mortuary rites. Buddhist lamas are also important in funerary rituals, as well as performing purification rites for infants and some seasonal agricultural rituals. Wealthier Gurungs occasionally call lamas in to perform house-blessing ceremonies. Brahman priests are summoned to cast horoscopes and perform divinations at times of misfortune. *Dammis* from the local service castes are believed to be particularly potent exorcists and are often called in cases of illness.

Arts.   Gurungs make nothing that they would identify as art. The goods that they produce, such as baskets and blankets, are useful and tend to be of a conventional plain design. The artistry of Gurungs is expressed in their folk music and dance and especially in the evanescent form of song exchanges between young men and women.

Medicine.   Gurungs often employ exorcists as well as scientific drugs when suffering from an illness. Scientific medicine is highly valued, but it is costly and is not easily available in rural areas. Herbs and plants are also used in treating illness and injury.

Death and Afterlife.   Death is of central symbolic importance for Gurungs. The funerary ritual (*pae*) is the main ceremonial occasion in Gurung society, involving two nights and three days of ritual activity. It is attended by kin, villagers, and a large number of people who come for the conviviality and spectacle. Buddhist lamas and the panju and klihbri priests of the pre-Buddhist religion may officiate at the pae. Death is believed to involve the dissolution of elements that make up the body, so that the earth element returns to earth, air to air, fire to fire, and water to water. This process leaves the *plah* or souls (nine for men and seven for women), which must be sent through the performance of the pae to the Land of the Ancestors. There life continues much as it does in the present world, and from there the spirit can take other rebirths.

See also Gurkha; Nepali

Bibliography

Macfarlane, Alan (1976). *Resources and Population: A Study of the Gurungs of Nepal.* Cambridge: Cambridge University Press.

Messerschmidt, Donald A. (1976). *The Gurungs of Nepal.* Warminister: Aris & Phillips.

Pignède, Bernard (1966). *Les Gurungs: Une Population himalayenne du Népal.* The Hague: Mouton.

ERNESTINE L. McHUGH

Hijra

ETHNONYM: Eunuch

Orientation

Identification. Hijras are a social group, part religious cult and part caste, who live mainly in north India. They are culturally defined either as "neither men nor women" or as men who become women by adopting women's dress and behavior. Hijras are devotees of Buhuchara Mata, a version of the Indian mother goddess. Through their identification with the goddess, ratified by an emasculation ritual, hijras are believed to be vehicles of the goddess's power. Although culturally defined as celibate, hijras do engage in widespread prostitution in which their sexual-erotic role is as women with men. Their traditional way of earning a living is by collecting alms, receiving payments for blessing newborn males, and serving at the temple of their goddess. Hijras are generally called eunuchs, and sexual impotence is central to the definition of a hijra and a major criterion for initiation into the group.

Location. Most hijras live in the cities of north India, where they have more opportunities to engage in their traditional occupations. Hijras are also found in rural areas in the north, as well as cities in south India where they work mainly as prostitutes.

Demography. The census of India does not list hijras separately; they are usually counted as men, but upon request they may be counted as women. It is thus impossible to say with certainty how many hijras there are in India. Large cities like Bombay or Delhi may have 5,000 hijras living in twenty or thirty localities; the national estimate may be as high as 50,000.

Linguistic Affiliation. Hijras speak the language of the regions of India in which they were born and lived before joining the community. There is no separate hijra language, although there is a feminized intonation and use of slang that characterizes their talk. Hijras come from all over India and those from south India who move to the north learn Hindi as well as the regional languages.

History and Cultural Relations

The history and cultural relations of the hijras are rooted both in ancient Hinduism, where eunuchs are mentioned in a variety of texts, including the epic *Mahabharata,* and in Islam, where eunuchs served in the harems of the Mogul rulers. The ritual participation of hijras in life-cycle ceremonies has a clearly Hindu origin, though they may perform for Muslims as well. Many aspects of hijra social organization are taken from Islam, and many of the most important hijra leaders have been and are Muslim. However, hijras differ from traditional Muslim eunuchs, who did not dress as women and were sexually inactive. Nor were Muslim court eunuchs endowed with the powers to bless and to curse that hijras derive from their ambiguous sexuality and connection with the mother goddess. In the eighteenth and nineteenth centuries Hindu and Muslim hijras did not live together, but in contemporary India they often do. Another historical connection of the hijras appears to be with the Magna Mata cults in ancient Greece, whose devotees also dressed in women's clothing and sometimes castrated themselves.

Economy

Like every caste in India, hijras are primarily associated with a few traditional occupations, foremost among them being ritualized performances at childbirth and marriage. The hijras' performance consists of dancing and singing, accompanied by a two-sided drum, and the blessing of the child or the married couple in the name of the mother goddess. In return for these blessings the hijras receive *badhai,* traditional gifts in cash and goods, always including some sweets, cloth, and grains. Hijras also beg in the streets for alms from passersby and from shops; these activities are regulated on a daily rotational basis by the elders of the hijra community. Although prostitution is considered deviant within the hijra community, as it is in India generally, many hijras earn a living from it. Prostitution is carried out within a hijra household, under the supervision of a house manager or "madam," who will collect part or all of the prostitute's earnings in return for shelter, food, a small allowance, and protection from the police and rowdy customers. Although many young hijra prostitutes feel that they are exploited by their "madams," few live or work on their own. Because of their historical role as performers, hijras sometimes dance in nonritual roles, such as at stag parties, for college functions, or in films. A small number of hijras also serve the goddess Bahuchara at her major temple in Gujarat, blessing visitors to the temple and telling them the stories of the goddess in exchange for a few coins. Hijras can also be found as household servants and cooks, and in some cities in India they run public bathhouses. Hijras complain that in contemporary India their opportunity to earn a living by the respectable means of performing at marriages and births has declined, due to smaller families, less elaborate life-cycle ceremonies, and a general decline in the respect for traditional ritual specialists. Hijras have effectively maintained economic predominance, if not total monopoly, over their ritual role. Defined by the larger society as emasculated men, they have clearly seen that it is in their interest to preserve this definition of their role. They do this by making loud and public gestures to denounce the "frauds" and "fakes" who imitate them. They thus reinforce in the public mind their own sole right to their traditional occupations. When hijras find other female impersonators attempting to perform where it is their right to do so, they chase them away, using physical force if necessary. Hijra claims to exclusive entitlement to perform at life-cycle rituals, to collect alms in certain territories, and even to own land communally receive historical support in the edicts of some Indian states that officially granted them these rights.

Hijras have also been successful in controlling their audiences in their own economic interest. Hijras identify with renouncers (*sannyasis*) and, like them, hijras have abandoned their family and caste identities in order to join their religious community. Like sannyasis, then, hijras transcend networks of social obligation. They occupy the lowest end of the Indian social hierarchy and, having no ordinary social position to maintain within that hierarchy, hijras are freed from the restraints of ordinary behavior. They know that their shamelessness makes ordinary people reluctant to provoke them or to resist their demands for money and hence they trade on the fear and anxiety people have about them to coerce compliance. A culturally widespread belief in India is that hijras have the power to curse people with sterility and bad fortune, most dramatically by lifting their skirts and exposing their mutilated genitals. The fear and anxiety this belief provokes are sufficient to compel most people to give in to their demands or at least to negotiate with them.

Kinship and Social Organization

Kinship and Descent. The major principle of social organization among the hijras is the relation between gurus (teachers) and their _chelas_ (disciples). This relationship is modeled both on the Hindu joint family and on the relationship of spiritual leader and disciple in Hinduism. The guru or senior person in the relationship is alternately conceived of as a father, a mother, or a husband, while the chela is regarded as a dependent. The guru, like an elder in a family, is expected to take care of the chela's material needs and the chela is expected to show respect and obedience to the guru and give the guru "her" earnings. Through the relationship of guru and chela, the chelas of a guru are like sisters. Every hijra joins the community under the sponsorship of a guru, who is ideally her guru for life. Hijras express the view that a hijra could no more live without a guru than an ordinary person could live without a mother. Gurus also provide the umbrella under which hijras earn a living, as economic territories among hijras all come under the control of a particular guru and are off-limits to the chelas of any other guru without explicit permission. Changing gurus, which involves a small ritual and an escalating fee, is possible, though frowned upon. In addition to the guru-chela relationship, there are other fictive kinship relations of which the guru is the center: a guru's "sisters" are called aunt, and guru's guru is called "grandmother" (mother's mother). A guru passes down her wealth and possessions to one or more of her chelas, usually the senior chela. Gurus and chelas belong to the same "house," a nonlocalized symbolic descent group similar to a clan. The hijra community is divided into approximately seven of these named houses (with some variation according to region). The heads of these houses within a particular city or geographical region form a council of elders, or _jamat_. This group makes important decisions for the community, is present at the initiation of new members, and resolves whatever disputes arise within the community. Hijra houses are not ranked and there are no meaningful cultural or social distinctions among them, but each house has its own origin story and certain rules of behavior special to itself. When a hijra dies, it is the members of her house who arrange the funeral. In addition to the regional groupings of hijras there is also a loose national organization, which mainly meets on the anniversary of the death of an important hijra guru.

Domestic Unit. The most relevant group in daily life is the hijra household. These are communally organized, and usually contain five to fifteen people, under the direction of a guru or house manager. Hijra households are structured around a core of relatively permanent members, plus visitors or short-term guests, often hijras from another city, who stay for variable periods of time. Every hijra in the household must contribute to its economic well-being by working and in return is given the basic necessities of life and perhaps a few luxuries. Older hijras who are no longer able or do not wish to work outside the house do domestic chores. Members of a household may have different gurus and belong to different houses.

Social Control. The hijra community has developed effective mechanisms of social control over its members, mainly through the near monopoly hijra elders have over the opportunities for work. When a hijra joins the community, she pays a "fee" which gives her the right to earn a living in the particular territory "owned" by her guru. Any hijra who is thrown out of the community by her guru forfeits her right to work as part of the group. Since all hijra performances are arranged by a guru, a hijra without a guru will not be invited to perform, nor can she beg for alms in any place already assigned to another hijra group. A hijra suspended from the community may attempt to form her own work group, but this is difficult as it requires finding an area not claimed by another hijra group. Hijras use both verbal and physical abuse to protect their territories and suspension severely inhibits one's ability to earn. Normally, suspension is the result only of severe misbehavior, such as attacking one's guru. For lesser offenses hijras may be warned, fined, or have their hair cut by the jamat. The most important norm in a hijra household is honesty with respect to property. With so much geographic mobility among hijras it is necessary that individuals be trustworthy. Quarreling and dishonesty are disruptive to a household and ultimately to its economic success. Furthermore, as ritual performers, hijras sometimes enter the houses of their audiences; therefore, maintaining a reputation for honesty is necessary for their profession. Because the hijra household is both an economic and a domestic group, pressures to conform are great. Serious conflicts are inhibited by the geographical mobility permitted within the community. Any hijra who cannot get along in one household can move to another for a while; a person who gets a reputation for quarrelsomeness, however, will be unwelcome at any hijra house. The national network of hijras can work as a blacklist as well as an outlet for diffusing the disruptive effects of conflict.

Religion and Expressive Culture

Religious Beliefs. The power of the hijras as a sexually ambiguous category can only be understood in the religious context of Hinduism. In Hindu mythology, ritual, and art, the power of the combined man/woman, or androgyne, is a frequent and significant theme. Bahuchara Mata, the main object of hijra veneration, is specifically associated with transvestism and transgenderism. All hijra households contain a shrine to the goddess that is used in daily prayer. Hijras also identify with Shiva, a central, sexually ambivalent figure in Hinduism, who combines in himself, as do the hijras, both eroticism and asceticism. One of the most popular forms of Shiva is Ardhanarisvara, or half-man/half-woman, which represents Shiva united with his _shakti_ (female creative power). The hijras identify with this form of Shiva and often worship at Shiva temples. The religious meaning of the hijra role is expressed in stories linking hijras with the major figures of the Hindu Great Tradition, such as Arjuna (who lives for a year as a eunuch in the epic, the _Mahabharata_), Shiva, Buhuchara Mata (the mother goddess), and Krishna, all of whom are associated with sexual ambivalence.

Ceremonies. The central ceremony of hijra life—and the one that defines them as a group—is the emasculation operation in which all or part of the male genitals are removed. This operation is viewed as a rebirth; the new hijra created by it is called a _nirvan_. For the hijras, emasculation completes the transformation from impotent male to potent hijra. Emasculation links the hijras to both Shiva and the mother goddess and sanctions their performances at births and weddings, in which they are regarded as vehicles of the goddess's creative power. Bahuchara has a special connection with the hijras as emasculated, impotent men. Hijras believe that any impotent man who resists a call from the goddess to emasculate himself will be born impotent for seven future births. Emasculation increases the identification of the hijras with their goddess, and it is in her name that the operation is ritually performed. A hijra, called a "midwife," performs the operation after receiving sanction from the goddess. The ritual of the surgery and many of the postoperative restrictions involving special diet and seclusion imitate those of a woman who has just given birth. At the end of the forty-day isolation period, the nirvan is dressed as a bride, is taken in procession to a body of water and subsequently to a ritual involving fertility symbolism relating to marriage and childbirth, becomes a hijra, and is then invested with the power of the goddess. In the hijra emasculation ritual, we have a culmination of the paradoxes and contradictions characteristic of Hinduism: impotent, emasculated man, transformed by female generative power into creative ascetics, becomes able to bless others with fertility and fortune.

Art and Performance. Hijras are performers at points in the life cycle related to reproduction, and thus much of their expressive culture employs fertility symbolism. Hijra performances are burlesques of female behavior. Much of the comedy of their performances derives from the incongruities between their behavior and that of ordinary women, restrained by norms of propriety. Hijras use coarse speech and gestures and make sexual innuendos, teasing the male children present and also making fun of various family members and family relationships. There are some songs and comedic routines that are a traditional part of hijra performances, most notably one in which a hijra acts as a pregnant woman commenting on the difficulties at each state of the pregnancy. In all the performances blessing the newborn male, the hijras inspect the infant's genitals. It is believed that any child born a hermaphrodite will be claimed by the hijras for their own. In addition to traditional elements hijra performances also include popular songs and dances from current favorite films.

Bibliography

Bradford, Nicholas J. (1983). "Transgenderism and the Cult of Yellamma: Heat, Sex, and Sickness in South Indian Ritual." *Journal of Anthropological Research* 39:307–322.

Freeman, James M. (1979). "Transvestites and Prostitutes, 1969–72." In *Untouchable: An Indian Life History.* Stanford: Stanford University Press.

Nanda, Serena (1990). *Neither Man nor Woman: The Hijras of India.* Belmont, Calif.: Wadsworth Publishers.

O'Flaherty, Wendy Doniger (1980). *Women, Androgynes, and Other Mythical Beasts.* Chicago: University of Chicago Press.

SERENA NANDA

Hill Pandaram

ETHNONYMS: Malai Pandaram, Malapaṇṭāram

Orientation

Identification. The Malapaṇṭāram (hereafter anglicized as the Hill Pandaram) are a Scheduled Tribe of the state of Kerala in south India and inhabit the forested hills of the Western Ghats between Lake Periyar and the town of Tenmali, about 9° N. Although they share the name "Pandaram" with a caste community of Tamil Nadu, there appear to be no links between the two communities. *Mala* (mountain) refers to their long association with the hill forests, the Western Ghats, which form the backbone of peninsular India and range from 600 to 2,400 meters. A nomadic foraging community, the Hill Pandaram loosely identify themselves with the forest and refer to all outsiders, whether local caste communities or forest laborers, as *nāṭṭukāraṉ* (country people).

Location. Centered on the Pandalam Hills, the Hill Pandaram primarily occupy the forest ranges of Ranni, Koni, and Achencoil. The Ghats are subject to two monsoon seasons; the southwest monsoon, falling between June and August, being responsible for the bulk of the rain. Rainfall is variable, averaging between 125 and 200 centimeters annually, precipitation being high at higher elevations around Sabarimala and Devarmala. The forest type ranges from tropical evergreen to moist deciduous. The foothills of the Ghats and the valleys of the major river systems—Achencoil, Pamba, and Azbutta—are cultivated and heavily populated by caste communities who moved into the Ghats during the past century.

Demography. A small community, the Hill Pandaram numbered 1,569 individuals in 1971, and had a population density of 1 to 2 persons per square kilometer.

Linguistic Affiliation. Living in the hills that separate the states of Kerala and Tamil Nadu, the Hill Pandaram also lie between two main language groups of south India—Tamil and Malayalam. They speak a dialect of one or the other of these languages, and divergences from standard Tamil or Malayalam seem to be mainly matters of intonation and articulation. Their dialect generally is not understood by people from the plains, and although there is no evidence available it is possible that their language may still contain elements of a proto-Dravidian language. Few Hill Pandaram are literate.

History and Cultural Relations

Although the Hill Pandaram live within the forest environment and have little day-to-day contact with other communities, they do have a long history of contact with wider Indian society. As with the other forest communities of south India, such as the Paliyan, Kadar, Kannikar, and Mala Ulladan, the Hill Pandaram have never been an isolated community; from earliest times they appear to have had regular and important trade contacts with the neighboring agriculturalists, either through silent barter or, since the end of the eighteenth century, through mercantile trade. Early Tamil poets indicate that tribal communities inhabited the forests of the Western Ghats during the Sangam period (around the second century B.C.); and these communities had important trade contacts with their neighbors and came under the political jurisdiction of the early Tamil kingdoms or local petty chieftains, who taxed forest products such as cardamom, bamboo, ivory, honey, and wax. The importance of this trade at the beginning of the nineteenth century is highlighted in the writings of the Abbé Dubois and in the economic survey of the former Travancore State made at that time by two British officials, Ward and Conner. Forest trade still serves to link the Hill Pandaram to the wider Hindu society.

Settlements

The Hill Pandaram have two types of residential grouping—settlements and forest camps—although about 25 percent of Hill Pandaram families live a completely nomadic existence and are not associated with any settlement. A typical settlement consists of about ten huts, widely separated from each other, each housing a family who live there on a semipermanent basis. The huts are simple, rectangular constructions with split-bamboo screens and grass-thatched roofs; many are little more than roofed shelters. Around the hut sites fruit-bearing trees such as mango and tamarind, cassava and small cultivations may be found. The settlements are often some distance from village communities (with their multicaste populations) and have no communal focus like religious shrines. Settlements are inhabited only on an intermittent basis. The second type of residential grouping is the forest camp, consisting of two to six temporary leaf shelters, each made from a framework of bamboo that is supported on a single upright pole and covered by palm leaves. These leaf shelters have a conical appearance and are formed over a fireplace consisting of three stones that were found on the site. Rectangular lean-tos may also be constructed using two upright poles. Settlements are scattered throughout the forest ranges except in the interior forest, which is largely uninhabited apart from nomadic camps of the Hill Pandaram. The majority of the Hill Pandaram are nomadic and the usual length of stay at a particular camping site (or a rock shelter, which is frequently used) is from two to sixteen days, with seven or eight days being the average, although specific families may reside in a particular locality for about six to eight weeks. Nomadic movements, in the sense of shifting camp, usually vary over distances from a half-kilometer to 6 kilometers, though in daily foraging activities the Hill Pandaram may range over several kilometers.

Economy

Subsistence and Commercial Activities. Although the Hill Pandaram occasionally engage in paid labor for the forest department, and a small minority of families are settled agriculturalists on the forest perimeter, the majority are nomadic hunter-gatherers, who combine food gathering with the collection of minor forest produce. The main staple consists of various kinds of yam collected by means of digging sticks, together with the nuts of a forest cycad, _kalinga_ (_Cycas cincinalis_). Such staples are supplemented with palm flour, and cassava and rice are obtained through trade. The hunting of small animals, particularly monkeys, squirrels, and monitor lizards, is important. These animals are obtained either during foraging activities or in a hunting party consisting of two men or a man and a young boy, using old muzzle-loading guns. Dogs, an aid to hunting, are the only domestic animals.

Trade. The collection of minor forest produce is an important aspect of economic life and the principal items traded are honey, wax, dammar (a resin), turmeric, ginger, cardamom, incha bark (_Acacia intsia_, one variety of which is a soap substitute, the other a fish poison), various medicinal plants, oil-bearing seeds, and bark materials used for tanning purposes. The trade of these products is organized through a contractual mercantile system, a particular forest range being leased by the Forest Department to a contractor, who is normally a wealthy merchant living in the plains area, often a Muslim or a high-caste Hindu. Through the contractor the Hill Pandaram obtain their basic subsistence requirements: salt, condiments, cloth, cooking pots, and tins for collecting honey. All the material possessions of the community are obtained through such trade—even the two items that are crucial to their collecting economy, billhooks and axes. As the contractual system exploited the Hill Pandaram, who rarely got the full market value for the forest commodities they collected, moves have been made in recent years to replace it by a forest cooperative system administered by forestry officials under the auspices of the government's Tribal Welfare Department.

Division of Labor. Although women are the principal gatherers of yams, while the hunting of the larger mammals and the collection of honey are the prerogatives of men, the division of labor is not a rigid one. Men may cook and care for children, while women frequently go hunting for smaller animals, an activity that tends to be a collective enterprise involving a family aided by a dog. Collection of forest produce tends to be done by both sexes.

Land Tenure. Each Hill Pandaram family (or individual) is associated with a particular forest tract, but there is little or no assertion of territorial rights or rights over particular forest products either by individuals or families. The forest is held to be the common property of the whole community. No complaint is expressed at the increasing encroachment on the forest by low-country men who gather dammar or other forest products, or at increasing incidences of poaching by them.

Kinship

Kin Groups and Descent. Unlike the caste communities of Kerala, the Hill Pandaram have no unilineal descent system or ideology and there are no recognized corporate groupings above the level of the family. The settlements are in no sense stable or corporate units, but like the forest camps they are residential aggregates that may be described as "transient corporations." The basic kinship unit is the conjugal family, consisting of a cohabiting couple and their young children. A forest camp consists of a temporary grouping of one to four such families, each family constituting a unit. There is a pervasive emphasis on sexual egalitarianism and women sometimes form independent commensal units, though these always are part of a wider camp aggregate. Many encampments consist only of a single family, and such families may reside as separate and isolated units for long periods.

Kinship Terminology. The kinship terminology of the Hill Pandaram is of the Dravidian type common throughout south India, though there is much vagueness and variability in usage. Apart from conjugal ties and close "affinal" relationships (which in contrast to the "kin" links have warmth and intimacy), kinship ties are not "load"-bearing in the sense of implying structured role obligations.

Marriage and Family

Marriage.   Both polyandrous and polygynous marriages have been recorded, but most marriages are monogamous. Cross-cousin marriage is the norm and marriages emerge almost spontaneously from preexisting kinship patterns, as camp aggregates center on affinally related men. There is little or no marriage ceremony and there is no formal arrangement of marriage partners, although young men tend to establish prior ties with prospective parents-in-law. Marriages are brittle and most older Hill Pandaram have experienced a series of conjugal partnerships during their lifetime. A cohabiting couple forms an independent household on marriage, but the couple may continue as a unit in the camp aggregate of either set of parents.

Domestic Unit.   The conjugal family is the basic economic unit. Members of a family may live in separate leaf shelters (though spouses share the same leaf shelter) and may form foraging parties with other members of a camp aggregate, but all food gathered by an individual belongs to his or her own immediate family, who share a simple hearth. Only meat, tobacco, and the proceeds of honey-gathering expeditions are shared between the families constituting a camp aggregate.

Inheritance.   As the Hill Pandaram possess no land and have few material possessions, little emphasis is placed on inheritance.

Socialization.   The Hill Pandaram put a normative stress on individual autonomy and self-sufficiency, and from their earliest years children are expected to assert independence. Children collect forest produce for trade and will often spend long periods away from their parents.

Sociopolitical Organization

Social Organization.   Organized as a foraging community, living in small camp aggregates of two to three families scattered over a wide area, the Hill Pandaram exhibit no wider structures of sociopolitical organization. There are no ritual congregations, microcastes, nor any other communal associations or corporate groupings above the level of the conjugal family. A lack of wider formal organization is coupled with a pervasive stress on egalitarianism, self-sufficiency, and the autonomy of the individual. Some individuals in the settlements are recognized as *muttukani* (headmen) but their role is not institutionalized, for they are essentially a part of the system of control introduced by administrative agencies of the Forestry and Welfare Departments to facilitate efficient communication with the community.

Social Control.   The Hill Pandaram have no formal institutions for the settlement of disputes, though individual men and women often act as informal mediators or conciliators. Social control is maintained to an important degree by a value system that puts a premium on the avoidance of aggression and conflict; like other foragers, the Hill Pandaram tend to avoid conflict by separation and by flight.

Religion and Expressive Culture

Although nominally Hindu, Hill Pandaram religion is distinct from that of the neighboring agriculturalists in being un-iconic (i.e., venerating not images of deities, but the crests of mountains) and focused on the contact, through possession rites, of localized *mala devi* (hill spirits). Hill Pandaram may occasionally make ritual offerings at village temples, particularly those associated with the gods Aiyappan and Murugan at the time of the Onam festival (December) or at local shrines established in forest areas by Tamil laborers; but otherwise they have little contact with the formal rituals of Hinduism.

Religious Beliefs.   The spiritual agencies recognized by the Hill Pandaram fall into two categories: the ancestral ghosts or shades (*chavu*) and the hill spirits (*mala devi*). The hill spirits are supernaturals associated with particular hill or rock precipices, and in the community as a whole these spirits are legion, with a hill deity for about every 8 square kilometers of forest. Although localized spirits, the hill spirits are not "family spirits" for they may have devotees living some distance from the particular locality. The ancestral shades, on the other hand, are linked to particular families, but like the hill spirits their influence is mainly beneficent, giving protection against misfortune and proffering advice in times of need. One class of spirits, however, is essentially malevolent. These are the *arukula*, the spirits of persons who have died accidentally through falling from a tree or being killed by a wild animal.

Religious Practitioners.   Certain men and women have the ability to induce a trancelike state and in this way to contact the spirits. They are known as *tuḷḷukara* (possession dancers, from *tuḷḷu*, "to jump"), and at times of misfortune they are called upon by relatives or friends to give help and support.

Ceremonies.   The Hill Pandaram have no temples or shrines and thus make no formal ritual offerings to the spirits, leading local villagers to suggest that they have no religion. Nor do they ritualize the life-cycle events of birth, puberty, and death to any great degree. The important religious ceremony is the possession seance, in which the tuḷḷukara goes into a trance state induced by rhythmic drumming and singing and incarnates one or more of the hill spirits or an ancestral shade. During the seance the cause of the misfortune is ascertained (usually the breaking of a taboo associated with the menstrual period) and the help of the supernatural is sought to alleviate the sickness or misfortune.

Arts.   In contrast with other Indian communities the Hill Pandaram have few art forms. Nevertheless, their singing is highly developed, and their songs are varied and elaborate and include historical themes.

Medicine.   All minor ailments are dealt with through herbal remedies, since the Hill Pandaram have a deep though unstructured knowledge of medicinal plants. More serious complaints are handled through the possession rites.

Bibliography

Fürer-Haimendorf, Christoph von (1970). "Notes on the Malapantaram of Travancore." *Bulletin of the International Committee for Urgent Anthropological and Ethnological Research* 3:44–51.

Krishna Iyer, L. A. (1937). "Malapantāram." In *The Travancore Tribes and Castes*. Vol. 1, 96–116. Trivandrum: Government Press.

Morris, Brian (1981). "Hill Gods and Ecstatic Cults: Notes on the Religion of a Hunting and Gathering People." *Man in India* 61:203–236.

Morris, Brian (1986). *Forest Traders: A Socio-Economic Study of the Hill Pandaram*. L. S. E. Monographs in Social Anthropology, no. 55. London: Athlone Press.

Mukherjee, B. (1954). *The Malapandaram of Travancore: Their Socio-Economic Life*. Bulletin of the Department of Anthropology, no. 3. Calcutta.

BRIAN MORRIS

Hill Tribes

ETHNONYM: Scheduled Tribes

This inexact term was long applied by British and American travelers and colonial authorities to the indigenous inhabitants of upland areas in South and Southeast Asia (and sometimes in other parts of the world). Although it would seem clear enough what a "hill tribe" is, the term finds little favor among modern anthropologists. First of all, it seems to have tones of racial inferiority; thus the term has never been applied, for example, to the Highland clans of Scotland, even though they do fit the usual mold of hill tribes. Second, Western writers have been inconsistent in their identification of hill tribes, usually defining them as somehow in opposition to other social categories. In the Indian subcontinent tribes or hill tribes have long been depicted as distinct from castes; in Southeast Asia they have often been presented as distinct from rice-cultivating peasants in the plains and alluvial valleys. The Nilgiri Hills of south India, to take a specific example, are home to several small, more or less indigenous groups, most notably the Todas, Kotas, Kurumbas, and Badagas (all dealt with elsewhere in this volume). British writers and administrators there during the nineteenth century always identified the Todas, Kotas, and Kurumbas as hill tribes or aboriginal tribes; whereas the Badagas, who had come up to the Nilgiri Hills from the Mysore Plains a few centuries before, were usually written about, even in legislation, as being something other than hill tribes. Yet they had lived within a few miles of the Kotas and Todas for centuries, and they were at a very similar level of economic development to the Kotas. The Nilgiri case leads to the conclusion that hill tribes are simply the indigenous communities that live above an elevation of 1,000 meters.

In traditional societies like those of India and Thailand one can still find discrete cultural units conventionally called tribes. These tend to be endogamous social units, occupying a distinguishable rural territory, bearing a tribal name and a distinct material culture, and often speaking their own language. But the same features characterize many dominant castes in South Asia as well (e.g., the Rajputs).

In this region the old categories will not simply disappear as anthropologists develop more useful ways of categorizing human societies. This is because the legal formulation in India soon after independence of two broad social categories, Scheduled Tribes and Scheduled Castes, has by now touched hundreds of millions of people who thereby have become eligible for special treatment by various branches of the government, in an effort to ameliorate the socioeconomic backwardness of these groupings. So valued have these government benefits become that the Indian authorities today find themselves unable to abandon the granting of special benefits, two generations after they were first instituted. There are even groups like the Badagas, who were never called hill tribes nor treated as Scheduled Tribes, who nonetheless today are clamoring for classification as Scheduled Tribes for the most obvious of reasons. The Badagas actually became a Scheduled Tribe in 1991.

Although many of the earlier accounts depicted hill tribes as "animists," or believers in spirit entities who did not follow one of the great South Asian religions (e.g., the Hill Pandaram), subsequent research has described hill tribes that are Hindu, Buddhist, Muslim, and even Christian (the Mizos, Garos). Along with these differences in belief, the hill tribes show a great variety of economic adaptations: while agriculture is preeminent among most, there are some who are pastoralists (such as the Todas), some who are artisans (Kotas), and some who are itinerant peddlers, magicians, and entertainers.

More than 500 named tribes can still be recognized in the countries of South Asia. Details about tribal demography are elusive. Most national censuses have not attempted (or at least have not published) a detailed tribe-by-tribe enumeration since gaining their independence. One has to go back to the British census of undivided India in 1931 to find the last set of reliable figures on individual tribes and castes throughout the entire region. But at that time, sixty years ago, the total population of the subcontinent was less than 400 million, compared with more than one billion today. Presumably the tribes have increased proportionally.

The future of the South Asian hill tribes is an uncertain one: while very few groups show any signs of dying out, most are in the process of rapid cultural and economic change that will eventually alter them, or their social boundaries, beyond recognition. Whether the government of India continues its special benefits for Scheduled Tribes into the indefinite future is one very big factor. Another is the alienation of "tribal" land—its seizure by immigrant settlers or timber merchants—which has long been reported in many hill areas, perhaps most notably in Andhra Pradesh. In general virtually all hill tribes are now changing greatly through the impact of Hinduism or Christian missionaries, as well as the effects of modernization, secularization, and sometimes industrialization. These factors, among others, are tending toward a weakening of tribal languages and tribal identity.

See also Scheduled Castes and Scheduled Tribes

Bibliography

Fried, Morton H. (1975). *The Notion of Tribe*. Menlo Park: Cummings Publishing Co.

Fuchs, Stephen (1973). *The Aboriginal Tribes of India*. New York: St. Martin's Press.

Fürer-Haimendorf, Christoph von (1982). *Tribes of India: The Struggle for Survival*. Berkeley: University of California Press.

Helm, June, ed. (1968). *Essays on the Problem of Tribe*. Proceedings of the 1967 Annual Spring Meeting of the American Ethnological Society. Seattle: University of Washington Press.

Mandelbaum, David G. (1970). *Society in India*. Vol. 2, 573–619. Berkeley: University of California Press.

Sahlins, Marshall D. (1968). *Tribesmen*. Englewood Cliffs, N.J.: Prentice-Hall.

Singh, K. S., ed. (1983). *Tribal Movements in India*. 2 vols. New Delhi: Manohar.

Singh, K. S. (1985). *Tribal Society in India*. New Delhi: Manohar.

PAUL HOCKINGS

Hindu

ETHNONYMS: Hindoo, Gentoo (eighteenth-nineteenth centuries)

While Hinduism is undoubtedly one of the world's major religions, whether gauged in terms of its ethical and metaphysical complexities or simply in terms of the numbers of adherents (estimated at 760 million in 1991), it defies easy description. It had no founding figure, like Jesus; it has no one sacred book, like the Quran, but many; it has no central doctrines; worship can be conducted anywhere; there is no principal spiritual leader, like a pope; and there is no hierarchy of priests analogous to a church. The very words "Hindu" and "Hinduism" are foreign terms with no ready translation into Indian languages.

"Hindu" is the Persian term that referred to the Indus River and surrounding country (Greek "Sindou," modern "Sindh"). As applied to people by the early Muslim invaders, it simply meant "Indian." Perhaps it was only in the nineteenth century that Europeans and educated Indians began to apply the word specifically to adherents of a particular, dominant South Asian religion.

Despite the great diversity in forms of Hindu worship, the hundreds of diverse sects, and the vast number of deities worshiped (conventionally 330 million), there are certain philosophical principles that are generally acknowledged by Hindus. In brief, there are four aims of living and four stages of life. The aims of living (and their Sanskrit-derived names) are: (1) *artha*, material prosperity; (2) *kama*, satisfaction of desires; (3) dharma, performing the duties of one's station in life; and (4) *moksha*, obtaining release from the cycle of rebirths to which every soul is subject. These aims are thought to apply to everybody, from Brahman to Untouchable. So too are the four stages of life, which are studentship, becoming a householder, retiring to the forest to meditate, and finally, becoming a mendicant (*sannyasi*).

Hinduism is more a "way of life," a cultural form, than it is a "faith," for its ethical and metaphysical principles pervade most acts of daily life: taking food, performing other bodily functions, walking around, conducting any business enterprise, farming, arranging marriages, bringing up children, preparing for the future, etc. These are just some of the things with which nearly everyone will be involved, yet all of them are tinged with religious rules. A "good Hindu" (not really an Indian concept) is one who strives to do his or her duty toward a person's family and caste traditions (dharma) and who shows devotion to certain gods. Regular attendance at temple is not required, nor is worship of a specific deity or study of a particular scripture; there are no rules about prayer being obligatory at certain hours or on certain days. It is almost true that one could follow any religious practice and, if an Indian, be considered a Hindu. Thus it should come as no surprise that many Hindus consider the Buddha and even Jesus Christ to be incarnations (avatars) of Vishnu, one of the three principal deities of Hinduism (the others being Shiva and Brahma). No doubt in historic times Hinduism absorbed local tribal deities into its large pantheon, by making them avatars or simply relatives (wife, son, daughter) of already established deities.

In summary, we may say that a Hindu is a South Asian person who recognizes a multiplicity of gods (though he or she may only be devoted to one); who practices either monogamous or polygynous marriage; who lives in some form of nuclear or extended patrilineal family; and who believes he or she has one soul, though it will normally be reincarnated after death.

Because of emigration beyond South Asia during the past century, Hindus are today to be found in considerable numbers in Canada, the United States, Trinidad, Jamaica, Surinam, and Guyana; in the United Kingdom and the Netherlands; in South Africa, Kenya, Tanzania, Réunion, Mauritius, and South Yemen; and in Myanmar (Burma), Malaysia, Singapore, Brunei, Hongkong, Australia, and Fiji. Over the past two decades many thousands of Hindu men and women have gone to take up menial jobs in the Persian Gulf nations, though they will probably not be allowed to become citizens of those (Islamic) nations. More than a thousand years ago Hindus also migrated to some parts of Indonesia, where they are still identifiable today on the islands of Java, Bali, and Lombok. There are also identifiable Hindus associated with the Thai royal court, especially Brahmans. In most of the above-mentioned countries there are at least a few Hindu temples.

Bibliography

Chaudhuri, Nirad C. (1979). _Hinduism, a Religion to Live By._ New York: Oxford University Press; London: Chatto & Windus.

Stutley, Margaret, and James Stutley (1977). _Harper's Dictionary of Hinduism: Its Mythology, Folklore, Philosophy, Literature, and History._ New York: Harper & Row.

Zaehner, R. C. (1962). _Hinduism._ London: Oxford University Press.

PAUL HOCKINGS

Indian Christian

ETHNONYMS: none

Indian Christians are believers in the divinity of Jesus Christ. Despite the persisting idea in South Asia that Christianity is the "white man's religion," it has a massive following today in the subcontinent. Still, it is very much a minority faith, accounting for nearly 8 percent of the Sri Lankan population but less than 3 percent in each of the other South Asian countries. In 1991 India had an estimated 21 million Christians, and the other South Asian countries together had another 3 million.

The idea that Christianity was introduced by the colonial powers—Roman Catholicism by the Portuguese and then Anglicanism by the English—is not strictly true. Kerala and some other parts of the west coast had certainly been evangelized by Nestorian missionaries since the sixth century, and many in south India believe that the apostle Thomas came to Tamil Nadu and was martyred and buried in what is now Madras city. These early religious connections were with Syria (cf. Syrian Christians). The Portuguese brought Portuguese and Italian priests with them, and in 1557 Goa, their major Indian colony, became an archbishopric. With the founding of the East India Company in 1600 the English introduced the Anglican faith, and as time passed other Protestant sects appeared. The years 1850–1900 were the high point of Protestant mission activity in South Asia, with ministers from America and virtually every country in Europe vying for converts, especially among the Untouchables, tribals, and downtrodden slum dwellers. In some areas they were dramatically successful at gaining converts: the Mizos of northeastern India are nearly all Christians today, thanks to the somewhat obscure Welsh Baptist mission. At the other end of the country, though, the Badagas are 97 percent Hindu after seventy years of concerted effort by the Basel Evangelical mission, followed by another seventy years of other missionary activity. The Roman Catholic missionaries have not fared any better among the Badagas; but elsewhere there are large Catholic congregations in many towns and cities. By the Congregation _de Propaganda Fide_ (1622) the Catholic church encouraged the training of Indian priests, and also brought in large numbers of European Jesuits in a supervisory capacity.

The year 1947 marked a landmark in Protestant church history, not just because this was the year of independence for both India and Pakistan but also because it was the year when the Church of South India came into being—the first unified Protestant church anywhere. It of course absorbed the former Anglican, Methodist, and several other sectarian institutions. In 1970 there followed a unified Protestant Church of North India and a Protestant Church of Pakistan.

These churches, both Protestant and Catholic, are now entirely in the hands of South Asian bishops and archbishops, with very few of the former European missionaries remaining. In Sri Lanka and south India, the greatest growths have recently been seen among the Roman Catholics, not primarily because of new conversions but rather because of a calculated avoidance of family planning. In Nepal Christian and Muslim missionary activity is prohibited by law.

The history of Christianity in South Asia has indeed been a checkered one, but it has been an important instrument of Westernization. The first printing presses and the first modern colleges were introduced by European missionaries. By the middle of the nineteenth century these people were making important contributions to the general social uplift of the country (and not only for Christian converts) by their promotion of rural and urban schooling, adult literacy, female education, colleges, hospitals and clinics, and modern urban careers. As a result the Christian population has wielded a disproportionate influence in modern Indian and Sri Lankan life. Little conversion is still taking place.

Indian Christians today tend to be urban, are always monogamous, and form nuclear families upon marriage (which takes place in a church). They usually follow Westernized professions, becoming teachers, nurses, bank clerks, and civil servants.

See also Europeans in South Asia; Syrian Christian of Kerala

Bibliography

Coutinho, Fortunato (1958). _Le régime paroissial des diocèses de rite latin de l'Inde des origines (XVIe siècle à nos jours)._ Paris: Éditions Béatrice-Nauwelaerts.

Gibbs, Mildred E. (1972). _The Anglican Church in India, 1600–1970._ Delhi: Indian Society for Promoting Christian Knowledge.

Nanjundayya, H. V., and L. K. Ananthakrishna Iyer (1930). "Indian Christian." In _The Mysore Tribes and Castes,_ edited by H. V. Nanjundayya and L. K. Ananthakrishna Iyer. Vol. 3, 1–76. Mysore: Mysore University.

Neill, Stephen (1984). _A History of Christianity in India._ 2 vols. Cambridge: Cambridge University Press.

Thomas, Abraham V. (1974). _Christians in Secular India._ Rutherford: Fairleigh Dickinson University.

PAUL HOCKINGS

Irula

ETHNONYMS: Erilagaru, Iraligar, Irulan, Kasaba, Kasava, Kasuba, Ten Vanniya, Vana Palli, Villaya

Orientation

Identification. Most Irula inhabit the state of Tamil Nadu, India. Although they form a Scheduled Tribe, the Irula are in many ways similar to their nearby Hindu caste neighbors. They have pantheistic and animistic tendencies of their own, but prolonged contact with more orthodox Hinduism has also had its indelible impact.

Location. Most Irula live in the northern districts of Tamil Nadu, where the majority are found in the Changalpattu, North Arcot, and South Arcot districts not far from Madras City. While the Irula in general merit additional fieldwork, it is only the Nilgiri Irula who are considered here. They live in the Nilgiri District in extreme northwestern Tamil Nadu, in the adjacent Coimbatore District, and in parts of Karnataka and Kerala states. Tamil Nadu is the southeasternmost state of India. It is thus a region within the tropics that is subject to westerly monsoonal rainfall, lasting mainly from mid-June through August, and to reverse monsoonal rainfall, which is heaviest from September into November. Some Nilgiri Irula occupy higher and cooler slopes, and others occupy plains that by April are hot and dry.

Demography. After the Malayali (who actually are not the speakers of Malayalam in Kerala) numbered at 159,426, the Irula at 89,025 formed the second-largest Tamil Nadu tribe in the 1971 census of India. There were over 12,000 Irula in the Coimbatore District. As the Nilgiri District had some 5,200 Irula in 1971, only about 6 percent lived there. By 1971, there were altogether 106,939 Irula in south India.

Linguistic Affiliation. Depending on the criteria used, the Irula have been identified as speakers of a distinct Irula language or speakers of a dialect of Tamil. In addition, Malayalam has influenced Irula speech in Kerala, and Kannada has influenced the speech of a subgroup of Irula, called Kasaba, in Karnataka.

History and Cultural Relations

Many of the lowland Nilgiri Irula live near impressive megalithic sites, so the question of whether they could possibly be descendants of inhabitants living in ancient times naturally arises. Particularly among the hoe-using Irula of the Nilgiri slopes, there are farming practices that may represent neolithic survivals. Our earliest description of the Nilgiri Irula in English, by Francis Buchanan who visited them in 1800, briefly provides an overview of how the Irula then survived. The descendants of these Irula ultimately were to be affected profoundly by the spread of plantation agriculture (mainly tea and coffee) by the British. Many lowland Irula, having more frequent contacts with urban centers, probably have long been a part of the lowland cultural continuum and changing civilization. The Irula are best understood as being primarily either lowlanders with many lowland ties or uplanders with both upland and lowland ties. The lowlanders, users of the plow and even cultivators of wet rice, often live with the members of other castes involved in similar agricultural pursuits. Because the upland Irula formerly lived on the forested outer slopes of the Nilgiris, they did not develop ties as close as those that existed between the upland Badaga, Kota, and Toda. However, they often lived with or close to the Kurumba (powerful magicians and doctors, in both the Alu and Palu groups), and they still do. After plantations spread over formerly forested outer slopes, most of the upland Irula became plantation laborers with ties to a plantation infrastructure. Many uplanders thus came to lead a dual existence: plantation laborers by day and Irula hamlet dwellers by night. Today, an efficient bus service enables lowlanders to travel more easily to lowland urban centers. While some uplanders may occasionally walk the long distances down and up that are necessary to visit lowland urban centers, it is generally far easier for an uplander to travel to a nearby upland urban center. Yet kinship and ritual ties still keep the upland and lowland Irula in close contact with each other.

Settlements

The Irula tend to place their houses together in hamlets or villages called *mottas*. After the British moved to end shifting (*kottukadu* or *kumri*) agriculture, starting at the time of the land settlements in the 1880s, it became increasingly difficult for the Irula to farm in this way. However, to the limited degree that some still manage to follow this practice in the wildest areas, there may be as a result scattered single houses next to temporary plots. Kasaba who live in a wildlife sanctuary are also likely to reside in separate houses. In hamlets, often with less than fifty people, there are separate houses, houses aligned into rows, or a combination of the two patterns. The alignment of houses was traditional, but the practice was reinforced when plantation managers had "coolie lines," houses built in rows for their laborers. Houses provided by the government also tend to be aligned. A courtyard fronting a house is the most common adjunct, and houses within a hamlet are invariably next to one or more courtyards. Some traditional Irula hamlets of the outer Nilgiri slopes might still have separate "pollution huts" or special rooms for women delivering infants, for women in the postpartum stage, or for women who are menstruating. In the traditional way, too, there is a tendency toward a proliferation of small huts to serve separate functions, and these huts are constructed next to courtyards. Apart from the common firewood storage huts and chicken, goat, or sheep huts, there may also be a separate hut just for drums. In these hamlets there is typically an absence of temples. In each of the main villages of Hallimoyar, Kallampalayam, and Thengumarahada, located on the lowland northeast of the Nilgiri massif and close to the Moyar River, there are over 100 Irula. Because caste people (of which the Badaga and Okkaliga are prominent) live with the Irula and because each of these settlements has considerable governmental investment, the Irula tend to be like their neighbors. Pollution huts or rooms and special purpose huts are thus usually absent, and temples are present. Because all the Irula still have a drive toward gardening, garden plants are usually planted in and adjacent to Irula settlements. Even a separate house next to a temporary millet field is thus likely to have some garden plants growing nearby. Jackfruit and mango trees typically gain a firm foothold in and close to permanent settlements, and the drought-resistant neem (*Mar-*

gosa) and tamarind are often present within lowland settlements. The lowland Irula who herd cattle for others, typically in drier areas with thorn forest, are associated with a distinctive settlement pattern in which a large cattle enclosure is surrounded by a thorny wall of piled branches. The Irula also have burial grounds with ancestral temples, called _koppa manais_, in which stones associated with the departed spirits of the dead are housed. Each patriclan has a burial place and a koppa manai, but the two are not necessarily together (for example, while Samban people are only buried at Kallampalayam, there are Samban koppa manais at Hallimoyar and Kunjappanai). Although a burial ground is usually close to a settlement, it can be farther away. As in many other parts of Asia and into the Pacific Basin, the sacredness of a burial ground is often associated with the pagoda tree (the Polynesian frangipani). Largely because many of the Irula are landless laborers, most of them live in one-roomed houses. Nevertheless, Irula plantation laborers inhabiting the Nilgiri slopes still occupy bipartite houses with the sacred cooking area formally separated (typically not with a wall but with a shallow earthen platform) from the living and sleeping areas. The Kasaba to the north of the Nilgiri massif, who herd cattle for others (Badagas included), occupy tripartite structures with living quarters for humans to one side of a room with an open front, and a calf room to the other side. The open front of the center room facilitates the watching of the enclosed cattle at night, and it is most useful when predators or wild elephants come near. While traditional Irula houses are made of wattle and daub, with thatched roofs (or in some instances banana sheaths for walling and roofing), more Irula are living in houses with walls of stone or brick and roofs with tiles, especially if the government has provided financial assistance.

Economy

Subsistence and Commercial Activities. The earliest reports indicate that the hoe-using Irula of the eastern Nilgiri slopes obtained one crop of millet in a year from shifted plots, involving a growing period that coincided with the westerly monsoon. They then depended upon garden produce, gathered edibles, and hunting for survival once the harvested grain had been consumed. That these Irula were probably named after a yam species is indicative of how important yams were to them when they turned to gathering. Several wild yam species were available. Irula are still well known for the gathering and supply of honey to their neighbors. Despite sculptured representations of bows and arrows in some Nilgiri dolmens at higher elevation, it is noteworthy that the Irula seem always to have used nets and spears when they hunted. Our record of at least eighty species of plants growing in Irula gardens testifies to the past and continuing significance of gardens to all the Irula. That at least twenty-five of the identified plants had a New World origin also proves the willingness of the Irula to incorporate introduced species into their economy. The continued cultivation of finger millet (_Eleusine corocana_), Italian millet (_Setaria italica_), and little millet (_Panicum sumatrense_) and no dry rice by the Irula on the higher slopes may in itself represent a Neolithic survival, because the cultivation of dry rice has in Southeast Asia widely replaced the earlier cultivation of the Italian and little millets from China. The Irula still commonly grow these two species of millet together and then harvest the Italian millet when the

little millet is far from maturation. Very small sickles are used for harvesting individual grain heads. When finger millet (grown apart from the other two) is to be harvested, the plants are visited periodically to permit the removal of grain as it ripens. Another economic pursuit that may have continued from Neolithic times, during which cattle rearing was widespread in southern India, is the manner by which lowland Irula in forested areas keep cattle for their neighbors (Kuruvas included). The few Irula who still manage to practice shifting agriculture set fire in April or May to the vegetation they have cut, so the cultivation of millet will then take place during the westerly monsoon. The barnyard millet (_Echinochloa_), bullrush millet (_Pennisetum_), common millet (_Panicum miliaceum_) and sorghum millet (_Sorghum_), all of the lowland, renowned for their drought resistance, and thus typically grown on dry fields, are cultivated with the aid of plows and mainly in the season of the westerly monsoon. Now with the cooperation of the Forest Department, the Irula gather forest produce (including medicinal plants) for sale. Since most Irula of the Nilgiri slopes currently work as plantation laborers, plantation managements starting with those in the time of the British Raj had to provide periodic release time for those Irula who needed to perform their own agricultural chores. The Gandhian quest to improve the lives of members of the Scheduled Tribes is demonstrated by the manner in which the government has enabled Irula of the eastern Nilgiri slopes to establish coffee and tea gardens of their own, and at Kunjappanai the Silk Board of the government of Tamil Nadu is now providing financial assistance to enable silkworm farming among the Irula. From 1974 the government gave small plots to Irula on the eastern slopes, and the Cooperative Land Development Bank (an agency of the Tamil Nadu government) at the nearest town (Kotagiri) was by 1979 helping to finance the growing of coffee and tea in nurseries, so that the Irula could have their own commercialized gardens. While a few Irula who wisely managed their granted lands and loans prospered, many did not manage their endeavors well and the return payment on loans at a low rate was eventually ended in many instances by a special bill passed in Madras by the Tamil Nadu government. It is primarily the cooperation of the government, with the Forest Department of Tamil Nadu playing an important role, that has enabled more lowland Irula to become involved in the annual cultivation of irrigated rice. Hallimoyar, Kallampalayam, and Thengumarahada (with its Cooperative Society), in which the Irula live close to the members of several castes, have irrigation networks. One rice crop started in March is harvested in June, and the second crop started in July is ready in December. In 1978 a newly constructed rice mill became operational at Thengumarahada. Irula living to the south of the Nilgiri massif are also involved in wet rice cultivation. There, apart from irrigation water from surface flow (Coonoor River is the most important), subsurface water is now being obtained with electric pumps. The main rice crop is grown from June into January or February, and the growing of short-maturation rice enables the production of a second crop from February to May. As lowland population increases, the majority of the lowland Irula (who own no land) are increasingly beset by the problem of obtaining work wherever possible. Some are employed in the irrigated areca groves near Mettupalaiyam, reputed to form the largest human-made forest of its kind in the world. Post–World War II dam projects, including that of Bhavani Sagar, created temporary work for others. Many Irula have entered the general job market in the Coimbatore-Mettupalaiyam-Ootacamund region and are employed in a wide array of jobs in the public and private sectors. Such jobs include positions in air force and army camps, nationalized banks, the income tax office, the Post and Telegraph Department, the Railway Department, the Sugarcane Breeding Institute and Pankaja Mill, both in Coimbatore (the only mill that employs Irulas, out of twenty surveyed), the cordite factory at Aruvankadu, and the Hindustan Photo-Film industry near Ootacamund. The Irula have cattle, chickens, dogs, goats, and sheep, and a few of them may keep buffalo, pigeons, or pigs. Pigs, dogs, and chickens serve as scavengers in some lowland hamlets. Jungle fowl, Nilgiri langurs, parrots, peacocks, quail, and assorted squirrels appear to be the most commonly tamed wild creatures.

Industrial Arts. The Irula make their own drums and wind instruments for their musical enjoyment. The Kota of the upper Nilgiris generally no longer supply music as they once traditionally did, so the Irula are now frequently employed as musicians at Badaga and Toda funerals.

Trade. A kind of bartering trade has persisted for generations between the Kina·ṛ Kota of the upper Nilgiris and the nearby Irula. The Kota obtain honey, brooms, winnowers and baskets made of bamboo and banana sheath strips, punk used to light fires (Kota priests may not use matches to light fires) and resin incense from the Irula in return for iron field and garden implements made by Kota blacksmiths.

Division of Labor. Women still perform all the household-related tasks. While males perform those agricultural tasks requiring more strength, such as plowing or hoeing the earth in preparation for the sowing of grain, women also perform many agricultural tasks. Males typically do the sowing, and women often do the most boring of tasks such as weeding, reaping, and the carrying of loads of harvested garden produce or grain. Both males and females are hired for a host of laboring tasks. Because infant care thus becomes a problem, it is not unusual for women to take their infants to workplaces. Older children not attending school are often taken care of by the elderly in extended families.

Land Tenure. Members of the Thengumarahada Cooperative Society cultivate allotted amounts of land. A few of the Irula own title to land, sometimes in the form of *patta* (land ownership) documents. Gaudas and Chettiars in particular have taken over Irula land through loan manipulation, and some thereby now also have Irulas working for them. Many Irula lease land from landowners.

Kinship

Kin Groups and Descent. The Irula form an endogamous caste with twelve exogamous patriclans (in Sanskrit *gotras*, in Tamil *kulams*)—Devanan (or Thevanan or Devala), Kalkatti, Koduvan (or Kodugar), Kuppan (or Koppilingam), Kurunagan, Ollaga, Peratha, Porigan, Pungan (or Poongkaru), Samban (or Chamban), Uppigan (or Uppali), and Vellagai (or Vellai)—and a clan represented by the *thudai* tree (*Ilex denticulata*). Nevertheless, because members of a patriclan cannot marry members in one or more "brother" patriclans, there are exogamous patriclan units among the Irula.

The overall size of these units varies from one area to another. Thus, the Irula kinship system is similar to the one that dominates in southern India. In addition, the Irula have a system whereby each patriclan is affiliated with a friendship patriclan whose members help when an event, typically a rite of passage, requires cooperative effort. The ideal marriage among the Irula is of a female with her father's sister's son (i.e., a male with the mother's brother's daughter). Also in conformity with the acceptable Dravidian norm, an Irula male should not marry the mother's sister's daughter. An Irula male may also marry his elder or younger sister's daughter, but this practice exhibits a departure from the Dravidian system, in which a male cannot marry his younger sister's daughter (the Irula do not differentiate between the two sisters).

Kinship Terminology. All near relatives are spoken of in terms of being older or younger in age than the person concerned, and generation thus plays a secondary role.

Marriage and Family

Marriage. Monogamous marriage is the rule, but a few polygamous marriages occur. Polyandry is extremely rare. Sororate and levirate remarriages are not the norm. By choice and consent, however, Irula men may occasionally marry sisters of their deceased wives. The old traditional marriage, started by parents negotiating and the young man then going to the young woman's village with a load of firewood to live with her on a trial basis for a few days, has almost disappeared. Nowadays the young man's parents go to the prospective bride's house, after they are certain that she is in a marriageable clan. The bride-price, now usually the standardized amount of Rs 101 and 50 paisa, is paid in the presence of elders from both sides and the facilitator (*jatthi*). Then the date for the marriage is jointly agreed to. The groom's sister will serve as the bridesmaid, and the bride's brother will serve as the best man. The bride is brought by her relatives and the groom's party to the groom's house on the wedding day. In the house or within a temporary shelter (*pandal*) erected near the house, the groom in the most pertinent act of the marriage ceremony and in conformity with the widespread practice in southern India, ties a necklace (*tali*, provided by his maternal uncle) around the bride's neck. A feast is then provided by the groom's people. Millet would in past times have been served, but it is now fashionable to serve rice with curry. The groom afterward bows to the feet of guests to receive their blessing and is followed in this act by his wife. Along with their blessing, the guests give money (typically Rs 1, 2, or 5) to the couple. All later go to the bride's house, and there is then another feast (again, with rice and curry), which runs into the night. All feasting is accompanied by the dancing of males and females (usually in separate groups but in one circle). The consumption of intoxicating beverages is also liable to take place. The establishment of a separate patrilocal household after marriage is the norm. Conforming with the widespread practice in southern India, the wife usually returns to her paternal home in her seventh month of pregnancy and remains there until after her infant is delivered. While a woman's inability to bear a child is not considered grounds for divorce, an Irula man may marry another woman if his first wife cannot conceive. He then is married to both women. The usual grounds for divorce are unfaithfulness or a husband's lack of provision for his wife. When a marriage is troubled, a member of the Samban patriclan will try to keep it intact, or a member of the Koduvan patriclan will help if a member of the Samban clan is involved. If three attempts at reconciliation do not work, a divorce is granted. The village headman and a group of males forming a council (_panchayat_) simply issue their consent for divorce. The bride-price and any gift jewelry must be returned to the husband's family. Then the husband's mother or husband's brother's wife smears some castor oil backward from the forehead of the wife along the part of her hair. After the tali is removed from her and returned to the husband, they are divorced. The children from the marriage will remain with the father.

Domestic Unit. The typical family whose members are served food from the same hearth averages four to five people, but it may reach a size of seven to nine people. Because the institution of the extended family still remains vital, those relatives beyond the nuclear family may assume residence, especially if they are left destitute in infancy or old age. If the wife dies, it is the responsibility of the husband to care for the children. He may remarry. While the constitution of India now enables a woman to remarry if her husband dies, an Irula widow seldom will. The brothers of a deceased husband are expected to care for the widow. The brothers of the widow may also care for her, if those of her deceased husband give their consent.

Inheritance. It is unfortunate that Irula tribal pattas are not more restricted by the government. Quite apart from their being taken over by unscrupulous outsiders, they also are divided equally among the sons upon the father's death. Purchased land units are similarly divided among the male descendants.

Socialization. Much of the infant and child rearing is done by adult females, including those among the elderly extended family members who might be present. Older siblings of both sexes play an important role in the care of their younger brothers and sisters. Government has now provided day and residential schools for the formal training of Irula children, and the related socialization process provides the main means for introducing the Irula into broader civilization. Unfortunately, most Irula have thus far abandoned the formal educational institutions in the lower stages.

Sociopolitical Organization

Social Organization. In the tribal manner, the Irula maintain an open and free society. Each hamlet or village has a headman (_gaundan_ or _muppan_) whose role is not to control from above but to help in the solving of problems and to act as a mediator among his people and between them and government officials or non-Irula neighbors. Following the ancient Indian tradition of the panchayat (the hamlet or village council), the headman can call a varying group of males together to help him. As Samban patriclan members (or Koduvan patriclan members, if a Samban person is involved) traditionally have acted as mediators for the Irula, a headman can also turn to one of them for counsel. There is also a local go-between person (_bandari_) who assists the headman. Any decision of a council is considered to be binding (_kattu manam_) on an individual or family. Each friendship patriclan in a hamlet or village is headed by a facilitator (_jatti_) who plays the vital role of organizing any cooperative effort. A local priest (_pujari_) is also present to take care of religious matters. Lastly, a Kurumba helps during ceremonial occasions. South of the Nilgiri massif, such an individual (a Palu Kurumba) also serves to protect the Irula from Muduga sorcery.

Political Organization. In the period of the British Raj, the lowest political division was a village unit with one or more villages and several hamlets. Along with several appointed officials, such as the _maniagar_ who was the representative to the Crown and the _tahsildar_ who kept the land records (and therefore the basis for taxation), there was a formal group of males who formed the village panchayat. The members of the panchayat then managed the affairs of the village. After independence, the village units were kept and the panchayat was envisioned as the grass-roots organization that would guarantee representation by the people. Its members were to be elected. Unfortunately, primarily because the Irula are so lacking in education, they are poorly represented in the larger panchayats. Also envisioned in the Indian constitution was the establishment of land units called blocks, each with a block development officer, in which economic development would be promoted with governmental assistance. Although some Irula—lowland Irula in particular—have benefited, including those living in Hallimoyar, Kallampalayam, and Thengumarahada, the general lack of Irula representation among block development officers has too frequently precluded Irula from obtaining the type of aid that would enhance them economically.

Social Control. The Irula as tribals place a premium upon the avoidance of conflict. They are in many ways rigidly controlled by their caste and patriclan standing. The possibility of being made an outcaste for unacceptable behavior normally causes members to abide by the mores. Even though they may have few actual contacts with officialdom, the Irula are subject to all the rules and regulations of the central and state governments.

Conflict. The Irula, beset by circumstances forcing change upon them from the outside world, are liable to come into conflict with their neighbors. Our best retrospective example of this is offered by the hamlet of Koppayur, on an eastern slope of the Nilgiris. The British managers on the nearby Kilkotagiri tea estate enabled the Irula to continue living at Koppayur and to cultivate the adjacent land. Irula worked on the estate and were considered to be dependable laborers who periodically needed time off for their own agricultural pursuits. Even after independence, the continued British management enabled the Irula at Koppayur to live in the same way until at least 1963. By 1978 the British had left. Because the Irula and their fields at Koppayur then occupied land in forest reserve, they began to be evicted. (By contrast, in the early 1800s, the Irula had usufruct use of all the surrounding land.) They were supposed to occupy a steep slope not far away. Under Indian management at the Kilkotagiri tea estate, coffee had already been planted right up to the Irula hamlet and over land once used by the Irula for the cultivation of millet. Originally, the dismal prospect of the move was alleviated by some possibility of government aid enabling 20.5 hectares of land to be opened to coffee and tea gardening near the new hamlet, but by 1988 this brighter prospect for the Irula had long since been extinguished. There were then fifteen Irula families living in the limited space (about ¼ hectare) covered by the new hamlet. The original hamlet, however, still had seven occupied houses. The only landowners are headmen Balan (1.6 hectares) and Masanan (3.6 hectares). Garden jackfruit and bananas are the main produce. The nearby ancestral temple, the koppa manai after which Koppayur is named, no longer has a roof, and the burial ground is choked by weeds. In that the estate management now restricts the access of the Irula to their hamlet, there is even more cause for ill will. The management considers the Irula to be a menace, because they stand accused of stealing coffee and selling it.

Religion and Expressive Culture

Religious Beliefs. The Irula are pantheists who make provision for the presence of spirits in humans and objects. In addition, a recurrent theme in their religious belief is the significance of the male and female principles as symbols of the ongoing creative process. It is rare for an Indian tribal people to be Vaishnavites, but the Irula, like the Beda of Karnataka, are ostensibly worshipers of Vishnu. They have thus gained fame for their temple dedicated to Ranga (also known as Vishnu) on the top of Rangaswami Betta. This is a peak that crowns the eastern Nilgiri slopes and that can be seen from many Irula hamlets and villages. In addition, the Irula seem to have a propensity for the worship of the god Muneshwar and the goddess Mari, both of whom are considered to be Hindu deities. Curiously, however, the Irula of Kallampalayam store their gilt image of Mari and the accompanying ritual paraphernalia in a rock shelter close by. They do this because they believe that the objects are too sacred to store in any structure made by humans. This practice perhaps may be prompted by a need to make Mari a part of the universal spirit that is everywhere. By dint of the accompanying bloody sacrifice, Mari is also related to earth and the fertility of plants springing from it. As Mari is the common goddess of smallpox in Tamil Nadu, the Irula have also worshiped her in that capacity. Like their Hindu neighbors, the Irula now watch nighttime performances of excerpts from the *Mahabharata* or the *Ramayana* acted into the early hours of the morning. There are benign and protective ancestral patriclan spirits and family ancestral spirits that may be petitioned for assistance; such a petition is called a *toga*. There are also roaming evil spirits (*pe*), and it is possible for one to possess a human. A virgin female demon (*kannipe*) must be treated with great care by any priest, and near Garkiyur there is a temple into which an Irula priest entices a kannipe for a month's stay (October to November) each year. She is enticed to come with a welcome song on one day, vegetarian food offering on another, and the sacrificial offering of meat from a sambar (an Asian deer) that must be hunted down on the third day. Because the Irula visit the temples of their Hindu neighbors, go on pilgrimages to Sabarimala in Kerala, and worship deities in the same manner as the Hindus, there is clear evidence that the Irula participate in polytheistic Hinduism.

Religious Practitioners. The Kalkatti (stone-offering) patriclan traditionally supplies priests, and the priests who serve on Rangaswami Betta come from a family that resides in Kallampalayam. The fact that a tribal Irula serves as priest to Ranga, which is a seeming departure from orthodoxy, is legitimized by a folktale in which an officiating Iyengar Brahman priest is convinced that an Irula should serve instead. The deity images and the ritual paraphernalia used in the recently constructed temple on Rangaswami Betta reveal a mixture of Shaivite and Vaishnavite imagery and symbolism. It thus seems probable that the officiating Irula priest is simultaneously and dualistically catering to Ranga and Krishna worship for Hindus and male principle worship for Irulas. The lowland Ranga temple at Karamadai offers interesting comparisons. In a folktale somewhat similar to one told about a stone associated with Ranga at Rangaswami Betta, a cow drops her milk on a stone in an anthill. When the cowherd discovers what is happening, he in a rage strikes the stone with a knife. He is amazed when blood comes from the stone. In a dream shortly thereafter, the god Ranga appears and asks to be worshiped with the stone as an image at the same place. The stone, a *linga*, became the centerpiece of worship in the temple that was eventually built on the site. But one of the most fascinating aspects of this temple is a belief that officiating Irula priests there were eventually replaced, ironically, by Iyengar Brahman priests.

Ceremonies. In January the Mattu Pongal festival (one of the main Hindu festivals held in Tamil Nadu), paying special homage to cows, is generally observed by the Irula. They also attend the annual festival at Karamadai, near Coimbatore, which takes place in the Tamil month of Masi (March–April). The annual one-week festival honoring Mari at Kallampalaiyam, with chicken, goat, and sheep sacrifices, climaxes on the full moon day of the Tamil month of Adi, on or close to 15 August. An Irula priest, wearing the "thread of the twice-born" (a loop of sacred thread hung over the right shoulder), officiates on the top of Rangaswami Betta on every Saturday for two months starting in mid-August. Shortly before the start of this period, the image of Ranga is carried between the Irula settlements and is the focus of worship at each nighttime halting place.

Arts. Irula women are tattooed and enjoy wearing jewelry, including earrings, nose rings and toe rings. Although the Irula do some doodlings on the walls of their houses, for example, there is a lack of any formal decorative art among them. They do however have a distinctive dance form called *arakkole atam*.

Medicine. Irula hamlets have a few members with an intricate knowledge of the medicinal values of plant species, so lowlanders in particular seek the counsel of Irula herbalists. Irula living near the Marudamalai temple, near Coimbatore, sell herbal cures to visiting Hindu pilgrims. A hospital founded by the late Dr. S. Narasimhan (who also founded the Adivasi Welfare Association) at Karikkiyur, the nearby dispensary at Kunjappanai, and a field hospital at Arayur on the Nilgiri massif have played a significant role in meeting the medical needs of the Irula. The Irula are also increasingly taking advantage of the widespread medical facilities provided by the government, including a mobile medical unit (first associated with the famous Toda nurse Evam Piljain). There is a dispensary with a midwife at Thengumarahada.

Death and Afterlife. When a death occurs, the relatives are informed by a Kurumba. Upon arriving at the place of the deceased, the heads of males are shaved by the jatti. Both males and females dance to music and about the cot upon which the deceased rests. After all those who should attend have arrived, the corpse is carried to the burial ground. Members of the deceased's brother-in-law's patriclan bear the prime responsibility for digging the grave, but the Kurumba present also assists. When all is ready, the body is placed in the grave so that it faces toward the north. The local Irula priest (pujari) then gazes at a lamp and goes into a trance. A member of the bereaved family asks him if the death was natural or the result of sorcery. If natural, the grave is filled in right away. If sorcery was the cause of death, elaborate ritual used to be performed; today, however, the priest says a simple and hasty prayer to ease any torment of the spirit and to enable it to depart peaceably. All the mourners then leave. A highlight in the ending of the seven days of ritual pollution among the close relatives of the deceased is the distribution of new clothing by the Kurumba to these relatives. As soon as possible after the funeral, preferably within a month, a stone (often waterworn and from a stream bed, but sometimes sculpted by non-Irulas) is placed in the ancestral temple to give the deceased a place to stay. Because of the belief that, without a stone, the spirit of the deceased wanders around and may become troublesome if it does so for too long, the time issue is understandable. After pouring a little oil on the stone as part of a prayer ritual and leaving food and drink for the spirit of the departed, the relatives leave. Once a year, all those who had a relative who died within the year participate in a final ceremony. Each family purchases a new cloth and rice gruel is prepared. At the nearby river or stream, the gruel is poured over the cloths, which are then set adrift. In addition to honoring the spirits of those who died within the year, the Irula thereby honor all the ancestral spirits of the related patriclans. After group feasting, dancing continues into the night.

See also Badaga; Kota; Kurumbas

Bibliography

Buchanan, Francis (later, Buchanan-Hamilton) (1807). *A Journey from Madras through the Countries of Mysore, Canara, and Malabar.* Vol. 2. London: W. Bulmer & Co.

Jebadhas, A. William, and William A. Noble (1989). "The Irulas." In *Blue Mountains: The Ethnography and Biogeography of a South Indian Region,* edited by Paul Edward Hockings, 281–303. New Delhi: Oxford University Press.

Nambiar, P. K., and T. B. Bharathi (1965). *Census of India, 1961.* Vol. 9, *Madras,* pt. 6. Village Survey Monographs, no. 20, *Hallimoyar.* Delhi: Manager of Publications, Government of India.

Nambiar, P. K., and T. B. Bharathi (1966). *Census of India, 1961.* Vol. 9, *Madras,* pt. 6. Village Survey Monographs, no. 23, *Nellithorai.* Delhi: Manager of Publications.

Zvelebil, Kamil V. (1973–1982). *The Irula Language.* 3 vols. Wiesbaden: Otto Harrassowitz.

Zvelebil, Kamil V. (1988). *The Irulas of the Blue Mountains.* Foreign and Comparative Studies/South Asian Series, no. 13. Syracuse, N.Y.: Maxwell School of Citizenship and Public Affairs, Syracuse University.

WILLIAM A. NOBLE AND A. WILLIAM JEBADHAS

Jain

ETHNONYMS: none

Possibly the oldest ascetic religious tradition on Earth, Jainism is followed today by about 3.5 million people, especially in Rajasthan, Madhya Pradesh, Gujarat, Maharashtra, and Karnataka. Along with Buddhism, Jainism was one of several renunciatory movements—the Sramana schools—that grew up in modern-day Bihar and southern Nepal in the sixth century B.C. The other Sramana movements (including Buddhism) gradually died out in India, leaving Jainism as the only one with an unbroken succession of Indian followers down to the present day. The Sramana schools, including Jainism, reacted against the contemporary form of Hinduism (known as Brahmanism) and posited that worldly life is inherently unhappy—an endless cycle of death and rebirth—and that liberation from it is achieved not through sacrifices or propitiating the gods but through inner meditation and discipline. Thus while Jains in India today share many social practices with their Hindu neighbors (indeed, several castes have both Hindu and Jain members), their religious tradition is in many ways philosophically closer to Buddhism, though distinctly more rigid in its asceticism than Buddhism has been.

The "founder" of Jainism is taken by modern scholars to be Mahavira ("great hero"), otherwise known as Vardhamana (c. 599–527 B.C.); but there is evidence that Jain practices were in existence for some time before him. The Jain texts speak of a succession of prophets (*tirthankaras*) stretching back into mythological time, of whom Mahavira was the twenty-fourth and last. The tirthankaras are distinguished by the fact that they are thought to have achieved liberation of their souls through meditation and austerities and then preached the message of salvation before finally leaving their mortal bodies. Jains today worship all twenty-four tirthankaras, not in the sense of asking them for boons or favors, but in memory of the path they taught. One of the most popular of the Jain texts is the *Kalpa Sutra,* at least part of which is canonical and may date back to the fourth century B.C., and which describes, among other things, the lives of all twenty-four tirthankaras.

The essential principle of Jain philosophy is that all living things, even the tiniest insects, have an immortal soul (*jiva*), which continues to be reincarnated as it is bound and constrained by karma—a form of matter that is attracted to the soul through good and bad desires in this and in past lives. Thus to free the soul one must perform austerities to strip away the karma-matter and cultivate in oneself a detachment or desirelessness that will not attract further karma. The principle means to this end is the practice of *ahimsa,* the lack of desire to cause harm to any living thing. From this principle arises the most characteristic features of Jain life: insistence on a strict vegetarian diet, filtering drinking water, running animal shelters and hospitals, never lying or causing hurt to others, temporarily or permanently wearing a gauze mask to prevent insects from entering the body, and sweeping the ground in front of one's every step.

For some Jains, their devotion to ahimsa leads them to be ordained as monks and nuns who live the life of wandering ascetics. Most Jains today, however, are laity, living worldly lives but seeking to adhere to the principle of ahimsa in as many ways as possible. The laity support the wandering ascetics, providing them with food and shelter; the ascetics in turn provide religious and moral guidance. Lay Jains include some of India's leading industrialists, jewelers, and bankers, concentrated particularly in the cities of Bombay, Ahmedabad, and Delhi. Because so many are businesspeople, the Jains are one of the few religious groups (along with the Parsis and Jews) who are more numerous in cities than in rural areas. Throughout western India Jains are to be found in every urban center, however small, working as merchants, traders, wholesalers, and moneylenders.

As so often happens in religious sects, the Jains are no strangers to schism. The most basic and widely known split within their community of believers, dating back to the fourth century B.C., separates the "sky-clad" (Digambaras) from the "white-clad" (Svetambaras); the names refer to the fact that the highest order of Digambara monks go naked to announce their complete indifference to their bodies, while Svetambara monks and nuns always wear simple white clothing. These two sects differ in their attitudes toward scripture, their views of the universe, and their attitudes toward women (the Digambaras believe that no woman has ever achieved liberation). Another major sectarian division, found particularly among the Svetambaras and dating back to fifteenth-century Gujarat, rejects all forms of idolatry. While *murti-pujaka* (idol-worshiping) lay and ascetic Svetambaras build and visit temples in which idols of the tirthankaras are installed, the Svetambara Sthanakavasi sect—like certain Protestant Christian sects—holds that such forms of worship may mislead the believer into thinking that idols, famous temples, and the like are sources of some mysterious power. Instead lay and ascetic Sthanakavasis prefer to meditate in bare halls.

Today, lay Jains—mostly of Gujarati origin—are to be found in east Africa, Great Britain, and North America, where they have migrated over the last century in search of business and trading opportunities. Temples have been established in several of these countries and the Jains are making themselves felt as a distinctive presence within the wider South Asian migrant community overseas.

See also Bania

Bibliography

Banks, Marcus (1992). *Organizing Jainism in India and England*. London: Oxford University Press.

Carrithers, Michael, and Caroline Humphrey, eds. (1991). *The Assembly of Listeners: Jains in Society*. Cambridge: Cambridge University Press.

Dundas, Paul (1992). *The Jains*. London: Routledge.

Fischer, Eberhard, and Jyotindra Jain (1977). *Art and Rituals: 2,500 Years of Jainism in India*. Delhi: Sterling Publishers Private Ltd.

Jaini, Padmanabh S. (1979). *The Jaina Path of Purification*. Berkeley: University of California Press.

Mathias, Marie-Claude (1985). *Délivrance et convivialité: Le système culinaire des Jaina*. Paris: Éditions de la Maison des Sciences de l'Homme.

Pande, G. C., ed. (1978). *Sramana Tradition: Its Contribution to Indian Culture*. Ahmedabad: L. D. Institute of Indology.

Sangave, Vilas A. (1959). *Jaina Community: A Social Survey*. Reprint. 1980. Bombay: Popular Book Depot

Vinayasagar, Mahopadhyaya, and Mukund Lath, eds. and trans. (1977). *Kalpa Sutra*. Jaipur: D. R. Mehta, Prakrit Bharati.

MARCUS BANKS

Jat

ETHNONYMS: Jāṭ, Jaṭ

Orientation

Identification and Location.   Primarily endogamous communities calling themselves and known as Jat live predominantly in large parts of northern and northwestern India and in southern and eastern Pakistan, as sedentary farmers and/or mobile pastoralists. In certain areas they tend to call themselves Baluch, Pathan, or Rajput, rather than Jat. Most of these communities are integrated as a caste into the locally prevalent caste system. In the past three decades increasing population pressure on land has led to large-scale emigration of the peasant Jat, especially from India, to North America, the United Kingdom, Malaysia, and more recently the Middle East. Some maintain that the sedentary farming Jat and the nomadic pastoral Jat are of entirely different origins; others believe that the two groups are of the same stock but that they developed different life-styles over the centuries. Neither the farmers nor the pastoralists are, however, to be confused with other distinct communities of peripatetic peddlers, artisans, and entertainers designated in Afghanistan by the blanket terms "Jat" or Jaṭ; the latter terms are considered pejorative, and they are rejected as ethnonyms by these peripatetic communities. In Pakistan also, among the Baluchi- and Pashto-speaking populations, the terms were, and to a certain extent still are, used to indicate contempt and lower social status.

Demography.   No reliable figures are available for recent years. In 1931 the population of all sedentary and farming Jat was estimated at 8,377,819; in the early 1960s 8,000,000 was the estimate for Pakistan alone. Today the entire Jat population consists of several million more than that.

Linguistic Affiliation.   All Jat speak languages and dialects that are closely connected with other locally spoken languages of the Indo-Iranian Group. Three alphabets are used, depending primarily on religion but partly on locality: the Arabic-derived Urdu one is used by Muslims, while Sikhs and Hindus use the Gurmukhi (Punjabi) and the Devanagari (Hindi) scripts, respectively.

History and Cultural Relations

Little is known about the early history of the Jat, although several theories were advanced by various scholars over the last 100 years. While some authors argue that they are descendants of the first Indo-Aryans, others suggest that they are of Indo-Scythian stock and entered India toward the beginning of the Christian era. These authors also point to some cultural similarities between the Jat and certain other major communities of the area, such as the Gujar, the Ahir, and the Rajput, about whose origins similar theories have been suggested. In fact, among both Muslims and Sikhs the Jat and the Rajput castes enjoy almost equal status—partly because of the basic egalitarian ideology enjoined by both religions, but mainly because of the similar political and economic power held by both communities. Also Hindu Jat consider the Gujar and Ahir as allied castes; except for the rule of caste endogamy, there are no caste restrictions between these three communities. In other scholarly debates about the origins of the Jat, attempts have been made to identify them with the *Jarttikā*, referred to in the Hindu epic the *Mahābhārata*. Some still maintain that the people Arab historians referred to as the *Zutt*, and who were taken as prisoners in the eighth century from Sindh in present-day southern Pakistan to southern Iraq, were actually buffalo-herding Jat, or were at least known as such in their place of origin. In the seventeenth century a (Hindu) kingdom was established in the area of Bharatpur and Dholpur (Rajasthan) in northern India; it was the outcome of many centuries of rebellion against the Mogul Empire, and it lasted till 1826, when it was defeated by the forces of the British East India Company. Farther north, in the Punjab, in the early years of the eighteenth century, Jat (mainly Sikh) organized peasant uprisings against the predominantly Muslim landed gentry; subsequently, with the invasion of the area—first by the Persian King Nadir Shah and then by the Afghan Ahmad Shah Abdali—they controlled a major part of the area through close-knit bands of armed marauders operating under the leadership of the landowning chiefs of well-defined territories. Because of their martial traditions, the Jat, together with certain other communities, were classified by British administrators of imperial India as a "martial race," and this term had certain long-lasting effects. One was their large-scale recruitment into the British-Indian army, and to this day a very large number of Jat are soldiers in the Indian army. Many Sikh Jat in the Indian part of Punjab are involved in the current movement for the creation of an autonomous Khalistan.

Settlements

The Jat as a whole are predominantly rural. Depending on whether they are sedentary or nomadic, the Jat of various regions live in permanent villages or temporary camps. Over the last 200 years there has been increasing sedentarization of nomadic Jat; this trend began in the last decades of the eighteenth century when many pastoralists settled in the central Punjab under the auspices of Sikh rule there, and it continued over a very large area with the expansion of irrigation in British imperial times. With the consequent expansion of cultivation all these pastoralists are facing increasing difficulties in finding grazing lands for their herds. The buffalo breeders face the maximum difficulties in this respect, since their ani-

mals need to be grazed in areas with plentiful water, and these are precisely the areas in which agriculture has expanded most. They still live in the moist region of the Indus Delta, but many have had to settle permanently. Formerly the camel breeders migrated over larger areas, but increasingly they are restricted to the delta region of the Indus River, the desert areas of the Thar and the Thal, and the semideserts stretching west of the Indus to Makran and Baluchistan. The camel drivers were, at least a few decades ago, fairly widespread in most parts of Sindh and the western Punjab, and Kachchh. While in some less densely populated areas each Jat clan has a compact geographic area of its own, elsewhere several clans may inhabit the same village. Most Jat peasants live in flat-roofed houses made of baked or unbaked bricks in large compact villages, with few open spaces within the inhabited area; all villages have cattle sheds, village commons, and wells or ponds. Depending on the region and the precise community, Jat nomadic pastoralists use a variety of huts, mostly made of reed mats and wood, that are fairly easy to dismantle. The reed mats are woven by the women.

Economy

Subsistence and Commercial Activities. The mainstay of sedentary Jat economy is and has always been agriculture, and there are several proverbs and sayings in local languages that emphasize both the skill and industry of the Jat peasant, as well as the traditional attachment of this community to the soil. Cereals such as wheat, maize, and types of millet, as well as pulses and the cash crop sugarcane, are grown by Jat cultivators; in certain areas they increasingly grow fruits and vegetables also. In most areas of India where the Jat farmers live cultivation is now fairly mechanized, but in some areas the plow is drawn by oxen and harvesting is done by hand. Most crops are grown both for subsistence and for commerce. In addition to land the peasant Jat own water buffalo and cows for milk; male buffalo are often used for carrying loads. Milk is for household consumption and is not generally sold. The cattle are grazed on the village commons. The pastoral Jat consist of three distinct groups of water buffalo breeders, camel breeders, and camel drivers (often known as Mir-Jat, rather than simply Jat). The buffalo breeders sell their herd animals for slaughter or as draft animals, especially for the Persian wheel; they also sell excess butterfat but never sell milk. The camel breeders do sell milk, but their main income is from the sale of young male camels, which are much in demand for purposes of transport. The camel drivers hire themselves out with their trained animals, either working for a fee or for a share of the profit. In many areas where former pastureland has come under the plow, due to irrigation facilities, they are obliged to ask local farmers for the rights to graze their herds on their lands; in return they often have to give their labor during the harvest. The women of the pastoral Jat of the north also sell mats and ropes made from the leaves of dwarf palms. The army has been a major source of income for the peasant Jat since the late nineteenth century, and in recent decades many Sikh Jat are in the motorized transport business. Remittances from Jat immigrants in North America and elsewhere also contribute much to the income of a very large proportion of the population.

Industrial Arts and Division of Labor. Among the agricultural Jat, traditionally only the men work in the fields, while the women are entirely responsible for the household. In recent times more prosperous families hire non-Jat, primarily landless labor from other regions, as farmhands, partly as full-time workers but especially as part-time workers in peak seasons. Among the buffalo-breeding nomads, the men graze and milk their animals, and they sell these animals and their butterfat. Their women prepare milk products and do all the housework—cooking, cleaning, fetching water and fuel, rearing the children, sewing and embroidering all textiles for household use, and weaving the reed mats for their huts. Among the camel breeders all work connected with the animals is carried out by the men—grazing the herds, milking, shearing, spinning and weaving the camel's wool into coarse blankets and bags, and selling animals. Household work is done by the women, and encompasses the same tasks as among the buffalo breeders. No food products are made from camel's milk, and in the months when the milk is plentiful enough to provide sole subsistence, little or no cooking is done.

Land Tenure. The landowners of a village stand collectively for the entire land of the village, but within the village each individual head of household has discrete rights within the various lineage segments. Generally, all landowners in a village are descended from a common ancestor who founded the village; his ownership of all the village lands is never forgotten, and by this token all individuated rights are successive restrictions of more general rights, applicable at all levels of genealogical segmentation. Common land is that which has not been brought under cultivation.

Kinship, Marriage, and Family

Kin Groups and Descent. All Jat are divided into several large, usually dispersed clans, whose localized segments are often geographically compact, but among peasants they are sometimes equally dispersed, due to the population pressure on land. Most clans are de facto maximal lineages, which are further segmented; among Jat peasants this segmentation takes place at four broad levels. The minimal lineage is composed of a group of households, which had formed a single household two or three generations previously; they may still share a common courtyard and have joint rights to a well.

Marriage. While among Muslim Jat the practice of exchange marriage takes place at various levels of lineage organization, among Hindu and Sikh Jat no such exchange marriages are allowed, and the rule of exogamy is such that a man may not marry a woman who has any of her four grandparental clans in common with his. Polygyny is allowed though not common, and the custom of adelphic polyandry, or the sexual access by an unmarried man to his brother's wife—which was often practiced by at least non-Muslim peasant Jat, in order to prevent further fragmentation of land—has declined in recent decades. Among all Jat, widow remarriage is permitted; either levirate is required or a widow is not allowed to remarry outside the maximal lineage, especially when she has children by her late husband. The practice of female infanticide, also known among the peasants, has dropped sharply. A woman's relationship with her husband's kin is organized according to a basic pattern of avoidance with seniors and of joking with those younger than the husband. Brothers share a common duty toward their sisters and their children.

Domestic Unit. Most Jat peasant households consist of lineal joint families, with the parents and one married son; many units are nuclear and some are collateral-joint, with two married brothers and their offspring living together. Among nomadic Jat the nuclear family and the lineal joint family are the most common domestic units.

Inheritance. Among those with land, all sons inherit equal shares in terms of both quantity and quality. Formerly, a man's wives shared equally on behalf of their sons, irrespective of the number of sons each had. Although in theory inheritance of land follows a strictly agnatic principle and daughters and sisters do not inherit, daughters' sons have been observed de facto to be among the inheritors in many cases.

Sociopolitical Organization

Social and Political Organization. All Jat are divided into patriclans; among the sedentary communities, each of these has a hereditary headman. By and large, the villages in which Jat farmers live, together with non-Jat, are under the jurisdiction of a clan council, and this council, of which every clan headman is a member, is the decision-making unit at the community level. Traditionally in these villages Jat farmers were integrated as patrons into the patron-client system prevalent in the area. Their clients were members of various service castes; however, this system has largely broken down today. Wealthy Jat landowners have entered local, regional, and even national politics since the beginning of this century, and in many areas they are still active as influential representatives of farmers and rural folk in general. Among the pastoral Jat of the Indus Delta, the clans are organized on the hierarchical principle of age, with the oldest man of the oldest lineage being at the head of the pyramid, followed by the eldest men of the younger lineages. Institutionalized authority over this entire group rests not with a Jat but with a Karmati-Baluch.

Conflict. A frequent source of conflict within the minimal lineage is land; such conflicts often take place between agnatic collaterals, since their lands usually border each other. Factional conflict is fairly common at a broader level.

Religion and Expressive Culture

Religious Beliefs and Ceremonies. A Jat can be Hindu, Muslim, or Sikh, and in 1931 over 50 percent of the entire Sikh population was constituted by Jat. Many ceremonies, especially those accompanying the rites of passage, are common to all Jat, irrespective of religious denomination. Among Hindu Jat there are in addition numerous local or more widely prevalent religious beliefs and observances. These include knowledge of certain but by no means all major mythological figures (gods and goddesses) of the Sanskritic tradition and the celebration of several festivals, both seasonal and annual, both of the all-Indian Hindu Great Tradition and of the localized Little Tradition. The Muslim Jat populations have a strong tradition of venerating a large number of local saints (*pīr*). Although most are officially Sunni, they have a large number of Shia traditions, and one group of Jat are Ismaelis. Till recently Sikh Jat, though very conscious of their distinct religious identity, were not very meticulous in their observance of the precepts of Sikhism. Most of them still observe Hindu marriage rites and till recently followed Hindu funeral customs; the majority also employed Brahmans as family priests. In most villages inhabited by Sikh Jat there is the shrine of a Sikh martyr of old that acts as an ancestral focus for the minimal lineage. Various supernatural beings play a role in Jat life and are common to most Jat irrespective of creed; belief in many of them is widespread in the region as a whole.

Arts. The women of the nomadic Jat are very skilled in needlework and embroider various textiles using threads of many colors in the delta region but mainly black and red in the north; tiny pieces of mirror are also used to decorate these textiles.

Death and Afterlife. Jat hold conflicting views on life after death. Some believe in the traditional Hindu concept of rebirth, others believe in going to Hell or Heaven, but many believe that there is no existence after death and that there is no form of life besides the present one on Earth.

See also Ahir; Baluchi; Gujar; Pathan; Punjabi; Rajput; Sikh

Bibliography

Heishman, Paul (1981). *Punjabi Kinship and Marriage.* Delhi: Hindustan.

Kessinger, Tom G. (1974). *Vilayatpur, 1848–1968: Social and Economic Change in a North Indian Village.* Berkeley: University of California Press.

Lewis, Oscar (1958). *Village Life in Northern India.* New York: Random House.

Pettigrew, Joyce (1975). *Robber Noblemen: A Study of the Political System of the Sikh Jats.* London: Routledge & Kegan Paul.

Pradhan, M. C. (1966). *The Political System of the Jats of Northern India.* Delhi: Oxford University Press.

Rao, Aparna (1986). "Peripatetic Minorities in Afghanistan—Image and Identity." In *Die ethnischen Gruppen Afghanistans,* edited by E. Orywal. Wiesbaden: L. Reichert.

Westphal-Hellbusch, Sigrid, and Heinz Westphal (1968). *Zur Geschichte und Kultur der Jat.* Berlin: Duncker & Humblot.

APARNA RAO

Jatav

ETHNONYMS: Jadav, Jatava, Jatua; also known as Chamar, Harijan, Scheduled Caste, Untouchable

Orientation

Identification. The Jatavs are an endogamous caste of the Chamar, or leather worker, category of castes in India. Because of the polluting occupation of leather worker they rank among the Untouchable castes close to the bottom of India's caste hierarchy. Some say the name "Jatav" is derived from the word *jat* (camel driver), while others say it is derived from "Jat," the name of a non-Untouchable farming caste. Many Jatavs themselves say it is derived from the term "Yadav," the lineage of Lord Krishna. They are also known as a Scheduled Caste because, as Untouchables, they are included on a schedule of castes eligible for government aid. Mahatma Gandhi gave to Untouchables the name "Harijans" or "children of god," but Jatavs reject the term and its connotations of Untouchable childlikeness and upper-caste paternalism.

Location. Jatavs live mostly in the states of Uttar Pradesh, Rajasthan, Haryana, and Punjab, as well as in the Union Territory of Delhi in northwest India. This is a semiarid area with rainfall mostly in the monsoon season of June to August and lesser rains in January–February. Temperatures range from 5.9° C in January–February to 41.5° C in May–June.

Demography. Jatavs are not listed separately in the census of India but along with other Chamars. In the four states mentioned above Chamars numbered 27,868,146, about 9.9 percent of the those states' population (1981).

Linguistic Affiliation. Jatavs speak related languages of the Indo-Aryan Family of languages including Hindi, Rajasthani, and Braj Bhasha, all using the Devanagari script, as well as Punjabi using the Gurmukhi script. Chamars in other parts of India speak other languages of the Indo-Aryan Family and languages of the unrelated Dravidian Family, such as Tamil and Telugu.

History and Cultural Relations

Origins of the Jatavs, as well as most other Chamar and Untouchable castes, are mythical. Some say the Jatavs are the product of marriage of upper-caste Jats with Chamar women. Jatavs themselves deny such origins. In preindependent India they claimed upper-caste Kshatriya or warrior origin. In postindependent India many have claimed to be descendants of India's ancient Buddhists. This claim is in part a rejection of Untouchable status and in part an assertion of a political identity of equality rejecting the caste system.

Settlements

In villages, where 90 percent of India's Untouchables live, Jatavs live in hamlets separate from non-Untouchable castes, while in cities they live in segregated neighborhoods. In larger settlements in cities these may be broken down into subsections with separate leadership. Houses are densely grouped in a nucleated pattern. Housing style is of two types: *kacca* and *pakka.* Kacca homes are generally one room made of mud, sometimes mixed with a special clay for strength, or of unbaked mud bricks. Roofs are flat, although some have sloping thatched roofs to protect against rain. Kacca homes are painted with a mixture of slightly antiseptic cow dung and mud. Pakka homes, mostly found in cities, are of baked brick and cement, the better ones with walls, floors, and flat roofs also coated with cement. Pakka homes frequently have more than one room, a small interior courtyard where cooking is done, and a second story.

Economy

Subsistence and Commercial Activities. Jatavs, and all other Chamars in India, are traditionally leather workers, tanners, and shoemakers. Nevertheless, in villages they are primarily agricultural laborers hereditarily attached to landowners (*jajmans*) for whom they work, often upon demand. Payment was traditionally in shares of grain, food, and items of clothing. In recent years increased payment in cash has weakened the obligations of landowners toward them and progressively reduced them to wage laborers. Population increase, the use of mechanical devices such as tractors, and land reform measures have caused further unemployment and destitution. Many migrate to cities where Jatavs are skilled shoemakers. A number of the educated younger generation have found jobs in government service where a certain percentage of jobs are reserved for Scheduled Castes. Differences based on class and education have begun to appear among, but not yet to divide, them. Those who can afford it may keep a cow or water buffalo for milk.

Industrial Arts. In addition to being skilled leather workers and shoemakers, Jatavs are also skilled masons and building contractors.

Trade. Shoes are manufactured, often on a putting-out system in which individual workers are given raw materials to make shoes in their homes, sold to wholesalers in a market. A few Jatavs in cities own large factories. Shoes are supplied to the domestic and a growing foreign market. However, since they do not control the wholesale and distributive networks, Jatavs do not reap the major profits of their craft.

Division of Labor. Division of labor by sex is strict. Males alone make shoes, plow and do heavy work in the fields, and freely move outside of the hamlet or neighborhood to shop in a market or attend caste councils and other public functions. Married women wear a veil (*ghunghat*) before their husband's elder male kinsmen and in his village or neighborhood; the women draw water, cook, and care for the home. They may also work at harvest time in the fields and separate scraps of leather.

Land Tenure. On the whole, Jatavs, like most Chamars, were until recently unable to own land in villages. In some villages a house tax is paid to the landowner. In cities, however, many have been able to purchase land for homes and factories.

Kinship

Kin Groups and Descent. Kin groups are formed patrilineally. The smallest coresidential unit is the nuclear or extended family (*parivar, ghar*). Extended families are most often composed of parent(s), married sons and their wives, and grandchildren. Otherwise they are composed of married brothers, their wives, and their children. Minimal patrilineages (*kutumb*) of nonresidential brothers and cousins are expected to support one another in conflicts. The maximal lineage (*khandan*) consists of all male descendants of a known or fictive ancestor. The "brotherhood" (*biradari*) consists of all members of the caste (*jati*). All members of the same neighborhood or village are real or fictive kin in an exogamous *bhaiband*. Descent is formally patrilineal, although the mother's role in procreation is acknowledged.

Kinship Terminology. Hawaiian-type cousin terms are used, while the first ascending generation uses bifurcate-collateral terms reflecting the lower status of girl-giving affinals (*nice rishtedar*) and the higher status of girl-receiving affinals (*unce rishtedar*). Affinals (*rishtedar*) are distinguished from agnates (*natedar*). Kin terms are fictively extended to all in a bhaiband.

Marriage and Family

Marriage. Most marriages are monogamous, but a very few polygamous marriages still occur. Parents arrange most marriages, although a few educated today may be allowed some say in the match. Totemically named categories (*gotras*) exist but their exogamic function is not strictly observed. Marriage is exogamous for the khandan but endogamous for the caste. As a practical rule, marriages are not allowed with anyone having a remembered relationship through both paternal and maternal patrilineages. Members of the village or city neighborhood are fictive kin for whom marriage is also exogamous. Also forbidden is giving girls to lower-ranked families, villages, or neighborhoods from which girls have previously been taken. A dowry must be offered to the boy's family on behalf of the girl. Divorce is possible at the instigation of either party, but it is infrequent and must be approved by the caste council. Widows, widowers, and divorced persons may remarry, but women may not remarry in a formal wedding ceremony (*shadi*). The ideal is patrilocal residence in the extended family of the husband; the reality is often a majority of nuclear families.

Domestic Unit. Those who live in the same house share living space, cooking, and expenses. When an extended family disintegrates—usually because of conflicts between brothers or their wives—separate living, cooking, and expense arrangements are made in the house if it is large enough; otherwise, new living quarters are sought. Sons are expected to care for aged parents who are unable to work.

Inheritance. Property is divided equally among sons; daughters because of the dowry customarily receive nothing. Inheriting brothers are expected to provide dowry for unmarried sisters. Eldest sons may succeed to any offices, such as headman, held by their fathers.

Socialization. Parents raise children affectionately, and elder siblings, usually sisters, are caretakers for younger siblings. Boys, however, are preferred and tend to receive better care and attention than girls. At around the age of 6 same-sexed parents become stricter disciplinarians. Children are not separated from most adult activities and easily move into adult occupations in early teens. Emphasis is on socialization for dependence upon the family, and boys are socialized especially to be dependent upon the mother, who may in turn become dependent upon them in old age.

Sociopolitical Organization

Social Organization. In India's villages the caste system is an organic division of labor, each caste having a traditionally assigned and distinct occupation and duty. Because Jatavs, as Chamars, do the polluting and polluted tasks of removing dead cattle from the village and of working with leather, they are ranked as Untouchables at the bottom of the system. Traditionally, their major occupation in the village was agricultural and other menial labor for landowners. In cities, where the traditional interdependencies of the caste system are virtually nonexistent, Jatavs are more like a distinct and despised ethnic group.

Political Organization. In preindependent India Jatavs gained considerable political expertise by forming associations and by developing a literate cadre of leaders. They tried to change their position in the caste system through "Sanskritization," the emulation of upper-caste behavior. Jatavs claimed Kshatriya or warrior-class origin and rank, and they organized caste associations to reform caste behavior and lobby for their claims. After independence India legally abolished the practice of untouchability, established the universal franchise, and developed the policy of "protective discrimination." That policy reserves electoral constituencies for Scheduled Caste candidates according to their percentages of population in the nation and the states; it does likewise for jobs in the national and state civil services; and it offers educational benefits to them. Jatavs have taken advantage of that policy and turned to active participation in India's parliamentary system of government. At times they have elected members of their caste to various state and national legislatures. In villages they have been less successful at influencing local political institutions and capturing funds meant for developmental projects. A major influence upon Jatavs was the Untouchable leader Dr. B. R. Ambedkar (d. 1956) who encouraged Untouchables to fight for their rights, and, as first minister for law in India, provided a powerful role model. Through their political efforts his statue and picture may be found in public parks and bus stations, symbolically asserting their quest for equal citizenship in the nation.

Social Control. Everyday control and leadership of local communities was traditionally in the hands of hereditary headmen (_chaudhari_). Serious cases of conflict, breaches of caste rules, and other caste-related problems were decided by councils of adult men (_panchayat_) in each locality. In the past, higher-level councils existed for more serious cases or for appeals. The council system and the powers of hereditary headmen have gradually eroded, especially in cities where the courts and the more educated and politically involved leaders and businessmen have become more prominent and influential.

Conflict. Conflicts arise within and between families and individuals over money, children, inheritance claims, drinking, insults, and the like. In recent years conflicts, both in cities and villages, have taken a political turn as Jatavs, and other Untouchables, have tried to assert their rights. Non-Untouchable castes have reacted negatively. Serious riots between Jatavs and upper castes have occurred in cities, such as Agra, and dangerous conflicts have also occurred in villages. Jatavs feel that the pace of change is much too slow, while upper castes have rejected it as too fast, unjustified, and contrary to orthodox Hindu teaching.

Religion and Expressive Culture

Religious Beliefs. In general, Jatavs and other Chamars are Hindus. They reject, however, the Hindu teaching that makes them Untouchables, as well as the Brahman priests who wrote the sacred texts so defining them. Most major Hindu festivals, particularly Holi, are observed, as are major life-cycle ceremonies. In postindependent India Jatavs may enter major Hindu temples and visit pilgrimage spots. Some Chamars are devotees of the Chamar saint Ravi Das. A number of Jatavs have followed Dr. Ambedkar and converted to Buddhism as a rejection of the caste system and as an assertion of the equality of all individuals. Buddhism for them is a political ideology in religious form. Ambedkar himself has been apotheosized as a bodhisattva; his birthday is the major public Jatav festival. Belief is in the major deities of Hinduism, especially in their localized forms. The Buddha and Dr. Ambedkar have become part of the pantheon. Ghosts of those who died before their time (_bhut_) and other spirits are believed to be able to possess or harm living people; fear of the evil eye is also widespread.

Religious Practitioners. Brahman priests traditionally have not served Jatavs and other Untouchables. Instead local headmen have officiated at rituals. Shamans (_bhagat_), who are sometimes Jatavs, have been known to be consulted in cases of spirit possession and other illnesses.

Ceremonies. Life-cycle ceremonies at birth, first hair cutting, marriage, and death are the major public ceremonies. Marriage is the most important ritual as it involves public feasts, the honor of the girl's family, cooperation of neighbors and specific kin, and gift giving over years to the families of married daughters. Death rituals also require participation of agnates and male neighbors to cremate the corpse immediately and of women to keen ritually. Very small children are buried. Memorial feasts or meals for the dead are given over a period of a year.

Arts. The verbal arts, particularly the composition of various forms of poetry, are cultivated, as is the skill in singing various forms of song.

Medicine. Folk remedies are used and practitioners of Ayurvedic, Unani, and homeopathic medicines are consulted. Modern medicines and physicians are used when affordable.

Death and Afterlife. Belief in transmigration of souls is widespread, and some believe in an afterlife in Heaven (Svarg) or Hell (Narak). A son to perform the funeral obsequies is essential. The dead soul lingers after death but passes on after a number of days.

See also Neo-Buddhist; Untouchables

Bibliography

Briggs, George W. (1920). _The Chamars_. Calcutta: Association Press.

Cohn, Bernard (1954). "The Camars of Senapur: A Study of

the Changing Status of a Depressed Caste." Ph.D. dissertation, Cornell University.

Lynch, Owen M. (1969). *The Politics of Untouchability: Social Mobility and Social Change in a City of India.* New York: Columbia University Press.

Lynch, Owen M. (1981). "Rioting as Rational Action: An Interpretation of the April 1978 Riots in Agra." *Economic and Political Weekly* 16:1951–1956.

OWEN M. LYNCH

Kalasha

ETHNONYM: Kalash Kafir

The Kalasha are a tribe of about 4,000, found in the Chitral District in North-West Frontier Province, on the western edge of Pakistan. They are unique among the tribes of the Hindu Kush in one respect: to this day they have resisted conversion to Islam. (Pakistan is 98 percent Muslim.) Instead they practice a form of Hinduism.

The Kalasha economy is based on agriculture, which is mainly women's work, and transhumant animal husbandry, which takes the men and their flocks to the lower pastures for winter and then to high mountain pastures in summer. The people grow maize, wheat, and millets on small irrigated fields. Goats are not only the main animal herded, they are also sacred: they are considered the gift of the gods, which men must protect against the pollution of females and demonic possession. Women have relative social freedom, as compared with the Muslim women of Pakistan, and there is certainly no purdah. There are many cases of marriage by elopement, involving already-married women. Much feuding and negotiation have to take place to resolve disputes over women.

During the 1950s several Kalasha villages were forcibly converted to Islam on grounds of the supposed "immorality" of the women. Since then other forms of antagonism have grown up between Kalasha and the surrounding Muslims. Recently the situation has somewhat improved through the building of schools in some valleys, which Kalasha children can attend. In the late 1970s some roads were also built into the area. As a result there has been an increase in tourism and timber exploitation, which have not really benefited the Kalasha thus far.

Bibliography

Parkes, Peter (1987). "Livestock Symbolism and Pastoral Ideology among the Kafirs of the Hindu Kush." *Man* 22:637–60.

Parkes, Peter (1990). *Kalasha Society: Practice and Ceremony in the Hindu Kush.* London: Oxford University Press.

PAUL HOCKINGS

Kanarese

ETHNONYMS: Canarese, Kannadiga

These are some 66 percent of the inhabitants of Karnataka, in south-central India, who speak the Kannada language. In 1991 they numbered about 31 million speakers (four percent of the national population). The Kannada language belongs to the Dravidian family. It has an ancient, mainly devotional, literature, stretching back to the ninth century A.D. The Kannada script, though similar to that of Telugu, is only used for writing Kannada and the closely related languages Tulu and Kodagu, both of which are spoken in the western parts of Karnataka.

The great majority of Kanarese (85.9 percent) are Hindus, but 11.1 percent of the state's population is Muslim and 2.1 percent Christian. There are also two important sects present: Jains and Lingayats. The Jains are a monastic sect often considered beyond the pale of Hinduism. The Lingayats are a Shaivite reformist sect of Hinduism, founded in the twelfth century A.D., and having a strong monotheistic tendency.

Most of the Karnataka state was from 1578 to 1947 the kingdom of Mysore, ruled by a maharaja based in Mysore City. Even before this kingdom there had been culturally brilliant Hindu kingdoms in the same area, as the temple art of the Hoysalas (1007–1336 A.D.) and the city polity of the Vijayanagar Empire (1336–1565) clearly attest. During the eighteenth century the Muslim adventurer Haidar Ali and his son Tipu Sultan fought four wars against the British, which culminated in Tipu's death in 1799; but after that the British never ruled Mysore directly, preferring to prop up the Hindu house of Mysore. It had a relatively efficient state administration and was one of the largest princely states in South Asia. As a result, in the twentieth century Karnataka has become one of the most prosperous and modernized Indian states.

Although its economy is still largely rural, the state includes the great city of Bangalore, one of the two major industrial centers in South India. Universities, technical colleges, and high-technology industries all abound in the Bangalore area. Aircraft, silk, and motorcycles are three of the best-known products. The important cultivated crops of the state are millet, rice, sorghum, tobacco, sugarcane, cotton, potatoes, onions, turmeric, cardamom, and chilies. The major plantation crops are coffee and coconuts, but there is some tea and rubber; and there are still extensive forests in the west. Gold is the major mineral product.

See also Coorg; Jain; Lingayat; Okkaliga

Bibliography

Beals, Alan R. (1974). _Village Life in South India: Cultural Design and Environmental Variation_. Chicago: Aldine.

Dubois, Jean-Antoine (1906). _Hindu Manners, Customs, and Ceremonies_. 3rd ed., edited by Henry K. Beauchamp. Oxford: Clarendon Press.

Epstein, T. Scarlett (1962). _Economic Development and Social Change in South India_. Bombay: Oxford University Press.

Epstein, T. Scarlett (1973). _South India, Yesterday, Today, and Tomorrow: Mysore Villages Revisited_. London and Basingstoke: Macmillan.

Nanjundayya, H. V., and L. K. Ananthakrishna Iyer (1928–1936). _The Mysore Tribes and Castes_. 4 vols. and appendix. Mysore: Mysore University.

Ross, Aileen D. (1961). _The Hindu Family in Its Urban Setting_. Toronto: University of Toronto Press; Bombay: Oxford University Press.

Srinivas, Mysore Narasimhachar (1976). _The Remembered Village_. Berkeley: University of California Press.

PAUL HOCKINGS

Kanbi

ETHNONYMS: Patel, Patidar

Orientation

The Kanbi are a large endogamous caste living in the Kheda District of Gujarat State, India. They are the most numerous of the high castes (e.g., Brahman, Bania, and Patidar) in this district. The name "Kanbi" is said to be derived from _katumbi_ (householder). In 1931 the caste name was changed from Kanbi to Patidar in recognition of an elevation in overall caste status. The information in this summary has been drawn from David F. Pocock's 1972 study of the Patidar in Gujarat. The Kanbi call their homeland Charotar (the pleasant land). The area is a flat alluvial plain of some 65 square kilometers within the Kheda District of Gujarat. In 1971 the Kheda District had a total population of slightly under 2 million. The lingua franca of this region is Gujarati, an Indo-Aryan language.

History and Cultural Relations

In the nineteenth century, the Leva Kanbi (one of the two large divisions of the Kanbi) were appointed by the Moguls and Marathas as revenue-collection officers. Some of these Kanbi had attained _patidari_ rights (i.e., ownership of cultivable strips of land, known as _pati_, that could be sublet for profit). Generally when revenue was being collected, an assessment was charged to a particular village. This assessment was divided according to the lineal divisions of the village, each of which paid a certain proportion of the fee. Senior members of divisions kept some land that was owned jointly by members of the division. The remainder was sublet as pati. Two classes of individuals rented these lands: tenants at will and hereditary tenants. Many of these hereditary tenants also had patidari rights. By the middle of the nineteenth century, some twenty-seven Kanbi villages had attained considerable wealth; of these, fifteen had an aristocracy of large landowners with developing interests in foreign commerce. These were considered to be Patidar; the remainder were considered to be Kanbi. These villages retained their wealth well into the twentieth century; they benefited extensively from British efforts to increase productivity in land yield through cultivation. In addition, twentieth-century foreign trade with east Africa brought an increase in revenue that was invested in land and property development in the Kheda District.

Settlements

Castes are assigned respective living areas within a typical Kanbi village, each of which has individual access to agricultural fields. Villages do not adhere to an established urban plan. A village square (containing temples, shrines, and offices for government officials) is located near the village entrance. A *talav* (tank) containing the water supply is located near the square. A typical house is constructed of mud, wood, and thatch. The home of a more affluent landowner is similarly constructed, but a superior grade of wood is used. Brick and iron are also used in the construction of homes for wealthy Kanbi.

Economy

Some Kanbi own land as shareholders while others work as tenant farmers. Agriculture is the major subsistence activity. Crops grown include several varieties of millet (including spiked millet), pigeon peas, rice, cluster beans, sesame, castor, chilies, and spices. Other vegetables are purchased from vendors locally and beyond the village confines. Cotton and tobacco are also cultivated. The more wealthy Kanbi supplement their income through investment, trade, industry, and commercial activities. The Kanbi have a cash economy and produce few implements. Wealthy Kanbi families engage in a variety of professional, industrial, and trade-related activities (foreign and domestic). In exchange for services rendered by several servant and specialized castes, the Kanbi settle their accounts in cash or by means of barter (e.g., with grain). Occupational specialization obtains in Kanbi villages. Specialized castes (e.g., Brahmans, barbers, washers, potters, carpenters, tailors, and shopkeepers) provide important services. Men work agricultural fields and women prepare meals, handle household chores, and care for domestic animals.

Kinship

The village, village division, and natal group are the most basic social units in Kanbi society. In leading Kanbi villages, the Kanbi are descendants of one man (a founding ancestor); in some villages, a minority lineage that predates the founding ancestor may also exist. In large villages, the descendants of a common ancestor build a compound (*chok* or *khadaki*) together. In wealthy villages, all members of the compound are agnatically related. At one time, these compounds may have served as home to several generations. By 1972, they housed little more than joint families of two generations' depth. Secession (and lineal segmentation) may take place; however, this is a rare occurrence. Compounds of this sort are not usually found in smaller Kanbi villages. The *bhayat* (small division consisting of four or five generations) also figures prominently in Kanbi social structure. It is the closest group of mutual cooperation outside the family. Patrilineal descent is the Kanbi norm.

Marriage and Family

Monogamous unions are normative. Extramarital liaisons of male and female spouses are not unusual. Hypergamy is practiced and *ekuda* (marriage circles) exist whose members must intermarry. The father of the bride is ceremonially and financially the inferior party in marital negotiations and is required to pay an exorbitant fee in order to secure a son-in-law of suitable social standing. Postmarital residence is patrilocal. The joint family, consisting of either a couple together with their children or a large group extending five or more generations, is the basic domestic unit. Male children inherit the parental estate. During his lifetime, a father is the manager of the ancestral estate, but no part of this estate may be encumbered without the consent of his sons. By birth they are entitled to be coparceners with their father. If the ancestral estate remains undivided after the death of the father, the eldest son becomes its manager and all family members have a right to maintenance from its proceeds. The responsibility for the raising of children is assumed largely by the mother, but it is shared to some extent by all members of the joint family.

Sociopolitical Organization

Gujarati society is rigidly stratified. The Kanbi are the most influential caste (below the Brahmans) in the Kheda District. Within the caste, social inequities obtain. These are based chiefly on wealth. In addition, the marital obligations enforced by the ekuda serve as the foundation for yet another level of social distinction within Kanbi culture. Regulations governing the nature and extent of social relations internally and between castes provide the basis upon which social control is maintained.

Religion and Expressive Culture

The Kanbi are adherents of Hinduism. Brahmans function in a sacerdotal capacity for the Kanbi family. They function as marriage priests and also officiate at ceremonies marking the beginning of the new year, etc. The nature of Kanbi religious ceremonies remains a mystery. It has been suggested by some that the origin of these rites is Vedic. Others believe them to be of syncretic origin. The confusion is due in part to the fact that the Kanbi are not served by a single Brahman caste. Whatever the case may be, it is likely that these ceremonies do contain a Brahmanic core to which additional elements have been added.

Bibliography

Pocock, David F. (1972). *Kanbi and Patidar: A Study of the Patidar Community of Gujarat.* Oxford: Clarendon Press.

HUGH R. PAGE, JR.

Kanjar

ETHNONYMS: Guguwālā, Jallad, Kanjari, Khānābādōsh

Orientation

Identification. Kanjar are an ancient, widely dispersed, and endogamous population of nomadic artisans and entertainers spread throughout Southwest Asia. They are widely known as singers, dancers, musicians, operators of carnival-type rides, and prostitutes; they are best known for the small terra-cotta toys they manufacture and hawk door-to-door through sedentary rural and urban communities.

Location.   Small nomadic groups of Kanjar are found throughout Pakistan and north India; they are most concentrated in the fertile and more densely populated areas of the Indus River valley and the Punjab. In 1947 the international boundary separating Pakistan from India divided the Punjab region between the two nations. Disputes between the two nations about irrigation resources and religious conflicts among Muslims, Hindus, and Sikhs keep tensions high on the frontier and prohibit free movement of nomadic peoples along traditional travel routes. Traditionally, Kanjar used to travel a circuit from Rawalpindi and Lahore in Pakistan to Amritsar and Delhi in India. This region lies in a warm temperate zone, generally arid, with hot summers and cool to cold winters. On the whole, rainfall is low. The five rivers feeding the Punjab and extensive systems of irrigation canals have sustained the development of relatively dense networks of agriculture-based villages and the growth of small towns and metropolitan centers. The human population of these communities forms the economic niche exploited by Kanjar.

Demography.   There are about 5,000 Kanjar in Pakistan and considerably more in north India. Unfortunately there is no accurate demographic or other census information on Kanjar in either nation. Small groups of one to three families travel extensively through rural areas following the wheat and rice harvests. Weddings and other festive occasions follow harvest activities in village areas and Kanjar capitalize on these patterns of seasonal wealth. During fallow and growing seasons they move into urban areas. By combining entertainment and handicraft skills with much spatial mobility the Kanjar exploit a peripatetics' niche—a constant demand for goods and/or services that local communities cannot internally generate or support on a full-time basis.

Linguistic Affiliation.   Kanjar are fluent in several languages and many regional dialects of Hindi, Urdu, Punjabi, and Sindhi. Their own language, Kanjari, has affinities with Indo-Aryan Prakrits and Romani. Linguistically, and in their cultural habits, contemporary Kanjar may share a common ancestry with Rōm (Gypsies) and other populations of Romani speakers throughout the world.

History and Cultural Relations

Ancient historical accounts indicate that nomadic groups like the Kanjar were firmly embedded throughout the fabric of sedentary social systems in South Asia by the late Vedic period (circa 1000–700 B.C.). Ongoing ethnoarchaeological research suggests that groups similar to or identical with contemporary Kanjar may have been responsible for the manufacture and distribution of terra-cotta figurines found throughout the ruins of the Harappan Civilization in the Indus Valley (circa 3000–1500 B.C.). Kanjar figure in local traditions and folklore and practically all villages and urban centers are visited by them at least twice each year. The nature of their peripatetic subsistence activities and ethnic pride govern Kanjar relations with client communities. Females peregrinate through narrow village lanes and urban streets calling out _Gugu ghoray lay lao_, "Come and take the toys." Responding to this beckoning refrain, children rush to parents for a few _annas_ (coins), measures of rice or wheat,

and/or items of cast-off clothing to exchange for some of the terra-cotta toys being offered for sale. Some will hold back cash or barter items knowing the Kanjar may also have carnival-type rides or _jhula_ (small merry-go-rounds and Ferris wheels) in their tent camps pitched in nearby fields or vacant lots. Adults anticipate a late afternoon or evening of music and dancing. Kanjar men surreptitiously smile while wives look scornfully at their husbands, knowing that Kanjar women also have sexual favors for sale. Senior females from client households with daughters about to marry will seek out older Kanjar women to come and quietly sing and joke before the bride-to-be about the wedding night, sexual intercourse, and relations with males, as part of the girl's enculturation into adulthood. Beyond these formalized roles and transactions, Kanjar relations with the membership of host communities are those of professional strangers. They have no bonds of kinship, they have not belonged to the community from the beginning, and they desire no contracts that might bind them in the future. They simply import goods and services that do not, and cannot, stem from the client community itself. Because relations with clients are confined to formalized transactions in structured settings, clients know very little about Kanjar life and cultural habits. Conversely, Kanjar constantly learn and understand a great deal about the roles and patterns of social structure and organization governing everyday activities in the communities and regions of their peregrinations. This knowledge is used and constantly updated in order to maintain timely and sensitive entertainment routines and to determine economic or political conditions affecting their travel routes and tenure in an area. Also by restricting their interactions with clients to public settings, Kanjar protect the sanctity of the private domains of their family and group activities. This strategy inhibits collection of accurate information about themselves that government, police, social service agencies, and others might be able to use in order to curtail their economic activities, group flexibility, and/or freedom of movement. In the larger sedentary world, Kanjar are often classified under the culturally nebulous term "Khānābādōsh." An ancient Persian term adopted into Hindi/Urdu, Khānābādōsh literally means "house-on-shoulder." It carries a negative semantic connotation and is similar in use to the English construct "Gypsy" or nomad. They are also inappropriately labeled as a caste (_ẕat_) of terra-cotta toy makers (Guguwālā).

Settlements

Kanjar own no land or permanent shelters. They survive by traveling from community to community through diverse regions, transporting their physical possessions on mule-drawn carts (_rehra_) or donkeys. The woven reed or _munj_ grass (_sirki_) walls of their tents are ideal for their peripatetic activities and contrast sharply with the mud and/or brick shelters of client settlements and the barrel-vaulted, patchwork cloth tents of other populations of nomadic artisans and entertainers. Tent walls are made by weaving and binding strands of sirki or split bamboo into long, flexible mats about 2 meters wide and up to 9 meters in length. This mat is wound around a rectangular frame of vertical poles or sticks to form a continuous wall that is rolled open to provide an entrance. Cloth or smaller grass-mat ceilings are supported by one or two ridgepoles secured to corner posts. The living area may be varied by adjusting the distance between corner posts. Each family maintains a separate tent and one seldom finds more than three tents traveling or camped together. In rural areas tent camps are pitched along canal banks and railway lines and in fallow or newly harvested fields around villages. In urban settings camps are located in vacant lots or undeveloped commercial sites. Because they are almost identical, Kanjar tents are frequently confused with tents belonging to the Changar. Changar are a totally different community of nomadic artisans who weave bamboo, reeds, and grass into mats, baskets, brooms, toys, and the like. While Kanjar are capable of manufacturing their own tents, it is common to contract with Changar to build or repair their tents.

Economy

Subsistence and Commercial Activities. Income-producing activities fall into three basic domains: (1) sale of *gugu* (terra-cotta toys); (2) entertainment routines including sale of jhula (carnival rides), singing, dancing, music-making activities, and prostitution; and (3) some begging strategies. Some families keep and train fighting dogs and roosters; however, income from wagers on animal fighting is not reliable. In rural areas Kanjar bargain for measures of wheat, rice, and other cereals as payment for their goods and services. In urban settings they are more inclined to accept cash, though even there many will negotiate for sugar, flour, and cast-off clothing as remuneration. Prostitutes demand cash. Occasionally, females will offer sexual favors in order to avoid harassment from local police or other authorities. Earnings in soft commodities are accumulated and transported until sufficient quantities justify visits to regional markets where the goods are sold for cash. Income not needed for immediate subsistence requirements is converted into silver and gold. Rice, *chappatis* (flat bread made from unleavened dough), dried lentils (*dal*), produce such as onions, potatoes, and chilies, occasional fresh meat, tea with milk and sugar, and yogurt comprise their basic diet. Enough of these items are usually earned daily; cash outlays for food generally are restricted to purchases of cooking oil, spices, tea, and luxury items such as fresh fruit and sweets. Family pack animals and goats are grazed in rural areas; however, in more crowded urban areas fodder is often purchased with cash. Seasonal income is influenced by local conditions in the diverse communities Kanjar service. Resourceful families may accumulate considerable wealth.

Industrial Arts. While the sale of terra-cotta toys accounts for only 24 percent of family income, the manufacture and hawking of *gugu-ghoray* give Kanjar their primary identity. Clay deposits are common throughout the Indus Valley and Punjab, and Kanjar are adept at finding local deposits of this raw material wherever they camp. Males generally dig up the clay; however, the entire group traveling together participate in making the clay figurines. Stylized yet consistent across the entire Kanjar population, the clay figurines represent dogs, sheep, goats, camels, cows, buffalo, birds, and elephants as well as miniature household items such as fireplaces, pots, plates, spoons, and bells. Hand-molded from damp clay, figurines are sun-dried before surface firing under grass, dried manure, and straw. Depending on local demand, families usually make gugu twice weekly. Surface firing ensures fragility and a relatively constant demand for these popular toys.

Trade. Kanjar avoid local markets and craft centers, preferring to hawk their wares and services door-to-door. In recent years the growth of inexpensive and durable plastic toys in the market has begun to affect sales of gugu-ghoray. Response to this competition has increased the number of toys a client may select for the same price.

Division of Labor. Kanjar females enjoy dominance over males in practically every sphere of daily activities. With the exception of income from jhula (carnival rides) operated exclusively by males, females generate the majority of income in both rural and urban settings. Door-to-door hawking, singing, dancing, and prostitution are exclusively female activities. Both sexes and all children beg. Daily provisioning of the family is provided by females and children. Males and elderly females prepare meals and tend infants. Dealings with outsiders are handled by females, and internally they tend to carry more weight when decisions are made about distribution and/or investment of family resources. Talented males are trained and skillful musicians; they accompany the singing and dancing routines of their mothers, sisters, and spouses with drums, flutes, harmoniums, cymbals, and a range of stringed instruments. Boys share tent-maintenance, livestock, and child-care responsibilities with fathers. Girls accompany mothers in their activities outside camps and concentrate on learning dancing and singing skills within the family domain.

Land Tenure. Most Kanjar avoid ownership of land or permanent property; however, some families may invest cash in professional entertainment establishments servicing urban centers.

Kinship, Marriage, and Family

Kin Groups and Descent. Contrary to popular belief and cursory historical records, Kanjar do not consider themselves to be a caste (zat). They refer to themselves as a *qam* and use this term to mean an endogamous "people" or society. Structurally they are divided into *biradari*. Kanjar use this term to define loosely organized, bilateral descent groups, the members of which can trace affiliation back to a common ancestor(s), usually a group of siblings. In turn, the apical siblings of each biradari are believed to be descendants of a common but unknown ancestor. The term biradari is also, and most commonly, used to indicate a group of families living and traveling together, regardless of actual kin ties among them. Biradari, as a descent group, is not an organizing principle and is only called upon when a specific kin link is disputed or perceived to be politically or economically profitable for a given Ego. Kanjar are related to each other in many involuted ways and each relationship has a distinct term. The closest kin ties are among siblings and their mother, Ego's father being the husband of his or her mother at Ego's birth.

Marriage. All females are highly valued, both as daughters and spouses, and the bride-price (*bovar*) is very dear, often amounting to more than three years' total earnings from the prospective husband's family. Kanjar prefer *wadi de shadi* (exchange marriages) between the children of siblings. Wadi de shadi enables a family to solidify alliances and accumulate cash for bride-price where exchange is impossible or undesirable. Marriages are arranged by members of the child's natal tent with an eye toward enhancing their own position, either through receipt of bride-price and/or through achievement of a more desirable alliance with other families. Divorce may be instigated by either spouse; however, reconciliation is always sought because otherwise bride-price must be returned. Disputes about marital tensions and bride-price are common sources of conflict.

Domestic Unit. The same term (_puki_) is used for tent and for the basic social unit of Kanjar society. Puki connotes the commensal group of a female, her spouse, and their unmarried children. Marriage creates a new tent and residence is either neolocal or with siblings or parental siblings traveling in other groups. Each tent is economically independent.

Inheritance. All material and animal resources are owned corporately by the tent or family unit. When a member dies, his or her portion of the tent's resources is equally divided among surviving members. Individual debts also become the responsibility of the bereaved tent if not settled before death.

Socialization. There is no separate world for children and adults and Kanjar believe that children learn best through a combination of example and specific training. Broadly speaking, males are enculturated to be cooperative and supportive, whereas females are encouraged to be more aggressive, self-reliant, and independent. Exceptionally attractive and talented girls are raised with expectation that they will be sold into professional entertainment establishments. Musically talented boys may be encouraged to leave their tents and work independently as professional musicians.

Sociopolitical Organization

Social Organization. Where each tent is an independent economic unit, families usually form temporary alliances with other tents forming a _dēra_. Dēra typically consist of two to four tents with a balance among skilled performers and jhula (carnival rides). While economic considerations are always a mediating factor, most dēra include tents involved in engagement or marriage negotiations.

Political Organization. While females tend to dominate, both tents and dēra are acephalous. Decisions affecting the group are reached through consensus, deference wisely being paid to older and/or more experienced individuals.

Social Control. Kanjar recognize that the independence of tents and freedom (_azadi_) to move are the most important forms of social control. Tents unwilling to abide with dēra consensus are encouraged to or simply move away in order to avoid serious conflict or violence. Among Kanjar, loss of mobility is loss of social control.

Conflict. Tension and disputes arise from bickering between spouses or entertainers working together about share and distribution of earnings, adultery or excessive sexual joking, disagreements about travel routes and tenure in an area, and bride-price negotiations, as well as individual transgressions such as drunkenness, excessive abuse, theft, physical attacks, serious injury, and murder. When group pressure and negotiated compromises fail, Kanjar have a formal legal system for hearing and resolving serious disputes. Since they lack institutions or formal roles for enforcing group sanctions, settlement of disputes ultimately devolves on the conflicting parties, their families, and their allies.

Religion and Expressive Culture

Religious Beliefs. As nomads Kanjar are familiar with a broad spectrum of religious beliefs and practices among the communities they service, and they don any sacred mantle that momentarily meets their practical needs. While they are essentially agnostic, they do protect themselves from spirits (_jinn_) by wearing amulets (_tabiz_) purchased from holy men (_fakirs_).

Arts. As professional artisans and highly skilled entertainers, their everyday subsistence activities are a form of expressive and creative art.

Medicine. Kanjar seek treatment from homeopathic practitioners, druggists or pharmacists, and fakirs (holy men) for serious illness. Chronic malaria is endemic and most suffer from seasonal bouts with typhoid and cholera. Greater energy and resources are spent on sick females than on sick males, especially as infants and young children. Males are constantly reminded that "_roti_ (bread) for your stomach" comes largely from the females in their lives.

Death and Afterlife. Kanjar are stoic about death and accept it as fate and a normal aspect of life. Individuals prefer to die in the company of family and siblings; however, they realize that their peripatetic life-style often prohibits dispersed kin from being present. Ideally, parents and/or siblings wash the body, wrap it in a new white cloth, sprinkle it with scented water, and bury it on its side facing east toward warmth and the rising sun. Burial takes place as soon as possible—the next day during the hot season, and after two or three days in winter, thus in cooler weather allowing any siblings who might be in the same area time to travel and be involved in the burial process. The body is considered polluting to females and therefore males prepare it for burial. Kanjar generally fear incapacitating diseases or long final illnesses more than the actual death itself. While a family will carry a sick individual on their carts and/or stop traveling when an individual becomes extremely ill or crippled, Kanjar fear loss of mobility more than death. Among Kanjar, freedom and mobility represent life.

See also Peripatetics; Qalandar

Bibliography

Berland, Joseph C. (1982). _No Five Fingers Are Alike: Cognitive Amplifiers in Social Context._ Cambridge, Mass.: Harvard University Press.

Berland, Joseph C. (1987). "Kanjar Social Organization." In _The Other Nomads: Peripatetic Minorities in Cross Cultural Perspective_, edited by Aparna Rao, 247–265. Cologne: Bohlau Verlag.

Berland, Joseph C., and Matt. T. Salo, eds. (1986). "Peripatetic Peoples." _Nomadic Peoples_ (Toronto) 21/22 (special issue).

Hayden, Robert (1979). "The Cultural Ecology of Service Nomads." _Eastern Anthropologist_ 32:297–309.

Misra, P. K., and Rajalakshmi Misra (1982). "Nomadism in the Land of the Tamils between 1 A.D. and 600 A.D." In _No-_

mads in India, edited by P. K. Misra and K. C. Malhotra, 1–6. Anthropological Survey of India. Calcutta.

JOSEPH C. BERLAND

Kashmiri

ETHNONYMS: none

The Kashmiris are the Hindu and Muslim inhabitants of India's most northerly state, Jammu and Kashmir, and of that fragment of land that is controlled by Pakistan and called Azad Kashmir (Gilgit, Baltistan, and four other districts, all thinly populated). The entire area is one of beautiful mountain ranges, high grazing valleys, and a large, central agricultural valley called the Vale of Kashmir, where Srinigar, the Indian state capital, is located. In point of fact some three-quarters of Kashmir, including most of Azad Kashmir and all of the Aksai Chin sector held by China, is permanently under snow and glaciers because of the extreme elevation.

The whole state has a major tourist potential, but for some years this has not been realized because of the continuing political and religious strife. This seemingly intractable situation arose from the fact that the majority of the Kashmiri population (77.1 percent in 1941) was Muslim, while the former maharaja of Kashmir and 20.1 percent (in 1941) of the population were Hindus. After Indian independence, India laid claim to the state (Pandit Nehru's homeland) and soon developed better communications with this region than Pakistan was able to develop with its own sector, Azad Kashmir. The Indo-Pakistan wars of 1948, 1965, and 1971 were largely fought over the issue of who should control Kashmir (although in 1971 Bangladesh was also a central issue), and today (1991) the political turmoil and "states of emergency" continue, prompted both by Pakistani shipments of arms across the border to sympathizers and by the agitation of Kashmiri Muslims who would prefer to live under the Islamic rule of Pakistan rather than the secular but sometimes repressive rule of India. Although involved in the issue from the beginning, the United Nations has been powerless to resolve it. Until this problem is resolved, the economic growth of the area will remain almost at a standstill.

The area is very large. Excluding that sizable part that is controlled either by Pakistan or by China at the present time, the Indian state of Jammu and Kashmir covers 222,236 square kilometers, most of it mountainous. It has a population estimated (in 1991) at 7.5 million. Although divided by religion and politics, the Kashmiris are united in one sense by their common language, Kashmiri. This is an Indo-Aryan tongue, written with a form of the Perso-Arabic script. It is the major language of the Dardic Subgroup, and it has a literature reaching back to the fourteenth-century poetess Lal Ded. Although the culture is predominantly Muslim today, prior to the Turkic incursions of the eleventh and twelfth centuries Kashmir was an important Buddhist territory, as some of its temple ruins testify. Later, under the Moguls, music, poetry, architecture, and garden design flourished there. The Hindus, though not very numerous, have been quite influential in the state, especially as landowners. The term "Kashmiri" is applied particularly to those who inhabit the Vale of Kashmir, which is the most populous area, and includes over two dozen Muslim and Hindu castes.

See also Pandit of Kashmir

PAUL HOCKINGS

Khasi

ETHNONYMS: Cassia, Cossyah, Kasia, Kassia, Kassya, Kasya, Khasía, Khasiah, Khassia, Khassu, Khosia, Ki Khási

Orientation

Identification and Location. The Khasi (who call themselves Ki Khási) live in two districts of Meghalaya State, India (21°10' to 26°05' N, 90°47' to 92°52' E), an area of some 16,000 square kilometers. This region is home to several Mon-Khmer–speaking groups. The Khasi themselves live in the upland center of this large area. The Khasi designation for the Khasi Hills section is Ka Ri Khási and that of the Jaintia Hills section is Ka Ri Synten. Other matrilineal and Mon-Khmer–speaking groups found in this region include the Lyngngams (Lynngam) who occupy the western part of the area, the Bhois who inhabit the north-central region, the Wars who occupy the district's southern expanse, and the Jaintia (also called Pnar or Synteng) in the southeast of the region.

Demography. According to P. R. T. Gurdon, who first studied the Khasi in 1901, the total population then numbered 176,614. Their number had risen to 463,869 by 1971.

Linguistic Affiliation. The Khasi speak a Mon-Khmer language (belonging to the Austroasiatic Family). Khasi is believed to form a link between related languages in central India and the Mon-Khmer languages of Southeast Asia. While dialectal variation may be noted within different villages, the major Khasi dialects are Khasi, Jaintia, Lyngngam, and War.

History and Cultural Relations

In the mid-sixteenth century there were twenty-five separate Khasi chiefdoms along with the separate kingdom of Jaintia. Before the arrival of the British, the Jaintia were vassals to a series of dominant kingdoms from the thirteenth to the eighteenth centuries (e.g., the Kachari, Koch, and Ahom). At the beginning of the sixteenth century Jaintia rule was extended to Sylhet and this marked the beginning of Brahman influence on the Jaintia. The annexation of Sylhet in 1835 (instigated by the seizing of British subjects for human sacrifice) preceded the subjugation of the Khasi states by some twenty or more years. By 1860, the British had annexed all of the Jaintia Hills region and imposed taxes on it as a part of British India. The Khasi states had limited cultural relations before the arrival of the British, characterized in large part by internal warfare between villages and states and raiding and trading in the Sylhet and Brahmaputra valleys. The incorporation of the markets at Sylhet into the British colonial economy in 1765 marked the beginning of Khasi subjugation. Khasi raids in the 1790s led to the rise of British fortifications in the foothills and an eventual embargo on Khasi-produced goods in Sylhet markets. In 1837 the construction of a road through Nongkhaw State linking Calcutta to the Brahmaputra Valley led to the eventual cessation of Khasi-British hostilities, and by 1862 treaties between the British and all of the Khasi states (allowing Khasi autonomy and freedom from British taxation) were signed. A significant amount of cultural change (e.g., an increase in wealth, decline of traditional culture, rise in educational standards, and frequent intermarriage) occurred after the British made Shillong the capital of Assam. In 1947 there was constituted an autonomous tribal area responsible to Assam's governor as an agent of the president of India. However, the native state system with its various functionaries remains intact, and Khasis now have their own state, Meghalaya, in which they predominate.

Settlements

Khasi villages are built a little below the tops of hills in small depressions to protect against storms and high winds, with houses built in close proximity to one another. In addition to individual houses, family tombs and memorial stones (*mawbynna*) are located within confines or nearby. Internal division of the village based on wealth does not obtain; rich and poor live side by side. Sacred groves are located near the village between the brow of the hill and the leeward side, where the village's tutelary deity is worshiped. Pigs wander freely through a village, and some villages (e.g., those of the high plateau) also feature potato gardens protected by dry dikes and hedges. Narrow streets connect houses and stone steps lead up to individual houses. The upper portion of a Khasi village may be as much as 100 meters higher in elevation than the lower portion. A village site is rarely changed. The typical Khasi house is a shell-shaped building with three rooms: the *shynghup* (porch for storage); the *nengpei* (center room for cooking and sitting); and the *rumpei* (inner room for sleeping). The homes of wealthy Khasi are more modern, having iron roofs, chimneys, glass windows, and doors. Some have European-style homes and furniture. A marketplace is located outside a Khasi village (close to memorial stones, by a river or under a group of trees, depending on the region). Within Khasi villages one may find a number of public buildings, Christian churches, and schools.

Economy

Subsistence and Commercial Activities. Cultivation is the major Khasi subsistence activity and the family farm (managed by a single family with or without the assistance of outside labor) is the basic operating unit in crop production. The Khasi are multioccupational and their economy is market-based. Marketing societies exist to facilitate trade and to provide aid in times of personal need. Crops are produced for consumption and trade. There are four types of land uti-lized for cultivation: forest; wet paddy land (*hali* or *pynthor*); homestead land (*ka 'dew kyper*); and high grass land (*ka ri lum* or *ka ri phlang*). Forest land is cleared by cutting trees, burning them, and planting seeds with hoes in the ground thus fertilized (*jhum* agriculture). Paddy land in valleys is divided into compartments by banks and flooded by irrigation channels. Proper soil consistency is obtained by using cattle and hoes. Crops produced by the Khasi include vegetables, pulses, sugarcane, maize, rice, potatoes, millet, pineapples, Job's tears, bay leaves, yams, tapioca, cotton, oranges, and betel nuts. Other crops known in the region include turmeric, ginger, pumpkins, gourds, eggplants, chilies, and sesame. The Khasi also engage in other subsistence activities such as fishing (by poisoning or with rod and line), bird snaring (quail, partridge, lapwings, coots, and wild geese), hunting (deer, wild dogs, wolves, bears, leopards, and tigers), and the raising of goats (for sacrifice), cattle (cows and oxen for manure, field cultivation, and dairy products), pigs, dogs, and hens (for sacrifice), chickens and ducks (largely for eggs), and bees (for larvae, wax, and honey).

Industrial Arts. Industrial specialization by village obtains to some extent among the Khasi, but generally they practice a great diversity of industrial arts. Cottage industries and industrial arts include cane and bamboo work, blacksmithing, tailoring, handloom weaving and spinning, cocoon rearing, lac production, stonecutting, brick making, jewelry making, pottery making, iron smelting, and beekeeping. Manufactured goods include: woven cloth, coarse cotton, *randia* cloth, quilts (made of beaten and woven tree bark), hoes, plowshares, billhooks, axes, silver work, miscellaneous implements of husbandry, netted bags (of pineapple fiber), pottery (made without the use of the potter's wheel), mats, baskets, rope and string, gunpowder, brass cooking utensils, bows, arrows, swords, spears, and shields.

Trade. Trade takes place between villages, with the plains areas, and between highland and lowland areas. Barter (though to a lesser extent now) and currency are the media of exchange. There are local markets (village-based) in addition to a large central market in Shillong, and a large portion of Khasi produce is exported. Within a typical Khasi market one may find the following for sale: bees, rice beer, rice, millet, beans, sugarcane, fish, potatoes, oranges, lemons, mangoes, breadfruit, pepper, bananas, cinnamon, goats, sheep, cattle (live and slaughtered), and housing and cultivation products (roofing grass, cut beams, bamboo poles, latticework, dried cow manure, spades, baskets, bamboo drinking cups, gourd bottles, wooden mortars, water pipes made of coconut, clay pipe bowls, iron pots, and earthen dishes). Large markets, like Shillong, contain goods from foreign markets (e.g., from Europe).

Division of Labor. Men clear land, perform jhum agriculture, handle cattle, and engage in metalworking and woodworking. Women weave cloth, act as vendors in the market, and are responsible in large part for the socialization of children. Women are credited with being the growers of provisions sold at market. Men also participate in market activities by selling articles which they manufacture and produce (e.g., ironwork), raise (e.g., goats, sheep), or catch (e.g., birds). They also bring provisions to women at market and exercise some degree of control over the market by acting as accountants. For example, a husband may be responsible to his own family (by working the fields for his wife) while at the same time keeping his sister's mercantile accounts. A woman's uncle, brother, or son may function in a similar capacity on her behalf, though this is more likely to be the case if the woman's business is on a large scale.

Land Tenure. There are four kinds of public land: *ka ri raj* (Crown lands); *ka ri lyngdoh* (priestly lands); *ki shong* (village lands for the production of thatching grass, firewood, etc.); and *ki 'lawkyntang* (sacred groves). There are two types of private land: *ri-kur* (land owned by a clan) and *ri-kynti* (land owned by families or acquired; it is inherited by a woman from her mother or is acquired by a man or a woman). Ancestral land must always be owned by a woman. Men may cultivate the land, but the produce must be carried to the house of the mother who divides it among the members of her family. Usually, if a man obtains land, upon his death it is inherited by his mother (i.e., if he is unmarried). There is, however, a provision made for a man to will land acquired after marriage to his children.

Kinship

Kin Groups and Descent. The Khasi are a well-known instance of matriliny. The maximal matrilineage among them is the clan (called *kur* or *jaid*). The Khasi speak of a family of great-grandchildren of one great-grandmother (thus, four generations) as *shi kpoh* (one womb). Clans trace descent from ancestresses or *kiaw* (grandmothers) who are called *ki lawbei-tynrai* (grandmothers of the root, i.e., of the clan tree). In some instances the actual name of the ancestress survives. She is revered greatly and her descendants are called *shi kur* (one clan). Below this division are the subclan or *kpoh* (as already mentioned, descendants of one great-grandmother) and the *iing* (house or family), usually made up of a grandmother, her daughters, and her daughters' children. Together these are said to be *shi iing* (one house).

Kinship Terminology. Kinship terminology employed for first cousins follows the Iroquois pattern.

Marriage and Family

Marriage. The Khasi are, for the most part, monogamous. Their social organization does not favor other forms of marriage; therefore, deviation from this norm is quite rare. Marriage is a purely civil contract. The ceremony consists of a betrothal, the pouring of a libation to the clan's first maternal ancestor, the taking of food from the same plate, and the taking of the bride to the house of the groom's mother where a ring is placed on the bride's finger by her mother-in-law. Males are between the ages of 18 and 35 when they marry, while women's ages range from 13 to 18. Although parentally arranged marriages do occur, this does not appear to be the preferred form. Young men and women are permitted considerable freedom in the choice of mates and in premarital sexual relations. Potential marriage partners are likely to have been acquainted before betrothal. Once a man has selected his desired spouse, he reports his choice to his parents. They then secure the services of a male relative (or other male unrelated to the family) to make the arrangements with the female's family (provided that the man's parent's agree with his choice). The parents of the woman ascertain her wishes and if she agrees to the arrangement her parents check to make certain that the man to be wed is not a member of their clan (since Khasi clans are exogamous, marital partners may not be from the same clan). If this is satisfactory, then omens are taken. If the omens are favorable, then a wedding date is set, but if the omens are negative, the wedding plans are abandoned. Divorce is frequent (with causes ranging from incompatibility to lack of offspring) and easily obtainable. This ceremony consists of the husband handing the wife 5 cowries or paisa which the wife then hands back to her husband along with 5 of her own. The husband then throws these away or gives them to a village elder who throws them away. According to Gurdon, postmarital residence is matrilocal, with the husband and wife leaving the wife's mother's residence after the birth of one or two children. C. Nakane makes a further distinction between two types of marriages, the first being marriage to an heiress, the second marriage to a nonheiress. The type of marriage is, for Nakane, the determining factor in marital residence. This practice is the result of rules and regulations governing inheritance and property ownership. These rules are themselves related to the structure of the Khasi iing. In short, postmarital residence when an heiress is involved must be uxorilocal, while postmarital residence when a nonheiress is involved is neolocal. Khasi men prefer to marry a nonheiress because it will allow them to form independent family units somewhat immune to pressures from the wife's kin. A Khasi man returns to his iing upon the death of his spouse (if she is an heiress). If she is not an heiress, he may remain with his children if they are not too young and if he plans to marry his wife's younger sister. Marriage to a deceased wife's elder sister is prohibited. This is the only form of the sororate found among the Khasi. The levirate does not obtain in Khasi society. It has been suggested that the increasing monetization of the Khasi economy and availability of jobs for men beyond village confines may have altered postmarital residence patterns.

Domestic Unit. Around the turn of the century, the basic Khasi domestic unit was a single household made up of a grandmother, her daughters, and her daughters' children (the grandmother being the head of the household during her lifetime). In mid-century, Nakane distinguished between four types of Khasi households: (1) a household comprised of wife, husband, their children, and wife's unmarried sisters and brothers; (2) a household composed of nearly all the iing members (but not including their spouses) or a larger household (including wives and husbands) that contains all descendants of three or more generations from one woman (in which case the iing corresponds to the kpoh); (3) an intermediate type of household, between types 1 and 2, that is popular among newly married couples before the birth of children, in which a husband is supposed to live in the wife's house but often returns to his sister's house for meals and to sleep, and in which the husband is responsible for working his wife's fields and may also work those of his mother and sister; and (4) one nuclear family unit (usually when the man marries a nonheiress). According to Nakane, most Khasi households are of types 1, 3, and 4. All three types are usually found in one village. Type 2 was prominent at one time among the Jaintias.

Inheritance. With regard to real property, inheritance goes to the youngest daughter of the deceased mother and upon the youngest daughter's death in turn to her youngest daughter. Other daughters are entitled to a smaller share of the inheritance of their mother, but the largest share goes to the youngest daughter. When the mother has no daughters, the inheritance goes to her sister's youngest daughter. If the sister has no daughters, then the mother's sisters and their female kin receive the inheritance. Men are prohibited from inheriting real property. All property acquired by a man before marriage belongs to his mother. Property acquired by him after marriage belongs to his wife and children. Of these children, the youngest daughter will receive the largest share of the inheritance upon the death of the man's wife. If the man has no daughters, then his sons receive his property upon the death of their mother. Christian conversion has had and may continue to have a deleterious effect on the Khasi system of inheritance. Khasi heiresses who converted to Christianity lost their right to inherit at one time in Khasi social history. With the gradual acceptance of Christianity, these rights were restored. However, there is a tendency for heiresses who convert to Christianity to discontinue their sacerdotal functions within the family. It has been suggested that this may threaten the institution of ultimogeniture. It has also been suggested that the availability of nonland-based employment for males may undermine the economic basis of matrilineal inheritance.

Socialization. Naming occurs one day after birth. Family activities center on the performance of religious rites, management of family property, and the maintenance and protection of kin relations. Men, women, and children participate fully in these and other labor-related activities. Women, however, are the chief agents of socialization.

Sociopolitical Organization

Social Organization. Khasi villages tend to be endogamous units, each one containing a number of matrilineal clans (kur). Members of these clans trace their descent from a common female ancestor. Solidarity is manifest largely on this level of social organization. There are three class-defined lineages—nobles, commoners, and slaves. Elderly men and men of importance wear turbans as a sign of status, and men who have sponsored a great feast may wear silver armlets above the elbows. Wealth can be demonstrated in a number of ways, including the size of the mawbynna (monument) one has constructed at the burial site of a deceased person and the ownership of decorative gongs (wiang). In some sense, the lyngdohship (priesthood) may also be treated as a sign of status. The matrilineal clan is perhaps the most important primary institution. The position of women is more prominent than that of men. As member of a clan, a man will be lost to his mother's clan when he marries, his status shifting from that of u kur (brother) in his clan to that of u shong ka (begetter) in his wife's clan. He is not allowed to participate in the religious observances of his wife's clan and when he dies he is not buried in his wife's family tomb. Women also assume leadership in secondary institutions (e.g., religion) as evidenced by their management of the family cults and the performance of its attendant rituals.

Political Organization. The Khasi state system arose originally from the voluntary association of villages or groups thereof. The head of state is the _siem_ (chief). He has limited monarchical powers. He may perform certain acts without the approval of his _durbar_ (an executive council over which he presides). He also possesses judicial powers. Those who sit on the durbar are called _mantris_. These individuals are charged with the actual management of the state. Some states have officials called _sirdars_ (village headmen) who collect labor, receive _pynsuk_ (gratification) for the siem, and settle local cases. In Nongstoin there is an official called a _lyngskor_ who acts as supervisor of a number of sirdars. In most states the siem is the religious and secular head of state. He conducts certain public religious ceremonies, consults oracles and acts as judge (the durbar being the jury) in legal cases, and in times past was the literal head of the army in battle. The siem was chosen by popular election in Langrim, Bhoval, and Nobosohpoh states. The British attempted to impose this system on all Khasi states but the results of their efforts were questionable. Little was accomplished save the confirmation of an electoral body that itself elected the siem. Succession to siemship is always through the female side. A new siem is elected from a siem family (of which there is one in every state) by an electoral body that may be composed of representatives from certain priestly and nonpriestly clans, village headmen, and _basams_ (market supervisors).

Social Control. Interpersonal tensions, domestic disagreements, and interclan disputes account for the major part of conflict within Khasi society. Other sources include the swearing of false oaths, incest, revenge, conversions to other religions, failure to maintain the family religious cults, adultery, rape, arson, and sorcery. Social control is maintained by clan, village, state, and national authorities. The traditional means used to maintain order included exile, monetary fines, curses, disinheritance, enforced servitude, imprisonment, capital punishment, confinement (e.g., in the stocks), imposition of fetters, and confinement to a bamboo platform under which chilies were burnt.

Conflict. Conflict between states and regions (e.g., between the Khasi and the peoples of the plains) was prevalent before the arrival of the British. The taking of heads (associated with the worship of the war god U Syngkai Bamon) was also practiced by the Khasi. In their conflict with British imperial forces, the Khasi relied heavily on ambush and guerrilla tactics. Little is known of traditional Khasi contacts with other groups.

Religion and Expressive Culture

Religious Beliefs. Christian missionary work among the Khasi began in the late nineteenth century with the efforts of the Welsh Calvinistic Methodist mission. The effects of their endeavors and those of other Christian bodies have been considerable. Today over half of all Khasis have adopted Christianity. The missionary impact may be noted on almost all levels of culture. However, the core of traditional Khasi religious beliefs remains intact. The Khasi believe in a creator god (U Blei Nong-thaw) who is considered feminine in gender (Ka lei Synshar). She is invoked when sacrifices are offered and during times of trouble. The propitiation of good and evil spirits is also part of this system, as is the worship of ancestors. The following major spirits are worshiped: Ulei Muluk (god of the state); Ulei Umtang (god of drinking water and cooking water); Ulei Longspah (god of wealth); and O Ryngkew or U Basa Shnong (tutelary deity of the village).

Religious Practitioners. The propitiation of the spirits is carried out by the *lyngdoh* (priest) or by old men knowledgeable in the art of necromancy. Other practitioners include the *soh-blei* and *soh-blah* (male functionaries with limited sacerdotal functions), the *ka soh-blei*, also called *ka-soh-sla* or *ka-lyngdoh* (female priests who must be present at the offering of all sacrifices), and the *nongkhan* (diviners). The lyngdoh—who is always appointed from a special priestly clan, who holds his office for life, and who may be one of several within a state—is the chief functionary of the communal cults. He also has certain duties in conjunction with marital laws and household exorcism. In some states, the lyngdoh subsumes the responsibilities of siem (chief) and rules with the assistance of a council of elders. The duty of performing family ceremonies is the sole responsibility of the head of the family or clan who usually fulfills them through the agency of the *kni* (maternal uncle). Female priests must assist at all sacrifices and, in fact, are the only functionaries in possession of full sacerdotal authority. The lyngdoh exercises his duties as appointed agent of the ka soh-blei (female priest). It is believed that this system is an archaic survival from a period in Khasi history when the female priest acted as her own agent in the offering of sacrifice. In some states (e.g., Nongkrem), there is a high priestess who functions sacerdotally and as head of state. She delegates temporal responsibilities to a son or nephew who then exercises them as a siem. The adoption of Christianity by a large segment of Khasi society has resulted in important changes. The sacerdotal function of the youngest daughter (responsible, in traditional Khasi culture, for conducting burial services on behalf of her parents and for acting as chief practitioner of the family cult) has been threatened by Christian teaching and practice (i.e., the youngest daughter, if a Christian, is less likely to fulfill her priestly responsibilities to her family).

Ceremonies. Dancing and music are important parts of Khasi ritual, and the Nongkrem Dance (part of the *pom-blang* or goat-killing ceremony) is the major festival on the Khasi calendar. It is dedicated to Ka lei Synshar, for the ruling of the Khasi. Its purpose is to ensure substantial crop yield and good fortune for the state. It is held in late spring (usually in May). A number of state and communal rituals are also performed, in addition to many ceremonies associated with the human life cycle (birth, marriage, death, etc.).

Arts. Examples of decorative art include metal gongs (with animal engravings), implements of warfare (arrows, spears, bows, and shields), and memorial slabs (with engravings). To a limited extent woodwork, jewelry, and other industrial manufactures may be so classified. Music is an important part of Khasi religious ceremonies (both communal and clan-related), hunting expeditions, and athletic events (e.g., archery contests). Musical forms include extemporaneous verse that is said to resemble, in form and content, magicoreligious incantations. Drums, guitars, wooden pipes and flutes, metal cymbals, and various harps are among the instruments used in Khasi musical performance. As was mentioned previously, dancing also accompanies most ceremonies in public and private life. With regard to literature, a considerable body of oral and written material exists. This includes proverbs, myths, legends, folktales, songs, and agricultural sayings.

Medicine. In traditional Khasi medical practice magicoreligious means are used to prevent and treat sickness. The only indigenous drugs used are chiretta (a febrifuge of the Gentianaceae order—*Swertia chirata*) and wormwood. Native medical specialists are not present. Generally illness is believed to be caused by one or more spirits as a result of a human act of omission. Health, within this system, can be restored only by the propitiation of the spirits or, if the spirits are not able to be appeased, by calling on other spirits for assistance. Divination is done by breaking an egg and "reading" the resulting signs.

Death and Afterlife. In Khasi eschatology, those who die and have proper funeral ceremonies performed on their behalf go to the house (or garden) of God, which is filled with betel-palm groves. Here they enjoy a state of endless bliss. Those who do not receive proper burial are believed to roam the Earth in the form of animals, birds, and insects. This idea of soul transmigration is believed to have been borrowed from Hindu theology. Unlike Christian eschatology, that of the Khasi is not characterized by a belief in any form of eternal punishment after death.

Bibliography

Assam, Department of Economics and Statistics (1955). *Report on Rural Economic Survey in United Khasi and Jaintia Hills*. Shillong: Government Press.

Becker, Cristofero (1924). "Familienbesitz und Mutterrecht in Assam." In *Zeitschrift für Buddhismus und verwandte Gebiete* 6:127–138, 300–310. Reprint. 1925. Munich and Neubiberg: O. Schloss.

Godwin-Austen, H. H. (1872). "On the Stone Monuments of the Khasi Hill Tribes, and on Some Peculiar Rites and Customs of the People." *Journal of the Anthropological Institute of Great Britain and Ireland* 1:122–143.

Gurdon, P. R. T. (1904). "Note on the Khasis, Syntengs, and Allied Tribes, Inhabiting the Khasi and Jaintia Hills District in Assam." *Journal of the Asiatic Society of Bengal* 73, pt. 3:57–74.

Gurdon, P. R. T. (1907). *The Khasis*. London: D. Nutt. 2nd ed. 1914. Reprint. 1975. Delhi: Cosmo Publications.

Hunter, William W. (1879). "Statistical Account of the Khasi and Jaintia Hills." In *Statistical Account of Assam*. Vol. 2, 201–255. London: Trübner.

McCormack, Anna P. (1964). "Khasis." In *Ethnic Groups of Mainland Southeast Asia*, edited by Frank M. Lebar et al., 105–112. New Haven, Conn.: HRAF Press.

Nakane, Chie (1967). *Garo and Khasi: A Comparative Study in Matrilineal Systems*. Paris: Mouton.

Roy, David (1938). "The Place of the Khasi in the World." *Man in India* 18:122–134.

Stegmiller, F. (1921). "Aus dem Religiösen Leben der Khasi." *Anthropos* 16–17:407–441.

Stegmiller, F. (1924). "Opfer und Opferbräuche der Khasi." *Anthropologischen Gesellschaft in Wien, Mitteilungen* 54: 211–231.

Stegmiller, F. (1925). "Pfeilschiessen und Jagdgebräuche der Khasi." *Anthropos* 20:607–623.

Stegmiller, F. (1928). "Das Marktleben der Khasi." In *Festschrift*. Publication d'hommage offerte au P. W. Schmidt. 76 sprachwissenschaftliche, ethnologische, religionswissenschaftliche, prähistorische und andere Studien.... Edited by Wilhelm Koppers, 703–710. Vienna: Mechitaristen-congregations-buchdruckerei.

HUGH R. PAGE, JR.

Khoja

ETHNONYMS: none

The Khojas are an ethnic group in India and Pakistan, formerly a Hindu trading caste, founded in the fourteenth century by a famous saint, and followers of the Agha Khan, the spiritual leader of the Ismaili sect. They live in the Punjab, in Sind, Kachchh, Kathiawar, and down the western coast of India; in Zanzibar and elsewhere on the east coast of Africa; and in scattered groups under the name of Mawalis in the Hindu Kush region and the North-West Frontier Province of Pakistan, in Afghanistan, in the Khanates of central Asia, in the hilly districts of eastern Persia, and in the Persian Gulf area. "Khoja" is the form used in India for the Persian term "Khwajah," meaning "a rich or respectable man; a gentleman; an opulent merchant."

Khojas are the major Muslim trading caste of western India. The Khojas of the Punjab are Sunni and are largely derived from the Hindu caste Khatri. The Khojas of Bombay, however, derive largely from the Hindu Lohana caste in Sind, and they are Shia and followers of the Agha Khan. The Punjab Khojas do not owe allegiance to the Agha Khan, but instead hold religious beliefs similar to those of the Bombay Khojas. They are, like the Bombay Khojas, converted Hindus, who are mainly engaged in commercial occupations, keep accounts in Hindi, and follow Hindu customs. The Punjab Khojas derive their origin from Hajji Saiyid Sadr al-Din, who came in the fifteenth century as an Ismaili preacher from Korasan in eastern Persia. He presented his doctrines to the Hindus in a form that would appeal to their own traditions. He is thought to be the author of *Das-Avatar*, in which the incarnations of Vishnu are described as leading toward Islam. The *Das-Avatar* is used to the present day by the Punjabi Khojas as well as by the Agha Khan's Indian followers and their offshoots in east Africa. The Punjab Khojas look to fakirs of the Kadriya and Cishtiya sects and other *pirs* (Muslim saints) for practical guidance because their religious beliefs are not identical.

The Khojas of western India and their offshoots in east Africa form a closely organized community and are in direct touch with the Agha Khan. Their religious ideas are in origin the same as those of the Punjabi Khojas, but their living contact with the imam in the person of the Agha Khan has isolated them from the influence of Muslim religious orders.

The Khojas are mainly governed by customary law. In 1847, the Bombay High Court held that the Muslim law of succession does not apply to them and that, as under Hindu law, their females are excluded from immediate succession. Khojas have many observances and customs differing from those of regular Muslims. The Chatti, a sixth-day ceremony after birth, differs from that performed by regular Gujarat Muslims. On that day, a *bajot* or wooden stool is placed near the mother's bed, on which the child and mother are bathed and dressed. On the evening of the sixth day the following items are placed on the stool: a red pen, an ink stand or blank book, a knife, and a garland of flowers. The pen, ink, and paper symbolize the goddess of fortune who is believed to write down the destiny of the newborn child. Along with the wooden stool, a *chaumukh* (a four-sided butter-fed dough lamp) is also placed there and lighted, and next to it a box of Chinese firecrackers. As each of the family relatives comes to visit, she strews a little rice near the stool, laying her present of gold or silver anklets and bracelets on the ground. Then each female bends over the mother and baby and takes their *balayen* or ills upon herself by passing her hands over them and cracking their finger joints against her temples. The baby is then laid on the ground on the strewn rice. Then the mother rises and worships the child by bowing toward it and the chaumukh on the stool. Then the firecrackers are ignited and the child is laid in its mother's lap.

The marriage, divorce, and funeral customs of the Khojas differ from the general law and customs of Islam. The fathers or male guardians of the marrying pair meet three or four days before at the *jama-at khana* or assembly lodge with their friends and relatives and the *mukhi* or another jama-at officer. The officer registers the name of the bride and the groom under the order of the Agha Khan. The father of the bridegroom gives a token 5.25 rupees to the father of the bride. The sum is received by the girl's father and handed to the jama-at officer as a contribution to the fund. The groom's friends place before the jama-at officer a copper or brass vessel containing from 5 to 10 seers of sugars. After repeating the hallowed names of the five holy persons, or the *Panj-tan*—the Prophet Mohammed, Ali (the Prophet's son-in-law), Fatima (the Prophet's favorite daughter and Ali's wife), Hasan and Husein (sons of Ali and Fatima)—the sugar tray is placed before the bride's father as a sign of acceptance of the compact. He tastes it, and then it is distributed among those present.

Next morning a written agreement is prepared. The jama-at scribe begins the writing with the names of the five holy persons and the names of the four archangels in the four corners: Diabrail, Israfil, Azra'il, and Mikail (except that in Bombay, this *nikah* ceremony used until recently to be celebrated by Sunni kadis [religious judges]). It is sometimes performed by the Agha Khan, or, outside Bombay, by his officers; a marriage certificate in due form is issued in Gujarati with the names of the four archangels on it.

No divorce is permitted without the jama-at's sanction, and the jama-at usually requires the consent of both parties. A second wife is not allowed in the lifetime of the first without the jama-at's sanction, which is however granted if 2,000 rupees are deposited for the first wife's maintenance. A curious custom followed on the approach of death is that of *samarchanta* or the sprinkling of holy water to the reading of *Das-Avatar*.

The organization of the community is in the form of a fiscal centralization around the sacred person of Agha Khan, but there is complete congregational independence in administrative matters, including even questions of excommunication. Every congregation has its own jama-at khana, which is both a meetinghouse and a mosque. The officers are sometimes appointed by the Agha Khan, but they are often elected. The offerings for the imam are collected through them. These comprise the fixed *dasandh* or tithe and various minor dues on special occasions, either recurring or occasional.

Khojas enjoy a good business reputation and are said to have a keen sense of competition. They are described as neat, clean, sober, thrifty, and ambitious, and enterprising, cool, and resourceful in trade. They are great travelers by land and sea, visiting and settling in distant countries for purposes of trade. They have business connections with the Punjab, Sind, Calcutta, Sri Lanka, Myanmar (Burma), Singapore, China, and Japan; with ports of the Persian Gulf, Arabia, and east Africa; and with England, the United States, and Australia. Khojah youths go as apprentices in foreign Khojah firms on salaries of 200 to 2,000 rupees a year with board and lodging. The Khojas now enjoy powerful positions in ivory, horn, cotton, hide, mother-of-pearl, grain, spice, fish maws, shark fins, cottonseed, furniture, opium, and silk trades. They have also gained high places in the professions as doctors, engineers, and lawyers.

See also Bania; Bohra

Bibliography

Enthoven, Reginald E. (1921). "Kojah." In *The Tribes and Castes of Bombay*, edited by Reginald E. Enthoven. Vol. 2, 218–230. Bombay: Government Central Press.

SARWAT S. ELAHI

Kiranti

ETHNONYMS: none

The Kirantis are composed of two distinct ethnic groups, the Rai and the Limbu, and number about 500,000 in eastern Nepal.

See also Limbu; Rai

Bibliography

Chemjon, I. S. (1952). *Kirati Itihas*. Gangtok.

Kohistani

ETHNONYMS: Dard, Duberwal, Killiwal ("villager"), Mayan, Mayr, Patanwal

Kohistan is a mountainous area lying between the Indus River and the Durand Line that forms the border between Afghanistan and Pakistan; it stretches northward from 35° N and the former kingdom of Swat as far as Gilgit. The Kohistanis have also been called Dards because they speak four languages of the small Dardic branch of the Indo-Aryan Subfamily: Torwali, Gawri, Eastern and Western Kohistani (but not Kashmiri, the most important language of this branch). Like the Gujars, who are also found in Kohistan, the Kohistanis practise transhumant pastoralism of sheep and goats; but in the fertile valley bottoms they are also able to plow and irrigate fields, growing maize, millet, and other crops. A few low-lying areas produce wheat or rice; but only one crop a year is possible. Thus Kohistanis move around seasonally between farmlands at about 1,000 meters and summer camps all the way up to 4,500 meters. Cattle and water buffalo are kept at the lower elevations.

The history of this area has been as varied as the terrain. The earliest mention of Swat can be found in the *Rig Veda*, and then in Greek (327 B.C.) and Chinese (A.D. 519) records. The area has successively been Buddhist, then Hindu, then (since A.D. 1000) Muslim. To some extent individual Pakhtuns have been absorbed in recent times into the Kohistani ethnic group, which perhaps numbers 50,000 today, although cultural influence has mostly flowed from the Pakhtun to the Kohistani.

Because the area is so diverse geographically, it tends to be politically fragmented, even anarchic, and control by the Pakistani government is minimal at best. Kohistani villages are made up of several minimal lineages, each of which has representation on a village council, which tends to be the highest authority. Aside from the farmers, a village population normally includes blacksmiths and carpenters (Pashto-speaking) and a few farm laborers or tenants.

The Kohistanis are Muslims. They are motivated by a reverence for the Quran and its teachings, as well as by *izzat* (male honor). The seclusion of women, however, is rather problematic because of their importance in farm work.

See also Dard; Pathan

Bibliography

Barth, Fredrik (1956). *Indus and Swat Kohistan: An Ethnographic Survey*. Studies Honouring the Centennial of Universitetets Etnografiske Museum, Oslo, 1857–1957, vol. 2. Oslo: Forenede Trykkerier.

Barth, Fredrik (1981). *Features of Person and Society in Swat: Collected Essays on Pathans. Selected Essays of Fredrik Barth*, vol. 2. London: Routledge & Kegan Paul.

Biddulph, John (1880). *Tribes of the Hindoo Koosh*. Calcutta: Superintendent of Government Printing.

Leitner, Gotlieb William (1877). *The Languages and Races of Dardistan*. Lahore: Government Central Book Depot.

PAUL HOCKINGS

Kol

ETHNONYMS: none

Orientation

Identification. The word "Kol" appears to have been derived from the Mundari word *ko*, meaning "they," or from *horo, hara, har, ho*, or *koro*—"the men"—by which the Kols identify themselves. The Kol lent their name to the language group formerly known as the Kolarian, and now better known as the Mundari or Austroasiatic Language Family. The Kol belonged to the Proto-Australoid ethnic stratum. The Santal, Munda, Ho, Bhumij, Kharia, Khairwar, and Korwa who are akin to the Kol were termed Kolarian tribes. The Kols are mentioned as a generic category of people in eastern India in medieval texts. In the imperial period, the word "Kol" acquired a pejorative meaning as it became a synonym for the savage, the lowly, those performing menial jobs, the militant, and the aggressive. The "Larka" (fighting) Kol was an appellation given by the British administration to the Ho and the Munda—both are related groups—who led the insurrection of 1831–1832 in Chota Nagpur. After this uprising, the word "Kol" appears to have faded out of the early ethnography of Chota Nagpur and was replaced by the names of the constituent tribes, such as Ho, Munda, etc. The Ho in Orissa still carry the name "Kolha," with a large population (326,522 in 1981), because they came from Kolhan in Singbhum District. There are also Kolha Lohar who practice blacksmithing in Orissa.

Location. The tribe that today bears the name Kol is restricted to a part of Madhya Pradesh and Uttar Pradesh. Earlier the Kols were described as one of the most widely spread and well-known tribes of the central uplands, extending from Kolhan to west of the Chittor Hills in Rajasthan. But now they are identified with the Kol tribe only, distributed in twenty-three districts of Madhya Pradesh and nine adjoining districts of Uttar Pradesh. In Maharashtra the Kol are found in Nagpur District, in small numbers, where they have settled down as migrant laborers. The habitat of the Kol is a very warm or quite cold climate with low humidity and medium rainfall.

Demography. In 1971 there were 489,875 Kols listed in the census (probably an undercount).

Linguistic Affiliation. The Kol no longer use their ancient language and have adopted Hindi and the Devanagari script. The Kol Lohar in Orissa speak Oriya but are bilingual in Kol as well. The speakers of this language (as of 1961) number only 64,465 persons, of whom 10,267 (15.93 percent) are bilingual. Among the bilinguals 7,937 persons (77.31 percent) know the Oriya language and 2,330 persons (22.69 percent) speak other languages.

History and Cultural Relations

The Kols consider themselves to be the descendants of Sahara Mata, a member of the Savaras of epic fame; she is known as the "mother of the Kol." The Kols of the Jabalpur-Katni area (of Madhya Pradesh) believe that they were earlier in Mewar (Rajasthan) and occupied its hills. They have inherited a martial character and believe that only with the help of the Kol and the Bhil peoples could Rana Pratap fight the Moguls. Nevertheless, while history has recorded the role of the Bhils, the Kols are not mentioned.

The Kols are an example of a tribe that has changed considerably over time. The earliest references relate to larger, generic conglomerates on the fringe of a Sanskritic culture and civilization. Their mention in the ethnography of the British imperial period was not very specific. Today the great Kols have disappeared, but their name clings to a small tribal population, which in 1946 was described as being very close to becoming a caste and to being Hinduized. Neither possibility has entirely materialized. The Kols have survived as a community, with an identity of their own and an adaptability that was underestimated by early ethnographers.

Economy

Subsistence and Commercial Activities. The Kols were once adept at unirrigated hill cultivation. Later, when they moved into the valleys, they could not easily adapt to wet rice cultivation. Therefore the Kol are not known today as agriculturists. They work more often as daily wage laborers, collectors of forest produce, and gatherers of wood fuel. They sell bundles of wood to their neighbors and at markets. The most important forest produce collected by them is the wood-apple, which is used for preparation of dyes and herbal medicine; it is dried and sold at a good price. In 1946, W. G. Griffiths identified three strata among the Kol: the factory workers who were fairly well-off; the forest people and agriculturists who had enough to eat but no cash; and the wood and grass cutters who were the poorest of the lot. Their condition has not markedly changed since.

Land Tenure. A few Kols own land, but most are landless. Those who have land enjoy free ownership rights over a patch of land for three years, and after the lapse of this period they become *bhumiswami* (lord of the patch of land). As a result they cannot sell their land without the express permission of the district collector. The forest where they collect wood fuel or wood-apples belongs to the government but they do not pay any taxes. They also graze their cattle on government land for which no tax is paid.

Kinship, Marriage, and Family

Kin Groups and Descent. The Kols are divided into a number of subdivisions such as the Rautia, Rautel, Dassao, Dahait, Kathotia, Birtiya, and Thakuria. In Jabalpur the Kol mainly belong to the Rautia and Thakuria subdivisions, whereas in Nagpur they are mainly Rautia. These subdivisions are endogamous units (*baenk*) that regulate marriage. Griffiths (1946) listed about twenty-two *kulhi* (baenk); William Crooke (1896) gave a list of nine septs, but now only seven are known. The members of the baenk do not inter-marry. There is a belief that one baenk is superior or inferior to another, and no intermarriage is thus possible between them. But in recent years a Rautel may marry a Kathotia and a Kathotia a Dassao. The members of Thakuria baenk who consider themselves superior to all others do not intermarry with members of other baenks.

Kinship Terminology.   The kin terms used by the Kol of Jabalpur are similar to those used by the local non-Kols. The terms are of a bilateral type in which there are different terms for father, father's brother, and mother's brother. Generation differences are explicit (e.g., *beta* = son, *pitaji* = father, *aja* = grandfather). Kinship terms are mostly denotative. Specific terms are used for kin of the same generation, such as mother = *dai*, wife's mother = *thakurain*, husband's mother = *didi*, or again father's sister = *fua*, mother's sister = *mosi*. There are classificatory terms too. A sister, mother's brother's daughter, father's sister's daughter, and husband's sister are all referred to as *baia*. The terminological system resembles the Hawaiian type.

Marriage.   Monogamy is the rule but polygyny also occurs. As there is an adverse sex ratio with the Kol females outnumbering males, the Kol keep concubines (*rakhelu*). A rakhelu may belong to any baenk. She is kept in a separate house if the wife is alive. Keeping a rakhelu is a status symbol, well publicized and recognized by throwing a feast for members of one's kin group (*biradari*). A widow cannot remarry but can be a rakhelu. The wife's younger sister can be kept as a rak-helu after the death of the wife, and after an elder brother's death his wife is often kept as a concubine. A wife's elder sister and younger brother's wife are avoided for such relation-ships. Girls marry between 14 and 18 years of age and the boys between 20 and 24 years. Marriage with cross cousins, parallel cousins, sisters and their daughters, or a wife's elder sister is strictly forbidden and persons contracting such mar-riages have to pay a fine and/or throw a feast to gain the com-munity's approval. The Kols pay a bride-price (*chari*), which consists of 20 rupees, a calf or a goat, and such ornaments as a bangle (*kangan*), toe ornament (*lacha*), etc. In recent years chari has given place to dowry (*dahej*), which comprises 50 rupees in cash and utensils. Giving dahej is a status symbol; nowadays educated boys get cash, a bicycle, etc. With the poorer Kols, chari is still in vogue. Wearing the color vermil-ion and bangles are the symbols of marriage for women. The rakhelu also use these symbols. Marriage by elopement for-merly was in vogue; this practice is now rare. Incompatibility, adultery, and barrenness are primary reasons for seeking a di-vorce. In the case of a divorce, older children stay with the fa-ther, but the babies may go with the mother. A divorced woman does not get any compensation nor can she claim any portion of the husband's property. The dahej or chari is never returned. Adoption (*godnama*) does not require any formal permission from the community nor is a feast to be given to seek approval of it. Only the village messenger (*kotwar*) has to be informed verbally and he in turn informs the leader (*sar-panch*). A child, male or female, taken on godnama gets a share of the inheritance (if there are other sons of the de-ceased) or else all of it (if the deceased has no son). The rak-helu and her children form an appendage of the family.

Domestic Unit.   Residence is patrilocal in general. Never-theless, there are instances when a man stays with his wife after marriage, to look after her inherited property.

Inheritance.   Both movable and immovable property is in-herited by sons equally and no extra share is given to the eld-est or the youngest son. After marriage, the daughters cannot claim any share of the deceased father's property; however, if the deceased left no son, then the daughters can claim his property. A childless widow owns her husband's property. The property of a dead bachelor goes to one of his siblings. A divorced woman cannot claim any share in property while staying at her natal house but can insist on maintenance for life.

Sociopolitical Organization.

Social Organization.   As described above, the Kol are di-vided into twenty-three endogamous subunits called baenk. In addition, status and wealth distinctions are based on occu-pation as described above.

Political Organization.   The Kol have a council compris-ing three elderly personages (*mukhobar*) including a *malik* (headman) selected by the villagers. In Kol society a malik is a highly revered man. His son may become malik if the villag-ers so decide. On the death of a malik, his wife may perform the duties of her husband (as malik) till the villagers choose a new one.

Conflict and Social Control.   The malik and mukhobars are competent to handle cases involving the Kols. Whenever a dispute arises between a Kol and a non-Kol, the village council (*panchayat*) is approached. If the conflict refers to two villages it has to be decided by a larger body (*nyaypanch*) that covers five or more villages. The *pradhan* who is the chief of the nyaypanch is assisted by an *upopradhan* and a few *panches*, one of whom may be a Kol. The mukhobars within a village are contacted whenever there is a dispute involving in-fringement of community norms.

Religion and Expressive Culture

Religious Beliefs.   The Kol mainly profess Hinduism. The 1961 census recorded 100 percent of them as followers of Hinduism. In the 1971 census 99.67 percent of the Kols were listed as Hindus and 0.32 percent as of "indefinite belief" (another name for the traditional tribal religion); 0.01 per-cent did not state their religion. The 1981 census recorded 99.7 percent of the Kols as followers of Hinduism, 0.28 per-cent as professing "other religions" (the tribal religion), and the remaining 0.01 percent as Christians, Muslims, or Jains. Thus there has been no significant change during the period 1961–1981.

Religious Practitioners.   The Kols' own priest (*panda*) is an important functionary in Kol society. He officiates at the rituals centering on the worship of Desai Dur in April and Sorokhi Devi at any appropriate time, for the welfare of the Kol villages and Kol households. The panda also serves as the exorcist (*ojha*) who drives away evil spirits that cause sick-ness. Both offices are often held by one and the same person.

Ceremonies.   The Kols continue to worship their family deities, Babadeo Baba and Marhi, and village deities such as Shankarji, Kherdai, Hardola Baba, Hanuman, and Bhain-saur, which are generally considered benevolent. Kols visit the sacred centers at Allahabad, Bandakpur, and Maihar Mata. For acculturated Kols living in multicaste villages the Brahman priest worships the deities belonging to the Hindu pantheon for the Kols and officiates at rituals connected with life-cycle ceremonies. The Kols celebrate festivals like Ramanavmi, Dassara, Rakhi, Holi, Diwali, Janmashtami, and Shabari Jayanti.

Arts. The Kols have no performing or graphic arts; however, they have a rich repertory of tribal legends.

Death and Afterlife. The Kols usually cremate the dead; burial is for persons who have died of snakebite. In the first case the period of pollution ends on the thirteenth day, while in the second case it lasts three days.

See also Bhuiya; Bondo; Kond; Munda

Bibliography

Crooke, William (1896). *The Tribes and Castes of the North-Western Provinces and Oudh.* Vol. 3. Calcutta: Government Press.

Das Gupta, Biman Kumar (1978). "The Kol as They Are Now." Paper presented at seminar, Tribal Customary Laws. held in Calcutta (sponsored by the Anthropological Survey of India.)

Griffiths, W. G. (1946). *The Kol Tribes of Central India.* Royal Asiatic Society Monograph Series, vol. 2. Calcutta: Royal Asiatic Society of Bengal.

Guha, B. S. (1946). Introduction to *The Kol Tribes of Central India*, by W. G. Griffiths. Royal Asiatic Society Monograph Series, vol. 2. Calcutta: Royal Asiatic Society of Bengal.

Hasan, Amir (1972). *The Kols of Patha.* Allahabad: Kitab Mahal.

Jagannathan, R. (1964). *Census of India 1961. Madhya Pradesh. District Census Handbook. Jabalpur.* Bhopal: Government of India.

Jha, J. C. (1964). *The Kol Insurrection of Chotanagpur.* Calcutta: Thacker, Spink.

Risley, Herbert H. (1915). *The People of India.* 2d ed., edited by William Crooke. London: Thacker & Co. Reprint. 1969. Delhi: Oriental Books Reprint Corp., Munshiram Mamoharlal.

Russell, R. V., and Hira Lal (1916). "Kol." In *The Tribes and Castes of the Central Provinces of India.* Vol. 3, 500–519. London: Macmillan & Co. Reprint. 1969. Oosterhout: Anthropological Publications.

K. S. SINGH

Koli

ETHNONYMS: Hill Kolis, Sea Kolis, Son Kolis

The name "Koli" (from which is derived the English word *coolie*) is explained in a dozen ways, among which the most plausible is that it comes from the Sanskrit word *kula*, meaning "clan." The Koli numbered only 336,000 persons in 1911, but their numbers were estimated at 1.5 million in Bombay State alone in 1969. The Koli constitute a tribe with many branches and two main subdivisions: the Hill Kolis; and the Sea Kolis or Son Kolis. The most popular explanation for the origin of the term "Son" is that turmeric, which is very sacred to Dhandoba, the family god, is *son*—"golden" or "yellow" in color. The Son Kolis represent the highest group of the many subgroups, and the Dhor Koli are generally considered the lowest. The Son Kolis traditionally inhabit the area in and around Bombay, which lies between 18° and 19° N and 72° and 73° E, on the west coast of India. The Hill Kolis are found in Madhya Pradesh and include the Suraivansi, Malhar, Bhilaophod, Singade, Magadeo (who are further subdivided into the Bhas or "pure" Kolis and the Akaramase or "impure" Kolis), Dshatreiga, Naiks, Nimar (soldiers), the begging Kolis, Watandars (village sentries), and the Muhammedan Kolis.

The native tongue of the Kolis is Marathi, an Indo-European language, of which there are many different dialects spoken among the different subdivisions of the tribe.

The origins of the Kolis seem to have been forgotten. One theory suggests they emigrated from Sind and were part of the White Huns; another says they are a western branch of the great Kol or Munda tribal group. In Nimar the Kolis, like the Bhils, made a reputation for themselves as bandits during the unsettled times of the eighteenth century, and hence the term "hill robbers" was used to designate them as a class. Among the Nimar Kolis there is a saying: "The Koli were born from Shiva's wallet." The Son Kolis whose headquarters is in Bombay are believed to have been there from very early times. The *Mahikavatichi Bakhar* (see Punekar 1959, pp. 3–4) refers to the Kolis and several other tribes as having moved onto the land in A.D. 1138, at the time Pratap Bimb invaded Mahim (now a suburb of Bombay).

Standards of housing differ from region to region, varying from simple shacks of thatched roofs, mud walls, and mud flooring to decorated homes with tiled roofs, brick walls, and paved or cement flooring.

As already stated, the Koli tribe is composed of two main subdivisions: the Son Koli, who are a fishing community; and the Hill Koli, who have many hereditary occupations. In the Burhanpur Tahsil and the Satpura Hills area many Hill Koli are village servants, village sentries, and baggage handlers. Most of the different subdivisions of the tribe eat fish, fowl, and pork, but abstain from beef, and drink liquor. The social status of the tribe is considered low but not impure, as indicated by the fact that many higher caste groups, such as the Gujars, Kunbis, and some Rajputs, accept water from them.

The tribe has exogamous septs. A man is forbidden to marry a girl of his own sept or the daughter of his maternal uncle. Girls generally marry at an early age. A Brahman performs the marriage ceremony, which is conducted at sunset; a cloth is held jointly by the couple, and as the sun fades it is removed and they clasp hands. Afterward the couple march seven times around a stone slab surrounded by four plow yokes. The remarriage of widows is allowed, the ceremony simply being the tying of a knot in the cloths of the couple. Divorce is permitted for a wife's misconduct, and if she marries the adulterer he must pay to the husband the sum spent on his wedding.

Most Koli are Hindus, with a small percentage being Islamic converts. The principal deity of the Kolis of Nimar is the goddess Bhawani, and nearly every family has a silver image of her. There is an important shrine dedicated to the goddess in Inchirapur, where members of the tribe traditionally perform the hook-swinging rite in honor of her. Centuries ago this ceremony was practiced with a human being; today, however, a bundle of bamboos covered with cloth is swung. Among the Son Kolis the god Khandoba is considered by some as an incarnation of Shiva. As fishers, the Son Koli consider the sea itself to be a deity. The Koli customarily either bury or burn their dead, although the former is more common.

Bibliography

Enthoven, R. E. (1921). "Koli." In *The Tribes and Castes of Bombay*, edited by R. E. Enthoven. Vol. 2, 243–360. Bombay: Government Central Press. Reprint. 1975. Delhi: Cosmo Publications.

Punekar, Vijaya (1959). *The Son Kolis of Bombay*. Bombay: Popular Book Depot.

Rose, H. A. (1970). "Koli." In *A Glossary of the Tribes and Castes of the Punjab and North-West Frontier Provinces*. Vol. 1, 553–557. Patiala: Punjab University Languages Department.

Russell, R. V., and Hira Lal (1916). "Koli." In *The Tribes and Castes of the Central Provinces of India*, edited by R. V. Russell and Hira Lal. Vol. 3, 532–537. Nagpur: Government Printing Press. Reprint. 1969. Oosterhout: Anthropological Publications.

JAY DiMAGGIO

Kond

ETHNONYMS: Kandh, Khand, Khond, Kondl, Kui

Orientation

The Konds are a Dravidian people traditionally inhabiting the hill country of the Eastern Ghats of India. In Phulbani District, central Orissa State, they occupy an area lying between 19° and 20° N and 83° and 84° E. Their population in 1971 was 911,239. The name "Kond" (plural Kondulu) means "mountaineer," from the Telugu word meaning "hill."

However, they refer to themselves in their Kui language as "Kui people." There are several different tribes of various origins who speak the Kui language; for clarity's sake the term "Kond" is used here to refer to members of that specific tribe.

Kui (and its closely related dialect, Kuvi) is a Dravidian language with strong resemblance to Telugu, Tamil, and Kannada in grammar. Although Kui does not have its own script, it has borrowed the Oriya script.

History and Cultural Relations

It is believed the Konds originally came from the richer coastal plains of eastern India before being driven away during the Aryan advance. Three separate groups of Konds emerged from history: the subjugated Bettiah Konds, who inhabit the plains below the Ghats; the Benniah Konds, who inhabit the foothills and lower slopes of the Ghats; and the Maliah Konds or Hill Konds, constituting the majority of the Kond population, who are situated on the central tableland of the Ghats. The Hill Konds have never been under foreign domination, and for centuries they raided Oriya villages in the plains. Until the early nineteenth century they practiced human sacrifice as a religious rite in order to avoid natural calamities. Their neighbors the Pans have always been indispensable to the Konds in their capacity as traders, moneylenders, musicians, and intermediaries in all transactions between Hindus and Konds. Certain aspects of funerals that are taboo to the Konds themselves are handled by the Pans.

Settlements

Kond homes are traditionally rectangular with hardened dirt floors, strong outer wall-planks of wood, and thatched grass roofs with wood supports. Doorposts are used to keep cattle from the sleeping quarters of the occupants, who are housed in the same dwelling; chickens and goats share another room, and a pigsty is also traditionally found in a separate part of the house. The houses of a village are generally scattered near the fields.

Economy

Rice is the staple of the Kond, and both dry and wet cultivation are practiced in the foothills; maize and lentils are also important crops. Turmeric and mustard seed for oil, as well as grain and legume surpluses, represent the cash crops. Cattle are domesticated both for their milk and as draft animals; occasionally they are slaughtered for their meat. Pigs are kept both for their meat and as sacrificial animals. Chickens and goats are kept as well for all their economic benefits; jungle products such as teak hardwood (the most valuable tree in the forest) are cut, collected, and sold to the Pan wholesalers. Cooking is very plain, featuring nothing like the rich curries found elsewhere in India. Except for linseed oil, which is used to grease pots for cooking vegetables, oil is not used in cooking; instead, everybody uses it on skin and hair. Wild boars, deer, and hares are occasionally hunted and their meat is dried in the hot sun and stored in earthen pots. Distilled spirit made of the *mahua* blooms is a popular alcoholic beverage.

The Kond's neighbors the Pan act as middlemen in all trade between the Hill Kond and the Hindus from the plains. Exchange relations between villagers are still more prevalent than money except near market towns. Reed sleeping mats and soft grass sweeping brooms are popular crafts the men engage in, during the off-season from work in the paddies; these are in demand on the plains.

The men of a household are responsible for the hill-plot preparation, such as deforesting the land and moving large rocks, and for the leveling of the wet paddy fields. Plowing is strictly a man's business; in fact, it is taboo for a woman to touch a plowshare, the male symbol that penetrates the female earth. Threshing the paddy is a man's job and is temporarily stopped if the wife is menstruating. Women generally do all the cooking, the planting and weeding in the paddies, and the raising of the young. Young and old generally patrol the fields to protect them from birds and deer that feed on the rice seedlings.

Kinship, Marriage, and Family

The Kond family is patrilineal in structure. Childhood is traditionally a time of preparation for marriage and civic responsibility. When a girl turns seven her ears are pierced many times and kept open with bamboo insertions, which upon marriage are filled with a dozen or more rings given to her by her husband. At ten years of age a girl's upper face is traditionally tattooed. Girls who don't submit are considered undesirable for marriage, and it was once widely believed that a girl without tattoos would turn into a tiger. According to the men, there was a raja of Gumsur who had such an eye for Kond women that the practice of tattooing was adopted to make them less desirable to him and to end his raids into their villages; however, today the custom is dying out. Cousin marriage on either side is considered totally impossible. The clan is completely exogamous. Although the caste system is absent in Kond society, in some villages there is a religious idea of defilement that extends into cooking, eating, and marriage customs. Priests and shrine keepers must keep themselves pure by avoiding others of lower religious status under certain circumstances, and this attitude in some villages extends into several lower degrees of social stratification as well.

Sociopolitical Organization

The traditional administration of the Konds is centered on the clan. Each clan is headed by a male who is representative of the common ancestor; succession passes on to whoever is most competent. Beyond the individual clan leaders, each village is led by a Kond headman, a lay ritual official, possibly also a priest, and a council of village family leaders including the priest and a lay ritual official.

Religion

The Kond religion has two different forms of ritual within the same tribe, based on two different interpretations of Bura (the supreme being) and his consort Tari (the earth goddess). The followers of Bura insist that Bura in his struggle with Tari (who rebelled against Bura) was victorious; Tari's followers maintain that Tari was never conquered. According to the Bura sect, Bura created three classes of lesser gods to regulate the powers of nature for man. According to the Tari sect, the beliefs are the same; however, Tari is supreme and must be appeased with her natural food, human sacrifice,

which has been replaced by animal sacrifices. Since the nineteenth century Christian missionaries have converted many Konds.

Bibliography

Bailey, Frederick G. (1960). *Tribe, Caste, and Nation.* Manchester: Manchester University Press.

Boal, Barbara M. (1982). *The Konds: Human Sacrifice and Religious Change.* Warminster: Aris & Phillips.

JAY DiMAGGIO

Korku

ETHNONYMS: none

The Korku are a tribe of 275,654 (in 1971). The Korku language, which is often called the Kolarian language, belongs to the Munda Family of languages. This is further divided into northern and southern groups. The general name for the northern languages is Kherwari: it includes Santali, Mundari, Bhumij, Birhor, Koda, Ho, Turi, and Asuri. The southern languages include Juang, Bondo, Sora, Gadaba, and Pareng. For territorial, social, and/or religious reasons the Korkus are divided into a number of endogamous sections: Bopchis, Mowasis, Bondhis, and Bondayas, for example. Depending on its degree of Hinduization or Sanskritization, the rank of a section varies. This splits the Korkus into two rough divisions: the Sanskritized Deshi Korkus and the Potharia Korkus.

People of the plains have two names for the most-used sections of territory: Muikal Hills for the easternmost range; and Satpura Hills for the westernmost section (outsiders use the name "Satpura" for the whole chain of hills). Most of the central portion of the Satpura range is occupied by Korkus, while at the same time they have extended their habitat into the regions north and south of the Satpuras.

Most recently, there has been increased pressure by excessive population and stricter governmental administration that is forcing shifting cultivators to abandon their traditional manner of cultivation for plow agriculture. This affects the Korkus because only those who were fully absorbed into Hinduism adopted plow cultivation and settled alongside Hindu farming castes. The staple food of the Korku is *joari* (or sorghum, made into wheat bread and eaten with vegetables or pulse) or rice with pulse and vegetables.

Most Korku housing consists of well-planned villages with two long rows of huts, hut on hut, with occasional space provided for passage in between them. The huts are constructed of wood and bamboo with fireplaces in front of every house; thus fire is an everyday danger. Wealthier Korkus have begun to use tile and corrugated iron sheets to cover their houses. There are no windows in the house: smoke escapes through the cracks in the walls, while fresh air comes in through the same cracks. The house is rectangular in shape and is generally one room.

Marriage among the Korku can be viewed as a social contract or as a religious rite; it is considered as an arrangement not only between a man and a woman but even more so between their families. Marriage also marks the final initiation for boys and girls into adulthood.

It is rare for a Korku household to consist merely of a nuclear family. The family norm is parents, adult sons, the sons' wives and children, and often also the families of daughters married to mates who are paying off the bride-price through service. This is known as a joint family. Women are largely responsible for the smooth and efficient functioning of the Korku household and family life.

Certain property rights are granted to children within the Korku family. Once maturity is reached, the child's father takes him or her to the side and points out an animal and says, "From now on this animal belongs to you!" With this saying the father passes on property to his son or daughter. The animal is still considered the child's even after marriage, whether or not the child continues to live with the joint family. The male head of the Korku family makes all the major purchases and sales of land, cattle, ornaments, and clothing for the entire family. The senior female purchases food, kitchen utensils, earthen pots, and iron pans at the local market.

Inheritance is dictated by detailed traditional laws. For example, on the death of a Korku, his eldest son usually inherits the property; but if he was not living at home prior to the father's death, then the next-oldest son who did stay with his father inherits all the property. There is another catch, however: in either case, if the surviving sons decide to dismantle the joint family, the family property is divided into equal parts. Daughters don't inherit; a widow receives equal amounts with the sons and hands over her share once she decides which son she will stay with. If the widow remarries she can keep only her private property and not her share of the inheritance, which is then redivided among her sons.

Bibliography

Deogaonkar, S. G. (1990). *The Korku Tribals*. Delhi: Concept Publishers.

Fuchs, Stephen (1988). *The Korkus of the Vindhya Hills*. New Delhi: Inter-India Publications.

LeSHON KIMBLE

Kota

ETHNONYMS: Cohatur, Kohatur, Kotar, Koter, Kothur

[*Editor's Note*: In this article the established spellings of Kota words have been retained, along with diacritical marks, to facilitate reference to M. B. Emeneau's seminal publications on the Kota language.]

Orientation

Identification.   The Kotas are one of several small communities thought to be indigenous to the Nilgiri Hills of Tamil Nadu in south India. The Indian government classifies the Kotas as a Scheduled Tribe. Their name "Kota" (Ko·ta) was given by outsiders. They call themselves Ko·v. Although the Kotas are few in number they have wide visibility in the urbanizing Nilgiris. Once looked down upon as servants and eaters of carrion and buffalo flesh, the Kotas have managed to succeed in a number of occupations outside their traditional domain. They often work as head postmasters, doctors, government employees, and bankers and in other professional positions. Educational standards are also rising. No doubt the Kotas' success in a modern Indian setting is somehow related to the jack-of-all-trades character they always seem to have maintained. By shunning service relationships with the Badagas and Todas they have also removed the source of what they considered ill treatment on the part of these two local communities.

Location.   They occupy seven villages distributed rather widely throughout the Nilgiris District. Each village is situated near present or former settlements of Badagas, Todas, or Kurumbas.

Demography.   By their own estimates in 1990 the Kotas number 1,500—less than one-quarter of one percent of the district population of 1981, and an even smaller percentage today. Of these roughly 1,500 Kotas, probably fewer than 100 live in cities outside the Nilgiri District. Epidemics and other unstable health conditions—and, possibly, endogamous marriage practices among so few people—have resulted in relatively stable population figures over the past 150 years. Kota proverbs and songs indicate a strong concern for this lack of growth. Present sanitary conditions and general standards of living in the village are higher than those of other tribes and are continuing to improve. The population is also growing, but not dramatically.

Linguistic Affiliation.   Kotas speak the Kota language or Ko·v Ma·nt, a Dravidian language closely related to Toda and also having strong linguistic affiliations with very early Tamil and Malayalam. All Kotas speak Badaga and Tamil also, as historically they have had to communicate with outsiders in languages other than their own.

History and Cultural Relations

While some scholars and members of Nilgiri communities maintain that the Kotas were placed in the Nilgiris to render services for their neighbors, the Kotas believe themselves to be autochthons. They describe a god who created the Kotas, Todas, and Kurumbas and taught them the skills they traditionally practiced in the Nilgiris. For the neighboring communities the Kotas provided music, iron articles and silver ornaments, baskets, pottery, and a variety of other specialized goods and services. With the change to a monetary and market economy these services are no longer required, and the vast increase in the Badaga population has made close reciprocal relationships impossible. The knowledge of many of these traditional practices among the Kotas is gradually being lost, and as yet no internal motivation has surfaced to replace lost contexts or encourage the maintenance of these arts and crafts.

Settlements

Six villages of the Kotas host 100–300 people in roughly twenty-five to sixty-five houses; while only a few families still inhabit the seventh village, Kala·c (or Gudalur Kokal). The houses are arranged in rows, called ke·rs, which correspond to exogamous social units. Kota villages are called ko·ka·l, literally "Kota leg," or the place where Kotas planted their feet. The pattern of settlement is believed to have been determined by a cow who led the Kotas through the Nilgiris and stopped in various places to indicate various sites for the villages. The following are the seven Kota villages listed in the order some Kotas believe they came into existence (Anglo-Badaga names as commonly rendered are given in parentheses): Me·na·r (Kunda Kotagiri), Kolme·l (Kollimalai), Kurgo·j (Sholur Kokal), Ticga·r (Trichigadı), Porga·r (Kotagiri), Kina·r (Kil Kotagiri), and Kala·c (Gudalur Kokal). In earlier times Kota houses were wattle and daub with thatched roofs, but these have been gradually replaced with modern houses identical to those of their Nilgiri neighbors. These newer houses are of whitewashed cement and brick with gabled roofs, made of corrugated zinc and/or baked clay tiles, or flat cement roofs such as those found on the plains. The number and arrangement of rooms has also changed in recent times. An old-fashioned Kota house consists of a front room, containing a raised platform on the left for sitting and sleeping and a hole in the floor for pounding, a kitchen, located to the right of the front room and containing a wood stove along the wall opposite the arched entrance, and a back room for bathing. Each room and parts of each room have particular names and functions. The walls have special crevices for oil lamps and wood, and other articles are often stored in rafters above the kitchen. In the past Kotas had no toilets and special huts were built for women to stay in while menstruating. Some of the earlier modern Kota houses are also built according to a relatively uniform pattern. These houses contain an entrance hall where shoes and other articles are kept, a small room on the right for entertaining guests, a main living room beyond the front room with a bedroom attached to that, and finally a kitchen with a bathing area in the rear. Some of these houses represent remodeled houses of the older type.

Economy

Subsistence and Commercial Activities. The Kotas, being agriculturalists, usually grow enough beans, potatoes, and carrots to suit their needs. Other vegetables and rice are purchased in the market. In earlier days the Kotas cultivated millet or relied on their Badaga neighbors for regular supplies of grain in return for their services. Now most Kotas own some land—even if they live in a nearby city—and cultivate tea, a commodity that fetches more than four times the price of any other cash crop. The Kotas, like most of India's cultivators, use chemical fertilizers with little concern for the effects on their health or the environment. Kotas keep buffalo and cows for producing milk, butter, and curds, but they no longer keep buffalo and never keep cows for meat or sacrificial purposes. Domestic dogs and cats are not uncommon and chickens can be seen about the village. Other animals used for food are usually purchased. Sheep raising and beekeeping have also been reported. The Kotas' traditional staple was a type of millet known as vatamk (Italian millet). This food is a must on ceremonial occasions today, but on a daily basis Kotas prefer rice. Idlis and dosais—the common light meals throughout the south of India—are rarely served. A typical day's menu comprises two to three meals of rice (or other grain) eaten with udk, a thick soup of pulses and vegetables in a tamarind broth flavored with chilies, salt, and other common south Indian spices. A meal is sometimes supplemented with an omelet, fruits, papadams (fried or grilled breads similar to tortillas), and pickles, especially if guests are present. Although the Kotas are not vegetarians they seldom eat beef. Mutton or chicken are regularly offered to some of the Hindu deities the Kotas have introduced into their villages. Raw vegetables are seldom eaten at meals but people commonly eat leaves and other vegetation while out walking or working in the fields. Alcohol abuse is a problem in some Kota villages but is not as widespread as among some of the other local tribes. Opium use is common but secretive. The government provides opium rations to the tribes but illegal cultivation also occurs. Other drug use is virtually absent. Cigarette and beedi (a small, leaf-rolled cigarette) smoking is common. Chewing tobacco is distributed at certain festival times but few people take it habitually.

Industrial Arts. Kota men have traditionally specialized in blacksmithing, silversmithing, roof thatching, basket making, wood- and leatherworking, and musical-instrument making. The skill for these crafts is often passed from father to son but almost anyone, except for priests in some cases, can do these jobs. Women make pottery for domestic and ceremonial purposes. In earlier times Kotas are said to have extracted ore from rocks quarried in the area; nowadays iron is purchased from the market in bar form or in various unrefined shapes, such as an unsharpened saw. Carpentry is still practiced but few artisans can carve with the skill displayed on old Kota door frames and on the stone pillars in front of their temples. A few artisans still produce fine hand-carved rifle butts and double-reed instruments (kol). Baskets are usually purchased from the market or from wandering merchants, but Kota-made baskets called kik are necessary on certain ceremonial occasions. Hides from goats and oxen are necessary for the production of their drums, the tabaṭk, e·rtabaṭk, kinvar, and do·par. Their long curved horns, called kob, used to be fashioned of buffalo horn. Now they are made of brass and purchased from the Coimbatore Plains.

Trade. Until the 1930s the Kotas maintained a close interdependent relationship with the Todas, Badagas, and Kurumbas. Each Kota village was located near settlements of other communities and each household had specific members of these communities on whom they depended and who depended upon them. Kota music was an essential at Badaga and Toda funerals and commonly performed on festive occasions as well. The Todas supplied dairy products and the Badagas provided grain and cloth. Kurumbas, who were feared for alleged witchcraft, were often village sentries and healers and also provided forest products for the other communities. Partly because the Kotas ate buffalo flesh—and reportedly even carrion—the Badagas and Todas looked down upon them, but the Kotas did not and do not accept the lowly position accorded them. They used to sacrifice buffalo at their own funerals and accept sacrificed buffalo as payment for their musical and other ritual services at Toda funerals. To explain this some Kotas claim they were originally vegetarians compelled to eat meat because the Todas had no other means of paying them for their services. Today, to show their rejection of this locally despised practice, the Kotas neither play for Toda funerals nor sacrifice buffalo themselves. In addition to those with the Todas, Badagas, and Kurumbas, some minor trade relations also existed with other Nilgiri tribes, but these transactions received little attention in the early colonial and anthropological literature. Items from the plains were procured from itinerant Chettis directly or through Badaga mediaries. Kota music has been largely replaced by Irula, Kurumba, Tamil, or Kanarese bands and sometimes by semi-Western bands or recorded film music. Musicians are remunerated in cash, food, and drink. Kotas are occasionally hired by Tamils and are usually paid more than other tribals for their services.

Division of Labor. In agricultural tasks the women ordinarily weed the fields, then the men till the soil, both sexes harrow and furrow, and finally women usually sow the seeds. Wood- and metalworking and the playing of musical instruments are the exclusive domain of men. In religious ceremonies both the priests and their wives, as well as other functionaries, have specific duties. Women's duties include collecting clay, making pottery, collecting water, preparing food for cooking, and cooking (though men also do cook). Men and women are further differentiated by the tunes used for their dances and by the dances themselves. Men always dance before women, and at the closing of larger festivals a day is devoted to women's singing and dancing. This is considered an auspicious ending (mangaḷam).

Land Tenure. The Kotas claim they have owned the land near their villages from time immemorial. Now they have also bought new lands some distance away from their villages. When Tipu Sultan's reign touched the Nilgiris the Kotas had to pay land tax to one of his ministers. Even today the rock can be seen in Kolme·l on which the Kota king and Tipu's minister sat while conducting their transactions. Fields are terraced or sloped and marked by boundaries of fencing, vegetation, embankments of soil, or other available means. Because land tends to remain with the family, the records of ownership also provide valuable genealogical information.

Kinship

Kin Groups and Descent. Each village comprises three exogamous divisions organized in three sets of house clusters called ke·rs. The clans do not extend beyond the village, though ke·r names may be common to several villages. Each ke·r shares a common ancestor, but only a few elders can recollect the relationships among the various families beyond two or three generations. Members of these ke·rs sometimes play specialized roles in ritual and compete against one another in ritual games. The ke·r as a spatiosocial entity is also highlighted in "green" and "dry" funerals (discussed later), where music and particular ceremonies are conducted while the corpse lies on a cot in the ke·r in which he or she lived. Although there is a strong connection between exogamous divisions and occupation of space in the village, some exceptions are possible. If space is a problem, sometimes a house is built in a ke·r other than a man's own; in this case the man still belongs to his natal division. The change in space does not alter his kin affiliations. Another system of kin groups revolves around the notion of family or kuyt. This classification seems to be largely defunct as a system of ritual differentiation except in a few villages—a situation further complicated by the fact that a kuyt size can range from a family of three or four members to the members of an entire ke·r. The head priests (mundika·no·n) and headmen (gotga·rn) usually belong to particular kuyts. Other principles of succession are less rigid.

Men belong to their father's ke·r, kuyt, and village; women, after marriage, belong to those of their husband.

Kinship Terminology. Kota kinship terminology, like most Dravidian systems, classifies relatives into those who are marriageable and those who are not. Because a father's brothers are classificatory fathers, the children of brothers cannot marry. Likewise the children of sisters cannot marry. Cross-cousin marriages, however, are common and indeed preferred. The following are a few Kota kinship terms of reference (sometimes kin are addressed by different terms): pe·ri·n—father's father, mother's father; pe·rav—father's mother, mother's mother; ayn—father, mother's sister's husband; av—mother, father's brother's wife; aṇ—elder brother; kara·l—younger brother.

Marriage and Family

Marriage. One cannot marry parallel cousins—that is, mother's sister's children or father's brother's children—because they are classificatory brothers and sisters. And because ke·rs are patrilineal and patrilocal units, this means Kotas are generally forbidden to marry anyone born in their natal ke·r. Kotas, like most communities in south India, prefer marriages between close cross cousins; but because most marriages are not arranged, young people have some leeway in choosing acceptable partners from other ke·rs or from other Kota villages. Traditionally the boy asks the girl's father for permission to marry. The father must ask his daughter whether she wishes to marry the boy, and if so, the boy must give a token 1.25 rupees to the father. Nowadays the girl's family may give money or goods to the married couple, but dowry is not part of the traditional system. In fact the entire ceremony is very simple. Unlike most south Indian communities music is not played, except to welcome the wedding party to the village. Some Kotas now host large receptions and broadcast film music to celebrate their weddings, but this is acknowledged to be a recent innovation.

Each of the three ke·rs or "streets" in each Kota village is exogamous. A man may marry a second wife if the first wife does not bear sons. In earlier days polyandry was also practiced. A bride generally moves to the ke·r of her husband, but now houses are being built in other ke·rs or even outside the confines of the ke·rs in a village, and a number of Kotas live in other Indian cities. In these situations patrilocality loses its relevance. If a husband dies, a young widow may sometimes remain in the household of or live with support from her husband's family. Divorce is common and no stigma is attached to it. Sometimes a divorced wife will live alone and sometimes she will remarry. Usually the children remain in the father's family and custody.

Domestic Unit.   Three generations sometimes live in the same house, especially if the house is big enough. But more commonly today, a young couple will move into a house of their own. The youngest son is likely to remain in the household of his parents because he inherits the house when his father dies (ultimogeniture). Four to five persons to a house is a probable average.

Inheritance.   Land and property are usually divided evenly among a man's sons or specified male or female heirs, but the youngest son inherits the house.

Socialization.   Women give birth either in a hospital or in a special hut called _kunpay_. The child is named about ten days after birth. This ceremony, which is considered in some ways more important than a marriage, is attended by the whole village and relatives from other villages. An elder tells the child his or her name while feeding it water and a few crumbs of cooked millet (_ta·ym ayk_). Then a lock of the baby's hair is placed in leaves and cow dung and the whole thing is tossed away. Head shaving is another rite of initiation. At the age of 16 all but a tuft (_kot_) of hair is shaved off a boy's head, and all but a rim (_mungol_) of hair is shaved from a girl's scalp. Ear piercing of several boys and girls of different ages usually occurs in the context of other festivals such as those honoring Hindu deities. Tattooing was a traditional practice, which, along with head shaving, is uncommon among modern Kotas. Children attend school from the age of about 6 to the age of 16, although an increasing number of men and women are completing higher studies. Young children usually stay around the village with their parents, relatives, or neighbors and help with household work when they are old enough. As marriages are not arranged, boys and girls are given some leeway to develop friendships, which may later develop into marriage. In the 1930s there were still special youth houses called _erm pay_ where young married and unmarried couples would sing, play music, tell stories, and become intimate with one another. Such houses are not in evidence today. Families living outside the seven villages maintain strong links with their village and the children of these families continue to learn the Kota language as a first language and Tamil as a second. Although Kota lullabies are sung to children there are no special Kota songs children themselves sing. Like many other Indian children they like to sing popular Tamil and Hindi songs and imitate film actors; their games include those common to the subcontinent and uniquely Kota games; some games are played only during particular festivals.

Sociopolitical Organization

Social Organization.   The Kotas are socially differentiated by families, clans (or ke·rs), and villages. The precise manner in which these differentiations are articulated varies from village to village. Certain families and/or clans share particular ceremonial responsibilities while others may or may not play particular ritual roles. Oral history indicates the nature of these responsibilities, and the assignment of ritual roles also varies with time. The Kotas do not perceive their community as divided by anything like Hindu castes (jati), so although social differentiation exists there is no formal hierarchy. Ritual responsibilities are not necessarily seen as a form of social power. Little formal differentiation exists at the village level, though each village has what might be called a "reputation," which may have social ramifications when villagers meet. For example, Ticga·r is famous for women's song and dance, the "dry" funeral is famous in Me·na·r, and the Kamatra·ya festival and instrumental music are famous in Kolme·l.

Political Organization.   Each village is led by a headman or treasurer called gotga·rn; in Me·na·r there is also a gotga·rn for all the seven villages. Whenever a dispute arises the gotga·rn calls a meeting (_ku·t_) and adjudicates. Within a village the gotga·rn and elders decide when festivals are to be held and how to solve problems in the community.

Social Control.   Justice is meted out within the larger Indian judicial system, but local decisions—especially those relating to the enforcement of Kota cultural dictates—are handled by the village ku·t.

Conflict.   There is no solid evidence of warfare in the Nilgiris involving the Kotas and other tribes. They claim, however, that the ritual drum, e·rtabatk, was originally used in battle.

Religion and Expressive Culture

Religious Beliefs.   Kotas consider themselves Hindus and no Kotas have gone on record as converting to any other religion, although one or two marriages have reportedly occurred between Kotas and Christians. The major Kota deities are A·yno·r (father god) and Amno·r (mother goddess). A·yno·r, also called Kamati·cvara or Kamatra·ya in some villages, is identified with the Hindu god Shiva. Some villages have a "big" and "small" A·yno·r (Doda·yno·r and Kuna·yno·r), but there is only one version of the goddess. Kana·tra·ya is a deity in the form of a stone and is found only in Ticga·r. Generally, Kota deities have no anthropomorphic representation, although once a year faces of silver ornaments are pasted onto the front of the A·yno·r and Amno·r temples. Today temples for the Hindu deities Krishna, Rangarama, Munisvara, Badrakaliamman, and Mariamman have also been erected by the Kotas, each in response to a particular need or supernatural event in the village.

Religious Practitioners.   For ceremonies relating to their indigenous deities the Kotas have two types of priest. The mundika·no·n, the primary priest, leads the Kotas in all important community activities. The other priest, the te·rka·ran, acts as a vehicle through which god (_so·ym_) communicates with the people. The te·rka·ran effects such communication by becoming possessed and responding to questions, which are usually posed by male elders. Possession occurs in established spatiotemporal contexts for which instrumental musicians (kolvar) play particular tunes (kol) and rhythms (da·k). The deity "chooses" the te·rka·ran initially through causing him to be possessed and speaking through him. Then the mundika·no·n is named by the deity via the te·rka·ran. Although there is a special te·rka·ran family (kuyt) in some villages, the te·rka·ran may also belong to a different family. The mundika·no·n can only come from the mundika·no·n family.

A village should have a te·rka·ran and mundika·no·n for each of their two or three indigenous Kota temples. For one reason or another several villages have been unable to replace all their priests in recent years. A peculiar feature of Kota priesthood is the participation of the wives of the priests. In fact these women are so important that a priest can no longer hold office if his wife dies. In major ceremonies not only the priests' wives, but also the gotga·rn's wife and those of the other ceremonial helpers (ca·tranga·rn) play instrumental roles. Whereas most practitioners are adults, young boys are essential in several ceremonies. For example, in death ceremonies a young boy called *tic vec mog* acts as head priest and, among other things, lights the funeral pyre. The Kota priests for widely recognized Hindu deities are not related to the te·rka·ran or mundika·no·n and have no ritual interaction with them. However, sometimes the wives of these priests, like those of their counterparts, play an integral role in the rituals performed by their husbands.

Ceremonies.   The major yearly festivals are the Kamaṭra·ya festival, which takes place in December or January and is three to thirteen days long depending on the village; and the annual *varalda·v* or "dry" funeral, which usually takes places before Kamaṭra·ya (recently this ceremony has been discontinued in some villages). Other festivals include Pabm, Ye·r ca·tram, Vei aytd ca·tram (agricultural festivals), and the milk ceremony (Pa·l ca·tram). This latter festival, seen as one of the most solemn, is not celebrated with music or dance. Ceremonies are enacted along Hindu lines for recently introduced Hindu deities, although the actual *ca·trams* or rituals are often revealed to the concerned priest during trance. There are yearly festivals for each Hindu god worshiped by the Kotas but not for each indigenous Kota deity individually—except for Kaṇa·tra·ya in Ticga·r. His festival is associated with the bringing of rain. While Kotas from outside villages may sometimes attend, there is no occasion that requires the attendance of all Kotas and no festival that is celebrated exactly the same way in two villages.

Medicine.   The Kotas have indigenous remedies for such ailments as broken bones, diarrhea, boils, and weariness. Many of the plants used in Kota medicine are becoming difficult to find because the Nilgiri ecology has been altered drastically in the last half-century. Kotas, like many educated Indians, have access to and place their trust in allopathic medicine, partly because it is associated with the West, science, and upward mobility. At this time no system of "faith" healing seems to be in existence, but stories are still told of various afflictions that were in fact signs that the deity wanted to speak through the patient, wished a temple to be built, or had some other request. Kotas do not consider themselves adept at magic but have traditionally feared the Kurumbas and Irulas for their sorcery. They still believe themselves to be the "guinea pigs" on which the Kurumba sorcerers test their spells.

Death and Afterlife.   The ordinary or "green" (*pac*) funeral is a rather simple ceremony led by a small boy known as the "fire-keeping boy" (*tic vec mog*), who is from the deceased's family. Kotas are cremated in a special place called the dav naṛ (death region), and a portion of the forehead bone is saved if the village of the deceased performs the annual "dry" funeral, or *varalda·v*. Each step of both the "green" funeral and the "dry" funeral is highly articulated by means of special musical tunes played on the double-reed instrument, koḷ, and rhythms on the barrel drums, do·par and kinvar, and the frame drum, tabaṭk. The tunes themselves are called *du·kd koḷ* (sad tunes), *ke·ṛ koḷ* (badness tunes), or *da·v koḷ* (funeral or death tunes). These tunes should not be played except at funerals. The "dry" funeral is an event of up to ten days, which is seen to remove *karmandram*, inauspiciousness or evil caused by death. Only after performing this festival can the yearly cycle of festivals begin. Due to the expense involved, and, possibly, an unwillingness to emphasize death-related rituals in front of Hindu neighbors, villages are beginning to discontinue the ceremony or to celebrate it only in extreme cases, such as after a priest has died. Before going to the dav naṛ or *varalda·v naṛ* (death region), the ceremonies are carried out in the ke·r in which the deceased lived.

See also Badaga; Toda

Bibliography

Emeneau, Murray B. (1944–1946). *Kota Texts.* University of California Publications in Linguistics, nos. 2–3 (in 4 pts.). Berkeley: University of California Press.

Hockings, Paul (1980). "Traditional Interchange (1)." In *Ancient Hindu Refugees: Badaga Social History, 1550–1975,* 99–110. The Hague: Mouton Publishers; New Delhi: Vikas Publishing House.

Mandelbaum, David G. (1941). "Culture Change among the Nilgiri Tribes." *American Anthropologist* 43:19–26.

Mandelbaum, David G. (1941). "Social Trends and Personal Pressures: The Growth of a Culture Pattern." In *Language, Culture, and Personality: Essays in Memory of Edward Sapir,* edited by Leslie Spier, A. Irving Hallowell, and Stanley S. Newman, 219–238. Menasha: Sapir Memorial Publication Fund.

Mandelbaum, David G. (1954). "Form, Variation, and Meaning of a Ceremony." In *Method and Perspective in Anthropology: Papers in Honor of Wilson D. Wallis,* edited by Robert F. Spencer, 60–102. Minneapolis: University of Minnesota Press.

Mandelbaum, David G. (1958). "Social Uses of Funeral Rites." *Eastern Anthropologist: A Quarterly Record of Ethnography and Folk Culture* 12:5-24.

Mandelbaum, David G. (1989). "The Kotas in Their Social Setting." In *Blue Mountains: The Ethnography and Biogeography of a South Indian Region,* edited by Paul Hockings, 144–185. New Delhi: Oxford University Press.

Verghese, Isaac (1965). "Priesthood among the Kota of Nilgiri Hills." *Vanyajati* 13:64–71.

Verghese, Isaac (1969). "The Kota." *Bulletin of the Anthropological Survey of India* 18:103–182. [Published in 1974].

RICHART KENT WOLF

Koya

ETHNONYMS: Dorla, Koi

Orientation

Identification.   The Koyas are a subdivision of the Gond tribes of central India. They are most closely related to the Bison Horn Maria Gonds of Bastar.

Location.   The majority of Koyas live in Andhra Pradesh, but significant numbers also live in Madhya Pradesh and Orissa. Their habitat is the alluvial plain of the Godavari River and its tributaries and the forested hills that rise up on both sides of the Godavari River. The hills range from 60 to 1,200 meters above sea level and are cut by numerous short streams that are dry for much of the year but become impassable in the monsoon. Approximately one-third of this habitat is reserve forest administered by the Forestry Department of the state government. The alluvial soils are rich and fertile, but the hill soils are thin and subject to erosion when deforested. Rainfall is abundant but dependent on the monsoon. Koyas recognize three seasons: the hot weather (April–June), with highs regularly above 38° C; the rains (June–November); and the cold weather (December–February), when night temperatures are frequently around 4° C. Communication within this area is poor. Only one major road parallels the Godavari River for approximately 160 kilometers, and it is unusable during most of the rainy season. The hills away from the river are reachable only by cart trails and footpaths. The area is also isolated by its reputation as a center for endemic malaria.

Demography.   In 1971 there were approximately 344,437 Koyas, of whom roughly 285,226 lived in Andhra Pradesh, 59,168 in Orissa, and the remainder in Madhya Pradesh and Maharashtra. Population density varies considerably between plains and hills, with the plains areas adjacent to the main road being much more densely populated.

Linguistic Affiliation.   The Koyas speak a Central Dravidian language closely related to Gondi. The language, both in vocabulary and grammar, has been strongly influenced by Telugu, the language of the neighboring Hindu population. Most Koyas are bilingual in Gondi or Telugu, and in the plains villages many are now literate in Telugu. Koya has no literature of its own aside from two books of the Bible translated into Koya and printed in Telugu characters by Christian missionaries in the nineteenth century.

History and Cultural Relations

Despite its relative isolation, the Koya area has been the object of numerous population movements, including those of the Koyas themselves, who are probably migrants from the north. Today increasing numbers of Hindu castes from the south have been moving in and displacing the Koyas, their movement into the area facilitated by the construction of a bridge over the Godavari at Bhadrachallam in the 1970s. Historically, the Koyas were subjects of Zamindars (landlords) holding royal grants from various outside rulers, but apart from taxation and corvée, the Zamindars had relatively little authority and were able to exercise control only over the plains villages, and even there only sporadically. British rule over the area came about as a result of their exploitation of the coal deposits at Singareni and from their attempts to make the Godavari River commercially navigable year-round. Christian influence dates from the 1860s, when missionaries were brought in during the construction of an irrigation canal at Dummagudem. Many Koyas in the area around Dummagudem were converted to Christianity and there is still a sizable population of Christian Koyas in the villages near Dummagudem. Many of the Koyas living in the most accessible villages are now indistinguishable from Hindu castes. Much of their land has been appropriated by non-Koyas and many of their villages now have mixed populations of Koyas, Christian Koyas, and Hindus. Acculturation has been a long-term process, and many aspects of Koya ritual and mythology are now informed by Hindu ideas and practices. Since independence, the Indian government has increased its influence over the Koyas, and its various programs and institutions have brought them more and more into the orbit of Indian culture. Koyas have from time to time attempted to free themselves from foreign domination, and have mounted numerous rebellions, most of which succeeded only for brief periods. The most recent rebellion occurred in the 1950s, when the majority of Koyas supported the Andhra Communist Party and joined in the violence that marked the relations between Congress and Communist parties in Andhra at that time. Koyas continue to be resentful of outside encroachment and are especially unhappy about land alienation, restrictions on the use of reserve forests, restrictions on the distillation of drinking alcohol, the unjust protection of rapacious moneylenders, and revenue assessments.

Settlements

Koya settlements are located near sources of dependable water supply such as ponds, streams, or a common well. Villages vary in size from three to more than sixty houses, but most often they consist of between thirty and forty houses with populations of approximately 200 persons. Larger villages are usually characteristic of the riverine plain, and smaller ones of the hills and jungle. Villages are sometimes nucleated, especially in the plains, but they are more often composed of scattered hamlets containing two or more houses occupied by members of a minimal lineage and/or by in-marrying affines. Koya houses are constructed of wood, thatch, clay, and wattle. Houses of wealthy families are larger, have several rooms, thick mud walls, and deep, well-maintained thatch roofs. Poorer families live in small, one-room houses with wattle walls and roofs thinly thatched with palm fronds rather than thatching grass. The average house has two rooms, a loft and a veranda. One room contains the hearth where the family cooking is done, and is strictly reserved to members of the family and minimal lineage. The ancestor pot, in which offerings are made to the ancestors, is kept near the hearth. Grain is stored in large baskets lined with mud and cow dung and kept in the loft. Houses are usually windowless and are ventilated only by an opening under the eaves and by open doors. Scattered about the rooms and hanging from the rafters are the Koya family's few material possessions—clay pots for storing water, brass pots for carrying water, woven baskets, winnowing fans, brooms, a drum, bow and arrows, a spear, a small metal box for valuables, wooden stringed cots, mortar and pestles, grinding stone, hoe, sickles, and an axe. Bags of seed grain, drying gourds, tobacco, chilies, garlic, balls of twine, and bits of cloth dangle from the rafters and roof beams. Night light is provided by a small kerosene lamp or by a shallow saucer containing an oil-soaked wick. Adjacent to the house is a bathroom constructed from four unroofed thatch walls. A pigsty, goat shed, and open-air sheds used for sleeping in the hot weather stand near the house. Kitchen gardens for growing herbs, gourds, squash, beans, tomatoes, corn, tobacco, greens, and root vegetables are planted next to the houses and are sometimes fenced to protect them from chickens, which run free, and from other wild and domestic marauders. Culturally, houses are divided into two areas: the inner rooms where only family and close kin are allowed entry, and the veranda where strangers and guests may gather.

Economy

Subsistence and Commercial Activities. A village consists of four culturally defined areas: houses and hamlets; cultivated and fallow fields; wasteland; and sacred places. Permanent fields are located near the water supply, below a dam, for example, where rice can be grown in fertilized and irrigated paddies. Away from the water source are the dry fields watered only by the monsoon where millets and legumes are grown. Each family typically has fields in both areas. Permanent wet field cultivation requires not only land but capital for plows, oxen, and hired labor at critical planting and harvesting times. It also necessitates extra labor in keeping up the dam, embankments, and irrigation channels. In the hills and jungles there are no permanent fields. Crops are grown in small clearings for two or three years; the clearings are then allowed to revert to jungle. The soil in these abandoned plots regenerates itself in about fifteen years and the plots can then be cleared and planted again. Axe, hoe, rake, and dibbling stick are the only tools required for this swidden cultivation. Koyas living in the permanent field areas of the riverine plain are nostalgic for this form of cultivation. They connect it with their tales, myths, gods, rituals, and freedom from money-lenders and government agents. As the Hindu population in Koya territory increases, Koyas are forced more and more to shift from swidden agriculture and subsistence production to permanent field agriculture and market production. Rice and tobacco are the main cash crops. Millets and legumes are the major subsistence crops even in the plains villages. Koyas cannot afford to eat much of the rice they grow. Koyas are herders as well as cultivators and pasture fairly large herds of cows, buffalo, and goats on the wasteland and in fallow fields. Cattle are kept for their dairy products, meat, fertilizer, and ritual uses. Goats are hardy, require little attention, and are important as sources of milk and meat. Wherever opportunity affords, Koyas supplement their food supply by hunting and gathering, and one of their chief complaints against outside government is its restriction of access to reserve forests, which Koyas regard as their own. Honey, roots, tubers, leaves, leafy plants, fiber, fruits, salt, spices, herbs, wood, nuts, fish, and small game provide a substantial addition to the diet and are the source of a variety of useful products that would otherwise have to be purchased from itinerant traders or in local weekly markets. Hunting, though much restricted, figures largely in Koya imagination, and a ritual hunt is an important part of the annual spring planting sacrifice performed for the village mother, even though the forest is somewhat outside her realm, being ruled instead by the "Lords of the Jungle," and the "Lord of Animals," who are the husbands of various disease goddesses. Inclusion of these jungle and animal deities in the planting ritual points again to the importance of swidden cultivation in the minds of Koyas.

Industrial Arts. Blacksmithing and weaving of baskets and mats, along with twine making, are the principal manufactures. Blacksmiths still make and repair traditional iron implements and tools such as plowshares, hoes, sickles, spear points, and wheel rims, but most other metal products are purchased from Hindu peddlers.

Trade. Most trade is carried out at weekly markets held in villages accessible by good cart tracks or roads. Itinerant Hindu peddlers bring cloth, oil, metal pots, and sundries to trade for cash or produce, usually the latter. Koya women also sell vegetables, twine, baskets, mats, and forest products independently, simply spreading their wares on a cloth in the market area. Where there are large Hindu villages nearby, Koyas trade these items with the Hindu merchants and shopkeepers in the bazaar.

Division of Labor. Koya society is divided into three hereditary, endogamous occupational groups: blacksmiths, bards, and funeral drummers and singers. These groups have no lineages of their own and assume the lineage name of a patron. Bards are not genealogists, but they sing the traditional lineage history and mythology during the lineage sacrifices. Funeral singers are panegyrists who sing songs of praise for the deceased and his or her family during funeral ceremonies. Blacksmiths, bards, and funeral singers are only part-time specialists, and they make most of their livelihoods from cultivation. Except for blacksmithing, plowing, hunting, village governance, and sacrificing, which are restricted to men, the sexual division of labor is not strict. Women do most of the cooking, washing, rice husking and pounding, weeding, and rice transplanting, but both sexes share in child care and in such activities as harvesting, fishing, gathering, twine making, basketry, and mat making. Women do much of the small-scale marketing of vegetables, forest produce, and household manufactures. Children are actively employed by age 4 or 5 as baby-sitters, rice huskers, food gatherers, errand runners, and crop watchers. By age 6 or 7 boys herd goats and cattle, and by age 10 they help in plowing, planting, and harvesting.

Land Tenure. Villages contain several different local lineages, one of which is usually recognized as the founding lineage, and all others are regarded as in-marrying affines. This practice may point to an earlier system of lineage territoriality, but nowadays rights to land are based on title and revenue is assessed on individual rather than corporate holdings.

Kinship

Kin Groups and Descent. All Koyas belong to one of five unranked exogamous patrilineal phratries called *gotrams*. Although Koyas agree that there are five phratries, they do not agree on their names, and different areas use different names. Each phratry is associated with a unique set of deities and a traditional sacred geography in the Bastar region. At five-year intervals, the phratry gods are brought down from Bastar and taken in procession through the whole Koya country. Phratries are subdivided into numerous named exogamous patri-lineages. There is no agreement from area to area or even from village to village about the phratry affiliation of different lineages. Many of the lineages are named for plants and animals, and there is a vague kind of totemism in some cases. An icon associated with a lineage god is kept in a village having a preponderant population belonging to its lineage. Such icons take the form of metal spear points. They are kept hidden in secret places near the "god shed," which houses other paraphernalia used in the lineage rituals. God sheds are usually located on the village outskirts. Lineages are neither political nor territorial units. Each is subdivided into many local branches scattered throughout the Koya area. They convene at a ritual center once a year to perform the lineage sacrifice, but apart from that have little in the way of corporate character. The local lineage consists of members of a lineage resident in the same village and tracing descent to a common named ancestor. They are sometimes multifamily land-holding groups, but these are more often divided into separate-family residential groups.

Kinship Terminology. Kinship terminology is Dravidian, distinguishing between cross and parallel relatives in Ego's generation and in the two generations above and below Ego's.

Marriage and Family

Marriage. Phratries and lineages are exogamous but have no preferred pattern of spouse exchange. Bilateral cross-cousin marriage is preferred and occurs among actual genealogical first cross cousins in approximately 18 percent of recorded marriages. Polygyny is permitted, but it is infrequent because of the high cost of bride-price. Widow remarriage is not stigmatized. The junior levirate is encouraged, but widows are just as likely to marry a man from another family. Koyas have considerable freedom of choice in mate selection and pay only a token compensation to the mother's brother in the event that they do not marry a cross cousin. Most first marriages are postadolescent. Postmarital residence is preferentially patrilocal, but bride-service is common and families without male heirs will often adopt a resident son-in-law. Divorce and remarriage are relatively easy and fairly frequent. The defecting spouse must pay compensation to the deserted spouse's family and pay a fine to the village council if it adjudicates the divorce.

Domestic Unit. The extended family is the main unit of cooperation, reproduction, and socialization. Many compromise family units arise from contingencies of the life cycle. Extended families split up after the death of the father or soon after the marriage of the youngest son.

Inheritance. The estate is subdivided equally among the male heirs and a portion is set aside for the dowry and marriage expenses of any unmarried female children. One of the brothers continues to live in the family home with the surviving mother and her unmarried children. Other married male children construct new dwellings within the compound or in a new nearby location.

Socialization. Authority within the family is determined by gender, age, and competence. The eldest male, as long as he remains competent, has authority over all the others in most family matters, but his wife or widowed mother supervise all work done by females and younger children. When the father dies or becomes incompetent, the eldest son assumes authority unless he is immature, in which case the father's eldest surviving brother will take control until the son is old enough. Children are seldom directly instructed in proper behavior or in how to perform tasks. They learn by direct observation and imitation. What little instruction they get comes almost entirely from older siblings and grandparents. Discipline for infractions is swift and certain and, in that coming from older siblings, often physical.

Sociopolitical Organization

Social Organization. The elements of Koya social organization are the family, the village, the phratry, and the lineage. Koya society is basically egalitarian, especially in the hill villages where there are few differences of rank and status other than those of age and personal reputation.

Political Organization. Although Koyas speak of themselves as a distinct group, no overall political organization holds them together. Traditionally they have had regional governing bodies consisting of the council of twenty-five villages under the authority of a headman and his assistant. The council's main functions were to oversee revenue collection and to try intervillage disputes.

Social Control. Social control is effected through the family, the lineage elders, and the village council. The council tries all cases involving villagers with the exception of murder or crimes against the state. Disputes over land inheritance, divorce, wife stealing, and payment of bride-price comprise the majority of cases. The council hears evidence, questions witnesses, and imposes fines on those whom it finds guilty.

Conflict. Apart from the village disputes noted above, most conflict today involves Hindus who encroach on Koya lands or use unfair practices in their dealings with Koyas. These cases are referred to the Indian judiciary and are almost always decided against Koyas.

Religion and Expressive Culture

Religious Beliefs. Koyas believe that numerous supernaturals influence all things and events and can be summoned to aid humans if they are propitiated by sacrificial offerings of animals, grain, and liquor. Many Koya deities are female, the most important being the earth mother, the smallpox goddess, and the goddesses of the lineages and phratries. Male deities, such as the Lord of the Jungle and the Lord of Animals, are consorts of these goddesses. Ancestors are also deities, as are many natural objects.

Religious Practitioners. Sacrifices are carried out by the village priest and the lineage priests. Shamans divine the source of uninvited supernatural interference and prescribe remedial sacrifices for it. Sorcerers are illicit practitioners who compel supernaturals to attack one's enemies.

Ceremonies. At the center of every ceremony is a sacrifice in which the deity consumes the essence and leaves the consecrated substance for humans to feast on.

Arts. Apart from singing and dancing and the drawing of decorative designs on the floor with rice powder, Koyas have little in the way of artistic expression.

Medicine. Koyas think most disease is caused by malevolent deities, and when an illness cannot be cured by home remedies, they consult the shaman. They also have recourse to Hindu Ayurvedic practitioners, and in rare cases they will visit a government-run dispensary.

Death and Afterlife. Koyas do not believe in Heaven or Hell, and they also do not profess to believe in reincarnation, even though some of their practices imply it. When someone dies, his or her spirit lingers about the ancestor pot, patrols the sky over the village, or wanders about the village interfering with daily life, sometimes benevolently.

See also Gond

Bibliography

Hajra, D. (1970). *The Dorla of Bastar.* Anthropological Survey of India Memoir no. 17. Calcutta: Government of India Press.

Ramaiah, P. (1981). *Tribal Economy of India.* New Delhi: Light & Life Publishers.

Subrahmanyam, P. S. (1968). *A Descriptive Grammar of Gondi.* Annamalai University, Department of Linguistics, Publication no. 16. Annamalai.

Tyler, Stephen A. (1968). *Koya: An Outline Grammar.* Berkeley: University of California Press.

Tyler, Stephen A. (1972). "Fields Are for Planting: Notes on Koya Agriculture." In *Proceedings of the Seminar on Tribal Studies,* edited by D. P. Sinha. New Delhi: Government of India Press.

STEPHEN A. TYLER

Kshatriya

ETHNONYMS: none

The Kshatriyas are a large block of Hindu castes, mainly located in the northern half of India. The Sanskrit term Kshatrā means "warrior, ruler," and identifies the second *varna,* ranking immediately below the Brahmans. No doubt, most of the many castes that claim to be Kshatriya are somehow descended from warriors who were in the service of princes and rulers or who were of royal families. Conversely, numerous rulers have legitimized their status, especially if usurpers, by claiming that their lineage was indeed Kshatriya. Most typical and best known of these groups are the Rajputs, who once formed the many princely houses of Rajasthan (former Rajputana) and neighboring areas. Of course, today most Kshatriyas are landowners or follow urban professions.

Although they rank high in the varna system, Kshatriyas may and commonly do eat meat (though never beef), and many also take alcoholic drinks; both of these characteristics set them apart from the Brahmans.

It is perhaps no mere coincidence that Mahavira and Gautama, the founders of Jainism and Buddhism respectively, were of this social category. It can be argued that their spiritual voyages in the sixth century B.C. were both prompted by reaction to the excessive ritualism that marked the Vedic sacrifice of the *purohita* (priests). Some centuries later there was a general understanding that Kshatriyas would abstain from wordly pleasures while they fought to protect the polity and the Brahmans' place in it. But in fact—if Rajput history can be taken as a guide—Kshatriya warriors when not actually on the battlefield surrounded themselves with luxurious palaces, multiple wives and concubines, fine horses and falcons, and all the pleasures of eating cooked meats.

See also Rajput

Bibliography

Fox, Richard G. (1971). *Kin, Clan, Raja, and Rule: State-Hinterland Relations in Preindustrial India.* Berkeley: University of California Press.

Tod, James (1829–32). *Annals and Antiquities of Rajast'han, or the Central and Western Rajpoot States of India.* Rev. ed., edited by William Crooke. 1920. London: Oxford University Press. Numerous reprints.

PAUL HOCKINGS

Kurumbas

ETHNONYMS: Alu-Kurumbas, Betta-Kurumbas, Jenu-Kurumbas, Kurubas, Mudugas, Mulla-Kurumbas, Palu-Kurumbas, Urali-Kurumbas

People identified as Kurumbas have been reported across a wide area in south India. Major settlements, however, are found in the Nilgiri area located between 11°10' and 11°30' N and between 76°25' and 77°00' E, at the junction of the Eastern Ghats and the Western Ghats. There the Kurumbas occupy the thickly forested slopes, glens, and foothills of the Nilgiri Plateau. The Nilgiri groups are seven in number: the Alu- (milk), Palu- (milk), Betta- (hill), Jenu- (honey), Mulla- (net), and Urali- (village) Kurumbas, as well as the Mudugas (no etymology). Each is a distinct ethnic group differing from the others in dialect, religious beliefs, and other cultural attributes. The 1971 Indian census counted 12,930 Kurumbas. In 1981 the Nilgiri District census reported 4,874 Kurumbas, most of whom are Muduga. Together the Kurumba groups compose the smallest proportion of the plateau population there, and the poorest.

Of the four tribes that occupy the Nilgiri Plateau, legend says that the Toda, Kurumba, and Kota tribes were brought into being simultaneously by a parent creator. There were three brothers who either transgressed against the parents or quarreled among themselves. As a result their father, a supernatural, assigned to each a different function in life and ordained that the three would exchange goods and services. The descendants of these three brothers became the three tribes and thus the three peoples have been bound in a common fate since the beginning of time.

Traditionally the Kurumbas have subsisted as hunters and gatherers. Living in jungles on the steep edges of the plateau, they practice shifting cultivation and the foraging and trapping of small birds and animals. Early settlements were usually isolated, with Kurumbas living in caves or rock shelters, in dwellings near forest clearings, or in houses or huts in small hamlets interspersed with garden patches. Bananas, mangoes, jackfruit, maize, and chilies were the usual garden produce. Today, with increasing population and deforestation, the Kurumbas have been forced to lower elevations of the plateau and subsist primarily by working on tea or coffee plantations.

Historically the Kurumbas have had a cooperative relationship with the other tribes that includes the exchange of goods and services. Kurumbas supply the tall poles used in Toda funeral rites, three types of baskets used by the Badagas, and often music for Badaga and Toda festivals. However, the activity for which the Kurumbas are best known has been the provision of sorcery. Traditionally each Badaga commune appointed a specific Kurumba man to act as guardian and watchman to certain constituent villages. This was a lifelong appointment that passed from father to son. In addition to guarding, the watchman took part in the sowing and harvest festivals as an adjunct priest (*kani-kuruma*). A number of other magical roles are played today by the Kurumbas. In the diviner (*kanigara*), exorcist (*devvagara*), and sorcerer (*odigara* or *odia*) roles a Kurumba, with the help of herbs, spells, and roots, can bring sickness or death to the enemy. The therapist (*maddugara*) functions as a medicine man and curer. As a wizard (*pilligara*) the Kurumba may turn himself into an animal. As a result of their knowledge of sorcery, the Kurumbas were feared; the other tribes frequently banded together against them. A number of massacres of Kurumbas were reported throughout the 1800s. These massacres were in retaliation for supposed deeds of sorcery inflicted on particular individuals or communities. Kurumba watchmen, however, no longer patrol the village fields, and the other tribes no longer fear the Kurumba as in the past. Their tradition for sorcery remains but personal fear is now little felt by neighboring tribespeople.

Today the question arise as to whether the Kurumbas are descended from ancient Nilgiri ancestors who were primarily gatherers or from far more recent farming immigrants. Their language belongs to the South Dravidian Subfamily. In general the groups have a clan organization that is exogamous and patrilineal. The tribes practice endogamy. Cross-cousin

marriages frequently occur. Traditionally there are a number of offices within the tribe including the village headman (*maniagara*) and priest (*mannugara*). The headman and assistant headman's offices are hereditary in the male line, while either a male or a female may be a priest or sorcerer. Traditional religious beliefs involve an ancestor cult with an emphasis on pollution and purity, which parallels other such beliefs upheld in Hinduism generally. Today young people are embracing both Hinduism and Christianity in addition to the traditional beliefs.

See also Irula; Nayaka

Bibliography

Kapp, Dieter B. (1978a). "Pālu Kurumba Riddles: Specimens of a South Dravidian Tribal Language." *Bulletin of the School of Oriental and African Studies* 41:512–522. London: University of London.

Kapp, Deiter B. (1978b). "Childbirth and Name-Giving among the Ālu Kurumbas of South India." In *Aspects of Tribal Life in South Asia*. Vol. 1, *Strategy and Survival*. Proceedings of an International Seminar held in Berne, 1977. Edited by Rupert R. Moser and Mohan K. Gautam, 167–180. Bern: Studia Ethnologica Bernensia 1.

Kapp, Dieter B. (1978c). "Die Kindheits-und Jugendriten der Ālu-Kurumbas (Südindien)." *Zeitschrift für Ethnologie* 103:279–289.

Kapp Dieter B. (1980). "Die Ordination des Priesters bei den Ālu-Kurumbas (Südindien)." *Anthropos* 75:433–446.

Kapp, Dieter B. (1982). "The Concept of Yama in the Religion of a South Indian Tribe." *Journal of the American Oriental Society* 102:517–521.

Kapp, Dieter B. (1985). "The Kurumbas' Relationship to the 'Megalithic' Cult of the Nilgiri Hills (South India)." *Anthropos* 80:493–534.

Kapp, Dieter B., and Paul Hockings (1989). "The Kurumba Tribes." In *Blue Mountains: The Ethnography and Biogeography of a South Indian Region*, edited by Paul Hockings, 232–248. New York: Oxford University Press.

Misra, Rajalakshmi (1989). "The Mullu Kurumbas." In *Blue Mountains: The Ethnography and Biogeography of a South Indian Region*, edited by Paul Hockings, 304–359. New York: Oxford University Press.

SARA J. DICK

Labbai

ETHNONYM: Kodikkalkaran ("betel-vine people")

Labbai are one of the four Muslim groups in Tamil Nadu State. The Ravuttan, Marakkayar, and Kayalan form the rest of the Islamic community. According to tradition, the name "Labbai" was given to them by the Arabs, meaning "Here I am." Previously the Labbais were few in number and were under the control of other Muslims and Hindus. In order to get their attention and be recognized, the Labbais traditionally would cry loudly, "Labbek," meaning "We are your servants."

Tamil is their main language, mostly spoken in the household. People living in the cities do speak Urdu, but they do not recognize it as their main language. In some Arab-influenced towns such as Nagapattinam and Kayalpatnam, Labbai Muslims write Tamil using Arabic script, the only people to do so.

The origin of the Labbais is not clear, but a few speculations have been recorded. The historian Mark Wilks suggests that in the early eighth century A.D. the governor of Iraq, Hijaj Ben Gusaff, drove a number of people, including fellow Muslim citizens, into exile by his barbaric actions. Some migrated to the western coast of India and others east of Cape Comorin. The Labbais are descended from the latter group. Another version says that the Labbais are descendants of Arabs who came to India in the eleventh and twelfth centuries for trade. But these Arabs were persecuted by the Moguls and were forced to flee the country, leaving behind their belongings and children born to Indian mothers.

Labbais are known as traders, although residents of different areas have different occupations. In the Mysore region, they are vendors of hardware, merchants, coffee traders, and owners of other profitable businesses. In the South Arcot District of Tamil Nadu, they grow betel nuts, manage a skin trade, are small shopkeepers, and trade at the seaports. The women of this district are expert at weaving mats, which are considered a valuable source of income. The Labbais of the Madurai District seem to have chosen a quite different means of subsistence: many are well known as smiths and others are boatworkers and fishers. In general, they are recognized as skilled and expert traders.

The Labbais worship as Muslims and recently this has had great influence on their life expectations. About 80 percent of the Muslims in Tamil Nadu are Muslim Tamils and the remaining 20 percent include the Mapillas and Urdu speakers such as Sheikh, Sayyid, Sharif, Pathan, Ismaili, Navayat, Daudi Bohra, and Wahabi. Labbais and Ravuttans follow the Hanafi school, a branch of the Sunni sect. Their religious practices demonstrate an orthodox way of living where men and their children go to the mosques to pray, while women stay at home to pray. Religious books are in Arabic and hold a sacred position. It is considered a duty to publish books in Arabic and distribute them among people. The Muslims do not recognize the caste system of Hindus, even though in the rural areas they are recognized as ethnically different from Hindus and are categorized as a separate caste. Girls do not marry before puberty. They practice the Islamic ritual except in some areas where they have adopted a Hindu wedding ceremony. Marriage with a mother's brother's daughter is the ideal, if and only if she is the right age. Kin marriages are common to hold together the ties between families, but no marriage occurs with parallel cousins. Family gatherings and visits are used by the older family members to find mates for their young ones.

Bibliography

Mines, Mattison (1984). "Labbai." In *Muslim Peoples: A World Ethnographic Survey*, edited by Richard V. Weekes. Vol. 1, 431–436. Westport, Conn.: Greenwood Press.

Thurston, Edgar, and Kadamki Rangachari (1909). "Labbai." In *Castes and Tribes of Southern India*, edited by Edgar Thurston and Kadamki Rangachari. Vol. 4, 198–205. Madras: Government Press. Numerous reprints.

SAIDEH MOAYED-SANANDAJI

Lakher

ETHNONYMS: Magha, Mara, Shendu

Orientation

Identification. The Lakher are a Kuki tribe located in the Lushai Hills of Mizoram (north of the Arakan Hills), in India. Lakher is the name given to this people by the Mizos (who live in that part of the region extending from 22°44' to 22°55' N and 92°35' to 92°47' E). Cultural affinities have been noted between the Lakher and the Mizos, Chin, and Naga. They are also called Shendu by the Arakanese. The Lakher refer to themselves as Mara and are composed of six groups: the Tlongsai, Hawthai, Zeuhnang, Sabeu, Lialai, and Heima. Much of what is known of Lakher culture has come from the work of N. E. Parry, who studied them early in this century, and his ethnography provides the basis for most of the information summarized below.

Location. The geographical locus of Lakher culture extends from approximately 22°00' to 23°00' N and from 92°45' to 93°25' E. Lakher settlements are found, in large part, within that area bounded on the north and east by the Kolodyne River (though some villages lie outside this boundary to the west and to the northeast). The area inhabited by the Lakher is hilly (the highest peak reaching in excess of 2,100 meters), damp (in winter), and fertile (accommodating the growth of rice, flowers, trees, and several varieties of bamboo).

Demography. According to Parry, the Lakher numbered some 10,000 in his day. The 1971 census of India reported a total of 12,871. A United Bible Societies survey revealed a total Mara Chin–speaking population of 14,000 in 1983.

Line

Linguistic Affiliation. The Lakher speak Mara Chin (Burmic Family, Tibeto-Burman Stock), a language belonging to the Sino-Tibetan Phylum.

History and Cultural Relations

The separate groups that make up the Lakher are all believed to have originated somewhere north of their present location, in the Chin Hills. The advancement of these peoples can be traced with some degree of certainty, and the original homeland of at least three of these groups (Tlongsai, Hawthai, and Sabeu) can be posited. The Tlongsai migration began in Leisai (between Leitak and Zaphai). The original homeland of the Hawthai is believed to have been Chira (in Haka). The Sabeu are found in Chapi, but it is believed that they migrated to that location from Thlatla, which is near Haka. Before the advent of British imperial domination, intervillage conflict was the Lakher norm. Individual Lakher villages fought against one another and against neighboring peoples (e.g., the Khumis and Chins). The relationship between the British and the Lakhers was characterized by intermittent conflict, extending from the middle of the nineteenth century to 1924, at which time all the Lakher tribes were brought under British control. British rule brought both political and economic stability to the region. Villages enjoyed a period of internal and external security, slavery was eliminated, and a new market for the sale of surplus goods appeared (with a resulting shift from barter to currency as the medium of exchange). This marked the beginning of the demise of the village chief's power and authority. With the advent of Indian home rule, the political structure of the Lakher region was reorganized. An administrative structure was established for the Lushai Hills (to which the Lakher Region sends one representative) and a regional council for the Pawi-Lakher regions (to which the Lakher Region is permitted to send four delegates). The office of village chief has been eliminated, and the Lakher are gradually being assimilated into the mainstream of Indian life as citizens of Mizoram state.

Settlements

Lakher villages are usually built on sloping terrain just below the apex of a hill or mountain. Village sites are more or less permanent, with the people preferring not to relocate because this would require abandoning ancestral burial grounds. Names are selected for villages that highlight some natural feature associated with the location (e.g., Lakai, "winding path," was so named because of the circuitous road that leads to it). Temporary habitations are established in fields during the cultivation season so as to eliminate the necessity of relocating as the need for additional _jhum_ land arises. The construction of individual homes is asymmetrical, and rarely is there found a major thoroughfare within village boundaries. Only the _tleulia_ area (reserved for community sacrifices) and the home of the chief are placed preferentially, the former being found in the center of the village and the latter usually being located nearby. In antiquity, each village had an internal fortress (_ku_) to which retreat was made in the event of external attack, with a network of sentry posts, strategically placed clearings to prevent covert attack, and stone traps (_longpa_) built along roads leading to the village. This system of fortification no longer exists in Lakher villages. The size and contents of individual homes vary according to the social status of the occupant. Building materials consist of wood, bamboo, cane rope, and palm (or bamboo) leaves.

Economy

Subsistence and Commercial Activities. The Lakher engage in most of the major subsistence activities (i.e., hunting, fishing, animal domestication, and agriculture). Jhum agriculture (in which jungle is cut, permitted to dry, burned, and seeded) is practiced. Three implements only are used in the process: the hoe, _dao_ (machete), and axe. While at least one report noted that the Lakher used terracing as a method, regional climate (which is dry) and terrain (which is quite steep) suggest otherwise. Maize, millet, cucumbers, pumpkins, rice, a variety of other vegetables, spices, cotton (for the manufacture of cloth), and tobacco (for personal use) are grown in the jhum fields. Rats, elephants, bears, snakes, dogs (eaten only by men), goats (eaten only by men), and various wild birds are hunted and consumed. Gayals (used as a means of monetary exchange and in festival sacrifices), cows (for meat only), pigs, dogs, cats, pigeons, and chickens (for meat and eggs) are domesticated by the Lakher. Fish, crabs (freshwater), and mussels are among the river creatures sought for consumption. Horses (because of their use as pack animals), leopards, tigers, and cats are not consumed.

Industrial Arts. Lakher manufactures include a variety of bamboo and cane baskets, mats, trays, and sieves (all produced by men), nonornamental metalwork (daos, knives, hoes, and axes), tools associated with cloth production (i.e., spindles, spinning wheels, and cotton gins), cotton cloth (plain), dyed cloth, various items manufactured by unmarried women and widows for domestic use (e.g., gourds, gourd spoons, plates, flasks), pipes (for smoking tobacco), jars, and certain implements of war (e.g., bows, arrows, daos, and spears before the acquisition of guns).

Trade. Trade is not a major part of the Lakher economy. During the imperial period, currency was acquired through the sale of rice to the British for military rations, the sale of cotton and sesame to the Arakanese, the transport of goods between Lungleh and Demagiri (for Lungleh merchants), and the sale of copper cooking pots (purchased, along with salt, from these same merchants) to the Chin. Bees' nests are also collected, with the wax being extracted and traded by the Lakher.

Division of Labor. Men and women participate fully in the economic life of the community. Parry has noted that women are as integral a part of the agricultural cycle as their male counterparts. He has also noted that Lakher women enjoy considerably more personal freedom than their counterparts who inhabit the Indian plains. Some tasks are reserved exclusively for either males or females. Textile manufacture (weaving and dyeing) is the province of women, and the production of earthenware items may be undertaken by unmarried women and widows only. Men produce baskets, hunt, fish, go fowling, cut jhum fields, and construct or repair houses. Women gather firewood and water, weave, feed and care for domestic animals (e.g., pigs), prepare meals, and participate fully in certain aspects of the agricultural cycle (weeding, cleaning, and harvesting).

Land Tenure. Village lands are owned by the village chief and are cultivated by members of the village only with the permission of the village chief. In exchange for the use of this land, there is a dues structure that each household must abide by. _Sabai_ is the fee (usually amounting to one basket of rice) that must be paid to the village chief in recognition of his chieftainship. The chief must also be paid a separate fee (*rapaw*) for the privilege of cultivating his land. If a household has jhum land within the territory of more than one chief, then these fees must be paid to each chief. These lands are passed on as an inheritance within the chief's family. His eldest son is his heir (thereby inheriting all village lands) and successor (assuming the mantle of rule upon the death of his father). Individual ownership of land does not appear to be permitted, though each household is allowed to select its jhum once the appropriate place for cultivation has been specified by the village chief and council of elders.

Kinship

Kin Groups and Descent. As has been mentioned above, the Lakher are composed of six groups, each of which consists of a number of clans. The dialects spoken by each group are mutually intelligible. Each clan is believed to have taken the name of an ancestor, though it is no longer possible to trace the lineage to its point of origin. Clan solidarity is manifest particularly during life-cycle events (e.g., marriage, birth, death) as well as at certain sacrificial occasions of a private nature. For most other purposes, the central sociopolitical unit is the village. There exist no clan-based marital prohibitions, and at least four clans (the Bonghia, Thleutha, Hnaihleu, and Mihlong) may be of totemic origin. Within the overall clan hierarchy, royal clans assume primacy of place. These are followed, in descending order, by the *phangsang* (noble) clans and the *machhi* (commoners') clans. There is a discernible relationship between clan status and material wealth. Descent is patrilineal.

Kinship Terminology. Omaha-type kinship terms are employed for first cousins.

Marriage and Family

Marriage. Young men and women are allowed considerable freedom in premarital relationships. Part of the courting procedure involves the male spending the day with the female with whom he would like to form a liaison. The two of them complete their daily chores together and then the male spends the night in the female's house. If the female is interested in initiating a physical relationship, she places her bed near that of the male suitor. Liaisons are also formed during those social events when males and females gather to drink and sing. Men usually marry between the ages of 20 and 25 while women marry after having reached 20 years of age. Parents play an important role in the betrothal process. A man's parents select his bride, and individual Lakher clans are not strictly endogamous or exogamous (though the paucity of marriages within Lakher clans suggests the presence of an earlier exogamous clan structure). Monogamous unions are the norm, but concubinage is permitted (though concubines do not enjoy the same status as wives). A bride-price (the amount of which is negotiated by representatives of the families involved) must be paid before the ceremony may take place. The marriage is not usually consummated on the first night of the wedding feast, a period of at least one month being required before this takes place (this practice does not obtain in all villages). During this time, the wife sleeps in the house of her husband while the husband sleeps elsewhere.

Postmarital residence is generally with the groom's father until the birth of the first child. After the birth of the first child, the new couple establish their own residence (though locational preference is not given). Parentally arranged child marriage, usually (though not always) involving two prepubescent children of the same age, is also permitted. These unions are generally consummated after both of the parties reach puberty. Marriage to a young woman belonging to a privileged clan and in general to a mother's brother's daughter, is preferred. Divorce is infrequent. It has been suggested that the traditionally high Lakher bride-price contributes to this (a woman's parents being required to refund payment to the husband in the event of a divorce). Divorce regulations favor the female, though it is more usual to find proceedings initiated by husbands than by wives. Impotence, madness, and adultery are all considered sufficient grounds for divorce.

Domestic Unit. Family size ranges from five to ten persons, with five being the norm. The typical household may be larger if a married son has not established separate residence for himself and his family.

Inheritance. A man's property is inherited by his eldest son. This son is then responsible for repaying all of the father's debts along with the father's death *ru* (a due paid to the mother's brother, called the *pupa*). A husband is responsible for paying the death ru of his wife. If he predeceases his wife, this responsibility must then be assumed by his youngest son. While it is not required, the eldest son may give a portion of the deceased father's estate to the youngest son. Other sons are allowed no share in their father's estate. Should a man leave no male heirs, his estate would pass first to his brothers, then (in descending order) to his uncles, first cousins, distant relations, and nearest clansmen. Women are forbidden to inherit, the one exception being if the woman is the last surviving member of her clan. An inheritance may not be refused, and one must be willing to assume the assets and debts of the deceased in full. A widow is allowed to remain in the home of her deceased husband until a memorial stone is set up. If she has children, she may remain in the marital home until she remarries. If the children are minors, the widow receives her husband's estate in trust for her eldest son. Should the widow prove unable to provide for herself and her family upon the death of her husband, either the eldest or youngest brother of her deceased husband would receive control of the estate and would provide for the needs of the surviving family.

Socialization. To a great degree, Lakher children are responsible for their own learning. There is no systematic program for the acquisition of basic life skills. Children are expected to observe the activities of their elders and imitate them. Parents appear to play an important part in the socialization process, though the pedagogical method employed allows children considerable autonomy once they are able to work independently. Male and female dormitories, which obtain in a number of other Indian tribal groups, are absent among the Lakher. Once children have matured to the point that they can accompany their male parent on jungle excursions, they observe the methods used in hunting, fishing, etc. and master these skills by imitation (e.g., by making model traps). Boys and girls are taught how to care for jhum fields and girls are taught how to weave. Magicoreligious rites are, for the most part, mastered by means of observation. The sole exception to this norm is the Khazangpina chant (which accompanies the sacrifice offered to the god Khazangpa), which children are taught.

Sociopolitical Organization

Social Organization. The social structure of the typical Lakher village consists of phangsang (patricians), macchi (plebeians), and _tlapi_ (regular citizenry). A special group exists within the phangsang called the _kuei_. These individuals have been excluded from the obligation of paying the chief the sabai (rice due) and sahaw (meat due). This privilege is awarded to the descendants of those who have extended some special service to the village or its chief (e.g., paying the indemnity owed to a conquering village after a military defeat or extending hospitality to a chief's guests).

Political Organization. The basic political unit in traditional Lakher society is the village, governed by the _bei_ (chief) with the assistance of the _machas_ (usually a noble or gifted plebeian). Other officials include: the _tlaawpa_ (village crier who dispatches the chief's business within the village); _seudaipa_ (blacksmith); _khireipa_ (village writer who handles the chief's correspondence); the _tleuliabopa_ (sacrificial priest) appointed by the chief who offers the _tleulia_ (sacrifice) to propitiate the spirits inhabiting the hill upon which the village is located); and the _cheusapathaipa_ (the cook for the Khazangpina sacrifice). In traditional Lakher society, the chief is the village's central political official during peacetime and war. He personally receives a variety of fees and services from the villagers and, along with the village elders, is empowered to levy such fees and services as are necessary to ensure the continued growth and safety of the community. With the abolition of chieftainship, the Lakher are being brought gradually into the mainstream of Indian political life.

Social Control. Social control is maintained by the Lakher jurisprudential system administered by the chief and his council of elders. The chief has final authority in all legal decisions, but provision is made for the expression of popular sentiment in these proceedings. If the chief is unable to render a legal decision, there is provision made for trial by ordeal. There is also a system of fines that may be imposed for various offenses. Capital punishment does not obtain in traditional jurisprudence. Murderers were required to pay fines—100 to 300 rupees according to Parry—and were excluded from performing clan-based sacrifices and participating in communal feasts. Other fines include those imposed for theft, assault, eavesdropping, trespassing, and character defamation. Control is also maintained by a series of _anas_. These are prohibitions against certain types of behavior that are believed to bring bad luck or death.

Conflict. As mentioned above, prior to British rule intervillage conflict was frequent. Resistance to British imperial authority was brought to an end by 1924. Since that time, the forces of acculturation have brought the Lakher closer to the mainstream of national life. The reorganization of the Lakher region, which began in 1947, has made it possible for the Lakher to have an impact on the government of their homeland and a voice in the administration of Mizoram, the larger state of which they are a part.

Religion and Expressive Culture

Religious Beliefs. The Lakher acknowledge one god (Khazangpa/Khazangleutha) who is believed to be the creator of the cosmos, the one who decrees the fates of all creatures. He is believed to live in the mountains or in the sky. His name means "father of all" and his alternate name, Pachhapa, means "the old man." The Lakher also believe that mountains, woods, and pools have _leurahripas_ (evil and beneficent spirits). It is also believed that every person has a _zang_ (tutelary deity/angelic guardian) charged with his or her protection. Some leurahripas are believed to be the source of all sickness and must be propitiated regularly.

Religious Practitioners. Magicoreligious rites may be performed by any member of a household. There is no hereditary Lakher priesthood, the sole exception being the tleuliabopa who is appointed by the village chief to perform the tleulia sacrifice. In most Lakher villages, this position is held for life. Misconduct can, however, result in dismissal and replacement. Upon the death of the tleuliabopa, the office passes to his son. The services of a _khazanghneipa_ (medium) may be obtained by those desiring fertility, cures for sickness, or knowledge of future events.

Ceremonies. Ceremonies accompany most of the major life-cycle events and other significant social events. Festival occasions are few in number and are usually associated with marriage and birth. A man of wealth may sponsor a feast upon the completion of a new home. Beer feasts may also be given by a man for his associates. The major Lakher festivals are Pazusata (a feast that marks the end of the year and during which behavioral restrictions on children are suspended), and Pakhupila (the "knee dance," occasioned by an excellent crop yield). The Siaha royal clan (the Khichha Hleuchang) departs from this norm. It has a series of six feasts designed to ensure favorable treatment in the afterlife (i.e., entrance into Paradise). In addition to these festivals, numerous additional magicoreligious rites (of a sacrificial nature) are associated with the subsistence cycle, matters of state, legal proceedings, medical practice, domestic affairs, ancestral worship, and the religious cults. Of these, the Khazangpina sacrifice (offered to Khazangpa), during which the sacrificer asks for blessings on himself and his family (e.g., wealth, health, abundance of children, good crops, and fertile domestic animals), is unsurpassed in importance.

Arts. Lakher visual art is represented by personal effects serving ornamental and other purposes (e.g., belts, hairpins, combs, earrings, bracelets, necklaces, pipes, guns, powder flasks, daos, swords, knives, nicotine-water flasks, syphons, and the lids of earthenware pots) and by tattooing. Music is of great importance and the Lakher have three classes of songs: those for daily usage; those accompanying the ia ceremony (performed over the head of a dead enemy or the carcass of a dead animal); and those accompanying the Pakupila festival ("knee dance"). Instruments include gongs, flutes, drums, violins, zithers, and the _chaei_ (a kind of mouth harp). Funerals, wakes, weddings, and feasts are all occasions for dancing. The Lakher claim that their dance patterns are based on movements characteristic of the fly. Lakher oral literature consists of a small number of proverbs, an ever-increasing corpus of folklore, and myths pertaining to cosmic origins, the exploits of primordial humanity, Khazangpa, and the nature of certain natural phenomena (earthly and celestial).

Medicine. Sickness is believed to be caused chiefly by leurahripas, who capture the soul of a person and prevent it from returning to the body. The ravages of sickness can be averted by individual or corporate sacrifice. The tleulia sacrifice (described above), the tlaraipasi ceremony (used to prevent the outbreak of an epidemic), and the sacrifice offered to a local *khisong* (spirit dwelling on a mountaintop, in a pool, or in a lake) are intended to ensure village health. Personal infirmities (e.g., swelling, minor illnesses, consumption, premature aging, and impotence) can be alleviated by a variety of individual sacrifices or through the ministrations of the khazanghneipa. Medicinal cures (both indigenous and Western) are also used, but they are considered of secondary importance to the sacrificial system of healing.

Death and Afterlife. Death results when Khazangpa or a leurahripa steals an individual's soul. The dead are believed to go to one of three domains in the afterworld. The habitation known as Athikhi (literally, "the village of the dead") is occupied by those who have had an average existence. Here they live lives similar in quality to those lived on Earth. Distinctions between the wealthy and the poor continue to obtain in Athikhi. Those who have killed certain animals in the wild and have performed the ia ceremony over them may attain to Peira, a domain near that of Khazangpa. Those who die unnatural deaths or perish because of terrible diseases are confined to Sawvawkhi. Men who have never had sexual intercourse are called *chhongchhongpipas*. These are fated to wander on the road between the earthly realm and Athikhi. As for those souls that have lived in Athikhi for an extended period, those of chiefs die, turn to warm mist, rise heavenward, and vanish. Those of the average person are transformed into worms and are consumed by chickens. It is believed that the spirits of those who die as children transmigrate and are reincarnated in the bodies of younger siblings.

See also Mizo

Bibliography

Barkataki, S. (1969). *Tribes of Assam*. New Delhi: National Book Trust.

LeBar, Frank M., et al., eds. (1964). *Ethnic Groups of Mainland Southeast Asia*. New Haven, Conn.: HRAF Press.

Löffer, L. G. (1960). "Patrilineal Lineation in Transition." *Ethnos* 1–2:119–150.

Parry, N. E. (1932). *The Lakhers*. London: Macmillan.

Shakespear, John (1912). *The Lushei Kuki Clans*. London: Macmillan.

HUGH R. PAGE, JR.

Lepcha

ETHNONYMS: none

Orientation

The Lepcha inhabit the southern and eastern slopes of Mount Kanchenjunga in the Himalayas, a land located in the districts of Sikkim and Darjeeling, India, lying between 27° and 28° N and 88° and 89° E. Their population in 1987 was estimated at 65,000 by the United Bible Societies, with 23,706 in Sikkim (1982), 1,272 in Nepal (1961), and 24,200 in Bhutan (1987), and others in India. The name "Lepcha" was originally given them by their Nepali neighbors, meaning "nonsense talkers." Although the Lepcha have no tradition of migration it is believed they originally came from either Mongolia or Tibet; their language is classified in the Tibeto-Burman Family.

History and Cultural Relations

For over three centuries the Lepcha were a subjugated people, absorbing invasions from the Nepalis, Tibetans, and Bhutanese, with consequent effects on their language and culture, and therefore their distinct ethnic identity was largely suppressed. Today few Lepchas speak their own language, and most have adopted the language and ways of life of their local neighbors, the Nepalis. Intermarriage with Nepalis is also very common in areas of mixed population. Although there was a brief revival of the Lepcha script during the nineteenth and early twentieth centuries by Christian missionaries, the script was never widely used and has now fallen into obscurity.

Settlements

The houses of a village are often scattered in isolated areas of the fields or the forests, and there are usually no more than three or four in a grouping. Thus it is possible to walk through a village without ever noticing it. Traditional Lepcha homes are rectangular buildings, raised 1 to 1.5 meters off the ground on stone piles, with the space underneath serving as shelter for farm animals; houses are often constructed of wood, plaster, and bamboo.

Economy

The principal crops raised by the Lepcha include wet rice, dry rice, buckwheat, maize, cardamom (their cash crop), and several varieties of millet. In the subtropical river valley, sugarcane and manioc are also grown. Fresh vegetables such as tomatoes and chili peppers are grown in backyard gardens and near the fields; wild vegetables and fruit are also collected. Hunting, once more common, is now seldom done, because of the time taken from working in the fields. The Lepchas have herds of cattle, which are generally kept for their dairy products and for plowing the fields; cattle are also occasionally slaughtered for meat. Goats are kept but never for their milk, only for their meat and for sacrifice. By far the most popular and numerous of the domesticated animals are pigs, kept for food and sacrifice.

The food of the Lepchas is not nearly as spicy as Indian

or Nepali dishes. Rice is the most popular staple of the Lepcha diet; wheat, maize, and buckwheat are also eaten but are not nearly as popular. Millet is grown for fermenting as an alcoholic beverage; this grain is never eaten by people. The Lepcha diet is rounded out with fresh fruits and vegetables; fish is occasionally caught but not often.

The traditional spartan nature of Lepcha life does not lend itself to secular art or painting, which (except for specially trained lamas) are completely alien to them. They are, however, outstanding carpenters, and many do find employment in this trade; they are also noted for their weaving and spinning abilities. The Marwari, an Indian merchant caste, are chiefly responsible for setting up shops and acting as moneylenders to the Lepcha. The principle cash crop of the Lepcha is cardamom, their main export.

There is no rigid division of labor based on sex; women, however, are strictly forbidden to kill any animals. Groups of women and men work side by side in the fields, and although men generally weave the baskets and mats, and women spin yarn, if one of the sexes were to try one or the other activity, no stigma would be attached to it.

Kinship, Marriage, and Family

The Lepchas are divided into groups based on birth and marriage; these are the patrilineal clan and the immediate nuclear and extended family. The Lepchas count descent for nine generations on the father's side and a minimum of four on the mother's. They have a very small number of kinship terms and exclude the whole category of cousins; and, except for the mother's brothers, they make no distinction between the paternal and maternal lines. For people younger than the speaker, they do not make any distinction based on gender. Only children's spouses have different terms for son-in-law and daughter-in-law.

Any sexual connection with blood relations for nine generations on the father's side and four on the mother's side is considered incestuous. Lepcha traditionally marry very young, girls usually before age 14 and boys by age 16. There are two stages in Lepcha marriage: betrothal and bringing home the bride. The betrothal phase is a validating ceremony at which the family of the groom presents the bride's family with gifts, called "the price of the bride," and once these are accepted the marriage is completed and the groom may have full access to his bride.

Sociopolitical Organization

Each Lepcha village is traditionally headed by a village leader, who is responsible for keeping order and collecting taxes. Crime is a very rare occurrence in a Lepcha village; murder is almost unheard of, although there have been accusations of poisoning. Theft is highly unusual because the Lepcha economy is founded on the belief that people do not steal, and when this does happen it is very disquieting. Any outbreak of a quarrel is handled immediately by neutral persons. The Lepcha attitude toward aggression is that it is not natural and that it is destructive to the community at large.

Religion

The Lepcha practice two mutually contradictory religions simultaneously, without any ambivalent feeling. The older Mun religion, named after the title of the priests, involves a special relationship with a family spirit. This spirit is appeased by animal sacrifices and by direct communication, as part of an effort to ward off evil spirits who cause illness and disaster. It is interesting to note that, among the many myths and legends of the Lepcha, there are many accounts of the Abominable Snowman (Yeti) in the glacial regions of the Himalayas, and he is worshiped as the god of the hunt, the owner of all mountain game, and the lord of all forest creatures. Tibetan Lamaism was introduced in the seventeenth century and is rooted in a priesthood and in sanctity gained by learning, not by inspiration; the sacrifice of animals is considered a terrible sin by members of this religion.

See also Sikkimese

Bibliography

Gorer, Geoffrey (1938). _Himalayan Village: An Account of the Lepchas of Sikkim_. London: Michael Joseph. 2nd ed. New York: Basic Books, 1967.

Hooker, Joseph D. (1891). _Himalayan Journals_. London: Ward, Lock, Bowden & Co. [Numerous earlier editions.]

Jest, Corneille (1960). "Religious Beliefs of the Lepchas in the Kalimpong District (West Bengal)." _Journal of the Royal Asiatic Society_ 1960:124–134.

Morris, John (1938). _Living with Lepchas: A Book about the Sikkim Himalayas_. London: William Heinemann.

Siiger, Halfdan, and Jørgen Rischel (1967). _The Lepchas: Culture and Religion of a Himalayan People_. Ethnographical Series 2. Copenhagen: National Museum of Denmark.

Tobias, Michael (1967). _Mountain People_. Norman: University of Oklahoma Press. 2nd ed. 1986. New York: Basic Books.

JAY DiMAGGIO

Limbu

ETHNONYMS: none

Orientation

The Limbu, one of the largest tribal aggregates in Nepal, live in the most easterly part of Nepal between the Arun River and the border of Sikkim District, India. The Limbu are of Mongolian descent and speak a Tibeto-Burman dialect. In 1970, the population was estimated at 245,000.

History and Cultural Relations

In the latter part of the eighteenth century Nepal was formed by uniting various ethnic groups and numerous principalities under a high-caste Hindu dynasty. This conquest resulted in a number of migrations of high-caste Hindu groups into eastern Nepal, causing an ethnic and cultural split with the Limbus. Limbus are considered the first settlers of east Nepal and are thought to be descendants of the Kiratis. Limbus became known to history in the eighteenth century, at a time when a number of small chiefdoms in Limbuan were under the authority of the kingdom of Bijayapur. The Limbus were expected to grant land to the immigrants for their support. The Nepalese government brought all tribal lands (with the exception of certain Limbus) under *raikar*, "a system of land-lordism under which the rights of an individual to utilization and transfer of the land are recognized by the state as long as taxes are paid." Before this system was enforced all Limbu groups held land under the system of *kipat*, in which "an individual obtains rights to land by virtue of his membership in a series of nesting kin groups." This change of land tenure caused Limbus to lose lands to the Hindu immigrants, who were mostly of Brahman caste. There were two reasons for this change. First, a shortage of lands was beginning to be felt, and therefore the government dissolved all the Limbuan rights to their kipat lands. A second factor was the absence of ownership documents, which led to legal conflicts over ownership and rent. Surrendered kipat lands helped to finance revenue settlements, postal services, and the army. The Limbus were left only with the land they were living on and cultivating. The Brahmans had some advantages over Limbus: they were skilled and had labor resources that the Limbus lacked and needed. They were also able to read and write, which qualified them for administrative jobs and forced the abolition of the kipat system. In the eyes of the Limbus, Brahmans were "ungrateful servants" who were trusted with their land but "stole" it instead. The Limbus are now determined to salvage their land under the kipat system and refrain from passing it on to members of other groups. Brahmans, at a cost to the Limbus, have become the most authoritarian ethnic group in east Nepal. Resentment is also felt by the Brahmans toward the Limbus; Brahmans regard the Limbus as "simple" and "concerned only for the present." Brahmans feel that if Limbus had looked to the future, they would not have granted their lands. The Limbuan struggle for land is an ongoing process that continues to affect social and political conditions in the region.

Economy

Agriculture is the main source of income. The abundance of land has made the cultivation of new agricultural lands possible, but insufficient knowledge of technology has limited their productivity. Limbu grow wheat, rice, and maize, and they trade some of the crops for goods that cannot be grown or made in their region. A sexual division of labor occurs in agriculture. Men plow the fields, women plant the seeds, and at the harvesting period both sexes join to complete the job. During cultivation families bring friends to help with the fields. These groups of people share labor with one another during especially busy times. Another source of income for Limbus is military service. Economic hardship has made it worthwhile to join the army both in Nepal and in India in return for a small amount of cash. Associated with military service is respect and honor, especially for those of higher military rank.

Kinship, Marriage, and Family

Marriage is defined as a legitimate union between a man and a woman so that they may produce legitimate children. In the past, marriages were arranged by families with neither the bride nor the groom having much comment on the marriage payments or ceremonies. After the wedding the girl would give up her last name for her husband's, in return for a bride-price. Modern times have changed this and now both parties have a chance to choose and decide on the matter. The gift giving continues after the wedding and marriage payments extend over many years. Women play a great and very active part in the marriage, in part because in many households the man serves in the army for many years and the woman is the decision maker concerning the house, children, marriage, and business. Women also influence the stability of a marriage. The mother-in-law phobia is strongly felt, and in most cases the mother-in-law is the prime reason for a bride's departure. Language is also a barrier if the bride is from a different region. The Limbus, like many Nepalese, are hesitant to address one another directly. Calling out a name in public is taboo and creates embarrassment; therefore the new bride is called "you" or "the wife of so-and-so" (teknonymy) and she does not have full status as a woman until she bears a child. Until full acceptance by the mother-in-law, the marriage is uncertain, as the wife can return to her natal home if she is made to feel uncomfortable. Polygamy is not widely practiced; it is practiced only if the wife is barren or has failed to produce sons. Kinship is very important in a marriage. A union with kin is considered successful and ideal. For the Limbus there are three types of marriages: adultery, arrangement, and "theft." All three are legal. In case of adulterous marriage a bride-price is not required. Some compensation is paid to the former husband by the new husband. Also, if the woman is single, the new husband visits the woman's natal home with offerings to form a closer bond with her family. "Theft" marriages are common. The term "theft" means that she has agreed to be taken without negotiations. Such elopement is one way to avoid the high cost of a bride-price. The women in these marriages are considered as weak subjects, labor resources, and child bearers. For the Limbus these undesirable marriages, especially theft of married women, are usually initiated at dances.

Families related "by the bone" make up patrilineal lineages and clans. Death of a member brings pollution on the local agnatic descent group. During this time adults refrain from eating meals cooked with salt and oil. Wives who have taken their husband's family name also take their impurities by eating leftovers from their meals. Lineage and clan groups are exogamous, so men and women with the same clan name are forbidden to marry or have sexual relations. Today, lineages do not have a great influence on marriage, though payments are made to the chief of the clan. In general Limbu families are economically and ritually independent of each other.

Religion and Expressive Culture

One area of difference between Limbus and Brahmans is religious. Limbus recognize and participate in many popular Hindu festivals but also have a number of their own practitioners. They worship by means of blood sacrifice. They believe that lineage divinities are not transmitted patrilineally.

Rather, a woman inherits her mother's gods and when she marries and lives with her husband, she brings with her the deities that will then be recognized as the gods of the household. Every time a bad thing or feeling is caused by the man, he will have to be washed clean of it. There are also forest deities that inhabit the area and have nothing to do with women. Limbu bury their dead and observe two to three days of pollution; the length of the period depends on whether the deceased is a female or a male, respectively.

Drinking and dancing are very important to the Limbus. Weddings, mourning, gift exchanges, and settlement of conflicts involve much consumption of liquor, especially beer. Dancing parties are given for visitors to the village. These affairs give the young Limbu girls and boys a chance to meet and enjoy dancing and drinking.

See also Brahman and Chhetri of Nepal; Kiranti; Rai

Bibliography

Caplan, Lionel (1970). _Land and Social Change in East Nepal: A Study of Hindu-Tribal Relations._ London: Routledge & Kegan Paul.

Jones, Rex L., and Shirley K. Jones (1976). _The Himalayan Woman: A Study of Limbu Women in Marriage and Divorce._ Palo Alto: Mayfield Publishing Co.

SAIDEH MOAYED SANANDAJI

Lingayat

ETHNONYM: Virasaiva

Orientation

Identification. The Lingayats speak Kannada, one of the four major Dravidian languages spoken in the south of India. They are called Lingayats because they worship _istalinga_, the symbol of Shiva, and they always wear it around their necks or across their chests. They are also called Virasaivas because of their deep love and commitment to their God, "the Omnipresent and Ever Compassionate."

Location. Lingayats live in all nineteen districts of Karnataka State in south India, which stretches from 11°05' N to 19°00' N and from 74°00' E to 78°06' E and along the Arabian Sea. The north and central regions are their heartland, although Lingayats are found also in the four neighboring states of Maharashtra and Goa to the north, Andhra Pradesh to the east, and Tamil Nadu to the south. The climate is basically a tropical monsoon type and the temperatures change periodically, varying between 15° and 40° C.

Demography. The census of 1981 places the Karnataka population at 37,135,714 with a population density of 194 persons per square kilometer. Assuming that the Lingayat population has grown at the rate of the general population of Karnataka, the Lingayat numbered about 5,600,000 then.

Linguistic Affiliation. The Kannada language is classified in the Dravidian Family, and the Lingayats fully identify with it. It is related to the Tamil, Telugu, Tulu, and Malayalam languages but it has its own script, which consists of thirty-four consonants and fourteen vowels. Its first poetics, _Kavirajamarga,_ and first grammar, _Bhasa Bhusan,_ were written in the early ninth and eleventh centuries, respectively, and its literary history spans well over 1,000 years.

History and Cultural Relations

The contribution of Lingayats to the cultural heritage of Karnataka is significant. Kannada literary historians have identified some 1,148 Kannada writers between the eighth and the end of the nineteenth century; of these, there are 453 Lingayats, 377 Brahmans, and 175 Jains, while the rest represent other groups. Basava, the founding father of Lingayat religion, was also in some ways the first to lead a successful crusade in the early part of the twelfth century A.D. against domination by the Sanskrit language in order to make Kannada, the language of the common man, the medium of literary expression. He set an example by recording his _Vacanas_ (sayings) in Kannada and the tradition set by him continues to flourish in modern Lingayat writings. The ideology of the Lingayat culture also begins with Basava, who rejected the feudal orientation of Hindu Brahmanism and substituted for it a new social order similar to Gandhian populism and based upon the principles of individuality, equality, and fraternity. The cooperative, communitarian movement initiated by Basava continues to flourish in the modern political life of Karnataka. The Lingayat monasteries, spread across contemporary Karnataka's small and large towns, run schools and colleges with free room and board for needy students. These monasteries serve not only as centers of religious culture but also as centers of education; they can claim a record of fifty years of contribution to the educational progress of the state, unrivaled by other educational institutions. The Shiva worshiped by the Lingayats does not belong to the Hindu pantheon. He is formless, qualityless, and an embodiment of love and compassion. Lingayats worship him as a symbolic manifestation of the universe and call him their personal God, istalinga. For them Sanskrit (like church Latin) is the vehicle of feudal values, inherited inequalities, and priestly prerogatives; so they identify with Kannada and contribute to its literary richness and variety. Their cultural heritage therefore follows neither the _marga_ (way of seeking) nor the _desi_ (way of instruction) traditions; it rejects the institutions, cultural prescriptions, notions, and values characteristic of both these Hindu traditions. It represents, in fact, partly a selective blending and partly a selective conflict between the two. It comes very close to a populistic tradition, with its own institutions and values rooted in the 27,000 villages and some 300 towns of Karnataka.

Settlements

Lingayat villages are usually nucleated with houses built close to each other. The population of a village may vary anywhere from 250 to 3,500 persons. Villages are dispersed and connected by paths and main roads that link them to the national highways. Farmers' houses are made of either mud, stone, or cement. A well-to-do Lingayat farmer's house, made out of mud and stone, consists of three sections. The first section is a porch with a raised platform, usually open but sometimes closed, which is used for visitors and resting. A threshold and a door frame with carved figures of Basava lead to the second section, which consists of units used for housing the cattle and for domestic purposes, including a kitchen, a storeroom, and a *puja* (worship) room. The third section of the house, the backyard, is used for storing hay, fuel, etc.

Economy

Subsistence and Commercial Activities. The economy of a Lingayat village, which is predominantly agricultural, reflects the Lingayat culture. Their social structure is populistic, with birth and occupation intertwined. Lingayats are engaged in an entire range of occupational activities—agriculture, commerce and trade, teaching and scholarship, blacksmithing, carpentry, weaving, oil pressing, hairdressing, etc. Traditionally, Lingayat farmers produced partly for local consumption and partly for a market economy, and plowed their land with metal-shod wooden plows powered by pairs of bullocks. Much of economic life was regulated by the *aya* system, in which exchange of goods and services took place. The local artisan groups and labor depended upon the farmers for their survival. With independence in 1947 and the launching of five-year plans and community development projects, the traditional mode of cultivation is being gradually modernized by the use of chemicals, fertilizers, lift pumps, irrigation, etc. Rural life, once characterized by exchange relationships, is giving way to competitive interests revolving around the economic realities of supply and demand. For example, the artisan community in the village has nearly closed its doors to local customers, as it now seeks new opportunities in the nearby city market in its traditional specialities. And the village washerman's family also is involved in the city electric laundering establishment, the cobbler in its shoe stores, the blacksmith in tool-making jobs, and the goldsmith in the jewelry store. So traditional work is becoming modern work, and traditional skills are becoming modernized in the process. The village farmers, who once produced primarily for domestic and local purposes, now prefer cash crops such as sugarcane, cotton, chilies, fruits, and vegetables for export. But such concerns do not seem to have eroded traditional values as indicated by the increasing number of cooperative societies in Lingayat villages. Urban Lingayats are found equally in all occupations and dominate small trade, commerce, and the textile industry in Karnataka.

Kinship

Kin Groups and Descent. The kinship universe of the Lingayats can be described in terms of two categories: effective and noneffective. Relationships among effective kin are close, intimate, obligatory, and reciprocal, whereas those among noneffective kin are less intimate and functionally insignificant. Effective kin are those closely related by descent and marriage, and mate selection among such kin is preferential. Noneffective kin are remotely related and rarely remembered, and meaningful interaction between them is absent. Ideally, Lingayat kinship emphasizes the patrimonial principle, but in reality matrilineal orientations prevail both in sentiments and obligations. Kin groups among rural Lingayats maintain and reinforce their kinship relations through uncle-niece, cross-cousin, and exchange marriages. Affinal relationships are recognized only if they are involved in preferential marriages.

Kinship Terminology. Lingayat kinship may be described as multilateral with partly descriptive and partly generic kin terms. Father's brothers and sisters, for example, are described as "big" or "little" "fathers" and "mothers" depending on relative age; terms for paternal and maternal grandfathers and grandmothers are treated in the same way.

Marriage and Family

Marriage. A common practice among Lingayat parents is to arrange their children's marriages. About five decades ago, a bride and bridegroom could see each other's face only at the marriage pedestal, but increasing education and widespread urbanization have crept into the villages and slowly affected the ways of traditional matchmaking. These days "love" marriages are heard of even in the countryside. In educated Lingayat families, younger generations enjoy some freedom in the choice of partners, a practice unheard of half a century ago. The use of horoscopes is conspicuously absent among the Lingayats. Divorce and separation are uncommon and marital breakdowns are frowned upon. Precautions against possible disintegration are taken by arranging interkin marriages, which help to strengthen the marital bonds. In the event of a breakdown, however, Lingayat attitudes toward divorce, especially in comparison with some other religious groups, are liberal and tolerant. They are equally liberal in encouraging widow remarriages, which are condemned by the Hindu-Brahmanic society. Residence is patrilocal among rural Lingayats. Upon marriage, the bride goes to live with the groom's household. Among urbanites they are expected to live independently. For an educated Lingayat couple, neolocal residence is the norm.

Domestic Unit. The extended family is regarded as the ideal arrangement among rural Lingayats, although the nuclear family is actually more common and there are occasional instances of conjugal family arrangements. Nuclear or conjugal, the family does not live in isolation, as it is always embedded in the larger kin group. Since the collective solidarity of the kin group is the prime value in the community, family autonomy and privacy are never its concerns. All related families are held together by a sense of mutuality and complementarity. Such interdependence is seen on occasions of births, weddings, fairs, and festivals. The urban Lingayat family is primarily nuclear but it too maintains its ties with its rural kin by providing shelter, hospitality, and employment opportunities, when needed.

Inheritance. Traditionally, legal rights favored the patrilineage. Upon marriage, a girl took her husband's surname and all the legal claims that went with it. Her loss of a share in her parental family property, however, was met through adequate gifts of jewelry and gold during her marriage and on successive visits to the natal family. Her parents and siblings fulfilled their moral obligations to her, especially in times of crisis. Such customs and conventions generally created an environment in which brother-sister relations continued even after the parents' deaths. The Succession Act of 1956 that gave guaranteed equal rights to surviving children of deceased parents altered the bonds that once united the conjugal and natal families and brother-sister relationships. It is not uncommon these days for brothers and sisters to behave like rivals over the sharing of parental property and to take their claims to court.

Socialization. The socialization of a Lingayat child begins immediately after birth when the priest, the _jangama_, visits the home, names the child, and initiates him or her into the Lingayat faith by tying a _linga_ around the child's neck. His role in communicating the values of his faith continues throughout the life of the named child, especially during some major life stages. Among other agents of socialization, mother, grandmother, father, siblings, and other extended relatives are significant, in that order. Among the nonfamilial agents, priest, peer group, elders, and teachers are effective. Socialization within the family is primarily informal and learning occurs there mostly by observation and imitation. Obedience and respect for elders, trust in their god and religion, hard work, and generosity are some of the values that Lingayat parents like to see in their children.

Sociopolitical Organization

Social Organization. The Lingayat system of social stratification is built largely around wealth, power, and prestige in both secular and religious spheres. Occupational and social mobility are open to everyone. Lingayats are therefore involved in all sectors of the economy. Their work ethic flows directly from their ethic of _kayaka_ (rites and observances performed with the body, hence the spiritual value of labor); their role in community building comes from their practice of _dashoha_ (community sharing of one's own labor), and their identification with society at large from their notion of _aikya_ (being with the linga is being with society). Lingayat economic behavior therefore stems from the values enshrined in their ideology.

Political Organization. Lingayats are actively involved politically through participation in the democratic establishment in Karnataka. Its political history records the successful mobilization of Lingayats in achieving power at the village level, in unifying a single united Karnataka that was divided among several adjoining states prior to 1956, and in promoting village links with the center. In carrying this out, they have long been aware that social mobilization could not be achieved without a political orientation. The hundreds of biographies of successful Lingayats (published by the Gadag Tontadarya monastery) provide ample evidence of this awareness. The secular and religious leaders steer their community, mediated by its middle- and lower-middle-class core, well beyond communal polities into the universal polity, and from premodern polities to a modern, liberal one.

Religion and Expressive Culture

Religious Beliefs. The Lingayat religion is the largest established religion in Karnataka. Other established religions include Brahmanism, Jainism, and Islam. Lingayats do not label themselves Hindus and claim an independent status for their faith. The Lingayat theological doctrine of sakti-visistadvaita (a qualified monistic philosophy characterized by Sakti, the spiritual power of Shiva); its socialization agents, the guru and the jangama (monk); and its notion of istalinga are distinctively Lingayat in character. Its system involving astavarnas (eight supportive systems), _panca acaras_ (five principles of conduct), and _sat stalas_ (six stages related to social and religious progress) has helped to transform Lingayatism into a distinct framework. Their ethical and behavioral norms have given them a capacity to coexist with other sociocultural groups and at the same time preserve their religious and cultural homogeneity and identity. The beliefs and behavioral patterns of Lingayats are expounded in the compositions of Basava, whom they regard as their founding father as well as a dominant influence in the works of his colleagues. These compositions, collectively known as the _Vacanas_, have the status of sacred literature, are taught to Lingayats from childhood, and are internalized by them. Lingayats believe in a one-and-only God and worship him in the form of istalinga, which resembles the shape of a globe. Lingayats are antimagic and antisupernatural in their religious orientation. They do not worship stone images and the deities of the desi tradition. They believe that devotion to Basava and the other Lingayat saints will bring them their blessings and guard their lives.

Religious Practitioners. They have their own priests who officiate at the various life-cycle rites, of which the prominent ones are those dealing with birth, marriage, and death. Priesthood among Lingayats is not ascriptive and is open to all irrespective of sex. Lingayats do not consider the world as _maya_, an illusion, and reject the Hindu notions of karma, rebirth, purity, and pollution.

Ceremonies. The Lingayat ritual calendar gives prominence to the birthdays of their saints, the first in importance being the birthday of Basava. In addition, they celebrate Hindu festivals such as Dipavali, Yugadi, and Sankramana. Their centers of pilgrimage are at Kalyan, Ulive, and Srisaila, the places where Basava, his nephew Cennabasava, Allama Prabhu, and Akka Mahadevi are laid to eternal rest.

Arts. Although Lingayats in past centuries were noted for their religious poetry and philosophical writings, today the chief arts are the singing and playing of hymns. There is no marked ability shown in the visual arts.

Medicine. Lingayat priests (called _ayya_ or _swami_) are also astrologers and medicine men, often dispensing herbal remedies to sick villagers. This is a useful craft for them to possess, rather than a learned profession.

Death and Afterlife. For Lingayats there is no life after death. They believe that there is one and only one life and that a Lingayat can, by his or her deeds, make this life a hell or heaven. At death, he or she is believed to have returned to God and to be united with him. They call this state _aikya_ (unity with linga). Since the dead person is believed to have attained the status of Shiva, the body is washed, clothed, decked with flowers, worshiped, and carried in a procession to the burial yard accompanied by singing in praise of Shiva.

See also Badaga; Kanarese

Bibliography

Beals, Alan R. (1967). "Pervasive Factionalism in Namhalli." In _Divisiveness and Social Conflict: An Anthropological Approach_, edited by Alan R. Beals and Bernard J. Siegel, 117–138. Stanford: Stanford University Press.

Chekki, D. A. (1974). _Modernization and Kin Network_. Leiden: E. J. Brill.

Desai, P. B. (1968). *Basveshwar and His Times*. Dharwar: Karnatak University.

Ishwaran, K. (1968). *Shivapur: A South Indian Village*. London: Routledge & Kegan Paul.

Ishwaran, K. (1977). *A Populistic Community and Modernization in India*. Monographs and Theoretical Studies in Sociology and Anthropology in Honour of Nels Anderson, no. 13. Leiden: E. J. Brill.

Ishwaran, K. (1983). *Religion and Society among the Lingayats of South India*. Leiden: E. J. Brill.

Ishwaran, K. (1989). *Basava and the Lingayat Religion*. Leiden: E. J. Brill.

Nandimath, S. C. (1942). *A Handbook of Viraśaivism*. Dharwar: The Literary Committee, Lingayat Education Association.

Nanjundayya, H. V., and L. K. Ananthakrishna Iyer (1931). "Lingāyat (Vīraśaiva)." In *The Mysore Tribes and Castes*, edited by H. V. Nanjundayya and L. K. Ananthakrishna Iyer. Vol. 4, 81–124. Mysore: Mysore University.

Parvathamma, C. (1972). *Sociological Essays on Veeraśaivism*. Bombay: Popular Prakashan.

Ramanujan, A. K. (1973). *Speaking of Siva*. Harmondsworth: Penguin.

K. ISHWARAN

Magar

ETHNONYMS: none

[*Editor's Note:* This entry is much longer and more detailed than others to provide a sense of the social, religious, economic, and interpersonal details that are typical of daily life in many Hindu village societies throughout South Asia. This description focuses on life in the early 1960s in a hamlet given the pseudonym of Banyan Hill.]

Orientation

Identification. People calling themselves Magar are concentrated in the middle Himalayas of west-central Nepal. The middle Himalayas are defined by the Mahabharat and Siwalik ranges to the south and the southern slopes of the highest Himalaya to the north. Small Magar settlements and individual farmsteads are also found elsewhere in Nepal, as well as in Sikkim and even in north India. This pattern of distribution in part reflects the excellence of Magar men as infantrymen. In the late eighteenth century Magars formed an important component in the armies raised by Prithivi Narayan Shah and his successors who created the modern nation of Nepal and for a time extended it well beyond its present borders both to the east and to the west. A number of families now living outside the area of Magar concentration occupy land given a forebear as a reward for his military service during these campaigns. Under the British Raj, when Magars served as mercenaries in the Gurkha Brigade, a few families settled permanently in north India around the cantonment areas. Magars in need of land have also been moving south to the low malarial Terai of Nepal, since it has been made more habitable by a mosquito eradication program.

Magars usually identify themselves as belonging through patrilineal inheritance to a named section or "tribe," which in the traditional Nepali system is also a caste. Some of these are Pun, Gharti, Rana, Thapa, Ale, Rokha(ya), Budha, Burathoki, and Jhankri. If a Magar man is asked to identify himself, he might say he is a Pun Magar.

Sections are subdivided into named subsections or clans. For example, one of the subsections of the Thapa section is the Sinjali clan. However, because some clans, such as the Ramjali, are widespread and found in more than one section, a person's identity might then be given as Ramjali Pun or Ramjali Gharti. Alternatively a Magar may choose to stress locality, saying "I am a Masali Gharti," with Masali referring to the specific small settlement in which he or she lives.

Location. Magar concentration in the middle Himalayas is roughly bounded on east and west by the drainage of the Kali Gandaki River at approximately the latitude of Pokhara up to and including the Bnuri Gandaki. It also includes much of the area drained by the Bheri River and its tributaries, notably the Uttar Ganga, Sano Bheri, and Thulo Bheri.

Demography. In the census of 1952–1954, the first after the restoration of the present ruling Shah family, the number of those identifying themselves as Magar was 273,800, or 3 percent of the total population of Nepal. Later censuses were based on mother tongue, and the census of 1981 gave the Magar population as 212,681, an underestimate that ignored

Magars whose mother tongue was Nepali. The total projected population for all of Nepal in 1991 is 19,370,300. If we take Magars as 3 percent of the population, we can estimate their population at 500,000.

Linguistic Affiliation. As their mother tongue Magars may speak one of three languages: Nepali, Magarkura, or Khamkura. The latter two both belong to the Bodish section of Sino-Tibetan, and though closely related, they are mutually unintelligible, (according to studies done by James F. Fisher). Nepali is the Sanskrit-based lingua franca and is the second language of almost all Magars.

History and Cultural Relations

Magars' Mongoloid physical type and their Sino-Tibetan languages suggest they entered Nepal from the north, through Tibet or southern China. The Magarkura speakers occupy the lower, warmer, and more desirable agricultural area and are known to have been there since at least the late thirteenth or early fourteenth century, so it is likely that they preceded the Khamkura speakers, who generally live in the higher, colder locations to the north.

Settlements

Banyan Hill lies in the heart of long-settled Magar territory. Other Magar hamlets elsewhere particularly those in the harsher northern areas, where food resources are both more limited and widely scattered and where Brahman influence is less—differ from Banyan Hill in various ways. The rapid changes of the last thirty years throughout Nepal have affected all Magar hamlets. Banyan Hill is one of seventeen hamlets comprising a traditional administrative district called Kihun Thum. Prior to the Gurkha conquest the Thum apparently was part of a petty kingdom ruled by the raja of Bhirkot. Like other Thums, Kihun had a fortification called a *kot*. Kihun's *kot*, now important solely as a ceremonial center, lies at the crest of the 1,500-meter ridge behind Banyan Hill.

In Kihun Thum there were about 600 households in the 1960s, and if one estimates 5 persons per household, the population as a whole numbered about 3,000. Brahmans were the most numerous caste and their 243 households comprised approximately 40 percent of the total number of houses. Magars' households numbered about 190, or approximately 32 percent. Caste groups such as the metalworkers (60 households), leatherworkers (36 households), ex-Slaves (36 households), and tailors (17 households) were less numerous. Other castes accounted for the remaining 18 households including seven Newars who were shopkeepers in the local bazaar.

The caste groups at that time tended to concentrate in separate hamlets. Practically all households in Banyan Hill were Magars, and Magars predominated in five other hamlets in Kihun Thum.

Banyan Hill consists of two house clusters, one dominated by a founding patrilineage and the second dominated by their wife receivers. Houses vary in size. Some are oval, and some rectangular. Most have two stories; a few have three. Despite variation in size and shape, the method of construction and basic layout are much the same. Walls are built up using stones and mud mortar. Next they are plastered with mud. The final coat that is applied dries to a warm reddish orange. Roofs are thatched. All houses have verandas. Interior ground floor plans, which may symbolically reflect the tripartite social system, consist of two side rooms flanking a comparatively large central room containing the fire pit. The single door of the house opens into the left-hand flanking room, making it an entrance hall. A notched pole ladder leads from the right-hand flanking room to the upper floor where clothing and valuables are stored in boxes and grain is stored in circular bins made of woven bamboo.

Other buildings and structures that are almost invariable parts of the farmstead include a thatched cattle shed, usually open on three sides, and a tall rack for storing ears of maize. The amount of maize on display is an indication of family wealth.

Economy

Banyan Hill's subsistence activities are carried out at elevations ranging from about 800 meters to 1,000 meters in a climatic zone classified as subtropical and characterized by deciduous broad-leaf trees such as *Shorea robustus*, as well as by banyans, pipals, bananas, and papayas.

Subsistence and Commercial Activities. The major crops on dry land terraces are maize, accounting for half of the harvest, wheat, and dry rice. With the exception of a small amount of maize, the irrigated terraces are planted to rice. Over the years the Magars have also made use of buckwheat, hulled barley, mustard, potatoes, sugarcane, bananas, arum lilies, radishes, sesame, lentils, beans, pumpkins, cucumbers, carrots, cauliflowers, cabbages, onions, tomatoes, yams, chilies, and tobacco. In addition there are many kinds of fruit and trees with leaves suitable for fodder, two plants providing leaves useful as plates, and three plants used for fencing.

All of Banyan Hill's tillage, dry or irrigated, is within a half-hour's walk from any house. The same is true of places where there are trees for firewood and grass for cutting hay or thatch. Water for irrigation and domestic use is spring-fed and plentiful. The cattle population includes buffalo, cows and calves, and bullocks. There are also goats, pigs, and horses, and a few families keep beehives and chickens. Buffalo are stall-fed and are seldom taken from their shed except to be bred.

The saying in Banyan Hill that "everyone gets enough to fill his belly" does not mean that every family obtains enough grain from its own land to meet even its minimum needs. It means rather that if the family does not have a sufficiently large grain income, it can make up the deficit by borrowing or by sending one or more family members to work as hired laborers. In the 1960s, only seven of Banyan Hill's families had tillage so large and productive that it provided a salable surplus. This problem still exists today. Families who are not among the fortunate few with adequate land have to purchase or borrow grain in amounts varying from what is required to support an adult for a year to the very little needed to feed a guest on ceremonial occasions. Even households that are comparatively well-off because they have dry landholdings that are more than adequate may lack paddy land and therefore have to buy rice. Most people prefer to sell jewelry rather than suffer the ignominy of serving riceless meals to guests. The majority of the families also need an income greater than their land can produce so that they can buy the services of specialists, cloth, supplemental ghee, salt, and occasional bazaar items such as powdered color, cigarettes, or soap.

The most important nonlocal source of income is army service. A young man wishing to enlist may join the Nepalese national army or any one of the regiments of Gurkha Brigade, divided in 1947 at the time of India's independence into four British and six Indian regiments.

Industrial Arts. Every household has rice-straw mats that women, and sometimes men, weave on looms pegged out in the courtyard. As a sign of hospitality and welcome such a mat is unrolled as seating for a Magar or other "Touchable" caste persons allowed on the veranda.

Sickles are one of the most widely used implements and are made by a neighboring man of the metalworker caste, but their wooden holsters are always carefully crafted by their Magar owners, who also decorate them with incised designs. Among other homemade articles of everyday use, the wicker carrying basket is one of the best-suited for an individual display of skill and appreciation for color patterning. The wicker can be more or less evenly woven, and color patterning can be obtained by varying the exposed side of the bamboo strips—green if exposing the outside of the strips, white if exposing the inside.

Banyan Hill Magars used to grow cotton to be spun and woven, but by the 1960s most clothing was of mill-made cloth. To show affection for a brother or favored young man, women often sew colorful embroidery on articles of their dressiest clothing.

Trade. Trade in livestock provides income for many families, even if the sales involve only a few chickens or an infrequent buffalo, goat, cow, or pig. A few families sell ghee or honey, but the chief local source of income for poorer families is field labor, done either for wealthier Magars or for neighboring Brahmans who believe plowing the earth is contrary to their religion and status. In absolute terms the most lucrative source of supplemental income in Banyan Hill is the interest earned on loans of cash and grain. By far the greatest part of such income goes to the headman because he makes the largest loans. Two other men who are pensioners have financed greater numbers of loans, but because the amounts of the loans are much smaller than those of the headman, the income from them is less.

Emergency sources of income are jewelry and land, usually in that order. For marginal families these are the two items with which they can keep themselves going through a series of bad years or finance a necessary ceremonial expense such as a father's funeral.

Along with funerals and similar expenses, plus purchases of livestock and grain, the other major drain on a family's resources is the purchase of bazaar goods mainly manufactured in India. Butwal was formerly the largest bazaar regularly visited, but by the 1960s it was being superseded by Pokhara, a town on an outwash plain beneath the Annapurna massif that is two easy days' walk away from Banyan Hill.

Division of Labor. The most common kind of work group is formed on the basis of labor exchange. Various families' fields are ready for planting, weeding, hilling, and harvesting at different times, and what needs to be done has to be done rapidly, requiring more labor than one family alone can provide. Participants in an exchange arrangement work on a daily basis. Generally the return of an equivalent number of days' work is made within a year, and often, though not necessarily, in kind: a day's weeding, for example, for a day's weeding. Work groups also form on the basis of wage payments.

Poor families with too few adults to participate in labor exchange seek help from relatives, often from another hamlet. The expected payment is a good rice meal, with meat and beer if possible, plus one tiffin (a light meal). Regardless of a family's wealth, roofs are almost always thatched on this basis.

A fourth kind of labor group is almost exclusively associated with carrying wood from the forest. Magars are reluctant to work on days of the full and new moon and on the day they do *puja* (worship) for the tiger deity, Mandale. But the ban does not apply to wood carrying, done out of neighborliness and for no return other than a tiffin. Nor does the taboo apply to community fishing, which requires enough people to dam and divert a large stream.

Work groups, especially those involved in labor exchanges, tend to be composed of a nucleus of persons who habitually work together. The usual group cuts across neighborhood and hamlet lines, as well as across caste lines from Untouchable to Brahman, and it encompasses wide differences in age. It also disregards gender, except in paddy and millet planting, where women do one task and men another, and roofing, which is done exclusively by men. Finally, it also includes members of families of varying wealth, from richest to poorest.

An exception to the flexible adaptation of the group size to its task is an occasional group that hires itself out as an unchanging unit. Its members work for payment in cash and at the end of the season use money they have saved to buy a feast. For example, a Banyan Hill group of this kind formed around a woman who was an exceptionally good singer.

Land Tenure. At the time of 1960s studies, only one Banyan Hill family did not own land. Most of the hamlet's tillage thus is owned by families individually. Exceptions are a small irrigated plot, the use of which rotates annually among the families of one particular lineage, and woodlots and places where thatch can be cut, which all lineages may use. Only well-to-do families purchase land. Obtaining land for use is much more common. Some is leased and paid for by a fixed sum. In other cases the user agrees to give the owner a share of the land's produce, usually two-thirds from a rice paddy and one-half from dry land.

Kinship

Kin Groups and Descent. Clans are made up of local patrilineages. A Magar man conceives of his local patrilineage as a group flanked on one side by one or more patrilineages that have provided his own lineage with wives and on the other side by one or more patrilineages to which his lineage has given wives. This configuration results from a rule that defines marriage to a woman from a wife-receiving lineage as incestuous. The rule is an important aspect of Magar identity, serving, for instance, to differentiate Magar society from Gurung society, which permits marriage with either flanking lineage. The configuration also serves to allocate to specific patrilineages a number of ceremonial duties connected, for example, with marriage, funeral, and certain other rites.

The Thapa clans of Sinjali, Makkim, and Sunari are represented in Banyan Hill. Members of the same clan believe they are all descended in the male line from a shared (but unknown) male ancestor, and clan members cannot marry one another.

Locally, the Thapa Sinjalis are divided into three patrilineages, each tracing descent through male links to a known ancestor. Lineage members share common pollution at the time of birth or death and observe related taboos. Birth pollution lasts eleven days, during which lineage members cannot participate in any kind of religious ceremony. The period of pollution after the death of an adult is thirteen days, and there is a taboo on eating salt. If a child dies before it is named, only the mother is polluted; a named child, dying when less than 3 years old, pollutes only the parents. The death of a child older than 3 years counts as an adult death and pollutes the whole lineage. An unmarried daughter living at home is not polluted by the death of her father or of her father's lineage members because she is not regarded as belonging to the lineage. When married, she becomes a member of her husband's lineage. She is polluted by death in the same way as its members and has to observe the same taboos they do.

A deceased man's sons, closest lineage brothers, and occasionally the husband of a daughter or sister take turns carrying his bier to the cremation site. When a wife dies, her sons and her husband's lineage brothers, but not the husband, perform this task.

Most lineages, as defined by men who are communally polluted by births and deaths, correspond to a group of men called _hukdar,_ which is determined by tracing male links from a common ancestor in the sixth ascending generation. The hukdar are important in the inheritance of land, especially if a widower dies without surviving sons and without previously willing some of his property to a daughter.

Banyan Hill Magars speak of daughters and sisters who have married and left home as _cheli-beti_ and call the men they have married _kutumba._ More broadly, they sometimes use the latter term to refer collectively to their married daughters and sisters, the husbands of these women and the husbands' lineage brothers, and even the hamlet areas where they all live. Girls refer to their fathers' lineages and their natal hamlets as _maita._ Magars say that when they celebrate an auspicious occasion such as the fall festival of Dasain, they call together the cheli-beti, but when it is a question of help to be rendered on an inauspicious occasion, such as a funeral, they call the kutumba.

When possible, a man prefers to marry a daughter of his mother's brother, or _mama._ If his mama has no daughter, the next choice is any girl from a family in mama's lineage who is younger than the prospective groom. Since any such girls are potential wives, their potential husbands are allowed and even expected to joke with them about sex and to touch them freely. Marriage to a mama's daughter is only a preference and is not in the same category as the strict rule forbidding marriage to a father's sister's daughter. As explained earlier, a patrilineage that becomes a source of wives cannot in the next generation become a receiver of wives, because such an exchange is regarded as incestuous. The rule sometimes is expressed using the metaphor of milk: a wife-giving patrilineage identified in the local context as the "milk side," the source of wives and mothers, is not a suitable source of husbands.

During the 1961 fieldwork in Banyan Hill, residents were queried about their kin relationship to each of their spouses, past or present, living or dead. Of the 58 marriages recorded, 17 were between a man and a woman who was either his mama's daughter or daughter of his mama's lineage. The remaining marriages were the result of a search for girls generally not more than a day's walk away, who belonged to a clan other than the potential groom's and to a lineage other than the one to which girls from the groom's lineage had in recent memory gone as wives. The result was a multiplex, fairly dense, and localized pattern of affinal ties. The groom who made such a marriage spoke of his wife's family, lineage, and hamlet as his _susural._ His son, though, spoke of it as his _mamali_—the family, lineage, and hamlet of his mother's brother. Both he and also his lineage mates now felt that they had a strong claim on marriageable girls in this lineage, which sometimes led to a run on brides from a particular and heretofore unallied patrilineage.

Kinship Terminology. Ego's descent group and his two flanking descent groups are the basic categories in the Magar system of kinship terminology. Whether the terms are in Magarkura, Khamkura, or Nepali—the increasingly usual language of Banyan Hill Magars—the terms that Ego uses clearly distinguish to which of these three descent groups a relative in his own and first ascending and descending generations belongs. In the third ascending and descending generations, the descent group distinction is lost and only two terms appear—one for males, the other for females. The system throughout is sensitive to gender difference and, in the middle three generations, to relative age, though an exception appears in the wife-receiving descent group. Here the same terms are used for two different categories of husbands: those married to Ego's descent group's sisters and those married to Ego's descent group's daughters.

Marriage and Family

Marriage. For a virgin girl the minimum ceremony generally regarded as sufficient to give her the status of a married woman consists of four rites. After securing permission from the prospective bride's family—usually through an intermediary—a representative of the groom's family goes to the bride's house and takes her to the groom's. There, in the first of the four ritual actions, one that only Vaishnavite Magars omit (see below), the man who accompanied the bride sacrifices a chicken at the entrance to the groom's farmstead. The bride and groom step on the blood for strength and wellbeing and to keep evil spirits at bay. The second action takes place at the entrance to the groom's house, when first the father and his lineage elders and then the mother, as tokens of their acceptance of the union and hopes for its auspicious future, each press a _tika_ (auspicious spot) of red-colored curd and rice on the couple's foreheads. Inside the house, as a symbol of their consummated union, the groom gives his bride some red powder for the part in her hair, usually applying some of it himself. The fourth and final step is the return of the couple and their party to the bride's house, carrying a gift of food for the bride's family. Each entering person is given a tika at the door, and then the bride's mother serves them a meal.

Marriages of virgin girls are sometimes made more elaborate, mainly by bringing more food to the bride's house and making the return procession more conspicuous. In such cases there is a tailor to beat a drum and, as companions and food carriers for the couple, a virgin girl from the bride's lineage and a man married to a girl from the groom's lineage. These two carry curd, fried bread, beer, and rice-based liquor. Further elaboration at the groom's house includes the use of one or more Brahmans to conduct Vedic rites.

Many Banyan Hill marriages are remarriages for both spouses. No social opprobrium is attached to the woman who marries a second time (*jari*), nor to the woman who marries for a third (*sari*), but one who marries for a fourth time is referred to by a term (*phundi*) that connotes sexual looseness. Second and third marriages enter the realm of politics. Before such marriages are recognized as legal, the deserted husband has to be compensated. The amount is negotiated by the couple's headmen. A deserted husband whose wife has married a fourth time cannot claim compensation.

To avoid the expense of a marriage ceremony the parents of a virgin girl sometimes arrange to have her abducted by a boy they approve of as a son-in-law. "Captures"—marriages that have not been arranged by the girl's parents—also occur, but not frequently. The abductor knows that the marriage is not legal and that if he is not approved of by the girl and her parents, they have legal recourse.

Husband and Wife. In many ways the relationship between husband and wife is biased in favor of the husband. When she marries, a wife leaves her natal home and moves to her husband's. In many daily situations she is expected to show her husband deference. For instance, if he is late in returning home, she feeds the children but herself refrains from eating until he comes home. In the morning she gets up before he does and carries out a ritual that implies she is worshiping him as if he were a god. She pours specially drawn water regarded as pure over one of his big toes and into one of her palms, and then she touches the water to her lips. Although in these and many other instances the wife has a subordinate role, some factors strengthen the wife's position in relation to her husband and his family. For a brief period the newly married couple live with the husband's parents, but soon they almost always move to a house of their own. This all but erases the possibility for a continuing servantlike relationship with an authoritative mother-in-law. Another important support for the wife is the gift (*pewa*) her parents usually present to her when she marries. Often it consists of livestock such as goats, cows, or buffalo. Chickens are also a common pewa. Wealthier parents sometimes give land, such as a paddy field. Whatever the gift, a husband has no right to it: it provides a wife with an independent source of income, small or large, and it may be transferred by her in her will or before her death to whomever she wishes. Further support lies in the fact that at marriage a woman acquires a share of her husband's property, to be hers if she is widowed or abandoned. The births of children diminish the size of her share, since at birth they also acquire rights to a portion of the estate. But so long as she does not remarry, a wife's share is hers until her death. Only then does it revert to her husband's estate. It is significant too that natal homes of most wives are not more than 8 kilometers distant. Wives go home often, and the tie to parents and brothers is frequently strengthened by exchange of gifts. A wife sometimes returns from a funeral

for someone in her natal lineage with a cow or a calf to be added to her pewa.

Two paths are open to a wife who is not happy with her husband: she may return to her natal home or run away with another man. Very often the first option is a precursor of the second.

The majority of the marriages are monogamous, but circumstances sometimes lead to polygyny. The most common reason is desire for a son in a sonless first marriage.

Gender-Based Division of Labor. Women's position in Magar society is enhanced by the essential and many-faceted part they play in the domestic economy. After men plow the fields, women break up the clods with mattocks. They plant and weed, carry wood, water, and manure. They care for the farm animals and do the milking. Although older women do not climb the tallest trees to collect fodder, they do gather heavy loads of leaves from the bushes and low-growing trees. From time to time women work heavy mills to extract oil from mustard seed. They spend much of every day processing food. In the very early morning they operate the grinding stones and hulling beams and winnow away the chaff. They also spend hours squatting by the firepit doing the cooking.

Other work, such as plowing, is strictly reserved for men, but many tasks may be done by either men or women and often are done by both together. Husbands and wives often join in group fishing, and although women mostly operate the hulling beams, when there is much hulling to be done, men frequently help. Men without daughters do the cooking when their wives are menstruating, and men also cook when traveling without women.

Socialization. Magar children are born into homes where tensions between adults are usually minimal and children are desired and liked. It is true that traditionally a boy was more wanted than a girl, yet daughters have always been highly regarded and treated with much affection. Unmarried girls of the family and lineage have high ritual value. Gifts given to them are considered to be like gifts to goddesses and are a way of obtaining religious merit. Daughters are also an important source of labor. It is hard to imagine some Magar farms operating successfully if daughters were not contributing many kinds of help.

Parents hope for as many children as possible. Their usefulness as labor and as supports in old age outweigh their costs as additional mouths to feed and bodies to clothe.

Children grow up in the center of the day-to-day life of the household. A nursing baby sleeps with the mother on a straw mat. During the day the baby spends many hours in a hammock slung between posts of the veranda. When the baby wakes or is fretful, the mother, or whoever else is nearby, gives the hammock a push. If rocking does not help, the infant is nursed and fondled. On trips away from the house, the mother carries the baby hung in a cloth across her back. Toilet training is gradual and without fuss. Weaning too is nontraumatic. A pregnant mother may try to hurry the weaning; otherwise a child is given the breast until the age of 3 or 4 years.

When a girl is about 3, her parents ceremoniously give her a new shirt, a rite of passage corresponding to the first haircutting of a 4- or 5-year-old boy. Both ceremonies honor the child and impress him or her with the parents' good wishes for the future. From the age of about 8 the child, whether girl or boy, is gradually asked to assist with household or farm tasks, which are divided among the children following the same pattern as among the adults. By the time children are about 12, they can do almost all adult tasks and have become genuine assets to the household economy.

Although children are taught the appropriate formal gestures to show respect for their parents, for the most part relations between parents and children are quite informal. They all sit together on the house porch, or, if children alone are sitting there when their father comes into the yard or up on the porch, they do not get up. Also, if they are smoking, they do not feel obliged to stop.

Birth order is recognized terminologically among brothers and sisters. It counts in some ritual contexts and becomes politically significant in that a headman's eldest son usually inherits the office. Despite instances such as that one that favor the eldest, there is no shyness or avoidance among siblings.

Brothers and sisters play together throughout childhood and remain close throughout life. Once a year their relationship is expressed ritually when a brother goes to the home of one of his married sisters and she gives him an especially good meal and paints a multicolored tika on his forehead.

Sociopolitical Organization

Caste Distinctions and Ranking. Banyan Hill Magars, who themselves comprise a distinctive caste group, live in two major kinds of relationships with the neighboring caste groups of Kihun Thum. One kind rests on ideas about ritual pollution, and the other involves exchanges of services for food or other payment.

A major split exists between those caste groups called Touchable (*chhune*) and those called Untouchable (*nachhune*). Members of a Touchable caste cannot ritually pollute those of any other local castes merely by touching them, but they are themselves subject to pollution by the touch of any Untouchable person.

From the Magar point of view, the major Touchable castes in the vicinity of Banyan Hill make up a hierarchical ritual order of Upadhyaya Brahman (Brahman of highest status), Jaisi Brahman (offspring of a Brahman and a Brahman widow), and Magar. The three Untouchable caste groups in the area, tailors (Dami), metalworkers (Kami), and leatherworkers (Sarki), are thought to have equal ability to pollute.

Magar Relationships with Brahmans. The relative status of Touchable caste groups is expressed in a variety of ways, as illustrated by a few kinds of interactions between Magars and Brahmans. When a Magar man meets an Upadhyaya Brahman man, the Brahman raises his foot and the Magar touches his forehead to it. A young Brahman meeting an older and respected Magar man first inclines his head and then lifts his foot to be touched. Before stepping on a freshly cleaned veranda of an Upadhyaya home, a Magar woman touches her forehead to one of the steps. Magars address Upadhyaya Brahmans as "grandfather" or "grandmother." If a Magar man boils rice in his own vessel he will not offer it to a Brahman because he knows that the Brahman may not accept it. In contrast, the Magar may take rice cooked in a Brahman's vessel.

Each Banyan Hill Magar family, except for that of the headman's plowman, is regularly served by one of seven Brahmans from four nearby Brahman hamlets. These Brahmans perform priestly functions and are referred to as *upret*. During the course of a year the upret visit their client families to help them observe a number of calendrical festivals, including the day in July or August when the "World Snake" (the "Bed of Vishnu" and the "Garland of Shiva") is worshiped; Tika Day in September or October, during the festival of Dasain, when they give each family member a tika to ensure good health and prosperity; and Thread Full Moon, usually in August or September, when they tie yellow and red yarn around their clients' wrists, partly to ensure that if they die within the next six months they will go directly to Heaven. Other occasions for which a Magar family may call their Brahman include: a ceremony to prevent an inauspicious disposition of the planets from harming a baby; the Satya Narayan puja for Vishnu; an elaborate marriage; and a baby's naming ceremony.

Upret are paid when they provide services; generally this payment consists of a small amount of money, plus food deemed appropriate for a person of such high caste to take from a Magar. Such food includes uncooked rice, ghee, salt, and spices.

Untouchable Service Castes. Magars regularly employ the services of the various Untouchable castes. The hamlet is served by seven tailor families, all but one of which had a sewing machine by the 1960s. At least once during the year, one or more members of a tailor family, often a man and his wife, come to their Magar client's family to sew. They work on the client's veranda and are given their meals. The items most in demand are blouses for men and women. A tailor who works for a regular client supplies his own thread, and if asked to make caps—usually a cap is required for each man in the family—he supplies the cloth. The client provides cloth for other garments. Magar families usually pay their tailors twice a year, after each harvest in the spring and fall, by giving them millet or maize. Wealthy families give additional payments at this time and, if possible, give rice, which is highly valued by groups like tailors who have no irrigated fields. A final set of payments may be made on major festival occasions such as Dasain in the fall. A tailor will come to a client's house on these occasions expecting a meal and liquor. If he has already eaten at another client's, he is given food and liquor to carry home.

In the 1960s, nine households of metalworkers provided services on a fairly regular basis for one or more Banyan Hill families. Four of the nine were ironsmiths; one, a coppersmith; four were goldsmiths. The most regular kind of work expected of the ironsmith is putting good cutting edges on plow tips, axes, mattocks, ditchers, and sickles. Pay for such usual work is the same as the tailor's: a measure of millet or maize twice a year plus food and drink on festival days. Ironsmiths also make a large variety of new implements for which they are paid on a piecework basis.

About half the Banyan Hill families regularly engage the coppersmith. (In the 1960s, one family gave him as much as 40 kilograms of paddy rice, but most gave a single payment of 18 kilograms of millet or maize.) In return for one such large payment, the smith repairs copper utensils such as water vessels, vessels for cooking buffalo mash, and vessels for making distilled liquor. Families who make regular payments think it cheaper to do this than to pay separately for each repair.

In the 1960s, four goldsmiths had a regular connection

with about a third of the Banyan Hill households. Goldsmiths devote their skills almost entirely to making and repairing women's jewelry—nose rings, earrings, necklaces, bracelets, finger rings, hair ornaments, and the small gold flowers women wear in one nostril. The goldsmith's work and pay is comparable to that of the coppersmith.

About half the hamlet's Magar families retain a leatherworker on a regular basis. Leatherworkers are from four neighboring leatherworking families. In return for annual payments of millet or maize and food or drink at major festival times, they are expected to remove dead animals—a service they usually perform whether or not they are retained, since they can sell the hides and, in the case of buffalo, the intestines, which are used as tie ropes.

Ferrymen and Messengers. Once a year representatives from members of the Untouchable ferryman caste living in a hamlet located at a much-used ferry point on the Kali Gandaki River come to Banyan Hill. They go from house to house asking at each for a number of kilograms of grain. Only those households whose members have crossed or expect to cross the river using ferryman services give to the ferrymen. It is said that the ferrymen remember who has given and do not charge them at the river.

In the 1960s, three messengers served all the hamlets in Kihun Thum, and all were members of an Untouchable caste. At that time the messenger who served the Banyan Hill households was a metalworker. Like the ferrymen the messenger annually goes from house to house in his constituency asking for bulk payments of grain. He also visits the houses at major festivals to get food and drink.

Song and Dance Groups. Singing is important in Magar life, and many songs are associated with the fieldwork of particular seasons. Some are sung when millet is being planted; others accompany rice planting. The songs, with lines sung by men and women alternately, make this stooping, difficult work go more easily. Other occasions also have their characteristic songs: those sung by boys and girls as they walk together, those sung by women ex-slaves during a marriage, and those sung by women during the days between Krishna's birthday and the following festival of Tij. There are also special songs for the day during Tivahar when offerings are made to Lakshmi, goddess of wealth, and songs for Brother-Worship Day.

Many times during the year, especially during festival seasons such as Dasain, boys and girls gather together in the evening at some centrally located sitting place. There are characteristic tunes, and the basic pattern is boy-girl question and answer. The boys' chosen song leader sings a question that all the boys then repeat three times. The subject matter seldom varies: all the questions and answers have to do with love, marriage, and a bantering sexual antagonism between boys and girls. The singing can go on indefinitely.

Besides the secular singing groups that come together on an ad hoc basis, there are two formally constituted singing groups composed of Magars from several hamlets. One tells of episodes in the life of Lord Krishna, the other of episodes drawn from the *Ramayana*. Each has a leader who tells the story, backed by a chorus, drums, and costumed male dancers, some of whom may be dressed as women. The atmosphere is intensely religious, for Saraswati, goddess of learning and music, is patron of both groups and indicates her

presence and approval by causing a member or members of a group to fall into a trance.

Political Organization. Kihun Thum is divided into eight jurisdictions, each with its own hereditary headman (*mukhiya*). Of the eight headmen, three are Brahmans, and five are Magars, one of whom is from Banyan Hill. In return for keeping the peace, acting as liaison officers between the government and the local people, and collecting taxes on unirrigated farmland, the eight headmen each receive 5 percent of what they collect. However, since taxes are extremely low, this form of income is not the major reward of the office. The real reward lies in the days of forced labor the headmen can claim from each household in their respective jurisdictions. Forced labor was legally abolished following the overturn of the extremely repressive Rana regime in 1951. Whether or not the abolition is observed depends, however, on the stature of the district's headman. In the 1960s, people continued to work as before for the exceptionally strong Banyan Hill headman because they recognized him as an outstanding community benefactor. He had studied law and knew how to write legal documents. Individuals thus could come to him for help with their legal problems. He was also a source for loans of cash or grain, keeping careful records and charging no more interest than community custom allowed. He was something of a water engineer and had laid out a series of channels to make water for drinking and irrigation more accessible.

The multifarious services expected of Kihun Thum's eight headmen contrast with what is expected of its two additional revenue collectors (*jimwal*). Both are well-educated Brahmans whose sole responsibility and source of a comparatively high income is to collect the taxes on irrigated rice-producing terraces.

Religion and Politics. During the course of his career as headman—an office that a member of his family has held for at least three generations—the Banyan Hill headman's major political opponents are neighborhood Brahmans. In the religious sphere he challenges them by hiring a learned Brahman as his religious retainer. Under his guidance the headman performs two elaborate pujas every day, morning and evening. He also follows a strict dietary regime and does not accept food from a Brahman known to drink liquor. In this and other ways he is more Brahman than many Brahmans.

The kot above Banyan Hill is the scene of two Dasain observances—both the major one which takes place during eleven days in the fall and a smaller one known as Chaitre Dasain that is held during a single day in March or April. The focus of both is the incarnation of Shiva's active female principle, or Shakti, who in one embodiment is called Chandi and in another is called Durga. The initial proceedings at the kot during the spring rite emphasize the importance of the Brahman community throughout the area. A group of Brahman men worship Chandi by reading aloud a Sanskrit text, the *Chandi-Patha*. This takes place in a small shedlike structure that is open on one side. The second part of the worship, the beheading of a young goat, takes place before a small stone building where Durga resides. (At one of these rituals observed by anthropologists in the 1960s, a Magar headman of a nearby hamlet was in charge. His young son was not yet strong enough to do the beheading, so the headman did that. But the boy was the one to wet his hands in goat blood and put his hand prints, one on each side, on the Durga temple door.) The remainder of the ritual symbolizes political aspects of the Thum. The three Thum messengers are given money. A leatherworker is designated to cut up the goat carcass according to traditional rules for distribution. Portions go to the Thum's eight headmen, with one for the raja of Bhirkot, and some to representatives of other Untouchable castes involved in Dasain—a tailor who with his band provided music, and a metalworker who sharpened the sword for the sacrifice.

Religion

Religious Beliefs. The Banyan Hill Magar's pantheon includes a great many deities, or spirit beings, most of whom a family at one time or another will try to influence. The most numerous deities are those who are pleased, or at least placated, by an offering of a live sacrifice.

Deities are usually thought to be invisible. The class of deities named _jhankri_ (male) and _jahkreini_ (female) are notable exceptions. They are often seen, and it is said that two humans from Kihun Thum were forced to live with them for a time in their underground home. Jhankris are hunters, requiring gifts that generally include a miniature bow and arrow for the male, and for his wife, miniature combs, baskets, tump lines (loops of cloth, about 2 meters long, placed over the head and used to carry a load on one's back), and the kind of bow used to shoot clay pellets at birds. Some Banyan Hill persons say that after dark they sometimes hear Jhankri hunting dogs and the bells they wear.

Some deities are the exclusive concern of a single family or, at most, of a few closely related families. Other deities may affect any family, or collectively a hamlet or a whole neighborhood, including its different caste groups. Sansari Mai, a female deity who causes cattle diseases, is generally placated with a communal sacrifice. Once, when an epidemic of cattle disease struck the cattle of one of Banyan Hill's neighboring hamlets, its thirty-two households combined to offer Sansari Mai a sacrifice.

Deities have varying degrees of power. Although all of them attract "promises" of gifts for granting specific boons, those with the reputation for exceptional power naturally attract the most. "Grandmother Satiwanti" is an example of a powerful hamlet deity. Following a common pattern, one soldier who was leaving Kihun Thum to complete his tour of duty promised her a sacrifice of five chickens, plus a carved pole to be set beside the shrine and a bell to be hung inside it. When the soldier returned safely from the Burma campaign, he promptly fulfilled the promise.

Two shrines, each a few hours' walk from Banyan Hill, are considered to be the most powerful in the vicinity. One to the west commands a sweeping vista from the top of a very high hill; the other, about the same distance away to the east, is a hot spring with a periodic flow. Both frequently attract soldiers seeking to protect their lives as well as others with a variety of requests—for a son, for a wife, for recovery from illness, for good crops, or for defeat of an enemy in a court case.

Some deities are believed to have originated in Banyan Hill itself as transformed humans. One of these, belonging to the class of deities called _mari_, is worshiped by two Magar families together with two neighboring metalworker families. This particular deity came into existence when a woman died in childbirth. In fact, most persons, male or female, who die

violent deaths become mari, although soldiers who die in battle are an exception. They are said to go directly to Heaven.

The pantheon worshiped in Banyan Hill with live sacrifices is dynamic, with some deities being added as others are forgotten. More than anyone else, shamans keep people informed of the pantheon's changing and locally relevant dimensions. Very frequently a shaman learns of a new and troublesome deity in a dream.

Three especially important Banyan Hill deities began their existence long ago as Magars. Two are believed to have become fearsome witches, so threatening that people avoid mention of them after dark. Called "Grandfather-Grandmother," they are conceived of as one, and once a year in the lunar month of Mangsir (November–December), the two are worshiped communally, often with the slaughter of two pigs. The sacrifice to Grandfather-Grandmother does not follow the pattern described earlier. Appropriately, it is more like the sacrifice to ancestors made by Magars without the help of a Brahman. Except for the autumn festival of Dasain, the day of annual offering to Grandfather-Grandmother is when relatives do the most visiting.

The third transformed Magar deity is Mandale. While still a human, he changed himself into a tiger, and thereafter he never reverted to human form. Many say that Grandfather-Grandmother are his maternal uncle and aunt. The major sacrifice to Mandale is a cooperative effort carried out by several neighborhoods, including Banyan Hill, in the month of Mangsir. The pig is considered the most appropriate live sacrifice. It is believed that tigers, all of whom are manifestations of this spirit, will not attack villagers or their cattle when Mandale is correctly propitiated.

Each Magar household has a male deity who comes to reside in the kitchen room whenever a new house is built. This deity's effects are limited to the family alone and it is the only deity to be propitiated by live sacrifice within the house. He looks to the well-being of family members and their cattle and crops, and he is regularly propitiated in the month of Jeth (May–June). The usual sacrifice is a cock promised during the ritual of the previous year. Besides the promised sacrifice of the "old cock," the central feature of the kitchen ritual is the offering of nine leaf plates containing rice and a piece of yeast used for making beer. A Magar's prayer during the ritual is the following: "I am remembering you every year. Please take care of my family."

Religious Practitioners. Most men in Banyan Hill follow a pattern of worshiping _pitri_ (spirits of dead ancestors) that does not require a Brahman. Once a year on the first day of the month of Magh (January–February) they go to a spring and make an offering there. This puja's major component is nine leaf plates containing hulled rice, black pulse, turmeric, barley, and sesame. The offerings are made to the ancestors generally, with the exact relationship remaining unspecified. A tenth plate with the same contents is set aside for the spirit porter who accompanies the ancestors. The ritual is repeated in the fall. Either or both rituals may be carried out in the house, in the place where the sacrifice to the "old cock" is made. When performed in the house, cooked food such as fish, crab, and chicken often are included.

Shamans are an important link between the people of Kihun Thum and the world of deities and spirits. During one of the studies done in the 1960s, there were three shamans in the Thum—two Magars and a Brahman. One of the two Magars was an ex-soldier living in a hamlet near Banyan Hill, and he was the one turned to most often by the people of Banyan Hill. He called himself a lama—implying that he was a Tibetan priest, though he was not—and he was most often referred to by that term. He would tell his clients the cause of a present trouble (for example, a sick buffalo) and would advise them on the steps to take to remedy the problem. But his practice was more than remedial. It was also prescient: he would foretell what misfortunes the future held and how to forestall them.

This shaman's special powers derived from his ability to enter a trance state. To do this he did not don any special costume other than an empowering necklace. While seated, he clasped a number of leafy branches in both hands and held them before his face while muttering a series of spells. When he became possessed by the spirit he had summoned, the branches shook violently, and he began speaking in the spirit's voice. The spirit would answer questions from the afflicted family and also those of any in the larger audience that usually assembled when it was known that the shaman would be holding a seance. His techniques were not limited to his ability to enter a trance state. When he deemed it appropriate, he provided medicines concocted from items he carried in an old army rucksack. His pharmacopoeia included the following: some Ayurvedic treatments available in the local or more distant bazaars; a bull's tooth; a human legbone; the navel of a musk deer; a shred of a leopard's tongue; a porcupine's jawbone, plus its stomach, still stuffed with the dried contents; a tortoise shell; a piece of red brick; a black stone; and numerous bits of leaf and bark. Often the patient was required to drink a concoction of selected ground-up bits from this array. Ground-up brick was a frequently used component. Harder, nongrindable items such as a bull's tooth were merely touched to the medicine.

Ceremonies. Disregarding small variations, the method of sacrifice generally follows a predictable pattern. The ritual takes place at a locality where the deity is thought to be present. It is carried out by a young unmarried boy who has bathed and dressed himself in a clean white loincloth. After sanctifying the ground with cow dung and water and constructing a small open-ended room from flat stones, he selects a small stone to represent the deity and provides it with new clothing by wrapping white string around it. He then sets the newly dressed deity in the stone room and fashions a cow-dung platform with a number of depressions in it. This he places before the deity to hold food offerings. Such offerings include rice flour fried in ghee, puffed rice, rice mixed with water and sage, and cow's milk. The deity is honored further by decorating the shrine with turmeric, bits of colored cloth, and flowers and by the presence of fire in the form of a mustard-oil lamp in a copper container.

Just before the sacrifice, the sacrificer makes an incense of ghee and sage and prays for whatever boon he wishes the deity to give. The animal to be offered is readied by sprinkling water, rice, and sage on its head until it shakes it, thus showing its willingness to be sacrificed. If the animal is small enough, it is then waved over the incense container. Otherwise the incense burner is waved under it. Next the animal is beheaded, and the blood that spurts from the carcass is directed toward the shrine and the image inside. The head is

then placed in front of the image. The sacrificer then gives tika to all who are present by pressing a small amount of rice mixed with blood onto their foreheads. One of the worshipers does the same for him. As a gift for his services, the sacrificer receives the head and whatever food is not needed for offering in the shrine. Sometimes the sacrificed animal is cooked near the shrine and everyone eats the food sanctified by its having been shared with a deity.

Death and Afterlife. A Magar who dies does not cease being a member of the family. He or she continues to be aware of descendants and can affect them. The descendants, in turn, continue to be aware of him or her and realize that what they do controls, at least partially, the way he or she treats them. There are two kinds of deceased ancestor. One kind, called *bai*, is a spirit being who wanders about on Earth and likes sacrificial blood. The other, called *pitri*, is in heaven and does not like sacrificial blood.

A deceased family member may become a bai for a number of reasons. Bai include those who performed no religiously sanctioned good deed during the course of their lives; those whose dead bodies were touched by some polluting animal, such as a dog; and those who were witches or shamans. In addition, those who in the ordinary course would not become bai may be intercepted on their way to Heaven by a witch or shaman and be made to return to Earth and trouble their family. Bai are somewhat like mari, the main difference being that mari trouble a wider range of persons than their own descendants.

Bai are honored once each year, and most families offer the sacrifice—generally a cock for a man and a hen for a woman—on the full-moon day in the month of Baisakh (April–May). To eliminate the necessity for making this annual sacrifice, a lineage member can go to Banaras (Varanasi, in India) where with a single offering he can placate the bai forever.

Bai can either cause trouble or refrain from doing so; pitri too can trouble their descendants or bring them good fortune, more frequently the latter. Pitri are honored in either of two ways. One way is through the ancient Hindu ceremony of *sraddha*. A Banyan Hill man who honors his mother and father in this way calls a Brahman to assist him and performs the rites on the anniversaries of their deaths. In the fall he repeats the ceremony on the appropriate day arrived at by calculations based on the Hindu calendar.

See also Brahman and Chhetri of Nepal; Sunwar

Bibliography

Fisher, James F., ed. (1978). *Himalayan Anthropology: The Indo-Tibetan Interface.* The Hague: Mouton.

Fisher, James F. (1986). *Trans-Himalayan Traders.* Berkeley: University of California Press.

Hitchcock, John Thayer (1961). "A Nepalese Hill Village and Indian Employment." *Asian Survey* 1:15–20.

Hitchcock, John Thayer (1963). "Some Effects of Recent Change in Rural Nepal." *Human Organization* 22:75–82.

Hitchcock, John Thayer (1965). "Subtribes in the Magar Community in Nepal." *Asian Survey* 5:207–215.

Hitchcock, John Thayer (1966). _The Magars of Banyan Hill_. Reprinted in 1980 as _Mountain Village in Nepal_. New York: Holt, Rinehart & Winston.

Kawakita, Jiro (1956). "Vegetation." In _Scientific Results of the Japanese Expedition to Nepal Himalaya, 1952–1953_, edited by H. Kihara. Vol. 2, _Land and Crops of Nepal Himalaya_, 1–65. Kyoto: Fauna and Flora Research Society, Kyoto University.

Nepal, National Planning Commission Secretariat (1988). _Statistical Pocket Book, 1988_. Kathmandu: Central Bureau of Statistics.

Tucker, Francis (1957). _Gorka: The Story of the Gurkhas of Nepal_. London: Constable.

Turner, Ralph L. (1931). _A Comparative and Etymological Dictionary of the Nepali Language_. London: Kegan Paul, Trench, Trübner & Co.

United Kingdom, Ministry of Defense (1965). _Nepal and the Gurkhas_. London: Her Majesty's Stationery Office.

Vansittart, Eden (1894). "Tribes, Clans, and Castes of Nepal." _Journal of the Asiatic Society of Bengal_ 63, pt. 1.213–249.

JOHN T. HITCHCOCK

Mahar

ETHNONYMS: Early British spelling was Mhar; nineteenth-century designation for military Mahars was Parwari; in Madhya Pradesh, India, Mahars are classed as Mehtars

Orientation

Identification. The name "Mahar" is of debatable origin. Explanations run from _maha rashtra_ (people of the great country, now the Indian state of Maharashtra) to _maha ari_ (great enemy) or _mrit har_ (he who takes away the dead animals). These various origins imply that the Mahar are the original inhabitants of Maharashtra State in western India, that they fought the Aryans or some invader, and that their traditional duties included the Untouchable work of removing dead carcasses from the village. General designations for Untouchable castes are: Dalit (oppressed), Depressed Classes, Scheduled Castes, Avarna (outside the _varna_ system), Antyaja (last-born), Outcastes (inaccurate, since they are in castes), or Harijans (people of god), a term coined by Mahatma Gandhi that most Mahars reject as being patronizing.

Location. Hindu Mahars and those Mahars who have converted to Buddhism may be found on the outskirts of every village and in every city of the Marathi-speaking area of India,

now the state of Maharashtra. There has been considerable migration to Madhya Pradesh and some to Baroda.

Demography. In the 1981 census of Maharashtra, 3,946,149 persons listed themselves as Buddhists, most of them being former Mahars, constituting 6.28 percent of the population of the state of Maharashtra; 1,648,269 listed themselves as Mahars. In the adjoining state of Madhya Pradesh, there were 75,312 Buddhists and 577,151 Mahars.

Linguistic Affiliation. The Marathi language, spoken by all people native to the Maharashtra region, is an Indo-European language, but it contains many elements from the Dravidian Family. Maharashtra is a bridge area between north and south India, and thus it reflects both zones.

History and Cultural Relations

It is clear that Mahars were among the earliest inhabitants of the Marathi-speaking area of India, if not the original dwellers. Their myths reinforce the epithet _bhumiputra_, "son of the soil," which implies original ownership of the land. The first Mahar to figure in history is Chokhamela, a fourteenth-century poet-saint in the devotional religious tradition that allowed participation by all castes. Chokhamela, the Untouchable Mahar, along with his wife, her brother, and their son are all historic figures in the _Warkari_ cult. The sixteenth-century Brahman poet, Eknath, wrote more than forty poems as if he were a Mahar, underlining their importance to the everyday world of that time. In the seventeenth century, Mahars were part of the armies of the Maratha king Shivaji, and in the late eighteenth century and the nineteenth century, Mahars joined the British armed forces and served until the army was reorganized on a "martial peoples" basis in the late nineteenth century. Former army Mahars were the first to petition the British government for redress and for equal treatment. Mahars who worked on the railways or in the ammunition factories, who were thus free from traditional village work, created a receptive body of urban workers who were ready to join a movement for higher status and even equality. There were a number of local leaders in Poona and Nagpur, but Bhimrao Ramji is still seen by Mahars, Buddhists, and many other educated Untouchables as the supreme example of Untouchable achievement. Statues of Dr. B. R. Ambedkar dot the landscape of Maharashtra, and he is often shown with a book in his hand, symbolizing the constitution of India, for his crowning achievement was to serve as chairman of the Drafting Committee of the Constitution and as law minister in independent India's first cabinet.

Mahars were the largest Untouchable caste in Maharashtra, comprising 9 percent of that area's population. Although the majority have converted to Buddhism, the cultural relations of those remaining in the villages have not changed. Mahars traditionally were in opposition to Mangs, an Untouchable caste of rope makers seen as lower than Mahars. The Chambhars, a caste of leather workers, were held to be of higher status than Mahars. The other two major blocks of castes in Maharashtra are Brahmans, who are seen as the theoreticians of the discriminatory practices against Untouchables and the basic enemy, and Marathas, landowning agriculturists who in the current period are the chief instigators of violence against Untouchables and Buddhists who attempt to free themselves from village duties.

Settlements

The Mahar quarters, called the *maharwada*, were always outside Maharashtrian villages, traditionally to the east, or downriver. In the nineteenth century, colonies of Mahars grew in railway towns, in mill towns, near ammunition factories, and in British army cantonment areas (where Mahars were servants), but city housing now is segregated more by economic level than by caste. The village pattern of segregation is still strictly observed. The Mahar village hut is typical of the poor in the Maharashtrian area. There are no special features.

Economy

Subsistence and Commercial Activities. Traditionally, the Mahars were servants to all the village, with a number of responsibilities. They were the deciding voices in land disputes, but they also brought wood to the burning grounds, carried off dead animals, took messages to other villages, cared for the horses of traveling government officials, mended the village wall, acted as village watchmen, and served the village headman as town criers. In this capacity they were *watandars* (leaseholders) and so held some land, but they were never primarily agriculturists. Mahars when not engaged in village duties served as agricultural laborers. In the eastern portion of the Marathi-speaking region, Mahars had more economic freedom, and they were sometimes weavers or contractors. Mahars kept no domestic animals, and they despised the Mangs for their pig keeping. Mahars were expected to eat the flesh of the cattle carcasses they dragged from the village, and this consumption of carrion beef became an early target for Mahar reformers.

Industrial Arts. The Mahar possessed no skill other than wall mending to carry them into the modern period. Some Mahars became masons in the early twentieth century.

Trade. The Mahar's untouchability prevented any "clean" trade, and the Chambhars had a monopoly on leather work, which the Mahar did not touch.

Division of Labor. Both men and women worked in the fields as agricultural laborers. Only men served as watandar village servants.

Land Tenure. The watandar land owned by the Mahars for their village service was not alienable.

Kinship

Kin Groups and Descent. Although the Mahars seem to be a fairly consistent caste group across the Maharashtra area, there were *potjat* divisions in various areas. These potjats were endogamous, ranked according to status, and to some extent based on occupation. From the 1920s on, Mahar reformers attempted to wipe out potjat differences, and the divisions today are largely ignored. The caste is patrilineal, but poverty dictated less stress on the joint family and more importance for women than among many higher castes.

Kinship Terminology. Mahar kin terms are the same as those used by Buddhists in Marathi.

Marriage and Family

Marriage. The cross-cousin marriage system of south India and of some castes in Maharashtra is common to the Mahars. Marriage to mother's brother's daughter or father's sister's son is allowed. There has never been a bar to widow remarriage. Residence is generally patrilocal, but this is less strictly observed than in higher castes. Divorce is and has been practiced informally among the lower castes in India, including the Mahars.

Domestic Unit. The joint family is the ideal, but poverty and mobility make this less common than in many castes.

Socialization. As is common in India, boys are raised permissively, girls much more strictly. In the modern period, there has been much stress on education, on pride, and on clean living, and many Buddhists credit their mothers with the stimulus to improve themselves.

Inheritance. Property descends patrilineally to male inheritors, although in point of fact it is rare for Mahars to own any land.

Sociopolitical Organization

Social Organization. Many features of Mahar caste organization that existed before the reform period have disappeared. There seems to have been a caste "guru" (a spiritual counselor not averse to speaking with Untouchables) in some areas, but there is little description of this practice. Local leadership seems to be determined now by merit, wealth, and political skill. There never was a caste center nor an overarching caste organization.

Political Organization. Dr. B. R. Ambedkar began his first political party, the Labour party, in 1935, and since that time, most Mahars and neo-Buddhists have considered themselves members of his successive parties: the Scheduled Castes Federation from 1942 and the Republican party from 1956. Since the parties have been unable to attract higher-caste members, they remain unimportant politically at the national and state levels. Ambedkar's followers are, however, very politically aware, and they do figure in local politics where they have the numbers and the leadership. An organization calling itself the "Dalit Panthers," after the Black Panthers of the United States, arose in the early 1970s, led by educated Mahars or Buddhists. After initial successes, the Dalit Panthers split into various groups, but militant local groups operate effectively even today in various slum localities. An issue such as the banning of one of Ambedkar's books in 1988 brought half a million Scheduled Castes into the streets of Bombay in one of that city's most effective political protests.

Social Control. There is no mechanism for control, other than the example or the chiding of local leaders.

Conflict. Competition and rivalry within the group are keen. Ambedkar was able to unify the Mahar through his exceptional qualifications, planning, and recognition by outside forces as well as by his charisma; no other leader has become acceptable to all. The Panther groups and the political parties are all factionalized. The Buddhist conversion movement has brought about efforts to unify on the basis of religious morality as well as a general disapproval of political infighting.

Religion and Expressive Culture

Religious Beliefs. The religious beliefs of those Mahars who have not converted now are basically those of most Hindu low castes in Maharashtra: a strong belief in possession, participation in the festival of the god Khandoba, active participation in the warkari cult and the pilgrimage to Pandharpur, and devotion to various non-Sanskritic gods. The Mahars were traditionally the servants of the village goddess Mariai, the goddess of pestilence. Since the conversion, many of the *potraj* class who served the goddess have given up that work. It is clear from the gazetteers of the British in the late nineteenth century that Mahars had many somewhat unusual religious practices, but the great rational reform movement has made any recent study of special caste practices impossible. There were *devrishis* (treatments of illness by ash and mantras) among the Mahars, and there still may be. Some potraj servants of the goddess still operate, but in many villages the care of the Mariai temple is now in the hands of the Mangs. The leadership of the caste discourages Hindu practices, and many that are still performed are done so without majority approval. For those who have converted to Buddhism, the rational, nonsuperstitious, egalitarian form of Buddhism promulgated by Ambedkar dominates. He died shortly after the initial conversion ceremony in 1956, and the converts have slowly built *vihāras* (monasteries) in which to meet for Buddhist worship, have created a *sangha* (community) of monks, have taught Pali and given moral lessons to the children, and have attempted to establish connections with Buddhists in other countries. The Theravada form of Buddhism is the base for Ambedkar's teaching. His grandson, Prakash Ambedkar, is now head of the Buddhist Society of India. Belief in god or ghost possession is common in India, and Mahars not firmly fixed in Buddhist rationality take part in possession rituals.

Ceremonies. No peculiarly Mahar ceremonies have been reported.

Arts. For the Mahar, the neo-Buddhist movement has produced a flowering of arts of all sorts. Mahars traditionally were part of *tamasha*, the village theater, and song was traditionally a Mahar property. Since the Buddhist conversion, literature has poured forth, creating a new school of Marathi literature called "Dalit Sahitya." Poetry, plays, autobiography, and short stories now are an essential part of the very important Marathi literary scene. There is also some emphasis on other arts, and most Dalit literary works are illustrated with Dalit art, but no one artist has yet achieved the fame of the writers such as Daya Pawar or Namdeo Dhasal. The latest trend in Dalit literature is writing by women, especially autobiographies of minimally educated women.

Medicine. The Mahar did not develop any particularly Mahar specialties in this area.

Death and Afterlife. Buddhist converts do not hold with the theory of rebirth. Mahars generally hold the standard beliefs of lower-class Hindus.

See also Maratha; Neo-Buddhist; Untouchables

Bibliography

Ambedkar, B. R. (1989). *Dr. Babasaheb Ambedkar: Writings and Speeches.* 6 vols. Bombay: Education Department, Government of Maharashtra.

Enthoven, Reginald E. (1922). "Mahār." In *The Tribes and Castes of Bombay.* Vol. 2. Bombay: Government Central Press.

Keer, Dhananjay (1954). *Dr. Ambedkar: Life and Mission.* Bombay: Popular Prakashan. 3rd ed. 1971.

Robertson, Alexander (1938). *The Mahar Folk.* Calcutta: YMCA Publishing House; Oxford University Press.

Zelliot, Eleanor (1978). "Dalit—New Cultural Context of an Old Marathi Word." In *Contributions to Asian Studies,* edited by Clarence Maloney. Vol. 9, *Language and Civilization Change in South Asia.* Leiden: E. J. Brill.

ELEANOR ZELLIOT

Malayali

ETHNONYMS: Keralite, Malabari (in north Kerala), Malayalee, Travancorean (in south Kerala).

Located on the far southwestern edge of India, Kerala is a state whose history has always been molded by its geography. In effect it consists of a long, narrow, but extremely fertile strip of coastland backed by the high mountain ranges of the Western Ghats, which are broken by very few passes. Numerous short and fast-flowing streams come down from these mountains to disgorge into the coastal backwaters that run for great lengths behind the ocean beaches. It has thus been natural that many of the Malayalis who inhabit the coastal area look to the sea for fishing and trade, and conversely that numerous foreign maritime powers have looked to the former principalities of Kerala for trade, religious converts, and sometimes slaves or loot. Thus the culture of the people has been formed by foreign contacts to a greater extent than was true for any other part of premodern India. Hellenistic traders from Alexandria and even Rome, Arab sailors, Chinese explorers, the Portuguese fleet of Vasco da Gama, the Dutch, and French and British imperialists represented the high points of a fairly constant commerce across the Indian Ocean; Kerala happens to lie almost in the center of that ocean. Ancient shipping that went from the Red Sea to Malakka, from Java to Madagascar, from China to Arabia, nearly always stopped in Kerala for water, food, and trading. Hence the extreme ethnic and religious diversity of the state.

It is one of the smallest Indian states, with 38,863 square kilometers and a 1981 population of 25,453,680 persons. Kerala produces irrigated rice, coconuts, pepper, cardamom, and other spices, as well as two valuable plantation crops, tea and coffee. Its other important economic resources are its fisheries, timber, iron ore, and tourism.

Malayalis, who may simply be defined as those people who speak the Dravidian language Malayalam (the Kerala state language, closely related to Tamil), include not only a diversity of Hindu castes but the Muslim Mappilas, the Syrian Christians, the Cochin Jews, and others besides. The basic Hindu culture of the area supposedly originated with the mythical sage Agastya, who, like the Yellow Emperor of China, is said to have invented various sciences and even dragged the arable land up from the sea. It is not impossible that the original of this great south Indian sage (ancient north India had what was probably a different Agastya) was none other than the Emperor Augustus and that Agastya's inventions were Roman innovations brought into the area. There certainly was a sizable Roman population, along with a legion of soldiers, in the Kerala seaport of Cranganur, and in the first century A.D. it did indeed have a temple to the god Augustus, the only Roman temple we know of in South Asia. Centuries after the Romans and Greeks had come from Alexandria, and with them the Jews and St. Thomas Christians, according to tradition, Arab Muslims came and sometimes settled, creating the first Muslim communities in southern India. The Chinese only came briefly, during the Ming expeditions of the early fifteenth century, and they had no lasting effect on the culture; but soon after their departure the Portuguese arrived, bringing Catholic missionaries and new trade opportunities. In later centuries the British and Dutch introduced Protestant missionaries.

The northern part of Kerala, called Malabar (now Malappuram), became a part of the British Indian Empire, whereas the south and central parts remained as the separate kingdoms of Travancore and Cochin until national independence in 1947. These principalities retained a conservative social structure with pronounced hierarchical differentiation; and Travancore was almost unique in this part of Asia because of its matrilineal royal family. Whether the matriliny practiced by Nayars was first introduced from the Minangkabau area of Sumatra in ancient times is a matter that remains to be demonstrated; but certainly the rest of south Indian society is patrilineal (with a few exceptions in Kerala and Sri Lanka).

In the twentieth century Kerala has become distinct in other respects, too. With an estimated population density of 763 persons per square kilometer for the whole state in 1990, Kerala has some of the densest rural occupation anywhere on earth, and certainly the highest state density in India. While this fact alone might imply abject poverty, the fertility of both land and sea has been so high that people are fairly well fed. Even more remarkable is the fact that Kerala has the highest literacy rate of any state: in 1980–1981, when India as a whole had 36 percent literacy, Kerala had 75 percent for males and 66 percent for females. The Malayalis are inveterate newspaper readers, with a well-developed political consciousness and a fairly extensive intelligentsia. This is one part of India where communist parties have done quite well, and in 1957–1958 Kerala had the distinction of possessing the world's first popularly elected Marxist government. In very recent years the appeal of Marxism has lessened somewhat, while the lure of employment in the Persian Gulf states has risen dramatically. Tens of thousands of Malayalis have worked there, bringing much-needed cash into their family economies. Huge numbers of skilled and white-collar workers have also migrated to other parts of south India, as well as to Western countries. These facts highlight the unemployment rate in Kerala itself, the highest of any Indian state. Partly it is

to be explained by another modern feature of Malayali society, the vast numbers of young people who are unemployed because they are college students. Incidentally, one final characteristic not unrelated to the extent of educational facilities here is that Kerala has a higher proportion of Christians in its population than any other Indian state except Mizoram, Manipur, and Nagaland. In 1981, 24 percent of all Malayalis were Christian—almost exactly the same number as were Muslim.

See also Cochin Jew; Hill Pandaram; Mappila; Nambudiri Brahman; Nayar; Syrian Christian of Kerala

Bibliography

Aiyappan, Ayinipalli (1965). *Social Revolution in a Kerala Village: A Study in Culture Change*. Bombay: Asia Publishing House.

Krishna Ayyar, K. V. (1966). *A Short History of Kerala*. Ernakulam: Pai & Co.

Krishna Iyer, L. A. (1968). *Social History of Kerala*. 2 vols. Madras: Book Centre Publications.

Rao, M. S. A. (1957). *Social Change in Malabar*. Bombay: Popular Book Depot.

Schneider, David M., and Kathleen Gough Aberle, eds. (1962). *Matrilineal Kinship*. Berkeley: University of California Press.

Woodcock, George (1967). *Kerala: A Portrait of the Malabar Coast*. London: Faber & Faber.

PAUL HOCKINGS

Mappila

ETHNONYMS: Mappilla, Moplah

Orientation

The Mappila are Muslims who live along the Malabar Coast (now known as Malappuram District) of Kerala State in southwestern India. They now number about 6 million. "Mappilla" was used in the past as a respectable title; *pilla* was also used among honorable Christians and continues to be to this day. This term was also used to welcome and honor foreign immigrants.

In Malappuram District, the temperature ranges up to about 27° to 32° C and drops to 21° C in the highlands. The southwest and northeast monsoons contribute to the average annual rainfall of 300 centimeters. Coconut palms and rice fields dominate the green scenery of the coastal area.

The language of the Mappila is Malayalam, a Dravidian

language that has absorbed loanwords from Sanskrit, Arabic, and European languages. Arabic is generally used for religious purposes. Kerala is the most densely populated state in India and the educational level there is quite high.

History and Cultural Relations

Mappila were evidently first converted to Islam in the seventh and eighth centuries A.D. by traders who arrived in Kerala. The arrival of the Portuguese began to disrupt Mappila life in 1498. The Portuguese sought both economic and religious domination. Economically, they sought a share of the spice trade and a sea connection with the Far East. Their religious goals stemmed from the desire of the pope to conquer Islamic and Hindu societies. The Portuguese had direct orders to establish their authority over the region so that the Catholic religion, business, and culture would flourish in a harmonious system that would be good for the church, the king and the people. The Portuguese period resulted in a decline in the indigenous economic system, estrangement from Hinduism, and increased bitterness and tension between the Christians and Muslims; finally, the Mappila became militant against the Portuguese. The area came under the political control of the British in the 1790s, and they ruled Malabar from 1792 to 1947. Mappila leaders agreed to pay the British for their protection of the territory and to accept advice from an appointed British administrator; but in 1921 the Mappila resistance began, continuing until India won its independence in 1947.

Economy

The overpopulation of Kerala, and especially of the Malabar area, has caused many economic problems. Today, most of the unemployed are educated people from universities or training schools. Another problem is that these people cannot find work in other states because each state wants to hire its own citizens first, before absorbing any outsiders. Agriculture is the main occupation of the Kerala, although land suitable for agriculture is limited. Cash crops earn a reasonable amount from export, but this has caused a shortage for local consumption. Rubber, pepper, cardamom, coconut, cashew nuts, tea, and coffee are the major cash crops. Food staples are rice, pulses, and sorghum. The area holds great forests that yield raw materials such as bamboo, charcoal, and gum. Industrial enterprises produce bricks and tiles and do oil milling. These factories employ a sizable percentage of the population. Still Malabar remains economically a primitive and stagnant area, and it is not surprising that in recent years tens of thousands of residents have sought work in the Persian Gulf countries.

Kinship, Marriage, and Family

Matrilineality was introduced to the Mappila from the Nayar community that is also located in Malabar. Leadership and property ownership were traditionally vested in the oldest sister, a practice that was and is very rare in Islamic societies. A majority of the Mappila now follow the patrilineal system; only some wealthy families carry on the matrilineal tradition. Families maintain strong bonds and mostly live under one roof. But modern conditions are forcing this practice to change, with each nuclear family now often striving to own a home and concentrate on its own survival and prosperity.

Islam plays a major part in childbirth, marriage, death, and burial ceremonies. At marriage, the marriage contract and blessing are signed and read by a _qazi_, a religious judge. Following death, the Koran is chanted in the mosque, and then the body is buried facing toward Mecca. Prayers are chanted at home on the anniversary of a death. Mappila life has been influenced by new attitudes and they have become greatly concerned about their health and surroundings. Head shaving is not practiced any longer by Mappila men. The dowry system is becoming less prominent as the Mappila women change their social status to that of citizens of Kerala. Women's position as property is also changing, as women are now seeking higher education and becoming schoolteachers, doctors, etc. Traditionally, the women of lower laboring castes in Kerala were relatively free compared to women of upper castes, because they could do any available work, whereas the upper-class women could not do anything inappropriate to their social status; this situation is also changing for the better. Polygamy is not practiced, even though Islam permits men to marry up to four wives.

Social Organization

There are various distinctions within the Muslim group. One major distinction is between those of Indian and those of foreign origin. Higher class status is enjoyed by those descended from the Prophet's family, the Sayyids. One internal distinction is between the Untouchables and the higher castes among the Mappilas. Another distinct group are all those of Arab descent.

Religion

Islam was introduced to Kerala in the seventh and eighth centuries by Sunni Arabs. Islam in all probability spread to peninsular India from Kerala. Arabs came through Kerala for the purchase of pepper and slaves. Kerala was also a very convenient rest stop for merchants passing east and west through the Indian Ocean. These Muslim merchants established a harmonious relationship and introduced Islam to the people. The Mappila were ready psychologically for new changes because of previous political and economic setbacks. Most Mappila today enrich their lives by prayers and Quranic readings. Mullahs (religious clergymen) are paid by families to visit and conduct special prayers or chant the Quran. Mappila attend a mosque for religious holidays and sometimes to listen to a preacher. Islam preaches that life is under one Lord and his command is one; but this idea has become perhaps less important for the Mappila as they struggle through life. Mappila culture is changing, with modern education and communist concepts playing a major role. The mullahs now can rely only on special occasions such as Ramadan for an opportunity to sermonize and strengthen the people's faith.

See also Malayali

Bibliography

Ananthakrishna Iyer, L. K. (1912). "The Jonakan Mappilas." In _The Tribes and Castes of Cochin._ Vol. 2, 459–484. Madras: Higginbotham & Co. Reprint. 1981. New Delhi: Cosmo Publications.

Miller, Roland E. (1976). *Mappila Muslims of Kerala: A Study in Islamic Trends*. Bombay: Orient Longman.

SAIDEH MOAYED-SANANDAJI

Maratha

ETHNONYMS: Kanbi, Kunbi, Mahratta

Orientation

Identification. Marathas are a Marathi-speaking people found on the Deccan Plateau throughout the present state of Maharashtra and nearby areas. The word "Kunbi" derives from the Sanskrit "Kutumbin" or "householder" (i.e., a settled person with home and land). Marathas/Kunbis are the dominant caste in Maharashtra State. They are landowners and cultivators, and they make up about 50 percent of the population. The distinction between Marathas and Kunbis is confused, and the former consider themselves superior to the latter. The Marathas were traditionally chieftains and warriors who claimed Kshatriya descent. The Kunbis are primarily cultivators. The distinction between them seems mostly one of wealth, and we may assume a common origin for both.

Location. Maratha territory comprises roughly one-tenth the area of modern India and is of interest as the southernmost area where an Indo-Aryan language is spoken in India. It is bounded on the west by the Arabian Sea, on the north by the states of Gujarat and Madhya Pradesh, on the east by tribal pats of Madhya Pradesh, and on the south by Andhra Pradesh and Karnataka states, as well as Goa. Maharashtra therefore is a culture contact region between the Indo-Aryan north and the Dravidian south, and so it reveals a mixture of culture traits characteristic of any region that is a buffer between two great traditions. Besides occupying the heartland of Maharashtra, Marathas have also penetrated southward through Goa into Karnataka. The area is watered by many rivers, including the Tapti, the Godavari, the Bhima, the Krishna, and their tributaries, which divide the land into subregions that have been important historically and culturally. There is also the fertile coastal plain of Konkan and thickly forested regions on the north and east.

Demography. According to the 1981 census, the population of Maharashtra was 62,784,171.

Linguistic Affiliation. All Marathas speak Marathi or a dialect of it. Historically Maharashtri, a form of Prakrit, became the language of the ruling house in the Godavari Valley; and from it modern Marathi is derived. People in the various subregions speak the following dialects: Khandesh has Ahirani, Konkan has Konkani, the Nagpur Plateau has Varhadi, the southern Krishna Valley has Kolhapuri, and an unnamed dialect that is found along the banks of the Godavari became the court language and rose to be the literary form of Marathi.

History and Cultural Relations

The early history of the Marathas is a tale of the rise and fall in the importance of the dynasties ruling the various regions. Over time the center of political influence shifted south from the Godavari Basin to the Krishna Valley. From the 1300s on, the Maratha rajas held territories under Muslim kings and paid tribute to them. Feuds among the local Muslim kingdoms and later their confrontation with the Mogul dynasty, which was eager to extend its power to the Deccan, allowed Maratha chieftains to become independent. One such successful revolt was that of Shivaji, a Maratha prince who fought against his Muslim Bijapur overlords in the name of establishing a Hindu kingdom. The local Muslim rulers, weakened by their fights with the Moguls, succumbed to the guerrilla attacks of Shivaji's light infantry and cavalry. Shivaji's military success also depended to a great extent on the chain of fortifications he built to guard every mountain pass in his territory and the system he devised for garrisoning and provisioning them. With the death of Shivaji (1680) the Maratha ranks were split between the claimants to his throne; his son Shahu set up his capital at Satara and appointed a chief minister with the title "Peshwa." The title and office became hereditary, and within a short time the Peshwas became the leading Maratha dynasty themselves. In the 1700s the Peshwas rose to be a powerful military force supported by the Maratha Confederacy, a group of loyal chieftains including the houses of Bhonsla, Sindhia, Holkar, and Gaekwar. With their support the Peshwas extended their territories all the way north to the Punjab. Their power came to an end with their defeat at the battle of Panipat in 1761. Infighting among the confederacy members at the death of the Peshwa led to the entry of the East India Company into the succession disputes among the Marathas. The British fought the three Maratha wars, supporting one faction against the other, and in each case the British gained territory and power over individual chiefs. At the end of the Third Maratha War in 1818 the British routed the Peshwas so completely that they abolished their position and directly incorporated vast areas of Maratha territory into the British Empire as a part of Bombay Presidency. In 1960 by an act of Parliament the modern state of Bombay was divided into the linguistic states of Maharashtra, with Bombay as its capital, and Gujarat. The legacy of the Maratha State lingers on in the memory of the people, who revere Shivaji as a modern hero. A more negative aspect of Maratha consciousness has led to intolerance of other communities who have settled in Bombay, the premier commercial, industrial, and cultural center of India. Political parties like the Shiv Sena, a labor union–based organization, have sought to politicize Maratha consciousness by demanding the ouster of "foreigners" like Tamils and Malayalis from Bombay.

Settlements

A Maratha village in the coastal lowlands is not a well-defined unit. A village (*kalati*) consists of a long street running north-south with houses on either side, each with its own yard. This street is also the main artery joining a village to the neighboring ones north and south. Hence the perimeter of the village is not well defined. Each house stands in its own walled or fenced enclosure; but the rice fields that stretch all around are bounded by narrow earth *bunds* zigzagging in all directions, which make communication between houses in the growing season difficult. In contrast, villages in the plateau ranges are tightly clustered, and the village boundaries are sharply defined. An outstanding structure in such a village might be a temple or the big house (*wada*) of a rich landlord. The typical house is a rectangular block of four walls, with the bigger houses being made up of more than one such rectangle. Frequently an open square in the center of the house serves as a sun court. Some of the rooms leading off this courtyard have no inner walls, so that there may be one or two rooms which can be closed and private and the rest of the house is a space with or without divisions for different purposes, like a kitchen, an eating area, etc. The houses had very small and very high windows and faced inwards onto the court. A village of such wadas is surrounded by fields with temporary shelters in them called *vadi*. Individual fields are large, and worked with draft animals. The use of the land has been dramatically affected in recent times by the building of dams for hydroelectric and irrigation purposes. Much of the previously arid inland areas can now grow sugarcane. Since Maharashtra is one of the most urbanized areas of India (35 percent urban in 1981), the Marathas have gravitated to the urban centers for jobs as well as farm-related services.

Economy

In general, the majority of Marathas are cultivators. They are mainly grant holders, landowners, soldiers, and cultivators. A few are ruling chiefs. For the most part the *patils* (village headmen) in the central Deccan belong to this caste. Some are traders, and many are in the army or other branches of government service. In the plateau region the fields are plowed with the help of bullocks. Almost every farmer except the poorest has cattle and takes great pride in them. The greatest agricultural festival is Bendur or Pola, when the cattle are decorated and taken in procession. The cattle are kept on the farm in a shed (*gotha*), and it is not unusual for them to share the house space with people, so that a corner of the sun court may be given over to them. This is to avoid both theft and predation by wild animals, which once were common on the plateau. Staple foods are wheat cakes, rice, lentils, clarified butter, vegetables, and condiments. Less affluent people usually eat *jowar* (sorghum), *bhajari* (spiked millet), and lentils, while the poorest will subsist on millets seasoned with spices. All Marathas eat flesh and fish, though not beef or pork. Marathas seldom drink liquor, though no caste rule forbids liquor or narcotics. *Beedi* smoking is common among the men.

Kinship, Marriage, and Family

Marathas practice *kul* or *devak* exogamy. Devaks are totemic groups that worship a common devak symbol. Kul is literally defined as a "family," and it is actually a lineage made up of extended families. Devak is an alternative name for this. Although they claim to have *gotras*, gotra exogamy is not essential. These are clan categories adopted from north India; but most of the Marathas do not know to which gotra they belong. Similarly, north Indian village exogamy is not practiced by Marathas. Cross-cousin marriage is allowed; so is marriage with a deceased wife's sister. Two brothers may marry two sisters. Polygyny is allowed and practiced, but polyandry is unknown. Boys are generally married between the ages of 12 and 25, and girls traditionally before they attain puberty. As in much of southern India, bride-wealth is paid to the bride's family, and gift exchange after the marriage between the two families is more reciprocal than in the north. Gifts are also required to fetch a wife back after visiting her natal home. The third, fifth, and seventh months of pregnancy are celebrated. A girl goes for her first confinement to her parents' home. Widow remarriage and divorce are strictly prohibited.

The laws of inheritance that prevailed in Maharashtra were governed by *Mitakshara*, a medieval commentary on *Yajnyavalkya Smriti*. The property was held and transmitted by males to males. When no male heir existed, adoption of one was the usual rule: a daughter's son could be adopted. Property was owned jointly by all male family members in certain proportions. Widows and unmarried daughters had rights of maintenance.

Sociopolitical Organization

Marathas claim to be Kshatriyas descended from the four ancient royal *vanshas*, or branches. In support, they point out that many of their kula, or family names, are common clan names amongt the Rajputs, who are indubitably Kshatriyas. In the past royal Maratha houses have intermarried with the Rajputs. They also observe certain Kshatriya social practices like wearing the sacred thread and observing purdah. These claims are made only by the Marathas proper (i.e., the chiefs, landowners, and fighting clans). The Maratha cultivators, known as Kunbis, and other service castes, such as Malis (gardeners), Telis (oil pressers), and Sutars (carpenters) do not consider themselves Kshatriyas. Nevertheless, the fact that the Kunbis and Marathas belong to one social group is emphasized by common occurrence of Maratha-Kunbi marriages.

Social Organization. Maratha social organization is based on totemic exogamous groups called kuls, each of which has a devak, an emblem, usually some common tree that is worshiped at the time of marriage. The devak may also be an animal, a bird, or an object such as an ax. The Maratha proper, who claim descent from the original four royal houses, belong to 96 named kulas, although much disagreement exists about which kula belongs to which vansha. Further, quite a few kulas have the same name as the Kunbi kulas with whom the aristocratic Marathas deny all identity. Some of the Marathas also claim to have gotras, which is a north Indian Brahman social category; but strict gotra exogamy does not exist, and this fact might suggest that the gotras, like the vanshas, might have been adopted at some time in the past to bolster Maratha social status.

Political Organization and Social Control. In the cities and small towns some Marathas have risen to very high positions in government service, which has given them political power. Positions of importance in the cooperative sugar mills, in the managing committees of schools, in the municipalities, and in the *panchayat samitis* are held by Marathas in most cases. As the Marathas are the majority agricultural community with smallholdings in this region, they still belong to the lower-income groups as a whole; but there has arisen among them a stratus of educated elite who are in higher administrative services and in industry and who hold political power.

This power to a great extent has its basis in the votes of the small rural landholder.

Religion

Marathas worship the god Shiva and his consort Parvati in her many guises as Devi or the mother goddess. At the same time, unlike other Shiva devotees in India, they may also worship Vishnu as Vitthal, by observing fast days sacred to both. Shiva worship is particularized by the worship of some of his specific incarnations, especially Khandoba, Bhairav, Maruti, etc., as family gods. The Devi or mother goddess is worshiped in many of her varying forms, such as Gawdi, Bhavani, Lakshmi, or Janni Devi. Marathas also worship as personal gods other Brahmanic, local, and boundary deities. They visit places of Hindu pilgrimage, such as Pandharpur. Maharashtra also has a whole line of saints who are worshiped, such as Namdev, Tukaram, and Eknath, who have written magnificent *bhakti* (devotional) poetry. Marathas also pay respect to holy men who may have been of humble origin but whose personal spirituality attracts reverence. An outstanding example of such a person was Sai Baba of Shiridi. In addition to the deities just mentioned, the Marathas believe in spirit possession and the existence of ghosts (*bhutas*).

Religious Practitioners. The village temple priest may be a Brahman or a man belonging to another caste, depending on the type of temple and the deity. Temples of Vishnu, Rama, Ganapati, and Maruti generally have Deshasth Brahman priests, whereas temples of Shankar (Mahadev) generally have a Lingayat or Gurav as a priest. Khandoba generally has a Maratha or Dhangar priest. Mari-ai or Lakshmi has a Mahar priest. Devi and Maruti also may sometimes have non-Brahman priests. At the village level, the priest at the main village temple is a recognized hereditary servant of the village. In the more important shrines, like the Vithoba temple at Pandharpur, there are different classes of priests serving a shrine, and these are all hereditary priests. The priesthood and the temple it serves are completely autonomous and not connected to any others.

Ceremonies. The life-cycle ceremonies regularly celebrated by the Marathas are birth, "mother's fifth and sixth" day after delivery, first hair cutting, an elaborate twenty-four-step marriage ceremony, of which the installation of the devak is the most important rite, and death ceremonies that follow the same rites as a Brahman funeral.

See also Kanbi

Bibliography

Carter, Anthony (1974). *Elite Politics in Rural India: Political Stratification and Alliances in Western Maharashtra.* Cambridge: Cambridge University Press.

Enthoven, Reginald E. (1922). "Marathas." In *The Tribes and Castes of Bombay*, edited by R. E. Enthoven. Vol. 3, 3–42. Bombay: Government Central Press. Reprint. 1975. Delhi: Cosmo Publications.

Karve, Irawati (1968). *Maharashtra State Gazetteer, Government of Maharashtra: Maharashtra—Land and Its People.* Bombay: Directorate of Government Printing.

Russell, R. V., and Hira Lal (1916). "Maratha." In *The Tribes and Castes of the Central Provinces of India*, edited by R. V. Russell and Hira Lal. Vol. 4, 198–214. Nagpur: Government Printing Press. Reprint. 1969. Oosterhout: Anthropological Publications.

W. D. MERCHANT

Mauritian

ETHNONYMS: Mauritians/Mauriciens/Morisien, Creoles/Créoles/Kreol, Indo-Mauritians/Indo-Mauriciens/Lendien, Sino-Mauritians/Sino-Mauriciens/Sinwa, Franco-Mauritians/Franco-Mauriciens/Blan, Hindus/Hindous/Lendu, Muslims/Musulmans/Mizilman, Gens de couleur/milat

Orientation

Identification. Mauritius has no indigenous population, and the island first appears on Arab maps from the sixteenth century. In the seventeenth century, it was briefly settled and abandoned by Portuguese and Dutch. The Dutch named it after their prince Maurits van Nassau; it was renamed Île-de-France by the French, the name Mauritius being restored subsequently by the British. Mauritius was a French colony from 1715 to 1814 and British from 1814 to 1968, and it has been independent since 1968. All Mauritians are descendants of immigrants who have arrived since 1715. Contemporary Mauritius is a nation-state comprising the island of Mauritius, the smaller island of Rodrigues, and a number of lesser dependencies. The ethnonyms above refer to the ethnic groups that make up national society, listed in the three main languages—English, French, and Kreol. The culture is multiethnic, but all groups are integrated into the labor market and the educational and political systems at a national level.

Location. The island of Mauritius, one of the three Mascareignes (the other two are La Réunion, a French department, and Rodrigues), covers 1,865 square kilometers at 19°55' to 20°30' S and 57°20' to 57°55' E, 805 kilometers east of Madagascar in the southern Indian Ocean. The land rises gently from the coast to the central plateau around Curepipe (about 500 meters above sea level). The climate is tropical with a dry season from April to October and a wet season from November to March, but there are local climatic variations. Mean annual temperature in coastal Port-Louis is 23° C; at Curepipe, it is 19° C. Precipitation is high; in some areas the annual rainfall is 500 centimeters. Mauritius is a volcanic island well suited for agriculture, and it is almost entirely surrounded by coral reefs. Its much smaller dependency Rodrigues is rockier.

Demography. Formerly high (3.5 percent in the 1960s), the population growth of Mauritius is now moderate at 1.4 percent per year. The latest population estimate (1989) is 1,081,669 (census figures from 1983 total 997,000); approximately 38,000 live in Rodrigues and the rest in insular Mauritius. Twenty-seven percent are Creoles of African descent; 42

percent are Hindus from northern India; 16 percent are Muslims of Indian descent; 9 percent are Tamils and Telugus (also Hindus) of southern Indian descent; 3 percent are of Chinese descent; less than 2 percent are of French and British descent; and about 2 percent are Mulattoes. The population density is roughly 500 persons per square kilometer, with 42 percent of the population urban.

Linguistic Affiliation. Officially, fourteen languages are spoken in Mauritius: French, English, Kreol, Bhojpuri, Mandarin, Hakka, Cantonese, Tamil, Telugu, Marathi, Urdu, Hindi, Arabic, and Bengali. The official language is English (no one's mother tongue), and the main literary language is French (the mother tongue of less than 3 percent of the population). A growing majority of the Mauritian population, almost regardless of ethnic affiliation, are truly fluent only in Kreol. Kreol, a French-lexicon creole language, is usually classified as a Romance language. Kreol tends to be regarded as inferior to English and French, even by its own speakers. English is associated with business and administration, and French is associated with journalism, literature, and the arts. The Indian languages, the most widely spoken being the Hindi dialect Bhojpuri, have declined steadily since World War II. Arabic, standard Hindi, Tamil, and Latin are used in various religious contexts. Most urban Mauritians are bi- or trilingual in Kreol, French, and (sometimes) English; most Sino-Mauritians can speak Hakka and read Mandarin. French is widely understood even in rural areas, where Kreol or Bhojpuri is the vernacular.

History and Cultural Relations

The ethnic groups that make up Mauritian culture arrived in the following order (dates are approximate): French and Creoles (1715–1830); British (1814–1900); Indian (1840–1910); Chinese (1900–1950). Economic and cultural links with France were strong until the British takeover in 1814. Culturally, the French influence remains strong, and the descendants of Britons are now Franco-Mauritians. Contacts with India are of increasing importance. Since the 1950s, emigration rates have been high, particularly in the direction of Australia, Canada, France, and Britain. At the time of Mauritian independence in 1968, many Franco-Mauritians settled in South Africa.

Settlements

There are three main kinds of settlements: towns, plantation villages, and autonomous villages. The main towns are located in an urbanized belt stretching from Port-Louis (population 160,000) through Beau-Bassin/Rose Hill (92,000), Quatre-Bornes (60,000), and Vacoas-Phoenix (57,000) to Curepipe (60,000). The only town outside this belt is Mahébourg (30,000) on the southeastern coast, but several villages are now the size of small towns. Plantation villages, formerly camps, are located close to the cane fields and sugar factories. Usually owned by the sugar estates, they are largely inhabited by Indians. Many of the coastal autonomous villages are fishing villages inhabited largely by Creoles. The new industrial, often "rurban," settlements, which are found in the north, are ethnically very mixed. Since Mauritius is a cyclone-ridden island (major cyclones struck in 1960 and 1976), most of its dwellings are one- or two-story concrete structures. A few villages, particularly on the coast, consist of houses constructed of mud and brick. Wood is used rarely. Most houses have electricity and piped water.

Economy

Subsistence and Commercial Activities. Historically strongly dependent on its sugar exports, Mauritius diversified its economy in the 1980s, through expanding its industrial base. The economy is thoroughly monetized. The majority of the adult population is engaged in wagework, the principal sources of employment being the manufacturing industry, the sugar industry, tourism, and the civil service. Subsistence activities include horticulture and fishing. Mauritius is a net importer of food, the staple being rice. Mauritius has developed the rudiments of a welfare state, which include old-age pensions and unemployment benefits.

Industrial Arts. Sugar, molasses, tea, knitwear, and other miscellaneous clothing are the main industrial products. Horticultural products (especially orchids and other flowers), handicrafts (made of wood, sharks' teeth, and seashells), and various industrial products are marketed domestically and internationally. Instruments of production that are produced locally include fishing nets, fish traps, and some machinery for the sugar and textile industries.

Trade. Petroleum products are imported from Persian Gulf countries; rice is imported from Madagascar and India, raw materials for the textile industry are imported from India and Europe; and advanced machinery is imported from Australia, South Africa, Japan, and Europe. The main export markets are Europe (particularly the United Kingdom and France) for sugar products, tea, knitwear, and other textiles. Other export markets, particularly for textiles, include the United States and South Africa. Tourism attracts Europeans. Exports in 1989 were U.S. $550 million; imports were U.S. $540 million (figures are estimates). The external debt in 1986 was U.S. $644 million.

Division of Labor. Traditionally, the Mauritian division of labor has been strongly ethnic in character, and this is still so to some extent. Most field laborers are Hindus and Muslims; most fishermen, dockers, and artisans are Creoles; most petty merchants are Sino-Mauritian; and the estate owners are Franco-Mauritian. Because of changes in the economic infrastructure, the current pattern is more ambiguous. The workforce in the manufacturing industry is multiethnic and largely female. The Hindus are overrepresented in the civil service, while the Creoles are overrepresented in the police force. Many of the lawyers, teachers, and journalists are Mulattoes. Two conflicting principles for recruitment to the labour market are applied. On the one hand, Mauritius is formally a meritocracy where educational attainment and relevant experience are criteria for employment. On the other hand, ethnicity, kinship and informal social relations are also frequently used as criteria for employment.

Land Tenure. More than 50 percent of the total surface of Mauritius is cultivated. Over most of this area sugarcane is grown; on the central plateau, tea is grown. Fifty-five percent of the cane lands are run by twenty sugar estates. One is state-owned, while the remaining nineteen are owned by Franco-Mauritian families. The remaining 45 percent of the cane land is shared by 33,000 small planters, most of them Hindus and Muslims. Much of the land (but not that owned by the estates) is Crown land, and the cultivator must pay rent to the state. In many villages, Creole and Hindu families grow vegetables and fruit for sale on private or rented plots.

Kinship

Kin Groups and Descent. Kinship is an important principle of social organization in Mauritius, but its form and content vary between the ethnic groups. The Sino-Mauritians are organized in patriclans, which are relevant as units of economic organization. Hindus and Muslims are also patrilineal; the clan feature is, however, less important there, except in very affluent or high-caste families. Among Hindus and Muslims, capital for investment is frequently pooled among relatives. Franco-Mauritians, Mulattoes, and Creoles have cognatic or undifferentiated kinship systems. Sino-Mauritian genealogies go back to one or two generations before arrival in Mauritius. Hindu and Muslim genealogies encompass three or four generations (sometimes more in the case of Brahmans and of Memons, and Surtees, Muslim "high castes"). Franco-Mauritian genealogies are usually detailed and profound; many can trace their ancestry back to several generations before 1789. Creole genealogies are inaccurate and shallow.

Kinship Terminology. The Kreol kin terms *maman, papa, ser, frer, tonton, tantinn, gran-mer, gran-per, kuzen, bo-frer,* and *bel-ser* (mother, father, sister, brother, uncle, aunt, grandmother, grandfather, cousin, brother-in-law, and sister-in-law) are universally used. Their significance can vary interethnically; particularly, the meanings of kuzen and tonton (or onk) are highly variable, and they can sometimes include relatives who would in other contexts be regarded as very remote (or not as relatives at all).

Marriage and Family

Marriage. All groups except Creoles and Mulattoes have ethnically endogamous ideologies of marriage. Sino-Mauritians forge economic alliances between clans through marriage, and their pattern of postmarital residence is patrilocal or neolocal. Hindus are endogamous at the level of caste and are generally patrilocal (but increasingly neolocal in urban settings). Muslims are endogamous at the level of religion; they accept marriages with non-Muslims provided the outsiders convert to Islam. They are also patrilocal, at least at the level of ideology. Memons and Surtees are endogamous in principle, but are too few to practice this consistently. Franco-Mauritians are endogamous at the level of race; aristocrats further tend to reject marriages with commoners. Postmarital residence is usually neolocal. Mulattoes and Creoles have no strong endogamous ideologies, but marriages with people with lighter skins are favored. The last two groups favor "love matches," whereas the other ethnic groups tend to favor marriages organized by the kin group. The divorce rate is low among all ethnic groups. Muslims and Hindus sometimes acquire wives from India.

Domestic Unit. The nuclear family is the norm among Franco-Mauritians, Creoles, and Mulattoes and is an increasingly common form among all urbanites. The average couple countrywide has two children; the number is slightly higher in rural areas and among Muslims. The largest extended families are rural Hindu and Creole families, where the nuclear family forms the core. The former may include the head of household's mother, unmarried siblings, and cousins. The latter may include relatives on both the husband's and the wife's side. Joint families are rarer but they do occur, particularly among Hindus. Nearly all heads of households are men.

Inheritance. Land is as a rule inherited by the oldest son in all ethnic groups. Creoles and Sino-Mauritians have practically no vested interests in land. Other means of production (shops, factories, etc.) are also usually inherited by the oldest son. All other property is partible and can be inherited by daughters as well as by sons. The strongest bilateral tendency in this respect is found among the Creoles. Caste is still important among Hindus, particularly in the three highest *varnas* (Brahmans, Rajputs, and Vaisyas).

Socialization. Patterns of socialization vary interethnically. Although fathers are expected to be harsh and mothers are expected to be loving in all ethnic groups, the authority of the father is strongest among Hindus, Muslims, and Franco-Mauritians. Among Creoles, the mother alone is responsible for primary socialization. Schools are ethnically mixed, and school attendance is nearly universal from 6 to 13 years. An important rite of passage in contemporary Mauritius is the passing of the certificate of primary education (CPE), since education is universally granted great importance. The literacy rate is about 85 percent. Mauritius has a small university, but many go abroad (to France, Britain, and India) for higher studies.

Sociopolitical Organization

Social Organization. Internal social differentiation operates according to three different principles: achievement-based class organization; ascription-based ethnic organization; and "feudal" patron-client relationships. The most powerful group are the landowning Franco-Mauritians, who have dominated the island's economy for more than two centuries. Others with great economic power include Muslim merchants and Sino-Mauritian industrialists and merchants. Most white-collar jobs in the public service are held by Hindus, although there are still many Mulattoes in this field. The most visible lumpen proletariat in Mauritius consists of immigrants from Rodrigues and Diego Garcia, who are usually underemployed or unemployed, sometimes illiterate, and usually poor. The interrelationship between ethnicity and class membership is strong but changing since social mobility is high. Mobility can be achieved through formal qualifications or through exploiting an informal ethnic network. As a rule, Creoles are the most stagnant group as regards economic and political power. Patron-client relationships, which entail commitments beyond the labor contract, can obtain between relatives, between employers and employees, and, most characteristically, between a prosperous family and their servants. Many middle-class families, particularly Franco-Mauritians, have servants; most servants are Creoles.

Political Organization. Mauritius is a parliamentary multiparty democracy under a constitutional monarch, Queen Elizabeth II. General elections for the seventy members of the legislative assembly (MLAs) are held every four years, and all citizens over the age of 20 are eligible to vote. Most political parties in independent Mauritius have been formed along ethnic lines. The Hindu-dominated Mauritius Labour party ruled the island from its independence to 1982, and its leader, Sir Seewoosagur Ramgoolam (1900–1985), was an important symbol of national unity. The most important political parties today are the Hindu-dominated "Mouvement Socialiste Mauricien" (MSM) and the ostensibly nonethnic, but in practice Creole-Muslim alliance, "Mouvement Militant Mauricien" (MMM). The so-called best-loser system, which supplements the Westminster electoral system, ensures the representation of ethnic minorities in the parliament. A main task for independent Mauritian society has been to create political consensus and some degree of cultural integration. This has been achieved in politics. Although parties remain ethnic in character, there is wide consensus regarding the rules of parliamentary democracy.

Social Control. Mauritius has no military force, and a specially trained segment of the police force is responsible for controlling violent conflict. Mauritian law is an amalgam of Napoleonic and British judicial principles. Although often accused of corruption, the court system functions effectively. At the village level, conflicts over property, adultery, or other minor crimes are often solved informally, sometimes involving respected elders as mediators. Ethnic conflicts are avoided or resolved through informal policies of avoidance and through a widespread ideology of tolerance, as well as for-mal policies of compromise.

Conflict. There have been two general strikes (1970 and 1979) since Mauritian independence. Strikes and other forms of protest are widespread among workers in the manufacturing industry, who feel they are underpaid and overworked. Ethnic conflicts, which turned violent through riots in 1965–1968, are usually mediated by, and expressed through, the formal judicial and political systems. In recent years, drug crimes have become common. Violent crimes are rare. The rapid rate of economic growth may help explain the comparative lack of manifest social conflict, especially ethnic conflict, in contemporary Mauritius.

Religion and Expressive Culture

Religious Beliefs. The religions of Mauritius are Hinduism (52 percent), Roman Catholicism (31 percent), Islam (16 percent) and Buddhism (1 percent). Within Hinduism there are many variants, which correspond to variants found in India itself. Low-caste practices of animal sacrifice are common in rural areas. Maratha and Tamil variants of Hinduism are also distinctive in relation to the dominant Bihari variety. Every year, the Maha Shivaratri is celebrated by Hindus, who march to a lake in southern Mauritius (since the Ganges is too distant). Most Muslims are Sunnis; a few are Shias and Ahmadis. A local Catholic custom is an annual pilgrimage to the tomb of Jacques-Désiré Laval, a now-beatified nineteenth-century priest. Syncretist beliefs are common, and traces of heterodox European and Indian beliefs and traditional African beliefs can be identified among Hindus and Creoles alike, particularly in rural areas. Belief in witchcraft is common, but it is rarely important socially.

Religious Practitioners. The Catholic church is led by the Archbishop of the Mascareignes and the Seychelles, the most powerful religious person in Mauritius. Catholic priests are highly respected and powerful in their local communities. Many are involved in social work. Hindu pundits and Muslim imams are also powerful, although their religions do not require formal leadership. Pundits and imams wield power in ritual and in the context of Hindu and Muslim youth clubs (_baitkas_ and _madrassahs_, respectively). Buddhism is of negligible importance in Mauritius; most of the Buddhists are also Catholics. The _longanis_ (French _longaniste_) is a sorcerer with considerable power in many locations. His or her magical power consists of the ability to heal the sick, divine the future, and influence people's character. The longanis is used by people of all ethnic groups; most longanis are Creoles or Hindus.

Ceremonies. There are three spectacular annual religious ceremonies. The Tamil festival Cavadi is a rite of passage involving fire walking; it is participated in by many non-Tamils. The Catholic Père Laval pilgrimage is exclusively Christian, and the Maha Shivaratri is exclusively Hindu. All major rituals and festivals of the largest religious traditions, including the Chinese New Year, are celebrated by their followers.

Arts. The only indigenous art form of Mauritius is the _séga_, a form of music similar to the Trinidad calypso, having been shaped in the encounter between French planters and African slaves. Now evolved into pop and dance music, the séga is very popular. Indian traditional and popular music are also widespread and are performed locally, but European classical music has only a limited appeal. The literature of Mauritius is comparatively rich; authors write mostly in French and Hindi, although radical nationalists have in recent years taken to writing in Kreol. Whereas Mauritian literature tends to deal with ethnicity and the search for cultural identity, the visual arts tend to be romantic and nature-worshiping in character.

Medicine. As many as seven distinctive traditional medical systems have been identified in Mauritius, in addition to scientific medicine. Mauritians tend to believe in, and use the services of, several different practitioners of medicine. Healing techniques may range from Indian Ayurvedic medicine to Chinese herbal medicine and the incantations of the longanis. Although the main killers are heart disease and diabetes, a common complaint is _move ler_ ("bad air"), which is perceived as psychosomatic. The general symptoms are giddiness and tiredness. Health services are free, and all major villages have a dispensary.

Death and Afterlife. The belief in an afterlife is universally common, and death is generally accepted as an inevitable fate. Hindus and Christians arrange wakes for their deceased. Muslim and Christian graveyards are visited around the time of important religious ceremonies, and flowers are planted on the graves. The Hindus cremate their deceased.

Bibliography

Arno, Toni, and Claude Orian (1986). _L'Île Maurice, une Société Multiraciale._ Paris: L'Harmattan.

Benedict, Burton (1961). _Indians in a Plural Society._ London: Her Majesty's Stationery Office.

Bowman, Larry W. (1990). _Mauritius: Democracy and Development in the Indian Ocean._ Boulder, Colo.: Westview.

Eriksen, Thomas Hylland (1988). *Communicating Cultural Difference and Identity: Ethnicity and Nationalism in Mauritius.* Occasional Papers in Social Anthropology, no. 16. Oslo: Department of Social Anthropology, University of Oslo.

Simmons, Adele Smith (1982). *Modern Mauritius: The Politics of Decolonization.* Bloomington: Indiana University Press.

Toussaint, Adolphe (1977). *History of Mauritius.* London: Macmillan.

THOMAS HYLLAND ERIKSEN

Meo

ETHNONYMS: Mewāti, Mina, Mina Meo

Representing the largest part of the Muslim population in Rajasthan, the Meos number approximately 600,000 (according to 1984 data). They are crowded into the Alwar and Bharatpur districts in the northeastern part of the state, as well as in the Gurgaon District of the adjacent state of Haryana. The areas of the three districts where they live are collectively called Mewat, a reference to their supremacy in the area. Meos speak Rajasthani, a language of the Indo-Iranian part of the Indo-European Family. The Meos pursue many different service occupations and are known as bangle sellers, dyers, butchers, water carriers, and musicians, among others.

Like most Indian Muslims, the Meos were originally Hindu; when and how their conversion to Islam came about is unclear. It seems probable they were converted in stages: first by Salar Masud in the eleventh century, by Balban in the thirteenth century, and then during Aurangzeb's rule in the seventeenth century. The Meos insist on Rajput descent for the entire community. For years the Meos blended both Hindu and Muslim customs in their culture. For example, the popular names for both males and females were Hindu, but Muslim names were given as well, and the Muslim title *Khan* was added to a Hindu name. Two major Islamic rituals observed by the Meos were male circumcision and burial of the dead. Most of the Hindu festivals and ceremonies were maintained. The Muslim festivals, such as the two Ids, Shab-e-barat, and Muharram, were practiced. Reading the Quran was less well liked than the Hindu epics *Ramayana* and *Mahabharata,* and Hindu shrines outnumbered the mosques in Mewat. Few Meos prayed in the Muslim manner but most worshiped at the shrines of the Hindu gods and goddesses. Since 1947, however, with the partition of India, a revival of Islamic tradition has forced many Meos to conform to Islamic norms. In addition, many Meos have emigrated to Pakistan.

Although the Meos today follow most Muslim customs, they still follow traditional Hindu marriage rituals and kinship patterns. Cousin marriage is still taboo among this group. Attempts to break this tradition have met strong opposition. In addition, Meos do not observe the Muslim tradition of secluding their women. Meo society is divided into at least 800 exogamous clans. Some of the clan organizations resemble those of the Rajputs, but others seem to have connections with Hindu castes such as Brahmans, Minas, Jats, and Bhatiaras. Apparently the Meos come from many Hindu castes and not just the Rajputs.

Bibliography

Aggarwal, Partap C. (1984). "Meos." In *Muslim Peoples: A World Ethnographic Survey,* edited by Richard V. Weekes, 518–521. Westport, Conn.: Greenwood Press.

Crooke, William (1896). "Meo." In *The Tribes and Castes of the North-Western Provinces and Oudh.* Vol. 3, 485–495. Calcutta: Government of India Central Printing Office.

Russell, R. V., and Hira Lal (1916). "Meo, Mewāti." In *The Tribes and Castes of the Central Provinces of India,* edited by R. V. Russell and Hira Lal. Vol. 4, 233–235. Nagpur: Government Printing Press. Reprint. 1969. Oosterhout: Anthropological Publications.

JAY DiMAGGIO

Mikir

ETHNONYM: Arleng

Orientation

Identification. The Mikirs are one of the more numerous of the Tibeto-Burman peoples inhabiting the Indian state of Assam. The major locus of their culture is within the Mikir Hills of Assam, but they are also dispersed throughout the Golaghat Subdivision of the Sibsagar District, Nowgong, Kamrup, the Khasi Hills, and the Cachar Hills. Mikir, a name of uncertain derivation, is the name given to this people by their Assamese neighbors. The Mikir call themselves "Arleng" (meaning "man" generally). Much of the detailed ethnographic data available on the Mikir was compiled by Edward Stack in the late nineteenth century. This information was edited, supplemented, and published by Charles Lyall in 1908.

Location. The Mikir homeland is an isolated and mountainous region situated between the Brahmaputra Valley (north), the Dhansiri Valley (east), the Kopili Valley (west), and the Jamuna Valley (south). Summits in the Mikir Hills reach as high as 1,200 meters, but the majority of the mountain peaks are of lower elevation. The entire area is densely forested. The plains at the base of these mountains, which are quite fertile, are also occupied by the Mikir. The climate is forbidding: there is little breeze and the air is quite moist. Malaria and leprosy are constant health threats.

Demography. In 1971 the Mikir population totaled 184,089 persons. However, a 1987 poll conducted by the United Bible Societies recorded some 220,000 Mikir speakers in the region.

Linguistic Affiliation. Mikir (also called Manchati, Mikiri, or Karbi), which belongs to the Tibeto-Burman Family of the Sino-Tibetan Phylum, is the native language of the people.

History and Cultural Relations

Some traditions point to the eastern portion of the Khasi and Jaintia Hills (near the Kopili or Kupli River) as the original Mikir homeland. The Mikir themselves designate this region as Nihang and call their current homeland Nilip. Before settling in their present locale, their history was dominated by intermittent conflict with Naga tribes, Kukis, and Khasis. After a brief period of conflict with the Ahoms (who occupied their present homeland) the Mikir placed themselves under the protection of the Ahom king in Sibsagar, and they are said to have refrained from armed conflict since that time. Unlike their more warlike neighbors, the Mikir have since occupied themselves with basic subsistence activities. Memory is retained of an early king, Sot Recho, who the Mikir believe will return to Earth one day. There are also architectural remains in the northern Mikir Hills, the construction of which is ascribed to the gods.

Settlements

Villages are located in forest clearings. Since the Mikir's chief subsistence activity is agriculture, the location of a village changes when cultivable land has been exhausted. The floor of a typical house is elevated a meter or so above ground level and the structure itself is built on supporting posts. Construction materials consist of bamboo and thatching grass. Each dwelling contains two doors (front and rear) affording access to the outside of the structure. Pigs are kept beneath the house. The *kam* (guest's/servant's chamber) and *kut* (family quarters) are the major sections of the house and are separated by a wall containing a doorway.

Economy

Subsistence and Commercial Activities. The major Mikir subsistence activity is slash-and-burn or *jhum* agriculture. Land used for cultivation is prepared by cutting trees, burning them, and planting seeds in the fertile ash residue. The Mikir make no use of the plow and their farmland is not artificially irrigated. Major crops are *maikun* (summer rice) and *phelo* (cotton). Additional crops include castor oil, *thengthe* (maize), turmeric, *hen* (yams), *birik* (red pepper), *hepi* (aubergines), *hanso* (ginger), and lac. Fowl, pigs, and goats are domesticated. Fishing (with rod and line) is also a subsidiary activity. Deer, wild pigs, iguanas, and tortoises are hunted. In addition, the chrysalis of the *eri* silkworm, crabs, and rats are also consumed. Rice beer, tobacco (smoked and chewed), and betel nuts are also used by the Mikir, as was opium until its use was prohibited by law.

Industrial Arts. Few items are manufactured by the Mikir. Among those found are dyed woven cloth of cotton and silk, metal implements (*daos* [adzes], knives, needles, and fishing hooks), ornaments of gold and silver (necklaces, bracelets, rings, ear adornments), and pottery (made without the use of the potter's wheel). Bamboo and wooden implements used within the household are also, one presumes, manufactured by the Mikir.

Trade. Little may be said of trade between the Mikir and their neighbors. It has been noted that the pressures of assimilation have led to a decrease in the indigenous manufacture of many items and a subsequent increase in the importation of foreign goods.

Division of Labor. The ethnographic literature does not contain much information on the Mikir division of labor. It is known that one task, the weaving of cloth, is the prerogative of women. Farming seems to be done exclusively by men.

Land Tenure. Village lands are apportioned by household, each house being allotted its own fields. Male members of a household limit their labors to their own fields.

Kinship

Kin Groups and Descent. The Mikir living in the hill country are divided into three groups: the Chintongm (living in the Mikir Hills), the Ronghang (occupying the Nowgong Plains), and the Amri (occupying the districts of the Khasi and Jaintia hills in Meghalaya and the Kamrup District of Assam). There is some question as to whether these names reflect true tribal divisions (derived from ancestral designations) or are simply place names. Each of these contains several subdivisions, or *kur*. Each of these kur is exogamous, and their number is reckoned variously by ethnographers. Among those cited by Lyall is the list of Stack, who reckons their number at four. These are Ingti, Terang, Lekthe, and Timung. These four are further subdivided into additional exogamous groups. All members of a kur are considered to be brothers and sisters. Patrilineal descent is the norm.

Kinship Terminology. Omaha-type kinship terminology for first cousins is employed.

Marriage and Family

Marriage. Monogamous unions are the Mikir norm, though polygyny also occurs (usually in the case of wealthy men able to afford more than one wife). Males are married between the ages of 14 and 25. Females are married between the ages of 12 and 15. Premarital sexual relations between males and females are uncommon, though in previous generations, when the *maro* (bachelors' house) was an active institution, liaisons are believed to have been more frequent. Marital infidelity is rare. Postmarital residence is patrilocal, a newly married couple taking up residence with the bridegroom's father. The only exception to this norm occurs if the female is an heiress or an only daughter. In such an instance, the couple reside with the bride's father. Divorce is permissible, though rare, and the remarriage of divorced persons is not prohibited. Widows are also allowed to remarry.

Domestic Unit. Small nuclear families are the Mikir norm. A typical household will consist of the members of a single family together with its male biological offspring and their families.

Inheritance. Sons inherit the property of their fathers, the eldest son receiving a greater share than his siblings. Daughters receive no inheritance from their father's estate. A widow may obtain control of the deceased husband's property by marrying another member of his kur. Otherwise, she is allowed to keep nothing more than her personal property (i.e., clothing, personal ornaments, etc.). Upon the death of a father, the surviving family usually remains undivided and adult sons support their widowed mother. A father may choose to divide his property during his lifetime.

Socialization. Little that is specific may be said of child-rearing practices among the Mikir. From the makeup of the typical domestic unit one may deduce that this is a responsibility shared by all family members. In the case of male youth, the maro (young men's dormitory) played an important part in the process of socialization at one time. The young men's association has survived as an institution, though the maro has been replaced by the home of the gaonbura (village headman). This organization is hierarchically structured and its members eat and work the village fields together.

Sociopolitical Organization

Social Organization. Mikir life is focused on the agricultural cycle. The young men's association plays an important part in this (e.g., by assisting in land cultivation) and in the maintenance of Mikir customs (e.g., in music and dance). There is no apparent evidence of a rigidly stratified social structure (e.g., by age, class, occupation, etc.); neither does there appear to be a ranked hierarchy of kur.

Political Organization. The autonomous village, headed by a gaonbura or sar-the (headman), is the central administrative unit. Village affairs are supervised by the headman and the members of the me (village council), made up of all male householders. The me mediates in disputes and has the power to levy fines. Villages belong to larger administrative districts called mauzas, which are administered by a me-pi (great council), membership in which is limited to gaonburas. A me-pi is headed by a mauzadar (head gaonbura). This body addresses issues having effects that extend beyond village boundaries.

Social Control. While vendettas (between families) are said to have been an element of prior Mikir history, the present state of internal cultural affairs is characterized by stability and order. Disputes are mediated by the me (village council), which is presided over by the gaonbura (village chief). The organizational structure of the young men's organization within a village is itself a mechanism of maintaining order. Oaths, corporal punishment, fines, and voluntary separation from the community are among the means used to maintain social control.

Conflict. Traditionally, the Mikir have not made armed conflict with their non-Mikir neighbors a priority. Furthermore, internal strife (e.g., between Mikir villages) has been absent historically. Periodic conflict between the Mikir and other neighboring peoples (e.g., Nagas, Kukis, and Khasis) may be noted, but it has not been a result of Mikir instigation.

Religion and Expressive Culture

Religious Beliefs. The Mikir acknowledge the existence of a number of divinities, though temples, shrines, and other places and objects of worship are lacking in their villages. Worship is not directed toward trees or animals. Individuals may be in the possession of bor (amulets or fetishes) of stone or metal that are believed capable of bringing good or bad luck. The gods are called upon and animals sacrificed to ensure good fortune and to avoid negative circumstances. Some of the more important members of the Mikir pantheon are: Arnam Kethe, the "Great God," who, though a household god, actually lives in Heaven and receives sacrifice once in three years; Peng, a household god who actually resides within the home; Hemphu, the "householder," who "owns" all of the Mikir people; Rek-anglong, the local deity identified with the hill upon which a village is located; and Arnam Paro, the "hundred god," who is, perhaps, a composite figure made up of all of the gods who are a prominent part of the annual Rongker festival. In addition to the aforementioned gods, there are others (e.g., Chomang-ase, "Khasi fever"; Ajo-ase, "night fever"; and So-mene, "evil pain") who are identified with specific diseases. In addition, natural features of an impressive nature (e.g., sun, moon, mountains, waterfalls) have divinities identified with them, though those of a celestial nature are not the objects of propitiatory sacrifice. Christianity has had little impact on the world view of the Mikir. Evidence of Hindu influence, however, may be noted.

Religious Practitioners. The diviner is the major Mikir religious practitioner. The generic designation for the office is uche, when held by a male, or uche-pi, when held by a female. Of these there are two classes. The first is the sang-kelang abang, or "man who looks at rice," who exercises this office after a period of instruction and practice. The second is the lodet or lodet-pi, a female practitioner who dispatches her duties while under the influence of supernatural forces.

Ceremonies. Communal celebrations include the following: the Rongker (annual village festival held either at the beginning of the cultivation season in June or in the cold season); a harvest-home celebration; and the occasional Rongker-pi ("great Rongker") held on special occasions (e.g., to expel man-eating tigers) and attended by an entire mauza. Several ritualized behavioral restrictions (called gennas in Assamese) are also observed.

Arts. In addition to articles that have a utilitarian or ornamental purpose (e.g., domestic utensils, clothing, and jewelry), musical instruments are also produced. Music and dancing are said to accompany the harvest-home celebration and burial rites. Tattooing is also practiced by Mikir women (a perpendicular line applied with indigo extending from the middle of the forehead to the chin). The oral literature of the Mikir includes myths and folktales.

Medicine. Prolonged illness is believed to be caused either by witchcraft or the malevolent action of supernaturals. The services of male and female diviners (the sang-kelang abang and the lodet or lodet-pi, respectively) are required to alleviate the malady, by discerning who has cast the spell or what the divine forces are that need to be propitiated.

Death and Afterlife. The burial cult of the Mikir is designed to insure that the deceased gain entrance into the underworld abode of the dead, which is ruled by Jom Recho, the "Lord of Spirits." Those whose burials are not accompanied by the proper ceremonies do not gain admittance. The deceased remain in Jom-arong, "Jom's town," until they are reborn on Earth as children. This belief in reincarnation is an apparent borrowing from the Hindu neighbors of the Mikir.

Bibliography

Barkataki, S. (1969). *Tribes of Assam*. New Delhi: National Book Trust.

Maloney, Clarence (1974). *Peoples of South Asia*. New York, Chicago, and San Francisco: Holt, Rinehart & Winston.

Stack, Edward. (1908). *The Mikirs*. Edited by Charles Lyall, London: D. Nutt. Reprint. 1972. Gauhati: United Publishers.

HUGH R. PAGE, JR.

Mizo

ETHNONYMS: Lushai, Zomi

Orientation

Identification. "Mizo," meaning "people of the high land," is a generic term for the related peoples who speak the Duhlian dialect and live mainly in Mizoram, Manipur, and Tripura states of India. In the earliest literature they were called "Kuki" by the neighboring Bengalis. The British called them "Lushai." Since 1950 the word "Mizo" has been accepted by the people as more comprehensive than "Lushai"; the name of their area of concentration has changed from Lushai Hills to Mizoram, meaning "country of the Mizo."

Location. Mizoram lies between 24° and 22° N and 93° and 92° E. It is bounded by three Indian states—Manipur, Assam, and Tripura—and by the countries of Myanmar (Burma) and Bangladesh. Mizoram consists of a mass of hill ranges averaging from about 1,000 to 1,800 meters running from north and south, with a small plateau at Champai; most are covered by thin jungles. Rivers are hardly navigable. The climate of Mizoram has two seasons—the hot, rainy period from April to September and the cold, dry period from October to March.

Demography. According to the 1981 census the population of Mizoram was 493,757; the Scheduled Tribes constituted 93.55 percent of this number, which included Mizo, Lakher, Pawi, Chakma, Riang, and others. The Mizo are currently about 80 percent of the population of Mizoram, but they are also found in neighboring states, for in the 1971 census they numbered 512,833 in all of the northeastern states.

Linguistic Affiliation. The Mizo language belongs to the Tibeto-Burman Family of the Sino-Tibetan Branch; its Kuki-Chin Subgroup is comprised of the Meitei, Lushai, Thadou, Halem, and Chin subgroups. The Mizo have no script of their own. The Mizo alphabet was printed by Christian missionaries in 1898 in Roman script on the basis of phonetics.

History and Cultural Relations

The Mizo believe that their ancestors once lived in China. Around A.D. 996 they migrated to the Chindwin belt of mountains through the Hukung Valley of Myanmar and lived for centuries in the Kabaw Valley. To avoid an onslaught of Shan influence they then migrated in groups to the Chin Hills. In about 1765 they established a large village in Myanmar called Selsih (Zopuii) 35 kilometers to the west of the Tiau River. The first historical mention of the Mizo (Lushai) is in 1777. In that year the chief of Chittagong, which had been ceded to the British under Lord Clive by Mir Kasim in 1760, applied for a detachment of soldiers to protect the people against an incursion of the Kuki, as they were then called. By 1810 Chief Lallula Sailo and other related chiefs controlled the whole of the country from the Tiau River to Demagiri. The pressure on the eastern Mizo chiefs from the Chin Hills chiefs such as Suktes was severe, as the latter were moving down from the hills to the plains in the Cachar and Sylhet areas. British punitive expeditions to Mizoram began in 1844. In December 1896 a resolution was passed to amalgamate the north and south Lushai Hills administratively at the Chin-Lushai Conference held at Lunglei. British administration continued until India gained independence in 1947. The Mizo, to safeguard their own identity and culture, became politically active in 1966, which resulted in 1983 in their recognition that the constitution of India was a mechanism for achieving socioeconomic development.

Settlements

In the past when the villages were under the control of chiefs their number and names were constantly changing. People were continually searching for land for cultivation and water. The villages were also split up among the sons of chiefs. A traditional village located on the spur of the hills was shapeless and clustered. In 1966 villages were reorganized under a project called "Operation Security," which involved 68 percent of the population. These new villages are of a linear cluster type: a main road bisects each village and all smaller streets radiate from a central plaza, with groups of houses arranged along the roadsides. Each village has at least one church, a school, a blacksmith's workshop, and shops. Villages range from 60 to 80 houses with a population of 400 to 700. Houses are constructed on raised bamboo or wooden poles. There are two major house types: those with two-sided roofs and those with four-sided roofs. A typical ordinary house is rectangular in shape with a thatched two-sided roof. Floor and side walls are made of split or plaited bamboo with one or two windows. Those who are well-off use wooden planks for the floor and corrugated iron for the roof. Generally an earthen hearth is constructed near the left side in the center of the roof. In the traditional houses the main bed occupied by the head of the house is at the rear side of the hearth. The large room is also partitioned to make cubicles for privacy. Storage of grain and food is in a corner of the room. Poultry and pigs are kept either in the front veranda or in a small enclosure behind the house.

Economy

Subsistence and Commercial Activities. The Mizos are now heavily involved in the money economy. About 80 percent of the people of Mizoram derive their sustenance from swidden cultivation on hill slopes. Wet rice cultivation was introduced in patches by non-Mizos—just after the annexation of the area by the British—in Thenzawl, Champhai, and Vanlaiphai villages, where a Burmese type of plow was used. Agricultural implements consist of axes, and hoes, and knives. Paddy, maize, cabbages, melons, cotton, and ginger are raised. Recently terracing has been introduced in Mizoram. The main cash crop is ginger. During lean months, the Mizo shoot birds with catapults and air guns, occasionally fish by poisoning water in hollows between the hills, and hunt animals. Domestic animals include pigs, poultry, and dogs; some people keep cattle. In the past every village had a number of gayals, which were killed for special festivals and ceremonies. Nowadays these animals are rarely kept.

Industrial Arts.   Each village has at least one blacksmithy where hoes, axes, and knives are made. Most of the households have a sewing machine. Each family has a number of loin looms (backstrap looms) used by women. They weave cotton yarn with attractive geometric designs. Men practice carpentry. All men weave baskets of various sizes, shapes, and designs. Lacquering and the *cire perdue* or "lost wax" process of casting bronze have died out. Earthen smoking pipes are still handmade by women.

Trade.   Since the regrouping of villages, shops are found in all villages. In the larger villages small markets are held. Otherwise people visit the few towns of Aizawl, Lunglei, Thenzawl, and Champhai for buying and selling. Bengali- and Hindi-speaking traders also do business with the permission of the administrative authorities. Peddlers move about in villages too.

Division of Labor.   The traditional division of labor is relatively fluid. Tasks such as weaving, winnowing, pottery making, etc. are women's jobs. Basketry, blacksmithy, carpentry, etc. are men's work. Nowadays educated urban women work as traffic police in Aizawl.

Land Tenure.   Before 1947, rights of the village communities and chiefs over their territory were recognized (the Chin Hill Regulation 5, 1896). With abolition of the rights of the chiefs, the authority of the village council over the land was finally established. It distributes land to each family for swidden cultivation and for residence. In the towns, plots of land for permanent ownership are distributed in response to individual application.

Kinship

Kin Groups and Descent.   There are two overall principles that govern kinship practices as they relate to social organization: (1) all females moving out of one's own family through marriage are categorized together and their husbands also stand as a group in relation to Ego; (2) the females who come into the agnate group of Ego form a group, and therefore male relatives of the incoming female group are designated by the same term, without making any distinction of generation and seniority, and all their spouses also form a group. All kin help in the construction of a house, assist in marriage and death ceremonies, and get their share of a bride-price and the meat of animals killed during a marriage. Descent is patrilineal.

Kinship Terminology.   Kinship terminology is of the Omaha type. Within the circle of closer kin the system works according to the bifurcate-merging principle. There are twenty-two kinship terms. The range of this terminology is limited to two generations above and two generations below.

Marriage and Family

Marriage.   Traditionally polygamy was allowed, but monogamy has been strictly enforced by the various churches. Marriage is by courtship, an institutionalized practice, with the choices of boys and girls approved by the parents. Premarital sex is common though not appreciated. Tribal endogamy is only normative; deviations do occur. Cross-cousin marriage is allowed but with less favor toward marriage with a father's sister's daughter. Payment of bride-price at marriage is a complicated affair. In certain areas a traditional practice of sharing portions of killed animals at a feast among the agnatic as well as affinal kin is still rigidly followed. Following marriage the married elder son has his house built and lives separately. The process goes on until the youngest son marries, after which he continues to reside with his parents. Divorce is common, easy, and favorable to the man, and it can be granted for almost any reason. In all divorces occurring before a woman bears a child, the bride-price is returned to the man. A divorced woman usually keeps an infant with her until there is a demand for the child from the man.

Domestic Unit.   Mizos do not distinguish between household and family. The people who live together under one roof and eat from the same hearth belong to one family. The average size of a family is between six and seven people. The nuclear family is the common type. The vertico-horizontal type of family tends to split into two sections, the nuclear family and the stem family. The life of the vertico-horizontal type of family is the shortest. This Ego-centered cyclic change is a unique feature. Usually the family consists of a parent of the male head of the family, the male head, his spouse, and his children.

Inheritance.   Mizos practice male ultimogeniture: the youngest son remains with his parents till death to become the heir. All movable and immovable property belongs to a male, except certain personal articles of females that remain women's property. Through matrifiliation a woman's property is passed to her daughter.

Socialization.   Children grow up with their parents and paternal grandparents. No serious distinction is made between boys and girls during early childhood. Female infanticide ended more than sixty years ago. Mizos put much emphasis on teaching the child to develop a sense of group cooperation and Christian values.

Sociopolitical Organization

Social Organization.   Mizo society is hierarchically organized on the basis of age, sex, standard of living, and knowledge. Those who work in high offices in urban and rural areas rank above those who work in the swidden. Those who are associated with the leading local church are held in high esteem.

Political Organization.   Mizoram is a state in the Republic of India. Mizoram has three districts: Chhimtuipui, Lunglei, and Aizawl. In the latter two, Mizo sociopolitical activities dominate. Each village has a council headed by a president.

He, his secretary, and members of his council are elected through adult franchise on the basis of political party. This democratic system replaces the traditional system based on privilege and nonprivilege. The village council manages the affairs of the village: matters concerning agricultural activities, allocation of agricultural plots, collection of taxes, distribution of water, control of the market, community activities, and welfare of the people. The religious activities are attended to by the different church denominations with the help of their members. The village crier and blacksmith are nominated by the village council. The state government manages such matters as communication, education, social welfare, law and order, hospitals, transport, food supply, industry, the judiciary, forests, etc.

Social Control. Mizo customary law is enforced through a village council that has judicial powers. The local church authority is another body that regulates the behavior of the people. In this matter clergy play an important role in religious and village issues. If an individual family is not happy with conditions in the village, it may leave the village for another, with the permission of the president of the village council.

Religion and Expressive Culture

Religious Beliefs. Mizos are ardent followers of Christianity. The great majority are Protestants. They generally donate a portion of the first product of the swidden to their churches during Sunday morning services in the harvest season. The Mizo churches get substantial gifts from followers for the support of their activities. Church denominations include the Welsh Presbyterian, United Pentecostal, Salvation Army, Seventh-Day Adventist, Roman Catholic, London Baptist, Sabbath Church, and cults or sects formed by the late preacher Khuangtua Vanawi, by Mizo Jews, and by other groups. Mizoram was 83.81 percent Christian in 1981.

Religious Practitioners. Each church denomination has its own clergy, trained in Mizoram or in neighboring states. Pastors are transferable from one area to the other. They preach, sing, bless people, and participate in life-cycle rituals. A few are now missionaries in Washington, D.C. In the village there are exorcists who treat the sick by invoking the blessings of the Holy Ghost and by warding off incursions of Satan. In this matter a belief in spirit possession is predominant.

Ceremonies. Mizos celebrate all Christian festivals, especially Christmas, New Year's Day, and Easter. Discarded traditional festivals (_kut_) are being revived not so much for their cultural content but as traditional identity markers. Carol singing and visiting houses in large groups are very common at Christmas and around New Year's Day.

Arts. Mizos weave designs in cloth, in baskets, and on the handles of their weapons and instruments. Geometric designs and motifs of flowers and plants are popular. Traditional lacquer work in red and black has gradually died out. Mizos are great lovers of Western music. In towns they organize Western music contests. The guitar is the most popular musical instrument. A traditional bamboo dance is very popular, as are church hymns. A big Mizo drum provides the musical accompaniment.

Medicine. Modern medicine as well as the use of native medicinal plants for sores and wounds are both common.

Death and Afterlife. Mizos bury their dead. The pastor performs the last rites according to the custom of the particular church denomination. They put memorial stones on the burial ground, engraving there the deeds of the deceased.

See also Lakher

Bibliography

Goswami, B. B. (1979). _Mizo Unrest: A Study of Politicisation of Culture._ Jaipur: Aalekh Publishers.

Goswami, B. B. (1987). "The Mizos in the Context of State Formation." In _Tribal Polities and State Systems in Pre-Colonial Eastern and North Eastern India,_ edited by Surajit Sinha 307–327. Calcutta: K. P. Bagchi; Centre for Studies in Social Sciences.

McCall, Anthony Gilchrist (1949). _Lushai Chrysalis._ London: Luzac.

Shakespear, John (1912). _The Lushei Kuki Clans._ London: Macmillan.

B. B. GOSWAMI

Mogul

ETHNONYMS: Moghul, Mugal, Mughal

Although the last Mogul emperor died in 1857, the Mogul people have not disappeared from India and Pakistan (especially the Punjab states). In 1911 there were some 60,000 Moguls. They have been variously called a tribe or a caste of Muslims, though neither term is exact and probably "descent group" would be more appropriate. Moguls are highly regarded, and their womenfolk still practice purdah. The name "Mogul" is derived from the Persian word for "Mongol."

Of the main Muslim groups in Pakistan and India, Sayyids rank highest, as being "descendants of the Prophet"; they are followed by Sheikhs; Moguls rank third; and Pathans are fourth. These four groups, which are largely endogamous, rank above other South Asian Muslims as being "Ashraf" (i.e., of foreign origin).

There is a broad continuity in the Muslim history of the subcontinent, but with the foundation of the Mogul Empire in A.D. 1526 we reach a political and cultural watershed. There was a much greater continuity in administration, as members of the same dynasty sat on the throne for more than 300 years, while Moguls also ushered in an era of a much richer cultural life. They were the first Muslim rulers of Delhi to patronize and encourage painting and music, and in the realm of architecture their monuments challenge comparison with similar achievements anywhere in the world.

In 1519 Babur, the founder of the Mogul Empire, first

appeared in India. In so doing he was following a family tradition. His ancestors, Chenghiz Khan and Timur the Lame, had both invaded India, the former in the thirteenth and the latter in the fourteenth century. Neither of these invasions had any lasting effects, though Babur declared that the principal object of his invasion was to recover the lost possessions of his family. Babur's rule started in 1526–1530. It shortly fell to Humayun (1530–1540), who lost control to an Afghan chieftain, Sher Shah (1539–1545). His son Akbar (1556–1605) fought the Afghan challenge at Panipat (1556) and extended the empire to include all land between Afghanistan and the Deccan. Akbar's time was a period of religious freedom, in which a policy of conciliation was pursued with the Rajput states. Akbar was succeeded by Jehangir (1605–1627) and Shah Jehan (1627–1658). Its last great emperor was Aurangzeb (1658–1707), who extended the limits of the empire farther south. The empire disintegrated under Maratha and British pressure. Its last emperor, Bahadur Shah II (1837–1857), was exiled by the British to Rangoon after the 1857 uprising.

The splendor and stability of the Mogul reign were due to the succession of those capable rulers. They attempted to build up an efficient administrative system, and they chose their principal officers with care and on the basis of merit.

A number of factors were responsible for what appears to have been the sudden collapse of the Mogul authority after the death of Aurangzeb, but one cause was predominant. The Moguls maintained a powerful empire for centuries and established a government and a social organization impressive by Asiatic standards, but they were not able to keep pace with the rapid, almost cataclysmic changes that were taking place in intellectual matters, military organization, instruments of offense and defense, and other factors that contribute to the stability and prosperity of a state. The intellectual revolution in western Europe, the new spirit and the new discoveries, and the wide diffusion of knowledge resulting from the introduction of printing had released forces that were bound to result in European domination.

See also Muslim; Pathan; Sayyid; Sheikh

Bibliography

Gascoigne, Bamber (1971). *The Great Moghuls.* New York: Harper & Row.

Haig, Wolseley, and Richard Burn, eds. (1937). *The Cambridge History of India.* Vol. 4, *The Mughul Period.* Cambridge: Cambridge University Press.

Hansen, Waldemar (1972). *The Peacock Throne: The Drama of Mogul India.* New York: Holt, Rinehart & Winston.

Majumdar, R. C., J. N. Chaudhuri, and S. Chaudhuri, eds. (1984). *The Mughul Empire.* The History and Culture of the Indian People, no. 7. Bombay: Bharatiya Vidya Bhavan.

ALLIYA S. ELAHI

Moor of Sri Lanka

ETHNONYMS: Marakkala, Musalman, Sonakar, Sonar

A consensus on the name for Sri Lanka Muslims has not been arrived at. The appellation "Moor" (from the Portuguese) is not used by the population to identify themselves. The Sinhalese use the term "Muslim" or "Marakkala" after a leading Muslim family name. Sri Lanka Muslims occasionally call themselves "Sonakar" or "Sonar," therefore setting themselves apart from the Muslims of south India. The Urdu appellation "Musalman" is used principally around the Colombo area (the Sri Lankan capital). In government publications the designation "Tamil" implies Hindu or Christian; Muslims are listed as Moors. The motivation is political, to represent a larger proportion of Sinhalese to Tamil speakers in the population.

Muslims represent 7.36 percent of the total population of Sri Lanka (1989). Sri Lanka Muslims represent a number of different ethnic groups, three of which are recognized in the 1984 government census: Sri Lanka Moors (1.1 million); Malays (60,000); and Indian Moors, the majority of whom are ethnic Tamils from southern India (40,000). Tamil is the established tongue of the Sri Lanka Moors. In recent years, because of political considerations, many have learned the Sinhala language and some children study it in school. A handful speak Sinhala in the hill areas at home; however, Tamil remains the language of education for the majority up through the university level. All religious literature and sermons are given in Tamil. Malays speak Malay at home, although they do not write it, and they prefer to educate their children in English. With the exception of the Bohras, who are Shiites, all of the other groups are Sunni Muslims.

Soon after settling in India, Muslim Arabs began arriving in the eighth century. According to legend, they established themselves in Bentotta and married Sinhala women. By the tenth century, they were a powerful merchant class. According to the historian Ibn Battuta, in the thirteenth century, Colombo was a Muslim city, while the Delhi sultanate's influence reached to the southern tip of India. An Arabized dialect written in Arabic script (not in use today) grew, and an epic of the life of the Prophet was popularized. The Malays were introduced by the Dutch from Indonesia as laborers. They are an urban population maintaining their own customs and language. The Indian Muslims came in the British period during the nineteenth century, mainly as traders. Few, however, are given Sri Lankan citizenship, and many have been sent back to India.

The majority of Muslims are involved in business ventures. Preeminent are the gem-trading families, who control the extraction and selling of gems almost exclusively. Most of them reside in Colombo and the other big city areas. Next in prominence are the city entrepreneurs, who change their businesses from time to time with the changes in limited manufactured goods and imports. The majority are small traders who run small shops in the rural and village areas. A few have gone into the professions; however, most have largely ignored modern secular education. There are some small Muslim fishing villages and masons on the island. On the east side of Sri Lanka there are some Muslim peasant farmers.

There are many caste, lineage, and family groups. The Maulanas or Sayyids claim descent patrilineally from the Prophet or those close to him. The Marakkayas (also Maraikkars or Marikkars) represent a leading business group in and around Colombo. An important Muslim caste in port towns is the Marakkalarayaras. They have a long tradition of trading in ships, dating back to King Solomon. The Lebbe or Lebbai serve principally as prayer leaders and preachers. These groups are like lineages but mostly without any great degree of lineage links. They also serve many of the functions of caste, although endogamy is not practiced as a cultural precept. Barbers form the most separate Muslim group. They are called Nasuvar in the west and Ostas in the east. They have the lowest social status and are practically endogamous, operating as a separate caste. Due to the proximity of Hindu neighbors many Muslim peasants have matrilineal clans.

Marriage and inheritance practices do not always follow Muslim tradition. Cross-cousin marriage is preferred and parallel-cousin marriage forbidden in keeping with Dravidian kinship rules and Tamil and Sinhala marriage conventions. A few urban Muslims today, however, permit parallel-cousin marriage. A girl's parents by custom look for a suitable groom. The two families bargain on a dowry. The girl's family assumes most of the expense of marriage, entertaining as many as several hundred people. The wedding ritual is simple, in accordance with Muslim custom; however, the bride must be present because in Sri Lanka the groom adorns her with a wedding necklace usually having a crescent on it. Postmarital residence is at the bride's house among all Sri Lankan Muslims, and the couple may remain there for some months or years. Divorce is rare, and polygyny insignificant. A large number of men take brides from any Muslim category except the barber caste.

Bibliography

Arasaratnam, S. (1964). _Ceylon_. Englewood Cliffs, N.J.: Prentice Hall.

Maloney, Clarence (1984). "Sri Lanka." In _Muslim Peoples: A World Ethnographic Survey_, edited by Richard V. Weekes, 723–727. Westport, Conn.: Greenwood Press.

Mauroof, Mohamed. "Aspects of Religion, Economy, and Society among the Muslims of Sri Lanka." _Contributions to Indian Sociology_, n.s. 6:66–83.

Robinson, Francis, ed. (1989). _The Cambridge Encyclopedia of India, Pakistan, Bangladesh, Sri Lanka, Nepal, Bhutan, and the Maldives_. Cambridge: Cambridge University Press.

Yalman, Nur (1967). _Under the Bo Tree: Studies in Caste, Kinship, and Marriage in the Interior of Ceylon_. Berkeley and Los Angeles: University of California Press.

JAY DiMAGGIO

Munda

ETHNONYMS: Hor, Kol, Kolarian

Orientation

Identification. Munda refers primarily to a group of languages, but the tribes that speak those languages have collectively become known to scholarship by the same name. Individually, ethnic designations are (with important alternatives in parentheses): Korku, Santal (including the Mahali subgroup), Munda, Ho, Bhumij, Birhor, Asur, Turi, Korwa, Kora, Kharia, Juang, Sora (Saora, Savara), Gorum (Parenga), Gadaba, Remo (Bondo, Bonda), and Gataq (Didayi, Dire). Some of these names (especially Kharia, Sora, and Gadaba) are shared with local groups of non-Munda speakers. The term "Munda" appears to be derived from a Sanskritic root meaning "substantial, wealthy," later "head," hence "headman"; it was thus originally a term applied by outsiders, a usage that became especially consolidated under the British regime. The word "Kol" (Kolarian), although pejorative, is probably really a corruption of their own _hor, kor,_ etc., meaning "man," common in the north of their area but replaced by _remo_ in southern Orissa, India.

Location. The Korku are located in southwest Madhya Pradesh and are isolated from other Munda. The last five groups in the list above are found mainly in the Koraput and Ganjam districts of southern Orissa. The remainder are found mainly on and around the Chota Nagpur Plateau—that is, in southern Bihar, northern Orissa, eastern Madhya Pradesh, and western West Bengal, with an outlier of Korwa in Mirzapur District, Uttar Pradesh. There are also some Santal in southeast Nepal (where they are called Satar), Bhutan, and northern Bangladesh.

Demography. There are just over 6 million Munda speakers, two-thirds of whom belong to just one tribe, the Santal, one of the largest tribes on earth. Other large groups of Munda speakers (with census figures in parentheses) are the Korku (275,654 in 1971), Munda (1,181,151 in 1971), Ho (538,124 in 1971), Kharia (274,540 in 1971), and Sora (521,187 in 1971). The rest number a few thousand each at the most, the Birhor 4,300 in 1971. Together they constitute well under 1 percent of the total Indian population.

Linguistic Affiliation. Munda is the westernmost branch of the Austroasiatic Language Family, which is otherwise associated mainly with continental Southeast Asia. The connection is remote and has been a matter of controversy but today is generally accepted: it manifests itself in common lexemes rather than any similarities in grammar, word morphology, or phonology. Literacy is generally low, and most literature is oral rather than written. However, missionaries and tribal educators have reduced many texts to writing, using the Roman script or one of the regional Indian scripts. There are also two dedicated tribal scripts, one for Santali (called _ol cemit_), the other for Ho.

History and Cultural Relations

The view that the Munda originally entered India from Southeast Asia is based mainly on their linguistic affiliations;

their own oral traditions give them instead a western origin (from Uttar Pradesh). There is some evidence of tribal kingdoms in pre-British times (e.g., the Ho/Munda kingdom of Chota Nagpur, and the Bhumij states, especially Barabhum). Mainly, however, the Munda have lived, often fairly autonomously, under the rule of outside powers. Most Munda are conventionally regarded as tribes rather than castes, despite the definitional problems this gives scholarship. It is an identity most of them promote themselves, partly because of the legal advantages they gain through being on the list of Scheduled Tribes, but mainly because of opposition to "Hindu" (i.e., upper-caste) officials and landowners, who, from early British times, have displaced many tribals from their land. This strongly tribal and anti-Hindu identity has led to rebellion in the past (the Ho rebellion of the 1830s, the Santal rebellion of 1855–1858, the Birsa Munda movement of 1895–1900), but today it has become translated into political action through the Santal-dominated Jharkhand Party, which agitates, among other things, for a specifically Adivasi (tribal) province. Despite this, there are a number of Munda groups who have sought to gain caste status by reforming customs (banning alcohol, public dancing, cross-cousin marriage) and acquiring a specialist occupation such as basket making. These attempts to improve their lot earn them the contempt of the "tribal" Munda and, since they are mainly artisan castes, ironically lower their status below that of the tribals in the eyes of the upper castes, since the tribals at least are not involved in a polluting occupation. Only the Bhumij, having been rulers, can convincingly claim a moderately high (Kshatriya) status.

Settlements

Most Munda live in villages, though some live and work in towns such as Ranchi and Jamshedpur, and some Birhor and Korwa, being seminomadic, have temporary forest camps. Traditionally, there was a tendency for villages to be fixed only temporarily because of the requirements of shifting cultivation, but with the government trying to discourage this form of agriculture, villages now tend to be more permanent. Villages may consist of detached dwellings or sometimes (as among some Sora) of dwellings connected into a longhouse. Houses are not generally oriented toward particular compass points, but they are usually symbolically divided internally according to principles of gender and age (the eldest members sleep nearest the hearth, male members on the right of the house, female members on the left, etc.). The hearth is especially important ritually and is the spiritual center of the homestead.

Economy

Subsistence and Commercial Activities. Most Munda are agriculturalists; increasingly, permanent irrigated sites are replacing the traditional swiddens. The other main traditional occupation is hunting and gathering, with which the Birhor and some Korwa are particularly associated, though all groups participate in these activities to some extent to supplement their agriculture. Today, however, government policy is to preserve the remaining forests, which are now much depleted, and this policy militates against both of the traditional forms of economic activity. The result is an increase in irrigated land and the development of other sources of in-

come, such as working in the tea plantations of the northeast, in mining, in the steel industry, etc., in the Ranchi-Jamshedpur area, or working as day laborers for local Hindu landowners.

Industrial Arts. Some groups, low castes rather than tribes, have a traditional artisan or other specialist occupation (e.g., the Asur are ironworkers, the Turi are basket makers, the Kora are ditch diggers, etc.). Some Birhor make and sell ropes. Generally, though, Hindu artisans supply most of the tribes' needs.

Trade. Few Munda live by trade, though they may occasionally sell forest products or some rice to wholesalers. The Birhor obtain their rice by selling ropes and forest products, and some Korwa, Turi, and Mahali sell their basketwork in local markets.

Division of Labor. Both men and women work in the fields, but the domestic burdens fall more on the women; many occupations (e.g., plowing, roof repair) are barred to them for ritual reasons. Men hunt; women gather. Specialist occupations are mainly men's work.

Land Tenure. Swiddens are normally owned by the dominant descent group in the village, though coresident nonmembers are usually granted access; the individual normally has use rights only while he cultivates. Irrigated land tends to be individually or family owned, primarily because of the extra labor involved in building terraces and irrigation ditches.

Kinship

Kin Groups and Descent. Descent is uniformly patrilineal, and all the Munda have patrilineal descent groups. Totemic, exogamous clans, mainly significant as regulators of marriage, and lineages, normally named after localities or village offices and mainly of ritual and economic significance, are identifiable in most tribes; subclans are also present in the larger Chota Nagpur tribes. Clans are not especially localized, though they are often identified with particular cemeteries or memorial stones, and each village will be dominated by the members of a particular clan. The Gadaba, Remo, Gorum, and Gataq also group their clans into phratries, and it is these that are totemic in those groups, though they are not necessarily strictly exogamous. No Sora descent groups are totemic. On the whole, a common totem, shared ritual food, or village coresidence are more important indicators of agnation than genealogy as such. Villages are often identified with a particular agnatic group, despite the frequent copresence of members of other clans. Clan members are not necessarily descended from their totem, but the totem usually plays some key role in the clan origin myth, and clan members must show respect to and avoid harming their own (though not others') totem species (most commonly an animal).

Kinship Terminology. Basically it is symmetric-prescriptive or bifurcate-collateral terminology, but Ego's genealogical level is normally generational, and the levels adjacent to it usually have affinal terms separate from those for cross kin. The terminologies of the Koraput tribes are less deviant in these respects.

Marriage and Family

Marriage. Apart from the Asur, Kora, Mahali, and possibly Turi, all Munda groups have positive marriage rules. Among the Koraput groups the prescribed category in marriage is the bilateral cross cousin (usually excluding first cousins), but farther north the prescribed category is more usually translatable as a "sibling's spouse's sibling"; often the indigenous term also covers referents belonging to the genealogical levels of the grandparents or grandchildren (though they nonetheless may be of roughly the same age as Ego). Preferences for a sibling's spouse's sibling usually go with a delay of one to three generations in renewing alliances between the same alliance groups. In most cases (but excluding the Ho and some Santal), spouse exchange is overall symmetric rather than asymmetric. Alliance groups are normally agnatically defined but may be villages rather than descent groups. Indeed, because of the agnatic identity of most villages, village exogamy is normally required, and negotiations, celebrations, and prestations frequently involve the whole village, not just the principals and their immediate families. Brideprice, not dowry, is the norm. How much choice of partner the principals are allowed varies from tribe to tribe: some tribes have youth dormitories for both sexes, though these do not necessarily take choice out of the hands of the parents (e.g., not among the Juang). There are numerous types of wedding ceremony, some simpler, others more "Hindu." Residence is normally virilocal, though all tribes allow a poor youth to live uxorilocally with (and eventually inherit from) his sonless father-in-law. Monogamy is the norm, though there is some polygyny, especially sororal (wife's classificatory younger but not elder sister). Junior levirate, or the inheritance of a man's widow by his classificatory younger (not elder) brother, is a commonly recognized and in some tribes virtually mandatory practice. Divorce and the remarriage of divorced and widowed people are normally allowed, even though, like the levirate, these are distinctly low-status practices in India generally.

Domestic Unit. Both nuclear and extended or joint families are found, though a single family often oscillates between the different forms, as new members are born and old ones die, or as quarrels split them up. For the hunting-and-gathering Birhor, the *tanda* (band) is the unit.

Inheritance. Irrigated land, use rights regarding swiddens, the family home, fruit trees, and most movables are inherited in the direct patrilineal line. The eldest son receives the most, though not normally everything, as the new head of the family (he may be responsible for the welfare, marriage expenses, etc., of his younger siblings, for example). In some cases, the sons who have remained at home are favored (the youngest sons among the Sora and some Santal, for instance). In default of sons, the closest collateral agnate or an uxorilocally living son-in-law (the *ghar-jawae*—see above) inherits. There is some matrilineal inheritance of female clothes and ornaments, but women cannot inherit land, because they marry out of the clan.

Socialization. Infants are brought up by their parents with the help of elder siblings, but it is the former who are mainly responsible for socialization. Other opportunities are provided by children watching and eventually helping with the daily work, and the elders play their part by telling myths and other folktales on ritual and other occasions.

Sociopolitical Organization

Social Organization. We have already seen that many tribes are internally divided because of some ritual fault or disagreement over custom, etc. The Birhor, Korwa, and some Asur distinguish settled groups from nomads. Most tribes distinguish landowning clans from tenant clans with use rights only, though since the clans involved vary with the village, this does not entail a tribewide class system. Santal clans are unusual in being ritually ranked, and there is some hypergamy between them. In all tribes, village officers command a marked degree of respect, though this rarely leads to a class system or to hypergamy between them and the ordinary villagers (the Sora are an exception in this regard). Kinship remains the basis of social organization, and there are a number of ritualized friendships for both men and women, between villages and even tribes, that are assimilated to it. Although all tribes distinguish affines from agnates (i.e., marriageable from nonmarriageable persons), these are relative designations only: despite the system of affinal alliance, there are no sociocentric categories of the sort associated with dual organization or four-section systems of some Australian Aboriginal peoples. The Juang and possibly other tribes have a system of generation moieties in which Ego's generation is linked with those of his grandparents and grandchildren in opposition to the set formed by those of his parents and children. This impinges on both stereotyped behavior and marriage choices: joking is only allowed with members of one's own moiety, which is also that from which one's spouse must come (and even then there are numerous exceptions in both regards), while avoidance or respect in behavior and avoidance of marriage and sexual relations is enjoined toward members of the opposite moiety.

Political Organization. The elected government *gram panchayat* was introduced in this region soon after Independence in 1947, but it often has to compete with the traditional village assembly or *panchayat*. This consists of the headman, other officials, and typically household heads at least, if not all males in the village. It is unusual but not unknown (e.g., among the Santal) for women to participate in decision making, though they are often called to give evidence in disputes. The headmanship and other offices (assistant headman, messenger, etc.) are mostly hereditary in the male line, though there may be an elective element in the choice, and the eldest son can always be replaced if believed to be unsuitable. Village headmen are no more than first among equals, for they have to consult the panchayat on all important matters and are removable for misconduct or incompetence. In Chota Nagpur, though not Koraput, villages are often grouped into federations (often called *pirh*), which may have originated as regional clan councils, especially since their main concern is breaches of the rule of clan exogamy. There is scarcely any institutional expression of tribal unity today (though some tribes had kingdoms or at least tribal assemblies in the past), and tribal identity is now only a matter of language or perhaps a common origin myth. Sovereignty and most authority now lie with the Indian government.

Social Control and Conflict.   The old sanction of expulsion from the community (*bitlaha*) has fallen into disuse, and fines, along with provision of a feast for the panchayat or even the whole village, are now the common penalties. Most conflicts concern land rights or marriage. Resort to violent direct action by an aggrieved party is by no means uncommon, though long-term feuding is less marked than among the neighboring Dravidian-speaking Kond, for example.

Religion and Expressive Culture

Religious Beliefs.   Hinduism is an influence, though the Munda are not among the main guardians of Hindu traditions as followed by the Brahmans. The great deity, as protector and judge—sometimes identified with the sun (e.g., Kharia Dharam, Remo Singi-Arke, the Singbonga of the Munda, Santal, etc.), sometimes depicted as a "diluted version" of Hindu gods (e.g., Mahadeo, Bhagwan)—should normally be distinguished from the creator (Munda Haram, Santal Marang Buru), especially since the former typically destroyed men through fire or flood in order to recreate them whole and pure; sometimes, however, the two deities are linked rather like the different incarnations of Hindu gods. There are in all tribes numerous spirits (called *bonga* in Chota Nagpur), both benevolent and malevolent. They include agricultural gods and goddesses, spirits of trees, hills, forests, the village, village boundaries, ancestral spirits (especially malevolent if uncared for or allowed to wander rather than being "brought back" to the hearth after their funeral), other household and lineage deities (some secret), clan deities, deities associated with snakes, tigers, monkeys, and other wild animals, the ghosts of women dead in childbirth or pregnancy, the ghosts of suicides or people killed by tigers, and shamans' tutelaries. Christians are in a minority in most tribes, though their proportion approaches 50 percent among the Kharia. There are hardly any Muslims.

Religious Practitioners.   Most tribes have both priests, concerned with village rituals and life-crisis rites, and shamans, concerned with illness, malevolent spirits, divining the fate of the dead, divining reincarnation, etc. Usually there is one of each to every village, though only the priest, not the shaman, sits on the village panchayat. Unlike the priests, whose offices are basically hereditary in the male line, shamans "emerge" by demonstrating their powers, becoming possessed, etc. Sometimes priests and shamans come from different tribes. Some shamans are female, but no priests. In most tribes domestic ritual is performed by male household heads.

Ceremonies.   The most important life-cycle rites are those concerned with birth, marriage, and death. Initiation and puberty are usually much less marked, if at all, and it is marriage, if not parenthood, which really makes one a full adult member of the tribe, with the right to sit on the panchayat, etc. There are also numerous agricultural rites (fertility, sowing, transplanting, harvesting), as well as rites to promote success in the hunt (usually in March), to safeguard the village against disease and other misfortune, to honor the supreme deity and clan deities, etc. Tribals often imitate, or take part in, local Hindu festivals.

Arts.   On the whole, the Munda are not renowned for artistic expression, though there are some exceptions, such as the wood carvings of the Kharia and Sora and the wall paintings of the Gadaba and Sora, mostly done for a ritual purpose.

Medicine.   Illness is attributed to the actions of malevolent spirits, who may be ancestors who have not been sufficiently appeased, or to the temporary withdrawal of soul substance from the body, etc. Shamans are frequently called in to divine the cause, often with the aid of their tutelary spirits, and to effect a cure through the sacrifice of a fowl, goat, or other animal.

Death and Afterlife.   There is no particular delay in disposing of the dead. Whether cremation or burial is followed depends on the tribe; the inauspicious dead (accidents, suicides, very young infants, etc.) are usually disposed of in a different manner from "normal" deaths; they are buried where cremation is the norm or buried with the opposite orientation from a normal burial. The person generally has at least two souls, sometimes more (e.g., a Juang has five). One is linked to the personality of the deceased and has to be "brought back" from the funeral ground to join the ancestors behind the domestic hearth. The other—commonly called *jiv*, really another term for "soul substance"—is usually reincarnated in a same-sex agnatic descendant, preferably a grandchild related in the direct line, though sometimes it is a collateral ascendant who is reincarnated, especially if there are several siblings. A person is usually given the name of the ancestor deemed to have been reincarnated in him or her.

See also Bhuiya; Bondo; Kol; Korku; Santal; Sora

Bibliography

Elwin, Verrier (1955). *The Religion of an Indian Tribe*. Bombay: Oxford University Press.

McDougal, Charles (1963). *The Social Structure of the Hill Juang*. Ann Arbor: University Microfilms.

Orans, Martin (1965). *The Santal: A Tribe in Search of a Great Tradition*. Detroit: Wayne State University Press.

Yamada, Ryuji (1970). *Cultural Formation of the Mundas*. Tokyo: Tokai University Press.

ROBERT PARKIN

Muslim

ETHNONYMS: Mahommedan, Mohammedan, Moslem, Musulman

Three countries in South Asia are among the largest Muslim nations: Bangladesh has about 98 million Muslims, India about 95 million, and Pakistan about 107 million. The entire subcontinental total can be estimated in 1989 as including about 301 million Muslims.

The first Muslims to reach this area from Arabia came in

A.D. 711, but while there were several other Muslim incursions from Persia and central Asia too in the succeeding 1,000 years it must not be thought that the huge numbers of Muslims living in the subcontinent today are all the descendants of invaders. The great majority of them are descendants of Hindus who were converted to Islam in the Middle Ages. This is important, for it goes some way toward explaining why the Islam of India, Pakistan, and Bangladesh is culturally different from and rather more tolerant of heterodoxy than the Islam of Arabia or Iran. While South Asian Muslims are in general orthodox believers, mostly of the Sunni sect (the party of Abu-Bakr), those aspects of their daily lives not directly related to religion tend to be more like the cultural practices of their Hindu neighbors than of their coreligionists in the Near East. And their languages are those of the regions where they live—Bengali, Urdu, etc.—not Arabic or Persian. Classical Arabic is studied, of course, by everyone who reads the Quran, for this holy book is not used in translation anywhere in South Asia.

South Asian Islamic religious practices are in no essentials different from those of Arabia or Iraq. Tradition states that Islam is built on five things: testimony that there is no god but Allah and that Mohammed is his apostle; prayer five times daily; giving alms for the poor (_zakat_); pilgrimage to Mecca (_hajj_); and fasting during the month of Ramadan. All this is fundamental in South Asia; but other aspects of Muslim society there are distinctively Indian. Even in those states—preeminently the Mogul Empire (1526–1858)—that were ruled and administered by Muslims in the past, the majority of the population always remained Hindu: they could hardly be offered the orthodox choice of conversion or death. Nor could these people be excluded from the army, the administration, education, or literature and other arts. Instead they commonly played their parts in what was always a multireligious society.

This can still be seen in microcosm in the innumerable villages having both Hindu and Muslim castes (perhaps with Sikhs or Christians too). The different religious communities share a common modus vivendi that allows them to interact with each other socially and economically while following their distinct religious practices separately.

Islam is an egalitarian religion in the sense that all believers are equal before God. But against this it may be argued that, from an outsider's point of view, Muslim women suffer certain disabilities—restrictions of freedom of movement, freedom of choice in marriage, freedom to divorce a spouse with the ease that men can, and freedom to become educated and pursue careers. Yet these strictures hold true also for all other non-Muslim communities of South Asia, with the modern exceptions of Christian and Parsi women. Muslims themselves see purdah and other restrictions placed on female activities as protective and thus in the best interests of the women themselves.

Despite the doctrine of equality and brotherhood in Islam, one finds that Muslim society in South Asia is in fact different from that of the Near East in one crucial respect, the existence of a caste hierarchy. Such divisions no doubt have persisted from the earlier Hindu caste society. Even the four-part _varna_ categories of Hindu society are roughly paralleled among the Muslims. Thus the highest category includes four castes of Near Eastern origin: Sayyid, Shaikh, Mughal, and

Pathan. Below them rank the Muslim Rajputs who will not marry above or below their own rank in Muslim society. Third is a group of occupational castes who again marry only people of equal rank. At the bottom of the hierarchy are Muslim sweepers, people whose ancestry presumably traces back to Hindu Untouchables. Even in Pakistan, where very few Hindus exist today, this caste-organized sort of society is still the model.

Perhaps no case emphasizes the Indianness of Muslim society more than that of the Mapillas (Moplahs) of northern Kerala. For while in Arab lands the family is patrilocal and indeed patriarchal, here is a case of a Muslim caste which, like neighboring Hindu castes, is both matrilineal and matrilocal. Something similar is to be found on the Laccadive (Lakshadweep) Islands too. Elsewhere in South Asia patriliny and patrilocality are the Muslim norm. Parallel-cousin marriage is practiced widely and is also found among Muslims of the Near East and North Africa. But cross-cousin marriage, so common among Hindus of southern India, is also widespread among the Muslims, although many take a spouse who is not a close relative at all.

The legacy of Islamic civilization is evident throughout the land, and most visibly so in the architecture of the Taj Mahal and many dozens of other Mogul monuments. Islamic science and medicine left their mark too, in a land where both disciplines were already well developed hundreds of years before the birth of Mohammed. At four points in northern India, including New Delhi, one can still see the huge astronomical observatories (_jantar mantar_) that Muslim scholars under the Maharaja Jai Singh II erected early in the eighteenth century. Even more pervasive was Arab-Persian medical knowledge, still widely in use as the Unani ("Greek") school of medicine. Large professional armies were introduced by the state. Mogul law and administration, first developed in India in the sixteenth century on the basis of four already established schools of Muslim jurisprudence, served as the basis for the British administration of India too. Persian was indeed the language of law courts and the civil service early in the British period. Painting, jewelry, calligraphy, and other minor arts were introduced by Persians and Turks. North Indian cuisine owes much to its Persian ingredients and methods of preparation. Muslim female dress has been widely adopted by Hindu women, for example in Punjab and Rajasthan.

Even in the religious sphere it is evident that Islamic mysticism (i.e., Sufism) had a wide impact on Hindu faith and literature: a medieval sect seeking immediate experience of God rather than academic understanding, Sufism in north India affected the rise of Hindu _bhakti_ (devotional) cults and the special worship of Krishna. Poetry, in the hands of such great Indian masters as Kabir (1440–1518), brought mystic insights from Sufism to the attention of a wide Hindu and Muslim public. Historical writing too was something that the Ghorid Turks introduced to India, starting a tradition that continued through the Mogul historians to the British, French, and South Asian historians of modern times. Sanskrit, Tamil, and other literatures that long predated the Muslim impact never managed to produce a tradition of historical writing that was distinct from epic poetry.

No theological originality marked the Islam of medieval India. Aside from the politic fiction of regarding Hindus as "people of the Book" (and thus, like Jews, Christians, and Zoroastrians, as eligible for the status of "protected unbelievers"), Muslim rulers and teachers propounded nothing in India that would have seemed out of place to the Sunni faithful in the Near East. Peter Hardy has succinctly summarized the ten fundamentals of Islamic belief as introduced to India:

1. God is One, without partners.
2. He is utterly transcendent, possessing no form and escaping all definition.
3. He is the Almighty Creator.
4. He knows and ordains everything that is.
5. God is all-powerful and in whatever he ordains, he cannot be unjust (that is, human concepts of justice and injustice cannot be applied to him).
6. The Quran is eternal.
7. Obedience to God is binding upon man because he so decreed it through his prophets.
8. Belief in the Prophet's divine mission is obligatory upon all.
9. Belief in the Day of Judgment is obligatory as revealed by the Prophet.
10. Belief in the excellence of the Prophet's companions and the first four caliphs is required by authentic tradition.

See also Mappila; Mogul; Sayyid; Sheikh

Bibliography

Ahmad, Aziz, ed. (1969). An Intellectual History of Islam in India. Islamic Surveys, no. 7. Edinburgh: University Press.

Ahmad, Imtiaz, ed. (1973). Caste and Social Stratification among Muslims in India. New Delhi: Manohar Publications. 2nd ed. 1978.

Ahmad, Imtiaz, ed. (1981). Ritual and Religion among Muslims in India. New Delhi: Manohar Publications.

Basham, A. L. (1975). A Cultural History of India. Oxford: Clarendon Press.

Eglar, Zekiye (1960). A Punjabi Village in Pakistan. New York and London: Columbia University Press.

Hardy, Peter (1958). "Part Four: Islam in Medieval India." In Sources of Indian Tradition, edited by William de Bary et al., 367–528. New York and London: Columbia University Press.

Qadir, Abdul (1937). "The Cultural Influences of Islam." In The Legacy of India, edited by G. T. Garratt, 287–304. Oxford: Clarendon Press.

Titus, Murray T. (1959). Islam in India and Pakistan. Calcutta: YMCA Publishing House.

Zaehner, R. C. (1969). Hindu and Muslim Mysticism. New York: Schocken Books.

PAUL HOCKINGS

Nagas

ETHNONYMS: none

Orientation

Identification. The designation "Naga" is applied to the numerous Indo-Mongoloid tribes living in the hill country at the convergence of the borders of India and Myanmar (Burma). Of these tribes, the following have received coverage in anthropological literature: the Kacha, the Angami, the Rengma, the Lhote, the Sema, the Ao, the Konyak, the Chang, the Sangtam, the Yachumi, the Tukomi, the Naked Rengma, the Tangkhul, and the Kalyo-kengyu or "slated-house men." The name "Naga" was first given to these tribal groups by the Ahoms in Assam and other neighboring peoples (e.g., early Indo-Aryans, Kamarupa and Bengali Mongoloids, as well as the Assamese Ahoms) occupying the regions immediately adjacent to the districts in which the Naga are found. The derivation of the name "Naga" is not known with any degree of certainty. According to John Henry Hutton, the most likely explanation is that it is the result of the European lengthening of the Assamese word naga, "naked" (Sanskrit nagna). Hutton also cites possibilities proposed by others for the meaning of the word, including "hill man" (from Hindustani nag, "mountain") and "people" (from nok, an Eastern Naga word of the same meaning). The Naga did not initially adopt this appellation; individual tribes preferred the use of their respective self-designations. It was not until nationalistic fervor grew with the decline of British imperial hegemony and the resultant advent of increased Indian authority over the Naga homeland that the name "Naga" gained widespread acceptance among the various tribes. Thus it was used in the names of the political organizations of the mid-twentieth century that championed the cause of Naga independence from India (i.e., the Naga National Council, which declared independence from India in 1947, and the Naga Peoples Convention, whose efforts resulted in the formation of the state of Nagaland in 1963). In this summary, the focus is on the Angami, with additional information provided selectively for other Naga tribes.

Location. The locus of Naga culture is the hill country of northeast India between Assam's Brahmaputra Valley to the west and the Myanmar (Burma) border to the east. It is a steeply ridged and densely forested area bordered by the states of Arunachal Pradesh on the north and Manipur on the south. The approximate geographic coordinates of the region are 24° 00' to 27° 30' N and 93° 00' to 95° 00' E.

Demography. The 1981 census of the state of Nagaland recorded a population of 774,930, three-quarters being Nagas. But Nagas live also in Arunachal Pradesh, Assam, Manipur, and Myanmar (Burma). In 1971 India had a total of 467,720 Nagas. Figures from 1982 record the following population estimates by tribe: 75,000 Ao Nagas, 18,000 Chang Nagas, 85,000 Konyak Nagas, 11,000 Maring Nagas, 21,000 Phom Nagas, 10,000 Rengma Nagas, 15,000 Rongmei Nagas, and 26,000 Zeme (Sema) Nagas.

Linguistic Affiliation. The Naga are characterized by a linguistic diversity that directly parallels their tribal diversity.

There are about as many Naga dialects as there are Naga tribes. The lingua franca of the state of Nagaland is Naga Pidgin (also known as Nagamese, Kachari Bengali, or Bodo) and is particularly prevalent in Kohima District. There are some twenty-seven known Naga dialects, all part of the Tibeto-Burman Family, which is itself part of the Sino-Tibetan Phylum. These include Angami Naga, Ao Naga, Chang Naga, Chokri Naga, Kheza Naga, Khiamngan Naga, Khoirao Naga, Konyak Naga, and many others.

History and Cultural Relations

While folk traditions regarding the history of the various Naga tribes abound, scholarly consensus has not been reached concerning their origin. Generally speaking, very little is known of the origin of any of the Mongoloid groups whose southwesterly migration brought them ultimately to the sub-Himalayan region and northeastern India (e.g., the Bondos and the Garos). Their presence is attested in these areas as early as the tenth century B.C. What is known is that these tribes spoke Tibeto-Burman dialects and that it is probable that their original homeland was in the region between the Huang-Ho and Yangtze (Ch'ang) rivers in northwestern China. These peoples came in successive migratory waves for several centuries (after the invasions of the Aryans in western India). The geographic extent of these migrations was quite considerable; Aryan-Mongoloid contact took place in the centuries that followed. The Mongoloid tribes were not homogeneous. Their languages, social structures, and cultures were diverse, and in the early centuries of the Common Era they began extensive expansion, from their initial settlements in the Irawadi and Chindwin river regions in northern Myanmar (Burma), throughout Assam, the Cachar Hills, and the Naga Hills. From the thirteenth century onward, the Ahoms—rulers of Assam from 1228 until the British annexation of the province in 1826—had extensive cultural contact with various Naga tribes. The nature of the relationship between these tribes and the Ahoms ranged from cooperative to antagonistic. Naga tribes living near the plains paid annual tribute to Ahom rulers as a sign of allegiance, for which the Nagas were given revenue-free lands and fisheries. These were granted with the understanding that the Naga would refrain from raids in the plains areas. Trade and commerce were also extensive, with the Nagas trading salt (a particularly important medium of exchange), cotton, medicinal herbs, ivory, bee's wax, mats, and _daos_ (adzes) for Assamese rice, cloth, and beads. At times, northern Ahom raiders attacked Naga villages, taking booty and demanding tribute. However, these incursions did not establish lasting Assamese rule over the Naga Hills region. The Naga retained their independence until the British annexation in the early nineteenth century. The British added Assam to the East India Company's territories in 1820. In 1832 they attempted to annex Naga country but met with sustained and effective guerrilla resistance from Naga groups, particularly the Angami tribe. The British responded by sending approximately ten military expeditions into Naga territory between 1835 and 1851. Guerrilla activity continued unabated and British posts were subsequently established in the Angami region. This marked an important point in the process of Nagaland annexation. A unified Angami response was mounted in 1878 with raids on British forces undertaken by villages and village clusters. The impe-

rial response involved the burning of offending villages. Angami resistance eventually met with failure and they eventually became an administered tribe under British rule. With the subjugation of this region, the extension of alien rule throughout Nagaland soon followed, further widening the cultural gap between the Naga and other hill peoples and the Indian inhabitants of the lowlands. British treatment of the Naga was favorable. They allowed no Indian to function as administrator of the hill districts and attempted to prevent exploitation of the hill peoples by plains folk. Christian missionary activity soon followed British annexation, with American Baptists assuming the lead. Rapid progress in conversion was made. Increased literacy and a growing sense of Naga solidarity—for which the official organ of expression was the Naga National Council (NNC)—resulted in the NNC's claim for regional independence in 1947. The departure of the British and the emergence of Indian self-rule made Naga political autonomy within a sovereign India a negotiable possibility. Total independence for the Naga homeland, however, was an impossibility. Violence erupted in Nagaland in 1955 as Indian forces tried to quell Naga secession efforts, and in 1956 the NNC declared the existence of the Federal Government of Nagaland. Conflict continued in spite of efforts to satisfy the call for Naga political freedom by the granting of statehood (a cause championed by the Naga Peoples Convention). In 1963 the efforts of this organization and the segment of the Naga populace which it represented resulted in the formation of the state of Nagaland. In spite of this action, hostilities continued. Under the sponsorship of the Baptist Church, a peace commission was formed and a cease-fire declared between the Nagaland federal government and the government of India on 24 May 1964. The cease-fire lasted until 1 September 1972 when an attempt on the life of the chief minister of Nagaland resulted in the Indian government's termination of the cease-fire and banning of the NNC. Armed resistance by the NNC continued into the 1970s and was not suppressed until the Shillong Accord was signed by representatives of the Indian government and the Nagaland federal government in November 1975. Isolated pockets of resistance persisted into the late 1970s, but effective resistance to Indian hegemony has since ceased. One very small Naga underground antigovernment operation existed in exile in Burma in the 1980s, but its influence in Nagaland at that time was minuscule.

Settlements

Naga villages are autonomous units situated on hilltops. The average elevation of the villages is between 900 and 1,200 meters. Because of the mountainous terrain and the threat of invasion by neighboring tribes, these small villages were originally intended to be self-sufficient and secure. Consequently early explorers reported that Naga villages were heavily fortified. However, with the cessation of both intertribal conflict and outside interference (chiefly from British and Indian forces), the need for security and the degree of village fortification has lessened considerably. Norms for construction varied somewhat within the constituent Naga tribes, yet a few general observations may be made. Villages have one or more entrances that were once guarded heavily and, at times, booby-trapped. Village fortifications included large wooden doors (latched from the inside of the village and hewn from a single piece of wood), pitfalls, and ditches filled with *panjis* (sharply pointed bamboo stakes of varying lengths and widths). Stone walls (whose thickness may reach some 3 meters) surround Angami villages. Ao villages are surrounded by fences composed of wooden stakes and reinforced with panjis. Villages are approached by narrow paths overhung with thorny growth and are constructed so that they must be traversed by walking single file. During time of war, roads leading to Angami villages would be studded with pegs (driven into the ground) to prevent attack. Paths leading to Ao villages were often paved with rough stones near the village gate. There are also roads leading from the village to the terraced fields and *jhum* land that the Naga use as farmland. Jhum is land cultivated by the clearing and burning of an area of jungle, which is then farmed for two years and subsequently allowed to return to jungle. An individual living in the village maintains a close attachment to the land of the village and to the family, clan, or village quarter (the *khel*). The khel (an Assamese word for an exogamous group that corresponds most closely to the Angami word *thino* and the Ao word *muphy*) is responsible for land cultivation, and each village is divided into several khels. The division of a village into khels is based largely on geography, but speakers of the same language, members of the same clan, or groups of immigrants (whose migration to the village may have taken place after the village's establishment) might occupy the same khel. Materials used in house construction vary somewhat among the Naga tribes. Angami practices contain many of the norms found in other Naga tribes and serve as an appropriate control group. A typical Angami house is a one-story structure with leveled earth used as flooring. It is from 10 to 20 meters in length and from 6 to 12 meters in width. Material used in home roofing is determined by individual status in the village, and there are four such degrees. A first-degree house may be roofed with thatching grass, a second-degree house with bargeboards, a third-degree house with bargeboards and *kika* (house horns), and a fourth-degree house with wooden shingles and kika (which differ at times in shape and placement on the house). The interior of each house contains three compartments. The front room (*kiloh*) is half the length of the house. Paddy is stored here in baskets along one or both walls and the room is furnished with a bench (*pikeh*) for rice pounding. The second compartment (*mipu-bu*) is separated by a plank partition containing a doorway. It is here that the hearth is located (consisting of three stones embedded in the ground to form a stand for cooking containers). This room also serves as sleeping quarters, and beds (raised ½ or 1 meter from the ground) are found here. The third compartment, 1 meter or so in depth and extending the entire width of the house, is the *kinutse*, where the liquor vat is located. This room also contains the rear entrance to the house. The house is usually home to no more than five persons. Houses are irregularly arranged in an Angami village, though there is a supposition that the Angami house should face east. Each house has an open space in front of it and houses are connected by irregular paths. Small gardens are frequently made near houses and may contain maize or mustard. Nearly every Angami village has an open space that serves as a meeting place and ceremonial locus for all of the village inhabitants. This area may also contain plinths for sitting made of stone masonry or wood. These stations (which often surmounted

village walls or other high points in the village and could rise as high as 9 meters) may have originally been used as posts for watchers whose purpose was to warn of impending enemy attack. The *morung* (dormitory, which serves as guardhouse and clubhouse for single men) is an important part of most Naga villages. However, it does not assume a place of prominence in Angami villages, some of which have no morung in the traditional sense; the house so designated is occupied by a family while simultaneously being recognized as the village morung. Villages are given names based on peculiar features of the village site, the memory of an ancient settlement that once stood where the village now stands (and which its current occupants wish to commemorate), particular events in the history of the village, or the whim of those living there.

Economy

Subsistence and Commercial Activities. Lhotas, Semas, Aos, and other Naga tribes use jhum cultivation almost exclusively. The Angami have a diversified agricultural system that involves jhum cultivation and terracing (steep hillsides are arranged in terraces, or *panikhets*, which are flooded and used as rice fields). Terraces are fed by channels (bearing water from streams) and hollow bamboo irrigation pipes. Crops are grown for consumption and sale. Rice and millet are the main staples. Additional crops grown are Job's tears, maize, great millet (*Sorghum vulgare*), beans, oil seeds, gourds, cucumbers, chilies, spinach, mustard, and *kachu* (a taro, *Colocasia antiquorum*). Cotton and jute for clothing, thatching grass for house construction, wood for housing and fuel, and bamboo are also grown. Agricultural implements include the following: ax (*merre*), spade or hoe (*keju*), mattock (*sivu*), rake (*paro*), hoe (*saro*), sickle (*zupfino*), and the marking stake (*kethi-thedi*) used for the marking of jungle or thatch for cutting or to prevent crop misfortune resulting from complimentary remarks about their condition. Domestic animals include: gayals (for trade), cows (for meat and trade), gayal/cow hybrids, pigs, dogs (for meat and hunting), cats (in limited number for food and magicoreligious purposes), fowl, bees, and goats. Hunting for food and sport is known among the Angami, frequent targets including serows (mountain goats), wild dogs, and deer. The usual hunting implements are spears and guns. Fishing by the use of poison, while frequent among many Naga tribes, is limited in use among the Angami. Iron, conch shells, Assamese *chabili* (carving knives used by the Ao), and barter were used as currency before the arrival of the British rupee.

Industrial Arts. Angami industrial arts include the following: the manufacture of black, blue, scarlet, pale terra-cotta, and yellow cloth (made of cotton, a species of nettle called *wuve*, or a species of jute called *gakeh*); blacksmithing (particularly the making of iron spear heads, brass wire, and brass earrings); the making of clay pots (a specialty confined to certain villages); basketry; the fashioning of bamboo mats; carving and woodwork; work in hard substances (e.g., shells, ivory, bone, and horns); the manufacture of musical instruments; and the production of salt (now a rarity among the Angami, but one of the chief products of the Kacha, Sangtams, Tangkhuls, and others).

Trade. The Angami and other Naga tribes trade in beads and other manufactured items with other Naga tribes and with their Assamese neighbors. The Ao trade _pan_, cotton, chilies, ginger, gourds, mats, and the gum of the _liyang_ tree to obtain salt and dried fish from traders in the plains. These commodities are then traded to the Phoms and Changs in exchange for pigs and fowl. The Ao also trade in wild tea seed with plains dwellers. Certain Ao villages grow cotton, the surplus of which is traded in the plains for salt. The decrease in intertribal conflict and the general political stabilization of the hill country in the late 1970s brought increased opportunities for trade.

Division of Labor. Weaving and cooking are the exclusive province of women among the Angami and the Ao, while hunting and warfare are men's activities. Agriculture and trade are carried on by members of both sexes. Among the Tangkhul, women manage most domestic affairs including the raising of children, the weaving of cloth (and the teaching of this art to female offspring), the storage and preparation of food, the brewing of rice beer and rice wine (_zam_), the drying of tobacco, the feeding of pigs, fowl, and cattle, the carrying of water, and the pounding of rice. Women also participate in agricultural tasks (e.g., jhuming). Among the Konyak, a husband is recognized as head of the household and the owner of the family home (since it is constructed on a site that belongs to his lineage). He is responsible for the upkeep of the house, its granaries, and its furnishings. The purchase of metal and wooden implements and baskets are his duties. The preparation of food and the weaving of textiles not purchased from other villages are the responsibilities of Konyak wives. Men claim personal ownership of implements associated with their activities (weapons, tools, etc.) as do women (cooking utensils, looms, textiles, etc.). Men are responsible for rice cultivation and storage while women plant, harvest, and dry taro.

Land Tenure. Among the Angami, individual ownership of terraced fields, wood plantations, gardens, building sites, and most jhum land is allowed. As such, its disposition is at the discretion of the owner. In the case of ancestral land, the seller retains a small parcel in nominal ownership to guard against death or misfortune. In several Angami villages, however, land on which thatching grass and cane (for bridge construction) is grown is the property of kindred, clan, or an entire village.

Kinship

Kin Groups and Descent. Descent among the Angami and all other Naga tribes is patrilineal (although possible evidence exists of the survival of a matrilineal descent system in the village of Kohima). The most distinct social unit is the exogamous clan. Clan loyalties generally supersede loyalties to other social groupings including the khel. Frequently, clans will splinter and new clans form, an indication of their fluid nature. The Angami believe themselves to be descended from two brothers (or cousins) born of the earth. The elder was named Thevo; the younger was named Thekrono. The Kepezoma issued from the elder of the two; the Kepefuma are the offspring of the younger. It is believed that the divisions bearing these names were exogamous originally. After settling into their present country these two exogamous _kelhu_ split, the result being the formation of the exogamous clans (or thino) making up Angami society. Originally exogamous, these thino have given way gradually to subdivisions called

putsa or "kindred" divisions (a more unified body than the thino). The Angami hold the thino and then the putsa responsible for the offenses of individuals. Hence, the putsa is in the process of replacing the thino as the exogamous group in Angami society. Neither kelhu, thino, nor putsa is totemic.

Kinship Terminology. Angami kin terms follow the Omaha terminological system.

Marriage and Family

Marriage. The Angami are monogamous. There are two forms of marriage—one ceremonial, the other nonceremonial. The ceremonial form is desired as a symbol of status and consists of an elaborate ritual involving the services of a marriage broker, the taking of omens, and the negotiation of a marriage-price (usually nominal). The nonceremonial form involves the taking of a woman to the house of a man where they remain _kenna_ (forbidden) for one day. Divorce is allowed and is common. The wife gets one-third of the couple's joint property, exclusive of land. The divorced and widowed are permitted to remarry (though a widowed woman may not remarry into her deceased husband's house). Polygamy is not allowed and women are allowed freedom of choice in the selection of mates. By contrast, the Lhota are polygynous, a husband having as many as three wives. Young girls are preferred and bride-prices are high; they are paid in installments over ten years. Divorce among the Lhota is also common. Arranged marriages are the norm with women having no freedom of choice in the selection of a spouse. A husband may also allow his brother or nearest relative on his father's side to have conjugal access to his wife when he is absent for any length of time. The Semas are also polygynous. A Sema husband may have as many as five to seven wives. Sema women have freedom of choice in mate selection. As is the case among the Lhota, marriage-prices are high. Marital residence practices seem to differ among the various Naga tribes. Part of the Angami marriage ceremony involves the giving of land to the new couple by the bridegroom's parents. The new couple work and eat on this land. This may be an indication of a patrilocal postmarital residence pattern. Part of the Ao betrothal process involves the husband's construction of a marital home (location not indicated) with materials gathered from the fields of his parents and the parents of his wife.

Domestic Unit. The typical Angami household contains about five persons: a husband, a wife, two to three children, possibly an aged and widowed parent, and perhaps a younger unmarried brother.

Inheritance. An Angami man cannot leave property to anyone outside of his clan or kindred without considerable complication. If no special provisions have been made, the next male heir within a kindred usually inherits a man's property (after the widow receives her third). The normal practice is for a man to divide his property during his lifetime. When sons marry, they receive their portions. When the father dies, the youngest son inherits all property including the father's house. At this time, the best field must be given to the eldest son in exchange for another field. This and all procedures governing inheritance may be modified by verbal agreement. The inheritance of adopted sons is determined at the time of adoption. Land may not be left permanently to daughters. It may be left for the daughter to enjoy during her lifetime, but it returns to the male heirs after her death. Very few exceptions to this general rule are known.

Socialization. After an elaborate postbirth ritual (part of which places the newborn in close relationship with the father's kindred), Angami children are suckled by their mothers for two to three years. Girls' ears are pierced six to twelve months following birth, while those of boys are pierced as soon as they are able to speak. At 4 to 6 years of age, an Angami boy leaves his mother's side of the house (where he has slept up to this point) and moves to his father's side of the house to sleep. From this point on he is considered a member of the male community and no longer remains with women when sex separation takes place at *gennas* (magicoreligious rites and ceremonies). Mothers are responsible for the upbringing of children and a nuclear family structure obtains. The Angami morung (young men's house), which functions as a guardhouse, clubhouse, and center of several communal activities in most Naga tribes (with the exception of the Sema), is of ceremonial importance only; it does not serve as an actual residence for young unmarried men (as it does among the Ao, for example). Girls' houses (found among the Ao, Memi, and other tribes) are also located in some Angami villages. Naga children generally share in all responsibilities assumed by their parents. The socialization of Naga girls includes instruction by their mothers in weaving, an industrial art belonging exclusively to women. Boys and girls are allowed a considerable amount of premarital sexual freedom in most Naga tribes.

Sociopolitical Organization

Social Organization. The basic Angami social unit is the exogamous patrilineal clan (thino), though the clan has been superseded by the kindred (putsa). Individual identity is bound chiefly to these groups. Clan and kindred are responsible for the behavior of constituent members. Social status is reflected in the roofing of houses. Prestige can be attained by the collection of trophies in war and in sponsorship of festivals. Status may also be based on a person's individual clan membership.

Political Organization. A council of elders functions as the administrative authority in a village, and individuals with grievances may voice them at council meetings. Chiefs are also part of the political structure of the village, but the delimitation of their powers varies among the several Naga tribes. The government appoints village officials today. In Angami villages these are called *gaonburas* and their authority and responsibilities are similar to those of the village chieftains (*pehumas*) of the past. The office of the gaonbura is not hereditary. The same was true, in most cases, of that of the pehuma. The gaonbura's major administrative responsibility is the collection of the house tax, though he may also act on behalf of his villagers as a go-between with government officials. The pehuma exercised most influence in the conduct of war, the settlement of disputes within the village being delegated to the elders' council.

Social Control. Conflicts are resolved within Angami villages by a council of elders who discuss matters of dispute among themselves, with the parties involved, and with the general public, until some resolution is reached. Issues centering on tribal custom are usually referred to the older men of a clan. Factual questions are decided by oath, and the authority of the oath (particularly when one party swears by the lives of family and clan members) is rarely questioned.

Conflict. Naga tribes maintained a high degree of isolation from neighboring peoples. Conflict between villages, tribes, and clans was frequent before annexation of the highland regions by the British, as were hostilities between the Naga and the Assamese living in the plains. Head taking was an important feature of warfare among the Naga generally, and weapons included spears, shields, and guns (acquired in large part after the coming of the British). Initial British incursions into Naga-held territories met with substantial resistance. The Angami in particular were actively involved in anti-British resistance, frequently conducting guerrilla raids on British outposts. In time, the conduct of war was augmented by diplomatic efforts to resolve issues of territorial sovereignty and independence. As a result, armed resistance seasoned with diplomacy has been the Naga method of conflict resolution, first with the British colonial authorities and then with the Indian government.

Religion and Expressive Culture

Religious Beliefs. Christianity has taken root in some Naga tribes, but it has by no means eclipsed traditional religious beliefs. The Angami religious system features belief in a number of spirits and supernatural forces associated with the cycle of life. Animate and inanimate objects may be regarded as embodied spirits, and there is a distinction drawn between the gods and the souls of dead humans. Among the vast number of *terhoma* ("deities") the following should be noted: Kenopfu (the creator god); Rutzeh (the giver of sudden death); Maweno (god of fruitfulness); Telepfu (a mischievous god); Tsuko and Dzurawu (husband and wife dwarf gods presiding over wild animals); Metsimo (guardian of the gate leading to paradise); Tekhu-rho (god of tigers); and Ayepi (a god who lives in Angami houses and brings prosperity). Supernatural forces are believed to possess both benevolent and malicious qualities and, when occasion demands, Angami belief provides for prayer to be made to them and for their propitiation or challenge by humans.

Religious Practitioners. Angami religious practitioners include the following: the *kemovo* (who directs public ceremonies and is the repository of historical traditions and genealogical information); the *zhevo* (who functions as integral part of the performance of personal gennas, and who also is called on in times of sickness to advise an appropriate ceremonial course of action to cure the disease); the *tsakro* (an old man who inaugurates the sowing of crops); and the *lidepfu* (an old woman who inaugurates the reaping of crops). All of these practitioners are public functionaries. Other religious specialists, whose realm of activity is confined to the private domain, are known as well. These include: the *themuma*, whose knowledge may range from competence in particular kinds of divination to knowledge of poisons; the *zhumma* ("invulnerables"), who reportedly can be harmed neither by bullet nor spear; the *kihupfuma* (individuals gifted with powers to cause illness and bad fortune); and the *terhope* (women who dream in order to foretell the outcome of various endeavors). A similar hierarchy of practitioners obtains in many other Naga tribes.

Ceremonies. Angami religious life centers on a series of eleven gennas (magicoreligious ceremonies accompanied by behavioral restrictions binding upon community and/or individual) performed during the year. These are connected with agricultural events that affect the life of the community. Gennas of less frequent occurrence include those for war dancing, interclan visitation, and preparation of a new village door. Individual gennas (i.e., those associated with the normal cycle of events in a person's life) include those for birth, marriage, and death. Some seven social gennas may be performed in order to gain status. Miscellaneous gennas for illness, rainmaking, head taking, and hunting may also be performed. Angami religious life also includes the observance of certain restrictions on individual behavior (called *kennas*) and corporate behavior (called *pennas*). The ceremony accompanying the genna (called *nanu*) involves the offering of flesh (part of which is offered to the spirits), the wearing of ceremonial garments, singing, dancing, the pounding of *dhan* (unhusked grain of the rice plant), the abstention from work, and the prohibition of any contact with strangers. Similarity in the structure of rites and ceremonies obtains in other Naga tribes.

Arts. Music and dancing are important components in Angami gennas. Oral literature includes numerous myths and legends (which are also accompanied by song). Images of spirits and gods are lacking in Angami visual art, but the representation of the human form in Angami woodwork is known. Wooden dolls of the human figure in miniature are made and dressed in traditional clothing. Originally these were produced for artistic purposes but their value was perceived by those who produced them, making them subject to sale. Life-size human figures are manufactured and placed over graves. The representation of the human head is a common feature of Angami wood carving (e.g., on village doors, house gables, and wooden bridges), as are the head of the gayal, the pig's head, and an image representing either a human breast or the top of a dhan basket. Proficiency in wood does not obtain among all Naga tribes.

Medicine. Magicoreligious ceremonies are the major cure prescribed for ills among the Angami. In addition to these rites, a number of medicinal herbs are used for their curative properties. The brain of the *khokhe* fish, the bile of the toad, the casts of earthworms, a dog's eyes and hairs, raw eggs, and the marrow of the serow are among the animal parts and by-products used for medicinal purposes by the Angami. Among other Naga tribes (e.g., the Ao), magicoreligious means for the cure of illnesses are also preferred, but the use of plant and animal by-products for medicinal purposes also obtains.

Death and Afterlife. Attitudes toward the burial of the dead vary among the various Naga tribes. The Angami place responsibility for the burial of the dead on the male relatives of the deceased. Burial usually takes place within the village. A grave is prepared either beside one of the village paths or in front of the deceased's house. The body of a man is interred in a coffin covered by a white cloth. With it are buried a fire stick, one or two spears, a dao, a young chicken (alive), and a *gadzosi* seed (placed between the teeth of the corpse). The gadzosi seed is provided so that the deceased's encounter with Metsimo in the afterlife will be a successful one. A woman is buried with a few beads, a new under-petticoat, a reaping hook, a young chicken (live), and the gadzosi seed. Once buried, the coffin is covered with flat stones. Onto the stones is poured the contents of the deceased's ceremonial *kang* ("carrying basket"): seed for wet rice, Job's tears, millet (and every other kind of edible grain), *zu* (rice beer), and the deceased's drinking cup. The grave is then covered with earth and leveled. Atop the grave are placed personal implements once belonging to the deceased. Angami eschatology distinguishes between the fates in the afterlife of those who live good lives and those who do not. The former join the sky god Ukepenopfu, while the latter are condemned to pass through seven existences beneath the Earth. Life with the sky god is presumed to be an extension of earthly life with hunting, headhunting, drinking, and feasting. The major requirement for entry into this blessed state is that one have performed the *zhatho genna* and abstained from unclean meat thereafter. Angami males must struggle with Metsimo on the narrow passage that leads to the gate of the sky god's domain. Failure results in the deceased's being forced to wander between Heaven and Earth as a wandering spirit. Similarities between the Angami and other Naga tribes regarding eschatology do obtain. Belief in the narrow road leading to Paradise is virtually universal among the Naga.

Bibliography

Anand, V. K. (1969). *Nagaland in Transition.* New Delhi: Associated Publishing House.

Elwin, Verrier, ed. (1969). *The Nagas in the Nineteenth Century.* London: Oxford University Press.

Fuchs, Stephen (1973). *The Aboriginal Tribes of India.* New York: St. Martin's Press.

Fürer-Haimendorf, Christoph von (1969). *The Konyak Nagas: An Indian Frontier Tribe.* New York: Holt, Rinehart & Winston.

Fürer-Haimendorf, Christoph von (1976). *Return to the Naked Nagas.* New Delhi: Vikas Publishing House.

Ganguli, Milada (1984). *A Pilgrimage to the Nagas.* New Delhi: Oxford and IBH Publishing Co.

Horam, M. (1977). *Social and Cultural Life of Nagas.* New Delhi: B. R. Publishing Corp.

Hutton, John Henry (1921). *The Sema Nagas.* London: Macmillan. 2nd ed. 1968. London: Oxford University Press.

Hutton, John Henry (1921). *The Angami Nagas.* London: Macmillan. 2nd ed. 1969. London: Oxford University Press.

LeBar, Frank M. (1964). *Ethnic Groups of Mainland Southeast Asia.* New Haven, Conn.: HRAF Press.

Majumdar, D. N. (1944). *Races and Cultures of India.* Allahabad: Kitabistan. 4th ed. 1961. New York: Asia Publishing House.

Maloney, Clarence (1974). *Peoples of South Asia*. New York: Holt, Rinehart & Winston.

Maxwell, Neville George Anthony (1973). *India and the Nagas*. Minority Rights Group Report no. 17. London. Rev. ed. 1980. *India, The Nagas, and the North-East*.

Mills, James Philip (1922). *The Lhota Nagas*. London: Macmillan. Reprint. 1979. New York: AMS Press.

Mills, James Philip (1926). *The Ao Nagas*. London: Macmillan. 2nd ed. 1973. London: Oxford University Press.

Mills, James Philip (1937). *The Rengma Nagas*. London: Macmillan. Reprint. 1979. New York: AMS Press.

HUGH R. PAGE, JR.

Nambudiri Brahman

ETHNONYMS: Bhattadiripad, Namboodiri Brahman, Namboodiripad

Orientation

The Nambudiri Brahmans are one of a number of caste groups living in Kerala State, India. Most of the description given in this article refers to Nambudiri society as it existed circa 1900. Traditionally, they were a wealthy aristocratic landed caste group of highest ritual and secular status, who maintained their position by the practice of primogeniture and a complex relationship with lower-ranking matrilineal castes including the Nayars. After the advent of the British toward the end of the eighteenth century they gradually lost their political power. They rejected Western education early on and, apart from those few who took to communism, became entrepreneurs in the second half of the twentieth century, or managed to get an advanced education, the majority in the 1990s are living in much-reduced circumstances.

Traditionally the Nambudiri Brahmans have lived on the southwest coast of India, in what is now the state of Kerala. (For a description of the area see the article on Nayars.) The Nambudiri Brahmans today make up less than 1 percent of the Hindu population of Kerala, but their status as the former elite of the state makes them important to document. The Nambudiri Brahmans speak Malayalam, a language belonging to the Southern Branch of the Dravidian Family of languages.

History and Cultural Relations

The early history of Kerala is very complex and there are many problems remaining to be resolved by historians. The history of the Nambudiri community still presents a number of puzzles. According to the legendary *Keralolpatty* (a traditional account of Kerala history, set down in writing in the eight-eenth century), Brahmans were brought to the southwest coast of India by the sage-warrior Parasurama, and they settled in thirty-two *grammam* (from Sanskrit *grama*, "community") in the South Kanara District of Karnataka State and in thirty-two grammam in what is now Kerala. Those who settled in Kerala are said to be Nambudiri Brahmans. Each grammam had its own temple and its own set of authorities for religious and secular law and its enforcement. Most of the grammam were localized geographically with their *illams* (large manorial homes) located within a 16- to 40-kilometer radius of the temple. However, the territory of one grammam might overlap that of another, as they were not communities in the usual sense. There is considerable argument among historians as to when the Nayars became matrilineal, some stating that this started in the tenth century A.D. and others seeing it as being rooted either in an earlier tribal matrilineal system or perhaps in an earlier bilateral system such as is found in Sri Lanka. There is some evidence from their customs and from physical characteristics that the Nambudiris came from outside the area.

The heyday of the Nambudiri system was between the twelfth and the seventeenth centuries. The majority of modern historians hold that they came to Kerala between the first and fourth centuries A.D., though there are some—such as E. K. Pillai—who believe they came later. Prior to the British, in some parts of Trichur Taluk (subdistrict) of Cochin State, which had the densest Nambudiri concentration, the area was ruled by the heads of the Vadakunnathan and Perumanam temple boards. Where they did not rule directly, or where their rule was weak, they would align themselves with different matrilineal rulers. When the Zamorin of Calicut was expanding his kingdom, he needed the allegiance of the heads of the two largest temple boards of Cochin to capture power. When the Maharaja of Cochin recaptured part of his kingdom, he had to break the power of the Nambudiri illams in Trichur.

Apart from their direct political control, Nambudiris were often able to exercise considerable indirect power because of their status as the highest spiritual authorities in Kerala.

Settlements

(For general details see the article on Nayars.) The geographic distribution of Nambudiris in Kerala was never completely uniform. Certain areas were noted for containing thick Nambudiri concentrations, particularly in parts of South Malabar and Cochin where they also had the most direct political control. This was the area where the greatest amount of land could be given over to rice cultivation. (With traditional tools and technology, control over paddy land was a major source of wealth.)

Nambudiri Brahmans had the unique role of being considered above and beyond territorial concerns. They would go from one ruler to another and carry messages. They had an essential communication function for the preservation of the then-existing political system, and they were considered to be good diplomats.

Economy

(For general details on the area see the article on Nayars.) Traditionally, the vast majority of the Nambudiris derived their subsistence from the income of their medium to large landed holdings. They were not expected to participate in the life-crisis ceremonies of castes lower than themselves, apart from the coronations in a few of the ruling houses. They all had at least a few servants in their homes. Some Nambudiris, slightly lower in rank, performed rituals at well-known temples (though many of these also had rituals performed by Embrandiri Brahmans from South Kanara District of Karnataka State and by Pattar Brahmans from Tamil Nadu).

Traditionally, the Nambudiri Brahmans lived off the income from their lands, although a few also worked in large temples. They spent considerable amounts of time learning and reciting Sanskrit _slokas_ and many of them were famous scholars and teachers of the Vedas. They also participated in sacrifices.

Under the traditional land tenure system, the Nambudiri Brahmans held land primarily as the rulers or as a direct grant from a ruler. They did not deal with that land directly, preferring to leave agricultural management to tenants and subtenants. Their land was held as an impartible inheritance by the eldest son, though younger sons and unmarried daughters were eligible to be supported by the income from the property. The land tenure laws passed in the 1920s and 1930s made the Nambudiri property partible. The major land reform law measures passed in the early 1970s plus a series of Supreme court decisions that provided for permanency of tenure for their tenants and gave ownership rights to the lowest rung of tenants have had the effect of causing many of the Nambudiri Brahman households to be severely impoverished.

Kinship

The Nambudiri Brahmans were patrilineal and practiced primogeniture. They were divided into various status groups, the most significant one being the division between the Adhyans and the Asyans. The Adhyans (recognized by the suffix -_pad_ at the end of their names) were the wealthiest and most powerful. There was a tendency for the eight most powerful of the Adhyans to be endogamous. The highest-ranking Asyans were the ones who had the right to recite the Vedas.

Kinship terminology follows a modification of the Dravidian pattern. There is a striking absence of terms to refer to affines not actually living in one's illam, indicating that affinity was not a critical principle of the system. Once a girl was married she was totally amalgamated into her husband's family and used the same terms that he used. The only affines even given a term are the mother's brother and mother's brother's wife. The other significant difference from the rest of south India is the absence of a distinction between cross and parallel cousins. Among Nambudiris both are considered to be similar to one's own brothers and sisters and both are forbidden as marriage partners.

Marriage and Family

Only the eldest son was allowed to take a wife or wives from his own caste. The younger sons either remained celibate or else formed permanent or semipermanent liaisons with women from the somewhat lower matrilineal castes (see the article on Nayars).

Although only the oldest son could marry, he was allowed up to three wives at a time. Girls tended to be married to households within a two- to three-days' walk from their native illam. Postpubertal marriage was most frequent. Dowries were quite high, and getting a girl married was considered a burden to her family. Sometimes a man might take a second wife in exchange in order to save on the dowry for his daughter. After marriage a girl had no rights in her natal home, and whether she was happy or miserable she simply had to bear it. Many Nambudiri women felt that being a Nambudiri woman was the worst fate any human being could have, and they sometimes prayed that no one should ever "be born a Nambudiri woman."

The size and composition of the domestic unit has varied over time. Traditionally it included a man and his wife or wives and their children, his unmarried brothers, and any unmarried sisters that might remain. It was often a three-generation unit with power and authority always vested in the oldest living male. When laws were passed permitting younger sons to marry, households sometimes came to include the wives and children of brothers, though by then these large households had begun to partition.

Traditional inheritance was in the male line and property was kept intact through the rule of primogeniture and impartibility. This has greatly changed since the 1920s and 1930s.

Sociopolitical Organization

(See the article on Nayars for general background information.) When at the end of the eighteenth century the British took over direct political control in Malabar and came to play a major role as advisers in Cochin and Travancore too, the Nambudiris, deprived of their political role but still maintaining their status as religious authorities, withdrew to their estates. They remained aloof, preferring to reemphasize their spiritual sanctity and purity. In the first quarter of the twentieth century some of the Nambudiri youth became involved in the Nambudiri reform movement. Through this activity they became directly involved in politics, with many of the older sons aligning themselves with the Congress party but most of the younger sons and women joining the Communists. The head of the Communist Party of India (Marxist) for the past twenty-five years, E. M. S. Namboodiripad, came out of the earlier Nambudiri reform movement.

Traditionally, social control was exercised through fear and shaming. Traditionally conflicts were handled by the caste elders. A special kind of court was held for females who were even suspected of committing adultery. These courts came to an abrupt end when one Nambudiri woman named sixty-four men (some quite well known) with whom she claimed to have committed adultery. Today, local conflicts are handled by the village _panchayats_ and more serious and wide-reaching matters by the civil authorities.

Religion and Expressive Culture

The Nambudiris are Hindus. The higher-ranking Nambudiris perform _pujas_ (individual worship rituals) and sacrifices in their own homes but do not work as ritual specialists for others. The main _pujaris_ (temple priests) are Tamil Brahmans or Brahmans from South Kanara, though in a few temples there are also Nambudiri or Kerala Brahmans. Kerala has been innovative in providing training and certification for well-trained lower-caste pujaris.

The most important ceremonies celebrated in Kerala among Hindus are Vishu, Onam, and Thiruvathira. In addition, traditionally there were numerous temple festivals, and on occasion Nambudiris were involved in performing important large Vedic sacrifices (Agnicayana), which could take as long as ten days and required months of preparation. Traditionally, no non-Brahmans were supposed to hear the words of the Veda or be present during a Vedic sacrifice. As among all Hindus, there is a strong belief in reincarnation.

See also Nayar

Bibliography

Logan, William (1887). Manual of Malabar. Reprint. 1961. Malabar. 3 vols. Madras: Government Press.

Mencher, Joan (1966). "Kerala and Madras: A Comparative Study of Ecology and Social Structure." Ethnology 5:135–171.

Mencher, Joan (1966). "Namboodiri Brahmans: An Analysis of a Traditional Elite in Kerala." Journal of Asian and African Studies 1:7–20.

Mencher, Joan (1966). "Namboodiri Brahmans of Kerala." Natural History Magazine, May, 15–21.

Mencher, Joan, and Helen Goldberg (1967). "Kinship and Marriage Regulations among the Namboodiri Brahmans of Kerala." Man 2:87–106.

Menon, Ramesh (1991). "The Namboodiris: Traumatic Decline." India Today (15 July): 90–92.

Pillai, Elamkulam P. N. Kujan (1970). Studies in Kerala History. Trivandrum: Privately printed.

JOAN P. MENCHER

Nayaka

ETHNONYMS: Jenu-Koyyo-Shola-Nayakas, Jenu Kurumba, Kattu Naikr, Kattu Nayaka, Naicken, Naiken, Naikr, Sola Nayaka

Orientation

Identification. The Nayaka are a tribal people. Their various names relate to the fact that they live in the forest and collect honey from wild bees' nests: kāṭṭu and sōla mean "forest," while jēnu means "honey." The names were given to them by outsiders. The name "Nayaka" probably originated in Malayalam. They refer to their own people by the phrase nama sonta, which roughly translates as "our family."

Location. The Nayaka live in the Nilgiri Hills in south India, at 11° N and 75° E, on the western jungle slopes, from 1,000 to 300 meters above sea level. The area, called the Wynaad (or Wainad), is divided administratively between the Nilgiris District of Tamil Nadu and the adjoining Malappuram District of Kerala. The Nayaka are scattered there amid other populations in small communities between which there are virtually no ties of any kind. The monsoon is at its height during July, while February is the middle of the dry period.

Demography. The Indian census of 1981 estimated their total number at 1,400. Local communities comprise three to thirty nuclear families each. The average number of children per family is probably about two.

Linguistic Affiliation. The Nayaka language, which the Nayaka call nama baśa, "our language," belongs to the Kannadoid Subgroup of the Nilgiri South Dravidian languages. It contains elements of Kannada, Tamil, and Malayalam, Kannada being predominant. There are linguistic differences between the various Nayaka local communities, reflecting their contact with different neighbors, but not to the point of mutual unintelligibility. Most Nayaka speak in addition to their own language at least one of these three major South Dravidian languages.

History and Cultural Relations

In the past, scholars suggested that the food-gatherer groups of the Nilgiris were the descendants of the powerful Kuruma (Pallavas), who fled to the wild during the ascension of the Cholla dynasty, around the ninth century A.D. More recently scholars have regarded them as the indigenous inhabitants of the area. The Wynaad itself, as part of the Nilgiris, was in the eighteenth century a part of the kingdom of Mysore, ruled by Haidar Ali, and later by his son Tipu Sultan. In 1803, British troops of the East India Company led by the (later) Duke of Wellington won it over. Infected by malaria, the Wynaad was not popular with immigrants, most of whom crossed it and settled higher up the hills; these immigrants included the agriculturalist Badaga in the late seventeenth and eighteenth centuries, the British during the nineteenth century, and after them Indians of various castes and religions. In the 1830s exploration for gold began in the Wynaad, building to a brief but devastating gold rush during the 1880s. In the 1860s some coffee, tea, and rubber plantations were opened; most remained marginal at these low elevations. The effects on the Nayaka varied from place to place. In some localities they took to wage labor as their main source of income. In other areas, they added casual wage labor to their traditional gathering in the forest, barter in forest produce, and labor for agricultural neighbors and forest contractors.

Nayaka, while they do not maintain close contact with Nayaka of other localities, do have close contact with neighboring non-Nayaka populations. They seem to have been in contact with non-Nayaka populations for a long time. They barter forest produce for simple agricultural and manufactured goods, such as tobacco, grain, and metal knives. They occasionally provide labor to their neighbors. They maintain friendly relations with neighboring populations and each party attends the other's festivals.

Settlements

A Nayaka community averages about five clusters of huts. The clusters, which we will call "hamlets", here are located in the jungle, near water sources, at a distance of a few miles from each other. Occasionally there are additional small hamlets at the fringes of the jungle near local Indian villages. The huts vary considerably. The most substantial have a framework constructed of wood on a mud platform. The walls are made of strips of split bamboo resting on a low mud base, leaving a small doorway. The hut has a roof of grass thatch. Occasionally several huts are joined to each other in a row. The more casual huts are simply lean-tos resting on a rock, or on another hut, with no walls. There is a little-used fireplace in each living space, and a few articles lie casually on the ground. Except during the rainy period, people mostly sleep, cook, and eat outside their huts.

Economy

Subsistence and Commercial Activities. The Nayaka know of many species of flora in the forest, whose various parts they utilize for culinary and medicinal purposes, as well as for barter and for fabricating their shelter, tools, and utensils. In the forest they gather roots (mainly of wild yams), nuts, berries, and fruit; they fish; they collect honey from wild bees' nests; occasionally they trap birds; and they sometimes hunt deer with their dogs. They collect forest produce such as soapnuts and spices to sell to their neighbors and to traders from the cities. Nayaka also take up a variety of casual employment, which usually requires expertise acquired through a food-gathering way of life (e.g., clearing jungle paths and guiding hunting expeditions). The nature of these jobs changes in response to changes in the surrounding environment. Viewing the forest as a generous provider of food and all other material requirements, Nayakas are flexible and opportunistic in their choice of occupations, and they frequently shift from one to another. Each family operates independently, and a heterogeneous economy arises around the core of the traditional food gathering, which is highly valued. The Nayaka have no tradition of animal husbandry or cultivation. A few families every now and then acquire a few chickens, or even a cow, which they keep for only a short period. Similarly, every once in a while a few families cultivate small plots of paddy, which they barely maintain and subsequently abandon. Most Nayaka plant some fruit trees near their huts. They keep dogs that feed on leftovers. Their children occasionally adopt as pets young monitor lizards and parrots found in the forest.

Industrial Arts. Nayaka manufacture various containers, baskets, and mats from bamboo and grass for their own use. Occasionally they make simple coconut spoons, wooden pots, and pestles and construct bamboo fences and huts for their non-Nayaka neighbors.

Division of Labor. The Nayaka have little division of labor based on gender. Spouses pursue most subsistence activities together and also share domestic pursuits to a considerable degree. Families, even single adults, are generally self-sufficient.

Land Tenure. Nayaka live and utilize resources wherever they wish to within the territory they occupy.

Kinship

Kin Groups and Descent. All the Nayaka of a local community consider each other kin. In everyday conversation they refer to and address each other by kinship terms. On the whole, families do not cooperate in work, share productive equipment, or exchange gifts; but people are expected to be generally friendly and hospitable toward one another. The Nayaka, though warm and friendly, are highly autonomous. They rarely cooperate with other members of their hamlet, and every six to eighteen months they move to another hamlet. Life-cycle events are celebrated, if at all, by ad hoc aggregates of people within the locality who are invited by the celebrants. The conjugal family is the only corporate and effective group among the Nayaka. Its members share possessions, work, and responsibility for each other. There are no descent groups. The Nayaka attach equal importance to matrilateral and patrilateral kin links.

Kinship Terminology. Nayaka use kinship terms that reflect a Dravidian kinship terminology. In everyday application of kinship terms, they do not strictly maintain the distinctions between affinal and consanguinal relations in the first ascending and first descending generations.

Marriage and Family

Marriage. Nayaka mostly find their spouses for themselves within the local community and sometimes among kin outside it. A courtship takes place, then the couple start sleeping together and establish their hearth, and then they increasingly share subsistence pursuits and domestic chores. There is no formal event to mark the marriage: it gradually emerges and is then publicly recognized. Some marriages, especially for long-standing single persons, are arranged. This is done by a maternal uncle or other relatives, and the spouse is usually from outside the local community. Such a union is sometimes celebrated by a meal that is offered to a small gathering of invitees and passersby. Nayaka express a preference for cross-cousin marriage (perhaps under the widespread Dravidian influence) and secondarily for spouses outside the close circle of relatives. Marriages are monogamous. A new conjugal family is independent and free to choose its place of residence. Some couples reside with the wife's parents during the initial period of marriage. Separation is common during the early years of marriage; it is effected by mutual agreement or by one of the parties leaving the other. A marriage that survives the early years is likely to endure.

Domestic Unit. A man, a woman, and their young offspring constitute the domestic unit and usually sleep, cook, eat, and work together. Single persons, young or old, are temporarily attached to families. Strict separation is maintained between the living spaces of the conjugal family and those of their long- or short-term visitors. The former, especially, keep their separate hearths, near where they sleep, eat their share of the food on their own, and frequently cook it themselves. Nayaka value their independence highly.

Inheritance. A Nayaka is frequently buried with the few possessions he or she used at the time of death. Children and other relatives sometimes take one or two of the deceased's possessions as remembrances. There is no individual ownership or inheritance of land.

Socialization. Young children are greatly indulged. They are rarely scolded or punished. They spend most of their time with their parents, though occasionally they stay with grandparents or older siblings. At about the age of 10, they start visiting other families in the local community, and later beyond it, for increasingly long periods. They become autonomous in their late teens, and they establish their own conjugal partnerships any time from then up to their mid-twenties. They acquire survival skills and knowledge through watching adults and by trial and error; there is no formal instruction.

Sociopolitical Organization

Social Organization. The Nayaka are highly egalitarian and individualistic. They have various leveling mechanisms to prevent the development of inequalities of wealth, power, and prestige. Very few persons maintain friendships, or other binding interpersonal ties, outside their own conjugal family. Cooperation and communication between the highly individuated conjugal families is facilitated by the still-single persons who move between the conjugal families. Conjugal families occasionally cooperate with such single persons in subsistence pursuits. The single persons are important channels of communication within the local community.

Political Organization. The Nayaka have a band society, with no overarching administrative or political organization. Its constituent units are autonomous families and individuals, who aggregate themselves voluntarily into ad hoc, fluid, and open-ended social groupings: the coresidents of a hamlet, for example, or the participants in a celebration. Neither Nayaka society itself, nor any of its local communities, constitutes a political community. There are no offices carrying authority or power. Today, there is external pressure on the Nayaka to organize themselves as a political unit or to appoint representatives.

Social Control. Valuing individual autonomy above all, Nayaka refrain from intervening in other people's affairs; even gossip is rare. When intervention is necessary, they appeal to outside agencies (neighbors or deities).

Conflict. Nayaka prevent conflicts by avoiding cooperation and competition and by moving away from potential confrontation. The few conflicts that occur are mainly over women.

Religion and Expressive Culture

Religious Beliefs. The Nayaka believe in natural spirits that reside on hilltops, in water sources, in high trees, and on the ground. They have added Hindu deities and the deities of neighboring people to their pantheon.

Religious Practitioners. There are a few individuals in each local community who are occasionally possessed by spirits and then mediate between humans and the spirit world. Most are men, but some are women. There are also diviners who can identify the supernatural causes of diseases.

Ceremonies. With the exception of death, which is celebrated quite elaborately, Nayaka barely mark life-cycle events, if at all. A communal celebration is held annually, in several locations in the area. During the celebration offerings are made to the ancestral and natural spirits. Through possession a sort of collective contract is renewed, by which the living undertake to preserve cultural continuity, to keep the "ways of the forefathers," and the deities undertake to preserve physical continuity, safeguarding the living from mortal diseases. The souls of the people who died during the preceding year are joined during the celebration with the other spirits.

Arts. A few individuals play the bamboo flute, or beat a drum, on their own. Only at the annual celebration is there any collective music making. Then dances are held, a band plays music, and a play is performed.

Medicine. Illnesses are classified into those for which a natural cause is obvious and those for which it is not. The former are treated by medicinal plants, known to all; the latter by establishing supernatural causes through divination or possession, and then by making offerings.

Death and Afterlife. A ritual is held in the place where the death occurred; the corpse is buried elsewhere. The spirit of the deceased, dangerous to meet, roams in the forest until it is brought back into the community of spirits during the next annual celebration.

See also Kurumbas

Bibliography

Bird, Nurit (1983a). "Conjugal Units and Single Persons: An Analysis of the Social System of the Food-Gathering Naiken of South India." Ph.D. dissertation, Cambridge University.

Bird, Nurit (1983b). "Wage-Gathering: Socioeconomic Changes, and the Case of the Naiken of South India." In *Rural South Asia: Linkages, Changes, and Development. Collected Papers on South Asia*, edited by Peter Robb, 57–89. London: Curzon Press for the School of Oriental and African Studies, London.

Bird, Nurit (1987). "The Kurumbas of the Nilgiris: An Ethnographic Myth?" *Modern Asian Studies* 24:173–189.

Bird-David, Nurit (1988). "An Introduction to the Naikens: The People and the Ethnographic Myth." In *Blue Mountains: The Ethnography and Biogeography of a South Indian Region*, edited by Paul Hockings, 249–280. New Delhi: Oxford University Press.

Francis, Walter (1908). *Madras District Gazetters: The Nilgiris*. Madras: Superintendent, Government Press.

NURIT BIRD-DAVID

Nayar

ETHNONYM: Nair

Orientation

Identification. The Nayars are one of a number of caste groups living in Kerala State, India. Most of the description given in this article refers to Nayar society as it existed around 1900. Traditionally they were warriors, landowners (who supervised but rarely worked the land), and rulers. Toward the end of the eighteenth century they began to abandon their role as warriors and gradually lost their political power. They took to Western education early on and came to form a significant proportion of the professional and white-collar class by the middle of the twentieth century.

Location. Traditionally Nayars belong to the southwest coast of India, in what is now the state of Kerala. It is a long, narrow area bounded on the west by the Arabian Sea and on the east by the high ranges of the Western Ghats. The area may be divided into (1) a narrow alluvial coastland extending only a few miles from the sea and mostly confined to the area south of Ponnani (the lower two-thirds of the coastline); (2) low lateritic plateaus and foothills between 75 and 200 meters above sea level, covered with grass and scrub; and (3) the highlands. The central region forms the main area of traditional village settlement as well as the main area for rice cultivation. It consists of a continually undulating countryside, with long, narrow, winding paddy fields surrounded by hills and slopes that were earlier covered by thick vegetation. The climate is monsoonal with heavy rains from both the southwest (oncoming) and northeast (retreating) monsoons. The average temperature is 27° C.

Demography. The state of Kerala has the highest rural population density in India with 1,244 persons per square kilometer in Alleppey District, 1,182 in Trivandrum District, 1,052 in Ernakulam District, and over 800 in Trichur and Kozhikode districts (1981). Despite an exceptionally successful family planning program, these densities are expected to be even higher in the 1991 census because of the demographic pyramid. Sex ratios in Kerala approximate those in the "developed world," with 1,032 females to every 1,000 males (1981 census). Extrapolating from the census of 1911, which gave great detail about caste, it can be estimated that the Nayars make up approximately 15 percent of the present population of Kerala, or a number close to 3.8 million (as of 1981) or 4.3 million (based on approximate figures for 1990).

Linguistic Affiliation. Nayars speak Malayalam, a language belonging to the Southern Branch of the Dravidian Family.

History and Cultural Relations

The early history of Kerala is very complicated and there are many problems remaining to be resolved by historians. The region was united between approximately A.D. 216 and 825, when the Malayalam era is said to have begun. By the beginning of the ninth century A.D. the area was divided into a number of small kingdoms, each ruled by a Nayar or Kshatriya (higher matrilineal subcastes related to Nayars) royal family. Those families were relatively autonomous, owing little allegiance to any overlord. Between the thirteenth century and 1498 (when the Portuguese arrived in Kerala) two Nayar chiefdoms, Kolattiri in the north and Travancore in the south, expanded into small kingdoms. In the central part of the coast the Zamorin of Calicut was in the process of establishing ascendancy over many of the petty rulers and was slowly expanding his territory through an alliance with the local Muslims and Arab traders. Although the Portuguese and later the Dutch and the British built up the ruler of Cochin (another central Kerala coastal kingdom), the Zamorin's kingdom remained powerful until the invasions of the Mysoreans in the eighteenth century. After defeating the Mysoreans in 1792, the British amalgamated the seven northern kingdoms (including the reduced domain of the Zamorin) to form the Malabar District of the Madras Presidency. The kingdoms of Cochin and Travancore remained independent, though each had a British resident and many British businesses. When India became independent in 1947, Malabar District became part of Madras Province and Travancore-Cochin became a separate state; in 1956 the state of Kerala was formed, uniting the district of Malabar with the state of Travancore-Cochin.

Settlements

In Kerala prior to the British period, communication was extremely difficult. There were no roads, wheeled vehicles, or even pack animals. Travel and the transportation of goods depended on human porters and boats plying the numerous rivers and backwaters as well as the seacoast. Only local rulers and petty chieftains could ride on elephants or horses, and even then their use was primarily confined to processions. Since Indian independence and especially since the formation of Kerala State, roads have been built linking all parts of the state and all villages by bus. A railroad now links the southern city of Trivandrum to Mangalore in the South Kanara District of Karnataka (apart from links to Madras and the rest of India); there is one international airport (at Trivandrum) and two regional airports (at Cochin and Calicut). By the mid-1980s all of the villages were electrified. The settlement pattern in Kerala has always been dispersed, with the house of each landowner standing on its own patch of higher ground. The actual physical features of the countryside do not encourage the formation of compact settlements, though today there is a tendency for some parts of settlements to hug the roads. It is impossible to tell where one village ends and another begins. The ideal Malayali house was set in its own compound with its food-producing trees, so that the dwelling space did not subtract from cultivation space. Formerly (prior to the twentieth century) the large Nayar house, set in its own compound with its walls for protection, was a veritable fortress. Nambudiri Brahman houses as well as middle-class Tiyyar houses followed the same pattern. Every home had a name and the individuals belonging to a given house were known by that name. The members of low and Untouchable castes attached to a Nayar house were known also by the name of that house. Today settlements are still dispersed, though because of population growth many of the spaces in between have been filled in.

Economy

Subsistence and Commercial Activities. Traditionally the Kerala economy was extremely complex. The main subsistence food was rice. It was supplemented by a wide variety of root vegetables and some leafy ones, eggs, fish, poultry, goat meat, and for most of the population (apart from Nayars and Nambudiri Brahmans) beef or water-buffalo meat. All of the Brahmans (about one percent of the population) and some of the higher-ranking Nayars (especially those that intermarried with Brahmans, see below) were vegetarian. Today, the diet includes bread and many other wheat products as well as Western vegetables such as carrots and potatoes. It is hard to separate commercial activities from trade, but it is important to note that every village supports a large number of tea shops, toddy shops, general stores, and rice mills, as well as numerous other enterprises. Kerala has probably more small-size printing and publishing establishments than anywhere in the world.

Industrial Arts. Industrial arts unique to Kerala include a wide variety of products made from coconut fiber, the very advanced manufacture of traditional Ayurvedic medicines for worldwide distribution, the crafting of exceptionally fine gold jewelry in intricate traditional designs, bell metalwork, until recently very delicate ivory work, and the construction of traditional seagoing boats and ships. The newer products made in the region are discussed in the next section.

Trade. Apart from the fact that the society was extremely hierarchical with several layers of nonworking overlords, the region was not self-sufficient in rice production (the main subsistence grain) even in the fifteenth century. (Vasco da Gama reported seeing ships carrying rice in the port of Calicut in 1498.) However, the port of Calicut and many lesser ports were grand emporiums for export by sea in this period. Traders came from China, from the Middle East, and even from Rome. Because of the great demand in Europe for black pepper (at that time grown only in Kerala), one of the places Columbus was trying to reach when he sailed west was the port of Calicut. Apart from black pepper, many other items were traded there: other spices, copra, gems of many kinds, peacock feathers, rice (used medicinally in ancient Rome), teak and mahogany, elephants and ivory, and cloth of various kinds, including both cotton and silk. Today Kerala exports pepper, cashew nuts, frozen freshwater fish and seafood, woven textiles, and (to other parts of India as well as many third-world countries) paper and paper products, condoms and other rubber products, coir rope and other coir products, radios and watches, fruits, and fertilizers. However, Kerala's major export today consists of people, primarily educated people, both to the Middle East and to the developed world. There are large numbers of Nayars working as doctors, lawyers, nurses, scholars, and other professionals in the United States, Canada, and Great Britain.

Division of Labor. Since the Nayars are part of an extremely hierarchical society with complex caste and class distinctions, it is hard to describe the division of labor simply. Traditionally, Nayars formed the militia of the countryside, as well as functioning as landlords. In some villages they were the highest level of landowners, in other villages they held the land on lesser tenures. In the extreme north of Kerala and in some parts of Cochin-Travancore, poor Nayar households actually worked the land. But in the rest of Kerala, while Nayars (both males and females) might supervise production, they did not work in the fields. This arrangement has changed to some extent in very recent times. Where Nayars worked in agriculture, the division of labor between the sexes was the same as that followed by other Malayali groups within a given region (though there were and are regional differences between the north and the south).

Land Tenure. Traditional Kerala land tenure resembled the feudal system in Europe, with several levels of subfeudation and infeudation. Land was owned either by an individual, an unpartitioned family, or a temple. The owners derived their income from rents or customary payments by their ten-

ants and lesser tenants or subtenants. Often the Nayars were the tenants, the Tiyyars or Ezhuvas the subtenants, and the agrestic slave castes the manual laborers. However, there were some Nayar owners and some Nayar subtenants. A series of land-tenure laws was passed starting in the late 1920s in Travancore, culminating in major land-reform laws in the early 1970s and a series of supreme court decisions that provided not only for permanence of tenure but also for the gift of actual ownership rights to the lowest rung of tenants in the former hierarchy. As a result, one finds today a large class of small landowners, an even larger class of landless laborers, and a small number of larger landowners (some of whom were former tenants and held land from a number of higher-ranking landowners) who have found ways to circumvent the legal land ceilings.

Kinship

Kin Groups and Descent. The Nayars were traditionally matrilineal. The traditional Nayar *taravad* consisted of all the matrilineally related kin, male and female, descended from a common female ancestor, living in one large taravad house and compound. The property was held impartible, and the several members each were entitled to maintenance within the taravad house but could not claim a separate share. This has all changed since the 1930s, when partition became legally possible. A traditional taravad was composed of a woman, her children, her daughters' and her granddaughters' children, her brothers, descendants through her sisters, and her relations through her dead female ancestors. Within each taravad a significant subgroup consisted of the set of individuals headed by a living female ancestor called a *tavari*. When partitions became possible, they originally occurred on tavari lines.

Kinship Terminology. Kinship terminology follows the Dravidian pattern, with the exception that kin terms traditionally were not used for paternal kin. Today, usage is completely of the Dravidian pattern with a clear distinction between matrilateral and patrilateral kin. Mothers' sisters are called elder or younger mothers, and cross cousins are distinguished from parallel cousins, who are equated with one's own brothers and sisters.

Marriage and Family

Marriage. Marriage customs among the Nayars have evoked much discussion and controversy in India among both jurists and social scientists. There was considerable subregional variation as well as variation by subcaste and family prestige. Details presented here refer to south Malabar and the former Cochin State. There were two kinds of marriage: *talikettu kalyanam* (tali [necklet]-tying ceremony); and *sambandham* (the customary nuptials of a man and woman). The tali-tying ceremony had to be held before puberty and often the ceremony was held for several girls at the same time to save on expenses. Depending on the group the tali could be tied by a member of a linked lineage (often two Nayar lineages that frequently intermarried were linked to one another and called *enangar* lineages), by a member of a higher subcaste of Nayars, by one of the matrilineal Ambilavasi (temple servant) castes, or by a member of a royal lineage. By the mid-1950s, it became common for some girls to have the tali tied by their mothers. It is still controversial as to whether this ceremony was ever a formal marriage or if originally it was simply an age-grade ceremony, since it often included a large number of girls ranging in age from 6 months to 12 or 14 years. Women did observe formal mourning practices for the men who tied their talis, and in some instances—for example, if the girl was close to puberty—it was possible that the marriage might be consummated during this ceremonial period. How often this occurred is unknown. By contrast, sambandan involved a man having a "visiting husband" relationship with a woman. While such relationships were considered to be marriages by the woman's family, especially when they occurred with males of higher subcastes or castes, the males tended to view the relationships as concubinage. Traditionally Nayar women were allowed to have more than one "visiting husband" either simultaneously or serially.

Domestic Unit. The size and composition of the domestic unit have varied over time. Before partition was permitted it could consist of as many as 50 to 100 people. However, once partition was allowed, the size of units decreased rapidly, so that by the late 1950s and 1960s the normal unit consisted of one or more married women with their children, their mother (if living), and possibly some adult male members of the matrilineage. Traditional Nayar family organization provided one of the relatively unique exceptions to the near universality of the nuclear family. The "visiting husband" had very little importance in his wife's family and had no responsibility for any children he might sire. His main responsibilities were for his sister's children. The practice of polyandry also placed a limitation on relationships between men and their own biological children. Today households are even smaller, consisting often of only the nuclear unit, though a matrilineal relative of the woman might often reside with a married couple.

Inheritance. Traditional inheritance was in the matriline only. Any property a man possessed went to his sisters and their children. As men took to modern, Western professions and started accumulating personal wealth as opposed to family property, they began passing it on to their own biological children. As a result, there are today slightly different laws regulating inherited and acquired wealth. However, even today it is customary for a man to put his self-acquired property in his wife's name so that it can then be inherited matrilineally. Furthermore, a man feels greater responsibility for his sister's children than for his brother's children. Even men living away from Kerala in Delhi or New York are more likely to sponsor a sister's son or daughter than a brother's.

Socialization. Traditional socialization patterns involved a strong emphasis on the use of shaming as a technique of control. Traditionally, in all but the poorest taravads, children (female as well as male) were expected to learn to read and write Sanskrit written in the Malayalam alphabet, and as soon as English education came to the region, boys started learning English. Girls only started learning English later. Socialization training strongly emphasized what people knew (i.e., keeping up appearances) rather than superego (i.e., internalized conscience and values).

Sociopolitical Organization

Social Organization. Society in traditional Kerala was highly hierarchical, with a fairly close (though not one-to-one) correlation between caste and class. Most of the landless, land-attached laborers were from the Untouchable castes and tribal groups. The semi-Untouchable Tiyyars or Ezhuvas tended to be tenants, and the Nayars (as noted above) generally held land on various levels of infeudation and subfeudation. Socially, each middle- or upper-class Nayar taravad was a core for social as well as political organization. Today this has all changed, as taravads have split into smaller and smaller units, as population increase has blurred village boundaries even more, and as there are now areas where the normal Indian rural/urban distinction does not apply. Social ties today tend to be closest among members of the same caste and socioeconomic position, though among the educated elite caste distinctions are less prevalent. The Nayars were divided into a number of subcastes all hierarchically placed, though the subdivisions varied from one place to another. In central Kerala, the highest-ranking ones were often referred to as Samantans. Some Samantans were powerful rulers. (The Zamorin of Calicut was a Samantan from the Eradi subcaste.) The Samantan women marry either other Samantans or Nambudiri Brahmans. The Nayars themselves included: Stani Nayars (local chieftains), high-caste Nayars who traditionally served in the military or in some other important capacity for Nambudiri Brahmans, Kshatriyas, or Samantans; the middle-ranking Nayars who did not intermarry or interdine with those higher than themselves, and who performed various tasks for the temple; and the small group of low-caste Nayars who served other Nayars as washermen, barbers, and oilmongers. The majority of Nayars belongs to the high-caste groups.

Political Organization. The traditional political organization was feudal in nature with many small states. Rulers had only limited control. After the British occupation of Malabar and the posting of British resident officers in Cochin and Travancore, the state came to have greater influence. Since Independence, large units of approximately 10,000 to 12,000 people have been governed by an elected _panchayat_ (village council). There is a large bureaucratic structure and an elected legislative assembly in the state. Politics and political parties, especially those of the left, have penetrated into every nook and cranny of the state.

Social Control. Social control is effected through the family, through a general concern about what people will think or what people will say and a strong emphasis on bourgeois values.

Conflict. Traditionally, conflicts were handled by the caste elders. In the Middle Ages, many of the Nayar men were warriors, fighting against neighboring principalities. Today, local conflicts are handled by the village panchayats, and large-scale ones by the police and the courts.

Religion and Expressive Culture

Religious Beliefs. The Nayars themselves are Hindus. However, in Kerala there are also many Christians (of various denominations) and Muslims.

Religious Practitioners. Nayars frequently attend Hindu temples. The main _pujaris_ (temple priests) are Tamil Brahmans or Brahmans from South Kanara, though in a few temples there are also Nambudiri or Kerala Brahmans. Kerala has been innovative in providing training and certification for well-trained lower-caste pujaris.

Ceremonies.   The most important ceremonies celebrated in Kerala among Hindus are Vishu, Onam, and Thiruvathira. Traditionally, these were the three ceremonial occasions when a "visiting husband" was expected to bring new clothes to his wife. Vishu occurs at the same time as the Tamil New Year in mid-April. It is a time for wearing new clothes and also is considered the beginning of the summer. The first things a person sees that morning upon arising are said to influence his or her life throughout the year. Onam (in August–September) is the harvest festival associated with the first paddy harvest. It is also the Malayali New Year. For Nayars it is extremely important not only as a time for getting new clothes but also because of the many rituals associated with it. Thiruvathira is in December, and it is said to be especially important for Nayar females, who have to take a bath in the family tank in the early morning before sunrise, sing a number of special songs, and perform a dance said to be especially beneficial as exercise for women.

Arts.   Nayar culture is closely associated with the Kathakali dance dramas that developed in the 16th century. They involve elaborate headdresses and makeup. It takes many years to master the intricate dance techniques (traditionally performed by males only, though today some females are involved in them). Other arts associated with Nayars include the famous Kalari *pattu* (Kalari or armed gymnasium play) and female Kaikuttikali (a kind of dance). All art forms traditionally were related to caste. Nayars were often patrons of art forms that they themselves did not practice.

Medicine.   The traditional medicine in Kerala is Ayurveda. It has been highly developed there, especially by the Variars, an Ambilavasi (temple servant) caste group that is also matrilineal and shares many traits with Nayars. Today they run Ayurvedic medicine factories, nursing homes, and dispensaries. In addition, Kerala has a well-developed scientific medical system. Kerala doctors (including many Nayar doctors) and nurses may be found all over the world. There is no clash between Ayurvedic and modern or allopathic medicine, as they tend to be used to treat different diseases.

Death and Afterlife.   As among all Hindus there is a strong belief in reincarnation. The dead are usually cremated.

See also Nambudiri Brahman

Bibliography

Fuller, Christopher J. (1976). *The Nayars Today.* New York: Cambridge University Press.

Gough, E. Kathleen (1959). "The Nayars and the Definition of Marriage." *Journal of American Folklore* 71:23–34.

Gough, E. Kathleen, and David M. Schneider (1961). *Matrilineal Kinship.* Berkeley: University of California Press.

Logan, William (1887). *Manual of Malabar.* 2 vols. Madras: Government Press. Reprint. 1961. *Malabar.* 3 vols.

Mencher, Joan P. (1965). "The Nayars of South Malabar." In *Comparative Family Systems*, edited by M. F. Nimkoff, 163–191. Boston: Houghton Mifflin.

Mencher, Joan P. (1966). "Kerala and Madras: A Comparative Study of Ecology and Social Structure." *Ethnology* 5:135–171.

Mencher, Joan P. (1978). "Agrarian Relations in Two Rice Regions of Kerala." *Economic and Political Weekly* 13:349–366.

JOAN P. MENCHER

Neo-Buddhist

ETHNONYMS: none

A central axiom of the religious history of South Asia is that Buddhism, which arose there in the sixth century B.C. and spread to become a world faith of inestimable influence, virtually died out in India, the land of its birth, many centuries ago. Buddhism is still one of the major religions of China, Japan, and Southeast Asia, and it is dealt with at length in later volumes of this encyclopedia. Yet on the South Asian subcontinent it has only been in the "fringe areas" of Sri Lanka in the far south, the mountain zones of Nepal, Sikkim, and Bhutan in the far north, and some tribal portions of northeastern India that are close to Tibet or Myanmar (Burma) where a tradition of Buddhist worship has been kept alive down to the present. So although vast tracts of India, Pakistan, Bangladesh, even Kashmir and Afghanistan, were once Buddhist, they are now predominantly Hindu or Muslim.

Quite unexpectedly, from the middle of the present century, large numbers of Untouchable Hindus, mostly Mahars and Jatavs (or Chamars), started converting to Buddhism. Their numbers grew rapidly; for example, in the decade 1951–1961 Indian Buddhists increased by 1,670.71 percent. By 1991 India had about six million Buddhists, the great majority of these being Neo-Buddhists living in or near Maharashtra. In that state Neo-Buddhists are now more numerous than Muslims or Christian converts.

The conversion of Untouchables to Buddhism was largely the work of one reformer, Dr. B. R. Ambedkar (1891–1956), who was himself a Mahar. He saw this as an avenue to greater respectability, beyond the pale of Hinduism. He also viewed Buddhism as a more desirable pathway to an egalitarian society than communism. Thus far, however, the move to Neo-Buddhism has certainly improved the self-esteem of Jatavs and Mahars, but it has done little to attract other Untouchable castes into the Neo-Buddhist ranks or to improve the status of this group in the eyes of higher-ranking Hindus.

See also Jatav; Mahar

Bibliography

Fiske, Adele M. (1977). "Caste among the Buddhists." In *Caste among Non-Hindus in India*, edited by Harjinder Singh, 91–106. Delhi: National Publishing House.

Zelliot, Eleanor (1966). "Buddhism and Politics in Maharashtra." In *South Asian Politics and Religion*, edited by Donald E. Smith, 191–212. Princeton: Princeton University Press.

PAUL HOCKINGS

Nepali

ETHNONYM: Nepalese

Orientation

Identification. The term "Nepali" refers to any person born within the borders of the kingdom of Nepal or from a group considered historically or territorially indigenous to the kingdom. As an ethnonym, this term roughly encompasses but does not describe the particularities of the multiple ethnic and caste groups that make up Nepal and have their own distinct ethnic identities. Through the cultural dominance of the state of Nepal following its emergence in 1769 and through a long history of political, economic, and cultural interactions between the peoples of this region, many ethnic groups share elements of a common pool of sociocultural attributes. Nevertheless, these groups also exhibit great variation in language, dress, and religion to the extent that certain groups on the northern and southern borders of Nepal are indistinguishable from the people of Tibet and north India, respectively. Nonetheless, there have been settlements in the foothills of the Himalayas since the fourth century B.C., and there is mention of ethnic groups in this region in the early Sanskrit epic literature.

The name "Nepala," referring to a frontier Himalayan kingdom, appears on inscriptions in India from the fourth century A.D. Nepal emerged as a unified nation-state in the eighteenth century with the conquests of the Shah dynasty, which ruled the Thakuri principality of Gorkha in west-central Nepal. In the early nineteenth century, following the confrontations with the British in India and the subsequent forced relinquishment of appropriated lands, the current borders of the country became established within a longitude of 80° and 88° E, with India on its eastern and western borders, and within a latitude of 27° and 30° N with India to the south and Tibet to the north. The country covers an area of 145,954 square kilometers (slightly larger than Arkansas). Social change is occurring very rapidly in Nepal with the influx of tourists and imported goods, the opening of new roads, and an increasing interest and investment in education. The country now has many doctors, engineers, and agronomists, a number of whom have been trained in the United States or Europe. Simultaneously, many old and elaborate social and cultural traditions are declining. The major political and social developments that Nepal is now undergoing are effecting many changes throughout the country. It is hoped that these developments will address the crucial problems of poverty and unemployment, soil degradation, and overpopulation that are currently troubling the country.

Demography. The population of the country is estimated to be between 19 and 20 million people (1991). With the control of epidemics and an expanding population since the 1930s, the rate of population growth has reached 2.7 percent. At this rate, the population will double in twenty-seven years and further increase the already severe pressure on the arable land available for cultivation. This situation has led to an increasing migration from the middle hills and mountain regions of Nepal to the cities and to lower-altitude Terai in the south, which has been viable for settlement for the last thirty years following the eradication of malaria. Nevertheless, the majority of Nepalis (53 percent) continue to live in the middle hill region of the country.

Linguistic Affiliation. There are more than twenty-six distinct languages spoken in Nepal that are related to Indo-European, Tibeto-Burman, and Austroasiatic language families. Nepali, the lingua franca of the country and an Indo-Aryan language related to Hindi, came to Nepal with Khas settlers who migrated into the western Himalaya region of northern India approximately 1500 B.C. The Nepali language is also known historically and colloquially as Khas Khura and Gorkhali because of its association with the early settlers of western Nepal and with the Gorkha dynasty. It is the native tongue of well over half of the inhabitants of the country. Many more people speak Nepali as a second language in administrative, commercial, and educational contexts. A number of important ethnic groups in the midland region of the country, including the Kathmandu Valley, speak Tibeto-Burman languages as their native tongues. Among this group are the first settlers and the architects of Nepal's cultural florescence in the Kathmandu Valley, the Newars. Other important ethnic groups such as the Tamang, Magar, Rai, and Limbu, who make up an important percentage of the population of the hills and mountain regions of Nepal, also speak Tibeto-Burman languages. There are a number of groups in the formerly malarial jungle valleys of the Siwalik and Mahabharat ranges in southern Nepal, such as the Tharu, Danuwar, and Darai, who speak languages that mix Austroasiatic linguistic elements with a number of words from North Indian and Tibeto-Burman languages. Along the southern plains of the Terai one also finds people whose languages (and customs) are indistinguishable from similar groups speaking Hindi, Bhojpuri, and Mithali in north India. Similarly, along the northern region of Nepal one finds various clusters of peoples (e.g., Sherpa, Manangi) whose language, religion, dress, and subsistence patterns closely resemble groups in Tibet, from which they had migrated during the last two millennia.

History and Cultural Relations

The geographic distribution and diversity of ethnic groups in Nepal reflect the migrations of groups displaced by or escaping adverse sociopolitical conditions in central, southern, and southeastern Asia. For instance, there is evidence that people from Southeast Asia moved into the Himalayan region in flight from the expanding Han dynasty during the first millennium B.C. It is also well documented that groups from north India moved into Nepal during various waves of the

Muslim invasions during the fourteenth century. Further, the military and administrative consolidation of the Gorkha regime in the eighteenth century united the eighty or so ethnically varied principalities in the region and asserted an orthodox, Hindu sociopolitical and religious order. This led to the legislative designation of singular ethnic groups such as the Tamang, which often encompass diverse peoples. The formation of the nation-state of Nepal and its need for resources of grain and labor also forced the expanded settlement of the region and led to migrations of families to India to escape the demands of the state.

Settlements

Throughout much of the hills and habitable mountainous ranges, most settlements consist of loosely clustered households surrounded by agricultural land. Households usually group on a hilltop or hillside and near a river or spring. They are connected by footpaths that often converge around a large pipal or banyan tree, which is surrounded by a stone platform and seating structure (*chautara*) that serves as a resting place for travelers and a meeting place for informal or village-council social gatherings. Most hamlets consist of a few clans (*thar*) of a particular group (e.g., Magar, Gurung) and often one or more households of artisan castes (e.g., metalworkers). There are also more densely compact settlements among the Brahmans and Chhetris, Sherpa, Newari, and others that may consist of over fifty households as well as small shops and schools. Throughout the hills there are a number of large towns consisting of several hundred or a few thousand people, especially where there is an important temple or monastery, a marketplace, a motorable road, or an administrative center. The Newari have typically lived in cities or large towns that each form a commercial, social, and ritual center surrounded by their terraced fields. Their settlements vary in size from large villages to the former city-states of Patan, Kathmandu, and Bhaktapur in the Kathmandu Valley. However, the most common houses in the middle hills are two-story, mud-brick houses with thatch—or, recently, tin—roofs. The bottom of each house is painted in red-clay ocher and the top half is whitewashed. The floor is cleaned regularly with a newly applied mixture of wet cow dung and clay. The kitchen must be kept pure, so it is often located on the second floor of the house in order to avoid the pollution of stray animals that might wander into it. Most houses have a veranda and a courtyard where people socialize and work on weaving, corn husking, and other chores. In the northern, mountainous regions of Nepal, such as among the Sherpa or people of Dolpo, houses are made of stone and wood. In the southern, lowland region of the country houses are made of bamboo matting, plastered with mud and cow dung, and covered with a thatch roof. In Newari towns and cities, houses are more elaborate three-story dwellings of stone or baked brick with tin or slate roofs, and they may have carved windows and courtyards in the middle of the house. Simplified versions of these houses are being made of cement or brick throughout the Kathmandu Valley to accommodate its current population boom.

Economy

Subsistence and Commercial Activities. Most Nepalis depend on agriculture for their main subsistence and as a source of cash. In the northern, mountainous regions of the country the Sherpa, Manangi, and others practice high-altitude agriculture. Their main crops are barley, wheat, buckwheat, and maize, along with potatoes—and, recently, squash—grown as vegetables. In these areas there is only one growing season, so that supplemental resources from trade, herding, and wage labor are needed. In the midland and southern regions of the country, the land has been terraced for generations, so that people are able to grow irrigated rice during the monsoon and dry rice, maize, millet, and wheat on more elevated dry land both in the summer and during the winter. They intercrop their fields with soybeans and chilies, and they have gardens of cauliflower, squash, turnips, and greens. Herding animals is an important and common economic activity in northern, Tibetan-oriented regions where people keep yaks, cows, and crossbreeds for butter, cheese, and meat. They also use ponies, sheep, and yaks as pack animals in their long-distance trading. In slightly lower elevations groups such as the Magar have a transhumant economy, and so they move seasonally between elevations for farming and herding. Most people in Nepal keep buffalo, goats, or cows for milk and buffalo or goats for meat, and, if the people are not orthodox Hindus, also pigs and chickens.

Industrial Arts. Most Tibetan-oriented peoples weave cloth and make sturdy and colorful clothes, bags, and carpets. Their carpets have become a desirable market item worldwide. Other groups such as the Gurung and Magar also weave cloth and rugs, but, as with most people today, they purchase commercial cloth, jewelry, and cooking utensils in markets. Most people build their own houses and many carve wooden containers for holding butter and yogurt. Also, most villages have artisan castes such as metalworkers and tailors. As the size of the settlement increases, other occupational castes such as barbers, butchers, potters, and launderers are found. Artisan specialization attained a high level of development among the Newars during the Malla period (twelfth to eighteenth centuries) in the Kathmandu Valley, where one still finds elaborate occupational specializations and refined traditions of painting, wood carving, and metal casting. However, the availability of inexpensive market goods and exposure to new cultural values have caused a decline in these traditions.

Trade. Since Nepal is at the crossroads of central and southern Asia, trade has always been an important facet of the economies of many peoples in the region. The trade between Tibet and India supported, in part, the rise of the great city-states in the Kathmandu Valley and allowed a number of Newar merchants to become very wealthy. Control of this major, regional trading network in the eighteenth century permitted Prithivi Narayan Shah, the first Shah king, to conquer and unify the country. Today, trade is crucial for most households for they sell a part of their produce, usually rice and milk, for cash to buy needed market items such as cloth, matches, and kerosene. Certain ethnic groups have specialized subgroups, such as the Uray among the Newar and the Daffali among Muslims, who are merchants and bangle sellers, respectively. With the closing of the border with China and the end of the Tibetan salt trade, many of the northern groups famous as traders, such as the Thakali and Sherpa, have had to travel to southern Nepal to trade for needed supplies. However, largely in the Terai, Indian merchants control the import of raw and commercial goods that are needed in

Nepal, and they likewise dominate capital investment in the country.

Division of Labor.   There is division of labor among most groups in Nepal, but it is rigid for only a few activities. Generally, women do the bulk of the work in the fields and at home. In many groups, women till the soil, plant, weed, and harvest the crops. They also dry, winnow, and often husk grains. Women also cut grass and collect leaves for animals and carry water. If impoverished, they may also perform wage labor. In the house they cook, clean, and care for children. Unless from a wealthy family, girls receive little education beyond elementary school and so rarely hold commercial or civil-service jobs, although this situation is changing. In a number of groups widowed or divorced women engage in trade or shopkeeping. Men do the heavier agricultural labor of plowing the fields and fixing terraces and irrigation works, but they may also help women in their fieldwork if necessary. Men engage in most major economic transactions, such as buying and selling land, animals, and produce. Many men temporarily travel to work sites or join the army in Nepal or India to make cash needed by their households. It is increasingly common for men to seek employment as wage laborers if poor, or in commerce or government jobs if somewhat educated. Occupational castes specialize in certain tasks such as cutting hair, fishing, priestly work, or butchering, which is largely carried out by men.

Land Tenure.   Almost all but the very poorest households own land. Land is classified according to its productive potential. In one classification, _khet_ is land that is irrigated and is the most valuable. _Bari_ is land that can be cultivated, but not irrigated. _Pakho_ is land that cannot be cultivated for it is usually steep or rocky. There are a number of forms of land tenure in Nepal relating to individual households, lineage ownership, mutual-aid ownership, or land designated as gifts or payment to religious institutions or for government service. In the _kipat_ system an individual has rights to land by virtue of membership in a lineage, although today only the Limbu are allowed to own this form of land. Gifts or payments of land by the government, though largely discontinued, still account for the ownership of large tracts of land and many landlord and tenant relationships. Most Nepalis possess land under the _raikar_ system, in which the utilization and transfer of land is recognized by the government as long as taxes are paid on it.

Kinship

Kin Groups and Descent.   Almost all Nepalis belong to patrilineal descent systems which organize marital, inheritance, and ritual behavior to varying degrees. A few groups along the Tibetan border recognize bilateral relations and function largely in terms of named households and kindreds. Most villages are dominated by one ethnic group and consist usually of a number of exogamous—and, in some northern regions, endogamous—patriclans. A few groups such as the Sherpa and Gurung have ranked, endogamous phratries or moieties, which consist of a number of clans that are associated with an aristocratic or ritual status. Members of clans consider themselves related through a common, though unknown, ancestor. Local descent groups or lineages form active, functioning agnatic units. Affiliation in a local descent group is marked by recognition of a common ancestor, observance of birth and death pollution, and, often, participation in mutual-aid groups. Men and women are born into their fathers' clans, though upon marriage a woman becomes a member of her husband's clan. Ties to matrilateral households and kindred may often be important sources of support, ritual relationships, and, at times, status (e.g., among Nyinba).

Kinship Terminology.   Among many Nepali-speaking and also some Tibeto-Burman–speaking groups siblings may be addressed according to an age order from oldest to youngest or simply as an older or younger sibling (e.g., Jetha, Kānchha). In many groups siblings address parallel and some cross cousins with sibling terms. In the first ascending generation parents' parallel siblings may be addressed with parental terms marked by their age rank (i.e., older or younger). Cross parental siblings may be addressed by particular terms and treated in a distinctively relaxed or more formal manner. Family and lineage relations almost always observe marital taboos. However, for some groups, such as high-caste Hindus, phratries or _gotra_ are exogamous, while for other groups, such as the Gurung, their moieties are endogamous.

Marriage and Family

Marriage.   All groups in Nepal follow some form of clan, lineage, or local descent group exogamy, at least through the fifth generation. Hypergamy is not commonly practiced except among some Rajputs in the Terai and a few interethnic marriages where trade-offs are made between ritual status and class. However, for many groups marriages entail hypergamous relations among families and lineages as a _post facto_ result of the higher status accorded wife takers over wife givers. For most high-caste Hindu groups dowry and bridewealth is an important factor in marriages and an indication of the status of the families involved. Nevertheless, for most Tibetan- and Tibeto-Burman–speaking groups a ritual and often substantial payment is made by the groom to the bride's family. Cross-cousin marriage is not practiced among many groups such as the Sherpa and Hindu caste groups. However, the Thakuri permit and prefer cross-cousin matrilateral marriage. Other groups such as the Tamang and Nyinba prefer bilateral cross-cousin marriage. In general, most marriages are made between couples of the same generation. However, the average age of marriage partners is increasing as education becomes more important and available. Monogamy is the most common form of marriage in Nepal, although a few individuals in most groups also practice polygyny. A number of Tibetan-speaking people, such as the Nyinba, Sherpa, and Baragaonli, practice variant forms of fraternal polyandry. Throughout Nepal most marriages are arranged by the parents of the couple, though with varying degrees of involvement and control. Among high-caste Hindus, marriages have typically been arranged wholly through the decisions of the couples' families. Young men and women of Tibeto-Burman–speaking groups in the middle hills, on the other hand, have more occasion to interact with one another and may induce their parents merely to arrange marriage ceremonies for them. An unusual, and perhaps more legendary than actual, practice among Tibeto-Burman–speaking groups is wife capture. In such a case, following the abduction of a woman, both she and her family need to agree to a marital arrangement or the relationship is dissolved. Eloping is mainly practiced among more impoverished families. After marriage, couples typically live with the husband's extended family for a number of years. However, among the Sherpa marriage takes place in stages, perhaps for years. Thus a husband and wife may continue to live with their respective natal families for years and only visit each other. Once the wife's dowry is arranged and/or they have children, they move in together. In groups throughout Nepal young wives look forward to visiting their natal families during their first few years of marriage. It is not uncommon for women to leave their husbands and return to their natal family or for men to leave their wives and form a union with a new wife. If bride-price has been paid it may have to be returned in part to the husband. Women are allowed to claim rights to their husband's property if they have been abandoned, especially if they have children. Second marriages are not condoned for high-caste Hindu women, and they result in a reduction in social and ritual status if they occur. Men also gain a bad reputation if they divorce their wives, but they do not lose ritual status if they remarry. For other groups divorce involves much less stigma for women. Among the Magar, for instance, women who leave their husbands and remarry lose a few ritual privileges, but this is nothing compared to what happens to high-caste women.

Domestic Unit. Most young couples live with the husband's parents for a number of years, usually until the father of the family dies. When this happens the brothers divide the patrimony. However, beforehand there may be many tensions and status considerations within the household among brothers and their wives. These conditions and the increasing need for household economic diversification often lead one of the brothers, with or without his wife, to seek employment or engage in trading outside the village, and sometimes outside the country, in order to provide cash and be able to act with a degree of autonomy. Polyandrous households appear to have more continuity and stability than extended families made up of monogamous couples.

Inheritance. Inheritance throughout Nepal generally is based on the traditional Mitakshara system, which is encoded in Nepalese law and which states that a legal right to an equal share of the household property goes to each son. In practice, of course, deciding equal shares of partible property is complicated and often fraught with tensions. There have been reforms in the inheritance law for women recently so that they supposedly have more equal rights to the property of their natal family, if they are unmarried, and to their husband's property if he dies. Formerly—and no doubt still today, in practice—they had to wait until they were 35 years old to claim an equal share of their father's property. If their husband had died, they only had been allowed rights to use the land, which reverted to their husbands' agnates.

Socialization. In general, Nepalis indulge and enjoy their young children. Toilet training and weaning are relaxed and breast-feeding may continue until children are 3 years old. Most Hindu and Buddhist groups have a number of rites of passage for children such as first rice feeding, first haircutting, puberty rites for girls, and sacred-thread or initiation ceremonies for boys. At about 8 years old, children are expected to begin to perform domestic chores. Girls carry water and fodder and care for young children and boys may be expected to tend animals.

Sociopolitical Organization

After a brief attempt at democracy in the 1950s, Nepal has had a constitutional monarchy based on a tiered system of representative government called the *panchayat* system. This system has largely been in the control of the king. Recently (1990–1991), Nepal has entered a period of major political transition in which a new constitution has been written and direct, democratic elections of representatives to the National Assembly has been instituted. These developments limit the power of the king.

Social Organization. There are a number of caste and secular hierarchies in Nepal that have a functional meaning in the context of local settings. However, for more than two hundred years high-caste Hindu Nepali-speaking groups have dominated in many sociocultural and institutional settings because of their control of the country's political economy. This cultural dominance was consolidated in the Legal Codes of 1859, in which all groups were broadly cataloged and ranked roughly according to caste principles with, of course, Brahman Chhetri at the top. However, in 1964 the king ended the government's legislation of social practices based on caste.

Political Organization. At the local level, villages have always been run by headmen and, often, a council of elders or influential men. The government had sanctioned the power of headmen by allowing them to collect taxes. The panchayat system, with its elected representatives at the ward and multivillage level, and the institution of government courts in administrative centers throughout the country have superseded, though not entirely replaced, this earlier system of political organization.

Social Control. At the village level there are no formal mechanisms of social control, although many groups have lineage or local-descent groups of elders that decide the meaning of inappropriate behavior. Yet, in the event of crime or legal disputes, these groups do not have real power other than to institute forms of ostracism or contact district courts or police.

Religion and Expressive Culture

Religious Beliefs. Nepal is a Hindu kingdom in which the king is considered an incarnation of the god Vishnu. Although the majority of the country is Hindu, a number of groups of sizable populations are Buddhist. There are a few groups of Muslims in the country and an even smaller number of converts to Christianity. Except for perhaps Christians, almost all groups participate in indigenous and syncretic shamanic, oracular, or pre-Buddhist Bon beliefs and practices that recognize the effects of local gods, godlings, spirits, and places of power. Generally, Hinduism in Nepal is based on the Dharmashastras, Puranas, and various developments in Vaishnavism and Shaivism that have largely originated in India. Buddhism in Nepal blends Mahayana, or the Great Vehicle, with Vajrayana, the Diamond Way. Whether Tibetans or Newars, Buddhists believe in the five Dhayani Buddhas, and along with Hindus they believe in the principles of dharma and karma. Hindus in Nepal worship the major gods of Hinduism, such as forms of Vishnu, Shiva, Durga, and Saraswati. In the Kathmandu Valley Hindus along with the Buddhists also worship powerful local goddesses and gods known as Ajima, Vajrayogini, Bhatbatini, and others who can be very powerful, protective, and punitive. There are also a number of local cults of particular deities throughout the country, such as the Masta cult in western Nepal. People believe that dangerous ghosts and demons, such as the _bhut_, _pret_, and _masan_, haunt crossroads and rivers and wherever they are made offerings of appeasement. Also, some people believe that snakes and frogs have supernatural powers.

Religious Practitioners.   Brahman priests and the Vajracharya Buddhist priests of the Newar are caste-specific roles that may be achieved only by caste members following initiations. These religious specialists perform important rites of passage and domestic rituals and provide important teachings and information on many subjects. Most shamans enter their role as practitioners through the onset of a sickness or possession, which serves as a calling. However, in some groups religious specialists, such as the _khepre_ and _pajyu_ among the Gurung, can achieve their roles only if they are members of one of the ranked divisions of their society.

Ceremonies.   Most of the major festivals and celebrations of Hinduism and Buddhism, such as Durga Puja (Dasain), Holi for Krishna, Shiva Ratri, and Buddha Jayanti are elaborately observed in Nepal. They take various forms in local ethnic communities, which also hold numerous other calendrical and deity festivals throughout the year. The blending of Buddhist and Hindu belief and practice, which is so common in Nepal, may be seen in the worship of certain deities and in large local festivals, such as the Machindranath Jatra in Patan in the Kathmandu Valley. These celebrations and ceremonies serve as rituals of renewal, reenactments of historical events, and the marking of powerful beliefs, practices, and relationships. The spectacular Mani Rimdu ceremony performed every year by the Sherpa in Khumbu has multiple meanings for the participants. Rites of passage, so crucial to the reproduction of social identities throughout Nepal, may be found in every community and entail activities such as those mentioned for child rearing, illness, marriage, and death.

Medicine.   People in Nepal often attribute a number of causes to illnesses. Most groups believe that humoral imbalance leads to physiological disturbances. They also believe that astrological disjunctions and the attack of ghosts and certain deities may also cause maladies. Witchcraft is also feared as a dangerous source of illness and death. It is not uncommon for people to seek treatment from many kinds of specialists as well as at an allopathic hospital or physician's clinic.

Death and Afterlife.   Most Hindus and Buddhists cremate their dead. For Hindus, this is done ideally by a river so that deceased's souls can have a swift passage to desirable realms in the afterworld. Many groups simultaneously believe in reincarnation and worship their ancestors. Among some of the remote Tibetan-speaking people, corpses are cut up and thrown into a river or left on a hilltop for vultures to eat. Members of the Jogi caste are some of the few people who bury their dead.

   See also Brahman and Chhetri of Nepal; Gurkha; Gurung; Lepcha; Limbu; Magar; Newar; Nyinba; Sherpa; Sunwar; Tamang; Thakali

Bibliography

Bista, Dor Bahadur (1967). _The People of Nepal._ Kathmandu: Ratna Pustak Bhandhar. Reprint. 1980.

English, Richard (1985). "Himalayan State Formation and the Impact of British Rule in the Nineteenth Century." _Mountain Research and Development_ 5(1):61–78.

Fisher, James F. ed. (1978). _Himalayan Anthropology: The Indo-Tibetan Interface._ The Hague: Mouton.

Fürer-Haimendorf, Christoph von (1973). _The Anthropology of Nepal._ Warminister: Aris & Phillips.

Hitchcock, John T. (1980). _A Mountain Village in Nepal._ New York: Holt, Rinehart & Winston.

Levine, Nancy E. (1988). _The Dynamics of Polyandry: Kinship, Domesticity, and Population on the Tibetan Border._ Chicago: University of Chicago Press.

Sharma, Prayag Raj (1983). "Nepali Culture and Society: An Historical Overview." _Contributions to Nepalese Studies_ 10:1–20.

ALFRED PACH III

Newar

ETHNONYMS: Newā (in Newari), Newār (in Nepali)

Orientation

Identification.   Most likely, the word "Newar," in use since the seventeenth century, is derived from the word "Nepal" and originally denoted the residents of the Kathmandu (or Nepal) Valley without regard to their ethnic affiliation.

Location.   Today, more than half of the Newars live in the Kathmandu Valley located at 27° 30' to 27° 50' N and 85° 10' to 85° 30' E. Most others live in commercial or administrative centers in the hills and the Terai Plain.

Demography.   According to the census of Nepal in 1981, the number of people speaking Newari as their mother tongue was 448,746 (3 percent of the total population of Nepal). Newars are also found in Darjeeling, Sikkim, and Bhutan and lived in Lhasa, Tibet, before 1959.

Linguistic Affiliation.   The Newari language belongs to the Tibeto-Burman Family. It has many classifiers and postpositions but is not tonal. Having a long history of contact with Indic languages such as Sanskrit, Maithili, and Nepali, it has many loanwords, especially from Sanskrit. The standard Newari is the Kathmandu dialect. Others are the Bhaktapur, Dolakha, and Pahari dialects. Newari is written in Devanagari script. There were several old Newari scripts derived from Indian alphabets.

History and Cultural Relations

Indian influence has been immense on the Newar culture and society. The oldest attested dynasty of the valley was the Licchavi dynasty (A.D. 464 to the ninth century) under which Indianized civilization developed with Buddhism and Hinduism, elaborate architecture, and Indic arts and crafts. Although the Licchavi rulers claimed an Indian origin and all the inscriptions of this period were in Sanskrit, the existence of non-Sanskrit words indicates that the bulk of the population consisted of people who later became the Newars. In the following transitional period, esoteric Vajrayana Buddhism with its monastic institution flourished and many new ritual elements were introduced. The Newar culture grew more distinct and full-fledged during the Malla period (1200–1769). In this period, Muslims conquered north India and caused many Hindus and Buddhists to flee to Nepal. With the help of Indian Brahmans, King Sthitimalla (1382–1395) is said to have codified the caste system and encouraged social stability. Nepalese Buddhism lost its source of inspiration in India, became more ritualized, lost celibate monks, and accepted the caste norms. Influence from Tibet increased around the century, but the trend toward Hinduization was stronger. Written Newari was used in the translation of religious texts and the writing of chronicles and literature of various genres. After Yaksamalla (1428–1482), who expanded the territory and supported the valley culture by donations and construction, the kingdom was eventually divided into the three small kingdoms of Kathmandu, Lalitpur, and Bhaktapur, which frequently quarreled with each other. This situation favored the Gorkhas to the west, a politically powerful group whose core consisted of Nepali-speaking high castes. They conquered the Kathmandu Valley in 1769 and established the present Shah dynasty. Under the Ranas (1846–1951), who set aside the Shah kings and monopolized power, the Newar culture was repressed. Unlike the former immigrants, the Gorkhas did not merge with the Newars. This led to the strengthening of Newari identity. Although Nepalization has been proceeding, many Newars still retain their culture and language.

Settlements

Most Newari settlements are built on elevated ground surrounded by agricultural fields. They appear to be urban with clusters and rows of brick buildings of three or more stories that often surround paved courtyards or border on narrow lanes. Kathmandu (235,000 people), Lalitpur (80,000), and Bhaktapur (48,000) stand out politicoeconomically and in terms of population. The populations of typical Newari settlements range from about one thousand to several thousand, though Kirtipur and Thimi are smaller. Newari settlements abound with temples and other religious places that form a sacred microcosm. These settlements are each divided into two major parts (e.g., upper and lower parts, male and female halves, etc.), which in some cases are named after the main temple in each part. This dichotomy is expressed in ritual processions, mock battles, distribution of socioreligious groups, and buildings. Major settlements have politicoreligious cen-

ters and are protected not only by surrounding walls but also by the temples of eight goddesses and other religious structures placed in proper directions. The agricultural population forms the majority in most of the Newar settlements except for modern Kathmandu and commercial towns outside the valley. A considerable commercial population can also be found in many settlements near the hills such as Sankhu, Capagaon, Lubhu, Banepa, and Dhulikhel, which are trade centers connecting the valley with points outside. Villages between these and the central cities are more agricultural. In some rural settlements, the Jyāpu (farmer) caste forms the overwhelming majority. Others have a multicaste structure.

Economy

Subsistence and Commercial Activities. Agriculture, commerce, and crafts have been the main sources of livelihood for the Newars. In recent years, there has been an increase in employment in government offices, schools, various companies, and construction work, mainly due to the development of the valley as a center of politicoadministrative activity, as well as tourism and commerce. Small shops and rice-flour mills are common even in rural areas. The main crop is rice, grown during the monsoon (June–September) in irrigated fields. Wheat, potatoes, and pulse in the dry season, vegetables, and maize are secondary crops. Since the 1960s improved varieties of rice, wheat, and maize have been introduced) and are cultivated with chemical fertilizers. Although some farmers now use hand tractors (cultivators), many still cultivate with a short-handled hoe called *ku*. Plowing is not popular, perhaps because it is not well suited for sloping fields. Agricultural labor from outside the household is recruited through the systems of *bwalā* (reciprocal exchange), *gwāli* (help without any direct repayment) and *jyāmi* (daily paid work). The last form has become more popular these days.

Industrial Arts. Crafts for which the Newars are famous are image casting in bronze, brass, copper, etc. and the making of ornaments and repoussé. Potting, weaving, wood carving, straw weaving, mask making, etc. are also popular. Potting in Thimi and oil pressing in Khokna are examples of localized caste-oriented work.

Trade. Newars are known to other ethnic groups of Nepal as *sāhu* or "shopkeepers." Both within and outside the valley, there are many Newar merchants. Kathmandu Valley was an important midpoint in the trade between India and Tibet. Carried out by merchants of high castes, it brought great wealth, which supported the high culture of the Newars. Although trade with Tibet ended in 1959, Kathmandu has been expanding as part of an international market in which Newar merchants are active participants.

Division of Labor. Both men and women work in agriculture and in shopkeeping. In agriculture, men use the hoe and women transplant rice. Child rearing and domestic work are mainly done by women. Both sexes weave. Sewing is a caste-specific job. The eldest male (*thakāli*) in each social group presides over its rituals, with the help of his wife. Newar society is divided into many occupational castes. There are both Buddhist and Hindu castes, though the distinction is not clear in many cases. The main Buddhist castes are: Gubhāju (in Sanskrit, Vajrācārya), Buddhist priest; Bare Sākya, gold-

and silversmith; Udāy (Udās), artisan; and Jyāpu (Maharjan), farmer. Among the Udāy there are, among others, Tulādhar, merchant; Kamsakār, bronze worker; and Tāmrakār, coppersmith, castes. Main Hindu castes are: Bramhu (Brahman), Hindu priest; Syesya (Sreṣṭha), merchant, clerk, etc.; and an unclean caste called Jugi (Kusle, Kapāli), tailor, musician. There are Hindu Jyāpus and Buddhist Syesyas also. Some examples of the castes below Jyāpu are: Kumhā (Prajapātī), potter; Nau (Nāpit), barber; Kau (Nakarmi), blacksmith; Sāymi (Mānandhar), oil presser; Pũ (Citrakār), painter; Chipā (Rañjitkār), dyer; Nāy (Kasāĩ), butcher; Kullu, drum maker; Po (Pode, Dyalā), fisherman, sweeper; Cyāme (Cyāmkhala, Kucikār), sweeper; and Hārāhuru, sweeper. Not all the members of a caste engage in their caste-specific occupation. In some castes, caste occupations are not clear-cut. There is much variation among castes in the extent to which caste occupations are followed. Some members of Nepali-speaking Damāĩ (tailor) and Kāmī (blacksmith) castes serve Newars. Division of roles by caste is more complex and actively observed in festivals. Remuneration for caste services is made in kind, in cash, by feasting, or by giving the usufruct of land. In terms of population, the Jyāpus outnumber others and the Syesyas follow. There are a considerable number of Buddhist priests but fewer Brahmans. The populations of lower castes are small in most cases.

Land Tenure. Most of the agricultural land is under the _raikar_ or state-owned tenure, under which farmers can utilize land by paying a tax. Old land-tenure forms, _bitrā_ and _jāgir_, have been changed to raikār since the 1950s. Some land is still owned as tax-exempt, such as land owned by socioritual organizations (_guthi_) and land owned by temples, much of which is also ultimately controlled by the semigovernmental guthi corporation. The amount of land held by a farming household seldom exceeds one hectare. Tenancy exists only to a limited extent.

Kinship

Kin Groups and Descent. Descent is patrilineal. Patrilineally related males call each other _phuki_, a term usually equated with dāju-kijā (brothers), but it is secondarily applied to brothers' and cousins' family members also. Those who call each other phuki form an exogamous lineage. The lineage members form a group to worship a common tutelary deity, _digu dya_ (represented by crude or carved stones), to observe birth and death pollution, and to carry out many rituals together. They may form the core of a labor exchange group in rural areas. In urbanized areas, there is a trend toward digu dya–worshiping units, often called _digu dya pūjā guthi_, splitting into smaller groups. Agnates split ritually and socially are called _bhu_ or _bā phuki_. Affines reciprocate by repeated prestations at life-cycle rituals and at some festivals.

Kinship Terminology. Contemporary cousin terms follow the Hawaiian system. Many terms are taken from Indo-Aryan languages.

Marriage and Family

Marriage. Marriage is generally monogamous and postmarital residence is virilocal. Polygyny is allowed in the absence of a son from the first wife. Caste endogamy is the rule. Contrary to what some authors claim, there are not all that many cases of divorce, intercaste marriages, or "climbing the [caste] ladder." Village endogamy occurs occasionally, but not in typical settlements. Cross-cousin marriage is forbidden. Marriage is usually arranged by parents who use a go-between. Marriage by elopement is popular in some peripheral villages.

Domestic Unit. A patrilineal extended family in which married brothers live with their parents is the ideal type of Newar household. In actuality, there are situations in which demographic, economic, and social conditions prevent the formation of these extended households.

Inheritance. Property is divided equally among the sons. Daughters are given a certain amount of the family property as _kwasa_ in the form of utensils, furniture, clothes, money, etc. at the time of marriage.

Socialization. Although children are taken care of by many members of the family, mothers have very close ties with their children. A child is often fed from his or her mother's breast for more than three years. Physical punishment is not common. Girls are required from the age of 7 or 8 to help in cooking, carrying water, and looking after small children. Boys are freer to play when small but they too work in agriculture, shopkeeping, etc. when the family is busy. Formal schooling has become more important recently.

Sociopolitical Organization

Social Organization. The intercaste relationship, which is hierarchical, is expressed in commensality, marriage, and other behavior as well as in the division of labor. Within a caste, there are socioritual groups categorized as guthi. A guthi is headed by several elders, has a particular name and function, often owns land and other property, and holds feasts, which are hosted in rotation by the members. Some priestly and artisan castes had or have guthis to cover one large area and control members' occupations, marriage, and conflicts. In many other castes, funeral associations control the caste members. They may extend beyond the settlement boundary, depending upon the demographic condition of the caste concerned. Castes tend to live in different quarters or wards (_twā_), which among some castes are given specific names. A quarter usually houses plural lineages, which may form a corporate ritual unit. There are many guthis of restricted membership to carry out rituals among higher castes. Musical groups and voluntary dance or drama groups are widely found both as intra-and intercaste organizations.

Political Organization. The present political system of the kingdom of Nepal is called the _panchayat_ system, under which there are local administrative units called town panchayat and village panchayat with elected heads. Each of the Newar settlements comprises one or more panchayats or is combined with others to form one. In the Rana period, the village head was appointed by the higher authority. One or two higher castes are usually dominant and tend to monopolize village leadership.

Social Control. A sense of conformity is pervasive. Violation of norms sometimes ends in ostracism. Each social group is led by elders who assume their seats according to seniority based on generation and age; but other members who have prestige and ability may emerge as practical leaders. The panchayat system with elections has been gaining legitimacy.

Conflict. In the late Malla period, there were frequent conflicts among the small kingdoms in the valley. Conflicts between castes often led to the weakening of service relations. The best-remembered one is the prolonged Gubhāju-Udāy conflict, which was brought before the court and even needed the king's intervention. A mechanism to split a group peacefully is absent in many cases; thus conflict, by creating fissures and splinter groups, helps maintain groups at an optimum size. Traditional social relations have been weakening in many respects recently.

Religion and Expressive Culture

Religious Beliefs. Buddhism, Hinduism, and indigenous beliefs coexist and are mixed among the Newars. The main form of Buddhism practiced here is Mahayana or Great Vehicle "Way," in which the Tantricized and esoteric Vajrayana, Diamond, or Thunderbolt "Way" is considered the highest. Theravada Buddhism is not as popular but there has been a moderate resurgence in recent years. Hinduism has benefited from stronger backing for several centuries. Shiva, Vishnu, and related Brahmanical deities are revered, but more characteristic is the worship of various goddesses called by blanket terms such as *mātrikā, devī, ajimā,* and *māī.* Indigenous elements are seen in the rituals of digu dya, *byāncā nakegu* ("feeding frogs" after transplanting rice), beliefs about supernaturals, and many other customs. The Newars believe in the existence of demons (*lākhe*), malevolent souls of the dead (*pret, agati*), ghosts (*bhut, kickanni*), evil spirits (*khyā*), and witches (*boksi*). Cremation grounds, crossroads, places related to water or disposal, and huge stones are their favorite haunting places. Mantras and offerings are used by priests and other practitioners to control and propitiate them.

Religious Practitioners. Gubhāju and Brahman are Buddhist and Hindu priests, respectively; they are married householders, as only Theravada monks are celibate. Buddhist and Hindu priests officiate at household rituals, festivals, and other rites. Tantric priests or Acāju (Karmācārya), funeral priests or Tini (Śivacārya), and Bhā are graded lower. Astrologers are also connected with funerals in some places. In certain localities, Khusah (Tandukār) serve the Nāy caste as their household priests.

Ceremonies. Main life-cycle rituals are: rituals at and after birth (*macā bu benkegu, jankwa,* etc.); two stages of initiation (*bwaskhā* and *bare chuyegu* or *kaytā pūjū* for boys; *ihi* and *bārā tayegu* for girls); wedding ceremonies; old-age celebrations (*budhā jankwa*); funeral and postmortuary rites. There are forty or more calendrical rituals and festivals practiced in a single locality. Some, such as *gathāmuga (ghantakarna), mohani dasāī, swanti,* and *tihār,* are common to all localities, but many other festivals are localized. Offering alms is an important religious act, of which the Buddhist *samyak* is the most festive. There are rituals repeated within a year. *Nitya pūjā* (daily worship of deities), *sālhu bhway* (feast on the first day of each month), and *mangalbār vrata* (Tuesday fasting) are examples. There are also rituals of which the date is not fixed, which are performed only when necessary or proposed.

Arts. Newar artistic talent is displayed in architecture and sculpture. Inspired by Indian tradition, unique styles of palaces, temples, monasteries, stupas, fountains, and residential buildings developed. They are often decorated with wood carvings and equipped with stone or metal sculptures. Religious paintings are found on the walls, scrolls, and manuscripts. Music with drums, cymbals, wind instruments, and sometimes songs is indispensable in many festivals and rituals. Most arts are practiced by males.

Medicine. Disease is attributed to evil objects, the ill will of mother goddesses, witchcraft, attack, possession or other influence of supernaturals, misalignment of planets, evil spells, and social and other disharmony, as well as natural causes such as bad food, water, and climate. People resort to both modern facilities and traditional medical practitioners. Among the latter are the *jhār phuk* (or *phu phā*) *yāyemha* (exorcist), *vaidya* (medicine man), *kavirāj* (Ayurvedic doctor), midwives, bone setters of the barber caste, Buddhist and Hindu priests, and *dyah waikimha* (a kind of shaman). Popular treatment methods include brushing off and blowing away ill objects in the body (*phu phā yāye*), reading or attaching mantras (spells), making offerings to supernaturals or deities, and using local herbal and other medicines.

Death and Afterlife. It is believed that the soul of the deceased must be sent to its proper abode through a series of postmortuary rites performed by male descendants. Otherwise, it remains in this world as a harmful *pret.* Two ideas about afterlife, that of Heaven and Hell and that of rebirth, coexist. Attainment of a good or bad afterlife depends upon the person's merit accumulated while alive and upon the proper performance of the rituals. The deceased are also worshiped and propitiated as ancestors.

See also Nepali

Bibliography

Gutschow, Niels (1982). *Stadtraum und Ritual der Newarischen Städte im Kathmandu-Tal: Eine architekturanthropologische Untersuchung.* Stuttgart: Kohlhammer.

Nepali, Gopal Singh (1965). *The Newars.* Bombay: United Asia Publications.

Slusser, Mary Shepherd (1982). *Nepal Mandala: A Cultural Study of the Kathmandu Valley.* Princeton: Princeton University Press.

Toffin, Gerard (1984). *Société et religion chez les Newar du Népal.* Paris: Centre National de la Recherche Scientifique.

HIROSHI ISHII

Nicobarese

ETHNONYMS: none

Orientation

The Nicobarese are the majority ethnic and linguistic group living in the Nicobar Island group, a district of India's

Andaman and Nicobar Union Territory in the Bay of Bengal. Located between 6°50' and 9°10'N and 92°10' and 93°55' E, the Nicobar group comprises 2,022 square kilometers of surface area, strung along a 262-kilometer NNW-SSE line. The principal islands are Car Nicobar (north); Kamorta, Chowra, and Nancowrie (center); and Great and Little Nicobar (south). The district population was 30,454 in 1981 including about 22,200 Nicobarese and Shampon.

Car Nicobar has the only important city of the district. Also on Car Nicobar is Big Laputi village, thought to be the parent village from which all other Nicobarese settlements originated. This island is flat, with fertile soils, and is home to the majority of the district's population. The other islands are hilly. The islands are densely forested under coconut and betel-nut trees, pandanus, mangoes, margosa, and casuarina. They receive heavy monsoon rains—230 to 330 centimeters annually—and because they lie along one of the Earth's major fault lines, they are subject to severe earthquakes.

Nicobarese is a Mon Khmer language of the Austroasiatic Family. There are three divisions: Car, Central, and Southern Nicobarese. Each of the latter two have four dialects. Chowra and Teressa are related but separate languages.

History and Cultural Relations

Tradition and linguistic evidence suggest that the Nicobarese originated in Myanmar (Burma). The first certain reference to them is in the 1050 Tanjore inscription of the Chola dynasty of south India, which calls the islands "Nakkavaram" ("Land of the Naked"). First and unsuccessfully missionized by the Jesuits, they also resisted Christianizing efforts by the Danish, Austrians, British, and French. In 1869, the British claimed the islands and held them until India gained independence in 1947. Christianity made real progress only on Car Nicobar, largely because of local respect for Bishop Richardson, a Nicobarese whose bravery during the 1942–1945 Japanese occupation of the islands inspired whole villages to convert. The Andaman and Nicobar Islands (Protection of Aboriginal Tribes) Regulation, passed in 1956, restricts entry of outsiders to tribal areas and regulates trade in the territory.

Settlements

Settlements are invariably located on the coast. Nearest the shoreline are three community houses. Behind these are a number of "birth" huts, in which a new mother, her husband, and their baby live for about a year after delivery. Behind these huts are the dwelling houses, usually on stilts, clustered around a sand-covered dance and sports ground. These huts are usually single-roomed and dome-roofed or rectangular with sloping roofs. Both house types are made of thatching woven through a frame of branches. There usually is a separate hut built near each dwelling that serves as a kitchen.

Economy

Nicobarese are agriculturalists and fisherfolk. Their main crops are rice, maize, fruits, vegetables, and, most importantly, coconuts and betel nuts. Their principal industries are copra making and oil pressing. Each Nicobarese household maintains a coconut and betel-nut plantation that can range in extent from one-quarter hectare to several hectares. The coconut tree is valued for more than its fruit: its wood is used for building, and its leaves are used for making mats, torches, and canoe covers. All Nicobarese households also raise pigs and poultry. Chowra Islanders specialize in the construction of canoes and earthenware pots. As the Chowra Islanders have a reputation for being great magicians, the Nicobarese will use only Chowra pottery for ritual food preparation and hold that canoes must be Chowra-made, or at least blessed by a Chowra ritual specialist (_menluana_). Men and women enjoy equal economic rights and position, although household tasks are largely performed by women and heavy work tends to be male-dominated.

Land Tenure. General rights to land are vested in the joint family, under the control of the household head. However, since land is abundant, use rights are easily gained by anyone willing to clear a bit of forest. As long as the land is worked, its use right may pass along from parent to child.

Kinship

The Nicobarese employ an extreme form of joint-family system. The family consists of a husband-wife pair, their children, brothers and/or sisters (and their offspring) of the core couple, and even cousins, uncles, etc.: the total number of household members can reach as high as a hundred, living in a cluster of neighboring dwelling houses.

Marriage and Family

Nicobarese select their own partners, but parental opinion of a prospective match carries some weight. There are no endogamous or exogamous groups other than the immediate nuclear family unit, and both cross and parallel cousins are appropriate marriage partners. Attitudes toward premarital sex are benign; marriages are often the simple regularization of a longstanding sexual relationship. Age at marriage is usually 20 to 28 for men, 16 to 20 for women. Marriage ritual involves the shaving of the couple's heads, after which the marrying pair don white clothes and are fed a meal of roast pig. A menluana then takes them to the sea for a ritual swim, and upon their return to the village there is a great feast. The pair goes into hiding for four to seven days, and then they return to the community as a married couple. There is no stigma attached to illegitimacy, and divorce seldom if ever occurs. Nicobarese are now monogamous, though they once were not. Widow remarriage is common. After marriage, the couple goes to live with whichever of their two joint-family groups has the fewer members.

Inheritance. Property is nominally vested in the joint family. Personal goods are not generally inherited, because they are buried with their owner upon his or her death.

Socialization. Traditionally, the child would not be named until it began to walk, when a naming ceremony and feast would be held. Today naming will often occur earlier, and among Christian Nicobarese a small feast is held at the infant's baptism. Children are highly valued by the Nicobarese, and both parents are engaged in their upbringing. Teaching is done by example and by admonition. Formal schools have been available on Car Nicobar for quite some time now, and in recent years have spread to some of the other islands.

Sociopolitical Organization

Village heads are chosen from among the joint-family heads. Headship is an achieved position, but it tends to remain in a single family for several generations. One of the village heads will serve as island head. Women are assumed to be fully as qualified for headship as men, but they are less frequently motivated to act as such. Village and island councils, formed of family and village heads, once had the sole formal authority to judge and punish offenses and only met to adjudicate specific problems. Today, serious crimes are no longer handled on the local level but are turned over to government representatives headquartered on Car Nicobar. Today, punishments are usually laid on in terms of fines (to be paid in pigs), or corporal punishment (caning).

Religion and Expressive Culture

Religious Beliefs. Although Christianity has achieved some success among the Nicobarese, traditional beliefs and practices are still strong. The Nicobarese are animists, and they have a rich tradition dealing with natural spirits and spirits of the dead.

Religious Practitioners. The menluana (witch doctor) is a ritual specialist and healer who begins as a disciple/apprentice to an established menluana. Although anyone can become a menluana if they express the desire and aptitude, ritual knowledge most often passes from parent to child. The most respected ritual specialists come from Chowra.

Ceremonies. There is an annual feast held to drive evil spirits away from the village and several seasonal festivals intended to promote the growth of crops. The biggest ceremonial event, involving several villages, is the ossuary feast, which honors the spirits of the dead. A great many pigs are killed for this feast, and it is the only time that pig fights are held. It occurs approximately every two or three years, whenever village heads agree that they have the necessary resources (in pigs) to host one.

Arts. Nicobarese songs are sung unaccompanied by instruments. Dancing is done in groups—on some islands males and females dance in separate groups. There is no Nicobarese traditional drama. Popular sports include canoe races, pig fighting, stick fighting, wrestling, and volleyball.

Medicine. The menluana cure sickness by controlling the spirits who cause it. Herbal remedies are used, as is curing by "sucking" out bits of stone or bone, etc., from the body of the ailing person.

Death and Afterlife. The Nicobarese believe in an afterlife in which the dead conduct themselves similarly to how they did in life. For this reason, the personal belongings of the dead are buried with the body and food is left at the burial site. Certain coconut palms of the deceased's former plantation are marked with a sign, designating their fruit as solely for the use of the dead person's spirit for about six months. The body of the deceased is interred, then exhumed and reburied after about a week, at the time of which final burial a feast is held.

Bibliography

Chak, B. L. (1971). *Andaman and Nicobar Islands.* New Delhi: Ministry of Information and Broadcasting, Publications Division.

Mathur, Kaushal Kumar (1967). *Nicobar Islands.* New Delhi: National Book Trust.

NANCY E. GRATTON

Nyinba

ETHNONYMS: Barthapalya (in Nepali), Bhotia, Bhutia, Tamang

Orientation

Identification. The Nyinba are one of many small, largely endogamous groups positioned along the northern borderlands of Nepal that can be identified as ethnically Tibetan by their language, by the Tibetan Buddhist religion, and other features of culture and social structure. The Nyinba live in Humla, a district of the Karnali Zone in far northwestern Nepal. Tibetan speakers in this region call their territory "Nyin Yul Tshan Zhi," literally, "the four villages on a south-facing [sunny] slope." Nepali speakers call the community "Barthapale," *thapale* referring to its high valley location. Government documents originally identified these people as "Bhotia," meaning Tibetan. Later, to affirm their Nepali nationality, they became classified as "Tamang," the ethnonym of Tibeto-Burman–speaking hill people from central Nepal.

Location. Nyinba villages are located at approximately 30° N and 81°51' E, in a valley carved out by the Humla Karnali and Dozam rivers. The terrain in this region is rugged and the arable land limited, creating strong competition for land. Nyinba control a narrow band of territory beginning at 2,550 meters and extending to the valley summit, with the villages located between 2,850 and 3,300 meters. This elevation is associated with a temperate climate. Much of the force of the summer monsoon is spent on mountains to the east and south, limiting annual rainfall. A second, western monsoon brings heavy snowfalls in winter.

Demography. In 1983, the Nyinba included 1,332 individuals, 716 males and 616 females. The high sex ratio, 116 males for every 100 females, can be attributed to a pattern of preferential treatment of male infants. Almost 35 percent of the population is less than age 15, and the intrinsic rate of natural increase appears to be relatively low: between 1 and 1.5 percent per year.

Linguistic Affiliation. The Nyinba speak a dialect of Tibetan similar to the dialects of other ethnic Tibetan groups in west Nepal. These seem most closely related to dialects spoken by western Tibetan agriculturalists. The Tibetan language is related to Burmese, with these two languages considered a branch of the Sino-Tibetan Language Phylum.

History and Cultural Relations

Nyinba believe that their ancestors are an amalgam of peoples mostly from western Tibet and also from elsewhere in Tibet, ethnic Tibetan regions in Nepal, and Byansi villages ("Byansi" refers to groups of Tibeto-Burman speakers found farther west in Nepal and India). Villagers state that their ancestors settled the region during the fifteenth century, thus after the collapse of the Malla Kingdom, which united western Tibet, western Nepal, and possibly Ladakh. Although the Mallas supported both Buddhism and Hinduism, their successors were high-caste Hindus hostile to Buddhist peoples. These rulers formed a feudal confederacy, which was conquered by and annexed to the kingdom of Nepal in 1789. The incorporation into a centralized state had little impact on daily life until recently. It principally affected matters of land tenure and taxation, intercaste relations, and serious legal offenses. Beginning in the 1950s, the government established a new district capital not far from where the Nyinba live and introduced a system of democratically elected, local _panchayat_ councils, which are linked to similar regional and national councils. Although Nyinba have long been citizens of Nepal, they also have provided support and had affiliations to Tibetan religious institutions. These relationships ended in 1959, with Chinese suppression of the revolt in Tibet.

Throughout their history, Nyinba have participated in a multiethnic society. Their territory stands at the intersection of the region's three major ethnic groups. To the south lie villages of high-caste Hindus, to the south and west are villages of Bura, a group of both Buddhists and Hindus citing Byansi antecedents, and to the north are the villages of ethnic Tibetans. Nyinba relationships with these other groups are oriented principally around economic transactions and religion. Nyinba trade extensively. They import commodities from Tibet and other Tibetan border regions into high-caste Nepali and Bura villages to the south and bring the latter's surplus grain back to Tibet. They also sponsor religious festivals with other ethnic Tibetans, send lamas to Buddhist Bura villages, and participate in regional cults of spirit possession. Otherwise, they are relatively insular and disapprove strongly of community exogamy.

Settlements

All four Nyinba villages include a main settlement at the center of village territory plus one or more small hamlets located nearer its borders. The largest village includes fifty-eight households, the smallest twenty-seven households (the constituent hamlets are two to seven households in size). The settlement pattern is nucleated; the houses are tightly clustered, with adjoining walls and roofs in the larger and older settlements. These houses are large and three stories tall; they are solidly built of fashioned stone and timber, often covered with a layer of mud plaster. At ground level is the barn, which is subdivided into compartments for different domestic animals. On the second story is the family's main quarters. This typically consists of a kitchen-cum-living room, a windowless storage room for valuables, another storage room also used for sleeping, and a long outer corridor, where a small, second hearth is placed. On the top story stand a number of storage sheds. The main living rooms have plank floors and carved pillars, while the other rooms have earthen floors and roughly cut pillars. Windows are small and closed by shutters; glass remains exceedingly rare. Villages and hamlets are surrounded by agricultural land, with the hamlets located adjacent to more recently reclaimed lands on the margins of village territory. Each village has rights to specific forest and grazing lands. Each village also includes its own _gompa_, the temple and domestic establishment of a noncelibate Buddhist lama. These buildings are set apart from the houses of lay people, typically located above village settlements and in a "pure" place.

Economy

Subsistence and Commercial Activities. Nyinba have a diversified economy and engage in agriculture, trade, and animal husbandry, in that order of importance. Agriculture is central, economically and symbolically. Due to the difficult terrain and the high elevation, however, it is both physically demanding and relatively unproductive. Villagers may double-crop their lowest-level fields with winter barley and buckwheat or plant a single crop of millet, amaranth, and beans. At middle elevations wheat and buckwheat are grown, whereas the highest fields are planted only with buckwheat. People grow vegetables—daikons (radishes), turnips, potatoes, peas, pumpkins, Hubbard squash, and cabbages—in small kitchen gardens. Households also own fruit and nut trees: apricot, walnut, apple, and the rare peach tree. On average, households produced approximately 84 bushels of unhusked grain in 1982, a disastrous agricultural year; in a year of good harvests, they expect to produce about 50 percent more. That yield was supplemented by the proceeds of trade and cattle herding. Nyinba do not have access to extensive grasslands, so that cattle herding is limited and continues to contract, as high lands are being converted into farmland. Nonetheless, households keep some cattle, for their milk products and manure.

Industrial Arts. Nyinba villagers employ low-caste Nepali speakers for metalwork and sewing cotton clothing. They employ Tibetan refugees for large carpentry jobs and for religious artwork. Woolen clothes, shoes, and coats are produced at home from their own or imported wool and sheepskins.

Trade. People rely on trade to cushion the inevitable fluctuations in agricultural productivity. This involves exchanging Tibetan and Indian salt for surplus grain produced in the Nepalese midlands. These goods are transported mostly on the backs of agile goats and sheep. Nyinba also trade in yak-cow crossbreeds and import high-pasture sheep and wool from Tibet and manufactured goods from India for their own consumption. Trade occupies nearly the entire year, taking its participants from the Tibetan plains through the Nepalese midlands to Indian border towns. In 1982 this trade resulted, on average, in take-home profits of 34 bushels of husked grain, 5 bushels of salt, and diverse commodities for each household with adequate manpower to engage in it.

Division of Labor. Some tasks, most notably plowing, are performed exclusively by men; others, particularly weeding, are performed exclusively by women. Nevertheless, many other subsistence tasks may be performed by either sex. This is quite practical in a society where the number of male and female household members varies widely. To generalize, women engage in a range of agricultural tasks over protracted periods of time, while men's contributions to agriculture are sporadic but very intense. Men are exclusively responsible for trade, while the relatively undemanding task of cattle herding may be entrusted to a child or elderly person of either sex. Women hold the major responsibility for domestic work, including child care.

Land Tenure.　Individual households have rights over farmland, while villages control forests and grazing lands. All Nyinba own some land, though the richer households have vastly more than the poorer ones. The state has ultimate rights over all this land, although they are realized in little more than the right to taxation. Nyinba buy and sell land rarely; it is in short supply and very expensive. In the past, when wastelands were reclaimed, each village household received an equivalent share.

Kinship

Kin Groups and Descent.　At the core of Nyinba kinship is the concept of *ru*—literally, "bone"—which describes hereditary substance transmission through men and provides the basis for a system of patrilineal clanship. Clan membership is important principally for marking social ranks within the community and for guiding marital choice through rules of exogamy. It has no economic and virtually no religious dimensions and does not generate any effective corporate groups. Although patrilineal descent appears important in several ethnic Tibetan societies in Nepal, it had minimal significance among agriculturalists in Tibet proper. Nyinba maintain that women transmit ru to their offspring through the medium of blood; these blood relationships provide a complementary, or matrifiliative, link to the mother's clan.

Kinship Terminology.　The system of kin classification incorporates Omaha-type skewing rules, classifies relatives via same- and opposite-sex sibling links differently, and features spouse-equation rules that accord with a system of cross-cousin marriage. It also includes special terms that distinguish parents by relative age in complex, multipartner polyandrous and polygynous marriages.

Marriage and Family

Marriage.　All Nyinba men who have brothers marry jointly in fraternal polyandry. Over time, these marriages may become monogamous, due to deaths of brothers and occasional divorce. Thus household histories show 70 percent of marriages to have been initially polyandrous, although only half the marriages in 1983 remained so. Postmarital residence is ordinarily virilocal. Only when a family lacks sons will a daughter marry uxorilocally. Most uxorilocal unions are monogamous, although sometimes a second sister joins the marriage, in sororal polygyny. Men whose wives are childless are encouraged to marry second wives and men extremely unhappy in their polyandrous marriages are sometimes permitted second wives by their families. This creates marriages that are both polygynous and polyandrous (less than 5 percent of extant marriages in 1983). In all such cases, the preference is for sororal polygyny. Polyandry is highly idealized in expressing fraternal unity; it is seen as economically advantageous, and it also confers political advantages in the village. Frictions between brothers seem to be minimized by practices ensuring equal sexual access to the common wife and by the designation of paternity, which gives brothers equal opportunity to father children within the common marriage. Divorce of men is rare, as is the divorce of women who have borne children.

Domestic Unit.　Households are large and multigenerational, including, on average, 7.7 members and 2.6 generations in 1983. The wealthier households tend to be larger and to include a relatively greater proportion of men than the poorer ones. Membership in households accrues only through marriage or by legitimate birth (due to polyandry and polygyny, the children may have different parents). Polyandry also has the effect of creating low dependency ratios. Household membership presumes cooperation in productive labor and a share in what the household produces, both of which vary with age and gender.

Inheritance.　Property is inherited jointly by all sons of the previous property-holding generation. When daughters marry, they receive a dowry of household goods, agricultural tools, and occasionally a domestic animal or rights to a small plot of land for lifelong use. Traditionally, never-wed women had rights to lifelong maintenance; now Nepali law entitles them to lifelong use rights in half the share given a son. In the rare cases of partition among brothers, property is divided according to *per stirpes* (equally between the branches of a family) reckoning, a custom that may be due to Hindu Nepali influence. Any household produced in partition that fails to maintain itself passes to the partitioners' brothers or their successors.

Socialization.　Boys and girls are raised differently, as are first and later-born sons. Girls, for example, begin productive work at an earlier age and are expected to help care for their younger siblings. First-born sons are encouraged to take a leadership role in the family, to prepare them for later household headship, and are taught to treat their brothers fairly, which is particularly critical for polyandry.

Sociopolitical Organization

Nyinba are citizens of the Nepalese state and subject to its legal code, which is Hindu-influenced but also gives recognition to traditional custom.

Social Organization.　Nyinba are socially stratified, with the major distinction between a class of slaveowners and the descendants of their slaves, freed in 1926. Slaves traditionally married monogamously and uxorilocally and lived in nuclear-family households. This family structure dovetailed with and augmented the polyandrous households of their masters, many of whom suffered chronic shortages of female labor. Today the poorer slave descendants serve as a dependent labor force, supplemented by hired laborers from ethnic Nepali villages. There also are minor status distinctions within the former slaveowner stratum: the older, village-founding clans have greater status than members of more recently arrived clans.

Political Organization.　In the past, the Nyinba were ruled by petty Hindu chieftains of high caste, whose descendants remain politically influential today. In 1789, they became subjects of the Nepalese state, which interfered little in the area, beyond regulating land usage and taxation, until the 1950s. The effect of these regimes has been to undermine Nyinba unity and indigenous institutions of leadership. The fact that villages successfully coordinate economic activities and religious ceremonials is due to a traditional system of village organization. This is based upon cooperative action between households related by past partitions and by the rotation of offices holding responsibility for collective events.

Social Control and Conflict. Today villages are highly factionalized, and prominent Nyinba anchor their power by affiliations with the descendants of their former rulers, who now participate in the national political arena. Although in law, Nepalese of all castes and classes now have equal political and legal rights, some elements of past inequality linger on. Thus slave descendants remain less powerful (as well as poorer) locally.

Religion and Expressive Culture

Religious Beliefs. Nyinba are Tibetan Buddhists of the Nyingmapa school, although people also give credence to certain cosmological beliefs held to antedate Buddhism and to the deities and ritual practices of their Hindu neighbors. The pantheon follows orthodox Tibetan Buddhism, with the addition of minor deities of local significance. Contrary to Buddhism, village founders become powerful ancestors who are thought to safeguard the village and to whom appeals for agricultural prosperity are addressed. People also fear the power of the evil eye and witchcraft.

Religious Practitioners. Each village includes one or more households of lamas, the most respected of whom trace descent to a hereditary lama lineage. These lamas are not monastics, although many have pursued advanced religious training in the monasteries of Tibet or in refugee centers in India and Nepal. Instead they marry, raise families, and serve the everyday ritual needs of villagers. A few women have become nuns; the esteem in which they are held depends on the rectitude of their lives and their religious accomplishments. Each village also includes several households of hereditary priests known as *dangri*, who are involved with the cults of local deities. These priests conduct from memory a simple liturgy modeled after Tibetan Buddhist ritual, preparatory to events of spirit possession. Finally there are the spirit mediums, or oracles, who are believed to incarnate local deities when possessed. The office of oracle rarely passes from father to son, but it does recur often among disadvantaged Nyinba, such as slaves and their descendants.

Ceremonies. Lamas celebrate Buddhist rituals at prescribed times in their household temples. In addition, they officiate at privately sponsored rituals, prompted by life-crisis events or the desire to acquire merit, and at public ceremonials. The ritual calendar includes both locally distinctive ceremonies and those known throughout ethnically Tibetan areas. Among the former are ceremonies held to propitiate clan gods, those seeking the blessings of founder ancestors, and rites associated with the growth and harvesting of the major crops. At these special local ceremonies, both lamas and dangris officiate, and there is public oracular possession.

Arts. The Nyinba are known for their finely made, beautifully executed textiles, including woven carpets, tie-dyed shawls, and embroidered boots. Religious artifacts used in their temples, such as drums, bells, statues, and paintings, are produced by artisans from Tibet.

Medicine. Certain lamas practice traditional Tibetan medicine, which relies on empirical and mystical treatments: herbal and animal remedies, moxibustion (cauterization), and the performance of special rituals. Oracles also may be called in to diagnose the mystical cause of illness and to exorcise malignant supernaturals deemed responsible. Nyinba have been exposed to scientific medicine only since the mid-1970s. As more facilities are established and sources of supplies become reliable, reliance on them increases.

Death and Afterlife. Following death are a series of ceremonies that culminate in a merit-creating feast for the entire village and close relatives of the deceased. Like other Buddhists, Nyinba believe in reincarnation, and one of the major goals of these ceremonies is to help the deceased attain the best possible rebirth. Funerals also include ceremonies designed to remove death pollution from relatives and those who have come in contact with the corpse. The funeral is accorded great importance, and rich and poor sponsor the same ceremonies, which is not the case for other life-crisis events.

See also Nepali

Bibliography

Bishop, Barry C. (1990). *Karnali under Stress: Livelihood Strategies and Seasonal Rhythms in a Changing Nepal Himalaya.* Geography research papers, nos. 228–229. Chicago: University of Chicago.

Fürer-Haimendorf, Christoph von (1978). "Trans-Himalayan Traders in Transition." In *Himalyan Anthropology: The Indo-Tibetan Interface,* edited by James F. Fisher, 339–357. The Hague: Mouton Publishers.

Levine, Nancy E. (1987). "Belief and Explanation in Nyinba Women's Witchcraft." *Man* 22:259–74.

Levine, Nancy E. (1987). "Caste, State, and Ethnic Boundaries in Nepal." *Journal of Asian Studies* 46:71–88.

Levine, Nancy E. (1988). *The Dynamics of Polyandry: Kinship, Domesticity, and Population on the Tibetan Border.* Chicago: University of Chicago Press.

NANCY E. LEVINE

Okkaliga

ETHNONYMS: Gangadikāra Okkalu, the peasant caste, Vokkaliga, Wokkaliga

The Okkaligas are the dominant landowning and cultivating caste in the multicaste population of southern Karnataka State in southwestern peninsular India. Among the hundreds of villages in which Okkaligas live is Rampura (population 1,523, 735 of whom are Okkaligas, ca. 1955), which is the focus of this entry and which displays many of the features typical of Okkaliga villages in India.

The village of Rampura is located on the Mysore-Hogur bus road about 32 kilometers from Mysore. The village is a cluster of houses and huts with thatched or tiled roofs; narrow, uneven winding streets running between the rows of houses. Surrounding the village are numerous plots owned by individual landowners. Rampura is an interdependent unit, largely self-sufficient, having its own village assembly (panchayat), watch, ward, officials, and servants. In the multicaste village of Rampura the relationship of castes appears to be determined more by the economic positions of the various members than by tradition. As agriculture is the primary way of life the peasants are the dominant caste. The hereditary headman (patel) and hereditary accountant (shanborg) are both peasants. The headman's responsibility is to represent the village to the government and vice versa. The accountant keeps a register of how much land each head of a family or joint family has and the amount of tax on the land. The elders of the dominant caste are spokespersons for the village and owe their power not to legal rights derived from the state but to the dominant local position of their caste. The elders of the dominant peasant caste in Rampura administer justice not only to members of their own caste group but also to all persons of other castes who seek their intervention.

Agriculture dominates village life. The cultivation of rice is the main activity in the village. Meticulous attention to and irrigation of the rice is necessary throughout the period of cultivation, the rainy season from June to January. The conclusion of the harvest is marked by the festival of Sankranti. During the dry season other social activities such as weddings occur.

Each of the seventeen castes living in Rampura has a distinctive tradition with strong ties with the same caste in villages nearby. The village has a vertical unity of many castes whereas each caste has a horizontal unity through alliances beyond the village. Other major castes and their traditional occupations include the Kuruba (shepherd), the Musalman (artisan and trader), Holeya (servant and laborer), and the Madiga (Harijans). Although paddy and millet grain were principally used in trade, money is used more frequently today. Maintenance of caste separation was achieved through ideas of purity and pollution. Beliefs and behaviors including diet, occupation, and ritual distinguish higher from lower castes. Two examples of this are the rules governing the acceptance of water or cooked food between castes and the rule of caste endogamy.

At one time it was customary for two families, one belonging to an upper caste and the other to an Untouchable caste, to be linked in a master-servant relationship (jajmani).

Independence has begun a process of social change in which many of the traditional forms and orders have been replaced.

The regional language is Kannada and the principal religion is Hindu. The principal temples in Rampura are the temples of Rama, Basava, Hatti Mari, and Kabbala Durgada Mari. These are endowed with agricultural land.

The kin group is agnatic with preference for cross-cousin marriage. Traditionally the Okkaligas live in joint families with the wife joining the home of her husband's family. Since Independence the joint families have tended to become smaller.

There is a fairly strict sexual division of labor with few women working outside the home. Boys work on the land early, while girls work in and around the house. An Okkaliga is buried on his or her ancestral land; and the land is an important part of one's life from an early age.

Bibliography

Banerjee, Bhavani (1966). *Marriage and Kinship of the Gangadikāra Vokkaligas of Mysore*. Deccan College Dissertation Series, no. 27. Poona: Deccan College.

Nanjundayya, H. V., and L. K. Ananthakrishna Iyer (1930). "Gangadikāra Okkalu." *The Mysore Tribes and Castes* 3:175–185. Mysore: Mysore University.

Srinivas, M. N. (1963). "The Social Structure of a Mysore Village." In *India's Villages*, edited by M. N. Srinivas, 21–35. Bombay: Asia Publishing House.

Srinivas, M. N. (1976). *The Remembered Village*. Berkeley: University of California Press.

SARA J. DICK

Oraon

ETHNONYMS: Dhangad, Dhangar, Dhanka ("farmworker"), Kisan, Kuda, Kurukh, Kurunkh, Orao, Uraon

The Oraons are one of the largest tribes in South Asia, numbering 1,702,663 persons at the 1971 census. About half of them live in Bihar, mainly on the Chota Nagpur Plateau; the remainder are in Madhya Pradesh, Orissa, and West Bengal. They speak a Dravidian language known as Kurukh. Oraons are closely related to the neighboring Munda tribe, and the headman of an Oraon village is called *munda*.

Although there are no subcastes among the Oraons, the Kudas ("navvies") and Kisans ("cultivators"), having their distinct occupations, tend to marry among themselves. Beyond this, Oraons observe village and clan exogamy. The patrilineal extended family is the ideal residential unit, but nuclear families are nearly as common. On the average a family contains five to seven coresident members.

Boys and girls marry after puberty, boys usually at 16–20 years. This follows a period in which both sexes sleep in a youth dormitory (*dhumkuria*). Boys are branded on the arm before being admitted to this institution. The dormitory provides a pool of agricultural labor that can be hired when necessary. Most Oraons are farmers, and in the past they practiced shifting cultivation. Hunting, formerly of major importance, has been reduced during the present century to the status of a ceremonial event; there is even a women's hunting ceremony, held every twelve years.

Although a small minority of the tribe are Christians, the great majority follow a Hindu form of worship. Their main deities are local, non-Sanskritic ones, such as Chandi, Chauthia, Dadgo Burhia, Gaon Deoti, and Jair Budhi, names one does not encounter elsewhere in India.

A remarkable feature of Oraon society is that it is one of the very few on earth (along with the neighboring Mundas and Marias) that practices human sacrifice (called *otanga* or *orka* by Oraons). Although extremely rare, evidence suggests the phenomenon is most prevalent in Ranchi District, Bihar. During the nineteenth century, British officials reported a much broader incidence, occurring among the Munda, Oraon, Gond, Kond, and Santal tribes.

Police records show that even as late as the 1980s there were a couple of sacrifices a year among the Munda, Maria, and Oraon tribes, and perhaps slightly more if one assumes that not all cases reached police attention. These sacrifices are of course illegal and are treated as homicide under Section 302 of the Indian Penal Code. Detection of culprits is made very difficult by the fact that some villagers believe the sacrifices are essential for the fertility of their fields, and hence they are not forthcoming with any information. The human sacrifices usually occur in remote places around the beginning of the sowing season and the associated festival of Sarhul. The reasons police can distinguish these sacrifices from other forms of murder are several: (1) the timing, to coincide with the sowing ceremony; (2) the victim is often an orphan or a homeless person, someone who will not be missed; (3) usually no personal animosities can account for the killing; (4) the victim's throat is cut with a knife; (5) signs of *puja* (worship) are normally found near the corpse; and (6) part of one little finger has been cut off and is missing. This last item is presumably a part of the human offering that the sacrificer (*otanga*) will bury in his field. Sometimes blood of the sacrificial victim is mixed with seed grain before it is sown. In earlier centuries the entire body was probably cut up and parceled out to the various fields around a village. The danger of detection now makes this too difficult. The sacrifice is normally offered to a vindictive goddess thought to control the fertility of the soil. If a human victim cannot be caught in time for the sowing ceremony, it is said that hair, sputum, or some other human bodily leavings are mixed with hen's blood as a token offering to this goddess.

See also Munda

Bibliography

Hermanns, Matthias (1973). *Die Oraon. Die religiös-magische Weltanschanung der Primitivstämme Indiens*, no. 3. Wiesbaden: Franz Steiner Verlag.

Roy, Sarat Chandra (1915). *The Oraon of Chota Nagpur*. Calcutta: Brahmo Mission Press.

Roy, Sarat Chandra (1928). *Oraon Religion and Custom*. Ranchi: Man in India Office.

Russell, R. V., and Hira Lal (1916). "Oraon." In *The Tribes and Castes of the Central Provinces of India*, edited by R.V. Russell and Hira Lal. Vol. 4, 299–321. London: Macmillan. Reprint. 1969. Oosterhout: Anthropological Publications.

Sachchidananda (1963). "Some Recent Evidence of Human Sacrifice." In *Anthropology on the March: Recent Studies of Indian Beliefs, Attitudes, and Social Institutions*, edited by L. K. Bala Ratnam, 344–351. Madras: The Book Centre.

Sachchidananda (1964). *Culture Change in Tribal Bihar: Munda and Oraon*. Calcutta: Bookland Private Limited.

PAUL HOCKINGS

Oriya

ETHNONYMS: Odia, Odiya; adjective: Odissi, Orissi (Orissan in English)

Orientation

Identification. In Orissa State in India, the Oriya constitute the regional ethnic group, speaking the Oriya language and professing the Hindu religion, to be distinguished from an Oriya-speaking agricultural caste called Odia found in central coastal Orissa. Some Oriya live in the adjoining states. The Oriya language and ethnic group are presumably derived from the great Udra or Odra people known since Buddhist and pre-Buddhist *Mahabharata* epic times.

Location. The state of Orissa is located between 17°49' and 22°34' N and 81°29' and 87°29' E, covering 155,707 square kilometers along the northeastern seaboard of India. The large majority of the Oriya live in the coastal districts and along the Mahanadi and Brahmani rivers. Orissa falls in the tropical zone with monsoon rains from June–July to September–October. Western Orissa is afflicted with recurring drought.

Demography. The last national census in 1981 records the population of Orissa as 26,370,271 persons, with a population density of 169 persons per square kilometer as compared to 216 for India as a whole. Of the total population of Orissa, 84.11 percent speak Oriya. Although rural, Orissa's urban centers with 5,000 or more persons rose from containing 8.4 percent of the population in 1971 (81 towns) to 11.79 percent in 1981 (108 towns). Most of the ninety-three Scheduled Castes, which constitute 15.1 percent of Orissa's population, speak Oriya. Of the 23.1 percent of Orissa's population categorized as Scheduled Tribes, many speak Oriya as their mother tongue. With 34.23 percent literacy in 1981 compared to 26.18 percent in 1971, Orissa trails behind many Indian states, especially in female literacy.

Linguistic Affiliation.   Oriya belongs to the Indo-Aryan Branch of the Indo-European Family of languages. Its closest affinities are with Bengali (Bangla), Assamese (Asamiya), Maithili, Bhojpuri, and Magahi (Magadhi). The Oriya spoken in Cuttack and Puri districts is taken as standard Oriya. The Oriya language has a distinctive script, traceable to sixth-century inscriptions. It has thirteen vowels and thirty-six consonants (linguistically, spoken Oriya has six vowels, two semivowels, and twenty-nine consonants).

History and Cultural Relations

Orissa has been inhabited since prehistoric times, and Paleolithic, Mesolithic, Neolithic, and Chalcolithic cultural remains abound. By the fourth century B.C. there was a centralized state in Orissa, though the hill areas often nurtured independent princedoms mostly evolving out of tribal polities. In 261 B.C., Orissa, then known as Kalinga, was conquered by the Emperor Ashoka after a bloody Kalinga war, leading to the conversion of the king into a nonviolent Buddhist who spread Buddhism in Asia. In the early second century A.D. Emperor Kharavela, a Jain by religion and a great conqueror, had the famous queen's cave-palace, Ranigumpha, cut into the mountain near Bhubaneswar, with exquisite sculptures depicting dancers and musicians. Both eastern and western Orissa had famous Buddhist monasteries, universities, and creative savants. Starting in the first century A.D., according to Pliny and others, there was extensive maritime trade and cultural relations between Orissa (Kalinga, Kling) and Southeast Asian countries from Myanmar (Burma) to Indonesia. Orissa was ruled under several Hindu dynasties until 1568, when it was annexed by the Muslim kingdom of Bengal. In 1590, Orissa came under the Mogul empire, until the Marathas seized it in 1742. In 1803 it came under British rule. As early as 1817 the agriculturist militia (Paik) of Orissa revolted against the British in one of the first regional anticolonial movements. In 1936 Orissa was declared a province of British India, and the princely states with an Oriya population were merged into Orissa in 1948–1949. The cultures and languages of south India, western India, and northern India—and also those of the tribal peoples—have enriched the cultural mosaic and the vocabulary of the Oriya.

Settlements

In 1981, 88.21 percent of the people of Orissa lived in villages. In 1971, 51,417 villages of Orissa ranged in population from less than 500 persons (71.9 percent), 500–900 persons (18.8 percent), 1,000–1,999 persons (7.5 percent), to more than 2,000 persons (1.78 percent). The Oriya villages fall into two major types: linear and clustered. The linear settlement pattern is found mostly in Puri and Ganjam districts, with houses almost in a continuous chain on both sides of the intervening village path and with kitchen gardens at the back of the houses. Cultivated fields surround the settlement. In the cluster pattern each house has a compound with fruit trees and a kitchen garden. The Scheduled Castes live in linear or cluster hamlets slightly away from the main settlement, with their own water tanks or, today, their own wells. In the flooded coastal areas one finds some dispersed houses, each surrounded by fields for cultivation. In traditional Orissa, two styles of houses (*ghara*) were common. The agriculturists and higher castes had houses of a rectangular ground plan with rooms along all the sides (*khanja-ghara*), leaving an open space (*agana*) in the center. Mud walls with a gabled roof of thatch made of paddy stalks or jungle grass (more durable) were common. The more affluent had double-ceiling houses (*atu ghara*) with the inner ceiling of mud plaster supported by wooden or bamboo planks. This construction made it fireproof and insulated against the summer heat and winter chill. The entrance room was usually a cowshed, as cattle were the wealth of the people. Men met villagers and guests on the wide front veranda. Poorer people had houses with mud walls and straw-thatched gable roofs, without enclosed courtyards or double ceilings. The smoke from the kitchen escaped under the gabled roof. The Oriya had, in common with eastern India, a wooden husking lever (*dhenki*) in the courtyard for dehusking paddy rice or making rice flour. Nowadays houses with large windows and doors, roofs of concrete (tiled or with corrugated iron or asbestos sheets), walls of brick and mortar, and cement floors are becoming common even in remote villages. In the traditional house, the northeastern corner of the kitchen formed the sacred site of the ancestral spirits (*ishana*) for family worship.

Economy

Subsistence and Commercial Activities.   Subsistence cultivation of paddy is ubiquitous as rice is the staple food. Double-cropping, sometimes even triple-cropping in irrigated fields, and single-cropping in drought-affected or rain-fed areas are all common. Large-scale farming with heavy agricultural machinery is still uncommon. Plowing with two bullocks or two buffalo is usual, with a wooden plow. Only recently have iron plows been coming into use. Cash crops like sugarcane, jute, betel leaves on raised mounds, coconuts and areca nuts (betel nuts) are grown in coastal Orissa, and pulses and oil seeds in drought-prone areas. Recently coffee, cocoa, cardamom, pineapples, and bananas have also been raised on a commercial scale. Fish are caught in traps and nets from village tanks, streams, rivers, coastal swamps, and also in the flooded paddy fields. Fishing boats with outboard motors and trawlers are nowadays used at sea. The domestic animals include cows, goats, cats, chickens, ducks, and water buffalo among the lowest castes, as well as pigs and dogs among the urban middle class.

Industrial Arts.   Most large villages had castes of artisans who served the agricultural economy in former times. Carpenters, wheelwrights, and blacksmiths were absolutely necessary. Some villages had potters with pottery wheels and weavers with cottage looms (cotton was formerly grown and yarn spun). Today, industrial products are displacing the village products except for the wooden plow and cart wheels. Some cottage industries, especially the handloomed textiles (including the weaving of *ikat*, cotton textiles that are tied and dyed), are producing for export. Brass and bell-metal utensils and statues and silver and gold filigree ornaments have a wide clientele.

Trade. In villages, peddling and weekly markets were the usual commercial channels. Since World War II ration shops have sold scarce essential commodities.

Division of Labor. Men plow, sow, and carry goods with a pole balanced on the shoulder, whereas women carry things on their head, weed, and transplant the fields. Harvesting is done by both sexes. While men fish and hunt, women perform household chores and tend babies. Traditionally, among higher-caste and higher-class families, women did not work outside home. Nowadays men and some women are engaged in salaried service, but only lower-caste and lower-class women undertake wage labor.

Land Tenure. Before Independence land under agriculture had increased substantially. However, because of the high rate of population growth and subdivision of landholdings, the number of marginal farmers and the landless increased sharply thereafter. Following Independence some land above the statutory ceiling or from the common property resources was distributed among the landless, weaker sections of society. Large-scale industrial and irrigation-cum-power projects displaced people and added to the ranks of the landless. All of this has resulted in various categories of tenancy and contractual lease of land for subsistence cultivation.

Kinship

Kin Groups and Descent. Traditionally and currently, three patterns of family organization have obtained: (1) the multihousehold compounds where the separate families of the sons of the common father are housed as an extended family; (2) joint families with all the brothers living together, with a common kitchen, with or without the parents living (more common in villages than towns); (3) several families belonging to a patrilineage among whom kin obligations continue, residing in neighboring villages. Descent is patrilineal.

Kinship Terminology. The social emphasis on seniority in age and differentiation by sex and generation are observed. Kinship terminology follows the Hawaiian system. Fictive or ritual kin terms are used widely and are expressed in respect and affection and also in meeting appropriate kin obligations.

Marriage and Family

Marriage. Although polygyny was practiced earlier, most marriages today are monogamous. Most marriages even now are also arranged by parents, though some are based on the mutual choice of the marriage partners. Only in western Orissa and southern Orissa is cousin marriage practiced. Marriage partners must not belong to the same _gotra_ (mythical patrilineal descent group). Bride-price among the lower and middle castes has been replaced by a more costly dowry for the bridegroom among all classes and castes. After marriage, residence is patrilocal, with the bride assuming the gotra of the husband. Nowadays residence tends to be neolocal near the place of work. The Hindu marriage was ideally for this life and beyond, but since 1956 divorce has been permitted under legal procedures.

Domestic Unit. Living in a family is considered normal and proper. Most families today in both villages and towns are nuclear, though some are joint families. Members working and living outside usually visit the residual family and shrines occasionally. Often land is cultivated jointly by sharing the farm expenses. Recently there has been a tendency to reduce the size of the rural household through family planning.

Inheritance. Traditionally only sons inherited land and other immovable properties. The eldest son was given an additional share (_jyesthansha_). Since 1956 the widow and daughters have been legal cosharers in all property.

Socialization. Parents, grandparents, and siblings care for infants and children and provide informal—and, recently, formal—education before school. Education of girls is still not common beyond primary school. Physical punishment to discipline a child is common, though infants are usually spared and cuddled. Respect for seniors in all situations and the value of education are emphasized, especially among the higher classes.

Sociopolitical Organization

Orissa is a state in the Republic of India, which has an elected president. The governor is the head of Orissa State, and the chief minister is the elected head of the government of Orissa.

Social Organization. Traditional Oriya society is hierarchically organized primarily on the basis of caste (and subcaste) and occupations and secondarily on the basis of social class. The highest castes, Brahman, are priests and teachers of the Great Tradition. Below them in descending order of status are: the Kshatriya, warriors and rulers; the Vaisya, or traders; and the Sudra, or skilled and unskilled workers and service holders. The occupations involving manual and menial work are low in status, and polluting occupations like skinning dead animals or making shoes are associated with the lowest castes, the Untouchables. Ascriptive status in the caste system is sometimes checked now by acquired status in the class system. In rural Orissa patron-client relationships are common and social mobility is difficult.

Political Organization. Orissa is divided into thirteen districts (_zilla_), and each district is divided into subdivisions (_tahsils_) for administrative purposes, into police stations (_thana_) for law-and-order purposes, and into community development blocs (_blok_) for development purposes. There are village-cluster committees (_panchayat_) with elected members and a head (_sarpanch_) for the lowest level of self-administration and development. The community development bloc has a _panchayat samiti_ or council of panchayats headed by the chairman, with all the sarpanch as members. Each caste or populous subcaste in a group of adjacent villages also had a _jati panchayat_ for enforcing values and institutional discipline. The traditional _gram panchayat_, consisting of the leaders of several important castes in a village, was for maintaining harmony and the ritual cycle.

Social Control and Conflict. Warfare between adjacent princedoms and villages came to a stop under British rule. The police stations (thana) maintain law and order in the rural areas.

Religion and Expressive Culture

Hinduism of various sects is a central and unifying force in Oriya society. The overwhelmingly important Vaishnava sect have their supreme deity, Jagannatha, who lords it over the religious firmament of Orissa. Lord Jagannatha's main temple is at Puri on the sea, where the famous annual festival with huge wooden chariots dragged for the regional divine triad—*Jagannatha, Balabhadra,* and *Subhadra* (goddess sister)—draws about half a million devotees. The famous Lingaraja temple of Lord Shiva at Bhubaneswar, the famous Viraja goddess temple at Jajpur, both in coastal Orissa, and Mahimagadi, the cult temple of the century-old Mahima sect of worshipers of Shunya Parama Brahma (the absolute soul void) at Joranda in central Orissa, are highly sacred for the Oriya people.

Religious Beliefs.   The people of Orissa profess Hinduism overwhelmingly (96.4 percent), with Christianity (1.73 percent), Islam (1.49 percent), Sikhism (0.04 percent) and Buddhism (0.04 percent) trailing far behind. Obviously many tribal groups have declared Hinduism as their religion. Apart from supreme beings, gods, and goddesses of classical Hindu religion, the Oriya propitiate a number of disease spirits, village deities, and revered ancestral spirits.

Religious Practitioners.   In the villages each Brahman priest has a number of client families of Kshatriya, Vaisya, and some Sudra castes. There are also magicians (*gunia*) practicing witchcraft and sorcery. *Kalisi* or shamans are consulted to discover the causes of crises and the remedies.

Ceremonies.   A large number of rituals and festivals mostly following the lunar calendar are observed. The most important rituals are: the New Year festival (Bishuba Sankranti) in mid-April; the fertility of earth festival (Raja Parab); festival of plowing cattle (Gahma Punein); the ritual of eating the new rice (Nabanna); the festival worshiping the goddess of victory, known otherwise as Dassara (Durga Puja); the festival of the unmarried girls (Kumar Purnima); the solar-calendar harvest festival (Makar Sankranti); the fast for Lord Shiva (Shiva Ratri); the festival of colors and the agricultural New Year (Dola Purnima or Dola Jatra); and, finally, the festival worshiping Lord Krishna at the end of February. In November–December (lunar month of Margashira) every Thursday the Gurubara Osha ritual for the rice goddess Lakshmi is held in every Oriya home.

Arts.   The ancient name of Orissa, Utkala, literally means "the highest excellence in the arts." The Oriya are famous for folk paintings, painting on canvas (*patta-chitra*), statuary and sculptures, the Orissan style of temple architecture, and tourist and pilgrim mementos made of horn, papier-mâché, and appliqué work. Classical Odissi dance, the virile Chhow dance, colorful folk dances with indigenous musical instruments (percussion, string, and wind) and also Western instruments, dance dramas, shadow plays (Ravana-Chhaya) with puppets, folk opera (*jatra*), mimetic dances, and musical recitation of God's names are all very popular. Orissi music, largely following classical (*raga*) tunes, and folk music, are rich and varied.

Medicine.   Illness is attributed to "hot" or "cold" food, evil spirits, disease spirits, and witches; and mental diseases to sorcery or spirit possession. Leprosy and gangrenous wounds are thought to be punishment for the commission of "great" sins, and, for general physical and mental conditions, planets and stars in the zodiac are held to be responsible. Cures are sought through herbal folk medicines, propitiation of supernatural beings and spirits, exorcism, counteraction by a gunia (sorcery and witchcraft specialist), and the services of homeopathic, allopathic, or Ayurvedic specialists.

Death and Afterlife.   Death is considered a transitional state in a cycle of rebirths till the soul (*atma*) merges in the absolute soul (*paramatma*). The god of justice, Yama, assigns the soul either to Heaven (*swarga*) or to Hell (*narka*). The funeral rites and consequent pollution attached to the family and lineage of the deceased last for ten days among higher castes. The dead normally are cremated.

Bibliography

Das, Binod Sankar (1984). *Life and Culture in Orissa.* Calcutta: Minerva Associates.

Das, K. B., and L. K. Mahapatra (1979). *Folklore of Orissa.* New Delhi: National Book Trust India. 2nd ed. 1990.

Das, M. N., ed. (1977). *Sidelights on History and Culture of Orissa.* Cuttack: Vidyapuri.

Eschmann, A., H. Kulke, and G. C. Tripathi (1978). *The Cult of Jagannath and the Regional Tradition of Orissa.* New Delhi: Manohar Publications.

Fisher, E., S. Mahapatra, and D. Pathy (1980). *Orissa Kunst und Kultur in Nordost Indien.* Zurich: Museum Rietberg.

Ganguly, Mano Mohan (1912). *Brissa and Her Remains—Ancient and Mediaeval (District Puri).* Calcutta: Thacker, Spink & Co.; London: W. Thacker & Co.

Mahapatra, L. K. (1987). "Mayurbhanj, Keonjhar, and Bonai Ex-Princely States of Orissa." In *Tribal Polities and Pre-Colonial State Systems in Eastern and Northeastern India,* edited by Surajit Sinha. Calcutta: K. P. Bagchi.

Marglin, Frédérique Apffel (1985). *Wives of the God-King: The Rituals of the Devadasis of Puri.* New Delhi: Oxford University Press.

Orissa, Government of. Revenue Department (1990). "History" and "People." In *Orissa State Gazetteer.* Vol. 1. Cuttack: Orissa Government Press.

L. K. MAHAPATRA

Pahari

ETHNONYMS: none

Orientation

Identification. "Pahari" can refer to any mountain-dwelling people, but in north India it generally designates the Indo-European–speaking peoples of the Himalayas who, however, generally prefer regional ethnic designations. In India these include, among many others (from west to east): Churachi, Gaddi, Kinnaura, Sirmuri (all in Himachal Pradesh); Jaunsari, Garhwali, Kumauni (all in Uttar Pradesh); etc. Crosscutting these are terms distinguishing religions (e.g., Hindu, Muslim), caste categories (e.g., for low castes: Dom, Kilta, Shilpkar; for high castes: Khas, Khasiya), and specific castes (e.g., for low castes: Bajgi, Lohar, Mochi, etc.; for high castes: Brahman, Baman, Rajput, Chhetri, Thakur). There are also terms associated with specific noncaste ethnic groups and livelihoods, such as Gujjar (transhumant cattle herders, some groups of which are Hindu, others Muslim). In Nepal distinctions among Paharis are more often reported to refer to caste than to region: that is, the high-caste category, Khas, and the low-caste category, Dom or Damai, with their specific caste names. These caste names distinguish them from Tibeto-Burman–speaking neighbors whom they identify by ethnic terms (e.g., Magars, Gurungs). The term, "Pahari" comes from the Hindi word *pahar*, meaning "mountain," and so literally it means "of the mountains."

Location. The Pahari occupy the outer, lower ranges of the Himalayas—generally between about 600 and 2,100 meters above sea level—adjacent to the Indo-Gangetic Plain, in a 1,600–kilometer crescent not more than 80 kilometers wide, stretching from Kashmir in the northwest to central Nepal in the southeast. These geologically young mountains are the result of the Indian tectonic plate pushing under the Asian one. This upthrust results in frequent landslides and rapid erosion, creating precipitous topography with sharp peaks and V-shaped ravines rather than alluvial valleys or lakes. The massive scarp, which even the lower Himalayas present to the flat Indo-Gangetic Plain, forces the northward-moving summer monsoon clouds abruptly upward, generating heavy precipitation each year and ensuring a rich postmonsoon harvest. Winters tend to be cold with moderate to slight snowfalls at the upper limits of Pahari habitation (at 1,800 to 2,400 meters) and comparable rainfall at lower elevations.

Demography. Reliable population figures on Pahari speakers are not available, but my estimate is in the neighborhood of 17 million: 6 million in Himachal Pradesh and Kashmir, 6 million in Uttar Pradesh, and 5 million in Nepal. Their population density is not great, perhaps 58 persons per square kilometer, but the annual growth must be around 2.5 percent.

Linguistic Affiliation. The people of the outer Himalayas are culturally and linguistically distinct from their plains-dwelling Hindi-, Punjabi-, and Urdu-speaking Hindu, Sikh, and Muslim neighbors to the south and from the higher-elevation–dwelling Tibetan-speaking Bhuddist Bhotias to the north. G. A. Grierson, in his classic *Linguistic Survey of India*, labeled their Indo-European language "Pahari" and identified its main sections: Western Pahari, found west of the Jumna River (i.e, now Himachal Pradesh) and into Kashmir; Central Pahari, between the Jumna and the Maha Kali rivers (i.e., in Garhwal and Kumaon, now comprising the Himalayan districts of Uttar Pradesh State; and Eastern Pahari (generally called Nepali), extending from Nepal's western border (the Maha Kali) into central Nepal. Less sharply drawn than the northern and southern linguistic boundaries are those to the east, where Pahari gives way to Tibeto-Burman, and to the west, where it meets Dardic languages, mainly Kashmiri. Also, along the southern border of the eastern half of the Pahari domain, in the *terai* (the narrow band where the Himalayas meet the plains), live the tribal Tharu with their distinctive language.

History and Cultural Relations

The Pahari people probably derive from population movements out of the plains into the mountains. It is widely believed that they have come during the past 3,000 years as refugees from population pressure, plagues, famines, droughts, political oppression, military and civil conflict, and the like. Muslim invasions, from about A.D. 1000 to 1600, may have accelerated such movements, which need not have been characteristically massive but likely included many small-scale, even familial, migrations. Residents of Sirkanda, the Garhwali village in which I have worked for many years, say that their ancestors began coming some 300 years ago in extended family groups from still-known mountain villages in the Pahari heartland to the northeast in search of new land and pastures. Whatever the sources, it is clear that over time the Pahari population has been geographically mobile and numerically variable. The very name of "Garhwal" suggests this, for it means "land of fortresses"— referring to the ruins that are to be found throughout the region (including two in Sirkanda) and that are as much a puzzle as the people who built them. The Eastern and Central Pahari languages form a dialectal continuum, but there is a relatively sharp break in mutual intelligibility between Central and Western Pahari. Other cultural differences between the Eastern/Central and Western speech communities, together with some demographic evidence, also suggest that long ago there was a frontier, located somewhere between the Jumna and Ganges watersheds. As recently as the first decade of the nineteenth century, the small princely principalities that comprised the Pahari region east of present-day Simla in Himachal Pradesh were conquered by the Nepalese. A decade later the British drove them back, decreed the Maha Kali River to be the western border of Nepal, and laid the foundation for the present administrative subdivisions of the Indian Himalayas.

Settlements

Throughout most of the Pahari region the population is clustered in small villages, usually of well under 350 people. These are situated adjacent to open hillsides, near pasturage, forested land, and a reliable water source—either a stream or a spring. The hillsides are terraced for agriculture, the terraces irrigated where possible from upstream sources through systems of canals and flumes that also serve to power water mills. Houses are rectangular, of two or occasionally more stories, made of 46-centimeter-thick stone and adobe mortar walls and reinforced by wooden beams (in some regions the upper stories are made largely or entirely of wood), with gabled (but in some areas flat) roofs of slate, heavy wooden shakes, or thatch. They are no more than two rooms deep, but vary greatly—up to six rooms—in length. In many regions, as in Sirkanda, they characteristically have a large open central living room (*tibari*) or veranda near the middle, on the front (downhill) side, supported by ornamentally carved columns. Doors, door frames, and windows—and often rafters and beams as well—are also likely to be ornately carved and sometimes painted. Next to the living room is a kitchen; other rooms serve as bedrooms and storage rooms. Occupants, comprising an extended family, live on the second floor in anywhere from two to six rooms reached by one or more external stone stairways; livestock live on the ground floor. Within a village houses tend to be arranged along the contour of the land in parallel rows of several houses each.

Many landowning families own additional houses (*chaan*) situated near fields or pastures at a distance from the village sufficient to make tending them difficult from there. Chaans are usually of a single story shared by livestock and people, separated by a wooden curb or sometimes a partition. They may be occupied seasonally or year-round depending upon circumstances: often a family will have a higher-elevation chaan for use in summer and a lower-elevation chaan for use in winter. The hills are alive with movement when the seasons change and people, goods, and animals are moved from one location (chaan, village house) to another. Chaans provide a way to separate family members without dividing the family. Clusters of chaans may evolve into villages as population increases—the names of many villages reveal their former chaan status.

Economy

Subsistence and Commercial Activities.   Pahari economy is based on subsistence agriculture, engaged in by landowning high castes (Brahmans and Kshatriyas). Extended joint families cultivate terraced fields that produce two crops per year. The winter crop, primarily wheat and barley, is planted in October–November and harvested in March–April; the rainy-season crop, primarily millets but also including substantial amounts of amaranth, maize, dry and wet rice (where irrigation permits), and a variety of lentils and vegetables, is planted in April–May and harvested in September–October. Fields are kept productive by intensive fertilizing with animal manure and systematic fallowing. Milk and milk products, along with potatoes, ginger, and some vegetables, are produced for sale as well as for consumption where markets are accessible. Apricots are a cash crop in some areas, and near Kotgarh, north of Simla, apples have also become so. Opium is another, notably in Himachal Pradesh.

Buffalo and cattle are kept both for the milk they produce and for the manure. In Sirkanda, agricultural households averaged three to four buffalo and sixteen to eighteen cattle. In villages more remote from markets, fewer of these livestock are kept. Buffalo produce more and richer milk than cows, but they are harder to maintain because they eat more, must be kept well watered and cool, and unlike cattle must be stall-fed and watered because they are regarded as too clumsy to fend for themselves. Most highly prized of all livestock are the small but sturdy Pahari bullocks used as draft animals: there are usually one to three pairs per household (depending

upon the size of landholdings). Goats and in some areas sheep are kept largely for sale but also for domestic sacrifice (and subsequent consumption). About half of Sirkanda households keep an average of fifteen of these animals per household. Horses or mules, one or rarely two, are kept by about a third of the landed families in Sirkanda, for transport of products to and from markets.

Industrial Arts.   What might be called "industrial arts" are engaged in only for domestic use, not sale or export. Low castes of artisans are to be found in most regions if not in most villages: smiths (blacksmiths, silversmiths, goldsmiths), carpenters, lathe turners, masons, weavers, tailors, rope makers, shoemakers. Traditionally they did their work not by the piece and not for cash but in the well-known South Asian *jajmani* relationship, as clients to a landed patron who compensated them for their service and loyalty with agricultural produce. Where no specialist caste is available to supply a required product or service, another low caste will generally be pressed into service or the high-caste community members will take the job. As transportation has enhanced contact with markets, piecework and cash purchases have impinged on this system, to the advantage of the consumers and the disadvantage of the providers (who are rendered superfluous by the availability of commercial products).

Trade.   See preceding subheadings under "Economy."

Division of Labor.   The fundamental divisions of Pahari labor are by sex and caste. The high castes are landowning farmers who do all of the work required to grow and process crops and to husband domestic animals. The low castes are their hereditary landless servants. The latter are defined as artisans, as is suggested by their derogatory-descriptive appellation, *shilpkar* (literally, "handworker"). They include, in addition to the artisan specialties described above, service specialties such as musician, entertainer, and barber. Service castes are required as well to perform any domestic service their patrons may demand of them. Among themselves, they exchange their special products and services. The one high-caste specialty is that of the Brahman priest. Most people of this caste are farmers like their Kshatriya village mates, but some men—often only one in an extended family or in a village—specialize in priestly activities. These men tend to rituals—annual or periodic rites, life-cycle rites, horoscopes, temple worship, etc—for their fellow high castes in the same jajmani relationship to those they service as is found among the artisan castes—except that here the Brahman server may be more accurately regarded as the patron and the person served as the client.

The sexual division of labor varies somewhat by caste. High-caste men and women share the agricultural labor, but men alone do the tasks entailing the use of draft animals (plowing, harrowing) and sow the seed, while women prepare the manure to be used as fertilizer, winnow and handmill the grain, and handle all phases in the preparation of food for eating. Men build and maintain houses and other structures and the terraces, transport goods into and out of the village, and handle the trading and all dealings with outsiders. Women care for the children, do the housekeeping, and handle most of the day-to-day maintenance and provisioning of persons and animals that farming households require. Among the service castes, the division of labor is the same except that men do most or all of the activities that their occupational specialty requires (essentially substituting such activities for the exclusively male agricultural activities of the high castes). Low-caste women perform a few special tasks to support their menfolk's caste specialties, but for the most part they have the same tasks and responsibilities as high-caste women: they process and prepare the food, care for the children, keep house, and do much of the care of animals.

It is important to note that the position of women in Pahari society is distinctly superior to the position of women in plains society. Both women and men are aware and proud of this feature of their society. Pahari women play an essential and recognized role in almost all aspects of the economy. They are not secluded, they are not limited in their movements within and around the village, and they participate fully in ritual and religious activities, except those reserved for priests and those which take place outside the village in which they live. They also participate fully in recreational activities including traditional dancing. Their marriage brings a bride-price to their family rather than costing a dowry. They can divorce and remarry as easily as men. Widows are not constrained by widowhood and routinely remarry. Pahari women are noticeably more outspoken and self-confident in the presence of others, including strangers, as compared to women of the plains. As the culture of the politically, economically, educationally, and numerically dominant plains society increasingly impinges upon Pahari people, their worldview is inevitably affected. Sanskritic standards of the plains distort or replace Pahari customs, to the point that not only plainspeople but expatriate Paharis as well become critical, even ashamed, of Pahari traditions. Thus traditional Pahari religious and ritual activities, which are matters of pride for many, have become matters of shame and denial for those seeking the approval of plainspeople. Among such customs are animal (especially buffalo) sacrifice, bride-price, marriage, female-initiated divorce, widow and divorcée remarriage, polygyny, polyandry (where it occurs), female singing and dancing in public—in fact, almost all expressions of female freedom of action, options, participation, and assertiveness in social life. Division of labor by age and familial status (e.g., daughter vs. daughter-in-law) also exists but harbors few surprises for those familiar with Indian society, and in any case it cannot be examined within the limitations of this space.

Land Tenure.   This topic is too complex to discuss in detail here. Suffice it to repeat that traditionally only the high-caste (Brahman and Kshatriya) categories were allowed to own land. Independent India has abolished this rule, and efforts have been made to provide land to the landless, but the overwhelming preponderance of low-caste people still own very little and very poor land, if any at all. The problem of bonded labor and "debt slavery" among low castes remains endemic in many Pahari areas.

In the vicinity of my research, there is very little in the way of sharecropping, renting, absentee landlordism, and the like. These are true extended joint-family subsistence farms, worked by the members of the owner families with the assistance of artisan castes and an occasional hired servant. But in other Pahari regions one can discover instances of virtually every conceivable alternative system of ownership and subsidiary rights to the land, as well as every manifestation of subinfeudation and exploitation.

Kinship

Kin Groups and Descent.   As with most South Asian societies, Pahari society is composed of named, ranked castes, membership in which is determined by birth (i.e., by ancestry). Castes are with few exceptions endogamous, and therefore they comprise very extended kin groups. Each caste is made up of exogamous patrilineal, patrilocal sibs (or clans). Each sib is made up of numerous extended joint families, usually including two generations but ranging from one to as many as three or even four. Brothers are expected to keep the family and its patrimony intact, but even if they succeed in doing so, upon their deaths their children, who are cousins, generally divide it up.

Kinship Terminology.   Kinship terminology reflects this social structure: there are detailed terminological distinctions on the basis of affinity and consanguinity, of seniority (generation, birth order, and age of self or husband), etc. But cousins are not terminologically distinguished from siblings, nor first from second cousins, etc. (i.e., all are regarded as siblings). Therefore, it is a system employing standard Hawaiian-type cousin terms. In short, Pahari kinship organization and terminology are typical of those found throughout north India.

Marriage and Family

Marriage and Domestic Unit.   Marriage must be within the caste and outside the patrilineal sib (clan). It is ceremonialized in a way well within the range of variation found through north India except that, unlike that of most high castes elsewhere, it does not entail a dowry. Rather, it entails a bride-price, which in fact is the traditional necessary component of a valid marriage. Polygyny is permitted (most often occasioned by the levirate), with an incidence of about 15 percent in the region of my work; about 20 percent of polygynous unions are sororal. Unmarried men never marry previously married women (although unceremonialized elopement occasionally occurs). Any subsequent marriage is ceremonialized only if the woman has not been previously married. Divorce, initiated by husband or wife, is easy and frequent, requiring only the return of the bride-price (by the wife's family or new husband). Children, however, belong to and stay with their father and his family, a major deterrent to divorce for women with children.

A major distinctive feature of the Western Pahari area is that fraternal polyandry—strictly prohibited in the Central and Eastern Pahari areas—is permitted and in fact is the preferred form of marriage in some regions such as Jaunsar Bawar and scattered localities in Himachal Pradesh.

Throughout the Pahari area, postmarital residence is prescriptively patrilocal (virilocal). Exceptions occur for economic reasons, but some stigma is attached to them.

Socialization.   Children are nursed to the age of 3 or 4 and are given the breast occasionally up to age 5 or 6. Socialization is permissive and relaxed, especially in the early years. Boys are socialized together with girls, in a largely female environment, up to the age of 7 or 8, at which time they begin to interact mainly with males. Never are the sexes as segregated as in the plains, however. Girls assume household responsibilities earlier and these are more taxing than for boys—in short, boys are indulged more than girls. Not until puberty are caste distinctions and restrictions rigorously enforced. The marriage ceremony may take place at an early age (8 to 10) but nowadays usually not until later, and in any case the couple does not begin to live together until puberty has been attained: girls by about age 13 or later, boys by age 16 or later. Schooling is a recent phenomenon, restricted primarily to high-caste boys from prosperous families and usually not pursued beyond the first three to five years. Learning for both sexes and all castes is by participation, in effect by apprenticeship.

Sociopolitical Organization

Social Organization. Most features of social organization have been covered above under the headings "Division of Labor," "Kinship," and "Marriage and Family." The remaining point requiring explanation is the Pahari system of caste categories. The pan-Indian system of castes and caste categories comprises innumerable localized castes (*jati*), hierarchically ranked according to their inborn purity. Castes, in turn, are grouped into five ranked categories called *varnas*: Brahman, Kshatriya, Vaisya, Sudra, and Achut. The first three are called "twice-born," indicating a higher order of ritual purity than the other two, while the Sudra, in turn, are purer than the Achut, who are regarded as woefully polluted (*achut* literally means "untouchable") and in fact are scripturally described as outside of the varna system, although structurally they comprise a fifth varna. Brahmans are traditionally the priestly castes; Kshatriyas are the royal, administrative, and warrior castes; Vaisyas are the yeoman farmer castes (who in historic times have come to be identified primarily as mercantile castes); Sudras are the "clean" artisan and service castes; and Achut are the castes that perform the most polluting tasks (e.g., scavengers, latrine cleaners, leatherworkers). In Pahari society, by contrast, generally only three varnas are represented—Brahman, Kshatriya, and Achut. Proportions in each category vary locally and regionally, but 75 to 90 percent of the Pahari population is Kshatriya. The Pahari social organization can be understood, in a rough way, by saying that there are no Vaisya castes, and all of those castes that in most of India are Sudra are in Pahari society classified as Achut, creating in effect a tripartite varna system. But indigenous terminology, at least in the Central Pahari region, suggests that the varna system is or in origin was in fact binary, comprising simply "twice-born" and "untouchable" categories. Pahari Brahmans and Kshatriyas are often collectively termed "Khas" or "Khasiya"; Pahari low castes are collectively termed "Dom." The social reality of this seems confirmed by the fact that marriage between Pahari Brahmans and Kshatriyas is tolerated (although reluctantly and without ceremony), something that plains society does not countenance, and marriage among low castes is similarly allowed.

Political Organization, Social Control, Conflict. At the village level, each caste is organized to handle internal conflicts and transgressions. However, heads of high-caste households (or some of them) traditionally constitute a council that decides matters of policy and social control for the village at large and intervenes as well in low-caste disputes or transgressions. Since independence, various kinds of councils have been established by the national governments of the nations in which Paharis live. In India, these are elected bodies, with an elected headman and with seats reserved for women and members of Achut castes. Their actual powers, however, tend to be limited to official matters, while social control remains with the traditional high-caste councils. As is true throughout India, low-caste individuals and collectivities are subject to stern measures, including violent physical sanctions of the most dire sort, to enforce the constraints placed on them by the high castes.

Religion and Expressive Culture

Religious Beliefs. Because the overwhelming preponderance of Paharis are Hindus, only that religion is described here. There are also Muslim Paharis, but they have been little described in the literature. Presumably their Islamic religion is that of the rest of South Asia, with a distinctly Pahari cast to it, notably as a result of beliefs and practices, pervasive in Pahari culture, that are neither identifiably Islamic nor Hindu in origin.

Pahari Hinduism shares most of its content with pan-Indian Hinduism, including some degree of belief in dharma (intrinsic individual and collective duty or "right behavior"), karma (just desserts contingent on fulfillment of dharma), samsara (reincarnation in accord with karma), maya (the illusory nature of existence), nirvana or *samadhi* (ultimate escape, if karma permits, from the wheel of reincarnation into oneness with the universe). Similarly there is an awareness of the scriptures, the great deities of Hinduism, the holy places, the holy days, the periodic and life-cycle rituals, the values, the prescriptions and proscriptions enjoined upon the faithful, etc. But there are also distinctive Pahari traditions regarded by their practitioners as the consequence of social and environmental circumstances of their alpine existence. In contrast to villages of the plains, there is little systematic difference among Pahari castes in religious belief and practice. In the eyes of outsiders, expatriates, and sophisticates, these traditions are often seen as rustic and therefore embarrassingly unorthodox and in need of reform. The dominant aspect of this rusticity is a lack of rigor in following the behavioral injunctions of Sanskritic Hinduism: dietary restrictions are virtually ignored, except for the taboo on beef; many of the great deities of Hinduism and the rituals associated with them are overlooked; niceties in the expression and maintenance of ritual purity are treated casually; most Sanskritic restrictions on high-caste women are not observed; and life-cycle rites and periodic rituals are understood and observed in a distinctly Pahari manner.

Supernaturals are of many types and innumerable manifestations—as suggested by the frequently quoted description of Hinduism as a "religion of 330 million gods." Deities (or gods) are the most powerful of supernaturals and must be placated to avoid their destructive wrath. Placation takes the form of honoring them with worship, especially by making offerings to them (prominently through animal sacrifice). In Sirkanda a number of household deities (associated with, affecting, and therefore worshiped by household members) are worshiped by each family at shrines in the dwelling. In addition, there are village deities, worshiped by most villagers on ritual occasions at a shrine in or near the village. Among the latter deities are the five Pandava brothers, known to every Hindu as heroic warriors of the *Mahabharata* epic, but to my knowledge worshiped as major deities only, and universally, by Paharis. Polyandrous Western Pahari societies cite the polyandrous Panduvas as the precedent for their own marriage rules. There are in addition a variety of other categories of supernaturals: ancestral spirits, ghosts or demons, sprites or fairies, etc. As with deities, each of these has dangerous powers that must be avoided, warded off, or properly attended to. Various diviners, exorcists, curers, and other specialists capable of dealing with the malevolence of such supernaturals are to be found in every locality.

Religious Practitioners. Pahari religious practitioners, as throughout Hindu society, are of two major types. The first type includes those of the priestly (Brahman) caste, exclusively entitled by birth to their profession, whose responsibilities are to convey, oversee, perpetuate, and perform the scripturally prescribed aspects of Hinduism necessary to the long-term maintenance of relations between the faithful and the supernatural. The second type includes the individually gifted and supernaturally inspired practitioners of folk traditions, who, while not incompatible with Hinduism and in fact universally associated with it, are not enjoined by it: namely, the shamans (called _baki_ in the Central Pahari region, and _bhagat_ in the north Indian plains), diviners, exorcists, curers, and a variety of other practitioners—most often of low caste but potentially of any caste and either sex—who serve the immediate, pragmatic needs of people by dealing via the supernatural with the fateful, unpredictable aspects of their lives.

Ceremonies. Ceremonies are numerous and often complex. They honor and placate deities and ancestors, celebrate or ward off the effects of astrological concordances, memorialize and celebrate life-cycle events, protect and perpetuate the well-being of individuals and groups, etc. Among several peculiar to the Pahari region (all well within the range of Hindu ceremonies) is the famous rope-sliding ceremony. Too complex to describe adequately here—and now outlawed—it is worth mentioning because it incorporates the features of all Hindu ceremonies in a unique and spectacular Pahari idiom. Basically, it is an attempt to appease the wrath of the most powerful deity of the region, who has wrought dire and persistent misfortune on a village, by offering him a magnificent and expensive entertainment accompanied by many subsidiary sacrifices and supplications carried out by scores of priests, shamans, and other specialists before hundreds of worshipful participants and spectators. The climactic event occurs when a ritually prepared low-caste man who has been secured to a saddle astride a gigantic oil-soaked rope that is stretched between a tree at the top of a cliff and another at a distance below to form a steep incline, is released to careen down the rope, smoke streaming behind, to an uncertain fate at the end of his ride. If the spectacle is successful, the rider survives, the god is pleased, the community is relieved of its misfortune, the many who contributed to the event are benefited in proportion to their material or financial contribution, and everyone who witnessed it is blessed.

Arts. Pahari artisan castes are the artists of this society, best known for wood carving of doors, windows, columns, rafters, etc. and ornamental stone carving. Carpenters and masons are noted for their architectural achievements through ingenious and beautiful use of wood and stone. The artistry of gold- and silversmiths, expressed primarily in women's jewelry, is also notable. Tailors and shoemakers are responsible for the colorful traditional Pahari clothing. The distinctive Pahari music has recently been selectively adapted to a popular idiom without entirely losing its traditional qualities, and it has achieved popular attention and commercial success in India. This music derives from folksongs known to all elements of Pahari society, rendered and preserved by the musician castes.

Medicine. Traditional practitioners employ a wide variety of herbal and ritual treatments for illnesses, injuries, and discomforts. In every village there are specialists known for their success in healing: herbalists, masseuses, curers of pustular diseases, bone setters, laceration healers, midwives, shamans, exorcists, etc. Elements of conventional Ayurvedic medical belief and practice are discernible but do not generally form a tightly organized system in rural villages. Government programs have brought medical personnel—employing variously Ayurvedic, Unani, and scientific medical treatments—to many villages and health clinics to many regions. Hospitals are available in major centers. Still, however, most treatment is by traditional, indigenous practitioners. When medicines are sought from outside they are almost always patent remedies rather than prescribed medicines. Mortality, especially infant mortality, remains extremely high in the Pahari areas.

Death and Afterlife. Among Hindu Paharis, death and afterlife are understood and dealt with in characteristically Hindu fashion. (Muslims bury their dead and attend to death in ways prescribed by Islam, but here I am able only to discuss Hindu customs in the matter.) Among Hindus, small children are buried, as are those who die of particular virulent diseases and the rare holy individual who has achieved samadhi. Others are cremated, preferably by the side of a stream, with the remains being committed to the water. The ceremonies attending death, cremation, and the postcremation period are complex but not notably different from those prescribed in Hinduism. Women do not attend the funeral cremation, but they, like all relatives, participate in mourning according to the closeness of their kinship to the deceased. It is believed that the station of one's next life in the cycle of reincarnation—one's karma—is a consequence of fulfillment of one's dharma—the donation to charities, the performance of austerities, etc.

See also Nepali; Tharu

Bibliography

Berreman, Gerald D. (1972). _Hindus of the Himalayas: Ethnography and Change._ 2nd ed. Berkeley: University of California Press.

Grierson, G. A. (1916). _Linguistic Survey of India._ Vol. 9, pt. 4, 1. Calcutta: Superintendent of Government Printing.

Majumdar, D. N. (1972). _Himalayan Polyandry: Structure, Functioning, and Culture Change, a Field–Study of Jaunsar Bawar._ New York: Asia Publishing House.

Newell, William H. (1967). _Census of India, 1961._ Vol. 20, _Himachal Pradesh,_ pt. 5-B, _The Gaddi and Affiliated Castes in the Western Himalayas,_ Report on Scheduled Castes and Scheduled Tribes. Delhi: Manager of Publications.

Parry, Jonathan P. (1979). _Caste and Kinship in Kangra._ London: Routledge and Kegan Paul.

Raha, Manis Kumar, ed. (1987). *The Himalayan Heritage*. Delhi: Gian Publishing House.

Raha, Manis Kumar, and Satya Narayan Mahato (1985). *The Kinnaurese of the Himalayas*. Memoirs of the Anthropological Survey of India, no. 63. Calcutta.

GERALD D. BERREMAN

Pandit of Kashmir

ETHNONYMS: Batta, Bhatta, Brahman, Saraswat

Orientation

Identification. The Pandits are natives of the Kashmir Valley in north India. They belong to the highest-ranked Brahman castes of Hindu society. Among Brahmans they are identified as Saraswats. The two most commonly offered interpretations of this appellation are: Brahmans who live west of the subterranean river Saraswati; or Brahmans who are devotees of Saraswati, the Hindu goddess of learning. The Sanskrit word *pandita* means a learned man. Although generally known as Kashmiri Pandits, they refer to themselves as Bhatta or Batta, which is the Prakrit word for "great scholars." There are no historical records of Pandits having come to Kashmir from elsewhere, though many lay observers have speculated about possible Jewish, Greek, or Persian origins.

Location. The Kashmir Valley is located approximately between 33°30′ and 34°30′ N and 73°30′ and 75°30′ E. It is famous for its scenic beauty. Surrounded by mountains of the Pir Panjal range, which rise up to 5,150 meters, the valley is 134 kilometers long and 40 kilometers wide and is situated at an average elevation of about 1,500 meters. Many rivers, streams, and lakes provide a rich source of water. Kashmir is marked by a temperate climate with four distinct seasons: spring, summer, autumn, and winter. Much of the annual precipitation of about 66 centimeters is snow and the mean temperature for January is about 0° C. Summer temperatures rarely rise above 35° C.

Demography. When all Hindus are counted together (there are some non-Pandit Hindus also in the valley), they add up to 117,431 persons (1981 census) constituting about 4.5 percent of the total population; the rest are Muslims. According to unofficial estimates there are about 100,000 Pandits in Kashmir. Men outnumber women. Of the total number of Pandits, nearly 65 percent live in urban areas. While there are numerous villages inhabited by Muslims alone, there is no village where only Hindus live or where they outnumber Muslims.

Linguistic Affiliation. Pandits speak Koshur (Kashmiri), an Indo-Aryan language with pronounced Central Asian (Dardic) affinities. The Koshur that Pandits speak contains a larger number of words of Sanskrit-Prakrit derivation than the Persianized/Arabicized Koshur of the Muslims. The original script of the language, Sharada, is akin to the Devanagari script (of Sanskrit) but has fallen into disuse. It is now used only by priests for writing horoscopes or copying traditional texts relating to domestic rituals. The script in use in schools and elsewhere is Persian.

History and Cultural Relations

The first recognizable historical narrative of India, the *Rajataringini* (*River of Kings*), composed in the middle of the twelfth century by a Kashmiri Brahman, Kalhana, speaks of the mythic origins of the valley in a sacred lake. Marine fossils found by modern researchers lend credence to the legends. According to the *Rajataringini*, early caste-based Hindu society was overlain by Buddhist elements but never completely displaced. Hindu dynasties continued to rule until the early fourteenth century when Islam was brought to Kashmir by kings and Sufi missionaries from central Asia, Afghanistan, and Persia. Tradition has it that only a handful of families of Brahmans survived the twin processes of conversion and elimination. These were the ancestors of the Pandits of today. Kashmir was incorporated into the Mughal Empire in the late sixteenth century. The liberal religious policy of the Mughals led to a gradual reassertion of the place of Kashmiri Brahmans in their native land. Many, however, migrated out of Kashmir. It was in response to the request from some of these Brahmans that the use of the appellation "Pandit" as an honorific title was approved by the Mughal emperor in the eighteenth century. There are today localized communities of Kashmiri Pandits in many Indian cities. According to estimates, there is one Kashmiri Pandit outside Kashmir for every three living there. The Nehru family were Pandits.

Settlements

In both urban and rural areas, Pandits live alongside of Muslims, receive goods and services from them in an asymmetrical relationship, but maintain social distance from them. The two communities do not intermarry or interdine with each other. The largest population of Pandits in any village is between 500 and 1,000. There are, however, many predominantly Pandit neighborhoods, particularly in the urban areas. Everywhere in the valley Pandits live in strongly built brick and timber houses with gabled roofs. Each house normally has three stories and about a dozen rooms. A yard, a kitchen garden, a granary, and a cattle shed may be attached to it.

Economy

Subsistence and Commercial Activities. Traditionally, rural Pandits were primarily dependent upon agriculture, the land being cultivated by the owners themselves or by their Pandit or Muslim tenants. Paddy, wheat, and maize are the main crops. Fruits and vegetables also are grown. Small-scale trade, shopkeeping, and civil or domestic service are additional sources of income. The traditional professions are priesthood, teaching, and the practice of traditional Unani (Greco-Arab) medicine. Pandits have never looked favorably upon working with their hands. All the village artisans (e.g., potters, blacksmiths, weavers) have been and are Muslims. Similarly, all menial services are provided by Muslim occupational groups (e.g., barbers, washers, scavengers). Like upper-caste Hindus elsewhere, Pandits consider cows and bulls sacred animals and every family that can afford it will have them at home. Ponies or horses also may be owned. Occasionally birds (parrots, mynahs) are kept as pets. Domestic cats are tolerated. Dogs, ducks, and poultry—though present everywhere (they are associated with Muslims)—are considered polluting and are avoided.

Trade. The grocery store is the typical shop. Trade on a larger scale in timber, fruits, milk products, etc., is also practiced.

Division of Labor. Subcaste, socioeconomic class, gender, and age comprise the bases of division of labor. Priestly work is the exclusive responsibility of the subcaste of Gor. Landed aristocracy and families of noble lineage do not themselves work on the land. Domestic chores are clearly divided between men (house repairs, grain storage, etc.) and women (cooking, washing, spinning, etc.). Children assist the elders.

Land Tenure. Land reforms enacted by the government in 1950 placed the ceiling on the ownership of agricultural land at 8.8 hectares. The rights of tenancy and the tenant's share in the produce are protected. Pandits employ fellow Pandits or more often Muslims as tenant farmers.

Kinship

Kin Groups and Descent. Pandit kinship is based on a well-articulated ideology of patrilineal descent. The widest category (maximal lineage) of agnates is called *kol*. In theory structural extension and territorial dispersal do not affect it. In practice, however, both these factors are important. Genealogical connections are rarely remembered beyond half a dozen generations. If collateral spread is combined with physical dispersal, interkin interaction and ultimately recognition fade away. The rule of *gotra* exogamy is sufficient protection against even an unwitting breach of the rule that agnates within six degrees of cousinship must not marry. Gotra refers to the ritual identification of families. While all families bearing the same gotra name are not agnatically related, all agnates invariably belong to the same gotra. The gotra and the kol are categories and not groupings of kin. The principal kin group is the extended family (*kotamb*), which has a core of agnatic kin, male and female, and includes the wives of the men.

Kinship Terminology. Kinship terms are of a descriptive type employing the following principal criteria of differentiation: gender, generation, and bilateral filiation. The only kin within two generations (ascendant or descendant) who are grouped together terminologically are the two sets of grandfathers and grandmothers. Age specification is achieved by prefixing words such as "older/elder" or "younger" to a kin term. Terms for Ego's spouse, parents, children, siblings, grandparents, grandchildren, parents' siblings, first-degree cousins, first-degree cousins once removed, and parallel categories of the spouse's kin provide the core of the terminology.

Marriage and Family

Marriage. Pandits consider marriage an indissoluble sacrament that binds two families and not merely two individuals. Marriages are therefore arranged by families. Subcaste endogamy is a prescription, and within the subcaste the rule of gotra exogamy is normally observed. The preferred type of marriage is between completely unrelated families. Bride givers accept a deferential role for themselves and offer dowry to bride takers. Owing to the shortage of women, however, marriages by exchange between bride givers and takers, though not well thought of, are about as frequent as the favored type of marriage. Very rarely a man may buy himself a wife, but such an arrangement is never publicly acknowledged. Relatively older widowers with resources resort to this practice. Traditionally widows did not remarry but in the last couple of generations some cases of widow remarriage have occurred, involving particularly young childless widows. Girls leave their parental home on marriage and go to live with the husband and his parents. If the husband is employed away from home, the bride begins her life as a married woman by living with her parents-in-law for about a year before joining her husband, who may however visit her at home. Occasionally, when a couple has no sons, they may arrange for their daughter (or one of their daughters, if there are several) to marry patriuxorilocally. Her husband then comes to live with his parents-in-law and looks after them. Since Pandits consider marriage a sacrament, the notion of divorce is absent.

Domestic Unit. The most important kin group of Pandit society is the household (*gara, chulah*). It is built around the three-generation minimal lineage. Every household has a history that is subject to the processes of augmentation (birth, adoption, marriage) and depletion (death, adoption, partition, marriage). Depending on the particular phase of the developmental cycle, a household may be either nuclear or extended in its composition.

Inheritance. Traditionally, property (land, house, cattle, fruit trees) goes from father to son, but it is now legally possible for daughters too to claim a share; they generally do not do so. In this limited sense dowry is treated as being equivalent to premortem inheritance, which it is not in principle. For purposes of ownership the household is a coparcenary. A man's sons have a right to equal ownership with him, on a per capita basis, in all his ancestral property; whatever he has earned and accumulated by his own efforts, without making use of anything inherited by him, is exclusively his property. The usual time for dividing property is after a man's death when his sons may no longer be willing to live together under the headship of the oldest among them. The widowed mother may serve as a cementing force: if she does so it is because of her moral authority and not because she has any property rights. The father has both. Occasionally, however, household dissensions may occur during the lifetime of the father and property may be divided between him and his sons. On his death his share would be divided equally among the sons.

Socialization. The bringing up of children is the collective responsibility of the household. A child's own parents are not expected to take any special interest—apart from breastfeeding of a child by the mother—nor do they have any special responsibility. In fact, grandparents play the principal role in socialization. For about the first six years or so, gender differences between children do not have any particular significance for socialization. Thereafter girls become more intimately associated with older women and boys with older men. Nowadays all boys and almost all girls begin school at about the age of 5 or 6.

Sociopolitical Organization

Pandits consider themselves to be a community (*gaum*) or "brotherhood" (*baradari*). They are divided into two endogamous subcastes, Gor (priests) and Karkun (workers). Socioeconomic standing and "noble" ancestry are important in the organization of social relations. For most goods and services Pandits are dependent upon Muslim artisan and service occupational groups. While these relations are governed by convention, the state too is increasingly involved in them as, for example, in the regulation of relations between landowners and tenants. Pandit society is fully integrated within the political and law-and-order frameworks of the modern state. They do not, therefore, have any independent institutions of political organization or social control. As in any other society, however, public opinion and social pressures are important as instruments of social control. Public esteem (*yash*) is a matter of deep social concern among Pandits; it is indeed a major cultural value.

Religion and Expressive Culture

Religious Beliefs. As Hindus, Pandits exhibit a repertoire of beliefs that include the notions of dharma (moral conduct, duty), karma (action, fruits of action), samsara ("flow," reincarnation), *ashrama* (stages of life), *purushartha* (instrumental and ultimate goals), *prarabdha* (fate), *anugraha* (divine grace), *punya* (meritorious action), and *papa* (moral evil). On a more abstract plane, they are legatees of the nondualistic school of philosophy known as Kashmir Shaivism. Rituals help people to relate to a hierarchy of supernaturals, ranging from local possession spirits, ghosts, and goblins, who cause illness and misfortune, to high Sanskritic deities (e.g., Vishnu, Shiva, Shakti) and regional gods and goddesses who are seen as being essentially benevolent.

Religious Practitioners. Householders are the practitioners par excellence of domestic rituals, whether these pertain to Sanskritic deities, locally recognized supernatural beings, or ancestors. While the performance of rituals is primarily the responsibility of men and women cannot be the principal officiants, the participation of the latter is nevertheless required in the roles of wife or mother. The presence of priests at Sanskritic rituals is essential.

Ceremonies. Religious ceremonies consist primarily of rites of passage (notably initiation and marriage rituals), rites for ancestors, devotional prayers, and pilgrimages. The annual pilgrimage to the cave of Amarnath (source of the Ganges) in the valley attracts pilgrims from all over India and from Nepal. In their worship of Sanskritic deities, Pandits follow the eclectic *smartha* mode. In domestic rituals they follow the school of Laugaksha.

Arts. The Pandit house is a well-designed building with carefully crafted wooden doors, windows, and ceilings. These are often embellished by carving, but this work is done by Muslim carpenters. Pandit women paint floral and geometrical designs on the facade of the house to symbolize domestic auspiciousness. They also chant auspicious songs at initiation ceremonies and weddings. Pandits have an old tradition of composing poetry, mostly devotional poems, and of group singing.

Medicine. Illness is believed to arise from a number of causes, physical as well as supernatural. Home remedies (mostly herbal brews and preserves) are combined with consultation with practitioners of traditional Unani (Greco-Arabic) and modern allopathic medicine. Priests and astrologers are consulted to determine supernatural and astral causes and to perform appropriate curative rituals.

Death and Afterlife. Deaths are classified as good, bad, or untimely. If one dies after successfully fulfilling legitimate worldly goals as a householder, without suffering a protracted illness or losing any essential faculties before passing away, then one is said to have "attained" the good death. The dead are usually cremated, though infants who die before they have cut teeth are buried. Cremation is followed by rituals spread over twelve days. These are performed to help the disembodied spirit to reach the "land" of the manes. There are daily "watering" and biannual "feeding" rituals for the manes. At the same time all except the most spiritually advanced people are believed to be reborn. To be freed from the bondage of rebirth and redeath is the goal of spiritual endeavor. Divine selection or grace is the ultimate source of such salvation (*moksha*).

Postscript. The above description is more applicable to the Pandits of rural Kashmir than to those living in urban areas. The latter are basically similar to the former in terms of, for example, the structure of kinship and the nature of religious beliefs and ceremonies. The character of economic life is very different, however, with the urban Pandits being prominent in civil services, the professions (engineering, law, medicine, teaching), business, and even manufacturing. Their higher educational attainments contribute to higher socioeconomic status. They hardly ever practice marriage by exchange of brides. In fact, they look down upon that and some other practices and the manners of the Pandits of rural areas. Nevertheless, at the level of the community (gaum) or "brotherhood" (baradari), all Pandits, rural and urban, consider themselves as one people, related to Kashmiri Pandits outside Kashmir but distinct from not only the Kashmiri Muslims but also non-Pandit Hindus living in Kashmir.

See also Brahman; Kashmiri

Bibliography

Bamzai, P. N. K. (1962). *A History of Kashmir*. Delhi: Metropolitan.

Chatterji, K. C. (1914). *Kashmir Shaivism*. Srinagar: Research Department, Kashmir State.

Madan, Triloki Nath (1965). *Family and Kinship: A Study of the Pandits of Rural Kashmir*. Bombay: Asia Publishing House. 2nd enl. ed. 1989. Delhi: Oxford University Press.

Sender, Henny (1988). *The Kashmiri Pandits: A Study of Cultural Choice in North India*. Delhi: Oxford University Press.

TRILOKI NATH MADAN

Paniyan

ETHNONYMS: Pania, Paniya, Panya

The word "Paniyan" means "laborer." They are among an unfortunate group of people who traditionally were bonded laborers. "Bonded labor" results from a social agreement between a debtor and creditor that stipulates that the debtor has a lifelong obligation to work for the creditor. These people are scattered in Kozhikode District, parts of Malappuram District on the outskirts of the Ghats, and also in some areas of Nilgiri District, in Tamil Nadu. They totaled 51,655 in 1971. The Paniyans' origins are unknown. To some Europeans they seem to be of African ancestry because of their dark skin, curly hair, large ear plugs, and broad noses. The people themselves have no notion of their ancestry or homeland.

Their housing consists of rows of huts made from bamboo with thatched roofs. They are either single- or double-storied. During the months of monsoon the Paniyan move near streams and cool places, and after the rain is finished they return to their main huts. The Paniyan speak a Malayalam dialect. People employed on estates also speak Kannada.

The main Paniyan occupation is working as cultivators for landowners. Traditionally, they were usually bought by the owners for small amounts of rupees, after which they could not leave at will; if such a bonded laborer left, the landowner made sure that he would not be hired by anyone else. Bonded labor is now illegal, and a few Paniyans own their own land and cultivate rice and ragi. Women and children usually participate in digging jungle roots or pot herbs for food. The Paniyans previously were often known as coffee thieves, because they were sometimes hired by wealthy landlords to go out during the night, strip bushes, and deliver the coffee beans to the landlord. Today they are frequently employed as farm and plantation laborers.

Marriage takes place with the help of parents. A girl is chosen by a man's family. The ceremony is very simple and is conducted by a _chemmi_ (priest). Sixteen coins and new clothes are given to the chemmi, who presents them to the bride's parents. Monogamy is usual, but there is no opposition to a man taking more than one wife if he can afford them.

Paniyan religion includes placating demons of various types with occasional offerings and worshiping deities in animal form, Kuli being the main one. They especially honor the Hindu divinity Kad Bhagavadi; this deity has no image, only a wooden box. Shrines dedicated to her are built in most inhabited places, with offerings.

Bibliography

Gopalan Nair, C. (1911). "Paniyans." In _Wynad: Its Peoples and Traditions_, 100–105. Madras: Higginbotham.

Thurston, Edgar, and Kadamki Rangachari (1909). "Paniyan." In _Castes and Tribes of Southern India_, edited by Edgar Thurston and Kadamki Rangachari. Vol. 6, 57–71. Madras: Government Press.

SAIDEH MOAYED-SANANDAJI

Parsi

ETHNONYMS: Parsee, Zoroastrian

Orientation

Identification. The Parsis are an immigrant community, possibly coming from Fars, Persia, and now located in Bombay, western India. They are distinguished by their adherence to the Zoroastrian faith.

Location. Parsis are found in the greatest numbers in the old Bombay Presidency, between 14° and 28° N and 67° and 77° E. They have also settled in recent times in all major cities and towns throughout India. Large immigrant communities are now found in the United States, Canada, Britain, and Pakistan. A similarly sized Zoroastrian community remains in Iran, but its members are not considered Parsis.

Demography. In 1901 there were 93,952 Parsis throughout India. There was a very slight population increase up to the midcentury; since then the population has decreased dramatically by almost 10 percent each decade. The birthrate is lower than the death rate, and emigration has long taken place, so that in 1976 the population was estimated at 82,000 in the Indian republic, plus 5,000 in Pakistan. Additional factors that have been cited for this decline are low fertility, late age at first marriage, and marrying outside the Parsi community.

Linguistic Affiliation. Virtually all Parsis today speak a Gujarati patois and English. The liturgical language is Avestan, and some of the religious literature is in Pahlavi.

History and Cultural Relations

Zoroastrianism had been in existence in Persia for well over a thousand years, usually as a state cult. When Muslim Arabs intent on spreading their new faith invaded and overthrew the last Zoroastrian king, Yazdagird III, in A.D. 651, numerous refugees fled, some following the Great Silk Route into China where they established trading communities and built fire temples in various cities. All traces of these Chinese Parsis had disappeared by the tenth century A.D. Others who had sought refuge in the mountainous region of Kohistan were finally driven to the port of Ormuz (Hormuz), from whence they sailed to India. The exact date of arrival is controversial, but it is traditionally put at A.D. 716. Recent research puts it as late as A.D. 936. The story of their flight and their landing on the west coast of India at Diu has since been romanticized. In reality, they eked out a subsistence on marginal land provided by their Hindu hosts. With the coming of the Europeans, Parsis moved into an intermediary niche between the foreigners and the natives in the cities. Today the Parsis are the most urbanized and Westernized community in India, having been the first to avail themselves of the opportunities that came from Western-style education and the growth of industry, commerce, and government under the British. Thus, the first Indians to become surgeons, barristers, pilots, and members of the British Parliament were all Parsis. Despite their long residence in the country Parsis have not been absorbed into the Indian caste system. Like the Europeans, they have been viewed as foreigners. The native Hindu and Muslim states accorded them positions of high authority and privilege, including prime ministerships and guardianship of the treasuries, on account of their education, relative incorruptibility, and impartiality toward caste allegiances.

Settlements

The Parsi population is concentrated in Bombay, where they arrived about 1750 from the small towns and cities of Gujarat. Today some 95 percent live in urban areas. They are usually found in exclusively Parsi housing estates endowed by Parsi charitable funds.

Economy

Unlike the caste Hindus, Parsis have not been bound to certain occupations or excluded from others by religious norms or taboos. This allowed them in the nineteenth century to adopt the modern professions that were emerging. The Parsis traditionally worked as entrepreneurs (ranging from the ownership of liquor shops to steel mills), in trade (especially with China), in finance (as bankers), or in government service. The modernization of Indian manufacturing and transportation owes much to individual Parsi wealth and genius. Families such as the Tatas, the Wadias, and the Petits were the owners of the largest private enterprises in the industrial economy of India. A decline in community wealth and therefore entrepreneurial capital has siphoned off highly educated younger Parsis to seek their fortunes overseas in every profession.

Kinship

Kin Groups and Descent. Most people today prefer to live in nuclear families. There are no larger kin-based groups such as lineages or clans. Descent is patrilineal.

Kinship Terminology. Kin terms follow the pattern found among other Gujarati speakers in the region.

Marriage and Family

Marriage. The Parsis are a strictly monogamous and endogamous group. At one time there was an avoidance of marriage between priestly and nonpriestly families. Given these restrictions and the small size of the community, it is not surprising that close consanguineal and affinal relatives are potential mates. Cross- and parallel-cousin marriages are permitted, as well as intergenerational marriages (e.g., between uncle and niece), though the occurrence of the latter is rare—less than 1 percent of all marriages in 1961. The greatest problem faced by the community today is a decrease in the number of marriages and a decreasing fertility rate. Since the 1950s deaths have consistently outnumbered births every year among Parsis, producing an aging population. This decline has two causes. Since independence in 1947 many younger Parsis have emigrated from India, thus strengthening the sense of crisis; and Parsi women who marry non-Parsis are strictly excluded along with their offspring from the community. The question of accepting children of such marriages, as well as converts to Zoroastrianism, is being vehemently debated among Parsis both in India and abroad. There appears to be a progressive attitude among the overseas Parsis that may in the future lead to a broadening of the definition of a

Parsi. Parsi divorce rates are higher than those for other Indian communities because, when compared to Hindu law, Parsi law has always made divorce easier. The education and economic emancipation of females also contributes to the high divorce rate. Remarriage after the death of a spouse is permitted for both sexes. Adoption is permitted and is common.

Domestic Unit. Parsis traditionally lived together as extended families. Owing to space constraints in the cities, however, nuclear families are common; and because of declining population, many elderly Parsis today live alone.

Inheritance. Both sons and daughters may inherit from both parents. There are no rules of primogeniture. Despite the above formal rules of inheritance, it is not uncommon for wealthy Parsis to leave their entire estates for charitable purposes: endowing schools, hospitals, fire temples, or the like. The stress on generosity and a sense of communal responsibility for the weak and needy fostered during childhood finds its expression in wills and trusts. Hence there has occurred a continuous redistribution of wealth from the rich to the poor.

Socialization. A great deal of conscious effort goes into the making of a Parsi child. Parsis were quick to grasp the value of Western education and were leaders in female education. It is no surprise then that the literacy rates among Parsis are extremely high (being 90 percent in 1961, when the average rate for Bombay was 57 percent). Both boys and girls are encouraged to prepare for careers. Child labor is not encouraged, and in 1961 only 0.06 percent of Parsis under age 15 were gainfully employed (as against 8.72 percent of all Maharashtrians). An essential part of a Parsi child's socialization is the nurturing of an awareness of his or her difference from other Indians. To this end there was a preference for Parsi schools endowed by Parsi charities and staffed entirely by Parsis, until the Indian government abolished sectarian education in the 1950s. The number of college graduates is extremely high. During the first half of the century the numbers of Parsis receiving professional degrees in law, medicine, and engineering were greatly out of proportion to their tiny numbers in the general population. Among overseas Parsis, Zoroastrian associations have been established with the explicit objective of instilling Parsi identity in the young. The Parsi child is constantly obliged to conform to a moral code derived from the Zoroastrian motto, "Good thoughts, good words, good deeds." Transgression of this code of conduct embodying the virtues of honesty, charity, and cleanliness is seen as not only a personal but also a communal failure. A child is inducted into the Parsi moral code through the ceremony of *naojot.* Such constant reminders of a child's Parsi identity are essential if the community is to enforce its rules of endogamy in a secular and nonsectarian world.

Sociopolitical Organization

The relationship of Parsis to the state of India has always been one of loyalty, since as a minority their survival depended on accommodation to the political authority. The Zoroastrian ideal state is one that is just and tolerant toward the practice of religion. The British enhanced this loyalty by elevating a number of Parsi families to noble rank: out of four hereditary barons in British India, three were Parsi. For a long time Parsis played a dominant role in local government, particularly in the Bombay municipality. They were also instrumental in forming the Bombay Presidency Association, which hoped to influence British policies in India. Later, with the movement for Indian independence, Parsis were a moving force in the Indian National Congress. In independent India Parsi political influence has waned somewhat, although eminent Parsis are still to be found in all branches of government, especially the judiciary. The internal affairs of the community relating to questions of membership, religious practice, and use of community funds are governed by Parsi _panchayats_. These are local bodies (of which Bombay's is the most important) made up of priests and wealthy laypeople. The juridical powers of the panchayats have slowly been yielded to Indian civil authorities, and the panchayats today are primarily involved in welfare activities and management of community trusts.

Religion and Expressive Culture

Religious Beliefs. Parsis follow the religion of Zoroaster, a prophet of the seventh century B.C. from the region between the Hindu Kush and Seistan. Their belief system includes ideas about a creator god, good and evil forces, individual choice, Heaven and Hell, the Last Judgment, and eternal life. These ideas are found in sacred texts that are fragmentary, including the _Avesta_ dating from the fourth or sixth century A.D. and attributed to the Prophet himself. This is supplemented by later Pahlavi texts written in Middle Persian, from around the ninth century A.D., which consist mostly of commentaries, interpretations, and selections. More modern sources are from India, written in Gujarati and English, beginning around the middle of the nineteenth century. Zoroastrianism may be viewed as one of the earliest monotheisms, since it postulates as First Cause Ahura Mazda, the Creator. It then introduces a radical dualism in the form of two opposing spirits who are both the offspring of Ahura Mazda. The presence of Spenta Mainyu, the beneficent spirit, and Angra Mainyu, the hostile spirit, explains the origins of good and evil; they are the prototypes of the choices between truth and lies that each individual must face in his or her own life. Human history then becomes a working out of these two antithetical principles in creation. Humans aid the victory of good over evil by the pursuit of good thoughts, good words, and good deeds. At the end of temporal existence evil will be completely vanquished, and only truth and happiness will prevail. To this basic tenet were added elements from the past, and we find other spiritual beings as well as ritual and magical practices incorporated into the original basic monotheistic belief.

Besides the above-mentioned Creator and his two offspring, there are seven beneficent immortals, which are entities as well as representations of Ahura Mazda's virtues, such as "best truth" and "immortality." Furthermore, Zoroastrianism absorbed some of the earlier Indo-Iranian gods who became Yazatas. The more important of these are seen to preside over aspects of the material world. Also considered worthy of reverence are the Fravashis or spirits of the soul, together with deceased mortals who led exemplary lives. Fire is the main symbol of Zoroastrianism: it receives the offerings of the priests and the prayers of individuals. Every ritual and ceremony involves the presence of the sacred fire. The fire in the place of worship called the fire temple is ritually consecrated and installed. Non-Zoroastrians are not permitted to set eyes on such a fire. Offerings of sandalwood and frankincense are made to it at least five times a day by ordained priests. It represents God's splendor and divine grace. A smaller ritual fire is also found in every Zoroastrian's home.

Religious Practitioners. The hereditary clergy is divided into Dasturs (high priests) and Mobeds. There are no monastic orders, nor are there women functionaries. Priests can marry. Becoming a priest is a long and arduous process involving several purification rituals and the memorization of texts. Sons of priests today prefer to enter the modern economy, and the community is facing a critical shortage of qualified functionaries.

Ceremonies. The major events of the life cycle that are ritually celebrated are birth, initiation, and marriage. Of these, the initiation or naojot is of special importance. It is performed for both boys and girls at about the age of 7, and consists of the investiture of the child with the sacred and symbolic shirt, _sadre_, and thread, _kasti_, which is tied around the waist. A Zoroastrian must always wear these two things, and the thread is to be untied and retied many times during the day as a prelude to prayers and meals and after bodily functions. The sadre is a shirt made of white muslin; its two halves, back and front, symbolize past and future, respectively. It is the earthly version of the garment made of light worn by the first creation of Ahura Mazda. The sadre has a small fold at the front neckline that forms a pocket. A Parsi child is exhorted to fill this purse with righteousness and good deeds. The kasti, made of undyed wool, is a hollow tube made up of seventy-two threads, ending in several tassels, their numbers either symbolizing religious precepts or referring to the liturgical texts. Wearing it is a sign of consent and obedience to Ahura Mazda. Once a child has had the naojot performed, he or she is spiritually responsible for his or her own salvation through an observance of the morality and rituals of the religion. The marriage ceremony is important in a religious sense because it leads to procreation, which will increase the number of soldiers in the cause of good. The ceremony shows a number of borrowings from Sanskritic Hinduism, as in the tying of the hands of the bride and groom and the recital of Sanskrit _shlokas_ (blessings) at the end of the ceremony. Certain purification rituals and the segregation of impure persons and things echo the strict Hindu dichotomy of pure and impure. Bodily substances like saliva, urine, and menstrual blood are considered to be defiling, while death and corpses are considered impure as well as spiritually dangerous. The practice of segregating menstruating and parturient females is falling into disuse in the urban setting, where space is at a premium. Daily worship involves recital of the basic credo while untying and retying the kasti. There are seasonal festivals known as _gahambars_ celebrated by the community as a whole, which were originally tied to the agricultural cycle. Commemorative ceremonies called _jashans_ may be held for family events or such historic occurrences as the death of a leader or the end of a war.

Arts. Parsi literature is to be found in languages that have been adopted, namely Gujarati and English. There are no indigenous visual or performing arts, although some modern artists follow Western models. Parsis have in recent years made serious contributions to Western classical music. In addition to numerous pianists and violinists of professional caliber, the community has produced Zubin Mehta, the internationally acclaimed conductor of the Israel Philharmonic, New York Philharmonic, and other orchestras. The composer Kaikhosru Shapurji Sorabji (1892–1991) may also be mentioned, if only because his 500-page piano composition, *Symphonic Variations*, which takes six hours to perform, holds the distinction of being the longest classical composition known.

Medicine.   There is no distinct Parsi medical system.

Death and Afterlife.   Parsis expose their dead to vultures on Towers of Silence (*dokhma*), although if a person dies where no such tower exists, then burial or cremation is practiced. Usually built on a hilltop, the dokhma is a round stone or brick structure about 15 meters high and perhaps 100 meters across, with an internal platform on which sit three ranks of stone slabs, for the bodies of men, women, and children, sloping down toward a central dry well. The bearers place a body there and within an hour or so vultures reduce it to bones. Some days later the corpse bearers return and throw the bones down the central well. It has sand and charcoal in it, the purpose of the charcoal being to protect the earth from the pollution of death. Zoroastrians believe in the immortality of the soul. It remains around the dead body for three days, during which time ceremonies are performed for the dead. At the beginning of the third night the soul will be judged by the spiritual judge Mitra at the Chinvat Bridge between this world and the next. If one's good actions outweigh one's evil actions one will proceed to Heaven; if they are equally weighted one will proceed to a place like Purgatory; and if one has been an evil person one will be cast down into Hell. At the end of time Zoroastrians believe that there will be a Last Judgment mediated by a future Savior, leading to the Transfiguration of the Dead, who will be resurrected in bodies clad in glory. The eschatological faith of this doctrine is one component of Zoroastrianism that has exercised a widespread and deep influence on other world religions.

See also Gujurati

Bibliography

Gnoli, Gherardo (1986). "Zoroastrianism." In *The Encyclopedia of Religion*, edited by Mircea Eliade. Vol. 15, 579–591. New York: Macmillan.

Kulke, Eckehard (1974). *The Parsees in India: A Minority as Agent of Social Change*. Munich: Weltforum Verlag.

Modi, Jivanji Jamshedji (1922a). "Parsis." In *The Tribes and Castes of Bombay*, edited by R. E. Enthoven. Vol. 3, 177–221. Bombay: Government Central Press. Reprint. 1975. Delhi: Cosmo Publications.

Modi, Jivanji Jamshedji (1922b). *The Religious Ceremonies and Customs of the Parsees*. Bombay: British India Press. 2nd ed. 1937. Bombay: J. B. Karani's Sons. Reprint. 1986. Bombay: Society for the Promotion of Zoroastrian Religious Knowledge and Education.

W. D. MERCHANT

Pathan

ETHNONYMS: Afghan, Pashtun, Pukhtun, Rohilla

Orientation

Identification.   The Pathan inhabit southern and eastern Afghanistan and western Pakistan. Their language is Pushto (Pashto) and, except for a small minority, they are Sunni Muslims. Pathan dynasties constituted and, until recently, have controlled the tribal kingdom of Afghanistan, and during some periods Pathan or Afghan monarchs established their rule on the Indian plains.

Location.   The Pathan inhabit an area roughly bounded by Kabul in the northeast and Herat in the northwest. It extends as far east as the Indus River and in the south an approximate boundary can be drawn from Sibi through Quetta to Qandahar. Pathan tribes like the Mohmand, Wazirs, Sulemankhel, and Achakzais actually straddle the international border. The topography of the area is primarily mountainous, consisting of a part of the Alpine-Himalayan mountain range in central Afghanistan and the Sulaiman range in Pakistan. To the east Pathan territory extends onto the Indus Plain and in the south onto the Iranian Plateau. The climate of Afghanistan is semiarid with cold winters and dry summers. The eastern Pathan areas are affected by the humidity and rain of the Indian monsoons. In addition Pathan live in and contribute to social life in certain areas of Indian such as Rampur (Rohilla) and cities like Bombay.

Demography.   The 1984 population of Pushto speakers was approximately 20 million. This includes 11 million native to Pakistan and 9 million originating in Afghanistan. Because of the civil war that has persisted in Afghanistan since 1979, roughly 2 million Pathans have left for Pakistan as refugees. The Pathan constituted from 50 to 60 percent of the population of prewar Afghanistan. As the largest and most influential ethnic group, the Pathan have dominated the society and politics of that country for the past 200 years. Other important ethnic minorities in Afghanistan include the Hazaras, Tajiks, and Uzbeks. Since the separation of Bangladesh from Pakistan, the Pathan constitute Pakistan's second-largest ethnic group. According to Pakistan's 1981 census 13 percent of the nation's households are Pushto-speaking. Punjabis make up the majority of Pakistan's population; other important linguistic groups are Sindhis, Baluchis, and Urdu speakers.

Linguistic Affiliation.   Pushto is in the Iranian Branch of the Indo-European Language Family. The two principal dialects, which differ in pronunciation, are Southwestern or Qandahari Pushto and Northeastern or Peshawari Pukhto. Most Pathans in Afghanistan speak Dari, a dialect of Farsi or Persian, as a second language, and it has had a strong influence on Pushto. Both languages are written in the Arabic script, modified to accommodate consonants that do not occur in Arabic.

History and Cultural Relations

The origin of the Pathan is debated. Linguistic evidence indicates Indo-European ancestry, while some tribal genealogies claim Semitic links. The regions of Afghanistan, eastern Iran, and western India have been some of the most heavily invaded in history and so the Pathan of today are probably a heterogeneous group. Among the invaders who have entered and established empires in the area have been Iranians, Greeks, Hindus, Turks, Mongols, Uzbeks, Sikhs, British, and Russians. The first historical reference to the Pathan (A.D. 982) refers to Afghans living in the Sulaiman Mountains. The first significant impact they had outside of that area was as troops in the armies of Mahmud of Ghazni, a Muslim Turk, who led a number of invasions against the Hindu kings in north India around the year 1000. Nearly 300 years later Afghan kings themselves took power in Delhi. The Pathan Khaljis and later Lodhis ruled there until displaced by Babur, the first of the Mogul emperors, in the early sixteenth century. It is ironic that Pathan kings ruled India before they ruled the mountainous areas to the west that are their homelands. That feat was not accomplished until 1747 when, from a base in Qandahar, Ahmed Shah Abdali fused together an empire that encompassed parts of Iran and India as well as Afghanistan. Members of his tribe ruled a more truncated Afghanistan until 1973. British involvement in Pathan areas was a consequence of efforts to protect the western borders of their Indian empire and check the southern advance of the Russians. In 1879, following the Second Anglo-Afghan War, the Afghan government conceded control of all the passes into India to the British and in 1893 the Durand Line was established, delineating the spheres of responsibility of the two governments. It is now the international border dividing the Pathan between two nation-states.

Settlements

While some Pathan are nomadic and others urban, the majority dwell in villages of 2 to 400 families. Frequently the villages cluster around a larger town and are always located with concern for the availability of water and for defense. Settlement patterns reflect lineage politics with dominant lineages holding the choice or strategic lands. Genealogical closeness determines a group's location relative to them. Nomadic groups are primarily cattle herders who move with the seasons to follow pasture. They follow set routes and have traditional camping sites. Like the villages, camps are structured around the tents of the senior lineages. Houses are generally constructed of mud or sun-dried mud bricks covered with mud plaster. The only valuable parts of the house are the doors and the wood beams that support a flat roof of mats covered with mud and twigs. In small villages households consist of high-walled compounds frequently resembling fortresses, complete with towers on the corners. A clear and strict demarcation is observed between the areas (*hujra*) where the public may enter and be entertained and the family's living space. Women are secluded from the former (according to the Islamic custom of purdah) and animals and grain stores are kept in the latter. In the traditional style nomadic tents are woven from black goat's hair and supported by posts or arched poles and guy ropes.

Economy

Subsistence and Commercial Activities. Agriculture, primarily grain farming, and animal husbandry are the most important activities in the Pathan economy. The practice of agriculture is largely limited by the rough terrain and arid climate to river valleys; elsewhere, it depends on the scant rainfall. The most important crop is wheat, followed by barley and maize. Cultivation is done primarily by hand or with animals, though, where possible, mechanization is taking place. Traditional irrigation techniques such as *kareezes*, a series of wells connected by an underground tunnel, are in many cases being replaced by tube wells. Other important agricultural products are fresh and dried orchard fruits, nuts, vegetables, opium, and hashish. In addition to raising stock, nomads as well as some farmers engage in trade and moneylending. The presence of the border dividing Pathan territory into two countries also makes smuggling a lucrative pursuit. Domesticated animals include both fat-tailed and short-tailed sheep, goats, cattle, water buffalo, chickens, camels, donkeys, and horses.

Industrial Arts. Many industrial activities such as carpentry, bricklaying, and shoemaking are done by part-time Pashtun specialists who also farm. However, in many areas non-Pathan occupational groups carry out these activities, as well as others such as weaving, blacksmithing, and goldsmithing. An exception is the manufacture of guns; in certain areas, notably Darra Adam Khel south of Peshawar, Pathans produce guns in small factories.

Trade. Villages in Pathan areas have until recently been largely self-sufficient. Traditionally trade and even farming were activities looked down upon by Pathans who saw raiding, smuggling, and politics as honorable pursuits. In areas where such attitudes persist, trade is carried out by non-Pathan (frequently Hindu) shopkeepers and peddlers or through barter with nomads. Despite these traditions, in large towns and urban areas Pathans have earned reputations as successful traders and businessmen.

Division of Labor. The strict observance of purdah results in a marked division of labor between the sexes. Although rural women may participate in the harvesting of crops, they remain primarily inside the compound where they are expected to do the traditional home tasks of rearing children, maintaining the house, cooking, etc. Indeed, purdah is frequently observed to such an extent that women are not allowed to go out in public to do the shopping; thus, the shopping is all done by men. Purdah is less strictly observed by nomadic groups.

Land Tenure. In the arid, low-yield regions the small landholdings are self-cultivated by the *malik* (petty chief or household elder) and his sons. In areas of greater productivity, where khans (village or tribal chiefs) own larger tracts, tenants do the work. Tenants receive about 20 percent of the product if they only supply labor and higher percentages if they supply implements or draft animals. Until early this century in the Swat and Mardan valleys the equality of the Pathan clans was underlined by the custom of *wesh* by which they periodically redistributed land between themselves. This involved physically shifting households and belongings to other parts of the valleys. Excess population from Pathan areas has traditionally left the area to serve as mercenaries in the armies of India, to work as tenants on the lands of others or, more currently, to act as laborers or entrepreneurs in the cities of Pakistan or the Persian Gulf states.

Kinship

Kin Groups and Descent. Segmentary tribal structure and unilineal descent define Pathan kin groups. Genealogical and geographic divisions generally coincide. The most pertinent division within the tribal structure is the clan subsection, that is, the children of one man, generally encompassing four or five generations. It is within this sphere that one marries, makes alliances, and is in conflict. The smallest unit is the *kor*, or household, and it implies cohabitation with a living grandfather. This is the major economic and social unit; its members may cohabit in a village, a single compound, or a nomadic group. Descent is patrilineal.

Kinship Terminology. Aspects of the Eskimo system, in which avuncular and cousin terms are uniform, are present, though certain collaterals are distinguished. For example, while all other female cousins carry the same term as do all other male ones, the father's brother's daughter (potential or preferred bride) and father's brother's son (rival for inheritance and thus potential enemy) are given distinct terms.

Marriage and Family

Marriage. Although polygamy with up to four wives is permitted under Muslim law, monogamy is prevalent. Marriages are overwhelmingly endogamous within the clan and to a large degree within the subsection. Parallel-cousin marriage with father's brother's daughter is preferred among some tribes. Marriages are arranged by the couple's parents and their plans are generally fulfilled. The union is commonly contracted on the basis of bride-price. Frequently the bride's parents spend the money received in bride-price as dowry to meet the future domestic needs of the couple. A common practice is exchange marriage between close agnatic kin in which a sister or daughter is given and one simultaneously taken. Residence after marriage is virilocal, the bride coming to live in a single compound with the son, who receives separate quarters within it. The death of the patriarch of a family is frequently the time when such joint or compound families divide themselves into separate compounds. Despite the ease of obtaining a divorce under Muslim law, it is very rare among Pathans. The bride-price and the man's honor are lost if the woman remarries.

Domestic Unit. The household (kor) is the primary unit of consumption and cooperation and is conceived of as those who share a hearth or as a man and/or his sons. Three main types of domestic unit are found: (1) the nuclear family; (2) the compound family, in which a patriarch and/or his sons and their wives live together and share expenses; and (3) the joint family, in which the nuclear families in a compound, frequently brothers, keep independent budgets.

Inheritance. Land is divided as inheritance only among the males and on the basis of equality. The eldest brother is generally given an extra share to be used for the upkeep of the family guest house (hujra). It is over the inheritance of land that rivalry develops between brothers and, in the next generation, cousins. Despite Islamic injunctions, neither wives nor daughters inherit property.

Socialization. With the separation of the sexes inherent in Islam, children are raised primarily by their mother and elder sisters. In the segregated atmosphere that prevails there is a great deal of competition for attention and affection, though men tend to be indulgent toward children. Boys are circumcised by their seventh year.

Sociopolitical Organization

The Pathan are divided into a number of different politicoadministrative structures. In Afghanistan the state, itself evolved from the tribal system, has historically exerted only loose control except in the major cities. In Pakistan several different systems prevail that are largely the legacy of British imperial administration. Although most Pathans live in districts where Pakistan's civil and criminal laws prevail, some tribes, such as the Mohmand and Wazirs, are within Federally Administered Tribal Areas (FATA), while others, such as those in Malakand in the North-West Frontier Province or those in Zhob Agency in Baluchistan, are within Provincially Administered Tribal Areas (PATA). In FATA and PATA tribal and customary law holds sway.

Social Organization. Despite administrative divisions Pathan maintain a conception of their cultural and ethnic unity. This idea stems from the segmentary tribal structure and the associated notion of descent from a common ancestor. A. S. Ahmed has identified two principles of social organization among the Pathan, *nang* (honor) and *qalang* (taxes or rent). In areas where nang prevails traditional values are practiced, there is little social stratification, and there is no central political authority. In qalang areas landownership, not lineage membership, gives status and social stratification is prevalent, along with political centralization in the hands of an aristocracy. In both contexts mullahs, Sayyids (descendants of the Prophet Mohammed), and occupation groups play their special roles in Pathan society but stand outside Pathan genealogy.

Political Organization. To varying degrees Pathans are assimilated into the administrative structure of the area in which they live. In the last twenty-five years Afghanistan has officially moved from being a constitutional monarchy to a republic and finally to a democratic republic. Despite these changes (and until the current civil war) the relationship between the government and the rural population changed little. Since the government's presence has usually been for the purpose of extracting taxes or conscripts, the villagers' attitude toward it has generally been defensive and noncooperative. To some extent the same was true on the other side of the border where there was ongoing resistance to British rule, though British administration was accepted in some areas and British subsidies in others. Although most Pathans supported the movement for the creation of Pakistan, others wanted to reunite Pathans on both sides of the border in a country to be called "Pakhtunistan." Since then the Pakhtunistan movement has smoldered in various forms in both countries. An important political role is played by indigenous decision-making councils called *jirgas*. They are made up of maliks and decide various intra- or intertribal matters on the basis of tribal custom and, to a lesser extent, Islamic law. In Afghanistan the institution extends to the national level where the Loya Jirga, made up of tribal, ethnic, and religious leaders, meets to decide important issues.

Social Control. Traditionally social control was maintained by a code of behavior and honor called Pakhtunwali. It combines the principles of revenge, hospitality to guests, defense of those who have sought protection in one's care, the chastity of married women, and restraint toward those considered weak or helpless (Hindus, women, and boys). Pakhtunwali in some cases contradicts and generally takes precedence over Islamic law. It is harsh—the penalty for illicit sexual behavior, for example, is death—and it is enforced by strong social pressure. Violations of law outside of the activities the code encompasses are dealt with by the jirga or the government administration.

Conflict. As noted, the rivalry with father's brother's son for property, power, and wives is a constant source of conflict, as is Pakhtunwali itself, since even petty quarrels can escalate to a point where honor is involved. Efforts to encapsulate the Pathan into political systems seen as alien are also a source of conflict. It is frequently at such times of external threat that religious leaders assume political importance since resistance takes the form of a holy struggle or jihad. Conflict resolution is done through the jirga or through the intervention of religious figures.

Religion and Expressive Culture

Religious Beliefs. Islam is an essential and unifying theme in Pathan life, and it also unites the Pathan with an international community of believers. The overwhelming majority of Pathan is Sunni Muslim of the Hanafi legal school. Some groups, notably in the Kurram and Orakzai agencies of Pakistan, practice Shia Islam. A number of supernatural figures reside among the Pathan. _Jinn_ are spirits born of fire that can enter and possess people. Other negative beings include the ghosts of disturbed or cursed souls, witches, and fairies. The souls of pious figures can also return to Earth to play a more positive role.

Religious Practitioners. While Islam has no ordained priesthood, religious leaders are recognized. At the village level this role is played by the mullah, a man who has attained some religious training. Besides tending the mosque and making the call to prayer five times a day, he officiates at the rites of passage that mark the stages of life, birth, circumcision, marriage, and death. Another important figure is the Sayyed who stands outside the tribal structure, since his genealogy extends to the Prophet himself and not to the ancestors of the Pathans. Not bound by the Pashtun code of honor, Sayyeds are saintly figures who can arbitrate between conflicting groups.

Ceremonies. Besides ceremonies at the various rites of passage, the religious calendar includes: three days of celebration at the end of Ramazan, the month of fasting; a day observed by the ritual slaying of sheep in memory of Ibrahim slaying a sheep in place of his son on Allah's order; and the birthday of the Prophet Mohammed.

Arts. Poetry is the art most esteemed by Pathans. Their greatest poet, Khushhal (d. 1689), wrote both love poems and patriotic poems. Embroidered waistcoats and elaborately decorated rifle butts were traditionally the major visual arts.

Medicine. While some medical facilities are being introduced, people customarily go to the mullah or traditional herbalist for cures. A jinn possessing the patient is commonly held to be the cause of disease. Indigenous treatment is in a tradition said to be of Greek origin or in a religious tradition worked out centuries ago. A common cure consists of the wearing of talismans around the neck composed of magic formulas or verses of the Quran sewn up in cloth or leather.

Death and Afterlife. In Islam the body is to be buried ritually pure so that the soul is prepared to enter Heaven on Judgment Day. After death the body is washed and wrapped in a white sheet. A mullah performs the death rites, leading the congregated mourners in a special prayer. The body is buried with the face pointing toward Mecca. Mourning obligations continue after the burial. The deceased's relatives gather at the grave on the first few Fridays and on the fortieth day after the death, and they observe the first year's anniversary of the death with a final memorial ceremony.

See also Kohistani; Sayyid

Bibliography

Ahmed, Akbar S. (1976). _Millennium and Charisma among Pathans: A Critical Essay in Social Anthropology._ London: Routledge & Kegan Paul.

Ahmed, Akbar S. (1980). _Pukhtun Economy and Society: Traditional Structure and Economic Development in a Tribal Society._ London: Routledge & Kegan Paul.

Barth, Fredrik (1972). _Political Leadership among Swat Pathans._ London School of Economics Monographs on Social Anthropology, no. 19. London: Athlone Press.

Caroe, Olaf (1958). _The Pathans 550 B.C.– A.D. 1957._ London: Macmillan; New York: St. Martin's Press.

Dupree, Louis (1980). _Afghanistan._ Princeton, N.J.: Princeton University Press.

AKBAR S. AHMED WITH PAUL TITUS

Peripatetics

ETHNONYMS: Gypsies, nonpastoral nomads

Orientation

Identification. The term "peripatetic" refers to spatially mobile groups who are largely nonprimary producers or extractors and whose principal economic resource is other people. They differ from pastoral nomads who mainly depend on biophysiotic resources. Peripatetics are referred to as nonpastoral nomads, other nomads, service nomads, commercial nomads, non–food-producing nomads, symbiotic nomads, wanderers, and travelers. Peripatetic groups have several common characteristics, the most important being flexible skills and knowledge of the residual resources and sensitivity to the social, cultural, linguistic, economic, and political environments of the larger social system from which they derive their subsistence. All complex societies have gaps in their service-delivery system, leaving some needs either unmet or only partially met. The peripatetic strategy is to identify such needs and adapt to them. Specific groups are identified with particular occupations. The number of peripatetic groups in India is quite large. A brief survey of two south Indian states in 1967 reported 88 different peripatetic groups as compared to 14 groups discovered over a six-month period in certain parts of Pakistan. Other studies have reported 172 groups in northern Karnataka, 40 groups in one north Indian village, and 23 in a south Indian village.

The existence of such a large number of peripatetic groups and the variety of roles they play can only be understood in the context of Indian society. In traditional India, goods and services were obtained via the *jajmani* relationship, weekly markets, periodical fairs, pilgrimages, and peripatetics. Thus, peripatetics were one part of the wider economic network.

Location. In India, peripatetics are found in almost all parts of the country.

Demography. According to a rough estimate made by the Nomadic Association of India, the number of peripatetics in India was 6 million in 1967, though the category of "nomad" was not specifically defined. This estimate as well as others may be wildly inaccurate, as no systematic count of peripatetics has ever been attempted. However, it can be safely assumed that the peripatetics constitute a large group in India.

Linguistic Affiliation. The native language of peripatetics is usually the language spoken in their "home village" or "camp," though most speak a number of languages and dialects. For instance, a peripatetic group with Andhra Pradesh as its "home village" will speak a dialect of Telugu as its native tongue but may also be conversant in Kannada, Marathi, and Hindi. The Gadulia Lohar, a peripatetic group of blacksmiths, in addition to speaking different dialects of Rajasthani and Hindi, speak a secret language of their own. This is typical of many peripatetics.

History and Cultural Relations

Peripatetic groups have been part of Indian civilization for hundreds of years. Evidence of peripatetic artisans and entertainers have been found for the early Vedic period. By the late Vedic period (circa 1000–700 B.C.) the *Rig Veda* refers to a number of specialized traders, artisans, entertainers, professional acrobats, fortune-tellers, flute players, dancers, jugglers, snake charmers, etc. Tamil literature from the first through sixth century A.D. has references to wandering musicians, dancers, fortune-tellers, and beggars. It also suggests that some of the peripatetics performed difficult tasks such as undertaking goodwill missions from one king to another or helping reconcile rival kings or brothers. In censuses, district gazetteers, and other dispatches written during the British period, the nomadic populations were often referred to as pastoralists, gypsies, or criminals. This situation has now changed somewhat, although the knowledge that the settled people of India have about peripatetics is still minimal. There are several reasons for this, including the settled people's typical suspicion of all those who are mobile, the nomads' effort to maintain an ambiguous posture with reference to the larger social system, and their attempt to cultivate a mystique about themselves.

The peripatetic groups are ethnically diverse and maintain their identities within the milieu of Indian society. Each peripatetic group has considerable autonomy to regulate its own affairs. Peripatetics adopt the style, dialect, and medium in performance of their services and supply of goods that best appeal to the imagination of the people of the region they serve. For themselves, peripatetics make conscious efforts to adopt appropriate regional customs and beliefs. They also claim a vague and ambiguous position in the *varna/jati* framework of the Hindu caste society. Within their own caste clusters they maintain a diffused hierarchy based on the concept of purity and pollution, and they also maintain some degree of exclusive rights to their occupations. For example, while one group of genealogists and bards serves only some middle-level castes, other groups serve only the lowest castes. Thereby, they reaffirm the hierarchical structure of the caste system but also enable even the lowest caste to have a place in the system. Myth, language, ritual, kinship, and specific occupations are used to legitimize a group's position in the caste hierarchy and to ensure its peripatetic niche. Caste endogamy and their caste *panchayats* (councils) play a pivotal role. People may wander far and wide yet they remain connected with their specific caste norms. In literature, peripatetics have been described as traveling specialists who provide cultural variety that is otherwise lacking in Indian villages, as popular religious instructors, as communicants of culture, and as those who carry the culture of the Great Tradition of Indian civilization to the local people.

Settlements

Some peripatetics travel during only part of the year and then return to their "home village," while others travel throughout the year. Between these two extremes a number of variations are possible. In "home villages" some live in houses typical of the region, while others continue to take shelter in their bullock carts, under cloth or reed tents, or out in the open under the sky as they do while on the move. Some take shelter on temple premises as well. Generally, peripatetics intensify their movements during the harvest season because they want to obtain grain as payment for their goods and services. They also believe that farmers are more generous at this time of year. During the rainy season, the lean season for peripatetics, they tend to remain in their "home villages." The time is used for settling disputes, negotiating marriage alliances, and planning for the next work season.

Economy

Subsistence and Commercial Activities. Peripatetics employ a variety of economic strategies. They generally have one or more occupations for which they are well known and may use a few additional skills to supplement their income. For example, hunting, trapping, and fishing peripatetic groups may also indulge in petty trade, craft making, and begging. The artisan category includes groups such as: makers of baskets, broomsticks, palm mats, iron tools, and needles; stoneworkers; and repairers of household utensils and farm tools. The mendicant category includes a variety of groups, such as those who sing devotional songs, chant incantations, beg in the name of a specific deity, wear special makeup and stand at public places in the posture of penance or as sadhus, or display a deity. Several of these groups beg only from the members of specific castes. According to Hindu belief a sadhu does not have to work for his livelihood. He can live by _biksha_ (religious begging). Seeing a mendicant at one's doorstep in the morning is considered auspicious. Giving alms is a charitable act but receiving alms is equally meritorious. Acrobats, magicians, musicians, snake charmers, displayers of tricks by animals like monkeys, bears, etc., puppeteers, storytellers, mimes, and those who wear different makeup all also have several other subsidiary occupations. Some of them may trade in animals, fix shoes on bullock and horse hoofs, or polish cattle horns. Some women may indulge in prostitution, serving members of specific castes. There are several other groups who have developed a variety of skills including tattooers, genealogists, fortune-tellers, buffalo-hair shavers, etc. Peddlers and traders also form a large group. However, if their exploitation of a particular resource niche becomes less profitable due to new technology or competition, they switch to a new activity or settle down. In short, for peripatetics, the human resource base is ubiquitous and exploitable with an infinite variety of strategies. Joseph C. Berland has called it "the most predictable and reliable of all the niches in the world today" (1983).

Peripatetics are able to avoid competition from the sedentary population or completely eliminate it through their choice of work, low overhead, variety of strategies, flexible work groups, family-based enterprises, potential for change of location, and ability to live on little income. The sedentary provider is further restricted by the caste-based restrictions. Although the peripatetic niche apparently is inexhaustible and reliable, peripatetics are generally poor. They are continuously under pressure as their occupations are taken over by modern industry and the number of places where they can camp diminishes. If fewer people were being forced out of villages, the number of peripatetics would be much less than it is.

Trade. Some peripatetic groups trade in cattle. Such groups intensify their activities at the beginning of the agricultural season, when the demand for cattle is high. They trade at weekly markets and fairs, where they can also socialize with relatives and friends. Some peripatetic groups have been able to find new avenues of trade. For instance, a group of Gadulia Lohar have started trading in scrap iron. Some other peripatetic groups have started producing decorative items such as chandeliers, papier-mâché, etc., and now peddle them in cities.

Division of Labor. Peripatetic enterprises are family-based. If females do not participate in the main occupation of the group they do some additional work to enhance the income of the household. However, domestic tasks such as cooking, fetching water, looking after infants, etc. are female jobs.

Land Tenure. Only a few peripatetic groups own land. Such people move out of their villages only when the land is fallow or they have been able to lease it. The government has made an attempt to settle some peripatetic groups by giving them houses and land.

Kinship, Marriage, and Family

Kinship. The most important kinship group after the household is the extended family, which may travel and camp together for a part of the year or for the entire year. Descent is traced patrilineally through a common ancestor. Members of the lineage have certain responsibilities and obligations that are expressed during life-cycle rituals and particularly in crisis situations. Some of the groups have bands, with membership determined by patrilineal, matrilineal, and affinal kin ties and by friendship.

Marriage. There are a wide variety of rules regarding marriage. While most of the groups based in central and southern India would allow or prefer cross-cousin and even uncle-niece marriage, groups in the north, west, and east prohibit such marriages. The age at marriage is generally low. Postmarital residence is always with the parents of the husband at first, but later the couple may establish their own home within the husband's father's band. Marriages are generally arranged by elders. In some groups, parents of a boy may have to pay to obtain a bride for their son.

Domestic Unit. The household is the smallest and most important domestic unit among the peripatetics. It is composed of husband, wife, and their unmarried children, and at times it may also include the husband's elderly parent(s). The composition of the household varies during different phases of its developmental cycle. Each household is economically independent and is responsible for meeting kinship obligations.

Inheritance. Inheritance is through the male line. In some of the groups it is the youngest son who inherits the household property. He also has responsibility for caring for the elderly parents.

Socialization. Children learn as they grow up and are given tasks according to their age and sex. In some groups, such as acrobats and animal displayers, children receive formal training starting in early childhood.

Sociopolitical Organization

Peripatetics are keenly aware of the need to maintain social and economic flexibility among themselves to maximize their economic returns. Each household is an independent unit and it must fend for itself. Its success depends upon the wisdom of its decisions regarding whether to break camp and move, which route to take, where to pitch a new camp, and how long to camp and with whom. While these are the crucial questions for each household's survival, the households must also maintain the ties among themselves for the survival of the group. Different peripatetic groups use different strategies to manage these critical tasks.

Social Organization. The factors that influence group cohesiveness are regional affiliation, agnatic ties in a ramifying descent system, matrilateral and affinal relations, ritual friendship, and resource potentials. Camps and bands are constituted on the basis of these factors.

Political Organization. Generally, peripatetics have been isolated from state and regional politics. Most of them do not know about or are unconcerned about political changes taking place in the country. They do not participate in any political activity and the majority of them probably do not vote. The only contact they have with governmental authority is with the subordinate police officers and sometimes with development officers.

Social Control. Social control is generally maintained by the council of elders. The council organization and its functions vary from group to group. The procedures it may adopt to resolve disputes are based on the traditions in each group. The objective is not merely to resolve a dispute per se but to arrive at a consensus in which the past behavior of the individuals and their families is also kept in view. In addition, the threat of excommunication and endogamy ensure conformity to the traditions of the group to a considerable degree. When disputing parties fail to reach a consensus, a camp band may dissolve, and different units involved in the case may travel on their own or seek to join other camps or bands.

Conflict. Conflicts and misunderstandings among peripatetics arise for a variety of reasons. Most common are those concerning marriage, sexual relations, travel routes, duration of a camp, and distribution of resources. Peripatetics generally avoid disputes with the settled populations on which they are dependent.

Religion and Expressive Culture

Religious Beliefs and Practitioners. The majority of the peripatetics are Hindus. There are also some Sikh and Muslim peripatetics. Their religious beliefs and practices reflect the influence of the traditions of the "home village."

Arts. Peripatetics' art is expressed through their subsistence activities. Numerous variety of *bhiksaks* (beggars) compose their songs and also employ different types of instruments and makeup. For example, one mendicant observed in a Mysore village wore more than 100 items on his body, and it took him a couple of hours to dress and paint himself with religious marks. Peripatetics try to be exclusive and try to remain in demand. For example, Budbudki, peripatetic fortune-tellers of Karnataka, use drums so tiny they can be held between their forefingers and thumbs; they play them while they visit houses in a locality in the morning to forecast the day's events for each household. The name of this group is taken from the sound of the drum. Leather puppeteers, acrobats, and displayers of animals continually express their creative urges through their professions.

Medicine. The majority of the peripatetics has not taken to scientific medicine. They use their own knowledge or that of the settled people to treat disease. Women give birth in their camps or at their "home villages." There are some groups that specialize in herbal medicines.

Death and Afterlife. Peripatetics accept death as part of life. They dispose of the dead body as quickly as they can, usually in the camp where the death has taken place. When they get together in the off-season, they may organize ceremonies for the dead.

See also Kanjar; Qalandar; Sadhu

Bibliography

Berland, Joseph C. (1983). "Peripatetic Strategies in South Asia: Skill as Capital among Nomadic Artisans and Entertainers." *Nomadic Peoples* 13.

Berland, Joseph C., and Matt. T. Salo, eds. (1986). "Peripatetic Peoples: An Introduction." *Nomadic Peoples* (Toronto) 21–22 (special issue).

Misra, P. K. (1970). "Study of Nomads." In *Research Programmes on Cultural Anthropology and Allied Disciplines*, edited by Surajit Sinha. Anthropological Survey of India. Calcutta.

Misra, P. K., and Rajalakshmi Misra (1982). "Nomadism in the Land of Tamils between 1 A.D. and 600 A.D." In *Nomads in India*, edited by P. K. Misra and K. C. Malhotra. Anthropological Survey of India. Calcutta.

Rao, Aparna (1987). "The Concept of Peripatetics: An Introduction." In *The Other Nomads*, edited by Aparna Rao. Cologne and Vienna: Boheau Verlag.

P. K. MISRA

Punjabi

ETHNONYM: Panjabi

Orientation

Identification. The term "Punjabi" signifies both an inhabitant of the Punjab and a speaker of the predominant language of that region, Punjabi. The name is from the Persian *panj*, "five," and *ab*, "river." The Punjab is defined by the Indus River and the five rivers to the south that flow out of the Himalayas to join it: the Jhelum, Chenab, Ravi, Beas, and Sutlej. These define five *doabs*, which differ culturally and linguistically. A doab is the land between two converging rivers. Culturally, Punjab actually extends southward still more, to the bed of the largely extinct Ghaggar, which also traces from the Himalayas to the Indus and joins it about where the Sutlej does. The Punjab culture region includes the states of Punjab in Pakistan and in India as well as portions of present-day North-West Frontier Province in Pakistan and Jammu, Rajasthan, and Himachal Pradesh in India.

Location. The region lies between 28° and 34° N and 70° and 74° E. It is mainly a nearly level plain, dropping in elevation from 300 meters in the northeast at the edge of the Siwalik range to about 100 meters at the point where the Indus becomes a single stream. Above the plain, the culture region includes the mountains of the Salt range in Pakistan and parts of the lower Himalayas in India. Its area is about 270,000 square kilometers. Of this, 205,344 square kilometers are in Pakistan Punjab and 50,362 square kilometers in Indian Punjab.

The climate is warm to temperate. The hottest season is May–June, when maximum daytime temperatures are about 40° C. The coolest months are January and February, when light nighttime frosts are common. Rainfall is monsoonal, with more than two-thirds falling in the summer rainy season. It is heaviest near the Himalayas. Along the Himalayan edge of the plains annual amounts of about 1 meter are normal. At Lahore, 100 kilometers out into the plain, rainfall is about 50 centimeters, and at Multan, about 500 kilometers from the mountains and in the center of the southeastern portion of the region, it is about 18 centimeters. There are two major agricultural seasons marked by two dry, hot harvest periods in April–May (_rabi_) and September–October (_kharif_). The winter monsoon, although light, is vital for the wheat crop that provides the traditional staple of the region.

Demography. The combined population of Indian and Pakistan Punjab in 1981 was about 64.1 million, compared to about 36.6 million in 1961. Population densities in rural areas range from over 1,900 persons per square kilometer in the highly urbanized Lahore District in Pakistan to about 10 persons per square kilometer in the desert of the Thal Doab between the Indus and the lower portion of the Chenab (Mianwala District). Indian Punjab had about 333 persons per square kilometer.

Linguistic Affiliation. Punjabi is Indo-European with close relations to surrounding languages, particularly to Pahari to the east. It is divided into six major dialects, localized in the major doabs. The Majhi and Malwa dialects are considered the most "pure." Majhi occupies the upper half of the Bari Doab, the plain region between the Ravi and the Sutlej rivers, which includes the cities of Lahore and Amritsar. The Malwa tract is just south of this between the Sutlej and Ghaggar, centering on Bhatinda. The other dialects are Doabi, spoken around Jalandhar between the Beas and the Sutlej; Powadhi, spoken in the eastern portion of the doab between the Sutlej and Ghaggar, centering on Sirhind; Dogri in Jammu District of Jammu and Kashmir and Kangra District of Himachal Pradesh; and finally Bhattiani, extending southeast from the Malwa tract across the eastern tip of Haryana State and into Ganganagar District of Rajasthan. North and west of Majhi, Punjabi gives way to Lahnda, also called Western Punjabi, which is spoken all across the western half of the Pakistani Punjab. While linguistically distinguishable, Lahnda speakers generally consider themselves Punjabi. Lahnda and Bhattiani have been attenuated further by large migrations to the canal colonies of Shahpur, Lyallpur, Montgomery, and Multan and to Ganganagar District in Rajasthan. These schemes comprised almost 2.5 million hectares of new agricultural land by 1930, and by far the largest numbers of settlers were Jat farmers from around Lahore, Amritsar, Ludhiana, and Jalandhar.

History and Cultural Relations

The Punjab is an ancient center of civilization. Historically it has been the main route of invasion and migration into India, going back beyond the Harappans. Harappa itself is on the Ravi in Punjab near present-day Montgomery, while Mohenjo Daro is on the Indus in Sindh just outside the natural gateway to Punjab that is formed as the Suliman range curves southward to squeeze the five rivers together. Remains of numerous Harappan communities extend from there to Gujarat in the west and to the upper Jamuna in the east. Invaders since the Harappans have included the ancient Aryans who are responsible for the _Rig Veda_, Scythians, Greeks (Alexander the Great came as far as the Ravi), Arabs, Persians, Afghans, Pathans, Baluchis, Mongols, and Europeans. Each group has left its marks.

The chief historic cities of Punjab are Lahore, Amritsar,

Ludhiana, Jalandhar, and Patiala. They are part of a line of commercial and military centers that lie along ancient routes from the Khyber Pass through the Ganges Plain. Along this route, rainfall is reliable, soils are deep, groundwater is accessible, and the climate is moderate. Cities in this belt south and east of Punjab include Delhi, Varanasi, Lucknow, Meerut, Allahabad, and Patna. These linkages keep Punjab in constant communication with surrounding regions. Punjabi culture has never been isolated.

Modern Punjabi culture has been shaped profoundly by the partitioning of India and Pakistan that accompanied independence in 1947. This event resulted in massive migrations that separated Muslims from Hindus and Sikhs, drove the Sikh cultivators who had been the backbone of the canal colonies to India, made Sikhs for the first time an actual majority in rural areas of central Indian Punjab, and initiated divergent government policies that have had far-reaching effects on all areas of life.

Settlements

Compared to surrounding regions, Punjab's population is evenly spread and dense, particularly in the central areas. In Indian Punjab the rural population is consistently 60–70 percent of the total. It is similar in the adjoining districts of Pakistani Punjab except for Lahore District, which is 84 percent urban. Urban settlements now are sprawling towns, growing rapidly in both Punjabs but faster in Pakistan. Formerly they were walled and compact, with many-storied houses and narrow lanes for defense and shade. The towns are educational and administrative centers, and they have active agriculture trading sectors as well as numerous and diverse types of manufacturing. The estimated 1981 populations of the principal towns were as follows: Lahore, 2,922,000; Lyallpur (Faisalabad), 1,092,000; Multan, 730,000; Sialkot, 296,000; Amritsar, 595,000; Ludhiana, 607,000; Jalandhar, 408,000; and Patiala, 206,000.

Villages in the Punjab plains are nucleated. In the older villages—apart from the canal colonies, where villages were laid out in blocks at crossroads—houses are built together in a compact area and the outer walls are joined together to make a common rampart, with limited points of entry. Houses abut one another along narrow lanes, sharing many common walls. One can reach much of the village by going over rooftops, but the only access to the rooftops is from the inside of houses. Close outside this wall are work areas and areas for storage, or perhaps a village mill. Beyond this the agricultural fields lie open; only valuable orchards would be fenced. At some distance in the fields there are always one or two cremation grounds and some ritual sites. In larger villages, there are commonly separate sides or neighborhoods for upper- and lower-caste groups, and there may be concentrations of households of specific caste or lineage groups in a particular lane or area.

Stereotypically, and commonly, the main entry to a village is through a masonry gateway, called the _durwaza_, which arches over the main road and limits the size of vehicles that can enter. It may be up to 20 meters long. Inside, along the roadway on both sides, it has wide raised plinths, where people can sit. The durwaza is always an important meeting place and the preferred stopping place for visiting artisans and traders.

The average population of a village in the central area is about 990 persons, but the distribution is highly skewed. About two-thirds of the villages are of less than average size.

Since independence many houses have been built outside the former rampart, and farmers have begun building houses directly in their fields, particularly at well sites. Many small new hamlets have also been established. The changes in settlement patterns reflect increased geographical mobility and regional integration. In India's Punjab all villages have been electrified and connected by paved roads. Almost all now have some kind of private motorized transport vans, motor rickshaws, or minibuses. Pakistani Punjab has a similar density of infrastructure in the central canal colonies, but it also has many areas that lack both electricity and paved roads.

Economy

Subsistence and Commercial Activities.   The Punjab has long been one of the world's most important agricultural regions. Pakistan's Punjab, which comprises 25.7 percent of its total land area, is its most important agricultural area by far. Its principal crops are cotton and wheat. Indian Punjab, although only about 1.7 percent of the total area of India, produces about 21 percent of India's wheat and 8.5 percent of its rice. The agriculture has several distinctive features, beginning with heavy reliance on irrigation and exceptionally high cropping densities and levels of investment.

Punjab agriculturalists cannot be divided into subsistence and commercial sectors. Even farmers who sell most of what they grow still obtain most of what they consume from their own fields. The agricultural system involves intensive multicropping and most of the major commercial crops are also traditional food crops. The diet is simple, based on winter and summer "typical" combinations of a bread made of grain from the last season with a pulse from the last season or a vegetable from the present season. Thus, for example, the typical meal in the cold months is a maize *roti* (a flat bread cooked on an iron skillet, without oil) with *sarson ka sag* (mustard greens with spices, onions, garlic, and clarified butter cooked into a thick soup). In the other months, the most common meal is wheat roti and a side dish such as curried lentils, chick-peas, potatoes, squash, or okra.

The main exceptions to the general rule that marketed crops are simply food crops produced in excess of the family needs are rice in Indian Punjab and cotton in Pakistani Punjab. Cotton is a historic cash crop grown for export; taking advantage of the dry climate and rich soils, it requires about the same amount of water as wheat and can be readily grown with canal irrigation. It has been largely abandoned in Indian Punjab because it carries about a 50 percent risk of loss. Rice was introduced as a response to widespread flooding in the Amritsar area in the mid-1960s, caused by new canals traversing the area. It has since spread to other areas as electrification has become available for private bore wells, but it has not been adopted into the diet.

From about 1965 to 1978, both parts of Punjab underwent a "green revolution." This is a blend of advanced university-based seed production, relatively small-scale machine and storage technologies, and a system of rural support institutions suited to family-owned peasant management. Since their consolidation in Punjab, these technologies and institutions have been steadily spreading outward. Punjabi migrants are prominent leaders of agricultural innovation in many surrounding regions. Punjab agriculture is also characterized by a large cattle population. Major animals are oxen (*Bos indica*), camels, and buffalo.

Cattle population densities are higher in Punjab than surrounding regions, and the cattle are generally larger and more productive, except that Haryana, to the south, is known for producing even larger oxen as plow animals. With mechanization accompanying the green revolution technologies, the densities have increased and the proportions have changed. The number of camels, oxen, and Indica cows has been reduced, and that of milk animals, mainly buffalo, has greatly increased. Their size and quality have also been increased by artificial insemination programs. Many farmers have also obtained new Indica-Jersey or Indica-Holstein cows.

Industrial Arts and Trade.   Associated with this agricultural base is an extensive economic infrastructure, including agroprocessing and agroservice industries, along with light and medium manufacturing. Ludhiana is widely known for very large scale bicycle manufacturing as well as the production of agricultural tools of many types. The infrastructure includes a vigorous truck transport industry, major agricultural universities in both Punjabs, and, in Indian Punjab, an extensive system of cooperatives engaged in obtaining input materials and distributing them to farmers as well as large-scale buying and transport of commodities on behalf of the national food-grain pools. Other cooperatives are engaged in sugar manufacturing, dairying, transport, and various small-scale industries such as the production of cotton and woolen textiles and clothing. Heavier production, both publicly and privately owned, includes farm tractors, railroad cars, cement, tools, and bicycles.

In Pakistani Punjab the agricultural infrastructure is weaker but heavy manufacturing is stronger. Major products include textiles, machinery, electrical appliances, surgical equipment, floor coverings, bicycles and rickshaws, and foodstuffs.

Division of Labor.   Urban areas in Punjab have the full range of occupations that exist in any comparable economic system: doctors, lawyers, teachers, government workers, engineers, mechanics, construction workers, shopkeepers, bankers, truck drivers, street sweepers, and so on. There is a high degree of industrial and craft specialization. Women as well as men participate in the labor force and in the professions. The proportion of women is lower in Pakistani Punjab.

In rural areas, the main occupational groups are: agriculturalists (landowner/farmer), about 50 percent; agricultural laborers, about 30 percent; and specialized artisans, about 20 percent—carpenters, masons, blacksmiths, mechanics, millers, operators of cotton gins. Large villages also have one or two shopkeepers, teachers, tailors, a mail carrier or postmaster, religious professionals, and perhaps a medical practitioner of some kind. Agriculturalists now commonly hire themselves out with their equipment for custom work such as plowing or harvesting with a combine.

The household division of labor is based on sex and seniority. In better-off households, men usually deal with the main property from which the family obtains its income: land, a shop, or the husband/father's individual vocation. The wife or mother of the senior man heads the women's side of the household. She takes direct charge of the internal household budget, oversees stores, takes care of young animals, directs the activities of other women and girls in the house, manages household servants, and oversees the daily preparation and distribution of food and the care of children. Sons are under the care of their mothers until about school age, when they begin to accompany their fathers at their work. In laboring households, both men and women work, although usually at different tasks. Men receive higher pay and do work that is physically more difficult. It is becoming common for women to take salaried work, but it would be considered very odd for a woman to set up an independent household.

Kinship

Kin Groups and Descent. The most important descent/ kinship groups in Punjab, in order of comprehensiveness, are caste (_jati_), clan (_got_), village (_pind_), division (_patti_), and family (_parivar_). In Punjab a caste is described as a group of families in an area, with common ancestry, who marry among themselves and have a common traditional occupation based upon a common type of inherited productive property.

Castes generally have origin stories that explain how they came into the area and/or into their present occupational position. Lower castes are described either as original landholders who were defeated and subordinated by later invaders (who became the present landholders), or alternatively as latecomers who were given their present occupation by the landholders in exchange for being allowed to settle. Higher castes are described as successful invaders or as a group given the land of an area by some past ruler for notable services.

In villages, castes commonly fall into higher and lower groups. Traditionally, members of the lower caste would have been considered unclean by the upper, and they might have been denied house sites and access to public wells on the upper-caste side of the village, and they also might have had to use different ritual specialists for marriages and other life-cycle rituals. Exactly which castes are put in each group varies by area, but the upper castes usually are Brahmans, landowners, and skilled artisans, while the lower groups do work such as handling dead animals and sweeping up offal. Landowning castes include Jats, Rajputs, Sainis, Kambohs, Brahmans, Gujars, and Ahirs. The term "Rajput" literally means "son of a king," but most of the other names are purely ethnic in connotation. There is no caste group literally named "landowner" or farmer. Artisan castes include carpenters, masons, blacksmiths, barbers, operators of cotton gins, and perhaps weavers. The lower group contains leatherworkers and sweepers. People often do not actually perform the work their caste name suggests. Leatherworkers, for example, are a numerous group who usually do agricultural labor. People of lower castes often use different caste names according to religion; for example, a Mazhbi is a leatherworker who is a Sikh.

In Punjab, caste discrimination is not generally supported by religion. It is specifically rejected in all forms of Islam and Sikhism. Many local Hindu sects and movements, such as Radhoswami, reject it as well. Each jati is divided into an indefinite number of clans (_got_). A got is a group descended from a common ancestor, not specifically known, whose members are more closely related to each other than to other members of the caste. Gots are exogamous; one must not marry a person from the gots of any of one's four grandparents. People commonly use the name of their got as part of their personal name.

Villages are also exogamous, and people of one's village are addressed with kinship terms as though they were people of one's own family, irrespective of caste or got. A patti— literally, a division—is the largest group of families with actual common ancestry within a caste or got in a single village. A family (_parivar_) is the basic and most important unit of Punjab society. The complementary roles of men and women in the household division of labor are based upon complementary rights and duties in terms of the kinship system, particularly complementary rights over property (see below).

Kinship Terminology. The Punjabi kinship terminology distinguishes just four superior generations and four inferior generations, but there is no limit to the relationships that may be considered collateral.

In Ego's own generation, all males are addressed as _bhai_ (brother) and all females are _bhain_ (sister). These terms include all of those who would be called "cousin" in English, and many more. In the first ascending generation, the terminology distinguishes mother, mother's brother, and mother's sister, and each of their respective spouses, all of which are further distinguished from father, father's elder brother, father's younger brother, and father's sister and their respective spouses. From an English speaker's point of view, Punjabi thus demarcates ten distinct relations where English has only "uncle" and "aunt." But the offspring of these relations are all either "brother" or "sister," according to sex.

The terms above +1 continue to separate the matrilateral and patrilateral sides: all the terms of the mother's side are built up on the stem _-nan-_. On the father's side the stem is _-dad-_. Prefixes and suffixes distinguish generation and sex only. Thus the father of the father is _dada_, mother of father is _dadi_. Dada also applies to any male relative through the dada or dadi, and dadi to any female through the dada or dadi. Thus dada is "grandfather," "great-uncle," and indeed all of their siblings, spouses, or siblings of spouses or spouses of siblings of whatever remoteness. _Nana_ and _nani_ are those similarly related on the mother's side. Father of dada is _pardada_, his wife/sister is _parnani_, and these terms too are similarly extended. Their counterparts on the mother's side are _parnana_ and _parnani_. The father or mother of parnana or parnani has no term (i.e., is not a relative). The term-pair superior to parnana-parnani on the father's side in turn is _nakarnana-nakarnani_. Above this no further relations are recognized on the father's side.

The system of terms for relatives below the generation of Ego is more complex. Each position is distinguished by generation, sex, and whether the person was brought into the family by birth or marriage. Further, lines of descent through males only are separated from those through females, beginning with distinguishing Ego's own sons and daughters from those of Ego's sister's on the one hand and Ego's brother's on the other. The line of direct descendants that remains with a man in his village is also separated out from all others. The terminology for men is the same as for women. In address, only terms for one's own and superior generations are used. Genealogical inferiors are addressed by name.

Marriage and Family

Marriage. Marriage is considered universal and necessary among all religious communities. Residence is patrilocal. The bride comes to live with her husband in his natal village and house. Marriages are arranged by parents, with wide consultation. Although there is no formal rule, families who have more than one son who in turn have sons will generally divide, and just one son and his family will remain with the parents. If a family has so many sons that its property cannot be divided and still be useful, it is customary in Punjab, particularly among Jats, for some of the sons to remain single and stay in the house with one of the brothers who marries. Dividing the house in marriage has no necessary connection to the division of ancestral property.

Although laws in both Punjabs provide for legally registered marriages, these are seldom used. Marriages generally occur according to customary forms, whether Hindu, Sikh, or Muslim. The ceremonies vary by caste and region, but generally they symbolically represent the ideal that a marriage is a free gift of the girl from the girl's family to the groom, with nothing taken back in exchange. Expenses of the wedding are borne by the girl's parents, and substantial gifts by way of dowry are given by the parents to the girl to take with her to her new house. They should be enough to provide for her upkeep (or the equivalent of it) for two or three years. By that time, having children will have established her permanently as part of her new household.

There is provision in the customary rituals for de facto divorce. Immediately after the marriage ceremony the girl returns to her parental home, and she should be fetched by her husband to return. She may refuse. Otherwise, she may in any case come home and refuse to return. The husband's family should then return her property. Once children are born, however, divorce is effectively impossible, since there is no way parental rights or responsibilities can be abrogated or reassigned. The parents' relations to each other are set by their common offspring. On the other hand, if children are not born, the marriage will probably dissolve. Since the only old-age security most people have is that which is provided by descendants who inherit their property and maintain it for them, the groom's family will be forced to send the bride away (although adoption is also common and easy). If sent away, her parents will have an obligation to receive her back, although this will be considered awkward for her brothers and their wives. In any case, from a traditional point of view it will be less a matter of divorce than a matter of the marriage not being completed.

Polygamy is accepted, but rare. There are no organized or legal sanctions against intercaste marriages.

Domestic Unit. The domestic unit is the parivar, as discussed above. A parivar is a group of related people who have a common interest in some ancestral property, which they jointly operate. Ideally and most commonly a parivar will consist of a senior man, his wife, perhaps his aged parents and unmarried brothers or sisters, his children, and some or all of their wives and children. There is no domestic cycle, or a changing sequence of forms for the family as a whole. Rather, the family structure is considered constant, and the members move through it according to their individual life cycles.

Inheritance. As with marriage, Punjabis may choose to be governed in matters of inheritance by custom or by religious laws as formalized in governmental acts: Christian, Hindu, or Muslim. Most follow custom, which varies by caste and/or region. This commonly makes all males equal sharers of their father's property from birth. If a man has one son, from the birth of that son they each have a half share in whatever was his ancestral property. If a second son is born, they all have a third, and so on. If there are four sons and one dies, all the survivors and the father divide his share equally. If a father sells his son's share or his own while the son is too young to formally agree, the son may, on reaching maturity, preempt the sale and reclaim the land by paying only the original purchase price.

Women have no birthrights in property, but they have a right to maintenance. In addition, a son's most sacred obligation is considered to be to his mother. For Hindus this idea is embodied in the notion of a sacred cow, worshiped simply because she is "like" mother. But the basic value is held by Muslims and Sikhs as well. For a son to refuse to care for his mother is almost unthinkable.

Within this general pattern, the customary laws of different communities differ in the way possible applications or interpretations are ordered. For example, in Hindu law generally, a son may demand a legal partition and take his share of the ancestral property at any time. In Jat customary law, the division will not take place unless the father agrees to it.

Socialization. Both Punjabs have modern school systems, although Indian Punjab's is more extensive. In 1981 rural Indian Punjab had a literacy rate of 38 percent; Pakistani Punjab had a rate of 17 percent. In addition to public education, each state has extensive religiously sponsored educational institutions. But in both, the main locus of socialization is still the family itself, and the discipline imposed by the knowledge that all family members are also part of a common economic enterprise, on which they are mutually dependent. Girls are trained in their economic tasks by accompanying their mothers; boys, after about age 5, accompany their fathers.

The different religious communities have various concepts of initiation to adulthood, but there is no general Punjabi concept as such.

Sociopolitical Organization

Social Organization. Both Punjabs have a multitiered administrative system with a centuries-long history. The basic units in this system are village, block or circle, *tehsil* (subdistrict), district, and state. For the last 150 years, the district has been the most important unit of administration and the lowest unit controlled by the elite national administrative service officers. In the imperial period, these district commissioners combined all the administrative functions: police, revenue, and judicial. Since independence the functions have been separated in both countries. Both governments also recognize an important legal distinction between villages, which are under direct state administration and in which land revenue is collected, and towns, which are under chartered municipal committees and which collect a wide range of property and business taxes, but not land revenue. (Information on caste is provided above in the section on kinship.)

Political Organization. Early writers on Punjab often reported that villages and caste groups in villages were governed by *panchayats*, village councils. Beginning in 1952, Indian Punjab built on this tradition by establishing an elected panchayat for every village. Representatives from the panchayats in turn met in *panchayat samitis* at block and district levels. This system grew to play an important role in the agricultural planning that produced Punjab's green revolution. But the panchayats had no power to change their own mandates or control their own elections. When Punjab came under central administrative control during the prime ministership of Indira Gandhi, the panchayats, along with other elected bodies, were legally disbanded. Although they had no legal power to continue on their own, many still did so informally.

Pakistani Punjab has not supported village-level government. Instead, in the 1960s the government established "Basic Democracies," a system of councils from the "circle" level up to the province that began with the election in each village of one "basic democrat" per 1,000–1,500 voters. The councils were remote from villages and dominated by large landlords and administrators. The result is that Pakistani Punjab continues to have a much less egalitarian distribution of power as well as resources, retaining a much clearer two-class system. Since independence both Punjabs have had provision for legislatures, although Pakistani Punjab, with the rest of Pakistan, has been under military rule for much of the time and the provincial assembly has been suspended. The chief executive is a governor, appointed by the president of Pakistan, assisted by an administrative secretariat. Indian Punjab established its legislature on the basis of direct elections, and electoral districts with large numbers of lower-caste voters are designated as "reserved" seats for members of those groups, to ensure minority representation. Except when under central rule, the chief executive of the state is the chief minister, elected by a majority of the legislative assembly. Both Punjabs have organized political parties, which go back historically to the late nineteenth century.

Both Punjabs also have active factional systems, beginning at the village level and extending upward to motivate much of the statewide party activity. In villages, these groups are considered "secret" and are not publicly acknowledged. They reflect alliances among households, commonly focusing on efforts to gain or protect land or other major resources. At higher levels, local factions engage with regional political figures or other influential persons in a complex and fluid system of exchanges that shows little regard for ideology.

Finally, organized religious establishments have an important role in social and political mobilization. They provide a public forum to discuss government policies that government itself cannot control. Each year, many tens of thousands of people customarily travel to attend religious fairs at major shrines, and those who speak on such occasions normally apply precepts of the religion to events of the day, including events involving government. In Indian Punjab, the most important forum of this type is the Sikh Gurdwara system. In Pakistani Punjab, mosques have similar functions.

Social Control and Conflict. There is no one system of social control. Rather, each system of institutions has its own set of sanctions and its own discipline: commerce, household management, politics, the civil administration, kinship, law and customary law, and the religious organizations.

Generally, village life is highly competitive even while it is cooperative. Villagers know each other well. Thus conflicts seldom arise by miscalculation. Slights are assumed to be deliberate, and they usually are. Such conflicts tend to persist. Village factions serve to structure and manage them; there is seldom a means for resolving them.

According to a Punjabi saying, the sources of all conflicts are land, women, and water. More exactly, it is the need to control the means to perpetuate one's family and property. Thus the sources of conflict are indistinguishable from the bases of social control.

Religion and Expressive Culture

Religious Beliefs. As of the 1981 census, the population of Indian Punjab reported itself as being 37 percent Hindu, 61 percent Sikh, 1 percent Muslim, and a little more than 1 percent Christian, with smaller portions of Buddhists, Jains, and others. Pakistani Punjab is about 97 percent Muslim and 2 percent Christian, with small numbers of others.

Religious Practitioners. Each religion has its own taxonomy of practitioners, and in addition there are many kinds of folk or customary practitioners. For example, a *jyotshi* would be a Brahman who professed some kind of ability to foretell the future, by astrology or other means. A *nai* is a barber. Since the last Sikh Guru enjoined his followers to leave their hair and beards uncut, nais in principle have little work in Sikh villages. But they commonly serve as ritual managers of weddings, while their wives work as midwives. There are Muslim and Hindu *sants* who obtain reputations for holiness and may attract supporters for activities such as maintaining or rebuilding a local shrine or for curing diseases. And there are storytellers, poets, singers, and preachers who go from village to village or from one religious event to another throughout the region.

Ceremonies. Rural Punjabis of all religions share many ceremonies considered customary, associated with the individual life cycle, village life, and the round of the seasons. Most of the specific ceremonies associated with marriages come under this heading, as do ceremonies of birth, naming, and death. An important sequence of annual rituals celebrates the successive roles a woman plays in her life. The ceremony of *tij* is celebrated as the rains begin by young girls and their brothers in the house of their parents; in the fall harvest season *karue* is celebrated by newly married and older married women in the house of the young woman's parents or in-laws; and in March (in Punjab a time of pleasant weather and steady growth of the all-important wheat crop) *behairi* is celebrated by mothers and their young children in the house of the husband. On the night of Diwali, in October/November, all buildings and structures of a village are outlined in little oil lamps (*diwas*) and people ask God for prosperity; and in midwinter there is a ceremony called "Tails" (meaning cattle), when men go in the evening to collect sweets from houses where boys have been born in the village, build a fire of dung (the traditional cooking fuel) at the village gate, pray to God for the health of the boys and more in the future, and distribute the sweets to the village children who come to collect them. Farmers commonly offer first fruits at village shrines, and almost any start of a venture or stroke of good fortune is an occasion for distributing sweets.

Arts. Punjab has generated distinctive forms of virtually all the arts, from dance to architecture, bawdy folk epics to sublime theological poetry. The best-known folk dance is lively and complex *bhangra*, named for *bhang* (marijuana). In architecture, the most distinctive major form is that of the Sikh Gurdwaras, which blend Mogul and Rajput elements. In literature, the most famous and prominent forms are romantic epic poems. The main ones are *Heer Ranjha*, *Sassi Punun*, and *Mirza Shahiban*, all by Muslim authors. Older than these are thirteenth-century theological *sufi* poems of Shaik Farid. In the Sikh tradition, closely allied in sentiment and style to the sufi, the most notable groups of poems are by Guru Nanak (1469–1539) and Guru Arjun Dev (1563–1606). There are also numerous modern poets and writers on both secular and religious topics and an active film industry that relies heavily on melodrama, folksong, and dance.

Medicine. Punjabis support all the forms of medical practice available in India, and when they can afford it, generally prefer the Western.

Death and Afterlife. The main formalized beliefs concerning death and the afterlife are those of the three major religious traditions, but the Punjabi versions of these traditions are generally austere, individualistic, and pragmatic. Religion is viewed as a source of strength and inspiration to meet the obligations of this world more than as a gateway to another. Funeral practices vary according to religion.

See also Sikh; Zamindar

Bibliography

Brass, Paul (1974). *Religion and Politics in North India.* Cambridge: Cambridge University Press.

Darling, Malcolm Lyall (1925). *The Punjab Peasant in Prosperity and Debt.* 4th ed. 1947. Bombay: Oxford University Press. Reprint. 1978. Columbia, Mo.: South Asia Books; New Delhi: Manohar Book Service.

Eglar, Zekiye (1960). *A Punjabi Village in Pakistan.* New York: Columbia University Press.

Kessinger, Tom G. (1974). *Vilayatpur, 1848–1968: Social and Economic Change in a North Indian Village.* Berkeley and Los Angeles: University of California Press.

Leaf, Murray J. (1984). *Song of Hope: The Green Revolution in a Panjab Village.* New Brunswick, N.J.: Rutgers University Press.

Michel, Aloys A. (1967). *The Indus Rivers: A Study of the Effects of Partition.* New Haven and London: Yale University Press.

Sims, Holly (1988). *Political Regimes, Public Policy, and Economic Development: Agricultural Performance and Rural Change in the Two Punjabs.* New Delhi: Sage Publications.

MURRAY J. LEAF

Purum

ETHNONYM: Burum

Orientation

Identification. The Purum are an Old Kuki tribe occupying the Manipur Hills area of India and Myanmar (Burma). In 1931 they were located in four independent villages: Purum Khulen, Purum Tampak, Purum Changninglong, and Purum Chumbang. The name "Purum" might mean "hide from tiger," as Tarakchandra Das and John Shakespear have suggested.

Location. The geographic extent of the region inhabited by the Purum ranges from 24°23' to 24°27' N and from 93°56' to 94°2' E.

Demography. As of 1931 there were 303 Purums living in Khulen, Tampak, Chumbang, and Changninglong. In 1977 the Purum population numbered 300.

Linguistic Affiliation. Purum (also called Puram) is a Tibeto-Burman language belonging to the Sino-Tibetan Phylum.

History and Cultural Relations

With regard to the origin of the Purum, their traditions state that they emerged from a subterranean region near Imphal. The original home of the Purum and other Old Kuki tribes is believed to have been in the Lushai Hills. They were forced to migrate to the hill country bordering the Imphal Valley by New Kuki tribes (who had been displaced by the Lushais or Mizos). The initial settlement of these Old Kuki peoples was short-lived as New Kukis forced them to scatter in many directions. Once in Manipur, independent communities began to develop. Once settled, they assimilated many aspects of Meithei culture (including some Hindu social and religious traits). The Purum and other Old Kuki tribes were also influenced by contacts with Naga tribes and New Kuki tribes whose migration followed their own. Of all of these, contact with the Meitheis has been most important.

Settlements

Khulen is located on a ridge some 1,200 meters above sea level, east of Waikhong. Tampak is found on the slope of a low hill north of Waikhong. Changninglong is situated atop a high hill east of Tampak. Chumbang is located in a valley on a ridge east of Khulen at the point where the Maha Turel and Timit Lok rivers converge. Purum villages are located near a readily available source of fresh water (e.g., spring or stream). A typical Purum house contains the following structures: a dwelling place for human occupants, a granary, a cowshed (optional), a pigsty, a pen for fowl, and courtyards. The design of the house is rectangular. In addition to individual habitations, the typical Purum village will also contain a *ruishang* (village assembly hall), *laman* (a shrine for the god Nungchungba and locus of certain magicoreligious ceremonies for the community), and raised platforms (remains of *thienhong-ba genna*) erected by community members for the purpose of obtaining social status.

Economy

Subsistence and Commercial Activities. Animal domestication (i.e., pigs, cows, buffalo, fowl, pigeons, ducks, dogs, and cats) and agriculture are part of the repertoire of Purum subsistence activities, though the latter is by far the most important. It is believed that the Purum economy was at one time largely self-sufficient and village-based (i.e., before the pressure to increase food supply). The availability of land suitable for _jhum_ (slash-and-burn) agriculture was probably one of the motivating factors in the selection of Khulen as a village site. Villages constructed after Khulen were founded in order to secure additional lands for cultivation with the plow. While a typical Purum village will control the lands on the slopes immediately below it, additional land in the valleys and at the base of the hills in the region belongs to the Meitheis, who occupy these areas. Purum agriculturalists lease some of these tracts for the growing of rice, sell their surplus produce to the Meitheis, and purchase additional agricultural land from them. Wet and dry agriculture are practiced by the Purum. The latter was a practice probably adopted from the Meitheis. Among the products grown by the Purum are plantains, sweet potatoes, rice, cotton, taro, gourds, cucumbers, _saukri_ (a local vegetable with bitter leaves), maize, onions, and sesame. Hunting and fishing (by means of traps in addition to the rod and line) are engaged in to a limited extent, but neither is an important part of the Purum cycle of subsistence.

Industrial Arts. With their raw materials obtained from the markets at Imphal, Purum smiths fashion essential tools and weapons (e.g. small hoes, spindles, vessel stands, spear and arrow heads, chisels, and hammers). Some of these items (e.g., plowshares, _daos_ [adzes], etc.) are purchased from the Meitheis. Purum women weave cloth from yarn spun from locally grown cotton. Spinning and weaving are activities engaged in chiefly by women.

Trade. The Meitheis and the markets at Imphal are the sources from which the Purum obtain essential and luxury items. Iron and steel are obtained in the markets at Imphal. High-quality fabric, metal ornaments, and other luxury items are purchased from the Meitheis. The Meitheis are major consumers of agricultural products grown by the Purum.

Division of Labor. Among those activities associated specifically with either gender, men manufacture baskets while women are responsible for the spinning and weaving of cloth, prepare meals, and gather firewood. There are no taboos reinforcing this task specialization. Women are also primarily responsible for the socialization of children. Men and women share agricultural duties.

Land Tenure. Inhabitants of a Purum village select parcels from the jhum land belonging to the village. Individuals are entitled to the use of this land but are not considered in any way to be its owners. Usufructuary rights may be inherited or transferred to another village member. Valley fields, which are owned individually, may be disposed of in any manner deemed appropriate by their owners. Areas that have not already been marked or cleared by others may be selected. There is no attempt at regulating the size or location of these plots by village officials. Once a site has been selected, a portion of it is cleared by the owner and a mark is made on a large tree (by removing part of the bark and attaching a crosspiece of wood in the body of the tree) by the claimant so as to prevent another from staking claim to it. Jhum land is farmed for four years and then allowed to lie fallow for ten years. Land disputes are mediated by village elders.

Kinship

Kin Groups and Descent. Three social groupings are of primary importance in Purum society: the family; the subsib (social unit composed of several families); and the sib (composed of several subsibs). The sib and the family are the oldest of these three constituent groups. The Purum are divided into five exogamous sibs: Marrim, Makan, Kheyang, Thao, and Parpa. Each of these (with the exception of Parpa) is divided into subsibs. Each sib is headed by a _pipa_ (leader or head) who functions in a similar capacity for one of the subsibs. Fourteen subsibs were noted by Das in 1945. Each one is headed by its own pipa. The sib has one major responsibility—the regulation of marriage. The members of a subsib consider themselves to be blood relatives: the relationship of its members to one another is more intimate than that between members of the sib. It has limited political, economic, and religious functions. At the time of Das's research, these units were no longer strictly exogamous; the rule of exogamy was strictly observed only at the level of the subsib. Exogamy at the subsib level is based on that at the sib level. Purum sibs are socially graded, but this gradation does not have an impact on the selection of marital partners (e.g., there is no evidence of hypergamy). Patrilineal descent obtains within the sib and subsib.

Kinship Terminology. Sudanese-type kinship terminology is employed for first cousins.

Marriage and Family

Marriage. Marital negotiations are instituted by either the parents of the male suitor or by the male suitor himself. Consent of the parties to be wed and the consent of their parents is required before the union may take place. Once an agreement has been made between the families, the male must work for a period of three years in the household of his father-in-law. This period of service is called _yaun-gimba_. Monogamous unions are the norm, though polygyny is not prohibited. When polygynous arrangements have been noted, the usual number of female spouses is two. Postmarital residence is patrilocal once the husband has completed his period of yaun-gimba service to his wife's father. At this time, the married son may choose to establish a separate household for himself and his wife. If he has no younger brother, then he and his spouse must remain in the home of his parents until the parents are deceased. This practice ensures that the son's parents will be cared for in their old age. Divorce may be obtained by either the husband or wife, though all cases must be decided by the village council and the _khullakpa_ (headman).

Domestic Unit. The principal domestic unit is the nuclear family made up of two parents and their unmarried offspring. Extended families consisting of parents and one or more married male children (together with their families) are uncommon.

Inheritance. Upon the death of a father, his property is inherited by his sons. Usually the youngest son receives the largest share as he has been responsible for caring for both parents during their lifetimes. The youngest son (if married) is also charged with the care of his unmarried sisters upon the death of his father. If the youngest son is not married, his older married brothers must assume this duty. The youngest son is also charged with the care of his widowed mother. Widows and daughters are not allowed to inherit property. A widow is entitled to maintenance from her husband's estate, provided that she remains in the house of her deceased husband and does not remarry. A daughter may be given use of valley land by her father during his lifetime; however, a father may not leave his house, animals, or other items to a daughter as an inheritance.

Socialization. The mother is the chief agent of socialization in the Purum family.

Sociopolitical Organization

Social Organization. Purum sibs are socially graded. Status may also be obtained by the performance of certain *gennas* (magicoreligious ceremonies). The *khullakpa* (village headman) and *luplakpa* (assistant to the village headman) are expected to perform the *to-lai-kong* genna in order to legitimize their community standing. Average citizens may perform the *thien-hong-ba* genna when they have attained wealth and wish to establish their place within the community. One of the distinguishing features of this celebration is the stone platform upon which the sponsor of the genna sits during the first day of the observance.

Political Organization. The village is the primary political unit in Purum society. Its affairs are managed by a council of elders and eight political officers: the khullakpa (headman); the luplakpa (assistant to the headman); *khunjahanba* (chief performer in magicoreligious rites associated with the god Nungchungba and the third most powerful political official); the *zupanba* (official who makes arrangements for the production of *zu*, "rice beer," on public occasions and in some instances acts as liaison between the village and the state); the *keirungba* (official who selects animals to be slaughtered in connection with the payment of fines); the *selungba* (official who collects fees for the performance of religious rites and acts also as the khullakpa's porter); and the *changlai* (official who collects rice at magicoreligious rites for the manufacture of zu).

Social Control. Traditional means of control have been limited largely to a system of fines for social offenses. Activities punishable by fine include theft, assault, marital infidelity, rape, divorce (in certain instances), violation of contracts, and damage to property by domestic animals.

Conflict. Das noted that there is an absence of warlike tendencies among the Purum. He gives no indication as to the nature of their relations with neighbors before his fieldwork. There are indications (e.g., the economic interdependence of the Purum and Meithei economic systems and the Purum reliance on Manipuri markets for essential and luxury items) that the Purum maintain cooperative relationships with neighboring peoples.

Religion and Expressive Culture

Religious Beliefs. Purum religion has been influenced on many levels by Hindu belief and practice. Hindu gods are present in their pantheon along with indigenous deities. The major gods in the Purum pantheon include the following: Nungchungba (the most important of the Purum deities—sometimes spoken of as the patron god of the village); Lamhel (a spirit connected with the jungle surrounding the village); Lamtaiba (a jungle spirit similar to Lamhel); Sabuhong (an agricultural god believed to preside over crops); Senamahi (a house and sib god); Panthonglakkpa (the god in charge of the gates of the village); the sun and the moon (two astral deities worshiped only in connection with the onset of labor during pregnancy); and the stars (worshiped for the purpose of securing recovery from sickness and ensuring village bounty). Spirits of a beneficent and capricious character (particularly disease-inflicting spirits) are also believed to inhabit human realms. Some of these represent the deification of forces in the natural world (e.g., forest, water, and the four compass directions). The spirits of deceased ancestors are also venerated periodically.

Religious Practitioners. Several classes of individuals officiate at various Purum magicoreligious ceremonies: village officials (e.g., the khullakpa and the khunjahanba); the oldest male in the village (also called the *thempu*, he plays an important role at the ceremony that accompanies the entering of a new house, the first hair-cutting ceremony of a child, the name-giving ritual, the cleansing of a house in which a death has taken place, the purification of those who have buried a woman dying in childbirth, and at the installation of a new village officer); individual male householders (who officiate at family-based ceremonies); the pipas (who officiate at the offering of first fruits to the god Senamahi); and the *maipa* (the medicine man, who, in addition to officiating at sacrifices offered to disease-causing supernaturals, also acts as priest when worship is directed toward Hindu gods brought into the Purum pantheon).

Ceremonies. Magicoreligious ceremonies accompany the major events in the individual life cycle (e.g., marriage, birth, child naming, ear piercing, first haircutting, and death).

Arts. Evidence of the visual arts is less well attested (unless note is taken of Purum industrial arts such as basketry and weaving) than that of music and dance, both of which are an important element in the magicoreligious ceremonies of the Purum. Among the genres represented within Purum oral literature must be noted magicoreligious incantations and myths of origin.

Medicine. Illness is believed to be caused by supernatural forces, and the maipa (medicine man) is the magicomedical official responsible for determining the nature of the sickness and prescribing the sacrificial measures necessary to alleviate it.

Death and Afterlife. The souls of those who have led exemplary lives and die natural deaths (i.e., who do not die because of misfortune, in childbirth, or by attack of wild animals) go to the Khamnung (the afterworld located in the sky). The souls of those who die of unnatural causes and those who have performed grave misdeeds in their lives are turned into evil spirits and roam the jungles for eternity.

See also Lakher; Mizo

Bibliography

Das, Tarakchandra (1945). *The Purums*. Calcutta: University of Calcutta.

Needham, Rodney (1958). "A Structural Analysis of Purum Society." *American Anthropologist* 60:75–101.

Shakespear, John (1912). *The Lushei Kuki Clans.* London: Macmillan.

HUGH R. PAGE, JR.

Qalandar

ETHNONYMS: Bandarwālā, Bhaluwālā, Khānābādōsh

Orientation

Identification. Qalandar (pronounced like the English word "colander") are a widely dispersed, endogamous population of nomadic entertainers found throughout South Asia. Practicing a variety of entertainment strategies, their name and ethnic identity are based on their skill in handling, training, and entertaining with bears and monkeys.

Location. Qalandar are scattered throughout Pakistan and North India, most heavily concentrated in the Punjab. The word "Punjab" is derived from Indo-Persian *panch* (five) and *āb* (water). The five rivers of the Punjab are, from north to south, the Jhelum, Chenab, Ravi, Beas, and Sutlej. The international boundary established in 1947 separating Pakistan from India cuts across four of these rivers and divided the Punjab politically between the two nations. Disputes over distribution of water and religious conflict among Hindus, Muslims, and Sikhs keep tensions high along the frontier, thus prohibiting free movement of Qalandar along their traditional travel routes from Peshawar to Lahore in Pakistan to Amritsar and Delhi in India.

Demography. There is no accurate demographic or census information on Qalandar in either Pakistan or India. Today, there are about 4,000 Qalandar in Pakistan and many times more in north India. Sufficient and predictable sources of

water have sustained the development of dense networks of small agriculture-based villages, towns, and trade and metropolitan centers. The high population density of the area (about 192 persons per square kilometer) forms an ideal economic niche for the Qalandar. The dense and perdurable membership of these sedentary communities forms a peripatetics' niche, where there is a constant demand for specialized goods and/or services that sedentary communities cannot, or will not, support on a full-time basis. Combining entertainment skills with spatial mobility, Qalandar have survived by exploiting these resources since earliest times.

Linguistic Affiliation. In both their language and cultural habits, contemporary Qalandar share common ancestry with Rom (Gypsies) and the Romany language of Gypsies and other traveler populations throughout the world. In addition to their own language, Qalandri (part unique, with some argot, and secret to the extent that it is only spoken among themselves), Qalandar are adept linguists, speaking as many as five languages and being familiar with many regional dialects. No Qalandar are literate. Their perpetually nomadic life-style precludes attending schools, and a strong sense of ethnic unity and strict adherence to traditional values outweigh for them the benefits of prolonged cultural contact necessary for formal education.

History and Cultural Relations

It is very likely that nomadic specialists such as the Qalandar may be as ancient as settled communities themselves. However, it is not until the late Vedic era (ca. 1000–700 B.C.) that we find historical confirmation of nomadic entertainers with performing bears and monkeys. Qalandar figure in sedentary folklore, traditions, and history. Their nomadic activities and pride in ethnic identity largely govern Qalandar relations with other communities. Qalandar prefer to limit relations with client communities to specific interactions and settings related to entertainment routines. Outside these situations they try to maintain a nondescript or "invisible" posture. This enables them unobtrusively to observe and gather information about community activities in order to adjust routines and determine their stay in an area. Practically every village and urban settlement is visited at least twice annually. Their relations with client communities are essentially those of professional strangers, people who are not "organically connected" to the membership of host settlements through traditional bonds of kinship, propinquity, or occupation. Thus, unlike nomadic populations of smiths, basket makers, or genealogists who benefit from regular bonds with clients, Qalandar understand that novelty rather than predictability is the key to their success. Thus groups vary their travel routes in order to maximize the productivity of established entertainment routines. Whereas Qalandar know a great deal about the structure and social organization of host settlements, clients understand very little about Qalandar life and cultural habits. Consequently members of the sedentary world tend to address and refer to Qalandar by names associated with entertainment skills or nomadic activities. For example, they are most often called Bandarwālā (monkey leaders) or Bhaluwālā (bear leaders). Today individuals, as well as cursory government census records, tend to classify Qalandar under these occupational designations and often impute separate domains of ethnic or cultural membership to each category. Qalandar are also lumped under the more inclusive and culturally nebulous ethnic rubric Khānābādōsh. An ancient Persian construct incorporated into Hindi and Urdu, Khānābādōsh glosses as "house-on-shoulder" and is comparable to English use of the terms "nomad" or "Gypsy." In dealing with the external world Qalandar also identify themselves by these ubiquitous but ethnically nebulous terms. They use this strategy in order to focus outsiders' attention on specific activities and to promote ambiguity about their private domains and actual group resources. This method of public posturing inhibits collection of accurate census, income, or other information sought by government, police, social service agencies, and others desiring access to, or control over, their private affairs or nomadic activities. Qalandar also realize that promoting ambiguous information about themselves neutralizes knowledge as an external source of power that might be used to curtail their freedom and cultural flexibility. Toward this end they actively cultivate inaccurate information about their income, traditions, origins, values, religion, and other cultural habits. To share valid information or otherwise involve outsiders with internal matters is a major source of shame and loss of pride for Qalandar. The nature of their peripatetic life-style and subsistence activities places Qalandar outside normative rules regulating caste and class interactions in the communities they service. Throughout South Asia, Qalandar and a few other populations of peripatetic specialists are the only groups that enjoy equal access to all levels of local social systems.

Settlements

Qalandar own no land or permanent shelters. They subsist by traveling from place to place, leading animals and transporting their limited physical possessions and tents on donkeys. Qalandar tents (*puki*) are the Bender type common to peripatetics throughout Asia and Europe: barrel-vaulted ribs supported by vertical endpoles and horizontal ridgepoles, covered with a patchwork cloth. In rural areas tents are pitched in fallow or newly harvested fields near villages, along canal banks, and along railway lines. In urban settings Qalandar camp in vacant lots and undeveloped industrial sites. Wherever located, tents and camps are considered private domains. Families keep vicious dogs to patrol the camp perimeters and Qalandar may assume unfriendly postures toward outsiders seeking entry, or passage through, these areas.

Economy

Subsistence and Commercial Activities. About 15 percent of Qalandar families own bears, the most common being the Kashmiri black bear with its distinctive white V on the chest. A few own the larger and more difficult to handle Asian brown bear. Both species adapt poorly to the hot, arid climate and the growing number of hard-surfaced roads connecting villages and urban centers. Easily irritable and prone to attack, a disturbed animal may kill its handler with a single blow. It is the danger and novelty of bear routines that appeal most to an audience, and this is therefore the most lucrative form of entertainment strategy. Because bears are dangerous and costly, especially since the Russian invasion of Afghanistan in 1979 and the proliferation of refugees in mountain areas where bears are found, most Qalandar keep and train performing rhesus monkeys (macaques). Like young bears, baby macaques are purchased from hill tribes and are trained to perform routines that mimic human situations—imitating police or soldiers, marital disputes, and relations among in-laws, as well as performing traditional feats of dancing and riding bicycles. Monkeys are less expensive to maintain and breed in captivity than bears. Qalandar also use trained dogs and goats to perform balancing acts. In addition to their animal-handling activities, Qalandar are also skilled jugglers, acrobats, magicians, impersonators, and beggars. They announce their presence in a community or neighborhood through small, highly resonant drums and/or goatskin bagpipes. These instruments are also used to provide rhythm and background music for their routines. Intensity of spatial mobility and entertaining schedules correspond with postharvest activities in rural areas: villagers are more affluent following the rice and wheat harvests and these periods mark marriage and other festive events on the rural scene. During these annual cycles Qalandar may travel and perform in as many as three villages daily. Payment is in kind and transported until they reach a market where it is sold for cash, silver, or gold. As postharvest resources diminish, Qalandar move toward urban settings where their activities are rewarded with cash, though many entertainers will strike bargains for sugar, fresh meat, cast-off clothing, and the like as recompense. Although prostitution is more common in an urban milieu, in rural areas females may exchange sexual favors for camping privileges and grazing rights. Along with young children, females also earn cash and considerable food working as professional beggars.

The staple diet throughout the year consists of rice, _chappatis_ (flat breads), cooked lentils and cereals, vegetables, goat's milk, and tea. If harvests have been plentiful Qalandar families often have sufficient resources to sustain them throughout the year. Following harvests, families that have been dispersed will gather to conduct intra-Qalandar business such as arrangement of marriages, repayment of loans, settlement of outstanding disputes, reaffirmations of relations among kin, and the forging of new alliances, before dispersing again.

Industrial Arts.   Qalandar invest their energies in entertainment skills and interpersonal relations. They manufacture no craft items for sale.

Trade.   Excess earnings of wheat and rice are sold for cash, which in turn is used to purchase silver and gold. The nail clippings and hair from bears may be sold as charms that villagers believe protect them from a host of diseases and evil spirits.

Division of Labor.   All members are expected to contribute labor and earnings toward the daily welfare of the tent family. Their division of labor is essentially one of situational pragmatism—that is, whoever is present when a task needs doing simply does it, depending on their level of experience and skill. Qalandar stress lifelong flexibility of individual skills and task performance rather than exclusive domains of influence or activities based on sex or age. While females may train animals within the confines of camps, they seldom perform in public as animal handlers, because bears and monkeys are more difficult to handle in public settings and Qalandar believe that men are better animal handlers overall. More importantly, Qalandar believe that females are more perceptive and aggressive and better suited for dealing with strangers and so will have greater success as beggars and gatherers. During periods of high mobility in the rural areas, females will guard tents and camps and accept the responsibility for meal preparation and child care. In urban settings, males perform these tasks, freeing females to beg and gather.

Kinship, Marriage, and Family

Kinship.   All Qalandar consider themselves kin to the extent that they trace themselves back to a common, but unknown, apical ancestor. They are related to each other in many different and involuted ways and the kin terminology is descriptive in nature (i.e., separate terms for each relationship). Qalandar often joke that no one actually knows for certain who his biological father really is. One's father (_pater_) is the husband of his or her mother at the time of birth. Children of the same mother or children who have nursed from the same breast are considered siblings. The children of successive generations of siblings are considered members of the same _zat_ or descent group. An individual may not marry his or her own sibling or a parental or grandparental sibling. Descent is traced bilaterally through the mother and pater at birth.

Marriage.   Qalandar are strictly endogamous and all marriages are arranged by parents and/or parental siblings. Engagements, marriages, and frequent divorces occupy a large part of Qalandar time and figure heavily in determining the alliances among families traveling together. All marriages and most divorces are arranged and involve payment of bride-price (_bovar_) for females. Either spouse and/or their parents

may negotiate a divorce and remarriage so long as reimbursement of the bride-price can be agreed upon. Qalandar prefer parallel-cousin marriage because they believe it helps to maintain sibling solidarity.

Domestic Unit.   Qalandar use the term _puki_ for both tent and family. Puki is the basic social and productive unit, structurally similar to Western notions of nuclear family. The tent is the commensal unit comprised of a female, her spouse, and their unmarried children. A new tent or puki is created by both marriage and divorce. Once betrothed, individuals never return to or reside in their natal tent. Each tent is self-sufficient; however, families usually form temporary alliances with other tents to travel and work together.

Inheritance.   Only the physical tent structure is corporately held by a family; all other physical and animal possessions are individually owned. Following death, possessions are distributed among tent members. Any livestock that has been purchased with loans is sold and the cash used to settle accounts with creditors.

Socialization.   From infancy, children are incorporated into income-producing activities, first as beggars, then as participants in entertainment routines. Qalandar believe that children learn best through imitation and example, and from birth they are carried or placed where they can observe tent and camp activities. There are no separate worlds for adults and children. Praise for appropriate behavior rather than corporal punishment for misadventures is most common. Children are encouraged to become economically independent as soon as possible and all are capable of supporting themselves by age 9.

Sociopolitical Organization

Social Organization.   A collection of tents in temporary alliance in order to work and travel together forms a _dēra_. Typical dēra contain three to seven tents with a balanced distribution of skilled performers and animal acts. Dēra membership involves complex social and economic considerations, including marriage-planning strategies and proximity to skilled individuals, especially bear leaders. Other considerations include common interests, friendship, kin loyalties, and efforts to maintain sibling solidarity. These motivations must be moderated by practical concerns related to the overall distribution of human skills and animal resources. Dēra organization is based on mutual agreements among tents to work and travel together in a spirit of _biradarana_, which prescribes mutual support, understanding, tolerance, and cooperation. Families unwilling to share biradarana are simply encouraged or forced to move on.

Political Organization.   Dēra are acephalous and decisions affecting the group, such as travel routes and tenure in an area, are achieved through consensus among tents. Deference is usually paid to opinions of older and/or more experienced individuals.

Social Control.   Group pressure and consensus among dēra members serve to regulate everyday activities. Tents unwilling to go along with group opinions break away, travel alone, or most commonly join other dēra or make new alliances to form new dēra. Freedom (_azadi_) to move is the most effective form of social control; however, Qalandar have an elaborate jural system comprised of their own lawyers, judges, and a complex trial process for resolving serious conflicts.

Conflict. Qalandar recognize that internal conflict and disputes among tents can seriously affect their survival. Major sources of conflict involve fights between spouses and among entertainers working together about the distribution of earnings, adultery, disagreements over travel routes, and excessive parental demands on married children, as well as individual acts of inappropriate behavior such as theft, drunkenness, excessive sexual joking, serious injury, murder, or involvement of outside authorities in any kind of internal Qalandar affairs. When senior members of a dēra cannot negotiate a compromise among disputing parties, adversaries and their supporters will seek out Qalandar lawyers (*waikel*), who in turn select judges (*surbara*), thus setting in motion an elaborate and prolonged legal proceeding culminating in a trial. Before proceeding to trial litigants and their supporters must agree to post a cash bond with judges binding them to the decisions (*karna*) or rulings of the jural body called for a particular dispute. Depending on the offense, sanctions involve public apologies, fines, banishment, or execution. Lacking institutions or specialized roles for enforcing legal decrees, enforcement devolves on the disputants, their families, and their friends. Conflict fuels perpetual processes of fission and fusion among tents and contributes to changing patterns of alliance and spatial mobility throughout the year.

Religion and Expressive Culture

Religious Beliefs and Practices. Rather than having a formal set of religious beliefs or practices, Qalandar rely on sacred activities and religious holidays in order to pursue their entertainment strategies. They are essentially agnostics or religious pragmatists, professing Muslim, Hindu, or Christian beliefs depending on whichever affiliation best serves their momentary purposes. They do believe in the "evil eye" and the effectiveness of charms or amulets (*tabiz*) in protecting them from a spectrum of spirits and ghosts.

Arts. Qalandar produce no art or artifacts, as they invest all their energies and pride in their knowledge and skills as professional entertainers.

Medicine. Excluded from access to modern hospitals, Qalandar rely on druggists and homeopathic practitioners for serious illnesses. Most suffer from chronic malaria and seasonal enteric diseases such as typhoid and cholera. Colostrum is considered "hot" and newborns are fed sugar water for the first three weeks after birth. This solution of water and brown sugar is readily contaminated by flies and infant mortality from enteric infections is very high. Senior females serve as midwives at birth, though strong women often deliver their own children.

Death and Afterlife. When an individual becomes too old or unable to walk he or she is considered dead, and left behind. Death is considered a part of life and bodies are simply washed, wrapped in a clean white cloth, sprinkled with perfume, and buried in an unmarked grave within thirty-six hours of death. Ideally siblings and parents care for the body; however, if not available, dēra members dispose of the body. Regardless of economic potential around a campsite following a death, Qalandar will immediately move on to their next destination. They are always aware that flexibility and freedom from both internal and external constraints are critical for their survival as nomadic entrepreneurs.

See also Kanjar; Peripatetics

Bibliography

Berland, Joseph C. (1982). *No Five Fingers Are Alike: Cognitive Amplifiers in Social Context.* Cambridge, Mass.: Harvard University Press.

Berland, Joseph C. (1983). "Behind Cloth Walls." *Natural History* 92:50–60.

Berland, Joseph C., and Matt. T. Salo, eds. (1986). "Peripatetic Peoples: An Introduction." *Nomadic Peoples* (Toronto) 21–22 (special issue).

Misra, P. K., and K. C. Malhotra, eds. (1982). *Nomads in India.* Anthropological Survey of India. Calcutta.

Rao, Aparna (1985). "Des nomades méconnus. Pour une typologie des communautés péripatétiques." *L'Homme* 25: 97–119.

JOSEPH C. BERLAND

Rai

ETHNONYM: Raji

Along with the Limbu, the Rai form the two subgroups of the Kiranti. The largest Tibeto-Nepalese group in eastern Nepal, the Rai are also found in India, Sikkim, and Bhutan. Subsisting primarily as rice agriculturalists, Rai also have a tradition of men migrating to cities for work and men serving as Gurkhas. The Rai are composed of two major subgroups, the Khambu and Yakhu, each of which is composed of patrilineal clans and lineages. The Rai speak a Kiranti dialect.

Unlike the Limbu, little is known about the Rai. In some areas, particularly in India, Rai have combined traditional shamanism and ancestor worship with beliefs and practices taken from Buddhism and Hinduism.

See also Kiranti; Limbu

Rajput

People who identity themselves as Rajputs are found across northwestern India, the Ganges plains, Madhya Pradesh, and Himalayan valleys. Following Indian independence, the twenty-three Rajput states that formed what was called Rajputana were consolidated into the modern state of Rajasthan. The great majority are Hindu, but more than one million are Muslim. In the past, Rajputs formed the fighting, landowning, and ruling castes. They claim to be the descendants of the Kshatriyas of ancient tradition, and from this association they derive their identity as a distinct group, superior to other groups in their traditional territory.

Rajputs are hereditary soldiers and landowners, but the demand for soldiers is now limited and few Rajputs have any occupation except as landowners. While some Rajputs farm their land themselves, many own enough land so that they can hire others to perform manual labor.

The chief feature of Rajput social organization is their division into hierarchically ranked clans and lineages. One hundred and three Rajput clans are well known. Additionally, rankings based on regional location, the degree of centralized political control within regions or Rajput states, and hypergamy were all important elements of the traditional Rajput social order. Since independence, Rajput power has been declining as other castes seek economic and political independence from Rajput control.

Still, the Rajput tradition and identity permit even poor Rajput farmers to consider themselves the equal of powerful landholders of their clan and superior to any high official of the professional classes. No people in India can boast of finer feats of arms or brighter deeds of chivalry, and Rajputs still form one of the main recruiting fields for the Indian army of today.

The Rajput courts were centers of culture; Sanskrit literature and drama flourished and the modern vernacular languages began to appear. The Rajput bards sang the praises of their overlords in Hindi; the earliest of these material ballads is the _Prithiraj Raso_, which tells how Prince Prithiraj carried off his bride. Rajput princes were great builders, and constructed magnificent palaces, fortresses, and stately shrines, of which the Saivite temples at Khajuraho in Bundelkhand and the Dilwara Jain temples at Mount Abu are outstanding examples in contrasting styles.

Rajput men and women are still much involved with elaborate ceremonies, especially weddings, for these are the rituals of Rajput identity. Suttee is no longer performed—indeed, it has long been illegal—but funerals are still cause for celebration of grandeurs past.

There are modern Rajputs who are followers of the Swaminarayan sect, of Ramanuja, or of Vallabhacharya. These groups are all vegetarians, but other Hindu Rajputs, the majority, are Shaivites. Not only do these Shaivites eat meat, but many are also partial to smoking tobacco, taking opium, or drinking liquor. Muslim Rajputs avoid these latter practices, although most of them are nonvegetarian.

See also Jat; Kshatriya

Bibliography

Enthoven, Reginald E. (1922). "Rajputs." In _The Tribes and Castes of Bombay_, edited by Reginald E. Enthoven. Vol. 3, 269–297. Bombay: Government Central Press. Reprint. 1975. Delhi: Cosmo Publications.

Minturn, Leigh, and John T. Hitchcock (1966). _The Rajputs of Khalapur, India_. New York: John Wiley & Sons.

Russell, R. V., and Hira Lal (1916). "Rajput." In _The Tribes and Castes of the Central Provinces of India_, edited by R. V. Russell and Hira Lal. Vol. 4, 410–470. London: Macmillan. Reprint. 1969. Oosterhout: Anthropological Publications.

Tod, James (1899). _The Annals and Antiquities of Rajasthan, or the Central and Western Rajpoot States of India_. Calcutta: Bengal Press. New ed., edited by William Crooke. 1920. London: Oxford University Press. [Numerous other editions.]

ALLIYA S. ELAHI

Reddi

ETHNONYMS: Bhumanchi Reddi, Kapu, Kil Reddi, Motad Reddi, Paknat Reddi, Pandava Reddi, Panta Reddi, Raja Reddi, Suryavanisa

The name "Reddi" is also the name of a section of Kapus, landowners of the Telugu country, who hold high-ranking positions in Hindu society and from whose martial branch the Reddi kings of Rajamundry are believed to have sprung. The number of Reddi clans is so great that a complete count is impossible. The information provided here pertains to the Reddis who live within Andhra Pradesh. The present habitat of the Reddis is the section of the Eastern Ghats that stretches from the confluence of the Mackund and Goperu rivers southward across the great Godavari gorges to the fringe of the deltaic plain between the Godavari and Kistna rivers. The Reddis' habitat can be divided into three distinct zones: the hill settlements, the riverside settlements, and the settlements of the Andhra Plains. The Reddis are essentially hill people; they make their home high in the valleys of the main ranges, on the slopes and spurs of the foothills, and in the narrow gorges of the Godavari. There is little variation in material culture and house construction among the many groups of Reddis; these features all remain more or less constant in occurrence and design. The language most prevalent is Telugu.

Berries, cucumbers, ripe fruit, and young tender maize are eaten raw. Most other foods are roasted, stewed, or made into gruel. A popular way of preparing meats is by roasting. The meats most commonly used are rats, mice, squirrels, small birds, and lizards. Meat, most vegetables, and fish are cooked in a highly spiced stew called *kura*. When serving meat stewed in this way the liquid is strained off and served separately. The most economical and most often eaten item in a Reddi household is *javoa*, a kind of gruel. It consists of flour made from grain, pulses, sago pith, dried mango kernels, or dried mushrooms cooked in a large pot of water.

Men and women do not remain single in Reddi society except in cases of serious and lasting illness or mental deficiency. Marriage age for boys is between 18 and 20; this is when a boy is first considered able to do the full work of a man. According to Reddi tradition neither the boy nor the girl voices an opinion in the selection of a mate. In the 1940s, prepuberty marriage was becoming quite popular, but now it is not so common—and indeed is illegal.

Bibliography

Fürer-Haimendorf, Christoph von (1945). *The Reddis of the Bison Hills*. London: Macmillian.

Fürer-Haimendorf, Christoph von (1982). *Tribes of India: The Struggle for Survival*. Berkeley: University of California Press.

LeSHON KIMBLE

Refugees in South Asia

While refugees in South Asian countries nowhere constitute a cohesive social group (with the possible exception of some groups from Afghanistan in western Pakistan), they are so numerous at the present time (1991) that an outline of their demography is appropriate in this volume. Three South Asian countries hold a total of about 4,085,800 refugees today, of whom only 293,000 are native to the region. Most do not live in formal refugee camps, but many do benefit, if only a little, from funds that have been funneled to them from Western nations and food provided by the United Nations High Commissioner for Refugees.

The countries of origin of refugees, estimates of their current numbers in each host country, and the main reason for their flight to that country are listed in the following table.

Host Country	Origin	Number	Reason for Flight
India	Sri Lanka	228,000	civil war between Sinhalese and secessionist Tamils
India	Tibet (China)	100,000	repression of Tibetan culture and religion by occupying Chinese forces
India	Bangladesh	65,000	mainly Biharis
India	Afghanistan	11,100	anticommunist freedom fighters (Mujaheddin)
India	Myanmar (Burma)	800	opponents of the military dictatorship
India	elsewhere	900	
Nepal	Tibet (China)	14,000	repression of Tibetan culture and religion by occupying Chinese forces
Pakistan	Afghanistan	3,666,000	anticommunist freedom fighters (Mujaheddin)
Pakistan	Iran	1,100	opponents of the fundamentalist Islamic government
Pakistan	Iraq	1,700	opponents of the Ba'ath government

To put these figures into perspective, we might add that although South Asia contains 23 percent of the world's population, it currently holds less than 10 percent of the world's refugees. Africa remains the region of biggest refugee movements across national boundaries at this time.

See also Tamil of Sri Lanka

Bibliography

Smyser, W. R. (1991). "New Priorities in Refugee Care." *The World and I* 6:142–149.

PAUL HOCKINGS

Sadhu

SYNONYMS: Baba, Jogi, Mahatma, Muni, Sant, Sanyasi, Swami, Tapasi, Tapsawi, Yati, Yogi

Orientation

Identification. The term *sadhu* is applied individually to any one of the millions of mendicant ascetics informally affiliated with the disparate Hindu religious orders of India. Most of these wandering holy persons are male, but women (called *sadhvin*, feminine of sadhu) are also represented in their ranks. At one time only Brahmans were able to be admitted to these ascetic orders. Later, admission was granted to members of any caste. Sadhus are expected to adopt ascetic practices, observe certain religious regulations, and teach or render service to those in need. Their ascetic practices include the departure from family and home, the application of bodily markings often associated with a particular sect, the wearing of attire associated with a particular sect (or being partially or totally naked), the growth of hair only on five important bodily parts (the head, upper jaw, chin, armpits, and pubic region) or the complete shaving of the body, the adoption of a mendicant or sedentary life-style, and the dependence on the goodness of others for daily survival. Their religious duties include acts of self-purification, worship, participation in religious discourses, the study of sacred literature, and the making of pilgrimages. The consolation of those in distress, preaching and teaching of religious tenets, the granting of assistance to the poor, and the opening of schools and hospitals are examples of the services that sadhus are expected to render to the larger society. Sadhus are found throughout India and Nepal and are not confined to any particular geographical locale. It is believed that there are some 5 million or more ascetics affiliated with several thousand "schools" or sects of sadhus living in various parts of South Asia. As mendicants, they do not form distinct communities.

History and Cultural Relations

There are three major Hindu religious orders: the Vaishnava, the Shaiva, and the Shakta. Of these, the Shaiva sect seems to have the largest number of devotees. These have spawned numerous subdivisions. It is believed by some that Shaivism represents the original religious faith of India, already in place before the arrival of the Aryans. The orders are much splintered, the result being the current existence of numerous "sects." Some are orthodox while others are reformist or radical. The roots of Hindu asceticism may be traced to the fourfold division of life outlined in Vedic literature. These stages are: *brahmacarin* (the life of the pupil); *grhastha* (the life of the householder, which includes marriage, procreation, and the practice of a craft); *vanaprastha* (the life of the forest hermit, resorted to when the transitory nature of worldly pleasures is realized); and *sannyasin* (the life of the wandering beggar who has renounced all worldly ties). One may claim to be an ascetic without having passed through all of the aforementioned stages of life. In modern times some ascetics have chosen to continue in the marital state. This represents a departure from earlier practice.

Settlements

Sadhus live either in monasteries (called *asrama*, *matha*, or *mandira*), if they have elected to lead a sedentary life-style, or at pilgrimage shrines as temporary residents. Each sect usually maintains at least one of these religious centers. The monastic life-style is austere, emphasis being placed on the cultivation of self-control and discipline. The daily routine includes exercises intended to purify the physical body, elevate mental capacity (e.g., through the reading of sacred literature), and enhance ecstatic experiences (e.g., through corporate prayer). Provision is also made so that the lay patrons of the monastery (who provide its chief means of support through *bhetapuja*, "honorific offerings") may receive the benefit of the spiritual counsel of the resident ascetics (by means of preaching and teaching). Monasteries have as their organizing concept the tradition (*sampradaya*) associated with a particular teacher (*acarya*) who first codified the belief system of the order. Monastic affiliation is usually indicated by the symbols applied to specific bodily parts, clothing color, and additional items in the ascetic's possession (e.g., rosary, water pot, and staff).

Economy

Sadhus are almost totally dependent on the alms of others for subsistence. In addition, they may also support themselves by engaging in any of the following activities: begging, serving as spiritual mentors to personal disciples, interpreting dreams, telling fortunes, reading palms, astrology, manufacturing amulets, performing exorcisms, casting spells, singing, conjuring, juggling, tattooing, or selling medicinal herbs and potions. Sadhus are particularly well known for the manufacture of the *kavacha* (talisman or amulet), which provides the bearer with protection from evil forces or guarantees the presence of beneficent ones.

Marriage and Family

The renunciation of family life and the married state are characteristic of the ascetic life. It has been suggested that marital breakdown is, in fact, one of the motivating factors in the adoption of mendicant life by some sadhus. Some may never have been married. An individual ascetic may, at his discretion, choose disciples who serve apprenticeships under him. Alternately, young children (orphans, runaways, and others) may be dedicated to the service of an order. After a period of training (which may last weeks, months, or years), they are sent out to fulfill their socioreligious duties within the context of the larger society. Yet a third route to socialization as a sadhu involves following the Vedic progression of life stages. An important part of the initiation process is the changing of the natal name. This may involve the addition of suffixes to it or the complete alteration of the name. In general, the new name identifies the place of the initiate within the order and as a votary of a particular god.

Religion and Expressive Culture

Generalizations with regard to the religious beliefs of sadhus are not easily made due to the heterogeneous character of Hindu asceticism. Their worship is directed to diverse gods of primary and secondary importance in the Hindu pantheon. Of the various sadhu religious rituals, that of the *dhuni* (sacred fire) seems more or less common to all sects. This fire is lit in a hollow pit wherever the ascetic camps. These sacred fires are also found in monastic centers and in the homes of household ascetics associated with certain sects. The liturgies, literature, and bodily adornment of the sadhu may be cited as manifestations of the artistic impulse within the various ascetic communities of India. With regard to options for medical treatment, the following are available to sadhus: Ayurvedic, allopathic, indigenous, homeopathic, Tantric, and naturopathic. At least one anthropologist has noted a decided preference for Ayurvedic medicines, there being some belief that these decrease the chance of medical relapse.

Bibliography

Ghurye, G. S. (1964). *Indian Sadhus*. Bombay: Popular Prakashan.

MacMunn, George Fletcher (1932). *The Religions and Hidden Cults of India*. New York: Macmillan. Reprint. 1982. Delhi: Neeraj Publishing House.

Miller, David M., and Dorothy C. Wertz (1976). *Hindu Monastic Life*. Montreal and London: McGill-Queen's University Press.

Tripathi, B. D. (1978). *Sadhus of India*. Bombay: Popular Prakashan.

Walker, Benjamin (1986). *The Hindu World: An Encyclopedic Survey of Hinduism*. Vol. 2. New York: Frederick Praeger Publishers.

HUGH R. PAGE, JR.

Santal

ETHNONYMS: Santhal, Saonta, Saonthal, Saunta

Orientation

Identification. The Santal are the largest of the tribal populations in South Asia. Santals are found in the three adjoining Indian states of Bihar, West Bengal, and Orissa. Migrants work in the tea plantations of Assam, with smaller groups elsewhere in India. There are also Santal communities in northeastern Bangladesh and in the Nepal Terai. Traditionally mixed farmers with a recent past of hunting and gathering, Santals have found their way to employment in agriculture and industry all over eastern South Asia. "Santal" is the only term currently used by outsiders for the tribe. It is also recognized as an ethnic term by the Santals themselves. *Hoṛ hopon ko* (human children) and *Hoṛ ko* (men) are used by them in a more traditional or ritual context.

Location. The Santal heartland is the area known as the Chota Nagpur Plateau, a hilly area of crystalline Cambrian rocks, strewn with laterite and covered by deciduous forest.

The area lies in northeastern India approximately between 22° and 24°30' N and stretches from 84° to 87° E. Elevation ranges from 200 to 500 meters with mountains over 1,000 meters. Rainfall, concentrated in the July monsoon, totals about 100 to 130 centimeters. Mean temperatures range from 15° to 21° C in January to 26° to 29° C in July.

Demography. The Indian census counted 3,640,946 Santals in 1971 (but did not count tea workers in Assam), and today the total number of Santals must be somewhat more than four million. It is difficult to say much about their population history, except that they are the largest tribal group in South Asia. The regions of the core Santal area seem to have been settled by different clans. Further migration led to a subdivision of land among subclans, still unevenly distributed over the area. In practice, however, each region today contains a number of clans, possibly the result of an ongoing process of migration.

Linguistic Affiliation. The Santal language, Santali, belongs to the North Mundari Group of languages, itself part of the Austroasiatic Language Family. Writing was introduced by Norwegian missionaries in the late nineteenth century, and so Santali literature uses Roman characters. More recently, Santali has been written in Devanāgari.

History and Cultural Relations

The original home of the Santals is believed to have been the Champa Kingdom of northern Cambodia, which explains their affinities with the Mon-Khmer groups. Physical anthropologists usually classify them under the Austro-Mongoloid type. They probably entered India well before the Aryan invasions and came by way of Assam and Bengal, as their traditions indicate. They assume the existence of a Santal kingdom, a tradition which is supported by the collections of medieval Santal weapons at the Oslo Ethnographic Museum and by the remains of what may be identified as Santal hill forts from the medieval period. Little else is known of this kingdom to which Santal mythic traditions allude. Moreover, the mythic tradition recalls a war between the Santals and a part-Hindu prince, Mandho Singh, who was born of a Santal mother. Mandho Singh succeeded in recruiting followers among the Santals who followed him to the south of Nagpur, settled there, and became more Hinduized. Early contacts with the British led to the Santal rebellion of 1854–1856, in which some ten thousand Santals were killed. They became an important source of plantation labor, while missionary efforts introduced writing and had some influence on their culture. Only small numbers were actually converted to Christianity. Today, the Santals are among the main sources of support for the Jharkhand "tribalist" movement, in which they collaborate to some extent with other Mundari-speaking groups.

Settlements

Santals typically live in their own villages, laid out on a street pattern, and numbering from 400 to 1,000 inhabitants each. While separate villages are preferred, various groups sometimes live more or less separately in the tribal or low-caste quarters of mixed villages or towns. Santals never live in Untouchable quarters. In the large industrial towns of the Indian coal and iron belt, there are separate Santal quarters.

Santal houses are mud structures, but they are sturdily built and often decorated with floral designs. Roofs are tiled and slope toward all four sides. Houses have verandas and at least two rooms; the "inner room" (_chitar_) contains the ancestors and the granary protected by them. The main post (_khunti_), located at the center of the house, to which sacrifices are made on building the house, is of considerable ritual importance.

Economy

Subsistence and Commercial Activities. It is probable that Santals originally were hunters and gatherers, as their near relatives and neighbors, the Birhors, still are. Their knowledge of plants and animals is reflected in their pharmacopoeia (see below). In hunting technology, their past is evidenced by the use of some eighty varieties of traps. Later, their main economic base shifted to slash-and-burn agriculture and husbandry. Today, wet rice is grown in terraced fields; on the plains, irrigation by canals and ditches is used. Several varieties of rice are grown along with some sixteen varieties of millet. Leguminous vegetables, fruit, mustard, groundnut (in Orissa), cotton, and tobacco are important crops. The Santals keep cattle, goats, and poultry and are nonvegetarian. Fishing is important whenever they have access to rivers and ponds. The economy of the Santals is biased toward consumption, but they sell or barter (in Bihar) goats, poultry, fish, rice and rice beer, millet, groundnut, mustard seed, vegetables, and fruits when a surplus is available.

Migrant labor plays an important role; many Santals have migrated to work in plantations, mines, and industries. In Bengal, some are gardeners or domestic servants. A small educated elite includes politicians, lawyers, doctors, and engineers, while considerable numbers of Santal women work as nurses. Seasonal or temporary migration is particularly important for women, who are working in construction or mining.

Industrial Arts. Santals are expert at wood carving, but this craft, like ironwork, is declining both in quality and importance. Such products were mainly made for their own ceremonial use. Basketwork, weaving of mats, and manufacture of dishes and cups from _sal_ leaves (_Shorea robusta_) are crafts still of commercial importance, as are rope making and the manufacture of string beds (_charpay_). Santal woodwork formerly included the building of impressive carts and advanced wooden utensils. They still make a large number of musical instruments. While industrial arts have declined, beautiful artifacts are still found, cherished as private heirlooms. Santal women also brew rice beer and alcohol, made from mohua flowers (_Madhuca indica_).

Trade. Santals sell their products for cash or barter at tribal markets; rice money was still in use in Bihar in the 1970s. Some trade is also done with Hindu villages and towns, mainly the marketing of agricultural and craft products. Women dominate this trade, while the main male preserve is the sale of goats and cattle.

Division of Labor. Hunting was always a male activity, gathering activities being dominated by women. In agriculture, men plow and sow, while women transplant and weed; division of labor by gender extends through most agricultural work. Boys and young men herd the cattle; women do the milking, collect the dung, and collect fuel in general. Poultry is tended by women, who also catch freshwater crabs, shrimps, etc. in the ponds; fishing by boat or with large land nets is done by the men. Women, as noted, dominate most trade. Ironwork, woodworking, and rope making are male activities; basketwork, weaving, and leafwork are done by women. Ritual specialists are traditionally male; women are formally excluded from such activities.

Land Tenure. Traditionally land was held by usufruct, for slash-and-burn agriculture. With the introduction of wet rice cultivation, local descent groups descended from the clans of the original settlers divided village lands between themselves. The village priest got an additional allotment. The British introduced individual holdings (_ryotwari_). Members of subclans, not represented among the village founders, were originally landless and are still accorded inferior status.

Kinship

Kin Groups and Descent. The Santals are divided into 12 clans and 164 subclans. They are patrilineal and strictly endogamous; their principal function is ceremonial and referential. The clans (_paris_) are ranked according to old functional divisions: the Kisku were kings, the Murmu priests, etc. There is an allusion to mythical wars between clans, ending in a ban on intermarriage. The ranking of clans is reflected in a slight tendency to hypergamy. Subclan hierarchy is expressed in terms of senior/junior distinctions as well as pure/impure; subclan identities focus on modes of sacrifice. On the village level, the local descent group is of major organizational importance. Here genealogical knowledge extends backward for only three to four generations. In some areas, there is a tendency for certain clans to intermarry unilaterally over several generations, forming a marriage alliance, but this practice never assumes the form of prescriptive marriage. Of greater importance, however, is the principle of alternate generations, which explains a whole range of joking and avoidance relationships. Politically, kinship is overshadowed by the functions of local chiefs and priests.

Kinship Terminology. The two main principles of the terminology are the distinctions between consanguine relatives and between affines. In address, there is a merging of all cousins into the sibling category. Despite the lack of a clear prescriptive alliance system, there is a tendency to marry the classificatory mother's brother daughter. The most distinctive Munda feature of the system is the alternation of generation (which recalls very clearly the Australian tribes). There is a slight tendency to have clan hypergamy—possibly a result of Hindu influence.

Marriage and Family

Marriage. Ideologically, the reasons given for marriage are to place offspring under the ancestor spirit (_bonga_) of the husband's clan and to secure labor for the land. Marriage may be of several types. William Archer notes fourteen forms, but the most important are bride-price and bride-service variants. Other alternatives are marriage by capture or elopement. The variations in form reflect the relative positions of spouses: bride-price leads to virilocal residence and is seen as the ideal form, but poor grooms performing bride-service reside uxorilocally. The openness of the system is reflected in the relative ease of divorce by mutual agreement, the provision for taking a second wife, the remarriage of widows, and the special arrangement of purchasing a groom for an unmarried mother.

Domestic Unit. Household units tend toward extended rather than nuclear families, with sons and their wives remaining in the paternal household. It is, however, common for sons to separate before the death of the father, sometimes at the latter's initiative. It is also common to extend nuclear households by the unmarried sister of the wife or through other arrangements. Nuclear households are an ever-present, though numerically relatively unimportant, alternative. Levirate and sororate are not uncommon in the case of the death of either spouse.

Inheritance. Inheritance rules are complex among the Santals, but land is usually divided among the brothers, with smaller portions going to daughters as dowry. In certain cases, unmarried girls may inherit land, but their land reverts to brothers on marriage.

Socialization. The most striking feature of socialization among Santals is the role of grandparents of both sexes. It is through them that children receive their cultural education, even sometimes to the extent of grandmothers initiating their grandsons sexually. Children are disciplined by teasing rather than punishment; while breast-feeding is prolonged, toilet training is achieved at an early age. Children have to work early; otherwise education is very liberal, with much emphasis on cleanliness.

Boys are initiated at the age of 8 or 10, when the five tribal marks are branded on their forearms by a maternal uncle. Girls are tattooed by Hindu or Muslim specialists at the age of 14, following the first menstruation ceremony, which shows Hindu features. At this age, girls are considered to be sexually mature.

Modern education is still a problem, because of a lack of teachers in outlying areas. There is, however, less difference in school attendance between boys and girls than among the nontribals. Christian children receive more and better education.

Sociopolitical Organization

Social Organization. Although, as noted, there is a traditional hierarchy of clans, the Santals are basically egalitarian, thus contrasting strongly with their Hindu neighbors. Economically, however, there are considerable differences in wealth and status. The clans and subclans, on the one hand, and the villages and regions, on the other, are the most important internal divisions. The senior male member of the local descent group enjoys a certain authority and prestige derived from ritual functions, as do the religious specialists (priests and *lojhas*) and the chiefs. Proficient hunters and orators likewise acquire prestige. Political leaders in the modern arena, like the charismatic leaders of the past, become sources of authority. District chiefs (*parganas* and *désmanjhis*) may enjoy a considerable status when successful in the settlement of disputes. Differences of wealth are expressed in the ability to employ servants. The well-to-do Santal families employ laborers on a contract basis and sometimes grant them land.

Political Organization. In general, authority tends toward a charismatic rather than a traditional pattern. At the village level, the most important political institution is the village assembly, which has no head. This institution directly confronts the "council of the five elders," who represent the "five brothers" of the Santal tradition and are the village chief, the messenger of the village, the one responsible for young people's morals, the village priest, and his assistant.

At the intervillage level, the pargana (chief of twelve villages), who is sometimes enthroned as a petty king, presides over the tribal court. He also leads intervillage ceremonial hunting, with the "hunting priest" at his side. The hunt is the occasion for a court. Likewise, the pargana is assisted by the "country chief" and the messenger who both carry out his orders.

For Indian Santals, villages and districts are subjects of *panchayati raj* (local government), sometimes overlapping and sometimes in competition with the traditional institutions.

Social Control. The sources of conflict among Santals can be summarized as: sexual offenses, land disputes, conflicts over money, cases of evil eye, jealousy, and witchcraft. Many cases are settled by compensation, usually through tribal assemblies, which still function parallel to, and sometimes in competition with, the Indian courts. The most general of these traditional assemblies is the Santal Lo bir Sendera, "the judgment of the burnt forest," which is convened at the time of the traditional intervillage hunts. Village assemblies likewise play an important role in the settlement of disputes. Witchcraft accusations are common. The witch is identified by ritual specialists, either a *janguru* or an ojha. Traditionally this naming led to the death of the witch.

While some sexual offenses, including rape, are usually settled by compensation through the mediation of the village assembly, the major offenses of incest and breach of tribal endogamy are primarily the responsibility of the local kin group, which excommunicates and—at least traditionally—kills the offenders. Excommunicates, like witches, are ostracized by their relatives. Land disputes may be cited as the main example of conflicts that are settled by Indian courts.

Conflict. The Santals have a long tradition of suspicion in regard to the *diku*, "foreigners," above all toward the dominant Hindu population of the area. This is clear not only from history (e.g., the Santal rebellion) but even more from the content of their myths and folklore, where the foreigner is the source of death, sickness, and other calamities. In practice, there has certainly been a history of exploitation by Hindu merchants, moneylenders, and labor brokers. Today this conflict continues mainly within the framework of the Indian political system, where Santals tend to support either the Jharkhand "tribalist" movement, working for a semiindependent state, or the Maoist Communist party, working for land reform and control of the means of producing, especially mines and plantations.

Religion and Expressive Culture

Religious Beliefs. The Santal pantheon includes about 150 spirit deities, generally called bongas. These deities include a large number of separate classes, impossible to enumerate here. Some relate to the subclan, but even here we must distinguish between the bonga of the place of origin of the clan and its ancestral bonga. Each village has a sacred grove, where we find represented the bongas common to the Santal tradition. They are generally benevolent. The forest bongas, however, are malevolent, and include the souls of people who died an unnatural death.

Hindu influence is particularly notable in the appearance of Hindu goddesses as tutelary deities of Santal ojhas. On the one hand, these goddesses patronize Santal witches and introduce disease; on the other hand, their patronage is necessary to combat the same evils. Hindu symbols, such as the trident, have become potent ritual paraphernalia of the Santal ojha.

Religious Practitioners. The village priest (_naeke_) is identified, with his wife, as representative of the original Santal couple. Their functions are mainly related to festivals and recurrent annual ceremonies. He consecrates the animals offered to the sacred grove deities. He often compares himself with the Brahman of the encompassing society.

The Santal ojha, a healer and diviner, has several functions. He drives away the malevolent deities, divines the causes of disease, administers remedies according to considerable medical knowledge, and expels pain from the body. He learns his basic magical formulas (mantras) from his master, but he also adds to them from his own experience. An important element in his repertoire is the sacrifice of his own blood (conceived as menstrual blood) to the boṅgas, for which he receives a fee. In the rationalization of his practice he employs several Hindu concepts, yet remains fundamentally within the Santal cultural framework. This position between two cultures enables him to interpret his own culture and society.

Ceremonies. Life-cycle rituals, such as initiation, marriage, and burial are celebrated individually. But after burial, the final ceremony of gathering the bones and immersing them in water becomes a collective rite. Other collective rites are related to the agricultural cycle: sowing, transplanting, consecration of the crops, and harvest festivals, as well as the annual festival of the cattle. Another cycle concerns the old hunting and gathering traditions, notably the seasonal hunts. The most important, however, of the festivals related to the old hunting and gathering society is the flower festival, which is also the festival of the ancestors and related to the fertility of women. Rainmaking rituals, held in the spring, involve the ritual participation of the village priest, who has the power to produce rain.

Arts. Santal oral literature is rich and includes folktales, myths, riddles, and village stories, and much of it has been recorded or written. Publication began in 1870 with the work of the Norwegian missionaries, who also left large archives of texts written by the Santals themselves. There is also a certain amount of literature in Santali: newspapers, Christian books, and schoolbooks.

Traditional songs are many and various, including ritual texts, dances in homage to the boṅgas, obscene songs sometimes related to hunting or the punishment of offenders, etc. They are classified according to tunes that in turn relate to content. Christian songs have been composed to the same pattern. Each type of song is accompanied by a particular type of traditional dance. The sexes dance separately except when love songs are performed.

More recently, a tradition of folk theater, often with political overtones, has developed. The main plays have been written by cultural reformers like Ragunath Murmu, and together they present a message of modernization and tribal uplift for the Santal tribe as a whole. Among the visual arts, we may mention the designs decorating houses, the traditional wood carving, and the traditional jewelery, sometimes made of iron and silver.

Medicine. Traditional medicine is highly developed among the Santals and implies a surprising range of botanical and zoological knowledge; more than 300 species each of plants and of animals are identified and used in the pharmacopoeia. There is even, in the organization of botanical knowledge, a hierarchization based on the morphology of plants. The making of remedies implies again a considerable practical knowledge of chemistry.

This medical knowledge is described in a Santal text from the turn of the century, which establishes a complete pathology defining and ranking symptoms and disease according to consistent criteria. Recent fieldwork data corroborates the value of this work, though there is a tendency nowadays to replace such remedies by ritual invocations.

For the Santals, modern medicine sometimes provides an alternative for healing without in any way replacing or superseding traditional medicine.

Death and Afterlife. Santal souls become boṅgas three generations after death, provided that the correct rituals have been performed. At cremation, some bones are collected by the main mourner (usually the eldest son) and kept for awhile under the rafters of the house. They are washed and fed ritually by female mourners with milk, rice beer, and sacred water. Thus, the mourning ritual displays the central Santal symbolism of flower and bone. The feeding of bones that are crowned by flowers expresses the complementarity of the principle of descent (bone) and the principle of affinity (flower = uterus). The chief mourner is possessed by and impersonates the dead and is questioned by the village priest. This dialogue aims at providing the deceased with the wherewithal of the other world. A year later, the bones are immersed in water, a ritual involving sacrifice of a goat. The dead now becomes an ancestor known by name; one month later the recitation of a ritual text releases him from identity to become a nameless ancestor. He now joins other ancestors in the ancestral room of the house and partakes in the offering of rice beer to the ancestors. Now his shadow, which was roaming between the worlds, goes to Hanapuri, the abode of the dead. Here Jom Raja, king of the dead, rules; the passage from there to the state of becoming a boṅga is never made explicit.

The land of the dead is conceptualized as a place where certain individuals acquire the source of magic powers, while others are simply rewarded according to the way they have acted during their life. While the yogi returns to the world and achieves immortality, simple men endure the justice of Jom Raja. The idea of afterlife shows both Hindu and Christian influence.

See also Kol; Munda

Bibliography

Archer, William G. (1974). _The Hill of Flutes: Life, Love, and Poetry in Tribal India; A Portrait of the Santals._ London: Allen & Unwin.

Archer, William G. (1984). _Tribal Law and Justice: A Report on the Santal._ New Delhi: Concept.

Bodding, P. O. (1927). *Santal Folk-Tales*. Vols. 1–3. Oslo: Aschehoug.

Bodding, P. O. (1932–1936). *A Santal Dictionary*. Vols. 1–4. Oslo: Det Norske Videnskaps Akademi.

Bouez, Serge (1985). *L'alliance chez les Ho et les Santal de l'Inde*. Paris: Société d'Ethnographie.

Carrin-Bouez, Marine (1986). *La Fleur et l'Os: Symbolisme et rituel chez les Santal*. Paris: École des Hautes Études en Sciences Sociales.

MARINE CARRIN-BOUEZ

Sayyid

ETHNONYMS: none

The Sayyids are descendants of Ali, the son-in-law of Mohammed by Fatima, Mohammed's daughter; and those found in South Asia today are the representatives of the Sayyids who, during the Muslim supremacy, flocked to India as religious teachers, soldiers, and adventurers, from Turkey, Arabia, and central Asia.

Sayyids, found widespread in South Asia, are Sunni Muslims, but in northern Gujarat many are Shia Muslims at heart, though all profess to be Sunnis. The Shia Sayyids there form a distinct community, their chief bond of union being the secret celebration of Shia religious rites. As a class, Sayyids are by their profession obliged to show that they are religious and are careful to observe all the rites enjoined by the Quran.

As a rule, a Sayyid's daughter marries only another Sayyid, preferably chosen from among some exclusive classes of Sayyids. Family trees are examined and every care taken that the accepted suitor is a Sayyid both on the father's and mother's side. But many take wives from any of the four chief Muslim classes and sometimes, though rarely, from among the higher of the local or "irregular" Muslim communities. Sayyid boys' names generally end in "Ali" or "Husain," and occasionally in "Shah."

Sayyids are landlords, religious teachers, soldiers, constables, and servants. In Gujarat there is a class of Sayyid beggars belonging to the Bukhari stock. They wander over Gujarat in groups of two to five, mainly during the month of Ramadan, and are famous for their creativity in inventing tales of distress.

Many of the Pathan tribes in the North-West Frontier Province of Pakistan, such as the Bangash of Kohat and the Mishwanis of the Hazara border, claim Sayyid origin. The apostles who completed the conversion of the Pathans to Islam were also called "Sayyids" if they came from the west, and "Sheikhs" if they came from the east; hence, doubtless, many Pathans falsely claim Sayyid origin. In Afghanistan the Sayyids control much of the commerce, as their holy charac-

ter allows them to pass unharmed where other Pathans would be murdered.

The Sayyids had a short-lived dynasty in India, which reigned at Delhi during the first half of the fifteenth century. Their name again figures in Indian history at the breakup of the Mogul Empire, when two Sayyid brothers created and dethroned emperors at their will. In 1901 the total number of Sayyids in India was 1,339,734. This number included many well-known and influential families. The first Muslim appointed to the Council to India and the first appointed to the Privy Council were both Sayyids.

See also Muslim; Pathan

SARWAT S. ELAHI

Scheduled Castes and Scheduled Tribes

ETHNONYMS: Adivasis, Backward Classes

The Indian constitution (1949) created broad categories of underprivileged groups in the Republic of India that were to be the object of special administrative and welfare efforts. Three categories were named, though not clearly defined: Scheduled Castes, Scheduled Tribes, and other Backward Classes. Very roughly, these were comprised respectively of (1) Untouchables or Harijans; (2) virtually all Adivasis or tribes; and (3) other economically disadvantaged groups not included in (1) or (2). In 1981 India had an estimated 105 million Scheduled Caste members and 52 million people in Scheduled Tribes. The category of other Backward Classes, always nebulous and fluctuating, is difficult to enumerate.

But which castes and tribes were to be singled out for this special attention, at the expense (literally and figuratively) of the remainder of the population? This burning and economically important question was solved for millions of concerned people by the publication of lists or schedules (which have been revised several times) that listed by name those castes and tribes that were to be eligible. These lists were created at the national level for Scheduled Tribes and Castes, and at the provincial level for other Backward Classes. Tribal and Harijan welfare departments were set up in each state to administer the benefits that were made available. Over the first forty years of operation they have no doubt done much to outlaw the practice of Untouchability, raise educational standards, and provide public health facilities. The framers of the Indian constitution thought that these benefits should be provided for twenty years; but, as it turned out, those eligible have fought tenaciously to retain their special benefits—and hence their "backward status"—right up to the present. The great weakness in the whole concept of special privileges for select categories of the population, especially today, is that no means test is required of an individual beneficiary. Thus, a Scheduled Caste youth, for example, whose father is a very wealthy timber merchant, will still be eligible for free university tuition and perhaps a hotly contested place in a medical college, while a Brahman girl from a poor family, who has much higher examination marks than he, may be denied admission.

Bibliography

Béteille, André (1969). "The Future of the Backward Classes." In _Castes: Old and New, Essays in Social Structure and Social Stratification,_ edited by André Béteille, 103–145. Bombay: Asia Publishing House.

Ghurye, G. S. (1963). _The Scheduled Tribes._ 3rd ed. Bombay: Popular Prakashan.

Mahar, J. Michael, ed. (1972). _The Untouchables in Contemporary India._ Tucson: University of Arizona Press.

PAUL HOCKINGS

Sheikh

ETHNONYM: Shaikh

The Sheikhs are Sunni Muslims, widespread in northern and central India as well as Pakistan and all of Bangladesh. Of the four main Muslim groups in South Asia, the Sheikhs rank second, below the Sayyids but above the Pathans and Moguls. While in theory there is no caste hierarchy in Islam, in practice people from these four groups do not usually marry one another; however, in some areas intermarriage may occur, with Sheikhs in particular marrying Sayyids. While the latter groups are "Ashraf" (of foreign, Middle Eastern origin), the Sheikhs are ultimately of local Hindu origin, although their ancestors may have converted to Islam many centuries ago. Sheikhs are engaged in a wide variety of urban and agricultural occupations. Men take the title "Sheikh" or "Mohammed" before their names, and women have "Bibi" after their names.

See also Mogul; Muslim; Pathan; Sayyid

Sherpa

ETHNONYM: Shar pa

Orientation

Identification. The Sherpas are one of the Bhotia, the Tibetan-related ethnic groups inhabiting several high valleys in northeastern Nepal. They practice the _Nying ma pa,_ or "old" version of Tibetan Buddhism. The name "Sherpa," Tibetan _shar pa,_ means "easterner," referring to their origin in the eastern Tibetan region of Khams.

Location. The main present homeland of the Sherpas is Solu-Khumbu in the northern part of the Sagarmatha District in eastern Nepal. The main valleys settled by Sherpas are the Khumbu, Pharak, Shorong (Nepali Solu), Arun, and Rolwaling. There are also permanent Sherpa settlements in the Nepali capital, Kathmandu, and in the Indian hill towns of Darjeeling, Kalimpong, Siliguri, and others. Most Sherpa villages in Nepal are at elevations between 2,400 and 3,600 meters, on the southern slopes of the Himalayan range, concentrated around the base of the Everest massif.

Demography. An estimate of Sherpa population places them at about 20,000 or 25,000, mostly living in the Solu-Khumbu area, but with colonies of several thousand each in Kathmandu and Darjeeling. They thus constitute less than 1 percent of the total population of Nepal. It appears that population in Solu-Khumbu is remaining stable or, if anything, declining, partly due to out-migration to the towns.

Linguistic Affiliation. The Sherpa language is a dialect of Tibetan, and thus it is a part of the Tibeto-Burman Family of languages, to which many of the other languages of Nepal also belong. All Sherpas speak Nepali, the official language of Nepal. While there is no Sherpa writing system, many Sherpas are literate in Tibetan, Nepali, and in some cases Hindi and English as well.

History and Cultural Relations

The present-day Sherpas are the descendants of a small group of families who emigrated from the Khams region of Tibet across the Himalayan range in the middle of the sixteenth century under the leadership of a great lama, or religious preceptor. The valleys into which they moved appear to have been sparsely settled at the time of their arrival. They lived by raising field crops in the cleared forest land and herding livestock, including yaks, cows, and yak-cow crossbreeds, prized for their excellent milk, in the higher pastures. During the nineteenth century, under the aegis of the British Raj in India and the Rana dynasty in Nepal, some Sherpas took advantage of their location near the Nana pa La, or "Inside Pass" between Tibet and Nepal, to establish themselves as intermediaries in trade routes linking China and the Indian subcontinent, using the yak as a transport animal ideally suited to alpine caravans. The introduction of the Irish potato into the region in the middle of the nineteenth century added prosperity to the region: this allowed for denser settlements in the high villages of Khumbu above the tree line but near the pass and the yak pastures. The potato is now the main staple crop of the Sherpas; before its introduction, they subsisted on grain, especially barley, and dairy products. In the years following the opening of Nepal to the west, after the restoration of the Shaha monarchy in 1952, mountaineering and tourism became major industries. Sherpas from Darjeeling had already established a reputation as able assistants on British surveying and mountaineering expeditions by the beginning of the century. The conquest of Mount Everest (in Nepali, Sagarmatha; in Sherpa, Chomolungma) in 1953 by a British team relying on Sherpa porters and guides—with a Sherpa climber, Tenzing Norgay, as one of the first two people on the summit, along with Sir Edmund Hillary—brought the Sherpas worldwide attention. Since then, work related to the tourist, trekking, and mountaineering trade has more and more dominated the economy of the Sherpas, who serve as guides, *sirdars* (expedition foremen), and service providers in the cash economy of tourism. The Sherpas in the towns, especially Darjeeling, are drawn there by wage labor in industries such as road building and tea planting. A few Sherpas made great fortunes as road-building labor contractors under the British and more recently since Indian independence. Although the Nang pa La is no longer an active trade route, trading, both within the region and over long distances throughout much of Asia, is an important Sherpa economic activity.

Settlements

In Solu-Khumbu, villages can range from just three or four households to more than a hundred houses in the large towns of Khumjung and Namche Bazaar. In higher valleys, where arable land is scarcer and fields are smaller, individual houses sit in the midst of their adjoining fields, which are separated by stone walls. In the lower, more fertile valleys, houses are usually clustered in central locations surrounded by the fields of the various village residents. Many villages may include a community temple, as well as a communal mill and the religious monuments called *chorten* (Tibetan *mchod rten*, Nepali *stupa*), a distinctively shaped reliquary mound. There are a few government schools in the region. Sherpa houses are substantial buildings of stone covered with plaster, worked with wood in the interior and with wooden shingles on the roof. Houses have at least two stories, the lower story usually serving as an animal shed and storage area. The main living quarters on the second story are built around a hearth area; there are shelves on the walls for the storage of kitchen and household items, as well as the family's collection of large copper kettles, heirlooms that serve as exchange and display items. There is no furniture, but the interior walls are lined with built-in platforms and benches for eating, sleeping, and entertaining guests.

Economy

Subsistence and Commercial Activities. The major part of Sherpa production consists of field agriculture. Potatoes are the main staple, along with barley, some wheat varieties, and more recently maize in the lower-elevation villages. Various garden vegetables are also grown, the most prominent being huge radishes the size of turnips (or larger) and cucumbers the size of watermelons. There is no mechanized farming; plowing is done with a single-bladed plow drawn by oxen. The other main component of the domestic economy is livestock herding for dairy products, especially butter and a form of yogurt. Butter is produced in surplus by some herders and is a major trade item. Imported tea, mixed with butter and salt, and *chang*, local beer made from maize or other grain, are drunk in great quantities. Rice and fruits are obtained from regional markets frequented by growers from lower-elevation regions. Sherpas, being Buddhists, do not slaughter animals and are not generally meat consumers, though they will eat meat slaughtered by non-Sherpas at the market or on special occasions.

Industrial Arts. The various crafts and industries necessary for Sherpa life are, at present, almost exclusively relegated to ethnic Nepalis of the artisan castes, including blacksmiths, goldsmiths, leather workers, and tailors. This pattern dates from the nineteenth century, when Nepali caste restrictions were accepted by the Sherpas as part of their incorporation into the expanding state.

Trade. Trade, including trans-Himalayan trade, has long been a leading Sherpa entrepreneurial activity and was the source of a number of very substantial fortunes. Sherpas like to make long trading expeditions, and men often go off on such journeys singly or in groups for many months, leaving both domestic chores and agricultural work in the hands of women. In recent times, merchants catering to the tourist trade have grown more numerous.

Division of Labor. Trading and wage labor are predominantly male activities. Agricultural and pastoral labor is shared by both sexes, and often women do the major share while men trek. Plowing is the only productive activity assigned exclusively to men.

Land Tenure. Most land is individually owned and worked by households. Threshing is sometimes done communally by cooperating households. Sherpas will not in general do agricultural work for wages, preferring to work the tourist trade or in the cities. A few Sherpa families who made great fortunes in trade own large tracts of land worked by wage laborers and tenant farmers coming from non-Sherpa ethnic groups. In recent years a land reform program of the government of Nepal has attempted to address major inequities in landownership.

Kinship

Kin Groups and Descent. The Solu-Khumbu Sherpas are divided into a number of named exogamous patrilineal clans, descended from the original founding families; the clans are subdivided into lineages. Clans can own common land, forests, mills, temples, or villages, though they do not necessarily do so. Agricultural fields are individual property. There are kindreds joined by mutual aid and participation in life-cycle ceremonies. These usually link several villages in a region.

Kinship Terminology. The terminology is a variant of the Omaha system. Relative ages of siblings are signified by distinct terms. The categories of mother's brother and of in-law are applied to a wide number of people. The standard term of address is "older brother" or "older sister."

Marriage and Family

Marriage. Most marriages are monogamous, though fraternal polyandry is allowed and has prestige. Polygyny is very rare. Marriage is supposed to be arranged, though the pattern is changing. Marriage is a long process involving many stages of betrothal and gift and labor exchange. Women receive a dowry when the marriage is finalized, and sons receive their fair share of the parental estate. Divorce is quite frequent, having been estimated as occurring in 30 percent of all Sherpa marriages.

Domestic Unit. The nuclear family residing in a single household sharing a joint economy is the basic domestic unit. Residence is neolocal. When all children have grown, married, and received their shares of the inheritance, parents are supposed to be housed by the youngest son.

Inheritance.   Land and herds are divided equally among all male heirs, who are also supposed to be given newly built or acquired houses on the finalization of their marriages. Monks and nuns receive their shares upon their ordination. Female heirs receive a fair division of movable property at marriage, including animals, jewelry, copperware, and cash. Families without male heirs may take in an adoptive son-in-law as heir. The youngest brother inherits the parents' house, while the oldest brother generally inherits offices or titles.

Socialization.   Child rearing is handled mainly by mothers and by older sisters if there are any. Fathers are nurturant to children, but Sherpa life entails long and frequent paternal absence because of expeditions, trade ventures, or wage-labor shifts. The treatment of children could be described as being on the indulgent-to-negligent side, though it varies by individual temperament. Girls are incorporated into the household economy earlier than boys, as child-care helpers and kitchen workers, while boys play in multiage groups.

Sociopolitical Organization

The Sherpas have never been organized into any coherent political unit as such. Throughout their history in Nepal, local headmen have established themselves as authorities on the basis of wealth, personality, religious status, and alliance with non-Sherpa centers of power including the Nepali state. More recently, the Sherpa region has been incorporated within the administrative system of the contemporary Nepali government.

Social Organization.   Sherpa society is notable for its stress on egalitarian values and on individual autonomy. Hierarchical relations exist within Sherpa society between "big" people with wealth or descent from an outstanding family and ordinary "small" people, but there are no real class distinctions. Descendants of the original settling ancestors of Solu-Khumbu are accorded higher status, while new immigrants and more distantly related people are relegated to marginal roles. Those threatened with poverty and debt have the option of going to Darjeeling or Kathmandu for wage labor. Patron-client relationships are established between Sherpas and the Nepali service castes who perform vital craft functions for them, but the Nepali are regarded as ritually impure and are viewed as occupying an inferior social position.

Political Organization.   There are few formal mechanisms for the exercise of power in Sherpa society. With the flow of surplus capital into the region through the exploitation of the monopoly on the Nang pa La trade route, some traders established themselves in the position of _pembu_, usually translated as "governor." With varying degrees of autonomy from or subordination to the overarching Nepali state, depending on different historical circumstances, these figures, by virtue of influence and wealth, became tax collectors, using some of the proceeds as investments in trade. The power of the pembus depended largely on personal authority and enterprise, and it was not readily transmissible from father to son. In more recent times, the Nepali governmental system has established more administrative control over the region, and the _panchayat_ system of local democratic village councils has been introduced.

Social Control.   Religious authority and values, the power of local headmen, tradition, and public opinion constrain action, but there are few indigenous mechanisms for enforcing social control or adjudicating complaints. Mediation or arbitration by neighbors, relatives, headmen, or lamas settles most disputes. Others can now be taken to Nepali law courts, though this is infrequently done. Nonviolent Buddhist values have helped keep Sherpa society almost entirely free of war and homicide. Few Sherpas join the Gurkha military forces. High mobility makes flight or avoidance a viable solution to conflict.

Religion and Expressive Culture

Religious Beliefs.   The Tibetan form of Mahayana Buddhism, sometimes called Vajrayana, "The Thunderbolt Vehicle," is universally observed among the Sherpas. In past centuries, religion was organized on a village and clan level; since the turn of the present century, celibate monasticism, imported from Tibet, has flourished in the Sherpa region. The Sherpa pantheon is vast, ranging from the great Buddhist divinities connected with the quest for enlightenment and salvation to local gods, spirits, and demons influencing health, luck, and day-to-day concerns. The former are the object of temple and monastic worship, the latter of exorcisms, commensal feasts, purification rites, and curing rites performed by married lamas and shamans.

Religious Practitioners.   On the village level, married lamas who are also householders preside over community and life-cycle ceremonies. Monks and nuns take lifetime vows of celibacy and live in institutions isolated from daily life. Their interaction with the community is mainly limited to the reading of sacred texts at funerals and annual monastic rituals to which the public is invited. The monks' and nuns' pursuit of merit in turn brings merit to the entire community. Sherpa monks and nuns are not supported by the state, as in Tibet, nor do they beg widely, as in Southeast Asian traditions, but rather support themselves from their own inheritance, through trade, or through donations by sponsors from wealthy households. Outstanding religious figures may be reincarnated, and the highest ecclesiastical offices at the present time are held by reincarnations of earlier religious figures. In addition, shamans perform exorcisms and cures, though this is now less prevalent than previously.

Ceremonies.   A spring first-fruits festival called Dumje and the great monastic masked dancing rituals, generically called Cham (in Tibetan, '_cham_; the specific Sherpa version, Mani Rimdu) and often held in fall or winter, are the major festivals. Individual households and villages sponsor exorcism, curing, and cleansing rites, often in connection with life-cycle events, especially funerals.

Arts.   An indigenous style of choral singing and line dancing is favored; as elsewhere in the hills, dancing parties with beer are a preferred social activity for the young people. Many Sherpas have become masters of the Buddhist ecclesiastical arts, including religious painting or iconography. The monastic dance dramas feature elaborate costumery and choreography. The traditional religious orchestra includes the drum, cymbals, telescopic horns, oboelike flageolets, conch shells, trumpets made from human thighbones, and hand drums made from the tops of two human skulls placed back to back.

Liturgical chanting is an art mastered by many laypeople as well as by monks and lamas.

Medicine. Indigenous cures include herbal medicines, shamanic exorcism, the reading of exorcism texts by lamas, and the use of amulets and medicines made or blessed by high religious figures. More recently, Western medicine has been widely sought.

Death and Afterlife. Funerals are the longest and most elaborate life-cycle ceremonies; the body is cremated, and the soul of the deceased is encouraged, through ritual action and instruction, to seek an advantageous rebirth. Rebirth is believed to occur forty-nine days after death; ideally the entire seven-week period is occupied with a rich cycle of ceremonies and the chanting of funerary texts from the Buddhist tradition. Although relatives and lamas do the best they can to influence future rebirth in a favorable body, it is generally agreed that the main determining factor is the working of karma, the principle by which meritorious and nonmeritorious behaviors are appropriately rewarded or punished in countless future lives.

See also Nepali

Bibliography

Fürer-Haimendorf, Christoph von (1964). *The Sherpas of Nepal: Buddhist Highlanders.* Berkeley: University of California Press.

Jerstad, Luther G. (1969). *Mani-Rimdu, Sherpa Dance Drama.* Seattle: University of Washington Press.

Oppitz, Michael (1968). *Geschichte und Sozialordnung der Sherpa.* Innsbrück and Munich: Universität Verlag Wagner.

Ortner, Sherry B. (1978). *Sherpas through their Rituals.* Cambridge: Cambridge University Press.

Paul, Robert A. (1982). *The Tibetan Symbolic World: Psychoanalytic Explorations.* Chicago: University of Chicago Press.

ROBERT A. PAUL

Sidi

ETHNONYM: Habshi

The Sidi, who are also known as Habshi, are descendants of Africans originally coming from the hinterlands of the East African coast. The term "Sidi" is supposed to derive from Sayyid, "Habshi" from the Arabic term for Abyssinia, "Habash." In the past, Black slaves stemming from the coastal strip from Ethiopia to Mozambique were carried by Arab slave traders to different parts of the Muslim world, including India. Here, their presence is recorded since the early establishment of Muslim rule during the Sultanate of Delhi (thirteenth-sixteenth centuries). African slaves continued to be imported to the western states of India until the late nineteenth century, though never in large numbers. They were mainly employed by local rulers as soldiers, bodyguards, and domestic servants. Today small groups of Sidi live in the west Indian coastal states of Karnataka, Maharashtra, and Gujarat as well as in Sindh in Pakistan. In Karnataka they belong to religious groups (Hindu, Muslim, and Christian). In Gujarat they presently form one of the lower Muslim castes of domestic servants and religious mendicants or fakirs.

The social life of the Sidi caste in Gujarat is closely related to the cult of Muslim saints. At the center of a cluster of related Sidi saints is the patron saint of the Sidi, Bava Gor, along with his younger brother, Bava Habash, and his sister, Mai Mishra. According to myth, the saint was originally an Abyssinian military commander who was sent by order of the Prophet to fight against a female demon in Hindustan; but it was his sister who eventually destroyed the female demon. The Sidi believe themselves to be descended from the Sidi soldiers and their wives who accompanied Bava Gor during his mission and who had become saints in the course of time. The shrines of these Sidi saints form a horizontal network connecting the geographically diffused Sidi caste in Gujarat. At the same time, the saints relate the Sidi to higher-ranking saints of the Sayyid and their representatives at the top of the regional hierarchy of Muslim castes. This ritual relation is further emphasized by one of the main functions of the shrine complex of Bava Gor, Bava Habash, and Mai Mishra, the exorcism of spirits, which connects it to similar regional centers.

As ritual specialists the Sidi are mediators between man and the supernatural. Many of them are engaged in the maintenance of shrines and related ritual activities. Their clientele, the devotees and cult adepts, stem from heterogenous social and economic backgrounds and belong to different religious communities (Muslim, Hindu, Parsi). The majority, however, is from a poor economic background and the lower rungs of the social hierarchy.

A salient feature of the syncretic saint cult as practiced by the Sidi is the existence of a male and a female sphere. The veneration of male saints is paralleled by that of female saints, whose shrines are cared for by Sidi women. While women are generally excluded from the most sacred part or the inner sphere of a Muslim saint's shrine, in the context of the cult, Sidi men are not allowed to enter the inner sphere of the shrine of a female saint. Sidi women perform ritual tasks specifically related to a female domain of the cult.

The central ritual activity of the Sidi consists of the performance of dancing and drumming called *dammal* or *goma*. The first term derives from dam, "breath," the latter from the Swahili term for dance, *ngoma*. This dance may be performed in various contexts, the most important being the annual celebration of *urs*, the death anniversary of the saint. Then the Sidi practice a form of divine possession. Men and women are said to become the vehicles of the saints; men are possessed by the male saints, women by the female saints. The dance also is performed with slight variation, especially without possession, in other social situations: at urs of higher saints; by wandering Sidi fakirs while begging for alms; in small groups, to the order of a devotee who sponsors a dance performance as part of fulfilling a vow; or simply because a wealthy patron wishes to entertain his guests. In these contexts another element is emphasized by the dance of the Sidi: that of clowning, obscene gesturing, and joking.

Within the caste-society of Gujarat the Sidi are part of the Muslim community, occupying special ritual roles in relation to the values of that society. They could be called the Muslim analogues of the Hindu Untouchables, but with the emphasis more on honor and dishonor than on purity and pollution. The activities of the Sidi violate in many respects the values of high-status Muslim groups and are at the same time indispensable to the maintainance of these values as well as to the expression of their appropriateness.

Bibliography

Basu, Helene (forthcoming). _Fool on a Hill: A Study of Social Experience and Religious Symbols._

Bhattacharya, D. K. (1970). "Indians of African Origin." _Cahiers d'études Africaines_ 10:579–582.

Chakraborty, Jyotirmay, and S. B. Nandi (1984). "The Siddis of Junagadh: Some Aspects of Their Religious Life." _Human Science_ 33:130–137.

Desai, G. H. (1912). _A Glossary of Castes, Tribes, and Races in the Baroda State._ Baroda: Government of Baroda.

HELENE BASU

Sikh

ETHNONYM: Sardarji (address)

The approximately 18,000,000 Sikhs who reside in the Punjab and in scattered communities across the world share a reverence for "the ten gurus" (from Guru Nanak to Guru Gobind Singh) and the teachings of their scripture, the _Adi Granth_ or _Guru Granth Sahib._ Worship is central for all devotees of Sikhism, India's youngest monotheistic religion, either in the form of daily observances at home or in corporate worship at the _gurdwara,_ a building designated for congregational ceremonies and social events such as communal kitchens (_langar_) providing free food. Many Sikhs also observe a code of conduct and discipline that includes males wearing recognizable marks of orthodoxy (unshorn hair, a comb, a dagger, a steel bangle, and a pair of breeches), a ban on tobacco, and the use of common titles for male and female converts (Singh, "lion," and Kaur, "princess," respectively). This orthodox group, which has gradually grown to dominate the public life of the community, consists of _amritdhari_ Sikhs (those who have undergone baptism). Other Sikhs in the community do not participate fully in the code of conduct but are accepted as Sikhs because of their devotion, participation in worship, and respect for the gurus.

The Punjab was and remains the homeland for Sikhs.

There Sikhism evolved, incorporating various tribes and castes including a preponderance of Jats, rural agriculturalists, who along with others have shown great courage in times of persecution and political turmoil. The first guru and founder of the faith was Guru Nanak (A.D. 1469–1539). By early in the seventeenth century the following had grown to such an extent in the Punjab area that it was seen as a threat to the Mogul rulers. Within a century the last of the ten gurus had died (by 1708), and open rebellion had broken out. By the middle of the eighteenth century bands of Sikh guerrillas were hastening the collapse of the Mogul administration in their area, while keeping Afghan invaders at bay (1747–1769). These military struggles continued, but by the end of that century Ranjit Singh had emerged as leader of the Sikhs and maharaja of the Punjab, a position he retained until his death in 1839. This continuing military activity had greatly encouraged a tradition of constant military readiness in the community, and it largely explains the role of Sikh men in the modern armies of India, Pakistan, and Great Britain.

The numerous shrines and holy spots associated with major events in Sikh history, most notably the Golden Temple at Amritsar, are primarily found in districts now in Pakistan or the Indian Punjab. In the late nineteenth century, Sikhs began migrating to Southeast Asia, Africa, Europe, and North America, and nowadays large and often very affluent and highly educated Sikh communities can be found in those areas. A new group of Western Sikh converts, the _gora_ or "white" Sikhs led by Harbajan Singh, are associated with many gurdwaras (houses of worship) in North America and also have their own organizations. Although the centrality of the Punjabi language and culture within the daily lives of Sikhs sometimes divides those with roots in the Punjab from these new converts, common worship, beliefs, and a shared code of discipline tend to overcome the divisions aroused by ethnicity.

Sikh identity and institutions have been strengthened and at times modified by experiences over the last century. Organizing themselves into Singh Sabhas in the late 1800s, Sikhs have emphasized their separateness from Hindus in areas such as theology, ritual, social practice, and politics. These efforts culminated in the dramatic, nonviolent campaign (1920–1925) to wrest Sikh gurdwaras from the hands of British-supported managers, often Hindu, and to place responsibility for all shrines in the hands of the community. Since 1925, the Sikh Gurdwara Protection Committee (a central management committee) has supervised the shrines and also played an important role in Sikh politics. The frustrations of their minority status, coupled with economic problems, helped foster growing Sikh militancy in the 1970s, culminating in the demands for a separate Sikh nation, "Khalistan." The resulting government attack on armed militants in the Golden Temple (1984) led to a period of continuing political chaos in the Punjab, sparked dramatic episodes such as the assassination of Prime Minister Indira Gandhi and the resulting massacres of many Sikhs, and fostered debate among Sikhs about ideology and strategy. Despite this turbulence, Sikhs still maintain a positive outlook and continue to provide leadership in public institutions and professions wherever they reside.

See also Jat; Punjabi

Bibliography

Barrier, N. Gerald (1970). *The Sikhs and Their Literature.* New Delhi: Manohar.

Barrier, N. Gerald, and Van Dusenbery, eds. (1990). *The Sikh Diaspora.* New Delhi: Chanakya.

McLeod, W. H. (1990). *The Sikhs.* New York: Columbia University Press.

McLeod, W. H. (1990). *Who Is a Sikh.* Oxford: Oxford University Press.

O'Connell, Joseph, et al., eds. (1988). *Sikh History and Religion in the Twentieth Century.* South Asia Series. Toronto: University of Toronto Press.

N. GERALD BARRIER

Sikkimese

ETHNONYMS: none

Orientation

The Sikkimese live in the Himalayan kingdom of Sikkim, with a population of 316,385 in 1981. Tibet, Nepal, India, and Bhutan all touch the borders of this kingdom. The Sikkimese live in villages of wooden buildings that hug the Himalayan slopes. The Sikkimese easily traverse passes that give access to the Tibetan Chumbi Valley. The country occupies a commanding position over the historic Kalimpong-Lhasa trade route. India and Tibet have frequently intervened in Sikkim's internal affairs. The British Indian government particularly put pressure upon the Sikkimese for access to central Asia. Sikkim is the political core of the larger former kingdom, and more recently the Sikkimese feel very strongly about keeping the Lhasa route between India and China under their control. Sikkim's location favors a dynamic role in international relations between the two great powers of Asia, India and China.

The mountainous environment of Sikkim is generally inhospitable. There are adverse surface features that seriously impede human development over large areas; cultivated land amounts to only a small proportion of the total area of the kingdom. The harsh climate damages economic development. The Sikkimese live in an enclosed basin nearly 65 kilometers wide, placed between two deeply dissected north-south transverse ridges stretching for 125 kilometers. A huge mountain mass some 19 kilometers south of the main chain of the Himalayas called the Kanchenjunga range constitutes a distinctive physical unit of Sikkim. The range receives heavy discharges from the monsoon, and it is covered with snow and ice as much as a hundred or more meters thick. These masses of snow and ice move downward slowly in the form of glaciers and great avalanches. The avalanches are an ever-present source of danger in northern Sikkim. The continuous creaking and groaning of the moving ice and the roar of avalanches combine to create a sense of instability and apprehension. The Sikkimese tribes regard Kanchenjunga as the seat of an all-powerful god. The outstanding feature of the physical landscape in the Sikkim Himalayas is the variety of temperature zones and vegetation. On the lowest level, less than 300 meters above sea level, tropical growth flourishes. From the bottom valleys, one moves north to the subtropical zone that finally leads to the alpine region.

The official language is English, though comparatively few speak it; Sikkimese and Gurkhali are the primary languages. Existing language divisions do not affect the overall political stability of Sikkim because the people are bonded together by what they call "a feeling of kinship."

Settlements

Nearly 50,000 people are concentrated near the kingdom's principal urban center and capital, Gangtok. The capital is important commercially as well as administratively. Gangtok is the center point of the state's political and economic core.

Economy

Agriculture has traditionally been the major feature of Sikkim's economy. Farming has been influenced by the nature of the terrain and by the diversity of climatic conditions. In Sikkimese agriculture attention is divided among staple cereal crops, commercial specialty crops, animals, and animal products. Rice and corn lead in hectares planted, but cardamom, citrus fruits, apples, and pineapples enter trade channels and so are better known. Potatoes are the major cash crop. Sheep, goats, cattle, yaks, and mules are abundant. The animals support the population in the high mountain valleys. The pastoral industries furnish wool, skins, hides, and surplus commodities.

About one-third of Sikkim's 7,096 square kilometers of mountainous territory is forested. Forests are considered one of the kingdom's greatest assets. There are valuable plantations of sal (*Shorea robusta*, a common timber tree that is a source of inexpensive building materials), sisal (a source of cordage), and bamboo. Since the 1960s Sikkim's mining corporation has been instrumental in sponsoring systematic mineral development. Copper, lead, and zinc are mined in large quantities. In Sikkim's forests there are raw materials for manufacture of paper pulp, matches, furniture, packing boxes, and tea chests. Sikkim's development has been severely slowed down by the lack of power supplies.

A major strategic road was built by the Indian army engineers and India's Border Road Development Board. This road is 240 kilometers long and is called the North Sikkim Highway. The highway that connects Gangtok with the northern border areas was completed in 1962 by India. Construction work on the road started in 1958, but several factors slowed the project. Besides the engineering problems, one of the main difficulties was supplying food for such a large labor force: there were about 6,000 workers during peak periods.

Sociopolitical Organization

The presence of culturally diverse groups within Sikkim hinders the kingdom's cohesiveness. The term "Sikkimese" indicates a resident of Sikkim, but it has no linguistic or ethnological implications. The citizens of modern Sikkim trace their ancestry to a variety of Asian people: Lepchas, Indians, and Nepalis. The native Lepchas comprise only 21 percent of the kingdom's population. Nepali settlers make up 60 percent of the present Sikkimese population. In about 1890 the British began to encourage immigration from neighboring Nepal. Until recently the Nepalese settler did not have the status of a citizen, but the Sikkim Subjects' Regulation legislation of 1961 gave citizenship to these inhabitants of Nepalese descent. Conflict between the Tibetan Bhutias and the Lepchas has led to considerable disturbances in Sikkim's past. The Lepchas have been pushed into the forests and lower valleys below 1,200 meters by Bhutias who have settled at higher elevations. Despite these distinctions of ethnicity, the religious factors and a common feeling of national consciousness have resulted in a certain degree of historic and cultural unity.

The two political aspects of Sikkim that merit special attention are: (1) the internal political problem of self-government and the country's ties to India; and (2) the broader problem of the relationship between India, China, and Sikkim. In theory, the maharaja of Sikkim controls the state's internal affairs. In 1963 he was 70 years old. At that time he was already delegating most of his power to his 39-year-old son, Prince Palden Thondup Namgyal. The Sikkimese prince was married to a 22-year-old American woman, Hope Cook of New York City. Their engagement was preceded by six months of negotiation between the governments of Sikkim and India because of the religious and political implications. Their marriage was the first between a member of the Sikkim royal family and any foreigner other than a Tibetan. In November 1961, the state elders met in Gangtok to give their formal approval to the match. In 1975, Sikkim became an Indian state, and the office of Chogyal (king) was abolished.

Religion

Tibetan Buddhism is the state religion and is followed by 28 percent of the population. Another 60 percent of the people are Hindu.

See also Lepcha

Bibliography

Karan, Pradyumna, and William M. Jenkins (1963). _The Himalayan Kingdoms: Bhutan, Sikkim, and Nepal._ Princeton: D. Van Nostrand.

BRENDA AMENSON-HILL

Sindhi

ETHNONYM: Sindi

Sind is a province in southeast Pakistan. It is bordered by the provinces of Baluchistan on the west and north, Punjab on the northeast, the Indian states of Rajasthan and Gujarat to the east, and the Arabian Sea to the south. Its name was derived from the Arabic word for the Indus River, which has long been known as the Sindhu. The province extends over the lower portion of that river valley. Its chief cities are Karachi, the former capital, and Hyderabad. It covers 140,914 square kilometers and had a population of about 19 million in 1981.

As in the rest of Pakistan, the economy is predominantly agricultural and depends almost entirely on irrigation. The principal source of water is the Indus River, on which there are three irrigation dams in Sind. They are the Ghulam, on the Punjab border; the Lloyd; and the Ghulam Muhammad, farthest south. Most Sindhis are engaged in irrigation agriculture, either as landlords who do not cultivate with their own hands or as tenant farmers and laborers. Sindh's principal crops are wheat, rice, cotton, oilseeds, sugarcane, and fruits (by double-cropping). Other ethnic groups in Sindh specialize in fishing in the Indus River and Manchar Lake, which is partly formed from Indus River overspill during the flood period, as well as on the southern coast in the Arabian Sea. Some make their living as merchants, physicians, lawyers, and teachers and by doing other professional jobs in industrializing towns and cities such as Karachi and Hyderabad. Karachi, Pakistan's chief port, has an oil refinery and also is the center of printing and publishing. Sindh culture is reflected in some of its fascinating handicrafts such as mirror embroidery, lacquerware, and exquisitely painted tilework.

The religion, family law and customs, food taboos, and art styles in Sindhi culture reveal the emphasis and importance of Islam. At least 80 percent of Sindhis are Muslim, mostly Sunni, while the other 20 percent consist of Indian Sindhis who are Hindu and who migrated from Pakistan to India after the partition in 1947.

Sindhi women are secluded behind the clay walls of house and compound; this practice of purdah is strict among landlords and other families who claim respectability accordingly. In some rural areas, when women leave their houses they not only go veiled but sometimes are followed by a small boy ringing a hand bell and calling out, "Pass!" Men hearing the signal turn toward a wall until the party has hurried past. However, Sindhi men center their social life in a special building called _otak_, which, unlike their homes, is not enclosed in compound walls. Here landlords who aspire to local power meet their followers. It is an honor to be a landlord, but among landlords further prestige comes from having family members, even daughters, who are formally educated and have professional careers or possess political power. Inside the otak, friends join together to drink refreshments, including betel-nut mixtures and alcoholic beverages. Here men also play cards, watch cockfights, and, in the evening, listen to professional musicians or watch hired female dancers.

The Sindhi language is spoken by less than 4 percent of the population of Pakistan. It has fewer dialects than Punjabi and has a small but important literary tradition of its own. There are four million people who claim it as a native tongue: they are concentrated in the former province of Sindh and Kharipur State as well as in the area around Karachi and in Baluchistan. The Sindhi script is similar to the Urdu script, yet different enough not to be easily read by a person who has learned to read in Urdu. The script is Arabo-Persian in its origin, but the language is Indo-Aryan.

Bibliography

Khan, Ansar Zahid (1980). *History and Culture of Sind.* Karachi: Royal Book.

Weekes, Richard V. (1964). *Pakistan: Birth and Growth of a Muslim Nation.* Princeton, N.J.: Von Nostrand.

SARWAT S. ELAHI

Sinhalese

ETHNONYMS: Singhlese, Sinhala

Orientation

Identification. The Sinhalese speak the Sinhala language, live in the southwestern portion of Sri Lanka (formerly Ceylon), and are predominantly of the Theravada Buddhist faith. The name derives from the term for "dwelling of lions," an allusion to the mythical founder, an Indian princess who mated with a lion.

Location. Sri Lanka is located between 5°55' and 9°51' N and 79°41' and 81°5.3' E. Sinhalese traditionally make their homes in the wet zone of the central, south, and west provinces of Sri Lanka, where they are divided into two regional subgroups, the Kandyan Sinhalese of the central highlands, and the Low Country Sinhalese of the maritime provinces. With the rise of government-sponsored internal colonization projects after 1945, considerable internal migration has occurred to the central and northeastern dry zone.

Demography. In 1989 the population of Sri Lanka was estimated as 17,541,000. The population density averages approximately 252 persons per square kilometer and the population is growing at the rate of 1.8 percent per year. Sinhalese constitute 75 percent of the population of Sri Lanka. Sri Lanka's principal ethnic minority, the Sri Lanka Tamils, comprise an additional 11 percent, while the Sri Lanka Moors, a Tamil-speaking Muslim group, constitute 6.5 percent. Other minorities include the so-called Indian Tamils, descendants of tea plantation workers imported by the British, who comprise 8 percent, and small communities of Malays and Europeans.

Linguistic Affiliation. Sinhala is an Indo-European language of the Indo-Aryan Group and was brought to Sri Lanka by North Indian settlers in approximately 500 B.C. Subse-

quently Sinhala evolved in isolation from its North Indian origins but in close proximity with the Dravidian tongues of southern India, which gave it a distinct character as early as the third century B.C.

History and Cultural Relations

Sinhalese dynastic chronicles trace their origins to the exile of Prince Vijaya and his 500 followers from his father's kingdom in north India. According to the chronicles, which portray Sri Lanka as a land destined to preserve Buddhism, Vijaya (the grandson of a Hindu princess and a lion) arrived in Sri Lanka at the moment of the Buddha's death. In the third century B.C., the Sinhalese king converted to Buddhism. By the first century B.C. a Sinhalese Buddhist civilization, based on irrigated rice agriculture, arose in the dry zone, with capitals at Anuradhapura and Pollunaruva. By the thirteenth century A.D., however, a major civilizational collapse occurred for reasons that are still debated (malaria, internal conflict, and South Indian invasions are possible causes), and the population shifted to the southwest. At the time of first European contact in 1505 there were two Sinhalese kingdoms, one in the central highlands at Kandy and one along the southwestern coast near Colombo. The Portuguese deposed the southwestern kingdom (but not Kandy) and won converts to Roman Catholicism among fishing castes along the coastal littoral, but they were driven out of Ceylon by the Dutch in 1656–1658. A legacy of Portuguese times is the popularity of Portuguese names such as de Silva, Fernando, and de Fonseca among Low Country Sinhalese. The Dutch instituted the Roman-Dutch legal system in the maritime provinces (but not Kandy, which remained independent) and cash-crop plantation agriculture, including coffee, cotton, and tobacco, but few Sinhalese converted to Protestant Christianity. The British took over the island's administration in 1798, brought down the Kandyan Kingdom in 1815, and favored the growth of a European-owned coffee and tea plantation sector in the central highlands. By the early twentieth century a new elite of English-speaking, largely Low Country Sinhalese rose to prominence in trading, petty industry, and coconut and rubber plantation agriculture. In 1932, universal adult suffrage and internal self-rule were granted. Without having to fight for its independence, Ceylon was granted freedom in 1948 becoming a constitutional democracy on the Westminster model. The country was governed for eight years by an ostensibly panethnic national party of unity, but in 1956 a Sinhalese populist politician won a landslide victory on a platform to make Sinhala the sole official language of government affairs. Tensions rose as Tamils resisted this move, and communal riots occurred in 1958. Sinhalese youths also grew disaffected as the economy stagnated and unemployment mounted in the 1960s. A 1971 insurgency by an ultraleftist Sinhalese youth group called the Janatha Vimukthi Peramuna (the "People's Liberation Army," or JVP) nearly toppled the government. There were significant Tamil-Sinhalese riots again in 1977, 1981, and 1983; by 1984 a violent Tamil separatist movement had all but driven Sinhalese security forces out of the Tamil north and east; a 1987 accord with India brought 60,000 Indian peacekeeping troops to the Tamil provinces but set off a violent antigovernment campaign by the JVP, which now articulates right-wing Sinhala-chauvinist ideology in addition to its ultraleftist doctrine. More than 17,000 Sri Lankans have died in communal and political violence since 1977.

Settlements

Only about one of five Sinhalese lives in a city; Sri Lanka is still predominantly rural country, and—unlike most Third World countries—its rural-urban balance has not changed significantly in this century. Educational and medical facilities are available in most rural areas and a very low rate of industrialization gives rural villagers little reason to migrate to the cities. In the traditional "one village, one tank" pattern, the village (_gama_) is situated downstream from an artificial reservoir. Ringed around the paddy fields are the traditional two- to four-room houses, each situated in its own garden and separated from others. Traditional houses are made of mud and plaster and thatched with woven palm fronds. Wealthier villagers construct stucco houses roofed with ceramic tiles.

Economy

Subsistence and Commercial Activities. Subsistence agriculture, supplemented by marginal employment in service-related occupations and government employment, characterizes the economic life of most rural Sinhalese villagers. Rice holdings are small and marginally economic at best. Plowing is often done with water buffalo; tractors are numerous but more often used for light transport. Seed is sown and the young shoots are transplanted by hand; harvesting and threshing are also done manually. "Green revolution" hybrids are widely used but are underfertilized. Additional subsistence food crops include fruit (jackfruit, breadfruit, and coconut), vegetables, and manioc, which has become a significant staple-of-last-recourse for the poor. Domestic animals include cattle, buffalo, goats, sheep, chickens, and pigs. There is significant nonplantation, as well as village-based cash-crop activity, especially in the highlands, that produces chilies and other spices, poultry and eggs, goats, honey, herbs employed in Ayurvedic medicine, onions, tomatoes, pulses, cereals, vegetables, _ganja_ (marijuana), and potatoes. A major supplement to the village economy is direct government income for schoolteachers and village officials. Low Country Sinhalese achieved early prominence in coconut, rubber, and low-elevation tea plantation agriculture as well as trade and light mining. Marginal employment is available for many in tea, rubber, and coconut processing.

Industrial Arts. The classical Sinhalese achieved remarkable feats in irrigation engineering, but the technology was lost in the collapse of the dry zone civilizations and Sinhalese today show little interest in engineering, mathematics, or science, preferring liberal arts subjects. "Hands-on" technical work is stigmatized by linkages to low-caste occupations, serving to inhibit children's hobbies, vocational education, and technological literacy, while Western imports have all but wiped out traditional arts and crafts. Efforts to industrialize Sri Lanka have met with little success, and the country shows one of the lowest rates of industrial growth of any South Asian country since its independence. Severe and growing unemployment and landlessness, particularly among rural youth, has contributed to the JVP youth militancy.

Trade. Apart from the prevalence of subsistence agriculture, the Sri Lankan rural economy is almost completely cash-based, with barter and reciprocity restricted to kin-group transactions. Village boutiques involve villagers in debt that frequently results in an impecunious farmer becoming little more than a tenant on his own land; village shopowners are thus able to amass large landholdings. Shops in town sell additional consumer items, and weekly village markets provide marginal economic niches for itinerant traders and village cash-crop agriculturalists. Transport is provided by bullock carts, tractors pulling flatbed trailers, old automobiles, and light trucks. Internal trade, foreign investment, tourism, and economic growth are all casualties of the Tamil rebellion and the JVP insurgency.

Division of Labor. Traditional Sinhalese society is male-dominated and patriarchal, with a strong division of labor by sex and a tendency to stigmatize female roles (women are considered to be ritually impure at times owing to the "pollution" of puberty, childbirth, and menstruation). Men are responsible for the provision of food, clothing, shelter, and other necessities, while women prepare food and care for children. Traditionally, a family lost status if it permitted its women to engage in extradomestic economic roles, such as menial agricultural labor or cash-crop marketing. Men and women led separate lives aside from the convergence brought about by their mutual obligations. The entry of women into higher education and the professions is beginning to alter this pattern.

Land Tenure. Traditionally the descendants of the village founder owned inheritable (but not marketable) shares (_panku_) of the village paddy lands. The actual holdings were sensitively adjusted to suit water availability and to reduce inequities in water distribution; when holdings were reduced below the economic level, a group of villagers hived off into the wilderness, constructed a new tank, and founded a new village. British reforms that defined all wilderness as Crown land and eliminated multiple claims to existing plots of land seriously eroded this system and, as land came on the market, a new class of rice land investors (called _mudalalis_) acquired substantial holdings but left the farming to clients holding the lands by a form of traditional sharecropping tenancy (_ande_ tenure). Population increase has led to severe and still growing landlessness.

Kinship

Kin Groups and Descent. The largest kin group is the "microcaste" (_pavula_), an endogamous and corporate bilateral kin group that represents the convergence of several families' bilateral kindreds. Pavula members share paddy lands, often dwell together in a hamlet, and cooperate in agriculture, trade, and politics. A pavula's members share a unique status within the caste; the group's internal equality is symbolized through life-cycle rites and communal feasts. Descent is fully bilateral in practice, but noncorporate agnatic descent lines linking families with aristocrats of the Buddhist kingdoms may be maintained for status purposes.

Kinship Terminology. The Sinhalese, including Moors, use Dravidian terms, which are associated with symmetrical cross-cousin marriage.

Marriage and Family

Marriage. Most marriages are arranged between the two families, with a strong preference for cross-cousin marriage. Marriage implies caste equality, but with a double standard: to preserve the status of a microcaste (*pavula*), women must marry men of equal or higher status within the caste; men, however, may have sexual relations with women of inferior status without threatening their family's status. Among the Kandyans, who are governed by Kandyan law, polyandry is rare, though villagers say it can be convenient for all concerned. Polygyny is also rare and may amount to no more than the husband's appropriation of sexual services from a low-ranking female servant. The bride normally comes to live with her husband, and this pattern (called *deega*) establishes a relationship of mutual aid and equality between the husband and his wife's kin. In the less common *binna* residence, in contrast, the groom—who is usually landless—goes to live with his wife's parents (matrilocal residence) and must work for his father-in-law. Dowry is rarely paid unless a woman marries a man of higher status within the caste (hypergamy). The marriage may not involve a ceremony if it occurs between equals and within a pavula. Among the Kandyans, property is held individually and is not fragmented by the dissolution of marriage, which is easy and common. Among the Low Country Sinhalese, who are governed by Roman-Dutch law, matrilocal residence is very rare and hypergamy, coupled with dowry, is more common. After marriage the couple's property is merged and in consequence the allied families resist the marriage's dissolution.

Domestic Unit. The smallest kin group is the commensal unit or nuclear family: a wife, unmarried children, and husband. Among traditional Kandyan Sinhalese, there may be more than one commensal unit in a house, but each has its own cooking area. Westernized families adopt the European pattern even for complex households.

Inheritance. In sharp contrast to Indian practices property is divided equally among all children, including women, although wealthy families control a daughter's property and use it as an instrument of marital alliance; among wealthy families, dowry may be paid in lieu of inheritance.

Socialization. There is a strong preference for male children, who may receive better care; the infant mortality rate for girls is higher. Girls are expected to work harder than boys and may be given significant household chores as young as age 5 or 6, and they may be taken out of school at an early age even though education is compulsory for all children aged 5 to 14. Children are cared for by their mother, with whom they sleep except in highly Westernized households. Children are expected to show respect to their elders. Curiosity, initiative, and hobbies are not encouraged. Schools repeat this pattern by emphasizing rote instruction and avoiding vocational subjects. Especially among the landed and high castes, the family is strongly authoritarian: deference to one's parents and acceptance of their decisions is required, on penalty of excommunication.

Sociopolitical Organization

Sri Lanka is a parliamentary democracy with a president as the head of the state. There is a strong two-party system in which politics are dominated by the centrist United National party (UNP, in power since 1977) and the center-to-left Sri Lanka Freedom party (SLFP). Both are dominated by Sinhalese politicians and appeal to Sinhalese sentiment.

Social Organization. The Sinhalese caste system is milder than its Indian counterpart; it lacks Brahmans and the stratifying ideology of Hinduism. Most Sinhalese villages lack caste organizations (*panchayats*) which, in India, punish transgressions of caste; enforcement of caste endogamy, for instance, is left up to families. Because property is inherited bilaterally, however, families have very strong incentives to enforce endogamy (this is one reason for their authoritarian nature). The Sinhalese ideology of caste is derived from precolonial feudalism, in which castes of almost all statuses were granted lands, contingent on their performing services for the king and local aristocrats. The highest caste, the agricultural Goyigama, comprise about half the population and count among their ancestors the aristocrats of the precolonial kingdoms. Among the Kandyans, additional castes include service castes, such as the Hena (washers), Berava (drummers), Navandanna (metalworkers), and the "lowest castes," such as the Rodiya, who were formerly itinerant beggars. Among the Low Country Sinhalese, three highly entrepreneurial maritime castes (Karava, Salagama, and Durava) have risen to economic and political prominence in this area, which has long been under European influence. Most Sinhalese continue to see caste as a positive principle of social affiliation but deny that castes should be ranked or given special privileges. A major consequence of the colonial period was the development of an achievement-oriented national elite based on education and especially knowledge of English. Persons of low caste have won membership in this elite. However, local elites continue to be dominated by high castes or locally powerful castes.

Political Organization. The Sri Lankan state, an artifact of colonial rule, is excessively centralized and politicized; the country's provinces are governed by agents appointed by the president, and virtually all services—roads, railways, education, health services, tax collection, government-owned corporations, land registry and allocation—are administered by centrally controlled ministries. Efforts to devolve power and resources to the provinces, including the Tamil Northern Province and Eastern Province, have been opposed by Sinhalese chauvinists who see devolution as an erosion of Sinhala sovereignty. Members of parliament select the candidates for government positions, including even the lowliest menial jobs, on the basis of political loyalty. Politicization has severely eroded the autonomy of the civil service and judiciary. The JVP insurgency and its popular support can be seen in part as a broad-based rejection of an unresponsive and corrupt political system, but the JVP offers few solutions.

Social Control. Within the village gossip and ridicule are strong forces for social conformity. The family regulates behavior through the threat of excommunication (deprivation of lands and family support in seeking employment). With growing landlessness and unemployment, however, many families are increasingly unable to deliver on their material promises and the threat of excommunication has become an empty threat. The JVP insurgency is in part a rejection of parental authority.

Conflict. Traditionally, violence occurred within families, often as the result of long-standing grudges and obsession with one's "enemies," real or imagined. In the absence of sustained economic growth, aspirations for social mobility cannot be fulfilled, and as competition and anomie grow more intense, ethnic and political violence occurs as various groups compete for state resources. A late-nineteenth-century riot occurred between Buddhists and Christians; later clashes pitted Sinhalese against Muslims (1915). After the "Sinhala only" language act of 1956, communal riots involving Tamils and Sinhalese occurred in 1958, 1977, 1981, and 1983. There was an aborted military coup in 1963, and violence often occurred during and after elections. Political violence has now become institutionalized in the form of youth insurgencies and government "death squads."

Religion and Expressive Culture

Sri Lanka is remarkable in that almost all major world religions are practiced there (Buddhism, Hinduism, Islam, and Christianity), but Buddhism has received special state protection under Sri Lankan constitutions since 1973. Nearly wiped out by Christian conversions and neglect in the late nineteenth century, Buddhism was revived by reformers who borrowed techniques of proselytization and political activity from Christian missionaries—and in so doing altered Buddhism by expanding the role of the laity and emphasizing a rigid Victorian morality.

Religious Beliefs. More than 70 percent of Sinhalese are Theravada Buddhists, but there are substantial (and largely non-Goyigama) Roman Catholic communities in the maritime provinces. Often thought by foreign observers to contradict Buddhist teachings, the worship of Hindu gods in their temples (_devale_) meets religious needs _bhikkus_ (Buddhist monks) cannot address, and the pantheon's structure symbolically expresses the pattern of traditional political authority. At the lower end of the pantheon are demons and spirits that cause illness and must be exorcised.

Religious Practitioners. In Theravada Buddhism, a true Buddhist—a monk, or _bhikku_—is one who has renounced all worldly attachments and follows in the Buddha's footsteps, depending on alms for subsistence. But few Sinhalese become bhikkus, who number approximately 20,000. Buddhist monastic organizations are known collectively as the _sangha_, which is fragmented into three sects (_nikayas_); most bhikkus live in the sect's temple/residence complexes (_viharas_). The largest and wealthiest sect, the Siyam Nikaya, is rooted in the precolonial Kandyan political order and is still limited, in practice, to Goyigama aspirants. The smaller Amapura Nikaya emerged from the nineteenth-century social mobility of the Karava, Salagama, and Durava castes of the maritime provinces. The smallest sect, the Ramanya Nikaya, is a reform community. Traditionally, the sangha was interdependent with Sinhalese kingly authority, which both depended on and supported the monastic orders, which in turn grew wealthy from huge land grants. The veneration of the famed Tooth Relic (a purported tooth of the Buddha) at Kandy was vital to the legitimacy of the Kandyan king. Bhikkus continue their tradition of political action today and are influential in right-wing chauvinist organizations. At village temples of the gods (_bandaras_ and _devas_), non-bhikku priests called _kapuralas_ meet the needs of villagers in this life.

Ceremonies. Holidays include the Buddhist New Year (April), Wesak (May), the anniversaries of the birth, death, and enlightenment of the Buddha, the annual procession (_perahera_) of the Tooth Relic at Kandy (August), and the Kataragama firewalking pilgrimage (August).

Arts. Classical Sinhalese civilization excelled in Buddhist architecture, temple and cave frescos, and large-scale sculpture. In colonial times artisans, now few in number, produced fine ivory carvings, metalwork, and jewelry. A mid–twentieth century school of Sinhalese painting called "The Forty-three Group" sparked an impressive renaissance of Sinhalese art, expressed in a traditional idiom in the temple paintings of George Keyt. A twentieth-century tradition of Sinhalese fiction and poetry has attracted international scholarly attention. A government-assisted Sinhala film industry produces many popular films, and a few serious ones have won international awards.

Medicine. The Indian-derived traditional sciences of Ayurveda (herbal medicine) and astrology, taught and elaborated at Buddhist schools (_piravena_) and practiced by village specialists, provide a comprehensive traditional explanation of health and illness.

Death and Afterlife. The possibility of enlightenment and freedom from rebirth is restricted to those withdrawn from the world; a layperson hopes for a more advantageous rebirth based on a positive balance of bad against good acts (karma) and performs meritorious acts (such as supporting the sangha) toward this end. In popular belief a person who dies without fulfilling cherished dreams may become a spirit and vex the living. The dead are cremated, unless Christians.

See also Moor of Sri Lanka; Tamil of Sri Lanka; Vedda

Bibliography

Gombrich, Richard F. (1971). _Precept and Practice: Traditional Buddhism in the Highlands of Ceylon._ Oxford: Clarendon Press.

Gunawardana, R. A. L. H. (1979). "The People of the Lion: The Sinhala Identity and Ideology in History and Historiography." _Sri Lanka Journal of the Humanities_ 5:1–36.

Roberts, Michael (1982). _Caste Conflict and Elite Formation: The Rise of a Karava Elite in Sri Lanka, 1500–1931._ Cambridge: Cambridge University Press.

Yalman, Nur (1967). _Under the Bo Tree: Studies in Caste, Kinship, and Marriage in the Interior of Ceylon._ Berkeley: University of California Press.

BRYAN PFAFFENBERGER

Sora

ETHNONYMS: Sahara, Saora, Saura, Savar, Savara, Sawar, Sawara

Orientation

Identification. The Sora are a "tribal" people living historically on the margins between shifting political centers in central India. They think of themselves as *adivasi* (tribal), but also as "Hindu," in conscious opposition to the small enclaves of Christian Soras. Culturally, Sora in the plains are similar to surrounding castes but in the hills they retain a distinctive character.

Location. The Sora live in Koraput and Ganjam districts of the state of Orissa and in neighboring parts of Andhra Pradesh, especially Srikakulam District. The Lanjia Sora, who have been studied mainly by Verrier Elwin and Piers Vitebsky, live in the hilly jungles, while several other virtually unstudied groups (e.g., Sarda, Kapu) live in the plains. This article refers to the Lanjia Sora. Within their territory there are settlements of various Oriya and Telugu castes, with some government employees. These settlements are dominated by the Oriya-speaking Pano (Pan, Dom), who trade with the Sora. The Sora lie just on the border between the North Indian and South Indian culture areas. To the northeast are the Indo-Aryan Oriya and to the south the Dravidian-speaking Telugu. To the northwest are the Dravidian-speaking but "tribal" Kond (Khond). The evidence of some place-names along the coast between Puri and Visakhapatnam, areas that now speak Oriya or Telugu, suggests that the Sora formerly were far more widespread and have since been forced into the interior or have survived only there as a separate group. Since early this century, Sora have migrated to the tea gardens of Assam for temporary wage labor and some have remained there. More recently they have migrated to road-building projects in Arunachal Pradesh, though conditions there are less conducive to settling.

Demography. The 1971 census lists about 521,187 Sora, of whom at least half speak the Sora language. The demographic picture is complicated because people around the edge of the Sora area may describe themselves variously. Many populations in the plains who are now nontribal were probably originally Sora.

Linguistic Affiliation. Sora belongs to the South Munda Branch of the Austroasiatic Family and is closely related to Bondo, Gadaba, and Juang. This family includes a number of Southeast Asian languages, especially Mon-Khmer. The Munda languages were perhaps present in India before Indo-Aryan and Dravidian. Sora has several dialects and contains loanwords from Hindi, Oriya, and Telugu. Yet in many areas it retains the power to assimilate these to Sora syntax and morphology. The language developed by Christian Soras as a legacy of Canadian Baptist missionaries already reflects the conceptual gulf between indigenous and Judeo-Christian worldviews.

History and Cultural Relations

Contact with the outside world is probably ancient. In British times the area formed the farthest northern tip of Madras Presidency. The hill area was brought under government control in 1864–1866 by a British expeditionary force that executed and transported Sora resistance leaders and established a permanent police presence. In Koraput District the British established the system of village headmen (*gomang*, also meaning "rich man") to collect revenue for the raja of Jeypore; in Ganjam District the Sora were ruled by march lords, or chieftains of the borderlands, of Paik (Kshatriya) caste. For a long time, and even up to the present, Sora have had a reputation for extreme fierceness, though this has not been the experience of anthropologists. However, every decade or so there are still violent uprisings, usually against Pano trading communities.

Many cultural features can be explained by the Soras' ancient association with Southeast Asia. (Their relation to Hinduism was explored inconclusively by Louis Dumont in his review of Elwin.) Sora are aware of Hindu values and use them in defining their own identity. As a nonliterate culture, they associate literacy with the power of the state; the power of shamans' familiar spirits is also associated with ideas about writing. The Sora have contributed to mainstream Hinduism: Oriyas say that they originally stole their god Jagannath (Juggernaut), an avatar of Krishna, from the Sora.

Settlements

The population of Sora villages varies from around 100 to 800. Villages generally contain several quarters (*longlong*), each inhabited by one patrilineage (*birinda*). Among close relatives, several houses are usually joined together in one terrace with a common veranda. Since the wall dividing these houses is not closed off at the top, the effect is somewhat like a longhouse and conversations can be held between houses over the dividing wall. In autumn, as the crops are ripening on the hillsides, the villages are largely deserted as people move to widely scattered "baby houses" (*o'onsing*) in order to guard their crops against wild animals. Some people prefer to remain permanently on these sites. Even at the edge of the villages new, freestanding houses are appearing. Houses are solidly built of stone plastered with red mud. Roofs are thatched. Inside there is generally a single room, though the layouts are highly variable.

Economy

Subsistence and Commercial Activities. Sora groups in the plains, such as the Kapu Sora, live by rice cultivation and work much like their caste-Hindu neighbors. In the hills, the only possible rice cultivation is rain-fed and small-scale, so that the population depends largely on shifting cultivation, or slash-and-burn agriculture, on hill slopes. Each year in the hot season (May–June) Sora cut down and burn an area of forest; at the start of the rains (July–August) they sow seeds. The main harvest is from November to February. Shifting cultivation gives a varied diet of gourds, millets, sorghum, wild rice, pulses, and edible leaves, which is both more nutritious and less dependent on rainfall than a diet based almost solely on rice. However, above a certain level of exploitation such cultivation causes irreversible degradation to the soil. This brings Sora into conflict with the Forestry Department, in whom ownership of nonirrigated land is vested. Sora eat most kinds of animals, either domestic animals sacrificed for rites or hunted wild animals. The Sora diet is based on a watery gruel or porridge, with a garnish of vegetables or meat when available. They use few spices and no oil, since cooking is done only by boiling. They drink palm wine and never milk. Tea is used by Christians, who have given up alcohol.

Industrial Arts. Sora manufacture most everyday articles themselves out of trees, leaves, stones, and earth. Houses are built entirely by work parties of friends and relatives. People make their own tools, bows and arrows, and other objects. Although Sora use store-bought aluminum dishes in the house, they stitch together large leaves with splinters of bamboo to form bowls for use outdoors.

Trade. Other necessities are bought in neighboring towns or in weekly markets (_hat_) held at sites where the plains meet the hills. Here, merchants from the plains sell clothing, iron axe heads and plow tips, salt, chilies, and jewelry. Recently the Sora have given up making their own pottery and mats and so now they buy these too. The local Pano population also travels around Sora villages selling soap, tobacco, and other small articles. Individual traders build up long-term relations with particular Sora villages and customers. The most important commodities sold in this way are buffalo for sacrifice, since these can supposedly not be bred in the Sora hills. In return, the Sora sell various millets and forest produce like tamarind, which is in great demand among caste Hindus for curries. The quantities sold are enormous and the prices received are low. The need to keep selling contributes to the ecological degradation of the Sora hills, since cultivation is not simply for subsistence.

Division of Labor. Poorer people work for hire in the fields, but the egalitarian ethos of reciprocal work parties (_onsir_) is strong. The most important specialized occupation is that of the shaman. There are also hereditary lineages of village heads, deputy heads, pyre lighters, and priests of the village deity (_kidtung_). All of these are male except for the occasional village head. The specialist lineages of potters, basket weavers, and blacksmiths have largely abandoned their craft and their customers now buy in the market. But the relations between these lineages and the rest of the population are still strongly expressed during rites. Although they perform conventional tasks, men's and women's roles are not as strictly divided as in many Indian societies and there is no task that cannot be done by either sex without embarrassment (except that women traditionally do not climb trees or play musical instruments). Thus, men can be seen fetching water for the household and women plowing with a team of buffalo. The role of women in ritual is striking: the most important shamans are female, and it is mostly the surrounding women who converse with the souls of the dead when they speak through the shaman in trance.

Land Tenure. Ownership of irrigated rice fields is recognized by law and such fields can be bought and sold. Behind this legalistic concept of land tenure lies another, in which ancestors reside after death in the sites that their descendants cultivate, thereby guaranteeing their heirs' rights. Because irrigated land gives a higher yield for the input of labor, it tends to be owned by relatively wealthy people, who thereby become wealthier. Although non-Sora are legally forbidden to own land in tribal areas, in practice outside traders and moneylenders control much of this land through complex webs of debt, mortgage, and fraud. All households practice shifting cultivation, and poorer households depend on it entirely.

Kinship, Marriage, and Family

Kinship Groups, Descent, Terminology. The basic unit of social organization is the birinda. This is an exogamous patrilineage in which the core of men stay put while women marry out. Parallel cousins within the lineage (father's brother's children) are called "sister" and "brother." Other parallel cousins and all cross cousins are called _maronsel_ (female) and _maronger_ (male). They can also be referred to as "sister" and "brother," implying the impossibility of marriage down to the third generation, after which they again become free to marry. However, there is much flexibility in the interpretation of this. In the Orissa hills, for example, a man's mother's brother is _mamang_ while his wife's father is _kiniar_. The terminology is thus of a North Indian type, resembling Oriya and Bengali in its patterning. In the Telugu plains, by contrast, it follows a South Indian pattern, in which _mama_ means both "mother's brother" and "father-in-law" (male speaking). But even in the Orissa hills, people often marry their cross cousins.

Marriage. In the hills there are two main ways of marrying. Among the wealthier families, who own paddy land, marriage (_sidrung_) may be arranged and a bride-price paid in buffalo or labor. But most marriages are by free choice (_dari_) with no payment. A woman and a man simply set up house together, though this often provokes difficulties with their families. Girls have considerable freedom to initiate relationships. Marriages are unstable in the early years and divorce is common. Marriage becomes more stable as children are born and grow up. Some wealthier men have more than one wife and the second wife is often the younger sister of the first (_aliboj_). If a woman's husband dies, she may marry his younger brother (_erisij_). There is no polyandry.

Domestic Unit. The basic household contains a married couple and their children. Many houses also contain unmarried siblings, aged parents, and sometimes other people's children who have decided to live there temporarily. Where a man has several wives they live together unless they quarrel, in which case he builds them separate houses and divides his time between them. Neighbors are usually very closely related and make quite free with each other's houses. During the season when they live in "baby houses" in the jungle, families are more isolated and live more intimately.

Inheritance. As each son marries he builds his own house. The youngest son stays behind with the parents and inherits the house. A man's irrigated fields, or the right to return to a shifting cultivation plot, are shared equally among his sons. As an ancestor spirit, he will eventually reside in one of these sites. Where there are no sons, they may be inherited by cousins in the closest branch of the lineage. Alternatively, they may be claimed by the lineage of his wife's brother if it is decided that the dead person has gone to reside in one of their plots. Personal possessions are likewise shared out equally. A woman may also have her own fields, provided by her own brothers. This woman's wealth (*keruru*) never passes under her husband's control and is usually inherited by her daughters. Inheritance is symbolized by planting a memorial stone, sacrificing a buffalo, and taking on the dead person's debts.

Socialization. A woman's child is closely associated with her body and only gradually socialized into her husband's lineage. One of the baby's first illnesses is diagnosed as caused by a dead patrilineal ancestor who wishes to give the child his or her name. If the child survives to the age of weaning, about age 3, it receives this ancestor's name in an elaborate rite. Children are carried, played with, and danced. They are rarely if ever struck. Very young children already have responsibility for infants. There are no rites associated with puberty or menstruation, though at that time a girl will start to grow her hair long.

Sociopolitical Organization

Social Organization. A village tends to contain several lineages, so that marriage may be inside or outside the village. A lineage is fixed in space by the sites of its cremation ground and memorial stones. The lineage affiliation of women remains ambiguous far into their married lives. Even after death, they are given a similar funeral by both their husband's and their father's lineage, and questions of inheritance may hinge on which group of ancestors the dead woman now resides with in the Underworld.

Political Organization. The British introduced a system of hereditary village heads (*gomang*) and other office holders. Each of these offices was assigned to a different lineage, and between them they formed the village council (*bisara*). Since Independence, this has been replaced by an elected *panchayat*. This is often dominated by representatives of the local trading castes. The hill Sora have become fully aware of Indian national party politics only during the 1980s. Lacking literacy and political power, they have been largely locked into old patterns of exploitation and intimidation. Younger Sora are learning to read and write their own language. They are also learning to speak Oriya or Telugu and so to dispense with Pano interpreters in their dealings with the government.

Social Control. Public opinion and gossip are important. Persons who are too solitary, greedy, or eccentric may be suspected of sorcery. Social embarrassment sometimes leads to suicide. Police and lawyers are used as weapons by factions who start cases against each other. Police proceedings are referred to by the same words as a sorcery attack. The principles of law and morality are upheld by the dead as they discuss the affairs of the living.

Conflict. The format of debate is pervasive in the old village council and the new panchayat. Both sides may end up shouting their cases, sometimes in a simultaneous monologue. This format is carried over into dialogues with the dead, where both sides argue their opposed cases about family relations, inheritance, and other contentious issues. Physical violence, or its threat, is never far below the surface, especially in conflicts involving the interests of wealthy Soras or the trading castes.

Religion and Expressive Culture

Religious Beliefs. Sora religion has aroused keen interest because of its wide variety of spirits and their importance in daily life. Creator spirits called *kintung* account for the origin of the world and of human society but have little direct effect on the living. The dead discuss their moods and motives with the living through the mouths of shamans in trance.

Religious Practitioners. The most important shamans are women, who achieve their powers through marriage in the Underworld with a high-caste (Kshatriya) Hindu spirit. This husband is the spirit child of the previous shaman. Since this predecessor is usually a patrilineal relative, the spirit husband is therefore a cross cousin and the marriage incestuous. A shaman marries in the Underworld very young. When she subsequently marries a living husband, he often persuades her to give up shamanism and she will not take it up again until middle age.

Ceremonies. Shortly after a death, the deceased is commemorated by planting an upright memorial stone and sacrificing buffalo. Further variants of this are repeated as part of a harvest festival for three years. Some years later, a ceremony celebrates the transmission of the name of the dead person to a new baby. Every time the deceased causes illness among his or her descendants, the living stage a rite to cure the patient. At every stage of existence, the dead person's state of mind is revealed through dialogue with the living.

Arts. The greatest Sora arts are verbal play and improvised song. In addition, the drama of the shaman's trance itself, if one does not believe that the spirits themselves are talking, must be seen as a subtle form of theater. Most ceremonies are accompanied by dancing. Wall paintings are made for spirits. Gold and silver jewelry is obtained from specialist castes in the plains.

Medicine. All illnesses and deaths are believed to be caused by the dead, who thereby repeat the form of their own suffering in another person. In doing this, they attack and eat the soul of their victim. Cure consists in offering the attacker the soul of a sacrificial animal as a substitute. If the spirit accepts this, the patient recovers. But spirits often cheat the living, and patients die. Sora use many amulets and rather fewer herbal remedies. Hospital medicine is used as a backup where available.

Death and Afterlife. Sora do not see "medicine" and the regulation of bodily states as separate from their relations with dead persons. As "spirits" (*sonum*), the dead endure emotional and material deprivation, but at the same time they are powerful causal agents among the living. Elwin portrays the dead as largely jealous and oppressive, but Vitebsky draws attention to their complementary role in granting fertility and social continuity. He distinguishes two aspects of the dead: their role as transmitters of suffering and their role as protective ancestors. He suggests that the drama of dialogues with the dead acts out the complex interplay between these aspects and that the dead may be understood as an objectification of living people's ambivalent memories of those whom they have known. The form in which a dead person affects a living person reflects how that living person remembers him. The sequence of funeral rites modifies the nature of this memory over time.

See also Bondo; Kol; Munda

Bibliography

Dumont, Louis (1959). "Possession and Priesthood." _Contributions to Indian Sociology_ 3:55–74. (Includes a review of Elwin 1955 on pp. 60–74).

Elwin, Verrier (1955). _The Religion of an Indian Tribe._ London and Bombay: Oxford University Press.

Singh, Bhupinder (1984). _The Saora Highlander: Leadership and Development._ Bombay: Somaiya Publications.

Thurston, Edgar, and Kadamki Rangachari (1909). "Savara." In _Castes and Tribes of Southern India._ Vol. 6, 304–347. Madras: Government Press.

Turner, Victor W. (1967). "Aspects of Saora Ritual and Shamanism." In _The Craft of Social Anthropology,_ edited by A. L. Epstein. London: Tavistock.

Vitebsky, Piers (1980). "Birth, Entity, and Responsibility: The Spirit of the Sun in Sora Cosmology." _L'Homme_ 20:47–70.

Vitebsky, Piers (1990). "Interview." In _The Ruffian on the Stair: Reflections on Death,_ edited by Rosemary Dinnage, 38–52. London: Viking.

Vitebsky, Piers (1992). _Dialogues with the Dead: The Discussion of Mortality, Loss, and Continuity among the Sora of Central India._ Cambridge: Cambridge University Press.

Zide, Norman H., ed. (1966). _Studies in Comparative Austroasiatic Linguistics._ The Hague, London, and Paris: Mouton.

PIERS VITEBSKY

Sudra

ETHNONYMS: Shoodra, Shudra, Ṣūdra

The Sudras are the lowest-ranking of the four _varnas_ into which Indian society was traditionally divided; but they are definitely higher in rank than the Untouchables or Panchamas, a category so demeaned in status that it is not even referred to in the classical varna model. Sudras are essentially rural laborers: the classical lawgiver Manu (c. 2nd century A.D.) defined their role as essentially to serve the three higher-ranking varnas. A racial justification for this state of affairs is implied in the earliest Sanskrit writings, which suggested that whereas the three higher varnas were originally the Indo-Aryan invaders, the Sudras were Dāsas, darker-skinned Aborigines (who probably spoke Dravidian languages). If there is any historic truth to this idea, then the Sudras may be viewed as the modern descendants of those who created the Indus (or Harappan) civilization.

Sudras are not entitled to wear a sacred thread, but they have normally been allowed to enter all Hindu temples (something that was not true for Untouchables). Today Sudras commonly are self-employed farmers, but they may also be found in all walks of modern life. They number several hundred million, and they include hundreds of castes in every part of the country.

See also Castes, Hindu; Scheduled Castes and Scheduled Tribes

Bibliography

Hutton, John H. (1963). _Caste in India._ 4th ed. London: Oxford University Press.

PAUL HOCKINGS

Sunwar

ETHNONYMS: Sunbar, Sunuwar, Sunwari

The Sunwar are a group of some 20,000 people located primarily in eastern Nepal. The Sunwar have frequent contact with the Gurung and Magar and are evidently culturally similar to these larger groups. The Sunwar are primarily agriculturalists, growing rice, wheat, and barley in river valleys and maize and millet in the hills. Their patrilineal clans are divided into the endogamous, high-status Bahra Thar and the exogamous, lower-status Das Thar groups. There is some evidence that the Bahra Thar are primarily Lamaist Buddhists and the Das Thar are mostly Hindu, although traditional beliefs of both religions are found in both groups.

Syrian Christian of Kerala

ETHNONYMS: Christians of St. Thomas, Nazarani, Suriyani Christiani

Orientation

Identification.   Syrian Christians live in Kerala State in the southwest corner of India and speak Malayalam, one of the four major Dravidian languages of south India. They can be considered a caste and are endogamous.

Location.   Kerala State lies at the southernmost extremity of the peninsula between 8°18' and 12°48' N and between 74°52' and 77°22' E and stretches along the shores of the

Arabian Sea for a distance of about 576 kilometers. It is a relatively narrow strip of land varying from 120 kilometers at its broadest to around 32 kilometers at certain points in the north and south. Kerala is only 38,863 square kilometers in area, forming distinct regions separated from the adjoining states by the Western Ghats, mountains that run parallel to the sea. The average elevation is 909 meters, with peaks soaring up to 1,800 to 2,400 meters in certain places. The plains are very humid and warm with an average temperature of 85° C. There are two monsoons providing adequate precipitation: the southwest monsoon from mid-June to early September and the northeast monsoon from mid-October to the end of November. The rest of the year is dry with occasional showers.

Demography.   The population of Kerala according to the estimate for 1987 is about 27.6 million, with Christians comprising about 21 percent of the population. In Kerala about 93 percent of the Christians are Syrian Christians; the rest have been converted by European missionaries.

Linguistic Affiliation.   Ninety-six percent of Kerala people speak Malayalam and about 2.37 percent speak Tamil. The latter reside mainly in the border areas adjacent to the state of Tamil Nadu. Those who are on the border of Karnataka State speak Tulu and Kannada. Malayalam was the last language in the Dravidian Group to develop a distinct form and literature. Until the ninth century A.D., Kerala was a part of Tamilakam and the language of the Kerala region was Tamil. Gradually Malayalam came under the influence of Sanskrit and Prakrit with the spread of Aryan influence. Sanskrit words and sentences are freely used in Malayalam. Kerala had its own scripts (*lipis*) from early days. The modern Malayalam script is adopted mainly from the grantha script (book script). Malayalam with its fifty-three letters perhaps expresses by proper marks the most extensive phonology among all the Indian languages. With more than 74 percent literacy, the highest in India, Kerala has developed a wealth of literature unmatched in any other region. The more than forty newspapers are read by intellectuals as well working-class farmers and factory laborers. The best known is *Malayala Manorama* (first published in 1888) with a readership of close to a million, the largest in India.

History and Cultural Relations

Those unfamiliar with the history of Christianity in India are likely to consider it a by-product of Western colonialism. The tradition is that Saint Thomas, the disciple of Jesus Christ, landed in A.D. 52 at Maliankara near Cranganore and preached the gospel. It is believed that he visited different parts of Kerala and converted a good number of local inhabitants, including many from the literate upper-caste Nambudiri Brahmans. It seems that Saint Thomas established churches in seven places in Kerala. The present Christian population claims descent from this early origin, though there has been much scholarly debate over the date of Saint Thomas's arrival. They are popularly known as Syrian Christians in view of the Syriac (classical form of Aramaic) liturgy used in church services since the early days of Christianity in India. They are also known as Nazaranis (followers of Jesus the Nazarene). The survival of the church in Kerala is very much a result of the development of an indigenous character

and adaptation to local traditions. Syrian Christians came to rank after the Brahmans and as equals of the Nayars. The survival of Syrian Christians in Kerala was also a result of the benevolence and tolerance of the rulers in Travancore, Cochin, and Malabar who donated land and helped financially to build churches. The early church received this aid partly because of the favorable impression created by the Christians, who served the rulers in various capacities, as well as respect for the religion. Syrian Christians remained an independent group and continued to get bishops from the Eastern Orthodox church in Antioch in Syria. After the Portuguese arrival in 1498, they gradually established their power and were eager to bring all Christians under the Church of Rome. With superior organizational skill and Portuguese help, Bishop Alexis de Menezes was successful in establishing the Roman Catholic church as the dominant church of the Malabar Coast (Kerala). However, when the Portuguese power declined by the early seventeenth century, the hold of the Roman Catholic church in Kerala weakened, and allegiance to the Syrian Orthodox tradition was reaffirmed in front of an improvised cross at Mattancherry in 1653, an event known as Coonan Kurisu Satyam. At present, Syrian tradition is quite well established, though Roman Catholic church members are more numerous.

Settlements

While most of rural India is a series of discrete villages separated by open fields, in Kerala there are no such concentrations. Instead, houses are scattered over the countryside in a dispersed pattern with some surrounding land intensively cultivated with rice and tropical vegetables and fruit trees. Every 5 to 10 kilometers, there are small and large towns ranging in size from 5,000 to 50,000 inhabitants. There is a railway running from north to south as well as paved roads crisscrossing the state, used for regular bus service run by the state as well as private companies. In the lowland areas, there are rivers, canals, and backwaters providing transport facilities with motor boats and manually operated small and large boats. There are schools, hospitals, and colleges in larger towns. People are conscious of a high level of hygiene; they wear clean clothes, brush their teeth before the first meal, and rinse their mouths after every meal. They bathe once a day or even twice in this humid climate. Towns as well as the countryside are fairly clean and people use private toilets rather than open fields (unlike the rest of rural India). The traditional construction of houses was similar to that of the upper-caste Hindus. The buildings were constructed mostly of wood; teak was commonly used. The front of the house always faced east. Every house had a storage room for rice (paddy). Furnishings were simple: cots were made of wood, and in traditional times, people squatted on the floor on woven palm-leaf mats. Modern houses are brick and of contemporary design, with electricity available to all. The well-to-do have modern amenities including color television.

Economy

Subsistence and Commercial Activities.   Agriculture remains the main occupation and nearly half of the population depends on agriculture, growing a variety of tropical vegetables, fruits, spices, and rice. Animal power is rarely used except for plowing in some rice fields. Bullock carts have mostly been replaced by small and large motorized vehicles. Cattle, buffalo, goats, chickens, and ducks are found in most rural areas. The quality of cattle has improved through interbreeding with Jerseys, resulting in more milk production and better nutrition. With the introduction of white Leghorns (Mediterranean fowls), egg production has multiplied, producing higher income as well as improved nutrition. Christians are leaders in modern education that was introduced by European missionaries in nineteenth century. They also took advantage of the lead given by British planters in the nineteenth century and thus they continue to dominate the plantation economy, owning cardamom, coffee, rubber, and tea plantations. These cash crops have made many Christians affluent. Other communities are emulating the Christians and are also getting actively involved in education and new economic enterprises contributing to the increasing prosperity of Kerala. As there are not enough employment opportunities in Kerala some Christians have moved to other regions and overseas and taken jobs in all professions. Most noteworthy is the near-monopoly Christian women from Kerala have on the nursing profession throughout India. With the rapidly expanding economies of the Middle East oil-producing nations, many Christians discovered all sorts of opportunities. They have also found well-paying jobs in Western countries.

Industrial Arts. There are few large-scale industries in Kerala. However, there are factories (many Syrian Christian-owned) that manufacture tiles and coconut fiber (coir) and process cashew nuts and rubber.

Trade. Many Christians own a variety of small businesses in towns, such as textiles, groceries, stationery, hardware, restaurants, etc. Some bring their farm produce—for example, bananas, pineapples, mangoes, and other tropical fruits—to weekly markets in town. The rest of the cash crops, such as coconut and pepper, are sold through large-scale dealers located in towns. Cashews, cardamom, coffee, tea, and rubber are sold through marketing boards.

Division of Labor. In farming areas, Christians own land and the manual labor is usually done by low-caste Hindus, members of Scheduled Castes, and also a small number of Christians. Men as well as women work in the farming areas. Many work in factories, as laborers, as technicians, on plantations, and in shops in towns, while others work in civil service. At home, men never get involved in household tasks because these are considered women's responsibility.

Land Tenure. Private ownership of land has been a special feature of the system of land tenure in Kerala from ancient times. Absolute ownership of land is known as the _jenmom_ system. Tenancy rights vary depending on the terms and conditions of the lease. Due to the high population density, there is a great shortage of land for individual families. Thus, the Communist party–dominated state government (1957–1958) passed the Kerala Agrarian Relations Bill, fixing a ceiling of about 6 to 10 hectares on family holdings, depending on the size of the family. All excess land is surrendered to the government, which then sells it for a modest price to landless tenants; however, the large plantations are exempted, as large-scale landholdings provide economic advantages for the state. The government has been somewhat successful in redistributing land.

Kinship

Kin Groups and Descent. Syrian Christians do not have the exact equivalent of the Hindu joint family. However, extended families are found in which parents live in the same household with married sons and their families. This is rapidly changing due to modern education. In a 1987 study on changing kinship in Kerala, I found that among the educated middle and upper classes, the majority of married sons have independent households, a situation almost always approved by the parents who themselves are well educated. However, they maintain close ties with lineal and collateral kin and provide financial help where necessary. They get together often to celebrate birthdays and religious festivals. Even so, due to the increasing emphasis on individualism, as a result of modern education, these ties are not as strong as they once were. Fortunately, the general improvement in the standard of living makes it less necessary to be economically dependent on kin. Descent is patrilineal. However, a 1987 Indian supreme court decision successfully challenged the exclusive right of sons to inherit.

Kinship Terminology. Depending on the age and rank of the immediate family members as well as other kin, there are different kin terms used to show respect and even older nonrelatives are addressed similarly to indicate respect.

Marriage and Family

Marriage. Syrian Christians are monogamous and strict community endogamy is maintained. Arranged marriage is still practiced, although prospective spouses are consulted about the marriage proposal. Today, quite a few marriages take place by self-choice and the families simply go through the formalities of arranging the marriages. There are no cross-cousin marriages. As residence is patrilocal, soon after marriage the wife will start living in the husband's house. Whenever they are able to move out to a separate household, they do so; but, if there is only one son in the family, parents may continue to reside with the couple. Divorce is rare due to the Christian tradition of permanent marriage. However, there are a few cases in which women are asserting their individuality by separating from their husbands, especially when they are well educated and not willing to accept a subservient role as housewives. Divorces are not yet statistically significant.

Domestic Unit. Husband, wife, and children constitute a family. Men as a rule take the responsibility of working outside the home and the women's role is primarily in the family home, except for professional women who have an active role outside the home. The nuclear family is now increasingly replacing the two- or three-generation extended family.

Inheritance. Property is traditionally divided among the sons. The youngest son is given the family home where he stays with the parents. However, in view of the recent Indian supreme court decision in favor of equal division of property, the future division of property will change.

Socialization. Both parents have responsibility for disciplining children. Fathers tend to be more strict than mothers. There is less emphasis on physical punishment due to modern education. Girls are more strictly controlled by the parents than the boys. Parents are willing to make a considerable effort to encourage children's education, especially professional education like medicine and engineering where competition for admission to schools is quite keen. Women are quite successful in all professions and compete on equal terms with men.

Sociopolitical Organization

Social Organization. Kerala society like the rest of India is divided into castes. Syrian Christians have enjoyed centuries of tolerance from the majority Hindu community by respecting the endogamous tradition of Hindu castes. They have not even tried to increase their numbers by proselytization. They rank themselves close to the Nayars in the caste hierarchy. It seems that most of the early Christians were converted from upper castes and even today they very rarely intermarry with Christians converted by European missionaries whom they consider inferior in social rank. Roman Catholics and non-Catholics rarely intermarry even if they are Syrian Christians. Non-Catholic Christians never use European names. Their names are Biblical names, as well as some Armenian and Greek names that are prevalent in the Middle East, making them distinctive. Examples of Armenian and Greek names are Kurian, Cherian, Alexander, Stephanos, and Markose.

Political Organization. India has a democratic federal constitution. Kerala was formed in 1956 from the two kingdoms of Travancore and Cochin ruled by maharajas and the district of Malabar in the north. Kerala is divided into districts administered by a collector who, though appointed by the state government, is a federal civil-service official. At the district level there are *taluks*, which are smaller administrative units under a *tahsildar*. Towns with both elected and appointed officials fall within the taluks. At the rural level the administrative unit is the *panchayat* with an elected council and appointed officials. The panchayat is responsible for revenue collection, supervision of the elementary school, medical care and public health, and the development of agriculture, animal husbandry, and cottage industries.

Social Control. Traditional social controls such as community pressure to conform to accepted values are still important. However, informal social control mechanisms are being increasingly replaced by the codified law of the state. Elders are no longer afforded the same level of respect as in the less urbanized times fifty years back. Today there is increasing reliance on the state police and the judiciary to resolve disputes, although the level of individual violence is lower than other states in India partly due to modern education and a sense of tolerance. However, people of Kerala spend an inordinate amount of time and money on long court cases.

Conflict. Kerala has been fortunate to have had a long period of relative peace. The last major war there was the invasion of Tipu Sultan of Mysore at the end of the eighteenth century, which only affected the northern areas of the state. This long history of relative tranquillity also changed the attitude of the people, although the Indian army is an important source of employment today.

Religion and Expressive Culture

Religious Beliefs. Syrian Christians as a community have strong and active religious organizations and a majority of the people attend Sunday church services. The church is divided into various denominations. Those who accept allegiance to the Roman Catholic pope are known as Syrian Roman Catholics. There are Roman Catholics converted by European missionaries known as Latin Roman Catholics. The rest are non-Catholics who are members of the Orthodox Syrian church, Jacobite Syrian church, Marthoma Syrian church, and Church of South India. Roman Catholics which include Latin and Syrian Catholics are 61.4 percent of the Kerala Christians, Syrian Orthodox and Jacobite Syrians are 21.4 percent, Marthoma Syrians 5.7 percent, Church of South India 5.2 percent, and others who are members of various Evangelical churches 6.3 percent. The Church of South India is a Protestant church uniting former Anglicans, Presbyterians, Methodists, and others. Syrian Christians, especially Syrian Orthodox and Jacobite Syrians, use the old Syriac language for their liturgy, as a means of maintaining contact with churches in the Middle East that provided bishops for a long time. Jacobite Syrians still consider the Patriarch of Antioch to be the head of their church. One cannot claim anything special about supernaturals in the context of Christianity. There are some parishes mostly of Roman Catholics, Orthodox Syrians, or Jacobite Syrians where some saints have special importance.

Religious Practitioners. Because the Syrian Christians are divided into several different sects, they have a diversity of priests. Those Catholics who are Romo-Syrians have two bishops assisted by a vicar-general and a council of four. At the parish level they, like all the other sects, have priests. The Latinite Catholics are governed by an archbishop and two bishops. The Jacobite clergy are organized under a metropolitan, and all except him are allowed to marry. The Protestants belong now to the Church of South India, with its own hierarchy of pastors and bishops. The Chaldean Syrians, centered on Trichur, have their own priests.

Ceremonies. Syrian Christians celebrate all Christian religious days. However, among the more orthodox people they maintain Lent for twenty-five days prior to Christmas and fifty days prior to Easter. Those who do so eat only vegetarian meals and refrain from consuming alcoholic beverages. Easter week is very important with special church services on Palm Sunday and also every evening including Good Friday. On Pesaha (Maundy) Thursday there is a special church service with Holy Communion. Good Friday is of great significance and church service starts at 9 a.m. and continues until about 3 p.m., when it is believed that Christ was crucified. On Easter Sunday, the church service starts at 4 a.m. and continues until 6:30 a.m., concluding with Holy Communion. Family members get together for Easter breakfast and break the Lenten fast by eating meat and special bread made for the occasion.

Arts. There are no special art forms at present that are typical of Syrian Christians. However, there used to be singing of folk songs and performance of some folk dances by men. One of them is *margam kali*, which is a kind of dance drama on a Christian theme. Another is *parisa muttu*, which is a martial dance from the time when Christians served in the army of the maharajas.

Medicine. Modern medicine has almost completely displaced traditional indigenous medicine, and there are many Syrian Christian physicians. However, there are some people who continue to learn Ayurveda, the Indian traditional medicine that is still widespread in Kerala.

Death and Afterlife. Many people prefer to bring their critically ill relatives to their family homes where a priest will administer the last rites and last communion. After death, the body is ritually washed, dressed up, and laid on a bed in a large room with lighted candles behind the head of the departed. All close relatives attend and sing hymns and read passages from the Bible. The funeral takes place within twenty-four hours. The body is taken to the church while people sing hymns. After the burial, close relatives and friends come to the house of the deceased for a simple vegetarian meal. In the case of older people like parents, there will be a memorial church service on the fortieth day after death and also an elaborate vegetarian lunch to which all relatives and people in the community are invited.

See also Indian Christians; Malayali

Bibliography

Brown, L. W. (1956). _The Indian Christians of St. Thomas._ Cambridge: Cambridge University Press.

Eapen, K. V. (1985). _Church Missionary Society and Education in Kerala._ Kerala: Kollett Publication.

Kurian, George (1961). _The Indian Family in Transition—A Case Study of Kerala Syrian Christians._ The Hague: Mouton.

Menon, Sreedhara A. (1978). _Cultural Heritage of Kerala: An Introduction._ Cochin: East-West Publications.

Miller, Peter (1988). "India's Unpredictable Kerala, Jewel of the Malabar Coast." _National Geographic_ 173:592–617.

Podipara, Placid J. (1970). _The Thomas Christians._ London: Darton, Longman & Todd.

Potham, S. G. (1963). _The Syrian Christians of Kerala._ Bombay: Asia Publishing House.

Thomas, P. (1954). _Christians and Christianity in India and Pakistan._ London: Allen & Unwin.

Woodcock, George (1967). _Kerala: A Portrait of the Malabar Coast._ London: Faber & Faber.

GEORGE KURIAN

Tamang

ETHNONYMS: Dhamang, Lama, Murmi

The Tamang, numbering some 500,000 in 1985, occupy mountainous regions and the hills surrounding the Kathmandu Valley in midwestern Nepal. The Tamang are composed of patrilineal exogamous clans that are classified into two endogamous status groups: those whose members have intermarried only with Tamangs or Sherpas and those whose members have intermarried with Magars, Gurungs, or Newars. In the mountains where the Tamang are the major ethnic group, they live in settled agricultural villages often subdivided into lineage-based hamlets. In these areas, each clan controls tracts of commonly owned land (_kipat_). The clan also appoints a village headman or tax collector who arbitrates disputes and manages the land. Each village also has one or more shamans (sometimes one for each clan) who conduct rites honoring ancestors and the annual agricultural rite. The Tamang have lamas too, with endogamous marriage to daughters of lamas preferred but not always practiced. Larger villages often have a Buddhist temple and perhaps a monastery. In the hills around the Kathmandu Valley, the Tamang are best described as a lower caste who work as tenant farmers, porters, and day laborers for the Pahari and Newar while retaining their Buddhist beliefs and practices.

See also Nepali; Nyinba

Bibliography

Fürer-Haimendorf, Christoph von (1956). "Ethnographic Notes on the Tamangs of Nepal." _Eastern Anthropologist_ 9:166–177.

Tamil

ETHNONYMS: Tamilar, Tamilian

Orientation

Identification. Indian Tamils are those who speak Tamil. Their homeland in India from ancient times was known as "Tamil Nāḍu" (land) or "Tamil akam" (home), now largely coterminous with the state of Tamil Nadu plus the small territory of Pondicherry. Tamils are also found in Sri Lanka, Malaysia, Fiji, Britain, and North America.

Location. Tamil Nadu is the southwesternmost state of India, extending from Madras city to the southern cape, between about 8° and 13° N and 76° and 80° E. The state is 130,058 square kilometers in area and was formed along with other linguistic states after the independence of India. It is mostly a sunny plain draining eastward with the Kaveri River basin in its center. The Western Ghats are mountains separating Tamil Nadu from Kerala; these rise to 2,400 meters in two places, near the mountain towns of Ootacamund and Kodaikanal. The rest of the state is tropical and moderately hot, with virtually no winter. Most of the rain comes with the northeast monsoon beginning in October, while the southwest monsoon begins in June. Rainfall is roughly 75 centimeters per year, but with the high evaporation and runoff, much of the state is semiarid, with large stretches of thorn-tree wasteland. There is no apparent source of more water for the state's agriculture, industry, and cities—nor is there enough water to support further population growth—and shortages are already occurring.

Demography.   There are about 60 million Indian Tamils. The 1991 census counted 55.6 million persons in Tamil Nadu and 8 million in Pondicherry, and it had an undercount of about 4 percent. There are perhaps 5 million Tamils around Bangalore and elsewhere in India, and a lesser number of Telugus and other ethnic groups in Tamil Nadu. The state has 1,024 males per 1,000 females, a marginal surplus compared with all of India. The density is 461 persons per square kilometer, compared with 267 for India as a whole. Literacy of persons above age 7 is 64 percent. Annual population growth has come down to 1.3 percent. Tamils are about 38 percent urban, the highest such percentage of any major ethnic group in India.

Linguistic Affiliation.   Tamil belongs to the Dravidian Language Stock, which includes at least 21 languages mostly in south and central India and is altogether different from the Indo-Aryan languages of north India. The four largest Dravidian languages are spoken in the four linguistic states comprising south India. The language and script of modern Tamil are directly descended from the Tamil of more than 2,000 years ago, and because of high consciousness about the purity of the language there has been some tendency to resist incorporation of Sanskrit or Hindi words. The modern regional spoken dialects of Tamil, including the Tamil of Sri Lanka, do not differ widely, but standard literary Tamil as taught in schools does differ grammatically. Malayalam, the language of Kerala, was considered in the ancient literature as Tamil, but in medieval centuries it gained status as a separate language.

History and Cultural Relations.   Tamils consider their language to be the "most pure" of the major Dravidian languages. Its roots are from western India, Pakistan, and further westward. Dravidian must have been spoken in the Indus Civilization around 2500 B.C., diffusing through Maharashtra to the south, especially after 1000 B.C. with adoption of the horse and iron and with the black-and-red pottery dating from a few centuries B.C. There is no hint of the earlier languages that might have been spoken in south India by cattle-keeping cultures or the hunters. The ancient literature defines Tamil Nadu as reaching from Tirupati (a sacred hill northwest of Madras) to Cape Comorin. Writing, urbanization, classical kingship, and other aspects of complex Indian civilization came to Tamil Nadu about the fifth to second centuries B.C. by sea, appearing on the southern coast in a progression parallel to diffusion of those features from Gujarat to Sri Lanka. There are also legends of early cities, including an ancient city of Madurai on the coast. The earliest Tamil inscriptions are in Buddhist and Jain caves of about the second century B.C. The present Madurai, capital of the enduring Pāṇḍiya kingdom, had an academy that produced the Tamil

Sangam literature, a corpus of unique poetical books from the first to third centuries A.D. that mention sea trade with Europeans. Other Tamil kingdoms were the Cōḷas in the Kaveri Basin, the Cēras of Kerala, and from the seventh to ninth centuries the Pallavas at Kanchipuram near Madras. The Cōḷas developed a magnificent civilization in the tenth to thirteenth centuries, and for a time they ruled Sri Lanka, the Maldives, and large parts of Indonesia. Tamils were never absorbed by a north Indian kingdom, but from the sixteenth century the land was ruled by Telugu-speaking dynasties from the Vijayanagar Empire. The British built a trading center, Fort Saint George, in Madras in 1639 and ruled all Tamil Nadu from 1801 to 1947. The French, having lost to the British in south India, held Pondicherry and Karikal, now administered as a separate Union Territory within India. The process of Sanskritization, partial assimilation into the overarching Indian pattern of civilization, progressed in late medieval centuries. But in the twentieth century the tendency has been to reject features ascribed to north India and to reemphasize Tamil identity in language, deities, foods, and state politics.

Settlements

The predominant settlement pattern is one of nucleated unwalled villages, often having 2,000 persons or even more than 5,000, while traditionally retaining a village character. The layout usually has well-defined streets, with sections for separate castes, each marked by one or more little temples for their respective deities. House types range from one-room huts of mud and coconut-leaf thatch of the laboring and low castes to larger houses with courtyards and two-story brick and tile houses of the higher castes or landowning families. Tamil villages look relatively neat, with most houses whitewashed. Early each morning the women of a house apply cowdung wash on the street before the front door and create a pattern design on the ground with chalklike powder. A large village usually has several open wells, one large temple, a common threshing floor with big trees, a piece of land or two for cremation or burials, and in many cases a catchment reservoir for irrigating its rice land. Now nearly all villages have electricity, but only a minority of houses use it.

Economy

Subsistence and Commercial Activities.   Land is classified into wet land growing mostly irrigated rice and dry land growing rain-fed or well-watered crops. Large irrigation systems were built from at least the second century B.C., especially on the Kaveri River, and there was an elaborate political economy supporting agricultural productivity especially developed by the medieval Cōḷas. The kings also built catchment reservoirs for growing rice and gave them to the villages to maintain, as recorded in temple inscriptions; there are 40,000 such reservoirs in Tamil Nadu. The main field crops are rice, pearl millet and several other millets, sorghum, several types of pulses and oilseeds, coconuts, bananas, Indian vegetables, and condiments. Mango and tamarind trees abound. The oxen plow and harrow, pull ox carts, draw buckets of irrigation water, and turn oilseed presses, while cows yield milk that is given to children and made into curds and buttermilk. A village may have chickens, buffalo, goats, sheep, and donkeys that carry the washers' clothes. Fishing castes occupy the long coast. Money was issued by ancient kings so there is a long tradition of moneylending, capitalism, and overseas trade; rural economic transactions became monetized in the nineteenth century. Since the 1960s farmers have installed many thousands of electric irrigation pumps and have taken up commercial crops such as sugarcane, cotton, and peanuts. But now agricultural growth is beginning to lag compared with industries and urbanization.

Industrial Arts. Artisan castes still make fine products of clay, leather, reeds, cotton, wood, iron, brass, silver, and gold. Ox carts are sturdy and still numerous. Tamils are known for their fine weaving, which even the ancient Romans imported, and today they have the most successful handweavers' cooperatives in India, though power looms are taking over. Great brass water vessels are given at weddings, though plastics are becoming popular. Bricks, roofing tiles, cement artifacts, and wooden furniture are now in demand everywhere.

Trade. The streets of large villages and towns are lined with shops, and there are still many weekly markets. Complex networks of wholesalers, agents, and financiers deal with all types of products. Now auctions are common for moving produce, and the trucking industry is intensively developed. Muslim traders are prominent in trade.

Division of Labor. Men plow, harrow, and handle the rice harvest, but women do transplanting and weeding for which their daily wage is less than that of men, and they may also milk cows. Tools of trade such as an ox cart, potter's wheel, fishing net, or nowadays a taxi are not handled by women. Women do kitchen work, cleaning, washing, and child care, but men may also do all these tasks, and professional cooks and washers are men. Women now may be teachers, nurses, and office employees.

Land Tenure. Landownership is well established with a system of official recording. Agricultural land is increasingly held by dominant farmer castes, while every village has its cadre of landless low-caste laborers available for fieldwork. There are few estates of great landowners, though temples and mosques still own some land for income. Sharecropping and tenancy are moderate, simply part of the socioeconomic dynamics. Because of population pressure and speculation, in many areas the market value of land now exceeds its productive economic value.

Kinship

Kin Groups and Descent. The Dravidian kinship system with its preference for cross-cousin marriage has been the subject of wide anthropological theorizing. The household is linked by a network of kin alliances established through marriage within the caste. Fictitious exogamous clans (*gotras*) are found in only a few Brahmanized castes. Lineage depth beyond three generations is not important in most families. Most Indian Tamils are patrilineal and patrilocal, though the Dravidian system equally accommodates matrilineal descent as among some Sri Lanka Tamils, including Muslims, and some castes in Kerala. But patriliny is less strong than in north India, and matrilateral links remain important. A woman is expected to go to her natal home for childbirth, especially for the first child, and may remain there for a few months for nurturance and to gain confidence and training in infant care.

Kinship Terminology. For a male, all females are classified as sister (or parallel cousin, unmarriageable) or as female cross cousin (marriageable). The preferred marriage for a male is generally to his mother's brother's daughter, while in some groups his father's sister's daughter and his own elder's sister's daughter are also quite acceptable, as are more distant cognates classifiable as female cross cousins. Kin terms are few compared with north Indian languages; for example, *māman* is wife's father/father-in-law, mother's brother (who may be the same person), and father of any female cross cousin or anyone so classified. For a man, *makan* is own son, brother's son, and son's male parallel cousin. Terms distinguish between elder and younger siblings, or those so classified, and between some elder and younger siblings of the parents, or those so classified. Some classical scholars tried to force explanations in terms of the north Indian system and Indo-Aryan languages, in which the bride's family is wife giver and hypergamy is built-in, but this misses the essence of the Dravidian system. About half of Tamil marriages now are between such kin, but the categories are so strongly maintained in the language that the kinship pattern is imposed on all interpersonal relations. This has been structurally analyzed by anthropologists. Louis Dumont sees it as essentially a matter of affinities established by marriage, in which women are exchanged among families that define the kin network; this has political and economic implications. Others see it as essentially a system of marriage rules that is an ideal or a mental representation. Still others have tried to explain it in terms of heritable body substances and biological ideas. The system has also been analyzed in terms of Freudian psychology: a man will want a marriage union enabling him to continue the warmth and protection of his mother, namely, through his mother's brother together with his daughter. For Tamils, as Thomas Trautman and others show, the whole conceptual structure is as much in the language as in the actual behavior. A recent approach proposed by Margaret Trawick is that the pattern itself is something like an art form that is perpetuated as any form of expressive culture; moreover, it creates longings that can never be fulfilled, and so it becomes a web of unrelieved tensions and an architecture of conflicting desires that are fundamental in the interpersonal relationships of Tamils.

Marriage and Family

Marriage. Marriages are arranged by elders, ideally by a sister and brother for their respective son and daughter. A girl is technically able to marry soon after the ceremony of her first menstruation, but now her marriage may be postponed a few years, and boys often do not marry until their twenties. The marriage is performed by a Brahman priest or by a caste priest in the home of the bride. Her family bears expenses and provides a modest dowry, though in some castes there is more bride-wealth given than dowry. Recently among educated classes the expectation of dowry has vastly increased, in line with the costs of education and the presumed benefits of the marriage for the girl and her family. Ideally a married couple sets up its own house, usually in the boy's village, but if necessary they may move in with the boy's or alternatively the girl's family until this is possible. Marriage is a religious ceremony and only a few register it with the state. Divorce is quite difficult for higher castes with strict social expectations, but separation and new alliances or marriages are common among castes whose prestige is not so damaged thereby. Widow remarriage is forbidden or rare among castes having Brahmanic values, but not among lower castes.

Domestic Unit. The average household size is five to six people, with preference for an extended nuclear family. It is not unusual for an old person or couple to live alone, especially if they have few assets. Occasionally there are joint families when there is land or a business to keep intact. Most influential families also have a live-in servant or servant family. When Tamil men migrate to a city for work, they try to take their wives and children along, so there is not a severe deficit of females in Tamil cities, but this means that urbanized families find their rural roots weakening.

Inheritance. Under Tamil Hindu tradition, sons divide the land because they may live by cultivating it, and daughters get the mother's gold and jewels either as dowry or as inheritance, but there are many exceptions and people can arrange their own wills.

Socialization. Tamils are a child-friendly society, and they socialize children so that they grow up with a firm sense of well-being. There is less tension than in many societies, and hospitality is often genuine. Men and women play with small children easily, pass them around, and may take in relatives' children temporarily or even adopt them. Several male gods have important child forms whose pictures are in houses everywhere, and Tamil literature creates abundant images of children. Toilet training is early and seemingly natural, with little use of diapers. The first rice is fed at about 6 months, and weaning is sudden after a year or so. Giving of food is important in relationships, and a mother may feed rice with her hand to a child up to the age of 6 or more. Adults frequently treat children with benevolent deceit and verbal ambiguity, and within the dynamic family context the child learns a wide range of verbal and emotional expression and body language. Children of school age are occasionally punished by tweaking of the ear or beatings given by the father. Girls are expected to help in household work as soon as they are able, and boys not in school may do agricultural activities or herd animals from about age 10. Most villages have their own elementary schools, and many now have middle schools also, so most children now become literate. There are no initiation rites except for high-caste boys at the time they put on the Brahmanic sacred thread. Girls have an important life-stage ceremony at the time of their first menstruation; a feast is given to relatives and friends, who bring presents. At this time the girl puts on a sari and is technically marriageable. This ceremony is found associated with the Dravidian kinship and marriage system.

Sociopolitical Organization

Social Organization. Within a village, society is ordered principally by caste. Particular castes or blocks of castes occupy sectors of a village, with the ritually lowest castes sometimes in satellite hamlets. Large villages or towns may have a Brahman street with a temple at the end, formerly off-limits to low castes, and in the past Brahmans would generally avoid eating food not prepared at home. Ritual pollution and purity differentiate a wide range of human interaction, though not as strongly as in the nineteenth century and hardly at all now in public life in towns. Village coffee shops until the 1980s had benches for middle castes, low seats for the low laboring castes, and places on the floor for the lowest sweeper caste; there were separate cups for these three groups. Now rank by caste ascription is slightly declining even in villages, while the more numerous agricultural castes are increasing their landholdings and using elections to enhance their political power. Brahmans have for decades used their education to enter urban life, while many landless laboring caste people also have migrated to cities for urban labor and service jobs. The urban educated class and government officers utilize English to preserve their power and privileges, so now even in small towns many Tamils are demanding that schools offer English-medium education for their children.

Political Organization. Traditionally many castes, or the larger ones, had caste *panchayats* (councils) that enforced caste behavioral norms, and sometimes there were informal village panchayats. In recent decades the state government has set up elected village panchayats, which were supposed to take over village government and development. But these have been neglected because state politicians tended to view them as threatening. Statewide political parties competing for people's votes have infiltrated most rural institutions, and in the main members of state-level parties espousing Dravidian identity are elected. Dominant and landholding families manage to enhance their economic and political power through these new mechanisms, while the relative position of the laboring and low castes remains about the same as before.

Social Control. Sources of tension in a village are family and caste norms of behavior, caste differences, and disputes over land. Caste or village elders can pronounce embarrassing punishment for violators of behavioral norms, particularly in sexual matters. Caste conflicts sometimes erupt over scarce resources, such as the rights of certain castes to use wells in time of water scarcity. Families basing prestige on land may engage in long litigation. An individual who feels wronged may wield a sickle against another, which may be occasion to call the police. The lowest administrative level is the *taluk*, usually centered in a particular town, with offices for police, land registration, and electricity supply, a local court, and usually high schools for boys and girls. The second level of administration is the district, of which there are twenty in Tamil Nadu; as throughout India, the district is headed by a collector, who has wide powers. The third level is the state, with Madras as its capital.

Conflict. Tamils have no destructive conflict with adjacent linguistic or ethnic groups, nor do Hindus have much conflict with the 6 percent Christian and 5 percent Muslim Tamil minorities. They tend to sympathize with the Sri Lanka Tamils in their struggle for political autonomy or independence. Tamils are suspicious of the overwhelming numbers and political power of north Indians and resent any attempts to "impose" Hindi on them, so Tamil Nadu does not require teaching of Hindi in schools. English is in fact favored over Hindi. The modern political system with its elections has provided a new arena for verbal conflict.

Religion and Expressive Culture

Religious Beliefs. Village Hinduism is vibrant, as are the imposing, large, and ancient temples in the center of all the old towns. Village beliefs are focused on a large number of deities, with most castes or social groups claiming a special deity. Female deities are more numerous and are worshiped for their power to intervene in healing, fertility, and other life situations. Male deities are protectors and dominate the landscape, especially Murugan, whose image stands on many stone hillocks and especially on Palani Hill, where people make special pilgrimages to him as protector of Tamil Nadu. By the process of Sanskritization over many centuries, most local deities acquired linkage with Sanskritic or Brahmanic deities. Among Brahman castes the distinctions between the sects of Shiva and Vishnu are maintained, but not always in village religion. It is very common that a person needing assistance of the power of the deity to solve some problem in life will make a vow to bend the will of the deity; for example, one may promise that if one's son passes his examination, if a disease is cured, or if an infertile woman gives birth, one will undertake some pilgrimage or make some gift to the deity. Tamil Catholics make similar vows. There is a strong stream of devotionalism (*bhakti*) in Hindu literature and in the practice of modern Hindus, Christians, and Muslims.

Ceremonies. Among the most important religious events in villages are the birthdays of the special deities, which are celebrated with processions in which the deity is taken from the temple and carried around the village and with night entertainment performances. Festival days of the deities of major temples, as of Madurai or Palani, are regional Tamil festivals in which hundreds of thousands of pilgrims throng those places. Pongal is a distinctive Tamil festival, in which kin groups boil rice in front of their special temple and eat it communally. This occurs in January, along with Māṭṭu Pongal, in which oxen are honored, their horns painted red and green, and garlanded. North Indian festivals such as Holi and Dassara are far less important, though Tamils celebrate Dīpāvali (Diwali), the festival of lights. The Tamil New Year is widely celebrated, in mid-April.

Arts. South Indian music, dance, and architecture were enhanced in Tamil Nadu in late medieval centuries by royal patronage, while north India was under the Moguls. There is no question that Bharatanāṭyam dance, preserved in the temples, along with south Indian classical instrumental and vocal music, are among the highest classical art forms anywhere; they are far too complex to discuss here. Tamil temples, immediately distinguishable by the soaring towers (*gōpuram*) above the gateways, are imposing living institutions. Large temples have tanks, thousand-pillared halls of stone, passages for circumambulating the deity, and an infinite number of sculpted images and figures, all done according to ancient architectural rule books. In villages today, troupes are commissioned to perform all-night musical narrations of epics such as the Tamil version of the *Rāmāyaṇa*, itinerant drama troupes are popular, and there may be magician entertainers, transvestite dancers, and fortune-tellers.

Medicine. The medical systems are: Ayurveda, based on Sanskrit texts; Siddha, a south Indian system using strong chemicals and herbs; Unani, the Muslim system; and Mantiravāti, the use of magical phrases (mantras) and herbal medicine that are found in villages everywhere, whose practitioners also prepare amulets many people use to ward off disease. Allopathic (scientific) medicine is available in towns in government hospitals and private clinics. Disease etiology may be analyzed as multiple, with proximate and ultimate causes. There are multiple possible cures including herbs, medicines, mantras, diet, psychological change, and divine intervention. Tamils believe that bodily qualities should be in balance, and they classify foods as "hot" or "cold." Vegetarianism is widely practiced by upper and middle castes on grounds of both religion and health.

Death and Afterlife. The doctrine of rebirth is not actively held by the majority of Tamils, though those who tend to orthodoxy are likely to assert that the doctrine is taught. But according to an old belief or longing, a child who dies has a soul that will be reborn in the same household, and therefore on death burial may be under or near the home. Many Tamil castes bury their dead, but those influenced by Brahmanic tradition cremate them. At a burial in a middle-rank caste, the corpse is wrapped in a cloth and lowered into the grave, whereupon the male relatives carrying pots of water circumambulate the grave counterclockwise (an inauspicious direction), then break their clay pots in the grave, while the women stand by watching. Death pollution lasts for a number of days that varies by caste; after that the house is cleansed and there is special food. For an important man, a brick structure may mark the grave, and there is an annual ceremony of offering food on the death anniversary.

See also Labbai; Tamil of Sri Lanka; Vellala

Bibliography

Clothey, Fred (1978). *The Many Faces of Murukan: The History and Meaning of a South Indian God*. The Hague: Mouton.

Daniel, E. Valentine (1987). *Fluid Signs: Being a Person the Tamil Way*. Berkeley: University of California Press.

Dumont, Louis (1983). *Affinity as Value: Marriage Alliance in South India, with Comparative Essays on Australia*. Chicago: University of Chicago Press.

Dumont, Louis (1986). *A South Indian Subcaste*. Delhi: Oxford University Press.

Trautmann, Thomas R. (1981). *Dravidian Kinship*. Cambridge: Cambridge University Press.

Trawick, Margaret (1990). *Notes on Love in a Tamil Family*. Berkeley: University of California Press.

Wadley, Susan, ed. (1980). *The Powers of Tamil Women*. South Asian Series, no. 6. Syracuse, N.Y.: Syracuse University.

CLARENCE MALONEY

Tamil of Sri Lanka

Orientation

Identification.   Linguistically and culturally related to the Tamil- and Malayalam-speaking peoples of southern India, Sri Lankan Tamils have long resided in their traditional homelands (the northern and eastern cultural regions of Sri Lanka), and interacted with the neighboring Sinhalese. The products of their unique geographical and historical circumstances are a distinct culture and society. Predominantly Hindus, Sri Lankan Tamils call their traditional homelands Tamil Eelam, a term that originally meant "Tamil Sri Lanka" but has now become virtually synonymous with the Tamils' quest for a separate state in the predominantly Tamil-speaking Northeastern Province. Sri Lankan Tamils distinguish themselves from the so-called "Indian Tamils," who are Tamil-speaking descendants of south Indian Tamil laborers brought to Sri Lanka to work nineteenth-century British tea plantations, as well as from the indigenous, Tamil-speaking Muslim population of Sri Lanka, the Sri Lankan Moors, who dwell in the eastern coastal region and in the central highlands.

Location.   Sri Lanka is located between 5°55' and 9°51' N and 79°41' and 81°53' E. Sri Lankan Tamils traditionally made their homes within the present Northern and Eastern provinces of Sri Lanka, within the dry zone. The center of Sri Lankan Tamil population and culture is the densely populated Jaffna Peninsula of the extreme north; other Tamil population concentrations are found on the island of Mannar and along the eastern coastal littoral, stretching from north of Trincomalee to Batticaloa. In recent times, many Sri Lankan Tamils have migrated to the North Central Province and to Colombo; almost half the Sri Lankan Tamil population dwells outside the group's traditional homelands. Significant overseas communities of Sri Lankan Tamils in London, Australia, and Malaysia maintain close ties with families back home; foreign remittances are a significant element in the Sri Lankan Tamil economy.

Demography.   In 1989 the population of Sri Lanka was estimated at 17,541,000, with an average population density of 252 persons per square kilometer and a growth rate of 1.8 percent per year. Sri Lankan Tamils constitute approximately 11 percent of the island's population. Many—perhaps as much as 60 percent of the population—are refugees from nearly a decade of fighting.

Linguistic Affiliation.   The Tamil spoken by Sri Lankan Tamils is a distinct regional dialect of mainland Tamil, but the two are mutually intelligible; Sri Lankan Tamils consider their dialect to be purer than that of the mainland. They fear that their language's survival is threatened by a Sri Lankan government that, in 1956, made Sinhala the sole official language of government affairs and, in 1973, elevated Sinhala to the status of the national language. Although subsequent measures were taken to allow for the legitimate administrative and educational use of Tamil within the predominantly Tamil areas and Tamil was also made a national language by the 1978 constitution, Tamils nevertheless believe that Tamil speakers are subject to rampant discrimination and cannot effectively participate in Sri Lanka's national affairs.

History and Cultural Relations

The unique culture of Sri Lankan Tamils took on distinctiveness early from its close proximity to the Sinhalese and from waves of immigration from diverse regions of southern India. Many features of Sri Lankan Tamil culture, including village settlement patterns, inheritance and kinship customs, and domestic and village "folk religion," stand in sharp contrast to mainland Tamil customs. One possible reason is that the immigrants who created the first Tamil settlements in Sri Lanka appear to have come not just from the Tamil region of south India but from the Kerala coast as well. It is not known when Tamils first settled in Sri Lanka; fishing folk doubtless visited the coasts, seasonally or permanently, from an early date, either for their own fishing needs or to engage in the pearl trade between Sri Lanka and Rome. During the period of the classical Sinhala dry zone civilizations (about the first twelve centuries A.D.), there is evidence that Tamil-speaking Buddhist merchants settled widely in the northern and eastern seacoast regions, where they built towns and shrines. By the thirteenth century, in the wake of the collapse of the Sinhalese dry zone civilizations, a Tamil Hindu kingdom arose in the Jaffna Peninsula, with a Hindu king and a palace. The Portuguese subdued the Hindu king in 1619, and as their geographic control was only over the coastal region, they left their legacy in coastal Catholic communities that persist today. In 1658, the Dutch followed the Portuguese. The Dutch codified the traditional legal system of Jaffna, but in such a way that they interpreted indigenous caste customs in line with Roman-Dutch definitions of slavery. Taking advantage of the situation, agriculturalists of the dominant Vellala caste turned to cash-crop agriculture using Pallar slaves brought from southern India, and Jaffna soon became one of the most lucrative sources of revenue in the entire Dutch colonial empire. In 1796, the British expelled the Dutch from the island. During the first four decades of British rule, few changes were made with the exception of granting freedom of religious affiliation and worship, a move that was deeply appreciated by the Tamil population. Slavery was abolished in 1844, but the change in legal status brought few meaningful changes to the status of Pallar and other low-caste laborers. More threatening to the structure of Tamil society was a sedulous conversion campaign by Christian missionaries, who built within the Tamil areas (especially Jaffna) what is generally considered to be the finest system of English-language schools to be found in all of Asia during the nineteenth century. In response to a tide of Christian conversions, Arumuka Navalar (1822–1879), a Hindu religious leader, reformulated Hinduism in line with austere religious texts so that it omitted many practices Christian missionaries had criticized as "barbarous," such as animal sacrifice. Navalar's movement was resented by many Hindus who felt that sacrifice and other practices were necessary, but his reformed Hinduism stemmed the tide of Christian conversions and gave educated Hindus access to a textual tradition of Saivism (called Saiva Siddhanta) that gave them pride in their religious traditions. Benefiting from the missionaries' English-language schools without converting to Christianity, many Sri Lankan Tamils (except those of low caste) turned away from agriculture—which became far less lucrative as the nineteenth century advanced—and toward government employment in the rapidly expanding British colonial empire. In this adaptation to foreign rule, an accommodative, utilitarian culture arose that stressed rigorous study in professional fields, such as medicine, law, and engineering, together with staunch adherence to Hindu tradition. Family support of educational achievement led to extraordinary success in the British meritocracy but to disaster later: after Sri Lanka's independence in 1948, many Sinhalese came to feel that Tamils were disproportionately present in Sri Lanka's esteemed civil service, professions, judiciary, and business affairs. In 1956, S. W. R. D. Bandaranaike won a massive electoral victory by appealing to these sentiments and promising to implement Sinhala as the sole official language of government affairs. Tensions over the language act led to the appalling 1958 riots, in which Sinhalese mobs attacked Tamils living in Sinhalese areas. The subsequent imposition of university and employment quotas radicalized Tamil youths; the first Tamil youth organizations included many unemployed graduates. In 1974, the Tamil political parties unified and called for the peaceful creation, though negotiation, of a separate Tamil state in the Northern and Eastern provinces, but largely because the Colombo government made few concessions and political moderates seemed content to wait the situation out, Tamil youths rejected their elders' politics and began a wave of violent assassinations, mainly aimed at Tamils who were suspected of collaborating with Sinhalese organizations. In 1981, Sinhalese security forces went on a brutal rampage in Jaffna, burning down Jaffna's library and terrorizing the population, which came to the conclusion that only the youth groups could protect them. The 1983 Colombo riots, which appeared to have the unofficial guidance and support of some sections of the government, effectively eliminated the Tamil business presence in Colombo and throughout the Sinhalese sections of the island, which further radicalized the Tamil people. After almost a decade of violence, the Colombo government has yet to make genuine concessions to the Tamil community and apparently believes the Tamil militants can be defeated by force. In the meantime, many Tamils have become refugees, hundreds of temples and schools have been destroyed, the Tamil middle class and intelligentsia have fled abroad, and tens of thousands of innocents have died, often in massacres of unspeakable brutality.

Settlements

Sri Lankan Tamil regions are predominantly rural; even the towns seem like overgrown villages. The rural-urban balance has not changed significantly in this century, thanks to Sri Lanka's vigorous rural social service program and to an almost complete lack of industrial development. Traditional villages are nonnucleated and are internally differentiated by hamlets, in which members of a single caste reside. The only obvious center of the village is the temple of the village goddess. Lanes wander chaotically through the village, and homes are hidden behind stout, living fences (trees), which provide copious green manure for gardens. Land is traditionally divided into three categories: house land, garden land, and paddy land. Traditional houses are made of mud and thatch; wealthier villagers construct stucco houses roofed with ceramic tiles. Houses are situated within a private, fenced, almost secretive compound, which is usually planted with mangoes, coconut palms, and palmyras.

Economy

Subsistence and Agricultural Activities. Subsistence agriculture, supplemented by marginal employment, characterizes the economic life of most rural Sri Lankan Tamils. A significant source of income for many families today is foreign remittances. Save in the eastern coastal region, where irrigation produces high rice yields, rice agriculture in Tamil areas is extensive but rainfall-dependent and only marginally economic at best. Under import restrictions following Sri Lanka's independence, Jaffna became a major source of garden crops, including tomatoes, chilies, onions, tobacco, gourds, pumpkins, okra, _brinjal_ (eggplants), betel, potatoes, manioc, and a variety of grams and pulses. Traditional agricultural practices make intensive use of green and animal manures, although the use of chemical fertilizers and pesticides is increasingly common. In coastal regions with limestone bedrock (and particularly in Jaffna), groundwater is intensively used to supplement rainfall; irrigation is rare, save in the eastern coastal region. Domestic animals include cattle and chickens. Significant foods of last recourse include manioc and the ubiquitous palmyra, which supplies starch from seedlings, molasses, jam, and a mildly alcoholic beverage called toddy. Rapid growth in the service section (especially retailing, transport, communications, banking, public administration, education, health services, repair, and construction) has created significant new employment opportunities.

Industrial Arts. Some members of the artisan castes (goldsmiths, blacksmiths, carpenters, potters, and temple builders) still create traditional goods, such as jewelry, ox carts, hoes, and cooking pots, although such goods face stiff competition from industrially manufactured plastic and aluminum goods, so that traditional goods are increasingly used only for ceremonial purposes. Very few industrial enterprises are located in Tamil regions, with the exception of the state-owned cement factory at Kankesanthurai along the northern coast, the chemical factory at Paranthan, and a paper factory at Valaichenei in the east. Private-sector ventures include manufacturing or assembly of garments, toys, candies, bottled juices, and soap. But indigenous goods are regarded as shoddy and receive stiff competition from imports and rampant smuggling.

Trade. The rural economy is thoroughly cash-based. Village boutique owners and wealthy villagers often engage other more impecunious villagers in what eventually becomes debt servitude. Shops in town sell needed consumer items, and weekly village markets provide marginal economic niches for itinerant traders and village cash-crop agriculturalists. Transport is provided by bullock carts, tractors pulling flatbed trailers, old automobiles, light trucks, and the ubiquitous Ceylon Transit Board (CTB), the nation's bus service.

Division of Labor. Traditional Sri Lankan Tamil society is male-dominated and patriarchal, with a strong division of labor by sex, arranged marriages, and a tendency to demean female roles. Female seclusion is a concomitant of family status, thus discouraging women from travel or work without a constant chaperone. However, significant new employment and educational opportunities for women cause many families to moderate the traditional division of labor as they seek additional income. In general, women are responsible for domestic affairs while men work outside the home in agriculture, transport, industry, services, and government.

Land Tenure.   Land is held outright but holdings tend to be both minute and geographically fragmented. Bilateral inheritance, coupled with population increase, compounds subdivision. Landlessness is increasingly common and delays or prevents marriage because traditional dowry customs require the married pair to be given lands and a house.

Kinship

Kin Groups and Descent.   The largest kin group is the "microcaste" (called "our caste people" in Tamil), a section of a larger caste category within which people recognize common descent and a shared status. The microcaste is often distributed among several hamlets or wards in adjoining (or in some cases separated) villages; within the hamlet microcaste members cooperate in agriculture, ritual, trade, and politics. In sharp contrast to south Indian Tamil culture, descent is fully bilateral, save in the eastern coastal regions, where matrilineal descent is common.

Kinship Terminology.   Dravidian terms, which strongly encourage symmetrical cross-cousin marriage, are used.

Marriage and Family

Marriage.   Marriages among the "respectable" castes are arranged by parents and are accompanied by a large dowry—which, again in sharp contrast to the mainland Tamil pattern, includes lands and a house as well as movables and cash. Boys are expected to delay marriage so that they can help their parents accumulate enough wealth to marry off their sisters. A girl is technically eligible to marry after puberty but marriages are increasingly delayed, often into a woman's mid- to late twenties, owing to the difficulties involved in assembling the dowry and finding a suitable groom. The ideal groom is an educated, English-speaking, and government-employed man from a good, respectable family of the same microcaste; again ideally, he is terminologically a cross-cousin of the bride, but this is by no means necessary. The traditional Hindu wedding is a lavish affair that proclaims the family's status. For most couples the marriage is strictly an unromantic relationship, though it may grow into love later; a "good wife" submits to her husband's authority and serves him humbly and obediently. If a boy's parents discover that he has fallen in love, they take offense at this erosion of their authority and try to break up the relationship; if a girl's parents discover that she has fallen in love, they express their disdain for her and take advantage of the situation by trying to strike a marriage deal that involves little or no dowry. More rarely, broad-minded parents may try to arrange what appears to be a traditional marriage even if the pair are in love. Residence after marriage is neolocal, the determining factor being the availability of lands and a house. "Love marriages" are increasingly common. Poorer and low-caste families can afford neither the dowry nor the ceremony, so their marriages are far more casual. Although wife abuse is thought to be common, it is publicly discouraged and, in strong contrast to India, women have a moderate degree of economic recourse in that they re-

tain property rights under traditional Tamil law (which is upheld in the courts). Divorce is exceptionally uncommon and quite difficult legally, but among the poor and lower castes desertion and new, casual relationships are common.

Domestic Unit.   The average household is five or six persons; a married couple may be joined by elderly parents after these parents relinquish their lands and homes to other children in a form of premortem inheritance.

Inheritance.   In contrast to the mainland Tamil pattern, property is divided equally among all children—if any property is left after paying dowry at the going rates.

Socialization.   Small children are treasured by most adults, who play with them, tease them, and create homes that are structured around their needs. A first rice-feeding ceremony takes place at approximately 6 months. Toilet training is relaxed and untraumatic. But there is a pronounced change at approximately age 5, when the parents begin the task of bending the child to their will. At this age there begins an authoritarian relationship in which the parents assume the right to determine the child's school interests, prospective career, friends, attitudes, and spouse. Tradition-minded families may force girls to leave school at puberty, following which there was formerly a ceremony (now done privately or not at all) that declared the girl to be technically eligible for marriage; she dons a sari and is no longer free to go about unchaperoned. Both the family and school declare to children, in effect, "Do what we tell you to do and we will take care of you in life." However, families and schools are increasingly unable to deliver on this promise. In the 1970s, Tamil youths found themselves receiving authoritarian pressure from their families to conform but faced bleak prospects; this double bind apparently contributed to a tripling of suicide rates, giving the Tamil areas of Sri Lanka one of the highest recorded suicide rates in the world. The rise of youthful Tamil militant groups is not only a political phenomenon but also a generational revolt; Tamil youths are rejecting not only Sinhalese rule but also the moderate politics and social conservatism of their parents.

Sociopolitical Organization

Sri Lanka is nominally a parliamentary democracy with a president as the head of state. The two-party parliamentary system is, however, dominated by Sinhalese, and the Sri Lankan Tamils are not sufficiently numerous to affect the outcome of elections. As a result moderate Tamil politicians who endorsed a parliamentary solution to Tamil grievances were ineffective and were swept away during the rise of Tamil youthful militancy.

Social Organization.   Sri Lanka's Tamil regions take on their distinctiveness owing to the presence of a dominant agricultural caste—the Vellala in the Jaffna Peninsula and the Mukkuvar in the eastern coastal region—on which the entire caste system is focused. In contrast to the Tamil mainland, Brahmans are few, and although they are considered higher than the dominant caste in ritual terms, they are generally poor and serve the dominant caste as temple priests or temple managers. Traditional intercaste services focused on the dominant caste and were both sacred and secular; the sacred services, such as the services provided by barbers and washers at life-cycle rites and by agricultural laborers at sacrificial rituals, served to define and regulate the low status of serving groups, while the secular ones created patron-client linkages that could endure for generations. Once bound to these sacred and secular relations, the artisan castes freed themselves by taking advantage of British liberalizations, the expanding service economy, and their urban residence. The rural service and labor castes remained in traditional relationships with the dominant castes until the mid-twentieth century, when the rise of a service economy created new marginal economic niches for these groups at the same time that mechanization rendered their labor unnecessary. Coastal fishing groups were never incorporated into the compass of agricultural caste solidarity, and in consequence they have long maintained their independence and resisted the stigma of low status. Prior to the twentieth century, caste statuses were upheld by a huge variety of sumptuary regulations, such as a rule prohibiting low-caste women from covering the upper half of their bodies. Caste discrimination in such matters, including temple entry and the use of public facilities and conveyances, is now illegal but persists in rural areas. In the face of the brutal occupation of Tamil areas by Sinhalese security forces in the early 1980s, caste rivalry diminished in intensity as the Tamil community pulled together. Prominent in many Tamil militant organizations are leaders from low or marginal castes; Tamil youthful militancy is thus a rejection of traditional caste ideology as well as a generational and ethnic revolt.

Political Organization. The Sri Lankan state is partly an artifact of colonial rule: excessively centralized, it was devised to suppress regional rebellions as the British were consolidating their power. The failure of this overly centralized political system to devolve power to the provinces is one of the reasons for the rise of militant Tamil separatism. Unable to win concessions from the Colombo government, Tamil parliamentarians lost credibility and were pushed out of the Tamil community by militant youth groups, which were composed mainly of unemployed graduates as well as unmarried and rootless youth. Fractious and focused on a single, charismatic leader, these groups competed with each other—sometimes violently—until the 1987 incursion by Indian troops under the provisions of an accord between Colombo and Delhi; the Marxist-oriented groups, unlike other factions, accommodated to the Indian security forces, whose presence and actions in the Sri Lankan Tamil community were resented as much as those of the Colombo forces. After the departure of the Indian troops, those Marxist groups lost credibility. At this writing the Liberation Tigers of Tamil Eelam (LTTE), a nationalist group, has effectively eliminated—through attrition, fear, assassination, and massacre—all other potential sources of political leadership within the Tamil community. They have won support among peasant folk who believe that no one else can protect them from the Sri Lankan security forces, but expatriate Tamils frequently voice concern that LTTE rule will amount to a brutal dictatorship.

Social Control. Within traditional Sri Lankan Tamil villages gossip and ridicule were potent forces for social conformity. The family backed its authoritarian control through threats of excommunication (deprivation of lands, dowry, and family support). With growing landlessness and unemployment, however, many families are unable to deliver on their material promises and the threat of excommunication has become increasingly empty. Suicide and youthful militancy are both manifestations of a general rejection by youth of traditional forms of authoritarianism.

Conflict. Traditionally, conflicts occurred within families and between castes. Interfamily conflict often arose from status competition, particularly when a wealthy ward attempted to cease relations with its "poorer relations" in pursuit of new, more lucrative ties with a similarly-endowed group. Long-standing grudges and obsession with "enemies," real or imagined, sometimes have led to violence. Dominant castes routinely used violence to punish subordinate groups that were taking on high-caste life-style attributes (such as using umbrellas), often by burning down huts or poisoning wells. Since the late 1970s, the ineffectiveness of moderate Tamil politicians has led many Tamil youths to conclude that the only solution to their problems lies in violence. The result has been the rise, not only in Tamil areas but throughout Sri Lanka, of a culture of violence, in which unspeakable acts of slaughter and massacre are commonplace. It has even spilled over into India where, in 1991, Sri Lankan Tamils assassinated the former prime minister, Rajiv Gandhi. Official estimates are that approximately 20,000 have died in Sri Lanka's decade-old civil war but unofficial estimates place the toll at two to three times that figure.

Religion and Expressive Culture

Religious Beliefs. Sri Lankan Tamils are predominantly Hindus, but there are significant enclaves of Roman Catholics and Protestants (mainly Methodists), who consider themselves to be full members of the Sri Lankan Tamil community. Discussed here is the Hinduism of Tamil Sri Lanka, a Hinduism that is at once utilitarian, philosophical, and deeply devotional. Shiva is the supreme deity but is not worshiped directly; Shiva bestows his grace by running your life so you aspire to nothing other than reunification with him. The perspective taken toward the other deities is frankly utilitarian: they are approached for help with mundane problems, such as illnesses, university exams, job applications, conflicts, legal problems, or infertility. Commonly worshiped deities include Shiva's sons Murukan and Pillaiyar, the several village goddesses (such as Mariyamman and Kannakiyamman), and a host of semidemonic deities who are thought to demand sacrifices. Of all deities, most beloved is Murukan, who bestows boons even on those who may be unworthy, to the extent that they devote themselves to him.

Religious Practitioners. In temples that conform to the scriptural dictates of the medieval temple-building manuals (called *Agamas*), the priests are Brahmans. A small caste of non-Brahman temple priests called Saiva Kurukkals performs the rites at non-Agama temples, particularly shrines of the goddess Amman. The officiants at village and family temples, called *pucaris*, are ordinary villagers with whom the temple's god has established a spiritual relationship, often through a form of spirit possession. Here and there one finds temple priests who open a shrine to the public and try to solve medical, legal, and social problems for all comers, without regard to caste. The very few holy men are revered but may attract more foreign than indigenous disciples. Astrologists are numerous and are routinely consulted at birth, marriage, and times of trouble; Hindus believe that one's fate is "written on one's head" (*talai viti*) and cannot be fully escaped, although some intelligent finessing and divine assistance can help one avoid some problems or calamities.

Ceremonies. Households celebrate a rich repertoire of calendrical and life-cycle rituals that bring the family together in joyous, festive holidays. Village temples offer annual "car" festivals, in which the deity is carried around the temple atop a huge chariot; these ceremonies occur on a much larger scale in regional pilgrimage, which used to attract visitors from all over the country.

Arts. With its utilitarian ethos, Sri Lankan Tamil culture does not encourage young people to pursue careers in the arts. Even so, young people today may receive instruction in traditional Tamil music or dance as a means of impressing on them the antiquity and greatness of Tamil culture; music and dance were formerly associated with low-caste status.

Medicine. There is a pronounced division of labor between scientific medicine and Ayurvedic medicine, which is thought to be more effective for mental illness, snakebite, paralysis, and listlessness.

Death and Afterlife. Westerners who believe Hindus are focused on a better life after reincarnation are inevitably surprised by the almost complete disinterest that Tamil Hindus show in the afterlife. It is thought, though, that someone who dies without having fulfilled a great longing will remain to vex the living. Cremation is the norm and is followed, for most castes, by a period of death pollution lasting thirty-one days; subsequently there is an annual death observance with food offerings. For the few highly educated Hindus familiar with the Saiva Siddhanta tradition, an oft-expressed goal of afterlife is reunification with Shiva.

See also Moor of Sri Lanka; Vellala

Bibliography

Banks, Michael Y. (1961). "Caste in Jaffna." In *Aspects of Caste in South India, Ceylon, and North-West Pakistan*, edited by E. R. Leach, 61–77. Cambridge: Cambridge University Press.

Helleman-Rajanayagam, Dagmar (1988–1989). "The Tamil Militants—Before the Accords and After." *Pacific Affairs* 61:603–619.

Holmes, W. Robert (1980). *Jaffna (Sri Lanka): 1980*. Jaffna: Jaffna College.

McGilvray, Dennis (1982). *Caste Ideology and Interaction.* Cambridge: Cambridge University Press.

O'Ballance, Edgar (1989). *The Cyanide War: Tamil Insurrection in Sri Lanka, 1973–1988.* London: Brassey's.

Pfaffenberger, Bryan (1982). *Caste in Tamil Culture: The Religious Foundations of Sudra Domination in Tamil Sri Lanka.* Syracuse: Maxwell School of Foreign and Comparative Studies, Syracuse University.

Schwarz, Walter (1988). *The Tamils of Sri Lanka.* 4th ed. London: Minority Rights Group.

Skonsberg, Else (1982). *A Special Caste? Tamil Women of Sri Lanka.* London: Zed Press.

BRYAN PFAFFENBERGER

Telugu

ETHNONYM: Andhra

Orientation

Identification. Speakers of the Telugu language inhabit Andhra Pradesh State in south India as well as border areas of the neighboring states of Orissa, Madhya Pradesh, Maharashtra, Karnataka, and Tamil Nadu. There are also substantial numbers of Telugu speakers in the interior of Tamil Nadu, especially in the central and northern regions. In addition there are small Telugu communities in the United States, the United Kingdom, and countries formerly part of the British Empire—Fiji, Guyana, Malaysia, Myanmar (Burma), Mauritius, Singapore, and South Africa.

Location. Andhra Pradesh is located in tropical latitudes (between 12° and 19° N and 76° and 86° E) similar to mainland Southeast Asia or southern Mexico. Important features of the land include a palmyra-dotted coastal plain extending 960 kilometers along the Bay of Bengal, lush deltas of the Godavari and Krishna rivers, a strip of forested hill country paralleling the coast, and a rolling upland plain strewn with eroded rocky outcrops. The major rainfall is supplied by the southwest monsoon, its winds prevailing between June and September.

Demography. In 1981 the population of Andhra Pradesh was 53,550,000, with an average density of 195 persons per square kilometer and a decennial growth rate of 23.1 percent. The population is mainly Hindu (87 percent) but with important Muslim and Christian minorities (8 and 4 percent, respectively).

Linguistic Affiliation. The Telugu language is a member of the Dravidian Language Family concentrated in the south of the Indian peninsula. Other related major languages are Tamil, Kannada, and Malayalam. Telugu possesses its own distinctive, curvilinear alphabet and a voluminous and venerable literary tradition. It is also the primary language of South Indian classical music.

History and Cultural Relations

Two millennia ago the Telugu country was a stronghold of Buddhism, a legacy of the empire of Asoka (ca. 250 B.C.). The Andhra Kingdom, with its capital in Paithan (now in Maharashtra), followed. Among the various dynasties that next held sway were the Pallavas, the Eastern Chalukyas, the Kalingas, the Kakatiyas, and the Cholas. The Muslim period saw the establishment of the Bahmani Kingdom and its successor, the sultanate of Golkonda. Hindu Vijayanagar in the southern part of the Telugu country was conquered by Muslims in 1565. European traders—Dutch, French, and English—attracted by textiles and spices began arriving on the scene in the sixteenth century. The British ultimately prevailed in the eighteenth century, acquiring control from the rulers of Golkonda over extensive tracts in the northeast coastal belt of the Telugu country. Later these territories were linked with those they acquired in the south and ruled from the city of Madras. The northwestern part of the Telugu-speaking lands remained in what became the state of the Nizam of Hyderabad, whose foreign affairs and defense came to be controlled by the British.

Political trends since Indian independence in 1947 include three decades of dominance by the Congress party. This was followed by the ascent of the regional Telugu Desam party, spearheaded by a former Telugu movie idol, N. T. Rama Rao.

Settlements

Telugu villages range in size from several hundred in population to many thousand, with larger ones resembling small towns. Frequently several "hamlets" are affiliated together as a single village. In some cases, the constituent settlements have been designated a village by the government for purposes of taxation, economic development, and political representation. Typically the main settlement of the village has the widest variety of castes (or _jatis_, endogamous groups often associated with particular occupations), with a temple, small shops, tea and drink stalls, a weekly market, a post office, and a village school. Quarters of former Untouchable castes are traditionally segregated from the other houses of a settlement.

Telugu house types vary considerably even within the same village. Differences in construction materials usually indicate differing economic statuses. Dwellings range from mud-walled, single-family houses with palm-thatched roofs to houses made of brick and mortar—or stone in some regions—with flat, cement roofs. All houses have at least one inner room where the family valuables are stored, ceremonial brass vessels (dowry) are displayed, and deities are worshiped at a small shrine. A roofed veranda with cooking nook lies outside this inner room. For the highest castes, for whom it is important that cooking take place beyond the polluting gaze of outsiders, the cooking area is adjacent to the back of the dwelling in a walled compound.

Economy

Subsistence and Commercial Activities. The food grain held in highest esteem is rice, cultivated intensively in the Krishna and Godavari deltas as well as extensively throughout other parts of the coastal zone and in scattered parts of the interior. Away from streams irrigation is by reservoirs known as tanks. These are formed with earthen dams that hold rainwater in the wet season. Other food grains, grown on nonirrigated lands, are also important. Mung beans, lima beans, and black-eyed peas are widely cultivated, as are sesame seeds and peanuts for oil. Popular garden vegetables, grown for home use and for sale, include tomatoes, eggplants, onions, garlic, chilies, bitter gourds, pumpkins, okra, yams, ginger, and corn. Widely grown fruits include mangoes, tamarinds, guavas, bananas, coconuts, custard apples, sapodillas,

limes, toddy-palm (palmyra, _Borassus flabellifer_), cashews, and pineapples. Turmeric root is also cultivated, as is mustard, fenugreek, coriander, and fennel. In addition to rice, important commercial crops are sugarcane, tobacco, and cotton. Chilies are cultivated throughout the state for sale. Fishing is important along the coast as well as in inland tanks.

Cultivation is mainly unmechanized, except for gasoline-powered pumps used by wealthier farmers to aid irrigation. Bullocks or water buffalo are used to pull wooden plows reinforced with iron tips. Crops are harvested by hand.

In addition to cattle and water buffalo—which are used not for meat but for dairy products—numerous other domestic animals are raised. These include chickens, ducks, turkeys, goats, sheep, and pigs. Dogs are kept by some villagers for hunting.

Industrial Arts. Telugu society with its Hindu caste system has a highly developed tradition of family transmission of manufacturing and food-processing skills. Among these are blacksmithing, carpentry, goldsmithing, cotton and silk weaving, basket making, pottery, and oil pressing. Many villagers weave their own baskets, make their own rope from palm fiber, and thatch their own roofs.

Trade. Village markets selling fresh vegetables, meat, spices, cloth, and bangles are typically held one day each week. Generally one particularly large weekly market on a main bus route serves as a magnet for an entire rural region. Women of farmer castes often bring produce from their families' farms, and their husbands engage in petty trading, offering chickens for sale. Potters and sellers of bangles and clothing also offer their wares. Professional merchant castes maintain small provision stores, which are open daily in the villages.

Division of Labor. To a great extent, women's time is taken up with child rearing and food preparation. However, among the middle and lower castes women engage in strenuous physical agricultural labor such as transplanting rice shoots and harvesting. In towns, women work on construction sites, carrying heavy baskets with cement or bricks or breaking rocks. But among the higher castes there are restrictions on women going out of their homes or even appearing in public unescorted.

In Telugu society labor is most strikingly divided by caste. Castes are economically interdependent endogamous groups often associated with particular occupations or crafts—barbering, washing, and oil pressing, for instance.

Land Tenure. Land is held by households and passes patrilineally along the male line, in equal shares between brothers. Land is not owned by all families but rather held mainly by members of farmer castes, as well as by members of higher castes who employ lower castes to cultivate it. Food is traditionally distributed throughout the rural population via exchange of grain or cash for services. Landless lower-caste members of society who cannot support themselves in the village economy frequently migrate to urban areas to work for wages. They then usually maintain ties with their home village.

Kinship

Kin Groups and Descent. An individual is a member of the following groups: (1) a family residing in a household generally headed by the eldest male; (2) an endogamous sub-clan or branch of a patrilineage; (3) an exogamous clan (sharing a patrilineally transmitted family name); and (4) an endogamous caste with a particular hierarchical status, customs of diet, prohibitions on food exchange with other castes, and often a traditional occupation. Descent is patrilineal.

Kinship Terminology.   Dravidian kinship terms are used; the terminology emphasizes relative age. For example, terms differ according to the ages of the speaker and the person spoken of; there are separate terms for "older brother" and "younger brother." The terminology also divides relatives into marriageable and unmarriageable categories. On the one hand, one calls one's parallel cousins "brothers" and "sisters." They are not considered to be potential spouses. On the other hand, one's cross cousins are designated by terms implying that they are potential affines.

Marriage and Family

Marriage.   Marriages are monogamous, polygyny having been prohibited since Indian independence. Marriages are generally arranged by parents and relatives, though potential mates may get to meet each other or may already be acquainted if they are related or live in the same village. As mentioned, marriage with cross cousins is common, and a man's maternal uncle is viewed as a preferred donor of a wife. Wives are considered responsible for the well-being of their husbands and are felt to be at fault if their husbands die before they do. The theme of the inauspiciousness of widowhood recurs in many ritual contexts. Marriages are generally patrilocal. The fission of individual households is a gradual process, beginning with a man's sons marrying and bringing their wives to live with him and his wife. Eventually separate hearths are established, followed later by a division of lands. A sharing of tasks around agricultural field huts near their lands is the last tie to be maintained. Different castes have varying attitudes toward divorce. The highest in status prohibit it entirely. Next down in the hierarchy are castes that permit divorce if no children have been born. These are followed by castes permitting divorce relatively unrestrictedly. Agreements are reached regarding the return of marriage gifts and property. Formal written documents of release are drawn up and exchanged by the parties, leaving them free to remarry.

Domestic Unit.   The basic unit is a nuclear family. A household, defined as those who share food prepared at a common hearth, is led by a household head. During the course of its development, a household can include additional members—spouses and offspring of sons, or widows and widowers.

Inheritance.   Property, such as land, is divided equally among brothers, though the less economically established youngest son also often inherits the family home.

Socialization.   Infants and small children are raised by the women of the household. Older siblings and other cousins also often tend children younger than themselves. Children are encouraged to accompany their parents everywhere and begin learning sex-specific tasks and caste occupations from an early age.

Sociopolitical Organization

Andhra Pradesh, one of the largest states in the Republic of India, is led by a chief minister and a governor and has an elected legislature. Its capital is Hyderabad.

Social Organization.   The primary organizing principle of Telugu society is hierarchy, based on age, sex, and social group. Each endogamous caste group reckons its relationship to other castes as either one of superiority, equality, or inferiority. While these relative rankings produce a hierarchy, this is in some cases a matter of dispute. To some extent the relative positions are perceived to be achieved on the basis of mutual willingness to engage in various sorts of symbolic exchanges, especially of food. Caste members do not accept food prepared by a caste they consider to be inferior to their own. In addition, castes maintain distinctive diets—the highest refuses to eat meat, the next level refuses to eat domestic pork or beef, and the lowest eats pork and beef. There are clusters of castes of similar status—such as farmers—that accept each other's food, as well as pairs of similar-status castes—such as the two major former Untouchable castes—that reject each other's food. There is also a group of castes—the Panchabrahma, artisans in gold, brass, iron, and wood—that claim to be higher than the highest Brahmans. But while they refuse food from all other castes, no other castes accept food from them.

Political Organization.   The state of Andhra Pradesh is divided into twenty-one districts (*zilla*). Districts were traditionally subdivided into *taluks* until 1985 when a smaller subdivision, the *mandal,* was instituted by the Telugu Desam party. The mandal, whose leader is directly elected, serves as a functionary of revenue administration and of government development projects. Towns with taluk headquarters are the seat of courts, police, and government health-care programs. The political culture of democracy among the Telugus is highly developed, with frequent elections for state and national representatives.

Social Control and Conflict.   In times of conflict the authority of elder males is respected. A male household head rules on a dispute within his household. Next, an informally constituted group of elder males of the same caste arbitrates difficult disputes within or between families in the caste. Cases involving members of different castes are often referred to higher castes for settlement, in a pattern of ascending courts of appeal. When conflicts begin there is often much commotion and shouting of accusations or grievances. This attracts the participation of bystanders and triggers the process of arbitration.

Religion

The vast majority of Telugus are Hindus. There are also some Telugu castes that have converted to Christianity and Islam. Each village has its main temple—often dedicated to a great Hindu god, usually Rama or Siva—as well as small shrines to numerous village deities, most of which are female. Preeminent among the regional shrines in the Telugu country is the temple of Sri Venkatesvara in the town of Tirupati, a major pilgrimage center.

Religious Beliefs.   Hinduism lacks a centralized ecclesiastical hierarchy or unified authority officially defining doctrine. The specifics of religious customs vary widely from one locality to another and even between different castes in the same village. Among the major types of ritual are family ceremonies, caste ceremonies, and village ceremonies. In addition the range of deities worshiped varies between localities. Many deities are associated with particular places or specialized powers or seasons. But a unifying theme is a system of worship called _puja_ in which offerings are presented to a deity in return for protection and help. The offerings imply a subordination by the worshipers and include the receiving back of part of the items offered—after their spiritual essence has been partaken of by the deity. Overarching the host of specific deities is a transcendent divinity, _bhagavan_ or _devudu_, responsible for cosmic order. People conceive of this deity in personified forms such as Vishnu and his associated circle of gods—including his ten incarnations, among whom are Rama and Krishna, and their various female consorts, such as Lakshmi, Sita, and Rukmini. Shiva and gods associated with him include his sons Ganapati and Subrahmaniam and his wife Parvati. Settlements, villages or towns, have a tradition of female "village deities" (_grama devatas_) who protect their localities as long as they are properly propitiated but cause illnesses if they are not. Ghosts of deceased humans, especially those of people who died untimely deaths, can hover about and interfere with people, as can other malevolent forces such as inauspicious stars and evil spirits. These thwart people's plans or render their children ill.

Religious Practitioners. A person acting as the officiant in a temple, conducting or assisting the worship, is known as a _pujari,_ or priest. Brahmans serve as priests in temples to deities associated with the scriptural deities known throughout India, such as Rama, Shiva, or Krishna. But members of many other castes, some of quite low social rank, act as priests for a wide range of lesser deities.

Ceremonies. There is little uniformity in the celebration of festivals across the Telugu country. Each region presents a kaleidoscopic variation of interpretations and emphases on common themes. In the northeast, Makara Sankranti is the principal harvest festival. It features castes worshiping the tools of their trades and a period of fairs featuring elaborate night-long operatic drama performances. In the northwest, Dasara and Chauti are the festivals during which castes worship their implements. Farther south, near the Krishna River, Ugadi is a time when artisans worship their tools. All regions have festivals that honor Rama, Krishna, Shiva, and Ganapati.

Village goddess festivals, celebrated on dates unique to individual settlements, are also among the most elaborate celebrations of the year. These rituals—entailing the offering of chickens, goats, or sheep—mobilize extensive intercaste cooperation to ensure the health of the whole community. Also important in the worship of village goddesses is the practice of making vows to achieve specific personal benefits, such as the curing of ailments or finding of lost objects. Periodically when emergencies arise—in the form of epidemics, a spate of fires, or sudden deaths—these goddesses are believed to require propitiation.

Life-cycle rituals vary greatly between castes and regions. All serve to define social statuses, marking the transitions between immaturity and adult (married) status, as well as between life and death. They also serve to define circles of interdependent relatives and castes. Weddings stand out as the most elaborate and significant life-cycle rites. They are highly complex, involve huge expenditures, last several days, and entail the invitation and feeding of large numbers of guests. Funerary rites are also highly significant, defining the lineal relatives who share ritual pollution caused by the death of a member. In addition, they mark social statuses by treating the body of a man differently from that of a woman (cremating it face up or face down, respectively) and by disposing of the body of an immature child differently from that of a married adult (by burial or cremation, respectively).

See also Reddi

Bibliography

Dube, S. C. (1967). _Indian Village._ New York: Harper & Row.

Hiebert, Paul G. (1971). _Konduru: Structure and Integration in a South Indian Village._ Minneapolis: University of Minnesota Press.

Tapper, Bruce Elliot (1987). _Rivalry and Tribute: Society and Ritual in a Telugu Village in South India._ Delhi: Hindustan Publishing Corp.

BRUCE ELLIOT TAPPER

Thadou

ETHNONYM: Thadu, New Kuki (in 19th century)

Orientation

The Thadou are a Kuki people located chiefly in the hill country adjacent to the Imphal Valley in the northeastern Indian state of Manipur. This area encompasses some 26,000 square kilometers. The Thadou share many cultural affinities with the Koms, Aimols, Khotlhangs, Lusheis, Chins, Pois, Suktes, Paites, and Gangtes.

In 1983 there were 125,100 Thadou living in India and 26,200 living in Myanmar (Burma). The Thadou language belongs to the Tibeto-Burman Family of the Sino-Tibetan Phylum. It shares many elements with Metei, Kachin, Garo, Lushei, and other Old Kuki dialects.

History and Cultural Relations

Thadou tradition links their origin with an area south of their current habitat. Intertribal conflict and the need for cultivable land are two of the reasons cited as possible causes for the northerly migration of the Thadou. However, Shaw believes that they originated in the north. It is his contention that they moved down the Imphal or Gun River, then proceeded down the Tuihat (Chindwin) River until they reached the sea. Since they were unable to traverse this obstacle, they retreated up the Tuihat until they reached that point where it merged with the Teo (Tyao) River. The retreat continued until they reached their present location. The Thadou feel that they are destined to be rulers of the Earth and eschew any yoke of domination. This attitude led to the Kuki rebellion of 1918–1919. In spite of their defeat then, the Thadou maintain the belief that a promising future awaits them. The impact of Christian missionary activity was felt early in the twentieth century. William Shaw believed that the Christianization of the area would improve relations between the Thadou and neighboring peoples (felt by the Thadou to be their inferiors). He also noted that Thadou participation in the Manipur Labour Corps altered significantly the Thadou worldview (i.e., revealing the world to be larger than the Thadou had thought it to be).

Settlements

Thadou settlements are located in dense jungle. Sites on the tops of ridges or just below ridges are preferred. Villages are not arranged according to an established urban plan and no method obtains for marking the perimeter of a village. The village chief's house is usually the largest dwelling within the village. Outside it (and outside the homes of wealthy villagers) there is a platform upon which men gather to discuss matters of importance and to mediate disputes. The typical Thadou dwelling is about 6 meters long and 5 meters wide. The rear of the house is elevated 1.5 to 2 meters above the ground while the front of the house rests on the surface of the sloping ground. Wooden posts and rafters are used for the household frame. Thatching grass held in place by split bamboo is used for the roof and bamboo matting is used for the walls. The house contains one large roof and a front veranda. The interior room is used for cooking, storage, general living, and sleeping. The veranda is used for the pounding of rice. An enclosure (of wood tied together by bamboo or cane) may surround the house to protect gayals and the household garden. Fruit trees (with the exception of banana plants) are not usually found in Thadou villages.

Economy

Thadou subsistence activities include animal domestication (i.e., gayals, buffalo, pigs, goats, dogs, and various fowl), cultivation (e.g., rice, taro, beans, millet, Job's tears, sesame, maize, chilies, mustard leaves, cotton, ginger, turmeric, onions, pumpkins, cucumbers, and gourds), hunting, and fishing. Jhum (slash-and-burn) agriculture is predominant. Small hoes are used to dig holes into which seeds are planted. Saw-edged sickles are used in crop harvesting. Guns and traps are used in hunting. Poison, bamboo rods, and various types of traps are used in fishing. Men and women share labor-related responsibilities. However, Thadou women assume a disproportionate share of these activities.

Industrial manufactures include the following: cloth, cups (of bamboo), plates (of wood), daos (adzes), and spearheads. Shaw reported that cooking utensils (of earthenware, aluminum, and iron) were purchased in Manipuri markets. He also noted that a number of indigenous metal implements once produced by the Thadou (e.g., gongs, basins, plates, head adornments, decorative iron racks, and knives) were, during his time, purchased from Burma.

The Thadou rely upon their market relationship with merchants in Manipur and Myanmar (Burma) to secure essential supplies that are not produced by Thadou artisans.

Little detailed information is available on the Thadou system of land tenure. In theory, all village land is owned by the village chief. Each village household pays an annual (changseo) fee of one measure of rice to the village chief for the privilege of cultivating land.

Kinship

The Thadou are subdivided into several exogamous clans among which are the Shitlhous, the Dongngels, the Kipgens, the Shingshons, the Chonglois, the Hangshings, and the Phohils. Patrilineal descent obtains. Omaha-type kinship terminology is employed for first cousins.

Marriage and Family

Four forms of marriage exist among the Thadou: chongmu, sahapsat, jol-lha', and kijam mang. The latter two are nonceremonial betrothal forms akin to elopement. The first of these forms involves the following elements: the negotiation of a bride-price between the parents of the groom and the parents of the bride; the establishment of a date for the removal of the bride from her parents' house to the home of her espoused; the sending (by the groom) of strong young men to retrieve the bride; ceremonial feasting and wrestling (with the throwing of mud, dung, and rotten eggs at the bridegroom's representatives); and the triumphant return of the groom's representatives with the bride. The sahapsat marriage form contains only the marital negotiations between families; the feasting and wrestling are absent. The jol-lha' marriage is resorted to in the case of a pregnancy resulting from premarital relations. In this case, a bride-price is usually agreed upon before cohabitation begins. When the pregnancy is discovered, cohabitation begins immediately. The kijam mang is a marital arrangement that results from the union of two parties without the consent of the parents of either bride, groom, or both. The bride-price is settled at some point after the union takes place. Postmarital residence is patrilocal. Divorce is frequent and permissible. Inheritance is exclusively through the male line. Thadou women are the chief agents of socialization. Children are permitted a great degree of independence once they are able to walk. Little structured education is provided by parents, thereby leaving the Thadou child to learn through experiential means.

Sociopolitical Organization

Shaw provided little information about the political structure of the traditional Thadou village. From what he has mentioned, the position of chief/headman was of primary importance. The chief was usually in possession of the largest domicile in a village. The gathering point for village males was adjacent to the chief's home. The chief also had the right to confiscate standing crops and stored grain belonging to any member of the village who migrated from there without his permission. Further, in regional intervillage combat, it was customary to take chiefs hostage rather than to kill them. It has been suggested that this was due to the belief that all chiefs were related by blood. The chief is owner of all village lands and receives the benefit of dues (e.g., annual cultivation due, migration due, and the due paid by anyone selling gayals, buffalo, or other cattle) and required services from his subjects (e.g., each villager must work one day each month in the chief's fields). Social control is maintained by the imposition of required service (i.e., to the village chief), dues, oaths, trials, and fines. Conflict between the Thadou and their immediate neighbors was intermittent in the early nineteenth century. However, the taking of life was not treated lightly in Thadou society: just cause had to be established before life could be taken. Village raiding was common and the taking of heads usually accompanied armed conflict. The taking of heads was associated closely with the cult of the dead. Heads secured in battle were placed on the graves of deceased relatives and it was believed that these captives would act as servants for these individuals in the afterlife. Raids were also conducted during this time for the purpose of securing heads for the burial of a village chief. In such an instance, village authorities would select a group for attack that had an unsettled debt or had committed an offense against the village.

Religion and Expressive Culture

Religious Beliefs. The god Pathen is believed by the Thadou to have created everything. He is also believed to be the ruler of the universe. Sacrifice is offered to Pathen for health or assistance in time of trouble. Thunder and lightning are manifestations of Pathen's anger. Beings of a more malevolent nature are also a part of Thadou cosmology. These are the Thailhas. Earthquakes, according to one myth, are believed to be caused by Chongja (elder brother of Chongthu, primordial ancestor of the Thadou), who failed to lead his party from the Underworld along with that of Chongthu in order to establish life on Earth. Chongja shakes the Earth from his Underworld home in order to make certain that the party of Chongthu is still alive.

Religious Practitioners. The *thempu* (medicine man/priest) is the chief religious practitioner of the Thadou. This individual functions in a variety of capacities and in a number of settings. He prepares charms, manufactures household gods, offers sacrifices, administers oaths, and participates in ceremonies associated with certain life crises (e.g., birth and death).

Ceremonies. A variety of Thadou magicoreligious ceremonies may be noted. Among the more important individually sponsored ceremonies are the following: Chang Ai (offered only by women and intended to secure a preferential place in Mithikho, the afterworld, after death); Sha Ai (a feast offered by men who have killed all, or at least some, of the various dangerous animals known to the Thadou); and Chon (a very important feast that may be offered only by those who have offered the Sha Ai feast three times; it ensures the sponsor eternal happiness in Mithikho). Additional village ceremonies are performed by the thempu for a variety of reasons (e.g., to secure the village from disease and to protect it from the incursion of evil spirits). Other ceremonies are associated with the agricultural cycle (e.g., the Daiphu ceremony that accompanies the burning of a field and the Changlhakou ceremony that follows the reaping and storing of the rice crop).

Arts. Thadou visual art is not well attested. Tattooing may be cited as one example, but it is practiced to a very limited extent. Thadou oral literature is, however, rich in folklore. As art forms, music (vocal and instrumental) and dance are important elements in the magicoreligious ceremonies of the Thadou.

Medicine. The Thadou believe that illness is caused by supernatural forces and resort to ceremonial (magicoreligious) methods of treatment almost exclusively. Medicinal plants are used to a very limited extent. The success of European medicine is accounted for, in the Thadou worldview, by the European discovery of odors that repel particular disease-bearing spirits.

Death and Afterlife. The Thadou believe that the spirits of the dead move on to Mithikho, the village of the dead, after their earthly existence has ended.

See also Mizo; Purum

Bibliography

Shakespear, John (1912). *The Lushei Kuki Clans.* London: Macmillan.

Shaw, William (1929). *Notes on the Thadou Kukis.* Calcutta: Asiatic Society of Bengal.

Simoons, Frederick J., and Elizabeth S. Simoons (1968). *A Ceremonial Ox of India: The Mithan in Nature, Culture, and History.* Madison: University of Wisconsin Press.

HUGH R. PAGE, JR.

Thakali

ETHNONYMS: Tamang, Tamu

Orientation

Identification. Thakali territory is called Thakhola or Thak-Satsae, in Jomson District in central Nepal. Thakola is sandwiched between the pastoral highlands in the north and the agricultural lowlands in the south. It is also the transitional zone between Tibetan Buddhist culture and Hindu culture.

Demography. According to the 1961 census there were 4,130 Thakali-speaking people. Accurate population figures are not available. Some Thakalis claim that their population is close to ten thousand. The majority of the Thakalis used to live in Thakhola until the end of the 1950s, but most of them migrated to cities and towns in the southern lowlands of Nepal after the events of 1959 in Tibet.

Linguistic Affiliation. The Thakalis are Himalayan Mongoloids whose mother tongue is of the Tibeto-Burman Family. It is called Thakali and belongs to the Tamang Group (including Tamang, Gurung, and Magar).

History and Cultural Relations

The origin of the Thakalis is not clear, although they claim to be the descendants of Hansraj, a Thakuri prince of the Jumla-Sinja dynasty in western Nepal. The Thakalis were agropastoral people who were engaged in local trade until the early nineteenth century like other neighboring Himalayan peoples. The rise of Thakali power goes back to the mid-nineteenth century. Nepal was at war with Tibet in 1857 and 1858. One of the Thakali leaders cooperated with the Hindu Rana regime and provided the central government in Kathmandu with valuable information about the Himalayan and Tibetan areas. After the Nepalese victory over Tibet, the Hindu Rana rulers allowed the Thakali leader to obtain a license to import rock salt from Tibet and also granted him the magistracy of the Upper Kali Gandaki Valley and neighboring Panchgaon, Baragaon, Lo, and Dolpo areas with the traditional and hereditary title of *Subba*. This prerogative was quite helpful in enabling the Subba and his family to carry on large-scale commerce in the Tibet-Himalayan regions. Thus, the Subba family and its descendants exercised political influence not only among the Thakalis but also over their neighboring ethnic groups in Panchgaon, Baragaon, Lo, and Dolpo. But the political influence of the Thakali leaders and their families gradually diminished after the mass migration of Thakali merchants from Thakhola toward the southern lowlands of Nepal following the 1959 Tibetan affair.

Many of the Thakalis have survived well in the cities and towns of southern Nepal as merchants, hotel owners, public servants, professors, teachers, medical doctors, and so forth, thanks to their hard-working efforts and businesslike attitude.

Settlements

The Thakali merchants live in the valley of the Upper Kali Gandaki, but some of the agropastoral Thakalis inhabit the slopes of the Annapurna and Dhaulagiri Himals. Their houses are either rectangular or square and were originally of Tibetan style. The houses of the Thakalis as a whole are large, spacious, and clean. Houses are made of slate stones with flat roofs. But the Thakalis have to build bamboo huts within the Tibetan-style houses during the rainy season in the comparatively humid area, like Lete and Ghasa villages, in the southern fringe of Thakhola.

Economy

Subsistence and Commercial Activities. In common with the rest of the Nepalese Himalayan region, Thakhola has a summer monsoon season that usually begins in July and ends in September. But as Thakhola is located on the northern side of the main Himalayan ridges, there is less summer precipitation and some snowfall in winter months. Therefore, rain-based farming is practiced only in summer, and the cultivation of winter crops in the upland fields is dependent on irrigation. Buckwheat is the summer crop, and barley and wheat are the winter crops; maize was introduced to Thakhola before World War II. The cultivation of garden vegetables is rather rare in Nepal outside the Kathmandu Valley, but the Thakalis are very fond of gardening, even growing both vegetables and flowers.

At present Thakalis are not so dependent on pastoralism (unlike Tibetan-speaking Bhotes in the northern high plateau), but it is still an indispensable part of their economy. On the steep slopes of the Annapurna and Dhaulagiri ranges, some of the Thakalis raise yaks, sheep, and goats from which they obtain meat, milk, butter, wool, fur, pelts, and hides. They also breed dzo (a hybrid of yak and cow), mules, horses,

and donkeys for use as pack animals in their trading operations. It would appear that the Thakalis have certain cultural traits usually associated with the rearing of domesticated animals for trading caravans.

Industrial Arts. The Thakalis are not very active in producing native artifacts for sale or trade, although they have developed a quite refined artistic sense. Some well-to-do Thakalis have started to operate a carpet factory on the outskirts of Kathmandu in recent times.

Trade. The Thakalis are one of the most famous trading communities in Nepal, having engaged in Himalayan trade between Tibet, Nepal, and India for many years. Although they were attracted by the foreign and native merchandise from the south and were interested in the potential market for trade goods, in the past they avoided trading operations in southern Nepal because of their dislike of the heat and humidity there during the summer monsoon season and their fear of the virulent forms of malaria and other tropical diseases prevalent there. Following the pioneer efforts of the group, through trial and error, they started traveling to the south in increasing numbers, where they came into contact with the Hindu inhabitants.

The trading center of the Thakalis was Tukuche, which is the largest "town" in the territory. Until the revolt in Tibet in 1959, the Thakali merchants had imported sheep, goats, yaks, dzo, hides, fur, pelts, butter, and cheese, as well as rock salt from the northern high plateau and Tibet, in exchange for Nepalese and Indian commodities such as rice, wheat, barley, maize, *dhal* (pulses), buckwheat, oil, tea, chilies, spices, Nepali paper, cotton, cotton cloth, metal utensils, guns, gunpowder, and some other commodities.

Frequently Thakali merchants organized caravans themselves, but they also functioned as intermediaries. Many Tibetan-speaking traders came to Tukuche from Dolpo, Lo, and Tibet, and Hindu lowlanders from southern Nepal. Cash was sometimes used in trading transactions but barter was more common until the end of 1950s. The barter was, in many cases, based on Tibetan rock salt and rice from the southern lowlands.

Since the 1950–1951 "democratic" revolution, Nepal has opened her doors to the outside world and thus more foreign goods, mainly Indian-made, have flowed into the kingdom. Among them the cheap salt from India dealt a blow to the Thakali economy. The price of salt declined by approximately 25 percent in Himalayan areas during a comparatively short period.

Another big blow hit the Thakali merchants in 1962 when the People's Republic of China closed the Himalayan border, owing to political unrest generated by Tibetan guerrillas sponsored by foreign countries. Many of the Thakali merchants had to leave Thakhola as the traditional trade of the Himalayan region was almost terminated by bad relations between China and Tibet.

Except for some rich Subba families, most of the middle-class and poor Thakalis migrated to the south and moved to smaller towns where they opened small shops and wayside inns. They were unable to survive well in a big city like Kathmandu. Thanks to their business acumen and industriousness, however, some of them have started their own profitable businesses and are forming a new class.

As for the trading activities of the Thakalis, a sort of financial cooperative called _dhikur_ (Tibetan _dri-kor_, or "rice rotation") was a very meaningful system for many Thakali merchants in Thakhola. But the system also seems to be changing in the urban settings by involving other castes and ethnic groups.

Division of Labor. Not only the adults but also the children work hard. The Thakalis in Tukuche have not developed a division of labor, except for work such as the caravan trade for males and housekeeping for females. However, the Thakalis living in the Hindu lowlands of Nepal have in recent times emulated the behavior of Hindu high castes and have secluded women from outside labor.

Kinship

Kin Groups and Descent. The Thakali community is endogamous and is composed of four exogamous patrilineages: Timtsen (Sherchan), Choeki (Gauchan), Burki (Bhattachan), and Salki (Tulachan). The four patrilineages are again subdivided into a number of family groups called _ghyupa_. Each of the four patrilineages has its own clan deities: the Lion for Timtsen, the Dragon for Choeki, the Yak for Burki, and the Elephant for Salki. Each respective patrilineage has its own "clan grave" called _khimj_ in which a throat bone is placed on the death of a patrilineage member. In spite of the high mobility of Thakali merchants, the ethnic identity has been well maintained thanks to the elaborate ritual activities based on family, patrilineage, and tribe levels.

Marriage and Family

Marriage. Marriage was traditionally initiated by capturing a bride with her informal consent, like the custom among some of the Himalayan groups. It is, however, the contemporary tendency for young Thakalis to prefer arranged marriages in the Hindu style. The rule of postmarital residence is generally patrilocal, and the youngest son tends to stay with the parents even after his marriage. In many cases, the elder sons go out and set up new families after their marriages (neolocal residence). Traditionally, divorce and remarriage were not encouraged but also not prohibited; today, however, the remarriage of widows is becoming somewhat unpopular among the Thakalis who have been brought up in the Hindu lowlands of Nepal.

Domestic Unit. The younger sons are apt to form extended families with their parents, but elder sons generally set up nuclear families in new localities after their marriages.

Inheritance. The property of the parents is inherited by the sons, but the younger sons obtain most of it.

Socialization. Traditionally, the socialization of the Thakali children was quite well balanced by a laissez-faire attitude and hard training systems in Thakhola. The _shoben lava_ initiation ceremony used to be performed in Thakhola. A similar rite is also performed in the Hindu lowlands in a modified fashion under the Hindu name of a _kumar jatra_. As for the modern education of Thakali children, the parents have been very active not only in urban settings but even in Tukuche. Formerly, only the affluent families could afford to send their children to the elite schools in urban centers, but many families have now started to send their children to such schools both in Nepal and foreign countries.

Sociopolitical Organization

Social Organization. The Thakalis claim that their society is egalitarian within the ethnic group. As a whole, intensive social stratification cannot be observed except for a certain kind of socioritual ranking.

Political Organization. The leadership of the Subba families was established in the mid-nineteenth century after the Nepal-Tibet wars. Under their leadership, the Thakali community had enjoyed semiautonomy within and without the group in the Upper Kali Gandaki Valley and neighboring areas, like Panchgaon, Baragaon, Lo, and Dolpo. It lasted almost until the end of the 1950s, when the majority of the influential Thakali merchants started their migration toward the south. The new leadership, however, has not been set up within the Thakali community yet in the urban areas nor even in Thakhola. Under a main Subba who administered Thakhola, there were thirteen _mukhiyas_, or village heads, who formed a "tribal" council and the village councils in thirteen Thakali villages of Thakhola.

Social Control. Among the Thakalis in Thakhola, social control was predominantly exercised by the Subba families. But it gradually shifted to the administration of the central government by social change among the Thakalis themselves and the nation building of the kingdom.

Conflict. The sources of conflict with other ethnic groups were mainly based on competition in trading transactions and the local political domination in the Upper Kali Gandaki Valley and neighboring areas. The conflicts, however, used to be compromised or solved under the leadership of the Subba families. In recent years, the Thakalis have had to deal with troubles with other ethnic groups on an individual basis and through legal measures. The same is true for conflicts within the Thakali community.

Religion and Expressive Culture

Religious Beliefs. Thakali religion represents a syncretism of Tibetan Buddhism, Hinduism, and a native belief called Dhom, a type of shamanistic animism common in all the Himalayan regions and Tibet. These three religions—Tibetan Buddhism, Hinduism, and Dhom—coexist not only in the villages but also in the minds of the Thakalis. The core of the Thakalis' animism is the worship of their ancestors, called _dhu-tin-gya_. In recent times cultural change among the Thakalis indicates a tendency toward Hinduism rather than Tibetan Buddhism, though the latter was more influential in the old days. Although the Thakalis started to style themselves Hindus in the mid-nineteenth century when the Thakali leader began to associate with the Hindu Rana regime in Kathmandu, there was not a single Hindu temple in Thakhola before the mass migration of Thakali merchants from Thakhola to the urban centers of southern Nepal in the 1960s. The reduction of Tibetan influence and increasing Hinduization of the Thakalis in Thakhola, which began even before the 1960s, is summarized as follows. (1) Changes in the Thakali way of life have been instituted, such as avoidance of eating yak meat (beef) and of drinking Tibetan beer. (2) Some of the Thakali leaders have discouraged the members of the community from wearing _bakus_ (Tibetan robes) and have encouraged them to wear Nepalese or Western dress instead. But many women still prefer to wear Himalayan-style costumes, partly because of cold weather in Thakhola and partly for convenience while working. (3) The people have been discouraged from using the Thakali language, a Tibeto-Burman dialect, in the presence of others. But in trading transactions, it may be usefully spoken as an argot among themselves while dealing with other ethnic groups. (4) Since the Thakalis have started claiming to be Hindus, nearly all of the pantheon in Tibetan Buddhism has been reshuffled. Now the old deities having Tibeto-Himalayan names are claimed to be the avatars (incarnations) of Hindu deities. (5) The Hinduization tendency has encouraged the claim of their Thakur (the caste of the present royal family of Nepal) origin in the Jumla-Sinja area of western Nepal. This trend parallels claims of Rajput origin among some of the castes in India.

The process of Hinduization and de-Tibetanization among the Thakalis has also been accelerated by the seasonal migration of Thakalis for trade and through frequent association with their relatives and friends already settled in Pokhara, Sasadhara, Butwal, and Bhairawa. The mass migration of influential merchants after the 1960s was vital in the process of cultural change. The declining salt trade in the Himalayan regions has also played an important role in Hinduizing and de-Tibetanizing the culture of the Thakalis. It goes without saying that the flexibility of Thakali culture is also responsible for this rapid cultural change. In this connection the upper stratum of the Thakali community as a whole has played a vital part in Hinduizing and de-Tibetanizing their culture, whereas the lower stratum has been somewhat more passive in these processes. It is also noteworthy that the tendency to revive native animism (Dhom) can be observed in urban areas such as Kathmandu, where the Thakalis seem to have suffered an identity crisis and anxiety because of the rapid urbanization of their culture. The Thakalis have been shamanistic animists, and the *dhoms* (shamans) have played important roles in treating and counseling patients.

Ceremonies. The native animism called Dhom has been influential in many aspects of Thakali life. Tibetan Buddhism once played an important part in rites of passage, but Hinduism has gradually replaced it in recent years.

Arts. The Thakalis are quite artistic people, loving not only the arts but also natural beauty such as the landscape and flowers. It is, however, very interesting that they show their artistic abilities more in secular aspects of life, such as commerce, cooking, interior designing, and so forth, rather than in the arts themselves.

Medicine. Due to the pragmatic tendency of Thakali culture, scientific medicines have been well accepted among them for many years. At the same time, they have also been utilizing Tibetan as well as Ayurvedic medicines and herbs.

Death and Afterlife. The influence of the Indic folk philosophy represented in Buddhism and Hinduism has been prominent among the Thakalis and so they believe in reincarnation. Traditionally, funeral ceremonies were performed in the Dhom style among the commoners in Thakhola, except for a few wealthy subba families who preferred Buddhist ceremonies and invited lamas from the monasteries to perform them. Many of the Thakalis, however, have started to hold funeral ceremonies in a Hindu style since they migrated to the south. Some revival of native shamanism is also observed in the funeral ceremonies of urban Thakalis.

Bibliography

Fürer-Haimendorf, Christoph von (1966). "Caste Concepts and Status Distinctions in Buddhist Communities of Western Nepal." In *Caste and Kin in Nepal, India, and Ceylon*, edited by Christoph von Fürer-Haimendorf, 140–160. Bombay: Asia Publishing House. Reprint. 1978. New Delhi: Sterling Publishers.

Iijima, Shigeru (1963). "Hinduization of a Himalayan Tribe in Nepal." *Kroeber Anthropological Society Papers*, no. 29, 43–52. Berkeley: Department of Anthropology.

Iijima, Shigeru (1975). *Himalayan Traders*. London: John Murray.

Iijima, Shigeru (1982). "The Thakalis: Traditional and Modern." *Anthropological and Linguistic Studies of the Gandaki Area in Nepal*. Monumenta Serindica, no. 10. Tokyo: Institute for the Languages and Cultures of Asia and Africa, Tokyo University of Foreign Studies.

Manzardo, A. E. (1978). *To Be Kings of the North: Community Adaptation and Impression Management in the Thakali of Western Nepal*. Ph.D. dissertation, University of Wisconsin, Madison.

Messerschmidt, Donald A., and N. J. Gurung (1974). "Parallel Trade and Innovation in Central Nepal: The Cases of the Gurung and Thakali Subbas." In *Contribution to the Anthropology of Nepal*, edited by Christoph von Fürer-Haimendorf. Warminster: Aris & Phillips.

SHIGERU IIJIMA

Thakur

ETHNONYMS: Tagore, Takara, Takur, Taskara, Thakara, Thakkar, Thakkura, Thakoor

The most contemporary of the remaining group of Thakurs can be found in at least the five districts of Pune, Ahmadnagar, Nashik, Thane, and Greater Bombay, in the state of Maharashtra. However, different people in different states of India are denoted by the term "Thakur." Coming from the Sanskrit *thakkura*, meaning "idol, deity," it has been used as a title of respect, especially for Rajput nobles. Even in Bengal the word "Tagore" is used as the name of a distinguished family of Brahman literary and artistic figures. But in other places *thakur* is the honorific designation of a barber. According to the Marathi *Encyclopedia*, this name refers to the people who are mainly in Gujarat, Maharashtra, Punjab, and Kashmir. They can be found among the ranks of Muslims, Hindus, Sikhs, and even Buddhists. In Bernard Cohn's study of Madhopur, the Thakurs are reported to have held predominant economic and political power there since the conquest of the village and the region by their ancestors in the sixteenth century. The Thakurs of today trace their ancestry to Ganesh Rai, who succeeded in conquering a tract around Madhopur that is now called Dobhi Taluka.

There seem to be two schools of thought on dress among the two separate groups of Thakurs (Ka and Ma). The Ka women normally do not wear a bodice with their saris, so they leave their breasts bare. Unlike the Ka, the Ma women wear bodices, but they too until a few years ago used to leave their breasts bare. After marriage, Ka women leave their left buttock uncovered as it is supposed to belong to the father's family.

The staple foods of the uplands are the millets, _vari_ (_Panicum sumatrense_) and _nagali_ (_Eleusine coracana_). Those who live at the foot of the mountains cultivate rented paddy lands, but most are unsuccessful at producing enough to exist on. Meat and fish when available are eaten, and sometimes wild onions are eaten for weeks at a time. The unavailability of required nourishment encourages nomadic tendencies. Milk is avoided by many Thakurs, as they say it makes them bilious. Exceptions are during monsoons, when they eat a delicacy called _kharvas_ which is prepared from new milk. Meals are eaten three times a day—breakfast, lunch, and dinner. Breakfast and lunch consist of bread with some complement, and for dinner rice, normally unpolished, and _dal_ are cooked; men and women eat apart.

The Hindu Thakur have assumed the religious views of life current in Hindu philosophy. Their folklore reveals glimpses into Vedantic philosophy and reflects the fatalistic passivism of the Indian way of life. In their dancing songs, prayers are offered to Shankar, Parvati, and other deities of the Hindu pantheon. The attitude toward such deities (_deva_) is one of fear and dread. Among them names such as Bhavani, Kanhoba, and Khanderav are worshiped by the more advanced classes. Others are Vaghya, thought to represent the tiger, and Thrava, who represents the peacock, while Munja and Vetal come from the spirit world. The Thakur deities are often housed in trees and worshiped according to the resources available to worshipers.

Not all Thakur are landlords; some are extremely poor and dwell in the jungles with little to eat. Thakur family structure usually consists of a man, who represents the head of the family, his wife, and their children. Married sons have the option of staying on with their father or making a new and separate home, while daughters are expected to live with their husbands. The Thakur have been slowly reshaping their family structures: in modern times the family ties have grown looser, and the importance of clan and village has declined. A lessened respect for the father's position is more common now, as are the tendencies to move away from formality, to allow more freedom between husband and wife, and to create smaller household units. The Thakur wife is coming out of seclusion, under the influence of the urban, Westernized family. This liberalization takes place in areas such as caste observance, religion, food habits, and many other aspects of social life.

Bibliography

Chapekar, L. N. (1960). _Thakurs of the Sahyadri_. London: Oxford University Press.

Cohn, Bernard S. (1955). _"Social Status of a Depressed Caste"_. In _Village India_, edited by McKim Marriot, 53–77. Chicago: University of Chicago Press.

Lewis, Oscar (1958). _Village Life in Northern India_. Urbana: University of Illinois Press.

LeSHON KIMBLE

Tharu

ETHNONYMS: none

The Tharus are the largest and most important of the various tribal groups occupying the Tarai zone of Nepal. (The Tarai is the lowest [300 to 800 meters above sea level] of the four ecological zones that run across the country from west to east.) In 1985 the Tharus numbered about 500,000 in Nepal, with a considerably smaller population in Uttar Pradesh, India (67,994 in 1971). The Tharus are sometimes described as containing two fairly distinct geographical subgroups, the Bhoksa in the west and the Mechi in the east. From the perspective of their high-caste Pahari and Newar neighbors, the Tharus are Untouchables, though higher than the official "unclean" Untouchable castes.

Contemporary Tharus are mainly wet-rice agriculturalists who live in permanent settlements integrated through kin ties and mutual economic obligations. Each village is governed by a council and a headman who collects taxes for the central government. There is some evidence that permanent settlements and wet-rice agriculture represent a shift from an earlier reliance on shifting horticulture. Traditionally, the Tharus were subdivided into two major groups of unequal status, each composed of a number of endogamous units called _kuri_. Today, the high-status group forms a single endogamous unit, while the low-status group continues to have a number of distinct endogamous units. Tharu religion is an amalgam of beliefs involving traditional supernaturals, Hindu deities, and Moslem saints, with the shaman as the central religious figure, calling on the power of supernatural forces from all three belief systems to exorcise evil spirits and cure the sick.

Bibliography

Srivastava, S. K. (1958). _The Tharus: A Study in Cultural Dynamics_. Agra: Agra University Press.

Thug

Political Service. Reprint. 1977. London: White Lion Publishers.

PAUL HOCKINGS

ETHNONYMS: Dacoo, Dacoit; formerly called Phansigar or Phanseegur, meaning "strangler"

The term "Thug" comes from *thag,* meaning "cheat, swindler, robber," and it refers to professional highwaymen who for centuries were the scourge of wealthier travelers throughout India. These men worked swiftly to win the confidence of their victims, then strangled them with a scarf or noose and robbed the bodies, which they immediately buried to avoid detection. They formed gangs of 10–200 men, organized into a sort of confederacy. *Thugee,* as this "trade" was called, was not simply a profitable criminal activity—it was a traditional calling. By wearing religious garb the Thug maintained an air of respectability. Under most Hindu and Muslim rulers this was regarded as a regular profession, and Thugs paid city taxes. Thugs believed that their crimes did honor to the goddess Kali (the Hindu goddess of destruction) whom they worshiped before each attempt to befriend and then kill travelers. Consecration of the pickax and the offering of sugar were important prior to an assassination, and after the deed some of the gains were set aside as a reward for Kali. In turn, the goddess expressed her wishes to Thugs through a complicated system of omens.

The earliest authentic reference to Thugs dates to about A.D. 1290, and India's Thugee and Dacoity Department was closed down only in 1904. Thugee was finally brought under control for the British administration of India around 1848 by Sir William Sleeman. Like organized crime elsewhere, the confederacy of Thugs persisted for so long because of its superior organization, secrecy, and the security offered everywhere by "retired" elderly Thugs, who continued to operate as spies or cooks. In his book, *Ramaseeana* (1836), Sleeman recorded the peculiar argot used by Thugs to maintain the secrecy of their intentions, and thus he introduced the word *thug* to English dictionaries. The crime of *dacoity,* however, still continues in some remote areas of South Asia. Now it is defined simply as brigandage committed by armed gangs of robbers, called *dacoits* or *dacoos.* By law there must be five or more in a gang for the robbery to be considered dacoity. Both thugee and dacoity were usually punished by hanging or banishment for life. Some of the criminals repented and converted to Christianity.

Bibliography

Russell, R. V., and Hira Lal (1916). "Thug." In *The Tribes and Castes of the Central Provinces of India,* edited by R. V. Russell and Hira Lal. Vol. 4, 558–587. London: Macmillan. Reprint. 1969. Oosterhout: Anthropological Publications.

Sleeman, William (1836). *Ramaseeana; or a Vocabulary of the Peculiar Language Used by the Thugs. . . .* Calcutta: G. H. Hultmann, Military Orphan Press.

Tucker, Francis (1961). *The Yellow Scarf: The Story of the Life of Thugee Sleeman or Major-General Sir William Henry Sleeman, K.C.B.: (1778–1856) of the Bengal Army and the Indian*

Toda

ETHNONYMS: O·ɣ, Todava, Ton, Tutavar

Orientation

Identification.   The Toda, a small, traditionally pastoral community of the Nilgiri Mountains in south India, call themselves O·ɣ (long rounded vowel, plus voiceless retroflex *l*), meaning simply "the men." Their Badaga neighbors call them Todava, while Tamil speakers call them Tutavar. To other Nilgiri neighbors, the Kota, they are Ton. "Toda" is an anglicization of the Badaga form. Today the Toda include traditionalists (the majority) and a small breakaway community of Christians.

Location.   The Nilgiri Mountains of India's Tamil Nadu State rise spectacularly to an elevation of 2,400 meters. The highlands, where the Toda live, enjoy a temperate monsoonal climate, very different from the tropical plains below. The natural vegetation of the highlands is rolling grassland, with patches of temperate forest known as *shola.* As the Nilgiri slopes are precipitous and the thickly forested foothills were once highly malarial, the Toda and their highland neighbors lived for centuries in considerable isolation from the South Indian mainstream cultures.

Demography.   Throughout recorded history the Toda community has been small. In 1603, a Jesuit priest who visited them wrote that the Toda numbered "about a thousand." The first government of India census in 1871 counted 693. In 1952 the parent, non-Christian community reached probably its all-time low of 475, and then it began slowly to increase. In August 1988 the author counted 1,042 Toda traditionalists (all but 35 living in Toda hamlets) and another 4 persons, born traditionalists but made outcaste for marrying non-Toda. The three Toda Christian settlements accounted for a further 133 people, but only 38 could claim pure Toda descent; kin and affines of these Toda Christians, living elsewhere in India and abroad, numbered at least 150, but only 35 were of pure Toda descent. Traditionalists, together with Christians and Outcastes of pure Toda descent, therefore totaled 1,119. Female infanticide (officially prohibited in 1819, but continuing sporadically for several decades) probably accounted for ancient population limits. More recently, venereal infections kept numbers low until a drive to eradicate these diseases, begun in the 1950s, succeeded in raising the birthrate.

Linguistic Affiliation.   A Dravidian language affiliated with Tamil-Malayalam, Toda may have emerged as a separate language in the third century B.C. It has no written form. Most Toda speak Tamil and Badagu in addition to their mother tongue. Literate Toda mostly write in Tamil; a few use English.

History and Cultural Relations

Despite much amateurish speculation about Toda origins in Greece, Rome, the Danube Basin, ancient Israel, Sumeria, and other unlikely places, the linguistic evidence points clearly to the people's South Indian roots. But because Toda emerged from the mother language before Tamil and Malayalam separated, we cannot be certain whether the community's ancestors ascended the Nilgiris from east or west, although west seems the better guess. (Toda say they were created on the Nilgiris.) Artifacts, seemingly unrelated to the Toda, from stone-circle burial sites in the highlands suggest that Toda were not there before the beginning of the Christian era. The first written evidence for Toda in or near the Nilgiris, an inscription on stone dated 1117, relates in Kannada how a Hoysala general "conquered the Toda" before dedicating the Nilgiri peak "to the Lakshmi of Victory." In 1799 the mountains became a British possession, though unadministered until after 1819. Before that time, Toda may have paid a grazing tax to overlords in the plains, but their physical isolation atop the high Nilgiris permitted a way of life mostly untrammeled by outside interference. After the assertion of British rule, Toda were never again to be quite free of state bureaucracy.

Linguistically, culturally, and economically distinct, the Toda are nonetheless an integral part of a traditional Nilgiri society whose affiliations—despite modifications due to physical isolation—are clearly with the wider civilization of south India. The Toda's traditional Nilgiri neighbors included: an artisan caste of potters, blacksmiths, and leather workers, the Kota; an immigrant group of Kannada-speaking castes with the common name of Badaga, who became the dominant food producers, hence political overlords, of the Nilgiris; and two forest-dwelling communities, Kurumba and Irula. These Nilgiri peoples maintained an interfamilial system of economic, ritual, and social interdependence very much within the tradition of multicaste rural communities throughout India. In typically Indic manner also, they recognized among themselves a social hierarchy based preeminently on considerations of relative ritual purity. In the early nineteenth century the isolation of the Toda homeland was shattered with the coming of the British administration. The resultant growth of an immigrant population, markets, and a cash-crop- and plantation-based economy disrupted the old economic interdependence of the Nilgiri peoples, while intensified contact with mainstream South Indian Hinduism eroded the foundations of the traditional ritual interdependence. Only vestiges of the old order now survive; modern Todas, several of them working in Nilgiri factories and a few college-educated, are as familiar with immigrant peoples as with their traditional Nilgiri neighbors, and they are far more conversant with the market economy than with the former system of intercommunity familial transactions.

Settlements

In 1988 there were 64 permanently occupied Toda hamlets (including the three Christian ones). Two dry-season hamlets also were still being used. Seasonal hamlets in the wetter parts of the highlands used to be occupied from December through March, when regular grazing grounds are parched. At least 26 have been abandoned in the past twenty years. The 61 non-Christian hamlets contained 214 households and 1,078 people, giving means of 4.7 houses and just under 16.5 persons per settlement. (Two Christian settlements follow the normal Toda pattern; the other has 18 households and 91 people.) A traditional Toda hamlet comprises 1 to 5 barrel-vaulted houses, a buffalo pen, calf sheds, and sometimes a separate calf pen. The site must have ample grazing ground for buffalo, running water, and a shola nearby for firewood and building materials. Most hamlets, until recently, had at least one sacred dairy building; a few had up to three. Toda house styles and settlements have been changing for more than a century and in 1988 only 13 of the 214 houses were of the traditional barrel-vaulted style. The dairies, where they exist, retain the traditional architecture, but as many as 26 hamlets (43 percent of the total) have no dairy building at all, or only a ruin. Buffalo pens mostly remain, but often only a fenced-in portion is still being used. Much of the surounding pasture has been dug up for potato and vegetable cultivation and several sholas have been felled. All hamlets now have electricity.

Economy

Subsistence and Commercial Activities. Traditional Toda economy revolves around their herds of female, long-horned, short-legged, and rather ferocious mountain water buffalo. Being vegetarians, Toda keep these animals for their milk and milk products, selling most male calves to Nilgiri butchers. In pre-British, premarket days, Toda exchanged milk products for grain (various millets) from Badaga, for pots and jewelry from Kota, and for forest products, mostly from Kurumba. These exchanges (involving also ritual and social obligations) took place between hereditarily linked families of the different communities, as is typical of Hindu *jajmani* relationships. Today, with the old economic interrelationships defunct, Toda who still keep enough buffalo mostly sell their milk through two cooperatives or directly to coffee shops, and they use cash to buy rice in the Nilgiri markets. Almost all Toda families are today involved in agriculture, if only as landlords. Growing numbers till the soil themselves, a radical departure for a proud pastoral people who once despised the agriculturalist's way of life. The principal crops are cabbages, carrots, and, above all, potatoes. Apart from their buffalo, traditional Toda, as vegetarians, had no need of domestic animals other than dogs, to watch over their settlements, and a few cats as house pets and vermin catchers. Toda Christians began to replace their buffalo with cattle early in this century; some traditionalists now also keep a few cows.

Industrial Arts. Toda obtain their clay pots, metal utensils, and textiles from outside their community (formerly through exchange, now in the markets). They are expert builders of their traditional (but not modern) houses and dairy temples, and they are skilled manufacturers of dairy appurtenances: herding and walking sticks, milking vessels, and churning sticks.

Division of Labor. Traditionally, care for the buffalo is an exclusively male concern and women are the principal housekeepers (although men cook on ritually important occasions). Women also devote much time to embroidery. When Toda take up agriculture, both men and women work in the fields.

Land Tenure. As buffalo pastoralists, Toda used rather than owned land. In 1843, however, the British administration began allocating land to the Toda, and by 1863 had alloted a little over 18 hectares to each hamlet and religious site. *Patta* (land titles) issued to Toda listed the names of household heads but stated that rights were communal, not individual. From 1871, the deeds also stipulated that Toda must not alienate their patta lands and, from 1881, that they could not lease them. These stipulations remain, although all along many Toda have leased land covertly to people more willing than themselves to farm. In 1975, the Hill Area Development Programme provided financial assistance to each Toda household to cultivate a maximum of 2 hectares of Toda patta land; the cultivated land was, for the first time, registered in the name of an individual, the family head. Since patta lands remain tied to the patriclans, any division for agricultural purposes has had to be made between household heads of the same patriclan. Not all patriclans have sufficient lands to permit every family its 2-hectare maximum.

Kinship

Kin Groups and Descent. The typically Dravidian classificatory system operates independently of any particular society's descent system. In the Toda case, it is found together with double-unilineal descent, for these people have a full-fledged patrilineal and matrilineal descent system, such that each Toda has both patriclan and matriclan membership, each one being exogamous.

Kinship Terminology. The Toda kinship system follows the classificatory principles common to most Dravidian-speaking peoples. Most importantly, a parent's siblings of the same sex as one's parent are classified as "parents"; those of opposite sex are termed "uncles" and "aunts" and belong to a completely different category of relative. The offspring of one's actual and classificatory parents are his or her siblings; marriage or sexual relations would then be incestuous. The children of uncles and aunts are "cousins," who are preferred marriage partners. All children of one's same-sex siblings, actual or classificatory, are classificatory children, a large category. A more restricted category in this first descending generation is that of the actual offspring of one's actual siblings of the opposite sex, the "nephews" and "nieces," who are the preferred spouses for Ego's own children. The Toda system thus distinguishes in three crucial generations two very different categories of relatives: parents, siblings, and children constitute the kin group, while uncles and aunts, cousins, and nephews and nieces (potential parents-in-law, spouses, and children's spouses) are the affinal or, more strictly, "potentially affinal" group.

Marriage and Family

Marriage. In Toda terms "marriage" must be defined as an alliance by which a female of any age, preferably a mother's brother's daughter or father's sister's daughter, is incorporated into the patriclan of a male, who is thereafter considered her husband, whether or not they live together. Marriages are negotiated and initiated usually before the partners are 2 or 3 years old and are completed at maturity, when the husband takes his wife from her home to his own hamlet. In ritual terms the children are as truly married as the adults. Traditionally, Toda practiced fraternal polyandry, younger brothers becoming cohusbands to the eldest's wife. Now abandoned, polyandry was necessary because of the sexual imbalance caused by female infanticide (also abandoned long ago). Some Toda, usually the wealthy older men, take a second or third wife. In the past this could result in two or more brothers sharing two or more wives. Some polygynous unions still exist among Toda, but monogamy is now the norm and, for most younger Toda, the ideal as well. Another consequence of the past shortage of women is the continuing institution of "marriage by capture," enabling men to take the wives of others and have the union regularized by payment of compensation in buffalo to the former husband. When a young man takes his wife from her parental home, they usually live first in his father's house. Subsequently they may build a house of their own in that hamlet or in another of the same patriclan. Inaugurated in infancy and easily broken by elopement, Toda marriages are rather brittle. Nonetheless, formal divorce (a man returns his wife to her father's home, proclaiming the union terminated) is a very rare event that brings disgrace to a woman and insults both her father and her children.

Domestic Unit. At the present time, the occupants of a single dwelling usually comprise a nuclear family: husband, wife, and their unmarried children. Except in the case of a widow with small children, the household head is always an adult male. In the past, with both polyandrous and polygynous marriages, households were often more complex.

Inheritance. The household head is custodian of the household's property: the house itself, domestic equipment, family heirlooms (personal jewelry, and ornaments and bells for buffalo), the buffalo, and, in recent times, a portion of the patriclan's patta lands as well. Some of this property, especially buffalo, may be distributed to a man's sons when he retires from active herding. On his death, all that remains is divided equally among his sons. Daughters receive nothing except a dowry. A widow with young sons is merely the guardian of the household property until her eldest son reaches manhood.

Socialization. Children are much desired and infants treated with indulgence by parents and elder siblings. Breast-fed for up to three years, they may have to be weaned by the mother applying the juice of an astringent plant to her nipples. Swaddled in pieces of old cloth, the infants are slowly toilet-trained. After a year or so, if they misbehave they will be reprimanded and perhaps stung on their buttocks with a nettle. For good behavior they are rewarded with candy and biscuits. From very young ages boys begin to play at being buffalo herders and girls at being mothers and housewives; slowly play merges into the real thing. More and more Toda children now attend school, but education is not compulsory.

Sociopolitical Organization

Social Organization. Toda society is divided into two endogamous and hierarchically ordered subcastes, with differing relationships to the community's sacred dairy cult: one ritually higher subcaste owns the most sacred of the dairies and the other subcaste alone may operate them. Each subcaste is again divided into named exogamous patriclans, which own the hamlets, funeral places, and sometimes an isolated dairy site. A patriclan has four subdivisions: _kwï·ṛ_, a ritual bifurcation; _po·lm_, an economic section, of which there may be more than two; hamlet and family. The two subcastes are also divided into exogamous matriclans, important descent categories for marital and ritual purposes but lacking corporate unity.

Political Organization. Toda society functions without formal headmen at any level, except the household, where the eldest male is dominant. A caste council makes political decisions affecting the whole community: all adult males may participate, debating each issue until a consensus is reached. Matters concerning one subcaste alone, or one patriclan, are debated by the subcaste or patriclan council respectively, comprising all adult male members who wish to participate. Because Toda have long recognized the politicoeconomic (but not ritual) dominance of the Badaga, they sometimes ask certain Badaga leaders to participate in their caste council.

Social Control. The household head is responsible for the good behavior of all who live under his roof. Disputes between households are mediated by the patriclan council; unresolved cases may be taken to the subcaste or, finally, caste council. Each patriclan oversees its own members, but disputes between patriclan members may go to a subcaste or ultimately a caste council for resolution. The subcaste also operates through its subcaste council to regulate its members, with the possibility of taking unresolved issues before the caste council. The caste council has the power to deal with any infringement of social conduct within the community and can fine or excommunicate offenders.

Conflict. The Toda have no weapons of war or martial institutions. Conflicts, either between individuals or groups, only occasionally provoke physical violence rather than the vitriolic verbal confrontation that is common. The various councils—clan, subcaste, and caste—are quick to intervene, defuse emotions, and argue for compromise.

Religion and Expressive Culture

Religious Beliefs and Practitioners. Traditional Toda cosmology identifies two worlds: that of the living, ruled by the goddess Tökisy, and that of the dead, where her brother, Ö·n, reigns supreme. There is no conception of an eternal Hell, but those who have led unmeritorious lives are said to suffer many indignities before they too eventually reach the other world. Toda also have appropriated much of the worldview of their Hindu neighbors, and concepts of ritual purity, pollution, hierarchy, and ritual specialization underlie even the most indigenous of Toda ritual practices. Pilgrimage to Hindu temples, no recent innovation, is increasingly popular among younger Toda. Toda religion finds ritual expression principally in the cult of the sacred dairies and their associated buffalo herds. Buffalo are categorized as secular (the mainstay of the traditional economy) or sacred (with several gradations). For the latter, ritual surrounds every task of the dairyman: herding, milking, churning, and preparing ghee (clarified butter) from butter, as well as seasonal or occasional activities such as burning the pastures (now discontin-

ued), naming a buffalo, giving salt to the herds, driving them to dry-season pastures, and rethatching or rebuilding a dairy building. Dairies, which Toda themselves identify as temples, are buildings kept in a state of ritual purity so that dairymen-priests (of comparable ritual purity) can process inside them the milk from associated herds of sacred buffalo. Ranked in a hierarchy, each grade of dairy has its associated grade of sacred buffalo and dairyman-priest. The higher the grade of a dairy, the greater is the need for ritual purity and the more elaborate the rituals that surround the daily tasks of the dairyman. Another category of religious specialist are the "god men," who in trance become mouthpieces of particular deities, frequently Hindu rather than Toda ones. Christian missionaries of several denominations have proselytized among the Toda, the most successful being those of the Church of England Zenana Missionary Society, whose first Toda convert in 1904 marked the beginning of a breakaway Toda Christian community. Now denominationally affiliated to the Church of South India, this community has churches in two of its three hamlets. Because of widespread intermarriage with non-Toda Christians and the use of Tamil, not Toda, as its principal language, this Christian community retains few traces of traditional Toda culture, although some of its members remain proudly conscious of their Toda ethnicity. The Toda populate their supernatural world with several anthropomorphic deities generically termed "gods of the mountains," because most of them are said to reside on Nilgiri peaks. The most important is the goddess Tökisy, creator of the Toda and their buffalo and ordainer of their principal social and ritual institutions. Other deities, the "gods of the sacred places," represent the divine essences of the more sacred of the dairy complexes; they too are sometimes conceived anthropomorphically. Most modern Toda worship Hindu deities, displaying lithographic icons of Shiva, Vishnu, Murugan, Aiyappan, etc. in their homes and sometimes even keeping an elaborate "gods' room" such as one finds among the Hindu mainstream.

Ceremonies. Apart from the intricate observances of the sacred dairy cult, the principal Toda ceremonies mark the passage through life. Pregnancy and birth traditionally involved periods of physical isolation for the women to prevent ritual defilement of a hamlet and particularly of its dairy. Paternity is a social fact determined by ritual rather than biology; a man acknowledges fatherhood of an unborn child by presenting the pregnant woman (in her seventh month) with a stylized bow and arrow. Important childhood ceremonies, more highly ritualized for boys than girls, are: the first uncovering of an infant's face outside the house and its subsequent naming; the marriage of infants; and the piercing of a boy's ears to mark ritual (not physical) maturity. Symbolic and actual defloration once initiated adulthood for a girl, but these customs probably have been abandoned. Ceremony also attends a man's taking of his mature wife from her parental home. Death occasions the greatest elaboration of Toda ritual (see below). Modern Toda actively participate in Hindu temple rituals, while Toda Christians follow the liturgical practices, mostly Anglican-derived, of the Church of South India.

Arts. The principal Toda arts are oral poetry, often but not necessarily sung to accompany dance, and embroidery. Women alone are the embroiderers, embellishing with geometric designs the large cloaks that Toda wear and producing tablecloths, placemats, etc. for sale. Both men and women compose songs about any noteworthy event in a rigidly conventionalized poetic language that uses parallelism to great effect. Practically every detail in Toda life has its special phrase that, in song, must be followed by a parallel phrase, either synonymous with or linked by convention to the first phrase: "all the hamlets / all the sacred places," "European in the courts / important man in the places," "child in the lap / calf in the pen," etc.

Medicine.   Toda may attribute sickness to natural causes, the malevolence of supernatural beings, or the sorcery of humans (especially Kurumba, traditionally feared for their supposed magical powers). They may take traditional herbal or modern pharmaceutical medicines, offer vows to Toda dairies, Hindu temples, Muslim mosques, or Christian churches, or seek the services of a Kurumba in countersorcery.

Death and Afterlife.   The death of an unnamed infant receives no public recognition, that of a named child some, and that of a respected elder a great deal. Traditionally two funeral rites were held and it was believed that the deceased could not enter the Land of the Dead until the second was complete. At the first funeral, the body was cremated; at the second, a relic (lock of hair or fragment of bone) was burned. The rituals of the two were very similar, the relic substituting for the corpse in the second. Today second funerals are no longer held, their concluding rites having been appended to the first ceremony. At a funeral, every major division of Toda society and every principal kinship and affinal role comes into play, and buffalo are sacrificed to accompany the dead to the afterworld: secular animals for females, sacred and secular ones for males. Reformists recently have opposed buffalo sacrifice and have, on occasion, prevented it. The Toda locate the world of the dead to the west and below the Nilgiri Plateau, possibly indicating Toda origins in Kerala. The several routes to this afterworld can actually be followed to the edge of the Nilgiri massif. Toda say that the world of the dead is much like that of the living, except that it has a harder surface. Instead of people and buffalo eroding the land, they wear down their own legs, and when their shortened limbs make life in "the other-side place" impossible, their spirits are reborn as Toda or Toda buffalo of the Nilgiri highlands.

See also Badaga; Kota; Kurumba

Bibliography

Emeneau, Murray B. (1967). *Dravidian Linguistics, Ethnology, and Folktales: Collected Papers*. Department of Linguistics Publication. Annamalainagar: Annamalai University Press.

Emeneau, Murray B. (1971). *Toda Songs*. Oxford: Clarendon Press.

Emeneau, Murray B. (1974). *Ritual Structure and Language Structure of the Todas*. Transactions of the American Philosophical Society, n.s. 63, no. 6. Philadelphia.

Nambiar, P. K. (1965). *Census of India 1961*. Vol. 9, *Madras*, pt. 5-C, *Todas*. Delhi: Manager of Publications, Government of India.

Rivers, W. H. R. (1906). *The Todas*. London: Macmillan.

Walker, Anthony R. (1986). *The Toda of South India: A New Look*. Delhi: Hindustan Publishing Corporation.

ANTHONY R. WALKER

Untouchables

ETHNONYMS: Adi-Dravida, depressed caste, external caste, Harijan, Panchama, Pariah, Scheduled Caste

The word "Untouchable" was first applied to this category of Hindus by the Maharaja Sayaji Rao III of Baroda in a lecture he gave in 1909, to describe their most essential characteristic vis-à-vis higher-ranking castes. Some twenty years later Mahatma Gandhi named them "Harijans," which means roughly "children of God." Later still the government of India drew up a list of the most disadvantaged castes, hence generating a new euphemism, "Scheduled Castes." Drawing on Sanskrit, Untouchables have called themselves "Panchama," or the "fifth _varna_," a term that is not often heard today; or, in South India, they are "Adi-Dravidas," meaning "original Dravidians." The British have long called them "Pariahs," in reference to a major Untouchable group of Tamil Nadu.

The Untouchables are collectively all those castes, in any part of South Asia, who are Hindus or former Hindus and rank below the Sudra varna. Their numbers are not known precisely, but in 1991 India probably had between 130 and 140 million Untouchables, and the subcontinental total would be close to 200 million.

The low rank of the Untouchables is explained by the general belief that their traditional occupations and other habits are or were polluting to higher castes in a spiritual way as they had something to do with blood, dirt, or death. Thus the families of leather workers, scavengers, and butchers are Untouchables, simply by reason of their traditional occupations. Furthermore, it is felt that this karma comes to Untouchables as a punishment for sins committed in a previous existence. Although these numerous castes all fall below the "pollution line," they are not undifferentiated in rank but rather recognize a range of social distinctions. Some, who rank higher than other Untouchables, serve as priests to the rest, at their own shrines, because it is impossible to get Brahmans or other priests of very high status to serve the religious offices of these people.

The marks of their supposed pollution were traditionally expressed in a variety of ways. Very commonly, a _cheri_ or separated, satellite hamlet was established for the Untouchables of a village; otherwise, they would inhabit a segregated quarter. The use of their own wells and even in some areas the use of their own footpaths and bridges were thought to be ways of protecting the rest of Hindu society from their polluting presence. In Kerala until a century ago there were various prescribed distances, ranging from 12 to 96 paces, closer than which the particular Untouchable castes could not approach higher-status Hindus. Some were said to be so polluting that they could pollute a corpse—itself considered highly polluting—or should only move around at nighttime. Some groups in Kerala polluted a Hindu of higher caste if only their shadow fell on him; others had to actually touch him or his food to do so.

In modern times the requirements of public transportation and daily living have made many of these observances anachronistic, if not quite unthinkable. Yet the Untouchables remain the most backward and least educated sector of the community. Various sorts of government uplift programs provided especially for the Scheduled Castes have gone some way toward improving the health, education, political representation, and employment opportunities for Untouchables. Yet they remain, in all South Asian countries, a somewhat despised and underprivileged category.

Sizable numbers of Untouchables have over the past century or so been converted to Christianity or Buddhism, partly in response to the relative egalitarianism of these faiths, and partly because membership in these communities might obscure one's Untouchable background and so improve the chances for better employment.

Untouchability is by no means confined to South Asia, for it has also been reported in Japan (the Buraku), Korea (the Paekchong), Tibet (the Ragyappa), and Burma (Pagoda slaves); in each case there is no association with Hinduism.

See also Castes, Hindu; Chamar; Mahar; Neo-Buddhist; Scheduled Castes and Scheduled Tribes

Bibliography

Fuchs, Stephen (1950). _The Children of Hari._ Vienna: Verlag Herold.

Mahar, J. Michael, ed. (1972). _The Untouchables in Contemporary India._ Tucson: University of Arizona Press.

PAUL HOCKINGS

Vaisya

ETHNONYM: Vaishya

The Vaisyas are the third-highest of the four *varnas* or categories into which Hindu society is traditionally divided, ranking above the Sudras. Vaisya includes a large number of distinct castes of similar ranking, traditionally traders, moneylenders, or farmers. They are entitled to wear a sacred thread. It is distinctly less common to encounter castes claiming Vaisya status in Sri Lanka and south India than in the north.

The category is certainly a very ancient one, for it is referred to in the *Rig Veda* (c. twelfth century B.C.). Vaisyas are clearly referred to in other early hymns as being Aryas, the Indo-European invaders, rather than Dasas, the Dravidian and other Aborigines of the subcontinent. According to the *Zend Avesta*, the Zoroastrian holy book, there was in ancient Persia a social category called "Vastrya," who ranked third in society below the Atharvas and Rethaesvas and bore a name that is cognate with the Sanskrit "Vaisya." The classical Indian lawgiver Manu (c. second century A.D.) spells out the duties of the Vaisya: "to keep herds of cattle, to bestow largesses, to sacrifice, to read the scripture, to carry on trade, to lend at interest, and to cultivate land." The economy depended on them, and the description of Manu still holds true

See also Bania; Castes, Hindu

Bibliography

Hutton, John H. (1963). *Caste In India*. 4th ed. London: Oxford University Press.

PAUL HOCKINGS

Vedda

ETHNONYMS: Vadda, Veddah, Veddha, Vaddo

Orientation

Identification. The Veddas are a small group of people living in the center of Sri Lanka, an island off the southern tip of India. "Vedda" is a Dravidian word meaning "hunter." Contemporary Vedda culture is strongly marked by prolonged interaction both with the Sinhalese and with the Tamils, the two largest ethnic groups in Sri Lanka, but the Vedda people themselves are generally reputed to be descended from the aboriginal population of the island and to have maintained until recent times a distinctive way of life based on hunting and gathering. The Veddas are divided into three regional groups (the Bintenne Veddas, the Anuradhapura Veddas, and the Coast Veddas) whose members have little or no contact with one another, although they acknowledge a remote kinship.

Location. Sri Lanka is located between 5° 55' and 9° 51' N and 79° 41' and 81° 53' E. Veddas formerly lived in all of the more isolated parts of the island, but today they are restricted to the arc of country between the predominantly Sinhalese areas in the west, south, and center of the island and the predominantly Tamil areas in the north and east. The Bintenne Veddas inhabit an area in the southeast of the island, inland from the towns of Batticaloa and Trincomalee and extending westward to the Verugal, Mahaweli, and Gal Oya rivers. The Coast Veddas live along the coast between Batticaloa and Trincomalee. The Anuradhapura Veddas live in the North Central Province. All three groups are located within Sri Lanka's dry zone, where the annual rainfall is normally less than 190 centimeters, most of which falls between October and December.

Demography. The Veddas constitute only a very small proportion of the total population of Sri Lanka, which was estimated at nearly 15 million by the 1981 census. There is, however, no consensus as to just how small this proportion is, because the criteria used to identify the Veddas vary widely. They were last enumerated separately in the census of 1963, at which time they numbered 400. In 1970, however, a census of the Anuradhapura Veddas, conducted as part of an ethnographic study, counted more than 6,600 of them. The main reason for this discrepancy is that government officials have tended to treat as Veddas only those who subsist from hunting and gathering—a criterion that would have excluded virtually all of the Anuradhapura Veddas—while the ethnographer's census included all those who identified themselves as Veddas. Estimates of the size of the Bintenne and Coast Vedda populations are not available, but both are probably much less than that of the Anuradhapura Veddas.

Linguistic Affiliation. Only faint traces of what might once have been a distinct Vedda language have been detected. Contemporary Veddas speak colloquial forms of either Sinhala or Tamil, depending on which of the two main ethnic groups predominates in their local area. The Bintenne and Anuradhapura Veddas mostly speak Sinhala, which is an Indo-European language, while the Coast Veddas speak Tamil, which is Dravidian. Peculiarities in the speech patterns of the Veddas can be attributed to their relative isolation, low level of formal education, and low socioeconomic status.

History and Cultural Relations

The weight of physical anthropological evidence is that certain groups of Veddas show stronger biological affinities with prehistoric inhabitants of the island than do any other groups in present-day Sri Lanka. This lends support to the common assertion that the Veddas are the remnant descendants of an aboriginal population that inhabited Sri Lanka before the emergence of a literate civilization in the later centuries of the first millennium B.C. The extent to which this civilization was an indigenous development and not just the creation of immigrant settlers remains a matter of controversy, but undoubtedly there was considerable exchange—both cultural and genetic—between the descendants of the prehistoric inhabitants and later immigrants. These relations are expressed in the popular myth that the contemporary Veddas are descended from a union between Kuveni, an aboriginal demoness, and Prince Vijaya, the legendary founder of the Sinhalese nation who came from India. In historic times, however, the most prominent feature—virtually the defining characteristic—of the Veddas has been their social marginality. They have made their living on the peripheries of Sinhalese and Tamil polities, in relation to both of which they came to represent the uncivilized element in society. Thus while actual Vedda culture reveals a variable pattern that merges readily with that of the rural Sinhalese, the categorical opposition between Vedda and Sinhalese radically distinguishes the former, as a group of savage and pagan foragers, from the more civilized, paddy-cultivating Buddhist Sinhalese. A similar pattern obtains between the Tamil-speaking Coast Veddas and the Hindu Tamils. In the last hundred years, however, with the rapid expansion of Sri Lanka's population, improved communications, and increased settlement in the dry zone, embodiments of the ideal or typical Vedda, defined in polar opposition to the civilized Sinhalese or Tamil, have become extremely hard to find. Nevertheless, because of its compatibility with the disposition of nineteenth-century European scholars to discover a pristine Vedda culture that was unambiguously associated with a distinct racial group, this idealized representation of the Vedda has exercised a commanding influence over the anthropological imagination. Recent studies of the Anuradhapura and Coast Veddas have encompassed groups that deviate significantly from the ideal, but representations of the Bintenne Veddas are still dominated by C. G. and Brenda Seligmann's classic study, published in 1911, which, in its ambition to describe the pure culture of pure-blooded Veddas, depicts a way of life that was followed only by a small minority of those who then identified themselves as Veddas.

Settlements

According to the Seligmanns, Bintenne Veddas lived both in permanent villages of up to 40 families and in temporary settlements, near their cultivation plots, which contained between 1 and 5 families of varying size. The Anuradhapura Veddas occupy 32 villages and 14 satellite hamlets that are scattered among the much more numerous Sinhalese villages in the region. In 1970 their largest village had a population of 552. Their settlement pattern is similar to that of the local Sinhalese, the core of the village being a cluster of houses built close to the village reservoir. The Coast Veddas live in small villages near the sea consisting of a cluster of compounds with two or three houses to a compound. Some of the Bintenne Veddas are reported to have been cave dwellers formerly, but by the Seligmanns' time they were mostly living in huts made of wattle and daub or in more temporary shelters consisting of a wooden frame covered with animal skins, bark, and/or leaves. The Anuradhapura Veddas live in wattle-and-daub houses with floors of packed earth. Coast Vedda houses are simple huts made of plaited palm. Some Veddas have recently received government-subsidized housing built of brick and plaster with concrete floors and tin roofs.

Economy

Subsistence and Commercial Activities. The distinction between "Wild," "Jungle," or "Rock Veddas," who live from hunting and gathering and sometimes also shifting cultivation, and "Village Veddas," who live in permanent settlements and subsist principally from cultivation, is long established, but already by the time of the Seligmanns' study there were very few Veddas who lived principally from foraging. The Anuradhapura Veddas until recently have derived their living mainly from shifting cultivation, supplemented where possible by wet-rice agriculture. Crops grown under shifting cultivation include millet, maize, beans, squashes, manioc, chilies, eggplants, tomatoes, and okra. Under present conditions of rapidly increasing population pressure and greater market involvement, many of the Anuradhapura Veddas now obtain the major part of their livelihood as agricultural wage laborers outside their own villages. At the same time an increasing proportion of what they produce in their own fields is now marketed rather than consumed at home. Coast Veddas put a greater emphasis on fishing, combining this with shifting cultivation and, less frequently, paddy cultivation. Fishing is done with nets cast from outrigger canoes, from rafts, or from platforms set up in the surf. Prawns are the principal catch. Like the Anuradhapura Veddas, many Coast Veddas now also work as casual wage laborers. A few individuals in all three groups hunt occasionally as a means of supplementing their income. Some Veddas also collect wild honey, one of their traditionally ascribed occupations. Veddas keep cattle, water buffalo, goats, chickens, and dogs, although the relative importance of these species varies greatly between different communities.

Industrial Arts. The Bintenne Veddas formerly made most of their own hunting equipment, such as bows and arrows, spears, axes, etc., although by 1900 those who hunted had already come to rely on metal for the heads of their spears, arrows, and axes, which they obtained through barter. Some had even begun to use guns to bring down their prey. The Anuradhapura Veddas obtain their agricultural tools in the market, as do the Coast Veddas. The Coast Veddas are, however, capable boat builders.

Trade. The Bintenne Veddas are reputed at one time to have engaged in "silent trade" with the Sinhalese. Exchange relations among the Veddas were formerly governed principally by rules of reciprocity, but in the last few decades all groups have become much more deeply involved in market relations. Only a few Veddas, however, have successfully established themselves as traders or shopkeepers.

Division of Labor. Men do most of the agricultural work, especially in paddy cultivation, while women gather wild foods and firewood, cook, care for children, tend domestic gardens, and assist in shifting cultivation and harvesting paddy. Among the Coast Veddas men do most of the fishing. Both male and female Veddas engage in wage labor. Occupational specialization and economic differentiation between households are not pronounced.

Land Tenure. Access to irrigated land is normatively obtained by inheritance, but sales and mortgages are common. Most of the jungle land on which shifting cultivation is practiced is claimed by the state, but Veddas see it as the communal property of the village it surrounds. Rapid population growth and the shift to cash cropping have intensified pressure on the land, resulting in increased landlessness and a dangerous reduction of the fallow period in shifting cultivation. A few Veddas have obtained land in development projects funded by the state. Some Bintenne Veddas who claim still to live from hunting and gathering have joined a movement to have a Vedda reservation established in the region.

Kinship

Kin Groups and Descent. The Seligmanns' claim that the Bintenne Veddas practiced matrilineal descent has been strongly challenged by other researchers. The Anuradhapura Veddas reckon kinship bilaterally. Above the level of the household their significant kin groups are the village community, all the members of which consider one another to be their kin, and the *variga*, a largely endogamous grouping that includes all the Anuradhapura Veddas. The Coast Veddas also reckon kinship bilaterally, but they do not recognize variga as a cultural category for regulating descent and marriage. They do, however, see themselves as related to all other Veddas in the vicinity and generally marry among themselves, forming loosely structured kindred groups. Traces of matrilineal descent and clan organization have also been noted among the Coast Veddas.

Kinship Terminology. Kinship terminology is Dravidian, both among the Sinhala-speaking and the Tamil-speaking Veddas.

Marriage and Family

Marriage. As is implied by Dravidian kinship terminology, the Veddas practice classificatory cross-cousin marriage. Among the Anuradhapura Veddas approximately 15 percent of marriages are between first cross cousins. The percentage is lower among the Coast Veddas, who also intermarry with outsiders more frequently than do the Anuradhapura Veddas. Almost all marriages within all three groups of Veddas are monogamous. The independent family household is the ideal. Most newly married couples, however, live for a while either in or close to the household of one of their parents. Divorce is common in the early years of marriage.

Domestic Unit. Among the Anuradhapura and Coast Veddas the normal unit is the nuclear family household whose members work together and eat from the same hearth. Among the Bintenne Veddas, it is common to find more than one related family living in the same shelter or house.

Inheritance. All sons and daughters have equal rights of inheritance, but among the Bintenne Veddas the daughter's inheritance, usually land, is typically given to her husband at the time of marriage, although this is not specifically referred to as dowry. Dowry is not significant among the Veddas as a whole, although some wealthier Veddas in all three groups give it in emulation of higher status Tamil or Sinhalese families living in the vicinity.

Socialization. Children are raised by parents and older siblings. Vedda children have comparatively poor access to the educational institutions in Sri Lanka.

Sociopolitical Organization

Social Organization. Social relations within Vedda villages are structured mainly by rules of kinship. Apart from hierarchies of age and gender, social relations are generally egalitarian. Caste also plays a role in regulating interaction between Veddas and their Tamil and Sinhalese neighbors, at least in the Anuradhapura and Coast regions. The caste specialization of the Veddas has been identified both as hunting and as spirit mediumship, although it is also claimed that the Veddas stand entirely outside either the Sinhalese or the Tamil caste system since they lack formal structural ties with other castes. The Anuradhapura Veddas collectively constitute a single variga (caste or subcaste), but their variga court, which used to regulate internal caste affairs, has not functioned since the 1950s. The Coast and Bintenne Veddas have apparently never had any kind of overarching caste court.

Political Organization. The Veddas formerly enjoyed considerable autonomy, being located at or beyond the effective limits of Sinhalese or Tamil political power. Within the villages leadership was provided by influential male elders. The Veddas were increasingly subordinated to state authority during the period of British colonial rule, a trend that has intensified since Sri Lanka became independent in 1948. Agricultural cooperatives, development societies, and other state-sponsored organizations have been established in many villages. In Anuradhapura and Bintenne the local officers of these organizations often are village leaders, but among the Coast Veddas the leadership is nearly always provided from among the Tamil elite in nearby Tamil villages.

Social Control. Everyday social life in Vedda villages is still largely governed by norms of kinship, although recourse is also made to state officials, and the police are a more frequent presence than in the past. Sorcery accusations can also act as an informal means of social control.

Conflict. Competition between kin-based factions has long been a prominent feature of village life. The Coast Veddas usually participate in local politics as subordinate members of Tamil-led factions. Today factional struggles typically appear in the guise of conflict between the local branches of the national political parties and focus on the distribution of welfare and development resources.

Religion and Expressive Culture

Religious Beliefs. The religious beliefs of the Veddas overlap considerably with those of Sinhalese villagers, who are predominantly Buddhists, and with those of Tamil villagers, who are mostly Hindus. All worship a hierarchical pantheon of deities, to whom offerings are made in the hope of gaining favors or relief from suffering. As described by the Seligmanns, the Bintenne Veddas had no knowledge of Buddhism. Their religion was apparently based on worship of recently deceased ancestors, various local demons, and other minor gods. In contrast, the Anuradhapura Veddas describe themselves as Buddhists, although their participation in Buddhist rites is infrequent. The Coast Veddas are more influenced by their Hindu Tamil neighbors and engage in various forms of temple worship associated with Hindu deities, as well as propitiating local deities and demon spirits. The pantheon extends from locally resident spirits and demons whose disposition is generally malevolent to powerful and benevolent, but more remote, major gods. For those who profess Buddhism, these major gods themselves derive their authority from the Buddha. The most important high gods for the Anuradhapura Veddas are Kataragama and Pulleyar. For the Coast Veddas they are Shiva, Murugan, Pillaiyar, and Valli. The Bintenne Veddas cut off the hierarchy at a lower level and attend only to more localized gods, demons, and ancestor spirits, although a few also worship the high god Kataragama.

Religious Practitioners.   Among the Anuradhapura and Bintenne Veddas one of the most important religious practitioners is the *kapurala*, who intercedes with a god on behalf of his fellow villagers. Among the Anuradhapura Veddas there is also the *anumatirala*, who becomes possessed by a minor god or demon and performs exorcisms. Specialized religious practitioners are rare among the Coast Veddas.

Ceremonies.   The Bintenne Veddas engage in many different ceremonial dances in which a specialized practitioner becomes possessed by a god or demon. These dances are always a part of an exorcism or an attempt to procure favors or information from the spirit being. The Anuradhapura Veddas hold an annual ceremony at which offerings are made collectively to the village's tutelary deity. Other ceremonies, such as exorcisms, are organized by individual households. The Coast Veddas observe the Hindu festival calendar, but their most important rituals are locally organized possession ceremonies, which are conducted jointly by all concerned Vedda villagers. Personal rites of propitiation and protection are also common among all groups of Veddas.

Arts.   Ritual performances, especially possession ceremonies that include dancing, chanting, instrumental music making, and the construction of temporary shrines, provide some of the principal occasions for artistic expression among all Vedda groups. The plastic arts are otherwise little emphasized beyond acts of individual decoration. The Seligmanns noted that the Bintenne Veddas were once adept at making artifacts and utensils from animal skins and also engaged in rock and cave drawings. Singing is a popular form of recreation among the Veddas.

Medicine.   Persons familiar with at least some aspects of the South Asian tradition of Ayurvedic medicine are found among both the Anuradhapura and the Coast Veddas. They use herbal compounds to adjust the balance of humors in the body. Some illnesses are attributed to demonic possession and are treated by exorcism. Among the Bintenne Veddas, almost all illness was treated through ritual ceremonies. Many Veddas now have access to the free medical care, based on Western science and technology, that is provided by the state.

Death and Afterlife.   Among the Anuradhapura and Coast Veddas, beliefs and practices regarding death are shaped by Buddhist and Hindu concepts of karma, reincarnation, and the transmigration of souls. The Bintenne and the Coast Veddas also practice rituals to propitiate and communicate with recently deceased ancestors who are believed to be able to influence events in the present life.

See also Sinhalese; Tamil of Sri Lanka

Bibliography

Brow, James (1978). *Vedda Villages of Anuradhapura District: The Historical Anthropology of a Community in Sri Lanka.* Seattle and London: University of Washington Press.

Dart, Jon (1985). "Ethnic Identity and Marginality among the Coast Veddas of Sri Lanka." Ph.D. dissertation, University of California, San Diego.

Kennedy, K. A. R., W. F. Roertgen, J. Chiment, and T. Disotell (1987). "Upper Pleistocene Fossil Hominids from Sri Lanka." *American Journal of Physical Anthropology* 72:441–461.

Seligmann, C. G., and Brenda Seligmann (1911). *The Veddas.* Cambridge: Cambridge University Press.

JAMES BROW AND MICHAEL WOOST

Vellala

ETHNONYMS: Mudaliar, Pandaram, Pillaimar (Pillai), Velalar (Velalan)

Orientation

Identification.   The Vellala are a major agricultural caste who live in Tamil Nadu, a state of southern India. They speak Tamil and are Hindu. The Velama and Ballal castes of the neighboring states of Andhra Pradesh and Karnataka, respectively, are believed to be historically related to the Vellala, but at present the three groups are separate and distinct. The Vellala are divided on a territorial basis and subdivided further into endogamous *jatis* or subcastes. As an integral part of an intercaste network, both ideologically and in daily life, Vellala culture is not an independent entity. It can be understood only in relation to other castes. The Vellala are a large heterogeneous category into which several upwardly mobile subcastes have successfully assimilated, at various points in time. They have done so by imitating a Vellala life-style. A popular saying throughout Tamil Nadu is: "Kallar, Maravar, Ahamudayar [three castes that rank lower than Vellala] gradually become Vellalar." Hence identity is a matter of great concern to "true" Vellala subcastes who take enormous pains to keep their purity intact through strict endogamy, extreme caution when forming marriage alliances, restrictions on women, and so forth. Broadly, the numerous Vellala subcastes constitute two major categories ranked hierarchically. Usually a subcaste's name has a prefix denoting a place, a further prefix, and an honorific suffix used in a particular region, together forming a term such as "Tondaimandalam Kondaikatti Vellala Mudaliar."

Location.   The Vellala live throughout Tamil Nadu. Different subcastes are localized in different regions. For example, Mudaliar subcastes are prominent in Tondaimandalam (with a concentration in Chinglepet), Choliya Pilli and Karkattar in Cholamandalam (concentrated in Thanjavur), Kongu Vellala or Kavundar in Kongumandalam (concentrated in Coimbatore), and Saiva Pillaimar, Karkattar, and Nangudi Vellala in Pandimandalam (concentrated in Madurai and Tirunelveli). In general, the first category of Vellala (who often call themselves vegetarian Vellala) predominate in the paddy-growing river-valley regions.

Demography. Since the Vellala are heterogeneous and live in multicaste environments, an estimate of the population is difficult. Current censuses do not provide statistics by caste. In some of the British period census reports, caste figures were given for some districts, and the Vellala constituted about 10 percent of the population. However, the criteria for defining Vellala seems to vary and there is no clear basis for interdistrict comparison.

Linguistic Affiliation. Among the living Dravidian languages, Tamil has the oldest recorded history and classical literary tradition. It is closely related to Telugu, Kannada, and Malayalam, which are spoken in the neighboring states. (Dravidian languages are also spoken in small pockets in central and eastern India, and in Pakistan.) The contemporary Tamil script is derived from the Brahmi script, which is also the source for the scripts of the Indo-Aryan Language Group. The Vellala speak a dialect that is common among high-caste non-Brahmans in Tamil Nadu. It is different from the highly Sanskritized language of the Brahmans and also from the language of the lowest castes. The Vellala of different districts flavor their speech with the local dialects.

History and Cultural Relations

Most Vellala subcastes share broadly similar origin myths that stress their links with the soil as agriculturists (as contrasted with artisans), their origin in the Ganga (Gangetic Valley) and migration from northern to southern India during the distant past, and their close relationship with the three ancient Tamil dynasties—Chera, Chola, and Pandya—in spite of the Vellalas' ineligibility for kingship. There is fairly strong literary and archeological evidence linking core Vellala subcastes with a group of chieftains called *velir*; the earliest references are found in the Sangam literature (first to third century A.D.). Until about the fourteenth century A.D., the velir were prominent in the Tamil polity, economy, and society, and they have been linked with virtually all the major ruling dynasties. They were autonomous and collectively wielded significant political influence. Although ineligible to be crowned as kings, they were bride givers to the three "crowned" kings. They were active militarily but also had a strong base as landholders of fertile, paddy-growing tracts. They were celebrated for their large and lavish charities and for their patronage of literature and poetry. In the post-Sangam period, velir autonomy decreased, although they continued as feudatories, with key civic and military positions. Their position as a landed elite with military and administrative power continued through the subsequent periods—the Nayak, the Nawab of Arcot, and the British. The Vellala served as revenue officers, temple trustees and managers, magistrates, administrative agents, rentiers, village chiefs, and village accountants. The literary sources on the Vellala make a distinction between those "who eat by plowing the land" and those "who eat by getting the land plowed (through others)." Even now, this distinction serves as an index of internal hierarchical differentiation.

Settlements

The Vellala live in all the districts of the state and in both urban and rural areas. In the latter, the settlement pattern is typically multicaste villages. Depending on the region, the Vellala may be the dominant caste, may share dominance with another caste, or may be a minority. In villages along the river basins, where wet rice cultivation is prominent, the dominant caste is often Vellala (of either category). Within a village, each Vellala subcaste, as indeed every subcaste, tends to live in a separate street. In larger villages and towns, this pattern gets blurred. There is no one distinct style of Vellala housing because house style is a function of wealth and location (rural or urban).

Economy

Most Vellala are engaged in agriculture full-time or as a side occupation. In areas of wet paddy cultivation, traditional techniques continue to be popular, both among small peasants and among noncultivating landholders who lease out to tenants. However, use of high-yielding varieties of seeds and chemical fertilizers is quite widespread. Tenancy is less favored now, because of the difficulties of getting the land back from tenants, but the traditional norm of having men and women of Untouchable castes perform the major labor is still intact. Some mechanization has been introduced by large landowners who have stopped tenanting out and started directly overseeing farming. Landholding Vellala had, in the past, an elaborate and complex patron-client relationship with subcastes who worked for them—both agricultural subcastes as well as artisan and service subcastes like priests, potters, barbers, etc. The relationship, in which economic and ritual dimensions are fused, approximates the *jajmani* relations that have been documented for other regions in India. Elements of jajmani continue to the present day. In areas where the Vellala of the second category predominate, cash crops, peasant proprietorship, and commercial agriculture are more common and there is greater mechanization. Women from the first category do not work in the fields. In the second, involvement with one's own family land is not uncommon, though working on another's field is considered undesirable and resorted to only in cases of extreme poverty. For various reasons, chief among which is the government's land reform policy, a sizable section of Vellala of the first category have taken to higher education and urban professional employment; however, they are less likely to enter entrepreneurial activities today than in the past.

Kinship

Kin Groups and Descent. The predominant Hindu pattern of patrilineal, patrivirilocal kinship in descent, inheritance, succession, and residence is the norm among the Vellala. Exceptions are the Nangudi Vellala and Kottai Pillaimar, who have matrilineal descent, patri-matrilineal inheritance, and uxorilocal residence. Exogamous units called *gotram*, membership in which is traced from a common ancestor or place, are found in some subcastes of the first category.

In other subcastes, the unit is called *kilai*. Members may be scattered over several villages. The local branch of the exogamous unit acts as a corporate entity for certain economic and ceremonial functions.

Kinship Terminology. Kin terms follow the Dravidian system.

Marriage and Family

Marriage. Although polygynous marriages were permitted and prevalent in the past, most marriages today are monogamous. With a few urban exceptions, marriage is usually arranged by elders, although some expression of disapproval may be available to the youth. The Dravidian pattern of preferential cross-cousin (both matrilateral and patrilateral) and maternal uncle-niece marriage is strongly adhered to. A breach of this norm often leads to an acrimonious dispute between families. Even traditionally, prepuberty or child marriage was not prevalent. Widow remarriage is not approved of, although it is now legal. Traditionally, divorce was not permitted. Despite modifications in Hindu law, divorce is still infrequent.

Domestic Unit. Various degrees of complexity of the extended patrilocal household are found both across Vellala subcastes and within any single Vellala subcaste. The neolocal or nuclear household is not uncommon, but it is embedded within the matrix of patrilineal kinship. It is thus different in character from the Western ideal type of nuclearity. Although patrilineal kinship places women in a weak structural position, there are aspects of the kinship system that leaven this situation. Upon marrying, a woman may join a family already related and known to her, she often lives in her natal village, and her natal and affinal relatives are continually interacting; all of these factors support her position in the family.

Inheritance. This follows the general principle of classical Hindu law, where land and immovables are inherited by sons. Daughters are given a dowry at marriage. Sometimes women are given small gifts of land (*manjal-kani*) but these are not treated as shares. One of the reasons for their strict endogamy and high rate of consanguineous marriage, say the Vellala, is their strong need to keep land in the family.

Sociopolitical Organization

Social Organization. The relation of the Vellala to other castes as well as Vellala internal ideology must be understood as both influencing all aspects of Vellala economic, political, religious, and kinship activities. The schematic division of Indian society into four hierarchical *varnas* (castes)—Brahman, Kshatriya, Vaisya, and Sudra—does not accurately reflect the situation in Tamil Nadu. While the Brahmans rank at the top and the Untouchables or Scheduled Castes at the bottom, between these two extremes are a wide range of castes and subcastes whose exact standing in relation to one another depends on the region and the village. Generally, a distinction is made between "clean" non-Brahmans, who adopt a Sanskritized life-style, and the others. The former are vegetarians, do not drink alcohol, eschew manual labor including plowing (if they are agriculturalists), and have very conservative attitudes and customs regarding women. The other category of upper non-Brahmans conforms to the Kshatriya ideal, which emphasizes manual strength, a land base, command over labor, political authority, more interaction with other castes, and so on. Although there is a greater emphasis on warriorlike qualities than on ritual status, concern with women's purity is high, especially in groups that were connected to royal dynasties of the past. In the twofold division of the Vellala, the second category (e.g., Kavundar, Nangudi Vellala, Tuluva Vellala) falls clearly into the Kshatriya model. The first category (e.g., Kondaikatti Vellala, Karkattar, Saiva Pillaimar) combines aspects of the two models: (1) high ritual status expressed through strict rules of interdining and intermarriage (according to a popular proverb, the Vellala are more orthodox than Brahmans), and (2) land base and political visibility (in traditional society). Thus the two Vellala categories occupy different structural positions in the social order.

Political Organization. The Vellala were, in the past, prominent in political networks constituted by the court, temple, and caste councils. They maintained their dominance through endowments to temples, charity to the poor, and patronage of the labor and service castes. In attempting to convert this prominence to secular political status, they have had mixed success. Often, they have been pushed out by lower castes, whose collective ethnic identity is perhaps stronger. The Vellalas' internal hierarchies and their fixed ideological positions have in part prevented the development of a unified political identity. One occasion when such an identity did develop was in the early twentieth century when the census classified the Vellala as Sudra. The Vellala responded angrily by citing evidence that as agriculturists they rightly belonged to the third varna (i.e., Vaisya). At about the same time, a journal, *Vellalan*, was also published for some years, focusing on the problems of the community and the need for educational and occupational advancement. Today many Vellala subcastes have their own associations, which are more social than political. The Justice party of Tamil Nadu, formed early in this century, was mainly a reaction to Brahman social and political domination. Considerable early support for the party came from Vellala subcastes. However, later developments based on Tamil linguistic identity (as exemplified by the D.K. and D.M.K. movements), blurred the distinctive Vellala component. In the state as a whole, the Vellala are politically weak, though they are very active in certain districts.

Religion

Religious Beliefs. A small minority of Vellala are Christians, via individual conversion rather than mass conversion of an entire subcaste. The majority are Hindu, and the operative principles of Hinduism pervade all spheres of life and activity. Although there is a division between Shaivites (followers of Shiva) and Vaishnavites (followers of Vishnu) there is no bar on intermarriage. While squarely within the orthodox Hindu tradition, the Vellala look to Tamil/indigenous forms in devotion, metaphysics, and philosophy. Thus *Shaiva Siddhanta*, a respected religious and philosophic system with Vellala as main figures, ultimately stresses Brahmanic values. However, the sources and metaphors are drawn from a Tamil cultural base. At one point in its history, Shaiva Siddhanta was used as a political weapon against Brahman domination. The Vellala owe allegiance to different *mathams* (apex religious organizations) that are wealthy, landed, and influential. The Vellala also maintain traditional links to the classical (Sanskritic) temples as trustees, donors, and receivers of temple honors.

Ceremonies.   The Vellala cycle of worship and festivals includes forms of worship of deities and other folk goddesses/ non-Sanskritic deities associated with lower castes. Vellalas' involvement is structured in such a way that their ritual status is not compromised, while the demands of powerful indigenous traditions are satisfied. Either a Brahman priest or a Vellala priest called a *gurukkal* can officiate. Life-cycle ceremonies are generally as prescribed for upper castes. The rules of purity and pollution for birth, menstruation, and death are elaborate. The grammar of these rules indicates the rank of Vellala as being immediately below that of Brahmans. The mantra (incantations in Sanskrit) component is relatively abbreviated, but the public display of status during ceremonies—especially puberty, wedding, and funeral rituals—is very important and includes large-scale feeding of relatives, service and labor castes, and the poor.

See also Tamil; Tamil of Sri Lanka

Bibliography

Arokiaswami, M. (1954). *The Early History of the Vellar Basin*. Madras: Amudha Nilayam.

Arunachalam, M. (1975). "A Study of the Culture and History of the Karkattar." *Bulletin of the Institute of Traditional Cultures* January–June:1–72.

Barnett, Stephen A. (1970). "The Structural Position of a South Indian Caste—Kontaikkatti Velalars in Tamilnadu." Ph.D. dissertation, University of Chicago.

Beck, Brenda E. F. (1972). *Peasant Society in Konku: A Study of Right and Left Subcastes in South India*. Vancouver: University of British Columbia Press.

Ponnambalam, M., ed. (1932–1933). *Veḷāḷan* (Tuticorin) [Tamil journal].

Thurston, Edgar, and Kadamki Rangachari (1909). "Vellala." In *Castes and Tribes of Southern India*, edited by Edgar Thurston and Kadamki Rangachari. Vol. 7, 361–389. Madras: Government Press. Reprint. 1975. New Delhi: Cosmos Publications.

KAMALA GANESH

Zamindar

ETHNONYMS: Landlord, Seth, Zemindar

Orientation

Zamindars are from the Muslim Rajput castes who settled in rural areas of the Indo-Gangetic Plain, from Pakistan to Bangladesh. Horsemen of these lineages were of higher status, while the foot troopers were from the lower castes. The root words, *zamin* and *dar*, are Persian, together meaning "landowner." Relationships of the Zamindars with the premodern state varied from region to region, as did the origin of the Zamindar class. Among examples mentioned by Tom Kessinger are caste or lineage groups that conquered an area, or at least became the dominant settlers there; officials who were able to make their land grants hereditary; rajas who had held on to some land after being deposed; and the descendants of holy men (Sadhus) who had received grants of land. In each case the crucial factor was state recognition of a responsibility on the part of Zamindars to collect and transmit revenue from a specified area. From a local point of view Zamindars, wherever they existed, were always a force to be reckoned with; for not only did they have an official sanction to collect revenue, but they could commonly back up their position with fortresses and small contingents of armed enforcers. These Zamindars were in charge of supervising new immigrants to the village and of organizing lands for cultivation. In return for their effort a share of the product was taken by them. The right of ownership of the land was through descent within the same family. Division of land was never marked specifically; therefore, land was jointly held and the income shared. Under the British, landownership was formalized for the organization of tax revenues. In 1857, permanent ownership was granted to those with land occupancy and Zamindars were held responsible to pay taxes to the government in cash and not in grain. In some areas, as in Dhanbad District, Uttar Pradesh, the amount of rent paid by cultivators to the Zamindars was not controlled by any law but rather was established at the will of the Zamindars. As time passed Zamindars gained power while the cultivators became weak and abused. Before the abolition of the Zamindari system in 1948, the Zamindars had the habit of spending money frivolously, often to the point of having to borrow more money to pay off their debts. The situation caused them loss of prestige and honor. In contrast to the district of Dhanbad is the village of Mohla in the district of Gujrat in Punjab State, where land and prestige go hand in hand. Zamindars there have certain obligations toward the farming people that make them trustworthy persons.

Economy and Social Organization

Social status ranges greatly according to the amount of land owned by any given Zamindar man. He is variously identified as a generous, authoritarian, logical, and friendly person, along with his patrilineage. A Zamindar man's chief concern is for his land and its productivity. He depends greatly on other people for their labor, especially on the artisans, because they make the tools needed for his land. The largest lands belong to the most powerful and influential Zamindars.

They spend, entertain, and associate with prominent people on occasions such as marriage, circumcision, and harvesting. Each such occasion can increase their status, honor, and prestige. The call by a Zamindar to *mang* (collective labor) is a test of people's loyalty. The main social effect of mang is the reinforcement of relations between the Zamindar and the community.

Zamindars are adopting new cultural changes and improvements. They are willing to go to the cities to learn new ways and introduce them to their village. New equipment for the cultivation of land is being bought, water glasses are now preferred, and tea sets are becoming fashionable. They are moving toward renewing business and raising the standard of living. At the same time, legal ceilings on landholdings in most states have been make it increasingly difficult in recent decades for the Zamindars to hold onto large tracts of land. Nevertheless, they try to do so, often by registering ownership of various plots of land in the names of different family members, whether male or female. Whatever they do, they never leave the village life behind and cannot be uprooted from it.

Kinship

Through *biraderi* (patrilineage), families maintain unity, which is very important in every aspect of life. Land is inherited from the male side by the sons; under normal circumstances none goes to the daughters. If a Zamindar dies without leaving any sons, then his daughters will inherit. The selling of land cannot occur without consultations with family members. A Zamindar must then establish a good reason, such as marriage or a need to pay off debts, and if the reason is accepted by others he may sell. The first option to purchase the land goes to his brother, then his brother's son, his father's brother's son, or any biraderi kinfolk. Zamindars are greatly attached to their biraderi and their village. They prefer to keep land and village in the family, because newcomers do not feel as reliable to them. The strong attachment within a patrilineage enhances the prestige of every member. Inheritance through a mother is called *nanki virsa*, and people who inherit from a mother are considered outsiders. This latter situation is not the only basis of a woman's dominance in a household. A chief needs the support of his wife and mother to develop his status among his people. Women are in charge of money and the food of the household. Currently women are voicing their own needs, even though they may be hesitant to do so. For a woman to ask for her share of inheritance is a very risky situation, even though the law permits it, because she is going against her brothers and traditionally such an action would destroy respect. The new law of equality in respect to inheritance has helped women to get their share and not feel guilty. Parents are also concerned about their daughters' education. It has become a strong prerequisite in choosing a respectable mate.

Marriage and Family

The major function of marriage is to form a bond between two families or to strengthen a previous bond. As in other parts of India the two families investigate the social and financial status of each other. They normally choose a mate close in age and skin complexion, the male being slightly older. Zamindars marry within their status category among other Zamindars. Marriage with other working-class people is disapproved of and done without paternal consent. The girl's parents are content when their daughter is treated well by her groom's family and is given a fair amount of gifts. The boy's family is pleased according to the amount of dowry brought and later gift giving by her family to the wife, her husband, and her children every time she visits her natal home.

Religion

Islam is devoutly followed by most Zamindars and it seems to be the uniting factor among them. They do not evaluate each other on the basis of caste. They believe that all belong to one caste and that it is Islam. To the Zamindars, the caste system borrowed from the Hindus is the equivalent of an occupational class structure. People celebrate every religious holiday and occasion. The wealthy Zamindars send food, sweets, and drinks to the mosque during the month of Ramadan (the fasting month). Prayers are said five times a day in the mosque over the loudspeakers. The people have put their faith in the hands of God, because they believe that God does not punish but helps. Zamindars also believe that while people must strive for a prosperous life, they must not let the material attachments of life hold them down. It is through prayers that they reach toward God and depend on his help. Zamindars in more easterly parts of the Indo-Gangetic plain tend to be Hindus, except for those in Bangladesh who again are Muslim.

See also Kambi

Bibliography

Eglar, Zekiye (1960). *A Punjabi Village in Pakistan.* New York: Columbia University Press.

Kessinger, Tom G. (1974). *Vilyatpur, 1848–1968: Social and Economic Change in a North Indian Village.* Berkeley: University of California Press. Reprint. 1979. Delhi: Young Asia Publishers.

Metcalf, Thomas R. (1979). *Land, Landlords, and the British Raj: Northern India in the Nineteenth Century.* Berkeley and London: University of California Press.

Rothermund, Dietmar, and D. C. Wadhwa, eds. (1978). *Zamindars, Mines, and Peasants: Studies in the History of an Indian Coalfield and Its Rural Hinterland.* New Delhi: Manohar.

SAIDEH MOAYED-SANANDAJI

Appendix
Additional Castes,
Caste Clusters,
and Tribes

The following caste and tribe names have been taken from the various sets of handbooks dealing with the castes and tribes of particular regions of South Asia. These volumes are nearly all more than a half-century old, but more recent information of this sort is not available. (Virtually all of the "Castes and Tribes" handbooks have, however, been republished in recent years.) Long as this list is, it is by no means exhaustive, and it merely represents those groups for which we have a certain amount of once reliable, if now outdated, information. Only monographs have been surveyed for this appendix, as space does not allow coverage of the massive amount of ethnographic material to be found in scholarly journals. For these, the interested reader should consult the excellent bibliographies by Ittaman et al. (1982) and Patterson (1981).

Most of these groups are internally divided into subcastes or tribal sections that have not been named in this appendix, which is essentially an index to the handbooks mentioned. It must be recognized that in many cases one named "caste" is actually a grouping of several endogamous units and, further, that changing economic conditions have made the traditional occupations listed here unimportant or even impossible to follow. In some cases, too, the locality where a caste is to be found has changed somewhat, particularly as a result of the partition of India and Pakistan in 1947. Modern district names are given in all entries.

Cross-references set in upper- and lower-case characters are to other headings in this appendix; those set in capitals and small capitals are to headings in the main body of the encyclopedia. An index of all ethnonyms given in this appendix is provided at the back.

Adi   A Paleo-Mongoloid tribal cluster found in central Arunachal Pradesh. The term embraces the Gallong, Korka, Shimong, Boker, Bori, Padam, Pasi, Minyong, and other agricultural tribes. They are related to the Abors. Partial total: 79,392 in 1971. *See also* ABOR. (Dalton 1872, 26–33; Roy 1960; Srivastava 1962; Chowdhury 1971)

Adiyan (Adiyar, Adigal)   A tribe found in northern Kerala. They are Hindus, speak Kannada, and work as farm laborers. Total: 7,192 in 1971. (Thurston and Rangachari 1909, 1:4; Gopalan Nair 1911, 97–100; Luiz 1962, 27–31)

Agamudaiyan   A Hindu cultivating caste found through-out much of Tamil Nadu. (Thurston and Rangachari 1909, 1:5–16)

Agasa (Asaga, Viraghata Madivala, Madiwal, Mallige Madevi Vakkalu)   A caste of washermen, found in southern Maharashtra and Karnataka. They are Hindus, though many are Lingayats, and those speaking Konkani are Christians. *See also* Dhobi. (Thurston and Rangachari 1909, 1:16–18; Enthoven 1920–1922, 1:1–5; Nanjundayya and Ananthakrishna Iyer 1928–1936, 2:1–31; Srinivas 1952)

Aghori (Aughar, Aghoripanthi, Aghorapanthi)   A class of Shaivite mendicants who used to feed on human corpses and excrement; in previous centuries they were even reputed to have engaged in cannibalism. Being a wandering people who have commonly been chased out of one district after another, they are now found widely scattered through India, although Varanasi (Benares) is thought to be their professional resort. (Risley 1891, 1:10; Crooke 1896, 1:26–69; Campbell 1901, 543; Russell and Hira Lal 1916, 2:13–17)

Agnihotri   A Brahman caste devoted to the maintenance of the sacred fire and found in northern India. (Crooke 1896, 1:30–33)

Agrahari (Agrehri).   A trading and cultivating caste, found in Bihar and Uttar Pradesh. (Risley 1891, 1:11–12; Crooke 1896, 1:33–35)

Agri (Ager, Agari, Agaria, Agle, Kharpatil)   A large caste found from northern Karnataka to Punjab. They are principally known as salt makers and farmers, but in recent years they have also gone into numerous other occupations. (Rose 1911, 1:3; Enthoven 1920–1922, 1:5–16; Kale 1952)

Aguri   A trading and cultivating caste, found in West Bengal. (Risley 1891, 1:12–13)

Ahar (Aheri, Heri, Ahari)   A herding and cultivating caste, found in Punjab and hilly northern parts of Uttar Pradesh. (Crooke 1896, 1:35–36; Rose 1911, 1:4)

Ahban   A Rajput caste, found in eastern Uttar Pradesh. Some are Muslim, others Hindu. (Crooke 1896, 1:37–39)

Aheriya (Aheri, Aheria)   A hunting, gathering and thieving tribe found in Uttar Pradesh. (Crooke 1896, 1:39–49)

Ahiwasi   A cultivating caste found in Uttar Pradesh. (Crooke 1896, 1:72–75)

Aka (Hrusso)   A Paleo-Mongoloid tribe of cultivators, found in the hills of western Arunachal Pradesh. Total: 2,345 in 1971. (Dalton 1872, 42–44; Sinha 1962)

Aka-Bale (Aka-Bala-wa)   A fishing, foraging, and gardening tribe of the Great Andaman group. (Radcliffe-Brown 1922, 12–19; Chakraborty 1990)

Aka-Bea   A fishing, foraging, and gardening tribe of the Great Andaman group. (Radcliffe-Brown 1922, 12–19; Chakraborty 1990)

Aka-Bo   A fishing, foraging, and gardening tribe of the Great Andaman group. (Radcliffe-Brown 1922, 12–19; Chakraborty 1990)

Aka-Cari   A fishing, foraging, and gardening tribe of the

Great Andaman group. (Radcliffe-Brown 1922, 12–19; Chakraborty 1990)

Aka-Jeru A fishing, foraging, and gardening tribe of the Great Andaman group. (Radcliffe-Brown 1922, 12–19; Chakraborty 1990)

Aka-Kede A fishing, foraging, and gardening tribe of the Great Andaman group. (Radcliffe-Brown 1922, 12–19; Chakraborty 1990)

Aka-Kol A fishing, foraging, and gardening tribe of the Great Andaman group. (Radcliffe-Brown 1922, 12–19; Chakraborty 1990)

Aka-Kora A fishing, foraging, and gardening tribe of the Great Andaman group. (Radcliffe-Brown 1922, 12–19; Chakraborty 1990)

Akali (Nihang) A class of Sikh devotees, found in northwestern India. They are a celibate sect. (Crooke 1896, 1:76–77; Rose 1911, 1:9–10)

Alkari (Shravagi, Golalare) A small caste of western Maharashtra, who claim to be Rajputs. They used to prepare red dye, but they are now mostly cultivators or day laborers. They are Shaivites. (Enthoven 1920–1922, 1:37–41)

Allar (Ollares) A tribe of Palghat District, in central Kerala. They are hunters and gatherers, some of whom still use caves for shelter. (Luiz 1962, 32–38)

Amat (Amath) A pair of Hindu cultivating castes found in Bihar; some are household servants. (Risley 1891, 1:17–19)

Ambalakkaran A caste of village watchmen, found in central Tamil Nadu. (Thurston and Rangachari 1909, 1:25–28)

Ambalavasi (Nambidi, Nampati, Adikal, Muttatu, Ilayatu, Elayad, Chakkiyar, Nambiar, Nambiyar, Nambiyassan, Variyar, Pisharoti, Pisharati, Pisharodi, Pothuval, Marar, Maran, Marayan, Gurukkal, Kurukkal, Samanthan, Unni) A group of castes in central Kerala who are traditionally temple servants. Many also cultivate. (Thurston and Rangachari 1909, 1:28–31; 2:7–11, 204–208, 309–313; 5:5–13, 149–151; 6:199–203; 7:221–228, 322–329; Ananthakrishna Iyer 1909–1912, 2:122–150)

Ambattan A Hindu caste of Tamil-speaking barbers and musicians; they were probably once surgeons. Their women are midwives. They are found in southern Kerala and throughout Tamil Nadu. *See also* Nai. (Thurston and Rangachari 1909, 1:32–44; Ananthakrishna Iyer 1909–1912, 3:364–366)

Amma Coorg (Amma Kodagi) A Hindu priestly caste found in Kodagu District, southern Karnataka. (Krishna Iyer 1948, 64–66; Srinivas 1952)

Andh A cultivating tribe of eastern Maharashtra and northernmost Andhra Pradesh. Many are farm laborers, and some work as village headmen. Total: 78,560 in 1971. (Russell and Hira Lal 1916, 2:38–40; Siraj ul Hassan 1920, 1:8–11)

Andhra Brahman (Telugu Brahman) A Brahman caste of Andhra Pradesh and adjoining states, with a very complex internal structure based on sectarian differences. (Siraj ul Hassan 1920, 1:121–130)

Apa Tani A Paleo-Mongoloid tribe found in central Arunachal Pradesh. They are about 13,000 people living in one valley of Upper Subansiri District. Total: 12,888 in 1971. (Fürer-Haimendorf 1956, 1962, 1980)

A-Pucikwar (Aka-Bojig-yab) A fishing, foraging, and gardening tribe of the Great Andaman group. (Radcliffe-Brown 1922, 12–19; Chakraborty 1990)

Aradhya (Aradhya Brahman) A caste of Brahman priests, found mainly in Andhra Pradesh. Some are now engaged in agriculture or medicine. (Thurston and Rangachari 1909, 1:50–54; Nanjundayya and Ananthakrishna Iyer 1928–1936, 2:32–46)

Arain (Rain) A caste of market gardeners, found from Punjab Province, Pakistan, to Uttar Pradesh. It includes both Hindus and Muslims. (Crooke 1896, 4:206–208; Rose 1911, 1:13–16)

Arakh A small caste of cultivators found from eastern Maharashtra to eastern Uttar Pradesh. (Crooke 1896, 1:81–85; Russell and Hira Lal 1916, 2:40–42)

Aranadan (Arandan, Eranadan) A tribe found in Kozhikode District, northern Kerala. They collect forest produce, and until recently they were also hunters. Total: 5 in 1971! (Luiz 1962, 39–43)

Arasu (Rajpinde) A caste that includes the former royal family of Mysore and ranks as Kshatriya. They are found in Karnataka, and many have been employed in the civil service or the army. (Thurston and Rangachari 1909, 1:55; Nanjundayya and Ananthakrishna Iyer 1928–1936, 2:47–73)

Arora (Rora) A caste of cultivators, traders, tailors, bankers, and contractors, found in Punjab and Sindh provinces, Pakistan. Most are Hindus, but some are Sikhs. (Rose 1911, 1:16–21)

Arya Samaj A modern Hindu sect found especially in Punjab and Uttar Pradesh. It was founded about 1847 and is strongly reformist. (Rose 1911, 1:21–24)

Asur An iron-smelting tribe found in much of central India, from West Bengal to Maharashtra. Total: 7,637 in 1971. (Leuva 1963)

Atari (Gandhi, Bukekari) A small Muslim caste selling scent, incense, and sundry personal necessities, living in central India. (Russell and Hira Lal 1916, 2:42–45)

Audhelia (Audhalia) A small caste of Bilaspur District, in Madhya Pradesh. They work as farm laborers and pig keepers, and, unlike most Hindus, they sacrifice pigs to their chief deities. (Russell and Hira Lal 1916, 2:45–48)

Audhiya (Audhya, Ajudhyabasi, Avadhapuri) An ex-criminal tribe who wander through north India, dealing in fake jewelry and counterfeit coins. (Crooke 1896, 1:87–91)

Awan A Muslim tribe found in Punjab Province, Pakistan. They are landowners. (Rose 1911, 1:25–28)

Babhan (Bhuinhar, Zamindar Brahman, Girhasth Brahman, Grihasth Brahman, Pachhima Brahman, Magahaya Brahman, Ajagyak Brahman, Zamindar, Chaudriji) A large landowning caste in Bihar and Uttar Pradesh. They are Shaivites and probably a class of Rajputs rather than Brahmans. (Risley 1891, 1:28–35; Crooke 1896, 2:64–70)

Babria (Durba, Ghardera) A small caste chiefly found in the Kathiawar Peninsula of Gujarat. They are Hindu landowners. (Enthoven 1920–1922, 1:44–48)

Bachgoti A section of the Rajputs, found in Uttar Pradesh. They are landlords. (Crooke 1896, 1:93–96)

Bachhil (Bachhal) A section of the Rajputs, found throughout Uttar Pradesh. They are landlords. (Crooke 1896, 1:96–99)

Badahāla (Badahela) A caste of potters found in Sri Lanka. (Ryan 1953)

Badhak (Badhik, Bagri, Baoria, Bawaria) Well-known in earlier times as a caste of Hindu Thugs who roamed north and central India as brigands devoted to the goddess Kali. *See also* THUG. (Crooke 1896, 1:100–101; Russell and Hira Lal 1916, 2:49–69)

Badhoyi A caste of carpenters and blacksmiths, found in Orissa. They are Vaishnavites. (Thurston and Rangachari 1909, 1:124–128)

Bagata (Bhakta, Bakta) A tribe of freshwater fishermen, found in Andhra Pradesh. Total: 71,919 in 1971. (Thurston and Rangachari 1909, 1:128–130)

Bagdi (Bagtit, Bagri, Mudi) A small peripatetic caste, with a home base in Kolhapur District, in southern Maharashtra, from which they wander throughout the state. They tell fortunes and beg, although their traditional occupations were fishing and weaving blankets. Another fishing and cultivating caste of the same name occurs in West Bengal. (Risley 1891, 1:37–43; Enthoven 1920–1922, 1:48–51)

Baghdadi Jew The smallest of the three Jewish communities in India (the others being Cochin Jews and Bene Israel). They left Baghdad in the eighteenth century, and their best-known family formed the international commercial house of Sassoon, based in Bombay. (Jackson [pseud.] 1968)

Baghel Rajput A Rajput caste found in Uttar Pradesh and central Madhya Pradesh, but probably of Gujarati origin. They were formerly brigands. (Crooke 1896, 1:102–104; Russell and Hira Lal 1916, 4:434–435)

Bagri Rajput A Rajput caste found in central Madhya Pradesh, former robbers who now cultivate. (Russell and Hira Lal 1916, 4:435)

Bahna (Pinjara, Pinjari, Dhunia) A caste of cotton cleaners in Maharashtra and Madhya Pradesh. They are Muslims, except for a few who are Hindus. (Russell and Hira Lal 1916, 2:69–76; Enthoven 1920–1922, 3:233–234)

Baidya (Vaidya, Vaidyan, Kabiraj, Ambastha, Bhisak, Chikitsak) A caste or profession practicing ayurvedic medicine and found from West Bengal to southern India. *See also* Vaidu. (Risley 1891, 1:46–50, 362–366; Thurston and Rangachari 1909, 7:267–270)

Bai Rajput (Bai) A Rajput caste found in Uttar Pradesh and northern Madhya Pradesh. (Crooke 1896, 1:118–126; Russell and Hira Lal 1916, 4:435–436)

Baiswar A tribe found in the hills of eastern Uttar Pradesh. They are singers and dancers; the women act as midwives. (Crooke 1896, 1:126–130)

Bajania (Dholi) A caste of Hindu musicians found throughout Gujarat. They make their living by performing at weddings or by making handicrafts and baskets. *See also* Mirasi. (Campbell 1901, 503–504; Enthoven 1920–1922, 1:52–54)

Bakkaru (Baggaru, Baga Holeya) A caste found in central Karnataka. They are tenant farmers. (Nanjundayya and Ananthakrishna Iyer 1928–1936, 2:94–98)

Balahi (Balai) A caste of Untouchable Hindu weavers and village watchmen found in parts of central India and Uttar Pradesh. (Crooke 1896, 1:134–135; Russell and Hira Lal 1916, 2:105–108; Fuchs 1950)

Balija (Balji, Banajiga, Linga Balija, Linga Banajiga, Pancham Banajigaru, Gurusthulu, Sivabhaktaru, Kavarai, Naidu). A large trading caste of south and central India. Although Hindus, many are of the Lingayat sect. Many are peddlers or farmers. *See also* Perika. (Thurston and Rangachari 1909, 1:134–145; 3:263–266; 4:232–236; Russell and Hira Lal 1916, 2:108–110; Nanjundayya and Ananthakrishna Iyer 1928–1936, 2:99–134)

Bam-Margi A Sakti sect who practice tantra and are found in parts of northern India. Intoxication and sexual cohabitation were part of their rituals. (Crooke 1896, 1:135–137)

Banaphar A section of the Rajputs, found in central Uttar Pradesh. (Crooke 1896, 1:137–139)

Bandhalgoti (Bandhugoti, Bandhilgoti, Banjhilgoti) A section of the Rajputs, found in Sultanpur District, Uttar Pradesh. (Crooke 1896, 1:140–143)

Bandhara (Galiara) A small caste of southern Gujarat, Vaishnavites who traditionally do indigo dyeing and silk folding. Some have converted to Islam. (Campbell 1899, 71; 1901, 181; Enthoven 1920–1922, 1:56–58)

Bandi A caste of bonded laborers, thought to be descended from slaves. Girls generally became prostitutes rather than marry. They are found in the coastal districts of Karnataka. (Enthoven 1920–1922, 1:58)

Bangali (Bengali) A section of Brahmans, found in northern India and originating in Bengal. In Punjab the name designates a vagrant ex-criminal tribe. (Crooke 1896, 1:145–149; Rose 1911, 1:56–57)

Banjara (Banjari, Brinjara, Wanjari, Wanjara, Vanjari, Labhana, Labana, Laban, Lambadi, Lambani, Lamani, Lamane, Mukeri, Ghor, Gohar Herkeri, Sugali, Sukali) A large and widespread tribe of grain and salt carriers, bullock-cart drivers, cattle dealers and breeders, but essentially Gypsies or peripatetics. In former times they were noted for such criminal customs as kidnapping children, slavery, traffic in women, and petty theft. Unlike most Indian castes, they are not wholly endogamous but accept wives from other groups, including girls that they have kidnapped. They are found throughout most of India, and they now may work as cultivators or farm laborers. Banjhara is also a Muslim trading caste in Gujarat, converted from the same Hindu caste. Partial total: 138,877 in 1971. *See also* PERIPATETICS. (Risley 1891, 1:59; Crooke 1896, 1:149–167; Campbell 1899, 85–86; Thurston and Rangachari 1909, 4:207–232; Rose 1911, 1:62–63; Russell and Hira Lal 1916, 2:162–192; Enthoven 1920–1922, 2:331–343; Siraj ul Hassan 1920, 1:15–27; 2:627–634; Nanjundayya and Ananthakrishna Iyer 1928–1936, 2:135–196)

Bant (Bunt) A Hindu caste found in Kodagu District and along the nearby Tulu coast of southern Karnataka. They are farmers. (Thurston and Rangachari 1909, 1:147–172; Krishna Iyer 1948, 67–70)

Bargujar A section of the Rajputs, found in Uttar Pradesh. (Crooke 1896, 1:187–190)

Barhai (Barhi, Badhi, Sutar, Suthar, Kharadi, Tarkhan, Mistri) A large caste of Hindu carpenters living in northern, central, and western India, from Bihar to Maharashtra. (Risley 1891, 1:66–68; Crooke 1896, 1:190–199; Russell and Hira Lal 1916, 2:199–202; Enthoven 1920–1922, 3:355–359)

Bari (Bargah, Bargaha, Bargahi, Panwale) A caste of household servants and makers of leaf plates, found in northern, western, and central India. Although they are Shaivites, a few claim to be Muslims. (Risley 1891, 1:68–69; Crooke 1896, 1:184–185, 201–206; Russell and Hira Lal 1916, 2:202–204; Enthoven 1920–1922, 1:59–65)

Barwar An ex-criminal tribe, found in eastern Uttar Pradesh. The same name identifies a section of Rajputs, found in western Uttar Pradesh. The article by Crooke includes a vocabulary of thieves' cant. (Crooke 1896, 1:206–221)

Basdewa (Wasudeo, Harbola, Kaparia, Jaga, Kapdi, Sanadhya, Sanauria Brahman) A caste of wandering beggars, who call themselves Sanadhya or Sanauria Brahmans. Although few in number, they are widely scattered through northern, central, and western India. (Russell and Hira Lal 1916, 2:204–207; Enthoven 1920–1922, 3:454–455)

Basor (Bansphor, Bansphod, Dulia, Dhulia, Balahar, Bulahar, Burud, Ghanche, Ghanchi, Ghache, Miyadar, Myadar, Medar, Medare, Medara, Medarlu, Medarakaran) A tribe of Hindu bamboo workers found widely in India. Some are Lingayats. There are also Muslim Ghanchis in northern Gujarat, converts from the Hindu caste, who sell oil. Partial total: 17,888 in 1971. (Crooke 1896, 1:132–134, 167–173, 222–228; Campbell 1899, 73; 1901, 181–183; Thurston and Rangachari 1909, 5:52–58; Russell and Hira Lal 1916, 2:208–212; Enthoven 1920–1922, 1:254–260; Siraj ul Hassan 1920, 1:135–142; Nanjundayya and Ananthakrishna Iyer 1928–1936, 4:191–205)

Batgam (Padu) A caste found in central Sri Lanka. They are farm laborers and in some areas funeral drummers. (Ryan 1953)

Batwal (Barwala) A caste of northern Punjab, who work as laborers. They are Hindus. (Rose 1911, 1:66–68)

Bavacha (Bamcha) A small tribe found in southern Gujarat. Traditionally they sell grass and work as grooms, but some are laborers. Total: 2,831 in 1971. (Enthoven 1920–1922, 1:65–67)

Bavuri (Baurio, Khodalo) A caste of basket makers, found in Ganjam District, Orissa. They are Hindus. (Thurston and Rangachari 1909, 1:175–180)

Bawariya (Bauria, Baori, Bauri, Bawaria) A hunting and thieving tribe, found in Muzaffarnagar and Mirzapur districts, Uttar Pradesh, and in Punjab. (Crooke 1896, 1:228–237; Rose 1911, 1:70–79)

Bedar (Bendar, Beria, Beriya, Bed, Berad, Bedia, Bediya, Bedea, Bejia, Bejea, Boya) A small but widespread Hindu tribe found in much of India, Untouchable in status. They are mainly involved in agriculture, but their name means "hunter," and they were once irregular troops. Some are village watchmen. Total: 51,360 in 1971. (Risley 1891, 1:83; Thurston and Rangachari 1909, 1:180–209; Russell and Hira Lal 1916, 2:212–214; Enthoven 1920–1922, 1:78–90; Siraj ul Hassan 1920, 1:34–43; Nanjundayya and Ananthakrishna Iyer 1928–1936, 2:197–230)

Beldar (Od, Ode, Odh, Ud, Odde, Odden, Vodden, Vodda, Vaddar, Waddar, Wudder, Wadu Rajlu, Odewandlu, Sonkar, Raj, Larhia, Karigar, Kalkola, Matkuda, Chunkar, Munurwar, Thapatkari, Pathrot, Takari, Takara, Dhondphoda) A grouping of earth- and stone-working castes found widely in India and parts of Pakistan. They are mostly Hindus who now engage in road making and other laboring activities; they used to make stone handmills. Those called Takara or Dhondphoda are Muslims. *See also* Sansia. (Risley 1891, 1:86–87; Crooke 1896, 1:237–240; Ananthakrishna Iyer 1909–1912, 3:390–393; Thurston and Rangachari 1909, 5:422–436; Rose 1911, 2:175–176; Russell and Hira Lal 1916, 2:215–220; Enthoven 1920–1922; 3:138–149, 359–361; Siraj ul Hassan 1920, 2:645–651; Nanjundayya and Ananthakrishna Iyer 1928–1936, 4:659–677)

Berava A caste of drummers, found in Sri Lanka. (Ryan 1953; Leach 1968)

Beria (Bedia, Bediya, Beriya, Kolhati, Dandewala, Bansberia, Kabutari) A peripatetic group of castes widespread in northern and central India. The article by Risley lists numerous specific occupations. They are Gypsies and former dacoits (thieves). Many of the women were once professional prostitutes and never married; some are tattooists and children's doctors. Beria are related to the Sansia and Nai, who had much the same occupations. *See also* PERIPATETICS. (Risley 1891, 1:83–85; Crooke 1896, 1:242–249; Russell and Hira Lal 1916, 2:220–224; 3:527–531; 4:286)

Beri Chetti A trading caste found in Tamil Nadu. Although Hindus, a few are Lingayat. (Thurston and Rangachari 1909, 1:211–218)

Besta (Bestha, Kabbaligar, Kabber, Kabher, Kabbera, Ambi,

Ambig, Ambiga, Ambekar, Barkar, Barekari, Bhillakabberu, Jad, Sungar, Sunnakallu Bestha, Durga Murgi, Parkitiwaru, Parivara, Toreya, Torea, Gangimakkalu, Gangemakkalu) A Hindu caste group, found in Maharashtra, Andhra Pradesh, Tamil Nadu, and Karnataka. Many work as domestic servants or porters, though they were formerly fishermen and palanquin bearers. The name "Toreya" comes from _tore_, "river bank," and is also used for the lowest phratry of Badagas in the Nilgiris District of Tamil Nadu. In Maharashtra they are a Kannada-speaking caste of fishers, ferrymen, and former palanquin bearers, now sometimes beggars or farmers. (Thurston and Rangachari 1909, 1:218–222; 3:1–6; 7:176–182; Russell and Hira Lal 1916, 1:348; Enthoven 1920–1922, 2:110–118; Siraj ul Hassan 1920, 1:77–82; Nanjundayya and Ananthakrishna Iyer 1928–1936, 2:239–258; 4:637–639)

Bhabra A Jain caste, mainly traders, found in the Punjab. _See also_ BANIA. (Rose 1911, 1:80–82)

Bhadauriya A section of the Rajputs, found in western Uttar Pradesh. (Crooke 1896, 1:250–252)

Bhagat (Bhakat) A class of Vaishnavite devotees in northern India. The term seems to be applied rather loosely: a section of the Oraon tribe is known as Bhakat. A tribe of eastern Uttar Pradesh is also called Bhagat or Radha. (Risley 1891, 1:91–92; Crooke 1896, 1:252–253; 4:195–196)

Bhaina A tribe found in the wild forest lands of Bilaspur District, in Madhya Pradesh. They worship a "noseless goddess" and are essentially Hindus. They may share some early ancestry with the Baigas. Total: 24,740 in 1971. (Russell and Hira Lal 1916, 2:224–233)

Bhale Sultan A section of Rajputs, found in much of Uttar Pradesh. (Crooke 1896, 1:253–256)

Bhamta (Bhamtya, Uchla, Uchlia, Takari, Ghantichor, Ganthachor) A small Hindu caste of western and central India. They were professional pickpockets, but now they are traders and cultivators, and they also make biers for the dead. (Russell and Hira Lal 1916, 2:234–238; Enthoven 1920–1922, 1:93–96; Siraj ul Hassan 1920, 1:48–50)

Bhandari (Bhondari, Bhand, Bhanr, Bhavaguna, Bhavaya, Targala, Madkar, Shingade, Sanaiwad, Naqqal) A caste of Hindu temple musicians and storytellers, found from Andhra Pradesh to western India. They are found in Pakistan under the name of Naqqal. In the latter area they are distillers and farmers. In southern Orissa there are barbers, of the name Bhandari. _See also_ Nai. (Crooke 1896, 1:256–259; Campbell 1901, 222–225; Thurston and Rangachari 1909, 1:230–237; Rose 1911, 1:83; 2:156–157; Russell and Hira Lal 1916, 1:349; Enthoven 1920–1922, 1:96–104; Siraj ul Hassan 1920, 1:51–52)

Bhangi (Bhangia, Mehtar, Hari, Kutana, Musalli, Dom, Olgana, Chuhra) A large caste of Untouchable sweepers and scavengers. They are found throughout northern, western, and central India. Although basically Hindus, many have converted to Christianity or Islam. _See also_ Lalbegi; UNTOUCHABLES. (Crooke 1896, 1:259–293; Campbell 1901, 334–338; Rose 1911, 1:182–210, 573; Russell and Hira Lal 1916, 4:215–233; Enthoven 1920–1922, 1:104–112 Fuchs 1950; Kolenda 1987)

Bhar (Rajbhar, Bharat, Bharadwaj, Bharpatwa, Kanaujiya) A tribe of eastern Uttar Pradesh. They are farmers, farm laborers, and former burglars. (Crooke 1896, 2:1–12)

Bharai (Pirhain) A Muslim caste found in Punjab. They were traditionally drummers. (Rose 1911, 1:84–86)

Bharbhunja (Bhadbhunja, Bhujari, Bhuj, Bhujua, Bhurji, Gonr, Kandu, Kanu) A Hindu caste of grain parchers and boatmen, found in northern, western, and central India, and in Punjab Province, Pakistan; they are especially numerous in towns. In Uttar Pradesh they work as stonemasons, farmers, and sweet makers, or they deal in grain. (Risley 1891, 1:414–418; Crooke 1896, 2:13–19; 3:130–133; Rose 1911, 1:86–88; Russell and Hira Lal 1916, 2:238–241; Enthoven 1920–1922, 1:90–93; Siraj ul Hassan 1920, 1:44–47)

Bharia (Bhar, Bharia-Bhumia) A Dravidian-speaking Hindu tribe found from West Bengal to Jabalpur District, in Madhya Pradesh. Among their many subgroups are Agaria and Ahir. They work as farm laborers. Total: 29,287 in 1971. _See also_ AGARIA; AHIR. (Risley 1891, 1:95–96; Russell and Hira Lal 1916, 2:242–250)

Bhat (Bhatt, Bhatrazu, Rao, Jasondhi, Thakur, Shivachandi Thakur) A caste of bards and genealogists found throughout northern, western, and central India. Some claim to have originally been Brahmans or Rajputs, but a few are Muslim. Some are religious mendicants and itinerant musicians. _See also_ Bhatraja; PERIPATETICS. (Risley 1891, 1:98–103; Crooke 1896, 2:20–33; Rose 1911, 1:94–101; Russell and Hira Lal 1916, 2:251–270; Enthoven 1920–1922, 1:123–133; Siraj ul Hassan 1920, 1:53–55; Nanjundayya and Ananthakrishna Iyer 1928–1936, 2:259–276)

Bhatia (Bhatiya) A caste of western and northwestern India and Sindh in Pakistan. They are merchants, bankers, and brokers. (Crooke 1896, 2:37–42; Campbell 1901, 116–121; Rose 1911, 1:91–93; Enthoven 1920–1922, 1:133–145)

Bhatiyara A caste devoted to the needs of travelers, they are innkeepers, cooks, fishermen, and tobacco sellers. They are Sunni Muslims, found throughout Uttar Pradesh. (Crooke 1896, 2:34–37)

Bhatra (Bhattra) A tribe of Bastar and Raipur districts, in eastern Madhya Pradesh, usually viewed as part of the Gonds. They practice shifting cultivation, or work as farm laborers. Total: 71,149 in 1971. _See also_ GOND; Ramaiya. (Russell and Hira Lal 1916, 2:271–277)

Bhatraja (Bhatrazu, Bhatraju, Bhat Murti, Bhatwandlu, Bhat, Bahrot, Bhato, Kannaji Bhat, Kani Razu, Battu Turaka, Padiga Raju, Magada) A caste group of northern Tamil Nadu and Andhra Pradesh but also found in Gujarat. They are traditionally bards and heralds; some are the hereditary bards of the Velma and Kapu castes and once attended at the courts of the Vijayanagar and Warangal kings. _See also_ Bhat. (Campbell 1901, 207–214; Thurston and Rangachari 1909, 1:223–230; Siraj ul Hassan 1920, 1:56–59)

Bhatti (Jaiswar) An agricultural caste found in the Punjab and Uttar Pradesh. They include both Hindus and Muslims. (Crooke 1896, 2:42–46; Rose 1911, 1:101–106)

Bhavaiya (Targala) A caste of northern Gujarat who perform comedies. They are Hindus and use Brahman priests. (Enthoven 1920-1922, 1:145)

Bhavin (Bavina, Devli, Naik, Naikin, Kalavant)   A caste who are found along the west coast of India from North Ratnagiri District in Maharashtra through Goa to Uttar Kannad District in Karnataka. They are traditionally Hindu temple sweepers. (Enthoven 1920-1922, 1:145-147; 2:130-133; Feio 1979, 98-99)

Bhilala   A Hindu tribe of central India, thought to have originated from the intermixing of Rajputs and Bhils. They are cultivators, farm laborers, and village watchmen. Total: 9,395 in 1971. (Russell and Hira Lal 1916, 2:293-297; Haekel and Stiglmayr 1961; Haekel 1963; Saxena 1964)

Bhishti (Bhisti, Beesti, Bijishti, Pakhali, Mashki)   A Hindu and Muslim caste cluster of water carriers, found in western and northern India. (Crooke 1896, 2:99-101; Campbell 1899, 89; Russell and Hira Lal 1916, 2:298-300; Enthoven 1920-1922, 1:179-181)

Bhoi (Kahar, Bundeli Bhoi, Kahar Bhoi, Kahar Bhui, Dhimar, Behara, Mahigir, Mahra, Dhebra, Palewar, Parivar, Baraua, Bauri, Machhandar)   A large caste bloc of fishermen, water carriers, and former palanquin bearers, found in much of western, northern, and central India. They are Hindus, and some work as farmers, earth movers, water carriers, or domestic servants for other Hindu castes; others raise silkworms or grow tobacco, vegetables, and water chestnuts. (Risley 1891, 1:78-82, 370-375; Crooke 1896, 3:92-104; Campbell 1901, 504-505, 520; Russell and Hira Lal 1916, 2:502-514; 3:291-296; Enthoven 1920-1922, 1:181-194; 2:125-126; Siraj ul Hassan 1920, 1:77; 2:300-302; Nanjundayya and Ananthakrishna Iyer 1928-1936, 3:502-503; 4:471-473; Patnaik 1960a)

Bhoksa (Bhuksa)   A tribe found in the hills of northern Uttar Pradesh. They cultivate, hunt, and fish. They have a reputation for sorcery and are mainly Hindus, though a few are Sikhs. (Crooke 1896, 2:55-61)

Bhoyar (Boyar, Bhoir)   A cultivating caste of central India. They claim descent from immigrant Rajputs. (Dalton 1872, 129-131; Russell and Hira Lal 1916, 2:300-304)

Bhuinmali (Bhuimali, Bhusundar)   A cultivating caste of Bangladesh, who formerly acted as palanquin bearers. They are Hindus. (Risley 1891, 1:105-107)

Bhulia (Bholia, Bhoriya, Bholwa, Mihir, Mehar)   A caste of Hindu weavers, who claim to have migrated to Orissa from Patna. (Russell and Hira Lal 1916, 2:319-322)

Bhunjia   A small Dravidian-speaking tribe in Raipur District, Madhya Pradesh. They are essentially Hindus, and they live by farming. Total: 14,245 in 1971. (Russell and Hira Lal 1916, 2:322-328)

Bhute (Bhope, Aradhi)   A caste of religious mendicants, originally recruited from among Brahmans and Marathas and devoted to the goddess Bhavani. There are even some Muslim ones. Many are eunuchs. They are usually beggars, found in Maharashtra. They marry; and their dead, if male, are buried in a sitting posture, whereas dead women are burned in a lying posture. *See also* HIJRA. (Enthoven 1920-1922, 1:41-43, 194-196; Siraj ul Hassan 1920, 1:88-90)

Bhutia (Butia, Bhot, Bhod, Bot, Bhotia, Bhotiya)   A tribal cluster of mountain cultivators, found from West Bengal to Nepal and Himachal Pradesh. Some are Lamaistic Buddhists, others Hindus. Their language, Bhotia, is a form of Tibetan. Indian total: 86,257 in 1971. *See also* Chhazang; Tibetan. (Dalton 1872, 93-98; Crooke 1896, 2:61-63; Srivastava 1966; Fürer-Haimendorf 1975; Das and Raha 1981; Bhasin 1989; Bishop 1990)

Biar (Biyar)   A Hindu tribe found in eastern Uttar Pradesh and Madhya Pradesh, employed in excavation. Partial total: 3,859 in 1971. (Crooke 1896, 2:128-140)

Bili Maggar (Bilimagga, Kuruvinna Setti, Kuruvina Banajiga)   A caste of Hindu weavers found in western Karnataka. (Thurston and Rangachari 1909, 1:239-243; Nanjundayya and Ananthakrishna Iyer 1928-1936, 2:277-287)

Billava (Billoru)   A caste of toddy tappers, who speak Tulu or Kannada and are found in Karnataka. Some of them cultivate. (Thurston and Rangachari 1909, 1:243-252; Nanjundayya and Ananthakrishna Iyer 1928-1936, 2:288-296)

Bind (Bin, Bhind, Bindu)   A fishing, hunting, and agricultural caste found from eastern Uttar Pradesh to Bangladesh, related to the Gonds. They are Hindus. *See also* GOND. (Risley 1891, 1:130-134; Crooke 1896, 2:106-115)

Binjhwar (Binjhia, Binjhoa, Binjhal, Birjia, Brijia)   A Dravidian-speaking tribe of eastern Madhya Pradesh, Bihar and parts of West Bengal, closely related to the Baiga. They are landholders. Total: 160,534 in 1971. *See also* BAIGA. (Risley 1891, 1:134-137; Russell and Hira Lal 1916, 2:329-336)

Birhor (Birhul)   A Munda-speaking tribe of hunters and gatherers, found in southern and central Bihar. Some accounts allege that they practiced cannibalism in the nineteenth century. Total: 4,300 in 1971. (Dalton 1872, 217-219; Risley 1891, 1:137-138; Roy 1926; Adhikary 1984)

Bisen   A Rajput group found in Uttar Pradesh. They are cultivators and landlords. (Crooke 1896, 2:116-120)

Bishnoi (Pahlad Bansi)   A Hindu sect, originating in the Panjab, that has become a caste. The name means "worshiper of Vishnu." They are traders. A few are found in central India, the remainder in the Punjab and Uttar Pradesh. (Crooke 1896, 2:120-127; Rose 1911, 1:110-114; Russell and Hira Lal 1916, 2:337-344)

Bohora (Bohra, Kasar)   A large Jain caste originally from Goa and found in nearby districts of Karnataka. They are landowners. Some are converts to Sunni Islam. *See also* BOHRA. (Enthoven 1920-1922, 1:197-207)

Bonthuk (Bonthuk Savara)   A caste found in Krishna and Guntur districts in Andhra Pradesh, where they are peripatetic. They collect and sell bamboo. (Thurston and Rangachari 1909, 1:258-262)

Borul (Burol)   A small caste of traders found in Parbhani and Beed districts of central Maharashtra. (Siraj ul Hassan 1920, 1:96-98)

Bottada (Bathudi, Bhottada, Dhotada)   A tribe of cultivators in Orissa; they are Hindus and probably related to the Murias. Total: 325,634 in 1971. (Thurston and Rangachari 1909, 1:264–266)

Brahma Kshatri   A small caste found in Gujarat. They are mostly scribes and government servants. (Campbell 1901, 55–59; Enthoven 1920–1922, 1:208–212)

Buna (Banua, Buno)   A group of castes or tribes found in Bangladesh. They were probably members of distinct tribes (e.g., Santal, Oraon, Bhuiya) who wandered eastward looking for farm-laboring jobs. (Risley 1891, 1:163–164)

Bundela Rajput   A Rajput caste found in northern Madhya Pradesh, formerly of great military power; they are now cultivators. (Russell and Hira Lal 1916, 4:438–440)

Chadar (Kotwar)   A small weaving caste of a few districts in central India. (Russell and Hira Lal 1916, 2:400–402)

Chain (Chai, Chaini, Barchain)   A cultivating and fishing caste, formerly thieves too, who are found from eastern Uttar Pradesh to western Bangladesh. In the west of this tract they cultivate, whereas in Bangladesh they are traders. (Risley 1891, 1:166–169; Crooke 1896, 2:167–168)

Chakkan   A Tamil-speaking caste of oil pressers found in Ernakulam and Trichur districts in central Kerala. (Ananthakrishna Iyer 1909–1912, 3:367–369)

Chakkiliyan (Chuckler)   A caste of Untouchable leather workers found in Tamil Nadu. They are Hindus. _See also_ UN-TOUCHABLES. (Thurston and Rangachari 1909, 2:2–7)

Chaliyan   A weaving caste found in northern and central Kerala, where they probably immigrated from Tamil Nadu. (Thurston and Rangachari 1909, 2:11–14; Ananthakrishna Iyer 1909–1912, 2:115–118)

Chandal (Chandala, Chanral, Chang, Karral, Nama-Sudra, Nama, Nishad)   A large caste of farmers and boatmen in West Bengal and Bangladesh. They also follow numerous urban trades. Most of them are Vaishnavites. (Risley 1891, 1:183–189, 428)

Chandel Rajput   A Rajput caste found in northern Madhya Pradesh and Uttar Pradesh, perhaps related to the Gonds. They are Hindu farmers. (Crooke 1896, 2:196–200; Russell and Hira Lal 1916, 4:440–443)

Charan (Gadhavi, Bahrot, Barath, Barahatta, Mangan)   A tribe of bards and genealogists, found throughout Gujarat. Total: 1,700 in 1971. (Campbell 1901, 214–222; Enthoven 1920–1922, 1:271–286)

Charandasi   A Vaishnavite sect founded in the eighteenth century by Charan Das, now found in western Uttar Pradesh. Some are mendicants, some merchants. (Crooke 1896, 2:201–204)

Chasa (Tasa, Sadgop, Satgop, Alia)   A Hindu cultivating caste found in Orissa, West Bengal, and Bangladesh. They are mostly Vaishnavite Hindus. (Risley 1891, 1:192–193; 2:212–214; Crooke 1896, 4:245; Russell and Hira Lal 1916, 2:424–426; Patnaik 1960b)

Chasadhoba (Chasadhopa)   A Hindu cultivating and trading caste, found in West Bengal. Some work as craftsmen or builders. (Risley 1891, 1:193–195)

Chatla   An itinerant caste of Muslims, found in parts of Gujarat. They are carriers and woodcutters. They bury their dead in a standing position. (Campbell 1899, 86)

Chaudhri   A large Hindu tribe found in Surat District, southern Gujarat. Most of them are farmers or farm laborers. Total: 177,155 in 1971. (Shah 1984)

Chauhan   A small caste of laborers and village watchmen in the Chhattisgarh area of Madhya Pradesh. They are Hindu and vegetarian, and they appear to have adopted their name from the prestigious Chauhan Rajputs. (Russell and Hira Lal 1916, 2:427–429)

Chauhan Rajput   A Rajput farming caste found from Punjab to Madhya Pradesh. (Crooke 1896, 2:207–213, Campbell 1901, 123–125; Rose 1911, 1:155–156; Russell and Hira Lal 1916, 4:443–446)

Chero (Cheru, Churu)   A tribe of cultivators, found from West Bengal to eastern Uttar Pradesh. They speak a Munda language and are Hindus. Some have taken up carting, trading, and other occupations. Total: 38,916 in 1971. (Dalton 1872, 121–123; Risley 1891, 1:199–203; Crooke 1896, 2:214–222; Mukherjee et al. 1973)

Cheruman (Cherumukkal, Cheruma, Pulayan)   A Hindu caste of former bonded laborers, found in northern Kerala. _See also_ Pulluvan. (Thurston and Rangachari 1909, 2:45–91)

Chet-Rami   A sect founded in the nineteenth century by one Chet Ram. It was based in Lahore, Pakistan, and acknowledges the Christian Trinity as well as a Hindu Trinity consisting of Allah, Parameswar, and Khuda (the first and last of these being Islamic terms). (Rose 1911, 1:157–158)

Chetti (Setti, Chetty)   A group of trading and money-lending castes, found throughout Tamil Nadu. The article by Thurston and Rangachari describes their secret trading language. _See also_ BANIA. (Thurston and Rangachari 1909, 2:91–97)

Chhalapdar (Mujawar)   A tiny caste in Delhi, probably recent converts to Islam from Hinduism. (Rose 1911, 1:160–163)

Chhapparband (Chapparband)   A tiny Muslim caste of western Maharashtra who formerly specialized in thatching roofs and making false coinage. They are also found in southern India. The article by Thurston and Rangachari describes their techniques. (Thurston and Rangachari 1909, 2:16–22; Enthoven 1920–1922, 1:286–287)

Chhazang   Buddhists of Lahul and Spiti District, Himachal Pradesh, who do not recognize caste; however, there are three classes among them. They are landowners and Tibetan in culture. (Rose 1911, 1:164–166)

Chhipa (Chhapgar, Chhapagar, Chhimba, Chhipi, Chhimpi, Charhoa, Calender, Rangari, Wannekar, Bhaosar, Bhavsar, Bhausagar, Bhavasagari, Paungar, Nirali, Nilari, Nilgar)   A caste of calico printers and dyers, found in lowland Pakistan and in northern, western, and central India, as far as northern Andhra Pradesh. Some are Hindus, some

Jains, some Sikhs, others Muslims. *See also* Rangrez. (Crooke 1896, 2:222–227; Campbell 1899, 71–72; 1901, 177–179; Rose 1911, 1:166–168; Russell and Hira Lal 1916, 2:429–431; Enthoven 1920–1922, 1:147–151; 3:135–138; Siraj ul Hassan 1920, 1:60–65)

Chibh   A Rajput caste of cultivators, found in Punjab and parts of Kashmir. (Rose 1911, 1:169–170)

Chingathan   A tribe found in Cannanore District in northern Kerala. Their main occupation is collecting wild honey. (Luiz 1962, 44–46)

Chishti (Chishtiya)   A Muslim sect found in the Punjab and much of Pakistan. Its founding saint, Abu Ishaq, is venerated by Hindus as well as Muslims. (Crooke 1896, 2:228–230; Rose 1911, 1:171–174)

Chitrakathi (Hardas)   A small caste of religious mendicants, storytellers, and puppeteers, found in Maharashtra and Madhya Pradesh; they are probably related to the Chitaris of central India. (Russell and Hira Lal 1916, 2:438–440; Enthoven 1920–1922, 1:287–289)

Chitrali   A Muslim people who live in Chitral, in the far north of Pakistan. They are of varied castes and occupations, and they are well adapted to the mountain conditions. (Rose 1911, 1:174–181)

Chodhra (Chodhara)   A tribe of southern Gujarat, who practice agriculture. Total: 11,767 in 1971. (Campbell 1901, 312–313; Enthoven 1920–1922, 1:289–293)

Churahi   People of the Churah area in Chamba District, Himachal Pradesh. They are Hindu landowners. (Rose 1911, 1:210–214)

Chutia (Deuri-Chutiya, Dibongiya)   A Paleo-Mongoloid tribe found in the easternmost parts of Assam, where they were historically the dominant people. (Saikia 1976)

Dabgar (Kuppesaz)   A caste that contains both Hindus and Muslims and makes rawhide jars for storing certain foods. They are found from Uttar Pradesh to West Bengal. (Crooke 1896, 2:235–236)

Dadupanthi   A Vaishnavite sect founded in the seventeenth century by Dadu, a cotton carder. They are found in the Punjab, Uttar Pradesh, and eastern Rajasthan. (Crooke 1896, 2:236–239)

Dafali (Darwesh)   A tribe of musicians and beggars, found throughout Uttar Pradesh. (Crooke 1896, 2:239–244)

Dafla (Daphla, Dophla, Nishi)   A Paleo-Mongoloid tribe of cultivators, found in western districts of Arunachal Pradesh. Total: 5,926 in 1971. (Dalton 1872, 40–42; Shukla 1959; Fürer-Haimendorf 1956, 1962)

Dahait (Dahayat)   A large tribe of village watchmen found in Jabbalpur and neighboring districts of Madhya Pradesh. They are related to the Kol, and they were once personal attendants and doorkeepers of a king, carrying his mace and, most importantly, the ceremonial umbrella. Total: 363,215 in 1971. (Russell and Hira Lal 1916, 2:444–453)

Daharia (Dahar)   A small caste claiming descent from Rajputs and found in Bilaspur and Raipur districts, Madhya Pradesh. Some are minor officials, but they refuse to handle the plow. Dahar are an agricultural clan of Jats, found in Punjab Province, Pakistan. (Rose 1911, 1:219; Russell and Hira Lal 1916, 2:453–457)

Dai   Not a caste, but the occupational category of midwife. These may be women of Muslim or Hindu castes, often Chamars. Their job is considered polluting. They are found all over northern and central India. (Risley 1891, 1:210–212)

Dakaut (Dak-putra, Jotgi, Panda, Dhaonsi)   A Brahman caste, found in the Punjab. (Rose 1911, 1:134–138)

Dandasi   A Hindu caste of village watchmen, noted also for thievery. They are found in Ganjam District, in southern Orissa. (Thurston and Rangachari 1909, 2:106–111)

Dangi   A cultivating caste found in Sagar District, Madhya Pradesh, and in Jhansi District, Uttar Pradesh. They are Hindus. The name probably comes from the Hindi word *dang*, meaning "hill," so they are "hill men." (Crooke 1896, 2:246–252; Russell and Hira Lal 1916, 2:457–463)

Dangri   A small caste of melon and vegetable growers, living in eastern Maharashtra. Their customs resemble those of the Kunbis. (Russell and Hira Lal 1916, 2:463–465)

Darzi (Darji, Shimpi, Simpi, Chhipi, Chipollu, Pipavasi, Merai, Meerolu, Sais, Suis, Sai Sutar, Suji, Thalavadi)   A caste of tailors, found throughout the towns of northwestern and central India, as far as Karnataka. The caste appears to be of fairly recent origin, and the word *darzi* is Persian. Many are Hindus of the Namdev sect; others are Muslim. Today some work as cloth merchants, writers, money changers, or cultivators. (Crooke 1896, 2:253–259; Campbell 1901, 179–181; Russell and Hira Lal 1916, 2:466–472; Enthoven 1920–1922, 1:295–297; 2:327–331; Siraj ul Hassan 1920, 1:153–156; Nanjundayya and Ananthakrishna Iyer 1928–1936, 3:77–100)

Dasa   A caste of Hindu and Lingayat beggars, found in Karnataka and Andhra Pradesh. (Enthoven 1920–1922, 1:298)

Dasri (Dasari, Tadan)   A class of Vaishnavite beggars who form several endogamous groups originally recruited from Telugu- or Kannada-speaking castes. Some catch fish and birds, and others are farmers. (Thurston and Rangachari 1909, 2:112–119; Siraj ul Hassan 1920, 1:157–161; Nanjundayya and Ananthakrishna Iyer 1928–1936, 3:101–117)

Dauri (Daur, Dawari)   A farming people found in Waziristan, North-West Frontier Province, Pakistan. They are Muslims. (Rose 1911, 1:225–232)

Davre Jogi (Davre Gosavi, Daure Gosavi, Bharadi)   A sect of Yogis who are professional mendicants. Some now work as laborers. They are Hindus, found in central and western India. *See also* Yogi. (Enthoven 1920–1922, 1:113–117; Siraj ul Hassan 1920, 1:278–281)

Demala-Gattara   A farming and laboring caste found in western Sri Lanka. (Ryan 1953)

Depala   A caste of western Gujarat, related to the Lohanas.

They are Hindu household servants and shopkeepers. (Enthoven 1920–1922, 1:299–301)

Deshastha Brahman (Deshasth, Grihastha, Bhikshuk)   A Marathi-speaking Brahman caste, found in Maharashtra and Karnataka. Many of them (Grihasthas) are householders with the usual urban jobs, such as clerk, moneylender, school-teacher; but some (Bhikshuks) are religious mendicants. (Enthoven 1920–1922, 1:244–245; Siraj ul Hassan 1920, 1:108–111)

Devadasi (Dasi, Bogam, Bhogam, Varangana, Calavantina, Colvonta, Kasban, Kasbi, Kalawant, Pathura Dawaru, Tawaif, Patar, Patoriva, Patur, Paturiya, Kanchan, Bailadeira)   A matrilineal caste of former dancing girls, musicians, and prostitutes, speaking the various regional languages. ("Bailadeira" is the Portuguese term.) They are Hindus, still to be found throughout India even though their occupations have changed. Girls were recruited into the caste by being dedicated to temples by their parents; and their children became members of this caste by matrilineal descent. Their sons were commonly temple musicians. In some areas (e.g., Andhra Pradesh and Uttar Pradesh) there were both Hindu and Muslim Bogams. (Crooke 1896, 4:364–371; Thurston and Rangachari 1909, 2:125–153; Russell and Hira Lal 1916, 3:373–384; Siraj ul Hassan 1920, 1:91–95; Feio 1979, 91–98; Marglin 1985)

Devanga (Devangalu, Devang, Devra, Jyandra, Jad, Koshti, Hatkar, Devanga Sale, Sali, Myatari)   A caste of weavers found all over central and southern India, from Maharashtra to Kerala. They speak Telugu, Kannada, or Marathi; most are Shaivites. Some have taken to farming, carpentry, or masonry. (Thurston and Rangachari 1909, 2:154–166; Ananthakrishna Iyer 1909–1912, 3:369–374; Enthoven 1920–1922, 1:301–310; Siraj ul Hassan 1920, 1:162–165; Nanjundayya and Ananthakrishna Iyer 1928–1936, 3:118–138)

Dewar   A small Dravidian-speaking caste of musicians and professional beggars, found in the Chhattisgarh area of Madhya Pradesh. (Russell and Hira Lal 1916, 2:472–477)

Dhakar   A small caste found in the Bastar area of Orissa. In 1911 their population was only 5,500, but almost two-thirds were female. The caste consists mainly of farm laborers. (Russell and Hira Lal 1916, 2:477–480)

Dhanuk (Dhanak)   An agricultural caste, mainly found in Bihar, in Uttar Pradesh, and in Narsimhapur District, Madhya Pradesh. Many people work as musicians at weddings, as village watchmen, and household servants. The women are midwives. (Risley 1891, 1:220–222; Crooke 1896, 2:271–276; Russell and Hira Lal 1916, 2:484–487)

Dhanwar (Dhenuar, Dhanuhar)   A tribe of Bilaspur District, in eastern Madhya Pradesh. They speak a dialect of Chhattisgarhi and work as hunters, gatherers, laborers, and cultivators. They worship in a Hindu manner and bury their dead. Total: 24,170 in 1971. (Russell and Hira Lal 1916, 2:488–501)

Dharkar (Bentbansi)   A section of the eastern Doms, found in much of Uttar Pradesh. They are Hindu cultivators. (Crooke 1896, 2:279–288)

Dheda (Dhed)   A large caste perhaps descended from local tribes in Gujarat. They were once spinners and weavers of cotton, but they are now small farmers. (Campbell 1901, 338–345; Enthoven 1920–1922, 1:322–328; Stevenson 1930)

Dhimal (Dhemal, Maulik)   A Tibeto-Burman–speaking tribe found near Darjeeling and in the eastern districts of Nepal. They are farmers and cattle keepers, but some fish, or pick tea near Darjeeling. (Risley 1891, 1:225–228)

Dhoba   A small caste of priests and cultivators, found in Mandla District, Madhya Pradesh. They probably had a Dravidian tribal origin. (Russell and Hira Lal 1916, 2:515–518)

Dhobi (Dhoba, Dhupi, Dhobhi, Warthi, Warathi, Madiyal, Baretha, Chakla, Chakala, Sakala, Tsakala, Rajak, Ramdu, Agesaru, Parit)   A large Hindu caste cluster of professional washermen. The word _dhobi_ is universally used in India for this occupation, and the caste is widespread throughout the country. Some have adopted cultivation. See also Agasa, Vannan. (Risley 1891, 1:229–236; Crooke 1896, 2:288–296; Campbell 1901, 228–230; Thurston and Rangachari 1909, 2:168–169; 7:197–202; Rose 1911, 1:239; Russell and Hira Lal 1916, 2:519–527; Enthoven 1920–1922, 1:329–330; 3:174–177; Siraj ul Hassan 1920, 1:143–148)

Dhodia (Dhodi, Dhundia)   A tribe of southern Gujarat, who work as farm laborers. Total: 379,895 in 1971. (Campbell 1901, 314–316; Enthoven 1920–1922, 1:330–336)

Dhor (Dohor)   A tanning caste of Maharashtra, now widespread in western and central India. They speak Marathi and are Shaivite Untouchables; but some are Lingayats. (Russell and Hira Lal 1916, 1:361; Enthoven 1920–1922, 1:336–340; Siraj ul Hassan 1920, 1:171–176)

Dhuldhoya   A Muslim caste who wash for gold in Gujarat. (Campbell 1899, 86–87)

Dhund   A Muslim caste of Punjab Province, Pakistan. They are primarily herdsmen. (Rose 1911, 1:240–241)

Dhuniya (Dhuna, Behna, Katera, Kandera, Naddaf)   A caste of cotton carders, found in Uttar Pradesh. Most are Muslim but some are Hindu. (Crooke 1896, 2:297–301)

Dhuri   A small caste of the Chhattisgarh area in Madhya Pradesh, who parch rice or follow other occupations, including that of household servant. (Russell and Hira Lal 1916, 2:527–530)

Dhurwa (Dhuru, Dharua)   A tribe found in Bastar District, in southeast Madhya Pradesh, and Orissa. Total: 8,791 in 1971. (Thusu 1965)

Didayi   An agricultural, Munda-speaking tribe of Koraput District, in southern Orissa. Total: 2,164 in 1971. (Guha et al. 1968)

Dikshit (Dikhit, Dikhshit)   A caste of Brahman priests, widespread in northern India. They are especially employed to initiate Hindu boys. The name is also applied to a clan of Rajputs found in Uttar Pradesh. (Crooke 1896, 2:305–309)

Dogar   A Muslim caste found in Punjab Province, Pakistan, and eastward into Uttar Pradesh. They are farmers and former cattle thieves, supposedly derived from the Chauhan Rajputs. (Crooke 1896, 2:310–312; Rose 1911, 1:244–246)

Dogra An inhabitant of the Dugra area in Jammu and Kashmir. They are mainly Hindu Rajputs. (Rose 1911, 1:246)

Doluva A caste found in Ganjam District, southern Orissa, who claim to be descended from the former kings by their concubines. They are Vaishnavites. (Thurston and Rangachari 1909, 2:171–173)

Domara (Dom, Dome, Doom, Domban, Dombara, Dumar, Dombo, Domra, Dombari, Dombar, Domar, Domahra, Domri, Dummna, Dum, Dhangad, Reddi Domara, Reddi Dhora, Kolhati) A vagrant tribe of acrobats and jugglers, formerly dacoits or brigands, found throughout central and northern India, from Uttar Pradesh to West Bengal, and in Nepal. They freely admit recruits from other castes. The women are also entertainers and prostitutes. Some families have taken to agriculture, trade, lending money, or making mats. Total: 5,254 in 1971. (Risley 1891, 1:240–251; Crooke 1896, 2:312–342; Thurston and Rangachari 1909, 2:173–190; Rose 1911, 1:250; Enthoven 1920–1922, 2:237–243; Siraj ul Hassan 1920, 1:176–181; Nanjundayya and Ananthakrishna Iyer 1928–1936, 3:139–174; Bishop 1990)

Donga Dasari A formerly criminal caste, found in Bellary District, Karnataka. They accept hypergamous marriages with Kabbera girls. (Thurston and Rangachari 1909, 2:191–194)

Dorla A tribe found in Bastar District, in southeast Madhya Pradesh. (Hazra 1970)

Dosadh (Dosadha, Dusadh, Dhari, Dharhi) A caste found in Bihar and West Bengal, who are watchmen, messengers, and grooms. (Risley 1891, 1:252–258)

Dubla (Talavia, Halpati) A large tribe of southern Gujarat, who work as farmers and were formerly bonded laborers. Total: 408,226 in 1971. (Campbell 1901, 316–318; Enthoven 1920–1922, 1:341–347; Shah 1958; Breman 1974)

Dudekula (Panjari, Panjukotti) A Muslim caste of cotton carders, who retain sundry Hindu practices. They are found in Andhra Pradesh. (Thurston and Rangachari 1909, 2:194–202)

Dudwala (Gadit) A Muslim caste of milkmen, converted from Hinduism; some are carters. They are found in Gujarat. (Campbell 1899, 35)

Dumal An agricultural caste of Sambalpur District, Orissa. They are Oriya-speaking Vaishnavites. (Russell and Hira Lal 1916, 2:530–537)

Durava (Chandos) A caste of toddy tappers found in Sri Lanka. (Ryan 1953)

Dusadh (Khasiya Rajput) A tribe found in eastern Uttar Pradesh. They are farm laborers and village watchmen, and they are Hindus. (Crooke 1896, 2:346–358)

East Indian A Roman Catholic community of mixed origin found in the environs of Bombay. They are cultivators and fishermen; they include Samvedi Christians, Koli Christians, Vadvals, and Salsette Christians. The term "East Indian" has sometimes been used indiscriminately in North America to distinguish all South Asians from American Indians. (Baptista 1967)

Edanadan Chetti A farming tribe of Ernad Taluk in Malappuram District, northern Kerala. (Gopalan Nair 1911, 53–55)

Elma A section of the Reddis who are household servants. *See also* REDDI. (Russell and Hira Lal 1916, 3:342–343)

Erakala (Yerukala, Yerukula, Kaikadi, Korwah) A nomadic Gypsy tribe of Andhra Pradesh, who used to subsist by stealing, begging, telling fortunes, and making baskets. They also used to traffic in their women. Total: 162,560 in 1971. *See also* PERIPATETICS. (Russell and Hira Lal 1916, 4:606–608; Siraj ul Hassan 1920, 1:185–195; Parthasarathy 1988)

Eravallan (Eravallar, Eravallen, Yeravallar, Villu Vedan) A tribe found in Palghat and Ernakulam districts, in central Kerala, and the nearby Coimbatore District of Tamil Nadu. They have an animistic religion and work as hunters or cultivators. Total: 678 in 1971. (Thurston and Rangachari 1909, 2:210–217; Ananthakrishna Iyer 1909–1912, 1:43–50; Luiz 1962, 47–51)

Ezhuva (Izhava, Izhuva, Irava, Illavan) A large and widespread caste of southern Kerala, possibly immigrants from Sri Lanka, who cultivate and also practice several trades and urban professions. They were formerly toddy tappers. There may be as many as five million today. (Ananthakrishna Iyer 1909–1912, 1:277–341; Thurston and Rangachari 1909, 2:392–418; Aiyappan 1965)

Fakir (Faqir) A widespread brotherhood of wandering Muslim mendicants. In theological terms and appearance, it is not always possible to distinguish them from Hindu Sadhus, and some are converts from Hinduism. They are more prevalent in Pakistan, northern and central India, and Bangladesh than in other parts of the subcontinent. Their name comes from the Arabic word *fakr*, "poverty"; some groups are celibate, while others marry. Most of the marrying groups or orders are not strictly endogamous. (Risley 1891, 1:262; Campbell 1899, 19–20; Rose 1911, 1:253–254; Russell and Hira Lal 1916, 2:537–540; Siegel 1991)

Gabit (Konkani Maratha) A caste of Goa and nearby coastal districts, mainly fishermen and sailors. (Thurston and Rangachari 1909, 2:242; Enthoven 1920–1922, 1:347–350)

Gadaria (Gadri, Gareri, Gadariya, Garariya, Gaderiya, Ganreriya, Bhenrihar, Bharvad) A large caste of Hindu shepherds and weavers widespread in northern, western, and central India. Many now keep cattle and sell dairy produce. Their three subcastes, Nikhar, Dhengar, and Barmaiyan, are of differential status. Gadarias not only breed goats and sheep but also weave woolen blankets. (Risley 1891, 1:271–274; Crooke 1896, 2:361–369; Campbell 1901, 267–285; Russell and Hira Lal 1916, 3:3–9; Enthoven 1920–1922, 1:118–122, 350–352)

Gadba (Garaba, Gadaba) A Munda-speaking tribe of laborers and cultivators, found in Bastar District, Madhya Pradesh, in Koraput District, Orissa, and in Vishakhapatnam

District, Andhra Pradesh. Their worship is Hindu, and they bury their dead. Total: 75,430 in 1971. (Thurston and Rangachari 1909, 2:242–252; Russell and Hira Lal 1916, 3:9–14; Thusu and Jha 1969)

Gaddi (Gadi)   A tribal group found in Himachal Pradesh, some of whom are Hindus, others Muslims. They claim descent variously from Brahmans, Thakurs, Rajputs, and others. They keep large flocks of sheep and goats. Total: 50,685 in 1971. (Rose 1911, 1:255–271; Newell 1960, 1967)

Gaduliya Lohar   A Hindu nomadic tribe found in Rajasthan. They work as blacksmiths and castrate bulls; they may originally have been Rajputs. (Ruhela 1968)

Gahala-Berava   A caste of former executioners, found in Sri Lanka. Today they are cultivators and prostitutes. (Ryan 1953)

Gaharwar Rajput (Gahadawala, Gherwal Rajput)   A small Rajput caste found in the Chhattisgarh area of eastern Madhya Pradesh. (Crooke 1896, 2:371–373; Russell and Hira Lal 1916, 4:446–448)

Gakkhar   A prominent Muslim caste of Punjab Province, Pakistan, who are soldiers and farmers. (Rose 1911, 1:274–277)

Gamadi (Gavandi)   A caste of masons found in western India and a section of the Reddis who are masons. Some of those in Gujarat are Muslims. (Russell and Hira Lal 1916, 3:342–343; Enthoven 1920–1922, 1:363–367)

Gamit (Gamta, Gavit, Mavchi, Padvi, Tadvi, Tetaria, Dhanka, Vasava, Vasave, Valvi)   A large tribe of farmers and woodcutters, found in eastern Gujarat. Total: 405,588 in 1971. (Campbell 1901, 318–319)

Gammala   A caste of toddy tappers and liquor sellers, found in Andhra Pradesh. They are Hindus. (Thurston and Rangachari 1909, 2:253–257)

Gam Vakkal (Gamgauda)   A cultivating caste of Uttar Kannad District, in Karnataka. Some are farm laborers, while others are in the timber business. (Enthoven 1920–1922, 1:352–354)

Ganda (Gandi, Gandia, Pan, Panwa, Panr, Pao, Pab, Panka, Panika, Chik, Chil-Baraik, Baraik, Mahato, Sawasi, Tanti)   A large Untouchable caste or tribe of the eastern Gangetic Plain, traditionally weavers, laborers, and musicians; they are Hindus and speak a Dravidian language. Remarkably, if their girls were not married by the advent of puberty, they were wedded to a spear stuck in the ground and then given away to anybody. Total: 104,390 in 1971. (Risley 1891, 2:155–159; Crooke 1896, 4:113–118; Russell and Hira Lal 1916, 3:14–17; 4:324–329)

Gandhabanik (Gandhabania, Putuli)   A caste of druggists, spice sellers, and grocers, found in Bangladesh and West Bengal. Most of them are Vaishnavites. (Risley 1891, 1:265–267)

Gandharia   Originally a caste of sailors, these people of the Kathiawar Peninsula in Gujarat are now tile makers. Some make ropes, weave, paint, or work as carpenters; they are a tiny Hindu caste. (Enthoven 1920–1922, 1:355–356)

Gandharv (Gandharb)   A caste of singers, dancers, and prostitutes, found in three districts of Uttar Pradesh. (Crooke 1896, 2:379–383)

Gandhmali (Thanapati)   A small caste of village priests in Orissa. "Thanapati" means "master of the sacred place." They are related to the Malis or gardeners. (Russell and Hira Lal 1916, 3:17–19)

Gangari   A caste of Brahmans who are found in Uttar Pradesh on the banks of the Ganges and who work as priests and farmers. (Crooke 1896, 2:389–391)

Gangeddu (Gangeddulu, Erudandi, Perumal Madukkaran)   A caste of Vaishnavite mendicants who wander around exhibiting bulls in Andhra Pradesh. (Thurston and Rangachari 1909, 2:258–263)

Gangota (Gangauta)   A cultivating caste found in Bihar, near the Ganges. They are Hindus. (Risley 1891, 1:268–269)

Ganiga (Gandla)   A Kannada-speaking caste of oil pressers, found in Karnataka. (Thurston and Rangachari 1909, 2:263–268; Nanjundaya and Ananthakrishna Iyer 1928–1936, 3:186–196)

Ganrar   A boating, trading, and fishing caste of Bangladesh. They are Hindus. (Risley 1891, 1:270)

Garpagari   A caste of village servants employed to avert hail damage magically. They are found mainly in eastern Maharashtra and western Madhya Pradesh. (Russell and Hira Lal 1916, 3:19–24)

Gauda (Gaudo, Gauddes, Gowder)   A very large caste of Hindu cultivators, found throughout Karnataka and Goa, and closely related to the Okkaligas; some are Lingayats. The term is also applied to the majority phratry of the Badagas, who are in the Nilgiris District of Tamil Nadu. _See also_ Okkaliga. (Thurston and Rangachari 1909, 2:269–272; Krishna Iyer 1948, 71–74; Srinivas 1952; Feio 1979, 76–85)

Gaudo   A herding caste found in Ganjam District, southern Orissa. (Thurston and Rangachari 1909, 2:273–276)

Gaur (Gauda)   One of the five divisions of Brahmans found in north India. (Crooke 1896, 2:393–399)

Gauria (Ghara)   A small caste of snake charmers and jugglers, related to the Gonds. They are only found in the Chhattisgarh area of eastern Madhya Pradesh and Orissa. But the name "Gauriya" is also applied to a Vaishnavite sect of Bengali origin, otherwise known as "Bangali Gusain." (Crooke 1896, 2:403–404; Russell and Hira Lal 1916, 3:24–26)

Gaur Rajput (Chamar Gaur)   A Rajput caste found in Uttar Pradesh and Madhya Pradesh. (Crooke 1896, 2:399–402; Russell and Hira Lal 1916, 4:448–450)

Gavada (Mith Gavada)   A Maratha caste originally of salt makers, who are now mostly farmers, laborers, petty traders, or carters. They are found in the coastal districts around Goa, from North Ratnagiri to Uttar Kannad. _See also_ MARATHA. (Enthoven 1920–1922, 1:359–363)

Gavli (Gouli, Gauliga, Dongore)   A herding caste found in parts of Karnataka, Goa, Maharashtra, and central India; they now sell dairy produce, though a few farm. They are

Lingayats. (Enthoven 1920–1922, 1:367–373; Siraj ul Hassan 1920, 1:196–200; Nanjundayya and Ananthakrishna Iyer 1928–1936, 3:514–515; Feio 1979, 85–90)

Ghadi A small caste of soothsayers, found on the coast of Karnataka. They also work as farmers and laborers. (Enthoven 1920–1922, 1:374–375)

Ghadshi A small caste of hereditary musicians, found in northern Karnataka. Many receive payments from temples they are attached to; they also work as farmers or farm laborers. (Enthoven 1920–1922, 1:375–376)

Ghasia (Ghasiya, Ghasi, Sais, Syce) A Hindu caste of northern and central India. Their occupation is to groom horses, cut grass for them, and perform music at festivals; some are cultivators or fishermen. (Risley 1891, 1:277–279; Crooke 1896, 2:408–419; Russell and Hira Lal 1916, 1:403; 3:27–32)

Ghermedi A caste of Muslim farmers located from Bombay north to Sindh, in Pakistan. Their name indicates that they disbelieve in the coming Mahdi, a prophet who will establish divine justice on earth prior to the ending of the world. (Campbell 1899, 62–64)

Ghirth A caste of cultivators in Kangra District, Himachal Pradesh. They are Hindu Rajputs. (Rose 1911, 1:287–295)

Ghisadi (Baiti Kamara, Bailne Kumbar) A caste of itinerant tinkers and knife grinders. Gujarati is their language, but they are found throughout western and central India. (Enthoven 1920–1922, 2:3–5; Siraj ul Hassan 1920, 1:201–203)

Ghosi A herding caste found in northern and central India. In northern India they are Muslim converts, whereas in Madhya Pradesh nearly all are Hindus. (Crooke 1896, 2:419–421; Rose 1911, 1:297; Russell and Hira Lal 1916, 3:32–35)

Goan (Goanese, Luso-Indian) Inhabitants of Goa, which is a small Union Territory on the west coast of India (and a former Portuguese colony). Their numbers are about 1.5 million (1991), but they are also found today in many other Indian cities, and a few live in Lisbon. They are especially numerous in the Bombay area, where they are esteemed as cooks. Goanese are nearly all Roman Catholics, bear Portuguese surnames, and are part Portuguese, part Konkani in ancestry. (Feio 1979)

Gola (Rana) A caste of rice pounders, found throughout Gujarat State. (Campbell 1901, 183–186; Enthoven 1920–1922, 2:6–9)

Golak Brahman (Govardhan) A Brahman caste of central Maharashtra. They have a variety of professions, being priests to the Kunbis as well as astrologers, hereditary village accountants, moneylenders, and farmers. (Enthoven 1920–1922, 1:245; Siraj ul Hassan 1920, 1:116–117)

Golapurab An agricultural caste, found only in Agra District, Uttar Pradesh. (Crooke 1896, 2:422–430)

Golla (Gollam, Golar, Gol, Gola, Gulla, Gullar, Uru Golla, Gollarajulu, Gollewar, Dhangar, Dhangad, Dhanka, Dhangar Mahratta, Kacha Gauliga, Gavada, Gavali, Gauliga, Golkar, Yadava-kula, Krishna-kula, Krishna Golla, Hanbar) A great shepherd tribal cluster, numbering several million. They are Hindus and are found throughout central and western India. They deal in cattle and sheep, weave blankets, and sell dairy products and medicines. Partial total: 192,234 in 1971. (Risley 1891, 1:219, Crooke 1896, 2:263–271; Thurston and Rangachari 1909, 2:284–296; Russell and Hira Lal 1916, 2:480–484; 3:35–38, 342–343; Enthoven 1920–1922, 1:311–321; 2:9–13, 56–60; Siraj ul Hassan 1920, 1:166–170, 204–215; Nanjundayya and Ananthakrishna Iyer 1928–1936, 3:197–218, 507–513)

Gond-Gowari A small caste of mixed Gond and Gowari ancestry; they are cultivators and laborers. Some marry women from certain other castes. They are mainly found in eastern Maharashtra. (Russell and Hira Lal 1916, 3:143–144)

Gondhali (Gondaliga) An order of wandering musicians, dancers, and beggars found in western and central India; they are Hindus. Some people leave their castes and become Gondhalis to fulfill a vow. *See also* SADHU. (Thurston and Rangachari 1909, 2:296–297; Russell and Hira Lal 1916, 3:144–147; Enthoven 1920–1922, 2:13–17; Siraj ul Hassan 1920, 1:233–236; Nanjundayya and Ananthakrishna Iyer 1928–1936, 3:243–249)

Gone (Goniga) A section of the Reddis; they make sacks. They are found in Andhra Pradesh and around Bangalore. *See also* Janappan. (Russell and Hira Lal 1916, 3:342–343; Nanjundayya and Ananthakrishna Iyer 1928–1936, 3:250–253)

Gonsavi (Motcare, Zogui) A caste of cultivators and carters, found in Goa. (Feio 1979, 75–76)

Gopal (Borekar) A small wandering criminal caste, now professional acrobats, street entertainers, and buffalo dealers, found in western and central India. They are Hindus; some speak Marathi, others Gujarati. *See also* PERIPATETICS. (Russell and Hira Lal 1916, 3:147–149; Enthoven 1920–1922, 2:17–19; Siraj ul Hassan 1920, 1:237–239)

Gorait (Korait, Baikar) A Hindu tribe of musicians, comb makers, and cotton carders, found in central Bihar and West Bengal. Total: 3,720 in 1971. (Risley 1891, 1:297–299)

Gosain (Gusain, Gosayi, Goswami) A caste of religious mendicants widespread in India. They are related to the Sadhus or Sannyasis but, unlike members of those groups, they are usually married. *See also* SADHU. (Crooke 1896, 2:469–472; Thurston and Rangachari 1909, 2:298–300; Rose 1911, 1:303–305; Nanjundayya and Ananthakrishna Iyer 1928–1936, 3:254–259)

Goundala (Gouda, Idiga, Kalal) A toddy-making and liquor-selling caste found in northern Andhra Pradesh. (Siraj ul Hassan 1920, 1:240–247)

Gowari A large herding caste of eastern Maharashtra, related to Ahirs. They are Hindus, for whom ancestor worship is important. (Russell and Hira Lal 1916, 3:160–165)

Goyigama The dominant cultivating caste in Sri Lanka. (Ryan 1953; Leach 1968; Obeyesekere 1974)

Gudikara (Gudigar, Gudigara, Rathakara, Gauda

Chitrakara) A tiny caste of sandalwood carvers, found in Goa and in northern Karnataka. (Thurston and Rangachari 1909, 2:302–306; Enthoven 1920–1922, 2:20–21; Nanjundayya and Ananthakrishna Iyer 1928–1936, 3:260–269)

Gujarati Brahman (Gurjara Brahman, Gurjar Brahman, Gujrati Brahman, Bias, Byas Brahman) A Brahman caste found in northern India and originally from Gujarat. They are Shaivites and work in a variety of professions. (Crooke 1896, 2:455–466; Rose 1911, 1:140–141, 318; Enthoven 1920–1922, 1:216–225)

Gulgulia A wandering tribe of beggars, gleaners, and thieves, who also hunt and sell herbal drugs. They are found in Bihar and have an animistic religion. (Risley 1891, 1:301–303)

Gunlodu (Nilbandhu) A section of the Bhoi group of castes, found in northernmost Andhra Pradesh. They are fishermen, whose name means "those of the riverbank." (Siraj ul Hassan 1920, 1:82)

Gurao (Gurav) A caste of village priests in Maharashtra. They claim to have formerly been Brahmans, worship Shiva, and wear the sacred thread; some are Jains. (Russell and Hira Lal 1916, 3:175–181; Enthoven 1920–1922, 2:22–34)

Gurava (Shiva Gurava) A caste of garland makers and musicians of eastern Maharashtra. (Siraj ul Hassan 1920, 2:600–602)

Habura A caste of peripatetic thieves, found in Uttar Pradesh. *See also* PERIPATETICS. (Crooke 1896, 2:473–481)

Haddi (Hadi) A Hindu caste whose members play drums in Orissa. (Thurston and Rangachari 1909, 2:313–320)

Haihaya Rajput (Haihaivansi, Kalachuri) A Rajput caste found in eastern Madhya Pradesh. (Russell and Hira Lal 1916, 4:450–452)

Halba (Halbi) A large tribe of farm laborers, found in Raipur and Bastar districts of eastern Madhya Pradesh. Total: 180,579 in 1971. (Russell and Hira Lal 1916, 3:182–201)

Hale Paika (Halepaik, Hakkipikki, Divaru, Billava, Billoru, Billuvaru) A tribe found in northern and central Karnataka, who practice agriculture and toddy tapping. Some have been hunters or timber cutters. Total: 2,561 in 1971. (Thurston and Rangachari 1909, 1:243–252; 2:320–322; Enthoven 1920–1922, 2:34–44; Nanjundayya and Ananthakrishna Iyer 1928–1936, 2:288–296; 3:278–295; Mann 1980)

Hallikar (Hallikararu, Hallikar Okkaliga) A caste of cultivators, found in southern Karnataka. They have also been employed as servants and postal runners by government. (Nanjundayya and Ananthakrishna Iyer 1928–1936, 3:270–277)

Hallir (Halleer) A caste of hereditary musicians, employed at marriages, and found in Uttar Kannad District, Karnataka. (Enthoven 1920–1922, 2:44–46)

Halvakki Vakkal A cultivating caste found only in Uttar Kannad District, Karnataka; some work as farm laborers. (Enthoven 1920–1922, 2:47–56)

Halwai (Mithiya) A caste of confectioners who have shops in Uttar Pradesh, Bihar, and Madhya Pradesh. They are Vaishnavites. (Risley 1891, 1:310–313; Crooke 1896, 2:481–490; Russell and Hira Lal 1916, 3:201–204)

Handi Jogi (Pandi Jogulu, Handichikka, Pakanati Jogi, Mandula Jogi, Pandula Gollalu, Mandula Gollalu) A class of Telugu-speaking beggars, who also practice pig breeding and herbal medicine. They are peripatetics, found in Andhra Pradesh and Karnataka. *See also* PERIPATETICS. (Thurston and Rangachari 1909, 2:323–324; Nanjundayya and Ananthakrishna Iyer 1928–1936, 3:489–501)

Hannali A small caste of tailors found in Sri Lanka. (Ryan 1953)

Harakantra A small caste of fishermen, found on the coast of Uttar Kannad District, Karnataka. (Enthoven 1920–1922, 2:61–67)

Hari (Har-Santan, Bhuimali, Mihtar) An Untouchable scavenger caste, found in Bengal. Their women are often midwives. (Risley 1891, 1:314–316)

Harni An ex-criminal tribe found in Punjab Province, Pakistan. They were expert burglars, but they now follow other occupations. (Rose 1911, 1:327–329)

Hasalar (Hasalaru, Hasala, Haslar, Hulsavar, Hasula, Agni Honnappana Matadavaru) A tribe found in northern parts of Karnataka. Many have been bonded laborers. Total: 11,213 in 1971. (Thurston and Rangachari 1909, 2:324–326; Enthoven 1920–1922, 2:67–68; Nanjundayya and Ananthakrishna Iyer 1928–1936, 3:296–308)

Hati A caste of Kathiawar District, in northern Gujarat. They are Hindus, working as farm laborers. (Enthoven 1920–1922, 2:68–71)

Hatkar (Hatgar, Bargi Dhangar) A small caste of Yavatmal District, in eastern Maharashtra. Formerly soldiers, they are now hunters and farmers. (Russell and Hira Lal 1916, 3:204–206; Siraj ul Hassan 1920, 1:248–255)

Havik Brahman (Embran, Havig, Havika, Haiga, Tulu Brahman) A Brahman caste of western Karnataka and northern Kerala. They work as temple priests, cooks, gardeners, and especially spice growers, and their women work in the gardens. They are both Shaivites and Vaishnavites. (Ananthakrishna Iyer 1909–1912, 3:344–345; Enthoven 1920–1922, 1:252–254; Nanjundayya and Ananthakrishna Iyer 1928–1936, 2:542–549)

Helava (Helav, Pichchuguntavallu, Mallabhatlu) A caste of beggars (literally "cripples"), who traditionally begged only from Okkaligas in return for telling their family histories, of which they were the custodians. They are found throughout Karnataka. (Thurston and Rangachari 1909, 2:328; Enthoven 1920–1922, 2:72–74; Nanjundayya and Ananthakrishna Iyer 1928–1936, 3:309–319)

Hena (Henaya, Rada, Dhoby) A caste of laundrymen found in Sri Lanka. *See also* Dhobi, Hinna. (Ryan 1953; Leach 1968)

Hinna Another caste of laundrymen found in the low country of Sri Lanka. They also weave baskets. *See also* Dhobi, Hena. (Ryan 1953)

Ho (Larka Kol, Larka Kolh) A Munda-speaking tribe of cultivators, found in Singhbhum District, Bihar; a few live in West Bengal. Total: 538,124 in 1971. (Dalton 1872, 176–206; Risley 1891, 1:319–335; Chatterjee and Das 1927; Das Gupta 1981)

Holeya (Holaya, Holar, Poleya, Valer, Adi-Dravida, Balagai, Chalavadi, Chalvadi, Kulavadi) A widespread Untouchable caste found in Karnataka, Kerala, and parts of Tamil Nadu. They are Hindus who work as farm and plantation laborers; formerly they were bonded laborers. (Thurston and Rangachari 1909, 2:329–351; Enthoven 1920–1922, 2:74–81; Nanjundayya and Ananthakrishna Iyer 1928–1936, 3:320–352; Krishna Iyer 1948, 29–37; Srinivas 1952)

Holia A small caste who claim relationship with Gollas or Ahirs. They were traditionally drummers and leather workers. They are found in central India. (Russell and Hira Lal 1916, 3:212–213)

Hunu A caste of lime burners found in Sri Lanka. (Ryan 1953)

Husaini Brahman (Musalman Brahman) A caste of Hindu beggars and astrologers who beg in the name of Husain, the prophet Mohammed's grandson. They adopt such Islamic tenets as are not contrary with Hinduism, and they are found in Gujarat, Delhi, and Punjab. The men dress like Muslims and the women like Hindus. (Crooke 1896, 2:499; Campbell 1899, 22; Rose 1911, 1:141–142)

Idaiyan A large shepherd caste, found in Tamil Nadu; many now follow diverse other occupations. (Thurston and Rangachari 1909, 2:353–366)

Idiga (Idigar) A toddy-tapping caste found throughout southern Karnataka. They are mainly Vaishnavites. (Thurston and Rangachari 1909, 2:366–368; Nanjundayya and Ananthakrishna Iyer 1928–1936, 3:353–377)

Injhwar A caste of farm laborers and fishermen, found in eastern Maharashtra and central Madhya Pradesh. Some of their women work as midwives. One section, the Sonjharias, wash for gold. *See also* Sonar. (Russell and Hira Lal 1916, 3:213–217)

Irani Inhabitants of Iran, now usually the Iranian Zoroastrians who arrived in India in the nineteenth century (and are therefore distinct from Parsis). An endogamous urban group, many of them now run restaurants. The term has also been used for peripatetics wandering between India and Turkey. *See also* PARSI. (Rose 1911, 1:335)

Iraqi (Iraki, Ranki, Raki, Kalal) A Muslim caste found in northern India. They are mostly shopkeepers. (Crooke 1896, 3:1–8)

Jadam A caste of western Madhya Pradesh. They are cultivators and farm laborers. (Russell and Hira Lal 1916, 3:217–219)

Jadua-Brahman (Jaduah-Brahman) A caste of confidence men, who probably originated in another caste of Brahman astrologers. The term "Jadua," meaning "magic," refers to their traditional trick of claiming to be able to turn metals into gold or find buried treasure. (Russell and Hira Lal 1916, 3:219–222)

Jaintia (Jyntia, Jayantia, Pnar, Sin-teng) A Paleo-Mongoloid tribe of cultivators, found in eastern districts of Meghalaya. (Dalton 1872, 60–61; Rymbai 1969)

Jalap An agricultural Hindu caste, found in Punjab Province, Pakistan. (Rose 1911, 1:350–351)

Jalari A caste of fishermen and former palanquin bearers, found from Ganjam to Vishakhapatnam districts, in eastern Andhra Pradesh. (Thurston and Rangachari 1909, 2:442–446)

Janappan A caste whose members make sacks from hemp. They are found in northern Tamil Nadu and Andhra Pradesh. *See also* Gone. (Thurston and Rangachari 1909, 2:447–450)

Jangama (Jangam) An order of wandering Lingayat monks, found throughout much of India. They eat only in the houses of Lingayats. *See also* LINGAYAT. (Crooke 1896, 3:16–20; Russell and Hira Lal 1916, 3:222–224)

Janjua A Rajput caste found in Punjab Province, Pakistan. They are farmers. (Rose 1911, 1:353–356)

Jarawa A hostile fishing, foraging, and gardening tribe of the South Andaman and Rutland Islands. (Radcliffe-Brown 1922, 11–19; Sarkar 1990)

Jati (Yati, Sewara) A class of mendicant Jain priests, found in northern India. *See also* JAIN. (Crooke 1896, 3:52–55)

Jaunsari A tribe found in the hills of Jaunsar-Bawar, northern Uttar Pradesh. Total: 56,699 in 1971. (Majumdar 1962)

Jetti (Malla Kshatriya, Chanura Malla) A caste of professional wrestlers, found in Andhra Pradesh and southern Karnataka. Their methods are described in the article by Nanjundayya and Ananthakrishna Iyer. (Thurston and Rangachari 1909, 2:456–460; Nanjundayya and Ananthakrishna Iyer 1928–1936, 3:472–482)

Jhadi Telenga A small caste of Bastar District, in eastern Madhya Pradesh. Their name means "Telugus of the jungles." They are Hindus who work as farmers or farm laborers. (Russell and Hira Lal 1916, 3:238–242)

Jhinwar (Jhiwar, Jhir, Kahar, Sodia, Mahra) A fishing, basket-making, and porter caste of the Punjab. They are both Hindus and Muslims. (Rose 1911, 1:381–387)

Jingar (Karajkar, Karanjkar, Lohar, Jadar, Chitrakar, Chitari, Chiter, Maharana, Dalsingar, Digwan, Tambatkar, Darji, Nakash Maistri) A Hindu caste of saddlers who now work as goldsmiths, carpenters, tailors, painters, wood-carvers, farriers, and metal, stone, or silk workers: hence their many ethnonyms. They were especially known as mural artists in Nagpur City. Evidently of mixed origin, they speak Marathi, Hindi, or Telugu and are widespread in central India, including Karnataka. (Russell and Hira Lal 1916, 2:432–438; Enthoven 1920–1922, 2:99–103; Siraj ul Hassan 1920,

1:273–277; Nanjundayya and Ananthakrishna Iyer 1928–1936, 3:483–488)

Johari (Jouhari, Joharia, Javheri, Javeri, Zaveri, Ramayye, Manyari) A small caste of peddlers and jewelers, found in central Maharashtra and some more easterly districts. They are Hindus, yet also honor the Sikh Guru Nanak. The names "Javeri" and "Zaveri" are also applied to wealthy Jain jewelers in Maharashtra. (Enthoven 1920–1922, 2:104–107; Siraj ul Hassan 1920, 1:286–289)

Joiya A Rajput caste found in Punjab Province, Pakistan. They are farmers. (Rose 1911, 1:410–413)

Joshi (Jyotishi, Bhadri, Budbudki, Budubudiki, Budubudikke, Budubudukala, Budubudukki, Dubaduba, Gibidki, Chudbudki Joshi, Parsai) A small caste of village priests, astrologers, peripatetic beggars, and fortune-tellers found throughout central India. They include both Muslims and Hindus. Russell and Hira Lal explain their astrological knowledge in some detail. (Crooke 1896, 3:64–69; Thurston and Rangachari 1909, 1:393–396; Russell and Hira Lal 1916, 3:255–279; Enthoven 1920–1922, 2:107–109; Siraj ul Hassan 1920, 1:290–296; Nanjundayya and Ananthakrishna Iyer 1928–1936, 2:550–559)

Juang (Patua) A Munda-speaking tribe of cultivators, found in Singhbhum District, Bihar, and northern Orissa. Total: 24,384 in 1971. (Dalton 1872, 150–156; Risley 1891, 1:350–355; Roy and Roy 1982)

Jugi (Jogi) A weaving caste of West Bengal and Bangladesh, many of whom have now taken up farming or other occupations. Most of them are Shaivites. (Risley 1891, 1:355–360)

Julaha (Julahe, Jolha, Jolaha, Momin, Paoli) A Muslim caste of weavers, found in much of northern India, Pakistan, and Bangladesh. (Risley 1891, 1:348–350; Crooke 1896, 3:69–72; Rose 1911, 1:413–416; Russell and Hira Lal 1916, 3:279–281)

Kabir-Panthi A community whose members follow the medieval mystic Kabir (1440–1518), probably a Sufi who combined Hindu and Muslim teachings. They are found in northern India. (Crooke 1896, 3:73–77; Rose 1911, 1:417–419)

Kabuli (Kabuliwallah) Afghan moneylenders who have settled throughout India. They are not actually from Kabul but from Katawaz District, Ghazni Province, and are Sunni Muslims. (Campbell 1899, 13–14)

Kachari (Dimasa, Dimasa Kachari, Semsa, Boro-Boro, Bodo) A large Paleo-Mongoloid tribe of cultivators, found in Cachar District, southern Assam, and Nagaland. Total: 853,585 in 1971. (Dalton 1872, 81–87; Endle 1911; Gilhodes 1922; Barkataki 1969; Danda and Ghatak 1985)

Kachera (Kachara, Manihar, Churihar) A caste cluster of glass-bangle makers found in Madhya Pradesh, and in Uttar Pradesh, where they are called Manihar or Churihar. Many of the latter have taken to agriculture or deal in hides and horns. Some are Hindu, others Muslim. (Crooke 1896, 2:230–233; 3:473–476; Russell and Hira Lal 1916, 3:281–284; 4:193–195)

Kachhi A large Hindu caste of vegetable and tobacco growers. They use irrigation for commercial-scale production, and they are to be found in Uttar Pradesh and Madhya Pradesh, especially in cities. Formerly they grew opium. (Crooke 1896, 3:77–86; Russell and Hira Lal 1916, 3:285–288; Enthoven 1920–1922, 2:119–121; Siraj ul Hassan 1920, 2:297–299)

Kachhia (Pastagia, Kunkara) A caste of Hindu fruit sellers and gardeners, found in Gujarat. (Campbell 1901, 153–154; Enthoven 1920–1922, 2:121–125)

Kachhwaha Rajput (Cutchwaha Rajput) A Rajput caste found in much of northern India. (Crooke 1896, 3:87–90; Russell and Hira Lal 1916, 4:453–455)

Kachi Meman (Cutchi Memon, Kachhi, Muamin) An important and wealthy class of Muslim merchants widespread throughout the cities of India, but originating in Kachchh District, western Gujarat. *See also* BANIA. (Russell and Hira Lal 1916, 2:440–443)

Kadar (Kadan, Kadir) A tribe that gathers food in the forests. They are animists, found in Palghat and Trichur districts, in central Kerala, and western Tamil Nadu. There is also a cultivating caste named Kadar in southern districts of West Bengal. Total: 1,926 in 1971. (Thurston and Rangachari 1909, 3:6–29; Ananthakrishna Iyer 1909–1912, 1:1–27; Ehrenfels 1952; Sarkar 1959; Luiz 1962, 59–64; Thundy 1983)

Kader A tribe found in Kozhikode and Cannanore districts, in northern Kerala. They cultivate pepper, coffee, and rice. (Gopalan Nair 1911, 80–82; Luiz 1962, 65–67)

Kadera (Kandera, Kadhera, Golandaz, Bandar, Hawaidar) A small caste of firework makers, found mainly in Narsimhapur District, central Madhya Pradesh. They are Hindus, but they worship the Muslim Lukman Hakim, believed by them to be the inventor of gunpowder. Kadhera is also reported as a caste of cultivators and boatmen in Uttar Pradesh. (Crooke 1896, 3:90–91; Russell and Hira Lal 1916, 3:288–291)

Kadia (Kadiya, Chunara) A Hindu and Muslim caste of bricklayers, found in Gujarat. (Campbell 1899, 74; 1901, 186)

Kadu Golla (Yadavakuladavaru, Krishnakuladavaru) A caste found in southern Karnataka, whose name means "wild cowherds." They are Vaishnavites, who rear animals and farm. (Nanjundayya and Ananthakrishna Iyer 1928–1936, 3:219–242)

Kadu Kuruba A general term for the two tribes of Betta Kuruba and Jenu Kuruba in southern Karnataka. Partial total: 14,848 in 1971. *See also* Kuruba. (Nanjundayya and Ananthakrishna Iyer 1928–1936, 4:68–73)

Kadupattan A caste of teachers, astrologers, and magicians found in Ernakulam District, in central Kerala. (Thurston and Rangachari 1909, 3:30–31; Ananthakrishna Iyer 1909–1912, 2:103–115)

Kafir A generic name for the tribes of Kafiristan, in the Hindu Kush. They are warriors and cultivators. The name means "infidel," although some are converts to Islam. (Robertson 1896; Rose 1911, 1:420–435; Jones 1967)

Kaghzi A caste of Muslim paper makers, found around Ahmedabad, in Gujarat State. (Campbell 1899, 73–74)

Kahut An agricultural caste, perhaps Rajput, found in Punjab Province, Pakistan. (Rose 1911, 1:435–436)

Kaikolan (Kaikkoolar, Sengunthar Mudaliyar) A caste of Tamil-speaking weavers, found in much of Tamil Nadu and in central Kerala. They make mats, practice palmistry, and are often peripatetics. (Thurston and Rangachari 1909, 3:31–44; Ananthakrishna Iyer 1909–1912, 3:374–384; Mines 1984)

Kakkalan (Kakkan, Kakka Kuravan) A peripatetic caste found in southern Kerala. They engage in begging, tattooing, palmistry, and other occupations. (Thurston and Rangachari 1909, 3:44–46)

Kalanady A Hindu tribe found in Kozhikode District, in Kerala. They are farm laborers. (Luiz 1962, 68–71)

Kalanga (Kalingi, Kalinji, Kalingulu) A small cultivating caste of northern Andhra Pradesh and eastern Madhya Pradesh. They are divided into a large number of exogamous totemic groups. (Thurston and Rangachari 1909, 3:47–52; Russell and Hira Lal 1916, 3:302–305)

Kalar (Kalal, Kalwar) A very large caste of distillers, liquor sellers, and traders found in northern and central India. The article by Russell and Hira Lal gives an outline history of alcohol and opium consumption in India. (Risley 1891, 1:385–387; Crooke 1896, 3:106–117; Russell and Hira Lal 1916, 3:306–322; Siraj ul Hassan 1920, 2:303–305)

Kallar (Kallan, Pramalai Kallar) Former cattle thieves, found in Madurai District, Tamil Nadu, where they now farm. They practice circumcision. When hunting deer in the last century, they used to use boomerangs. (Thurston and Rangachari 1909, 3:53–91; Dumont 1986; Dirks 1987)

Kamar (Karmakar) A metal-working tribe found from Madhya Pradesh to Bangladesh. They work in all kinds of metal, including gold. Partial total: 19,758 in 1971. (Risley 1891, 1:388–392)

Kamar A small Dravidian-speaking tribe found in eastern Madhya Pradesh. They are Hindus, who formerly practiced swidden agriculture but more recently took up basket weaving or farm labor. Some were living in caves in the nineteenth century. (Russell and Hira Lal 1916, 3:323–330; Dube 1951)

Kamboh A cultivating caste found from Punjab Province, Pakistan, to western Uttar Pradesh. They are Hindu. (Crooke 1896, 3:118–122; Rose 1911, 1:447–446; 2:524)

Kami (Kamia) A Hindu caste of blacksmiths found in Nepal and West Bengal. (Risley 1891, 1:393–395)

Kamma An agricultural caste found in Andhra Pradesh. They are Hindus, allied to the Reddis. (Thurston and Rangachari 1909, 3:94–105)

Kammalan (Kammala, Kammara, Kamsale, Kamsala, Panchal, Panchala, Panchalan, Nanku Parisha, Panchadayi, Punyavachan, Vishva Brahman, Acharji, Achari) A widespread tribe of blacksmiths, carpenters, stonemasons, brass smiths, and goldsmiths found in central, western, and southern India, from northern Andhra Pradesh to Kerala; but in Maharashtra, at least, these five occupational categories form five endogamous groups. They are Hindus. Partial total: 36,376 in 1971. (Ananthakrishna Iyer 1909–1912, 1:342–353; Thurston and Rangachari 1909, 3:106–149; Russell and Hira Lal 1916, 1:373; Enthoven 1920–1922, 3:156–159; Siraj ul Hassan 1920, 2:544–554; Nanjundayya and Ananthakrishna Iyer 1928–1936, 4:452–470)

Kanada Brahman (Karnatic Brahman) A landowning caste of Karnataka and adjoining states. (Siraj ul Hassan 1920, 1:118–119)

Kanakkan A Tamil-speaking caste of accountants, found throughout northern Tamil Nadu. A clan of this name and traditional occupation is also found among the Badagas of the Nilgiris District. *See also* BADAGA. (Thurston and Rangachari 1909, 3:150–159)

Kanaladi A tiny tribe of Ernad Taluk in Malappuram District, northern Kerala, who earn their living as oracles, fire walkers, and "devil dancers." (Gopalan Nair 1911, 95–96)

Kandha (Kandha Ganda) An agricultural tribe found in Koraput District, southern Orissa. Total: 7,185 in 1971. (Banerjee 1968)

Kanet (Kanaura, Kinner, Kinnara, Kanaurese, Kunawara, Kinnaurese) An agricultural tribe of Kinnaur and elsewhere in northwestern India. In some areas they are polyandrous; elsewhere they claim descent from Rajputs. Partial total: 35,120 in 1971. (Crooke 1896, 3:133–134; Rose 1911, 1:456–472; 2:525; Rosser 1960; Chandra 1981)

Kangra Brahman A Brahman caste, found in northern Punjab State. (Rose 1911, 1:127–130)

Kanikkar (Kanikar, Kanikaran, Kanikkaran, Kani, Kanakkan, Malayarayan) A Hindu tribe of southern Kerala and southern Tamil Nadu, who speak a dialect of Malayalam and farm. Those on the coast are fishermen. They seem to be related to the Mala Vedan. Total: 14,292 in 1971. (Ananthakrishna Iyer 1909–1912, 1:138–144; Thurston and Rangachari 1909, 3:162–177; Krishna Iyer 1937–1941, 1:1–79, 226–265; Luiz 1962, 72–77)

Kaniyan (Kanyan, Kalari Panikkan, Panikkan, Ganikan, Kanisan, Kurup, Asan) A tribe of astrologers found in much of Kerala and western Tamil Nadu, who were also teachers of martial arts and umbrella makers. Polyandry is common. Total: 1,265 in 1971. (Ananthakrishna Iyer 1909–1912, 1:185–230; Thurston and Rangachari 1909, 3:178–200; Srinivas 1952)

Kannadiyan A caste of cattle breeders and farmers found in northern Tamil Nadu, who were originally from Karnataka. Most of them are Lingayats. (Thurston and Rangachari 1909, 3:200–214)

Kanphata (Gorakhnathi, Darshani) A class of religious mendicants, who live by begging and selling amulets. *See also* SADHU. (Crooke 1896, 3:153–159)

Kanyakubja Brahman (Kanaujiya, Kanaujia Brahman) A caste of Brahmans originating in Kanauj (ancient Kanyakubja), capital of the seventh-century emperor Harsha Vardhana. Those of central India practice hypergamy, eat meat, and plow their own lands. In Uttar Pradesh the child of a second wife can marry the child of the same man's first wife. (Crooke 1896, 3:124–129; Russell and Hira Lal 1916, 2:390–391)

Kapali A Hindu weaving and farming caste of Bangladesh. (Risley 1891, 1:421–423)

Kapariya (Khapariya) A peripatetic tribe found in Uttar Pradesh, who deal in goats and ponies or beg. *See also* PERIPATETICS. (Crooke 1896, 3:160–163)

Kappiliyan (Karumpuraththal) A caste of Kannada-speaking farmers, found in southern Tamil Nadu. (Thurston and Rangachari 1909, 3:215–222)

Karan (Karama, Karnam, Mahanti) The Hindu writer caste of Orissa; some are found in eastern Madhya Pradesh. Some wear the sacred thread. (Risley 1891, 1:424–426; Russell and Hira Lal 1916, 3:343–345; Mohanti 1975)

Karava The main fishing caste of Sri Lanka. (Ryan 1953; Raghavan 1962)

Karavazhi A tribe found in Kottayam District, in central Kerala. They are Hindu farm laborers. (Luiz 1962, 78–81)

Kare Okkalu A caste related to the Okkaligas, found in Uttar Kannad District, northern Karnataka. They are tenant farmers and laborers. *See also* OKKALIGA. (Nanjundayya and Ananthakrishna Iyer 1928–1936, 3:504–506)

Karhada Brahman (Karhade Brahman, Karhataka Brahman) A Maratha Brahman caste (named after the town of Karhad) now found widely in central and western India. They are probably related to the Deshashta Brahmans, and many are government officers. Until the nineteenth century, a few of them engaged in human sacrifice. (Enthoven 1920–1922, 1:246–247; Siraj ul Hassan 1920, 1:111–115)

Karimpalan (Karimbalan) A tribe found in Cannanore and Kozhikode districts, in northern Kerala. They are former hunters and shifting cultivators, who now farm small plots. (Gopalan Nair 1911, 77–79; Thurston and Rangachari 1909, 3:250; Luiz 1962, 82–85)

Karna Sale (Seniyan) A Telugu-speaking caste of weavers, found in Tamil Nadu and Andhra Pradesh. (Thurston and Rangachari 1909, 3:252–253)

Kasai (Kassab, Are Katika, Katika, Khatik, Lad Kasab, Suryachelad, Arewaru) A small caste of Muslim butchers, found in central India from Gujarat to Andhra Pradesh. They speak Marathi. (Campbell 1899, 74–75; Russell and Hira Lal 1916, 3:346–369; Enthoven 1920–1922, 2:163; Siraj ul Hassan 1920, 1:12–14)

Kasta Brahman A small Brahman caste found in central Maharashtra. They are priests, moneylenders, and shopkeepers. (Siraj ul Hassan 1920, 1:119–120)

Kastha A farming caste found in the southern part of West Bengal. (Risley 1891, 1:431–432)

Katalarayan (Katakoti) A tribe of sea fishermen found in Ernakulam District, central Kerala. (Ananthakrishna Iyer 1909–1912, 1:261–266)

Kathak (Kathik) A caste of storytellers and musicians, found in Uttar Pradesh. (Crooke 1896, 3:172–176)

Kathi (Kathia) A tribe found in Kathiawar District, Gujarat, and in Punjab and western Uttar Pradesh. They are Hindus, mostly Shaivites; they work as cultivators and farm laborers. The Kathia, cultivators found in the Punjab, seem to be identical to the Kathaioi recorded as being there by the ancient Greeks. (Crooke 1896, 3:178–179; Campbell 1901, 252–262; Rose 1911, 1:482–483; Enthoven 1920–1922, 2:164–170)

Kathiyara A small caste of bricklayers and carpenters, found in Aligarh District, Uttar Pradesh. They are Hindus. (Crooke 1896, 3:179–181)

Katia (Katwa, Katua) A caste of cotton spinners and village watchmen, found in western districts of Madhya Pradesh. They are Hindus, who either burn or bury their dead, according to convenience. (Russell and Hira Lal 1916, 3:384–388)

Katike (Katikilu) A caste of Telugu-speaking butchers, found in Andhra Pradesh. They observe both Muslim and Hindu customs. (Thurston and Rangachari 1909, 3:259–261)

Katkari (Kathkari, Kathodi, Kathodia) A tribe found in the Western Ghats of western Maharashtra and Gujarat. They work as farm laborers or cultivators, or sell firewood and honey. Total: 150,303 in 1971. (Campbell 1901, 319–320; Enthoven 1920–1922, 2:170–183)

Kavara A Tulu-speaking caste found in northern and central Kerala. They do wicker work. (Ananthakrishna Iyer 1909–1912, 3:384–386)

Kavikara (Kaikara, Malavara) A caste of Sri Lankan female dancers and male chanters, like Indian Devadasis. (Ryan 1953)

Kawar (Kanwar, Kur, Kaur, Chewara, Cherwa, Rathia Tanwar, Chattri) A large tribe found from eastern Madhya Pradesh to West Bengal. They claim descent from the Kauravas, who are important in the *Mahabharata*. They are cultivators and farm laborers. Their religion is animistic, with witchcraft a prominent feature. Total: 417,739 in 1971. (Dalton 1872, 132–134; Russell and Hira Lal 1916, 3:389–403)

Kayalan A caste of Tamil-speaking Muslims who sell beads, toys, and other trinkets or act as petty moneylenders. They are found in Madras and other cities of Tamil Nadu. (Thurston and Rangachari 1909, 3:267)

Kayasth (Kayashta, Kaith, Kaet, Kaeth, Kait, Kayath, Kaya, Lala) A large and influential caste of writers and village accountants, found throughout northern, western, and eastern India; they are especially important in Bengal society and in Hyderabad. They occupy a high social position, are Hindus of the Shakta cult, and possibly originated from some Brahman caste. (Dalton 1872, 300–302; Risley 1891, 1:438–453; Crooke 1896, 3:184–216; Campbell 1901, 59–68; Rose

1911, 1:436–437; Russell and Hira Lal 1916, 3:404–422; Enthoven 1920–1922, 2:184–190; Siraj ul Hassan 1920, 2:322–335; Leonard 1978)

Kehal A nomadic tribe of Muslim fishermen, found on the Indus River in Punjab Province, Pakistan. (Rose 1911, 1:486–488)

Kewat (Khewat, Keot, Keyot, Kiot, Khyan, Jaliya, Jele, Jalo, Jalwa, Jeliya, Jalia Kaibartta, Jalia Kaibarta, Kaibartta, Kaibartta-Das, Chasi-Das, Halia-Das, Parasar-Das, Dhivara) A group of castes of fishermen, boatmen, grain parchers, and cultivators, found from Uttar Pradesh and eastern Madhya Pradesh to Bangladesh. Each such caste has its own name (e.g., Bagdi). (Risley 1891, 1:340–342, 375–382, 454–458; Crooke 1896, 3:217–220; Russell and Hira Lal 1916, 3:422–426)

Khairwar (Kherwar, Kharwar, Khaira, Khairwa, Khayra, Kora, Kaora) A Hindu tribe found throughout much of the Gangetic Plain. They are cultivators, pig farmers, catechu makers, and basket makers; they speak a Munda language and are related to the Gonds and Soras. Partial total: 62,909 in 1971. *See also* GOND; SORA. (Dalton 1872, 123–126; Risley 1891, 1:506–511; Crooke 1896, 3:221–225; Russell and Hira Lal 1916, 3:427–436)

Khambu (Jimdar, Rai) A Hindu warrior tribe found in Nepal. They claim to have gone there from Varanasi. (Risley 1891, 1:459–461)

Khamti (Tai) A Paleo-Mongoloid tribe of cultivators, found in eastern Arunachal Pradesh. Total: 4,078 in 1971. (Dalton 1872, 9–13; Sarkar 1987)

Khandait (Khandayat) A military caste of Orissa, formerly swordsmen. *See also* Paik. (Risley 1891, 1:461–464; Russell and Hira Lal 1916, 3:436–438; Mohanti 1975)

Khant A caste found in Kathiawar District, northern Gujarat. They are cultivators and farm laborers. (Enthoven 1920–1922, 2:194–196)

Kharak A caste of farmers found in parts of Gujarat. They are Hindus. (Enthoven 1920–1922, 2:196–199)

Kharia (Kheria, Kharian, Kharria) A large Munda-speaking tribe of eastern Madhya Pradesh and southern Bihar. They are hunters and cultivators, and they also collect forest produce. Their language is closely related to Sora, Korku, and Juang. Total: 274,540 in 1971. *See also* BHUIYA, KORKU and SORA. (Dalton 1872, 156–159; Risley 1891, 1:466–472; Russell and Hira Lal 1916, 3:445–453; Roy and Roy 1937; Vidyarthi and Upadhyay 1980; Sinha 1984)

Kharral A Rajput caste of Punjab Province, Pakistan, who are landowners. (Rose 1911, 1:495–499)

Kharva (Kharvi) A caste of coastal sailors, fishermen, and boat builders, found from Kathiawar to Bombay. (Campbell 1901, 520–522; Enthoven 1920–1922, 2:200–205)

Kharwar (Kherwar) A large cultivating tribe found in northeastern India. They speak a Dravidian language and are Hindus. Total: 142,580 in 1971. (Risley 1891, 1:472–476; Crooke 1896, 3:237–253)

Khasiya (Khasa) Name applied to Brahmans and Rajputs found in the hills of Jaunsar-Bawar, northern Uttar Pradesh, and Nepal. (Crooke 1896, 3:253–257; Majumdar 1944, 110–184; Saksena 1962; Bishop 1990)

Khatik (Sultankar, Alitkar, Pardeshi Alitkar) A Hindu caste of tanners, skin dyers, mutton butchers, and vegetable sellers. They are found throughout northern and western India, and they are usually considered Untouchables. Some, however, do employ Brahmans as their priests. (Risley 1891, 1:477; Crooke 1896, 3:257–264; Rose 1911, 1:500–501; Russell and Hira Lal 1916, 3:453–456; Enthoven 1920–1922, 1:34–37; Siraj ul Hassan 1920, 2:326–327)

Khatri (Khattri, Chhatri) A large Hindu merchant caste primarily of the Punjab and Gujarat, but found all over India. They claim to be of Rajput origin and derive their name from Kshatriya, the second-highest varna. Some are silk weavers in Gujarat. (Risley 1891, 1:478–484; Crooke 1896, 3:264–277; Campbell 1901, 188–189; Thurston and Rangachari 1909, 3:282–287; Rose 1911, 1:501–526; Russell and Hira Lal 1916, 3:456–461; Enthoven 1920–1922, 2:205–208; Siraj ul Hassan 1920, 2:328–331)

Khattak (Khatak) A tribe of Pathans, found in the North-West Frontier Province of Pakistan. They are Muslims and herd their animals in a dry land. (Rose 1911, 1:526–532; Caroe 1958)

Khattar (Kathar, Kahtar) A Muslim caste, recently converted from Hinduism, who are found in Punjab Province, Pakistan. (Rose 1911, 1:532–534)

Khava (Gola, Hajuri, Vajir, Lunda) A caste of servants and personal attendants, found throughout Gujarat. They also work as farmers and day laborers. (Campbell 1901, 234–236; Enthoven 1920–1922, 2:208–212)

Khetri (Chhetri, Mustigar) A cultivating caste, found in northern Karnataka. (Enthoven 1920–1922, 2:212–217)

Kho (Ko, Koo, Khaa) A group of tribes of cultivators, found in the hills of northeastern India. (Dalton 1872, 112–113)

Khokar (Khokur) A caste of Rajput origin, found in Punjab Province, Pakistan. They are Muslim landowners. (Rose 1911, 1:539–549)

Killekyata (Killekyatha, Killikiyata, Kiliket, Katabu, Chhatri, Shillekyata, Bombe Atadavaru, Bomalatavallu, Togalubombeyavaru) An itinerant group of picture showmen and entertainers, found in Karnataka and recruited from several castes. Some are swimmers and fishermen. (Enthoven 1920–1922, 2:231–236; Nanjundayya and Ananthakrishna Iyer 1928–1936, 3:516–535; Morab 1977a)

Kingriya (Kingariya, Kingriha) A caste of dancers and singers found in eastern parts of Uttar Pradesh. They are Sunni Muslims. (Crooke 1896, 3:280–282)

Kinnara A caste of cultivators and mat weavers, found in central Sri Lanka. (Ryan 1953)

Kir (Keer) A farming tribe found in Hoshangabad District, in western Madhya Pradesh. They are Hindus, who grow market vegetables; some act as family priests to local

Marwaris. Total: 6,099 in 1971. (Russell and Hira Lal 1916, 3:481–485)

Kirar (Kirad)   A cultivating caste found in Uttar Pradesh and northern parts of Madhya Pradesh. They are Hindus, some of whom traditionally worked as village headmen. The term "Kirar" is also applied to traders in the Punjab and Himachal Pradesh. (Crooke 1896, 3:282–285; Rose 1911, 1:552; Russell and Hira Lal 1916, 3:485–493)

Kochh (Kocch, Koch, Cooch, Koch-Mandai, Rajbansi, Paliya, Polia, Pola, Desi)   A caste of cultivators, found in northeastern India and Bangladesh. They practice hypergamy. (Dalton 1872, 88–92; Risley 1891, 1:491–500)

Kochuvelan (Kochuvelanmar)   A tiny tribe found in Quilon and Kottayam districts, in southern Kerala. They are farmers. Total: 10 in 1971. (Luiz 1962, 91–94)

Kohli   A small caste of cultivators, found in eastern parts of Maharashtra, where they once built great irrigation tanks in Bhandara District. (Russell and Hira Lal 1916, 3:493–499)

Koil Tampuran (Koil Pantala)   A caste found in Kerala, where they are linked with the former royal family of Travancore. (Thurston and Rangachari 1909, 3:296–299)

Koiri (Kocri, Murao)   A large cultivating caste found in Uttar Pradesh and Bihar. They are Vaishnavite Hindus. (Risley 1891, 1:500–505; Crooke 1896, 3:287–294; 4:7–11)

Kolam   A Dravidian-speaking tribe found in Yavatmal District, in eastern Maharashtra. They are cultivators and farm laborers and are related to the Gonds. Total: 82,910 in 1971. (Russell and Hira Lal 1916, 3:520–526; Hazra 1983)

Kolgha (Koli Dhor, Tokre Kolcha, Kolcha)   A tribe found in eastern Gujarat; they work as servants, farm laborers, and woodcutters. Total: 75,958 in 1971. (Campbell 1901, 320–321)

Koliyan   A weaving caste found in central Tamil Nadu. (Thurston and Rangachari 1909, 3:302–304)

Kollia   A Paleo-Mongoloid tribe of cultivators, found in central Assam.

Kolta (Kolita, Kulta)   An agricultural caste found in northern Orissa. They are Hindus, and good cultivators. (Russell and Hira Lal 1916, 3:537–542; Patnaik 1960d)

Komarpaik   A caste only found in Uttar Kannad District, Karnataka. They are farmers and carters; some are Lingayats. (Enthoven 1920–1922, 2:260–264)

Komati (Komti, Setti, Chetty, Chetti, Vaishya, Gavara, Baqal, Bania, Sahukar)   A caste of traders and moneylenders widespread in southern and central India. Poorer members are cooks or confectioners. They are Hindus and wear a sacred thread. (Thurston and Rangachari 1909, 2:277–279; 3:306–348; Russell and Hira Lal 1916, 3:542–545; Siraj ul Hassan 1920, 2:340–356; Nanjundayya and Ananthakrishna Iyer 1928–1936, 3:536–582)

Konda Dora (Kondadora, Konda Kapu, Muka Dora, Oja)   A large tribe of cultivators, found mainly in Vishakhapatnam District, eastern Andhra Pradesh. Total: 149,249 in 1971. (Thurston and Rangachari 1909, 3:349–356; 5:103–106)

Konga Malayan   A Tamil-speaking tribe found in Ernakulam District, central Kerala. They are woodcutters and farm laborers. (Ananthakrishna Iyer 1909–1912, 1:38–42)

Konga Vellala   A caste of Hindu cultivators, found in western parts of Tamil Nadu. See also VELLALA. (Thurston and Rangachari 1909, 3:417–421)

Konkani Brahman   A caste of Brahmans found in Goa and southward through the Konkani-speaking districts to central Kerala. They work as priests and cultivators. (Ananthakrishna Iyer 1909–1921, 3:346–364; Feio 1979, 24–72)

Konkna (Kokna, Kokni, Kukna)   A large tribe found in eastern Gujarat. They are Hindu farmers. Total: 420,883 in 1971. (Campbell 1901, 321–323)

Korava (Korva, Korua, Kora, Korar, Korgar, Kormar, Korama, Korga, Koraga, Karanga, Karenga, Koranga, Koracha, Korchar, Koragar, Kuravan, Kuraver, Kaikari, Kaikadi, Bargandi)   A peripatetic tribe of basket makers, hunters, fortune-tellers, and thieves, found throughout India and Sri Lanka. Koraga is a settled tribe of Cannanore District, in northern Kerala, with much the same occupations; they speak Tulu. Total: 130,835 in 1971. (Thurston and Rangachari 1909, 3:424–504; Russell and Hira Lal 1916, 3:296–302; Enthoven 1920–1922, 2:126–130, 266–270; Hatch 1928; Nanjundayya and Ananthakrishna Iyer 1928–1936, 3:583–619; Ryan 1953; Luiz 1962, 95–99)

Kori   A Hindu weaving caste widespread in northern India. They trace their origin to the poet Kabir, but they may well have branched off from the Kols. (Crooke 1896, 3:316–321; Russell and Hira Lal 1916, 3:545–549)

Korwa (Korua)   A Munda-speaking tribe of Bihar, West Bengal, and southern parts of Uttar Pradesh. They are shifting cultivators of vegetables, but they were also expert hunters and dacoits at one time. Total: 89,242 in 1971. (Dalton 1872, 219–224; Risley 1891, 1:511–513; Crooke 1896, 3:322–334; Russell and Hira Lal 1916, 3:571–580; Majumdar 1944, 1–64)

Koshti (Koshta, Mahara, Salewar)   A large caste of Hindu weavers of silk and fine cotton, found throughout central India from Maharashtra to Andhra Pradesh. See also Padma Sale. (Risley 1891, 1:513–514; Russell and Hira Lal 1916, 3:581–589)

Kottai Vellala   An interesting cluster of tiny castes only found living inside a fort (_kottai_) at Srivaiguntam, Tirunelveli District, in the far south of Tamil Nadu. Tradition has it they have been there for a thousand years, totally cut off from all intercourse with other Vellalas. Their women never leave the mud enclosure, and no strangers may enter, although Brahmans and other familiar workers do so. Until recently the fort also contained slaves. The castes apparently survive through their landownership. See also VELLALA. (Thurston and Rangachari 1909, 4:33–36)

Kotte Okkalu (Kot Vakkal)   A Vaishnavite caste found in central Karnataka. They are gardeners and farm laborers. (Enthoven 1920–1922, 2:271; Nanjundayya and Ananthakrishna Iyer 1928–1936, 4:1–3)

Kotwal (Kotal, Kotwar, Khangar, Khagar, Jemadar, Darbania)   A caste of village watchmen and gatekeepers, found throughout much of north India. Some were formerly thieves. They are Shaivite Hindus. (Risley 1891, 1:514–515; Crooke 1896, 3:228–233, 335; Russell and Hira Lal 1916, 3:439–444)

Koupui   A tribe of cultivators, found in the hills of northeastern India. (Dalton 1872, 57–60)

Krishnavakakkar   A caste of southern Kerala, who are Hindu temple servants. (Thurston and Rangachari 1909, 4:74–79)

Kuchband (Kooch Band, Kuchbandhia)   A Hindu tribe of Rajasthan and Punjab, who hunt and cultivate. (Rose 1911, 1:558–560)

Kudan (Koodan, Kootan)   A tribe of Ernakulam District, in central Kerala, who work as farm laborers. (Thurston and Rangachari 1909, 4:91–96; Ananthakrishna Iyer 1909–1912, 1:134–138)

Kudavakkal   A Hindu and Lingayat cultivating caste, found in southern Maharashtra and northern Karnataka. (Enthoven 1920–1922, 2:272–274)

Kudiya (Male Kudia, Male Kudiya, Melakudi)   A tribe of Cannanore District, northern Kerala, and Kodagu District, southern Karnataka. They rear farm animals and cultivate, or work at drawing palm sap to make toddy. Total: 7,136 in 1971. (Thurston and Rangachari 1909, 4:96–99; Krishna Iyer 1948, 23–28; Luiz 1962, 100–104)

Kudubi (Kaluvadi)   A caste found in Dakshin Kannad District, on the coast of Karnataka. They used to practice swidden cultivation; now some extract catechu from the cutch tree. They are Hindus, and they bury their dead in a sitting posture. (Thurston and Rangachari 1909, 4:99–106)

Kudumi Chetti (Goa Chetti, Konkani Sudra, Kudumi, Kudumikkar)   A caste of domestic servants to the Konkani Brahmans, found from Goa southward to central Kerala. (Ananthakrishna Iyer 1909–1912, 3:386–387; Thurston and Rangachari 1909, 4:106–110)

Kudumo (Kurumo)   A Hindu cultivating caste found in Ganjam District, in southern Orissa. (Thurston and Rangachari 1909, 4:177–181)

Kuki (Aimol, Anal, Chiru, Chothe, Sahte, Balte, Biate, Biete, Changsan, Chhalya, Chongloi, Doungel, Fun, Gamalhou, Gangte, Guite, Hajango, Hanneng, Haokip, Haupit, Haolai, Hengna, Hongsungh, Hrangkhwal, Rangkhol, Jangtei, Jongbe, Khawchung, Khawathlang, Khareng, Khothalong, Khelma, Khephong, Kholhou, Kipgen, Koirao, Koireng, Kom, Kuntei, Lamgang, Laifang, Lengthang, Lenti, Lhangum, Lhoujem, Lhouvun, Lupheng, Mangjel, Misao, Mizel, Namte, Paitu, Paite, Rangchan, Rangkhote, Riang, Sairhem, Salnam, Singson, Sitlhou, Sukte, Thangluya, Thangngen, Uibuh, Vaiphei, Vaiphui)   A Paleo-Mongoloid tribal cluster; they are cultivators, found in south-central Assam, Meghalaya, Nagaland, Tripura, and Manipur. Total: 137,870 in 1971. See also THADOU. (Dalton 1872, 50–54; Shakespear 1912; Barkataki 1969)

Kumhar (Kumbhar, Kummara, Kumar, Kumbaran, Kumbara, Kumbaro, Kumbhakar, Ghumiar, Ghumar, Khubar, Khuhar, Kubhar, Kubar, Telugu Kummaravadu)   A large caste of potters and pig breeders, widespread in India. They also manufacture bricks and tiles. Although mainly Hindus, some are Lingayats; but there are also Muslim Kumhars, and a few are Sikhs. (Risley 1891, 1:517–526; Crooke 1896, 3:335–344; Campbell 1901, 189–190; Ananthakrishna Iyer 1909–1912, 3:387–390; Thurston and Rangachari 1909; 4:112–117; Rose 1911, 1:562–570; 2:526–528; Russell and Hira Lal 1916, 4:3–15; Enthoven 1920–1922, 2:275–284; Siraj ul Hassan 1920, 2:357–361; Nanjundayya and Ananthakrishna Iyer 1928–1936, 4:4–16; Patnaik 1960c)

Kunchitiga (Kunchigar, Kunchiliyan, Kunchati Okkalu)   An agricultural caste of the Okkaliga group, found in southern Karnataka and northern Tamil Nadu. See also OKKALIGA. (Thurston and Rangachari 1909, 4:118–119; Nanjundayya and Ananthakrishna Iyer 1928–1936, 4:17–26)

Kundu Vadiyan (Kunduvatiyan)   A tiny tribe found in Kozhikode District, in northern Kerala, who cultivate rice. (Gopalan Nair 1911, 74–77; Luiz 1962, 105–108)

Kunjra (Karunjra, Mewa-farosh, Sabz-farosh, Sabzi-farosh)   A caste of Muslim greengrocers, found from Madhya Pradesh to the Punjab. (Crooke 1896, 3:345–346; Rose 1911, 1:571–572; Russell and Hira Lal 1916, 4:50–52)

Kunnuva   A cultivating caste found on the Palni Hills, in Madurai District, Tamil Nadu. They are Tamil-speaking Hindus. (Thurston and Rangachari 1909, 4:119–122)

Kunte (Bhiksha Kunte)   A section of the Reddis who are bards and beggars. (Russell and Hira Lal 1916, 3:342–343)

Kurichchian (Kurichchan, Kuricchiyan, Kurichiyar, Kurichiya, Kurichiyan, Kowohan, Kuruchan)   A former hunting tribe found in northern Kerala. Thought to be descendants of Nayar warriors, they are now shifting cultivators. Total: 16,869 in 1971. (Thurston and Rangachari 1909, 4:125–130; Gopalan Nair 1911, 59–64; Luiz 1962, 109–115; Aiyappan and Mahadevan 1990)

Kuruba (Kurumba, Kuruman, Kuruma, Kurava, Kuramwar, Prathama Sudra, Indra Sudra, Kanakajatiyavaru)   A shepherd tribe of southern India, especially Karnataka and Andhra Pradesh. Many weave blankets or deal in milk; poor members work as day laborers or were bonded laborers. They are Hindus, though some, called Hande Kuruba or Hande Vazir, are Lingayats. Total: 38,319 in 1971. See also Kadu Kuruba. (Thurston and Rangachari 1909, 4:122–125, 133–155; Russell and Hira Lal 1916, 4:52–54; Enthoven 1920–1922, 2:316–323; Siraj ul Hassan 1920, 2:362–369; Nanjundayya and Ananthakrishna Iyer 1928–1936, 4:27–67)

Kuruvikkaran (Nakkalvandlu, Jangal Jati, Kattu Mahrati)   A caste of Marathi-speaking bird catchers and beggars, who wander widely with pack bullocks in central India. (Thurston and Rangachari 1909, 4:181–187)

Kusuvar   A caste of Tamil-speaking potters who are Hindus wearing the sacred thread. They are found throughout Tamil Nadu. (Thurston and Rangachari 1909, 4:188–197)

Labana A caste found from Punjab Province, Pakistan, to Himachal Pradesh. In some areas they are Sikhs, whereas elsewhere they claim to be Brahmans. They are farmers, and normally they are monogamous. (Rose 1911, 2:1–9)

Ladakhi A Mongoloid people found in Ladakh, northernmost India, who are essentially Tibetan in culture and speak a Tibeto-Burman language. (Mann and Ghosh 1986)

Ladar (Lad) A merchant caste found in cities of Karnataka. Some are now butchers or landholders but originally they were cavalrymen, probably originating in Gujarat. (Enthoven 1920–1922, 2:324–328; Nanjundayya and Ananthakrishna Iyer 1928–1936, 4:74–80)

Lahula (Lahuli, Lahaula, Lahauli) The inhabitants of Lahul, the mountainous northernmost part of Himachal Pradesh. They are landowners, and they include several castes, such as Thakur, Brahman, and Kanet, who are linked by instances of hypergamous marriage. Total: 3,144 in 1971. (Rose 1911, 2:10–19)

Lakhera (Lakheri, Laheri) A small caste making bangles and other lac objects. Found in Bihar, Uttar Pradesh, and parts of Madhya Pradesh, they are Hindus devoted to Bhagavati and claim a Rajput origin. The name is also used for a clan in Punjab Province, Pakistan. (Risley 1891, 2:1–2; Crooke 1896, 3:361–362; Rose 1911, 2:19; Russell and Hira Lal 1916, 4:104–111; Enthoven 1920–1922, 2:329–330)

Lalbegi A caste of sweepers, often working as servants, who though Muslim follow many Hindu customs. They are treated as Untouchables and are found from Bengal to Punjab and in central India. They worship Lalbeg, a mythical high priest of the Chuhras. _See also_ Bhangi; UNTOUCHABLES. (Risley 1891, 2:3–4; Rose 1911, 2:20–24; Siraj ul Hassan 1920, 2:380–382)

Lal Dasi A Muslim sect found in the Punjab, whose worship approaches Hinduism. It was founded by Lal Das in the sixteenth century. (Rose 1911, 2:24–25)

Lalung A tribe found in the plains of Assam, in Nagaon District. They are cultivators. Total: 95,609 in 1971. (Syamchoudhuri and Das 1973)

Lama The Lamas are not a caste but rather the priesthood of Tibetan Buddhism. Many are found in the Buddhist communities of India and Nepal in their Himalayan areas. Some are celibate, others married. Their spiritual leader, the Dalai Lama, currently resides in Dharamsala, Himachal Pradesh. (Rose 1911, 2:26–30)

Lodhi (Lodha, Lodhe, Shabar, Kheria, Kharia) A large agricultural tribe found widespread in northern and central India. Many work as petty traders, carters, charcoal dealers, or moneylenders. Some clans invest boys with a sacred thread made by Brahmans. Total: 290,141 in 1971. (Crooke 1896, 3:364–371; Russell and Hira Lal 1916, 4:112–120; Enthoven 1920–1922, 2:377–381; Siraj ul Hassan 1920, 2:400–403; Bhowmick 1963; Ray 1965)

Lohana (Lavana, Luvana) A large caste of Hindu merchants found in Gujarat and Sindh. Originally soldiers, they now follow a variety of urban occupations. (Campbell 1901, 121–122; Enthoven 1920–1922, 2:381–384)

Lohar (Luhar, Khati, Ghantra, Ghisari, Panchal) A large caste of Hindu blacksmiths widespread from West Bengal to western India and Pakistan. (Risley 1891, 2:22–24; Crooke 1896, 3:372–385; Campbell 1899, 75; 1901, 90–92; Rose 1911, 2:36–38; Russell and Hira Lal 1916, 1:396; 4:120–126; Enthoven 1920–1922, 2:384–392)

Lonari (Lonaria, Lonmali, Lonkar) A Hindu caste of lime and charcoal burners, cement and salt makers, found in central Maharashtra. (Enthoven 1920–1922, 2:392–397; Siraj ul Hassan 1920, 2:404–408)

Lorha (Lohra, Lohara) A cultivating tribe found in the western part of Madhya Pradesh, Orissa, and Bihar. They grow the hemp used in sacking. Total: 130,270 in 1971. (Russell and Hira Lal 1916, 4:126–128)

Macchi (Machinde Bhoi, Machhi, Machchhi, Tandel, Koli Machhi) A section of the Bhoi group of castes, found in northern Andhra Pradesh. They are fishermen and former palanquin bearers. Some work as domestic servants, and their women parch grain. There are also Muslim converts from the Bhois, who are fishermen and are found in eastern Gujarat. Some are found as far west as Peshawar, in the Punjab Province of Pakistan. _See also_ Bhoi. (Campbell 1899, 87; 1901, 519–520; Rose 1911, 2:41–43; Enthoven 1920–1922, 2:397–400; Siraj ul Hassan 1920, 1:85–87)

Madari (Mdariya) An unorthodox order of Muslim holy men who take their name from the saint Zinda Shah Madar. They are found in Uttar Pradesh. Some are farmers, while others are wandering mendicants. (Crooke 1896, 3:397–401)

Madhunapit (Madak) A caste of Hindu confectioners, found in Bangladesh. (Risley 1891, 2:26–27)

Madiga (Madigowd, Madigaru, Madgi, Madru, Dher, Chandal, Chambhar, Antyaja, Ettiwandlu, Peddintiwandlu, Panchamollu, Matangi Makallu, Gosangi, Kamathi, Bendar) A very widespread caste of leather workers, corresponding to the Chamar of northern India. They are found throughout much of India. Their girls sometimes became Devadasis. (Thurston and Rangachari 1909, 4:292–325; Russell and Hira Lal 1916, 1:384–385; Enthoven 1920–1922, 1:260–271; Siraj ul Hassan 1920, 2:409–420; Nanjundayya and Ananthakrishna Iyer 1928–1936, 4:125–169)

Mahabrahman (Acharaj, Mahapatra, Kantaha, Kataha, Karataha) A caste of low-ranking Brahmans in northern India who receive funeral gifts. (Crooke 1896, 3:402–405; Rose 1911, 2:133–134)

Mahdavia Musalman A Muslim community found widespread in South Asia and the Middle East. They are followers of the Mahdi, an expected Redeemer who will come before the ending of the world. They are found as far south as Karnataka and Andhra Pradesh, where they are traders and cultivators. (Nanjundayya and Ananthakrishna Iyer 1928–1936, 4:374–384)

Mahesari Marwadi (Mahesri, Maheswari, Mesri Marwadi) A caste of shopkeepers and moneylenders found in northwestern and central India. They are Vaishnavites, who claim Rajput ancestry. (Crooke 1896, 3:407–409; Rose 1911, 2:46–47; Siraj ul Hassan 1920, 2:492–496)

Mahia   A small caste found in Kathiawar District, Gujarat, who farm or work as servants. (Campbell 1901, 263; Enthoven 1920–1922, 2:418–422)

Mahli (Mahali, Mahili)   A Dravidian-speaking tribe of farm laborers, bamboo workers, and former palanquin bearers, found in southern Bihar, Orissa, and West Bengal. Total: 132,314 in 1971. (Risley 1891, 2:40–43; Russell and Hira Lal 1916, 4:146–148; Sengupta 1970)

Mahtam (Matam)   A caste found in Punjab Province, Pakistan. They are rope makers. Most are Hindu, but some are Muslim. (Rose 1911, 2:49–51)

Mahton   A Rajput caste, originally Hindu, though some are now Sikhs or Muslims. They are found in Punjab State. (Rose 1911, 2:51–54)

Mailari (Bala-Jangam, Kanchaviralu, Virabhatalu)   A caste of beggars found in eastern Karnataka and nearby. (Nanjundayya and Ananthakrishna Iyer 1928–1936, 4:181–184)

Majhwar (Majhi, Manjhi, Gond Majhwar, Majhia)   A tribe derived from the Gonds, Mundas, and Kawars, it would seem. They are found in the hilly area where Orissa, Madhya Pradesh, and Bihar meet, and in Mirzapur District, Uttar Pradesh. They practice swidden agriculture or work as farm laborers. Partial total: 37,627 in 1971. (Crooke 1896, 3:413–450; Russell and Hira Lal 1916, 4:149–153)

Mala (Mal, Dher, Telugu Dher, Antyaja, Panchama, Telangi Sadar Bhoi)   A large caste of laborers, village watchmen, and cotton weavers, found from West Bengal and central India to southern India, especially Andhra Pradesh. They are Untouchables. Some now cultivate or fish. (Risley 1891, 2:45–50; Crooke 1896, 3:450–451; Thurston and Rangachari 1909, 4:329–387; Russell and Hira Lal 1916, 4:156–158; Siraj ul Hassan 1920, 2:428–438)

Mala Arayan (Malai Arayan, Malayarayan, Malayarayar)   A tribe found in central Kerala. They collect forest products, grow pepper, engage in swidden agriculture, or work on plantations. Total: 18,007 in 1971. (Thurston and Rangachari 1909, 4:387–393; Krishna Iyer 1937–1941, 1:161–201; Luiz 1962, 120–125)

Malakkaran   A tribe found in Kozhikode District, in northern Kerala. Their traditional occupations were hunting, foraging, and shifting cultivation; but now many are plantation laborers. (Luiz 1962, 126–130)

Mala Kuravan (Malakkuravan, Malankuravan, Mala Koravan)   A tribe found in central Kerala who hunt, gather forest produce, or farm. Total: 274 in 1971. (Krishna Iyer 1937–1941, 1:80–95; Luiz 1962, 131–135)

Mala Panikkar (Mala Panickar)   A tribe found in Kozhikode District, northern Kerala, who perform forest work or cut stones. (Luiz 1962, 147–150)

Malapulaya (Mala Pulayan, Pulayan)   A group of tribes found in central Kerala who are shifting cultivators; some were bonded laborers. Some appear to be of the Kurumba group. See also KURUMBAS. (Ananthakrishna Iyer 1909–1912, 1:87–127; Krishna Iyer 1937–1941, 1:117–134)

Malasar (Maha Malasar, Malha Malasar, Malai Malasar, Mala Malasar, Malacharivan Malasar, Nattu Malasar, Nattu Malayan)   A tribe found in the districts of central Kerala and the neighboring Coimbatore District of Tamil Nadu, who work as laborers in plantations and forests. Some collect honey and other forest produce, but they do not cultivate. Total: 3,185 in 1971. (Ananthakrishna Iyer 1909–1912, 1:28–38; Thurston and Rangachari 1909, 4:394–405; Luiz 1962, 136–139, 151–154)

Mala Vedan (Malai Vedam, Malai Vedan, Malavetan, Malaveder, Mala Vettuvan, Vettuvarn, Vettuvan, Vettuva Pulayan)   A tribe found throughout Kerala and in parts of Tamil Nadu. They are Hindus. Former hunters and gatherers, many now labor on plantations or farms. They seem to be related to the Kanikkar and Vedan. Total: 1,343 in 1971. (Thurston and Rangachari 1909, 7:333–335, 394–404; Ananthakrishna Iyer 1909–1912, 1:128–134; Krishna Iyer 1937–1941, 1:135–160; Luiz 1962, 155–163)

Malayadiar (Mala Adiyar)   A tribe found in Kottayam District, southern Kerala. Some collect forest produce, but most are farm laborers. (Luiz 1962, 164–167)

Malayalar   A tiny tribe found in Cannanore District, northern Kerala. Although formerly shifting cultivators, they are now settled farmers. (Luiz 1962, 168–171)

Malayali (Malayalee)   A Tamil-speaking hill tribe found in various western districts of Tamil Nadu, where in 1971 159,426 were counted as undifferentiated members of Malayali Scheduled Tribes. See also MALAYALI. (Thurston and Rangachari 1909, 4:406–436)

Malayali Kshatriya   A small caste of Ernakulam District, in central Kerala. They include the former Raja of Cochin. (Ananthakrishna Iyer 1909–1912, 2:151–168)

Malayan   A tribe found widespread in Kerala. Their name simply means "hill people." They collect forest produce or work as exorcists, elephant drivers, and farm laborers. Total: 3,616 in 1971. (Thurston and Rangachari 1909, 4:436–439; Luiz 1962, 172–176)

Maler (Maleru, Male, Mal, Samaria Mal, Mal Paharia, Paharia, Savar Paharia, Sauria, Sauria Paharia, Samil Paharia, Asal Paharia, Sangi)   A Dravidian-speaking tribe of the Rajmahal Hills, on the eastern edge of Bihar, probably related to the Sora; some are found in West Bengal. Long ago they were raiders, but now they are engaged in agriculture. A tribe of the same name is also found in northern Karnataka. Total: 140,180 in 1971. See also SORA. (Dalton 1872, 253–265; Risley 1891, 2:51–60, 66–72; Russell and Hira Lal 1916, 4:153–156; Nanjundayya and Ananthakrishna Iyer 1928–1936, 4:185–187; Vidyarthi 1963; Singh 1981; Narayan 1986)

Mali (Malakar, Marar, Maral)   A great Hindu caste of gardeners and vegetable growers. Traditionally they made garlands for the temples. There are several millions of them in western, central, and northern India and in Punjab Province, Pakistan, speaking a variety of languages. (Risley 1891, 2:60–63; Crooke 1896, 3:452–459; Campbell 1901, 172; Thurston and Rangachari 1909, 4:440–443; Rose 1911, 2:57–61; Russell and Hira Lal 1916, 4:159–171; Enthoven 1920–1922, 2:422–426; Siraj ul Hassan 1920, 2:439–446)

Mali Gujarati   A group of religious mendicants who wander in central India. They are Hindus, devoted especially to the smallpox goddess, Sitala. *See also* SADHU. (Siraj ul Hassan 1920, 2:447–449)

Mallah (Malha, Machhua, Gourhi, Guriya, Gunrhi)   A caste of Hindu boatmen and fishermen, found in central and northern India; many are farmers. (Risley 1891, 1:294–297; 2:63–64; Crooke 1896, 3:460–471; Rose 1911, 2:62–63; Russell and Hira Lal 1916, 4:171–172)

Malo (Jhalo, Jhalo Malo, Malo-Patni)   A caste of boatmen and fishers, who are Vaishnavites. They are found in West Bengal and Bangladesh. (Risley 1891, 2:64–66)

Mana   A caste of Dravidian-speaking farm laborers, found in central Madhya Pradesh. They are evidently a former tribe who adopted Maratha customs and came to be regarded as a caste. (Russell and Hira Lal 1916, 4:172–176)

Manbhao (Manbhav, Mahanubhao, Mahatmana)   A Vaishnavite sect, now a small caste, found in eastern Maharashtra. Their religious respect for all forms of animal life makes them similar to the Jains. They are not celibate, but many lead a wandering life as mendicants. *See also* SADHU. (Russell and Hira Lal 1916, 4:176–183; Enthoven 1920–1922, 2:427–433; Siraj ul Hassan 1920, 2:450–457)

Mandadan Chetti (Mandatan Chetti, Mauntadan Chetty)   A cultivating tribe found in lower parts of the Nilgiris District, Tamil Nadu. They are closely related to the neighboring Wyndadan Chettis. (Thurston and Rangachari 1909, 4:444–446; Gopalan Nair 1911, 57–59)

Mang (Manga, Mangela, Madig, Mang Raut)   An Untouchable caste of western India. They work as musicians, castrate bullocks, and make ropes and mats; their women are midwives. They are closely related, by marriage, to the Ramosi. (Campbell 1901, 323–324; Russell and Hira Lal 1916, 4:184–189; Enthoven 1920–1922, 2:434–447; Siraj ul Hassan 1920, 2:458–462; Feio 1979, 118–119)

Mangala (Bajantri, Kalyanakulam, Angarakudu)   A Hindu caste of barbers, found in Andhra Pradesh. (Thurston and Rangachari 1909, 4:448–451)

Mangela (Dhivar, Tandel)   A Hindu caste of fishermen and laborers. They are found in western Maharashtra and southern Gujarat. (Enthoven 1920–1922, 3:1–3)

Mang-Garori (Mang Garodi, Mang Garudi, Rangidas Garodi, Firaste Mang, Pendhari Mang, Pahilwan)   A formerly criminal section of the Mang caste, found in the same area. Some of them are wandering acrobats and snake charmers. *See also* Mang. (Russell and Hira Lal 1916, 4:189–193; Siraj ul Hassan 1920, 2:469–472)

Manipuri   Hindu inhabitants of the state of Manipur, in northeastern India. (Dalton 1872, 54–57; Johnstone 1896)

Mannan   A tribe found in the hills of central Kerala, who formerly practiced shifting cultivation. They now have settled farms, though some collect forest produce. Total: 4,270 in 1971. (Thurston and Rangachari 1909, 4:452–455; Krishna Iyer 1937–1941, 2:202–225; Luiz 1962, 177–180)

Mannewar   A small Telugu-speaking tribe found in Chandrapur District, eastern Maharashtra. They are Hindus, related to the Koya Gonds, and practice agriculture. (Russell and Hira Lal 1916, 4:195–197)

Marakkayar   A trading caste of Tamil Nadu, including both Hindus and Muslims. They engage in overseas trade around the Bay of Bengal, using their own vessels. They speak a language called Arab-Tamil and write Tamil with the Arabic script. (Thurston and Rangachari 1909, 5:1–5)

Maratha Bhoi   A section of the Bhoi group of castes, Marathi-speaking fishermen. They are found in eastern Maharashtra. They are Hindus, and ancestor worship is prominent among them. (Siraj ul Hassan 1920, 2:82–84)

Marati   A nontribe, if ever there was one. In the 1971 census, enumerators recorded 48,840 persons in Karnataka (then Mysore) and a further 17,556 persons in Kerala as belonging to this "Scheduled Tribe," under a name that does not appear in any of the previous handbooks. The word in fact means "forgotten" in Kannada and Malayalam.

Maravan   A caste of Hindu landowners, found in southern Tamil Nadu. When hunting deer in the last century, they used to use boomerangs. (Thurston and Rangachari 1909, 5:22–48)

Marma (Mug, Magh, Mag, Mogh, Maramagri, Bhuiya Magh, Barua Magh, Rajbansi Morma, Myam-ma, Roang Magh, Thongtha, Thongcha, Jumia Magh)   A group of Paleo-Mongoloid tribes of Bangladesh, Tripura, and West Bengal who are Buddhists. The name means "Burman." They are mainly plow cultivators, and many have intermarried with Bengalis. Total: 16,530 in 1971. (Dalton 1872, 108–110; Risley 1891, 2:28–37; Bessaignet 1958; Mey 1981)

Marwadi Brahman   A Brahman caste found in northern and central India. They are traders, moneylenders, and priests. (Siraj ul Hassan 1920, 1:130–133)

Marwari Shravak   A caste of traders, found in Surat District, Gujarat. (Campbell 1901, 103–115)

Marwat   A tribe of Pathans, found in the North-West Frontier Province, Pakistan. (Rose 1911, 2:70–72; Caroe 1958)

Matha   A tribe found in Kozhikode District, in northern Kerala. They are farm and road laborers. (Luiz 1962, 186–189)

Matia Kanbi   A Muslim caste found in southern Gujarat, who in many respects still follow Hindu practices. They are cultivators. (Campbell 1899, 66–68)

Maulik (Laya, Naya)   A Dravidian-speaking caste of West Bengal, perhaps related to the Maler. They collect forest produce, work as Hindu priests, or are employed as farm laborers. (Risley 1891, 2:82–83)

Mavilan (Mavillon)   A tribe found in Cannanore District, in northern Kerala. They have recently become elephant drivers and farm laborers, but traditionally they were hunters and gatherers of forest produce. (Luiz 1962, 190–192)

Mayara (Modak, Maira, Kuri)   A caste of confectioners, found in West Bengal and Bangladesh. They are mostly

Vaishnavites. Many are now farmers or civil servants. (Risley 1891, 2:84–86)

Mech (Mechi) A Paleo-Mongoloid tribe of shifting cultivators, found in the hills of western Assam and northern West Bengal. Total: 13,432 in 1971. (Dalton 1872, 87–88; Risley 1891, 2:86–91)

Meghval (Menghwal, Meghwal, Menghvar, Meng, Megh, Mihngh, Ganeshia, Rishia, Rikhia, Rakhia, Dhedha, Dheda) A Hindu caste found from northern Gujarat to the Punjab. They are weavers, tanners, and farmers. (Rose 1911, 2:77–79; Enthoven 1920–1922, 3:43–52)

Meithi A Paleo-Mongoloid tribe found in Manipur. They speak Manipuri. (Hodson 1908)

Melakkaran Two castes of musicians, one speaking Tamil, the other Telugu. They are Hindus, found in Tamil Nadu and Andhra Pradesh. (Thurston and Rangachari 1909, 5:59–60)

Mer (Mhed, Mand, Mher) A small caste found in the Kathiawar Peninsula, in Gujarat. They are farmers, and they were once a feudal militia. (Campbell 1901, 285–286; Enthoven 1920–1922, 3:55; Trivedi 1986)

Mian A caste of Rajputs found in the hills of Punjab and Himachal Pradesh. They are farmers. (Rose 1911, 2:87–100)

Mina (Maina, Bhil Mina, Deswali) A Rajasthani tribe also found from Punjab to western Madhya Pradesh. They were originally a famous tribe of brigands, with a gory history. They are now cultivators. Total: 1,554,785 in 1971. (Rose 1911, 2:102–104; Russell and Hira Lal 1916, 4:235–242)

Mirasi (Mir, Langha, Dholi, Dom, Dom Mirasi, Dum Mirasi, Pakhawaji, Kalawant, Qawwal) A caste of Muslim singers and genealogists, found mostly in northwestern India. *See also* Bajania. (Crooke 1896, 3:496–497; Campbell 1899, 83; Rose 1911, 2:105–119; Russell and Hira Lal 1916, 4:242–243; Enthoven 1920–1922, 3:110–111)

Miri (Hill Miri, Mi-shing) A Paleo-Mongoloid tribe of cultivators, found in central Arunachal Pradesh. Total: 271,084 in 1971. (Dalton 1872, 33–40; Fürer-Haimendorf 1962)

Mishmi (Idu-Mishmi, Chulikata Mishmi, Kaman Mishmi) Tribes of Paleo-Mongoloid cultivators, found in the hills of eastern Arunachal Pradesh. Total: 8,944 in 1971. (Dalton 1872, 17–26; Baruah 1960; Sarkar 1987)

Mochi (Muchi, Mochavaru, Mochigar, Machigar, Multani, Konai, Matial, Chambhar, Chammar, Samgar, Rishi, Jingar, Jirayat, Jildgar, Chitrakar, Chitevari, Musabir, Arya Somavansi Kshatriya) A widespread caste of saddlers and cobblers. Some repair guns, bind books, or make clay idols. They are Hindus and are found throughout India; some have converted to Islam (Risley 1891, 2:95–99; Crooke 1896, 3:497–500; Campbell 1899, 77–78; 1901, 192–195; Thurston and Rangachari 1909, 5:82–84; Rose 1911, 2:123–124; Russell and Hira Lal 1916, 4:244–250; Enthoven 1920–1922, 3:56–59; Siraj ul Hassan 1920, 2:508–514; Nanjundayya and Ananthakrishna Iyer 1928–1936, 4:206–211)

Moger A caste found in the coastal districts of Karnataka, who were originally fishermen. They are Vaishnavites, and

most now work as traders, servants, cultivators, clerks, or brokers. (Thurston and Rangachari 1909, 5:65–70; Enthoven 1920–1922, 3:59–62)

Mohmand (Bara Mohmand, Mahmand) An agricultural caste of Pathans, found in the North-West Frontier Province, Pakistan. They are Muslims, speaking a dialect of Pashto. (Rose 1911, 2:125–128; Caroe 1958)

Molesalam A caste of "half-converts" to Islam from the Rajput castes. They are cultivators, found in southern Gujarat. (Campbell 1899, 68)

Momim (Momna) A Muslim caste of Gujarat; though converted several centuries ago, some still observe Hindu festivals. They are farmers, weavers, and cloth dyers. (Campbell 1899, 76–77; Enthoven 1920–1922, 3:62–64)

Mondaru (Mondi, Mondiwadu, Banda, Landa, Landawadu, Kalladi-siddhan, Kalladi-mangam) A peripatetic caste of beggars, found in Tamil Nadu and Andhra Pradesh. Some have now settled down to farm. They are Shaivites. (Thurston and Rangachari 1909, 5:71–73; Siraj ul Hassan 1920, 2:515–517; Nanjundayya and Ananthakrishna Iyer 1928–1936, 4:217–224)

Morasu Okkalu (Morasu, Hosadevara Okkalu) A section of the Okkaligas, who are found in eastern Karnataka and Andhra Pradesh. They are primarily farmers. They formerly would amputate some of the finger joints of their girls prior to betrothal. *See also* OKKALIGA. (Thurston and Rangachari 1909, 5:73–80; Nanjundayya and Ananthakrishna Iyer 1928–1936, 4:225–278)

Mowar A small caste of cultivators found in the Chhatisgarh area, in eastern Madhya Pradesh. They are related to Kurmis and Kols. (Russell and Hira Lal 1916, 4:250–252)

Mudaliyar (Modaliyar) A Tamil-speaking agricultural caste of Tamil Nadu and eastern Karnataka. They are related to the Vellalas. *See also* VELLALA. (Nanjundayya and Ananthakrishna Iyer 1928–1936, 4:212–216)

Muduga (Mudugar, Muthuvan, Muthuwan, Muduvan, Mudukkan, Muduvar, Thaggappanmargal) A tribe found in central Kerala and western districts of Tamil Nadu. They intermarry with the Urali Kurumbas and are one of the Kurumba tribes. Some are still hunters and gatherers, while others are farm laborers. Total: 8,858 in 1971. *See also* KURUMBAS. (Thurston and Rangachari 1909, 5:86–103; Krishna Iyer 1937–1941, 2:1–48; Luiz 1962, 193–196, 203–208)

Muhial A Saswa Brahman caste, found in the northern Punjab. They formerly practiced female infanticide. (Rose 1911, 1:121–122; 2:132–136)

Mukkuvan (Mukkava) A caste of sea fishermen found in northern and central Kerala, and also in Sri Lanka, where they are either Catholic or Muslim. Some now farm or have urban professions. (Ananthakrishna Iyer 1909–1912, 1:266–276; Thurston and Rangachari 1909, 5:106–117; Ryan 1953)

Mukri (Hebbe-Gauda) A caste of Uttar Kannad District, in western Karnataka. They speak Kannada and are Hindus.

They make shell lime or work as farm laborers. (Enthoven 1920–1922, 3:65–69)

Mullukurumba (Mulla Kuruman, Mullakurumber) A tribe found in the Nilgiris District of Tamil Nadu and in the Kozhikode and Cannanore districts of northern Kerala. They are one of the several Kurumba tribes who cultivate or do farm labor. _See also_ KURUMBAS. (Gopalan Nair 1911, 64–71; Luiz 1962, 197–202; Misra 1971, 1989)

Munur (Munnur, Munnurwad, Munurwar, Munnud Kapu, Kapewar) A widespread cultivating caste in central India. A few have become village headmen or landlords. (Siraj ul Hassan 1920, 2:518–524)

Murha A Dravidian-speaking caste of earth diggers and farm laborers, found in central Madhya Pradesh. They are Hindus. (Russell and Hira Lal 1916, 4:252–257)

Muriari (Mariyari) A boating, fishing, and cultivating caste of Bihar. (Risley 1891, 2:109–110)

Musahar (Mushahar, Mushera) A tribe found from eastern Uttar Pradesh to West Bengal. They work as watchmen and farm laborers and were once palanquin bearers. They collect and sell jungle produce—including, interestingly, the live lizard used by burglars to fix a rope to a roof. Their huts are very rudimentary. (Crooke 1896, 4:12–37)

Mussad (Muttatu, Potuval, Poduval, Akapotuval) A caste found throughout much of Kerala; they rank below the Brahmans but follow the Namboodiri Brahmans in their rituals and in their rule that only the eldest son of a family may marry. Mussad are custodians of the temple images. (Thurston and Rangachari 1909, 5:119–126)

Mutrasi (Mutrasa, Muthrasi, Mutracha, Muttaracha, Muttirajulu, Muttarasan, Mutratcha, Mut-Raj, Muttiriyan, Modi-Raj, Koli, Naik, Bantu, Palaiyakkaran, Telgaund, Tengaud, Telaga) A large farming caste, some of whom are hunters or laborers; others are traders, carters, fishermen, and collectors of jungle produce. They are found in Andhra Pradesh and speak Telugu. (Thurston and Rangachari 1909, 5:127–131; Russell and Hira Lal 1916, 1:392; Siraj ul Hassan 1920, 2:525–531)

Muttan A Hindu trading caste of northern Kerala. (Thurston and Rangachari 1909, 5:131–133)

Myasa Beda (Myasa Nayakar) A tribe of Chitradurga District, in central Karnataka, related to both the Bedars and the Chenchus. They cultivate and collect forest produce. Unusual for South Asia, they are animists who practice circumcision. (Nanjundayya and Ananthakrishna Iyer 1928–1936, 2:231–238)

Nadar (Shanan, Shanar) A great toddy-tapping caste, found in Tamil Nadu. (Caldwell 1850; Thurston and Rangachari 1909, 6:363–378; Hardgrave 1969)

Nador (Nadu Gauda, Gauda) A Hindu caste of northern Karnataka. They speak Tulu and are farmers or laborers. Some are moneylenders. (Enthoven 1920–1922, 3:117–119; Nanjundayya and Ananthakrishna Iyer 1928–1936, 4:397–401)

Nagar Brahman A caste of Brahmans found in Gujarat.

They work as clerks, moneylenders, or landlords. (Enthoven 1920–1922, 1:234–237)

Nagartha (Nagarata, Nagarattar, Nagarakulam) A caste found near Bangalore, in Karnataka. They are urban professionals, such as merchants, bankers, contractors, or jewelers, or are dealers in bullion, grain, etc. (Nanjundayya and Ananthakrishna Iyer 1928–1936, 4:402–421)

Nagasia (Naksia, Nagesar, Nagesia, Kisan, Kisada) A large Hindu agricultural tribe found from central Uttar Pradesh to West Bengal. Total: 243,778 in 1971. (Dalton 1872, 127–128; Risley 1891, 2:122; Crooke 1896, 3:285–287; Russell and Hira Lal 1916, 4:257–259; Ekka 1984)

Nagbansi (Vais, Vayasa) A caste of cultivators, found in Bihar and easternmost Uttar Pradesh. (Dalton 1872, 131–132; Crooke 1896, 4:39–40)

Nagori A Muslim caste of carters, found in Gujarat. (Campbell 1899, 88)

Nahal (Nihal, Nahul) A tribe closely related to the Bhils and Korkus. They are found in the southwestern districts of Madhya Pradesh and Maharashtra. Total: 8,686 in 1971. (Russell and Hira Lal 1916, 4:259–261)

Nai (Nayinda, Nao, Nau, Naua, Naherna, Nhavi, Napik, Napit, Nadig, Nayadaru, Warik, Varik, Valand, Vavdichaski, Ghaijo, Matko, Mahali, Mhali, Mangala, Hajjam, Hajam, Turki Hajam, Bhandari, Kshaurak, Karagir, Kelasi, Sanmukh) A very large group of castes of barbers found throughout most of India. They have numerous duties at marriages and festivals. Many perform surgery in their villages. While most are Hindu, some are Muslim. The article by Russell and Hira Lal has much information on beliefs concerning hair. _See also_ Ambattan. (Risley 1891, 1:92–94, 306–309; 2:124–129; Crooke 1896, 4:40–49; Campbell 1899, 84–85; 1901, 230–234; Thurston and Rangachari 1909, 2:320; 3:68–78; 5:413; Rose 1911, 2:140–150; Russell and Hira Lal 1916, 4:262–283; Enthoven 1920–1922, 3:127–135; Siraj ul Hassan 1920, 2:463–468; Nanjundayya and Ananthakrishna Iyer 1928–1936, 4:429–451)

Nalke (Nalakeyava, Panara) A Tulu-speaking caste of mat and umbrella makers, found in the coastal districts of Karnataka. (Thurston and Rangachari 1909, 5:141–149)

Nanakpanthi (Nanakshahi) A category of Sikh holy men, found in northern India. The name refers to Guru Nanak. _See also_ SIKH. (Crooke 1896, 4:51–54)

Nanchinad Vellala A caste of southern Kerala; they are Hindu cultivators. _See also_ VELLALA. (Thurston and Rangachari 1909, 5:241–246)

Naoda A small caste of boatmen, found in western Madhya Pradesh. They are Hindus. (Russell and Hira Lal 1916, 4:283–285)

Naru A caste of Rajputs found in the hills of the Punjab. Many of them are Hindu cultivators, while others are Muslim. (Rose 1911, 2:160–161)

Nat (Nut, Navdigar, Kubutar, Badi, Bajgi, Dang-Charha, Karnati, Bazigar, Garudi, Kolhati, Sapera) A tribe of wandering entertainers in central, northern, and western India. "Badi" and "Bazigar" mean "rope walker," "Dang-Charha" means "rope climber," while "Sapera" is a "snake charmer." They are closely related to the Beria, Domara, or Kanjar castes, which have similar occupations. Some are Muslims, but most are Hindus. Partial total: 7,492 in 1971. *See also* KANJAR. (Crooke 1896, 1:130–132; 4:56–80; Campbell 1899, 88–89; Rose 1911, 2:163–165, Russell and Hira Lal 1916, 4:286–294; Siraj ul Hassan 1920, 1:181–184)

Nattukottai Chetti   An important Hindu caste of Tamil moneylenders, native to Madurai District in Tamil Nadu but widespread throughout south India, Sri Lanka, Malaysia, Fiji, and, until recently, Myanmar (Burma). (Thurston and Rangachari 1909, 5:249–271)

Nattuvan   A community of musicians, drawn from the Kaikolan and Banajiga castes. They were dancing masters to Devadasis. (Nanjundayya and Ananthakrishna Iyer 1928–1936, 4:422–428)

Naumuslim   Term for any recent Indian convert to Islam. (Crooke 1896, 4:81–85)

Navandanna (Acari)   A caste of carpenters, blacksmiths, and other craftsmen found in Sri Lanka. (Ryan 1953)

Nayadi (Nayady)   A tribe or Untouchable caste found throughout Kerala; their name may mean "dog eaters." They collect forest produce, make baskets, straps, etc., and until recently were hunters also. (Ananthakrishna Iyer 1909–1912, 1:50–58; Thurston and Rangachari 1909, 5:274–283; Aiyappan 1937; Krishna Iyer 1937–1941, 2:49–67; Luiz 1962, 209–213)

Nikumbh   A Rajput clan, found in Uttar Pradesh. (Crooke 1896, 4:86–88)

Nunia (Noniar, Noniyan, Nuniya, Rauniar, Raunia, Luniya, Lunia)   A caste of traders, cultivators, salt makers, and earth workers, found in West Bengal and much of northern India. (Risley 1891, 2:135–137, 198–199; Crooke 1896, 3:386–395; Russell and Hira Lal 1916, 4:294–296)

Occhan   A caste of Hindu temple priests, found in Tamil Nadu. (Thurston and Rangachari 1909, 5:419–420)

Ojha   A caste or subtribe who work as soothsayers and minstrels to the Gonds in Uttar Pradesh and Madhya Pradesh. Some are Tantric Brahmans. They are said to divine from the entrails of sacrificed animals. (Crooke 1896, 4:93–94; Russell and Hira Lal 1916, 4:296–298)

Oko-Juwoi   A fishing, foraging, and gardening tribe of the Great Andaman group. (Radcliffe-Brown 1922, 12–19; Chakraborty 1990)

Oli (Oliya, Olee)   An agricultural caste found in Sri Lanka. (Ryan 1953)

Omanaito (Omanatya, Omaito)   A Hindu cultivating tribe found in Orissa. Total: 17,671 in 1971. (Thurston and Rangachari 1909, 5:443–445)

Onge (Ongee)   A fishing, foraging, and gardening tribe of the Little Andaman group. Total: 98 in 1987. *See also* ANDAMANESE. (Radcliffe-Brown 1922, 12–19; Basu 1990)

Orakzai (Wrukzai)   A Pathan tribe, found in the North-West Frontier Province, Pakistan. They are Muslim farmers. (Rose 1911, 2:176–189; Caroe 1958)

Otan   A Shaivite caste of Tamil-speaking potters, found in Ernakulam District, central Kerala. Some work as farm laborers. (Ananthakrishna Iyer 1909–1912, 3:393–395)

Otari (Watari, Watkari)   A tiny caste of smelters, found in central India. Their traditional occupation was to make toe rings, but some make religious images. (Russell and Hira Lal 1916, 1:394; Enthoven 1920–1922, 3:150–152; Siraj ul Hassan 1920, 2:532–535)

Padma Sale (Sale, Salewar, Channewar, Julaha, Tantunayakadu)   A widespread tribe of Telugu-speaking weavers, from Andhra Pradesh. Although mostly Shaivite Hindus, some have become Lingayats. They are related to the Koshti caste. Partial total: 3,971 in 1971. *See also* Koshti. (Thurston and Rangachari 1909, 5:448–453; Siraj ul Hassan 1920, 2:536–543)

Padti   A small caste found in Goa and northern Karnataka. They are cultivators, but a few make salt. (Enthoven 1920–1922, 3:152–155)

Paidi   A cultivating caste, found in Vaishakhapatnam District, eastern Andhra Pradesh. Many are now traders. (Thurston and Rangachari 1909, 5:454–458)

Paik   A small Oriya-speaking caste, found in Orissa and eastern Madhya Pradesh; originally they were foot soldiers. Probably they once served local rulers, under the command of Khandaits. *See also* Khandait. (Thurston and Rangachari 1909, 5:458–459; Russell and Hira Lal 1916, 4:321–323)

Pali (Paliya, Palie, Palee)   A caste of laundrymen to the lower castes, found in Sri Lanka. (Ryan 1953)

Pallan   A caste of farm laborers, found in western districts of Tamil Nadu. (Thurston and Rangachari 1909, 5:472–486)

Palli (Vanniyan, Vannia, Agnikula, Pallilu, Palle)   An agricultural caste found throughout Tamil Nadu and parts of Andhra Pradesh. They also work as carpenters, fishermen, beggars, etc. (Thurston and Rangachari 1909, 6:1–28)

Palliyar (Paliyan, Palliyan, Palleyan, Palayan)   A tribe found in Kottayam District, in southern Kerala, and in southern Tamil Nadu. They are former hunters and gatherers who now farm. Total: 4,316 in 1971. (Thurston and Rangachari 1909, 5:461–472; Krishna Iyer 1937–1941, 2:68–81; Luiz 1962, 214–217; Gardner 1969, 1972, 1982)

Palwar (Paliwar)   A Rajput clan found in eastern Uttar Pradesh. (Crooke 1896, 4:111–113)

Panan (Koravan, Mestri)   A caste of central Kerala and southern Tamil Nadu who are tailors, umbrella makers, and barbers. (Ananthakrishna Iyer 1909–1912, 1:171–180; Thurston and Rangachari 1909, 6:29–42)

Panchkalshi (Somvanshi Kshatriya Pathare)   A caste found in Bombay city and the coastal districts to the north. Although some are house or boat builders, the majority are farmers. (Enthoven 1920–1922, 3:159–168)

Pando   A tribe mainly found in Surguja District, Madhya

Pradesh. It is usually considered a branch of the Bhumia tribe. *See also* BHUIYA. (Sinha 1981)

Pangul A small caste of beggars, mat makers, and buffalo dealers, found in Maharashtra. Some have become farmers or petty traders. (Siraj ul Hassan 1920, 2:555–557)

Pangwal (Pangwala) Any high-caste inhabitant of Pangi, a part of Chamba District, in Himachal Pradesh. They include Brahmans, Rajputs, and Thakurs, all of whom are said to intermarry. Total: 9,291 in 1971. (Rose 1911, 2:195–198)

Panikki (Embatteo) A caste of barbers found in Sri Lanka. (Ryan 1953)

Panisavan A Shaivite mendicant caste found in Tamil Nadu. They also include farmers. (Thurston and Rangachari 1909, 6:55–57)

Panna (Panna-Durayi, Durayi) A former grass-cutting caste, now engaged in agriculture in Sri Lanka. (Ryan 1953)

Pano (Pan, Sawasi) A weaving caste found from Ganjam District, southern Orissa, to West Bengal. Some of their unmarried girls sleep in separate dormitories; in other respects the culture is similar to that of the Khonds. (Thurston and Rangachari 1909, 6:72–76)

Panwar Rajput (Puar, Ponwar, Pramara Rajput) A famous Rajput clan, now widespread in western and central India. They are Hindus, good farmers, and skilled tank builders. (Crooke 1896, 4:120–125; Russell and Hira Lal 1916, 4:330–351)

Paracha (Paraicha, Parachi, Parancha, Parachagi, Paraichi, Rachi, Tattar) A Muslim trading caste found in Punjab and North-West Frontier provinces, Pakistan. (Rose 1911, 2:200–202)

Paradesi (Tamil Brahman) An immigrant caste of Brahmans from Tamil Nadu who have long been settled in Ernakulam District and elsewhere in central Kerala. They are thus distinct from the indigenous Namboodiri Brahmans. Although some are priests, many have adopted cultivation or urban professions. (Ananthakrishna Iyer 1909–1912, 3:289–343)

Parahiya (Parhaiya, Parahaiya) A Dravidian-speaking tribe found in Mirzapur District, southern Uttar Pradesh; a few live in Bihar and West Bengal. They are Hindu cultivators. Total: 14,759 in 1971. (Crooke 1896, 4:125–133; Prasad 1981)

Paraiya (Parayan, Paraiyan, Paria, Pariah, Sambavar) A category of Untouchable Hindu castes, widespread in southern India. They are usually farm laborers, speaking Tamil. Their name is the origin of the English word "pariah." (Ananthakrishna Iyer 1909–1912, 1:68–86; Thurston and Rangachari 1909, 6:77–139; Krishna Iyer 1937–1941, 2:82–116; Feio 1979, 119–124; Moffatt 1979)

Paravan (Parava) A fishing caste found on the east coast of Tamil Nadu and southern Kerala. They formerly controlled the pearl fisheries. (Thurston and Rangachari 1909, 6:140–155; Roche 1984)

Pardhan (Pathari, Panal, Saroti) A section of the Gond tribe, widespread in central India. They are priests to the Gonds, and they also work as village musicians. Total: 531,950 in 1971. *See also* GOND. (Russell and Hira Lal 1916, 4:352–358; Hivale 1946)

Pardhi (Phanse Pardhi, Phans-Pardhi, Chita Pardhi, Langoli Pardhi, Takia, Bahelia, Bahellia, Baheliya, Adivichanchar, Advichincher, Mirshikar, Moghia, Shikari, Takankar) A tribe of wandering fowlers and hunters, found in western, northern, and central India, from Gujarat to West Bengal and Andhra Pradesh. Russell and Hira Lal describe their techniques. Many now work as farm laborers. Partial total: 42,239 in 1971. (Crooke 1896, 1:104–112; Russell and Hira Lal 1916, 4:359–370; Enthoven 1920–1922, 3:169–177; Siraj ul Hassan 1920, 2:558–561)

Pargha (Parigha) A small cultivating caste, found in southern Bangladesh and West Bengal. (Risley 1891, 2:163–164)

Parihar A Rajput clan, found in Uttar Pradesh. (Crooke 1896, 4:133–136)

Parivaram A caste found in western Tamil Nadu, where they were formerly palanquin bearers. (Thurston and Rangachari 1909, 6:156–158)

Pasi (Passi) A great Hindu caste cluster of northern and central India, numbering several millions. Their traditional occupation was tapping palms for the sap, but they also used to be thieves. Now some are hunters and fowlers; most are farmers. (Risley 1891, 2:166–168; Crooke 1896, 4:138–152; Thurston and Rangachari 1909, 6:158–159; Rose 1911, 2:204; Russell and Hira Lal 1916, 4:380–385)

Patari (Pathari) A caste of priests to the Majhwar tribe, found in Uttar Pradesh. (Crooke 1896, 4:153–155)

Patharvat A caste of stonecutters and image carvers, unusual in that they include Vaishnavites, Shaivites, Lingayats, and Muslims. They are widespread in Maharashtra and Karnataka. (Enthoven 1920–1922, 3:222–223)

Pathiyar (Pathiyan) A tribe found in Kozhikode District, northern Kerala. They cultivate or work as farm laborers. (Gopalan Nair 1911, 82–85; Luiz 1962, 222–224)

Patni (Patuni, Patauni, Dom-Patni) A trading and farming caste of West Bengal and Bangladesh, who also engage in fishing and basket making. (Risley 1891, 2:170–172)

Patnulkaran A weaving caste found in parts of Tamil Nadu, especially Madurai. They originated in Gujarat. (Thurston and Rangachari 1909, 6:160–176)

Pattanavan (Karaiyan) A caste of fishermen on the coast of Tamil Nadu. (Thurston and Rangachari 1909, 6:177–186)

Patwa (Patwi, Patra, Patua, Patvekari, Patvegar, Ilakeband, Ilaqeband, Alaqeband) A caste of weavers in silk and makers of body ornaments, found in much of central and northern India. Most are Hindus, but some are Muslims. There are also Muslim Patwas in West Bengal, who are peddlers. (Risley 1891, 1:83–85; Crooke 1896, 4:172–176; Thurston and Rangachari 1909, 6:176–177; Russell and Hira Lal 1916, 4:385–387; Enthoven 1920–1922, 3:224–226; Nanjundayya and Ananthakrishna Iyer 1928–1936, 4:476–481)

Pawi (Poi)   A Paleo-Mongoloid tribe found in the south of Mizoram. They practice swidden agriculture. Total: 20,669 in 1971. (Das 1969)

Penta   A Tamil-speaking farming caste, found in southern Andhra Pradesh. They are Hindus, originally soldiers from Tiruchchirappalli District in Tamil Nadu. (Siraj ul Hassan 1920, 2:562–564)

Pentiya (Pentia, Pantia, Holva, Halaba, Halba, Holuva) An Oriya-speaking tribe of betel-leaf sellers, found in Orissa. Total: 11,994 in 1971. (Thurston and Rangachari 1909, 6:189–191)

Perika (Periki, Perike, Perki, Perka, Perike Shetti)   A Telugu-speaking caste of sack makers. Some now cultivate or sell wood and *mahua* flowers. They are found in northern Andhra Pradesh and nearby; they are a section of the Balijas. *See also* Balija. (Thurston and Rangachari 1909, 6:191–194; Russell and Hira Lal 1916, 1:399; Siraj ul Hassan 1920, 2:565–567)

Phudgi   A small Hindu caste, only found in Thane District, western Maharashtra. Once wandering beggars or thieves, they are now cowherds, cultivators, and laborers. They are reported to use many words common also in the European Romany language. (Enthoven 1920–1922, 3:231–233)

Pichakuntala (Pichagunta, Pichigunta, Pichai, Bhaktollu, Gollakulam)   A caste of beggars who serve as genealogists to the Gollas, Kammas, and Kapus. Some also make mats. They are found in Andhra Pradesh and northern Tamil Nadu. (Thurston and Rangachari 1909, 6:195–196; Siraj ul Hassan 1920, 2:568–572)

Pindari (Pindara, Pendhari)   A former caste of brigands and freebooters, now cultivators and animal dealers, found widespread in central India. They are thought to be descendants of Bhil, Gond, and Korku children who were carried off in raids, circumcised, and brought up to the profession; but others claim descent from Pathans, Marathas, and Jats, three martial peoples. Some today are Hindus, while others are Muslims. (Thurston and Rangachari 1909, 6:198–199; Russell and Hira Lal 1916, 4:388–399; Enthoven 1920–1922, 3:228–231; Nanjundayya and Ananthakrishna Iyer 1928–1936, 4:393–395)

Pod (Poundra, Padmaraj, Chasi)   A fishing, cultivating, and trading caste found in the south of West Bengal. (Risley 1891, 2:176–177)

Polegar (Poligar, Palayakkaran)   Not a caste, but feudal chieftains who formerly ruled over small territories in the south of India, especially the Tamil country. Although an important factor in local history for some centuries, those who survive today are usually landlords. (Thurston and Rangachari 1909, 6:205–206)

Poraja (Paroja, Porja, Poroja, Parja, Parangiperja)   A group of Hindu agricultural tribes found in southern Orissa and in Bastar District, Madhya Pradesh. They grow rice and other crops, and some work as village headmen. They used to have youth dormitories. Total: 232,788 in 1971. (Thurston and Rangachari 1909, 6:207–222; Russell and Hira Lal 1916, 4:371–379; Thusu 1977)

Prabhu (Parbhu)   A Marathi-speaking caste of clerks and accountants, found in Maharashtra and Gujarat. Some are landlords, but most are in government service. (Campbell 1901, 68; Russell and Hira Lal 1916, 4:399–403; Enthoven 1920–1922, 3:235–252)

Pujari (Poojaree, Pucari)   Not a caste, but the title of Hindu priests in most of India. They are either sacrificers or performers of *puja* (worship). (Thurston and Rangachari 1909, 6:225)

Pulluvan (Pulaya, Hill Pulaya, Pulayan, Thantapulaya, Thanda Pulayan, Kanapulaya, Padinjaran Pulaya, Kizhakkan Pulaya, Southern Pulaya, Valluva Pulaya)   A tribe found throughout Kerala. Formerly beggars, they are now astrologers, priests, or farm laborers. Total: 90,558 in 1971. *See also* Cheruman. (Ananthakrishna Iyer 1909–1912, 1:145–154; Thurston and Rangachari 1909, 6:226–235; 7:19–27; Gopalan Nair 1911, 105–108; Krishna Iyer 1937–1941, 2:117–196, 295–326)

Pushkarna   A Brahman caste, found only in Punjab Province, Pakistan. (Rose 1911, 1:117–118; 2:240)

Qassab (Qassai)   A caste of Muslim butchers, found in Uttar Pradesh. They also deal in hides. (Crooke 1896, 4:190–193)

Quraishi (Qureshi, Quraish, Navayat)   A Muslim clan of Punjab Province, Pakistan, who claim descent from the Prophet's own clan, the Quresh. Some are quite influential; some are guardians of a shrine. (Rose 1911, 2:260–261; D'Souza 1955)

Rabari (Mogha, Raika, Bhopa, Vishotar, Sinai)   A large tribe of herdsmen found in Sindh, Pakistan, and in Gujarat. They rear cattle, goats, sheep, and, in Kachchh District, camels. They are Hindus, and some are temple servants. Partial total: 4,693 in 1971. (Campbell 1901, 286–289; Enthoven 1920–1922, 3:252–258)

Rabha (Datiyal Kachari)   A Paleo-Mongoloid tribe of cultivators, found in western Assam and West Bengal. Total: 141,096 in 1971. (Das and Raha 1967)

Raddi   A Hindu caste of farmers, found in northern Karnataka and southern Maharashtra. About half of them are Lingayat. (Enthoven 1920–1922, 3:258–267)

Ra-Deo (Raja Deo)   People found in the village of Malana, in Kullu District, Himachal Pradesh. They were originally hunters who came into the valley, and they claim to have been Kanets. (Rose 1911, 2:263–268)

Raghuvansi (Raghubansi, Raghbansi, Raghvi)   A caste of supposed Rajputs who now cultivate in Madhya Pradesh. But they are also found in Uttar Pradesh and the hills of Punjab State. (Crooke 1896, 4:198–200; Rose 1911, 2:268; Russell and Hira Lal 1916, 4:403–405)

Rahbari (Rahwari, Riwari, Raewari)   A Hindu caste of camel drivers, hunters, and carters. They are found in northwestern India. (Crooke 1896, 4:200–202; Rose 1911, 2:269–271)

Raikari (Gal Bhoi)   A tiny caste of fishermen, found only in Thane District, western Maharashtra. (Enthoven 1920–1922, 3:267–269)

Raikwar A Rajput clan, found in Uttar Pradesh. (Crooke 1896, 4:202–205)

Raji (Rawat) A tribe found in the lower ranges of the Himalayas in Uttar Pradesh. They are Hindus who practice swidden cultivation. Total: 1,918 in 1971. (Crooke 1896, 4:210–215)

Rajjhar (Rajbhar, Rajaur, Rajwar, Lajjhar) A caste of farm laborers found from northern Madhya Pradesh to West Bengal. They are Hindus, probably related to the Gonds, and speak a Dravidian language. (Risley 1891, 2:192–194; Russell and Hira Lal 1916, 4:405–409)

Rajwar (Rajuar, Rajawar, Rachewar) A farming tribe of West Bengal, Orissa, and Bihar, probably related to the Bhuiyas. They are Hindus; some are also found in Karnataka. Those in Bengal claim descent from Kurmis and Kols. Partial total: 1,478 in 1971. (Russell and Hira Lal 1916, 4:470–472; Nanjundayya and Ananthakrishna Iyer 1928–1936, 4:482–488)

Ramaiya (Bhatra) A caste of peddlers and small traders, found in western Uttar Pradesh and the Punjab. _See also_ Charandasi. (Crooke 1896, 4:223–227; Rose 1911, 1:93–94)

Ramosi (Ramoshi, Naik, Naiklok) A caste of former robbers found mainly in Maharashtra. More recently they have been employed as village watchmen or cultivators. They are closely related, by intermarriage, with the Mangs. (Russell and Hira Lal 1916, 4:472–476; Enthoven 1920–1922, 3:297–304)

Rana (Rajanaka) Descendants of petty kings who ruled in the western Himalayas in ancient times. They are considered Rajputs, and they are mainly found in Himachal Pradesh and the Punjab. (Rose 1911, 2:307–318)

Randhawa A widespread caste of Jats found in Punjab State, India, and Punjab Province, Pakistan. They are cultivators, mainly Sikhs. (Rose 1911, 2:318–321)

Rangrez (Rangari) A Muslim caste of dyers found in Gujarat and northern districts of Madhya Pradesh. Their art differs considerably from that of the Hindu dyers. However, the Rangari of Andhra Pradesh and elsewhere are Hindu dyers. _See also_ Chhipa. (Crooke 1896, 4:229–232; Campbell 1899, 79; Thurston and Rangachari 1909, 6:242–243; Russell and Hira Lal 1916, 4:477–479)

Rastaogi (Rastaugi) A Hindu trading caste found in Uttar Pradesh. (Crooke 1896, 4:234–235)

Rathi A caste of Jat cultivators found in Punjab State and Himachal Pradesh. They are related to the Rajputs and Thakurs. (Rose 1911, 2:324–329)

Rathor Rajput (Rathaur Rajput) A Rajput caste found in eastern Rajasthan and central Madhya Pradesh. Some, called Rathor, have been converted to Islam and are found in northern Gujarat and Punjab, where they work as farmers and messengers. (Crooke 1896, 4:236–240; Campbell 1899, 69; Rose 1911, 2:329–330; Russell and Hira Lal 1916, 4:458–461; Enthoven 1920–1922, 3:114)

Rautia A farming caste of the Chhota Nagpur Plateau, in southern Bihar. (Risley 1891, 2:199–209; Russell and Hira Lal 1916, 4:479–482)

Raval Jogi (Raval, Rawal, Ravalia, Raul Jogi, Shiv Jogi, Kanialanath Raval) A large sect of Yogis who are professional mendicants; but many are farmers, traders, tailors, or weavers. They are mostly Hindus, found in central and western India; but some in Punjab State are Muslims. (Campbell 1901, 508–509, 541–542; Rose 1911, 2:330–331; Enthoven 1920–1922, 3:304–310; Siraj ul Hassan 1920, 1:281–285)

Razu (Raju) A caste of former soldiers, who now cultivate. They are found in Andhra Pradesh and northern parts of Tamil Nadu. (Thurston and Rangachari 1909, 6:247–256)

Rodi (Rodiya) An Untouchable caste of farmers and scavengers, found in Sri Lanka. (Ryan 1953; Raghavan 1957)

Rona (Rena) A tiny tribe of cultivators, found in the hills of Orissa. They are Hindus. Total: 12 in 1971. (Thurston and Rangachari 1909, 6:256–259)

Roshania A heterodox Muslim sect, found in Punjab Province, Pakistan. (Rose 1911, 2:335–338)

Sada (Sadaru) A cultivating caste of Karnataka. Some are Hindus, some Lingayats, some Jains. (Thurston and Rangachari 1909, 6:260; Nanjundayya and Ananthakrishna Iyer 1928–1936, 4:526–535)

Sadh (Satnami) A Hindu sect found in Punjab and Uttar Pradesh. (Crooke 1896, 4:245–252, 299–301; Allison 1935)

Sagar A Hindu caste of northern Gujarat. They are cultivators, though some work as stonecutters. (Campbell 1901, 174–175; Enthoven 1920–1922, 3:311–315)

Sahariya (Saharia, Saharya, Sosia, Sor, Saur, Seharia, Sehria) A large Dravidian-speaking tribe found in Rajasthan, southern Uttar Pradesh, and western Madhya Pradesh. They are Hindus, and they collect forest produce. Total: 260,164 in 1971. (Crooke 1896, 4:252–255; Saxena 1964)

Sakadwipi (Sakaldwipi) A Brahman caste found in Uttar Pradesh, who work as family priests and astrologers. (Crooke 1896, 4:260–263)

Salagama (Halagama, Chalia) A caste of former weavers of Sri Lanka, mainly found in the cinnamon-producing areas. (Ryan 1953)

Salahuva Vakkalu (Salapu Kapulu) A caste of iron workers and farmers, found in Karnataka. (Nanjundayya and Ananthakrishna Iyer 1928–1936, 4:536–558)

Salat A small grouping of three stone-cutting castes, found in Gujarat. (Campbell 1901, 195–197; Enthoven 1920–1922, 3:316–317)

Sale (Sali, Salvi, Saliyan) A group of weaving castes of mixed origin found in central and southern India, many of whom also cultivate. They are Hindus. (Campbell 1901, 197; Thurston and Rangachari 1909, 6:265–279; Siraj ul Hassan 1920, 2:577–581; Nanjundayya and Ananthakrishna Iyer 1928–1936, 4:559–570)

Samantan   A group of rulers and chieftains in Kerala. They seem to include several castes, including Nayar. *See also* NAYAR. (Thurston and Rangachari 1909, 6:280–288)

Sanadh   A Brahman caste found in Uttar Pradesh. They are landowners and priests. (Crooke 1896, 4:266–271)

Sanaurhia (Sanaurhiya, Sanorhiya, Chandravedi)   A small community of former criminals, possibly of Brahman origin, found in southern Uttar Pradesh. (Crooke 1896, 4:271–272; Russell and Hira Lal 1916, 4:483–487)

Sangar   A Hindu caste of blanket weavers, found in Gujarat and western Maharashtra. Some work as laborers. (Enthoven 1920–1922, 3:318–320)

Sankhari (Sankhakar, Sankhabanik)   A caste of shell cutters found in West Bengal and northern Orissa. They are Vaishnavites. (Risley 1891, 2:221–223)

Sansia (Sansi, Sansiya, Saonsi)   A small caste of wandering dacoits and former executioners, now beggars, genealogists, and cattle dealers. Some have settled down in the Punjab and elsewhere. They are widespread in northern India. (Crooke 1896, 4:277–286; Rose 1911, 2:362–379; Russell and Hira Lal 1916, 4:488–496)

Sansia (Uria, Wadewar, Waddar)   A caste of masons and earth movers of Orissa, related to the Beldar. *See also* Beldar. (Russell and Hira Lal 1916, 4:496–499).

Sarai   A caste of Jat cultivators, found in Punjab Province, Pakistan. (Rose 1911, 2:381–384)

Sarak (Srawak)   A small caste of the Chhota Nagpur Plateau, in southern Bihar. They are sugarcane farmers. They are Hindus, though they claim a Jain ancestry. (Risley 1891, 2:236–237)

Saraswati (Shenavi, Saraswat Brahman, Sarsut)   A Brahman caste found in northwestern India, who take their name from the Saraswati River, which is lost in the Thar Desert. They are family priests. They are known as Shenavi in Gujarat. (Crooke 1896, 4:286–292; Rose 1911, 1:122–127; Conlon 1977)

Sarvade (Sarvade Joshi)   A small caste of fortune-tellers, only found in North Ratnagiri District, Maharashtra. (Enthoven 1920–1922, 3:321)

Sarwariya   A caste of Kanaujia Brahmans, found in Uttar Pradesh. They are said to eat a variety of meats. *See also* Kanyakubja Brahman. (Crooke 1896, 4:293–299)

Satani (Chatani, Chatali, Sattadavil, Sameraya, Ayyawar, Vira Vaishnava, Khatriya, Khadri Vaishnava, Vigha, Vishnu Archaka, Kulsekharam)   A Vaishnavite sect, who work as priests or temple servants. Some are also wandering musicians or farmers. They claim descent from Brahman disciples of Ramanuja and are found in Andhra Pradesh. (Thurston and Rangachari 1909, 6:297–304; Russell and Hira Lal 1916, 1:406–407; Siraj ul Hassan 1920, 2:585–589; Nanjundayya and Ananthakrishna Iyer 1928–1936, 4:586–591)

Sathwara (Sathvara)   A caste found throughout Gujarat; they work as farm laborers and bricklayers. (Campbell 1901, 175–176; Enthoven 1920–1922, 3:322–324)

Segidi   A caste of toddy tappers and distillers, found in southern Orissa. (Thurston and Rangachari 1909, 6:348–350)

Sejwari   A small caste found only in Lalitpur District, in southern Uttar Pradesh. They are Hindus, and they work as village watchmen and guards for bankers. (Crooke 1896, 4:310–312)

Sembadavan   A fishing caste of Tamil Nadu, who only work in tanks, ponds, and rivers. They are Shaivite Hindus. (Thurston and Rangachari 1909, 6:350–359)

Sengar Rajput   A clan of Rajputs, found in Uttar Pradesh. (Crooke 1896, 4:312–314)

Sesodia Rajput (Sisodiya, Gahlot, Aharia, Ahariya)   A Rajput caste, thought to be preeminent among all Rajputs. They are found from southern Rajasthan and Madhya Pradesh to Uttar Pradesh. (Crooke 1896, 2:374–377; Russell and Hira Lal 1916, 4:461–465)

Sheoran   A caste of Jat cultivators, found in Punjab Province, Pakistan. (Rose 1911, 2:403–405)

Sherdukpen   A Paleo-Mongoloid tribe found in western Arunachal Pradesh. They are craftsmen, farmers, and fishermen. Total: 1,639 in 1971. (Sharma 1961)

Shin   A Muslim tribe that is widespread in the Indus Valley of Pakistan. They practice hunting and agriculture. (Rose 1911, 2:405–407)

Shiranni (Shirani, Sherani, Sheorani)   A Pathan tribe found in the north of Baluchistan Province, Pakistan. They are farmers. (Rose 1911, 2:407–416; Caroe 1958)

Shishagar   A Muslim caste of glass makers, found in central Gujarat. (Campbell 1899, 89–90)

Sholiga (Sholaga, Sholega, Solaga, Soliga, Soligaru)   A tribe found in the hills that separate Karnataka from Tamil Nadu. They collect forest produce and honey or work as laborers. Total: 21,932 in 1971. (Thurston and Rangachari 1909, 6:379–386; Nanjundayya and Ananthakrishna Iyer 1928–1936, 4:592–599; Morab 1977b, 1981)

Shom-Pen   A tiny tribe living in the interior of Great Nicobar Island. They appear to be related to the Malays—if indeed they still exist. They are hunters and gatherers, who make baskets and other forest products, including dugout canoes. Some of these items they barter with outsiders in return for cloth, beads, knives, axes, tobacco, and other requirements. Total: 214 in 1982. (Lal 1969; Singh 1974; Rizvi 1990)

Sial (Syal)   A Muslim caste of Punjab Province, Pakistan. They claim to be Rajputs. (Rose 1911, 2:417–420, 529)

Sidi (Siddi, Habshi, Habashi)   A caste that is now both Muslim and Hindu and that has some Christian converts in Karnataka. They work as farm laborers and sometimes as thieves, and they are found throughout western India. The name is also applied to former African slaves, who are found in parts of Gujarat and are Muslim. *See also* SIDI. (Campbell 1899, 11–12; Enthoven 1920–1922, 3:332–336)

Sindhava (Sindhva, Shenva, Senva, Chenva)   A caste

found only in central Gujarat, who make brooms, ropes, and mats. Some are now messengers or barbers. (Campbell 1901, 346–347; Enthoven 1920–1922, 3:336–338)

Sindhu   A large caste of Jat cultivators, found in Punjab Province, Pakistan, and in Punjab State. The term is also applied to Madiga drummers in Tamil Nadu and nearby. (Thurston and Rangachari 1909, 6:388–389; Rose 1911, 2:423–425)

Singe   A mendicant caste of Andhra Pradesh. They are Lingayats. (Siraj ul Hassan 1920, 2:590–591)

Singpho (Ching-po, Kakhen)   A Paleo-Mongoloid tribe of cultivators, found in eastern Arunachal Pradesh. Total: 1,567 in 1971. (Dalton 1872, 13–17)

Sipahi (Sepoy)   A caste of Muslim soldiers, found in Gujarat. The term "sepoy" was also used in general for native soldiers in the British Indian Army. (Campbell 1899, 83–84)

Soeri (Soiri, Surir)   A small tribe found in parts of central Uttar Pradesh. They are probably related to the Soras. They are Hindu farmers. (Crooke 1896, 4:320–325)

Sombansi   A Rajput clan found throughout Uttar Pradesh. (Crooke 1896, 4:327–330)

Sonar (Sunar, Sunara, Suniar, Suniari, Sunera, Soni, Sona, Sonr, Shamsi, Hon-Potdar, Kain, Kamya, Zargar, Aksali, Agsali, Pattar, Potadar, Shet, Saraf)   A Hindu caste of gold- and silversmiths, widespread and numerous from West Bengal to Punjab and Karnataka. Those called Soni are found in Gujarat; unlike most Sonars they are vegetarian, and some are Muslim, as are the Sunars found in the Punjab. They were once employed to count and test money in treasuries. Partial total: 1,149 in 1971. See also Injhwar, Sonjhara. (Risley 1891, 2:256–258; Crooke 1896, 4:332–344; Campbell 1899, 79; 1901, 197–202; Thurston and Rangachari 1909, 6:393–394; Rose 1911, 2:439–444, 530–532; Russell and Hira Lal 1916, 4:517–534; Enthoven 1920–1922, 3:338–348; Siraj ul Hassan 1920, 2:592–596)

Sonjhara (Jhara, Jhora, Jhira, Jalagadugu)   A small caste who wash for gold from eastern Madhya Pradesh and southern Bihar to Madras City. Some now sweep up and sift the refuse of goldsmiths and brass smiths, others have become cultivators or fishermen. See also Sonar. (Thurston and Rangachari 1909, 2:439–442; Russell and Hira Lal 1916, 4:509–514)

Sri Vaishnava Brahman   A cluster of Vaishnavite Brahman castes found in south India. They are traditionally temple priests and are divided into two castes, Tengalai Sri Vaishnavas and Vadagalai Sri Vaishnavas. (Rangachari 1931)

Sudh (Sudha, Sudho, Suda)   A small Hindu cultivating caste of Orissa. (Risley 1891, 2:267–268; Russell and Hira Lal 1916, 4:514–516)

Sudir (Shudra)   A caste found in Uttar Kannad District, in coastal Karnataka. They are Hindus who engage in farming or work as laborers. (Enthoven 1920–1922, 3:349–352)

Sudugadu Siddha   A caste of peripatetic mendicants,

found in southern Karnataka. (Nanjundayya and Ananthakrishna Iyer 1928–1936, 4:600–604)

Sultani (Sultania, Sarwaria)   A Muslim follower of Sultan Sakhi Sarwar, found in Punjab Province, Pakistan. He was essentially the patron saint of the Jats. (Rose 1911, 2:435–437)

Sundi (Sondi, Sounti, Sundhi, Sunri, Sondhi, Saundika, Sundaka, Shaha)   A Hindu liquor-distilling tribe widespread in northeastern and central India. Many are now traders. Partial total: 55,178 in 1971. (Risley 1891, 2:275–280; Thurston and Rangachari 1909, 6:394–401; Russell and Hira Lal 1916, 4:534–536)

Suppalig (Devadig, Devadiga, Moyili, Moili)   A caste of temple musicians, found in Uttar Kannad District, in coastal Karnataka. They are Hindus. (Thurston and Rangachari 1909, 5:80–82; Enthoven 1920–1922, 3:353–355)

Suraj-Bansi (Surajbans, Bansi)   A jungle-dwelling caste of Bangladesh who cultivate. The name "Suraj-Bansi" is also applied to a Rajput clan in Uttar Pradesh. (Risley 1891, 2:285–286; Crooke 1896, 4:345–348)

Suthra Shahi   A sect of Sikh mendicant devotees, among them some Hindus, found in the Punjab and Uttar Pradesh and dating back to the seventeenth century. See also SIKH. (Crooke 1896, 4:348–349; Rose 1911, 2:445–448)

Sutradhar (Chhutar, Suthar)   A caste of carpenters, found in West Bengal and Bangladesh. Many are engaged in making images of Hindu gods or in cutting conch shells. They are also found in Gujarat, where they are called Suthar. (Risley 1891, 2:287–290; Campbell 1901, 202–206)

Taga   A cultivating caste found in western Uttar Pradesh. Some are Hindus, others Muslims. (Crooke 1896, 4:351–355)

Tai   A Muslim caste of silk weavers, found in Gujarat. (Campbell 1899, 80)

Tamdi (Baraiya, Barui, Tamboli, Tambala, Tambuli, Tamuli, Tamoli, Tamli, Thammadi, Phulari, Pansari, Barai, Tamliwandlu, Shiva Brahman, Shivarchaka)   A caste of beggars, betel-leaf sellers, temple servants, and musicians, found from central India to northern India and Bangladesh (where they are traders). They are Shaivites, though some are Lingayats; and a few have become Muslims. (Risley 1891, 1:71–76; 2:292–295; Crooke 1896, 1:177–182; 4:355–360; Thurston and Rangachari 1909, 7:5–6, 9; Rose 1911, 2:454–455; Russell and Hira Lal 1916, 2:192–198; Enthoven 1920–1922, 3:364–369; Siraj ul Hassan 1920, 1:28–33; 2:597–600; Nanjundayya and Ananthakrishna Iyer 1928–1936, 4:605–608)

Tamera (Tambat, Tamhera, Thathera, Tambatkar, Kasar, Kansar, Kansara, Kansari, Kansabanik, Twashta Kasar, Kasera, Bharewa)   A caste dealing in brass or copper vessels and selling bangles, found throughout western, northern, and central India. They are Hindus and are served by Brahman priests. Some have taken up modern urban professions. (Risley 1891, 1:419–420, 429–430; Crooke 1896, 3:167–171; 4:407–410; Campbell 1901, 186–188; Russell and Hira Lal 1916, 3:369–372; 4:536–539; Enthoven 1920–1922, 2:159–160; 3:361–364; Siraj ul Hassan 1920, 2:320–321)

Tandan   A caste of toddy tappers and carpenters, found in southern Kerala. (Thurston and Rangachari 1909, 7:9–12)

Tangsa   A Paleo-Mongoloid tribe of Tirap District, in eastern Arunachal Pradesh, who practice agriculture. Total: 13,546 in 1971. (Dutta 1959)

Tanti (Tantrabaya, Tantubaya, Tatwa, Tantwa)   A weaving caste of Bihar, West Bengal, and Bangladesh. They are Hindus. (Risley 1891, 2:295–304)

Taonla   A small caste of Orissa, derived from the Khond tribe. They are Hindus who work as farm laborers. (Russell and Hira Lal 1916, 4:539–541)

Tarakan   A caste of warehouse keepers or brokers, found in central Kerala. (Ananthakrishna Iyer 1909–1912, 2:118–121)

Tarkhan (Tarkhanr, Takhan, Darkhan)   A caste of carpenters, found in villages throughout Pakistan, at least prior to independence. They are Hindus. (Rose 1911, 2:457–460)

Tarkihar   A caste of western Uttar Pradesh who make women's ear ornaments from palm leaf. They also sell spices and sundry items at fairs. (Crooke 1896, 4:362–364)

Taru   A small caste of ferrymen found in some coastal districts of Maharashtra and Goa. Most are now farmers or petty traders. (Enthoven 1920–1922, 3:369–371)

Telaga (Mendicant Telega, Masan Jogi, Katibaglodu, Katipappla, Sharadakani, Balasantosha, Bahurupya, Jathikarta, Gorpalwad, Tolubomalawaru, Katti Bomalawaru, Katbo, Manda Buchawad, Bhagwat, Vipranoru, Bairagi)   Various castes of mendicants that are found in Andhra Pradesh and Karnataka; some are herbal therapists. They are Vaishnavites. The term "Telaga" has been applied to several categories of dancing girls, temple prostitutes, and the illegitimate offspring of the Kapu, Mutrasi, and Munur castes. *See also* Devadasi. (Thurston and Rangachari 1909, 7:13–15; Siraj ul Hassan 1920, 2:503–507, 603–610; Nanjundayya and Ananthakrishna Iyer 1928–1936, 2:87–93)

Teli (Gandla, Ganig, Ganiga, Ganigaru, Ghanchi, Chaki, Chaqi, Roghangar, Roghankash, San Teli, Taili, Tili, Telli, Tailika, Tailakar, Tailpal, Kalu, Tilwan, Tilghatak)   A great caste of oil pressers and sellers, numbering several million. They are widespread in northern, western, and central India. Most are Shaivite Hindus; some are Lingayats, and some are Muslims. Many have become shopkeepers or moneylenders. (Risley 1891, 2:305–310; Crooke 1896, 4:371–379; Thurston and Rangachari 1909, 7:15–17; Rose 1911, 2:461–464; Russell and Hira Lal 1916, 4:542–557; Enthoven 1920–1922, 1:356–358; 2:1–2; 3:371–374; Siraj ul Hassan 1920, 2:611–618; Nanjundayya and Ananthakrishna Iyer 1928–1936, 3:186–196; Patnaik and Ray 1960)

Thachanaden (Thacchanaden, Thachanad Muppan)   A tribe found in Kozhikode District and perhaps Palghat District, in northern Kerala. They are farm laborers and cultivators. (Gopalan Nair 1911, 89–95; Luiz 1962, 225–228)

Thakar (Bagde Thakar, Togata, Neyigeyavaru)   A Hindu caste of fishermen and weavers, often found begging, in Goa, Karnataka, and Andhra Pradesh. Those inland are only weav-

ers and occupy a higher status. (Thurston and Rangachari 1909, 7:170–172; Enthoven 1920–1922, 3:374–376; Nanjundayya and Ananthakrishna Iyer 1928–1936, 4:625–636)

Thori (Aheri)   A small peripatetic tribe who speak Gujarati and are found from eastern Gujarat to the Punjab hills. They have a varied economy, making and selling bedsteads, stealing cattle, making baskets, or playing music. They only worship Bechra, but some are converted to Islam. (Campbell 1899, 90; 1901, 109–110; Rose 1911, 2:466; Enthoven 1920–1922, 3:382–383)

Tibetan   Although fully dealt with in volume 6, *Soviet Union and China*, the Tibetans are listed here too because they are found as refugees in Nepal, Himachal Pradesh, Delhi, and Karnataka, and they have long been settled in the Lahul and Spiti District of Himachal Pradesh. Their spiritual leader, the Dalai Lama, currently resides in Dharamsala, Himachal Pradesh. (Rose 1911, 2:467–471; Fürer-Haimendorf 1975)

Tigala (Tilgar, Tilvai, Vanneru, Vannikuladavaru)   A caste of Vaishnavites found in Karnataka and parts of Maharashtra who speak a Tamil dialect. They are gardeners and farmers. (Thurston and Rangachari 1909, 7:29–32; Enthoven 1920–1922, 3:383–387; Nanjundayya and Ananthakrishna Iyer 1928–1936, 4:609–624)

Tirgar (Tirbanda)   A small Hindu caste of former arrow makers who now farm. They are found in eastern Gujarat. (Enthoven 1920–1922, 3:387–390)

Tirgul Brahman (Trigarth, Trigul Brahman)   A Brahman caste of central Maharashtra and northern Karnataka; they usually speak Kannada. Most of them grow betel vines, though there are many who have now adopted a wide variety of modern urban occupations. (Enthoven 1920–1922, 1:249; Siraj ul Hassan 1920, 1:115–116)

Tirmali (Kashikapdi)   A caste of bullock showmen, found in northwestern Maharashtra. They are petty traders and beggars. (Enthoven 1920–1922, 3:390–391)

Tiyan   A toddy-tapping caste found in Kerala. (Thurston and Rangachari 1909, 7:36–116)

Tiyar (Tiar, Tior, Rajbansi, Rajbanshi, Machhua)   A Vaishnavite tribe found from Bangladesh to eastern Uttar Pradesh. They are fishermen and boatmen. (Risley 1891, 2:328–331; Crooke 1896, 4:411–412)

Tomara Rajput (Tomar, Tuar, Tunwar)   A Rajput caste found in central and eastern Madhya Pradesh and Uttar Pradesh. (Crooke 1896, 4:412–415; Russell and Hira Lal 1916, 4:468)

Toto   A Paleo-Mongoloid tribe found in the hills in the north of West Bengal. They speak a Tibeto-Burman language and formerly practiced shifting cultivation. They still farm their land, as well as hunt and fish. (Das 1969)

Tottiyan   A Telugu-speaking caste of cultivators, found in Andhra Pradesh and Tamil Nadu. *See also* Reddi; Telugu. (Thurston and Rangachari 1909, 7:183–197)

Tripura (Tripuri, Tippera, Tipperah, Tipra, Tripra, Mrung,

Morung, Mro, Mru) A large peripatetic tribe of Tripura and adjoining parts of Bangladesh. They practice swidden cultivation. Total: 251,381 in 1971. (Risley 1891, 2:323–327; Bessaignet 1958)

Turi (Toori) A caste of farmers, bamboo workers, and basket makers, found from southern Bihar to West Bengal. They are Munda speakers. A Pathan tribe of this name is found in the North-West Frontier Province of Pakistan. They have no historical connection with each other. (Risley 1891, 2:333–335; Russell and Hira Lal 1916, 4:588–593; Caroe 1958)

Turi A caste of drummers, found from Gujarat to Himachal Pradesh. They are Hindus, devoted to two goddesses. They are also cultivators. (Campbell 1901, 225–227; Rose 1911, 2:474–476; Enthoven 1920–1922, 3:392–393)

Udaiyan A farming caste found throughout much of Tamil Nadu. (Thurston and Rangachari 1909, 7:206–213)

Udasi (Nanakputra) The principal religious sect of the Sikhs, concentrated in Punjab State and Uttar Pradesh. (Crooke 1896, 4:417–420; Rose 1911, 2:479–481)

Ulladan (Ullatan, Kattalan, Kattan, Nadi, Nayadi, Mala Ulladan) A small tribe that is widespread in Kerala. They are mainly wandering hunters and gatherers, but many work as farm laborers. On the coast they cut timber and make boats. Total: 3,692 in 1971. (Ananthakrishna Iyer 1909–1912, 1:58–67; Thurston and Rangachari 1909, 7:214–220; Krishna Iyer 1937–1941, 2:197–222; Luiz 1962, 229–235; Nandi et al. 1971)

Uppar (Uppara, Uppaliga) A caste of salt makers, who speak Kannada and are found throughout Karnataka. They have now taken to masonry, stonecutting, and making lime from shells. (Enthoven 1920–1922, 3:394–396; Nanjundayya and Ananthakrishna Iyer 1928–1936, 4:640–656)

Upparwar (Uppara, Uppiliyan, Uppaliga, Matadi, Memar, Chunnar, Beldar, Sagar, Sagarollu) A section of the Reddis who are earth diggers. They are Hindus and speak Telugu. _See also_ REDDI. (Thurston and Rangachari 1909, 7:228–241; Russell and Hira Lal 1916, 3:342–343; Siraj ul Hassan 1920, 2:619–623)

Urali (Uraly, Urali Kuruman, Oorali Curumaru, Urali Kurumaru, Urali Kurumba, Urali Kurumber, Vetta Kuruman, Betta Kurumba, Bettu Kurumba, Betta Kuruba) A tribe found in central Kerala, western Tamil Nadu, and in Maisur District, southern Karnataka. They are swidden farmers, and they also collect honey and other forest produce, as well as practicing various handicrafts. Total: 2,685 in 1971. (Thurston and Rangachari 1909, 7:242–257; Gopalan Nair 1911, 71–74; Nanjundayya and Ananthakrishna Iyer 1928–1936, 4:68–73; Krishna Iyer 1937–1941, 2:223–247; 1948, 19–22; Luiz 1962, 236–248)

Uridavan Gowdalu (Uridavan) A tribe found in Kozhikode District, northern Kerala. They originated in Karnataka and speak Kannada. They are cultivators or farm laborers. (Gopalan Nair 1911, 85–89; Luiz 1962, 249–252)

Vada A Telugu-speaking caste of fishermen, found on the coast of Andhra Pradesh. They are Hindus. (Thurston and Rangachari 1909, 7:258–265)

Vader (Wodeya, Odeya) Priests of the Lingayat community, found in southern Karnataka and among Badagas in the Nilgiris District of Tamil Nadu. _See also_ BADAGA. (Nanjundayya and Ananthakrishna Iyer 1928–1936, 4:657–658)

Vagher A caste of Jamnagar District, in Gujarat. They were a warlike people, involved in piracy and dacoity, but now they are farmers, fishermen, and sailors. Some are Hindus, while others are Muslim. (Campbell 1901, 522–523; Enthoven 1920–1922, 3:397–399)

Vaghri A tribe found throughout Gujarat, who are Hindus. They work as farmers, market gardeners, hunters and fowlers, herdsmen, laborers, etc. Total: 4,637 in 1971. (Campbell 1901, 510–518; Enthoven 1920–1922, 3:399–406)

Vahumpura (Kandeyo, Hakuru) A very large toddy-tapping caste found in Sri Lanka. (Ryan 1953)

Vaidu A class of itinerant herbalists, their name coming from the Sanskrit word _vaidya_, meaning "physician." They also hunt and beg for alms. They are recruited from the Bhois, Dhangars, Kolis, Malis, and Phul-Malis and are found in central India. _See also_ Baidya. (Enthoven 1920–1922, 3:406–410; Siraj ul Hassan 1920, 2:624–626)

Vaiti A caste of fishermen, sailors, and farm laborers, found only in Thane District, north of Bombay. (Enthoven 1920–1922, 3:410–412)

Valaiyan (Valan) A Hindu hunting and fishing caste found in central Tamil Nadu and central Kerala. The article by Ananthakrishna Iyer describes their fishing techniques. (Ananthakrishna Iyer 1909–1912, 1:231–260; Thurston and Rangachari 1909, 7:272–298)

Vallabacharya (Gokulashta Gusain) A Vaishnavite sect found in Uttar Pradesh, named after the sixteenth-century Hindu philosopher Vallabhacharya. (Crooke 1896, 4:425–428)

Vallamban A small caste of Tamil farmers, found in the central part of Tamil Nadu. (Thurston and Rangachari 1909, 7:299–303)

Valluvan (Valuvan, Pandaram, Valluva Pandaram) A caste of Tamil priests, astrologers, and therapists. (Thurston and Rangachari 1909, 7:303–310)

Vaniyan A Tamil-speaking caste of oil pressers found in Tamil Nadu and parts of Kerala. (Thurston and Rangachari 1909, 7:312–315)

Vanjha A small weaving caste, who have now taken up carpentry and farming. They are found in parts of Gujarat. (Enthoven 1920–1922, 3:442–445)

Vannan A caste of laundrymen found in Tamil Nadu and Kerala. _See also_ Dhobi. (Thurston and Rangachari 1909, 7:315–321)

Varaich A large Jat caste of cultivators, found in Punjab State. Nearly all are Muslims. (Rose 1911, 2:485–486)

Varli (Warli) A large Marathi-speaking tribe who are found in Thane District, north of Bombay, and nearby areas of Maharashtra and Gujarat. They are Hindus, with no traditional craft or occupation. Many are bonded laborers or tenant farmers. Total: 461,562 in 1971. (Campbell 1901, 328–329; Enthoven 1920–1922, 3:445–454; Save 1945)

Vasudeva Joshi   A wandering caste of beggars and minstrels, found in central India. *See also* PERIPATETICS. (Siraj ul Hassan 1920, 1:293–294)

Vedan   A hunting caste found in Tamil Nadu. Formerly they were also soldiers and brigands, but now they commonly cultivate. They are probably related to the Mala Vedans and the Veddas of Sri Lanka. (Thurston and Rangachari 1909, 7:331–335)

Ved-Patr   A Brahman caste, found in the Punjab. They practice palmistry. (Rose 1911, 1:139–140)

Velama (Elama, Yelama, Yelma)   A small Telugu-speaking caste of farmers, found in southern Orissa and northeastern Andhra Pradesh. They are Vaishnavite Hindus. (Thurston and Rangachari 1909, 7:336–342; Russell and Hira Lal 1916, 4:593–595; Siraj ul Hassan 1920, 2:635–640)

Velan   A caste found in Ernakulam District, central Kerala, who practice sorcery and make umbrellas, beds, etc. Some are now farmers. (Ananthakrishna Iyer 1909–1912, 1:155–170; Thurston and Rangachari 1909, 7:342–359)

Velli-Durayi   A tiny caste of temple caretakers, found in North-Central Province, Sri Lanka. (Ryan 1953)

Vellutedan   A caste of laundrymen found in northern Kerala. They are Hindus. (Thurston and Rangachari 1909, 7:389–392)

Vidur (Vidur Brahman, Bidur)   A Maratha caste found in eastern Maharashtra and western Madhya Pradesh. They are landowners, government officials, and shopkeepers, and they claim to be Brahmans. (Russell and Hira Lal 1916, 4:596–603; Siraj ul Hassan 1920, 1:117–118)

Vilkurup   A caste found in Ernakulam District, central Kerala, who engage in shampooing and teach martial arts and gymnastics. (Ananthakrishna Iyer 1909–1912, 1:181–184)

Viramushti (Vir, Virabhat, Vastad, Bhadrapad)   A caste of Telugu-speaking religious mendicants and acrobats, mainly found in northern Andhra Pradesh. They are Lingayats. (Thurston and Rangachari 1909, 7:406–411; Enthoven 1920–1922, 3:456; Siraj ul Hassan 1920, 2:641–644)

Vishavan (Malankudi)   A tribe found in Ernakulam and Trichur districts, in central Kerala. They collect forest produce, or grow rice and tapioca, and raise animals; some work as laborers. (Krishna Iyer 1937–1941, 2:248–260; Luiz 1962, 253–257)

Vitolana (Wansphoda, Palvada Kotwalia, Barodia, Vitolia, Vitola, Vitoria)   A small tribe only found in Surat District, Gujarat. They were traditionally basket and mat makers. Total: 13,972 in 1971. (Campbell 1901, 329–330; Enthoven 1920–1922, 3:457–459)

Waghya (Vaghe, Murli, Waghe Joshi, Murli Joshi)   An order of mendicants devoted to Khandoba, an incarnation of Shiva. They are found in Maharashtra, where childless Marathas vowed to dedicate their first child to this sect. Their dead are buried in a sitting posture. *See also* SADHU. (Russell and Hira Lal 1916, 4:603–606; Enthoven 1920–1922, 3:70–72; Siraj ul Hassan 1920, 1:294–296)

Wahabi (Ahl-i-Hadi)   A sect of Muslim purists, founded by Muhammad ibn Abdul Wahhab in the eighteenth century. They are found in Pakistan and in parts of India. (Thurston and Rangachari 1909, 7:412–413; Rose 1911, 1:8)

Wattu   A Rajput caste of agriculturalists, found in Punjab Province, Pakistan. (Rose 1911, 2:491–493, 533)

Wazir   A Pathan tribe found in Waziristan, in the North-West Frontier Province, Pakistan. They are cultivators and cattle keepers. (Rose 1911, 2:493–507; Caroe 1958)

Wynadan Chetti (Wynaadan Chetti, Wainad Chetti)   A farming caste of Ernad Taluk in Malappuram District, northern Kerala, and in the neighboring Nilgiris District of Tamil Nadu. They are Hindus. (Thurston and Rangachari 1909, 7:413–415; Gopalan Nair 1911, 55–57)

Yadu Rajput (Yadava, Yadu-Bhatti, Jadon)   A Rajput caste found in eastern Rajasthan. (Russell and Hira Lal 1916, 4:469–470)

Yanadi (Yenadi)   A large tribe found in Andhra Pradesh who are hunters and gatherers. They have Australoid features. Total: 239,403 in 1971. (Thurston and Rangachari 1909, 7:416–434; Raghaviah 1962; Bhaskar 1990)

Yata   A caste of toddy tappers found in northern districts of Andhra Pradesh. (Thurston and Rangachari 1909, 7:435–437)

Yerava   A tribe found in Kodagu District, southern Karnataka. They are farm laborers and Hindus. Total: 13,743 in 1971. (Krishna Iyer 1948, 8–14)

Yogi (Jogi, Dhoddiyan, Tottiyan)   An order of Shaivite religious mendicants found throughout India. There is a yogic system of philosophy, founded by Patanjali, which these men follow. They are noted for acts of self-torture. Although traditionally beggars, they now sell trinkets, tell fortunes, or sell magical cures; some are swindlers. *See also* SADHU. (Crooke 1896, 3:58–63; Campbell 1901, 543; Thurston and Rangachari 1909, 2:494–499; Rose 1911, 1:388–410; Russell and Hira Lal 1916, 3:243–254; Enthoven 1920–1922, 2:103–104; Siraj ul Hassan 1920, 1:278; Siegel 1991)

Bibliography

Adhikary, Ashim Kumar (1984). *Society and World View of the Birhor: A Nomadic, Hunting, and Gathering Community of Orissa.* Anthropological Survey of India, Memoir no. 60. Calcutta.

Aiyappan, Ayinipalli (1937). *Social and Physical Anthropology of the Nayadis of Malabar.* Bulletin of the Madras Government Museum, [New Series, general section, vol. 2, no. 4] Madras: Government Press.

Aiyappan, Ayinipalli (1965). _Social Revolution in a Kerala Village: A Study in Culture Change._ Bombay: Asia Publishing House.

Aiyappan, Ayinipalli, and Kuttan Mahadevan (1990). _Ecology, Economy, Matriliny and Fertility of Kurichiyas._ Delhi: B. R. Publishing Corp.

Allison, W. L. (1935). _The Sadhs._ Calcutta: Y.M.C.A. Publishing House.

Ananthakrishna Iyer, L. K. (1909–1912). _The Tribes and Castes of Cochin._ 3 vols. Madras: Higginbotham & Co. Reprint. 1981. New Delhi: Cosmo Publications.

Banerjee, S. (1968). _Ethnographic Study of the Kuvi-Kandha._ Anthropological Survey of India, Memoir no. 24. Calcutta.

Baptista, Elsie W. (1967). _The East Indians: Catholic Community of Bombay, Salsette and Bassein._ Bombay: Bombay East Indian Association.

Barkataki, S. (1969). "Tribes of North Cachar Hills." In _Tribes of Assam,_ edited by S. Barkataki, 63–80. New Delhi: National Book Trust.

Baruah, Tapan Kumar M. (1960). _The Idu Mishmis._ Shillong: Adviser's Secretariat.

Basu, Badal Kumar (1990). _The Onge._ Calcutta: Seagull Books; Anthropological Survey of India.

Bessaignet, Pierre (1958). _Tribesmen of the Chittagong Hill Tracts._ Dacca: Asiatic Society of Pakistan.

Bhaskar, S. (1990). _Prehistoric and Primitive Hunter-Gatherers of South India._ New Delhi: Discovery Publishing House.

Bhowmick, P. K. (1963). _The Lodhas of West Bengal: A Socio-Economic Study._ Calcutta: Punthi Pustak.

Bishop, Barry (1990). _Karnali under Stress: Livelihood Strategies and Seasonal Rhythms in a Changing Nepal Himalaya._ Geography Research Paper nos. 228–229. Chicago: University of Chicago.

Breman, Jan (1974). _Patronage and Exploitation: Changing Agrarian Relations in South Gujarat, India._ Berkeley: University of California Press.

Caldwell, Robert (1850). _The Tinnevelly Shanars: A Sketch of Their Religion, and their Moral Condition and Characteristics, as a Caste._ London: Society for Promoting Christian Knowledge.

Campbell, James M. (1899). _Gazetteer of the Bombay Presidency._ Vol. 9, pt. 2, _Gujarát Population: Musalmans and Parsis._ Bombay: Government Central Press. Reprint. 1990. _Muslim and Parsi Castes and Tribes of Gujarat._ Gurgaon: Vintage Books.

Campbell, James M. (1901). _Gazetteer of the Bombay Presidency._ Vol. 9, pt. 1, _Gujarat Population: Hindus._ Bombay: Government Central Press. Reprint. 1988. _Hindu Castes and Tribes of Gujarat._ Gurgaon: Vintage Books.

Caroe, Olaf (1958). _The Pathans, 550 B.C.-A.D. 1957._ London: St. Martin's Press.

Chakraborty, Dilip K. (1990). _The Great Andamanese._ Calcutta: Seagull Books; Anthropological Survey of India.

Chandra, Ramesh (1981). "Ecology and Religion of the Kinner, Mountain Dwellers of North-Western Himalayas." In _Nature-Man-Spirit Complex in Tribal India,_ edited by R. S. Mann and Vijoy S. Sahay, 273–293. New Delhi: Concept Publishing Co.

Chatterjee, Anathnath, and Tarakchandra Das (1927). _The Hos of Seraikella._ Pt. 1. Anthropological Papers, n.s. 1. Calcutta: University of Calcutta.

Chowdhury, J. N. (1971) _A Comparative Study of Adi Religion._ Shillong: North-East Frontier Agency.

Conlon, Frank E. (1977). _A Caste in a Changing World: The Chitrapur Saraswat Brahmans, 1700–1935._ Berkeley: University of California Press.

Crooke, William (1896). _The Tribes and Castes of the North-Western Provinces and Oudh._ 4 vols. Calcutta: Superintendent of Government Printing.

Dalton, Edward Tuite (1872). _Descriptive Ethnology of Bengal._ Calcutta: Superintendent of Government Printing. Reprint. 1960. Calcutta: Indian Studies, Past & Present. [Pagination cited from 1960 edition.]

Danda, Dipali G., and Sanchita Ghatak (1985). _The Semsa and their Habitat._ Anthropological Survey of India, Memoir no. 64. Calcutta.

Das, Amal Kumar (1969). _The Totos._ Special series, no. 11. Calcutta: Scheduled Castes and Scheduled Tribes Welfare Dept., Government of West Bengal.

Das, Amal Kumar, and M. K. Raha (1967). _The Rabhas of West Bengal._ Calcutta: Scheduled Castes and Scheduled Tribes Welfare Dept., Government of West Bengal.

Das, Jagdish Chandra, and Manish Kumar Raha (1981). "Divergent Trends of Transformation among the Kumaon Bhotia." In _Asian Highland Societies in Anthropological Perspective,_ edited by Christoph von Fürer-Haimendorf, 250–265. New Delhi: Sterling Publishers.

Das, S. (1969). "The Lesser Known Tribes of South Lushai

Hills." In *Tribes of Assam,* edited by S. Barkataki, 99–110. New Delhi: National Book Trust.

Das Gupta, Amitava (1981). "A Study in Nature-Man-Spirit Complex." In *Nature-Man-Spirit Complex in Tribal India,* edited by R. S. Mann and Vijoy S. Sahay, 41–55. New Delhi: Concept Publishing Co.

Dirks, Nicholas B. (1987). *The Hollow Crown: Ethnohistory of an Indian Kingdom.* Cambridge: Cambridge University Press.

D'Souza, Victor (1955). *The Navayats of Kanara.* Dharwar: Karnatak University.

Dube, S. C. (1951). *The Kamar.* Lucknow: Universal Publishers.

Dumont, Louis (1986). *A South Indian Subcaste.* Delhi: Oxford University Press.

Dutta, Parul (1959). *The Tangsas of the Namchick and Tirap Valleys.* Shillong: North-East Frontier Agency.

Ehrenfels, Uma R. von (1952). *Kadar of Cochin.* Madras: University of Madras.

Ekka, William (1984). *The Nagesia of Chhattisgarh.* Anthropological Survey of India, Memoir no. 58. Calcutta.

Endle, Sidney (1911). *The Kacharis.* London: Macmillan.

Enthoven, Reginald Edward, ed. (1920–1922). *The Tribes and Castes of Bombay.* 3 vols. Bombay: Government Central Press. Reprints. 1975. Delhi: Cosmo Publications. 1990. New Delhi: Asian Educational Services.

Feio, Mariano (1979). *As Castas Hindus de Goa.* Estudos de Antropologia Cultural, no. 11. Lisbon: Junta de Investigações Científicas do Ultramar, Centro de Estudos de Antropologia Cultural.

Fuchs, Stephen (1950). *The Children of Hari: A Study of the Nimar Balahis in the Central Provinces of India.* Vienna: Verlag Herold.

Fürer-Haimendorf, Christoph von (1956). *Himalayan Barbary.* New York: Abelard-Schuman.

Fürer-Haimendorf, Christoph von (1962). The *Apa Tanis and Their Neighbours: A Primitive Civilization of the Eastern Himalayas.* London: Routledge & Kegan Paul.

Fürer-Haimendorf, Christoph von (1975). *Himalayan Traders.* New York: St. Martin's Press.

Fürer-Haimendorf, Christoph von (1980). *A Himalayan Tribe: From Cattle to Cash.* Berkeley: University of California Press.

Gardner, Peter M. (1969). "Paliyan Social Structure." In *Contributions to Anthropology: Band Societies,* edited by David John Damas, 153–167. National Museums of Canada, Bulletin no. 228. Ottawa.

Gardner, Peter M. (1972). "The Paliyans." In *Hunters and Gatherers Today,* edited by Marco G. Bicchieri, 404–447. New York: Holt, Rinehart & Winston.

Gardner, Peter M. (1982). "Ascribed Austerity: A Tribal Path to Purity." *Man* 17:462–469.

Gilhodes, Charles (1922). *Kacharis: Religion and Customs.* Calcutta: Catholic Orphan Press.

Gopalan Nair, C. (1911). *Wynad: Its Peoples and Traditions.* Madras: Higginbotham & Co.

Guha, Uma, M. K. A. Siddiqui, and P. R. G. Mathur (1968). *The Didayi: A Forgotten Tribe of Orissa.* Anthropological Survey of India, Memoir no. 23. Calcutta.

Haekel, Josef (1963). "Some Aspects of the Social Life of the Bhilala in Central India." *Ethnology* 2:190–206.

Haekel, Josef, and E. Stiglmayr (1961). "Bericht über die Oesterreichische Zentralindien–Expedition 1960/1961." *Wiener Völkerkundliche Mitteilungen* 9:25–44.

Hardgrave, Robert L., Jr. (1969). *The Nadars of Tamilnad: The Political Culture of a Community in Change.* Berkeley: University of California Press.

Hatch, W. J. (1928). *The Land Pirates of India.* London: Seeley, Service & Co. Reprint. 1976. Delhi: Concept Publishing Co.

Hazra, Durgadas (1970). *The Dorla of Bastar.* Anthropological Survey of India, Memoir no. 17. Calcutta.

Hazra, Durgadas (1983). *The Kolam of Yeotmal.* Anthropological Survey of India, Memoir no. 49. Calcutta.

Hivale, Shamrao (1946). *The Pardhans of the Upper Narbada Valley.* London: Geoffrey Cumberlege, Oxford University Press.

Hodson, T. C. (1908). *The Meithis.* London: Macmillan.

Ittaman, K. P., et al. (1982). *Bibliography on Scheduled Castes and Scheduled Tribes.* Census of India Occasional Paper no. 1 of 1982. New Delhi: Office of the Registrar General.

Jackson, Stanley [pseud.] (1968). *The Sassoons.* New York: E. P. Dutton & Co.

Johnstone, James (1896). *My Experiences in Manipur and the Naga Hills.* London: Sampson Low, Marston & Co.

Jones, Schuyler (1967). *The Political Organization of the Kam Kafirs: A Preliminary Analysis.* Det Kongelige Danske

Videnskabernes Selskab Historiskfilosofiske Meddelelser 42, no. 2. Copenhagen.

Kale, D. N. (1952). *Agris: A Socio-Economic Survey*. Bombay: Asia Publishing House.

Kolenda, Pauline M. (1987). "Living the Levirate: The Mating of an Untouchable Chuhra Widow." In *Dimensions of Social Life: Essays in Honor of David G. Mandelbaum*, edited by Paul Hockings, 44–67. Berlin: Mouton de Gruyter.

Krishna Iyer, L. Ananthakrishna (1937–1941). *The Travancore Tribes and Castes*. 3 vols. Trivandrum: Superintendent, Government Press.

Krishna Iyer, L. Ananthakrishna (1948). *The Coorg Tribes and Castes (with 27 Illustrations)*. Madras: Gordon Press. Reprint. 1969. New York: Johnson Reprint Corp.

Lal, Parmanand (1969). "The Shompens of Great Nicobar." *Bulletin of the Anthropological Survey of India* 18:247–254.

Leach, Edmund Ronald (1968). *Pul Eliya: A Village in Ceylon*. Cambridge: Cambridge University Press.

Leonard, Karen I. (1978). *Social History of an Indian Caste: The Kayasths of Hyderabad*. Berkeley: University of California Press.

Leuva, K. K. (1963). *The Asur: A Study of Primitive Iron-Smelters*. New Delhi: Bharatiya Adimjati Sevak Sangh.

Luiz, A. A. D. (1962). *Tribes of Kerala*. New Delhi: Bharatiya Adimjati Sevak Sangh.

Majumdar, Dhirendra Nath (1944). *The Fortunes of Primitive Tribes*. Lucknow: Universal Publishers.

Majumdar, Dhirendra Nath (1962). *Himalayan Polyandry: Structure, Functioning, and Culture Change: A Field-Study of Jaunsar-Bawar*. Bombay: Asia Publishing House.

Mann, Rann Singh (1980). *Hakkipikki: Trapper and Seller*. Anthropological Survey of India, Memoir no. 51. Calcutta.

Mann, Rann Singh, and T. K. Ghosh (1986). *The Ladakhi: A Study in Ethnography and Change*. Anthropological Survey of India, Memoir no. 69. Calcutta.

Marglin, Frédérique Apffel (1985). *Wives of the God-King: The Rituals of the Devadasis of Puri*. Delhi: Oxford University Press.

Mey, Wolfgang E. (1981). "Political Systems in the Chittagong Hill Tracts, Bangla Desh: A Case Study." In *Asian Highland Societies in Anthropological Perspective*, edited by Christoph von Fürer-Haimendorf, 214–222. New Delhi: Sterling Publishers.

Mines, Mattison (1984). *The Warrior Merchants: Textiles, Trade, and Territory in South India*. Cambridge: Cambridge University Press.

Misra, Rajalakshmi (1971). *Mullukurumbas of Kappala*. Anthropological Survey of India, Memoir no. 30. Calcutta.

Misra, Rajalakshmi (1989). "The Mullu Kurumbas." In *Blue Mountains: The Ethnography and Biogeography of a South Indian Region*, edited by Paul Hockings, 304–317. New Delhi: Oxford University Press.

Moffatt, Michael (1979). *An Untouchable Community in South India: Structure and Consensus*. Princeton: Princeton University Press.

Mohanti, Prafulla (1975). *My Village, My Life*. Nanpur: A Portrait of an Indian Village. London: Davis–Poynter.

Morab, S. G. (1977a). *The Killekyatha: Nomadic Folk Artists of Northern Mysore*. Anthropological Survey of India, Memoir no. 46. Calcutta.

Morab, S. G. (1977b). *The Soliga of Biligiri Rangana Hills*. Anthropological Survey of India, Memoir no. 45. Calcutta.

Morab, S. G. (1981). "The Soliga: A Study in Ecology, Society, and Religion of a Hill Tribe in South India." In *Nature-Man-Spirit Complex in Tribal India*, edited by R. S. Mann and Vijoy S. Sahay, 127–178. New Delhi: Concept Publishing.

Mukherjee, Bhabananda, B. C. Roy Chaudhury, and Deepali Ghosh (1973). *The Chero of Palamau*. Anthropological Survey of India, Memoir no. 32. Calcutta.

Nandi, Santibhushan, C. R. Rajalakshmi, and I. Verghese (1971). *Life and Culture of the Mala Ulladan*. Anthropological Survey of India, Memoir no. 26. Calcutta.

Nanjundayya, H. V., and L. K. Ananthakrishna Iyer, eds. (1928–1936). *The Mysore Tribes and Castes*. 4 vols. and appendix. Mysore: Mysore University. Reprint. 1988. New Delhi: Mittal.

Narayan, Sachindra (1986). *A Dwindling Hill Tribe of Bihar: A Development Approach*. Calcutta: Naya Prokash.

Newell, William H. (1960). "Goshen: A Gaddi Village in the Himalayas." In *India's Villages*. 2nd ed., edited by M. N. Srinivas, 56–67. Bombay: Asia Publishing House.

Newell, William H. (1967). *Census of India 1961*. Vol. 20, pt. 5-B, *Himachal Pradesh: Report on Scheduled Castes and Scheduled Tribes (A Study of Gaddi—Scheduled Tribe—and Affiliated Castes)*. Delhi: Manager of Government of India Press.

Obeyesekere, Gananath (1974). "A Village in Srī Lankā: Mādagama." In *South Asia: Seven Community Profiles*, edited by Clarence Maloney, 42–80. New York: Holt, Rinehart & Winston.

Parthasarathy, Jakka (1988). *The Yerukula: An Ethnographic*

Study. Anthropological Survey of India, Memoir no. 79. Calcutta.

Patnaik, Nityananda (1960a). "Bhoi or Bauri of Puri District." In *Data on Caste: Orissa,* edited by Nirmal Kumar Bose, 173–174. Anthropological Survey of India, Memoir no. 7. Calcutta.

Patnaik, Nityananda (1960b). "Caste of Cultivators (Chasa)." In *Data on Caste: Orissa,* edited by Nirmal Kumar Bose, 119–127. Anthropological Survey of India, Memoir no. 7. Calcutta.

Patnaik, Nityananda (1960c). "Kumbhara—Potter Caste—Puri." In *Data on Caste: Orissa,* edited by Nirmal Kumar Bose, 149–151. Anthropological Survey of India, Memoir no. 7. Calcutta.

Patnaik, Nityananda (1960d). "Regulations of the Kulta Caste of Orissa, Kulta Jati Mahasabha, Sambalpur." In *Data on Caste: Orissa,* edited by Nirmal Kumar Bose, 129–148. Anthropological Survey of India, Memoir no. 7. Calcutta.

Patnaik, Nityananda, and Ajit Kishore Ray (1960). "Oilmen or Teli." In *Data on Caste: Orissa,* edited by Nirmal Kumar Bose, 9–79. Anthropological Survey of India, Memoir no. 7. Calcutta.

Patterson, Maureen L. P. (1981). *South Asian Civilizations: A Bibliographic Synthesis.* Chicago: University of Chicago Press.

Prasad, R. K. (1981). "The Parahaiyas: A Study in Nature-Man-Spirit Complex." In *Nature-Man-Spirit Complex in Tribal India,* edited by R. S. Mann and Vijoy S. Sahay, 57–67. New Delhi: Concept Publishing Co.

Radcliffe-Brown, Alfred Reginald (1922). *The Andaman Islanders: A Study in Social Anthropology.* Cambridge: Cambridge University Press. Reprint. 1948. Glencoe: Free Press.

Raghavan, M. D. (1957). *Handsome Beggars: The Rodiyas of Ceylon.* Colombo: Colombo Book Centre.

Raghavan, M. D. (1962). *The Karava of Ceylon: Society and Culture.* Colombo: K. V. G. de Silva & Sons.

Raghaviah, V. (1962). *The Yanadis.* New Delhi: Bharatiya Adimjati Sevak Sangh.

Rangachari, Kadamki (1931). *The Sri Vaishnava Brahmans.* Bulletin of the Madras Government Museum, [n.s., general section, vol. 2, pt. 2]. Madras: Government Press

Ray, P. C. (1965). *The Lodha and Their Spirit-Possessed Men: A Psycho-Socio-Cultural Study.* Anthropological Survey of India, Memoir no. 15. Calcutta.

Risley, H. H. (1891). *The Tribes and Castes of Bengal: Ethnographic Glossary.* Calcutta: Secretariat Press. Reprint. 1981. Calcutta: Firma K. L. Mukhopadhyay.

Rizvi, S. N. H. (1990). *The Shompen, a Vanishing Tribe of the Great Nicobar Island.* Calcutta: Seagull Books; Anthropological Survey of India.

Robertson, George Scott (1896). *The Kafirs of the Hindu Kush.* London: Lawrence & Bullen. Reprint. 1970. New York: Johnson Reprint Corp.

Roche, Patrick A. (1984). *Fishermen of the Coromandel: A Social Study of the Paravas of the Coromandel.* New Delhi: Manohar.

Rose, H. A. (1911). *A Glossary of the Tribes and Castes of the Punjab and North-West Frontier Province.* 2 vols. Lahore: Superintendent of Government Printing. Reprints. 1970. Patiala: Languages Department of Punjab University. 1990. New Delhi: Asian Educational Services.

Rosser, Colin (1960). "A 'Hermit' Village in Kulu." In *India's Villages.* 2nd ed., edited by M. N. Srinivas, 77–89. Bombay: Asia Publishing House.

Roy, Jitendra Kumar, and B. C. Roy (1982). *Hunger and Physique: A Study of the Juang Population of Orissa.* Anthropological Survey of India, Memoir no. 55. Calcutta.

Roy, Sachin (1960). *Aspects of Padam-Minyong Culture.* Shillong: North-East Frontier Agency.

Roy, Sarat Chandra (1926). *The Birhors: A Little Known Jungle Tribe of Chota Nagpur.* Ranchi: Man in India Office.

Roy, Sarat Chandra, and Ramesh Chandra Roy (1937). *The Kharias.* 2 vols. Ranchi: Man in India Office.

Ruhela, Satya Pal (1968). *The Gaduliya Lohars of Rajasthan—A Study in the Sociology of Nomadism.* New Delhi: Impex India.

Russell, R. V., and Hira Lal, eds. (1916). *The Tribes and Castes of the Central Provinces of India.* 4 vols. London: Macmillan. Reprint. 1969. Oosterhout: Anthropological Publications.

Ryan, Bryce (1953). *Caste in Modern Ceylon: The Sinhalese System in Transition.* New Brunswick, N.J.: Rutgers University Press.

Rymbai, T. (1969). "The Jaintias, Also Called Pnars." In *Tribes of Assam,* edited by S. Barkataki, 42–49. New Delhi: National Book Trust.

Saikia, Paban Chandra (1976). *The Dibongiyas: Social and Religious Life of a Priestly Community.* Delhi: B. R. Publishing Corp.

Saksena, R. N. (1962). *Social Economy of a Polyandrous People.* Rev. ed. Bombay: Asia Publishing House.

Sanyal, Charu Chandra (1965). *The Rajbansis of North*

Bengal: A Study of a Hindu Social Group. Calcutta: Asiatic Society of Bengal.

Sarkar, Jayanta (1987). *Society, Culture, and Ecological Adaptation among Three Tribes of Arunachal Pradesh.* Anthropological Survey of India, Memoir no. 68. Calcutta.

Sarkar, Jayanta (1990). *The Jarawa.* Calcutta: Seagull Books; Anthropological Survey of India.

Sarkar, S. S., et al. (1959). *A Physical Survey of the Kadar of Kerala.* Anthropological Survey of India, Memoir no. 6. Calcutta.

Save, Khanderao Jagannath (1945). *The Warlis.* Bombay: Padma Publications.

Saxena, Ranvir Prakash (1964). *Tribal Economy in Central India.* Calcutta: Firma K. L. Mukhopadhyay.

Sengupta, Syamal Kanti (1970). *The Social Profiles of the Mahalis, the Tribal Basketmakers of Midnapur.* Calcutta: Firma K. L. Mukhopadhyay.

Shah, Ghanshyam (1984). *Economic Differentiations and Tribal Identity.* Delhi: Ajanta Publications.

Shah, P. G. (1958). *Dublas of Gujarat.* New Delhi: Bharatiya Adimjati Sevak Sangh.

Shakespear, John (1912). *The Lushei Kuki Clans.* London: Macmillan.

Sharma, R. R. P. (1961). *The Sherdukpens.* Shillong: North-East Frontier Agency.

Shukla, Brahma Kumar (1959). *The Daflas of the Subansiri Region.* Shillong: North-East Frontier Agency.

Siegel, Lee (1991). *Net of Magic: Wonders and Deceptions in India.* Chicago: University of Chicago Press.

Singh, Pradip (1981). "Nature-Man-Spirit Complex of a Hill Tribe: A Restudy." In *Nature-Man-Spirit Complex in Tribal India,* edited by R. S. Mann and Vijoy S. Sahay, 9–40. New Delhi: Concept Publishing Co.

Singh, Sheetal Prasad (1974). "The Vanishing 'Shompen' Tribe of Great Nicobar: Current Problems and Remedies for Survival." *Vanyajati* 22(2):50–58.

Sinha, Dikshit (1984). *The Hill Kharia of Purulia: A Study on the Impact of Poverty on a Hunting and Gathering Tribe.* Anthropological Survey of India, Memoir no. 59. Calcutta.

Sinha, R. K. (1981). "A Note on the Nature-Man-Spirit Complex of a Tribe (Pando)." In *Nature-Man-Spirit Complex in Tribal India,* edited by R. S. Mann and Vijoy S. Sahay, 69–115. New Delhi: Concept Publishing Co.

Sinha, Raghuvir (1962). *The Akas.* Shillong: Adviser's Secretariat.

Siraj ul Hassan, Syed (1920). *Castes and Tribes of the Nizam's Dominions.* 2 vols. Bombay: Times Press. Reprint. 1990. Gurgaon: Vintage Books.

Srinivas, Mysore Narasimhachar (1952). *Religion and Society among the Coorgs of South India.* Oxford: Clarendon Press. Reprint. 1965. Bombay: Asia Publishing House.

Srivastava, L. R. N. (1962). *The Gallongs.* Shillong: Adviser's Secretariat.

Srivastava, Ram P. (1966). "Tribe-Caste Mobility in India and the Case of Kumaon Bhotias." In *Caste and Kin in Nepal, India, and Ceylon: Anthropological Studies in Hindu-Buddhist Contact Zones,* edited by Christoph von Fürer-Haimendorf, 161–212. New Delhi: Sterling Publishers.

Stevenson, Margaret Sinclair (1930). *Without the Pale: The Life Story of an Outcaste.* Calcutta: Association Press.

Syamchoudhuri, N. K., and M. M. Das (1973). *The Lalung Society: A Theme for Analytical Ethnography.* Anthropological Survey of India. Calcutta.

Thundy, Zacharias P. (1983). *South Indian Folktales of Kadar.* Meerut: Archana Publications.

Thurston, Edgar, and Kadamki Rangachari, eds. (1909). *Castes and Tribes of Southern India.* 7 vols. Madras: Government Press. [Numerous reprints.]

Thusu, Kidar Nath (1965). *The Dhurwa of Bastar.* Anthropological Survey of India, Memoir no. 16. Calcutta.

Thusu, Kidar Nath (1977). *The Pengo Porajas of Koraput: An Ethnographic Survey.* Anthropological Survey of India, Memoir no. 39. Calcutta.

Thusu, Kidar Nath, and Makhan Jha (1969). *Ollar Gadba of Koraput.* Anthropological Survey of India, Memoir no. 27. Calcutta.

Trivedi, Harshad R. (1986). *The Mers of Saurashtra Revisited and Studied in the Light of Socio-Cultural Change and Cross-Cousin Marriage.* New Delhi: Concept Publishing Co.

Vidyarthi, Lalita Prasad (1963). *The Maler: A Study in Nature-Man-Spirit Complex of a Hill Tribe in Bihar.* Calcutta: Bookland.

Vidyarthi, Lalita Prasad, and V. S. Upadhyay (1980). *The Kharia: Then and Now, a Comparative Study of Hill, Dhelki, and Dudh Kharia of the Central-Eastern Region of India.* New Delhi: Concept Publishing Co.

Ethnonym Index to Appendix

Bajania
Bajantri—**Mangala**
Bajg—**Nat**
Bakkaru
Bakta—**Bagata**
Balagai—**Holeya**
Balahar—**Basor**
Balahi
Balai—**Balahi**
Bala-Jangam—**Mailari**
Balasantosha—**Telaga**
Balija
Balji—**Balija**
Balte—**Kuki**
Bamcha—**Bavacha**
Bam-Margi
Banajiga—**Balija**
Banaphar
Banda—**Mondaru**
Bandar—**Kadera**
Bandhalgoti
Bandhara
Bandhilgoti—**Bandhalgoti**
Bandhugoti—**Bandhalgoti**
Bandi
Bangali
Bania—**Komati**
Banjara
Banjari—**Banjara**
Banjhilgoti—**Bandhalgoti**
Bansberia—**Beria**
Bansi—**Suraj-Bansi**
Bansphod—**Basor**
Bansphor—**Basor**
Bant
Bantu—**Mutrasi**
Banua—**Buna**
Baori—**Bawariya**
Baoria—**Badhak**
Baqal—**Komati**
Barahatta—**Charan**
Barai—**Tamdi**
Baraik—**Ganda**
Baraiya—**Tamdi**
Bara Mohmand—**Mohmand**
Barath—**Charan**
Baraua—**Bhoi**
Barchain—**Chain**
Barekari—**Besta**
Baretha—**Dhobi**
Bargah—**Bari**
Bargaha—**Bari**
Bargahi—**Bari**
Bargandi—**Korava**
Bargi Dhangar—**Hatkar**
Bargujar
Barhai
Barhi—**Barhai**
Bari
Barkar—**Besta**
Barodia—**Vitolana**
Barua Magh—**Marma**
Barui—**Tamdi**
Barwala—**Batwal**
Barwar
Basdewa
Basor
Batgam

Bathudi—**Bottada**
Battu Turaka—**Bhatraja**
Batwal
Bauri—**Bawariya**
Bauri—**Bhoi**
Bauria—**Bawariya**
Baurio—**Bavuri**
Bavacha
Bavina—**Bhavin**
Bavuri
Bawaria—**Badhak**
Bawaria—**Bawariya**
Bawariya
Bazigar—**Nat**
Bed—**Bedar**
Bedar
Bedea—**Bedar**
Bedia—**Bedar**
Bedia—**Beria**
Bediya—**Bedar**
Bediya—**Beria**
Beesti—**Bhishti**
Behara—**Bhoi**
Behna—**Dhuniya**
Bejea—**Bedar**
Bejia—**Bedar**
Beldar
Beldar—**Upparwar**
Bendar—**Bedar**
Bendar—**Madiga**
Bengali—**Bangali**
Bentbansi—**Dharkar**
Berad—**Bedar**
Berava
Beria
Beria—**Bedar**
Beri Chetti
Beriya—**Bedar**
Beriya—**Beria**
Besta
Bestha—**Besta**
Betta Kuruba—**Urali**
Betta Kurumba—**Urali**
Bettu Kurumba—**Urali**
Bhabra
Bhadauriya
Bhadbhunja—**Bharbhunja**
Bhadrapad—**Viramushti**
Bhadri—**Joshi**
Bhagat
Bhagwat—**Telaga**
Bhaina
Bhakat—**Bhagat**
Bhakta—**Bagata**
Bhaktollu—**Pichakuntala**
Bhale Sultan
Bhamta
Bhamtya—**Bhamta**
Bhand—**Bhandari**
Bhandari
Bhandari—**Nai**
Bhangi
Bhangia—**Bhangi**
Bhanr—**Bhandari**
Bhaosar—**Chhipa**
Bhar
Bhar—**Bharia**
Bharadi—**Davre Jogi**

Bharadwaj—**Bhar**
Bharai
Bharat—**Bhar**
Bharbhunja
Bharewa—**Tamera**
Bharia
Bharia-Bhumia—**Bharia**
Bharpatwa—**Bhar**
Bharvad—**Gadaria**
Bhat
Bhat—**Bhatraja**
Bhatia
Bhatiya—**Bhatia**
Bhatiyara
Bhat Murti—**Bhatraja**
Bhato—**Bhatraja**
Bhatra
Bhatra—**Ramaiya**
Bhatraja
Bhatraju—**Bhatraja**
Bhatrazu—**Bhat**
Bhatrazu—**Bhatraja**
Bhatt—**Bhat**
Bhatti
Bhattra—**Bhatra**
Bhatwandlu—**Bhatraja**
Bhausagar—**Chhipa**
Bhavaguna—**Bhandari**
Bhavaiya
Bhavasagari—**Chhipa**
Bhavaya—**Bhandari**
Bhavin
Bhavsar—**Chhipa**
Bhenrihar—**Gadaria**
Bhiksha Kunte—**Kunte**
Bhikshuk—**Deshastha Brahman**
Bhilala
Bhillakabberu—**Besta**
Bhil Mina—**Mina**
Bhind—**Bind**
Bhisak—**Baidya**
Bhishti
Bhisti—**Bhishti**
Bhod—**Bhutia**
Bhogam—**Devadasi**
Bhoi
Bhoir—**Bhoyar**
Bhoksa
Bholia—**Bhulia**
Bholwa—**Bhulia**
Bhondari—**Bhandari**
Bhopa—**Rabari**
Bhope—**Bhute**
Bhoriya—**Bhulia**
Bhot—**Bhutia**
Bhotia—**Bhutia**
Bhotiya—**Bhutia**
Bhottada—**Bottada**
Bhoyar
Bhuimali—**Bhuinmali**
Bhuimali—**Hari**
Bhuinhar—**Babhan**
Bhuinmali
Bhuiya Magh—**Marma**
Bhuj—**Bharbhunja**
Bhujari—**Bharbhunja**
Bhujua—**Bharbhunja**
Bhuksa—**Bhoksa**

Gangeddulu—**Gangeddu**
Gangemakkalu—**Besta**
Gangimakkalu—**Besta**
Gangota
Gangte—**Kuki**
Ganig—**Teli**
Ganiga
Ganiga—**Teli**
Ganigaru—**Teli**
Ganikan—**Kaniyan**
Ganrar
Ganreriya—**Gadaria**
Ganthachor—**Bhamta**
Garaba—**Gadba**
Garariya—**Gadaria**
Gareri—**Gadaria**
Garpagari
Garudi—**Nat**
Gauda
Gauda—**Gaur**
Gauda—**Nador**
Gauda Chitrakara—**Gudikara**
Gauddes—**Gauda**
Gaudo
Gaudo—**Gauda**
Gauliga—**Gavli**
Gauliga—**Golla**
Gaur
Gauria
Gaur Rajput
Gavada
Gavada—**Golla**
Gavali—**Golla**
Gavandi—**Gamadi**
Gavara—**Komati**
Gavit—**Gamit**
Gavli
Ghache—**Basor**
Ghadi
Ghadshi
Ghaijo—**Nai**
Ghanche—**Basor**
Ghanchi—**Basor**
Ghanchi—**Teli**
Ghantchor—**Bhamta**
Ghantra—**Lohar**
Ghara—**Gauria**
Ghardera—**Babria**
Ghasi—**Ghasia**
Ghasia
Ghasiya—**Ghasia**
Ghermedi
Gherwal Rajput—**Gaharwar Rajput**
Ghirth
Ghisadi
Ghisari—**Lohar**
Ghor—**Banjara**
Ghosi
Ghumar—**Kumhar**
Ghumiar—**Kumhar**
Gibidki—**Joshi**
Girhasth Brahman—**Babhan**
Goa Chetti—**Kudumi Chetti**
Goan
Goanese—**Goan**
Gohar Herkeri—**Banjara**
Gokulashta Gusain—**Vallabacharya**
Gol—**Golla**

Gola
Gola—**Golla**
Gola—**Khava**
Golak Brahman
Golalare—**Alkari**
Golandaz—**Kadera**
Golapurab
Golar—**Golla**
Golkar—**Golla**
Golla
Gollakulam—**Pichakuntala**
Gollam—**Golla**
Gollarajulu—**Golla**
Gollewar—**Golla**
Gondaliga—**Gondhali**
Gond-Gowari
Gondhali
Gond Majhwar—**Majhwar**
Gone
Goniga—**Gone**
Gonr—**Bharbhunja**
Gonsavi
Gopal
Gorait
Gorakhnathi—**Kanphata**
Gorpalwad—**Telaga**
Gosain
Gosangi—**Madiga**
Gosayi—**Gosain**
Goswami—**Gosain**
Gouda—**Goundala**
Gouli—**Gavli**
Goundala
Gourhi—**Mallah**
Govardhan—**Golak Brahman**
Gowari
Gowder—**Gauda**
Goyigama
Grihastha—**Deshastha Brahman**
Grihasth Brahman—**Babhan**
Gudigar—**Gudikara**
Gudigara—**Gudikara**
Gudikara
Guite—**Kuki**
Gujarati Brahman
Gujrati Brahman—**Gujarati Brahman**
Gulgulia
Gulla—**Golla**
Gullar—**Golla**
Gunlodu
Gunrhi—**Mallah**
Gurao
Gurav—**Gurao**
Gurava
Guriya—**Mallah**
Gurjar Brahman—**Gujarati Brahman**
Gurjara Brahman—**Gujarati Brahman**
Gurukkal—**Ambalavasi**
Gurusthulu—**Balija**
Gusain—**Gosain**

Habashi—**Sidi**
Habshi—**Sidi**
Habura
Haddi
Hadi—**Haddi**
Haiga—**Havik Brahman**
Haihaivansi—**Haihaya Rajput**

Haihaya Rajput
Hajam—**Nai**
Hajango—**Kuki**
Hajjam—**Nai**
Hajuri—**Khava**
Hakkipikki—**Hale Paika**
Hakuru—**Vahumpura**
Halaba—**Pentiya**
Halagama—**Salagama**
Halba
Halba—**Pentiya**
Halbi—**Halba**
Halepaik—**Hale Paika**
Hale Paika
Halia-Das—**Kewat**
Halleer—**Hallir**
Hallikar
Hallikararu—**Hallikar**
Hallikar Okkaliga—**Hallikar**
Hallir
Halpati—**Dubla**
Halvakki Vakkal
Halwai
Hanbar—**Golla**
Hande Kuruba—**Kuruba**
Hande Vazir—**Kuruba**
Handichikka—**Handi Jogi**
Handi Jogi
Hannali
Hanneng—**Kuki**
Haokip—**Kuki**
Haolai—**Kuki**
Harakantra
Harbola—**Basdewa**
Hardas—**Chitrakathi**
Hari
Hari—**Bhangi**
Harni
Har-Santan—**Hari**
Hasala—**Hasalar**
Hasalar
Hasalaru—**Hasalar**
Haslar—**Hasalar**
Hasula—**Hasalar**
Hatgar—**Hatkar**
Hati
Hatkar
Hatkar—**Devanga**
Haupit—**Kuki**
Havig—**Havik Brahman**
Havika—**Havik Brahman**
Havik Brahman
Hawaidar—**Kadera**
Hebbe-Gauda—**Mukri**
Helav—**Helava**
Helava
Hena
Henaya—**Hena**
Hengna—**Kuki**
Heri—**Ahar**
Hill Miri—**Miri**
Hill Pulaya—**Pulluvan**
Hinna
Ho
Holar—**Holeya**
Holaya—**Holeya**
Holeya
Holia

Holuva—**Pentiya**
Holva—**Pentiya**
Hongsungh—**Kuki**
Hon-Potdar—**Sonar**
Hosadevara Okkalu—**Morasu Okkalu**
Hrangkhwal—**Kuki**
Hrusso—**Aka**
Hulsavar—**Hasalar**
Hunu
Husaini Brahman

Idaiyan
Idiga
Idiga—**Goundala**
Idigar—**Idiga**
Idu-Mishmi—**Mishmi**
Ilakeband—**Patwa**
Ilaqeband—**Patwa**
Ilayatu—**Ambalavasi**
Illavan—**Ezhuva**
Indra Sudra—**Kuruba**
Injhwar
Iraki—**Iraqi**
Irani
Iraqi
Irava—**Ezhuva**
Izhava—**Ezhuva**
Izhuva—**Ezhuva**

Jad—**Besta**
Jad—**Devanga**
Jadam
Jadar—**Jingar**
Jadon—**Yadu Rajput**
Jadua-Brahman
Jaduah-Brahman—**Jadua-Brahman**
Jaga—**Basdewa**
Jaintia
Jaiswar—**Bhatti**
Jalagadugu—**Sonjhara**
Jalap
Jalari
Jalia Kaibarta—**Kewat**
Jalia Kaibartta—**Kewat**
Jaliya—**Kewat**
Jalo—**Kewat**
Jalwa—**Kewat**
Janappan
Jangal Jati—**Kuruvikkaran**
Jangam—**Jangama**
Jangama
Jangtei—**Kuki**
Janjua
Jarawa
Jasondhi—**Bhat**
Jathikarta—**Telaga**
Jati
Jaunsari
Javeri—**Johari**
Javheri—**Johari**
Jayantia—**Jaintia**
Jele—**Kewat**
Jeliya—**Kewat**
Jemadar—**Kotwal**
Jetti
Jhadi Telenga
Jhalo—**Malo**
Jhalo Malo—**Malo**

Jhara—**Sonjhara**
Jhinwar
Jhir—**Jhinwar**
Jhira—**Sonjhara**
Jhiwar—**Jhinwar**
Jhora—**Sonjhara**
Jildgar—**Mochi**
Jimdar—**Khambu**
Jingar
Jingar—**Mochi**
Jirayat—**Mochi**
Jogi—**Jugi**
Jogi—**Yogi**
Johari
Joharia—**Johari**
Joiya
Jolaha—**Julaha**
Jolha—**Julaha**
Jongbe—**Kuki**
Joshi
Jotgi—**Dakaut**
Jouhari—**Johari**
Juang
Jugi
Julaha
Julaha—**Padma Sale**
Julahe—**Julaha**
Jumia Magh—**Marma**
Jyandra—**Devanga**
Jyntia—**Jaintia**
Jyotishi—**Joshi**

Kabbaligar—**Besta**
Kabber—**Besta**
Kabbera—**Besta**
Kabher—**Besta**
Kabiraj—**Baidya**
Kabir-Panthi
Kabuli
Kabuliwallah—**Kabuli**
Kabutari—**Beria**
Kacha Gauliga—**Golla**
Kachara—**Kachera**
Kachari
Kachera
Kachhi
Kachhi—**Kachi Meman**
Kachhia
Kachhwaha Rajput
Kachi Meman
Kadan—**Kadar**
Kadar
Kader
Kadera
Kadhera—**Kadera**
Kadia
Kadir—**Kadar**
Kadiya—**Kadia**
Kadu Golla
Kadu Kuruba
Kadupattan
Kaet—**Kayasth**
Kaeth—**Kayasth**
Kafir
Kaghzi
Kahar—**Bhoi**
Kahar—**Jhinwar**
Kahar Bhoi—**Bhoi**

Kahar Bhui—**Bhoi**
Kahtar—**Khattar**
Kahut
Kaibartta—**Kewat**
Kaibartta-Das—**Kewat**
Kaikadi—**Erakala**
Kaikadi—**Korava**
Kaikara—**Kavikara**
Kaikari—**Korava**
Kaikkoolar—**Kaikolan**
Kaikolan
Kain—**Sonar**
Kainya—**Sonar**
Kait—**Kayasth**
Kaith—**Kayasth**
Kakhen—**Singpho**
Kakka Kuravan—**Kakkalan**
Kakkalan
Kakkan—**Kakkalan**
Kalachuri—**Haihaya Rajput**
Kalal—**Goundala**
Kalal—**Iraqi**
Kalal—**Kalar**
Kalanady
Kalanga
Kalar
Kalari Panikkan—**Kaniyan**
Kalavant—**Bhavin**
Kalawant—**Devadasi**
Kalawant—**Mirasi**
Kalingi—**Kalanga**
Kalingulu—**Kalanga**
Kalinji—**Kalanga**
Kalkola—**Beldar**
Kalladi-mangam—**Mondaru**
Kalladi-siddhan—**Mondaru**
Kallan—**Kallar**
Kallar
Kalu—**Teli**
Kaluvadi—**Kudubi**
Kalwar—**Kalar**
Kalyanakulam—**Mangala**
Kaman Mishmi—**Mishmi**
Kamar
Kamar
Kamathi—**Madiga**
Kamboh
Kami
Kamia—**Kami**
Kamma
Kammala—**Kammalan**
Kammalan
Kammara—**Kammalan**
Kamsala—**Kammalan**
Kamsale—**Kammalan**
Kanada Brahman
Kanakajatiyavaru—**Kuruba**
Kanakkan
Kanakkan—**Kanikkar**
Kanaladi
Kanapulaya—**Pulluvan**
Kanaujia Brahman—**Kanyakubja Brahman**
Kanaujiya—**Bhar**
Kanaujiya—**Kanyakubja Brahman**
Kanaura—**Kanet**
Kanaurese—**Kanet**
Kanchan—**Devadasi**

Kanchaviralu—**Mailari**
Kandera—**Dhuniya**
Kandera—**Kadera**
Kandeyo—**Vahumpura**
Kandha
Kandha Ganda—**Kandha**
Kandu—**Bharbhunja**
Kanet
Kangra Brahman
Kani—**Kanikkar**
Kanialanath Raval—**Raval Jogi**
Kanikar—**Kanikkar**
Kanikaran—**Kanikkar**
Kanikkar
Kanikkaran—**Kanikkar**
Kani Razu—**Bhatraja**
Kanisan—**Kaniyan**
Kaniyan
Kannadiyan
Kannaji Bhat—**Bhatraja**
Kanphata
Kansabanik—**Tamera**
Kansar—**Tamera**
Kansara—**Tamera**
Kansari—**Tamera**
Kantaha—**Mahabrahman**
Kanu—**Bharbhunja**
Kanwar—**Kawar**
Kanyakubja Brahman
Kanyan—**Kaniyan**
Kaora—**Khairwar**
Kapali
Kaparia—**Basdewa**
Kapariya
Kapdi—**Basdewa**
Kapewar—**Munur**
Kappiliyan
Karagir—**Nai**
Karaiyan—**Pattanavan**
Karan
Karana—**Karan**
Karanga—**Korava**
Karanjkar—**Jingar**
Karataha—**Mahabrahman**
Karava
Karavazhi
Karenga—**Korava**
Kare Okkalu
Karhada Brahman
Karhade Brahman—**Karhada Brahman**
Karhataka Brahman—**Karhada Brahman**
Karigar—**Beldar**
Karimbalan—**Karimpalan**
Karimpalan
Karmakar—**Kamar**
Karnam—**Karan**
Karna Sale
Karnati—**Nat**
Karnatic Brahman—**Kanada Brahman**
Karral—**Chandal**
Karumpuraththal—**Kappiliyan**
Karunjra—**Kunjra**
Kasai
Kasar—**Bohora**
Kasar—**Tamera**
Kasban—**Devadasi**
Kasbi—**Devadasi**
Kasera—**Tamera**

Kashikapdi—**Tirmali**
Kassab—**Kasai**
Kasta Brahman
Kastha
Katabu—**Killekyata**
Kataha—**Mahabrahman**
Katakoti—**Katalarayan**
Katalarayan
Katbo—**Telaga**
Katera—**Dhuniya**
Kathak
Kathar—**Khattar**
Kathi
Kathia—**Kathi**
Kathik—**Kathak**
Kathiyara
Kathkari—**Katkari**
Kathodi—**Katkari**
Kathodia—**Katkari**
Katia
Katibaglodu—**Telaga**
Katika—**Kasai**
Katike
Katikilu—**Katike**
Katipappla—**Telaga**
Katkari
Kattalan—**Ulladan**
Kattan—**Ulladan**
Katti Bomalawaru—**Telaga**
Kattu Mahrati—**Kuruvikkaran**
Katua—**Katia**
Katwa—**Katia**
Kaur—**Kawar**
Kavara
Kavarai—**Balija**
Kavikara
Kawar
Kaya—**Kayasth**
Kayalan
Kayashta—**Kayasth**
Kayasth
Kayath—**Kayasth**
Keer—**Kir**
Kehal
Kelasi—**Nai**
Keot—**Kewat**
Kewat
Keyot—**Kewat**
Khaa—**Kho**
Khadri Vaishnava—**Satani**
Khagar—**Kotwal**
Khaira—**Khairwar**
Khairwa—**Khairwar**
Khairwar
Khambu
Khamti
Khandait
Khandayat—**Khandait**
Khangar—**Kotwal**
Khant
Khapariya—**Kapariya**
Kharadi—**Barhai**
Kharak
Khareng—**Kuki**
Kharia
Kharia—**Lodhi**
Kharian—**Kharia**
Kharpatil—**Agri**

Kharral
Kharria—**Kharia**
Kharva
Kharvi—**Kharva**
Kharwar
Kharwar—**Khairwar**
Khasa—**Khasiya**
Khasiya
Khasiya Rajput—**Dusadh**
Khatak—**Khattak**
Khati—**Lohar**
Khatik
Khatik—**Kasai**
Khatri
Khatriya—**Satani**
Khattak
Khattar
Khattri—**Khatri**
Khava
Khawathlang—**Kuki**
Khawchung—**Kuki**
Khayra—**Khairwar**
Khelma—**Kuki**
Khephong—**Kuki**
Kheria—**Kharia**
Kheria—**Lodhi**
Kherwar—**Khairwar**
Kherwar—**Kharwar**
Khetri
Khewat—**Kewat**
Kho
Khodalo—**Bavuri**
Khokar
Khokur—**Khokar**
Kholhou—**Kuki**
Khothalong—**Kuki**
Khubar—**Kumhar**
Khuhar—**Kumhar**
Khyan—**Kewat**
Kiliket—**Killekyata**
Killekyata
Killekyatha—**Killekyata**
Killikiyata—**Killekyata**
Kingariya—**Kingriya**
Kingriha—**Kingriya**
Kingriya
Kinnara
Kinnara—**Kanet**
Kinnaurese—**Kanet**
Kinner—**Kanet**
Kiot—**Kewat**
Kir
Kirad—**Kirar**
Kirar
Kisada—**Nagasia**
Kisan—**Nagasia**
Kizhakkan Pulaya—**Pulluvan**
Ko—**Kho**
Kocch—**Kochh**
Koch—**Kochh**
Kochh
Koch-Mandai—**Kochh**
Kochuvelan
Kochuvelanmar—**Kochuvelan**
Koeri—**Koiri**
Kohli
Koil Pantala—**Koil Tampuran**

Luvana—**Lohana**

Macchi
Machchhi—**Macchi**
Machhandar—**Bhoi**
Machhi—**Macchi**
Machhua—**Mallah**
Machhua—**Tiyar**
Machigar—**Mochi**
Machinde Bhoi—**Macchi**
Madak—**Madhunapit**
Madari
Madgi—**Madiga**
Madhunapit
Madig—**Mang**
Madiga
Madigaru—**Madiga**
Madigowd—**Madiga**
Madiwal—**Agasa**
Madiyal—**Dhobi**
Madkar—**Bhandari**
Madru—**Madiga**
Mag—**Marma**
Magada—**Bhatraja**
Magahaya Brahman—**Babhan**
Magh—**Marma**
Mahabrahman
Maha-Brahman—**Acharaj**
Mahali—**Mahli**
Mahali—**Nai**
Maha Malasar—**Malasar**
Mahanti—**Karan**
Mahanubhao—**Manbhao**
Mahapatra—**Mahabrahman**
Mahara—**Koshti**
Maharana—**Jingar**
Mahatmana—**Manbhao**
Mahato—**Ganda**
Mahdavia Musalman
Mahesari Marwadi
Mahesri—**Mahesari Marwadi**
Maheswari—**Mahesari Marwadi**
Mahia
Mahigir—**Bhoi**
Mahili—**Mahli**
Mahli
Mahmand—**Mohmand**
Mahra—**Bhoi**
Mahra—**Jhinwar**
Mahtam
Mahton
Mailari
Maina—**Mina**
Maira—**Mayara**
Majhi—**Majhwar**
Majhia—**Majhwar**
Majhwar
Mal—**Mala**
Mal—**Maler**
Mala
Mala Adiyar—**Malayadiar**
Mala Arayan
Malacharivan Malasar—**Malasar**
Malai Arayan—**Mala Arayan**
Malai Malasar—**Malasar**
Malai Vedam—**Mala Vedan**
Malai Vedan—**Mala Vedan**
Malakar—**Mali**

Malakkaran
Malakkuravan—**Mala Kuravan**
Mala Koravan—**Mala Kuravan**
Mala Kuravan
Mala Malasar—**Malasar**
Malankudi—**Vishavan**
Malankuravan—**Mala Kuravan**
Mala Panickkar—**Mala Panikkar**
Mala Panikkar
Malapulaya
Mala Pulayan—**Malapulaya**
Malasar
Mala Ulladan—**Ulladan**
Malavara—**Kavikara**
Mala Vedan
Malaveder—**Mala Vedan**
Malavetan—**Mala Vedan**
Mala Vettuvan—**Mala Vedan**
Malayadiar
Malayalar
Malayalee—**Malayali**
Malayali
Malayali Kshatriya
Malayan
Malayarayan—**Kanikkar**
Malayarayan—**Mala Arayan**
Malayarayar—**Mala Arayan**
Male—**Maler**
Male Kudia—**Kudiya**
Male Kudiya—**Kudiya**
Maler
Maleru—**Maler**
Malha—**Mallah**
Malha Malasar—**Malasar**
Mali
Mali Gujarati
Mallabhatlu—**Helava**
Mallah
Malla Kshatriya—**Jetti**
Mallige Madevi Vakkalu—**Agasa**
Malo
Malo-Patni—**Malo**
Mal Paharia—**Maler**
Mana
Manbhao
Manbhav—**Manbhao**
Mand—**Mer**
Manda Buchawad—**Telaga**
Mandadan Chetti
Mandatan Chetti—**Mandadan Chetti**
Mandula Gollalu—**Handi Jogi**
Mandula Jogi—**Handi Jogi**
Mang
Manga—**Mang**
Mangala
Mangala—**Nai**
Mangan—**Charan**
Mangela
Mangela—**Mang**
Mang Garodi—**Mang-Garori**
Mang-Garori
Mang Garudi—**Mang-Garori**
Mangjel—**Kuki**
Mang Raut—**Mang**
Manihar—**Kachera**
Manipuri
Manjhi—**Majhwar**
Mannan

Mannewar
Manyari—**Johari**
Marakkayar
Maral—**Mali**
Maramagri—**Marma**
Maran—**Ambalavasi**
Marar—**Ambalavasi**
Marar—**Mali**
Maratha Bhoi
Marati
Maravan
Marayan—**Ambalavasi**
Mariyari—**Muriari**
Marma
Marwadi Brahman
Marwari Shravak
Marwat
Masan Jogi—**Telaga**
Mashki—**Bhishti**
Matadi—**Upparwar**
Matam—**Mahtam**
Matangi Makallu—**Madiga**
Matha
Matia Kanbi
Matial—**Mochi**
Matko—**Nai**
Matkuda—**Beldar**
Maulik
Maulik—**Dhimal**
Mauntadan Chetty—**Mandadan Chetti**
Mavchi—**Gamit**
Mavilan
Mavillon—**Mavilan**
Mayara
Mdariya—**Madari**
Mech
Mechi—**Mech**
Medar—**Basor**
Medara—**Basor**
Medarakaran—**Basor**
Medare—**Basor**
Medarlu—**Basor**
Meerolu—**Darzi**
Megh—**Meghval**
Meghval
Meghwal—**Meghval**
Mehar—**Bhulia**
Mehtar—**Bhangi**
Meithi
Melakkaran
Melakudi—**Kudiya**
Memar—**Upparwar**
Mendicant Telega—**Telaga**
Meng—**Meghval**
Menghvar—**Meghval**
Menghwal—**Meghval**
Mer
Merai—**Darzi**
Mesri Marwadi—**Mahesari Marwadi**
Mestri—**Panan**
Mewa-farosh—**Kunjra**
Mhali—**Nai**
Mhed—**Mer**
Mher—**Mer**
Mian
Mihir—**Bhulia**
Mihngh—**Meghval**
Mihtar—**Hari**

Mina
Minyong—**Adi**
Mir—**Mirasi**
Mirasi
Miri
Mirshikar—**Pardhi**
Misao—**Kuki**
Mi-shing—**Miri**
Mishmi
Mistri—**Barhai**
Mith Gavada—**Gavada**
Mithiya—**Halwai**
Miyadar—**Basor**
Mizel—**Kuki**
Mochavaru—**Mochi**
Mochi
Mochigar—**Mochi**
Modak—**Mayara**
Modaliyar—**Mudaliyar**
Modi-Raj—**Mutrasi**
Moger
Mogh—**Marma**
Mogha—**Rabari**
Moghia—**Pardhi**
Mohmand
Moili—**Suppalig**
Molesalam
Momin
Momin—**Julaha**
Momna—**Momin**
Mondaru
Mondi—**Mondaru**
Mondiwadu—**Mondaru**
Morasu—**Morasu Okkalu**
Morasu Okkalu
Morung—**Tripura**
Motcare—**Gonsavi**
Mowar
Moyili—**Suppalig**
Mro—**Tripura**
Mru—**Tripura**
Mrung—**Tripura**
Muamin—**Kachi Meman**
Muchi—**Mochi**
Mudaliyar
Mudi—**Bagdi**
Muduga
Mudugar—**Muduga**
Mudukkan—**Muduga**
Muduvan—**Muduga**
Muduvar—**Muduga**
Mug—**Marma**
Muhial
Mujawar—**Chhalapdar**
Muka Dora—**Konda Dora**
Mukeri—**Banjara**
Mukkava—**Mukkuvan**
Mukkuvan
Mukri
Mulla Kuruman—**Mullukurumba**
Mullakurumber—**Mullukurumba**
Mullukurumba
Multani—**Mochi**
Munnud Kapu—**Munur**
Munnur—**Munur**
Munnurwad—**Munur**
Munur
Munurwar—**Beldar**

Munurwar—**Munur**
Murao—**Koiri**
Murha
Muriari
Murli—**Waghya**
Murli Joshi—**Waghya**
Musabir—**Mochi**
Musahar
Musalli—**Bhangi**
Musalman Brahman—**Husaini Brahman**
Mushahar—**Musahar**
Mushera—**Musahar**
Mussad
Mustigar—**Khetri**
Muthrasi—**Mutrasi**
Muthuvan—**Muduga**
Muthuwan—**Muduga**
Mutracha—**Mutrasi**
Mut-Raj—**Mutrasi**
Mutrasa—**Mutrasi**
Mutrasi
Mutratcha—**Mutrasi**
Muttan
Muttaracha—**Mutrasi**
Muttarasan—**Mutrasi**
Muttatu—**Ambalavasi**
Muttatu—**Mussad**
Muttirajulu—**Mutrasi**
Muttiriyan—**Mutrasi**
Myadar—**Basor**
Myam-ma—**Marma**
Myasa Beda
Myasa Nayakar—**Myasa Beda**
Myatari—**Devanga**

Naddaf—**Dhuniya**
Nadi—**Ulladan**
Nadig—**Nai**
Nador
Nadu Gauda—**Nador**
Nagarakulam—**Nagartha**
Nagarata—**Nagartha**
Nagarattar—**Nagartha**
Nagar Brahman
Nagartha
Nagasia
Nagbansi
Nagesar—**Nagasia**
Nagesia—**Nagasia**
Nagori
Nahal
Naherna—**Nai**
Nahul—**Nahal**
Nai
Naidu—**Balija**
Naik—**Bhavin**
Naik—**Mutrasi**
Naik—**Ramosi**
Naikin—**Bhavin**
Naiklok—**Ramosi**
Nakash Maistri—**Jingar**
Nakkalvandlu—**Kuruvikkaran**
Naksia—**Nagasia**
Nalakeyava—**Nalke**
Nalke
Nama—**Chandal**
Nama-Sudra—**Chandal**
Nambiar—**Ambalavasi**

Nambidi—**Ambalavasi**
Nambiyar—**Ambalavasi**
Nambiyassan—**Ambalavasi**
Nampati—**Ambalavasi**
Namte—**Kuki**
Nanakpanthi
Nanakputra—**Udasi**
Nanakshahi—**Nanakpanthi**
Nanchinad Vellala
Nanku Parisha—**Kammalan**
Nao—**Nai**
Naoda
Napik—**Nai**
Napit—**Nai**
Naqqal—**Bhandari**
Naru
Nat
Nattukottai Chetti
Nattu Malasar—**Malasar**
Nattu Malayan—**Malasar**
Nattuvan
Nau—**Nai**
Naua—**Nai**
Naumuslim
Navandanna
Navayat—**Quraishi**
Navdigar—**Nat**
Naya—**Maulik**
Nayadaru—**Nai**
Nayadi
Nayadi—**Ulladan**
Nayady—**Nayadi**
Nayinda—**Nai**
Neyigeyavaru—**Thakar**
Nhavi—**Nai**
Nihal—**Nahal**
Nihang—**Akali**
Nikumbh
Nilari—**Chhipa**
Nilbandhu—**Gunlodu**
Nilgar—**Chhipa**
Nirali—**Chhipa**
Nishad—**Chandal**
Nishi—**Dafla**
Noniar—**Nunia**
Noniyan—**Nunia**
Nunia
Nuniya—**Nunia**
Nut—**Nat**

Occhan
Od—**Beldar**
Odde—**Beldar**
Odden—**Beldar**
Ode—**Beldar**
Odewandlu—**Beldar**
Odeya—**Vader**
Odh—**Beldar**
Oja—**Konda Dora**
Ojha
Oko-Juwoi
Olee—**Oli**
Olgana—**Bhangi**
Oli
Oliya—**Oli**
Ollares—**Allar**
Omaito—**Omanaito**
Omanaito

Omanatya—**Omanaito**
Onge
Ongee—**Onge**
Oorali Curumaru—**Urali**
Orakzai
Otan
Otari

Pab—**Ganda**
Pachhima Brahman—**Babhan**
Padam—**Adi**
Padiga Raju—**Bhatraja**
Padinjaran Pulaya—**Pulluvan**
Padmaraj—**Pod**
Padma Sale
Padti
Padu—**Batgam**
Padvi—**Gamit**
Paharia—**Maler**
Pahilwan—**Mang-Garori**
Pahlad Bansi—**Bishnoi**
Paidi
Paik
Paite—**Kuki**
Paitu—**Kuki**
Pakanati Jogi—**Handi Jogi**
Pakhali—**Bhishti**
Pakhawaji—**Mirasi**
Palaiyakkaran—**Mutrasi**
Palayakkaran—**Polegar**
Palayan—**Palliyar**
Palee—**Pali**
Palewar—**Bhoi**
Pali
Palie—**Pali**
Paliwar—**Palwar**
Paliya—**Kochh**
Paliya—**Pali**
Paliyan—**Palliyar**
Pallan
Palle—**Palli**
Palleyan—**Palliyar**
Palli
Pallilu—**Palli**
Palliyan—**Palliyar**
Palliyar
Palvada Kotwalia—**Vitolana**
Palwar
Pan—**Ganda**
Pan—**Pano**
Panal—**Pardhan**
Panan
Panara—**Nalke**
Panchadayi—**Kammalan**
Panchal—**Kammalan**
Panchal—**Lohar**
Panchala—**Kammalan**
Panchalan—**Kammalan**
Panchama—**Mala**
Pancham Banajigaru—**Balija**
Panchamollu—**Madiga**
Panchkalshi
Panda—**Dakaut**
Pandaram—**Valluvan**
Pandi Jogulu—**Handi Jogi**
Pando
Pandula Gollalu—**Handi Jogi**
Pangul

Pangwal
Pangwala—**Pangwal**
Panika—**Ganda**
Panikkan—**Kaniyan**
Panikki
Panisavan
Panjari—**Dudekula**
Panjukotti—**Dudekula**
Panka—**Ganda**
Panna
Panna-Durayi—**Panna**
Pano
Panr—**Ganda**
Pansari—**Tamdi**
Pantia—**Pentiya**
Panwa—**Ganda**
Panwale—**Bari**
Panwar Rajput
Pao—**Ganda**
Paoli—**Julaha**
Paracha
Parachagi—**Paracha**
Parachi—**Paracha**
Paradesi
Parahaiya—**Parahiya**
Parahiya
Paraicha—**Paracha**
Paraichi—**Paracha**
Paraiya
Paraiyan—**Paraiya**
Parancha—**Paracha**
Parangiperja—**Poraja**
Parasar-Das—**Kewat**
Parava—**Paravan**
Paravan
Parayan—**Paraiya**
Parbhu—**Prabhu**
Pardeshi Alitkar—**Khatik**
Pardhan
Pardhi
Pargha
Parhaiya—**Parahiya**
Paria—**Paraiya**
Pariah—**Paraiya**
Parigha—**Pargha**
Parihar
Parit—**Dhobi**
Parivar—**Bhoi**
Parivara—**Besta**
Parivaram
Parja—**Poraja**
Parkitiwaru—**Besta**
Paroja—**Poraja**
Parsai—**Joshi**
Pasi
Pasi—**Adi**
Passi—**Pasi**
Pastagia—**Kachhia**
Patar—**Devadasi**
Patari
Patauni—**Patni**
Pathari—**Pardhan**
Pathari—**Patari**
Patharvat
Pathiyan—**Pathiyar**
Pathiyar
Pathrot—**Beldar**
Pathura Dawaru—**Devadasi**

Patni
Patnulkaran
Patoriva—**Devadasi**
Patra—**Patwa**
Pattanavan
Pattar—**Sonar**
Patua—**Juang**
Patua—**Patwa**
Patuni—**Patni**
Patur—**Devadasi**
Paturiya—**Devadasi**
Patvegar—**Patwa**
Patvekari—**Patwa**
Patwa
Patwi—**Patwa**
Paungar—**Chhipa**
Pawi
Peddintiwandlu—**Madiga**
Pendhari—**Pindari**
Pendhari Mang—**Mang-Garori**
Penta
Pentia—**Pentiya**
Pentiya
Perika
Perike—**Perika**
Perike Shetti—**Perika**
Periki—**Perika**
Perka—**Perika**
Perki—**Perika**
Perumal Madukkaran—**Gangeddu**
Phanse Pardhi—**Pardhi**
Phans-Pardhi—**Pardhi**
Phudgi
Phulari—**Tamdi**
Pichagunta—**Pichakuntala**
Pichai—**Pichakuntala**
Pichakuntala
Pichchuguntavallu—**Helava**
Pichigunta—**Pichakuntala**
Pindara—**Pindari**
Pindari
Pinjara—**Bahna**
Pinjari—**Bahna**
Pipavasi—**Darzi**
Pirhain—**Bharai**
Pisharati—**Ambalavasi**
Pisharodi—**Ambalavasi**
Pisharoti—**Ambalavasi**
Pnar—**Jaintia**
Pod
Poduval—**Mussad**
Poi—**Pawi**
Pola—**Kochh**
Polegar
Poleya—**Holeya**
Polia—**Kochh**
Poligar—**Polegar**
Ponwar—**Panwar Rajput**
Poojaree—**Pujari**
Poraja
Porja—**Poraja**
Poroja—**Poraja**
Potadar—**Sonar**
Pothuval—**Ambalavasi**
Potuval—**Mussad**
Poundra—**Pod**
Prabhu
Pramalai Kallar—**Kallar**

Sembadavan
Semsa—**Kachari**
Sengar Rajput
Sengunthar Mudaliyar—**Kaikolan**
Seniyan—**Karna Sale**
Senva—**Sindhava**
Sepoy—**Sipahi**
Sesodia Rajput
Setti—**Chetti**
Setti—**Komati**
Sewara—**Jati**
Shabar—**Lodhi**
Shaha—**Sundi**
Shamsi—**Sonar**
Shanan
Shanar—**Shanan**
Sharadakani—**Telaga**
Shenavi—**Saraswati**
Shenva—**Sindhava**
Sheoran
Sheorani—**Shiranni**
Sherani—**Shiranni**
Sherdukpen
Shet—**Sonar**
Shikari—**Pardhi**
Shillekyata—**Killekyata**
Shimong—**Adi**
Shimpi—**Darzi**
Shin
Shingade—**Bhandari**
Shirani—**Shiranni**
Shiranni
Shishagar
Shiva Brahman—**Tamdi**
Shivachandi Thakur—**Bhat**
Shiva Gurava—**Gurava**
Shivarchaka—**Tamdi**
Shiv Jogi—**Raval Jogi**
Sholaga—**Sholiga**
Sholega—**Sholiga**
Sholiga
Shom-Pen
Shravagi—**Alkari**
Shudra—**Sudir**
Sial
Siddi—**Sidi**
Sidi
Simpi—**Darzi**
Sinai—**Rabari**
Sindhava
Sindhu
Sindhva—**Sindhava**
Singe
Singpho
Singson—**Kuki**
Sin-teng—**Jaintia**
Sipahi
Sisodiya—**Sesodia Rajput**
Sitlhou—**Kuki**
Sivabhaktaru—**Balija**
Sodia—**Jhinwar**
Soeri
Soiri—**Soeri**
Solaga—**Sholiga**
Soliga—**Sholiga**
Soligaru—**Sholiga**
Sombansi
Somvanshi Kshatriya Pathare —

Panchkalshi
Sona—**Sonar**
Sonar
Sondhi—**Sundi**
Sondi—**Sundi**
Soni—**Sonar**
Sonjhara
Sonkar—**Beldar**
Sonr—**Sonar**
Sor—**Sahariya**
Sosia—**Sahariya**
Sounti—**Sundi**
Southern Pulaya—**Pulluvan**
Sowar-**Komati**
Srawak—**Sarak**
Sri Vaishnava Brahman
Suda—**Sudh**
Sudh
Sudha—**Sudh**
Sudho—**Sudh**
Sudir
Sudugadu Siddha
Sugali—**Banjara**
Suis—**Darzi**
Suji—**Darzi**
Sukali—**Banjara**
Sukte—**Kuti**
Sultani
Sultania—**Sultani**
Sultankar—**Khatik**
Sunar—**Sonar**
Sunara—**Sonar**
Sundaka—**Sundi**
Sundhi—**Sundi**
Sundi
Sunera—**Sonar**
Sungar—**Besta**
Suniar—**Sonar**
Suniari—**Sonar**
Sunnakallu Bestha—**Besta**
Sunri—**Sundi**
Suppalig
Surajbans—**Suraj-Bansi**
Suraj-Bansi
Surir—**Soeri**
Suryachelad—**Kasai**
Sutar—**Barhai**
Suthar—**Barhai**
Suthar—**Sutradhar**
Suthra Shahi
Sutradhar
Syal—**Sial**
Syce—**Ghasia**

Tadan—**Dasri**
Tadvi—**Gamit**
Taga
Tai
Tai—**Khamti**
Tailakar—**Teli**
Taili—**Teli**
Tailika—**Teli**
Tailpal—**Teli**
Takankar—**Pardhi**
Takara—**Beldar**
Takari—**Beldar**
Takari—**Bhamta**
Takhan—**Tarkhan**

Takia—**Pardhi**
Talavia—**Dubla**
Tambala—**Tamdi**
Tambat—**Tamera**
Tambatkar—**Jingar**
Tambatkar—**Tamera**
Tamboli—**Tamdi**
Tambuli—**Tamdi**
Tamdi
Tamera
Tamhera—**Tamera**
Tamil Brahman—**Paradesi**
Tamli—**Tamdi**
Tamliwandlu—**Tamdi**
Tamoli—**Tamdi**
Tamuli—**Tamdi**
Tandan
Tandel—**Macchi**
Tandel—**Mangela**
Tangsa
Tanti
Tanti—**Ganda**
Tantrabaya—**Tanti**
Tantubaya—**Tanti**
Tantunayakadu—**Padma Sale**
Tantwa—**Tanti**
Taonla
Tarakan
Targala—**Bhandari**
Targala—**Bhavaiya**
Tarkhan
Tarkhan—**Barhai**
Tarkhanr—**Tarkhan**
Tarkihar
Taru
Tasa—**Chasa**
Tattar—**Paracha**
Tatwa—**Tanti**
Tawaif—**Devadasi**
Telaga
Telaga—**Mutrasi**
Telangi Sadar Bhoi—**Mala**
Telgaund—**Mutrasi**
Teli
Telli—**Teli**
Telugu Brahman—**Andhra Brahman**
Telugu Dher—**Mala**
Telugu Kummaravadu—**Kumhar**
Tengalai Sri Vaishnava—**Sri Vaishnava Brahman**
Tengaud—**Mutrasi**
Tetaria—**Gamit**
Thacchanaden—**Thachanaden**
Thachanaden
Thachanad Muppan—**Thachanaden**
Thaggappanmargal—**Muduga**
Thakar
Thakur—**Bhat**
Thalavadi—**Darzi**
Thammadi—**Tamdi**
Thanapati—**Gandhmali**
Thanda Pulayan—**Pulluvan**
Thangluya—**Kuki**
Thangngen—**Kuki**
Thantapulaya—**Pulluvan**
Thapatkari—**Beldar**
Thathera—**Tamera**
Thongcha—**Marma**

Thongtha—**Marma**
Thori
Tiar—**Tiyar**
Tibetan
Tigala
Tilgar—**Tigala**
Tilghatak—**Teli**
Tili—**Teli**
Tilvai—**Tigala**
Tilwan—**Teli**
Tior—**Tiyar**
Tippera—**Tripura**
Tipperah—**Tripura**
Tipra—**Tripura**
Tirbanda—**Tirgar**
Tirgar
Tirgul Brahman
Tirmali
Tiyan
Tiyar
Togalubombeyavaru—**Killekyata**
Togata—**Thakar**
Tokre Kolcha—**Kolgha**
Tolubomalawaru—**Telaga**
Tomar—**Tomara Rajput**
Tomara Rajput
Toori—**Turi**
Torea—**Besta**
Toreya—**Besta**
Toto
Tottiyan
Tottiyan—**Yogi**
Trigarth—**Tirgul Brahman**
Trigul Brahman—**Tirgul Brahman**
Tripra—**Tripura**
Tripura
Tripuri—**Tripura**
Tsakala—**Dhobi**
Tuar—**Tomara Rajput**
Tulu Brahman—**Havik Brahman**
Tunwar—**Tomara Rajput**
Turi
Turi
Turki Hajam—**Nai**
Twashta Kasar—**Tamera**

Uchla—**Bhamta**
Uchlia—**Bhamta**
Ud—**Beldar**
Udaiyan
Udasi
Uibuh—**Kuki**
Ulladan
Ullatan—**Ulladan**
Unni—**Ambalavasi**
Uppaliga—**Uppar**
Uppaliga—**Upparwar**
Uppar
Uppara—**Uppar**
Uppara—**Upparwar**
Upparwar
Uppiliyan—**Upparwar**
Urali
Urali Kuruman—**Urali**
Urali Kurumaru—**Urali**
Urali Kurumba—**Urali**
Urali Kurumber—**Urali**
Uraly—**Urali**

Uria—**Sansia**
Uridavan—**Uridavan Gowdalu**
Uridavan Gowdalu
Uru Golla—**Golla**

Vada
Vadagalai Sri Vaishnava—**Sri Vaishnava Brahman**
Vaddar—**Beldar**
Vader
Vadval—**East Indian**
Vaghe—**Waghya**
Vagher
Vaghri
Vahumpura
Vaidu
Vaidya—**Baidya**
Vaidyan—**Baidya**
Vaiphei—**Kuki**
Vaiphui—**Kuki**
Vais—**Nagbansi**
Vaishya—**Komati**
Vaiti
Vajir—**Khava**
Valaiyan
Valan—**Valaiyan**
Valand—**Nai**
Valer—**Holeya**
Vallabacharya
Vallamban
Valluvan
Valluva Pandaram—**Valluvan**
Valluva Pulaya—**Pulluvan**
Valuvan—**Valluvan**
Valvi—**Gamit**
Vaniyan
Vanjari—**Banjara**
Vanjha
Vannan
Vanneru—**Tigala**
Vannikuladavaru—**Tigala**
Vanniya—**Palli**
Vanniyan—**Palli**
Varaich
Varangana—**Devadasi**
Varik—**Nai**
Variyar—**Ambalavasi**
Varli
Vasava—**Gamit**
Vasave—**Gamit**
Vastad—**Viramushti**
Vasudeva Joshi
Vavdichaski—**Nai**
Vayasa—**Nagbansi**
Vedan
Ved-Patr
Velama
Velan
Velli-Durayi
Vellutedan
Vetta Kuruman—**Urali**
Vettuvan—**Mala Vedan**
Vettuva Pulayan—**Mala Vedan**
Vettuvarn—**Mala Vedan**
Vidur
Vidur Brahman—**Vidur**
Vigha—**Satani**
Vilkurup

Villu Vedan—**Eravallan**
Vipranoru—**Telaga**
Vir—**Viramushti**
Virabhat—**Viramushti**
Virabhatalu—**Mailari**
Viraghata Madivala—**Agasa**
Viramushti
Vira Vaishnava—**Satani**
Vishavan
Vishnu Archaka—**Satani**
Vishotar—**Rabari**
Vishva Brahman—**Kammalan**
Vitola—**Vitolana**
Vitolana
Vitolia—**Vitolana**
Vitoria—**Vitolana**
Vodda—**Beldar**
Vodden—**Beldar**

Waddar—**Beldar**
Waddar—**Sansia**
Wadewar—**Sansia**
Wadu Rajlu—**Beldar**
Waghe Joshi—**Waghya**
Waghya
Wahabi
Wainad Chetti—**Wynadan Chetti**
Wanjara—**Banjara**
Wanjari—**Banjara**
Wannekar—**Chhipa**
Wansphoda—**Vitolana**
Warathi—**Dhobi**
Warik—**Nai**
Warli—**Varli**
Warthi—**Dhobi**
Wasudeo—**Basdewa**
Watari—**Otari**
Watkari—**Otari**
Wattu
Wazir
Wodeya—**Vader**
Wrukzai—**Orakzai**
Wudder—**Beldar**
Wynaadan Chetti—**Wynadan Chetti**
Wynadan Chetti

Yadava—**Yadu Rajput**
Yadava-kula—**Golla**
Yadavakuladavaru—**Kadu Golla**
Yadu-Bhatti—**Yadu Rajput**
Yadu Rajput
Yanadi
Yata
Yati—**Jati**
Yelama—**Velama**
Yelma—**Velama**
Yenadi—**Yanadi**
Yerava
Yeravallar—**Eravallan**
Yerukala—**Erakala**
Yerukula—**Erakala**
Yogi

Zamindar—**Babhan**
Zamindar Brahman—**Babhan**
Zargar—**Sonar**
Zaveri—**Johari**
Zogui—**Gonsavi**

Glossary

Akbar, Jalal-ud-din Mohammed Mogul emperor (1542–1605) and son of Humayun. He extended the imperial power over most of what is now Pakistan and Northern India, stabilizing the administration and promoting learning and commerce. Although a Muslim, he was tolerant of other religions and encouraged debate between them.

Alexander the Great King of Macedon (now northern Greece; 356–323 B.C.), he led his army through the Middle East, and in 326 he invaded what is now Pakistan, traveling through the Hindu Kush and much of the Indus Valley. Although his forces did not stay long, the Greeks had a lasting impact on Indian art, astrology, medicine, and coinage.

areca nut. _See_ paan, pan

arranged marriage The prevalent mode of marriage in South Asia, in which a marriage partner is chosen for a young person by his or her parents.

Austroasiatic. _See_ Munda

Ayurvedic medicine A Hindu system of medicine of great antiquity, based on a theory of humors, and of seasonal effects on the human body, and on the control of these by diet, herbal medicines, and even changing the body's microenvironment.

bajra Spiked millet (_Pennisetum typhoideum_), a tall grass, probably of African origin, cultivated throughout much of South Asia for grain and fodder. Bajra flour is mixed with buttermilk and made into cakes or bread.

banyan A tree (_Ficus bengalensis_) that is widespread in India and Sri Lanka. It yields an inferior rubber, but it is chiefly valued for its shade.

betel. _See_ paan, pan

bhakti Devotion to a personal Hindu god, especially through communal hymn singing.

bhikkhu, lama A Buddhist monk. Always male, he can occupy varying ranks from that of lowly wanderer to the unique position of the Dalai Lama. _Bhikkhu_ is the Sri Lankan term, _lama_ the Tibetan one. _See also_ "Lama" in the Appendix

Brahma The Creator, who with Shiva and Vishnu forms the Hindu Trinity of gods. There are very few temples in his honor, however.

British Raj. _See_ Raj

Buddha The Enlightened One, a common title of Siddhartha Gautama or Sakyamuni, who was a prince of Kapilavastu in the Nepalese _terai_, until he renounced his family and this world and began to preach the path of enlightenment that so many hundreds of millions have followed since and that we call "Buddhism." The forty-five years of his religious life were spent in Uttar Pradesh and Bihar, traveling as a teacher. According to Chinese tradition, he lived from about 563 to 483 B.C.

caste, jati An endogamous hereditary group, usually with a distinct hereditary occupation, who have a virtually immutable position in a hierarchy. Although the caste system is most elaborated throughout South Asia, castes have also been reported in Tibet, Japan, Korea, Burundi, and the American South. _See the article_ Castes, Hindu

chapati Flat, unleavened cake of wheaten bread.

chela A student or acolyte.

curry Any vegetable or meat stew made on a base of fried onions and sundry condiments or spices; served with rice in Bangladesh, southern India, and Sri Lanka and with _chapatis_ in the north and in Pakistan.

dacoit A brigand, bandit, highwayman. _See the article_ Thug

dall. _See_ dhal

Deccan Triangular-shaped plateau in the southern part of India. It is bounded on the north by the Satpura range, on the west by the Western Ghats, and sporadically on the east by the Eastern Ghats.

dhal, dall Split pulse or lentil.

dharma The duties proper to one's station in Hindu life.

Divali, Dipavali Hindu festival in October–November, when lamps are lit and presents exchanged.

Dravidian The language family of the darkest-skinned people in South Asia, mainly found in southern India and Sri Lanka. _See the article_ Tamil

Eurasian Person of mixed European and South Asian ancestry; now usually called Anglo-Indian. _See the article_ Anglo-Indian

evil eye The belief that a certain person can perform harm to another simply by wishing him or her harm (casting the evil eye). In South Asia mothers are especially fearful for their young children and may use amulets or other devices as protection against the evil eye.

fakir A wandering Muslim holy man. _See the Appendix_

gaur, Indian bison A huge wild ox (_Bos gaurus_) found in the forests of India, Myanmar (Burma), and Malaysia. It may weigh up to 1,000 kg.

Gautama Buddha. _See_ Buddha

gayal, mithan A species of semiwild cattle (_Bos frontalis_) that are herded by tribes of northeastern India.

ghat Landing place or steps on a riverbank; also the mountains that flank the east and west coasts of India.

ghee, ghi Clarified butter.

Great Tradition, Little Tradition Terms first used by the anthropologist Robert Redfield to contrast the formal, literate tradition of a civilization with its variant manifestations at a local and rural level. In Hinduism the Great Tradition centers on such universal deities as Shiva and Vishnu, on such national pilgrimage centers as Benares (Varanasi), and on the use of Sanskrit prayers and scriptures. By contrast, the Little Tradition in Hinduism is likely to be nonscriptural, to acknowledge local deities and other spirits, and to conduct worship in a regional vernacular. Elements of the Little Tradition are thought to be continually absorbed into the Great Tradition through a process called _universalization_.

gurdwara   Sikh house of worship.

guru   Hindu spiritual teacher.

haj   Muslim pilgrimage to Mecca.

Himalayas   The world's highest mountain range, stretching over 2,200 kilometers eastward from Kashmir through Nepal, Sikkim, Bhutan, and northeast India to form the boundary between South Asia and Tibet.

Hindu Kush   A mountain range that covers the northeast portion of Afghanistan and joins with the Karakoram in the northernmost parts of Pakistan.

Holi   A Hindu spring festival marked by much merriment, especially the throwing of colored water or powders at passersby.

hookah, hubble-bubble   A complex pipe used for smoking tobacco or cannabis through water.

hypergamy   A marriage system in which women marry men of higher social or caste status than themselves.

hypogamy   A marriage system in which men marry women of higher social or caste status than themselves.

Id   Muslim festival to commemorate Abraham's offer to sacrifice his son Ishmael. The festival breaks the fast after Ramadan.

Indian bison.   *See* gaur

Indo-Aryan   The easternmost subfamily of the Indo-European language family. Its ancient languages were first introduced into South Asia by the Aryans, and today Indo-Aryan languages are spoken throughout most of Pakistan, Nepal, Bangladesh, Sri Lanka, and northern India. Seventy-four percent of the Indian population speak an Indo-Aryan language; Hindi, with over 200 million speakers, is one of the world's leading languages.

Indo-Gangetic Plain   The vast, flat area of the Indus and Ganges valleys, which join around Haryana State. The area covers much of Pakistan, northern India, and Bangladesh. It is fertile and heavily populated.

Islam, Mohammedanism   Mohammed the Prophet chose the name "Islam" for the new faith he began preaching in Arabia in A.D. 622 (A.H. 1). The term signifies "submitting oneself to God." The faithful are called "Muslims," "Moslems," or "Mohammedans." *See also* Mohammed

izzat   Honor, respect, or prestige in Islamic societies.

jaggery   Crude brown sugar.

jajmani   A system of economic exchange of goods and services between castes, without using money as the intermediary. The system is now little used.

jati *See* caste

jhuming *See* swidden cultivation

jowar   Sorghum or great millet (*Sorghum vulgare*), which is widely grown in Pakistan and India, although not in the northeast or in Bangladesh.

jungle   The English word is derived from Sanskrit and Hindi *jangala*, which means "dry or desert; waste, uncultivated ground," and certainly not "thick forest."

Karakoram   The northernmost mountain ranges of South Asia, primarily the area of Pakistani Kashmir. Of many peaks, the highest is K2 (8,611 meters).

karma   The effect of former deeds, whether done in this life or in a previous existence. These are thought to determine a Hindu's future and his or her social condition.

kin terms   The words that any particular language uses to describe specific kin relationships.

Koran. *See* Quran

lama. *See* bhikkhu; *see also* the Appendix

lamaistic Buddhism   A form of Mahayana Buddhism practiced by Tibetans. It acknowledges as its supreme earthly head the Dalai Lama, formerly also political ruler of Tibet, and it recognizes many minor demons and deities.

Little Tradition. *See* Great Tradition, Little Tradition

Mahābhārata   The world's longest poetic miscellany, this Hindu poem deals with the war between the Pandavas and the Kauravas. There are numerous versions, the oldest perhaps dating to a period between 200 B.C. and A.D. 200.

maharaja. *See* raja, rajah

mahout   Elephant driver

mantra   A verse or phrase believed to have magical or religious efficacy, especially as a protection.

mithan. *See* gayal

Mohammed   The Arab prophet of Islam, who received the Quran from the Angel Gabriel. Although most venerated, he is not considered a deity, for in Islam there is no god but Allah. He lived from about A.D. 570 to 632. *See also* Islam; Quran

Mon-Khmer. *See* Munda

monsoon   Regular and persistent winds that blow in the Indian Ocean, coming from the southwest between June and August and from the northeast between October and December. The southwest monsoon is the main rain-bearing one.

mulla   Muslim preacher, one learned in the Quran.

Munda, Mundari, Austroasiatic, Mon-Khmer   A language family, formerly called "Kolarian"; its main distribution is throughout Southeast Asia. In India the family is represented by only a number of tribal languages spoken in the east-central parts of the country, notably Santali, Munda, and Oraon.

Muslim, Moslem, Mohammedan. *See* Islam

neem, nim   The margosa tree (*Melia azadirachta*), the sap of which is extracted to make a liquor called *toddy*. The timber and leaves also have many uses. *See* toddy

Nestorians   Founded on the heresy that Jesus Christ had two distinct persons, this Christian sect was established by Nestorius, an abbot of Antioch, in about A.D. 431. Although the issue was virtually a dead one by 451, the Nestorian Church has continued down to the present, with over 100,000 adherents today, mainly in Iraq, Iran, Kerala State, and the United States. From the seventh to the tenth centuries, Nestorian missionaries were active in western India and went as far as China. *See also the article* Syrian Christian of Kerala

paan, pan The leaf of the betel vine (*Piper betle*), chewed after meals with slaked lime, catechu, and *betel* or *areca* nut, as a savory.

paddy The rice plant (*Oryza sativa*), grown either in irrigated fields (wet rice) or in rain-fed fields (dry rice). Rice is the staple food of Sri Lanka, Bangladesh, Kashmir, and Dravidian India. Elsewhere wheat is more important.

panchayat Literally, a "council of five," but in fact a village or caste council of any size.

peepul, pipal The Indian fig tree (*Ficus religiosa*), much venerated by Hindus and very long-lived; called "Bo-tree" in Sri Lanka, where it is associated with Buddhist sites. The tree produces a useful gum.

pir A Muslim saint, especially a Sufi master, whose tomb is often venerated by Muslims and Hindus alike.

Prakrit The common Indo-Aryan languages of South Asia in ancient times, as contrasted with Sanskrit.

puja Act of making an offering to a Hindu deity during worship.

pujari A Hindu priest. *See* the appendix

purdah Seclusion of women; mainly a Muslim custom in South Asia and Middle East. *See also* zenana

pyre The pile of logs on which a Hindu is cremated.

qadi, qazi A judge of Islamic law.

Quran, Koran Divinely inspired holy book of Islam, written down by the Prophet Mohammed at the dictation of the Angel Gabriel in about A.D. 610–630. *See also* Islam; Mohammed

ragi The thick-spiked eleusine (*Eleusine coracana*), grown in most parts of India except the northeast and northwest as a food staple.

Raj Government or rule, especially the period of British rule in much of South Asia. Although the East India Company had been in existence since 1599, it was only after the eighteenth century that it directly administered vast conquered territories in the subcontinent, primarily the presidencies of Bengal, Bombay, and Madras. From 1858 to 1947 India (which has since become India, Pakistan, and Bangladesh) was ruled by a viceroy and council, and this was an extension of British government centered on London. Much of the higher civil service consisted of British professionals. India was never constitutionally a British colony, but it was proclaimed a separate empire by its first empress, Queen Victoria, in 1877.

raja, rajah Hindu king or ruler; also called *maharaja*.

Ramadan, Ramazan Month of fasting during daylight observed by Muslims; it concludes with the festival of Id.

Ramayana Epic Hindu poem whose hero is Rama, one of the incarnations of Vishnu. Its date is variously placed between 500 B.C. and A.D. 200.

rupee Standard unit of currency in South Asian countries since Mogul times. It used to be made up of 16 annas, and now it consists of 100 paise. Currently, the Indian rupee is worth about one U.S. nickel.

sacred thread A continuous cotton thread worn across the right shoulder by males of the Brahman *varna*, once they have undergone initiation (*upanāyana*). It should be worn at all times, and it is highly symbolic. A sacred thread may also be worn by Kshatriyas and Vaishyas, but in these latter two cases it should be made of wool and linen, respectively. *See the articles* Castes, Hindu; Brahman

Sadhu A Hindu holy man. *See the article* Sadhu

sal A tree (*Shorea robusta*) found in the *terai* and lower Himalayas, as well as in central India. The tree yields aromatic resin, its seeds are eaten, the bark is used as a dye, and the timber provides railroad sleepers.

Sannyasi A wandering ascetic. *See also* Sadhu

Sanskrit The sacerdotal Indo-Aryan language of South Asia in ancient times, as contrasted with the Prakrits or common speech. Sanskrit is still used by Brahmans in their prayers, but otherwise is hardly spoken.

Sanskritization The emulation of the ritual behavior of higher-ranking castes, especially Brahmans, in an attempt to achieve higher social status. It normally includes more attention to the universal deities of Hinduism, switching from praying in a vernacular to Sanskrit, adopting a vegetarian diet, abandoning blood sacrifices, and if possible engaging Brahman priests to perform the main religious ceremonies of a caste.

sari, saree Seamless length of cloth, generally worn by South Asian women draped over a bodice and petticoat. Another style of dress, *salwar* and *kamis*, is usual among Muslim women.

Shaivism Following Shiva as the preeminent Hindu deity.

Shiva The Destroyer, who with Brahma and Vishnu forms the Hindu Trinity of gods.

slash-and-burn cultivation. *See* swidden cultivation

subcaste A section or major part of a caste or jati. It is commonly endogamous.

Sufism Islamic mysticism. *See also* pir

swidden cultivation A form of horticulture in which plots of land (*swiddens, jhums*) are cleared and planted for a few years and then left to fallow for a number of years while other plots are used. The system is now mostly used in certain tribal areas of central and northeastern India. Also called shifting or slash-and-burn cultivation, or jhuming.

tahsil, taluk A subdivision of an administrative district in India, where in 1981 there were 412 districts divided into 3,342 *taluks*. Reorganization had created 452 districts by 1989.

tamarind A large evergreen tree (*Tamarindus indica*), yielding a fruit that is very popular in curries and chutneys and in ayurvedic medicine. The leaves are used in dyeing.

terai Name for the low-lying tract of land along foothills of the Himalayas, bordering India and Nepal. It has always been highly malarial and thus not heavily populated.

terraced fields   A technique of forming narrow but more or less level fields along steep hillsides. Where the fields are for irrigated rice they have to be absolutely level to hold the water, but for other grain crops and potatoes they simply hold the soil to prevent erosion and allow access by the farmers and their equipment.

Tibeto-Burman   A subfamily of languages found mainly in Tibet, Myanmar (Burma), Nepal, and northeastern India. The larger family is called Sino-Tibetan and also includes the Chinese languages.

toddy   Palm wine, the fermented sap of the palmyra (*Borassus flabellifer*) and other palms, such as date, coconut, or sago.

universalization.   *See* Great Tradition, Little Tradition

Vaishnavism   Following Vishnu as the preeminent Hindu deity.

varna system.   *See the article* Castes, Hindu

Vedas   The four oldest documents of Hinduism, written in early Sanskrit in north India. They are the *Rig Veda* (perhaps 1200–900 B.C.), the *Yajur Veda*, the *Sama Veda*, and the *Atharva Veda*. Collectively these books are known as "Samhitas."

Vishnu   The Preserver, who with Brahma and Shiva forms the Hindu Trinity of gods.

zenana   Women's quarters or harem in a Muslim household. *See also* purdah

Zoroastrianism   Monotheistic religion worshiping Ahura Mazda, which was formalized by the prophet Zoroaster (or Zarathustra) in the sixth century B.C. at the latest. The modern followers include about 85,000 Parsis in western India and perhaps another 100,000 Zoroastrians in Iran and Tadzhikistan. *See the article* Parsi

Filmography

The following list of films is not exhaustive, but it does represent what is currently (1992) available for rental in the United States. The cultural groups or subjects are indicated in parentheses and noted in the index at the end of the list of films. Included are a few feature films that have significant anthropological or historical interest. In many cases, only a selection of distributors has been indicated, at most one on the West Coast, one in the Midwest, and one on the East Coast. In most cases, too, there are also prints of these films available for sale, and not necessarily with the rental distributors indicated here. (Abbreviations are indicated at the end of the filmography.) To find the appropriate sales organization, one should either approach a rental distributor or film librarian, or check for further details available in the references listed at the end of the filmography.

A wider range of films on South Asia is available in the United States than in any other country. Unfortunately, the U.S. distributors listed below do not lend their films and videotapes overseas, not even to Mexico. Users in the British Isles should inquire about the following film titles of the Film Librarian, Royal Anthropological Institute, 50 Fitzroy Street, London W1P 5HS. Those in central Europe might inquire at the Institut für den Wissenschaftlichen Film, 3400 Göttingen, Germany. French readers may write to the Comité des Films de l'Homme, Musée de l'Homme, Place du Trocadéro, 75116 Paris. In Japan readers should contact the Managing Director, Nippon Audio-Visual Library, Eizo Kiroku Building, 6-27-27 Shinjuku, Shinjuku-ku, Tokyo 160; telefax numbers are 0462-480947 for the London office, and 3204-0117 for the Tokyo office.

1. *About the Jews of India: Cochin.* (Cochin Jews) 1976. Johanna Spector. Color, 30 minutes, 16mm. (JMS)
2. *About the Jews of India: Shanwar Telis or Bene Israel.* (Bene Israel) 1978. Johanna Spector. Color, 10 minutes, 16mm. (JMS)
3. *Ahimsa, Non-Violence.* (Jains) 1987. Marion Hunt, Michael Tobias. Color, 58 minutes, 16mm. (MnU)
4. *Ahmedabad: Life of a City in India.* (Gujarat) 1983. Howard Spodek. Color, 27 minutes, 16mm. (UWSAAC, MoU, TxU)
5. *Ajuba Dance and Drama Company.* (Indian theater) 1979. Color, 20 minutes, 16mm, VHS. (UWSAAC)
6. *Altar of Fire.* (Nambudiri Brahmans) 1975. Robert Gardner, Frits Staal. Color, 45 minutes, 16mm, VHS, U-Mat. (IU, CU)
7. *Amir: An Afghan Refugee Musician's Life in Peshawar, Pakistan.* (Music in Pakistan) 1985. John Baily. Color, 52 minutes, VHS. (DER)
8. *Amjad Ali Khan.* (Music) 1973. Inter-Culture Associates. Color, 25 minutes, 16mm. (IU, MoU)
9. *Amra Dujon (Together).* (Bangladesh) 1984. John Riber, Alamgir Kabir. Color, 30 minutes, 16mm, VHS. (DSR)
10. *And Who Shall Feed This World?* (Indian agriculture) 1975. Color, 54 minutes, 16mm. (CU)
11. *Aparajito.* (Bengali family) 1956. Satyajit Ray. B&W, 108 minutes, 16mm. (BF, FF, FI)
12. *An Appointment with the Astrologer: Personal Consultants in Hindu Society.* (Astrology, Varanasi) 1985. Color, 40 minutes, 16mm, VHS. (UWSAAC)
13. *Asian Earth.* (Village life) 1954. J. Michael Hagopian. Color, 22 minutes, 16mm. (IU, CLU, CtU)
14. *The Avatar: Concept and Example.* (Hinduism) 1977. Robert A. McDermott, Nuala O'Faolain. Color, 25 minutes, 16mm, VHS. (MG)
15. *The Awakening.* (Neo-Hinduism) 1975. Anthony Hixon. Color, 30 minutes, 16mm. (LB)
16. *Balasaraswathi.* (Dance) 1963. Color, 20 minutes, 16mm. (JFCAWU)
17. *Banaras.* (Varanasi) 1970. Michael Camerini. B&W, 22 minutes, 16mm, VHS. (UWSAAC, MoU, WaPS)
18. *Bangladesh Nationhood: Symbols and Shadows.* (Bangladesh) 1975. Color, 49 minutes, 16mm, VHS. (UWSAAC)
19. *Benares: Steps to Heaven.* (Varanasi) 1984. Richard Riddiford. Color, 30 minutes, 16mm, VHS. (Wombat)
20. *Between Time: A Tibetan Village in Nepal.* (Tibetans) 1984. Ken and Ivory Levine. Color, 20 minutes, 16mm. (OrPS, TxU, WAU)
21. *Bhimsen Joshi Sings Rag Miya Malhar.* (Music) 1971. Color, 29 minutes, 16mm. (IU)
22. *Bishmillah Khan.* (Music) 1967. James Beveridge, Tom Slevin. B&W, 29 minutes, 16mm. (CU, InU, WaU)
23. *Bombay: Our City.* (Urban life) 1985. Anand Patwardhan. Color, 82 or 57 minutes, 16mm, VHS, Beta. (FRIF, MiU)
24. *Calcutta.* (Urban life) 1968. Louis Malle. Color; 13, 99, 105, or 115 minutes; 16mm. (13 min.: CtU; 99 min.: WaU, MtU, CU; 105 min.: IU; 115 min.: BF, Swank)
25. *Caste and Class.* (Caste) 1980. Color, 23 minutes, 16mm. (OKentU)
26. *Circles-Cycles: Kathak Dance.* (Dance) 1989. Robert S. Gottlieb. Color, 28 minutes, VHS, U-Mat. (CU)
27. *Classical Music of North India.* (Music) 1969. Color, 33 minutes, 16mm. (WaU)
28. *Consecration of a Temple.* (Hinduism) 1979. Fred Clothey. Color, 25 minutes, 16mm. (UWSAAC, TxU)
29. *A Contemporary Guru: Rajnish.* (Neo-Hinduism) 1975. David Knipe. Color, 30 minutes, VHS. (UWSAAC)
30. *Courts and Councils: Dispute Settlement in India.* (Panchayats in Uttar Pradesh and Maharashtra) 1981. Ron Hess. Color, 30 minutes, 16mm. (UWSAAC, PSt, TxU)
31. *Courtship and Marriage.* (Arranged marriage) 1962. B&W, 60 minutes, 16mm. (MnU, PSt, CoU)
32. *Dadi and Her Family: A Rural Mother-in-Law in North India.* (Haryana joint family) 1979. James MacDonald, Michael Camerini. Color, 45 minutes, 16mm, VHS. (MoU, NhU, UWSAAC)
33. *Dadi's Family.* (Haryana joint family) 1981. James MacDonald, Michael Camerini. Color, 59 minutes, 16mm, VHS. (Pst, TxU, WaU)

34. *The Dam at Nagarjunasagar.* (Modernization) 1972. Gene Searchinger. Color, 10 minutes, 16mm. (CU, MiU, PSt)

35. *Death and Rebirth in Hinduism.* (Hinduism) 1975. David Knipe. Color, 30 minutes, VHS. (UWSAAC)

36. *Devi.* (Bengali family) 1960. Satyajit Ray. B&W, 96 minutes, 16mm. (BF, FI)

37. *Dhrupad.* (Singing) 1974. V. M. Jain, Sheldon Rochlin. Color, 50 minutes, 16mm. (NK)

38. *Discovering the Music of India.* (Music) 1969. Bernard Wilets. Color, 22 minutes, 16mm. (IU, WaPS, NSyU)

39. *Distant Thunder.* (Bengali caste and family) 1973. Satyajit Ray. Color, 100 minutes, 16mm. (AC5)

40. *Edge of Survival.* (India) 1982. Color, 58 minutes, 16mm. (CU, WU, PSt)

41. *Evolution of a Yogi.* (Neo-Hinduism) 1970. Elda Hartley. Color, 28 minutes, 16mm. (CU, IU)

42. *Family of India.* (Family) 1955. B&W, 13 minutes, 16mm. (MnU, OKentU)

43. *Floating in the Air, Followed by the Wind: Thai Pusam, a Hindu Festival.* (Hinduism in Malaysia) 1973. Gunther Pfaff, Ronald A. Simons. Color, 33 minutes, 16mm. (CU, InU, PSt)

44. *The Flute and the Arrow.* (Oraon) 1958. Arne Sucksdorf. Color, 78 minutes, 16mm. (FI)

45. *Forest of Bliss.* (Hinduism in Varanasi) 1987. Robert Gardner, Ákös Östör. Color, 89 minutes, 16mm. (AC)

46. *Fountains of Paradise.* (Sri Lanka) 1985. Color, 57 minutes, VHS. (CU, InU, PSt)

47. *Four Families, Part 1: India and France.* (Family) 1959. Margaret Mead. B&W, 30 minutes, 16mm. (CU, IU, PSt)

48. *Four Holy Men: Renunciation in Hindu Society.* (Hinduism) 1976. Mira Binford, Michael Camerini. Color, 37 minutes, 16mm. (UWSAAC, WaU)

49. *Four Men of India.* (Modernization) c. 1970. Color, 31 minutes, 16mm. (IU, MnU, NSyU)

50. *Four Religions, Part 1: Hinduism, Buddhism.* (Hinduism, Buddhism) 1961. James Beveridge, Arnold Toynbee. B&W, 30 minutes, 16mm. (IU, NSyU, MtU)

51. *The Fourth Stage: A Hindu's Quest for Release.* (Sannyasi) 1985. Color, 40 minutes, 16mm, VHS. (TVKC, UWSAAC)

52. *The Fragile Mountain.* (Mountain ecology) 1982. Sandra Nichols. Color, 55 minutes, 16mm. (IU, MtU)

53. *Freak Street to Goa: Immigrants on the Rajpath.* (Westernization) 1987. John Caldwell, John Pudaite. Color, 60 minutes, 16mm. (FL)

54. *Frontiers of Peace: Jainism in India.* (Jains) 1986. Color, 40 minutes, VHS. (TVKC, UWSAAC)

55. *Gandhi.* (Independence) 1959. Color and B&W, 25 minutes, 16mm. (CU, IU, PSt)

56. *Gandhi.* (Independence, British) 1983. Richard Attenborough. Color, 188 minutes, VHS. (WaPS, MiU, CoU)

57. *Gandhi: A Profile in Power.* (Independence) 1977. Color, 25 minutes, 16mm. (CU, MnU, NSyU)

58. *Gandhi's India.* (Independence) 1969. B&W, 58 minutes, 16mm. (CU, InU, MnU)

59. *Ganges River.* (Geography, Hinduism) 1955. Edward Levonian. Color, 17 minutes, 16mm. (IU, WaPS, FTS)

60. *Ganges—Sacred River.* (Hinduism) 1964. Color, 27 minutes, 16mm. (CU, IU, PSt)

61. *Gazipur.* (Village life) 1975. Bruce Holman. Color, 20 minutes, 16mm. (IB)

62. *Given to Dance: India's Odissi Tradition.* (Orissan dance) 1985. Ron Hess. Color, 57 minutes, 16mm. (UWSAAC)

63. *Glory That Remains, No. 4—Imminent Deities.* (Tamil Nadu temples) 1969. Color, 31 minutes, 16 mm. (WaU, IU)

64. *The Goddess Bhagavati: Art and Ritual in South India.* (Hinduism) 1976. Clifford Jones. Color, 15 minutes, 16mm. (SACCU)

65. *God with a Green Face.* (Kathakali drama) 1972. Bruce Ward, Myron Emory. Color, 25 minutes, 16mm. (MoU)

66. *Growing Up in Benares.* (Varanasi) 1970. Color, 17 minutes, 16mm. (WU)

67. *Gurkha Country.* (Gurkhas, Nepal) 1966. John and Patricia Hitchcock. Color, 19 minutes, 16mm. (CU, PSt, IFB)

68. *Hail Mother Kali: A Tribute to the Traditions and Healing Arts Brought to Guyana by Indentured Madrasi Laborers.* (Hinduism in South America) 1988. Stephanos Stephanides. Color, 60 minutes, 16mm. (SSP)

69. *Hajari Bhand of Rajasthan: Jester without Court.* (Rajasthan) 1985. John and Ulrike Emigh. Color, 40 minutes, VHS. (DER)

70. *Hare Krishna People.* (Neo-Hinduism) 1974. John Griesser, Jean Papert. Color, 30 minutes, 16mm. (CU)

71. *He Touched Me.* (Neo-Hinduism) Color, 45 minutes, super-8mm. (KYR)

72. *Himalayan Journey.* (Nepal) 1985. Color, 14 minutes, 16mm. (CU, IU)

73. *Himalayan Shaman of Northern Nepal.* (Shamanism) 1966. John and Patricia Hitchcock. Color, 15 minutes, 16mm. (CU, PSt, WU)

74. *Himalayan Shaman of Southern Nepal.* (Magar, Shamanism) 1966. John and Patricia Hitchcock. Color, 14 minutes, 16mm. (CU, PSt, WU)

75. *Hindu Devotions at Dawn.* (Brahmans in Madras) 1969. H. Daniel Smith. Color, 10 minutes, 16mm. (NSyU, WaU, WU)

76. *Hindu Family Celebration: 60th Birthday.* (Brahmans in Madras) 1969. H. Daniel Smith. Color, 9 minutes, 16mm. (WaU)

77. *Hinduism.* (Hinduism) 1962. B&W, 18 minutes, 16mm. (CU, IU, PSt)

78. *Hinduism and the Song of God.* (Hinduism) 1975. Elda Hartley. Color, 30 minutes, 16mm, VHS. (WaU, PSt, FTS)

79. *Hinduism in South India.* (Hinduism) 1977. David Knipe. Color, 30 minutes, VHS. (UWSAAC, MoU)

80. *Hinduism: Parts 1–3.* (Hinduism) 1955, 1962. Huston Smith. B&W, 30 minutes each part, 16mm. (InU, OKentU)

81. _Hinduism: The Many Paths to God._ (Hinduism) 1973. Howard Enders. Color, 29 minutes, 16mm. (IU, WaU)

81a. _Hindu Loaves and Fishes._ (Sadhus) 1985. Philip Singer, Bill Sharrette. Color, 20 minutes, 16mm, VHS. (SSP)

82. _Hindu Procession to the Sea._ (Hinduism in Madras) 1969. H. Daniel Smith. Color, 8 minutes, 16mm. (NSyU, WaPS)

83. _The Hindu Ritual Sandhyā._ (Hinduism in Maharashtra) 1973. Doris Srinivasan. Color, 19 minutes, 16mm. (CU, WU, PSt)

84. _Hindu Sacrament of Surrender._ (Brahmans in Madras) 1969. H. Daniel Smith. Color, 8 minutes, 16mm. (NSyU, WaU)

85. _Hindu Sacrament of Thread Investiture._ (Brahmans in Madras) 1969. H. Daniel Smith. Color, 14 minutes, 16mm. (NSyU, IaU, WaU)

86. _Hindu Sacraments of Childhood: The First Five Years._ (Brahmans in Madras) 1969. H. Daniel Smith. Color, 25 minutes, 16mm. (NSyU, WU, WaU)

87. _Hindu Temple Rites: Bathing the Image of God._ (Brahmans in Madras) 1965. H. Daniel Smith. Color, 13 minutes, 16mm. (NSyU, WU, WaPS)

88. _The Hindu World._ (Hinduism) 1963. Robert M. Perry. Color, 10 minutes, 16mm. (IU)

89. _How a Hindu Worships: At the Home Shrine._ (Brahmans in Madras) 1969. H. Daniel Smith. Color, 18 minutes, 16mm. (NSyU, WU, WaU)

90. _India and the Infinite: The Soul of a People._ (Hinduism) 1979. Elda Hartley. Color, 30 minutes, 16mm, VHS. (MoU, MtU, PSt)

91. _India: An Introduction._ (India) 1981. Michael Camerini, James MacDonald. Color, 25 minutes, 16mm. (CU, WU, PSt)

92. _India Cabaret._ (Modern Bombay) 1986. Mira Nair. Color, 60 minutes, 16mm, VHS. (FL)

93. _Indian Holy Men: Darshan._ (Hinduism) 1972. Satyam Shivam Sundaram, Florence Davey. Color, 28 minutes, 16mm. (FI)

94. _An Indian Pilgrimage: Kashi._ (Hinduism in Varanasi) 1976. Michael Camerini, Mira Binford. Color, 29 minutes, 16mm, VHS. (UWSAAC, WaPS)

95. _An Indian Pilgrimage: Ramdevra._ (Hinduism in Rajasthan) 1974. Michael Camerini, Mira Binford, Color, 25 minutes, 16mm. (UWSAAC, WaPS)

96. _Indian Village Life—Two Villages in Orissa Province._ (Orissan villages) 1972. Julien Bryan. Color, 16 minutes, 16mm. (PSt, OrPS)

97. _An Indian Worker: From Village to City._ (Urban migration) 1977. Michael Camerini, Mira Binford. Color, 18 minutes, 16mm. (CoU, InU)

98. _India's Sacred Cow._ (Hinduism) 1980. Color, 28 minutes, 16mm. (CU, InU)

99. _Indira Gandhi of India._ (Indian politics) 1973. Color, 60 minutes, 16mm. (MnU, WaU)

100. _In India the Sun Rises in the East._ (Scenery) 1970. Color, 14 minutes, 16mm. (WaU)

101. _In Search of a Holy Man._ (Hinduism) 1988. Color, 30 minutes, VHS. (PSt)

102. _Iramudun._ (Sri Lankan shamanism) 1984. Barrie Machin. Color, 45 minutes, VHS. (PSt, WaPS)

103. _Jhaoo Chowdhari: A Tongawallah from Delhi._ (Urban life, Delhi) 1975. Yavar Abbas. Color, 28 minutes, 16mm. (WaU)

104. _Journey's Battle-Victory._ (Neo-Hinduism) 1977. Color, 15 minutes, 16mm. (LB)

105. _Juggernaut._ (Modernization) 1968. Eugene Boyko. Color, 28 minutes, 16mm. (IU, NSyU, WaU)

106. _The Kalasha: Rites of Spring._ (Non-Muslim tribe in Pakistan) 1990. Peter Parkes. Color, 52 minutes, VHS. (FI)

107. _Kaleidoscope Orissa._ (Orissan arts) 1967. Robert Steele. Color, 35 minutes, 16mm. (CU, MiU, NSyU)

108. _Kamala and Raji: Working Women of Ahmedabad._ (Gujarati women) 1990. Color, 46 minutes VHS. (For sale only—UWSAAC)

109. _Kamban Ramayana._ (Puppet drama) 1974. Clifford Jones. B&W, 30 minutes, 16mm. (SACCU)

110. _Kanchenjungha._ (Westernized family) 1962. Satyajit Ray. Color, 102 minutes, 16mm. (FI)

111. _Kataragama._ (Sri Lankan Hinduism) 1987. Gananath Obeyesekere, Charlie Nairne. Color, 52 minutes, VHS. (FL)

112. _Kathputli: The Art of Rajasthani Puppeteers._ (Puppet theater) 1988. Color, 28 minutes, VHS. (PSt)

113. _Kheturni Bayo: North Indian Farm Women._ (Gujarati women) 1980. Sharon Wood. Color, 18 minutes, 16mm. (InU, PSt)

114. _Krishnamurthi: A Dialogue with Huston Smith._ (Neo-Hinduism) 1971. Color, 63 minutes, 16mm. (BI)

115. _Kundalini._ (Yoga) 1973. Yale Medical School. Color, 28 minutes. 16mm (PSt)

116. _Kuttiyattam: Sanskrit Drama in the Temples of Kerala._ (Kerala drama) 1974. Clifford Jones. Color, 27 minutes, 16mm. (SACCU)

117. _Lady of Gingee: South Indian Draupadi Festivals._ (Tamil festival) 1988. Color, 16mm, VHS. (UWSAAC)

118. _Land of the Indus._ (Pakistan) 1974. John Frank, John Herr. Color, 27 minutes, 16mm. (NBuU)

119. _Living Yoga._ (Yoga) 1970s. Color, 20 minutes, 16mm. (HP)

120. _The Long Search, Part 2—Three Hundred Thirty Million Gods._ (Hinduism) 1977. Peter Montagnon. Color, 54 minutes, 16mm, VHS. (CU, IU, PSt)

121. _Loving Krishna._ (Bengali Hinduism) 1985. Robert Gardner, Ákos Östör. Color, 37 minutes, 16mm. (IU, NSyU)

122. _Mahanagar._ (Urban Bengal) 1964. Satyajit Ray. B&W, 122 minutes, 16mm.. (FI)

123. _Maharishi Mahesh: Jet-Age Yogi._ (Neo-Hinduism) 1960s. Yavar Abbas. Color, 28 minutes, 16mm. (NYU)

124. _Mahatma Gandhi: Silent Revolution._ (Independence) 1968. Color, 38 minutes, 16mm. (NSyU, WaU, InTI)

125. _Major Religions of the World—Development and Rituals._ (Hinduism, Buddhism, Islam) 1954. B&W and Color, 20 minutes, 16mm. (IU, PSt, WaU)

126. _Manifestations of Shiva._ (South Indian Hinduism) 1980. Malcolm Leigh. Color, 61 minutes, 16mm. (AS)

127. *Modern Brides: Arranged Marriage in South India.* (South Indian family) 1985. Happy Luchsinger. Color, 30 minutes, 16mm, VHS. (UWSAAC, WaU)
128. *The Monk, the Village, and the Bo Tree.* (Sri Lankan Buddhism) 1987. Color, 28 minutes, VHS. (CU, MiU)
129. *Monthly Ancestral Offerings in Hinduism.* (Brahmans in Madras) 1969. H. Daniel Smith. Color, 9 minutes, 16mm. (WaU)
130. *Mother Teresa of Calcutta.* (Christians, Calcutta life) 1971. Malcolm Muggeridge. Color, 50 minutes, VHS. (UPB, WaPS)
131. *Munni ("Little Girl"): Childhood and Art in Mithila.* (Bihari painting) 1983. Raymond Owens, Ron Hess. Color, 29 minutes, 16mm, VHS. (UWSAAC)
132. *The Muria.* (Gonds) 1982. Melissa Llewelyn-Davies. Color, 55 minutes, 16mm, VHS. (PSt, FI)
133. *A Musical Tradition in Banaras.* (Music) 1973. Roger Hartman. Color, 40 minutes, 16mm. (UWSAAC, WaPS)
134. *A Nation Uprooted—Afghan Refugees in Pakistan.* (Pathans, Pakistan) 1986. Judith Mann, Debra Denker. Color, 29 minutes, 16mm. (OrPS)
135. *Nehru: Man of Two Worlds.* (Indian politics) 1966. B&W, 24 minutes, 16mm. (IU, NSyU, WaPS)
136. *Non-Violence—Mahatma Gandhi and Martin Luther King: The Teacher and the Pupil.* (Nonviolence) 1971. C. Grinker, M. Koplin. Color, 15 minutes, 16mm. (PFDC)
137. *North Indian Village.* (Uttar Pradesh) 1959. John and Patricia Hitchcock. Color, 30 minutes, 16mm. (CU, IU, NSyU)
138. *Of Grace and Steel.* (American Sikhs) 1984. Phyllis Jeroslow. Color, 20 minutes, VHS. (CLU, MoU, PSt)
139. *Our Asian Neighbours: India Series—The Village Economy.* (Village life) 1977. William V. Mayer. Color, 15 minutes, 16mm. (PSt, TxU)
140. *Padma, South Indian Dancer.* (Dance) 1976. Color, 20 minutes, 16mm. (TxU)
141. *Pakistan: Mound of the Dead.* (Indus civilization) 1972. Color, 27 minutes, 16mm. (IU, FTS, WaPS)
142. *Pandit Jasraj.* (Music) 1971. Color, 30 minutes, 16mm. (IU)
143. *Pankuni Uttaram: Festival of Marriage and Fertility.* (Festival in Tamil Nadu) 1970. Fred Clothey. Color, 20 minutes, 16mm. (DRSUP)
144. *A Passage to India.* (British in India) 1984. David Lean. Color, 163 minutes, 16mm, VHS. (FI)
145. *Patal Ganga: River of the Gods.* (Geography, Hinduism) Color, 24 minutes, 16mm. (CU, InU, CtU)
146. *Pather Panchali.* (Bengali family) 1955. Satyajit Ray. B&W, 112 minutes, 16mm. (BF)
147. *Phantom India, Part 2: Things Seen in Madras.* (Daily life) 1967–1968. Louis Malle. Color, 52 minutes, 16mm. (NYF, MtU)
148. *Phantom India, Part 3: The Indians and the Sacred.* (Hinduism) 1967–1968. Louis Malle. Color, 52 minutes, 16mm. (NYF)
149. *Phantom India, Part 5: A Look at the Castes.* (Caste) 1967–1968. Louis Malle. Color, 52 minutes, 16mm. (NYF)
150. *Phantom India, Part 6: On the Fringes of Indian Society.* (Jews, Christians, tribals) 1967–1968. Louis Malle. Color, 52 minutes, 16mm. (MtU, NYF)
151. *Pilgrimage to a Hindu Temple.* (Brahmans in Madras) 1969. H. Daniel Smith. Color, 14 minutes, 16mm. (WaU, MoU)
152. *Pilgrimage to Pittsburgh.* (Temple festival) 1990. Color, 25 minutes, VHS. (For sale only—UWSAAC)
153. *Puppeteer.* (Udaipur, Rajasthan) 1976. Color, 20 minutes, 16mm. (TxU)
154. *Radha's Day: Hindu Family Life.* (Women in Madras) 1965. H. Daniel Smith. Color, 17 minutes, 16mm. (NSyU, WaU)
155. *Raga.* (Ravi Shankar's music) 1970. Howard Worth. Color, 96 minutes, 16mm. (FI)
156. *Raj Gonds.* (Gonds) 1982. Melissa Llewelyn-Davies. Color, 55 minutes, 16mm, VHS. (PSt, FI)
157. *Raju: A Guide from Rishikesh.* (Pilgrimage) 1960s. Yavar Abbas. Color, 28 minutes, 16mm. (NYU)
158. *Rich Man, Poor Man, no. 3: Food.* (Sri Lankan farming, fishing) 1972. Color, 53 minutes, 16mm. (IU, MnU)
159. *The River.* (Ganges, British) 1952. Jean Renoir, Hari Das Gupta. Color, 90 minutes, 16mm. (BF, FI)
160. *Salaam Bombay!* (Urban life, Bombay) 1988. Mira Nair. Color, 114 minutes, 16mm. (CEG)
161. *Sectarian Hinduism: Lord Śiva and His Worship.* (Hinduism) 1977. David Knipe. Color, 30 minutes. (WaU has VHS; MoU has Beta)
162. *Sectarian Hinduism: Lord Vishnu and His Worship.* (Hinduism) 1977. David Knipe. Color, 30 minutes. (WaU has VHS; MoU has Beta)
163. *Sectarian Hinduism: The Goddess and Her Worship.* (Hinduism) 1977. David Knipe. Color, 30 minutes, Beta. (MoU)
164. *The Serpent Deities: Art and Ritual in South India.* (Kerala ritual) 1976. Clifford Jones. Color, 18 minutes, 16mm. (SACCU)
165. *Serpent Mother.* (Mythology) 1986. Color, 27 minutes, 16mm, VHS. (Centre)
166. *Shakespeare Wallah.* (Westernization, Anglo-Indians) 1966. James Ivory, Ismael Merchant. B&W, 115 minutes, 16mm. (CF)
167. *Shamans of the Blind Country.* (Nepali shamanism) 1980. Michael Oppitz. Color, 224 minutes, 16mm, VHS. (TxDas)
168. *Shelter for the Homeless.* (Sri Lanka) 1987. Color, 27 minutes, 16mm. (CU, IU)
169. *Sherpa.* (Sherpas) 1985. Robert Godfrey. Color, 29 minutes, 16mm, VHS. (IU, NSyU)
170. *Sherpa High Country.* (Sherpas) 1977. Xenia Lisanovich. Color, 20 minutes, 16mm, VHS. (CU)
171. *Sherpas.* (Sherpa family) 1977. Sherry Ortner, Leslie Woodhead. Color, 52 minutes, VHS. (FI)
172. *Sitala in Spring: Festival of the Bengali Goddess of Health and Illness.* (Bengali festival) 1986. B&W, 40 minutes, 16mm, VHS. (UWSAAC)
173. *Skanda-Sasti: A Festival of Conquest.* (Festival in Tamil Nadu) 1970. Fred Clothey. Color, 17 minutes, 16mm. (WaU)
174. *So Far from India.* (Gujaratis in New York) 1982. Mira Nair. Color, 49 minutes, 16mm, VHS. (FL)

175. _Song of Ceylon._ (Sri Lankan Buddhism, British, modernization) 1934. Basil Wright. B&W, 40 minutes, 16mm. (CU, MiU, NSyU)

176. _Sons of Shiva._ (Bengali Hinduism) 1985. Robert Gardner, Ákos Östör. Color, 27 minutes, 16mm. (IU)

177. _Southern Asia: Problems of Transition._ (Sri Lankan politics) 1967. Color, 16 minutes, 16mm. (NSyU)

178. _Spark of Life._ (Science and Hinduism) Color, 24 minutes, 16mm. (ISKCON)

179. _The Spiritual Frontier._ (Neo-Hinduism) 1976. John Griesser, Jean Papert. Color, 27 minutes, 16mm. (ISKCON)

180. _Sunseed._ (Neo-Hinduism) 1971. Frederick Cohn, Ralph H. Silver. Color, 87 minutes, 16mm. (CoF)

181. _Swami Karunānanda: From Wallaroo, Australia._ (Neo-Hinduism) 1971. Yavar Abbas. Color, 28 minutes, 16mm. (NYU)

182. _Swami Shyam._ (Neo-Hinduism) 1976. Color, 20 minutes, 16mm. (TxU)

183. _The Sword and the Flute._ (Mughal painting) 1959. James Ivory. Color, 24 minutes, 16mm. (MnU, WaU)

184. _Tantra._ (Tantric Hinduism) 1968. Nik Douglas, Robert Fraser, Mick Jagger. Color, 26 minutes, 16mm. (CoF)

185. _The Tantric Universe._ (Nepalese tantrism) 1976. Mike Spera, Sheldon Rochlin. Color, 22 minutes, 16mm. (FII)

186. _Textiles and Ornamental Arts of India._ (Indian cloth) 1955. Paul Zils. Color, 11 minutes, 16mm. (InU, CU, NSyU)

187. _Therayattam._ (Kerala dance) 1972. K. T. John. Color, 18 minutes, 16mm. (CLU)

188. _Tibetan Buddhism: Cycles of Interdependence._ (Ritual in Ladakh) 1983. Edward W. Bastian. Color, 59 minutes, 16mm, VHS. (UWSAAC, WaU)

189. _Tibetan Buddhism: Preserving the Monastic Tradition._ (Tibetans in Karnataka) 1982. Edward W. Bastian. Color, 29 minutes, 16mm, VHS. (UWSAAC, WaU)

190. _Tibetan Heritage._ (Nepalese Buddhism) 1976. Mike Spera, Sheldon Rochlin. Color, 19 minutes, 16mm. (FII)

191. _Tragada Bhavai: A Rural Theatre Troupe of Gujarat._ (Drama, Gujarat) 1981. Roger Sandall, Jayasinhji Jhala. Color, 42 minutes, 16mm, VHS. (DER)

192. _Trip to Awareness: A Jain Pilgrimage to India._ (Jains) 1974. Color, 29 minutes, 16mm, VHS. (PSt, WaU)

193. _Two Daughters._ (Bengali family) 1961. Satyajit Ray. B&W, 114 minutes, 16mm. (FI)

194. _Undala._ (Rajasthani village) 1967. Marek Jablonko. Color, 28 minutes, 16mm. (CU, InU, PSt)

195. _The Universal Flame._ (Theosophy) 1974. Color, 27 minutes, 16mm. (IU)

196. _Vijay Raghav Rao (Flute)._ (Music) 1974. Color, 29 minutes, 16mm. (IU)

197. _The Village, A Village in Tanjore._ (Tamil family) 1976. Color, 16 minutes, 16mm. (TxU, PSt)

198. _Village in India: Fifty Miles from Poona._ (Maharashtra) 1963. Faili Bilimoria. B&W, 20 minutes, 16mm. (NSyU, WaU)

199. _Village Man, City Man._ (Urban migration) 1975. Mira Binford, Michael Camerini. Color, 38 minutes, 16mm. (WU, WaU)

200. _Viney._ (Hindu family) 1976. Color, 17 minutes, 16mm. (TxU)

201. _Vinoba Bhave: Walking Revolutionary._ (Landownership in India) 1970. Kirby Steele. Color, 39 minutes, 16mm. (IFB, MnU, WaU)

202. _Vishnu's Maya._ (Hinduism) 1975. Thomas Ball. Color, 30 minutes, 16mm. (CU, InU)

203. _Voices of the People: The Elections in India 1977._ (Indian politics) 1978. Color, 30 minutes, 16mm, VHS. (WaU, UWSAAC)

204. _Vṛndavan: Land of Kṛṣna._ (Hinduism) 1978. Color, 24 minutes, 16mm, VHS. (ISKCON)

205. _The Wages of Action: Religion in a Hindu Village._ (Hinduism near Varanasi) 1979. David Thompson. Color, 47 minutes, 16mm. (UWSAAC, NhU)

206. _Wedding of the Goddess (Parts 1 and 2)._ (Hinduism in Madurai) 1976. Mira Binford, Michael Camerini. Color, 36 minutes (Pt. 1) and 40 minutes (Pt. 2), 16mm. (UWSAAC, WaPS)

207. _William Rivers: Everything Is Relatives._ (Toda, Torres Straits Is.) 1990. BBC. Color, 52 minutes, 16mm, VHS, Beta, U-Mat. (FFHS)

208. _The Work of Gomis._ (Sri Lankan shamanism) 1972. Yvonne Hannemann. Color, 48 minutes, 16mm. (CLU, PSt)

209. _The World of Apu (Apur Sansar)._ (Bengali family) 1959. Satyajit Ray. Color and B&W, 104 minutes, 16mm. (IdU, WaU)

210. _The Worship of the Deity Ayyappan: Art and Ritual in South India._ (Hinduism in Kerala) 1976. Clifford Jones. Color, 20 minutes, 16mm. (SACCU)

211. _Yakam—A Fire Ritual in South India._ (Festival in Tamil Nadu) 1970. Fred Clothey. Color, 10 minutes, 16mm. (WaU)

212. _A Zenana: Scenes and Recollections._ (Rajputs) 1982. Roger Sandall, Jayasinhji Jhala. Color, 36 minutes, 16mm, VHS. (DER)

ADDENDA

18a. _Being Muslim in India._ (Islam in India) 1984. Color, 40 minutes, 16mm, VHS. (UWSAAC)

118a. _Life and Death of a Dynasty._ (Indian Politics) 1991. Anne and Robert Drew. Color and B&W, 90 minutes, VHS. (DC)

189a. _Tibetan Buddhism: The Wheel of Life._ (Buddhist philosophy) 1991. Color, 30 minutes, 16mm, VHS. (UWSAAC)

Index to Filmography

Bibliography

Binford, Mira Reym (1971). _Films for Study of India._ New Delhi: Educational Resources Centre.

de Cunha, Uma (1973). _India on Film._ New Delhi: Educational Resources Centre.

Dell, David J., et al. (1981). _Focus on Hinduism: A Guide to Audio-Visual Resources for Teaching Religion._ 2nd ed. Revised by H. Daniel Smith and Robert A. McDermott. Chambersburg, Pa.: Anima Books.

Heider, Karl (1983). _Films for Anthropological Teaching._ 7th ed. American Anthropological Association Special Publication no. 16. Washington.

Directory of Distributors

AC	Arthur Cantor, Inc., 33 W. 60th St., New York, NY 10023
AC5	Almi-Cinema 5, 1900 Broadway, New York, NY 10023
AS	Asia Society, Inc., 725 Park Ave., New York, NY 10021
BF	Budget Films, 4590 Santa Monica Blvd., Los Angeles, CA 90029
BI	Blaisdell Institute, 143 E. 10th St., Claremont, CA 91711
CEG	Cinecom Entertainment Group, 1290 Avenue of the Americas, New York, NY 10019
Centre	Centre, Barr Films, 12801 Schabarum Ave., P.O. Box 7878, Irwindale, CA 91706-7878
CF	Corinth Films, 34 Gansevoort St., New York, NY 10014
CLU	Instructional Media Library, Powell Library, University of California, Los Angeles, CA 90024
CoF	Cornerstone Films, 12 W. 27th St., New York, NY 10001
CoU	Colorado Media Collection, Stadium 360, University of Colorado, Box 379, Boulder, CO 80309
CtU	Center for Instructional Media and Technology, University of Connecticut, 249 Glenbrook Rd., Storrs, CT 06269
CU	Extension Media Center, 2176 Shattuck Ave., University of California, Berkeley, CA 94720
DC	Direct Cinema Ltd., P.O. Box 10003, Santa Monica, CA 90410
DER	Documentary Educational Resources, 5 Bridge St., Watertown, MA 02172
DRSUP	Dept. of Religious Studies, 2604 Cathedral of Learning, University of Pittsburgh, Pittsburgh, PA 15260
DSR	DSR, Inc., P.O. Box 281, Columbia, MD 21045
FF	Festival Films, 2841 Irving Ave. S., Minneapolis, MN 55408
FFHS	Films for the Humanities and Sciences, P.O. Box 2053, Princeton, NJ 08540
FI	Films, Inc., 5547 N. Ravenswood Ave., Chicago, IL 60640
FII	Focus International, Inc., 14 Oregon Dr., Huntington Station, NY 11746
FL	Filmmakers Library, 124 E. 40th St., New York, NY 10016
FRIF	First Run/Icarus Films, 6th floor, 153 Waverly Place, New York, NY 10014
FTS	Film and Video Library, University of South Florida, 4202 Fowler Ave., Tampa, FL 33620
HP	Hartley Productions, Inc., Cat Rock Rd., Cos Cob, CT 06807
IaU	Audio-Visual Center, C-5 Seashore Hall, University of Iowa, Iowa City, IA 52242
IB	Interbook, Inc., 131 Varick St., New York, NY 10013
IdU	Media Center, University of Idaho, Moscow, ID 83843
IFB	International Film Bureau, 332 S. Michigan Ave., Chicago, IL 60604
InTI	Audio-Visual Center, Stalker Hall, Indiana State University, Terre Haute, IN 47807
InU	Audio-Visual Center, Indiana University, Bloomington, IN 47405
ISKCON	International Society for Krishna Consciousness, Bhakti Vedanta Book Trust, 3764 Watseka Ave., Los Angeles, CA 90034
IU	Film Center, University of Illinois, 1325 S. Oak St., Champaign, IL 61820
JFCAWU	John Frazer Center for Arts, Wesleyan University, Middletown, CT 06457
JMS	Jewish Media Service, 15 E. 26th St., New York, NY 10010
KYR	Kripalu Yoga Retreat, Box 120, Summit Station, PA 17979
LB	Lewis Buchner, 455 Utah St., San Francisco, CA 94110
MG	Media Guild, Suite E, 11722 Sorrento Valley Rd., San Diego, CA 92121
MiU	Film and Video Library, University of Michigan, 400 Fourth St., Ann Arbor, MI 48103
MnU	University Film and Video, University of Minnesota, Suite 108, 1313 Fifth St. S.E., Minneapolis, MN 55414

MoU	Film and Video Library, University of Missouri, 505 E. Stewart St., Columbia, MO 65211	SSP	Singer-Sharrette Productions, 336 Main Street, P.O. Box 68, Rochester, MN 48063
MtU	Instructional Media Services, University of Montana, Missoula, MT 59812	Swank	Swank Motion Pictures, Inc., 910 Riverside Dr., Elmhurst, IL 60126; or 350 Vanderbilt Motor Parkway, Hauppauge, NY 11787
NBuU	Media Library, 24 Capen Hall, State University of New York, Buffalo, NY 14260	TVKC	TVKC, P.O. Box 404, Mendham, NJ 07945
NhU	Dept. of Media Services, Dimond Library, University of New Hampshire, Durham, NH 03824	TxDas	Media Services, University of Texas at Dallas, P.O. Box 830643, Richardson, TX 75083
NK	Navin Kumar, Inc., 967 Madison Ave., New York, NY 10021	TxU	Film Library, General Libraries, University of Texas, Box W, Austin, TX 78713
NSyU	Film Rental Center, Syracuse University, 1455 E. Colvin St., Syracuse, NY 13210	UPB	Audio-Visual Services, 101 Harvey Fletcher Building, Brigham Young University, Provo, UT 84602
NYF	New Yorker Films, 16 W. 61st St. New York, NY 10023	UWSAAC	Dept. of South Asian Studies, 1269 Van Hise Hall, University of Wisconsin, Madison, WI 53706
NYU	Film Library, New York University, 26 Washington Place, New York, NY 10003	WaPS	Instructional Media Services, Washington State University, Pullman, WA 99164
OKentU	Audio Visual Services, 330 Library Building, Kent State University, Kent, OH 44242	WaU	Instructional Media Services, 23 Kane Hall, DG-10, University of Washington, Seattle, WA 98195
OrPS	Continuing Education Film and Video Library, Portland State University, 1633 S.W. Park, P.O. Box 1383, Portland, OR 97207	Wombat	Wombat Film & Video, Inc., Suite 2421, 250 W. 57th St., New York, NY 10019
PFDC	Pictura Films Distribution Corp., 111 8th Ave., New York, NY 10011	WU	Bureau of Audio-Visual Instruction, University of Wisconsin, 1327 University Ave., P.O. Box 2093, Madison, WI 53701
PSt	Audio Visual Services, Special Services Building, Pennsylvania State University, University Park, PA 16802		
SACCU	South Asia Center, School of International Affairs, Columbia University, New York, NY 10027		

Ethnonym Index

This index provides some of the alternative names and the names of major subgroups for cultures covered in this volume. The culture names that are entry titles are in boldface.

The Editors

Editor in Chief
David Levinson (Ph.D., State University of New York at Buffalo) is vice-president of the Human Relations Area Files in New Haven, Connecticut. He is a cultural anthropologist whose primary research interests are in social issues, worldwide comparative research, and social theory. He has conducted research on homelessness, alcohol abuse, aggression, family relations, and ethnicity. Among his dozens of publications are the award-winning text, *Toward Explaining Human Culture* (with Martin J. Malone), *The Tribal Living Book* (with David Sherwood), and *Family Violence in Cross-Cultural Perspective*. Dr. Levinson also teaches anthropology at Albertus Magnus College in New Haven, Connecticut.

Volume Editor
Paul Hockings (M.A., University of Toronto; Ph.D., University of California, Berkeley) is also editor of the journal *Visual Anthropology*. He is a professor of anthropology at the University of Illinois, Chicago. Although primarily a cultural anthropologist and linguist, he has done archaeological and bibliographic work, and he also has made anthropological films. Among those films is *The Village*, made in Ireland with Mark McCarty. He has written or edited nine books and dozens of articles, most of them dealing with the Badagas and related South Indian peoples. His most recent books are *Blue Mountains: The Ethnography and Biogeography of a South Indian Region* (written with several collaborators), and *A Badaga-English Dictionary* (with Christiane Pilot-Raichoor). Paul Hockings is a Fellow of the Royal Anthropological Institute of Great Britain and a life member of the American Anthropological Association.